BOLTON WANDERERS

THE COMPLETE RECORD

BOLTON
WANDERERS
THE COMPLETE RECORD

SIMON MARLAND

First published in Great Britain in 2011 by The Derby Books Publishing Company Limited, Breedon House, 3 The Parker Centre, Derby, DE21 4SZ.

© Simon Marland, 2011

The images contained in this book have been reproduced with kind permission of Action Images and *Bolton News*.

ISBN 978-1-85983-792-0
Printed and bound in Poland.
www.polskabook.co.uk

CONTENTS

FOREWORD

By John McGinlay

I am both delighted and honoured to be asked to write a few words about *The Complete Record of Bolton Wanderers Football Club*. When I first joined the club I became quickly aware of the heritage and history of the club, and while we all need to look to the future we don't want to forget what has gone before.

We have all experienced the highs and lows, the tears of joy and disappointment, the firsts and lasts over the years, and the facts, figures and information in this book will bring back some very memorable performances of both players and teams that have been fortunate to represent this special football club.

I count myself as one of those fortunate to have pulled on that famous shirt and am grateful that I became a part of a special journey that the club were making, both on and off the field, when I joined in September 1992.

I realised that I had to do something special to win over the supporters, but from my debut at Leyton Orient, my first goal at Chester to my last goal, also against Orient at The Reebok Stadium in September 1997, I always gave 100 per cent. In return I received some fantastic support, even if I missed an easy goalscoring opportunity, of which there were a few, the crowd would still support me and that gave me the confidence to go out and enjoy the game which in turn produced some memorable results.

I was fortunate to be a member of three promotion-winning sides, took part in some fantastic Cup victories that made national news, played twice at Wembley and played for Scotland at full international level, fulfilling a boyhood dream. I couldn't have managed any of this without your support alongside that of my family and teammates.

There are so many special memories, but if I was to select just three to reminisce about with those that were around. Firstly, my early headed goal against Liverpool at Anfield from David Lee's cross that sent us on our way to knocking out the holders of the FA Cup, as a Second Division side, in 1993. The sight of seeing 8,000 happy Bolton supporters behind the goal proved we were about to witness something special.

How about the epic Play-off semi-final second-leg success against Wolves at Burnden in 1995? I had a special relationship with their supporters, they didn't like me, but it showed the spirit we had in our side to come back from a first leg deficit to win through and then again showed that spirit in the Final at Wembley to win promotion to the Premier League.

Finally, it has to be the last game at Burnden Park. It was always a special atmosphere on the ground, more so for evening games, but this had everything

Happiness, because we were about to be presented with the First Division Championship, yet sadness because 102 years of history at the ground was coming to an end.

I still get a buzz when I talk about that evening and am privileged that I managed to score the final goal on the ground in front of some of the illustrious players that had gone before me such as the great late Nat Lofthouse.

I'm sure you will all have your personal favourite players and moments in the club's illustrious history, and this book brings them all together and I am proud to have been involved in a small part of it.

Although I'm now living in the States, I get to watch most of the Wanderers games on TV, along with my family who are staunch Wanderers supporters and still get that special feeling that comes with belonging to a special club.

(Super) John McGinlay

Nat Lofthouse OBE
The Lion of Vienna
27 August 1925–15 January 2011.

INTRODUCTION

When I first put pen to paper to write the *Bolton Wanderers Complete Record* in 1989, to coincide with the club's 112th anniversary, we had just been successful at Wembley in the Sherpa Van Trophy Final and had consolidated a position in the old Third Division. In the 22 years that have followed there have been so many changes, not only to the club but also within the game itself, and it is a source of much pleasure to everyone involved from supporters up to the chairman that Bolton Wanderers have, just like previous times in their history, kept up to hold a place within the elite in English football after a number of years in the doldrums.

Those intervening years have produced so many twists and turns that could have only been dreamt of back then. Twelve seasons in the Premier League, the last 10 consecutively, the move to the Reebok Stadium after a record-breaking Championship-winning final season at Burnden Park and, of course, two seasons in the UEFA Cup competition.

Added to that have been two major Cup Finals, two FA Cup semi-finals, five trips to Wembley, four promotions and two relegations to leave any supporter with more memories than at any time in the club's history.

The founders of Christ Church in 1874, and those who got together to form Bolton Wanderers three years later, could scarcely have imagined the growth of the game as a pastime the world over and, through all those years that followed, the Wanderers' history has produced many dramatic moments that are covered in this book.

The Trotters' motto, *Supera Moras* – overcome all difficulties – has always prevailed, even in times of disappointment and despair and now, having been labelled as 'fighting above our weight' in relation to League position, attendances and wage bill, the challenge is to reach the next level. Unfortunately, such is the gap that has now emerged in the Premiership between the top clubs and the rest that the next level seems so far away, just as the top flight and European football had seemed way back in 1989!

I hope this book will bring back some great memories, just as it did for me putting it together, and here's to the future, but let's not forget the past.

Simon Marland

THE BOLTON WANDERERS STORY

Bolton Wanderers had its beginnings from the desire of the scholars and teachers to participate in outdoor recreation, and in particular at Christ Church Sunday School. The game of Association football in the town, however, had its roots in the village of Turton, situated to the north of the town.

The game was introduced to the villagers by John Kay, who had learned his footballing skills at Harrow Public School, and this proved to be a significant move in the history of the game in the County of Lancashire. In December 1871 the first general meeting of the Turton Club was held and Kay's father, James, the squire of Turton, was elected as its first President. John James Bentley was one of the club's first players, and he was later to become an influential figure in the game, becoming Secretary of Bolton Wanderers and the President of the Football League.

During 1871 the Revd Joseph Farell Wright was appointed the vicar of Christ Church while the headmaster, Thomas Ogden, had been appointed two years previous. Both shared a great interest in football, with Ogden himself partaking in the game on a regular basis. There was a popular Christian belief at the time that taking part in sport, and in particular team sport, led to a great development of character, fair play and self control.

In July 1874 Ogden, who had witnessed the game played at Turton, persuaded Wright to form a team, and so Christ Church FC came into being with the sole purpose of providing a wholesome pastime for their members and the Boys School became the headquarters. Wright was elected president, Ogden assumed the captaincy and Tom Rawsthorne became secretary, with subscriptions set at a penny a week. Money was collected to buy a football, and on the first Saturday of the month a practice match was arranged on Bob Wood's field which forms part of Heaton Cemetery, the game being postponed for a week due to heavy rain.

It is believed that Christ Church FC played their first game against Farnworth on a field called Smithfield, situated between Green Lane and Plodder Lane, and the game took place under rugby rules. Many games began to take place under both rugby and association rules against other local clubs with The Recreation Ground, opposite the Cross Guns Inn and known as Dick Cockle's field, becoming home with changing taking place at the school.

Christ Church FC prospered and served the purpose for which it was established but, in 1877, a split developed when Wright demanded that, as president, he had to be in attendance at all committee meetings held at the school. The players and other members saw this as authoritarian and decided to part company with Wright and his church.

The last meeting to take place at Christ Church Boys School was on 28 August 1877 and from there the committee 'Wandered' to the Gladstone Hotel where it was unanimously agreed to become 'the Bolton Wanderers' and so set in motion a club that has figured prominently in English football for almost 135 years.

As for Wright, his legacy was the formation and foresight to establish such a club, but unfortunately he was not to see the fruition of his endeavours when he died in 1883 at the age of 56. His grave is situated at Christ Church, Walmsley, and his part in being the club's founding father was recognised in 2008. His able assistant in the formation, Thomas Ogden, passed away the following year at the age of just 38 after serving the school for 15 years.

The Britannia Hotel, on the corner of Deane Road, became the club's headquarters and the rules of the club were strict. Fines were issued for not turning up at meetings, and players were treated likewise if they did not give notice of their unavailability to play for the team. Swearing on the field was unacceptable, and any offender was fined the sum of two old pence. At first the players and honorary members paid subscriptions, while players had the additional burden of paying their own railway fares and for their own kit. Less well-off members were subsidised by a whip-round although, as the club prospered, gate receipts warranted an allowance towards their expenses.

Bolton Wanderers were one of a number of teams in the locality. Farnworth, Bolton Association, St James', All Saints, Eagley, Halliwell, Astley Bridge Gilnow Rangers, Bolton Olympic, Bolton Hornets, Emmanuel, Great Lever and Turton were all competing to be the most successful club in the town.

In 1878, Mr Peter Parkinson, who was the manager of a mill in the town, became an honorary member and he saw the advantages of Bolton having a successful football team, and it was through his efforts that Bolton Wanderers grew rapidly to such prominence.

Turton FC organised the Turton Challenge Cup in the same year which was the first knock out cup organised in Lancashire. The Wanderers entered, but the inaugural winners were Eagley. The Lancashire Football Association was also formed, with 30 members, of which only the Wanderers and Blackburn Rovers were to later become members of the Football League.

In 1879 the Lancashire FA Cup was born, although the Wanderers were eliminated by Blackburn who were the county's leading club at that time. The following year Tom Naylor became the first Trotters player to be recognised for representative honours when he was selected for Lancashire to play against North Wales.

In 1881 the Wanderers moved home again, this time making the short journey down Pikes Lane. A sum of £150 was spent on improving the pitch, a grandstand, in reality a timber shed, was erected and admittance to games was set at sixpence (3p) and four pence (2p) with season tickets costing one guinea (£1.05). At the annual meeting that year Peter Parkinson was elected President of the club, and he was instrumental in introducing Scottish players to the club. Billy Struthers from Glasgow Rangers and Jim Devlin from Arbroath were the first to arrive. Struthers was seen as one of the best centre-forwards of the day, while Devlin was a full-back who unfortunately had his career cut short when an accident at his work in Woods Foundry deprived him of his sight in one eye.

The club first entered the FA Cup in 1881–82 but were defeated in the second round by Blackburn Rovers. The games in the earlier round against The Druids were to prove

1883 Back row: Kennedy, Dobson, Bromley, McKernon, Steel, Parkinson. Front row: Howarth, Fallon, Struthers, Gleaves, Davenport, Scholes.

beneficial for the Wanderers, who made strong ties in Wales to secure the services of the likes of Bob Roberts, Jacky Vaughan, Jack and Albert Powell, Dai Jones and 'keeper Jimmy Trainer, who was to later become Preston's double-winning custodian.

The club were fortunate to receive nothing more than a censure in 1883 after a referee was given some rough verbal treatment as he left the field at Pikes Lane and was later assaulted at the railway station. It was recommended that Bolton be expelled from the Lancashire FA for failing to protect him.

Although professionalism was illegal, it was no secret that players were being paid. Goalkeeper Jim Trainer was earning 50 shillings (£2.50) per week, while the other players were earning anything between £1.50 and £2 per week. They were also found 'jobs',

Match report from Bolton v 3rd Lanark RV, 1883.

BOLTON WANDERERS v. 3RD LANARK R.V.

After being defeated on Saturday by the Rovers, the Volunteers appeared at Pike's Lane on Easter Monday. Snow, which fell somewhat heavily just for an hour before the game, helped to make the ground wretchedly soft and treacherous, and fast play was entirely out of the question. In fact, the mud flew about in showers, and the slipperiness of the ground caused frequent spills and many free kicks from "hands." Dobson, who played well all the time, returned a straight shot of the Rifles, which Struthers got hold of, and rattling down the straight and passing to Steel, the latter at the second attempt got the first goal in a very few minutes. Then Lanark had a close chance, the ball just missing the post. The heavy charging often found Struthers on his back, but despite the way he was carefully watched, he eluded his wily opponents and again landed a shot, but the goal was disallowed off-side. Shortly afterwards the same player, by a long low shot after his own peculiar style, scored the second goal for the Wanderers. A very sharp tussle occurred in the visitors' quarters, where the dexterity of C. Campbell cleverly saved, amidst due applause. Stewart, unfortunately, got kicked in the stomach, and had to retire. The rest of the game, with the exception of good runs by Struthers, who scored the third goal, and Weir for their respective sides, was dull, slow, and very monotonous, the Riflemen apparently having "shot their bolt." Muir played a fine back game all through.

WANDERERS.—Wilson (goal), Kerman and Dobson (backs), Gleaves and Kennedy (half-backs), Howarth and Fowler (rights), Steel and Schole (lefts), Struthers and Christie (centres).

LANARK.—Campbell (goal), McLachlan and Muir (backs), Kennedy and Lang (half-backs), Fraser and Rae (rights), Stewart and Weir (lefts), Pearson and King (centres).

Referee: R. Kirkham (Darwen).

although they did not perform their duties and kept fit purely for football. The players held the upper hand as they could move clubs whenever they felt like it as clubs were hardly in a position to complain. A commission from the FA paid a visit to the Wanderers, who were suspected of paying their players, and they commenced an audit of the books. They left complimenting the secretary, Tom Rawsthorne, on the manner in which they were kept, unaware that he had been up all night preparing a set of new books for inspection.

In 1883–84 the Wanderers reached the fourth round of the FA Cup and drew 2–2 at Notts County. The town stirred for the replay, with the stand being extended and special preparations put in place at Pikes Lane. The crowd paid then record receipts of £468, but the attendance was unknown due to the number of people who got in without paying with local farmers earning a pay day by charging admission to watch from adjoining fields.

In 1884 Preston North End, Burnley and Great Lever were suspended by the Lancashire FA as they were suspected of paying their players. On 10 October a meeting took place at the Commercial Hotel in Bolton with clubs and the Lancashire FA in which Peter Parkinson suggested a British FA be formed to compete against the FA who wished the game to remain as an amateur pastime. Consequently, Bolton were not involved in the 1884–85 FA Cup. They had been drawn against Preston Zingari, but both clubs were embroiled in the political issue of professionalism and withdrew from the competition. Prestigious friendly games against the likes of Notts County and Aston Villa were also cancelled as the Wanderers' opponents attempted to avoid the issue by claiming amateur status.

The FA put up a stern fight, but the advent of the British FA ensured that professionalism would be established and, now realising they were defeated, the FA held a meeting in July 1885 to ratify the issue of payments to players. The meeting lasted 10 minutes, the persistence of the Lancashire clubs having brought an end to the charade.

J.J.Bentley had been appointed secretary of the Wanderers the previous February, and his knowledge of the game's finer points was to be of immense value in the coming months. The FA decreed that a professional player could only partake in the FA Cup if he had been born within a six-mile radius of the club's headquarters or ground or had lived in the area for at least two years.

This had immediate repercussions on Bolton Wanderers. After defeating Eagley and Rawtenstall, with weakened teams, they were drawn against Preston North End. Both clubs fielded ineligible players and were subsequently disqualified from the competition. In Bolton's case it was Jack Powell who had taken a job in Ruabon without telling the club of his whereabouts.

The Cup competition became farcical, with clubs spying on their opponents players. In 1887–88 the Wanderers played Everton in a long-running saga. A goal from Bob Roberts appeared to have won the game for Bolton, but Everton successfully appealed against the qualification of Bob Struthers who proved to be ineligible by three days. The replayed game was drawn and a second replay also failed to produce a winner before Everton won a fourth game.

Everton were then beaten by Preston who went on to defeat Halliwell in the third round. Meanwhile, the Wanderers protested that Everton had fielded two professionals against them who were registered as amateurs. The FA found Everton had infringed the rules and

A pre-League match programme, March 1888. Preston won 5–1 at Deepdale.

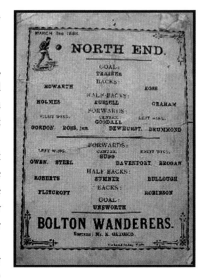

suspended the club for a month. Preston, therefore, had to come back from the fourth round to face Bolton. North End ran out 9–1 winners, a result that still stands as Bolton's worst-ever defeat in the FA Cup.

In 1885–86 the Wanderers enjoyed their most successful season to date, winning the Lancashire Cup by defeating Blackburn and also lifting the Bolton Charity Cup and the Derbyshire Charity Cup. Despite this on-field success, things were far from rosy off it.

Peter Parkinson resigned, along with treasurer William Barnes and committee member Ellis Parkinson. The annual meeting was a stormy affair, with second-team players, who were not members, being told to vote against the old guard. The result was that Billy 'Masher' Struthers was appointed secretary in place of J.J.Bentley. Struthers, however, showed no inclination for the job, and in February 1887 he was replaced by Fitzroy Norris.

Bolton soon missed Bentley's administrative skills and to compound their problems they were forced to discharge all their players at the season's end. Many returned for the following season but the exceptions were Davie Weir and Jim Trainer. Trainer was snapped up by Preston North End despite being on the wrong end of a 12–1 scoreline when North End had hammered the Wanderers on Christmas Day 1886. He later went on to earn the title the 'prince of goalkeepers'.

In October 1887 the Wanderers persuaded Bentley to return as secretary, his temporary exclusion showing just how indispensible he was. By now the club were in debt and the following year organised a prize draw with a first prize of £100. The police objected to the draw and stationed officers at the secretary's house on the planned date of the draw. The club went ahead with the draw at a shop of one of the committee with the winner coming from the Manchester area. The draw had, however, cleared the debt for now.

In March 1888, Bolton Wanderers were one of a number of clubs invited to attend a meeting to consider a proposal from Aston Villa's William McGregor to form a 'Football League'. On 17 April 1888, at a meeting in Manchester, the Football League was founded. Accrington, Aston Villa, Blackburn Rovers, Burnley, Derby County, Everton, Notts County, Preston North End, Stoke, West Bromwich Albion and Wolverhampton Wanderers were the other clubs chosen to constitute the League which would end the non-stimulating games of friendlies between clubs.

On 8 September 1888 the Football League got underway, with all the founder members except Blackburn and Notts County playing their first game. Pikes Lane had seen new dressing rooms installed, which had been paid for by private benefactors, who were given five-year season tickets in return.

Derby County were the first visitors, arriving late, and so the game kicked off half an hour after the advertised time. The Wanderers' first international player Kenny Davenport, born and bred in Bolton, had the distinction of scoring the club's first League goal after only two minutes play. He scored again and, a minute later, Jim Brogan, who had been with the club since 1883, found the goal to put Bolton three up inside five minutes. The visitors came back to lead by half-time and eventually won 6–3.

A week later, Burnley were the visitors to Pikes Lane, and circumstances were again similar. The visitors arrived late, Bolton took a three-goal lead but went down 4–3, with the winner coming in the 75th minute. After losing to the invincibles of Preston at Deepdale, the Wanderers recorded their first League win at the fourth attempt, with a 6–2 success against Everton at Pikes Lane.

On 22 November 1888, the League Committee decided to award points to decide the Championship, two points for a win and one for a draw. Clubs were also ordered to prevent disruption and improper demonstrations by supporters.

Although there was now 22 League games to be played, the club completed a total of 64 fixtures during the season. A crowd of 7,000 saw Glasgow Celtic defeated 2–0 at Pikes Lane on their first-ever Lancashire appearance, while another top Scottish club, Battlefield, were beaten 5–0.

Davie Weir scored the Wanderers first League hat-trick during a 4–1 defeat of Accrington in December 1888, and he was one of five players who appeared in every League game in that inaugural season, the other being Kenny Davenport, Bob Roberts, Jim Brogan and Jim Milne.

In 1890 the Wanderers finished fourth from bottom of the League on goal average, the difference of one-hundredth of a goal being in favour of Aston Villa, thus leaving the Wanderers having to apply for re-election. At the League meeting, the Wanderers stated that their home defeat by Notts County had been by three goals and not four, therefore placing Bolton above Villa. The League settled the matter by stating that only Bolton and Burnley had complied with the secretary's request for an official return of results. It was agreed that both Bolton and Villa should remain in the League without going to re-election, this being the closest the Wanderers have ever come to losing their League status.

The same season saw Bolton reach the semi-finals of the FA Cup for the first time where Sheffield Wednesday came out on top at Perry Bar. In an earlier round the Wanderers had defeated Sheffield United 13–0 to register the Wanderers record victory in a major competition. Jimmy Cassidy scored five of the goals to equal the feat set by Bob Struthers in an FA Cup tie against Bootle in 1882. It was not until 1983 that Tony Caldwell became the third Wanderer to equal the feat during an 8–1 Third Division defeat of Walsall.

During 1891–92 the Wanderers played against Nottingham Forest in a friendly that saw goal nets used for the first time, initially for one half of the game, the idea coming from a Liverpudlian engineer named Brodie. At the end of the season the Wanderers became the 46th member of the Manchester Football Association allowing them to compete in their Senior Cup competition.

It was in Cup football that success looked more likely as the Wanderers reached both the Lancashire and Manchester Cup finals in 1893 and the FA Cup Final a year later. A mediocre attendance of only 23,000 saw Bolton go down 4–1 to Second Division Notts County at Goodison Park in their first major Cup Final, and incredible as it may seem, the club actually lost money by not playing League fixtures at the best times due to the Cup commitments. Extravagant bonuses paid to players for reaching the Final did not help matters.

On 5 October 1894 it was decided that Bolton Wanderers Football & Athletic Company should be incorporated under the Company Acts of 1862 and 1880, whereby the liability of each shareholder is limited to the amount of his shares. A capital of £4,000 was to be raised and a plot of land at Burnden was to be leased. All this came with the club lying in the bottom four and only the teams form late in the season, seven wins and one draw in the final eight Pikes Lane appearances, prevented any worries about relegation.

The first season at Burnden Park saw the Wanderers chasing the Championship, lying second for a long period before finishing fourth. They also missed out on another Cup Final appearance with a semi-final defeat against Sheffield Wednesday in a replay at Nottingham.

Only two defeats in the first 15 games of the 1896–97 season saw the Wanderers head the League. On New Year's Day 1897 a crowd of 19,000 paid then record receipts of £512 at Burnden to see Liverpool end the Wanderers undefeated home record. This was followed by a second-round FA Cup defeat to Derby, Steve Bloomer getting a hat-trick in their 4–1 win, and things went downhill from there.

After such a great start to the season it was worrying how the team could suffer such a dramatic decline in the New Year. Supporters were crying out for a manager to take over the running of team affairs rather than it being left to a number of the directorate who disagreed among themselves over team selection. The players themselves were on a state bordering mutiny. They complained long and hard with a number vowing to leave at the season's end. The players were badly managed with too many people in authority over them. Things came to a head when Jim McGeachan was suspended for a month when he flatly refused to accompany the team to Sheffield.

The club began to stumble from one crisis to another. Seven of the main players left, including Welsh International David Jones, while goalkeeper James Sutcliffe re-signed only after he received an increased offer of £5 per week. This, however, caused problems with the rest of the playing staff as there was a reduction in the amount available for players' wages, and this crisis was to manifest itself in the club suffering its first-ever relegation.

Towards the end of the 1898–99 season money was found to sign players, but it proved to be too late. Four wins in the final eight games, including victories over Cup finalists Derby and League runners-up Liverpool, was not enough to save the club from relegation to Division Two.

The directorate offered the team £500 to win promotion at the first attempt, which they duly did as runners up to Sheffield Wednesday who had suffered relegation with the Wanderers 12 months earlier. Only four League games were lost, a record that was not equalled until 1997, and a club record defensive tally of just 25 goals conceded was set.

Off the field, however, the price of Second Division football had been high. The poor attendances had plunged the club into a deficit of £2,900, while the £500 bonus paid to the

Cover and first page (below) of the brochure from Bolton's fundraising bazaar, 1900.

players for promotion was funded by a local iron-foundry owner. The club organised an amateur athletics festival and, in October 1900, a bazaar in the Albert Halls to raise money for the club.

The club commenced life back in the top flight practically out of debt, and they kept their heads above water on the field after a slow start and a disappointing home FA Cup defeat to Southern League Reading. Ironically, Burnden Park staged the FA Cup Final replay

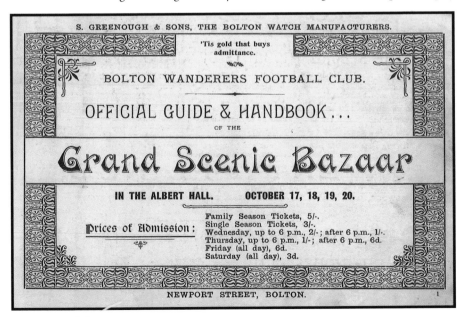

Dai Davies signed from Swinton RLFC.

PROMINENT FOOTBALLERS.

D. DAVIES,
BOLTON WANDERERS.

in April 1901 when only 20,470 saw non-League Tottenham defeat Sheffield United, the day becoming known as Pie Saturday due to the local caterers' over estimation of the crowd.

The 1902–03 season was met with new markings on the football pitch, the penalty area being described as we know it today and not a continuous 12-yard line. Wanderers stalwart 'keeper James Sutcliffe joined Millwall for a £400 fee after 364 first-class games for the club, and he was replaced by another rugby international in Dai Davies, a stalwart of the League code with Swinton.

Unfortunately, the Wanderers made their worst-ever start to a season. The first seven games were all lost, and the only respite came in a Lancashire Cup win at Barrow. The first point came in the eighth game, a 1–1 draw with Liverpool at Burnden. And so the dire form continued, 16 games without a win, and three heavy defeats over Christmas making relegation a certainty with 15 games still to play.

On 7 January 1903 the Wanderers registered their first win of season at the 23rd attempt. A 3–1 success at Notts County lifted the gloom, and 16 points were taken from the final 12 games, but the improvement came too late to save the Wanderers from relegation for the second time in their history.

Once again the club went all out to regain their place in the top flight, but it was to be their away form and interest in the FA Cup that saw them finish in seventh place. After accounting for Southern League sides Reading and Southampton in the FA Cup the Wanderers were drawn to face First Division Sheffield United at Bramall Lane. Bolton were clear underdogs not only due to the divisional difference but also because of their poor away form.

The Wanderers created the sensation of the round in winning 2–0 to go into the semi-finals. A goal from Bob Taylor, 13 minutes from the end against Derby County at Molineux, put Bolton into their second FA Cup Final. The Final was an all-Lancashire affair against Championship-chasing Manchester City, but the Cup once again eluded the Wanderers thanks to a disputed goal from Billy Meredith.

The chase for promotion during 1904–05 became a three-cornered affair between the Wanderers, Liverpool and Manchester United. The Anfielders took the title by winning their final five games without conceding a goal,

Action from the 1904 FA Cup Final againt Manchester City.

BOLTON WANDERERS' LEAGUE TEAM.   Copyright

Members of the 1908 team.

while the Wanderers finished runners-up, leaving United to drag themselves through another season of weary existence in the Second Division.

Bolton did not have any problems scoring goals on their return to the top flight, with the forward line of Stokes, Marsh, Shepherd, White and McEwan becoming the most feared in the country. They helped the Wanderers become the League's leading scorers with a total of 81 goals.

Shepherd earned international recognition with England, while White was similarly honoured by Scotland, but after two successful seasons the Wanderers found themselves involved in a relegation cliffhanger. A draw from the club's final game in April 1908, against fellow strugglers Notts County at Burnden, would have ensured safety, but Notts took maximum points, thanks to a goal from Cantrell. Bolton's last chance of survival hinged on Chelsea avoiding defeat against Notts at Stamford Bridge but a dubious penalty sealed Bolton's fate, and relegation was suffered alongside Birmingham.

John Somverville became the Wanderers first secretary-manager for the start of the 1908–09 season and the Second Division Championship came to Burnden Park for the first time at the end of that term. The final 12 games produced 21 points but the quick return had cost the club over £3,000 in transfer fees, while the wage bill of £6,472 was the highest of all the Lancashire clubs.

Bolton were quickly earning a reputation as a 'see-saw' club, for in 1910 they again suffered relegation to Division Two. The club's finances were again stretched with rumours of a delay in paying players wages. To help matters Marshall McEwan was sold to fellow strugglers Chelsea, the Londoners, despite their poor League position, were commanding the best attendances in the country, but they were to accompany the Wanderers through the trap door.

Promotion was won at the first attempt, although runners'-up spot was not secured until the final day of the season, but season 1910–11 was to prove a platform that saw the formation of the left wing of Ted Vizard and Joe Smith. It was a combination that was to serve the club for more than 16 years and to national success.

For the next few seasons the Bolton public were treated to 'scientific' football, a clever, thrilling game, not the crashing sort associated with the Second Division. They saw players in Wanderers colours produce a class of football that was normally associated with the likes of Aston Villa and Newcastle United to whom they had 'lost' players of the ilk of Tom Barber and Albert Shepherd respectively.

During 1914–15, due to the outbreak of war, attendances slumped by 59,000 over the first five games, with people putting everything into the war effort. During the season the record away League win, 7–1 at Aston Villa was set and worst away League defeat, 7–0 at

Tom Buchan one of nine players who played twice in one day.

Sheffield Wednesday, was equalled. The FA Cup semi-finals were also reached, but a final appearance was denied by eventual winners Sheffield United who won 2–1 at Ewood Park.

The following season saw the introduction of regional Leagues due to the Great War, with games only being allowed to take place on Saturdays and public holidays. Midweek matches were banned so as not to interfere with the work of making munitions. The police kept watch at football matches in an attempt to catch men shirking their responsibility to their country, and the Wanderers had great difficulty in fielding teams, which was made harder when compulsory military service was introduced in 1916.

The main concern during this era was keeping the club alive. During 1917–18, fixtures were arranged on a home and away basis so that clubs played each other on successive Saturday's and a 20 per cent split of the takings could be taken immediately to help the financial hardships. Stalwarts such as Tom Buchan, who played in every position apart from full-back, and was one of nine players who played twice in one day on Good Friday 1917, proved invaluable to keep the spirit of the players and supporters intact.

For the return of normal League football the club appointed Charles Foweraker as secretary-manager on 12 July 1919. George Eccles was re-appointed trainer and Joe Smith was handed the captaincy and this 'team' were to push the club into the most successful part of their history.

The game was, however, plagued with further problems due to the railway strike. Some of the less important games had to be postponed on account of teams being unable to get to their destinations. The Wanderers managed to reach Derby by means of private cars and two taxis in September 1919. They defeated The Rams 2–1, and in goal for the home side was James Kidd who, four days earlier, had been sold to County by Bolton.

In 1920–21 the Wanderers went all out to secure their first League Championship. In the space of a few weeks they twice broke their transfer record in securing full-back John Elvey for £2,500 from Luton Town and David Jack for £3,500 from Plymouth. Attendances were also on the up, with the average increasing by some 5,000 on the previous season.

Despite always being in the race for the title and losing only three of the final 13 League games, they had to settle for third place behind Burnley and Manchester City, but it was enough to equal the club's best-ever position, while Joe Smith set a club record and equalled a Football League record with his 38 goals.

A sixth-place finish in 1921–22 was credible, but it was the FA Cup that caught the imagination of the Bolton public, with a then record attendance of 66,442 witnessing a 3–1 fourth-round defeat to Manchester City at Burnden. At the time, the receipts of £5,220 were the fourth largest ever in English football.

In 1923 Bolton Wanderers were ensured a permanent place in the annals of football with victory in the first-ever FA Cup Final to be held at Wembley Stadium. The season had

Dick Pym was ever present in 1922–23.

begun with poor results and disruption when centre-forward Frank Roberts joined Manchester City after being suspended by the Wanderers for taking over the management of licensed premises which was against club policy. The club acted swiftly to replace Roberts with the signing of John Smith from Glasgow Rangers, and he scored an 89th-minute winner against Manchester City on his debut.

The FA Cup run began with a 2–0 success at Norwich City in what was the Wanderers' first away win in the competition since 1905. Leeds were defeated and then Huddersfield Town knocked out after a replay. Walter Rowley, later to manage the club, was sent off in the original game and received a six-week ban from the FA.

David Jack netted the only goal of the game against Charlton and then scored in the 46th minute to secure a 1–0 semi-final win over Sheffield United at Old Trafford before a crowd of 72,000. After reaching the Final, only five League points were taken from nine games, 'keeper Dick Pym being the only ever-present in those and throughout the season.

On 28 April 1923 Bolton took to the field with then Second Division West Ham United for what became the White Horse Final at the new Wembley Stadium. The greatest-ever crowd at an FA Cup Final, estimated to be over 150,000, were pushed back behind the touchline by a

John Smith, the second player to score at Wembley Stadium.

police horse named Billy. David Jack became the first player to score in the new stadium and a second from John Smith brought the FA Cup back to Bolton for the first time.

Clubs were falling over themselves in an eagerness to entertain the FA Cup winners. A week after the Wembley success, the Wanderers won 8–0 at Chorley, where the home side paraded the Lancashire Combination Championship trophy alongside the FA Cup. A tour to Switzerland

Captains meet before the first FA Cup Final at Wembley. Joe Smith meets former Wanderer George Kay captain of West Ham.

The three Cups in Wanderers possession in April 1923; The Manchester Cup, The Lancashire Cup and The FA Cup.

was undertaken, with seven victories and a draw resulting, while back at Burnden Tom Buchan, a stalwart who had served throughout World War One, was given a free transfer for services rendered.

Seasons 1923–24 and 1924–25 saw the club chasing the elusive Championship but on both occasions fell just short of the mark, with a fourth and third placing respectively. Both seasons began poorly which in the final analysis cost the club the opportunity of winning

The Wanderers make their way down the steps at Wembley with the FA Cup.

the League. The closest they came was in 1925 when they finished just three points behind champions Huddersfield Town, losing just once in the final 10 League games of the season and stringing together 17 consecutive home League victories. Ironically, the Wanderers defeated Huddersfield at Burnden, drew at Leeds Road and knocked them out of the FA Cup just for good measure.

During this period the club continued to strengthen the playing staff. Rollo Jack, David's brother, arrived from Plymouth Argyle and £4,400 was spent on bringing centre-forward Joe Cassidy from Glasgow Celtic. His stay at Burnden was to be short-lived, he failed to displace John Smith and after 12 months was sold to Cardiff City for £3,500.

It was to be in the FA Cup that the Wanderers again excelled during 1926. Goals from David Jack were to prove invaluable in the early rounds. His strike defeated Accrington, although Bolton were down to 10 men for a long period after Ted Vizard had been sent off, and Jack's late equaliser earned a draw at Bournemouth. The South Coast club were beaten in the replay, and South Shields were shown the exit in the fifth round.

It needed three games for the Wanderers to see off Nottingham Forest and reach the semi-final where three first-half goals against Swansea Town sent the club to Wembley for the second time. Bolton were to face Manchester City, giving them the opportunity to avenge the Cup Final defeat of 1904, and it was Jack who once again proved his worth by scoring the only goal to again secure the FA Cup. On this occasion, however, the manic scenes of three years previous had been consigned to the history books with an all-ticket crowd of 91,447 at the game.

Joe Smith, who had captained the Wanderers to their two Cup successes, netted his 250th League goal for the club early the following season, but a Cup defeat by Cardiff City heralded changes in 1927. After 19 loyal years, Smith was transfer listed and joined Stockport County. His replacement was George Gibson, who came to Lancashire from Hamilton Academicals. Harold Blackmore was secured from Exeter City, the centre-forward being signed after scoring twice against Bolton in a friendly.

After seven years of consistent League position sprinkled with Cup success things took a turn for the worse during 1927–28 when, after 10 games and only one victory, the Wanderers found themselves at the bottom of the League for the first time since 1909–10.

Incredibly, there was a dramatic revival that lifted the club to fourth place by early February 1928, but it did not last and the slump heralded another change when John Smith was transferred to Bury for £1,590. He was replaced by Jim McClelland from Middlesbrough who joined for a fee of £6,800, and he netted eight goals in the final 10 games of the season.

Billy Butler, scorer in 1929
FA Cup Final.

Champion clogwalker Bob Carr
sets off to Wembley in 1929.

Bolton again secured the FA Cup in 1929. Such was the confidence among their own supporters that they would succeed, by the time they had reached the quarter-finals against Blackburn the club had already received £500 worth of Wembley ticket applications. In the Final they defeated Portsmouth thanks to two goals in the final twelve minutes from Billy Butler and Harold Blackmore.

Despite the Cup success, it had been a poor League campaign. The club had sold David Jack to Arsenal in a then record £10,750 transfer and were accused of financing the new Burnden Stand with the proceeds. They had again spent time at the bottom of the League before a late revival and had Harold Blackmore to thank as he was the major source of the team's goals that had steered them clear of relegation and to the Cup Final.

The early 1930s became a transitionary period for Bolton Wanderers, with comings and goings of younger players who were expected to immediately fill the boots of the 1920s 'old school', which in reality was an unenviable task. The halcyon days of the 1920s had been enjoyed but were now over as the star players' careers came to an end.

Dick Pym, Bob Howarth and 41-year-old Ted Vizard all came to the end of their Bolton careers during 1931, and this left the club with a number of positions requiring immediate attention if they were once again to become a force to be reckoned with. It was difficult to attract top players to Burnden with many of the staff being offered reduced terms. Only the top players could command £8 a week during the winter, whether playing or not, and summer wages were to cut to the bone.

Two players who arrived to take part in the fall and rise of the club during this period were Jack Milsom, a £1,750 buy from Rochdale and who eventually took over from Harold Blackmore who was sold to Middlesbrough, and Ray Westwood, a future England international.

Season 1932–33 proved to be a crossroads for the club. Burnden Park held its largest recorded crowd when 69,912 saw Manchester City run out 4–2 winners in a fifth-round FA Cup tie, yet four days later only 3,101 turned up to see the Wanderers defeat Portsmouth 4–1. This proved to be the lowest recorded crowd for a League game on the ground until 1983.

After some near misses the club were relegated, thus ending a run of 22 years in the top flight. The Wanderers went into the last game of the season needing to defeat Leeds United at Burnden and hope results elsewhere went in their favour to have a stay of execution.

Leeds were crushed 5–0, Jack Milsom netting a first-half hat-trick, but all three struggling rivals also won leaving the Wanderers and Blackpool to face Second Division football. Despite relegation the club had made a profit and announced that an open cheque book was available to sign players.

Promotion at the first attempt was missed by a solitary point as the Wanderers finished third behind Preston North End and Grimsby Town. An FA Cup run which saw the club reach the sixth round had meant some focus had been lost on the League front, but after an exit at the hands of Portsmouth at Burnden, the Wanderers played out their final 12 League games without defeat.

Records tumbled during 1934–35 as the club made their way back to the big time as runners up to Brentford. The first seven games of the season were all won with just two goals being conceded. The first six had equalled a feat set in 1899 when the club had also won promotion and those, along with the last 12 from the previous season, set a then club record of 19 League games without defeat. Centre forward Jack Milsom had also set off well by scoring in 11 of the opening 12 games.

During this spell, on 6 October 1935, the Wanderers recorded their best ever League victory when the previous season's Third Division North champions Barnsley were thrashed 8–0 at Burnden. They were three down inside 39 minutes to a Ray Westwood hat-trick, the Wanderer having won his first England international cap the previous week against Wales. Incredibly, the final five goals did not arrive until the final six minutes of the game.

The team seemed to take their eye off the ball concerning the League with an impressive FA Cup run, and it needed three games to defeat Tottenham Hotspur in the fifth round. After winning at Everton in the sixth round, a home League game to Hull was lost along with leadership of the League.

The Wanderers lost out on a Wembley appearance when they went down 2–0 to West Brom in a semi-final replay at Stoke. The defeat had repercussions in that the following three League games were lost but, just as it seemed that they were again going to miss out, form returned and they secured the point needed on the final day of the season at Blackpool in a 1–1 draw. Ray Westwood scored Bolton's goal which set a then club record 96th League goal of the season and which was not bettered until 1997.

Burnden Park's capacity was increased to 70,000 for the return to Division One thanks to the concreting of the Great Lever End and the removal of what remained of the cycle track. Local brewery, Magee's, supplied clocks that were installed on top of the Manchester Road and Burnden Stands. They remained there for 40 years.

The following seasons saw the Wanderers back to their inconsistent form and battles to hold on to their newly won status. In March 1936 a 7–0 reverse at Manchester City equalled the club's worst-ever League defeat. The experienced Harry Goslin and Alec Finney had been left out of the side, while Fred Swift, in the Wanderers goal, was opposed by his more illustrious brother, Frank, in goal for City. Bolton got over the shock to take five points from the next three games which virtually guaranteed survival.

A spate of injuries was to cause problems during 1936–37. The jinx even struck G.T. Taylor when he ended a consecutive run of 290 first-class games for both Notts County and Bolton. To stem the problem the Wanderers made four major signings. Alf Anderson and Alec Carruthers arrived from Hibernian and Falkirk, while centre-forward John Calder,

Autographs from the 1938 team.

who was the most expensive at £4,000, signed from Morton. Harry Hubbick, who was to be a wartime stalwart also arrived from Burnley.

It proved effective in keeping the club in the top flight by a two-point margin, but the loss for the year of £12,000 was the largest in the Football League and to help offset this George Eastham was sold to Brentford for £4,500.

The club had early-season Championship aspirations in 1937–38, heading the table for a number of weeks, but in the final analysis they fell short of the mark, although a finishing position of seventh proved to be a marked improvement. Jack Milsom left the club at his own request to join Manchester City, and he was replaced by England international George Hunt for a £4,000 fee from Arsenal, and he scored six minutes into his debut in a 3–0 home win over West Brom. The club were intent, however, on keeping their star players, turning down a £12,000 offer for Ray Westwood from Chelsea after he had scored a hat-trick against them in a 5–5 draw at Burnden.

Further team strengthening continued but was to prove for nothing when, after three games of the 1939–40 season, war was declared. The previous season had seen many professional footballers join the Territorial Army or other National Service organizations, spending their leisure time preparing for what appeared to be the inevitable.

On 6 September 1939 the Football League Management Committee met at Crewe and officially suspended League activities. Contracts between players and clubs were automatically terminated. The Government placed a ban on the assembly of crowds, but on 14 September it was announced that friendly matches could be arranged, even in areas banned by the Home Office under defence regulations, providing the local police gave their approval. Therefore, football ceased for only a matter of days.

Two clubs had signed up for army or service duty virtually en masse, one being the Wanderers, the other being West Ham. Fifteen professionals from the Wanderers had enlisted in May 1939 and, when war was declared, all were immediately called up with the exception of Syd Jones and Charlie Hanks who were too young. They joined up with the 53rd field regiment RA (Bolton Artillery) and spent much of the war together virtually as a team on many foreign fields, being involved in the Dunkirk evacuation and the Middle East and Italian campaigns. Of the 35 players on the staff, 32 eventually went into uniform, the other three going into either the coal mines or munitions factories.

The Wanderers joined the North West Regional League, but interest was minimal. In December 1939 just 1,509 were at Burnden to see Bolton entertain the 53rd RA who had returned home on leave. The current Wanderers against the Old Wanderers ended in a 3–3 draw, but the footballing public of Bolton wanted nothing short of proper League Football and the FA Cup to give them excitement and interest.

At this time the club were taken to court by a season ticket holder who had claimed a refund due to not being able to see Football League games for which he had paid. The

Wanderers won the test case, allowing ticket holders into the regional tournament. If they had lost it would have cost many clubs up and down the country thousands of pounds they could ill afford.

A loss was sustained on every home game, and it was increasingly difficult to recruit a team to represent the club. The club announced that they would not take part in any organised competition in 1940–41, effectively closing down, although the players continued to play by guesting for other clubs, while Burnden Park was used by the Education Authority and the stands by the Ministry of Supply to store food.

The Wanderers returned to action on Christmas Day 1940 with a friendly at Blackpool who were also opening again after closure. On 22 March 1941, a surprise change was made in the Wanderers attack for the visit of Bury. Nathaniel Lofthouse, a former Folds Road and Bolton town team centre-forward appeared for the first time, aged 15 years 207 days. Bolton won 5–1, with Lofthouse grabbing his side's fourth and fifth goals to begin a relationship with the club that continued for the rest of his life.

The job of recruiting a team each week fell on the shoulders of Charles Foweraker and he had numerous problems. He had to rely to a great extent on amateurs under military age or soldiers on leave. A game at Bradford in March 1942 had to be cancelled when only Lofthouse and Hubbick could be recruited with the release of guest players in the services being impossible.

Match return for the game versus Bury, Nat Lofthouse's debut, 1941.

THIS FORM TO BE COMPLETED AND POSTED TO THE LEAGUE SECRETARY WITHIN SIX DAYS OF THE GAME BEING PLAYED

WAR TIME MATCHES

THE FOOTBALL LEAGUE

PERCENTAGE OF NETT TAKINGS IN ACCORDANCE WITH RULE

RECEIPTS.	£	s.	d.	PAYMENTS.	£	s.	d.			
Date *March 22nd 1941*				Amusement Tax	18	11	9			
Match: *Bolton Wndrs v. Bury*				Referee and Linesmen ...	1	8	6			
				Printing, Posting and Advertising	2	17	·			
Gross Taking—Ground, Stands, Enclosures, etc. (including Tax)	84	15	2	Gatemen	3	6	6			
				Police		12	·			
				Visiting Team's Expenses	1	7	·			
				Home Club	26	17	11			
				Visiting	26	17	11			
				Football Lge 5%	2	16	7			
								5% to League £ 2 s. 16 d. 7		
TOTAL	84	15	2	TOTAL ...	84	15	2			

I herewith enclose Cheque value £ ; : : A separate Cheque to be forwarded for each Match.
"Percentage Cheques **must** be paid to the League Secretary within six days of the game being played."

Secretary ___C C Foweraker___ Club ___BOLTON WANDERERS___

Date ___March 22/41___

THE GUARDIAN PRESS, FISHERGATE, PRESTON

In the same year the Wanderers recruited the services of a young Tom Finney from Preston North End as a guest for game at Burnley. Another Preston player, Bill Shankly, had promised to give the Wanderers the benefit of his services, but he was transferred to Scotland with his unit. While there he turned out for East Fife but wrote to Foweraker explaining his disappointment in his inability to become a wartime Wanderer. The following season he managed to appear in two games in a Bolton shirt while on leave.

The Wanderers of the 53rd RA had built up a stout reputation and in the spring of 1943 were challenged to a game by a team of Poles, the self-styled champions of Persia and Iraq, the game taking place at Kifri in Iraq. The team, captained as usual by Harry Goslin, ran out 4–1 winners, providing valuable entertainment for the excited crowd of sport-starved soldiers.

Unfortunately, this was to be one of Goslin's last games. Lieutenant Goslin was wounded in action while with the 8th Army Central Mediterranean Forces and died on 18 December 1943. He was a popular captain and exemplary athlete who had inspired the Wanderers staff to join the Territorial Army in 1939. He had since led a bunch of them in France, escaping from Dunkirk in 1940, Africa and Italy, and his influence was not only a loss to the club but also to King and Country. Another fatality that struck the club was that of young winger Walter Sidebottom, who lost his life when his ship was torpedoed in the English Channel.

In August 1944, Charles Foweraker handed over the reigns to Walter Rowley, and six months later the club were attracting record wartime crowds as they won the Football League North Cup by defeating Manchester United over two legs. Lofthouse had now made his mark with some important goals but the discovery of the likes of Willie Moir and Malcolm Barrass also bode well for the future and the return of League normality.

On the 2nd June 1945 the Wanderers visited Chelsea for the North v South Cup winners Final. A crowd of 45,000 saw Bolton come from behind to win 2–1 although no trophy was presented for winning the game and the players received savings certificates instead of medals.

Football in general ran into a boom period after the war and the Wanderers were no exception. Despite a successful season on the field, the 1945–46 campaign can only be remembered for the loss of 33 lives on 9 March 1946 when, during an FA Cup sixth-round second-leg tie at Burnden against Stoke City, barriers collapsed causing not only death but injury to many. A final League position of third and an FA Cup semi-final appearance were overshadowed by those events.

The Football League returned to normality in August 1946 when the Wanderers opened the season with a 4–3 defeat at Chelsea before a crowd of 62,850 which was the best of the day. After a midweek win at Stoke, Portsmouth were the first visitors to reopen League proceedings at Burnden. A crowd of 33,597, compared to the 12,992 who attended the fixture in 1939, saw Willie Moir hit the winner two minutes from time. Five Bolton players remained from the pre-war team.

Despite some initial promise, the seasons immediately after the war were disappointing, with poor FA Cup performances and worrying League positions prevailing. Defeat to Second Division Manchester City in the Cup prompted a crowd of only 4,280 for the next game against Leeds in February 1947, and that gate stood as a post war low record until 1983.

News of the World reports the 1946 disaster.

In 1948 a Willie Moir hat-trick helped secure the Lancashire Cup with a 5–1 success against Southport at Haig Avenue. The County Cup did not appear in the Wanderers trophy cabinet again until 1988. Moir scored 25 League goals during 1948–49, a total that made him the First Division's leading goalscorer. Indeed, individually, the club's playing staff began to gain recognition.

Bobby Langton, who had joined the club for a record £20,000 fee from Preston, was selected for the Football League alongside Nat Lofthouse. Moir and Langton opposed each other in the Scotland v England clash at Hampden, while in the close season of 1950, Lofthouse and goalkeeper Stan Hansen went on the FA tour of Canada. Trainer Bill Ridding also went to Brazil with the England World Cup party as his country's chief trainer.

In October 1950 the directors accepted the resignation, due to ill health, of secretary-manager Walter Rowley. It had been Rowley's 39th season at Burnden and, ironically, his last had seen the foundations laid for the club to go on to greater things, especially after ending a run of almost two years without an away win in the League the previous month, when a Moir goal had secured a 1–0 victory at Aston Villa.

Nat Lofthouse was recognised at full international level when he led England's forward line against Yugoslavia at Highbury in November 1950. He fulfilled his promise by scoring both England's goals in a 2–2 draw in a game that was to be the first of 33 international appearances.

Bill Ridding was put in temporary charge and took over officially in February 1951 with the duties of chief coach going to ex-Bolton stalwart George Taylor. His assistant was another ex-Wanderer in George Hunt, who had returned to the coaching staff at Burnden after his playing days had ended at Sheffield Wednesday in 1948.

The Wanderers again put themselves in the Championship frame in 1951–52 by taking 11 points from the opening six games before having to settle for a finishing place of fifth. Further spending came in the shape of George Higgins from Blackburn and Harold Hassall from Huddersfield Town for a then club record fee of £27,000.

Nat Lofthouse, 1953 Footballer of the Year.

There was also the introduction of two home-grown players who were to serve the club admirably. Firstly, Doug Holden appeared on the left wing, having signed as a part-time professional before completing his National Service. Then there was Ray Parry, who began the season in the fourth team before progressing through the ranks to make his debut in a 5–1 defeat at Wolves in October 1951 when only 15 years 267 days old to become the Wanderers' youngest player to appear in a League game.

In 1953 the Wanderers fielded an all international forward line for the first time since the 1924–25 season. Hughes (Northern Ireland), Moir (Scotland), Lofthouse (England), Hassall (England) and Langton (England) were the players, with only Hassall having failed to win a cap while with the club, a fact that was rectified later in the year.

It was in the FA Cup that the Wanderers gained recognition that year in what became known as the legendary 'Matthews Final' when Blackpool ran out 4–3 winners at Wembley. On the evening prior to the Final, Nat Lofthouse was awarded the Footballer of the Year trophy, having scored in every round of the FA Cup, a record he kept the following day. But, after the Wanderers had led 3–1 with 20 minutes remaining, it was a disappointed Bolton team that returned home for the first time from Wembley without the Cup.

The mid-1950s saw Bill Ridding have to make changes from some of the old guard. Stan Hansen and Willie Moir departed, while Harold Hassall had to retire through injury. Fortunately the club's youth policy was starting to pay dividends with a Central League Championship success for the first time in the club's history in 1955 and, a semi-final appearance in the FA Youth Cup the following year, losing to eventual winners Manchester United.

Season 1956–57 saw Eddie Hopkinson make the first of his record 578 first-class appearances for the club, while Manchester United, the Busby Babes, who were to win the League Championship, were defeated 2–0 in both League games by the Wanderers.

The floodlights at Burnden Park were officially opened on 14 October 1957 when a crowd of 21,058 saw a 1–1 draw with Heart of Midlothian. The lights, which were switched on by club chairman Harry Warburton, saw further renowned visitors the following month when Russian Army side CDSA were beaten 3–0 before a crowd of 34,139.

It was in the FA Cup that the Wanderers, with a team that had been put together by Ridding and had cost nothing but the £10 each

Nat Lofthouse lifs aloft the FA Cup with Bryan Edwards and John Higgins.

FA Cup and Charity Shield winners, 1958.

signing on fees, once again tasted success in 1958. The sixth-round tie against Wolves was perhaps the greatest hurdle that Bolton got over on their way to Wembley. The game was a great battle, with neither side giving anything away and, despite being outplayed for long periods, Bolton held on to their 2–1 advantage in an epic struggle against the team that won the League that year.

In the semi-final the Wanderers were without the injured Nat Lofthouse against Second Division Blackburn Rovers at Maine Road. His stand in, Ralph Gubbins, performed admirably in his captain's absence by scoring both goals as they came from behind to register a 2–1 win.

In the Final at Wembley they took on a decimated Manchester United side that had a wave of national sympathy backing them after the Munich air disaster. Nat Lofthouse became the club's Wembley hero by scoring both goals in a 2–0 win, the second of which became a major talking point when he charged both the ball and the United 'keeper into the back of the net. The Cup was back in Bolton for the fourth time.

Despite the Wembley success, the opening game of the 1958–59 season attracted a crowd of only 25,922 to Burnden, the second lowest in the First Division, for the Wanderers 4–0 defeat of Leeds United. In October 1958 the FA Charity Shield was added to the FA Cup when League champions Wolves were beaten 4–1 at Burnden.

In 1959 the Wanderers reached the sixth round of the FA Cup before losing to eventual winners Nottingham Forest at the City Ground, while in the League Bolton only failed to equal their best ever position of third to Arsenal, the Gunners having a better goal average thanks to a 6–1 win over the Wanderers at Highbury.

The following season Nat Lofthouse, Bryan Edwards, Tommy Banks and Eddie Hopkinson were all missing for long periods through injury, in Bank's case he injured his ankle in a friendly at Hibernian. Despite this, and a poor start in the opening six games, the club managed to finish in sixth position, only seven points behind champions Burnley. Lofthouse's presence would surely not have left the Wanderers with a goals for record that saw only Nottingham Forest and Luton Town score fewer, yet defensively only Tottenham had a better record.

The early 1960s were a time of change not only at Bolton Wanderers but also for football in general with the abolition of the maximum wage. Wanderers youth product, Freddie Hill, scored the only goal of the game at Blackpool in September 1960 in what was the first televised Football League game to be shown live. The Football League Cup competition also commenced with the Wanderers reaching the fourth round in the inaugural season.

Lofthouse returned to the side for the first time in over a year in October 1960, but on 17 December 1960 he received a leg injury in a 2–2 draw at Birmingham and it effectively ended his illustrious playing career. One of his last goals for the club came the previous month in a 3–1 home win against Manchester City. In the same game a 16-year-old

Wyn Davies, signed from Wrexham, 1962.

youngster, Francis Lee, made his debut and also got his name on the scoresheet. Other promising youngsters who that were thrown into the rigours of First Division football were Warwick Rimmer and Charlie Cooper.

The forward line went through a transitional period after the retirement of Lofthouse. Results were also anything but stable, and there were a number of comings and goings. Irish international forward Bill McAdams came to Burnden for £15,000 from Manchester City and, despite scoring 26 goals in 44 League appearances, he remained for only one year before moving to Leeds United. Two other signings that were less successful were Brian Pilkington from Burnley and Ron McGarry from Workington. A record fee of £35,000 was received by the Wanderers from Everton for the services of Dennis Stevens, his subsequent success at Goodison included a League Championship medal.

Within two days of Stevens's departure, 19-year-old centre-forward Wyn Davies was recruited from Wrexham for £20,000, with the Wanderers reserve striker Ernie Phythian going to the Racecourse Ground as part of the deal.

Season 1962–63 proved to be another difficult one for the Wanderers as they fought tooth and nail to hold on to their First Division status. The season, however, is best remembered not for football but for the weather, the game virtually closing down between the middle of December and beginning of March due to the arctic conditions.

After a 1–0 home win over Championship-chasing Tottenham on 8 December 1962, Peter Deakin netting an 88th-minute winner, Bolton did not kick a ball in anger again until 16 February 1963 at Arsenal. Three days prior to the visit to Highbury the Wanderers visited the Republic of Ireland for some match practice, losing a friendly game against Manchester United in Cork.

The third round of the FA Cup saw the Wanderers drawn against Sheffield United at Bramall Lane. The game was played at the 13th attempt on 6 March 1963 the Blades winning 3–1. Bolton had the opportunity to get quick revenge as United visited Burnden for a League game three days later. It was the first game on Burnden for three months, and a Freddie Hill hat-trick secured the points as the Wanderers fielded their youngest-ever forward line. Lee (18), Hill (23), Davies (20), Bromley (16) and Butler (18) took to the field, with Bromley making his League debut after just six Central League games.

Bolton were saved from relegation with two home victories in the space of three days. FA Cup finalists Leicester City were defeated 2–0 and Liverpool by 1–0, but it had been too close for comfort. It was obvious that, while the club's youngsters were full of potential, they were not, as yet, ready to play regular First Division football. Attendances were not big enough to produce the income for the club to go out and buy experienced players while the abolition of the maximum wage was now causing a problem as the younger players were being courted by bigger clubs where they could earn more money.

Only four victories in the opening 26 League and Cup games of 1963–64 were to prove decisive in ending the club's First Division status. Of the team that opened the season, only Roy Hartle proved to be consistent, missing only one game. A number of players lost form and no fewer than eight sustained long-term injury.

An early season game at Arsenal perhaps typified the situation. Bolton held a 3–1 half-time lead before the Gunners struck back to level matters. Brian Pilkington then missed a penalty, Arsenal scored a last-minute winner and 'keeper Eddie Hopkinson received a kidney injury that was to keep him out for almost two months.

A Francis Lee penalty saved the Wanderers' blushes in the FA Cup at Southern League Bath City, but the replay at Burnden proved more comfortable. Back in the League, the Wanderers found themselves cut adrift in 21st position during March 1964 until a last-ditch attempt to stave off relegation was put together when 10 points from a possible 12 were won.

The Wanderers needed to win their final home game, against a mid-table Wolves side, to avoid the drop. The game took place on a Friday evening, so as not to clash with the local Holcombe Brook races. Just when it mattered Bolton slumped, going down 4–0, and Birmingham took the initiative the following day by defeating Sheffield United to assure their safety and to end Bolton's run of 29 years in the top flight. Ipswich Town accompanied the Wanderers into the Second Division.

For the first season out of the top flight since 1935 the team was built upon a young side supported by the experience of Hopkinson, Hartle and Edwards. The challenge to make a quick return was impressive for, after losing the first home game, nine consecutive wins at Burnden were put together with 30 goals finding the opponents' net. Francis Lee proved to be in good form with 16 goals in 14 games.

A fifth round FA Cup tie against Liverpool at Burnden attracted 57,207 and was only settled four minutes from time in favour of the visitors by a goal from Ian Callaghan, and they went on to win the trophy. Unfortunately, the team's worst run of the season coincided with the promotion run in and, with only two victories in the final eight games, it left them six points adrift of runners up Northampton Town in third place.

In 1965 the Football League allowed a substitute to be brought on at any time for an injured player, and the first such appearance was at Burnden Park when Charlton Athletic's Keith Peacock took to the field as the Wanderers ran out 4–2 winners on the opening day

of the season. Gordon Taylor was Bolton's first number 12 to appear on the field when he came on in the club's 11th game of the season, a 3–2 home defeat by Southampton. Both Bolton goals were scored by local discovery Roy Greaves, who had made his debut the previous week at Leyton Orient.

Gordon Taylor, the Wanderers' first substitute, heads a 1965 team photograph.

The lack of success in regaining First Division status led to a number of major transfers involving the club. In 1966, John Byrom came in from Blackburn Rovers for £25,000, Wyn Davies left for Newcastle United for £80,000, having scored 12 goals in as many games and, a year later, Francis Lee moved to Manchester City for £60,000. Lee's last game in a Bolton shirt was in a 3–2 League Cup victory against Liverpool, having previously scored in six consecutive League games.

The sale of Lee prompted the Wanderers to go into what was then the biggest spending spree in the club's history. Half-back Gareth Williams was recruited from Cardiff City for £50,000 and, a fortnight later, a then club record of £70,000 was spent on Bolton-born winger Terry Wharton from Wolves.

Any thoughts of returning to the top flight had long since evaporated, and it was now a case of doing everything to avoid dropping into the Third Division for the first time ever.

For the start of the 1968–69 season Nat Lofthouse took over as temporary manager from Bill Ridding who retired to concentrate on his physiotherapy business. Another former player, Ted Rothwell, became secretary. Lofthouse was officially appointed team manager on 18 December 1968, with the club producing a late flurry to avoid the drop.

Bolton changed to an all white kit for 1969–70 season in which Eddie Hopkinson ended his League career through injury after clocking up 519 League appearances for the club. A major coup was the signing of World Cup-winner Roger Hunt from Liverpool in December 1969, for a fee of £32,000, but he could do little to prevent the slump.

The following year proved to be traumatic. In November 1970, Jimmy McIlroy was appointed team manager, with Lofthouse taking over administrative responsibilities.

1968 team line up. Back row: Jones, Hulme, Farrimond, Hill, Cooper, Hopkinson. Middle row: D. Hatton, R. Hatton, Rimmer, Byrom, Williams. Front row: Taylor, Wharton, Ritson, Bromley, Phillips, Lennard, Greaves.

1973 Third Division champions.

McIlroy resigned 18 days after taking the job, leaving Lofthouse again in charge of team affairs. Off the field, financial problems hung over the club, there had been a poor response to the share and loan notes issue and the board of directors had to give personal guarantees to keep the club afloat.

On 15 January 1971 the Wanderers fielded one of their youngest-ever sides with an average age of 20. It included seven teenagers, one of whom, Paul Jones, made his debut. They came from behind to defeat promotion chasing Sheffield United at Burnden, but it proved to be the last League victory of the season.

Jimmy Meadows came and went in the managerial merry-go-round and relegation to the Third Division for the first time was finally confirmed with a 4–1 defeat at Charlton Athletic with two games of the season remaining. Local rivals Blackburn Rovers accompanied the Wanderers into the lower reaches.

During the summer Jimmy Armfield was appointed manager, and he instilled some confidence back into the club, reverting back to the traditional white shirts and navy shorts and making some experienced signings to add to the young talent that was to prove the backbone of the team in the next few seasons.

In his first season Armfield built a strong defence, the Wanderers' goals against record being bettered only by champions Aston Villa and third place Bournemouth as the free fall was halted. The best Cup receipts for over 10 years were also collected with an inspiring League Cup run which included a 3–0 win over Manchester City at Burnden before 42,039.

The 1972–73 season saw the tide turn with the club returning to the Second Division as champions and also reaching the fifth round of the FA Cup. The youth policy, having been established by Lofthouse through a financial need, proved to be the foundation of the promotion drive. The Third Division Championship trophy was presented to Warwick Rimmer after the last game of the season in which the club had collected a then record of 61 points.

In October 1974, having re-established the club in the Second Division, Jimmy Armfield left to take on the challenge of managing Leeds United and Ian Greaves took over the reigns. Greaves twice took the club to within a whisker of a return to the top flight, to a successful FA Cup run and an appearance in the 1977 League Cup semi-finals where Everton edged them out of a Wembley trip.

It all came together in 1977–78 when Greaves complimented the team with the signing of Frank Worthington, after a loan spell, from Leicester City for a then club record £90,000. He secured his place in Bolton folklore when on 26 April 1978 he scored the goal that earned a 1–0 win against Blackburn Rovers at Ewood Park that took the club back into the First Division.

The environs of Ewood and all routes back to Bolton became the location for late-night parties as two years of near misses were put to rest. The following Saturday the Second

Frank Worthington, First Division leading goalscorer in 1979.

Division Championship was won with a goalless draw against Fulham at Burnden.

In the latter weeks of the season the club record transfer fee was extended when Alan Gowling joined for a £120,000 fee from Newcastle United. He teamed up well with Worthington to cause numerous problems for First Division defences the following season, and it was Worthington who won the golden boot for topping the Division goalscoring charts at the end of what was a satisfactory return to the big time thanks to some consistent home results. Worthington also won the Goal of the Season for his spectacular effort against Ipswich Town at Burnden.

For 1979–80, experienced campaigners in defender Dave Clement, for £150,000 from Queen's Park Rangers, and midfielder Len Cantello, for a record £350,000, from West Brom looked to have strengthened the squad to consolidate the club's position in the top flight. After taking four points and being unbeaten in the opening three games the wheels came off and the season turned out to be a disaster.

Departures included Worthington, Meil McNab, Roy Greaves and Willie Morgan, while the big-money transfers failed to produce the performances that had been their trademark at previous clubs. A number of youngsters got their chance but could not force any results on a consistent basis.

After an FA Cup fourth-round win over Halifax Ian Greaves was replaced by his assistant Stan Anderson, with former full-back Tony Dunne appointed as coach. A run of 24 League games without a win finally came to an end when a Neil Whatmore goal defeated Nottingham Forest at Burnden Park but relegation, after just two seasons back in the top flight, was confirmed with five games remaining.

The club never looked like bouncing back quickly, despite spending £150,000 on Brian Kidd from Everton and £180,000 on Dusan Nikolic from Red Star Belgrade, and it was not until the penultimate game of the season that the Wanderers were mathematically safe from a consecutive relegation. In November 1980 the club wore sponsored shirts for the first time when 'Knight Security' adorned them in a 1–1 draw with Grimsby Town at Burnden.

George Mulhall, who had returned as coach, took over the managerial reigns from Anderson but the

Len Cantello became Wanderers' record signing in 1979.

The first team shot with sponsored shirts in 1980.

financial realities of attempting to halt the slide were kicking in. Neil Whatmore was sold to Birmingham City to join his former teammate Frank Worthington for what was then the clubs record transfer receipt of £340,000. Some of that was spent on bringing in Tony Henry from Manchester City and Jeff Chandler from Leeds United, but it was again a difficult season.

A disastrous League run culminated in a 7–1 defeat at FA Cup finalists Queen's Park Rangers on their plastic pitch at Loftus Road leaving the Wanderers to win their last two home games to stand any chance of avoiding the drop. Both Derby County and Sheffield Wednesday were defeated in nervous fashion as relegation was avoided by two points and this prompted a further change in the manager's chair.

John McGovern, who had played under Brian Clough at Derby and Nottingham Forest, where he captained the European Cup-winning team, became the Wanderers' player-manager in June 1982. Unfortunately, little changed in terms of results, and relegation to Division Three came on the final day of the season. It was a bitter coincidence that relegation was suffered at Charlton Athletic and by an identical 4–1 scoreline as had been inflicted in 1971.

It was a young and inexperienced squad that opened the club's Third Division campaign in August 1983. The emergence of Tony Caldwell, a £2,000 buy from Horwich RMI, was a highlight with his five goals in an 8–1 home win over Walsall equalling the club record for goals in a game. The performances and results kept the club on the fringe of promotion for a long period but that evaporated late in the season and that form continued into 1984–85.

After a first-round FA Cup defeat at Hull City, and the club lying in 18th place in the Third Division, McGovern parted company in January 1985, with former Wanderers 'keeper Charlie Wright taking over after a temporary period in charge. After a poor start to the following season, despite bringing in experienced players at that level, Wright left the club in November 1986.

The Wanderers then appointed former Liverpool and England full-back Phil Neal as player-manager, who took on his first managerial job. At the end of his first term in charge he took the club to Wembley for the first time in 28 years in the Freight Rover Trophy Final. Despite defeat to Bristol City, confidence was high for the start of the 1986–87 season, but it proved to be a false dawn when the club finished in a relegation Play-off position after scoring just seven goals in the final 17 League games.

Aldershot won the two-legged tie to send the Wanderers into the Fourth Division for the first time in their history. Neal made a number of changes on the playing front with Asa Hartford, Tony Caldwell and George Oghani all leaving Burnden while old boys John Thomas and Jeff Chandler returned. The experienced Mick Brown came in as coach and £30,000 was invested in bringing in Robbie Savage from Bradford City. It was to be his goal in the final game of the season that gave Bolton victory at Wrexham to win the third promotion spot out of the basement Division after losing just twice in the final 13 League games.

The momentum continued into season 1988–89. A run of 20 undefeated League and Cup games saw a top-half finish and took the club to Wembley in the Sherpa Van Trophy, the Wanderers coming from behind to win 4–1 against Torquay United.

The Play-offs were reached in 1990, but the form shown to reach them evaporated by the time Notts County ran out 3–1 winners in the two-legged semi-final.

For the second season in succession the Wanderers reached the Play-offs and put together a club record 23 unbeaten League games to get there. On this occasion they went one better by reaching Wembley after defeating Bury 2–1 on aggregate in the semi-finals, only to lose to Tranmere where the winning goal came in extra-time to condemn Bolton to another season in Division Three.

The failure at Wembley carried over into 1991–92 and, despite a good FA Cup run that saw a fifth round extra-time defeat at Southampton, the final 11 games of the season produced just one win, and Phil Neal ended his six and a half years tenure in charge.

Bruce Rioch was appointed manager for 1992–93 and Colin Todd as assistant, but by the middle of October the Wanderers were lying in 16th place in Division Three. The turnaround came when John McGinlay, who had arrived from Millwall to partner Andy Walker up front, scored his first goal for the club in a 2–2 draw at Chester City after being two down at half-time. That result set the Wanderers off on a 15-game unbeaten run in League and Cup.

A fantastic FA Cup run saw them reach the fifth round before losing at Derby County but not before knocking out holders Liverpool at Anfield in a third-round replay and Wolves at Molineux in the fourth round.

That form carried over into the League and a magnificent run of consistency that produced fifteen wins and just one defeat in the final 19 games saw the Wanderers win promotion as Second Division runners-up to Stoke City on the final day of the season. A crowd of 21,720, the clubs best League gate since April 1980, saw a John McGinlay penalty win promotion and create a then club record points haul of 90.

John McGinlay scores the penalty against Preston to win promotion in 1993.

John McGinlay, David Lee and Andy Walker after the 2–0 FA Cup third-round replay win at Liverpool.

The team was strengthened with the arrival of Alan Thompson and Owen Coyle, along with a return for Jimmy Phillips. It was to be in the FA Cup that the club again received national acclaim by reaching the sixth round after a near miss in the first round when non-League Gretna led 2–1 at Burnden with 11 minutes remaining. Wins against Everton at Goodison and Arsenal at Highbury in replays were followed by a Burnden win over Aston Villa before the run came to an end in the quarter-finals against Oldham Athletic.

The club also had their first taste of competitive European football in 1993–94 when they played in the Anglo-Italian tournament and, despite being unbeaten, just missed out on a Final appearance at Wembley.

Once again there was some Cup success in 1995 when the Wanderers reached the Final of the Coca-Cola Cup. On this occasion, however, it was mixed with League success built on a superb home record, a run of 26 consecutive unbeaten League and Cup games being registered in what was Burnden Park's 100th season.

Liverpool ran out winners 2–1 at Wembley in the Coca-Cola Cup Final, but the Wanderers recovered to qualify for the Play-offs. Wolves were beaten in the semi-final thanks to a memorable performance in the second leg at Burnden to overcome a 2–1 deficit from Molineux in a game that saw Peter Shilton become the oldest player to wear a Bolton shirt at 45 years, 239 days of age.

The Play-off Final became one of the most memorable games in the club's history when Reading stormed into a two-goal lead inside 12 minutes. They had the opportunity of making it three from the penalty spot just before half-time, but Keith Branagan's save from

Gudni Bergsson, Owen Coyle and John McGinlay celebrate the Play-off win over Reading.

Stuart Lovell's spot-kick proved to be the watershed as the second half saw Bolton take command. Goals from Owen Coyle and Fabian De Freitas levelled the scores late on, and the Wanderers went on to win 4–3 in extra-time with further goals from De Freitas and Mixu Paatelainen.

For the club's return to the top flight, and first season in the Premier League, Colin Todd and Roy McFarland were put in charge after the departure of Bruce Rioch to Arsenal during the close season. Despite some good home successes against the likes of champions Blackburn Rovers and Arsenal, the Wanderers found themselves at the foot of the League by New Year. McFarland left the club, Todd taking sole charge and, despite a late flurry, the club's relegation was confirmed after the penultimate game, a 1–0 home defeat to Southampton, and the last top-flight game to be played on Burnden Park.

The disappointment of just one season back in the top level was tempered in 1996–97 in what was the final season at Burnden Park. Colin Todd led the Wanderers to what could arguably be described as the club's most enthralling season in the 102 years at the ground.

Only four League defeats all season, Ipswich being the only League winners at Burnden, along with a club record 100 League goals, 98 points and 28 League wins. All this culminated in the First Division League Championship trophy being presented after the final game at Burnden when the Wanderers came back from a half-time deficit to win 4–1 against Charlton, with John McGinlay scoring the last-ever Burnden goal.

There was a mixed set of results in Cup competitions at Burnden. The Coca-Cola Cup saw Chelsea despatched by 2–1, and Tottenham by 6–1, to set a club record victory in the competition before Wimbledon ended the run in the quarter-finals. In the FA Cup it was giant killers Chesterfield who became the last visiting club to win at Burnden when a Kevin Davies hat-trick ended Bolton hopes with a 3–2 fourth-round win.

John McGinlay scores the final goal at Burnden Park.

The Reebok Stadium opened on 1 September 1997 when Everton were the opponents, just as they had been the first League visitors to Burnden back in 1895. A scoreless draw resulted, but a TV audience of millions saw Gerry Taggart's second-half header go over the line before being cleared, but of more concern at the time was the broken leg sustained by Robbie Elliott who had joined in a club record £2.5 million transfer from Newcastle.

The Reebok Stadium at night.

Dean Holdsworth extended that transfer record when he joined from Wimbledon for £3.5 million, and home results kept the Wanderers in with a chance of holding their Premier League place right up until the final day of the season. Unfortunately, the Wanderers went down 2–0 at Chelsea, while Everton drew at home to Coventry to save themselves and send the Wanderers down on goal difference.

Season 1998–99 saw debuts to two players who were to prove stalwarts and were still playing Premier League football for the club in 2011. Jussi Jääskeläinen had joined from Vaasa in 1997, playing the first of over 500 games in a 2–2 draw at Crystal Palace in August 1998, and Ricardo Gardner, who joined from Harbour View after the 1998 World Cup, scored on his League debut in a 3–2 win at West Brom in September 1998.

An unbeaten 11-game start to the season augured well for a quick return to the Premier League, but Bolton had to settle for the Play-offs where a semi-final success on away goals against Ipswich Town sent them to Wembley where Watford ran out 2–0 winners to end any hopes of a swift return.

A season of change followed. Colin Todd resigned in September 1999. The club had taken just six points from seven games and crowds had dipped to below 12,000. The

Team line up for the start of the 2000–01 season.

financial implications of not getting back into the Premier League were kicking in with Per Frandsen being sold to Blackburn for £1.75 million. Chairman Gordon Hargreaves stepped down and Phil Gartside took over, Eddie Davies joined the board and was to take overall control four years later. Sam Allardyce was appointed as manager on 19 October 1999, coincidentally the 45th birthday of the former Wanderers centre-half.

On the field the Wanderers had an incredible season but ended with nothing to show for it. In the semi-final of the Worthington Cup, Tranmere ran out 4–0 winners over the two legs, but Bolton recovered to have a great FA Cup run. An Eidur Gudjohnsen goal defeated Charlton at the Reebok to secure a first FA Cup semi-final since 1958 against Aston Villa at Wembley. A goalless draw after extra-time saw Villa run out 4–1 winners on penalties with Dean Holdsworth, who had missed a fantastic chance to win the game in the dying minutes of normal time, the only Bolton player converting.

The final disappointment came when, after reaching the First Division Play-offs, they again lost out in a semi-final, this time by 7–5 on aggregate to Ipswich Town. The second leg at Portman Road went into extra-time and saw the home side awarded three penalties while the Wanderers ended the game with nine men after two red cards.

There was plenty of summer trading in 2000 as the club looked to balance the books. Eidur Gudjohnsen and Claus Jensen left for fees of almost £8 million to Chelsea and Charlton respectively, while Per Frandsen returned and Michael Ricketts joined from Walsall for a fee that was to rise to £500,000. It was to be another season of Play-off nerves after Fulham and Blackburn had secured the automatic promotion places.

In the semi-final the Wanderers found themselves two down at West Brom, pulled it back to 2–2 and then ran out 3–0 winners in the second leg at the Reebok. Victory set up a clash with Preston North End at the Millennium Stadium in Cardiff and this time the Wanderers made no mistake. Gareth Farrelly settled the nerves early on and late goals from Michael Ricketts, his 24th of the season and Ricardo Gardner made it a 3–0 success.

The team celebrate Play-off success after the defeat of Preston.

Bolton were the bookies' favourites to be relegated from the Premier League in 2002, but the season got off to a great start with the club's best-ever opening-day result, a 5–0 success at Leicester City and, after seven Premier League games, were on top of the League. By February the Wanderers had slipped into the bottom three, but it was to be the arrival of French World Cup-winner Youri Djorkaeff, from Kaiserslautern, that proved the catalyst to a revival. He was joined by another loan signing, Fredi Bobic, on loan from Dortmund, and he scored a hat-trick, the club's first in the top flight since Freddie

Ivan Campo salutes the Reebok crowd after his goal against Manchester City in 2002.

Team line up in the 125th anniversary kit prior to a 0–0 draw at home to Fulham in January 2003. Back row: Jääskeläinen, Bergsson, Barness, Pedersen, Campo, Gardner. Front row: Charlton, Frandsen, Djorkaeff, Facey, Okocha.

Hill in 1962, to help defeat relegation rivals Ipswich 4–1 at the Reebok. Premiership safety was assured two weeks later.

A final-day success in May 2003 against Middlesbrough at the Reebok extended the Wanderers' Premier League membership, by which time the mercurial Jay Jay Okocha had become a crowd favourite. Other overseas players that joined to become household names at the Reebok were Ivan Campo and Stelios Giannakopoulos, and it was from a base of players of that ilk, along with youth product Kevin Nolan and free transfer signing Kevin Davies that the Wanderers finished eighth in 2004. This included a run of five consecutive wins in the final weeks, a feat not matched by the club in the top flight since 1928.

Also in 2004, the Carling Cup offered the opportunity of some silverware. After defeating Aston Villa 5–4 on aggregate in the semi-finals the Wanderers went down to Middlesbrough 2–1 in the Final at Cardiff, with Kevin Davies getting onto the scoresheet.

Despite suffering a run of six consecutive League defeats during November and December 2004, the Wanderers recovered to finish sixth and with it qualification for the UEFA Cup. The Wanderers managed to combine a successful Premier League season, finishing eighth, with an impressive run in Europe that ended in the last 32 and a narrow two-legged defeat to Marseille.

In August 2006 the club smashed their transfer record when Nicolas Anelka was signed for £8 million from Fenerbahçe, and by the end of the year he was the leading scorer in a side lying third in the Premier League. In the end the club again qualified for the UEFA Cup by finishing seventh, but there was a change in the managerial chair when, after a 2–2 draw

Record signing Nicolas Anelka scores against his former club Arsenal.

at Chelsea at the end of April, Sam Allardyce announced he was resigning. Within 24 hours his assistant Sammy Lee took over, and he was in charge when the Wanderers earned the point, from a 2–2 draw with Aston Villa, which matched results elsewhere to secure European qualification on the final day.

The Wanderers had five players making their debut on the opening day the 2007–08 season which saw Newcastle United visit the Reebok and win 3–1 under the charge of Sam Allardyce. After just one victory in the first nine League games, Sammy Lee came to the end of his managerial tenure and Gary Megson was appointed with one objective...to keep the Wanderers in the Premier League.

During the January transfer window Nicolas Anelka was sold for a club record £15 million to Chelsea while Gary Cahill, Matt Taylor and Gretar Steinsson joined the fight. The European campaign, hampered somewhat by the League worries, produced some magnificent results including draws at Bayern Munich and Atletico Madrid before Sporting Lisbon ran out narrow winners in the last 16.

With just one point to show from eight games, the Wanderers went into the last five games of the season as favourites for the drop. In an incredible turnaround they registered three wins, two draws, and with it, safety.

A club record £8.2 million was spent on signing Johan Elmander from Toulouse in July 2008, and he scored on his debut in an opening-day 3–1 win over Stoke at the Reebok. A steady mid-table season was a relief after the previous 12 months.

The final game of 2009 saw the Wanderers lose a two-goal lead to draw at home to Hull City and, finding themselves in the bottom three, ended Gary Megson's two years in the manager's chair. Former

2007. Kevin Davies celebrates his equaliser at Bayern Munich.

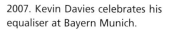

2010. Kevin Davies's England cap.

England v Montenegro
UEFA Euro 2012™ Qualifier
October 2010

Wanderers striker Owen Coyle was appointed and he galvanised the team and support to lift the club away from the relegation zone.

Further improvement came in 2010–11 with a first visit to the new Wembley Stadium for the club's 14th FA Cup semi-final, earned after three successive away wins at Premier League clubs in previous rounds, albeit that it ended in a disappointing 5–0 reverse to Stoke. Both Gary Cahill and Kevin Davies made their full England debut, while there were milestones for Jussi Jääskeläinen, who made his 500th appearance for the club, and Ricardo Gardner who took part in his 400th Wanderers game.

Jussi Jääskeläinen's 500th appearance for the club.

FROM PIKES LANE TO BURNDEN PARK

The old ground at Pikes Lane, situated in the Deane area of the town, had been the Wanderers home from 1881 and had seen the club rise to become a much respected founder member of the Football League. Prior to moving to Pikes Lane the club had played on the Park Recreation Ground and Cockle's Field.

Pikes Lane had a grandstand capable of holding 750 spectators and was a scenic spot considering its close proximity to town, flanked by houses down one side and the open moors on the other with a large oak tree situated no less than three yards from the touchline. As the game began to get more popular the facility began to show that it was not capable of future demands.

The largest crowd on the ground had been 18,000 in February 1884 to see the Wanderers lose 2–1 to Notts County in a fourth-round FA Cup replay, but many had seen the game from outside the boundaries of the stadium. Indeed, a local farmer had attempted to sue the Wanderers for damage to his fields by trespassers, but his case fell apart when it was revealed he had collected cash from those wanting to see the game.

Moves were made by the club to relocate in 1893 when, in the space of five years, the rent had risen from £35 to £175 per annum. Indeed, the owners of the land were also looking to

A full house at Pikes Lane.

sell, with building speculators showing a keenness to buy. In August that year the club's followers were informed that the secretary, Mr J.J. Bentley, had made an offer to the Gas Committee for land at Burnden which had been secured some years earlier by the Corporation for extending their gas works. This land was now no longer required for that purpose and was offered to Bolton Wanderers on a 14-year lease for a rent of £150 per annum.

In July 1894 the club sent a deputation to meet with the gas committee and thrashed out an agreement that saw the club take on the 14-year lease at £130 per annum. On 26 October 1894, a general meeting of the club was called with the object of raising funds to complete works at the ground. It was decided at this meeting to turn the club into a limited liability company, and issue 4,000 shares of £1 each, the title of the new company being The Bolton Wanderers Football and Athletic Company Limited. The Athletic part of the name being derived form the fact that it was decided to have, in addition to a football pitch, a cycling and running track.

The new company was incorporated on 15 January 1895 under company registration number 43026. Mr J.W. Makant was elected president and chairman, the other directors being, Mr J.J. Bentley, Mr F.W. Kenyon, Mr J. Magee, Mr T.H. Gregson, Mr J.T. Atkinson, Mr R. Isherwood and Mr R.H. Jackson. Mr A.H. Downs, who had been Bentley's assistant was elected first secretary.

Only 1,500 of the shares were taken up at the initial meeting, but these were later snapped up when subscribers of £25 were awarded with two stand tickets in perpetuity.

Prior to work commencing at Burnden, the site was a miserable place. One end was bound by a railway, and the smell of dumped refuse and chemicals did little to enhance the area. In the early 1800s the area had been part of the countryside with several small bleaching crofts and works carrying on a thriving industry in the valley. In 1838 the Bolton to Manchester railway had been constructed and, 10 years later, a branch line to Bury cut the Burnden area into two. The discovery of several rich coal seams led to a number of collieries being established which in turn brought further industry and housing thus robbing the area of it's country image forever.

The Great Lever Colliery was situated on the site of what became the Greyhound Stadium at Raikes Lane with the pit yard fronting Manchester Road. The Rose Hill Colliery site was eventually covered by the car and coach park on the front of Burnden Park which in turn led to the odd case of subsidence. In 1870, what later became the car park was fronted by a collection of cottages, whilst the playing pitch itself was occupied by a chemical works with numerous heaps of slag covering the area.

The total area of the Burnden enclosure was almost six acres, but an enormous amount of tipping had been necessary to level the area, thus making the ground well elevated. Within a few months during 1895 the area was transformed by the contractors who were J.O. McQuone from Scarborough.

The turf was laid on a bed of cinders of between 12in and 18in deep, with the area being 118yds by 80yds. The contractor advised that drainage would be perfect, but this was to prove a problem with the onset of winter. The cycle track was 22ft in width, 28ft on the bends, and was banked up 6ft at the corners, with one lap being the equivalent of a quarter of a mile.

The Manchester Road side ran for 120 yards and was uncovered with a facility for 5,000 spectators to stand up for an admission of 9d (4p). The plan was at a later date that the area would be roofed. The grandstand was on the Darcy Lever side and was capable of holding 1,600 in 10 rows of seats with the central area reserved for 400. The standing area in front of the seats had a facility for 2,500 while two dressing rooms were constructed along with a referee's retiring box.

Pikes Lane was last used for League football on 13 April 1895 when the Wanderers defeated West Bromwich Albion 5–0. A crowd of 10,000 saw the Wanderers thrash the FA Cup finalists who were reduced to 10 men late in the game when the goalkeeper Reader was given his marching orders for a kneeing offence. Pikes Lane was a happy place in those final months at the old ground for, after losing to Small Heath in November 1894, the Wanderers won seven and drew one of the final eight games there. Away form cost the club any chance of winning the League, but the Manchester Cup was secured to leave the club with something to show in the last season there.

Burnden Park was used for the first time on 17 August 1895 when the Wanderers held their ninth annual Athletic Festival, the competition carrying over onto the Bank Holiday Monday. The crowd on the Saturday was almost 20,000, perhaps the largest ever for an athletic meeting in Lancashire. On the Monday a crowd of 15,000 attended, but the incomplete turnstiles struggled on both days to cope with the crowds who were eager to see not only the proceedings but also the new surroundings.

The ground presented a fine appearance, the holiday crowd packing the stands and almost covering the side of the railway embankment, which afforded a grand view. The new track was rewarded with a splendid class entry, and the spectators were unstinting in their praise for the visiting athletes who seemed well pleased with their reception. Some splendid sport was witnessed, especially the cycle races, with prizes up to the value of £230 being made available. The 100yd sprint was won in 10.25 seconds by J.H. Bradley and the final of the one-mile cycle race was won by John Owen in a time of 2 minutes 30 seconds.

The gala programme consisted of a paddock troupe of lady cyclists, Sister St Lava wire performers, Pannell's performing dogs, Comies stilt walker and a dive by Professor J. Bracken, enveloped in a sack from a trapeze suspended 100ft from the ground into an eight foot tank containing only five feet of water. The Halliwell Brass band performed while all the acts were in progress.

The Wanderers finally got to use the ground on Tuesday 27 August when a public practice match took place. The event was repeated two days later, with around an hour's play being indulged in on both evenings. Burnden Park officially opened for football on Wednesday, 11 September 1895 when Preston North End were the visitors for a benefit game for Di Jones. The Lillywhites won the game 1–0 with a crowd of 3,000 seeing David Smith score the first goal at the new stadium.

Burnden Park on its opening in August 1895.

BURNDEN PARK

'Burnden' – Scottish terminology for a brook or stream is a burn. 'Den' comes from an old English word dene or denu meaning a valley. Thus in liberal terms Burnden is a valley with a stream running through it. The particular stream was Burnden Brook which originally flowed from Rose Hill. Later culverted, it then ran underneath both Manchester Road and the ground itself.

Billy Joyce kicked off the Wanderers League career at Burnden on 14 September 1895. Kicking off towards the Embankment, James Martin scored the first League goal after 25 minutes to help the Wanderers to a 3–1 win against Everton.

Within a month the ground saw its first addition when a reporters' box was erected on the Manchester Road side of the ground. This was built to save messengers dashing all the

Burnden's first League team.

The Athletics programme from 1895.

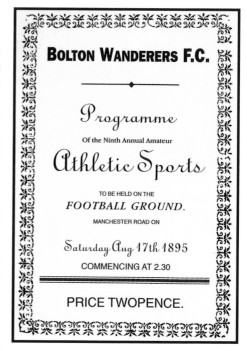

BOLTON WANDERERS F.C.

Programme

Of the Ninth Annual Amateur

Athletic Sports

TO BE HELD ON THE

FOOTBALL GROUND.

MANCHESTER ROAD ON

Saturday Aug 17th 1895

COMMENCING AT 2.30

PRICE TWOPENCE.

way around the ground and was in action for the visit of Bury in October 1895. The following month the pitch began to deteriorate when water collected up to 6in deep in places. Some of the club's reserve games were switched to a derelict Pikes Lane, while emergency work was carried out on both the pitch and cycle track which was breaking up.

The first postponement came against Small Heath, while in December 1895 Preston North End refused to play the second half with the game scoreless due to the waterlogged pitch. At the end of that first season work began on the pitch with the centre, which had sunk during the bad weather, raised in the hope that it would withstand future downpours. The ground had also seen its first 20,000-plus attendance that first season, a New Year's Day holiday crowd watching two goals from Jimmy Gunn help defeat Derby County 2–1.

The fog and mist from the River Croal proved to be a continual problem, but the pitch and cycle track were at last holding up. On Christmas Day 1896 Motherwell became the first non-English side to play on the ground as part of the transfer arrangement for goalkeeper Paddy Smith, Bolton running out 6–0 winners.

Burnden held the World Mile Championships in January 1897 and a month later the 400 yards Championships of the World with a crowd of 9,007 turning up to witness the event. Cycling, lacrosse and brass band contests all took place before the FA bestowed an FA Cup semi-final in 1899. Liverpool and Sheffield United contested a replay that ended 4–4 and later in the same year, despite the Wanderers being in the Second Division, Burnden was the venue for a Football League representative game against the Irish League. Wanderers half-back Jack Fitchett was selected for the English League, being the only representative from outside the top division and also the youngest player.

In April 1901 the FA Cup Final replay was held on Burnden between Tottenham Hotspur and Sheffield United. The occasion became known as 'Pie Saturday' as a crowd of 50,000 had been expected and only 20,470 actually turned up, leaving many local caterers with mountains of left-over pies. The lack of cheap railway facilities was blamed for the poor attendance.

The bank holiday weekend of August 1904 saw the 18th and final amateur athletic festival. A crowd of 8,000 saw a total of 1,037 entries at differing events with prizes totalling £200. In the summer of 1905 the cycle track was removed to create more space for spectators, and the lease on the ground was renewed with the Corporation for a further 10

Action from the 1901 FA Cup Final replay at Burnden between Tottenham and Sheffield United.

years. The Manchester Road stand was erected at a cost of £3,658 which provided accommodation for 6,000 spectators, 3,420 seated, 2,000 on the terrace and 580 along the track. A year later 32 terraces were laid on the slope of the Embankment and the Great Lever End was also terraced.

Burnden hosted its second FA Cup semi-final in March 1907 when Everton took on West Bromwich Albion. Everton had already won an FA Cup tie at Burnden that season, having defeated the Wanderers 3–0 in a third-round replay, and it proved to be a lucky omen as the Toffees won 2–1 only to go down in the Final to Sheffield Wednesday at Crystal Palace.

The Great Lever End of the ground was covered in 1912, which enabled spectators to view the game on three sides under shelter from the elements, while in November 1913 the

The Manchester Road Stand in 1906.

A frost-bound Burnden Park in 1926.

first crowd of over 50,000, 53,747, paid then record receipts of £1,700 to see the Wanderers defeat First Division leaders Blackburn Rovers by virtue of a goal from George Lillycrop.

In July 1914 the club purchased the freehold of Burnden Park at a cost of £8,021 and 15 shillings after the shareholders had received a dividend of five per cent. The club wanted to keep the large space between the ground and the Manchester Road clear and free from new buildings to facilitate the gathering of large crowds.

In 1915 a wing stand was added to the Manchester Road main stand and in 1928 the Burnden Stand was built to replace the Darcy Lever Stand at a cost of £17,712. The new structure seated 2,750 but was built in controversial circumstances, with the proceeds of the sale of David Jack going towards the building cost.

The largest official crowd on the ground came in February 1933 when 69,912 witnessed Manchester City win a fifth-round FA Cup tie. Four days later only 3,101 attended a League game against Portsmouth to set a record League low until November 1985 when 2,902 saw a Third Division game against Darlington.

Two landmarks were put up during 1935. Clocks were placed on top of both the stands which had been supplied by Magees the brewery. These remained in use until 1973 on the Burnden Stand and 1975 on the Manchester Road Stand. Record crowds were also set during the 1930s for League football. In May 1935 46,554 became the highest on the ground for a Second Division fixture when the

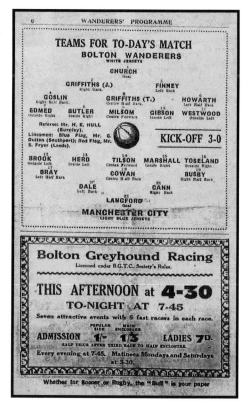

A programme from Burnden's record gate versus Manchester City in 1933.

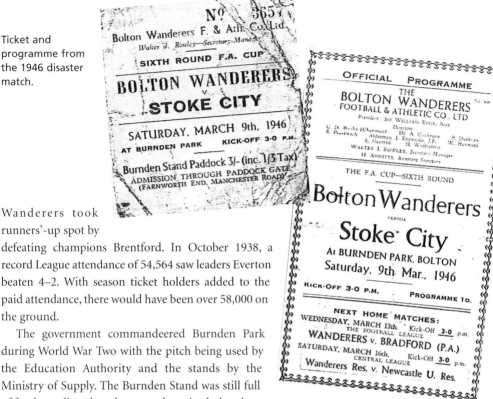

Ticket and programme from the 1946 disaster match.

No 3655

Bolton Wanderers F. & Ath. Co. Ltd.
Walter J. Rowley, Secretary-Manager

SIXTH ROUND F.A. CUP

BOLTON WANDERERS
v.
STOKE CITY

SATURDAY, MARCH 9th, 1946
AT BURNDEN PARK   KICK-OFF 3-0 P.M.

Burnden Stand Paddock 3/- (inc. 1/3 Tax)
ADMISSION THROUGH PADDOCK GATE
(FARNWORTH END, MANCHESTER ROAD)

OFFICIAL   PROGRAMME

THE
BOLTON WANDERERS
FOOTBALL & ATHLETIC CO. LTD
President: SIR WILLIAM EDGE, Bart.

THE F.A. CUP—SIXTH ROUND

Bolton Wanderers
VERSUS
Stoke City

At BURNDEN PARK, BOLTON
Saturday, 9th Mar., 1946
KICK-OFF 3-0 P.M.   PROGRAMME 1D.

NEXT HOME MATCHES:
WEDNESDAY, MARCH 13th.   Kick-Off 3-0 p.m.
THE FOOTBALL LEAGUE
WANDERERS v. BRADFORD (P.A.)
SATURDAY, MARCH 16th.   Kick-Off 3-0 p.m.
CENTRAL LEAGUE
Wanderers Res. v. Newcastle U. Res.

Wanderers took runners'-up spot by defeating champions Brentford. In October 1938, a record League attendance of 54,564 saw leaders Everton beaten 4–2. With season ticket holders added to the paid attendance, there would have been over 58,000 on the ground.

The government commandeered Burnden Park during World War Two with the pitch being used by the Education Authority and the stands by the Ministry of Supply. The Burnden Stand was still full of food supplies when the ground saw its darkest hour on the afternoon of 9 March 1946.

An estimated 85,000 swarmed into Burnden Park, the official gate being 65,419 for the second leg of an FA Cup sixth-round tie against Stoke City. Half an hour before kick-off many people were in a crush outside the ground, attempting to gain entry to the Embankment from the Manchester Road terraces. Unfortunately, once inside the ground it was impossible for spectators to move along the terraces to find a position where they could see.

The turnstiles remained open until 20 minutes before kick-off as the head checker could not be located. Instructions from outside the ground could not be passed to the police inside due to the density of the crowd and, as the turnstiles closed, people began climbing over the walls to get in.

There was an invasion over the railway line fence at the Embankment end, but the Police were reluctant to send any officers to that area as they were guarding the stockpiles of food underneath the Burnden Stand.

Panic began to set in and, inside the ground, a father and son wanting to escape the crush picked a padlock off an exit gate. They slipped out, but the open gate allowed more people to rush in. An estimated 1,000 climbed into the ground over the boys entrance, and the railway police were helpless to prevent people climbing onto a stationary train to get a view of the pitch.

People were being passed down to the track and, as the teams entered the field, two barriers near the north-west corner flag collapsed under the pressure. The crowd sunk and

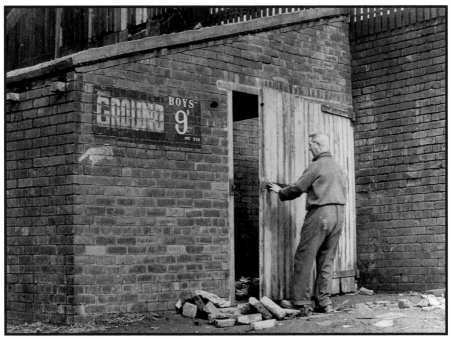

1923 FA Cup-winner Harry Nuttall makes repairs to the boys entrance in 1946.

a number of people were smothered. Hundreds spilled onto the track as the game commenced, but it was not apparent to many what had happened.

It was not until 12 minutes into the game that there was a realisation that people had actually died. In all 33 bodies were found and laid out on the pitch while first aid was given to hundreds.

Spectators were moved to other parts of the ground with the Burnden stand being opened to accommodate some of them. After consultation, both the referee and the police

The entrance to the Embankment in 1946 showing where the new concrete entrances were to be bulit after the disaster.

decided to re-start the game and proceeded without any interval ending in a scoreless draw, the Wanderers going through to the semi-final on a 2–0 aggregate.

The Mayor of Bolton opened a relief fund which raised almost £40,000, while a shocked community came to terms with the loss of life. Charity matches such as England v Scotland at Maine Road helped the fund while the enquiry into the disaster was far reaching and lasted for five days. The report of R. Moelwyn Hughes KC, appointed by the Home Secretary, Chuter Ede, found the expectation of a 50,000 gate reasonable. It also made recommendations relating to the reception and control of crowds not only at Burnden, but also at football grounds in general.

The enquiry determined that the crowd had inflicted the disaster on itself, and the club made alterations to the Embankment at a cost of £5,500 to enhance safety. In 1986 the area in which the disaster had unfolded was covered with the building of the Normid Superstore.

In June 1957 work began on erecting four floodlight pylons. The new Bolton landmarks were 160ft tall and the installation saw the end of early Saturday afternoon and midweek afternoon kick-offs. On 14 October 1957, unbeaten Scottish First Division leaders Hearts were the first club to play the Wanderers under the new lights. They were switched on by chairman, Mr H. Warburton, and a crowd of 21,058 saw a 1–1 draw, with Terry Allcock getting the Trotters goal.

Burnden in 1956.

The signal box at the Embankment end.

The following month CDSA Moscow became the first European side to play on Burnden Park in the second game under the new lights. A crowd of 34,139, bettered only once in League games at Burnden that season, saw Bolton run out 3–1 winners.

Although the club had slipped out of the top flight, the ground was selected for two FA Cup semi-finals during the 1960s. In 1966 Everton defeated Manchester United, and in 1970 Leeds United also beat Manchester United in a second replay.

The frontage of Burnden Park changed in 1967 when a supporters' club was erected. This was originally built as first-floor premises over the players entrance with a drive through underneath but was later boxed in to create offices. In 1971 the famous signal box behind the Embankment was destroyed by fire to change the face of the ground forever.

Sunday football was first witnessed in January 1974 when Stoke City were beaten 3–2 in a third-round FA Cup tie, and in February 1977 the last crowd of over 50,000; 50,413 saw a League Cup semi-final defeat by Everton. The following season segregation and fences were in evidence, and the Great Lever End was made all seater on the club's promotion to the top flight in 1978, with 4,342 plastic seats being placed on the old terracing.

Despite the antiquated surroundings, the stadium managed to keep up with the times. In the close season of 1980 undersoil heating was installed at a cost of £70,000 for the 14 miles of heating pipes under the pitch, while in 1984 another landmark disappeared when the half-time scoreboard was demolished after it had fallen into disrepair.

The entrance to the Embankment in 1982 before the Normid Superstore was built.

Burnden and its environs in the eary 1990s.

In October 1985 the go-ahead was given for a multi-million pound development on the Embankment side of the ground, which was to include a superstore. The scheme was to include converting the pitch from grass to an artificial surface, and the club received permission to do so. However, the League voted to put a freeze on the spread of artificial pitches, and so Burnden remained a real grass pitch. The following year, however, the superstore was built, cutting the Embankment in half.

The Burnden Stand in the ground's only Premier League season in 1995.

View from the visitors section on the Embankment.

November 1985 saw the grounds lowest-ever League attendance when 2,902 saw a Third Division 3–0 defeat at the hands of Darlington. In fact, during the 1980s the biggest crowds at Burnden were for Rugby League, the largest being 21,144 for the John Player Trophy Final between Wigan and Warrington.

Burnden's lowest crowd for a first-class game came in December 1991 when 1,507 saw a David Reeves hat-trick help Bolton defeat Rochdale 4–1 in the Autoglass Trophy. During the 1990s the crowds came back as the club climbed through the League's and returned to the top flight in 1995.

The curtain finally fell on the ground in April 1997 when the First Division Championship trophy was presented after the Wanderers had defeated Charlton Athletic 4–1 in the final game of a record-breaking season. John McGinlay netted the last goal on an emotional evening that saw Bolton come back from a half-time deficit.

The ground was vacated and, after a fire in the main stand, Burnden Park was finally pulled down. A lengthy period in which the site was derelict followed before the old ground finally became home to a Big W superstore and is now an Asda store.

The final fixture advertised on the hoarding outside the ground.

The last act at Burnden. The Championship trophy is presented.

Burnden just prior to its final demolition.

October 1996.

THE REEBOK STADIUM

Although discussions concerning the club's relocation took place as early as 1986, with the club heading for Division Four, it was not until the early 1990s that the Taylor report and the lack of space to rebuild Burnden Park forced the issue. From the 14 sites that were looked at for a new facility it was the 200-acre site at Lostock that proved to be the most feasible and work got underway in November 1995.

At a cost of £35 million, the Reebok Stadium, with an initial capacity of 25,000 became the focal point of the Middlebrook development, with a retail park, community facilities, indoor/outdoor tennis arena, athletics track, rail halt, hotel and housing all added to the area.

The sweeping curves of the upper tiers create a bowl effect which means no spectator is ever more than 90m from the centre of the field. The stand roofs are some 88ft high, while the floodlights are 182ft high. The stadium maximises spectator comfort with wider than normal terrace units giving more leg room, concourses with concession units and TV screens, all a million miles away from considerations that were undertaken in the construction of Burnden Park.

At the end of August 1997 over 10,000 spectators turned up for a 'dry run' to look around the inside of the stadium for the first time and watch a short game between the club's youngsters. On 1 September 1997 the first game took place when Everton were the

March 2007.

first visitors for a Premier League game, 102 years after they had been the first visitors for a League game to Burnden Park.

The game became famous for the goal that never was, with Gerry Taggart's header crossing the line for the Wanderers but not being given by the referee Steve Lodge, a 0–0 draw resulting. Alan Thompson became the first player to score in the stadium, converting a penalty in a 1–1 draw with Tottenham, Chris Armstrong, later to have a spell with Bolton, scored for the Londoners to give him the distinction of scoring the first goal from open

May 1997, the floodlights ready to be mounted.

July 2007.

play. Aston Villa were the first team to win a game in the stadium, 1–0 on 4 October 1997, with Bolton's first victory coming at the fifth attempt when Wimbledon were beaten in extra-time in the League Cup.

The stadium has since hosted international Rugby League games with visits from both New Zealand and Australia, the World Club Championship won by St Helens and a number of major concerts, the first being in the summer of 2000 when Oasis played over two evenings.

September 1997.

The Reebok Stadium from the north-west corner.

The FA also granted recognition by hosting internationals at Under-17, Under-20 and Under-21 level along with a full women's international.

The record attendance at the Stadium to date for a Wanderers game came in December 2003 when 28,353 saw a 2–2 draw with Leicester City in the Premier League. The lowest gate for a League game was 10,180 who witnessed a 3–1 Championship defeat of Queen's Park Rangers in October 2000, while just 3,673 were there in September 1999 to see a 2–0 League Cup win over Gillingham in what was Colin Todd's final game in charge.

The stadium saw further milestones during 2010–11. Martin Petrov scored the Wanderers' 250th Premier League goal in the stadium during the 2–2 draw with Manchester United in September 2010, and the Boxing Day 2–0 win against West Brom was the stadium's 200th Premier League game.

FIFTY MEMORABLE MATCHES

1 February 1890

BOLTON WANDERERS 13 SHEFFIELD UNITED 0

Sheffield United must have taken leave of their senses when they agreed to switch this FA Cup second-round tie from Bramall Lane to the dour Pikes Lane enclosure. The loss of home advantage, switched for financial reasons as Wednesday were at home, gave them an impossible task.

On a mud bath of a pitch, the Wanderers went one up inside 90 seconds when Davie Weir scored, five minutes later the Scot added a second. Jim Brogan and Jim Cassidy kept the crowd of around 4,000 happy with further goals, and just before the interval Brogan netted the Trotters' fifth.

A short passing game was impossible, but Bolton adapted superbly and Cassidy scored the sixth just after the restart. Cassidy again hit the target, and the eighth came from Weir. The ninth and tenth were crashed home by Cassidy, Brogan shot the 11th and Weir the 12th before the baker's dozen was completed by Bethel Robinson with the crowd shouting, 'you only need another seven to make the score'.

The result still stands as the club's record win in a competitive game, and Jim Cassidy's five goals equalled the feat set by Bob Struthers in 1882 during a 6–1 first-round success against Bootle.

31 March 1894

BOLTON WANDERERS 1 NOTTS COUNTY 4

Bolton's first appearance in an FA Cup Final ended in disaster when Second Division Notts County took full advantage of the Trotters' off-field problems.

Davie Weir was not selected due to his individualistic temperament that caused arguments with other members of the team, while James Turner and David Willocks were out injured. Also suffering from injury were Sandy Paton, Handel Bentley and Harry Gardiner, while John Somerville had raging toothache. All four played, and it showed in the performance.

The 23,000 present at Goodison Park saw Watson put County ahead after 20 minutes, Wanderers centre-half Archie Hughes suffering injury in the incident to become the fifth passenger in the side. Logan scored the second before the interval, and he wrapped things up when he hit two more in a three-minute spell during the second half.

Wanderers' only consolation was a goal from Jim Cassidy late in the proceedings and the performance of 'keeper John Sutcliffe who prevented a complete rout.

11 September 1895

BOLTON WANDERERS 0 PRESTON NORTH END 1

The opening match at Burnden Park took place for the benefit of the Wanderers captain Di Jones, the Welsh international full-back, who had served the club for seven years. A crowd of 3,000 saw Bolton test former Wanderers international goalkeeper Jim Trainer on a number of occasions, but the North End custodian held firm. The only goal of the game came in the final minutes as darkness began to fall, with David Smith claiming the distinction of Burnden Park's first goal.

Three days later the Wanderers took on Everton in the first League game on the ground and ran out 3–1 winners.

23 April 1904

BOLTON WANDERERS 0 MANCHESTER CITY 1

The club's second appearance in the FA Cup Final saw them as underdogs when they came up against First Division Championship chasers Manchester City, while the Wanderers had had an indifferent season in Division Two.

A crowd of almost 62,000 at Crystal Palace saw City set off the better, and it was during this spell that they went ahead in controversial fashion. The scorer, Billy Meredith, was standing two yards behind Bob Struthers, in an offside position, before racing clear to shoot home.

In the second half the Wanderers produced some of the fine form that had seen them defeat other First Division sides in the competition but their shooting left a lot to be desired. They had a good 30-minute spell where they bossed the game but could not come up with a goal. In the end, the affair was settled by the questionable goal to leave the Wanderers disappointed, despite being admired for their dogged persistence.

1 January 1906

BOLTON WANDERERS 6 WOOLWICH ARSENAL 1

After a gruelling series of four First Division away games in a week that had failed to produce a win, the Wanderers were welcomed back to Burnden by a crowd of around 21,000. Both Bolton and Arsenal had been struggling at the wrong end of the League table, but this game was to set the Wanderers off on a run of nine consecutive League wins that would propel them to a top-six finish.

The game was only four minutes old when Walter White let fly with a bouncing shot that Ashcroft, in the Arsenal goal, allowed to go past him and just inside the upright. Sam Marsh made it two four minutes later when he got onto the end of a Marshall McEwan corner. White hit the third from a David Stokes corner but the visitors did not seem dispirited and Bert Baverstock had to be on his mettle to clear off his own line.

The fourth goal came in the 21st minute when Albert Shepherd sent David Stokes away. His cross found Marsh who was on it like a flash with a lightening ground shot. Upon the restart, after an unusually long break, the Londoners could not prevent Shepherd from heading the Trotters fifth goal from McEwan's corner.

The half dozen was made up two minutes later when McEwan converted a Stokes corner but Arsenal responded almost immediately when Satterthwaite headed past Dai Davies. After such a flurry of goals, the final 40 minutes seemed pedestrian, but Bolton were comfortable and the goals fest was to continue in the upcoming League games.

26 April 1911

BOLTON WANDERERS 2 CHELSEA 0

A Second Division game of Cup tie proportions brought Burnden Park's largest attendance since an FA Cup tie against Everton in 1907. The race for promotion to the First Division was a three-horse affair between the Trotters, Chelsea and West Brom, who were all level on 49 points from 36 games with two left to play for the two promotion places.

The attendance of 38,613 was all the more remarkable in view of the many who were lured away to Old Trafford for an exceptional treat in the shape of an FA Cup Final. There were, however, hundreds who spared neither expense nor inconvenience with the object of witnessing both games.

As soon as the state of the game would warrant the conclusion that Bradford City would beat Newcastle United, hundreds of people made, by every conceivable mode of transport, for the evening kick-off at Burnden Park. Here they saw a contest that was streets ahead of the Cup Final in the quality of football on show. The decision of the Wanderers management to delay the kick-off long enough to enable mill and other workers to see the start brought forth a tremendous response.

The footwork of Vivien Woodward and the dash and shooting power of Whittingham was a pronounced feature of the game, but there was nothing in the Pensioners' play to come up to the work of Bolton's tried and trusty left wing of Joe Smith and Ted Vizard.

Six minutes from the start Ernie Whiteside placed in a delightful free-kick that found Harold Hilton, who forced it straight into the corner of the net. The second goal came in the 67th minute and followed an admirable centre by Vizard, with Hilton again dashing the ball into the goal.

There was a lively demonstration of admiration for the Wanderers as they made for the dressing room at full-time with several players being carried off by crowds of supporters who believed promotion was won.

West Brom went on to win their final two games to secure the Championship and, although the Wanderers lost their final game at Birmingham, they accompanied the Throstles into Division One as Chelsea lost at Gainsborough Trinity.

25 December 1920

BOLTON WANDERERS 6 SUNDERLAND 2

The Wanderers gave a crowd of over 40,000 (39,521 plus tickets) a rare Christmas box with Sunderland receiving the full weight of an unexpected avalanche in the final quarter of an hour when their defence collapsed like a pack of cards.

After Jimmy Seddon and Joe Smith had put Bolton into a comfortable lead, the storm suddenly burst when Sunderland drew level with goals from Buchan and Moore.

It was principally due to Joe Smith, who recorded a hat-trick in the space of five minutes that caused the air to become charged with excitement after the visitors had cast a gloom over the crowd by their recovery. Directly after scoring his last goal Smith had to be helped from the field as he was so dazed in heading the heavy ball that he was oblivious as to what was going on around him.

Sunderland's new 'keeper Dempster was helpless to stop Smith's canonball shots, and these went towards his tally of 38 League goals during the season that remain a club record. Frank Roberts rounded off the scoring for Bolton who were to finish the season in third spot in Division One, a position never bettered.

28 April 1923

BOLTON WANDERERS 2 WEST HAM UNITED 0

The first FA Cup Final at Wembley Stadium was unquestionably the most unsatisfactory match ever decided in the history of the competition. An official crowd of 126,047 passed through the turnstiles, with between a further 70,000 and 100,000 gaining admission by rushing the barriers.

It was remarkable that nothing more serious than encroachment onto the pitch took place, with almost a quarter of a million people shoehorned into a space designed to hold

Joe Smith receives the FA Cup from the king.

only half that number. A white horse named Billy helped clear the pitch while the arrival of the King helped keep a calm in the sea of people.

The kick-off was delayed for forty minutes but once underway the Wanderers wasted no time against their Second Division opponents. Two minutes in, David Jack put his name into folklore by scoring the first-ever goal on the ground, although West Ham went close to equalising soon after when Watson missed in front of an open goal.

John Smith scored Bolton's second after the interval with a shot that was so strong it hit the net and bounced out to secure the FA Cup for the Wanderers. The Final came to be remembered more for what happened off the pitch than on it, but the club had at last won some major silverware.

26 December 1923

WEST BROMWICH ALBION 0 BOLTON WANDERERS 5

The Wanderers completed a holiday double over Albion, having defeated them 2–0 at Burnden on Christmas Day.

A crowd of 12,148 at The Hawthorns saw Bolton totally outplay their hosts. David Jack opened the scoring when he converted a Billy Butler corner and then Jack became provider for Joe Smith. Despite their superiority, it was not until the final 10 minutes that Bolton ran out of sight.

John Smith applied the finishing touch to a clever piece of skill by Jimmy Seddon, and then Jack completed a hat-trick with two goals set up by Ted Vizard's perfect crosses.

The Albion defence had been unable to deal with the passing skills of the Smiths, Jack and Vizard, while Seddon had dominated the centre of the field to earn a win that put the Wanderers into second place in the First Division after a run of just one defeat in 11 games.

David Jack scores the winner against Manchester City.

24 April 1926

BOLTON WANDERERS 1 MANCHESTER CITY 0

A crowd of 91,447 passed calmly through the Wembley turnstiles in complete contrast to the scenes three years earlier and to witness the Trotters' opportunity to gain revenge for the perceived wrong of their defeat in the FA Cup Final of 1904.

The first half saw Bolton hold the balance of the play, but they wasted a number of openings. The second period was vigorously contested but was finally settled 12 minutes from time when David Jack scored the only goal from a Ted Vizard pass.

City went all out to force an equaliser, but Dick Pym was in top form and kept a clean sheet to make sure that Joe Smith received the FA Cup from the king for the second time in three years.

27 April 1929

BOLTON WANDERERS 2 PORTSMOUTH 0

By beating Portsmouth, the ambitious but forlorn hope of the south, Bolton Wanderers created something of a minor record by securing their third FA Cup success in six seasons at Wembley.

Most of the neutrals in the 92,576 crowd favoured Bolton due to their consistent Cup form and, with six players in their line up that had previous experience of Wembley, started as favourites although 'keeper Dick Pym was carrying an injury.

The 1929 FA Cup winners.

While Bolton played well within themselves the breakthrough, as three years earlier, was late in coming. Twelve minutes were left to play when Billy Butler scored the first goal with a terrific shot, and almost immediately Harold Blackmore made the game safe with the second to bring the Cup back to Bolton again.

1 January 1930

BOLTON WANDERERS 7
HUDDERSFIELD TOWN 1

An early New Year's Day kick-off failed to deter the Wanderers support for this First Division fixture, and they were to be rewarded with a goal fest.

It took only six minutes for Bolton to go ahead when Billy Butler's shot went in off the underside of the Great Lever End goal. Butler netted the second from a Jimmy Seddon knockdown, and in the 23rd minute the winger completed his hat-trick.

Four minutes after the interval Mangnall pulled one back for the Terriers, but Bolton went down the other end and restored the advantage through Billy Cook. In the next attack Harold Blackmore made it five with a high cross shot, and he then made it three goals in a four-minute spell with a shot from the edge of the area.

George Gibson rounded off the scoring with a simple seventh to make it a very happy New Year for Bolton supporters.

25 January 1947

BOLTON WANDERERS 3 MANCHESTER CITY 3

The Wanderers' reward for defeating Stockport County 5–1 in the third round of the FA Cup was a home tie against Second Division Manchester City. It gave them the opportunity of avenging defeats in the Cup against City at Burnden in 1933 and 1937.

Bolton made a great start when Billy Wrigglesworth scored inside 30 seconds without a City player having touched the ball. Nat Lofthouse made it two when he headed home a Harry Hubbick cross after nine minutes, and it stayed that way until Black pulled one back for City after 55 minutes. Eight minutes later City were level when Black scored again from close range.

City made it three goals in 12 minutes when Capel put them ahead after a poor clearance from Stan Hansen. Bolton fought back to level with 10 minutes remaining when Malcolm Barrass tapped the ball over the line after a shot from Tom Woodward had struck the inside of the post.

Four days later City won the replay 1–0 to keep up their FA Cup hoodoo over the Wanderers.

18 August 1951

BOLTON WANDERERS 5 ASTON VILLA 2

The opening day of the season saw Aston Villa race into a two-goal lead. Thompson opened the scoring after 10 minutes, and they increased the lead while down to 10 men after 'keeper Rutherford had left the field for attention to an injured hand.

The 'keeper returned to the action but could not prevent Harry Webster pulling one back. Willie Moir levelled before half-time, but the Wanderers took command in the second half. Nat Lofthouse put Bolton ahead from a Billy Hughes centre, and he also provided the fourth for Webster.

Bolton's fifth goal came from the penalty spot after Lofthouse had been brought down by Moss. Langton converted to complete the recovery in a season that was to see Bolton finish fifth.

25 December 1952

BOLTON WANDERERS 4 ARSENAL 6

A Christmas Day goalfest was served up for the 45,432 Burnden crowd who saw Willie Moir set things off with an early opening goal. Milton levelled for the Gunners in the 12th minute, and they went in ahead at half-time thanks to a powerful drive from Holton.

Two goals in five minutes after the break, from Roper and Logie emphasised the Gunners superiority at that stage of the game before Nat Lofthouse made it 2–4. Arsenal promptly added two more through a penalty kick from Daniel and a shot from Holton and the game looked to be over. The spirit of the Wanderers came to the fore, and goals from Lofthouse and Moir, in the 78th and 80th minutes, produced a grandstand finish.

Five minutes from time Bobby Langton won a penalty and the crowd went wild, but their excitement was doused when Langton's spot-kick was saved by Kelsey, and with that the issue was settled despite another fantastic save from Kelsey to deny Lofthouse in the dying moments.

2 May 1953

BLACKPOOL 4 BOLTON WANDERERS 3

The nationwide sympathy fell with Blackpool in the 1953 FA Cup Final and especially Stan Matthews who was looking to win an elusive Cup-winners' medal after defeats in the 1948 and 1951 Finals. Bolton got off to a great start when, with just 75 seconds on the clock, the Footballer of the Year Nat Lofthouse opened the scoring from 28 yards out.

Fate then played a hand that was to have a detrimental effect on Bolton's performance. An injury to Eric Bell saw him switched to the left wing and in the latter stages saw him become a passenger. Blackpool levelled after 37 minutes when a Stan Mortenson shot was

Eric Bell scores Wanderer's third against Blackpool in the 1953 FA Cup Final.

deflected into the net off Harold Hassall, but the Wanderers regained the lead thanks to Willie Moir.

Ten minutes into the second half the Wanderers went 3–1 up when the heroic Bell flung himself to get onto the end of a Doug Holden cross but the drama that was about to unfold had not yet begun. In the 66th minute Stan Hanson failed to hold a Matthews cross and Mortenson snapped up the chance to reduce the arrears.

It was Mortenson who struck the equaliser to complete his hat-trick with a free-kick from just outside the area, and with a minute to go Matthews dribbled to the goalline to pull the ball back to the unmarked Bill Perry who smashed the ball home from five yards out. The Wanderers had taken part in one of the most exciting FA Cup Finals in history, but only two of their players were to make up for the disappointment of losing five years later.

10 November 1956

Bolton Wanderers 2 Manchester United 0

The Wanderers faced a Busby Babes line up that had not been beaten away from home and came out on top before Burnden's best League gate of the season. After soaking up United pressure Bolton broke to take the lead after 10 minutes when Doug Holden placed an inch-perfect shot past Ray Wood.

After this both defences got on top, but early in the second half Bolton gave themselves breathing space against the champions with a second goal. Bryan Edwards sent the ball across to Dennis Stevens who set up Terry Allcock to turn it past the advancing Wood.

The Wanderers went on to keep up their fine form against United by completing the double with a 2–0 win at Old Trafford the following March.

1 March 1958

BOLTON WANDERERS 2 WOLVERHAMPTON WANDERERS 1

Bolton started as underdogs in this FA Cup sixth-round tie at Burnden, but they managed to come out on top against the champions but rode their luck along the way.

Dennis Stevens opened the scoring in the 27th minute, but the lead lasted only two minutes when Bobby Mason levelled for Wolves. What turned out to be the winning goal came in the 56th minute. Wolves 'keeper Malcolm Finlayson handled outside the area, and Ray Parry stepped up to float the perfect free-kick into the corner of the net.

Bolton then faced the 'Alamo', with Wolves striking the woodwork no less than half a dozen times and both Roy Hartle and Tommy Banks having to clear off their own goalline. Bolton were further hampered when, with eight minutes to go, Parry was carried off with concussion. Bolton managed to hold on, and when he awoke after the final whistle he realised he had fired his team into the semi-final of the FA Cup.

3 May 1958

BOLTON WANDERERS 2 MANCHESTER UNITED 0

Bolton's £110 team, none costing more than the signing on fee, defeated a Manchester United side rebuilding after the Munich tragedy to bring the FA Cup back to Burnden Park for the first time in 29 years.

It was to be Nat Lofthouse's Final. The captain stabbed the Wanderers ahead after just three minutes, and United seldom offered any serious challenge to Bolton's all-round strength and unity. The nearest they came was a shot from Bobby Charlton that struck the post in the 54th minute, but three minutes later Bolton wrapped it up with probably the most controversial goal scored in an FA Cup Final.

Dennis Stevens sent in a shot that United's 'keeper Harry Gregg could only push into the air, and as he turned Lofthouse stormed in to send both Gregg and the ball into the back of the net.

8 December 1962

BOLTON WANDERERS 1 TOTTENHAM HOTSPUR 0

The Wanderers proved they could be a match against anyone on their own patch by defeating a classy Tottenham side on the back of a five-goal defeat at Aston Villa the previous Saturday.

It was a contrast in styles, with the Londoners preferring the close passing game. Jimmy Greaves proved a threat, while the Wanderers trusted more to the long pass. Bill Brown in the Tottenham goal was much the busier of the 'keepers, but as the game wore on it was the visitors who began to dominate the proceedings.

With only five minutes remaining Bolton struck to defeat the Cup holders. Freddie Hill pushed through a delightful pin-point pass to Peter Deakin, who side stepped a defender before shooting low into the net. Over two months were to pass before the Wanderers played another League game as one of the worst winters on record set in.

27 September 1967

Bolton Wanderers 3 Liverpool 2

Bolton's first 'giantkilling' in the League Cup came against a full-strength Liverpool side at Burnden. A fortnight earlier the sides had drawn 1–1 at Anfield in the second-round tie, and 30,669 turned up to see the replay that fluctuated, with both sides having dominating spells throughout the game.

It was Second Division Wanderers who took the lead in the 26th minute when a shot from the skipper Dave Hatton was parried by Tommy Lawrence. Hatton headed the rebound across the face of goal and Gordon Taylor was on hand to put the ball into the net.

Ten minutes from half-time Liverpool levelled when Tommy Smith converted a penalty, awarded after Peter Thompson had been brought down. It was not until the 70th minute the Bolton regained the lead, Freddie Hill being on hand to follow up a Francis Lee shot that had been blocked. The Burnden crowd went wild when, five minutes later, Taylor latched onto a through ball from Hill and planted a powerful shot beyond Lawrence for Bolton's third goal.

Liverpool made it an anxious final 10 minutes when Ian Callaghan scored with a spectacular swerving shot that left Eddie Hopkinson rooted but Bolton held on for a famous victory.

29 NOVEMBER 1969

Bolton Wanderers 6 Queen's Park Rangers 4

A crowd of only 7,253 witnessed this Second Division 10-goal thriller on a frost-bound Burnden pitch. The conditions proved to be a nightmare for defenders, and the ball was difficult to control. It took only 45 seconds for Rangers to open the scoring when Mick Leach headed in a Rodney Marsh cross. The Wanderers had to wait until the 24th minute to level with a goal from Gordon Taylor and two minutes from half-time John Byrom nudged the home side ahead.

Play swung from end to end in the second half. John Manning headed Bolton's third in the 51st minute, but within seconds Barry Bridges pegged one back only for Terry Wharton to restore the two-goal margin in the 55th minute. Full-back Dave Clement, later to play for the Wanderers, smashed home Rangers third in the 68th minute before Manning got his second with a header.

Byrom brought up the half dozen for Bolton, and Marsh scored Rangers' fourth six minutes from time. Bolton enjoyed their games against Rangers this particular season, winning the return 4–0 at Loftus Road the following March.

John Byrom takes on the Queen's Park Rangers defence, November 1969.

5 October 1971

BOLTON WANDERERS 3 MANCHESTER CITY 0

A crowd of over 42,000 saw Third Division Bolton produce a major shock in this League Cup third-round tie against a City side fielding former Wanderers in Wyn Davies, Francis Lee and Freddie Hill. City had won the League, FA Cup and European Cup-Winners' Cup in recent seasons and were clear favourites, but the Wanderers had 'form' in the competition having defeated First Division Huddersfield Town 2–0 at Leeds Road in the previous round.

The hero of the hour was 20-year-old striker Garry Jones who notched a hat-trick. His first came after 16 minutes when he headed an Alan Waldron cross out of Joe Corrigan's reach. It was not until the 65th minute that he increased the lead when he was played in by Roy Greaves, and Jones raced clear to slip the ball beyond Corrigan.

Eleven minutes from time, the tie was wrapped up when Willie Donachie brought down Waldron and Jones stepped up to send Corrigan the wrong way from the spot-kick.

28 April 1973

BOLTON WANDERERS 2 BRENTFORD 0

The Wanderers said 'goodbye' to the Third Division with a two-goal blast that secured the Championship and sent Brentford into Division Four.

After a slow start, in which part of the 21,646 crowd were slow handclapping, the Wanderers produced a scintillating second-half performance. With a £250-a-man winning bonus to spur them on, they tore Brentford open with two goals in 11 minutes. Leading scorer John Byrom got the first after 51 minutes before Peter Nicholson netted his third goal in as many games.

The 61 points secured were then a club record, while 18 home wins with only nine goals conceded on home territory equalled previous club records.

6 January 1974

BOLTON WANDERERS 3 STOKE CITY 2

Soccer on a Sunday was voted an overwhelming success at Burnden Park when 39,138, twice as big as the club's best that season and the best of the entire third round of the FA Cup, saw the Wanderers defeat First Division Stoke City 3–2.

A three-day week was the cause for the switch, and the Wanderers became the first club to make the switch to the Sabbath, with supporters willingly paying 40p and 60p for teamsheets to enable them to gain admission to the ground to keep in line with the Sunday Observance Act.

John Byrom proved to be Bolton's hero with a spectacular hat-trick. His first came in the 25th minute when he stooped to head home a Garry Jones cross, the second arrived just after the interval with a shot that flew underneath the advancing 'keeper, John Farmer. He put the Wanderers three goals to the good in the 62nd minute when he casually flicked the ball up to send a left-foot half volley into the net.

Stoke got back into the game two minutes later with a John Ritchie goal and, with five minutes to go, City won a penalty when John Ritson brought down Ritchie. Sean Haslegrave converted and in the dying moments Byrom put the icing on his Man of the Match performance by clearing off his own goalline to deny Stoke a replay.

John Byrom completes his hat-trick against Stoke City.

14 February 1976

BOLTON WANDERERS 3 NEWCASTLE UNITED 3

First Division Newcastle United visited Burnden for this FA Cup fifth-round tie unbeaten in Cup football, having already reached the League Cup Final. The Wanderers headed the Second Division and were to twice come from behind in one of the most exciting ties ever seen on the ground.

Bolton got off to a great start by taking the lead after only five minutes when Sam Allardyce headed home Peter Thompson's cross. Newcastle hit back to level when Tommy Cassidy sent Malcolm Macdonald away to outpace the Wanderers defence and round Barry Siddall before putting the ball into the net. A minute before half-time Macdonald put the Magpies ahead with a goal of incredible quality. The striker had his back to the Bolton goal when he collected a throw in from Tommy Craig. He dummied Paul Jones, swivelled and hammered a superb bending right-foot shot into the top corner of the net from 25 yards out.

Many sides would have crumbled having conceded such a goal, but six minutes after the interval Bolton levelled when Roy Greaves set up Garry Jones to score from close range. Eight minutes from time United scored what they thought would be the winner when Alan Gowling netted, but the crowd of 46,584 saw further drama when three minutes later Paul Jones rose to head home a Greaves corner for a spectacular ending to a full-blooded Cup tie.

The sides played out a scoreless draw in the replay at St James' Park before Newcastle ran out 2–1 winners in a second replay at Elland Road.

26 April 1978

BLACKBURN ROVERS 0 BOLTON WANDERERS 1

Bolton returned to the First Division after 14 years out of top-class football and after two frustrating seasons in which promotion had been snatched from them at the last gasp. It was a goal from Frank Worthington after 34 minutes that settled the issue before 27,835 at Ewood Park that in honesty was too taut to ever be a classic, but that did not matter to the thousands of Wanderers supporters who had travelled 'over the hill'.

Although John Radford had struck the post for Rovers early in the first half Bolton had the better of things. The winner came when Worthington got free on the left, and he waited patiently, almost aware that this was to be a special moment, before driving the ball past John Butcher.

John Ritson celebrates with the crowd at Ewood Park.

Bolton urgently needed another goal to ease the tension but, though they had control of the match, they were denied a second breakthrough as much by their own shortcomings as by Blackburn's defence.

At the final whistle hundreds of Bolton supporters spilled on to the pitch and swamped the players, hoisting them high as the despair and disappointment of the previous two seasons was washed away. Rarely can a single victory have released so much pent-up emotion and the party continued through the night.

The following Saturday the Second Division Championship was won with a scoreless draw at Burnden against Fulham, Tottenham and Southampton accompanying the Wanderers into the top flight.

11 April 1979

MANCHESTER UNITED 1 BOLTON WANDERERS 2

The Wanderers went into their first top-flight visit to Old Trafford for 16 years full of confidence, having won four of the previous five games, along with the fact they had defeated United 3–0 at Burnden the previous December.

United dominated the first half, their 'keeper Gary Bailey scarcely laying a glove on the ball, and Bolton went in at half-time trailing to a headed goal from Martin Buchan. Having soaked up so much pressure in the first 45 minutes the Wanderers threw everything forward and levelled in the 53rd minute when Frank Worthington struck his 23rd goal of the season.

This storming, fluctuating contest swung again on the hour when Paul Jones handled a cross from Sammy McIlroy and Gordon McQueen stepped up to put the spot kick into the corner of the net. The referee, Pat Partridge, interrupted the Stretford End's rejoicing by instructing the kick to be retaken. This time McQueen saw his kick hit the post and roll across the face of the goal before going out for a goal kick.

Having ridden their luck it was now Bolton's turn to dominate and Bailey became the busier of the two 'keepers, but he was helpless when, in the final seconds, Brian Smith broke away to outstrip a now ragged United defence and set up Worthington for the winner.

10 September 1983

BOLTON WANDERERS 8 WALSALL 1

No one could have expected the goal avalanche that the Wanderers produced in this Third Division fixture before just 4,375 spectators. Part-timer Tony Caldwell, an electrician by trade, put himself into the record books by equalling the club's record of five goals scored in a game set by Billy Struthers and Jim Cassidy in the previous century.

Tony Caldwell scores his fourth goal of five against Walsall at Burnden.

Caldwell, signed from Horwich RMI for £2,000, began the blitz in the 18th minute when he hammered home from five yards out and four minutes later he was first to a long clearance from 'keeper Simon Farnworth to volley past Ron Green in the Walsall goal.

Seconds later the Wanderers went three up, Caldwell's drive being blocked before falling to Ray Deakin who converted the opportunity. Caldwell completed a 27-minute hat-trick just before half-time when he got onto the end of a Jeff Chandler free-kick.

It was a case of stick or twist for the Wanderers and the early action proved they had gone for the latter. Caldwell scored the fifth in the 59th minute after Neil Redfearn's shot had been parried into his path, and the striker went into the record books with his fifth after 79 minutes.

A 25-yarder from Simon Rudge made it seven, and in the 87th minute centre-half Peter Valentine scored his first goal for the club with the best effort of the afternoon, a thundering left-foot volley. In the dying seconds Ally Brown scored Walsall's consolation but it was enough to deny the Wanderers the opportunity of equalling their best-ever League victory set in 1934.

9 May 1986

Bolton Wanderers 2 Wigan Athletic 1

The Wanderers had put themselves 90 minutes away from Wembley by winning 1–0 in the first leg of the Freight Rover Trophy Northern Final at Wigan and a crowd of 12,120 created an atmosphere not seen at Burnden for many years for the second leg.

An opportunity to visit the twin towers for the first time since 1958 seemed to evaporate when Wigan, who had not lost away since the previous December, levelled the aggregate scores inside nine minutes through Paul Jewell.

It was not until after the interval that Bolton got a foothold, and the equaliser finally came midway through the half when a poor clearance from Colin Methven fell to George Oghani who rounded Roy Tunks to put the ball into the net. Bolton kept on the front foot, aided by the crowd, and with two minutes remaining Tony Caldwell got onto the end of an Oghani cross to spin and crash the ball home to set up a visit to the Wembley for the first time in a generation.

24 May 1986

BOLTON WANDERERS 0 BRISTOL CITY 3

The Wanderers' sixth visit to Wembley proved to be the most disappointing as it resulted in their heaviest defeat there, coupled with a poor performance on the day.

A crowd of 54,502 watched the two Third Division sides and helped put the Freight Rover Trophy, a once maligned competition, onto the football map, with many sampling the Wembley atmosphere for the first time.

Tony Caldwell produced Bolton's best effort early in the first half when his shot struck the crossbar, but from then on City took command. Glyn Riley put them ahead just before the interval and, although the second did not come until 17 minutes from time, Bristol were never really tested. Howard Pritchard scored the second and Riley completed the scoring.

Bolton's poor record in the capital during this period continued with just two draws to show for their last 29 visits.

17 May 1987

BOLTON WANDERERS 2 ALDERSHOT 2

The Wanderers' failure to defeat Aldershot sent them into the Fourth Division for the first and only time. Trailing 1–0 from the first leg of this League Division Three-Four Play-Off semi-final the Wanderers got themselves level on aggregate five minutes after the interval when Tony Caldwell converted a penalty awarded after Mark Gavin had been brought down.

It was Caldwell's first goal since the previous February and lifted some of the tension, but Aldershot restored their aggregate lead in the 75th minute when substitute Darren Anderson was first to react to a loose ball from a free-kick.

There were nine minutes remaining when Caldwell swooped to fire past Shot's 'keeper Tony Lange to level the aggregate scores and take the game into extra-time. Unfortunately, the final 30 minutes of the season produced nothing for Bolton and after Glenn Burvill scored Aldershot's second goal in the first period it became obvious why the team had won just twice in 19 games.

The Wanderers, one of the League's founder members, would be spending the League's centenary season in the basement division.

7 May 1988

WREXHAM 0 BOLTON WANDERERS 1

The Wanderers managed to get out of the Fourth Division at the first attempt in a most dramatic final day promotion scramble. Wolves and Cardiff City had secured the first two places and the final spot was between the Wanderers, Torquay, who needed just one point from their final two games, and Scunthorpe United.

Torquay lost their penultimate game and faced Scunthorpe on the final day leaving the Wanderers requiring a win and the Iron to win in Devon. The scene was set and the occasion became one that all the players and supporters will never forget.

The all important match winner came from Robbie Savage midway through the second half and when Wrexham's Geoff Hunter was sent off it looked to be Bolton's day. The Wanderers became nervous in the final stages with some wayward passing, and with five minutes left they too were reduced to 10 men when John Thomas was sent off for his second yellow card.

The final five minutes seemed an eternity, but when the news filtered through that Torquay had lost, the final whistle sparked scenes of jubilation that brought back memories of Blackburn in 1978.

Robbie Savage scores the goal that wins promotion from the Fourth Division.

Phil Brown and Steve Thompson celebrate the Sherpa Van Trophy success at Wembley.

28 May 1989

BOLTON WANDERERS 4 TORQUAY UNITED 1

The Wanderers made up for the disappointment of 1986 by winning the Associate Members' competition, known as the Sherpa Van Trophy. Victory over Blackpool, with a

2–1 aggregate win, secured Bolton's seventh visit to the twin towers were they faced Fourth Division Torquay United.

The underdogs took the lead after 23 minutes when Dean Edwards headed past Dave Felgate, but it took only four minutes for Bolton to respond. Julian Darby levelled when he swung a low right-foot shot past Kenny Allen's despairing dive.

A slice of luck swung the game Bolton's way in the 63rd minute when Jeff Chandler's shot took a deflection off John Morrison to wrong foot Allen and end up in the net. Felgate was in fine form to deny Torquay's attempted fight-back, but two well-worked goals in three minutes made it an enjoyable day in the sunshine for Bolton supporters.

Dean Crombie started and finished a move by racing clear to score with his first goal for the club in the 79th minute, and then Stuart Storer used his pace to link up with John Thomas for Trevor Morgan to score the fourth and the first by a Bolton forward in that season's competition. The result established a then new club record of 20 games without defeat.

13 January 1993

LIVERPOOL 0 BOLTON WANDERERS 2

Many thought that Bolton had missed their chance of defeating Liverpool in the third round of the FA Cup, having been pulled back from a two-goal advantage at Burnden Park, but Bruce Rioch's spirited and highly committed team made the two-division gap between the sides a mockery in the replay at Anfield.

It took only three minutes for the Wanderers to go ahead when John McGinlay rose to meet an exquisite cross from David Lee to direct a powerful header past the helpless Mike Hooper. Bolton's defence found answers to any questions they were asked by Liverpool and came out stronger and more determined after the break.

Indeed, it was the Wanderers who looked most dangerous several times as the match drew towards a tense finale notably when Scott Green and Andy Walker hurried their shots when they had more time than they realised. With 12 minutes remaining the Wanderers wrapped up the tie to inflict Liverpool's worst defeat in the competition since 1959 when Walker rose to clinically head home at the far post from McGinlay's curling cross.

For 8,500 Bolton supporters who were at the game it was a memorable night that brought back memories of days of when the club were at the same playing level and hopes that one day they would return.

8 May 1993

BOLTON WANDERERS 1 PRESTON NORTH END 0

The Wanderers went into this final day of the Second Division season as favourites to defeat Preston and regain the status they had lost 10 years previously. With just one defeat in 18 games and with a victory over champions Stoke City the previous Tuesday, they needed to keep their nerve to finish off the job.

It was a day that saw quality come second to spirit as John McGinlay carved himself a piece of Burnden folklore with the winning goal from the penalty spot. News had come through that the only club that could pip Bolton, Port Vale, were winning 3–2 at Blackpool, but the decisive moment came 16 minutes from time when the referee awarded a penalty for handball by Simon Burton.

Up stepped the ice-cool McGinlay, shut himself off from the pressure of the 21,720 crowd and the fact that an entire season's work rested on his kick, to keep his nerve to fire past former Wanderers 'keeper Simon Farnworth.

The goal sent Bolton up as runners-up, just three points behind one-time runaway leaders Stoke, sending North End into Division Three as thousands cascaded onto the Burnden pitch at the final whistle to celebrate the promotion in a carnival atmosphere.

13 November 1993

GRETNA 2 BOLTON WANDERERS 3

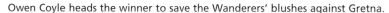

The Wanderers late, late show avoided an embarrassment in this first round FA Cup tie played at Burnden due to safety issues at Raydale Park. The crowd of 6,447 saw the Northern Premier League part-timers take the lead through Derek Townsley, before John McGinlay converted a penalty awarded for a blatant push on Owen Coyle.

In the 25th minute Gretna restored their advantage when Mark Dobie's left-foot shot evaded Aidan Davison and from then on Gretna 'keeper Jason Priestley produced the game of his dreams to keep Bolton out.

Owen Coyle heads the winner to save the Wanderers' blushes against Gretna.

Gretna were on the brink of national acclaim, and it looked like it was not going to be Wanderers' day in the 76th minute when Jason McAteer rattled the crossbar. With 11 minutes remaining it was Coyle who stepped up to the plate when he side-footed the equaliser after a strong run from McAteer much to the relief of the Burnden crowd.

Five minutes later the Scot rose to head home the winner after McGinlay had flicked on David Lee's cross, but this close encounter was to set the club off on their best run in the FA Cup since 1958.

9 February 1994

ARSENAL 1 BOLTON WANDERERS 3

The Wanderers produced their most stunning Cup result of modern times by knocking the holders of the Cup out of the competition for the second successive season. It appeared that the Wanderers had missed their chance after drawing 2–2 at Burnden in the original fourth-round tie but their performance at Highbury stunned most of the 33,863 crowd.

The Wanderers soaked up early pressure with Aidan Davison making two great saves before John McGinlay pounced to head his 21st goal of the season after twenty minutes of the game. Alan Smith equalised for the Gunners 15 minutes later but, undaunted, it was in extra-time that Bolton turned the screw.

Jason McAteer exploited a Nigel Winterburn error nine minutes into overtime, shooting Bolton ahead after an Owen Coyle effort had struck the post. Substitute Andy Walker,

Jason McAteer, John McGinlay and Andy Walker celebrate after the FA Cup win at Arsenal.

returning after 10 months out with injury, completed the scoring, but it should have been more as Tony Kelly fired home a free-kick a minute from time. The referee ordered a re-take and sent off Arsenal defender Martin Keown for encroaching having previously been booked.

For several minutes at the end of the game the Wanderers stood dancing in front of their 5,000 supporters at the Clock End as they celebrated inflicting what was only Arsenal's second defeat in 29 Cup ties.

8 March 1995

Bolton Wanderers 3 Swindon Town 1

The Wanderers reached their first major Final in 37 years by coming back from the dead in this Coca-Cola Cup semi-final second leg that sent the 19,851 crowd through a spectrum of emotions. Losing 2–1 from the first leg to their First Division rivals, Jan Fjortoft increased the Robins advantage eight minutes after the break, and it appeared that the Wanderers were to fail at the final hurdle.

The resilient Bolton side turned this with a tactical switch when Jason McAteer was given a free role in midfield, and he levelled the second leg scoreline after 64 minutes, tapping home after a shot from Alan Thompson had come back off the post.

This was the lifeline that the Wanderers needed, and just 10 minutes after entering the action Mixu Paatelainen levelled the aggregate scores by hammering a ferocious 25-yard drive into the roof of the net. The noise inside Burnden was deafening as they went in pursuit of the goal that would take them to Wembley.

Three minutes from time that goal came. Thompson's free-kick cannoned off a Swindon defender and fell to John McGinlay. The Scottish striker kept his nerve, controlled the ball and calmly placed it past the advancing 'keeper Fraser Digby.

2 April 1995

Liverpool 2 Bolton Wanderers 1

Two goals from Steve McManaman won him the Man of the Match trophy and the Coca-Cola Cup for Liverpool in a Wembley Final that that lived up to its quality billing, especially in the second half. The Wanderers made the Premiership side fight all the way for their sixth success in the competition.

Liverpool drew first blood in the 37th minute. John Barnes fed McManaman who set off on a run that took him past Alan Stubbs and cut inside before drilling a low shot beyond Keith Branagan. It was a stunning blow for the Wanderers who had created the two best chances of the half.

Although Liverpool had been in control for long periods of the opening half, it was Bolton who were on top after the interval. Jason McAteer began to take control in the middle and Dutch midfielder Richard Sneekes had three shots within minutes to demonstrate how much possession Bolton enjoyed. Despite this, it was Liverpool who went further ahead when McManaman again created and finished a goal from a pacey run.

Within two minutes the Wanderers were back in it. From Mark Seagraves's cross, Mixu Paatelainen flicked on to Alan Thompson who spun and blasted a left-foot shot into the top-right-hand corner of David James's goal. Unfortunately, despite a final flourish they could not find one more to take the game to extra-time and returned to the Premiership promotion push.

29 May 1995

BOLTON WANDERERS 4 READING 3

It looked like the Wanderers' second visit to the twin towers in eight weeks was going to end in a similar manner when Reading took a two-goal advantage inside the opening 12 minutes in this First Division Play-off Final. Lee Nogan put The Royals ahead in the fourth minute, and Adrian Williams increased the advantage when he knocked a near-post shot past Keith Branagan from a free-kick. The turning point of the game came in the 35th minute when Reading were awarded a penalty after Jason McAteer took away Michael Gilkes's heels. Branagan pulled off a marvellous save from Stuart Lovell's kick to keep Bolton in the game

Bolton came out for the second half with greater purpose and better organisation. Bruce Rioch brought on Fabian de Freitas, and his pace began to cause problems. The Lancashire section of the 64,107 crowd erupted when Owen Coyle climbed to head a magnificent goal past Shaka Hislop in the 75th minute to set up a nail-biting finale.

Keith Branagan's penalty save against Reading.

There was just four minutes left on the clock when Bolton completed the comeback. Alan Thompson released De Freitas, and his pace got him away to drive past Hislop's groping dive for a dramatic equaliser. Bolton set about imposing their growing superiority in extra-time. Fourteen minutes into the extra half hour, McAteer swept past two tiring defenders, back heeled to Coyle who crossed for John McGinlay to set up Mixu Paatelainen to head home for Bolton to take the lead.

There was just three minutes left when Paatelainen supplied De Freitas who saw his shot come back of the post but the Dutchman put away the rebound. Reading's player-manager Jimmy Quinn volleyed his side back into the game with a minute to go, but it was no more than a gesture as Bolton returned to the top table after 15 years.

27 November 1996

BOLTON WANDERERS 6 TOTTENHAM HOTSPUR 1

The Wanderers demolished Tottenham to reach the quarter-finals of the Coca-Cola Cup, producing their most emphatic victory in the competition and leaving the Premier League side humiliated. First Division leaders Bolton were led to victory with a hat-trick from John McGinlay, his first goal coming after just six minutes.

Spurs drew level completely against the run of play in the 19th minute thanks to a refereeing error. Paul Danson ruled that John Sheridan had touched the ball with his arm rather than his shoulder, and from the resulting free-kick Teddy Sherringham struck.

It was not until the 37th minute that Bolton regained the lead, McGinlay tapping home from close range after 'keeper Ian Walker had missed his punch. On the hour Gerry Taggart headed the Wanderers third, and McGinlay completed his hat-trick from the penalty spot after he had been pushed over by Steven Carr.

Nathan Blake struck the fifth goal in the 79th minute, holding off Colin Calderwood before striking a low shot from the edge of the area into the bottom corner. Substitute Scott Taylor rounded off the scoring with his first touch, but Spurs were spared an even greater humiliation in the dying seconds when the officials failed to spot that a Scott Sellars corner had gone over the line.

John McGinlay wheels away after scoring the opening goal against Tottenham.

25 April 1997

BOLTON WANDERERS 4 CHARLTON ATHLETIC 1

One hundred and two years of history came to an end at Burnden Park, but with it came a memorable game in which to see off the old ground, and for the finale came the presentation of the First Division Championship. The team became the highest scoring in Wanderers' history and were runaway leaders in the League, but no one could have planned a better send off.

Charlton had not appeared to have read the script and held an interval lead through a Mark Kinsella goal. The final half to be played was one that no Wanderers supporter wanted to end. A minute into the second period Bolton were level when Alan Thompson, who had changed his boots during the break, fired home with an unfamiliar right-foot shot.

Gerry Taggart put Bolton ahead with a sweet volley in the 63rd minute, but it was not until the final minutes that John McGinlay stole the show with two late goals to bring the curtain down. In the 88th minute he converted a penalty awarded after Scott Sellars had been brought down, and in the final minute he tapped in at the far post to convert a cross from Jimmy Phillips.

The final two goals took the Wanderers to 98 League goals for the season, eclipsing the

record set by the 1933–34 side and they were to reach the century in the final game of the season at Tranmere Rovers.

A fitting end to Burnden. The Wanderers are presented with the First Division Championship after the 4–1 defeat of Charlton.

1 September 1997

BOLTON WANDERERS 0 EVERTON 0

After all the planning and build up for the first-ever match in the Reebok Stadium the actual 90 minutes proved to be something of an anti-climax. It did, however, have its moments and controversy that was to have repercussions later in the season and is still a talking point years afterwards.

In the 54th minute referee Steve Lodge waved play on after Gerry Taggart's header fell behind the line before Terry Phelan bundled the ball away. TV evidence proved the ball was

Everton's Terry Phelan clears Gerry Taggart's effort from behind the line.

over the line and by the season's end the Wanderers were relegated from the Premier League on 40 points while Everton stayed up with the same total by virtue of their better goal difference.

And so Taggart, who scored in the final game at Burnden, missed out on having the honour of scoring the first goal at the £35 million showpiece stadium and despite that chance, Bolton had other efforts that could have secured the points. Scott Sellars missed a near open goal, while Nathan Blake forced Neville Southall into a couple of decent saves.

The crowd of 23,131 saw history made, along with a TV audience of millions, but the club saw it as a satisfactory night's work that gave them a steady if unspectacular start after the season began with three away games.

17 May 2000

IPSWICH TOWN 5 BOLTON WANDERERS 3

The second leg of the Nationwide League First Division Play-off semi-finals proved to be a cruel way for the Wanderers to end a season that had seen them also knocked out at the semi-final stages of both the League Cup and FA Cup. The official for the evening, Barry Knight, awarded three penalties to the home side, and to the Wanderers he showed 12 yellow cards and two red but not so much as a single caution to Ipswich.

After leading 2–0 at the Reebok Stadium in the First leg, Ipswich fought back to earn a 2–2 draw to set up a winner-takes-all tie at Portman Road. The Wanderers, without 21-goal Eidur

Allan Johnston scores the Wanderers' third goal at Ipswich.

Gudjohnsen through injury, went ahead in the sixth minute when Dean Holdsworth poked home after a mistake by 'keeper Richard Wright. Ipswich levelled from the penalty spot through Jim Magilton as tempers began to fray due to his theatrical tumble to win the kick.

In the 39th minute Bolton regained the lead when Holdsworth sent in a free-kick that went in off the post, but on the stroke of half-time Ipswich won another controversial penalty. This time Jussi Jääskeläinen saved Magilton's kick, but he could not prevent him levelling three minutes after the interval with a rising shot.

Ipswich were still celebrating when Allan Johnston put Bolton 3–2 up with a screaming 20-yard shot, and it was a lead that was held until a minute from time when Magilton completed his hat-trick. Two minutes into injury time Mike Whitlow was sent off for a second bookable offence leaving Bolton to face extra-time a man down.

Four minutes into extra-time Ipswich were awarded their third penalty of the evening which was converted by Jamie Clapham, and three minutes later Bolton were left with a mountain to climb when they were reduced to nine men after Robbie Elliott was shown a second yellow card. Martin Reuser's goal late in the second period of extra-time was academic as substitute Franck Passi became the recipient of the Wanderers' 12th yellow card with virtually the last kick of the game.

28 May 2001

Bolton Wanderers 3 Preston North End 0

After two successive Play-off failures, Bolton returned to the Premier League with victory over their Lancashire rivals at the Millennium Stadium in Cardiff. Superior for all but the opening exchanges, the Wanderers led from the 16th minute as Preston failed to clear their lines and Gareth Farrelly swooped to drive a low shot into the net from the edge of the area.

Anthony Barness and Dean Holdsworth celebrate after the Play-off victory against Preston, 2001.

Chances came and went for Bolton and Preston were grateful to be still in it at half-time. With 20 minutes left, 'keeper Matt Clarke made a terrific save from David Healy that made sure Bolton did not pay dearly for those missed chances.

In the 89th minute Farrelly released substitute Michael Ricketts to score his 24th goal of the season to rubber stamp Bolton's return to the top flight and, within seconds, Ricardo Gardner scampered down the left to release a left-foot shot for the goal of the afternoon to put the icing on the cake.

18 August 2001

LEICESTER CITY 0 BOLTON WANDERERS 5

Sam Allardyce and his Bolton team made a memorable opening day start after winning promotion. The Wanderers, heavily backed for the drop and without any new signings for their Premiership return, played more like title contenders in a four-goal first-half blitz at Filbert Street.

Bolton were stronger, smarter, more committed and might easily have doubled their first half tally. Kevin Nolan started the romp after 15 minutes, heading past Tim Flowers before Michael Ricketts smashed a shot into the bottom corner for the second on 33 minutes.

Four minutes before the break Nolan claimed his second, and the first-half rout was completed in added time when Per Frandsen scored directly from a free-kick. The fifth goal did not come until the 83rd minute, Frandsen curling the ball around the wall with another free-kick.

29 December 2001

BOLTON WANDERERS 2 LEICESTER CITY 2

Bolton pulled off an astonishing comeback from two goals down with just nine men for three quarters of the game to battle back to earn a point against Leicester City at the Reebok Stadium. The match had everything expected from an old fashioned panto – villains, heroes, excitement, drama and moments of pure comic farce.

Cast in the role of villain was referee Mike Riley who controversially sent off Paul Warhurst and Dean Holdsworth. Cast in the role of Riley's sidekick was Leicester's Robbie Savage. He seemed to make a meal of Warhurst's challenge that produced the first red in the 18th minute.

Michael Ricketts and Kevin Nolan celebrate the late equaliser against Leicester City.

Worse was to follow for Bolton when Michael Ricketts headed into his own net after 22 minutes, and a minute later Holdsworth was dismissed for grabbing Savage around the neck. Brian Deane increased City's lead in the 26th minute, but incredibly Bolton pulled a goal back in the 34th minute when Kevin Nolan nodded past Ian Walker.

Riley continued to brandish cards and livened things up in the 69th minute by showing a second yellow to City's Muzzy Izzet and this gave the Wanderers fresh heart for the final minutes. Per Frandsen hit the post with a free-kick, but in the final seconds Ricketts rose to head home Nicky Southall's cross to take the roof of the Reebok Stadium.

11 May 2003

BOLTON WANDERERS 2 MIDDLESBROUGH 1

The Wanderers extended their stay in the top flight to three years for the first time since 1963–64 after an afternoon of high tension. They came into the game knowing that victory would ensure safety and send West Ham into the Championship.

If it was billed as a day when the Wanderers multinational squad would be forced to display a traditional British fighting spirit, it proved nothing of the sort. Always in control of their destiny from the 10th minute when Per Frandsen opened the scoring with a spectacular goal, Jay Jay Okocha and the team played, as always, with smiles on their faces and a carefree abandon.

Boro 'keeper Mark Schwarzer was again clutching thin air on 21 minutes as Okocha's delightful free-kick sailed past his right hand. A threat of a twist in the tale came in the 61st minute when Michael Ricketts came off the bench to score his first goal for Middlesbrough since his acrimonious transfer from the Wanderers. News that West Ham were winning filtered through, and for 15 minutes the Wanderers lost their composure.

Middlesbrough's momentum was lost when Franck Queudrue was sent off for two senseless lunges on Ivan Campo in as many minutes, and news of Birmingham's fightback against the Hammers made sure the final five minutes were played out in a carnival atmosphere.

15 May 2005

BOLTON WANDERERS 3 EVERTON 2

For the second year in succession the Wanderers went into the final game of the season free of any nerves, having secured a UEFA Cup place the previous week in a 1–1 draw at Portsmouth, while Everton had won the fourth Champions League qualification place. All was set for an end of season kickabout but what both teams produced was a scintillating action-packed 90 minutes.

Tim Cahill put Everton into a ninth-minute lead and once Bruno N'Gotty received his marching orders for cuffing Cahill on the stroke of half-time the game had a 1–0 scoreline written all over it. Bolton stuck with three forwards and were rewarded with three set piece goals.

Stelios scores the winner against Everton.

Eight minutes after the break Radhi Jaidi sparked the fightback with a towering header from Fernando Hierro's free-kick. Bolton took the lead eight minutes later when Stelios set up Kevin Davies for a crisp shot that flew past Richard Wright. The game took a twist two minutes later when Lee Carsley lashed the ball into the net for Everton's equaliser.

The pendulum swung again two minutes later, Davies crashing in a header direct from a corner that Wright saved on the line but could not hold on to and Stelios flew in like a flash to the score the winner. A minute later, Man of the Match, 37-year-old Hierro, was substituted in his final game before retirement to rapturous applause.

The home support in the 27,701 crowd enjoyed the Wanderers making history by qualifying for the UEFA Cup, producing a magnificent comeback with 10 men and then staging a great end-of-season party.

HIGHLIGHTS OF 2011–11

Daniel Sturridge heads the Wanderers ahead against Arsenal at the Reebok.

Chung Yong Lee scores the winner in the FA Cup quarter-final at Birmingham City.

A-Z OF BOLTON PLAYERS

SAM ALLARDYCE

Born: Dudley, 19 October 1954

Spotted playing in his native West Midlands, Sam Allardyce began his professional football career after serving his apprenticeship at Burnden Park. He soon made his mark in the Wanderers' youth team, in a central-defensive line up that also included Paul Jones and Don McAllister, and was a member of the team that won the Lancashire Youth Cup in 1971. In November 1973 Allardyce made his League debut for Bolton against Notts County at Burnden and then spent the remainder of the season as understudy to his former youth team colleagues. The following season, soon after the departure of McAllister to Tottenham, 'Big Sam' won a regular place in the Trotters' League line up. He scored a memorable powerful header against Sunderland at Burnden in December 1975 and a long-range

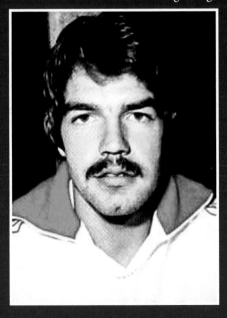

thunderbolt at home to Orient in April 1978, both efforts going into folklore, and won a Second Division Championship medal in 1978. Unfortunately both Allardyce and the club failed to establish themselves in the top flight and, after the Trotters were relegated in 1980, he joined Sunderland for a £150,000 fee. After one season at Roker Park, Allardyce was transferred to Third Division Millwall for £95,000. A spell in the NASL with Tampa Bay was followed by brief spells at Coventry City and Huddersfield Town before he returned to Burnden for a £10,000 fee in 1985. Injury hindered his second spell with the club and in August 1986 he moved to Preston, where he helped them to win promotion from Division Four in 1987. He ended his playing career at West Bromwich Albion, playing his only game for them in November 1989, having been appointed assistant manager to Brian Talbot the previous February. He later set off on his own managerial career (see 'Managers').

	League		FA Cup		FL Cup		Total	
	A	G	A	G	A	G	A	G
1973–74	7	-	-/1	-	1	-	8/1	-
1974–75	17/1	3	-	-	-	-	17/1	3
1975–76	40	5	6	1	1	-	47	6
1976–77	41	6	-	-	8	-	49	6
1977–78	41	4	4	-	3	1	48	5
1978–79	18/2	1	-	-	2	-	20/2	1
1979–80	16/1	2	4	1	-	-	20/1	3
1985–86	14	-	-	-	3	-	17	-
	194/4	21	14/1	2	18	1	226/5	24

NICOLAS ANELKA

Born: Versailles, France, 14 March 1979

Nicolas Anelka became Bolton's record signing in August 2006 when £8 million

was paid to Feberbahçe. He began his career at Paris Saint-Germain before moving to Arsenal in February 1997 at the age of 17 for a £500,000 fee. He was a member of the Arsenal double-winning team in 1998 and scored their second goal in the 2–0 FA Cup Final win over Newcastle United. He scored 28 goals in 90 first-team games for Arsenal and won the PFA Young Player of the Year in 1999 before a £22.3 million move to Real Madrid that summer. It was a love/hate relationship between Anelka and the club ensued, which included a 45-day suspension for refusing to train, but he helped the club to secure the Champions League in 2000. A move back to Paris Saint-Germain for £20 million followed in the summer, and in January 2002 he spent six months on loan at Liverpool. Manchester City kept him in the Premiership that summer after paying £13 million, and in two and a half seasons there he netted 37 League goals. In January 2005 Fenerbahçe secured his services for £7 million and he helped them to the title that season. He returned to the Premier

League at the Reebok Stadium making his Bolton debut against Watford and scored his first goal for the club against Arsenal. He ended the 2006–07 season as the Wanderers' top scorer with 12 goals. Anelka signed a new four-year deal in August 2007 but the following January became Bolton's record transfer sale when he joined Chelsea for £15 million, making him the most expensive player in history in relation to transfer fees paid. At the time he led the Trotters' scoring charts with 11 goals. Anelka was a member of the side that reached the 2008 Champions League Final, but he saw his penalty saved in the shoot-out that resulted in Manchester United winning the trophy. During 2008–09 he led the Premier League goalscoring charts and the following season won the double with the London club. While at the Reebok he won 12 of his 69 international caps for France, his final appearance coming in the 2010 World Cup Finals in South Africa, where he was banned by the FFF after falling out with coach Raymond Domenech.

	League		FA Cup		FL Cup		UEFA Cup		Total	
	A	G	A	G	A	G	A	G	A	G
2006–07	35	11	2/1	-	1	1	-	-	38/1	12
2007–08	18	10	-	-	-	-	2/2	1	20/2	11
	53	21	2/1	-	1	1	2/2	1	58/3	23

JACK ATKINSON

Born: New Washington, 20 December 1913
Died: 1977

Spotted by Bolton playing for Washington Colliery, Jack Atkinson was immediately snapped up by Bolton, who allowed him to remain in the North East to continue his football education with his old club. Signed for nothing, the Wanderers made a number of donations to the colliery club's funds and Atkinson finally came to Burnden Park in August 1931. He graduated through the Lancashire

1934–35	40	2	8	1	48	3
1935–36	39	1	2	-	41	1
1936–37	17	-	5	-	22	-
1937–38	37	-	1	-	38	-
1938–39	38	-	2	-	40	-
1945–46	-	-	2	-	2	-
1946–47	25	-	-	-	25	-
1947–48	5	-	1	-	6	-
	240	4	23	1	263	5

JOHN BALL

Born: Ince, 13 March 1925

John Ball began his career with his home-town club, Wigan Athletic, during World War Two, guesting for Gravesend during the hostilities. In February 1948 he joined Manchester United, for whom he made 22 First Division appearances as understudy to Johnny Carey. Ball joined the Wanderers in September 1950 as Bolton attempted to fill the problem position of full-back. He took over the right flank and was joined soon after on the left by George Kennedy from Blackpool. He was a regular for five seasons, being ever present during

Combination and Central League sides at centre-half and his first-team opportunity arose after the departure of Tom Griffiths to Middlesbrough towards the end of the 1932–33 season. He became the defensive kingpin of the side that reached the semi-finals of the FA Cup in 1935 and won promotion to the First Division the following year. Many of his best years were lost due to the war, during which he guested for Everton and Blackpool as well as turning out for the Trotters whenever possible. After the war he managed just one full season before losing his place to Lol Hamlett, and in April 1948 he was given a free transfer. A month later he became player-manager at New Brighton, playing 52 League games before retiring from the game to take over licensed premises in Bolton.

	League		FA Cup		Total	
	A	G	A	G	A	G
1932–33	3	-	-	-	3	-
1933–34	36	1	2	-	38	1

1953–54 and 1954–55. His only lapse came during the early part of 1953 when a young Roy Hartle took over, but Ball fought his way back into the side to win a Cup Final place after Hartle had played in every other round. Hartle eventually won the full-back spot from Ball after two games of the 1955–56 campaign, but Ball continued to be on hand to fill in at either full-back positions until his retirement in May 1958. While with the club he represented the Football League in both 1952 and 1954. He returned to Wigan and in 1960 was appointed manager of the then Cheshire League side, where he remained for three years before retiring from the game.

	League		FA Cup		Total	
	A	G	A	G	A	G
1950–51	35	-	2	-	37	-
1951–52	39	-	1	-	40	-
1952–53	26	-	1	-	27	-
1953–54	42	-	6	-	48	-
1954–55	42	-	2	-	44	-
1955–56	2	-	-	-	2	-
1956–57	10	1	-	-	10	1
1957–58	4	1	-	-	4	1
	200	2	12	-	212	2

RALPH BANKS

Born: Farnworth, 28 June 1920
Died: Bolton, October 1993
Ralph Banks was born and bred in Farnworth, less then three miles from Burnden Park. He began his career with Farnworth St Thomas' as a left-back. After a spell with South Liverpool just before the war, he joined the Wanderers and made his debut in their opening Football League North game in January 1941, after the club had been closed for six months. Without doubt Banks lost his most promising years through the war and his career was curtailed even further after the cessation of hostilities because he was called up for National service. During the war he served

with the Royal North Lancashire Regiment in both Italy and Palestine, where he played in the Canal Zone team. The 1948–49 season was his most consistent for the club when he missed only four games. He became understudy to George Kinsell, then to George Kennedy and George Higgins, but he outlasted them all. His last appearance for the Wanderers came at Wembley in the 1953 FA Cup Final, when he wore the number-three shirt before seeing his brother, Tommy, take it from him for the start of the following season. He joined Aldershot in January 1954 and ended his playing days with Weymouth. The Banks brothers played in only three League games together for Bolton, which all came in the early part of the 1950–51 season.

	League	FA Cup	Total
	A	A	A
1946–47	2	2	4
1947–48	16	-	16
1948–49	38	3	41

1949–50	22	3	25
1950–51	11	1	12
1951–52	4	1	5
1952–53	11	4	15
	104	14	118

TOMMY BANKS

Born: Farnworth, 10 November 1929

Tommy Banks was one of the great 'hard men' of the Bolton defence of the 1950s, when the mere mention of his name was enough to frighten opposition wingers. Banks played local football with Partridges and signed for the Trotters in 1947 while still working down the pit at Mossley Common. He made his debut in a First Division game at Wolves in May 1948, but his first-team opportunities were few and far between, with his older brother Ralph occupying one of the full-back berths. It was to be five seasons before Tommy became a regular, but it did not take long for his reputation as a tough-tacking left-back to spread. His threat to opponents that they would end up with gravel rash from the Burnden Park track if they attempted to get past him became

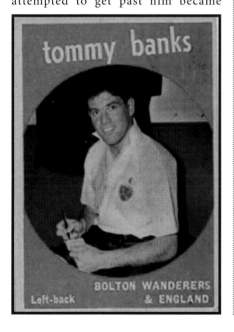

synonymous with the club's defence of the day, but Banks was a quality full-back. His most memorable times at Burnden came towards the end of his career. In 1958 he won an FA Cup-winners' medal and, in May of that year, made his England debut against the Soviet Union in Moscow. He went on to win a further five caps, all in the space of five months, and also represented the Football League against the Scottish League. He played his last League game for the club in February 1961 and at the end of that season joined Altrincham in the Cheshire League. He took part in the 1964 Welsh Cup Final for a Bangor City side who took Cardiff to a Play-off before losing. He later retired from the game to concentrate on the building trade in his home town, where he still resides today.

	League		FA Cup		Total	
	A	G	A	G	A	G
1947–48	1	-	-	-	1	-
1948–49	1	-	-	-	1	-
1949–50	3	-	-	-	3	-
1950–51	3	-	-	-	3	-
1952–53	4	-	-	-	4	-
1953–54	40	-	6	-	46	-
1954–55	25	-	-	-	25	-
1955–56	39	-	2	-	41	-
1956–57	21	-	-	-	21	-
1957–58	28	-	7	-	35	-
1958–59	37	-	6	-	43	-
1959–60	20	1	-	-	20	1
1960–61	11	1	1	-	12	1
	233	2	22	-	255	2

TOM BARBER

Born: West Stanley, 22 July 1886

Died: Nuneaton, 18 September 1925

Born within 100 yards of St James's Park in Newcastle, Tom Barber began his footballing career at Todd's Nook boarding school and Hamotley FC before joining West Stanley. The Wanderers secured his transfer for a fee of £75 in May 1908 and Barber made his League debut at Fulham

	League		FA Cup		Total	
	A	G	A	G	A	G
1908–09	20	2	-	-	20	2
1909–10	15	1	1	-	16	1
1910–11	17	5	1	-	18	5
1911–12	38	4	3	-	41	4
1912–13	12	2	-	-	12	2
	102	14	5	-	107	14

MALCOLM BARRASS

Born: Blackpool, 13 December 1924

Malcolm Barrass signed amateur forms for the Wanderers in 1944, following in the footsteps of his father, Matt, who had played League Football for Blackpool, Sheffield Wednesday and Manchester City. Malcolm had been spotted while playing for Manchester Works' team, Ford Motors, and had previously played three trial games for Wolves. He had been offered terms but joined Bolton, where he turned professional in November 1944. He showed no signs of being overawed by the

in October that year. He became a reliable half-back and inside-forward, securing two promotions and suffering one relegation while with the Wanderers, which included an ever-present season in 1911–12. On Christmas Eve 1912 Aston Villa paid £1,950 for his services, and it was with them that he recorded his greatest success in scoring the winning goal in the 1913 FA Cup Final against Sunderland. The profits from his transfer to Villa went towards a roof to cover the Great Lever End at Burnden. Barber was wounded during World War One but recovered to guest for Celtic, Partick Thistle, Linfield and Belfast Celtic. He also represented the Footballers' Battalion and later had spells with Stalybridge Celtic, Crystal Palace, Merthyr Town and Pontypridd after the war. He ended his career at Walsall in 1921 before his untimely death in 1925 due to tuberculosis.

big step up into wartime League football and during 1945–46 scored 22 goals in 40 games at inside-forward. Two of those goals came in the second leg of the North War Cup Final against Manchester United, which the Wanderers won on aggregate, and he also appeared in the North/South success against Chelsea. Selected to play for England in the Victory international against Wales at West Brom in October 1945, Barrass went on to win three full England caps, the last of which came in 1953 against Scotland at Wembley. He became a versatile player, representing his country at centre-half, and in 1948 he scored four goals for the Wanderers at centre-forward in a 5–1 win against Manchester City. Barrass won an FA Cup runners'-up medal in 1953 against his home-town club, but his 12-year association with the Wanderers ended in September 1956 when he was signed by Joe Mercer for Sheffield United. In August 1958 he became player-manager at Lancashire Combination side Wigan Athletic but resigned on New Year's Day 1959. He joined Southern League Nuneaton Borough, where he spent two and a half years before settling in the Bury area. He became a sales rep while helping out Pwllheli, then Hyde United, as trainer.

	League		FA Cup		Total	
	A	G	A	G	A	G
1946–47	8	3	2	2	10	5
1947–48	23	6	1	-	24	6
1948–49	37	7	2	-	39	7
1949–50	36	2	3	-	39	2
1950–51	38	-	2	-	40	-
1951–52	37	-	1	-	38	-
1952–53	38	-	8	-	46	-
1953–54	38	-	6	-	44	-
1954–55	40	5	2	-	42	5
1955–56	32	2	1	-	33	2
1956–57	2	-	-	-	2	-
	329	25	28	2	357	27

HERBERT BAVERSTOCK

Born: Cradley Heath, 13 January 1883
Died: Bolton, December 1951

One of several Bolton players to hail from the Dudley area, Herbert Baverstock began his career with Netherton St James before joining Brierley Hill Alliance, from whom the Wanderers secured his signature in May 1905. And so began a 16-year association with the club. Baverstock become a major part of the defence, one of a long line of outstanding defenders who gave the team its dogged prominence. Capable of playing in either full-back berth, it was at right-back that he excelled. After missing the opening game of the 1905–06 season Baverstock made his League debut in the next game, a 3–3 draw at Notts County, and did not miss another game for two years as the Wanderers finished sixth in Division One in consecutive seasons. He missed only one game during the Second Division Championship season in 1908–09 and, to show how versatile he was, played the majority of the 1910–11 season, in which promotion was won again, on the left flank. During World War One he served with the Royal Flying Corps, and he continued to hold down a regular place in the side after the hostilities despite the arrival of record signing John Elvey from Luton Town in 1920. He played his final full season at Burnden in 1920–21 as the club finished in third place in the First Division, but it was another stalwart-to-be in the form of Bob Haworth who eventually displaced him. Baverstock's last game for the club came at Huddersfield in October 1921, and the following month he joined Blackpool on a free transfer. He played 18 League games for the Seasiders before retiring from the game to take up the licence at the Lever Arms in Bolton.

	League		FA Cup		Total	
	A	G	A	G	A	G
1905–06	37	-	1	-	38	-
1906–07	38	-	4	-	42	-
1907–08	24	-	5	-	29	-
1908–09	37	1	1	-	38	1
1909–10	34	3	1	-	35	3
1910–11	36	-	1	-	37	-
1911–12	26	-	3	-	29	-
1912–13	25	-	-	-	25	-
1913–14	31	-	3	-	34	-
1914–15	27	-	2	-	29	-
1919–20	17	-	-	-	17	-
1920–21	33	-	1	-	34	-
1921–22	1	-	-	-	1	-
	366	4	22	-	388	4

ERIC BELL

Born: Clayton, Manchester, 27 November 1929

Eric Bell began his career as a forward with Manchester United in October 1949 but his time there lasted only one month before he joined the Wanderers, who had spotted him playing for the RAF. Bell became a regular in the reserves, hitting a hat-trick against Preston on Christmas Eve 1949. Disaster struck in the return fixture when he broke his leg, which ruled him out of touring with

the FA that summer. He made his Bolton League debut as an inside-right in a 4–1 home defeat to Tottenham in August 1950 but was to become a regular in the side at wing-half from January 1953. He took over from Tommy Neill and was ever present in the team's run to the FA Cup Final against Blackpool that year. Unfortunately Bell was struck by injury after just 18 minutes of the game and was despatched to outside-left, from where he managed to score Bolton's third goal. The following season was his most consistent, and he missed just two games as the club finished fifth in the First Division and reached the sixth round of the FA Cup. Bell also won two England B caps, against Scotland at Roker and Yugoslavia in

Ljubljana, and was selected for the Football League against the Scottish League. In February 1955 he scored what was his only goal in League football in a 6–1 win over Wolves at Burnden, but between April 1955 and February 1957 he languished in the reserves, having lost his place to Bryan Edwards. He returned for a short swan-song before retiring through injury in July 1958.

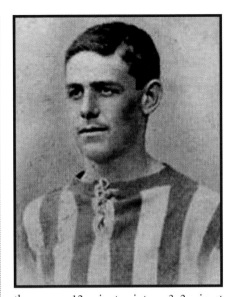

	League		FA Cup		Total	
	A	G	A	G	A	G
1950–51	1	-	-	-	1	-
1951–52	5	-	-	-	5	-
1952–53	15	-	8	1	23	1
1953–54	40	-	6	-	46	-
1954–55	21	1	2	-	23	1
1955–56	-	-	-	-	-	-
1956–57	12	-	-	-	12	-
1957–58	8	-	-	-	8	-
	102	1	16	1	118	2

LAURIE BELL

Born: Langbank, May 1875
Died: 1933

Laurie Bell was one of a number of Scottish players who travelled the familiar crowded road over the border in the late 19th century. He began with his home-town side, Langbank, in Renfrewshire, and made his name as a centre-forward with Dumbarton. In 1895 he joined Third Lanark and spent two years there, representing the Scottish League, before joining Sheffield Wednesday. He scored 10 goals in 47 League appearances for the Yorkshire club before moving over the Pennines to Everton. His debut for the Toffees came on the opening day of the 1897–98 season in which he hit two goals against the Wanderers, and he went on to be the club's leading scorer that term. The Wanderers recruited Bell in the close season of 1899 for what was the club's first season in the Second Division. Bell wasted no time, scoring the opening goal of

the season 12 minutes into a 3–2 win at Loughborough and went on to lead the club's scoring charts as they swept to promotion at the first attempt. He had the satisfaction of scoring the winning goal against Everton the following season, but disaster struck in April 1902 when he broke a leg during a Manchester Senior Cup semi-final against Newton Heath. After recovery he was used more as a winger but could not prevent the Wanderers being relegated in 1903. He joined Brentford before returning to the Football League with West Bromwich Albion in 1904, where he played 16 times before ending his career at Hibernian. His brother, Jack Bell, a League player with Everton, New Brighton Tower and Preston, became chairman of the first Players' Union and Preston's first manager-coach in 1909.

	League		FA Cup		Total	
	A	G	A	G	A	G
1899–1900	32	23	1	-	33	23
1900–01	33	8	2	1	35	9
1901–02	22	9	1	0	23	9
1902–03	12	4	-	-	12	4
	99	44	4	1	103	45

TAL BEN HAIM

Born: Rishon LeZion, Israel, 31 March 1982
Tal Ben Haim joined the Wanderers on trial in the summer of 2004 and was taken on the pre-season tour to Portugal. He impressed enough to earn a three-year contract with the club, transferring from his first club Maccabi Tel Aviv. He had begun with Maccabi in 1998, winning the Israeli League with them in 2003 and going on to play 147 League games. An Israeli Under-21 and full international by the time he made the 250,000 euro move to the Reebok, Ben Haim made his Bolton debut against Charlton and proved to be capable in either full-back position or in the centre of defence. His only goal for the club came in that first season, heading home a free kick from Stelios in the 3–1 win against Tottenham at the Reebok Stadium in February 2005. Ben Haim went on to earn 16 full international caps while with Bolton and attracted the interest of a number of clubs towards the end of his contract, which culminated in him joining Chelsea in June 2007 on a Bosman. Ben Haim made his competitive debut for the Londoners in the FA Community Shield against Manchester United, but as the season wore on he slipped to fourth-choice centre-back at the club. After just 13 Premier League games he returned to the North West in a £5 million transfer to Manchester City, becoming Mark Hughes's second signing of the summer. In January 2009 he joined Sunderland on loan before

making a move to Portsmouth. He missed the FA Cup Final through injury and joined West Ham on loan in July 2010 before returning to the south coast in January 2011.

	League		FA Cup		FL Cup		UEFA Cup		Total	
	A	G	A	G	A	G	A	G	A	G
2004–05	19/2	1	4	-	2	-	-	-	25/2	1
2005–06	32/3	-	4	-	3	-	7	-	46/3	-
2006–07	30/2	-	1	-	1	-	-	-	32/2	-
	81/7	1	9	-	6	-	7	-	103/7	1

GUDNI BERGSSON

Born: Reykjavik, Iceland, 21 July 1965
A stalwart of the Bolton defence as the club looked to establish itself in the Premier League, Gudni Bergsson became an adopted Boltonian as a member of three successful promotion-winning sides under three different managers. He had begun with his local club, Valur, playing 94 League games, and had been on a short loan spell at TSV 1860 Munchen before Terry Venables paid £100,000 to take him to Tottenham in December 1988. Bergsson played 72 League games for Spurs and in

1994 returned to Valur on loan, where he began studies to become a lawyer. In 1995 he returned to England, having trial games at Crystal Palace and in the Wanderers' reserves before Bruce Rioch signed him for an initial fee of £65,000. His debut came as substitute in the 1995 League Cup Final and he helped the club win promotion to the Premier League at the end of that season by winning the Play-off Final against Reading at Wembley. He missed only four games in that first Premier League season for the club, but unfortunately he could not prevent relegation after just one season. He was a vital member of the Championship-winning side of 1996–97 in the last-ever season at Burnden as the club broke numerous records and lost only four games. Two of his League goals that season came in a 7–0 defeat of Swindon at Burnden. In the first season at the Reebok Stadium Bergsson was a regular in the side that suffered relegation on the last day of the season on goal difference. Injuries curtailed his games the following season but he bounced back to be part of the side that reached the Play-offs in 2000 and 2001. His goals in the latter season, especially in the semis against West Brom, were vital in helping the club reach what became a successful final at Cardiff in 2001. Bergsson was persuaded to sign for another season that summer and, in his last term, he helped the club remain in the Premier League for the first time, safety being assured in his final game, which came in the 2–1 home success against Middlesbrough on the last day of the season. He won 21 of his 80 Iceland international caps while with the Wanderers, the final coming against Lithuania in June 2003, and is second in his country's appearance list behind Runar Kristinsson. After retirement from the game he became a certified lawyer in his home country and also a football show host on TV. He still visits the club a few times each season to keep in touch.

	League		FA Cup		FL Cup		Total	
	A	G	A	G	A	G	A	G
1994–95	11	-	-	-	-/1	-	11/1	-
1995–96	34	4	-	-	6	-	40	4
1996–97	30/3	3	2	-	3	-	35/3	3
1997–98	34/1	2	1	-	3	-	38/1	2
1998–99	15/4	-	1	-	3	-	19/4	-
1999–2000	39/1	4	4	-	7	1	50/1	5
2000–01	47	10	2	-	1/1	-	50/1	10
2001–02	30	1	2	1	-	-	32	2
2002–03	31	1	-	-	-	-	31	1
	271/9	25	12	1	23/2	1	306/11	27

BRIAN BIRCH

Born: Southport, 9 April 1938

A winger who made his First Division debut for the Wanderers at 16 years old and went on to serve the club for 10 years, Brian Birch was snapped up from Southport Boys and made his way through the junior ranks, representing Lancashire and England Boys during 1952–53. His League debut came in September 1954 when he replaced the injured Doug Holden and figured at outside-left in a 3–3 draw with Aston Villa at Burnden. It was not until 1957 that he became a regular in

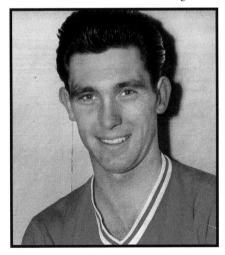

the side and the following year he played in every round of the FA Cup as the Wanderers went on to win the trophy. At 20 years old Birch was considered the 'baby' of the side, but he was serving with the RAF at the time. For the next two seasons he shared the outside-left position with another Bolton youth discovery, Neville Bannister, but the arrival of Brian Pilkington from Burnley put Birch further down the pecking order, with Doug Holden reverting to the number-seven shirt in 1961. His last game for the Wanderers came in the League Cup in October 1963 in a 3–0 third-round defeat at Stoke City. In July 1964 Birch joined Rochdale, where he played 61 League games in two seasons before ending his footballing days at Ellesmere Port.

	League		FA Cup		FL Cup		Total	
	A	G	A	G	A	G	A	G
1954–55	2	-	-	-	-	-	2	-
1955–56	11	-	-	-	-	-	11	-
1956–57	5	1	-	-	-	-	5	1
1957–58	34	4	7	1	-	-	41	5
1958–59	28	6	6	2	-	-	34	8
1959–60	30	6	3	1	-	-	33	7
1960–61	27	3	3	-	3	1	33	4
1961–62	12	1	-	-	2	-	14	1
1962–63	11	2	-	-	1	-	12	2
1963–64	5	-	-	-	1	-	6	-
	165	23	19	4	7	1	191	28

HAROLD BLACKMORE

Born: Silverton, 13 May 1904
Died: 1989

Harold Blackmore followed his fellow Devonian, Dick Pym, to Burnden Park from Exeter City. Like Pym, he was to become a Cup-winner and produce a magnificent goal return for the club. The centre-forward had scored twice in a 3–2 win against the Wanderers in March 1927 when they visited Exeter to play the Grecians in a benefit game for Robert Pollard, and, immediately afterwards, the

Wanderers handed over £2,150 to take him to Burnden Park. He had scored 45 goals in 71 appearances for Exeter and got off to a great start for Bolton with a goal five minutes into his debut, a 3–2 win against Sheffield Wednesday at Burnden. He became the regular centre-forward in the team in 1928 after the departure of John

Smith. During 1928–29 Blackmore hit 30 goals in 35 League games and another seven in the FA Cup, the last of which came in the Final when Bolton defeated Portsmouth 2–0. He topped the Wanderers' goalscoring charts the following two seasons before losing his place to Jack Milsom. In June 1932 Blackmore moved to Middlesbrough, having bagged a hat-trick against them the previous season, and hit nine goals in 19 League games in his only season in the North East. The following summer he moved to Bradford Park Avenue, scoring 32 goals in 60 games, and he then had a short spell with Bury before returning to Exeter in 1935 where he opened a butchers shop with his brother-in-law.

	League		FA Cup		Total	
	A	G	A	G	A	G
1926–27	5	3	-	-	5	3
1927–28	12	8	-	-	12	8
1928–29	35	30	8	7	43	37
1929–30	38	30	-	-	38	30
1930–31	40	27	3	3	43	30
1931–32	23	13	1	1	24	14
	153	111	12	11	165	122

NATHAN BLAKE

Born: Cardiff, 27 January 1972
Nathan Blake joined the Wanderers from Sheffield United in December 1995 for a £1.35 million fee but managed only one goal that term, in a 4–1 win at Middlesbrough, as the club dropped out of

the Premier League after a solitary season. He had started his career at Newport County before joining Chelsea as a trainee and had then moved back to his home-city club, Cardiff City, in 1990, where the striker helped them win the Third Division Championship in 1993. Blake went on to score 35 goals in 131 League games before a £300,000 move to Sheffield United in February 1994. His five goals could not keep the Blades in the Premier League that season, but he went on to become their leading scorer in the following two seasons. He struck up a fruitful striking partnership with John McGinlay in 1996–97, hitting 19 League goals to help Bolton to the First Division Championship. The following year Blake was the club's leading League goalscorer but it was not enough to prevent relegation after one season in the Premiership. The goals continued to flow for him at the start of 1998–99, including a hat-trick at Hartlepool in the League Cup, and it was in that competition that he made his final appearance for the club in a third-round win on penalties at Norwich in October 1998. He returned to the Premier League in a £4.25 million deal with Blackburn Rovers but again suffered relegation and managed only 13 goals in his spell at Ewood. In September 2001 Wolves paid £1.5 million and the goals again began to come, including one against his former club, Sheffield United, in a 3–0 Play-off win in 2003. Blake unfortunately suffered his fifth relegation from the Premier League as Wolves lasted just one season, and he joined Leicester City in 2004. He failed to find the net for the Foxes and the last League goal of his career came while on loan at Leeds United against Coventry City in January 2005. He was suspended for six months in August 2005 after failing a drug test and spent two months playing non-League with Newport County before retiring to concentrate on his property management company in South Wales. He won 29 caps for Wales, five of which came while with the Wanderers, his only goal in that spell coming in a 6–4 World Cup qualifying defeat in Turkey in August 1997.

	League		FA Cup		FL Cup		Total	
	A	G	A	G	A	G	A	G
1995–96	14/4	1	2	-	-	-	16/4	1
1996–97	42	19	3	2	5	3	50	24
1997–98	35	12	1	-	3	2	39	14
1998–99	11/1	6	-	-	2/1	3	13/2	9
	102/5	38	6	2	10/1	8	118/6	48

KEITH BRANAGAN

Born: Fulham, 10 July 1966

Keith Branagan began his goalkeeping career at Cambridge United, where he made 110 League appearances before joining Millwall for a £100,000 fee in March 1988. He played 46 League games for the Lions and had loan spells at Brentford and Gillingham before his former manager at the Den, Bruce Rioch, brought him to Burnden on a free transfer in 1992. He was an ever-present in 1992–93, playing in all 60 first-class games as the Wanderers won promotion from the Second Division and reached the fifth round of the FA Cup. Injury curtailed his appearances the following season, but he returned to miss just three games in 1994–95 and make two Wembley appearances. Branagan made some sterling saves in the League Cup Final defeat to Liverpool, but it was his penalty save from Reading's Stuart Lovell in the Play-off Final that proved to be a springboard for Bolton's comeback from two down to win 4–3 and promotion to the Premier League. He also gained international recognition that season when he represented the Republic of Ireland B team in a 2–0 reverse against England, in a side that also contained club teammates Owen Coyle and Jason McAteer. Branagan was first choice in the club's first season in the Premier but missed the run-in after suffering a training injury in March 1996. He won a First Division Championship medal in 1996–97 and his only full international cap when he kept a clean sheet in a goalless draw against Wales in Cardiff. He was again a model of consistency during Bolton's first season at the Reebok, missing just four Premier League games through injury, but it was the emergence of Jussi Jääskeläinen that kept his appearances to a minimum thereafter with the Finn starting the 1998–99 season. He regained his place for the start of the 1999–2000 season but suffered injury during a 1–0 win against Huddersfield at the Reebok in October 1999 in what was his last appearance for the club. In the summer of 2000 he joined Ipswich Town, playing three League games before retiring from the game in October 2002 following a long battle with a shoulder injury. He has subsequently gained his coaching qualifications and has instructed goalkeepers at Crewe, Stockport and Bolton Wanderers Academy and had a coaching role at Bolton School.

	League	FA Cup	FL Cup	Autoglass Trophy/Auto Windscreens Shield	Anglo– Italian Cup	Total
	A	A	A	A	A	A
1992–93	46	6	4	4	-	60
1993–94	10	-	4	-	1	15
1994–95	45	1	8	-	-	54
1995–96	31	2	6	-	-	39
1996–97	36	-	4	-	-	40
1997–98	34	-	3	-	-	37
1998–99	3	-	1	-	-	4
1999–2000	11	-	3	-	-	14
	216	9	33	4	1	263

JAMES BROGAN

Born: Beith, 1865
Died: 1951

A Scotsman of Irish decent, James Brogan became one of the Wanderers' first professional players in the days before the Football League. His first club was his home-town side, Beith, from where he later joined Edinburgh Hibernians and Heart of Midlothian. It was while Hearts

were on tour in Lancashire that Brogan attracted the attention of the Wanderers, and he signed in December 1884. He helped the club win the Bolton Charity Cup at both inside and outside-left in that first season and went on to become a useful goal-getter for the club. Brogan took part in the club's first League game in September 1888, scoring one of the goals in a 6–3 defeat by Derby County and, the following December, hit five goals in a 10–1 friendly win against Sunderland at Pikes Lane. That form earned him recognition when he was selected for Lancashire, and he became the club's leading League scorer in that first season and also an ever present. He was the Wanderers' oldest player at 26 years old when the Wanderers won the Lancashire Cup against Darwen in 1891, having taken a benefit the previous year against Everton. The emergence of James Turner in 1892 restricted Brogan's appearances, and his last League game for the club came in defeat at Sunderland in March that year. He left the game and returned to Scotland to work in the shipyards, where he continued to work until he was 85 years old.

	League		FA Cup		Total	
	A	G	A	G	A	G
1887–88	-	-	5	2	5	2
1888–89	22	13	-	-	22	13
1889–90	21	8	4	4	25	12
1890–91	21	4	1	-	22	4
1891–92	10	1	2	-	12	1
	74	26	12	6	86	32

BRIAN BROMLEY

Born: Burnley, 20 March 1946

A product of the Wanderers' youth scheme, having been spotted playing for Burnley Schools at inside-forward, Brian Bromley was only 16 years old when he made his League debut in one of the club's

First Division goal, in a 1–0 home win against Chelsea, until the club regained their place in the top flight in 1978. Injury prevented Bromley being ever present during 1964–65, when he missed the last four games, but he continued to be a regular until Bolton accepted an offer of £25,000 from Portsmouth in November 1968. His last game for the club came in a 2–1 defeat at Crystal Palace. His three years at Fratton Park brought little success and in November 1971, after 89 League games and three goals, he moved along the coast to Brighton. At the Goldstone he became a member of their Third Division promotion-winning side, but unfortunately they were relegated the following season and he joined Reading in September 1973. Bromley's final appearances in the Football League came in March 1975 during a three-game loan spell with Darlington. He finished his career with Wigan Athletic in the Northern Premier League, where he played 23 games, scoring one goal, before returning to reside on the south coast.

	League		FA Cup		FL Cup		Total	
	A	G	A	G	A	G	A	G
1962–63	3	-	-	-	-	-	3	-
1963–64	18	4	-	-	-	-	18	4
1964–65	38	7	3	-	1	-	42	7
1965–66	31	4	3	1	2	-	36	5
1966–67	37	6	3	-	1	-	41	6
1967–68	21/1	2	1	-	3	-	25/1	2
1968–69	17	2	-	-	1	-	18	2
	165/1	25	10	1	8	-	183/1	26

PHIL BROWN

Born: South Shields, 30 May 1959

Phil Brown was brought to Bolton by Phil Neal in June 1988 for a bargain £17,500 fee from Halifax Town. The right-back had turned professional 10 years earlier with Hartlepool, where he played 217 League games before making a move to Halifax in

youngest-ever forward lines. His first appearance came in March 1963, when Bolton entertained Sheffield United in the First Division, their first home game in three months due to the big freeze that winter. A Fred Hill hat-trick gave Bolton a 3–2 win, and Bromley went on to play a further two games that season until Billy Russell was signed from Sheffield United. In 1964 he was selected for the England Youth team and won a regular spot in the Bolton side towards the end of that season, which ended in relegation to the Second Division. Bromley scored the club's last

July 1985. He made 135 League appearances for the Shaymen and was club captain. Brown's Wanderers' League debut came on the opening day of the 1988–89 season, a 2–0 reverse at Southend, but he had already helped the club win the Lancashire Cup for the first time in 40 years in the pre-season competition. He was an ever present that season, which ended when he collected the Sherpa Van Trophy at Wembley after the Wanderers had defeated Torquay United 4–1. He captained the club to the Play-offs in both 1989–90 and 1990–91, but in April 1991 a run of 134 consecutive League appearances (including Play-off games) for the club came to an end when injury caused him to miss a 1–0 reverse at Bournemouth. Three days later he returned to help the side win at Crewe Alexandra. During 1992–93 Nicky Spooner put Brown under pressure for the full-back slot, but Brown missed only six League games as the club won promotion from Division Two with just one defeat in the final 19 games. He ended his Bolton career in May 1994, his only season in the

First Division, again showing great consistency when he was absent for just four League games. His last game for the club came in the final-day 3–2 home defeat to Barnsley and that summer he joined Blackpool, where he went on to play 44 League games. He became assistant to Sam Allardyce at Bloomfield Road, returning to the Wanderers in 1996 as assistant to Colin Todd. Following Todd's departure in 1999 Brown took charge of the team, winning four of the five games until the appointment of Sam Allardyce, who Brown served as assistant for six years before taking his first management position at Derby County in June 2005. Brown was sacked after seven months in charge but became first-team coach at Hull, under Phil Parkinson, in October 2006. After serving Hull as caretaker manager alongside Colin Murphy, Brown was appointed manager in January 2007, keeping them in the Championship. A year later he led them to the Premiership, via the Play-offs, for the first time in the club's history. He was placed on gardening leave in March 2010 before formally leaving in June that year and returned to management with Preston North End in January 2011.

	League		FA Cup		FL Cup		Autoglass Trophy		Anglo–Italian Cup		Total	
	A	G	A	G	A	G	A	G	A	G	A	G
1988–89	46	4	3	-	2	-	8	1	-	-	59	5
1989–90	48	1	1	-	8	1	5	-	-	-	62	2
1990–91	48	-	4	-	4	-	2	-	-	-	58	-
1991–92	35/2	2	2	-	4	-	2	-	-	-	43/2	2
1992–93	40	5	5	-	3	-	4	-	-	-	52	5
1993–94	42	2	8	1	4	-	-	-	2	-	56	3
	259/2	14	23	1	25	1	21	1	2	-	330/2	17

TOM BUCHAN

Born: Plumstead, September 1889
Died: 1952

Although not as illustrious as his brother, Charles, Tom Buchan was a mainstay of

the Wanderers' side that spanned World War One. He was captain of the club throughout the hostilities while working in the munitions factory. He had begun with Woodhall Thistle and had then been on the books of Sunderland, Leyton and Sunderland Rovers before joining Blackpool in 1913, where he made his League debut. He signed from the Seasiders in May 1914 and made his Bolton debut in a goalless home draw with Everton the following October. It was during the war that Buchan really came to the fore, missing only four games in a three-season spell between 1915 and 1918 in the Football War Section games. He played in every position apart from full-back, even turning out as emergency goalkeeper in a 4–2 reverse at Stockport County in November 1915 and in a 3–2 win on the same ground exactly two years later. Buchan was one of nine players who took part in two games on the same day for the Wanderers in April 1917, losing at Stockport in the morning and winning at Oldham in the afternoon. His younger brother, John, also appeared for the club during the war. When League Football resumed in 1919, Buchan was the only ever present in the side as the club finished sixth in Division One. His experience of

various positions proved valuable in what was essentially a season of transition for most clubs. After two more successful seasons in the League, Buchan found it difficult to command a regular place and he made his last appearance for the Wanderers in March 1923, in a 2–1 reverse at Burnley, after which he was allowed to join Tranmere Rovers on a free transfer. There he teamed up with another ex-Wanderer, Harold Hilton, making 36 League appearances before joining Runcorn. In October 1924 Buchan joined Atherton, where he ended his career.

	League		FA Cup		Total	
	A	G	A	G	A	G
1914–15	3	1	-	-	3	1
1919–20	42	8	-	-	42	8
1920–21	40	2	1	-	41	2
1921–22	22	2	-	-	22	2
1922–23	9	1	-	-	9	1
	116	14	1	-	117	14

BILLY BUTLER

Born: Atherton, 27 March 1900
Died: Durban, July 1966

A member of the great Wanderers side of the 1920s and a winner of three FA Cup-winners' medals in his 13-year spell with the club, Billy Butler had been spotted playing for Atherton in the Bolton Combination and was signed in April 1920. Butler had joined the Royal North Lancashire Regiment at 19 years of age, having never taken part in any organised football, and became a centre-forward. It was in that position that he subsequently played for Howe Bridge and Atherton Collieries, but he was switched to outside-right, where he was to become prolific when he made his Bolton debut in a 2–0 home reverse to Chelsea in January 1921. Butler became a regular thereafter and was included in the first Wembley final in 1923. He won an England cap in April 1924

	League		FA Cup		Total	
	A	**G**	**A**	**G**	**A**	**G**
1921–22	13	1	-	-	13	1
1922–23	30	2	7	-	37	2
1923–24	36	2	2	-	38	2
1924–25	33	-	3	-	36	-
1925–26	32	5	7	2	39	7
1926–27	39	10	4	-	43	10
1927–28	39	5	2	1	41	6
1928–29	38	6	8	5	46	11
1929–30	35	7	1	-	36	7
1930–31	41	8	3	-	44	8
1931–32	36	9	2	-	38	9
1932–33	35	10	3	1	38	11
	407	65	42	9	449	74

JOHN BYROM

Born: Blackburn, 28 July 1944

John Byrom began his career with his home-town club in 1959 and was selected for England Youth before becoming a regular in the Ewood Park line up in 1963. He scored 45 goals in 108 League games for Rovers before the Wanderers snapped him up for £25,000 in June 1966. He made his Bolton debut in a 1–0 win at Rotherham in August 1966, but it was not until the 1969–70 season that he began to fulfil his promise.

partnering David Jack against Scotland, also at Wembley, and his second Cup-winners' medal in 1926. He scored the Wanderers' opening goal in the 1929 FA Cup Final success over Portsmouth, but relegation in 1933 hit Butler hard and he went onto the transfer list at his own request. The last of his 449 games for the club came in a 5–0 home win over Leeds, but it was unfortunately too little, too late. Butler was reunited with his former teammate Joe Smith, who was in charge at Reading, and made 56 League appearances for them before taking over as manager after Smith's departure to Blackpool in August 1935. Reading never finished below sixth place in Division Three South during Butler's tenure and were heading for a top-five finish when he resigned in February 1939. He took over at Guildford City and served in the RAF as a PT instructor during the war. He took over at Torquay United in August 1945 but left before League football resumed and later emigrated to South Africa, where he managed Johannesburg Rangers. He later coached at Pietermaritzburg & District FA and the Rhodesian FA.

Two hat-tricks in the space of four days at the start of the season, in a 4–1 opening day success over Millwall and a 6–3 League Cup win over Rochdale, set Byrom off on what was to be his best goalscoring season while at the club. It was a remarkable performance, considering the team were struggling at that time. After relegation to the Third Division in 1971 Byrom was put up for sale, but he remained to lead the goalscoring charts again. During 1972–73, when he won a Third Division Championship medal, he hit another profitable spell that continued upon the club's return to Division Two. He completed the set of scoring a hat-trick in the League and both major cups when Stoke were defeated 3–2 in the third round of the FA Cup in January 1974, which was also the club's first ever Sunday game. Leading scorer for the fifth time in six seasons in 1973–74, Byrom scored his 100th League goal for the club in a 3–2 win at Nottingham Forest in February 1975. His final goals for the club came in his last League appearance in a 3–1 win at Bristol Rovers after the Wanderers had been pipped to promotion by West Brom. Byrom took part in the pre-season games of 1976–77 before retiring, only to put in one more season with Blackburn after Bolton had given him a free transfer. His testimonial took place at Burnden, fittingly against Blackburn, in November 1978.

	League		FA Cup		FL Cup		Total	
	A	G	A	G	A	G	A	G
1966–67	25	6	1/1	-	-	-	26/1	6
1967–68	23	9	1	-	3	1	27	10
1968–69	21	6	1	-	-	-	22	6
1969–70	40	20	1	-	4	5	45	25
1970–71	22/1	3	1	-	1/1	-	24/2	3
1971–72	37/1	11	3	1	4	1	44/1	13
1972–73	39/1	20	5	1	2	1	46/1	22
1973–74	32/1	18	3	5	5	1	40/1	24
1974–75	28	10	-/1	-	2	-	30/1	10
1975–76	29/4	10	6	-	1	1	36/4	11
	296/8	113	22/2	7	22/1	10	340/11	130

GARY CAHILL

Born: Dronfield, 19 December 1985

A £5 million signing from Aston Villa in January 2008, Gary Cahill forced his way into the England squad by displaying some great form while in his Wanderers' shirt, which culminated in his full debut as a substitute in a 4–0 UEFA qualifying win over Bulgaria at Wembley in September 2010. The centre-half had started his career with AFC Dronfield while training with Derby County before joining Aston Villa's academy, where he progressed through the youth ranks to turn professional in December 2003. In November 2004 Cahill joined Burnley on loan, playing 27 League games for the Clarets and going on to win the club's Player of the Year award. His Villa debut came as a substitute in a 5–0 defeat at Arsenal in April 2006, but he kept his place for the final six games of the season and also netted his first League goal in a 3–1 win over local rivals Birmingham City. In

September 2007 he joined Sheffield United on loan, spending three months at Bramhall Lane, during which he played 16 League games. While at Villa Park he was called into the England Under-20s and, in March 2007, made his England Under-21 debut in a 3–3 draw with Italy in what was the first game at the new Wembley Stadium. Cahill went on to play 49 League games for Villa before his move to the Reebok Stadium, with his Bolton debut coming in a 2–0 Premier League win at Reading. He became a regular in the club's defence, netting his first goal in a 3–1 win at West Ham in October 2008 and built up a good understanding with his former Villa teammate Zat Knight.

	League		FA Cup		FL Cup		UEFA Cup		Total	
	A	G	A	G	A	G	A	G	A	G
2007–08	13	-	-	-	-	-	4	-	17	-
2008–09	33	3	-	-	1	-	-	-	34	3
2009–10	29	5	2	1	3	1	-	-	34	7
2010–11	36	3	5	-	-	-	-	-	41	3
	111	11	7	1	4	1	4	-	126	13

TONY CALDWELL

Born: Salford, 21 March 1958

Tony Caldwell hit the headlines only four games into his League career when he scored five goals in an 8–1 win over Walsall at Burnden Park in September 1983 to equal James Cassidy's and Billy Struthers record, which had stood since the late 1800s. He had played local football with Irlam Town and was with Horwich RMI when the Wanderers snapped him up for a £2,000 fee at 25 years of age, although he had already had unsuccessful trials at other League clubs. At the end of his first season with the club Caldwell was the leading scorer, a feat he repeated in each of the following three seasons. In 1986 his goals in the two-legged Northern Final of the Freight Rover Trophy against Wigan took Bolton to Wembley for the first time in 28 years. The final was lost to Bristol City, and it was the Robins who snapped Caldwell up for a tribunal set £27,500 fee after Bolton had been relegated to Division Four in 1987. He played only 17 League games for City and was loaned to Chester before joining Grimsby in September 1988. He was there only a matter of weeks before returning to the North West with Stockport County.

	League		FA Cup		FL Cup		Frieght Rover Trophy		Total	
	A	G	A	G	A	G	A	G	A	G
1983–84	32/1	19	3	1	1	2	1	1	37/1	23
1984–85	29/2	18	-	-	4	1	5	3	38/2	22
1985–86	38/2	10	-	-	2/1	1	7	5	47/3	16
1986–87	34/3	13	5	3	1	-	4	1	44/3	17
	133/8	60	8	4	8/1	4	17	10	166/9	78

MARK CAME

Born: Exeter, 14 September 1961

Mark Came joined the Wanderers in March 1984 from North West Counties League side Winsford United. He became one of a number of players who made the transition from non-League to the professional ranks at that time, but the

centre-half's first full game for the club was one to forget. It came in a third-round Milk Cup tie against Notts County at Meadow Lane in October 1984 and Bolton found themselves six goals down at half time before losing 6–1. After the departure of Gerry McElhinney, Came made the position his own and missed only three games during 1987–88 as the Wanderers won promotion from the Fourth Division at the first attempt. He became club captain for the following season, lifting the pre-season Lancashire Cup after Bolton had defeated Preston in the Final to win the trophy for the first time since 1948. He then suffered a broken leg in a Littlewoods Cup tie at Chester, which ended his season prematurely. Came returned to take part in the Third Division Play-offs in 1990 but his appearances became limited, including some at centre-forward, notably in the League Cup marathon against Swindon Town. His final game came in a 2–1 reverse at Plymouth in September 1992. In December 1992 Came joined Chester City, suffering relegation to Division Three that

season but winning promotion the following term. In July 1994 he moved to his home town of Exeter, becoming Player of the Year in his two seasons at St James Park, playing 70 League games before rejoining Winsford United. Came retired through injury in 1998 and became manager for 1999–2000 season. In 2005 he had a spell as manager of Cheshire side Barnton.

	League		FA Cup		FL Cup		Frieght Rover Trophy		Total	
	A	G	A	G	A	G	A	G	A	G
1984–85	22/1	1	1	-	1/1	-	3	-	27/2	1
1985–86	35	1	1	-	4	-	7	1	47	2
1986–87	44/1	-	5	-	1	-	3	1	53/1	1
1987–88	43	5	3	-	2	-	3	-	51	5
1988–89	2	-	-	-	2	-	-	-	4	-
1989–90	17/4	-	-/1	1/2	2	3	-	-	21/7	2
1990–91	8	-	2	-	1/1	-	1	-	12/1	-
1991–92	18	-	4/1	-	2	-	3	-	27/1	-
1992–93	3/1	-	-	-	1	-	-	-	4/1	-
	192/7	7	16/2	-	15/4	2	23	2	246/13	11

IVÁN CAMPO (RAMOS)

Born: San Sebastien, 21 February 1974
A mainstay of Bolton's steady improvement in the Premier League, Iván Campo became a cult hero during his six-year spell with the club. He began in youth football at Logroñés before joining Deportivo Alavés in 1993, who were in the third level of Spanish football. Valencia CF signed him in 1995 as a central-defender and loaned him to Real Valladolid. In 1997 he joined Real Mallorca, who had just been promoted, and played 33 games that season as they finished fifth. His performances earned him international honours and he went on to represent Spain on four occasions, becoming a member of their 1998 World Cup squad. Real Madrid secured his services and he made 60 League appearances for the Bernabéu side, and in May 2000 played in their

Champions League Final success against Valencia in Paris. In August 2002 Campo joined the Wanderers on a season-long loan, an eventful introduction to English football. His debut came as a substitute in a 1–0 win at Manchester United the following month. In the next game he again appeared off the bench and found the net in a 3–2 home defeat to Liverpool, but he was sent off at Arsenal on his first start as the Wanderers went down 2–1 to an injury-time goal. The following season he joined Bolton permanently and went on to be involved in every Premier League game that season for the club, the majority in a defensive midfield role. One of his most consistent seasons with the club was in 2006–07, when he scored with a 40-yard shot against Tottenham on the opening day of the season and helped the club to secure UEFA Cup qualification for the second time. It was also against Tottenham that he made his final Bolton appearance in April 2008 as the club earned a vital point on the way to Premier League safety. At the end of that season his contract expired, and the following August he signed for Ipswich

Town in the Championship. In December 2009 Campo joined AEK Larnaca in the Cypriot Second Division before retiring at the end of that season.

	League		FA Cup		FL Cup		UEFA Cup		Total	
	A G		A G		A G		A G		A G	
2002–03	28/3	2	2	-	1	-	-	-	31/3	2
2003–04	37/1	4	-	-	6	-	-	-	43/1	4
2004–05	20/7	-	1/1	-	-	-	-	-	21/8	-
2005–06	8/7	2	1	-	-/1	-	1	-	10/8	2
2006–07	31/3	4	2	-	1/1	1	-	-	34/4	5
2007–08	25/2	1	-	-	-/1	-	2/1	-	27/4	1
	149/23	13	6/1	-	8/3	1	3/1	-	166/28	14

JAMES CASSIDY

Born: Kilmarnock, 1869
Died: unknown

One of the shortest centre-forwards in the club's history at 5ft 7in tall in 1893, James Cassidy was still the tallest player in the Wanderers' forward line. He began his career with his home-town side before joining Glasgow Hibernians. He was recommended to the Wanderers when 20 years old and he went on to win over the partisan crowd at Pikes Lane. Cassidy's first goal for the club came under the

floodlights at Bramhall Lane in November 1889 when the Wanderers won an exhibition game 2–0 against Sheffield United. At the end of that month he opened his League account with four goals in a 7–1 win over Derby County and then netted five in the club's record win in a major competition when Sheffield United were thrashed in the FA Cup in 1890. He equalled the feat set by Billy Struthers in 1882, and it was not equalled again until 1983 when Tony Caldwell netted five against Walsall. Cassidy was the first player to score from a penalty for the club, which came against Notts County at Pikes Lane in 1892, and he netted at Burnden Park in the first League game there against Everton. He went on to top the club's scoring charts in five seasons.

	League		FA Cup		Total	
	A	G	A	G	A	G
1889–90	15	13	4	7	19	20
1890–91	16	8	1	1	17	9
1891–92	26	18	1	-	27	18
1892–93	27	9	2	0	29	9
1893–94	29	11	5	4	34	15
1894–95	26	9	3	2	29	11
1895–96	22	7	3	1	25	8
1896–97	9	2	3	1	12	3
1897–98	24	7	3	1	27	8
	194	84	25	17	219	101

JEFF CHANDLER

Born: Hammersmith, 19 June 1959
Jeff Chandler began his professional career with Blackpool and made his debut for the Seasiders at Blackburn in 1977. He made 37 League appearances before joining Leeds United and it was while at Elland Road that the winger won his two Republic of Ireland caps, against Czechoslovakia and the USA. In October 1981 the Wanderers paid £40,000 for his signature and he made his debut in a 3–0 home defeat at the hands of Leicester City. He

was ever present for the club in 1983–84 and his 20 goals in League and Cup the following season put him top of the club's charts. He joined Derby County for a tribunal set fee of £38,000 and was a member of their side that won promotion from the Third Division. After a short spell on loan at Mansfield Town, Chandler returned to the Wanderers in 1987 for £20,000. He missed most of the Fourth Division winning campaign through injury but recovered to play his part in the Wembley Sherpa Van Trophy success in 1989. In November 1989 he signed for Cardiff City for £15,000, where he ended his League career through injury. Chandler returned to the North West to work as a counsellor for youth offenders in Preston.

	League		FA Cup		FL Cup		Frieght Rover Trophy		Total	
	A	G	A	G	A	G	A	G	A	G
1981–82	32/1	2	2	-	-	-	-	-	34/1	2
1982–83	35/2	4	1	-	3	-	-	-	39/2	4
1983–84	46	14	4	3	2	-	1	-	53	17
1984–85	39/2	16	-	-	5	4	4	-	48/2	20
1987–88	2/1	2	-	-	2	1	-	-	4/1	3
1988–89	16/4	2	-	-	-	-	4/1	-	20/5	2
1989–90	-/1	-	-	-	-/1	-	-	-	-/2	-
	170/11	40	7	3	12/1	5	9/1	-	198/13	48

SIMON CHARLTON

Born: Huddersfield, 25 October 1971

A member of the promotion-winning side of 2001, Simon Charlton was capable of playing at left-back, centre-back or the left side of midfield. He served his apprenticeship at his home-town club, Huddersfield Town, turning professional in 1989 and going on to play 125 League games for the Terriers. In the summer of 1993 he joined Southampton for a £250,000 fee and played 115 Premier League games before joining Birmingham City on loan, making the move permanent in 1998 for an identical fee. He figured in 72 League games for the St Andrews side as they twice reached the Championship Play-offs. Charlton joined the Wanderers in the close season of 2000 on a free transfer, making his debut in a 1–1 opening day home draw with Burnley. He played in the Play-off Final victory over Preston and missed only two Premier League games the following season. Charlton continued to produce some

consistent performances, which culminated in him winning the Player of the Season award in 2004. Norwich City paid £250,000 for him in the summer of 2004 and he played 45 League games before being released. Charlton joined Oldham and retired in May 2007, moving into coaching at Norwich. In April 2009 he became manager of Eastern Counties League side Mildenhall Town before leaving in June 2010.

	League		FA Cup		FL Cup		Total	
	A	G	A	G	A	G	A	G
2000–01	21/4	-	3/1	-	-	-	24/5	-
2001–02	35/1	-	-	-	1	-	36/1	-
2002–03	27/4	-	-	-	-	-	27/4	-
2003–04	28/3	-	-	-	5/2	-	33/5	-
	111/12	-	3/1	-	6/2	-	120/15	-

WILLIE COOK

Born: Dundee 11 March 1906
Died: 1981

Willie Cook began his working life as a clerk with a timber firm in his home town of Dundee while appearing for Dundee North End. In 1924 he joined Forfar Athletic and then Dundee a year later, where he was watched by a number of English clubs before signing for the Wanderers for £5,000 in December 1928. The 5ft 4in outside-left made his League debut in a 5–0 home win against Leicester City the same month, and by the end of his first season he had collected an FA Cup-winners' medal in the 2–0 success over Portsmouth. Cook gained the first of his three Scottish international caps against England at Wembley in 1934, when the Wanderers were playing in the Second Division. His other caps came the following season, when he was a member of the Bolton's promotion-winning team. In April 1936 he joined Blackpool and also helped them win promotion to the First Division before spending a short time at

Reading. He returned to Dundee in 1938 to end his playing days and took over as licensee of a public house there.

	League		FA Cup		Total	
	A	G	A	G	A	G
1928–29	16	-	8	-	24	-
1929–30	41	6	1	-	42	6
1930–31	26	7	3	-	29	7
1931–32	34	4	1	-	35	4
1932–33	27	3	2	2	29	5
1933–34	30	2	5	2	35	4
1934–35	29	6	6	1	35	7
1935–36	31	7	2	-	33	7
	234	35	28	5	262	40

JULIAN DARBY

Born: Farnworth, 3 October 1967

A product of the Wanderers youth team, Julian Darby went on to serve the club throughout the drop into the Fourth Division and the subsequent rise up the Leagues. Capable of playing in a number of positions, primarily at right-back, midfield or central defence, he represented England at Schoolboy level and first appeared for the Wanderers' reserves as a 15-year-old in September 1983. Darby made his League debut at right-back against Blackpool at Burnden in March 1986, while the following season he played in no fewer than nine different positions, failing only to pull on the goalkeeper's shirt and the number-nine jersey. He was a member of the team that won promotion from the Fourth Division on the final day of the season at Wrexham in 1988 and 12 months later scored at Wembley for the successful Sherpa Van Trophy team. He missed only one game in two seasons, helping the side to two unsuccessful Play-off attempts in 1990 and 1991. Although he did not feature as much in the Second Division promotion-winning side of 1993, Darby came up trumps towards the end of the season when he appeared at centre-forward and scored the vital goal to beat Stoke at Burnden to set up the final-day success against Preston. In October 1993 he joined Coventry City for £150,000, playing 55 Premier League games before a £200,000 move to West Brom in November 1995. He returned to the North West in June 1997 with a £150,000 transfer to

Preston. He subsequently had a loan spell at Rotherham and ended his League career at Carlisle. Darby began his coaching career at Preston, becoming first-team coach, and joined Billy Davies at Derby County in 2006. After leaving Pride Park he returned to the Wanderers, coaching in the Academy before again teaming up with Davies at Nottingham Forest in 2009.

	League		FA Cup		FL Cup		Autoglass Trophy		Anglo–Italian Cup		Total	
	A	G	A	G	A	G	A	G	A	G	A	G
1985–86	2	-	-	-	-	-	-	-	-	-	2	-
1986–87	24/4	-	3	-	2	-	4	1	-	-	33/4	1
1987–88	34/1	2	3	-	1	-	3	-	-	-	41/1	2
1988–89	44	5	3	1	2	1	8	3	-	-	57	10
1989–90	48	10	1	-	8	1	5	1	-	-	62	12
1990–91	48	9	4	1	4	3	2	-	-	-	58	13
1991–92	42/2	6	5	1	4	3	3	-	-	-	54/2	10
1992–93	18/3	4	-	-	3	-	-/1	-	-	-	21/1	4
1993–94	3/2	-	-	-	1	-	-	-	1	-	5/2	-
	263/12	36	19	3	25	8	25/1	5	1	-	333/13	52

KENNY DAVENPORT

Born: Bolton, 23 March 1862
Died: 1908

James Kenyon Davenport was a Wanderer born and bred. He was born in the Deane area of the town, a stone's throw away from the Pikes Lane ground where he was to become a household name. He began his career with Gilnow Rangers and joined the Wanderers in 1883. Two years later he became the club's first England international when he was selected to play against Wales at Blackburn. He didn't win his second cap until 1890, when he scored twice in a 9–1 win over Ireland in Belfast. During this time he was selected in almost every county match by the Lancashire FA and in 1886 he was a member of the Bolton side that won the Lancashire Cup, Derby Charity Cup and Bolton Charity Cup. Davenport has the distinction of scoring the club's first League goal when he put Bolton

ahead against Derby County at Pikes Lane on 8 September 1888. He also grabbed another goal, but unfortunately Derby ran out 6–3 winners. Davenport spent most of his career in the inside-left position but would often appear on the wing or even in defence, such was his versatility. He missed only one game in the two inaugural League seasons and was given a benefit against Blackburn in 1889. In 1892 he joined Southport Central but returned to Bolton in 1894, where he assisted the reserves in the Lancashire Combination.

	League		FA Cup		Total	
	A	G	A	G	A	G
1882–83	-	-	1	-	1	-
1883–84	-	-	5	4	5	4
1884–85	-	-	-	-	-	-
1885–86	-	-	1	1	1	1
1886–87	-	-	3	3	3	3
1887–88	-	-	5	1	5	1
1888–89	22	11	-	-	22	11
1889–90	21	8	4	2	25	10
1890–91	12	5	-	-	12	5
1891–92	-	-	2	-	2	-
1892–93	1	1	-	-	1	1
	56	25	21	11	77	36

DAI DAVIES

Born: Llanelli, 1880
Died: 1944

Dai Davies followed in the footsteps of John Sutcliffe as a goalkeeper, successfully making the transition from rugby to football. Davies had made his name in the rugby world with Blackwatch Llanelli and Swinton Rugby League Club as a threequarter-back. He was with the Lions when they won the Challenge Cup in 1900 and scored a try in the defeat of Salford. Davies came to Bolton in May 1902 and made his debut against Preston in the Ibrox Disaster Fund game. His prominence quickly spread and he made his Welsh international debut against Scotland at Dundee in March 1904. This forced him to miss his only game for Bolton during the season, but he won another international appearance against Ireland and an FA Cup runners'-up medal when beaten by a dubious goal from

Manchester City's Billy Meredith. Davies remains as the only player to have competed in both an FA Cup Final and a Challenge Cup Final. In 1905 he broke his collarbone in an FA Cup tie with Newcastle and unfortunately was never the same again. He did, however, win another Welsh cap when, in March 1908, he came on as a substitute at half-time for Sunderland 'keeper, Roose, in a 7–1 defeat by England at Wrexham. Davies returned to Rugby League with Swinton in November 1909, just as his brother, Dan, had done some years earlier after a spell at half-back with Bolton. He went on to play for a further four seasons, taking his total appearances for Swinton to 173 and gaining a Welsh international cap when Wales were defeated by England in December 1910.

	League	FA Cup	Total
	A	A	A
1902–03	6	-	6
1903–04	33	6	39
1904–05	21	4	25
1905–06	35	1	36
1906–07	14	1	15
1907–08	13	2	15
1908–09	-	-	-
1909–10	1	-	1
	123	14	137

KEVIN DAVIES

Born: Sheffield, 26 March 1977

Kevin Davies made his name as a centre-forward with Chesterfield. He signed professional in 1994 but came to prominence during the club's run to the semi-finals of the FA Cup in 1997. In the fourth round that season he netted a hat-trick against the Wanderers and the Spireites went on to win 3–2. They became the last visiting side to win at Burnden and Davies the last player to score a hat-trick. After 129 League games for the Derbyshire outfit, Southampton paid £750,000 for him in May 1997 and he netted nine goals

in 20 Premier League starts, prompting Blackburn to pay £7,250,000 for him a year later. He found the net just once in the League for Rovers and in August 1999 returned to Southampton in exchange for Egil Ostenstad. Davies went on to win three England Under-21 appearances but struggled to gain a regular first-team place on the south coast and scored only 10 goals in four years. In September 2002 he had a loan spell at Millwall, scoring three times in nine League games before joining the Wanderers in July 2003 on trial. He put in an eye-catching performance in a pre-season win at Ballymena United and subsequently signed a contract. Davies rediscovered his best form at the Reebok Stadium, playing every Premier League game in 2003–04 and scoring nine goals. He subsequently became the club's talisman – while not a prolific goal-getter, he epitomised the club's hard-working style and helped the Wanderers to European football for the first time.

During 2008–09 Davies scored his 50th goal for the club in a 2–1 win over West Ham United and, after Kevin Nolan's departure to Newcastle United, he became club captain. In October 2010 he became the oldest English international debutant since Leslie Compton in 1950 when he appeared as a substitute in a scoreless draw against Montenegro at Wembley.

	League		FA Cup		FL Cup		UEFA Cup		Total	
	A	G	A	G	A	G	A	G	A	G
2003–04	38	9	-	-	4/1	1	-	-	42/1	10
2004–05	33/2	8	4	1	1/1	-	-	-	38/3	9
2005–06	37	7	3	1	2	-	4/1		46/1	8
2006–07	30	8	2	1	1	-	-	-	33	9
2007–08	31/1	3	-	-	1	-	8	1	40/1	4
2008–09	37/1	12	1	-	-/1	-	-	-	38/2	12
2009–10	37	7	3	1	2	1	-	-	42	9
2010–11	38	8	4/2	2	1	-	-	-	43/2	10
	281/4	62	17/2	6	12/3	2	12/1	1	322/10	71

WYN DAVIES

Born: Caernarfon, 20 March 1942

An archetypal target man, Wyn Davies earned the nickname 'Wyn the Leap' because of his heading ability. He began with Llanberis and Caernarfon before

joining Wrexham in April 1960. He scored 22 goals in 55 League games and, in March 1962, Bolton paid £20,000 for his services with Wrexham also taking Ernie Phythian. He took over the number-nine shirt and grabbed his first goals in a 4–2 First Division win over Chelsea. His best season with the Wanderers came in 1964–65 when he scored 25 goals in 38 games, and it was in 1964 that he won the first of 34 full Welsh international caps, 16 of those being earned while with the Wanderers. He became linked with a number of First Division clubs and his final game for Bolton came in October 1966, where he scored the Wanderers' goal in a 2–1 defeat at Bury, taking his tally to 12 goals in as many games for that season. Newcastle United paid a club record £80,000 for him and he was a member of their 1969 Fairs Cup-winning team. In August 1971 he returned to the North West with Manchester City, playing alongside ex-Wanderers Francis Lee and Freddie Hill, and a year later he moved across the town to Old Trafford. Davies later had spells at Blackpool, Crystal Palace and Stockport before ending his League career at Crewe in 1977. He spent some time in South Africa before returning to England and non-League football before becoming a baker in Bolton.

Hadji Diouf began his professional career in France with Sochaux in November 1998. He moved to Stade Rennais in 1999, but his career took off at Lens, where he scored 18 goals in 55 games between 2000 and 2002. Liverpool paid £10 million for his transfer, originally as a striker but he was mainly used on the right wing while at Anfield. He won a League Cup-winners' medal in 2003 but the following season he became the first Liverpool player to wear the number-nine shirt and fail to score in an entire season. In September 2004 he joined the Wanderers on loan for the season and made his debut as a substitute in a 2–2 home draw with Manchester United, netting his first goal the following month in a 2–1 win over Newcastle. The Wanderers agreed a £5.5 million fee for Diouf, although he remained on loan until November 2005 due to outstanding off-the-field issues. In September 2005 he scored Bolton's first-ever goal in the UEFA Cup when he equalised against Lokomotiv Plovdiv at the Reebok Stadium, and Bolton went on to win 2–1. His final goal for the club came against Sunderland, in a 2–1 win at the

	League		FA Cup		FL Cup		Total	
	A	G	A	G	A	G	A	G
1961–62	12	3	-	-	-	-	12	3
1962–63	40	10	1	-	-	-	41	10
1963–64	23	7	4	1	2	-	29	8
1964–65	34	21	3	3	1	1	38	25
1965–66	34	13	3	2	1	1	38	16
1966–67	12	12	-	-	-	-	12	12
	155	66	11	6	4	2	170	74

EL HADJI DIOUF

Born: St Louis, Senegal, 15 January 1981
A member of the Senegal team that reached the quarter-finals of the 2002 World Cup, El

Reebok in May 2008, a result that secured Premiership status, and his final game for the club came the following week at Chelsea. In July 2008 he joined Sunderland for £2.6 million but failed to score in 14 League games. He joined Blackburn, initially on loan, in January 2009. In January 2011 he joined Glasgow Rangers on loan where he won League Championship and League Cup winners' medals.

	League		FA Cup		FL Cup		UEFA Cup		Total	
	A	G	A	G	A	G	A	G	A	G
2004–05	23/4	9	1/2	-	2	-	-	-	26/6	9
2005–06	17/3	3	-	-	-/1	-	4/2	1	21/6	4
2006–07	32/1	5	1	-	-/1	-	-	-	33/2	5
2007–08	30/4	4	1	-	1	-	2/4	2	34/8	6
	102/12	21	3/2	-	3/2	-	6/6	3	114/22	24

YOURI DJORKAEFF

Born: Lyon, France, 9 March 1968
The capture of Youri Djorkaeff by the Wanderers in January 2002 turned many heads in the footballing world. A World Cup-winner with France in 1998 and a European Championship-winner in 2000, Djorkaeff moved to the Reebok with the intention of resurrecting his career, which had stalled at Kaiserslautern, and gaining a place in the French 2002 World Cup Finals squad. The son of a former professional player, Jean Djorkaeff, Youri had begun his career with French club Grenoble in 1984, where he became an effective forward or attacking midfield player. In 1989 he moved to Strasbourg, scoring 25 goals in 35 games

before signing for Monaco, where he netted 65 times in 177 games. He moved north to Paris Saint-Germain in 1995, winning the Cup-Winners' Cup with them and then the 1998 UEFA Cup a year later when he joined Inter. Kaiserslautern secured his signature in 1999 and he remained there until he joined Bolton. Djorkaeff made his debut in a 0–0 draw at Southampton and quickly began to show his superb technique and silky skills. He scored two fantastic goals at Charlton in March 2002 and helped the Wanderers retain Premiership status. After appearing for France in the 2002 World Cup Finals he retired from international football, having won 82 caps, six of which while with Bolton. He extended his contract with the Wanderers missing only two League games during 2002–03, and he was a member of the side that reached the Carling Cup Final in 2004. He netted both goals in a 2–1 win at Everton in the final away game of that season as the club recorded five consecutive wins in the top flight for the first time since 1928. His contract was not renewed, though, and he joined Blackburn. He played three games for them before joining the MetroStars in the MLS in February 2005. Djorkaeff continued in the States with the rebranded Red Bull New York and retired in October 2006.

	League		FA Cup		FL Cup		Total	
	A	G	A	G	A	G	A	G
2001–02	12	4	-	-	-	-	12	4
2002–03	36	7	1	-	-	-	37	7
2003–04	24/3	8	-	-	4/1	1	28/4	9
	72/3	19	1	-	4/1	1	77/4	20

ALEX DONALDSON

Born: Barrhead, 4 December 1890
Died: Unknown
The history books were almost rewritten when, in April 1914, Alex Donaldson was invited to the North v South England trial, nearly becoming the first Scotsman to play

for England. Unknown to the FA, he was actually born north of the border and moved to Leicestershire when he was 10 years old. The error was eventually realised, but he didn't have to wait too long for his first taste of international football when he was selected for Scotland against Wales the same year, the first of six caps all earned while with the Wanderers. Donaldson's early clubs were Belgrave, Balmoral United and Ripley Athletic, and he had a trial with Sheffield United but returned to Ripley before Bolton paid £50 for his transfer in December 1911. His 9st 9lb frame was ideal for a fast and tricky outside-left but the war cut short his best years. Donaldson worked in a munitions factory during the conflict, and after the war he was dogged by injury, fracturing his right kneecap against Preston in February 1921. The emergence of Billy Butler then restricted his appearances, and he made his final Bolton appearance in a 2–0 reverse at Burnley in February 1922. The following month he joined Sunderland, playing 43 League games before returning to the North West with Manchester City. He only played seven games for them before brief spells with Crystal Palace and two spells at

Chorley either side of a season at Ashton National. During the 1950s he became licensee of the Gardeners Arms in Bolton.

	League		FA Cup		Total	
	A	G	A	G	A	G
1912–13	27	3	-	-	27	3
1913–14	33	2	3	1	36	3
1914–15	15	-	-	-	15	-
1919–20	30	-	1	-	31	-
1920–21	26	-	1	-	27	-
1921–22	8	-	2	-	10	-
	139	5	7	1	146	6

BRYAN EDWARDS

Born: Woodlesford, Leeds, 27 October 1930
Excelling at football and cricket, Bryan Edwards had trials with both the Wanderers and Yorkshire County Cricket Club. He was spotted by Bolton playing at Under-16 level for Oulton Youth Club in Leeds and signed amateur forms. The club had no hesitation in offering him a professional contract on his 17th birthday as he showed good promise as a wing-half in the A team. Edwards progressed through the reserve side and made his League debut in a 3–3 draw at Liverpool in September 1950. He went on to become a regular in the side, but his call up for National service stopped his progression and this ultimately cost him a place in the 1953 FA Cup Final line up. He won his place back in the side in 1954–55 and such

was his consistency that he missed only two League games in four seasons between 1955 and 1959. Edwards was a member of the 1958 Cup-winning side and he maintained his reliability after switching to centre-half. He completed 500 first-team appearances for the club during 1964–65 before retiring at the end of that term, his National service probably having cost him the club's appearance record. He joined Blackpool as assistant trainer-coach before becoming first-team coach at Preston. After a spell at Plymouth in a similar capacity he became manager at Bradford City in November 1971, where he stayed until January 1975. He became a qualified physiotherapist and served at Huddersfield and Leeds before returning to Bradford, where he also worked in a number of other roles, including assistant manager and general manager.

	League		FA Cup		FL Cup		Total	
	A	G	A	G	A	G	A	G
1950–51	30	-	2	-	-	-	32	-
1951–52	40	-	1	-	-	-	41	-
1952–53	14	-	-	-	-	-	14	-
1953–54	2	-	-	-	-	-	2	-
1954–55	38	1	2	-	-	-	40	1
1955–56	42	2	2	-	-	-	44	2
1956–57	42	-	1	-	-	-	43	-
1957–58	41	-	5	-	-	-	46	-
1958–59	41	4	6	-	-	-	47	4
1959–60	17	-	-	-	-	-	17	-
1960–61	33	1	3	-	1	-	37	1
1961–62	42	-	1	-	2	-	45	-
1962–63	41	-	1	-	-	-	42	-
1963–64	23	-	4	1	1	-	28	1
1964–65	36	-	3	-	1	-	40	-
	482	8	31	1	5	-	518	9

SYD FARRIMOND

Born: Hindley, Wigan, 17 July 1940
One of a number of players to progress through the youth ranks of the club during the late 1950s, Syd Farrimond was spotted playing for Moss Lane Youth Club in 1956.

He won England Youth honours in 1958 and played in the same England Amateur Youth team as Warwick Rimmer. Farrimond went on to represent the Wanderers for 13 years, beginning his League career against Preston at Deepdale in October 1958. He became understudy to regular left-back Tommy Banks, a position he took over after Bank's departure, and was an ever present during 1961–62 season. His only goal for the club came in a 1–1 home draw with Norwich in March 1967, and he continued to hold down his place despite other youngsters making a claim. His last game for the club came at Millwall in November 1970, and he was given a free transfer after a dispute over a loyalty bonus. After a short spell at Shrewsbury, Farrimond joined Tranmere Rovers, where he made 134 League appearances. He left Prenton Park to become player-coach at Halifax Town before joining Sunderland as a coach and then Leeds in a similar capacity. After retiring Farrimond returned to the Wanderers as a member of the corporate matchday staff.

	League		FA Cup		FL Cup		Total	
	A	G	A	G	A	G	A	G
1958–59	1	-	-	-	-	-	1	-
1959–60	23	-	3	-	-	-	26	-
1960–61	27	-	2	-	3	-	32	-
1961–62	42	-	1	-	2	-	45	-
1962–63	30	-	1	-	1	-	32	-
1963–64	31	-	4	-	-	-	35	-
1964–65	38	-	3	-	1	-	42	-
1965–66	33	-	3	-	2	-	38	-
1966–67	37	1	3	-	1	-	41	1
1967–68	41	-	1	-	3	-	45	-
1968–69	38	-	1	-	1	-	40	-
1969–70	5/1	-	-	-	-	-	5/1	-
1970–71	18	-	-	-	3	-	21	-
	364/1	1	22	-	17	-	403/1	1

JAMES FAY

Born: Southport, 29 March 1884
Died: Southport, 1957

Jimmy Fay began his career in his home town with local sides Southport Crescent, Southport Blue Star and Southport Working Lads. He moved up to Chorley and Oswaldtwistle Rovers before entering League football with Oldham Athletic in 1907. Between 1907–08 and 1910–11 he didn't miss a League game and was the Latics leading scorer in 1909–10 with 26 goals from inside-forward, helping them to runners'-up spot in Division Two. In September 1911 he joined the Wanderers and made his name at the club as a centre-half but was laid up for most of 1913 with a hernia. At the outbreak of World War One Fay was to be found playing for Southport Central, having lost his place in the Bolton line up to Walter Rowley. In March 1917 he guested for the Wanderers at Preston, having been unable to get to Bury to represent Southport. At the end of the war he rejoined Bolton and represented the Football League against the Scottish League at Ibrox in April 1919, when he was 35 years old. He played his last game for the club in a 1–1 home draw against Burnley in March 1921, just short of his 37th birthday before

ending his career at Southport in 1922. He then became secretary of the PFA, a position he held until 1952, and was chairman from 1922 until 1929, having been a founder member of the old Players' Union in 1907. Fay continued to operate his sports outfitting business and became a JP, earning himself the title of Gentleman James Fay.

	League		FA Cup		Total	
	A	G	A	G	A	G
1911–12	29	2	3	-	32	2
1912–13	14	-	-	-	14	-
1913–14	27	2	3	-	30	2
1914–15	22	1	-	-	22	1
1919–20	25	-	1	-	26	-
1920–21	11	-	1	-	12	-
	128	5	8	-	136	5

JACK FEEBURY

Born: Hucknall, 10 May 1888
Died: Nottingham, 1960

Noted for his powerful shooting, Jack Feebury started his career at Hucknall and Bulwell White Star before joining the Wanderers in 1908. After a season in the reserves he forced his way into the first team, replacing Jack Slater at left-back,

and at 6ft tall was the tallest player in the side. In August 1913 he won a Players' Union kicking contest with an 80-yard right-foot punt. He was challenged by a spectator to do the same with his other foot and duly obliged. Feebury received a £500 benefit from a game against Sunderland in April 1914 and during the war guested for Notts County. In 1919 he scored in four successive games from full-back. A couple of those goals were from penalties, but Feebury then went the way of all penalty artists and missed one, handing the job to Frank Roberts. In May 1920 he joined Exeter City, playing 42 League games, before ending his League career at Brighton in 1923 and moving to Mid-Rhondda United.

	League		FA Cup		Total	
	A	G	A	G	A	G
1909–10	22	-	-	-	22	-
1910–11	19	1	-	-	19	1
1911–12	26	2	3	-	29	2
1912–13	35	5	1	-	36	5
1913–14	37	4	3	-	40	4
1914–15	16	-	4	-	20	-
1919–20	25	4	1	-	26	4
	180	16	12	-	192	16

DAVID FELGATE

Born: Blaenau Ffestiniog, 4 March 1960

Goalkeeper David Felgate began his career with Bolton but left in September 1980, two years after turning professional and without playing a first-team game. He had gathered experience in loan spells at Rochdale, where he played 47 times in two spells, and at Crewe, where he played 14 games. He joined Lincoln City for a £25,000 fee and it was while with the Imps that he won his only Welsh cap when he appeared as a substitute for Neville Southall in a 5–0 win over Romania at Wrexham. In December 1984 Felgate had a loan spell at Cardiff followed by one at Grimsby, which persuaded them to sign him for £27,000 in June 1985. He played only 12 games before joining the Wanderers for a three-month loan period in February 1986, his debut coming in a 4–0 home win over Newport County. Felgate returned to Blundell Park but the following February he came back to Bolton again, initially on loan and then in a permanent £15,000 transfer. His first full season ended in relegation to Division Four, but he was an ever present in the side that won promotion in 1988 and he won

the club's Player of the Year award. Having missed out on a Wembley appearance in 1986 because his loan period had run out, Felgate made up for it in 1989 when the club won the Sherpa Van Trophy while he appeared in goal. Felgate's last game for the club came in May 1992 at home to Stoke, and the following season he had spells at Bury and Wolves before joining Chester City. He played 71 games for Chester, scoring one goal, before ending his League career at Wigan. He then had a non-League spell at Leigh RMI, which included a famous FA Cup draw at Fulham, followed by Hyde United, Radcliffe, Chorley and Bacup. He turned to coaching and after spells at Rossendale and Stockport joined Manchester City.

	League	FA Cup	FL Cup	Frieght Rover Trophy	Total
	A	A	A	A	A
1985–86	15	-	-	4	19
1986–87	22	-	-	-	22
1987–88	46	3	2	3	54
1988–89	46	3	2	8	59
1989–90	42	1	6	5	54
1990–91	49	4	4	2	59
1991–92	25	6	-	2	33
	245	17	14	24	300

ALEX FINNEY

Born: St Helens, 13 March 1892
Died: May 1982

A former barber's lather boy and miner in his home town of St Helens, Alex Finney went on to become a stalwart of the Wanderers halcyon days in the 1920s. He started with Sutton Juniors and Peasley Cross before joining South Liverpool. He then moved to New Brighton and it was while playing for the Rakers in the Lancashire Junior Cup Final against Chorley at Burnden in 1922 that the left-back was noticed by the Wanderers. He was snapped up after New Brighton had forgotten to put his name on their retained list, and he made his Bolton debut in September 1922. At 22 years old Finney was the youngest member of the 1923 FA Cup-winning side and the following year he was the only ever present as the Wanderers finished fourth in Division One. He represented the Football League in a 9–1 win against the Irish League at Newcastle in 1924–25 but missed most of the following season, including the Cup Final, due to a cartilage operation. He returned, however, and won another Cup-winners' medal in 1929. Finney's last game for the club came in 1937 – he was the last player at the club from those Cup successes of the 1920s – and in August of that year he joined Darwen. He ended his footballing days back at New Brighton, where he assisted Jack Atkinson in coaching the team. He then worked for the parks department in Wallasey, where he lived, until his retirement.

	League		FA Cup		Total	
	A	G	A	G	A	G
1922–23	26	-	6	-	32	-
1923–24	42	-	3	-	45	-
1924–25	31	-	3	-	34	-
1925–26	5	-	2	-	7	-
1926–27	33	-	4	-	37	-
1927–28	33	1	1	-	34	1
1928–29	32	-	7	-	39	-
1929–30	38	-	-	-	38	-
1930–31	39	-	3	-	42	-
1931–32	38	-	2	-	40	-
1932–33	41	-	3	-	44	-
1933–34	40	1	5	-	45	1
1934–35	38	-	6	-	44	-
1935–36	40	-	2	-	42	-
1936–37	7	-	-	-	7	-
	483	2	47	-	530	2

PER FRANDSEN

Born: Copenhagen, Denmark, 6 February 1970

A midfield stalwart of two promotion campaigns in two separate spells with the club, Per Frandsen was secured from FC Copenhagen for a £350,000 fee in July 1996. He began his career with BK Skjold and B.93 but made his debut in senior football with B1903 and earned the first of 28 Danish Under-21 caps while there. In November 1990 he joined OSC Lille, playing 109 games and representing Denmark in the 1992 Olympics before returning to his home country in 1994 with FC Copenhagen. Frandsen was a member of Copenhagen's 1995 Danish Cup-winning side and joined the Wanderers a year later for the last season at Burnden Park, missing just six games as the club stormed to the First Division Championship. He played in all the Premiership games the following season, the first at the Reebok Stadium. After another consistent campaign that saw the Wanderers reach the Play-offs, Frandsen was sold to Blackburn for £1.75 million in September 1999. His stay at Ewood lasted less than a year, though, and he returned for £1.5 million to help Bolton to promotion via the Play-offs at Cardiff. He netted two goals at Leicester in a 5–0 opening day Premier League win at Filbert Street in August 2001, and his performances helped the club to hold on to their status that term. He also scored a vital goal in the final game of the 2002–03 season against Middlesbrough at the Reebok, helping the club to a 2–1 win and securing premiership status. 2003–04 proved to be Frandsen's last with the club, his final game coming against Fulham on the last day of the season. That summer he joined Wigan Athletic, but injuries unfortunately cut short his stay and he retired in January 2005. Frandsen won 23 full caps for Denmark, 19 while with the Wanderers, including appearances in the 1998 World Cup Finals. After retirement he became an agent before joining HB Koge as assistant manager in June 2009.

	League		FA Cup		FL Cup		Total	
	A	G	A	G	A	G	A	G
1996–97	40/1	5	2/1	-	4/1	-	46/3	5
1997–98	38	2	1	-	4	1	43	3
1998–99	47	9	1	-	4	1	52	10
1999–2000	7	2	-	-	3	2	10	4
2000–01	37/5	8	2/2	-	1/1	-	40/8	8
2001–02	25/4	3	-	-	1	-	26/4	3
2002–03	34	2	-	-	-	-	34	2
2003–04	22/10	1	1/1	-	3	-	26/12	1
	250/21	32	7/4	-	20/2	4	277/27	36

ARCHIE FREEBAIRN

Born: Glasgow, 1873
Died: Unknown

Archie Freebairn had the distinction of scoring one of the goals in the 5–0 win over West Bromwich Albion in April 1895 in what was the final League game at Pikes Lane. He had joined the Wanderers the previous season, having been with Wheatburn and Partick Thistle prior to making the half-back position his own. Between 1894 and 1899 he was a model of consistency, missing only two games throughout that period. In 1899 he was appointed captain, taking over from Di Jones, but he could do little to prevent the club's relegation for the first time. He played his part in securing promotion at the first attempt, though, and continued to be a

regular in the team, only missing matches through injury. By the time the 1904 FA Cup Final came round, Freebairn was back in the side at 31 years old, despite injury earlier in the season. Although he remained at the club for a further three years before his retirement, he was only called on when other players were injured, and he spent most of his final days at Burnden in the reserves. His 135 consecutive League appearances between 1894 and 1899 remain a club record for an outfield player.

	League		FA Cup		Total	
	A	G	A	G	A	G
1894–95	29	1	3	-	32	1
1895–96	30	-	5	-	35	-
1896–97	30	-	4	-	34	-
1897–98	30	-	4	-	34	-
1898–99	33	1	2	-	35	1
1899–1900	29	2	-	-	29	2
1900–01	29	2	2	-	31	2
1901–02	23	1	2	-	25	1
1902–03	23	1	1	-	24	1
1903–04	18	1	6	1	24	2
1904–05	-	-	-	-	-	-
1905–06	11	-	-	-	11	-
1906–07	1	-	-	-	1	-
	286	9	29	1	315	10

RICARDO GARDNER

Born: St Andrews, Jamaica, 25 September 1978

Capable of playing at full-back or in midfield, 'Bibi' made his debut for Harbour View when only 14 years old, representing Woolmer's Boys High School, and was still there when he made his international debut two years later. He has gone on to represent his country more than a hundred times, including all the World Cup Final games in France 1998, and is now the Wanderers' most-capped player. It was while playing in the 1998 Finals that he came to the club's attention and his signature was secured for a £1 million fee. Gardner made his League debit... debut as a substitute at West Brom in September 1998, coming on to score the winning goal in a 3–2 success. He made a Wembley appearance in his first season with the club, a 2–0 Play-off Final defeat to Watford, and quickly became a crowd favourite. Injuries have limited his appearances, the first of three major setbacks coming at Barnsley in February 2000, but each time he has recovered and forced his way back into the line up. He grabbed one of the Wanderers' goals in the 3–0 success over Preston in the 2001 Play-off Final at Cardiff and, although he has popped up with other important goals, his early opener in the UEFA Cup at Bayern Munich is one that will be remembered.

	League		FA Cup		FL Cup		UEFA Cup		Total	
	A	G	A	G	A	G	A	G	A	G
1998–99	22/11	2	-/1	-	2/1	1	-	-	24/13	3
1999–2000	26/3	5	2/2	-	9	1	-	-	37/5	6
2000–01	30/5	5	2	-	-	-	-	-	32/5	5
2001–02	29/2	3	2	-	-/1	-	-	-	31/3	3
2002–03	31/1	2	-	-	-	-	-	-	31/1	2
2003–04	20/2	-	-	-	2/2	-	-	-	22/4	-
2004–05	30/3	-	3/1	-	1	-	-	-	34/4	-
2005–06	27/3	-	4	-	3	-	7	-	41/3	-
2006–07	13/5	-	3	-	-	-	-	-	16/5	-
2007–08	25/1	-	-	-	-	-	4	1	29/1	1
2008–09	18/11	4	1	-	1	-	-	-	20/11	4
2009–10	11/10	1	3	-	2	-	-	-	16/10	1
2010–11	3/2	-	-	-	1	-	-	-	4/2	-
	285/59	22	20/4	-	21/4	2	11	1	337/67	25

STELIOS GIANNAKOPOULOS

Born: Athens, Greece, 12 July 1974

The son of former Panathinaikos player Alekos Giannakopoulos, Stelios started his career at semi-professional club Ethnikos Asteras, making his debut in 1991. The club won promotion to Division C of the Greek League and he turned professional, scoring six goals in 1992–93. The winger was snapped up by Paniliakos that summer and he spent three years there establishing himself in the Greek Under-21 team. In the summer of 1996 Olympiacos signed him, and in his seven seasons with them they won the Championship on each occasion. He scored their first-ever Champions League goal and helped them reach the quarter-finals in 1999, going on to score 49 goals in 161 League games. He joined the Wanderers in May 2003, having 'Stelios' emblazoned on the back of his shirt and helping the club reach the Carling Cup Final with a goal in the semi-final 5–2 first-leg victory over Aston Villa. After playing his part in Greece's successful 2004 Euro' Championship success, he returned to have two further successful seasons. He netted eight goals in 2004–05, including a final-day winner against Everton that secured sixth place, and the following season his 12 goals included an FA Cup fourth-round winner against Arsenal. His final two seasons at the club saw him suffer with some injuries and a loss of form, but his two League goals in 2008 proved vital, securing a last-minute home win over Derby and a point at Tottenham. It was ironic that he was also to score in the UEFA Cup against his fellow countrymen

from Aris FC to secure a 1–1 draw, again in the final minute. Stelios's contract expired in the summer of 2008, and that September he joined Hull, but he only featured in three games before returning to Greece with Larissa in January 2009. His international career also came to an end in Euro 2008 with 77 caps to his name, 47 of which were won while at Bolton. After retiring he worked for the Greek PFA.

	League		FA Cup		FL Cup		UEFA Cup		Total	
	A	G	A	G	A	G	A	G	A	G
2003–04	17/14	2	2	-	4/2	2	-	-	23/16	4
2004–05	28/6	7	2	1	1/1	-	-	-	31/7	8
2005–06	29/5	9	4	2	2	-	6	1	41/5	12
2006–07	11/12	-	3	-	2	-	-	-	16/12	-
2007–08	1/14	2	1	-	1/1	1	4/4	1	7/19	4
	86/51	20	12	3	10/4	3	10/4	2	118/59	28

HARRY GOSLIN

Born: Willington, 9 November 1909
Died: Italy, 18 December 1943
A captain until the end, Harry (Henry) Goslin is a player whose name is written large in Bolton history, not because he hit the headlines like Smith or Lofthouse but for his style, gentlemanly conduct and untimely death. He lost his life in the Italian campaign in the battle of the River Sangro when a bomb exploded on his observation point. He was serving in the

53rd Field Regiment RA (Bolton Artillery), having already fought in both France and North Africa, along with the majority of his Wanderers teammates. He joined the Wanderers in August 1930 for a £25 donation to Boots Athletic of Nottingham and succeeded Fred Kean at half-back the same year, making his debut in a 7–2 reverse at Liverpool. Goslin ran a cycle shop in the Churchgate area of the town, and in 1936 he took over the captaincy from Alec Finney, an honour he held to the last. On 8 April 1939, with war inevitable, Goslin made a rousing speech at Burnden before the assembled crowd, telling them that after the game the Bolton team would be signing up at the Territorial Army Hall. Goslin was promoted to sergeant and then lieutenant for his actions on the battlefield. While on leave he represented both Chelsea and Norwich and gained well-earned, if deferred, recognition from the selectors in England's wartime team. His last appearance for Bolton was at York in March 1942, and that summer, along with many of his team, he played for the British Army in a 4–2 win against their Polish counterparts in Egypt.

	League		FA Cup		Total	
	A	G	A	G	A	G
1930–31	33	1	3	-	36	1
1931–32	10	-	1	-	11	-
1932–33	26	4	3	-	29	4
1933–34	32	2	5	-	37	2
1934–35	42	2	8	-	50	2
1935–36	41	3	2	-	43	3
1936–37	37	3	5	-	42	3
1937–38	40	5	1	-	41	5
1938–39	42	3	3	-	45	3
	303	23	31	-	334	23

ALAN GOWLING

Born: Stockport, 16 March 1949

Alan Gowling became the Wanderers' record signing in March 1978 when he joined the club for a £120,000 fee from Newcastle United. His role in Bolton's push towards the Second Division Championship that year was minimal, but he proved his worth the following season in a magnificent striking partnership with Frank Worthington, which kept them in the top flight and also included the club's first goal at that level for 14 years. Gowling had begun his career at Manchester United, by way of County Schools and

Manchester University, where he gained a degree in economics. He had also won England Schoolboy and Amateur honours and represented the British Olympic side at the 1968 Summer Olympics. He played 71 League games for United, both in attack and midfield, and won an England Under-23 cap before joining Huddersfield Town for £60,000 in June 1972. Although he became a regular goalscorer at Leeds Road under Ian Greaves, the club still suffered two relegations. In August 1975 Gowling joined Newcastle for £70,000, where he formed a potent attack with Malcolm Macdonald, and Gowling scored at Wembley in the 1976 League Cup Final defeat by Manchester City. He moved to Burnden in 1978 and teamed up again with Ian Greaves, but after a successful 1978–79 season in goalscoring terms he became a dual-purpose player, either leading the attack or marshalling the centre of defence. Gowling was elected chairman of the PFA in November 1980 and, in May 1982, after missing only three games in the previous two seasons for the Wanderers, he was given a free transfer. He joined Preston North End and retired from the game in 1984. He now regularly summarises the Wanderers games on BBC Radio Manchester.

	League		FA Cup		FL Cup		Total	
	A	G	A	G	A	G	A	G
1977–78	6/2	-	-	-	-	-	6/2	-
1978–79	36	15	1	-	2	1	39	16
1979–80	24	1	3	-	2	1	29	2
1980–81	41	10	2	-	2	-	45	10
1981–82	40	2	2	1	2	-	44	3
	147/2	28	8	1	8	2	163/2	31

ROY GREAVES

Born: Farnworth, 4 April 1947

Roy Greaves was just three games short of equalling the club's appearance record when, in March 1980, he left to join Seattle

Sounders in the North American Soccer League. The local player had served his apprenticeship at Burnden and had made his League debut in October 1965, aged 18, in a 1–0 defeat at Leyton Orient. He had played at centre-forward for his first home game and scored twice as Southampton were beaten 3–2. Greaves then settled at inside-forward, becoming a regular in 1967 and the club's leading scorer in 1967–68 and 1968–69. After relegation to the Third Division, Greaves was played in a deeper position by manager Jimmy Armfield and attracted interest from a number of First Division clubs. He was ever present in the team that won the Third Division Championship in 1973 and a cornerstone of the side that spent the next five years in Division Two. He was awarded a testimonial in May 1976 before getting into the top flight in 1978. By then he was captain of the club, and he lifted the Second Division Championship aloft prior to Peter Thompson's testimonial game. Greaves missed only one game in his debut season in the top flight but, the following

season, injuries and a lack of form heralded changes as the club slumped to relegation. Greaves's last appearance for the club was in an FA Cup defeat at Arsenal in February 1980, but after his stint in the NASL he returned to England and became player-coach at Rochdale during 1982. He played 21 League games, giving him the distinction of having played in every division of the League. After leaving Spotland Greaves continued to play local football and is regularly in attendance at the Reebok Stadium.

	League		FA Cup		FL Cup		Total	
	A	G	A	G	A	G	A	G
1965–66	9/3	3	-	-	1	1	10/3	4
1966–67	2/1	1	-	-	-	-	02/1	1
1967–68	36/1	10	1	-	3	-	40/1	10
1968–69	32	11	2	1	1	-	35	12
1969–70	37	4	1	1	4	2	42	7
1970–71	34	2	1	-	1	-	36	2
1971–72	38	7	4	4	6	2	48	13
1972–73	45/1	1	9	2	2	-	56/1	3
1973–74	41	4	3	-	5	1	49	5
1974–75	29/1	2	2	-	2	-	33/1	2
1975–76	42	7	6	-	1	-	49	7
1976–77	41	4	1	-	9	2	51	6
1977–78	40	7	4	1	2	1	46	9
1978–79	41	1	1	-	2	-	44	1
1979–80	20/1	2	4	1	2	-	26/1	3
	487/8	66	39	10	41	9	567/8	85

SCOTT GREEN

Born: Walsall, 15 January 1970

Scott Green proved to be a bargain £50,000 buy from Derby County at the back end of the 1989–90 season and went on to become a great utility player, capable of playing at full-back, midfield or as a striker. He had had spells at Stoke, West Brom and Walsall as a schoolboy before signing for the Rams, but he failed to make a first-team appearance for them. He also spent a summer in Finland with Euran Pallo. Green made his Bolton debut in a 1–0 home Third Division defeat to

Shrewsbury Town in April 1990 but grabbed the winner a week later against Bristol City. He made a Wembley appearance as a substitute in the 1991 Third Division Play-offs and was an integral part of the team that won promotion as runners-up in 1993. By the time promotion to the Premier League came around in 1995, Green had switched to full-back and played in both the League Cup Final defeat to Liverpool and the Play-off win over Reading at Wembley. He played in the majority of the club's first season in the Premier League, but his appearances became curtailed the following year. He scored the club's last-ever FA Cup goal at Burnden Park in a 3–2 reverse to Chesterfield and in June 1997 made a £300,000 move to Wigan Athletic. He helped the Latics win the Auto Windscreens Shield at Wembley in 1999 and the Second Division Championship in 2002. The following year he joined Wrexham, spending a season with Telford United before returning to the Racecourse. In 2005 Green joined Ashton United in the Unibond League, becoming player-

manager before leaving in 2007. In 2009 he became head of youth at Yeovil Town.

	League		FA Cup		FL Cup		Autoglass Trophy		Anglo–Italian Cup		Total	
	A	G	A	G	A	G	A	G	A	G	A	G
1989–90	6/1	2	-	-	-	-	-	-	-	-	6/1	2
1990–91	33/10	6	2/1	-	4	-	2	-	-	-	41/11	6
1991–92	26/11	2	5/1	1	2	-	3	-	-	-	36/12	3
1992–93	33/8	6	5	1	4	1	3	-	-	-	45/8	8
1993–94	11/11	4	3	-	-/1	-	-	-	3/2	1	17/14	5
1994–95	29/5	1	1	-	6	-	-	-	-	-	36/5	1
1995–96	26/5	3	2	-	3/2	-	-	-	-	-	31/7	3
1996–97	7/5	1	2/1	2	-/1	-	-	-	-	-	9/7	3
	171/56	25	20/3	4	19/4	1	8	-	3/2	1	221/65	31

SAM GREENHALGH

Born: Eagley, July 1882
Died: 1955

Sam Greenhalgh turned out for both Eagley and Turton before joining the Wanderers in June 1902. He became a regular at centre-half, one of the few successes in the team that failed to register a League win until January and were duly relegated. He was a member of the 1904 FA Cup Final side that narrowly went down to Manchester City, and he missed only two games throughout 1904–05 as Bolton won promotion from the Second Division. That year he was selected for the Football League against the Scottish League and in October 1905 Aston Villa secured his services. He spent his time in the Midlands at wing-half and played 46 League games before returning to Burnden Park in September 1907. Greenhalgh won a Second Division Championship medal in 1909 and was captain two years later when promotion was won again after a swift relegation from the top flight. He fell out of favour with the club in March 1912 when he refused to play on the wing in an emergency and was suspended for six weeks. However, he returned to the side after issuing an apology and continued playing until 1913, his final game coming on the opening day of the

season, a 1–0 home reverse to Sheffield Wednesday. He joined Chorley the following season and became licensee at the Cheetham Arms in Dunscar.

	League		FA Cup		Total	
	A	G	A	G	A	G
1902–03	30	1	1	-	31	1
1903–04	30	2	6	-	36	2
1904–05	32	2	4	-	36	2
1905–06	4	1	-	-	4	1
1907–08	28	-	5	1	33	1
1908–09	32	3	1	-	33	3
1909–10	23	-	-	-	23	-
1910–11	36	5	1	-	37	5
1911–12	13	2	-	-	13	2
1912–13	30	3	1	-	31	3
1913–14	1	-	-	-	1	-
	259	19	19	1	278	20

EIDUR GUDJOHNSEN

Born: Reykjavik, Iceland, 15 September 1978

Eidur Gudjohnsen played his first game in Bolton colours in a 3–2 defeat in a pre-season game at Waterford in July 1998. Looking unfit, he grabbed one of the goals and manager Colin Todd offered the Icelandic striker a contract. He had begun

with FC Valur before joining PSV Eindhoven in 1994, entering the record books in April 1996 when he came on as a substitute for his father, Arnor, for Iceland in Estonia. Unfortunately he suffered injury playing for the Icelandic Under-18s side and joined KR Reykjavik in the summer of 1998. Most of his first season at Bolton was spent regaining his fitness, but he forced his way into the first team after Dean Holdsworth suffered injury, playing at Wembley in the Play-off defeat to Watford. The following season Gudjohnsen was the club's leading goalscorer, again making a Wembley appearance in the FA Cup semi-final penalty defeat to Aston Villa. His last appearance for the club came in a 2–2 Play-off semi-final first-leg draw against Ipswich at the Reebok. He grabbed one of the goals but received the injury that kept him out of the controversial second-leg defeat. In the close season of 2000 Chelsea paid £4 million, and Gudjohnsen formed a deadly partnership with Jimmy Floyd Hasselbaink. Gudjohnsen played a significant role in helping Chelsea to the Premier League title in 2005 and after 182

games and 54 goals he joined Barcelona for an initial 12 million euros in June 2006. In the summer of 2009 he moved to Monaco before returning to England with Tottenham in January 2010 and Stoke City at the start of the 2010–11 season. In January 2011 he joined Fulham on loan.

	League		FA Cup		FL Cup		Total	
	A	G	A	G	A	G	A	G
1998–99	11/6	5	-	-	-/1	-	11/7	5
1999–2000	41/1	14	4/1	4	8	4	53/2	22
	52/7	19	4/1	4	8/1	4	64/9	27

STAN HANSEN

Born: Bootle, 27 December 1915
Died: Bolton, November 1987

Stan Hansen had a 50-year association with the Wanderers that began in August 1935 when, as a 19-year-old goalkeeper, he appeared in trials at Burnden and the Wanderers signed him on amateur forms. He had represented Bootle Schoolboys and had spells with both Liverpool and Southport before joining Litherland in 1934. Aston Villa were keen to sign him, but after just two months with the Wanderers he turned professional, making his League debut in September 1936 against Huddersfield. He became a regular in 1938 when he displaced Fred Swift. In 1940 Hansen was one of 13 Wanderers players involved in the retreat at Dunkirk. He played regularly throughout the war and appeared for the Eighth Army in their 4–2 win over Yugoslavia. Hansen was demobbed in 1945 and helped the club reach the semi-finals of the FA Cup the following year. He toured Canada with the FA in 1950 and played in the famous 1953 FA Cup Final against Blackpool. He left Burnden as a player in 1956 and played part-time for Rhyl while taking charge of the Wanderers B team. He also became the sub-postmaster at the Burnden Post Office opposite the ground. Hansen retired in October 1986.

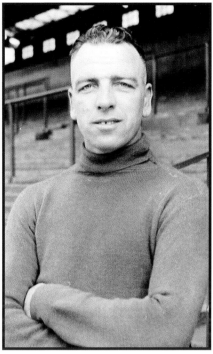

	League	FA Cup	Total
	A	A	A
1936–37	4	-	4
1937–38	14	-	14
1938–39	30	3	33
1945–46	-	9	9
1946–47	42	3	45
1947–48	41	1	42
1948–49	15	-	15
1949–50	39	3	42
1950–51	42	2	44
1951–52	40	1	41
1952–53	42	8	50
1953–54	40	6	46
1954–55	33	2	35
1955–56	2	1	3
	384	39	423

ROY HARTLE

Born: Bromsgrove, 4 October 1931

Roy Hartle signed amateur forms for the Wanderers when he was 16 years old and gained experience by playing on a regular basis while doing his national service in Oswestry. He had begun with local side

Bromsgrove Rovers and signed professional forms for Bolton in 1952. Hartle made his League debut on New Year's Day 1953, a 2–1 reverse at home to Charlton, taking over at right-back from the injured John Ball. He went on to play in every round of the FA Cup but missed out on the Final against Blackpool when Ball returned. He didn't appear again in the first team until 1955, when he displaced Ball two games into the season, and from then on he became a fixture in the side for over 10 years. He missed only 20 League games in a 10-season spell. Hartle made up for the disappointment of 1953 by winning a Cup-winners' medal in 1958, and he was rated as one of the finest full-backs never to win an England cap, although he did win Football League representative honours. Hartle ended his Bolton career in 1966, one appearance short of 500 games for the club, and had a spell with Buxton in the Cheshire League before hanging up his boots. He successfully ran for election to Bolton Borough Council, served on the executive of the PFA and earned his FA coaching badge. He spent a year as coach to the New York Generals in the fledgling North American Soccer League and

in 1969 the Wanderers awarded him a testimonial. Hartle also had a spell as chief scout at Bury and in recent times has worked at the Reebok Stadium, where a corporate lounge is named after him.

	League		FA Cup		FL Cup		Total	
	A	G	A	G	A	G	A	G
1952–53	17	-	7	-	-	-	24	-
1953–54	-	-	-	-	-	-	-	-
1954–55	-	-	-	-	-	-	-	-
1955–56	40	1	2	1	-	-	42	2
1956–57	41	-	1	-	-	-	42	-
1957–58	39	-	7	-	-	-	46	-
1958–59	41	-	6	-	-	-	47	-
1959–60	35	5	3	-	-	-	38	5
1960–61	40	2	3	-	5	1	48	3
1961–62	41	2	1	-	2	-	44	2
1962–63	41	1	1	-	1	-	43	1
1963–64	41	-	2	-	2	-	45	-
1964–65	41	-	3	-	1	-	45	-
1965–66	29/1	-	3	-	2	-	34/1	-
	446/1	11	39	1	13	1	498/1	13

HAROLD HASSALL

Born: Tyldesley, 4 March 1929

Harold Hassall played with both Mossley Common and Astley & Tyldesley Collieries before being spotted by Huddersfield Town. He signed for the Terriers in 1946, making his League debut in 1948 and, while at Leeds Road, had the distinction of saving a penalty from the great Tom Finney when he took over as an emergency 'keeper. The inside-forward won the first of five England caps in 1951, scoring against Scotland at Wembley and, after 74 League games for Town, joined Bolton for £27,000 in January 1952. Hassall became a member of the club's all-international forward line and played in the 1953 FA Cup Final. The following season he scored a number of vital goals to help the club to fifth place in the First Division. On New Year's Day 1955 he sustained a serious knee injury against Chelsea at Burnden that ended his career. His benefit game

DAVE HATTON

Born: Farnworth, 30 October 1943

Graduating through the Wanderers' junior sides, Dave Hatton made his League debut at half-back against Leicester City at Filbert Street in April 1962. The following season he took over from Syd Farrimond at left-back for a long spell, but it was not until the club had been relegated in 1964 that Hatton became a regular in the side. He missed just one game in 1964–65, as Bolton just failed to win promotion at the first attempt, and his consistency was rewarded with the captaincy. In September 1969 Hatton made a £40,000 move to Blackpool and was a member of their Second Division promotion-winning side that season. The Seasiders were relegated after one season, but Hatton continued to be a regular in the side, playing 250 League games until he joined Bury in August 1976. After a year at Gigg Lane Hatton was appointed player-manager and went on to play 97 League games before being sacked after the club narrowly escaped relegation to Division Four in May 1979.

attracted 20,000 spectators and he then fell back on his qualifications as a teacher. In 1958 he was appointed manager-coach of the England Youth team and in 1966 was appointed by FIFA to report on the World Cup games and submit findings on all aspects of the games played during the competition. He later became a lecturer in physical education and was appointed secretary of the Amateur Swimming Association. He still resides in Bolton.

	League		FA Cup		Total	
	A	**G**	**A**	**G**	**A**	**G**
1951–52	17	3	-	-	17	3
1952–53	33	7	7	-	40	7
1953–54	28	16	-	-	28	16
1954–55	24	8	-	-	24	8
	102	34	7	-	109	34

	League		FA Cup		FL Cup		Total	
	A	G	A	G	A	G	A	G
1961–62	2	-	-	-	1	-	3	-
1962–63	14	-	-	-	1	-	15	-
1963–64	29	3	4	-	2	-	35	3
1964–65	41	1	3	-	1	-	45	1
1965–66	33	4	3	-	2	-	38	4
1966–67	40	-	2	-	1	-	43	-
1967–68	35	-	-	-	3	-	38	-
1968–69	31	-	2	-	1	-	34	-
1969–70	6	-	-	-	2	-	8	-
	231	8	14	-	14	-	259	8

BOB HAWORTH

Born: Atherton, 26 June 1897
Died: March 1962

Bob Haworth became part of Bolton Wanderers folklore as a member of the team that won three Wembley FA Cup Finals in the 1920s. He was a collier in Atherton and had started his footballing career as a centre-forward with Howe Bridge. He joined Atherton Collieries, where he won the Bolton & District League Championship and the Junior Shield. In 1921 he became Charles Foweraker's first professional signing, turning down offers from both Plymouth, who were managed by ex-Wanderer Bob Jack, and Oldham. Haworth made his debut in November 1921 in a 1–0 win at West Brom and kept his place at full-back for the remainder of the season. In 1923 Haworth shared the right-back position with Walter Rowley but won the place for that year's famous 'White Horse' Cup Final, where he played alongside his fellow Athertonian Billy Butler. In 1930 Haworth succeeded Jim Seddon as captain, having missed only two League games in two seasons. In February 1931 he suffered a broken leg at Grimsby Town and, at 34 years old, it ended his Bolton career. After his recovery he had a spell at Accrington, making three League appearances, but the injury hastened his retirement and left the game to take over a newsagent's shop.

	League	FA Cup	Total
	A	A	A
1921–22	29	2	31
1922–23	30	5	35
1923–24	36	3	39
1924–25	35	2	37
1925–26	39	9	48
1926–27	14	-	14
1927–28	28	2	30
1928–29	40	8	48
1929–30	42	1	43
1930–31	29	3	32
	322	35	357

DEREK HENNIN

Born: Prescot, 28 December 1931
Died: January 1989

Derek Hennin had started his career at his home-town club Prescot Cables before he signed for the Wanderers in June 1949, the same year he won England Youth international honours. But he had to wait until March 1954 for his first-team debut, a 3–2 reverse against Tottenham at White Hart Lane. He took over the right-half position from injured John Wheeler for the remainder of that season as the club finished fifth in the First Division. Wheeler returned to the side after recovering from injury, and Hennin was a regular in the reserve side that won the Central League for the first time in 1955. In 1957 Wheeler left for Liverpool and Hennin became a regular in the first-team side. The following year he won an FA Cup-winners' medal and proved his worth as an emergency centre-forward when he grabbed a hat-trick in a Good Friday victory against Aston Villa. The emergence of Graham Stanley curtailed Hennin's appearances in 1960–61, and in February 1961 he joined Chester. He made 54 League appearances for the Sealand Road club and in July 1962 moved to Wigan Athletic, where he ended his career.

	League		FA Cup		FL Cup		Total	
	A	G	A	G	A	G	A	G
1953–54	11	-	2	-	-	-	13	-
1954–55	9	-	-	-	-	-	9	-
1955–56	2	-	-	-	-	-	2	-
1956–57	39	2	1	1	-	-	40	3
1957–58	32	5	5	-	-	-	37	5
1958–59	38	-	6	-	-	-	44	-
1959–60	27	1	3	-	-	-	30	1
1960–61	6	-	-	-	2	-	8	-
	164	8	17	1	2	-	183	9

FERNANDO HIERRO

Born: Vélez-Málaga, Spain, 23 March 1968
Although he spent only one season with the club, Fernando Hierro made such an impression in that time that he received a hero's send-off in his final game. Comfortable at either centre-half or as a holding midfielder, it was in the latter position that he came to the fore at the Reebok Stadium. Hierro had begun with Real Valladolid in 1987, playing 58 League games before joining Real Madrid, where he became one of the most famous players to don the white shirt. He won La Liga five

times and the Champions League three times, scoring 102 goals in 439 games and making 89 appearances for Spain in that time. In 2003 he was released by Madrid and joined Al Rayyan in Qatar, playing there for one season before joining the Wanderers on a free transfer. Hierro made his debut as a substitute in a 2–0 reverse at Fulham, but it was not until the latter stages of the season that he became a regular in the starting line up. He played his part then, as the club lost just twice, against Liverpool and Chelsea, in the final 10 games to finish sixth in the Premier League and secure a UEFA Cup spot. Hierro's final game came in the last game of the season, a 3–2 home win over Everton, being substituted late on to rapturous applause. He decided to retire from playing and, after a short spell back with Madrid in an advisory capacity, became sporting director of the Spanish Football Federation.

	League		FA Cup		FL Cup		Total	
	A	G	A	G	A	G	A	G
2004–05	15/14	1	4	-	2	-	21/14	1
	15/14	1	4	-	2	-	21/14	1

JOHN HIGGINS

Born: Bakewell, 15 November 1932
Died: Macclesfield, 22 April 2005

The son of a Buxton baker, John Higgins followed in a long line of outstanding centre-halves at Burnden. He joined the club from Buxton in 1950 and in his early days played at full-back, but he developed into a centre-half while on National service. His debut came in March 1953 when he stood in for the injured Malcolm Barrass in a 1–0 win at Burnley. He became a regular in 1956 after Barrass departed for Sheffield United and was appointed vice captain to Nat Lofthouse in 1957–58. He was ever present in both the League and Cup that season, playing his part in the FA Cup success, and his strength proved invaluable in the following seasons as the club twice finished in the top six in the top flight. Higgins was the first Wanderer since the war to be sent from the field when he received his marching orders at Hillsborough in February 1960. His three-week suspension caused his only absence that season. Higgins retired from League football in 1961, his last game coming in a 2–2 draw at Birmingham in December 1960, which coincidentally was also Nat Lofthouse's final game for the club. Higgins joined Wigan Rovers and during the late 1980s was at Stockport County as commercial and general manager. His son, Mark, followed in his footsteps as a centre-half with Everton, Manchester United, Bury and Stoke City.

	League A	FA Cup A	FL Cup A	Total A
1952–53	2	-	-	2
1953–54	4	-	-	4
1954–55	2	-	-	2
1955–56	10	-	-	10
1956–57	29	1	-	30
1957–58	42	7	-	49
1958–59	38	4	-	42
1959–60	39	3	-	42
1960–61	17	-	4	21
	183	15	4	202

FREDDIE HILL

Born: Sheffield, 17 January 1940

Freddie Hill made his First Division debut at 18 years old for the Wanderers in April 1958, standing in for the injured Ray Parry in a 4–0 reverse at Aston Villa. The inside-forward had been spotted playing in junior football in Sheffield and the Wanderers acted quickly to secure his signature after he had turned down offers from Sheffield Wednesday. After only three seasons in League football, Hill was selected for the England Under-23 side, and in October 1962 he won his first full cap against Northern Ireland in Belfast. He won another cap the following month against Wales to add to his 10 Under-23 caps. He also represented the Football League in various fixtures. Hill became a regular in the Wanderers' side and attracted the interest of a number of clubs. Between 1962 and 1964 he asked for a move on no less than four occasions and a bid of £60,000 was accepted from Liverpool, but Hill failed a medical due to high blood pressure. Hill went on to score against Liverpool in a famous 3–2 League Cup victory at Burnden and in July 1969 he joined Halifax Town for a £5,000 fee. In May 1970 he was back in the First Division, when he joined Manchester City for £12,000, and he teamed up with other former Bolton favourites Francis Lee and Wyn Davies. Hill only managed 35 League

games in a three-year spell at Maine Road and ended his League career with Peterborough United before playing local football with Droylsden and Radcliffe Borough.

	League A	League G	FA Cup A	FA Cup G	FL Cup A	FL Cup G	Total A	Total G
1957–58	1	-	-	-	-	-	1	-
1958–59	18	7	-	-	-	-	18	7
1959–60	40	8	3	-	-	-	43	8
1960–61	31	3	2	-	3	3	36	6
1961–62	41	14	1	-	2	-	44	14
1962–63	38	7	1	-	1	-	40	7
1963–64	29	2	4	-	1	-	34	2
1964–65	41	15	3	1	1	-	45	16
1965–66	38	8	3	-	1	-	42	8
1966–67	25	1	3	-	1	-	29	1
1967–68	36	3	1	-	3	1	40	4
1968–69	35/2	6	2	-	1	-	38/2	6
	373/2	74	23	1	14	4	410/2	79

JIMMY HOGAN

Born: Nelson, 19 October 1882
Died: Burnley, January 1974

Jimmy Hogan became one of the most influential coaches in Europe after ending

his playing career with the Wanderers in 1912. He had begun with local sides Burnley Belvedere and Nelson before playing for Rochdale and Swindon Town. The inside-forward signed for Burnley in 1903, playing 50 League games before suffering a long-term injury. After recovery he moved to Fulham but played only four games before joining Bolton in October 1908. He made his debut for the club in a 2–0 win at Chesterfield in November 1908, scoring both goals, and became a regular in the side that won the Second Division Championship that season. After promotion Hogan's appearances were more spasmodic, and in May 1910 he moved to Holland, where he began his coaching. He returned to Burnden a year later, replacing the injured Harold Hilton, but his final game came in a defeat at Manchester City in September 1912. After leaving the club he coached the Austrian national side before being interned in Budapest during World War One. By 1921 he was working in Switzerland and, two

years later, the Wanderers played his club, the Young Boys of Berne. Hogan returned to England in 1934 to manage Fulham, and he then guided Austria to the 1936 Olympic Final before taking Aston Villa back to Division One in 1938. After World War Two Hogan was involved with both Celtic and Brentford, and he became youth-team coach at Aston Villa when he was 70 years of age.

	League		FA Cup		Total	
	A	G	A	G	A	G
1908–09	24	11	1	-	25	11
1909–10	14	2	1	1	15	3
1911–12	13	4	2	-	15	4
1912–13	3	1	-	-	3	1
	54	18	4	1	58	19

DOUG HOLDEN

Born: Manchester, 28 September 1930

Doug Holden began his career in his native Manchester with Princess Road School before joining Lancashire Amateur League side Manchester YMCA, where his three brothers also played. He joined the Wanderers as an amateur in 1948 and went on to play for the England Youth team before completing his national service. He had played in just 12 Central League games when he made his first-team debut in November 1951, replacing Bobby Langton in a 1–1 draw at Liverpool. Holden began his League career on the left wing, but it was on the opposite flank that he became a regular in the side, appearing in the 1953 FA Cup Final in that position. Five years later, however, when the Wanderers returned to Wembley, he had reverted back to the left wing. In March 1959 Holden was selected for the Football League against the Irish League in Dublin, and a month later he won the first of five England caps playing against Scotland at Wembley. In November 1962, after 11 seasons as a regular, Holden moved to Preston North

Outside-left BOLTON WANDERERS & ENGLAND

End, his final game for the Wanderers coming at the same venue as it had started, at Anfield. In his time at Deepdale Holden helped Preston reach the 1964 FA Cup Final, where he scored in a 3–2 defeat to West Ham United. He ended his League career with Preston and emigrated to Australia in 1965, becoming player-coach at Sydney Hakoah and Auburn. Holden also played in the Australian national side and returned to England in 1970, having a spell as trainer at Grimsby and as manager at Dartford.

	League		FA Cup		FL Cup		Total	
	A	G	A	G	A	G	A	G
1951–52	25	4	1	-	-	-	26	4
1952–53	33	2	8	2	-	-	41	4
1953–54	42	1	6	-	-	-	48	1
1954–55	39	1	2	-	-	-	41	1
1955–56	40	4	2	-	-	-	42	4
1956–57	42	4	1	-	-	-	43	4
1957–58	37	3	7	-	-	-	44	3
1958–59	37	2	6	1	-	-	43	3
1959–60	42	4	3	-	-	-	45	4
1960–61	39	3	3	-	4	1	46	4
1961–62	32	11	1	-	-	-	33	11
1962–63	11	1	-	-	-	-	11	1
	419	40	40	3	4	1	463	44

DEAN HOLDSWORTH

Born: Walthamstow, 8 November 1968

Dean Holdsworth became the Wanderers' record signing when, in October 1997, he moved to the Reebok from Wimbledon for a £3.5 million fee. The striker had begun his career with Watford, having loan spells with Carlisle United, Port Vale, Swansea City and Brentford before making the move to Griffin Park permanent for £125,000 in September 1989. He won the old Third Division Championship with the Bees in 1992 and went on to score 76 first-class goals for them before moving to Wimbledon for £720,000 in July of that year. He was a regular with the Dons' 'Crazy Gang', hitting the net 58 times in 169 League games, and went on to win England B honours while with them. Holdsworth's Bolton debut came in a 1–0 home defeat to Aston Villa but three weeks later he netted his first goal, which was enough to beat Chelsea and register the club's first ever League win at the Reebok. He formed successful striking partnerships with both Eidur Gudjohnsen and Michael Ricketts after the club's relegation to the

149

First Division, and scored the Wanderers' only goal in the 4–1 FA Cup semi-final shoot-out defeat against Aston Villa at Wembley, although he rued his miss during normal time. He was a member of the side that won promotion back to the Premier League at Cardiff in 2001 and he became a regular substitute in the top League. He hit the headlines when he hit the winner against Liverpool at the Reebok to put Bolton on top of the Premier League. Holdsworth played alongside his twin brother, David, in the Wanderers' Worthington Cup home defeat by Bury in October 2002 and two months later he joined Coventry City on loan before making the move permanent. He followed that up with spells at Rushden & Diamonds, Milton Keynes, Havant & Waterlooville, Derby County (as assistant manager alongside Phil Brown), Weymouth, Heybridge, Cambridge United, Newport County and Redbridge (as player-manager). In May 2008 Holdsworth became manager at Newport County and won the Blue Square South Manager of the Month award in April 2009. He led the club to promotion to the Conference as champions. In January 2011 he became manager at Aldershot.

	League		FA Cup		FL Cup		Total	
	A	G	A	G	A	G	A	G
1997–98	17/3	3	-	-	-	-	17/3	3
1998–99	22/10	12	1	-	3/1	-	26/11	12
1999–20	24/13	14	2	-	3/2	1	29/15	15
2000–01	25/9	11	2/1	3	2	1	29/10	15
2001–02	9/22	2	-/1	-	3/1	2	12/24	4
2002–03	5/4	-	-	-	-/1	-	5/5	-
	102/61	42	5/2	3	11/5	4	118/68	49

EDDIE HOPKINSON

Born: County Durham, 29 October 1935
Died: 25 April 2004
Appearing in a club record 519 League games for the Wanderers, Eddie

Hopkinson became a 'naturalised' Lancastrian when his family moved from the North East to Royton. He signed as an amateur for Oldham Athletic and was only 16 years old when he played in three Third Division North games in 1951–52. He joined the Wanderers in August 1952 and signed professional forms the following November. 'Hoppy' bided his time in the reserves and completed his national service but, at the start of 1956–57, regular 'keeper Ken Grieves could not be released by Lancashire CC and Hopkinson took the opportunity. He made his Bolton debut in a 4–1 home win over Blackpool and went on to play every game that season. At 5ft 9in he was one of the smallest 'keepers in the League, but that did not prevent him from furthering his career. In 1957 he won the first of six England Under-23 caps and, in October that year, made his full international debut in a 4–0 victory over Wales at Ninian Park. He went on to win 14 full caps and kept a clean sheet at Wembley in the 1958 FA Cup Final success. He remained first choice throughout the 1960s, missing only five League games in as

many seasons, until injury forced his premature retirement in November 1969. He became an assistant trainer at Burnden and, in May 1971, was awarded a testimonial, a game which saw Portuguese World Cup stars Eusébio and Simões appear at Burnden. In 1974 Hopkinson left Burnden to join Stockport County as assistant manager, returning in 1979 as a goalkeeping coach. He then left the game to become a representative for a chemical company. His son, Paul became a 'keeper at Stockport County, and Eddie kept his connections with the Wanderers by becoming a hospitality host at the Reebok Stadium. He was an inaugural member of the club's Hall of Fame.

	League	FA Cup	FL Cup	Total
	A	A	A	A
1956–57	42	1	-	43
1957–58	33	7	-	40
1958–59	39	6	-	45
1959–60	26	3	-	29
1960–61	42	3	5	50
1961–62	42	1	2	45
1962–63	39	1	1	41
1963–64	31	4	1	36
1964–65	40	3	1	44
1965–66	42	3	2	47
1966–67	41	3	1	45
1967–68	40	1	3	44
1968–69	42	2	1	45
1969–70	20	-	4	24
	519	38	21	578

DON HOWE

Born: Wakefield, 26 November 1917
Died: 1978

Don Howe spent his entire League career, which spanned World War Two, with Bolton, having joined from Whitehall Printeries in 1933. He had initially joined the groundstaff at Burnden before he turned professional. He was 18 years old when he made his League debut in October 1936, taking over the right-wing

position from Jack Rimmer in a 0–0 draw at Liverpool. Rimmer returned to the side, but the versatile Howe was always found a place and by the end of the season had played in every forward position apart from centre-forward. His appearances were curtailed with the arrival of Tom Grosvenor, but Howe went on to prove capable of filling in any position in the team before settling in at wing-half after the war, taking over from Harry Goslin as captain. He was one of Bolton's Territorials who fought in France, the desert and Italy with the 53rd RA, and he rose to the rank of Battery Sergeant Major. He guested for both Norwich City and Newcastle United during the war. Howe's final game for the Wanderers' came as an emergency left-back in February 1952 in a 2–0 win at Sunderland. He was a qualified FA coach and was offered a coaching role at Burnden, but he elected to leave the game and joined a local firm of paper merchants.

	League		FA Cup		Total	
	A	G	A	G	A	G
1936–37	30	6	-	-	30	6
1937–38	14	3	-	-	14	3
1938–39	36	9	3	-	39	9
1945–46	-	-	7	-	7	-
1946–47	23	-	1	-	24	-
1947–48	33	3	1	-	34	3
1948–49	40	2	3	-	43	2
1949–50	38	5	3	-	41	5
1950–51	42	4	2	-	44	4
1951–52	10	3	-	-	10	3
	266	35	20	-	286	35

HARRY HUBBICK

Born: Jarrow, 12 November 1910
Died: Bolton, 1992

Harry Hubbick left school at 14 years of age and went to work in the mines. During that time, he played football for Jarrow, Blyth Spartans and Spennymoor United before signing for Burnley in March 1935. The left-back quickly got into the side and went on to play 58 League games before joining the Wanderers in February 1937 as a replacement for Alex Finney. He became 'Mr Consistent', missing only three games

before the outbreak of the war, during which he resumed his career down the pits. This enabled him to continue playing for the Wanderers in the Football League Northern competition. In all he played 227 League games, missing just two games in six seasons in matches that are not counted as official. In 1943 Hubbick guested for Blackpool when they won the League North War Cup and the North v South Final. Two years later he captained the Wanderers to success in the same competition against Manchester United and Chelsea respectively. In 1947 Hubbick joined Port Vale, making 50 League appearances before leaving for Rochdale, where he served two years before ending his career at Lancaster City and Caernarfon Town. During the latter stages of his career, while working at De Havilland at Horwich, Hubbick qualified as an FA coach. In 1953 he was appointed trainer-coach at Accrington Stanley and, apart from a short spell when he became second-team trainer at Bury, remained at Peel Park until Accrington withdrew from the League in 1962. He later took on the same role at both Halifax Town and Preston North End until his retirement.

	League	FA Cup	Total
	A	A	A
1936–37	13	-	13
1937–38	40	1	41
1938–39	41	3	44
1945–46	-	9	9
1946–47	34	3	37
	128	16	144

BILLY HUGHES

Born: Stourbridge
Died: Unknown

Billy Hughes started his career at his local club, Stourbridge, before joining Bolton in 1908. He led the Wanderers' League goalscoring charts in three of his five seasons with the club, starting his tally with a goal on his debut, a 3–0 win over Oldham Athletic at Burnden, as a replacement for Albert Shepherd in December 1908. His 16 goals that season went a long way to earning the Second Division title, but the following year things proved more difficult and the club were relegated. In 1910, back in the Second Division, the centre-forward formed a productive partnership with Harold Hilton that helped reinstate the club to the top flight. Over four consecutive home games in December 1910 and January 1911, Hughes scored 11 goals, netting hat-tricks in three of the games. In September 1911 he lost his place to Alf Bentley and his appearances were further

curtailed when George Lillycrop was secured from Barnsley. In September 1913 he signed for Wolves, although Bolton were later fined £25 by the League for misleading Hughes into assuming he would receive £200 in lieu of a benefit if he left. He went on to score 10 goals in 21 League games for Wolves.

	League		FA Cup		Total	
	A	G	A	G	A	G
1908–09	21	16	1	-	22	16
1909–10	31	12	-	-	31	12
1910–11	28	21	1	-	29	21
1911–12	13	-	-	-	13	-
1912–13	7	2	-	-	7	2
	100	51	2	-	102	51

JOHN HULME

Born: Mobberley, 6 February 1945
Died: Macclesfield, 26 May 2008

Spotted by the Wanderers while playing for Stockport and Cheshire Boys, centre-half John Hulme was signed after leaving school and went on to serve the club for 10 seasons. He made his League debut at 17 years old, in a 1–0 First Division home win over Nottingham Forest at Burnden. He vied for the position with both the experienced Bryan Edwards and another Bolton youth product, John Napier. Hulme became a regular in January 1967 but was a member of the side that were relegated to the Third Division for the first time in 1971. Paul Jones and Warwick Rimmer became the defensive partnership and in March 1972 Hulme joined Notts County on loan. A £12,000 fee was later agreed between the clubs, but Hulme could not agree personal terms, and so he remained on the transfer list until he signed for Reading, managed by former Wanderer Charlie Hurley, in July 1972 for £10,000. Hulme found a new lease of life at Elm Park, winning a PFA divisional award in 1973–74 and playing 87 League games. His final game for the club came at

Chester in April 1974 and he skippered the side as substitute. He tossed the coin but played no further part in the game. Hulme returned to the North West with Bury, making 86 League appearances before joining La Chaux-de-Fonds in Switzerland as player-manager in July 1976. He retired in 1978 and set up his own successful building development business in the Stockport area.

	League		FA Cup		FL Cup		Total	
	A	G	A	G	A	G	A	G
1962–63	1	-	-	-	-	-	1	-
1963–64	20	-	-	-	2	-	22	-
1964–65	4	-	-	-	-	-	4	-
1965–66	3	-	-	-	1	-	4	-
1966–67	18/1	-	3	-	-	-	21/1	-
1967–68	34	2	1	1	3	-	38	3
1968–69	32/1	3	2	-	1	-	35/1	3
1969–70	15	1	-	-	3	1	18	2
1970–71	37	1	1	-	2	-	40	1
1971–72	22	-	2	-	6	-	30	-
	186/2	7	9	1	18	1	213/2	9

ROGER HUNT MBE

Born: Golborne, 20 July 1938
Roger Hunt joined Liverpool from Stockton Heath in May 1959, and he went on to win many of the game's top honours as well as legend status at Anfield. A Bolton supporter as a youngster, Hunt scored on his Liverpool debut, a 2–0 home Second Division win over Scunthorpe United. He won a Second Division Championship medal in 1962, scoring 41 goals in as many League games, League Championship medals in 1964 and 1966 and an FA Cup-winners' medal in 1965. He was also selected for the Football League representative side and won 34 England caps, scoring 18 goals between 1962 and 1968. His greatest prize of all was to be a member of England's World Cup-winning team in 1966, playing in all six games through the tournament. Bolton first made moves to sign him early in 1969–70 but he refused to leave Anfield. However, in December 1969, the striker was persuaded to make the trip to Burnden in a £32,000 deal. 'Sir' Roger made his Bolton debut in a Boxing Day win at Preston, but he could do little to revive the club's flagging fortunes. In October 1970 he was dropped but returned after six weeks to hit a hat-trick against Birmingham. The club, however, were

relegated to the Third Division in 1971, and 1971–72 proved to be Hunt's last in football. He contributed 11 goals in the club's first season at that level, helping to stabilise Bolton's slide. In April 1972 over 56,000 attended his testimonial at Anfield, after which he retired to concentrate on his family haulage business. He also became a sitting member of the Pools Panel and in 2000 was awarded the MBE.

	League		FA Cup		FL Cup		Total	
	A	G	A	G	A	G	A	G
1969–70	17	5	1	-	-	-	18	5
1970–71	22/2	8	-	-	1/1	-	23/3	8
1971–72	33/2	11	1/1	1	2/1	-	36/4	12
	72/4	24	2/1	1	3/2	-	77/7	25

JUSSI JÄÄSKELÄINEN

Born: Mikkeli, Finland, 19 April 1975
Goalkeeper Jussi Jääskeläinen joined the Wanderers from VPS Vaasa for a £350,000 fee in November 1997, having begun his career at Mikkeli at the age of 17. After spending a period of time in the Wanderers' reserves, he came through the ranks to make his debut on the opening day of the 1998–99 season in a 2–2 draw at Crystal Palace. He missed out on the Play-off Final that season after losing his place in the side to Steve Banks, but he bounced back to become number one the following season and played at Wembley in the FA Cup semi-final. Jääskeläinen again missed out on the Play-off Final of 2001 after suffering a ligament injury against Tranmere in January of that year, but he was absent for just four games of the Wanderers' 2001–02 Premier League campaign. He was ever present in the League during 2002–03, keeping six clean sheets in the final nine games to keep the club's top flight status, and again during 2003–04. His consistency continued as the club qualified for Europe 12 months later. In October 2006 Jääskeläinen saved two penalties in as many

minutes to help the Wanderers secure a 1–0 win at Blackburn and that season won the club's Player of the Year award along with the Players' Player award. In August 2009 he was awarded a testimonial when Hibernian visited the Reebok Stadium. Jääskeläinen won 15 Under-21 caps for Finland and made his full international debut in March 1998 against Malta. He now has 56 caps to his name. His 500th wanderers appearance can=me in Bolton's FA Cup quarter-final win at Birmingham in March 2011.

	League	FA Cup	FL Cup	UEFA Cup	Total
	A	A	A	A	A
1998–99	34	1	5	-	40
1999–2000	35/1	3	2	-	40/1
2000–01	27	-	-	-	27
2001–02	34	1	3	-	38
2002–03	38	-	-	-	38
2003–04	38	-	3	-	41
2004–05	36	4	-	-	40
2005–06	38	3	2	5	48
2006–07	38	2	-	-	40
2007–08	28	-	1	6	35
2008–09	38	1	1	-	40
2009–10	38	3	2	-	43
2010–11	35	3	-	-	38
	457/1	21	19	11	508/1

BOB JACK

Born: Alloa, 4 April 1876
Died: Southend, 6 May 1943

Bob Jack began his career with home-town club Alloa Athletic, making his debut at 15. The outside-left joined the Wanderers in 1895, his first appearance coming in a 2–1 win at Small Heath in September of that year. He quickly established himself with his exciting wing play and was a member of the team that reached the FA Cup semi-final in 1896. A year later he was the club's leading scorer. He helped the club win promotion to the First Division in 1900 but the following year he lost his place to William Tracey and joined Preston in August. A year later Jack moved to Glossop and Burslem Port Vale before joining Plymouth Argyle in 1903, where he became the club's first professional player. He became player-manager and in 1906 moved to Southend United in a similar capacity, guiding them to the Southern League Division Two title. Jack became secretary-manager at Plymouth in 1910 and remained in charge until his retirement in 1938. In that time he took them to the Southern League title in 1913 and into the Football League in 1920. Jack's three sons, David, Rollo and Donald, all appeared for the Wanderers at different points in their careers. Jack also represented England at bowls and after his death his ashes were scattered over Home Park in Plymouth.

	League		FA Cup		Total	
	A	G	A	G	A	G
1895–96	15	5	5	-	20	5
1896–97	28	11	4	-	32	11
1897–98	19	4	3	-	22	4
1898–99	27	2	2	-	29	2
1899–1900	19	7	1	-	20	7
1900–01	2	-	-	-	2	-
	110	29	15	-	125	29

DAVID JACK

Born: Bolton, 3 April 1899
Died: 10 September 1958

David Jack is perhaps most famous for scoring the first-ever goal in a Wembley Cup Final, but he contributed far more to the game. The son of former Wanderer Bob Jack, David's football career took him from Leigh Road School, Southend, to Plymouth Presbyterians, the Royal Navy and Plymouth Argyle, where his father was manager. Arsenal and Chelsea, with whom he had played as a guest during World War

One, wanted to sign him, but in December 1920 he chose to join the Wanderers for a fee of £3,500, a record for both Argyle and Bolton. Jack made his debut at inside-forward in a goalless draw at Oldham the following month and became a regular thereafter. He shared the goalscoring responsibilities with Joe Smith for the next five seasons and was the Wanderers' top League scorer in all five, again following in his father's footsteps; Bob Jack had been top scorer in 1896–97. David netted in six of Bolton's seven FA Cup ties on their way to winning the trophy for the first time in 1923. A year later he won the first of four England caps, a 2–1 defeat to Wales, and in 1926 scored the only goal against Manchester City to secure the FA Cup for a second time. In October 1928 Jack joined Arsenal for a record £10,750. The Gunners wanted him to replace Charles Buchan, who had retired, and Jack went on to win the League Championship with them in 1931, 1933 and 1934, along with FA Cup success in 1930. In all, he scored 113 goals in 181 League games for Arsenal. In May 1934 Jack joined Southend United as manager and remained until August 1940. He served as Middlesbrough boss from September 1944 to April 1952 before resigning due to ill health. He became manager of League of Ireland club Shelbourne in August 1953 and worked as a sports journalist before retiring in April 1955.

	League		FA Cup		Total	
	A	G	A	G	A	G
1920–21	19	4	1	-	20	4
1921–22	39	24	2	-	41	24
1922–23	41	11	7	7	48	18
1923–24	39	24	3	3	42	27
1924–25	42	26	3	1	45	27
1925–26	37	14	7	5	44	19
1926–27	38	16	4	1	42	17
1927–28	33	24	2	-	35	24
1928–29	7	1	-	-	7	1
	295	144	29	17	324	161

BILLY JENNINGS

Born: Barry, 25 February 1893
Died: 1968

Billy Jennings was capped by Wales Schoolboys in 1907 while playing for Bethel Baptists in Barry. Bolton signed him in 1912, and he made his debut at left-back against Derby County in November that year. In February 1914 he won the first of 11 full international caps for Wales when he played against Scotland in Glasgow. At the time he was a regular in the Central League side but not yet the first team. That changed the following season, in which he frequently switched between left-back and left-half and appeared in the FA Cup semi-final defeat by Sheffield United. During the war Jennings served in the Royal Flying Corps, and after hostilities he resumed the half-back role. In the years that followed he suffered with a number of injuries, which curtailed his appearances. He did, however, play in all seven FA Cup ties when Bolton won the trophy in 1923, and he and the team were again victorious in 1926. Jennings played his last game for the club in November 1929 and retired in 1931. Two years later he became a coach at Notts County and then took a similar role at Cardiff City. In April 1937 he was appointed manager at Ninian Park and faced the job of rebuilding the team with little money after a fire had destroyed the stand and offices.

	League		FA Cup		Total	
	A	G	A	G	A	G
1912–13	5	-	-	-	5	-
1913–14	10	-	-	-	10	-
1914–15	24	-	2	-	26	-
1919–20	34	1	1	-	35	1
1920–21	18	-	-	-	18	-
1921–22	20	-	2	-	22	-
1922–23	32	1	7	-	39	1
1923–24	34	-	3	-	37	-
1924–25	23	-	-	-	23	-
1925–26	29	-	4	-	33	-
1926–27	10	-	-	-	10	-
1927–28	18	-	1	-	19	-
1928–29	9	-	-	-	9	-
1929–30	1	-	-	-	1	-
	267	2	20	-	287	2

BOB JONES

Born: Everton, 9 January 1902
Died: 1989

Goalkeeper Bob Jones admirably took over from legend Dick Pym to become the club's number one for seven seasons in the 1930s. His career started at Everton, where he had applied for a trial as a left-half. At the session the goalkeeper failed to turn up and Jones took the flat cap and gloves, making such an impression that the Toffees signed him. He made his debut in a Merseyside derby but made only three League appearances before signing for Southport. Jones spent three seasons in the reserves before forcing his way into the first team, and the Wanderers secured his signature in 1929, initially as cover for Pym and Jimmy Gill. Jones made his Bolton debut at Birmingham in March 1930 and

established himself the following season. In 1931–32 he was ever present, a feat that had only been achieved once since the war, by Pym in 1922–23. Jones looked capable of repeating the feat the following year until he was struck down with appendicitis in February 1933 and Harry Church took over. Jones recovered to become a member of the Wanderers' side that won promotion from the Second Division and reached the FA Cup semi-finals in 1935. In 1937 he joined Cardiff City on a free transfer, and two years later he re-signed for Southport, where he became assistant trainer. He played for them during the war and became first-team trainer in 1947, continuing to play for the reserves until he was 48. Jones's son, also Bob, was a professional 'keeper with Southport, Chester, Blackburn and Great Harwood.

	League	FA Cup	Total
	A	A	A
1929–30	7	-	7
1930–31	37	3	40
1931–32	42	2	44
1932–33	27	2	29
1933–34	19	5	24
1934–35	41	8	49
1935–36	21	-	21
1936–37	25	5	30
	219	25	244

DAVID JONES

Born: Trefonen, 1867
Died: August 1902

David 'Di' Jones started his career at Oswestry, helping them to win the Shropshire Cup, before moving to Chirk when he was 17 years old and becoming a member of their Welsh Cup-winning side of 1885. He worked as a miner while at Chirk and, after a couple of games for Newton Heath, he signed for the Wanderers in 1888. Earlier that year he had won the first of 14 Welsh international caps in an 11–0 defeat of Ireland at Wrexham. Jones was noted for his strong tackling and ability to kick with either foot, and he was capable of playing in either full-back position, though he normally appeared at left-back. By 1890 he was the Wanderers' captain and a fixture in the side. In January 1892 Jones missed the club's first-ever penalty kick, awarded in a League match at Everton. He captained the 1894 FA Cup Final side and in September of the following year was awarded a benefit, which was the first game to take place at Burnden Park,

against Preston. In October 1898 Jones joined Manchester City, helping them to the Second Division Championship in his first season. He went on to play 114 games for City. During a practice game in August 1902, he gashed his knee and contracted tetanus, the infection taking his life 11 days later. The affection for Jones in Bolton was highlighted by the large crowds that turned out to pay their respects as his funeral passed through en route to the railway station for a burial in his home town.

	League		FA Cup		Total	
	A	G	A	G	A	G
1888–89	12	-	-	-	12	-
1889–90	21	1	4	-	25	1
1890–91	21	-	1	-	22	-
1891–92	26	1	2	1	28	2
1892–93	30	-	2	-	32	-
1893–94	28	-	5	-	33	-
1894–95	26	1	3	1	29	2
1895–96	27	-	3	-	30	-
1896–97	22	1	4	2	26	3
1897–98	15	-	3	-	18	-
	228	4	27	4	255	8

GARRY JONES

Born: Wythenshawe, 11 December 1950

Forward Garry Jones joined the Wanderers as an apprentice in 1966, having caught the club's attention while representing Manchester Schoolboys. He made his League debut as a 17-year-old in a Second Division game against Huddersfield Town and, although he played one more game that term, he did not appear again until September 1970. At the time he was one of a number of Bolton youngsters thrown into the first team in an unsuccessful attempt to avoid relegation to the Third Division. In October 1971 he hit the headlines with a hat-trick in a 3–0 League Cup victory against Manchester City in front of over

	League		FA Cup		FL Cup		Total	
	A	G	A	G	A	G	A	G
1968–69	2	-	-	-	-	-	2	-
1969–70	-	-	-	-	-	-	-	-
1970–71	22	2	1	-	1	-	24	2
1971–72	41/1	5	4	-	6	3	51/1	8
1972–73	39	14	9	4	2	2	50	20
1973–74	30	6	3	1	3	-	36	7
1974–75	5/1	-	2	-	1	-	8/1	-
1975–76	36/1	11	6	2	1	-	43/1	13
1976–77	14/4	3	-	-	1	-	15/4	3
1977–78	6	-	-/2	1	1/1	1	7/3	2
1978–79	-/1	-	-	-	-	-	-/1	-
	195/8	41	25/2	8	16/1	6	236/11	55

PAUL JONES

Born: Ellesmere Port, 13 May 1953

A stylish centre-half who came through the club's junior ranks, Paul Jones was a member of the two Bolton sides that won promotion during the seventies. He played for Ellesmere Port Boys, Cheshire Boys, Wirral Youth and Shell, before joining the Wanderers in 1969 as an apprentice and progressed through the Lancashire and Central League sides to make his League debut as a 17-year-old in January 1971 against Sheffield United at Burnden. During 1971–72 he had a spell

42,000 at Burnden, but it was not until the following season, when he struck up a partnership with John Byrom, that he began to find the net on a regular basis at League level and guided the club to the Third Division Championship. In February 1975 Jones had a three-game loan spell at Sheffield United after struggling to get into the Wanderers' line up, but he returned to have a successful 1975–76 season, being joint scorer with Neil Whatmore as the club just missed out on promotion to Division One. The emergence of Steve Taylor and then the arrival of Frank Worthington kept Jones in the role of understudy, but his last appearance for the club came in the top level as a substitute in a defeat at West Brom in August 1975. Jones moved to Blackpool in November 1978, scoring five goals in 27 League games and, in August 1980 he went to Hereford, where he ended his League career. He later turned out for Northwich Victoria and Prescot.

in midfield before taking over at centre-half from John Hulme and the following season was the only player to start every League game as the club won the Third Division Championship. He also chipped in with some vital goals in that memorable season. Don Revie selected Jones for the England squad but Jones missed out when Revie stuck with his old guard. Jones missed only one game in three seasons as the Wanderers pushed for promotion to the First Division. Injury curtailed his appearances during 1977–78, and although a number of transfer requests followed, Jones stayed on at Burnden, making a number of appearances at right-back in the First Division. He continued to remain consistent, despite the club's fall during the early 1980s, and he made his 500th appearance for the club at Rotherham in February 1983. He played only another six games before ending his 14-year association with the club by joining Huddersfield, where he played 73 League games before joining Oldham. In March 1987 Jones joined Blackpool and later had spells in South Africa and with Rochdale, Atherton LR, Stalybridge Celtic, Wigan and Stockport County.

	League		FA Cup		FL Cup		Total	
	A	G	A	G	A	G	A	G
1970–71	4	-	-	-	-	-	4	-
1971–72	37/1	1	4	-	1	-	42/1	1
1972–73	46	7	9	-	2	-	57	7
1973–74	38	-	3	-	4	2	45	2
1974–75	42	5	2	-	2	1	46	6
1975–76	41	6	5	1	1	-	47	7
1976–77	42	11	1	-	9	1	52	12
1977–78	19/2	4	2	-	1	-	22/2	4
1978–79	31/1	1	1	-	-	-	32/1	1
1979–80	32	1	-	-	2	-	34	1
1980–81	35	-	1	-	2	-	38	-
1981–82	41	1	2	-	2	-	45	1
1982–83	33	1	1	-	4	-	38	1
	441/4	38	31	1	30	4	502/4	43

WARREN JOYCE

Born: Oldham, 20 January 1965

Warren Joyce followed his father's footsteps into professional football. Walter Joyce had played for Burnley, Blackburn and Oldham before turning to management and coaching. He was coach at Burnden when his son came into the first team. Warren was at Burtonwood when he was offered the chance to play for Bolton's reserves. He signed professional forms at 17 years old, quite a feat considering he had broken a bone in his neck while playing rugby in Australia the year before. He became a member of the team that won promotion from the Second Division of the Central League in 1983, making his League debut at Carlisle as a substitute in April that year. The battling midfielder missed only two games between 1983 and 1985, showing his versatility with the occasional game at full-back. In October 1987 Preston paid £35,000 for his services, and he played over 200 games for them before Plymouth signed him in May 1992 for £160,000. He was there only one season before returning to the North West with Burnley paying £140,000 for him. He remained at Turf Moor for three years and, after a loan spell at Hull City in January 1995, he moved to Boothferry Park permanently in July 1996. He became club captain and later player-manager. In 1998–99 Joyce became a Hull legend by keeping them in the Football League after they had looked doomed. After his playing days were over he held coaching roles at Leeds, Stockport and Tranmere and Royal Antwerp. In May 2008 he became manager of Manchester United reserves along with Ole Gunnar Solskjær.

	League		FA Cup		FL Cup		Frieght Rover Trophy		Total	
	A	G	A	G	A	G	A	G	A	G
1982–83	5/3	-	-	-	-	-	-	-	5/3	-
1983–84	45	3	4	1	2	1	1	-	52	5
1984–85	45	5	1	-	5	-	5	2	56	7
1985–86	31	4	1	-	3/1	-	1	-	36/1	4
1986–87	45/1	5	5	-	2	-	2	-	54/1	5
1987–88	11	-	-	-	2	-	-	-	13	-
	182/4	17	11	1	14/1	1	9	2	216/5	21

TONY KELLY

Born: Prescot, 1 October 1964

Midfielder Tony Kelly began his career as an apprentice at Liverpool before joining Prescot Cables in 1983. In January 1984 he signed for Wigan Athletic, helping them to win the Freight Rover Trophy at Wembley in 1985. He played 101 League games for Wigan, scoring 15 goals, before joining Stoke City in April 1986 for £80,000. He played 36 League games for Stoke and in July 1987 joined West Brom for £60,000. While at the Hawthorns Kelly had loan spells at both Chester and Colchester before he joined Shrewsbury Town in January 1989. He made 101 League appearances for Town before moving to Bolton for £100,000 in August 1991. He

was joined at Burnden by his Town teammate, Michael Brown. Kelly made his debut in a 1–1 home draw against Huddersfield on the opening day of the season, but his best football came during 1992–93 as the Wanderers won promotion from the Second Division and reached the fifth round of the FA Cup, knocking out Liverpool at Anfield along the way. One of Kelly's two League goals that memorable season came at his old club, Wigan Athletic, as Bolton ran out 2–0 winners. His last game for the club came in September 1994, against Portsmouth at Burnden, and later that month he joined Port Vale on a free transfer. Kelly played only four games for the Valiants before having spells with Millwall, Wigan and Peterborough that season. He rejoined Wigan for the start of 1995–96, playing two games, and in February 1996 he signed for Altrincham. He ended his playing days with Sligo Rovers in 1997. In 2008 Kelly rejoined the Wanderers as fans' liaison officer and is now an Academy coach with the club.

	League		FA Cup		FL Cup		Autoglass Trophy		Anglo–Italian Cup		Total	
	A	G	A	G	A	G	A	G	A	G	A	G
1991–92	31	2	6	-	4	1	3	-	-	-	44	3
1992–93	33/3	2	4/1	-	1	-	3	1	-	-	41/4	3
1993–94	35	1	5/2	-	4	1	-	-	3	-	47/2	2
1994–95	4	-	-	-	-	-	-	-	-	-	4	-
	103/3	5	15/3	-	9	2	6	1	3	-	136/6	8

BOBBY LANGTON

Born: Burscough, 8 September 1918
Died: Burscough, 13 January 1996
Bobby Langton came to prominence with Blackburn Rovers after they had paid £50 to secure his services from Southport League side Burscough Victoria in 1937. He played outside-left in his second season and became Rovers' leading scorer. He spent a period of the war as an infantryman in India and also helped Glentoran win the Irish Cup in 1945 while stationed in Northern Ireland. In September 1946 he won the first of 11 England caps in a 7–2 defeat of Northern Ireland and in August 1948 was transferred

to Preston North End for £16,000, having played 107 games for Rovers. He appeared 58 times for Preston and in November 1949 joined Bolton for a then club record of £20,000. Langton became a regular in the number-11 shirt until 1953, when he was placed on the transfer list at his own request. He appeared in the 1953 FA Cup Final defeat by Blackpool but that proved to be his last game for the club, and in September 1953 he rejoined Blackburn. He remained at Ewood for three years before seeing out his professional career with Ards in Northern Ireland. Langton subsequently moved into non-League, having two spells at Wisbech Town, where he became a publican, Kidderminster Harriers and Colwyn Bay. In 1962 he became trainer at Kings Lynn and a year later returned to Wisbech in a similar capacity. In 1968 he returned to Burscough, becoming manager and guiding them to the Lancashire Junior Cup. In 1998, two years after his death, a road that goes past Burscough's ground was renamed Bobby Langton Way.

	League		FA Cup		Total	
	A	G	A	G	A	G
1949–50	23	1	3	1	26	2
1950–51	40	6	2	1	42	7
1951–52	35	5	1	-	36	5
1952–53	20	4	8	0	28	4
	118	16	14	2	132	18

DAVID LEE

Born: Whitefield, 5 November 1967
Right-winger David Lee began his career at Bury, making 208 League appearances and scoring 35 goals between 1986 and 1991. He helped the Shakers to the Third Division Play-offs in 1990 and 1991 but they lost out to Tranmere and Bolton respectively in the semi-finals. Southampton signed him for £350,000, but he played only 20 games for the Saints before joining the Wanderers on

had a loan spell at Blackpool in 1999. Lee moved to Carlisle United and ended his career at Morecambe in 2001. He became youth coach at Wigan until returning to the Wanderers in 2008 as assistant Academy director.

	League		FA Cup		FL Cup		Autoglass Trophy		Anglo–Italian Cup		Total	
	A	G	A	G	A	G	A	G	A	G	A	G
1992–93	32	5	4	-	-	-	4	1	-	-	40	6
1993–94	35/6	5	7	-	4	-	-	-	3/1	-	49/7	5
1994–95	36/4	4	-/1	-	8	2	-	-	-	-	44/5	6
1995–96	9/9	1	1	-	3/1	-	-	-	-	-	13/10	1
1996–97	13/12	2	1/1	-	4	-	-	-	-	-	18/13	2
	125/31	17	13/2	-	19/1	2	4	1	3/1	-	164/35	20

FRANCIS LEE

Born: Westhoughton, 29 April 1944

Francis Lee had an explosive eight years at Burnden Park, during which time he averaged a goal every two games and was rarely out of the headlines. He made his League debut partnering 35-year-old Nat Lofthouse as a 16-year-old amateur in November 1960 after playing in only eight Central League games. The Wanderers ran out 3–1 winners against Manchester City at Burnden, Lee scoring a goal and getting booked for foul play. He signed professional forms in May 1961, but his volatile nature caused problems off the field when he refused to play after being dropped to the A team. A number of transfer requests were turned down as clubs began to chase the goalscoring winger who had also become one of the game's most deadly penalty takers. At the start of the 1967–68 season Lee scored in seven consecutive games, including one at Liverpool in a League Cup second-round tie. His last game for the club proved to be a 3–2 replay win against the Anfield side and in September 1967 he joined Manchester City for £65,000. At Maine Road he won the 1968 League

loan in November 1992. Lee made his debut in a 3–1 win at Exeter City and the following month the move was made permanent for £275,000. He played in all the remaining games that season as the Wanderers won promotion from the Second Division. He produced a number of great displays as the club got established in the higher League but in 1995 he missed out on the Play-off Final success against Reading, having suffered injury against Wolves in the semi-final. He did, however, get a Wembley appearance in the League Cup Final defeat to Liverpool that year. Lee was part of the squad that won promotion back to the Premier League in the final season at Burnden in 1997, but his last appearance for the club came in a 1–0 home success against West Brom in March that year. He joined Wigan Athletic for £275,000, playing 84 games for them, and

	League		FA Cup		FL Cup		Total	
	A	G	A	G	A	G	A	G
1960–61	6	2	-	-	-	-	6	2
1961–62	5	-	-	-	-	-	5	-
1962–63	23	12	1	1	1	-	25	13
1963–64	34	12	4	2	1	2	39	16
1964–65	38	23	2	1	1	-	41	24
1965–66	34	13	3	3	2	2	39	18
1966–67	40	22	3	1	1	1	44	24
1967–68	9	8	-	-	2	1	11	9
	189	92	13	8	8	6	210	106

NAT LOFTHOUSE OBE

Born: Bolton, 27 August 1925
Died: Bolton, 15 January 2011

Centre-forward Nat Lofthouse was undoubtedly Bolton Wanderers' most illustrious personality, becoming the club's post-war hero. He signed for the club in September 1939, having previously played for Brandwood and Castle Hill Schools and Lomax's. His first game for the club was in March 1941 when, aged 15 years and 207 days, he scored twice in a 5–1 win against Bury at Burnden in a Football League North game. Lofthouse was a member of the 1945 War Cup-winning team and was on the field when 33 people lost their lives in the Burnden disaster of

Championship and the 1969 FA Cup. In 1970 he scored a penalty in the successful European Cup-Winners' Cup Final and in 1971–72 set a British record for the number of penalties converted in a season, with 15 of his 35 goals coming from the spot. In August 1974 Lee joined Derby County and won the League Championship with them before retiring in 1976. He had won 27 England caps in his time, some of which came from the 1970 World Cup Finals in Mexico, and scored 10 international goals. After retiring Lee returned to the successful paper business he had started while at Burnden, and he also bred and trained racehorses near his Cheshire home. In 1994 he became chairman at Manchester City, stepping down four years later.

1946. He won 33 England caps and scored what was then a record 30 goals for his country, including two on his debut against Yugoslavia in November 1950. In May 1952 he earned the tag 'The Lion of Vienna' after his heroic performance against Austria, when he scored twice in England's 3–2 win. The following September he scored six goals for the Football League against the Irish League at Molineux and in 1953 he won the Footballer of the Year award, having scored in every round of the FA Cup. In 1956 Lofthouse topped the First Division scoring charts and two years later captained Bolton to their FA Cup Final victory over Manchester United, scoring both goals in the 2–0 Wembley win. He was injured during the club's South African tour and missed most of the following season, but he fought back to regain his fitness. Another injury, in December 1960 at Birmingham City, ended his career and he was appointed assistant trainer. In 1967 he became chief coach and later manager, succeeding Bill Ridding. Lofthouse left the club in 1971 but later returned to become executive club manager and in 1986 club president. In 1989 he became a Freeman of Bolton and in 1994 was awarded an OBE (see 'Managers').

	League		FA Cup		FL Cup		Total	
	A	G	A	G	A	G	A	G
1945–46	-	-	6	2	-	-	6	2
1946–47	40	18	3	3	-	-	43	21
1947–48	34	18	1	-	-	-	35	18
1948–49	22	7	3	1	-	-	25	8
1949–50	35	10	3	3	-	-	38	13
1950–51	38	21	2	1	-	-	40	22
1951–52	38	18	1	-	-	-	39	18
1952–53	36	22	8	8	-	-	44	30
1953–54	32	17	6	1	-	-	38	18
1954–55	31	15	2	-	-	-	33	15
1955–56	36	32	2	1	-	-	38	33
1956–57	36	28	1	-	-	-	37	28
1957–58	31	17	5	3	-	-	36	20
1958–59	37	29	6	4	-	-	43	33
1959–60	-	-	-	-	-	-	-	-
1960–61	6	3	-	-	2	3	8	6
	452	255	49	27	2	3	503	285

DON McALLISTER

Born: Radcliffe, 26 May 1953

Local player Don McAllister represented Lancashire Schoolboys before joining the Wanderers in 1968. The following year he established himself in the reserves at centre-half or left-half, and in 1971 he skippered the club to victory in the Lancashire Youth Cup against Blackpool. He was part of a youth team defence that included Barry Siddall, Paul Jones and Sam Allardyce. McAllister made his League debut in the final game of the 1969–70 season, a goalless draw at home to Norwich City, and in November 1971 he took over the left-back position from Syd Farrimond. McAllister missed only one game as the Wanderers won the Third Division Championship in 1973 and was a regular in the defence in the higher level. In February 1975 Tottenham Hotspur paid £80,000 for his services and

he was a member of their side that won promotion as runners-up to the Wanderers from the Second Division in 1978. McAllister grabbed Spurs' winning goal against the Wanderers that season before more than 50,000 at White Hart Lane and played over 200 games for Tottenham before moving to Charlton Athletic in July 1981 for £40,000. There, he made 55 League appearances, the last of which came in May 1983 against Bolton at The Valley, the home side winning 4–1 to relegate the Wanderers to the Third Division. He joined Tampa Bay Rowdies in the NASL before having a short spell in Portugal with Vitória de Setúbal. McAllister returned to the North West to end his career with three League games for Rochdale before emigrating to Australia, where he works as a finance manager.

	League		FA Cup		FL Cup		Total	
	A	G	A	G	A	G	A	G
1969–70	1	-	-	-	-	-	1	-
1970–71	24	-	1	-	-	-	25	-
1971–72	21/1	2	2	-	-	-	23/1	2
1972–73	45	-	9	-	1	-	55	-
1973–74	38	-	-	-	5	-	43	-
1974–75	26	-	2	-	1	-	29	-
	155/1	2	14	-	7	-	176/1	2

JASON McATEER

Born: Birkenhead, 18 June 1971

Spotted while playing for Marine Reserves, Jason McAteer was given a trial for Bolton's visit to Leek Town to open their new stand in January 1992. He impressed enough to be offered a contract and his League debut came the following December as a substitute in a 4–0 home win over Burnley. A week later he started in a second-round FA Cup tie against Rochdale, scoring a goal in another 4–0 win. The midfielder became a regular in the side that won promotion from Division Two in 1993 and the following season he was involved in every League game as Bolton consolidated

in the higher division. In March 1994 he was called up for Ireland and made his debut against Russia in Dublin, going on to become the first Bolton player to play in the World Cup Finals since Tommy Banks in 1958. He went on to win 52 caps, 14 of which were won while with Bolton. In 1995 McAteer helped the club to the League Cup Final and promotion to the Premier League, but he played only four games for the club in the top flight. His last game for the club came in a 1–0 defeat at Aston Villa in August 1995, and a few days later he joined Liverpool for £4.5 million. He played 100 League games for the Reds and helped them reach the FA Cup Final in 1996. In January 1999 he joined Blackburn Rovers for £4 million and was a member of their side that won promotion to the Premier League in 2001. He made a £1 million move to Sunderland in October 2001 and ended his League career with Tranmere Rovers, where he was made captain. McAteer was released in May 2007 and became a coach at Chester City. He returned to Prenton Park in June 2009 as assistant manager to John Barnes, but the pair left in October 2009.

	League		FA Cup		FL Cup		Autoglass Trophy		Anglo–Italian Cup		Total	
	A	G	A	G	A	G	A	G	A	G	A	G
1992–93	19/2	-	2	1	-	-	1/1	-	-	-	22/3	1
1993–94	45/1	3	8	2	4	-	-	-	4	1	61/1	6
1994–95	44/2	6	1	-	7	2	-	-	-	-	52/2	8
1995–96	4	-	-	-	-	-	-	-	-	-	4	-
	112/5	9	11	3	11	2	1/1	-	4	1	139/6	15

JIM McCLELLAND

Born: Dysart, 11 May 1902
Died: unknown

Jim McClelland made his name at Middlesbrough, having started his career with Raith Rovers before joining Southend United in 1923. He led United's goalscoring charts in 1924–25 and moved to Ayresome Park in March 1925. He was ever present in Boro's team in 1925–26, scoring 32 goals, five of them coming against Leeds to equal a club record, and the following season was a member of their side that won promotion to Division

One. In March 1928 Bolton paid £6,300 for his transfer, allowing John Smith to move to Bury at the same time. McClelland took over at centre-forward and started well, scoring on his debut, at Burnley, and grabbing eight goals in the last 10 games of the season. After a slow start to 1928–29 he moved to inside-right and was an important member of the side that won the FA Cup that season. In 1929 he moved to Preston North End for £5,000, scoring 22 goals in 53 games before joining Blackpool in February 1931, scoring against the Wanderers on his debut. McClelland later played for Bradford, alongside former Wanderer Harold Blackmore, and he ended his League career in 1936 at Manchester United, who had just won promotion to the First Division.

	League		FA Cup		Total	
	A	G	A	G	A	G
1927–28	10	8	-	-	10	8
1928–29	39	9	8	1	47	10
1929–30	8	1	-	-	8	1
	57	18	8	1	65	19

JIM 'SEAMUS' McDONAGH

Born: Rotherham, 6 October 1952

Goalkeeper 'Seamus' McDonagh began with his home-town club, Rotherham United, in December 1970, serving his apprenticeship and winning England Youth honours while at Millmoor. He had a short loan spell at Manchester United, although he never got a game, and went on to play 121 League fixtures for the Millers, including an ever-present term in 1974–75, winning promotion from Division Four. He suffered a broken leg and lost his place after recovery, joining the Wanderers on loan in August 1976 and making the move permanent a month later in a £10,000 deal. McDonagh's first game for Bolton came in the Anglo-Scottish Cup at Partick Thistle in September 1976, and

became a goalkeeping coach and has held positions at Coventry City, Leicester City, Celtic and Aston Villa.

	League		FA Cup		FL Cup		Total	
	A	G	A	G	A	G	A	G
1976–77	35	-	1	-	7	-	43	-
1977–78	42	-	4	-	3	-	49	-
1978–79	42	-	1	-	1	-	44	-
1979–80	42	-	4	-	2	-	48	-
1981–82	39	-	2	-	2	-	43	-
1982–83	42	1	1	-	4	-	47	1
	242	1	13	-	19	-	274	1

GERRY McELHINNEY

Born: Park, Northern Ireland, 19 September 1956

Gerry McElhinney's rugged approach to his central-defensive duties eventually earned him international honours for the successful Northern Ireland side. He initially made his name playing Gaelic football, having been part in the 1975 and 1976 Ulster Senior Championship-winning Derry side. He was also a boxer of some note, winning mid-Ulster titles in both middleweight and light heavyweight categories. His football career saw him play with Derry City, Limavady United and Dungiven Celtic before Scottish giants Celtic took him to Parkhead. Unfortunately, he did not force his way

he became the club's first-choice 'keeper later that month when Barry Siddall moved to Sunderland. McDonagh's best season came in 1977–78, when he set a club record of conceding only 33 goals in a 42-match season as the club won the Second Division Championship. Between 1976 and 1980 McDonagh made a club record 161 consecutive League appearances and in July 1980, after the Wanderers had been relegated, he joined Everton for £250,000. He won the first of 24 Ireland international caps while at Goodison and a year after leaving Burnden he returned, exchanged for Mike Walsh and £90,000. McDonagh scored against Burnley at Burnden in January 1983 with a long clearance but could not help prevent the club suffering relegation to Division Three. He moved to Notts County and then had spells with Birmingham City, Gillingham, Sunderland, Wichita Wings, Scarborough, Huddersfield and Charlton Athletic. In 1988–89 he became manager of Galway United before leaving the game to run a pub in Nottingham. McDonagh

into the first team and returned to Ireland with Finn Harps before a stint in the States with Chicago Sting. He went back to Ireland to join Distillery, and it was from there that the Wanderers paid £25,000 to bring him to Burnden in September 1980. McElhinney's early days were blighted with injury, and in November 1982 he was loaned out to Rochdale, where he played 20 games before being recalled in April 1983 after Paul Jones suffered injury. The Irishman played a major part in Bolton's four consecutive clean sheets, but he could not prevent the club being relegated to the Third Division. McElhinney became a regular in 1983–84, and in November 1983 he won the first of six Northern Ireland international caps in a 1–0 win over West Germany in Hamburg. The following year he helped his country win the last-ever British Home International Championship. In January 1985 he was sold to Plymouth Argyle for £32,500, captaining the club as they won promotion to Division Two in 1986. In August 1988 he moved to Peterborough before joining the club's coaching staff. McElhinney later played with Corby Town, becoming joint player-manager, and in 2006 was manager of Central Midlands League club Graham Street Prims for a spell before leaving the game to concentrate on his business, which he runs from his base in Derby.

	League		FA Cup		FL Cup		Frieght Rover Trophy		Total	
	A	G	A	G	A	G	A	G	A	G
1980–81	17	-	2	-	-	-	-	-	19	-
1981–82	18-/1	1	2	-	1	-	-	-	21/1	1
1982–83	16	-	-	-	2	-	-	-	18	-
1983–84	43	1	4	-	2	-	1	-	50	1
1984–85	13/1	-	-	-	4	-	-	-	17/1	-
	107/2	2	8	-	9	-	1	-	125/2	2

MARSHALL McEWAN

Born: Rutherglen, 1885
Died: 1966

A canny Scottish winger, Marshall McEwan began his League career with Blackpool, making his debut for them in a 5–0 defeat at Bristol City in December 1903. He missed only one game in the following 13 months, and in February 1905 he moved to Burnden Park. His first appearance was in a 2–0 home win over Bradford City, but that proved to be his only game that season as the club won promotion from Division Two. However, he displaced Tom Wilson after only one game of the 1905–06 season, going on to play at outside-left in the remaining 37 games. With David Stokes on the right flank, the wing positions were consistently filled for over four seasons. Unfortunately, McEwan missed out on Bolton's Second Division Championship glory in 1909 after sustaining injury in the run-in. The following year the Wanderers were struggling against relegation and, two weeks before the end of the season, Chelsea paid £750 to take McEwan to Stamford Bridge. The Londoners were also struggling, and it transpired that both clubs went down. As a result of Chelsea's

action the FA brought in a new rule, the transfer deadline, set as the fourth Thursday in March. McEwan remained in London until 1911 when he joined Linfield. He ended his career at Fleetwood.

	League		FA Cup		Total	
	A	G	A	G	A	G
1904–05	1	-	-	-	1	-
1905–06	37	7	1	-	38	7
1906–07	35	1	4	-	39	1
1907–08	32	1	5	2	37	3
1908–09	21	1	1	-	22	1
1909–10	26	3	1	-	27	3
	152	13	12	2	164	15

JOHN McGINLAY

Born: Inverness, 8 April 1964

John McGinlay became a cult hero during his five-year spell at Bolton as the club won two promotions, reached a major Cup Final and produced a number of Cup shocks thanks to his goals, which led to him winning international honours. He began with Nairn County in 1982 while working as a part-time builder before having spells with North Shore United, Nairn, Yeovil Town, Hanimex Sports and Elgin City. In 1989 Shrewsbury Town gave him an opportunity at League level and he repaid them with 27 goals in 60 League appearances. Bury secured his services in July 1990 and during his spell there he netted a hat-trick against the Wanderers at Burnden in March 1991. Later that month he moved to Millwall, playing 34 games before the Wanderers paid £120,000 for him in September 1992. He made his Bolton debut in a 1–0 defeat at Leyton Orient but went on to form a lethal partnership with Andy Walker that season as the club won promotion from Division Two, both strikers also scoring in the famous FA Cup win at Liverpool. In 1993–94 McGinlay scored 25 League goals and also found the net in FA Cup wins at

Everton and Arsenal. In April 1994 he made the first of 14 international appearances for Scotland, scoring in a 2–1 win against Austria in Vienna. His final appearance for his country came three years later against the same opponents at Celtic Park. McGinlay led the Bolton's goalscoring charts in the 1994–95 season as promotion to the Premier League was won, and he also scored the goal that defeated Swindon to take the Wanderers to the League Cup Final against Liverpool, from which Bolton returned empty-handed. McGinlay formed a partnership with Nathan Blake in 1996–97 that rocketed the Wanderers back to the Premier League after just one season's absence. He was again leading scorer, and it was fitting that he should score the last ever goal at Burnden Park in a 4–1 win over Charlton in April 1997. After the move to the Reebok Stadium, McGinlay struggled to find some form and netted his last goal for the club from the penalty spot in a 4–4 home League Cup draw against Leyton Orient in September 1997. In November that year he moved to Bradford City for £625,000 and later had spells at Oldham Athletic and Cincinnati Riverhawks before turning his hand to

management at Ilkeston Town and Gresley Rovers. He then returned to the States to become a coach at Cincinnati Kings. In May 2000 McGinlay was awarded a testimonial, which saw the Wanderers take on Preston North End.

	League		FA Cup		FL Cup		Autoglass Trophy		Anglo–Italian Cup		Total	
	A	G	A	G	A	G	A	G	A	G	A	G
1992–93	31/3	16	5	5	-	-	4	1	-	-	40/3	22
1993–94	39	25	8	3	3	1	-	-	4	4	54	33
1994–95	37/3	18	1	-	7/1	4	-	-	-	-	45/4	22
1995–96	29/3	6	1/1	1	6	2	-	-	-	-	36/4	9
1996–97	43	24	1	1	5	5	-	-	-	-	49	30
1997–98	4/3	-	-	-	2/1	2	-	-	-	-	6/4	2
	183/12	89	16/1	10	23/2	14	4	1	4	4	230/15	118

SAM MARSH

Born: Westhoughton, 1879
Died: Unknown

Discovered in the early 1900s playing in the Atherton area, Sam Marsh was another local player who came through the ranks to serve the Wanderers for 10 seasons. He was capable of playing at centre-forward, inside-right and right-half, and began his career at Daisy Hill in the Wigan League before joining Hindley. He then played for Atherton Church House, and his 35 goals for them secured his move to the Wanderers in 1902. Marsh made his debut that November, while his first goal for the club came in the infamous first win of the 1902–03 season, at the 23rd attempt at Notts County in January 1903. Despite relegation he was the club's leading scorer, a feat he repeated the following season when he collected an FA Cup runners'-up medal. During 1904–05 Marsh struck up an effective strike force with Albert Shepherd and Walter White, the three players hitting 65 goals between them as Bolton won promotion from Division Two, Marsh leading the way. He took a back seat to the others in 1905–06, but the

strike force still scored more goals than any other club in the League. His appearances thereafter became sporadic. He captained the reserves to Manchester Cup success in 1909 before returning at half-back to help secure promotion to the First Division in 1911. In May 1912 he joined Bury, making three appearances before retiring to become the publican at the Ainsworth Arms in Bolton.

	League		FA Cup		Total	
	A	G	A	G	A	G
1902–03	15	9	1	-	16	9
1903–04	30	16	6	5	36	21
1904–05	32	26	4	1	36	27
1905–06	33	12	1	-	34	12
1906–07	15	6	-	-	15	6
1907–08	9	1	2	3	11	4
1908–09	7	-	-	-	7	-
1909–10	21	1	1	-	22	1
1910–11	16	1	1	-	17	1
1911–12	7	-	-	-	7	-
	185	72	16	9	201	81

JACK MILSOM

Born: Bedminster, 22 February 1907
Died: Ashton, 1977

Centre-forward Jack Milsom is the only player to have been the Wanderers' leading scorer in six consecutive seasons. He registered this feat between 1932 and 1937 after fighting his way into the side at the expense of another West Country born player, Harold Blackmore. Milsom began his career with Hopewell Hill Mission and joined Bristol Rovers after being turned down by Exeter City. Kettering was his next club before moving to the North West, where he joined Rochdale. Thirty-eight goals in 54 League games prompted the Wanderers to pay £1,750 for him in December 1929, but he struggled to make an impact with Blackmore in good form. Milsom netted six in a reserve game and managed three goals in his four appearances in his first season before he fractured a leg in October 1930 during a Lancashire Cup tie against Manchester City. Early in 1932 he recovered to become the club's regular centre-forward, and with

it came plenty of goals. Although he netted 25 League goals in 1932–33, they were not enough to prevent relegation. He was, however, a member of the team that won back their First Division place in 1935. Milsom's last game for the club came in February 1938, a 1–1 home draw with Sunderland in which he netted the Wanderers' sole goal. The following week he joined Manchester City for £4,000, where he played until retiring from the game in 1940.

	League		FA Cup		Total	
	A	G	A	G	A	G
1929–30	4	3	-	-	4	3
1930–31	6	3	-	-	6	3
1931–32	22	19	1	-	23	19
1932–33	39	25	3	2	42	27
1933–34	38	23	5	4	43	27
1934–35	40	31	6	4	46	35
1935–36	34	20	-	-	34	20
1936–37	35	13	4	1	39	14
1937–38	17	5	1	-	18	5
	235	142	20	11	255	153

WILLIE MOIR

Born: Aberdeen, 19 April 1922
Died: May 1988

Willie Moir was capable of playing in any position in the forward line and began his career with the 25th Old Boys FC before joining Bucksburn Juniors. During the war he was in the RAF and was posted to Kirkham, where he was spotted playing for the station team by Wanderers scout Bob Jackson. In April 1943 Moir was taken on by the Wanderers as an amateur but within a fortnight he had been signed on professional forms. During the war Moir guested for both Dundee and Aberdeen, and he played for the Wanderers in the successful 1945 North v South Cup Final. After the resumption of League football Moir played mostly at outside-left, although he was a naturally right-footed

1951–52	39	16	1	–	40	16
1952–53	37	17	8	5	45	22
1953–54	39	18	6	5	45	23
1954–55	32	8	2	3	34	11
1955–56	2	–	–	–	2	–
	325	118	33	16	358	134

WILLIE MORGAN

Born: Alloa, 2 October 1944

Willie Morgan earned himself a new lease of life when he joined the Wanderers on a free transfer from Burnley in March 1976. He had started his career at Turf Moor, signing as an amateur in May 1960 after playing for Alloa Schoolboys and Fishcross. He turned professional in October 1961, making his debut in 1963 and going on to win the first of 21 Scottish international caps, against Northern Ireland in 1967. The winger played 231 games for Burnley and in August 1968 Manchester United paid £115,000 to take him to Old Trafford. He played 236 games for United, winning a Second Division Championship medal in 1975, and in the summer of that year he returned to Burnley. He managed only 13 League appearances before joining the Wanderers in March 1976. Morgan's talent was renewed at Burnden under Ian Greaves, and was absent from just three League games from the date

player. At the beginning of the 1948–49 season he moved to inside-right and scored all the Wanderers' goals in a 4–2 win at Aston Villa. That season he played in every game and finished top of the First Division scoring charts with 25 goals. In April 1950 Moir won his only Scottish international cap, playing against England in Glasgow, and in 1953 he captained the side in the FA Cup Final defeat to Blackpool. He joined Stockport County in September 1955 and in June the following year was appointed their player-manager. Moir retired from playing in 1958, remaining as manager until July 1960. In March 1961 he became manager at Nelson in the Lancashire Combination before becoming a sales rep. He was also a keen cricketer, playing for Bolton CC, and retained his links with Burnden, helping out on the commercial side until his death.

	League		FA Cup		Total	
	A	G	A	G	A	G
1945–46	–	–	4	1	4	1
1946–47	31	8	3	–	34	8
1947–48	31	5	1	–	32	5
1948–49	42	25	3	–	45	25
1949–50	31	9	3	–	34	9
1950–51	41	12	2	2	43	14

he signed until May 1979 as the Wanderers produced some classy performances, just missing out on promotion to Division One on two occasions. He was instrumental in the season promotion was finally won in 1977–78 but missed the penultimate game of the season at Blackburn, when promotion was secured, due to injury. Morgan twice played in the NASL in the summer months while at Bolton, with Minnesota Kicks and Vancouver Whitecaps. His final game for the Wanderers came in February 1980 at Manchester United, and in September 1980 he joined Blackpool, where he played 42 League games before retiring from the game.

	League		FA Cup		FL Cup		Total	
	A	G	A	G	A	G	A	G
1975–76	10/1	-	-	-	-	-	10/1	-
1976–77	41	1	1	-	8	2	50	3
1977–78	41	4	4	-	2	-	47	4
1978–79	41	2	1	-	2	-	44	2
1979–80	21	3	4	-	1/1	-	26/1	3
	154/1	10	10	-	13/1	2	177/2	12

BRUNO N'GOTTY

Born: Lyon, France, 10 June 1971
Central-defender Bruno N'Gotty began his career in his home city with Olympique in 1988 and played 143 times, scoring 10 goals, before joining Paris St Germain in 1995. There he became a hero, scoring the winning goal that defeated Rapid Vienna in the 1996 European Cup-Winners' Cup Final. During this period he won all six of his French international caps, the last being in 1997. His towering strength attracted AC Milan and in 1998 he moved to the San Siro, being part of the team that won the 1999 Serie A title. He had a spell on loan at Venezia as his chances in the Milan side diminished, and he joined Olympique Marseille in 2001. He played only 31 games for the French club before joining the Wanderers on loan in January 2002. N'Gotty made his debut as a substitute in a 1–1 draw at Blackburn Rovers and became a regular as the club retained Premier League status. The move became permanent that summer for a £400,000 fee, and he became a steady performer in the centre of defence or occasionally at right-back. He played his part in helping the club reach the 2004 League Cup Final, scoring in the semi-final against Aston Villa, and the following season he was voted the supporter's Player of the Year, missing just one Premier League game. His final game for the club came in April 2006, a scoreless draw at West Brom, and that summer he joined Birmingham City, where he helped them win promotion to the Premier League. In June 2007 N'Gotty joined Leicester City, playing 38 games, and in September 2008 signed for Hereford United on loan before suffering a ruptured Achilles tendon.

	League		FA Cup		FL Cup		UEFA Cup		Total	
	A	G	A	G	A	G	A	G	A	G
2001–02	24/2	1	-	-	2/1	-	-	-	26/3	1
2002–03	23	1	1	-	-	-	-	-	24	1
2003–04	32/1	2	-	-	6	1	-	-	38/1	3
2004–05	37	-	4	-	-	-	-	-	41	-
2005–06	27/2	-	2	-	-/1	-	6/1	1	35/4	1
	143/5	4	7	-	8/2	1	6/1	1	164/8	6

PETER NICHOLSON

Born: Cleator Moor, 12 January 1951

Peter Nicholson was a servant of the club for 11 years in the top three divisions after joining the club from Blackpool in 1971 for a £4,000 fee. 'Nico' began his career with Carlisle United as an apprentice and moved to Blackpool in August 1969. He made his First Division debut at 18 years old but managed only six appearances for the Seasiders. He became Jimmy Armfield's first signing and went on to play in every position apart from goalkeeper, such was his versatility, although it was to be at right-back that he made most of his appearances for the Wanderers. He played his part in the promotion-winning sides of 1973 and 1978 and was a regular in the club's two seasons in the top flight in the seventies. In 1981 Nicholson was given a free transfer,

only to be reinstated by new manager George Mulhall, and he began 1981–82 as first-choice right-back. A broken wrist kept him out of action for a long period, and his last game for the club came in a defeat at Cambridge in March 1982. The following season he played seven games for Rochdale before playing in local football, which he continued to do until 1987. Nicholson returned to the club to assist on the commercial side and has coached in the Academy. He is still a regular at the Reebok, where he works with corporate guests on matchdays.

	League		FA Cup		FL Cup		Total	
	A	G	A	G	A	G	A	G
1971–72	40/1	2	2	1	6	-	48/1	3
1972–73	36/2	5	7/1	1	2	-	45/3	6
1973–74	33/3	-	3	-	4	-	40/3	-
1974–75	36/1	2	2	-	2	-	40/1	2
1975–76	15/3	2	1	-	-	-	16/3	2
1976–77	34	-	1	-	7	-	42	-
1977–78	21/2	1	3/1	-	2	-	26/3	1
1978–79	34	-	1	-	-	-	35	-
1979–80	30	-	2	-	1	-	33	-
1980–81	18/1	-	1/1	-	-	-	19/2	-
1981–82	6/2	-	-	-	2	-	8/2	-
	303/15	12	23/3	2	26	-	352/18	14

KEVIN NOLAN

Born: Liverpool, 24 June 1982

Kevin Nolan represented Liverpool Schoolboys and was on Liverpool's books before joining the Wanderers Academy primarily as a central-defender. He progressed through the reserve team quickly and switched to midfield, making his League debut as a substitute in a 2–0 home defeat against Charlton in March 2000. His first start came in a 2–2 draw at Gillingham the following October, and he was a member of the side that won promotion that season in the Play-off Final against Preston North End. Nolan netted twice in his first Premier League game, a 5–0 opening day win at Leicester

were relegated to the Championship, but he helped them bounce back by winning the League at the first attempt.

	League		FA Cup		FL Cup		UEFA Cup		Total	
	A	G	A	G	A	G	A	G	A	G
1999–2000	-/4	-	-	-	-	-	-	-	-/4	-
2000–01	27/6	1	3/1	2	-	-	-	-	30/7	3
2001–02	34/1	8	1/1	-	1/1	-	-	-	36/3	8
2002–03	15/18	1	1/1	-	-/1	-	-	-	16/20	1
2003–04	37	9	-/2	1	4/1	2	-	-	41/3	12
2004–05	27/9	4	2/2	-	2	-	-	-	31/11	4
2005–06	35/1	9	3	-	2	-	4/3	2	44/4	11
2006–07	31	3	2	1	-/1	1	-	-	33/1	5
2007–08	33	5	-	-	1	-	5	-	39	5
2008–09	20	-	1	-	-/1	1	-	-	21/1	1
	259/39	40	13/7	4	10/5	4	9/3	2	291/54	50

HARRY NUTTALL

Born: Bolton, 9 November 1897
Died: Bolton, May 1969

Harry Nuttall was Burnden born and bred. His father, Jack, who served the club as both trainer and groundsman, lived in a cottage at the corner of the railway embankment at the ground, and his brother, James, played for the Wanderers during the war. Harry began his career with St Mark's in the Bolton League before playing for Fleetwood and Atherton. In December 1920 Harry signed

in August 2001, and his status with Bolton supporters rose further as he scored one of the goals in a 2–1 win at Manchester United, ending the campaign with a total of eight. The following season he managed only one goal, which proved to be the winner at Old Trafford, but his form dipped during that second Premiership season. Nolan produced his best performance with the club during 2003–04, when he missed just one League game, helped the club reach the League Cup Final and rediscovered his scoring touch to head the club's scoring chart. He reproduced that form during 2005–06, netting two goals in the club's first ever UEFA Cup campaign, and there were calls for him to be included in the England squad, which would add to his appearances at Under-18 and Under-21 level. Nolan's final game for the club came at Blackburn Rovers in January 2009, and his only goal that season – his 50th for the club – came in a League Cup defeat by Northampton Town. He joined Newcastle United for £4 million before the transfer deadline. Nolan's start at St James' Park proved to be disappointing as the Toon

for the Wanderers, making his League debut in September 1921 in a 1–0 win over Cup holders Tottenham Hotspurs at Burnden. He played at half-back, a position in which he was to capture both Cup medals and international caps. The middle line of Nuttall, Seddon and Jennings remains as the most successful in the club's history, with only Jennings missing out on a hat-trick of FA Cup-winning medals. Nuttall won the first of three England caps in October 1927 in Belfast and was selected as 12th man for his country on three occasions in 1929. He played his last game for the club in March 1932, a 3–0 reverse at Sunderland, and in May that year joined Rochdale. He spent a season there before becoming coach at Nelson and in 1935 he returned to Bolton as second-team trainer. He remained with the club until his retirement in 1964, in the latter years taking on the responsibility for the kit and dressing rooms.

	League		FA Cup		Total	
	A	G	A	G	A	G
1921–22	10	-	-	-	10	-
1922–23	20	-	5	-	25	-
1923–34	30	2	-	-	30	2
1924–25	41	-	3	-	44	-
1925–26	22	-	6	-	28	-
1926–27	35	-	4	-	39	-
1927–28	36	2	1	-	37	2
1928–29	31	-	8	-	39	-
1929–30	27	1	1	-	28	1
1930–31	20	1	3	-	23	1
1931–32	22	-	1	-	23	-
	294	6	32	-	326	6

JAY-JAY OKOCHA

Born: Enugu, Nigeria, 14 August 1973
Jay-Jay Okocha joined the Wanderers in July 2002 after appearing in the 2002 World Cup Finals in Japan. In doing so he lifted Bolton's profile both at home and abroad – the attacking midfielder was one of the most recognisable players in the world. Okocha had begun his career with local side Enugu Rangers before moving to Germany and signing for Third Division Borussia Neunkirchen in 1990. In 1992 he signed for Eintracht Frankfurt, playing 90 Bundesliga games, but could not prevent them being relegated in 1996. He moved to Fenerbahçe, where he was to have his most prolific goalscoring spell, netting 30 goals in 63 games. In 1998 he joined Paris St-Germain for a £12 million fee, becoming the most expensive African player ever. He spent four years in the French capital, playing 84 League games. Okocha's Wanderers debut came on the opening day of the 2002–03 season in a 4–1 defeat at Fulham, but the midfielder found the game tough and was substituted at half-time. It was not until the following November that he found his feet in the Premier League, and with it came some vital goals to keep the club in the top flight, including a spectacular winner against West Ham at the Reebok. He became club captain and led the team to the 2004 League Cup Final, netting two goals in the home semi-final against Aston Villa before departing to represent Nigeria in the African Nations Cup. He scored the first

goal of the 2004–05 season, a 4–1 home success against Charlton, and the Wanderers finished the campaign in sixth place to qualify for the UEFA Cup. The following season, however, Okocha's influence diminished and his last game for the club came as a substitute in the final game of the 2005–06 season against Birmingham City. He joined Qatar SC in the Middle East but returned to England with Hull City in 2007, playing 18 games for the Tigers as they won promotion to the Premier League for the first time. He represented Nigeria on 75 occasions, 15 of which came while with the Wanderers, and in 1996 was a member of their successful Olympic gold-winning side in Atlanta.

	League		FA Cup		FL Cup		UEFA Cup		Total	
	A	G	A	G	A	G	A	G	A	G
2002–03	26/5	7	-/1	-	-	-	-	-	26/6	7
2003–04	33/2	-	-	-	5/1	3	-	-	38/3	3
2004–05	29/2	6	1	-	1	1	-	-	31/2	7
2005–06	18/9	1	3	-	1	-	6/1	-	28/11	1
	106/18	14	4/1	-	7/2	4	6/1	-	123/22	18

RAY PARRY

Born: Derby, 19 January 1936
Died: Bolton, 23 May 2003

Ray Parry became the youngest player to appear in the First Division when, on 13 October 1951, he played for the Wanderers against Wolves at Burnden aged 15 years 267 days. The inside-forward came from a footballing family – brothers Jack and Cyril played League football for Derby and Notts County respectively. Parry represented England Schoolboys at 14 years of age, playing alongside Johnny Haynes, and signed for Bolton in May 1951, making just six reserve appearances before his first-team debut. He became a regular in the team during 1953, missing just one game during 1953–54, and was a member of the 1958 FA Cup-winning side. After appearing twice for the England

Under-23 side Parry won the first of two full caps in November 1959, scoring in a 2–1 win over Northern Ireland at Wembley. In October 1960 he moved to Blackpool, spending four years at Bloomfield Road before joining Bury, where he made his debut against Bolton. He played his 500th League game in August 1968 and remained with the Shakers until 1972, when he joined New Brighton for a short spell before retiring. Parry was a qualified FA coach and a popular figure around Bolton, where he owned a newsagent's in the town centre until his retirement.

	League		FA Cup		FL Cup		Total	
	A	G	A	G	A	G	A	G
1951–52	2	-	-	-	-	-	2	-
1952–53	15	1	1	-	-	-	16	1
1953–54	41	6	6	1	-	-	47	7
1954–55	28	9	2	1	-	-	30	10
1955–56	33	7	2	-	-	-	35	7
1956–57	31	5	1	-	-	-	32	5
1957–58	38	14	7	4	-	-	45	18
1958–59	37	12	6	2	-	-	43	14
1959–60	33	12	3	3	-	-	36	15
1960–61	12	2	-	-	1	-	13	2
	270	68	28	11	1	-	299	79

ALEX PATON

Born: Scotland

Died: Unknown

Alex Paton was one of the few players to have the distinction of having played in both the Scottish and English FA Cup Finals, unfortunately ending up on the losing side on each occasion. He had begun his career with Vale of Leven, appearing at centre-forward in the 1890 Scottish FA Cup Final against Queens Park, who won after a replay. He moved south to join West Manchester and moved to Bolton in the close season of 1890. He became a regular in the half-back line, ever present in his first season with the club. It was not until Boxing Day 1893 that he missed his first game when injury forced him to step down. The Wanderers reached the 1894 FA Cup Final with a number of injuries, including Paton, who took to the field swathed in bandages, but the ploy failed as Notts County ran out 4–1 winners at Goodison. Paton then went on another consistent run in the side, missing only one game in three seasons, and he played in the first game at Burnden Park in 1895. In

1898 there was a disagreement over pay and he refused to re-sign. Although the dispute was eventually resolved Paton only played another six games for the club as First Division status was lost for the first time.

	League		FA Cup		Total	
	A	G	A	G	A	G
1890–91	22	-	1	-	23	-
1891–92	26	-	2	-	28	-
1892–93	30	2	2	-	32	2
1893–94	21	1	5	-	26	1
1894–95	30	6	3	-	33	6
1895–96	30	4	5	-	35	4
1896–97	29	1	4	-	33	1
1897–98	22	1	3	-	25	1
1898–99	5	-	1	-	6	-
	215	15	26	-	241	15

MARK PATTERSON

Born: Darwen, 24 May 1965

A battling midfield player, Mark Patterson joined Blackburn Rovers as an apprentice and turned professional in May 1983. He helped Rovers win the Full Members' Cup in 1987 and went on to score 30 goals in 101 League appearances before a £20,000 move to Preston North End in June 1988. He played 55 League games for Preston and in February 1990 joined Bury, where he played alongside a number of players who were to later join Bolton, such as David Lee, John McGinlay and Tony Cunningham. Patterson was at Gigg Lane for less than a year as the Wanderers paid £65,000 to take him to Burnden. He made his debut in a 1–1 draw at Bradford City in January 1991 but missed out on a Wembley appearance in the Play-off Final that season through injury. Patterson was a regular in the side that won promotion in 1992–93, and he scored his only FA Cup goal for the club the following season in a 1–1 home third-round draw with Everton. His three League goals during 1994–95 all

	League		FA Cup		FL Cup		Autoglass Trophy		Anglo–Italian Cup		Total	
	A	G	A	G	A	G	A	G	A	G	A	G
1990–91	18/1	2	-	-	-	-	-	-	-	-	18/1	2
1991–92	36	2	4	-	2/1	1	1	-	-	-	43/1	3
1992–93	35/2	2	6	-	4	-	4	-	-	-	49/2	2
1993–94	34/1	1	6	1	3	-	-	-	4	-	47/1	2
1994–95	23/3	3	1	-	2/2	-	-	-	-	-	26/5	3
1995–96	12/4	1	-	-	5/1	1	-	-	-	-	17/5	2
	158/11	11	17	1	16/4	2	5	-	4	-	200/15	14

secured vital 1–0 wins, but he again missed out on Wembley appearances in both Cup and Play-offs. He did, however, start as a regular in the club's first ever Premier League season. Patterson's last game for the club came in a 0–0 League Cup fourth-round replay at Burnden against Norwich City, and it was unfortunate that his last kick came in the penalty shoot-out. He missed and City ran out winners. Two days later he joined Sheffield United for £300,000, subsequently having a loan spell at Southend before rejoining Bury for £125,000 in December 1997. He played only 31 League games in his second spell, being loaned out to Blackpool before moving to Southend in March 1999 on a free transfer. He later had spells with Accrington and Scarborough, where he became manager in 2006. Patterson spent time with Leigh, Chorley, Rossendale and Hednesford Town before taking up a coaching post at Accrington in 2009.

HENRIK PEDERSEN

Born: Kjellerup, Denmark, 10 June 1975
Henrik Pedersen began his career with Silkeborg IF in Denmark, scoring 62 goals in 122 games. The striker helped the club win the 2001 Danish Cup and in July of that year he joined the Wanderers for an initial £650,000, which rose to £1,080,000 based on games. He made his Bolton debut as a substitute in an opening day 5–0 Premier League win at Leicester City in August 2001 but failed to find his feet in that first season. In 2002 he returned to Silkeborg on loan, but afterwards he became a regular in the Bolton team during 2002–03, when he scored seven Premier League goals. He matched the feat the following term, hitting the net in three consecutive games in April 2004. His game developed, with appearances in a wide-midfield position and at left-back. The last occasion that the Reebok saw his 'peacock' goal celebration was in January 2007, when he netted his last goal for the club against Charlton in a 1–1 draw. Pederson's final appearance came in March 2007 in a 4–1

reverse at Manchester United. In May 2007 he signed for Hull City, playing 21 games as they won promotion to the Premier League, and the following year he returned to Denmark to re-sign for Silkeborg. He won three full international caps for Denmark, two of which came while he was with the Wanderers.

	League		FA Cup		FL Cup		UEFA Cup		Total	
	A	G	A	G	A	G	A	G	A	G
2001–02	5/6	-	2	1	1/1	1	-	-	8/7	2
2002–03	31/2	7	-	-	-/1	-	-	-	31/3	7
2003–04	19/14	7	2	-	4/3	2	-	-	25/17	9
2004–05	13/14	6	3/1	2	1/1	1	-	-	17/16	9
2005–06	15/6	1	-/1	-	-/1	-	2/1	-	17/9	1
2006–07	10/8	1	-/2	-	1	-	-	-	11/10	1
	93/50	22	7/4	3	7/7	4	2/1		109/62	29

JIMMY PHILLIPS

Born: Bolton, 8 February 1966

Jimmy Phillips played for Bolton Schoolboys at Under-14 and Under-15 before joining the Wanderers after leaving school with 10 O Levels under his belt. Capable of playing at left-back or on the left side of midfield, Phillips had his first taste of League football in April 1984 when he appeared as a substitute against Gillingham at Burnden. The following season, after the departure of Ray Deakin, he made the number-three shirt his own and in 1986 appeared at Wembley for the club in the Freight Rover Trophy Final against Bristol City. He was ever present the following season until he joined Rangers in March 1987 for a £95,000 fee. Phillips played 19 League games for the Glasgow club and four games in the European Cup but returned to England in 1988 when Oxford paid £110,000 for his signature. He made 86 League appearances for the Manor Ground side and in March 1990 joined Middlesbrough for £250,000. There he played 145 League games, being part of the side that won promotion to the

inaugural Premier League in 1992. In July 1993 Phillips rejoined the Wanderers for £250,000, playing every game in the successful 1995 side that won promotion in the Play-off Final and reached the League Cup Final. He was a member of the 1996–97 First Division Championship side and played in the final League game at Burnden. In August 1998 he was awarded a testimonial with Celtic, visiting the Reebok Stadium and attracting a crowd of almost 18,000. His final first-team appearance came as a substitute in the infamous 5–3 Play-off defeat at Ipswich Town in May 2000. Phillips later had spells as a youth coach and reserve-team coach at the club before being appointed Academy manager in 2008.

	League		FA Cup		FL Cup		Freight Rover Trophy		Anglo–Italian Cup		Total	
	A	G	A	G	A	G	A	G	A	G	A	G
1983–84	-/1	-	-	-	-	-	-	-	-	-	-/1	-
1984–85	37/3	1	1	-	4	-	3	-	-	-	45/3	1
1985–86	33	1	1	-	2	-	7	-	-	-	43	1
1986–87	33/1	-	5	-	2	-	4	-	-	-	44/1	-
1993–94	41/1	-	7	-	4	-	-	-	6	2	58/1	2

1994–95	49	1	1	-	8	-	-	-	-	-	58	1
1995–96	37	-	2	-	6	-	-	-	-	-	45	-
1996–97	36	-	-	-	4	-	-	-	-	-	40	-
1997–98	21/1	1	-	-	1/1	-	-	-	-	-	22/2	1
1998–99	14/1	-	-	-	3/1	1	-	-	-	-	17/2	1
1999–2000	15/10	1	-	-	3/1	-	-	-	-	-	18/11	1
	316/18	5	17	-	37/3	1	14	-	6	2	390/21	8

RONNIE PHILLIPS

Born: Worsley, 30 March 1947
Died: Cumbria, 18 April 2002

Ronnie Phillips joined the Wanderers from local football and signed professional in October 1965, having served an apprenticeship in industry at Dobson & Barlows in Bradley Fold. His League debut came in January 1967, replacing Gordon Taylor on the left wing in a 3–1 win against Cardiff City at Burnden. Phillips flirted in and out of the side, with both Taylor and then Terry Wharton vying for the position. Although Phillips struggled to make headway during the late 1960s he came to the fore in 1972–73, when he missed just one game as the Wanderers won the Third Division Championship. That year saw him hit a personal best for number of goals in a season, and the diminutive winger also provided many a chance for the potent strike force of John Byrom, Garry Jones and Stuart Lee. Towards the end of 1973 Peter Thompson joined the club from Liverpool and Phillips was the one to make way. In January 1975 he joined Chesterfield on loan for a month, and he made his last appearance for the Wanderers as a substitute in a 2–0 home defeat to Sunderland in April 1975. That summer he joined Bury for £12,000, playing 72 games before signing for Chester in September 1977. There he played in a successful side on 130 occasions until 1981, when he had a spell at both Chorley and Barrow before retiring from the game. Phillips later worked in insurance and then set up a newsagent's, which he ran until his death.

	League		FA Cup		FL Cup		Total	
	A	G	A	G	A	G	A	G
1966–67	11/1	2	3	-	-	-	14/1	2
1967–68	3/1	1	-	-	-	-	3/1	1
1968–69	13	2	-	-	-	-	13	2
1969–70	13	2	-	-	3/1	-	16/1	2
1970–71	20/4	1	1	-	2	-	23/4	1
1971–72	13/1	4	-	-	1/1	1	14/2	5
1972–73	45	5	9	1	2	-	56	6
1973–74	13/1	-	-/1	-	3/1	-	16/3	-
1974–75	4/2	-	-	-	1/1	-	5/3	-
	135/10	17	13/1	1	12/4	1	160/15	19

TONY PHILLISKIRK

Born: Sunderland, 10 February 1965

Known as the 'Ice Man' during his three-year spell at Burnden Park, Tony Philliskirk formed a productive goalscoring partnership with David Reeves that helped the club reach the Play-offs in successive seasons in 1990 and 1991. Philliskirk had begun his career at Sheffield United, having represented England Schoolboys before turning professional at 18, and had been a member

play his final game for the club in October 1992 when Hartlepool won 2–1 at Burnden. Philliskirk's 75th and last goal for the club came in a 1–0 League Cup win at Wimbledon the same month. Peterborough United secured his signature for £90,000 before he returned to the North West with Burnley in 1994. He later had spells with Carlisle United, Cardiff City, Halifax Town and Macclesfield Town before ending his career at Oldham Athletic in 1998. Philliskirk became youth coach at Boundary Park and had spells as assistant manager and manager before returning to the youth role. He also had a spell as a referee, progressing as far as the Northern Premier League.

	League		FA Cup		FL Cup		Autoglass Trophy		Total	
	A	G	A	G	A	G	A	G	A	G
1989–90	47	19	1	-	7	5	4	1	59	25
1990–91	46	21	3	2	4	5	2	-	55	28
1991–92	42/1	12	6	5	3	1	2	1	53/1	19
1992–93	9/1	2	-	-	4	1	-	-	13/1	3
	144/2	54	10	7	18	12	8	2	180/2	75

of the Blades side that won promotion from the Third Division in 1983–84. In 1986 he had a brief loan spell at Rotherham United, and after scoring 20 goals in 80 League appearances for Sheffield he joined Oldham Athletic in July 1988. He only had a short stay before joining Preston in February 1989, and in June of that year he joined the Wanderers for £50,000. Philliskirk scored on his Wanderers debut, a 2–0 win at Cardiff City at Ninian Park on the opening day of the 1989–90 season, and he topped the club's scoring charts with 25 League and Cup goals that term. The following season he again led the way with 28, netting a goal in each game against Bury, which sent the Wanderers to Wembley in the 1991 Play-off Final. He led the scoring charts again in 1992, but the arrivals of Andy Walker and John McGinlay saw him

DICK PYM

Born: Topsham, 2 February 1893
Died: Exeter, 16 September 1988

Nicknamed 'Pincher' Pym, the Topsham fisherman earned his living from the sea and played as an amateur centre-forward with Topsham before becoming a goalkeeper. In 1911 Pym signed for Southern League Exeter City and went on to make 186 consecutive appearances before breaking a collarbone in a Cup tie against Watford. In 1916 he joined the Devonshire Regiment and became a Sergeant PTI. Two years later he was transferred to the 8th Surrey Regiment and was wounded in action. After the war he returned to football with Exeter and in July 1921, after weeks of negotiation, Pym signed for Bolton for £5,000. The fee was a record for both clubs and for any goalkeeper. He made his debut in a home 2–2 draw with Preston North End on the opening day of the 1921–22 season and the following year played every game as the club won the FA Cup for the first time in the famous 'White Horse' Final. His performances were recognised and he appeared for the Football League in Belfast. Incredibly, despite his seafaring background, he was seasick on the crossing from Liverpool. In February 1925 Pym won the first of three England caps, against Wales in Swansea. The following year he collected another FA Cup-winners' medal and, despite injury, made it a hat-trick of Wembley wins and clean sheets in 1929. He played his last game in 1930 and returned to his home in Topsham to work in the fishing industry, although he played some non-League football with Yeovil & Petters United and Topsham. Pym was the last surviving member of the historic 1923 team.

	League	FA Cup	Total
	A	A	A
1921–22	23	-	23
1922–23	42	7	49
1923–24	41	3	44
1924–25	39	3	42
1925–26	39	9	48
1926–27	37	4	41
1927–28	21	-	21
1928–29	32	8	40
1929–30	24	1	25
1930–31	3	-	3
	301	35	336

DAVID REEVES

Born: Birkenhead, 20 November 1967

The striker began his career with Heswall before signing for Sheffield Wednesday in August 1986. While at Hillsborough he had two loan spells with Scunthorpe United and in November 1987 scored eight goals in 16 League games in another loan period at Burnley. He played only 17 League games for the Owls and in August 1989 he joined Bolton for £80,000. At Burnden he formed a prolific partnership with Tony Philliskirk, Reeves's first goal being a winner against

Bristol Rovers. In December 1991 he netted a hat-trick in a 4–1 defeat of Rochdale in the Autoglass Trophy before Burnden Park's lowest ever crowd for a Bolton game of 1,507. He proved to be a fans' favourite due to his working ethos, although the arrival of Andy Walker in January 1992 limited his appearances. Reeves's last League goal for the club came at Chester in October 1992, John McGinlay scoring his first in the same game, and his last appearance came in a 1–1 draw at Blackpool in February 1993. The following month Notts County signed him for £80,000, but he was only at Meadow Lane for six months before Carlisle United paid £121,000 to take him to Cumbria. There he scored 48 goals in 127 League games and helped them win the Third Division in 1995. In October 1996 Reeves moved to Preston and a year later joined Chesterfield. He scored 46 goals in 168 League games and proceeded to Oldham in December 2001. He rejoined Chesterfield in August 2002 and played his 600th League game in January 2004. Reeves ended his playing career with spells at Ards, Scarborough and Gainsborough Trinity before becoming assistant manager at Alfreton Town. He had a period as player-coach at Sutton Town before rejoining Gainsborough as assistant manager in 2008. He now works as a players' agent.

full England international and play in the World Cup Finals. He joined the Wanderers as an apprentice, turning professional in May 1974. He made his debut the following October as a substitute in a 2–0 home win over Orient in what was Ian Greaves's first game in charge. Within two months Reid was a regular in the side and matured with the team that narrowly missed promotion to Division One in 1976 and 1977. Between December 1974 and April 1978 Reid missed only four games, three due to suspension. He collected a Second Division Championship medal in 1978 and appeared for England Under-21s on six occasions. Unfortunately, injury struck in a pre-season game in July 1978 and he missed the club's return to the top flight. He recovered but suffered a broken leg on New Year's Day 1979 when he collided with Everton 'keeper George Wood on a snowbound Burnden pitch, the game later being abandoned. Reid was out for a year and his return came too late to save the club from relegation. Contractual issues saw him left out of the side after he had failed to agree terms with Everton, Arsenal and Wolves, who had offered £600,000 for his transfer, and he was later placed on a weekly contract. In September 1981 Reid suffered another broken leg in a League game at Barnsley. He

	League		FA Cup		FL Cup		Autoglass Trophy		Total	
	A	G	A	G	A	G	A	G	A	G
1989–90	43	10	1	-	7	1	3	2	54	13
1990–91	36/9	10	4	1	3	-	2	1	45/9	12
1991–92	24/12	8	2/3	3	4	-	2	4	32/14	15
1992–93	10/4	1	1/2	1	-/1	-	-/1	-	11/8	2
	113/24	29	8/5	5	14/1	1	7/1	7	142/31	42

PETER REID

Born: Huyton, 20 June 1956
Peter Reid saw many highs and lows at Burnden Park before going on to become a

again recovered to return to action, and his last game for the Wanderers came in a 4–1 home win over Charlton in December 1982 before a £60,000 fee took him to Everton. At Goodison he won two League Championship medals, an FA Cup-winners' medal and a European Cup-Winners' Cup medal, along with 13 England caps. In 1987–88 he was appointed player-coach at Everton, and after 159 League games for the Toffees he moved to Queen's Park Rangers in February 1989. He joined Manchester City in December 1989 and later became player-manager after the departure of Howard Kendall. Reid resumed his playing career with Southampton in October 1993 after his dismissal at City and saw out his playing career with Notts County and Bury. He returned to management in March 1995 with Sunderland and in 1996 led them to the First Division Championship, a feat that was repeated in 1999. He spent eight years in charge on Wearside and in March 2003 took over at Leeds United, keeping them in the Premier League after relegation looked inevitable. He was fired in November 2003 and joined Coventry City in May 2004, but he was there for only six months. In September 2008 he took charge of the Thailand national team while also appearing regularly on TV as a football pundit. Reid returned to England and joined the coaching staff at Stoke City and in June 2010 became manager at Plymouth Argyle.

	League		FA Cup		FL Cup		Total	
	A	G	A	G	A	G	A	G
1974–75	24/3	-	2	-	-	-	26/3	-
1975–76	42	2	6	1	1	-	49	3
1976–77	42	5	1	-	9	1	52	6
1977–78	38	9	4	-	3	-	45	9
1978–79	14	-	-	-	-/1	-	14/1	-
1979–80	17	3	4	-	-	-	21	3
1980–81	18	2	-	-	-	-	18	2
1981–82	12	1	-	-	1	-	13	1
1982–83	15	1	-	-	4	-	19	1
	222/3	23	17	1	18/1	1	257/4	25

MICHAEL RICKETTS

Born: Birmingham, 4 December 1978

Michael Ricketts became Bolton's first England international since Freddie Hill in 1962 thanks to his goalscoring exploits on the Wanderers' return to the Premier League in 2001–02. He had started his career with Walsall in 1996 and had gone on to score 14 goals in 76 League appearances. In July 2000 he joined the Wanderers for £500,000 and made his debut as a substitute in a 2–0 home win over Preston in which he netted the second goal. That set the tone for the season as the 'super sub' went on to score 14 of his 24 goals from the bench. One of those goals came in the Championship Play-off Final success against Preston at Cardiff, and he continued in the same vein the following season with a goal on the opening day Premiership 5–0 win at Leicester City. He scored the winner against Manchester United at Old Trafford in October 2001, and his international breakthrough came

when he played the first half against Holland in Amsterdam in February 2002. All of his goals for the Wanderers that season came before his call up, and he found himself relegated to the bench for the latter part of that season. The following season Ricketts again struggled to regain his form, with three of his six League goals coming from the penalty spot. His final game for the club came in January 2003, a 2–1 home defeat to Everton, and three hours before the transfer deadline struck he joined Middlesbrough for £3 million. During his spell on Teesside Ricketts managed to score only three League goals in 32 appearances but did appear as a substitute in the League Cup Final success against the Wanderers in 2004. In July 2004 he joined Leeds United on a free transfer and had subsequent loan spells at Stoke, Cardiff and Burnley. In June 2006 he signed for Southend United but was released with the club questioning his level of fitness. He later had spells with Preston, Oldham and Walsall without rediscovering the form he had produced for the Wanderers. Ricketts rejoined Walsall for a third spell in 2008, scoring nine goals that season, and began 2009–10 season at Tranmere, appearing as a substitute against the Wanderers in a second-round League Cup tie.

played for Tranmere. In his own career, Warrick Rimmer bridged the gap between the Wanderers' slump of the 1960s and the long haul back to the top flight during the 1970s. He was selected for Cheshire Boys and in 1956 played five times for England Boys before signing for Bolton as an amateur, aged 15. He went on to represent England Youth at both amateur and professional level and turned full-time with the Wanderers in March 1958. His first-team debut came in the club's first ever League Cup tie, in October 1960 at Hull, and he quickly won a regular place in the half-back line. In 1961–62 he was ever-present in Division One and in the years that followed he became a firm favourite, with his strong tackling and no-nonsense approach to the game. He twice suffered relegation with the Wanderers, but in 1973 he captained the club as they won the

	League		FA Cup		FL Cup		Total	
	A	G	A	G	A	G	A	G
2000–01	25/17	21	2/2	2	-/1	1	27/20	24
2001–02	26/11	12	1/1	1	-/3	2	27/15	15
2002–03	13/9	6	1	1	-	-	14/9	7
	64/37	39	4/3	4	-/4	3	68/44	46

WARWICK RIMMER

Born: Birkenhead, 1 March 1941
Warwick Rimmer had football in his blood – he was the nephew of former Sheffield Wednesday and England player Ellis Rimmer and the son of Syd Rimmer, who

Third Division Championship, and that year he was awarded a testimonial against Burnley. Rimmer played his last game for the club in December 1974, a 3–1 home win over Oxford, and the following March he joined Crewe Alexandra. He went on to play 128 games for the Gresty Road club, which was followed by a spell as manager. He left in 1979 and became coach to the Sierra Leone national side, but on his return to England he concentrated on the commercial side. Rimmer rejoined the Wanderers in 1981 and in 1983 became commercial manager at Tranmere. He founded the Rovers' youth section in 1987 and has had a successful career producing a number of players who have progressed through the ranks at Prenton Park.

	League		FA Cup		FL Cup		Total	
	A	G	A	G	A	G	A	G
1960–61	20	-	-	-	2	-	22	-
1961–62	42	2	1	-	1	-	44	2
1962–63	40	2	1	-	-	-	41	2
1963–64	24	2	2	-	1	-	27	2
1964–65	42	1	3	-	1	-	46	1
1965–66	42	3	3	-	2	-	47	3
1966–67	40/2	3	3	-	1	-	44/2	3
1967–68	24	2	1	-	1	-	26	2
1968–69	19/3	2	-	-	-	-	19/3	2
1969–70	36	-	1	-	4	-	41	-
1970–71	27/1	-	1	-	2	-	30/1	-
1971–72	39	-	2	-	6	-	47	-
1972–73	42	-	9	-	2	-	53	-
1973–74	23	-	3	-	5	-	31	-
1974–75	2/1	-	-	-	1	-	3/1	-
	462/7	17	30	-	29	-	521/7	17

JOHN RITSON

Born: Liverpool, 6 September 1949
John Ritson served his apprenticeship with the Wanderers, playing in the A team and reserves regularly and turning professional in September 1966. His first-team debut came in a 1–0 reverse at Queen's Park Rangers in October 1967, Ritson playing in the number-seven shirt left by Francis Lee,

who had joined Manchester City. Although capable of playing in midfield, it was at right-back that Ritson came to the fore, and in 1968 he became a regular in the side. After missing the early part of the 1972–73 season through injury, Ritson returned to become a member of the Third Division Championship-winning team. The following season he missed just one game as the Wanderers consolidated their place in Division Two, and he was later appointed captain. In 1976 Ritson struggled with injury but played a part in helping the club return to the top flight two years later. Known for his powerful shot, two of his goals during the 1977–78 season – a third-round FA Cup replay success against Tottenham at Burnden and a winner in a League game at Mansfield Town – were priceless. Unfortunately, he failed to make an appearance in the First Division, his last game for the club coming in the Second Division Championship-winning game against Fulham, and in September 1978 he moved to Bury for £25,000. Ritson played 41 games for the

Gigg Lane side before returning to the Wanderers on a non-contract basis, playing a handful of reserve games before returning to local football.

	League		FA Cup		FL Cup		Total	
	A	G	A	G	A	G	A	G
1967–68	7/2	-	-	-	1	-	8/2	-
1968–69	29	-	2	-	1	-	32	-
1969–70	39	-	1	-	4	-	44	-
1970–71	32	1	1	-	2	-	35	1
1971–72	32	1	3	1	6	-	41	2
1972–73	37/1	-	8	2	-	-	45/1	2
1973–74	41	2	3	-	4	-	48	2
1974–75	38	1	2	-	2	-	42	1
1975–76	32	3	6	-	1	-	39	3
1976–77	15	-	-	-	2	-	17	-
1977–78	19	1	4	1	1	-	24	2
	321/3	9	30	4	24	-	375/3	13

FRANK ROBERTS

Born: Sandbach, 3 April 1893
Died: Crewe, 23 May 1961

Frank Roberts would almost certainly have been a member of the Wanderers successful Cup sides of the 1920s but for his insistence on taking over the management of licensed premises in 1922, which was against club rules. He had begun his career with Sandbach Villa and Sandbach Ramblers before joining Crewe. Roberts had been a regular in the side at

either inside-forward or centre-forward and the Wanderers paid £200 to secure him in May 1914. He made his First Division debut the following October, spearheading the Wanderers' attack with Joe Smith as they reached the FA Cup semi-finals. During the war Roberts served in the North Lancashire Regiment and guested for West Ham United, scoring 18 goals in 20 appearances. In the first season of peacetime football he was Bolton's leading goalscorer and in 1920–21 was ever present as the club finished third in the First Division. Between them, Roberts and Smith scored 62 goals, Smith being the Division's highest scorer. The arrival of David Jack added another dimension to Bolton's attacking options, but for Roberts it all went sour in 1922 when he was suspended. He joined Manchester City in October 1922 for £3,400 and was their leading scorer in 1925, 1926 and 1928. He played in the 1926 FA Cup Final against the Wanderers and helped City win promotion to the First Division in 1928. He concluded his time at City with 130 goals in 237 games along with four England appearances. In June 1929 Roberts joined Manchester Central and ended his career with Horwich RMI before becoming a licensee.

	League		FA Cup		Total	
	A	G	A	G	A	G
1914–15	28	10	7	-	35	10
1919–20	40	26	1	-	41	26
1920–21	42	24	1	-	43	24
1921–22	39	18	2	1	41	19
1922–23	8	1	-	-	8	1
	157	79	11	1	168	80

JOHN ROBERTS

Born: Swansea, 30 May 1918
Died: 2001

John (Jackie) Roberts joined the Wanderers from his only junior club, Cwmburia, in

	League		FA Cup		Total	
	A	G	A	G	A	G
1937–38	1	-	-	-	1	-
1938–39	17	8	2	-	19	8
1946–47	32	6	1	-	33	6
1947–48	37	-	1	-	38	-
1948–49	36	2	2	-	38	2
1949–50	37	3	3	-	40	3
1950–51	2	-	-	-	2	-
	162	19	9	-	171	19

WALTER ROWLEY

Born: Little Hulton, 14 April 1891
Died: Shrewsbury, 22 March 1976

Walter Rowley spent all his working life in football, including 38 years with the Wanderers as player, coach and manager. He began with local sides Farnworth Wednesday, Walkden Wednesday and Little Hulton Wednesday, playing at half-back or centre-half. His first professional club was Oldham Athletic, where he spent two seasons in the reserves. Rowley joined the Wanderers in August 1912 and made his League debut as a centre-half in

April 1936, having represented Wales at schoolboy level, and made his League debut in February 1938. He played at inside-forward against Sunderland at Burnden and it was in that position that he made most of his appearances the following season. He hit a purple patch, scoring six goals in as many games, including a hat-trick against Everton. During the war Roberts served with the 53rd Field Regiment (RA), playing a number of games abroad and guesting for Norwich City. In May 1944 he was caught in the blast of an enemy shell while serving in Italy. He returned to Bolton and recovered to play in some of the Football League North games during 1945–46. In 1946–47 he was switched to right-back when Lol Hamlett moved to centre-half. Roberts became a consistent performer in that position and was awarded the captaincy. His only Welsh international appearance came in May 1949 against Belgium in Liege. He played the opening two games of 1950–51, but the arrival of John Ball limited his appearances. In September 1950 Roberts signed for Swansea, making 16 League appearances before joining Llanelli, continuing to work in a Swansea steel works.

February 1913 at West Brom. He helped the club to reach the FA Cup semi-finals in 1915. He guested for Port Vale during the war and returned to the Wanderers afterwards. He was 12th man for the 1923 FA Cup Final, having just completed a six-week suspension for being sent off in the fifth round against Huddersfield Town. In May 1925 injury forced Rowley to retire from playing, and he was appointed coach to the reserves, succeeding Fred Scotchbrook. Rowley continued to work behind the scenes until 1945, when he was appointed secretary-manager after Charles Foweraker's retirement. Rowley retired in 1950 through ill-health but later recovered to manage both Middlesbrough, from 1952 to 1954, and Shrewsbury Town, from 1955 until 1957. He was made a life member of Bolton Wanderers (see 'Managers').

	League		FA Cup		Total	
	A	G	A	G	A	G
1912–13	9	-	-	-	9	-
1913–14	24	1	3	-	27	1
1914–15	29	1	7	-	36	1
1919–20	26	2	-	-	26	2
1920–21	16	1	-	-	16	1
1921–22	13	1	1	-	14	1
1922–23	33	1	5	-	38	1
1923–24	14	-	-	-	14	-
1924–25	11	-	-	-	11	-
	175	7	16	-	191	7

MARK SEAGRAVES

Born: Bootle, 22 October 1966

Mark Seagraves began his career at Liverpool, where he came through the Anfield youth system to win England Youth honours but failed to reach the first team in the Football League. The centre-half did appear in both major Cup competitions but made his League bow while on loan at Norwich City in November 1986. In September 1987 Manchester City paid £100,000 to take him to Maine Road, and he went on to play 42 League games before Phil Neal secured his signature in September 1990 for an identical fee. Seagraves made his Wanderers debut in a 2–1 defeat at Wigan Athletic and became a regular in the side, where he partnered both Alan Stubbs and Mark Winstanley for the rest of the season. Seagraves was a member of the side that won promotion from Division Two in 1993 and also scored against his former club Liverpool in an FA Cup third-round tie at Burnden. Injury kept him out for a large proportion of the 1994–95 promotion season but he played in the League Cup Final at Wembley against Liverpool. His final game for the club came in May 1995, at Stoke City, and the following June he moved to Swindon Town for £100,000. He helped them win the Second Division Championship in 1996 and went on to play 61 League games before ending his career at Barrow. Seagraves remained in the game as a coach, assisting Blackpool, and in 2006 he joined Wigan as coach. In November 2007 he followed manager Paul Jewell to Derby County until resigning in December 2008. In 2009 Seagraves rejoined the Wanderers as a scout.

	League		FA Cup		FL Cup		Sherpa Van Trophy		Anglo–Italian Cup		Total	
	A	G	A	G	A	G	A	G	A	G	A	G
1990–91	35	-	2	-	1	-	1	-	-	-	39	-
1991–92	39/1	1	6	-	2	-	2	-	-	-	49/1	1
1992–93	36/1	5	5	1	2	-	3	-	-	-	46/1	6
1993–94	32/3	1	4	-	1	-	-	-	4	1	41/3	2
1994–95	13	-	-	-	2	-	-	-	-	-	15	-
	155/5	7	17	1	8	-	6	-	4	1	190/5	9

JIMMY SEDDON

Born: Bolton, 20 May 1895
Died: October 1971

Jimmy Seddon was yet another of the club's local 'finds' in the Golden Twenties who went on to gain three FA Cup-winners' medals with the club. He began his football career with Trinity School and Hamilton Central, and it was while at the railway station in 1913 going to play for Hamilton that Seddon was asked to play for the Wanderers' reserves, who were a man short. He accepted and made his League debut in February 1914 against Middlesbrough at Burnden, giving a penalty away for handball. The central-defender served his country for three and a half years in France during the war and contracted trench foot, an affliction that was to trouble him throughout his career. He did not turn professional until 1919, leaving his job in a local mill and going on to become a regular in the side for the next 13 years. In 1923, after collecting his first FA Cup-winners' medal, Seddon was selected as England's centre-half against France in Paris. He went on to win six caps, but the peak of his career came when he captained the Wanderers to their 1929 FA Cup success against Portsmouth. The last of his Bolton appearances came in January 1932 at Middlesbrough, and later that year he became coach at Dordrecht. In 1935 he took a similar post with Altrincham. A year later Seddon joined Southport and after the war was trainer to Liverpool reserves. His son, Ken, played for Liverpool before becoming a League referee. After retiring from the game Seddon became manager of the Scarisbrick Hotel in Southport.

	League		FA Cup		Total	
	A	G	A	G	A	G
1913–14	1	-	-	-	1	-
1914–15	6	-	-	-	6	-
1919–20	24	1	1	-	25	1
1920–21	32	2	1	-	33	2
1921–22	27	-	1	-	28	-
1922–23	16	-	6	-	22	-
1923–24	29	-	3	-	32	-
1924–25	35	-	3	-	38	-
1925–26	29	-	8	-	37	-
1926–27	35	1	3	-	38	1
1927–28	21	-	-	-	21	-
1928–29	26	-	8	1	34	1
1929–30	32	-	1	-	33	-
1930–31	21	-	3	-	24	-
1931–32	3	-	-	-	3	-
	337	4	38	1	375	5

ALBERT SHEPHERD

Born: Great Lever, 10 September 1885
Died: 8 November 1929

Centre-forward Albert Shepherd became only the second Boltonian to win an England cap while playing for the Wanderers when he scored England's goal in a 2–1 defeat by Scotland in April 1906. He had started his footballing career with Bolton Schools, St Mark's and Bolton Temperance before joining Blackburn Rovers. He had failed to make an appearance for them and in 1902 signed for Bolton. The Wanderers saw his potential but allowed him to join local side St Luke's, where his scoring record persuaded Bolton to give him a professional contract in 1904. Shepherd made his League debut in a 5–1 win over Gainsborough Trinity, and he quickly made the centre-forward position his own. In his first season he helped the Wanderers to win promotion from the Second Division. In 1905–06 Shepherd set the First Division alight with 26 goals, which included four in each game against Nottingham Forest and Sunderland at Burnden. His form earned him

international recognition, but injury dogged him in 1906–07, although his goal ratio was still one of the best. In 1907–08 he struck 25 League goals but could not prevent the club from being relegated. Bolton supporters never really appreciated him, and his decision to join Newcastle United after a poor start to the season resulted in him receiving abuse from supporters. His final game for Bolton came in November 1908, and he scored his side's goal in a 1–1 draw. Shepherd went on to lead Newcastle's scoring charts in 1909 and 1910, and in 1911 he was top not just of the Toon's but of the First Division's goal tally. He won the Championship with Newcastle in 1909 and scored both goals to help them win the 1910 FA Cup Final against Barnsley. In that game he became the first player to score a penalty in an FA Cup Final. Shepherd scored 74 goals in 104 League games on Tyneside and won another international cap before joining Bradford City in 1914, where he scored 10 goals in 22 League games before ending his career. He returned to Bolton, where he became a publican until his death.

	League		FA Cup		Total	
	A	G	A	G	A	G
1904–05	24	15	4	2	28	17
1905–06	31	26	1	-	32	26
1906–07	21	16	3	3	24	19
1907–08	29	25	-	-	29	25
1908–09	10	3	-	-	10	3
	115	85	8	5	123	90

BARRY SIDDALL

Born: Ellesmere Port, 12 September 1954

Barry Siddall became an apprentice with the Wanderers in 1970, having appeared for the club's Central League side while still at school. He was part of the successful youth set-up and came from the area that also produced Paul Jones and Neil Whatmore during the same period. Siddall

McDonagh. Siddall's last game for the club came in a 1–1 draw at Plymouth Argyle in September 1976, and he signed for Sunderland for a fee of £80,000. He made 167 League appearances for the Wearsiders and, after a loan spell at Darlington, joined Port Vale in August 1982, where he helped them win promotion from the Fourth Division. Loan spells at Blackpool and Stoke City followed before a permanent move to Stoke for £20,000 in March 1985. While there he was sent on loan to Tranmere Rovers and Manchester City, and in July 1986 he signed for Blackpool, where he played 110 League games and made his 500th League appearance in January 1988. Siddall later played for Stockport County, Hartlepool United, Carlisle United, Chester City and Preston North End, where he ended his League career in 1993. He later played for Northwich Victoria and Horwich RMI before becoming a freelance goalkeeping coach.

	League	FA Cup	FL Cup	Total
	A	A	A	A
1972–73	4	-	-	4
1973–74	42	3	5	50
1974–75	42	2	2	46
1975–76	42	6	1	49
1976–77	7	-	2	9
	137	11	10	158

JOE SMITH

Born: Dudley, 25 June 1889
Died: Blackpool, 11 August 1971

Inside-forward Joe Smith was Bolton's most consistent goalscorer until Nat Lofthouse, and his 38 League goals in 1920–21, which equalled Bert Freeman's League total, remain a club record. Smith had played for Crewe as a youth and was with Newcastle St Luke's when he was awoken one August morning in 1908 by Bolton trainer George Eccles. Smith was

became understudy to the experienced Charlie Wright and in January 1972 turned professional, winning England Youth honours and making his League debut at Walsall in October 1972. He became first-choice 'keeper at the end of the 1972–73 season after Wright's retirement and made an impact on the club's return to the Second Division. Siddall went on to play 133 consecutive League games for the Wanderers, a record only beaten by three other players, including his successor Jim

offered 50s (£2.50) a week to sign, and he made his League debut at West Brom in April 1909. His left-wing partnership with Ted Vizard played a major part in the Wanderers' success in that era. Smith helped the club reach the FA Cup semi-finals in 1915 and during the war struck 48 goals in 51 in unofficial games. He guested for Port Vale and Chelsea, along with Vizard, while serving in the RAF and in 1918 they helped the Londoners win the London v Lancashire Cup Final. Smith, who won his first England cap in February 1913, continued his international career after the war but was limited to five appearances overall, but he toured South Africa with the FA in 1920. Smith's greatest honour came in 1923 when he was the first FA Cup Final captain to receive the trophy at Wembley. Three years later he lifted the trophy again, but his career at the club was coming to an end. After leading the club's scoring charts for the sixth time, he joined Stockport County in March 1927 for £1,000. He scored 61 goals in 69 League games for County and in 1929 became player-manager at Darwen. There he scored 42 goals in 51 games and guided

them to the Lancashire Combination Championship on two occasions. Smith then had a short spell with Manchester Central before being appointed manager at Reading in July 1931. In his four seasons there they never finished outside the top four in the Third Division South, and in August 1935 he became Blackpool's manager, a position he held until April 1958. He won promotion to Division One in 1937 and took the club to three FA Cup Finals in 1948, 1951 and 1953, the latter being the most notable for their success against the Wanderers.

	League		FA Cup		Total	
	A	G	A	G	A	G
1908–09	1	-	-	-	1	-
1909–10	6	-	-	-	6	-
1910–11	32	11	1	-	33	11
1911–12	37	22	3	2	40	24
1912–13	33	22	1	-	34	22
1913–14	35	17	3	4	38	21
1914–15	38	29	7	7	45	36
1919–20	27	18	1	-	28	18
1920–21	41	38	1	-	42	38
1921–22	39	18	2	-	41	18
1922–23	37	17	7	2	44	19
1923–24	39	16	3	-	42	16
1924–25	36	24	3	2	39	26
1925–26	36	15	8	6	44	21
1926–27	12	7	3	-	15	7
	449	254	43	23	492	277

JOHN SMITH

Born: Pollockshaws, 2 April 1895
Died: Cardiff, September 1946

John Reid 'Jack' Smith arrived at Burnden in November 1922 from Glasgow Rangers as a replacement centre-forward for Frank Roberts, who had joined Manchester City. Smith had begun his career with Battlefield Juniors and Albion Rovers before joining Kilmarnock, where he had helped them claim the Scottish FA Cup in 1920 by scoring the winning goal. He had a disagreement with Kilmarnock and joined Cowdenbeath, where he scored 45 goals during 1921–22, taking them to the runners'-up spot in the Second Division. Rangers paid £3,000 to take him to Ibrox and he scored on his debut in a 2–0 win over Alloa in August 1922. Smith played only two more games for Rangers, and Bolton were quick to secure his signature. He scored an 89th-minute winner against Manchester City on his debut and Bolton's second goal in the 1923 FA Cup Final defeat of West Ham. Smith gained a reputation for being a 'crock' due to the fact he always appeared to be limping, but he continued to get his fair share of the goals to compliment the likes of Joe Smith and David Jack. He won another FA Cup-winners' medal in 1926, but the arrival of Harold Blackmore gave the club more depth in the striking department and in March 1928 Smith joined Bury for £1,500. Jim McClelland joined the club from Middlesbrough at the same time. At Bury, Smith scored a hat-trick on his debut against Sheffield Wednesday, and he went on to score 108 goals in 157

League games for the Shakers before joining Rochdale in August 1933. He ended his career at Ashton National. In 1939 Smith was appointed assistant trainer at Cardiff City, who were being managed by ex-Wanderer Billy Jennings.

| | League | | FA Cup | | Total | |
	A	G	A	G	A	G
1922–23	22	7	7	2	29	9
1923–24	32	17	3	4	35	21
1924–25	21	13	3	-	24	13
1925–26	22	12	8	4	30	16
1926–27	32	13	4	4	36	17
1927–28	18	10	2	1	20	11
	147	72	27	15	174	87

JOHN SOMERVILLE

Born: Ayr
Died: 1917

John Somerville formed part of the Wanderers' immaculate defensive line up of the 1890s, which invariably read Sutcliffe, Somerville and Jones. His performances at right-back earned him the name 'Johnny Surefoot'. Somerville had started out with Ayr Parkhouse and had joined the Wanderers in March 1890, making his debut

in a Good Friday match against Celtic, which Bolton won 4–0 despite starting with only 10 players. His first League appearance came on the opening day of the 1890–91 season in a 4–2 win against Notts County at Pikes Lane. He played in the 1894 FA Cup Final and the very first League game at Burnden Park in 1895. Somerville was a member of the side that won promotion in 1899 and remained a regular until April 1901, his last game being a 3–2 success at Everton. During 1898 he was appointed secretary after Frank Brettell had left to join Spurs, and he continued in that role alongside his playing duties until his retirement from the football field. He then became the club's first secretary-manager in 1908 (see 'Managers').

	League		FA Cup		Total	
	A	G	A	G	A	G
1890–91	19	-	1	-	20	-
1891–92	26	-	2	-	28	-
1892–93	26	-	2	-	28	-
1893–94	25	-	4	-	29	-
1894–95	29	1	3	-	32	1
1895–96	29	-	5	-	34	-
1896–97	28	-	4	-	32	-
1897–98	29	-	4	-	33	-
1898–99	25	-	2	-	27	-
1899–1900	20	1	-	-	20	1
1900–01	9	-	1	-	10	-
	265	2	28	-	293	2

GARY SPEED

Born: Mancot, 8 September 1969
Welsh international midfielder Gary Speed joined the Wanderers for a £750,000 fee from Newcastle United in July 2004 and appeared in every Premier League game the following season to help the club secure a sixth-place finish. His career had started with Leeds United, making his debut at 19 years old, and he became a member of the side that won the League Championship in 1992. He played 248 League games for Leeds, scoring 39 goals before moving to Everton, who he had supported as a youngster, in July 1996 for £3.5 million. He played 58 League games for the Goodison club before joining Newcastle United for £5.5 million in February 1998. While on Tyneside Speed helped them reach the FA Cup Final in both 1998 and 1999 and qualify for the Champions League in 2002. He played 213 League games before making his move to the Reebok Stadium. Speed made his Bolton debut in a 4–1 home success against Charlton Athletic on the opening day of the 2004–05 season, and in December 2006 became the first player to reach 500 Premier League appearances when he played in the Wanderers' 4–0 victory over West Ham United. In August 2007 he scored the opening goal against Reading at the Reebok to keep up his record of having scored in every Premier League season, a record he shared with Ryan Giggs at the time. After having a spell as player-coach under Sammy Lee, Speed returned to playing and made his final

start in a Bolton shirt in the 1–0 UEFA Cup win against Red Star Belgrade in December 2007. His last appearance came as a substitute in the Wanderers' 4–1 win over Wigan Athletic the following weekend in what was the club's 100th Premier League win. In January 2008 Speed joined Sheffield United, initially on loan, before making a £250,000 move, and he made 29 League appearances before a back injury forced him out. He took over a coaching role and was a member of their staff when the club reached the Play-off Finals in 2009. In August 2010 he was appointed manager at Bramall Lane. Speed won 85 full caps for Wales, a record only bettered by Neville Southall, and he retired from international football in 2004 after losing to Poland in a World Cup qualifier. In December 2010 he left his post at Sheffield United to become the Welsh international manager.

	League		FA Cup		FL Cup		UEFA Cup		Total	
	A	G	A	G	A	G	A	G	A	G
2004–05	37/1	1	2	-	-	-	-	-	39/1	1
2005–06	29/2	4	2	-	2	-	2/3	-	35/5	4
2006–07	38	8	2	-	2	-	-	-	42	8
2007–08	11/3	1	-	-	-	-	3	-	14/3	1
	115/6	14	6	-	4	-	5/3	-	130/9	14

DENNIS STEVENS

Born: Dudley, 30 November 1933

Dennis Stevens was only 15 years old when he was signed by the Wanderers after being spotted playing for Worcestershire Boys. He came from the same area that had produced the great Joe Smith and was a cousin of the late Duncan Edwards. Stevens turned professional in 1950 and made his League debut at Preston in September 1953. He became a regular at inside-forward after Harold Hassall was forced to retire through injury and went on to represent the Football League. Stevens also won two England Under-23 caps, but although he was selected for the full England squad in 1957 he failed to win a full cap. He was a member of Bolton's 1958 FA Cup-winning side and, in 1959–60, was the club's leading goalscorer after taking over at centre-forward from the injured Nat Lofthouse. Steven's 100th goal for the club came in January 1962 against Cardiff at Burnden but, in March 1962, Bolton accepted a fee of £35,000 from Everton for his transfer, which at the time was the club's largest fee received. He went on to play 120 League games for the Toffees and won a League Championship medal in 1963. In December 1965 he moved to Oldham Athletic, and then in March 1967 he joined Tranmere Rovers, where he helped them win promotion to Division Three. Stevens retired from the game in 1968 when a back injury forced him to quit, and he returned to Bolton to open a gents' outfitters in the Harwood area of the town. He continues to be a regular at the Reebok.

	League		FA Cup		FL Cup		Total	
	A	G	A	G	A	G	A	G
1953–54	12	4	6	1	-	-	18	5
1954–55	14	3	2	-	-	-	16	3
1955–56	39	13	2	1	-	-	41	14
1956–57	39	13	1	-	-	-	40	13
1957–58	37	13	7	3	-	-	44	16
1958–59	32	13	5	-	-	-	37	13
1959–60	39	14	3	1	-	-	42	15
1960–61	31	10	3	2	5	1	39	13
1961–62	30	7	1	1	2	1	33	9
	273	90	30	9	7	2	310	101

DAVID STOKES

Born: Ketley, 1880
Died: Unknown

David Stokes represented the Wanderers for almost 20 years, including a period that straddled World War One. He began with Kingswinford Albion, Wordsley Olympic and Halesowen before joining Brierley Hill Alliance. Both Aston Villa and Small Heath sought his signature, and he joined Villa on Birmingham & District League forms. Although he was on Villa's books, he continued to play for Brierley Hill, and in

December 1901 the Wanderers signed the winger. Villa reported the Wanderers to the League for poaching, but it was ruled that Villa had to give Stokes a free transfer because he was not signed on Football League forms and the Wanderers were fined 10 guineas. Stokes made his Bolton debut in February 1902 on the right wing and scored his first goal the following month against Aston Villa. He made the right-wing position his own and appeared in the 1904 FA Cup Final for the club. In October that year he played for the Football League in Belfast and missed only two games as the Wanderers won promotion to Division One in 1905. He was ever present in 1905–06 and 1907–08, and in 1909 he won a Second Division Championship medal as well as collecting further representative honours. Stokes was in the Bolton team for a third promotion success in 1911, but his position was then challenged by Alec Donaldson. During the war Stokes worked in a local munitions factory and in November 1919, at the age of 39, he returned to the Wanderers' League side. He played his final game for the club in April 1920 before returning to his old club, Brierley Hill Alliance. In September that year Wolves brought him back into the Football League and he made seven League appearances in the Second Division side during 1920–21 at the age of 40.

	League		FA Cup		Total	
	A	G	A	G	A	G
1901–02	12	2	-	-	12	2
1902–03	16	3	-	-	16	3
1903–04	32	8	6	-	38	8
1904–05	32	5	4	1	36	6
1905–06	38	6	1	-	39	6
1906–07	33	5	4	1	37	6
1907–08	38	1	5	1	43	2
1908–09	34	1	1	-	35	1
1909–10	24	1	-	-	24	1
1910–11	34	3	1	-	35	3

1911–12	37	3	3	-	40	3
1912–13	18	-	1	-	19	-
1913–14	7	1	-	-	7	1
1914–15	21	3	7	-	28	3
1919–20	11	1	-	-	11	1
	387	43	33	3	420	46

ALAN STUBBS

Born: Kirkby, 6 October 1971

Alan Stubbs came through the Wanderers' youth ranks in the late 1980s, proving his versatility by playing for the reserves at full-back, midfield and centre-half. He made his Bolton debut as a substitute in a 1–0 home defeat to Bradford City in the Third Division on the opening day of September 1990. Three days later he made his full debut as a centre-half, scoring a goal in a 2–1 home League Cup win against Huddersfield Town. He became a regular at the back end of the season after Mark Winstanley suffered injury, and he played in the Play-off Final defeat to Tranmere at Wembley. Stubbs spent most of the following season in midfield but was back in the centre of defence for the promotion from Division Two in 1993, being absent for only four games. He quickly made the transition to the higher level and scored some vital FA Cup goals in 1994, one coming in a 3–2 third-round replay success against his boyhood club, Everton, at

Goodison and a fifth-round winner against Aston Villa at Burnden. His only international honour came in May 1994 when he won an England B cap against Northern Ireland at Hillsborough. Stubbs played in both the 1995 League Cup Final defeat and the Play-off success against Reading, forming defensive partnerships with Simon Coleman, Mark Seagraves and Gudni Bergsson throughout the season. His final game for the club came in the last game of the 1995–96 season, the club's first season in the Premier League, a 2–1 defeat at Arsenal, who were managed at the time by Stubbs's former boss Bruce Rioch. In July 1996 Stubbs joined Celtic for £3.5 million, winning the League in 1998 and 2000, and he twice beat testicular cancer during his time north of the border. He played 106 League games for the Glasgow club before joining Everton at the end of his contract in July 2001. Stubbs was a consistent performer for the Toffees and clocked up 124 Premier League appearances before joining Sunderland in August 2005. His stay on Wearside was short and after 10 League games he returned to Everton, helping them to qualify for the UEFA Cup. In January 2008 he moved to Derby County, playing nine games before retiring from the game in August 2008 with a recurring knee injury. The following month he was back at Goodison as a coach, assisting with the reserves and Under-18 sides.

	League		FA Cup		FL Cup		Sherpa Van Trophy		Anglo–Italian Cup		Total	
	A	G	A	G	A	G	A	G	A	G	A	G
1990–91	19/7	-	-	-	2	1	-	-	-	-	21/7	1
1991–92	26/6	1	3/2	-	4	-	1	-	-	-	34/8	1
1992–93	37/5	2	2	-	4	2	1/1	-	-	-	44/6	4
1993–94	41	1	8	2	4	-	-	-	4	-	57	3
1994–95	40/2	1	1	-	6	1	-	-	-	-	47/2	2
1995–96	24/1	4	2	-	3	-	-	-	-	-	29/1	4
	187/21	9	16/2	2	23	4	2/1	-	4	-	232/24	15

JOHN SUTCLIFFE

Born: Shibden, 14 April 1868
Died: Bradford, 7 July 1947

John Sutcliffe was a capable all-round sportsman, beginning his career in rugby union, where he played at either centre three-quarter or full-back for both Bradford and Heckmondwike. He won an England cap against New Zealand in 1889, but when Heckmondwike were suspended from the RFU for professionalism Sutcliffe turned to football, joining the Wanderers to strengthen the forward line. He was the fastest player in the team over 120 and 440 yards, a fact he proved in the club's sports day in 1890. He also had the best batting average for Great Lever cricket club. Sutcliffe had started for Bolton in the reserves, his first match coming against Accrington. His rugby instincts were obvious and he switched to goalkeeper. He made his League debut in a 7–0 win against West Brom at Pikes Lane in December 1889. The following year Sutcliffe became the club's regular custodian, brushing aside all challengers to the position for the following 11 years. In

March 1893 he made the first of five England appearances in a 6–0 win over Wales, becoming one of only three players to win England honours at both rugby and association football. He was fortunate to always be on the winning side for his country. He also represented the Football League on three occasions. Sutcliffe played for Bolton in the 1894 FA Cup Final defeat, in the first game at Burnden Park, and in January 1902 he became the first Bolton player to be sent off at Burnden Park, for showing dissent in a game against Sheffield Wednesday. After problems over his wages and a benefit, he joined Millwall Athletic in the Southern League for £400 in May 1902, helping them reach the FA Cup semi-finals the following year. In May 1903 he joined Manchester United after his request to rejoin the Wanderers was turned down. He played 21 League games for United and a year later moved to Plymouth Argyle, where he played 166 Southern League games before becoming coach at Southend United in 1911. Sutcliffe moved abroad to coach at Arnhem in 1914 and after the war he became trainer at Bradford City for a spell. His brother, Charles, who was 22 years younger, kept goal for Leeds City, Rotherham and Sheffield United.

	League A	FA Cup A	Total A
1889–90	2	-	2
1890–91	18	1	19
1891–92	26	2	28
1892–93	30	2	32
1893–94	29	5	34
1894–95	29	3	32
1895–96	28	5	33
1896–97	27	3	30
1897–98	25	4	29
1898–99	31	2	33
1899–1900	33	1	34
1900–01	26	2	28
1901–02	28	2	30
	332	32	364

GEORGE TAYLOR

Born: Ashton-under-Lyne, 23 April 1908
Died: Unknown

George Taylor served Bolton Wanderers for over 50 years as a player, coach and scout. He joined the club as an amateur in February 1926, having played for his native Ashton-under-Lyne team and Lancashire Schoolboys. He had won England Schoolboy honours against Wales and had captained the side against Scotland. After leaving school he had served his apprenticeship as a plumber and signed for Bolton in a disused tramcar in a tram shed where his father worked. Taylor made his League debut in April 1931 at Blackpool, where he appeared at inside-left. After some useful performances in the reserves, he made that position his own in the first team. An ankle injury kept him out of the whole of the 1932–33 season, when Bolton were relegated, but two years later he missed only one game as they returned to the top flight. During 1935–36 Taylor was chosen as a reserve for the full England

team and in 1938 injury robbed him of an appearance for the Football League side. When war broke out he became a sergeant-instructor in the Army PT Corps, assisting the Wanderers whenever he could. He played his last game for the club in December 1945 in a Football League North war game at Stoke and was later appointed coach. Taylor became chief coach, a position he held when Bolton won the FA Cup in 1958, and in 1967 he was awarded a testimonial for his long service. Even after retirement he continued to work for the club on a part-time basis.

	League		FA Cup		Total	
	A	G	A	G	A	G
1930–31	2	-	-	-	2	-
1931–32	9	2	2	-	11	2
1932–33	-	-	-	-	-	-
1933–34	37	-	5	-	42	-
1934–35	41	-	8	-	49	-
1935–36	34	-	2	-	36	-
1936–37	31	-	4	-	35	-
1937–38	37	1	1	-	38	1
1938–39	29	-	2	-	31	-
	220	3	24	-	244	3

GORDON TAYLOR OBE

Born: Ashton-under-Lyne, 28 December 1944

Gordon Taylor was destined to play for the Wanderers as he had supported the club as a boy, while his grandfather was a season ticket holder. As a schoolboy he scored 97 goals in a season, representing Ashton Boys in the run to the sixth round of the English Schools Trophy, playing at inside-forward. He also made three appearances for Lancashire Boys, and clubs such as Manchester United and Arsenal began to make overtures for his signature. He joined Bolton as a youth player and signed professional forms in January 1962, making his League debut in March 1963 at Wolves. After a seven-game spell in

	League		FA Cup		FL Cup		Total	
	A	G	A	G	A	G	A	G
1962–63	1	-	-	-	-	-	1	-
1963–64	24	6	3	1	2	-	29	7
1964–65	42	5	3	-	1	-	46	5
1965–66	37/1	9	3	-	2	-	42/1	9
1966–67	32	2	2	-	1	-	35	2
1967–68	41	9	1	1	3	2	45	12
1968–69	29	5	2	-	1	1	32	6
1969–70	28/3	3	-	-	1	-	29/3	3
1970–71	19/1	2	-	-	3	-	22/1	2
	253/5	41	14	2	14	3	281/5	46

JOHN THOMAS

Born: Wednesbury, 5 August 1958

A carpenter by trade, striker John Thomas joined Everton in August 1977 but failed to make the first team. He was loaned out to Tranmere in March 1979 and later that year had a spell with Halifax Town. In June 1980 he was recommended to Bolton by Brian Kidd and he signed on a free transfer, making his debut as a substitute against Orient at Burnden. He replaced Brian Kidd, in the Wanderers' line up towards the end of the 1980–81 season as a run of seven League games without defeat kept the club in the Second Division. Thomas struggled with injury the following season, but he fought back and claimed the distinction of scoring the

1963–64 he was left out of the side, only to return in the New Year at outside-right. He later switched to the left but was more than capable of playing on either wing. Taylor was ever present in 1964–65 as the Wanderers just missed out on an immediate return to the top flight, and he continued to be a regular throughout the late 1960s. His final game for the club came in a 1–0 defeat at Middlesbrough in December 1970, and he was transferred to Birmingham City for £18,000. He helped the St Andrews' club to win promotion to Division One in 1972 and reach the FA Cup semi-finals that year and again in 1975. After 166 League games Taylor returned to the North West when he joined Blackburn Rovers in March 1976. He made 64 League appearances and had a summer spell at Vancouver Whitecaps before ending his playing career with Bury in 1980. He then joined the Professional Footballers' Association on a full-time basis and rose to become the chief executive. In 2008 he was awarded an OBE.

club's 5,000th League goal, which came against Grimsby Town in October 1981. At the end of the season he moved to Chester City on a free transfer. He was the top scorer there, with 21 goals, and in July 1983 he joined Lincoln City for £22,000. Thomas netted 21 goals in 71 games before signing for Preston North End for £15,000 in July 1985. He led the scoring charts at Deepdale as they applied for re-election to the League in 1986 and then won promotion from Division Four in 1987. The Wanderers paid £30,000 to bring him back to Burnden in July 1987 and his 22 goals ensured his second promotion from the basement division in a year. He netted two hat-tricks that season, the goals at Peterborough in January 1988 being the first by a Bolton player on an away ground since Francis Lee in 1967. Thomas appeared at Wembley with the club in the successful 1989 Sherpa Van Trophy Final against Torquay, but that proved to be his last appearance in a Bolton shirt. In July 1989 he joined West Brom for a tribunal set fee of £30,000 but managed only one League goal for the Baggies before rejoining Preston for £50,000. He later had spells with Hartlepool and Halifax Town, where he ended his League career in 1993. Thomas moved into non-League and had a spell with Bamber Bridge, where he played against the Czech Republic prior to the 1996 European Championships in England. He continues to live in Bolton and works as a pre-match host at the club.

ALAN THOMPSON

Born: Newcastle upon Tyne, 22 December 1973

Alan Thompson began his career at Newcastle United, coming through the ranks to make his League debut in November 1991. In all he played 16 times for the Magpies, two appearances coming in 1992–93 as they won the First Division Championship. Capable of playing on the left side of midfield or at left-back, he joined the Wanderers for £250,000 in July 1993, and it proved to be a shrewd signing. Thompson made his Bolton League debut in a scoreless draw at Grimsby in August 1993 and notched his first goal for the club a month later in a 4–3 televised win over Nottingham Forest at Burnden. He scored the Wanderers' goal in their 2–1 reverse to Liverpool in the 1995 League Cup Final and played in the Play-off Final success against Reading the following May. A week after the Play-offs he earned his first taste of international football when he played for England Under–21s against Latvia at Burnley. 'Tomo' scored the Wanderers' first-ever Premier League goal, a penalty conversion in a 3–2 defeat at Wimbledon, and notched some great goals with his sweet

	League		FA Cup		FL Cup		Autoglass Trophy		Total	
	A	G	A	G	A	G	A	G	A	G
1980–81	15/2	5	-	-	-	-	-	-	15/2	5
1981–82	3/2	1	-	-	1	1	-	-	4/2	2
1987–88	43/1	22	2	3	2	1	2/1	2	49/2	28
1988–89	28/1	9	-	-	2	-	4/1	-	34/2	9
	89/6	37	2	3	5	2	6/2	2	102/8	44

left foot as the Wanderers romped to the First Division Championship in 1997. One of his goals that season came in the 4–1 defeat of Charlton in the club's last game at Burnden. He continued his list of firsts by becoming the first player to score at the Reebok Stadium, a converted penalty against Tottenham Hotspur in September 1997. Thompson's last game for the club came in the 2–0 reverse at Chelsea in May 1998 that sent the club down from the Premier League, and that summer he joined Aston Villa for £3 million. He played 46 games at Villa before joining Celtic for £2.75 million in July 2000 and spent almost seven years at Parkhead. During that time he won the Scottish Premier League on four occasions, the Scottish FA Cup three times and the Scottish League Cup twice. He also earned a full England cap against Sweden in 2004. In January 2007 Thompson joined Leeds United on loan, moving permanently in August 2007, but suffered with injury. He had a loan spell at Hartlepool before returning to Elland Road, where he retired in the summer of 2008. In July 2008 he was appointed academy coach at Newcastle United and in June 2010 he returned to Celtic as first-team coach.

	League		FA Cup		FL Cup		Anglo-Italian Cup		Total	
	A	G	A	G	A	G	A	G	A	G
1993–94	19/8	6	3	1	3/1	-	4/1	1	29/10	8
1994–95	37/3	7	-/1	-	8	2	-	-	45/4	9
1995–96	23/3	1	1	-	5	1	-	-	29/3	2
1996–97	34	11	1/1	1	4	1	-	-	39/1	13
1997–98	33	9	1	-	4	1	-	-	38	10
	146/14	34	6/2	2	24/1	5	4/1	1	180/18	42

PETER THOMPSON

Born: Carlisle, 27 November 1942

Peter Thompson proved to be one of the club's bargain buys when Jimmy Armfield persuaded Liverpool to part with the tricky winger for a fee of £18,000 in January 1974.

Thompson's skilful play and the ease at which he went past defenders won him England Schoolboy honours before he signed for Preston North End in November 1959. He had made 121 League appearances for North End before Bill Shankly took him to Anfield in August 1963. At Liverpool he won a League Championship medal in his first season, an FA Cup-winners' medal in his second and another League Championship in 1966. By this time he had already won England Under-23 and full international honours, although he earned just 16 caps as Alf Ramsey's age of 'wingless wonders' dawned. After playing 323 League games for Liverpool, Thompson found himself languishing in the reserves and he joined the Wanderers on loan in December 1973, when he had been considering retirement from the game. The move revitalised both player and club. Thompson made his debut against Second Division League leaders Sunderland at Burnden in a game played on a Wednesday afternoon due to the power strike, helping the Wanderers to a 1–0 win. He thrilled supporters with his performances and signed permanently the following month, going on to become a regular for the following two seasons and helping the club through an exciting period, which culminated in promotion to Division One. Thompson retired from the game in

April 1978, after a crowd of 20,516 attended his testimonial at Burnden against a combined Liverpool and Everton side. He went on to run a hotel in the Lake District.

	League		FA Cup		FL Cup		Total	
	A	G	A	G	A	G	A	G
1973–74	24	-	3	-	-	-	27	-
1974–75	41	1	2	-	2	-	45	1
1975–76	38	1	5	-	1	-	44	1
1976–77	6/5	-	-	-	1	-	7/5	-
1977–78	2/1	-	-	-	1	-	3/1	-
	111/6	2	10	-	5	-	126/6	2

STEVE THOMPSON

Born: Oldham, 2 November 1964

Steve Thompson was spotted playing for Poulton and joined the Wanderers as an apprentice, turning professional in 1982. He was a member of the reserve side, along with the likes of Neil Redfearn and Warren Joyce, that won promotion in 1982–83. He made his League debut in a scoreless draw at Derby County in November 1982, taking part in three League games as the Wanderers fell from Division Two. The following season he became a regular in midfield, chalking up his first League goal at Bournemouth in November 1983. He was a member of the side that reached Wembley in the Freight

Rover Trophy in 1986 and was the only player with the club to make up for that defeat when he played in the successful Sherpa Van Trophy Final in 1989. In between he suffered relegation to Division Four but missed only two games to help the club win promotion from the basement at the first attempt. He helped the Wanderers to reach the Play-offs in both 1990 and 1991 and was the longest-serving player at the club at that time. Thompson's last game for the Wanderers came in a 1–1 draw at Swansea in August 1991, during which he was sent off for a professional foul. Days later he joined Luton Town for £220,000 but was there only six weeks before moving to Leicester City in a swap deal with Scott Oakes and Des Linton. He played 127 first-class games for City, helping them reach the First Division Play-offs in three successive seasons between 1992 and 1994, the last of which was successful when they defeated Derby County. In February 1995 he joined Burnley for £200,000, playing 49 League games before heading to Rotherham in August 1997. He later had spells at both Halifax Town and Leigh RMI before retiring. Thompson coached at Blackpool's Centre of Excellence and in 2006 became first-team coach. He has since become assistant manager to both Tony Parkes and Ian Holloway.

	League		FA Cup		FL Cup		Sherpa Van Trophy		Total	
	A	G	A	G	A	G	A	G	A	G
1982–83	3	-	-	-	-	-	-	-	3	-
1983–84	40	3	4	-	1	-	1	-	46	3
1984–85	34	4	1	-	4	1	4	-	43	5
1985–86	35	8	1	1	4	-	5	-	45	9
1986–87	41/5	7	5	2	2	-	4	-	52/5	9
1987–88	43/1	7	2	-	2	-	3	-	50/1	7
1988–89	43	9	3	-	2	-	8	2	56	11
1989–90	47	6	1	-	8	1	5	-	61	7
1990–91	48	5	4	1	4	-	2	-	58	6
1991–92	2	-	-	-	-	-	-	-	2	-
	336/6	49	21	4	27	2	32	2	416/6	57

TED VIZARD

Born: Cogan, 7 June 1889
Died: Wolverhampton, 25 December 1973

Outside-left Ted Vizard had a meteoric rise with the Wanderers. He was recommended by an old school-friend and invited for a month's trial. He was signed on in a fortnight and made his League debut within two months. Vizard had begun his footballing career with Barry Town, also playing rugby for Penarth, before coming to Bolton in September 1910. He made his League debut with Bolton the following November against Gainsborough at Burnden. Vizard became a regular in the side for the next 18 seasons and went on to win 22 caps for Wales. The first came in January 1911, only two months after his League debut, and his last in October 1926, when he was 37. During World War One Vizard served in the RAF and guested for Chelsea alongside his Wanderers' teammate Joe Smith, the pair forming a formidable partnership. In February 1919 the management of the Bolton side was placed in the hands of Vizard until normal

League football resumed and Charles Foweraker was appointed. The Welshman was a member of the Wanderers' FA Cup-winning sides of 1923 and 1926, and he made his final appearance for the club in March 1931. He was then 41 years of age, making him the oldest outfield player to have appeared in a first-team game for the club. After retiring from playing he took charge of the club's A team before leaving in April 1933 to take charge of Swindon Town. Vizard took over at Queen's Park Rangers in 1939 but did not manage them in a competitive game due to the outbreak of war. In 1944 he became manager at Wolverhampton Wanderers, taking them to third place in 1947 before being replaced by Stan Cullis in June 1948. He later had a spell in charge at Cradley Heath before managing a pub in Tattenhall.

	League		FA Cup		Total	
	A	G	A	G	A	G
1910–11	23	4	1	-	24	4
1911–12	33	2	3	-	36	2
1912–13	31	3	1	-	32	3
1913–14	31	5	3	-	34	5
1914–15	38	5	7	4	45	9
1919–20	39	4	1	-	40	4
1920–21	29	2	1	-	30	2
1921–22	35	3	2	1	37	4
1922–23	38	2	7	-	45	2
1923–24	40	1	3	-	43	1
1924–25	31	4	3	1	34	5
1925–26	38	13	9	-	47	13
1926–27	29	9	4	-	33	9
1927–28	18	4	-	-	18	4
1928–29	7	3	-	-	7	3
1929–30	4	-	-	-	4	-
1930–31	3	-		-	3	-
	467	64	45	6	512	70

ANDY WALKER

Born: Glasgow, 6 April 1965

The diminutive Scottish striker became a prolific goalscorer during his spell at Burnden Park, forming a formidable

against Huddersfield at Burnden and going on to claim 26 League goals in 32 games as the club stormed to promotion. Walker also scored in the famous FA Cup win at Liverpool, but disaster struck when he suffered a ligament injury against Swansea at Burnden in April 1993. He didn't return to action until the following February, scoring at Highbury in the FA Cup defeat of Arsenal. At the end of the season Walker returned to Celtic for £550,000, helping them win the Scottish FA Cup in 1995. In 1996 he came back to England when Sheffield United paid £500,000 for his signature. He hit 20 goals in 52 games for the Blades and in 1998 had loan spells at both Hibernian and Raith Rovers. He then joined Ayr United and had short spells with Carlisle United, Partick Thistle and Alloa Athletic. Since retiring Walker has worked as a TV pundit and writes a column for the *Sunday Mail*. He also appears in the Masters competitions and has represented both Bolton and Celtic.

partnership with fellow countryman John McGinlay that propelled the club out of the Second Division and onto famous FA Cup victories. Walker had started with Baillieston Juniors and had turned professional with Motherwell in 1984, scoring 17 goals in 77 games before joining Celtic for £350,000 in 1987. There he helped them win the double in his first season, and he earned the first of three full Scottish international caps. However, he could not keep up the form that he produced in that first season at Celtic Park and by 1991 was out of the first team. He had a loan spell at Newcastle United and in January 1992 joined the Wanderers on loan. Walker made his debut as a substitute in a 2–2 draw at Exeter City, scoring the Wanderers' second goal with his first touch. He ended that first season with 18 League and Cup goals and joined the club permanently for a £160,000 fee. The following season continued in the same vein, with the goal-poacher netting after just 47 seconds of the 1992–93 campaign

	League		FA Cup		FL Cup		Sherpa Van Trophy		Total	
	A	G	A	G	A	G	A	G	A	G
1991–92	23/1	15	3	3	-	-	1	-	27/1	18
1992–93	31/1	26	6	4	3	1	4	2	44/1	33
1993–94	7/4	3	-/3	1	-	-	-	-	7/7	4
	61/6	44	9/3	8	3	1	5	2	78/9	55

MIKE WALSH

Born: Manchester, 20 June 1956

Mike Walsh joined the Wanderers straight from school, graduating through the youth and Central League teams to sign professional in July 1974. He started his career at left-back but could also play as a central-defender or in midfield. His League debut came in February 1975 when he appeared as a substitute for the experienced Tony Dunne in a 3–2 win at Nottingham Forest. For the next two

seasons Walsh continued to act as an understudy but made the headlines with a late equaliser against Fulham in the League Cup, and he played in the first leg of the semi-final against Everton in place of the suspended Sam Allardyce. During the Wanderers' Second Division Championship success of 1977–78 Walsh missed only one game and appeared in three different positions. He was an ever present in Bolton's two seasons back in the top flight and a run of 126 consecutive League appearances came to an end in December 1980 through injury. His last Wanderers League appearance came in May 1981, a final day home defeat to Luton Town, and during the close season he joined Everton for £90,000, Jim McDonagh returning to Burnden as part of the deal. Walsh made only 22 appearances for the Goodison club but became a full Republic of Ireland international, going on to win five caps. He had loan spells with Norwich City and Burnley before spending a summer with Fort Lauderdale Strikers. He later played with Manchester City and Blackpool, where he helped them win promotion

from Division Four in 1985. He became club captain and played 153 League games before ending his career with Bury in 1989. He became first-team coach there, taking over as manager in September 1990, and he saw the club to three Play-offs, including their first appearance at Wembley. He spent five years at Gigg Lane and then had a spell in charge at Barrow before becoming assistant at Swindon Town in 1997. Walsh later had a spell as chief scout at Sunderland and took charge of Southport before retiring from the game altogether to run a restaurant in Javea, Spain.

	League		FA Cup		FL Cup		Total	
	A	G	A	G	A	G	A	G
1974–75	4/1	-	-	-	-	-	4/1	-
1975–76	6/3	-	-/1	-	-	-	6/4	-
1976–77	5/3	-	1	-	4	1	10/3	1
1977–78	40/1	1	4	-	3	-	47/1	1
1978–79	42	1	1	-	2	-	45	1
1979–80	42	1	4	-	2	-	48	1
1980–81	30	1	-	-	2	-	32	1
	169/8	4	10/1	-	13	1	192/9	5

DAVID WEIR

Born: Aldershot, 1863
Died: Bolton, December 1933
David Weir learned his footballing skills in Scotland, despite being born in England. He played with Hampton, Glasgow Thistle and Maybole before joining local rivals Halliwell in 1887. He joined the Wanderers as a half-back in June 1888 and became an ever-present in that first League season, scoring his first League goal in a defeat to eventual League champions Preston North End at Deepdale. He went on to play in six different positions that year and also scored the club's first League hat-trick in a 4–1 defeat of Accrington at Pikes Lane in December 1888. In 1889 he won his two England caps, the first against Ireland at Everton in March, where he played centre-

temperament caused a rift between the players the following season, and they refused to play alongside him. He therefore missed out on an FA Cup Final appearance in 1894, although fit, when at least half the team that played were struggling with injury. He played his last game for the club in January 1895 in a 5–0 reverse at Stoke before returning to Maybole. After retiring he took charge of Glossop North End between 1909 and 1911.

	League		FA Cup		Total	
	A	G	A	G	A	G
1888–89	22	10	-	-	22	10
1889–90	21	11	4	10	25	21
1892–93	8	7	-	-	8	7
1893–94	24	3	2	-	26	3
1894–95	11	-	-	-	11	-
	86	31	6	10	92	41

half, and the second a month later as he appeared at inside-forward in a 3–2 defeat to Scotland at Kennington Oval. He found the net in both games. Later that year he scored for the Wanderers in a floodlight game against Sheffield United at Bramhall Lane and was appointed captain. In February 1890 he contributed four goals in the club's record 13–0 FA Cup victory against Sheffield United. The following month proved to be his final appearance in the League for Bolton, a 2–2 home draw with Burnley. He was enticed away from the club in May 1890 by Ardwick, who promised him £3 a week and the licence of a pub. Ardwick, not a League club at the time, later became Manchester City, and Weir scored their first-ever FA Cup goal in October 1890. At Hyde Road he helped them win the Manchester Cup two seasons in succession and was their top scorer in their first season as founder members of the Second Division. In February 1893 Weir returned to the Wanderers, immediately going into the team and netting seven goals in his first eight appearances. Unfortunately, his individualistic

RAY WESTWOOD

Born: Brierley Hill, 14 April 1912
Died: Brierley Hill, January 1982
Ray Westwood was a 'box office' footballer who drew the crowds with his speed, body swerve and superb ball control, his famed sparkling runs making him a matchwinner. Born on the day the Titanic sunk, he played for Brierley Hill in the English Schools Trophy semi-final and then joined Stourbridge and Brierley Hill Alliance, where his father was a committee member. A trial at Aston Villa came to nothing but he was recommended to Bolton by former centre-half Jack Round. Westwood signed amateur forms in May 1928, turning professional in May 1930, and he proved to be one of several top-class players to hail from the Brierley Hill area. In March 1931 he made his League debut against Manchester City, playing at outside-left in place of Ted Vizard. He later moved inside to form a formidable partnership with Willie Cook. During 1934–35, when the Wanderers won

	League		FA Cup		Total	
	A	G	A	G	A	G
1930–31	8	1	-	-	8	1
1931–32	21	7	1	-	22	7
1932–33	37	12	1	1	38	13
1933–34	37	21	5	4	42	25
1934–35	38	30	8	3	46	33
1935–36	40	17	2	-	42	17
1936–37	29	6	5	1	34	7
1937–38	33	23	1	-	34	23
1938–39	18	6	-	-	18	6
1945–46	-	-	9	8	9	8
1946–47	29	4	-	-	29	4
1947–48	11	-	-	-	11	-
	301	127	32	17	333	144

TERRY WHARTON

Born: Bolton, 1 July 1942

Bolton-born winger Terry Wharton became the Wanderers' record signing when they paid Wolves £70,000 for his signature in November 1967. He was to hold that record for 10 years until the Wanderers signed Frank Worthington for £90,000. Terry had followed his father into the game. John Wharton, also born in

promotion from the Second Division, he netted 30 goals in 38 League games, one less than leading scorer Jack Milsom. In September 1934 Westwood won the first of six England caps, helping his country to a 4–0 defeat of Wales. He also represented the Football League on six occasions. A month after his international debut he scored his first League hat-trick in Bolton's record 8–0 defeat of Barnsley at Burnden. Westwood, who served in the wartime Territorial Army and the 53rd Bolton Field regiment at Dunkirk and Egypt, was a member of the Wanderers sides that reached the FA Cup semi-finals in 1935 and 1946, and he played in the 1946 Burnden disaster. His last game for the club was in October 1947 and the following December he moved to Chester, scoring 13 goals in 38 League games before ending his career at Darwen. He later became a newsagent in Brierley Hill.

Bolton, had played more than 250 games for Plymouth, Preston, Manchester City, Blackburn and Newport between 1939 and 1954. Terry Wharton joined Wolves at 15 years old and scored on his debut in a 2–0 First Division win over Ipswich Town in November 1961. He became Wolves' first-choice right-winger for over five seasons, scoring 69 goals in 224 League games. At Bolton, Wharton replaced Francis Lee, who had been sold to Manchester City, and he made his debut in a 1–1 draw at Preston. He became the Wanderers' penalty taker, although injuries prevented him from performing consistently. His best season was 1969–70, when he missed only four League games, and he began the following term by hitting his first hat-trick for the club in a 4–2 win over Luton at Burnden. Unfortunately he failed to live up to that promise and in January 1971 became one of a number of the more experienced players who were sold to keep the club alive. Crystal Palace paid £12,000 to take him to Selhurst Park. Wharton played 20 League games for them before ending his League career with Walsall, where he made one appearance in December 1973. After that he travelled to South Africa, where he played for Durban City.

	League		FA Cup		FL Cup		Total	
	A	G	A	G	A	G	A	G
1967–68	19	5	-	-	-	-	19	5
1968–69	35	10	1/1	-	1	1	37/1	11
1969–70	38	9	1	-	4	1	43	10
1970–71	9/1	4	-	-	-	-	9/1	4
	101/1	28	2/1	-	5	2	108/2	30

NEIL WHATMORE

Born: Ellesmere Port, 17 May 1955
Striker Neil Whatmore joined the Wanderers straight from school and was a member of the successful Lancashire Youth Cup-winning side of 1971. He turned professional in May 1973, having already

enjoyed a headline-making debut when he scored two goals in a 3–2 Third Division win at Swansea. He quickly adapted to the higher level after promotion, playing alongside the likes of experienced campaigners John Byrom and Hugh Curran. Whatmore was joint top scorer with Garry Jones in 1976 and led the way himself in the following two years. After promotion to Division One, Whatmore took on more of a midfield role as Frank Worthington and Alan Gowling became the main strikeforce. During 1980 and 1981 he again led from the front to become the club's leading scorer, and he notched his 100th League goal for the club in a 3–2 win at Cambridge United in April 1981. In August 1981 Birmingham paid a then club record fee of £340,000 to the Wanderers, with Whatmore teaming up again with Frank Worthington. Whatmore made only 26 League appearances before returning to Burnden on a two-month loan in December 1982. He then joined Oxford United on loan before signing permanently for £25,000, but once again he came back to the Wanderers on loan in March 1984. Unfortunately, the Wanderers could not afford the £15,000 fee to sign him permanently and he joined Burnley before teaming up again with his old boss Ian Greaves at Mansfield Town. Whatmore played at Wembley in the successful 1987 Freight Rover Trophy Final for the Stags and at the start of the 1987–88 season he found himself back at Burnden for a fourth time when an anonymous benefactor offered to pay his wages. He therefore became the only player to have been on the club's books through their membership of all Divisions of the Football League, but he failed to force his way into the side and in December 1987 returned to Mansfield as reserve coach. At the end of the season he joined Worksop, where he ended his playing days. Whatmore continues to live in the Nottinghamshire area while working as a school caretaker and has been a regular visitor to the Reebok.

	League		FA Cup		FL Cup		Total	
	A	G	A	G	A	G	A	G
1972–73	1/1	2	-	-	-	-	1/1	2
1973–74	31/3	9	3	-	2/1	-	36/4	9
1974–75	14/3	3	-	-	2	-	16/3	3
1975–76	35	11	6	2	-	-	41	13
1976–77	40/1	25	1	-	9	6	50/1	31
1977–78	42	19	4	1	3	1	49	21
1978–79	23/6	3	-	-	2	-	25/6	3
1979–80	40/1	16	4	2	2	-	46/1	18
1980–81	36	14	2	1	2	-	40	15
1982–83	10	3	1	1	-	-	11	4
1983–84	7	2	-	-	-	-	7	2
	279/15	107	21	7	22/1	7	322/16	121

JOHN WHEELER

Born: Crosby, 26 July 1928.

John Wheeler became Bill Ridding's first signing as Bolton manager in February 1951 when he was transferred from Tranmere Rovers, with Vince Dillon going in the opposite direction with a cash adjustment. Wheeler had started with St Leonard's School and Bootle before joining Carlton. From there he joined Tranmere, where Bill Ridding was trainer, and went on to play 101

League games, mainly at wing-half. Wheeler played his first match for the Wanderers in a 2–1 home success over Liverpool and made rapid progress, establishing himself at right-half and appearing in the 1953 FA Cup Final against Blackpool. In January that year he turned out as an emergency centre-forward against Blackpool at Burnden and hit a hat-trick in a 4–0 win. International honours came his way with five appearances for England B, along with Football League representative games. In October 1954 he won his only full England cap in a 2–0 win against Northern Ireland in Belfast. In September 1956 Second Division Liverpool paid £9,000 to take Wheeler to Anfield, where he became captain in 1958–59. He went on to play 164 League games for Liverpool and played his last two seasons under Bill Shankly. In May 1963 he was appointed player-manager of New Brighton but did not take up the post, becoming assistant trainer at Bury instead. Wheeler remained at Gigg Lane in that capacity until 1969 and still resides in the town.

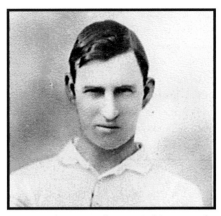

	League		FA Cup		Total	
	A	G	A	G	A	G
1950–51	13	1	-	-	13	1
1951–52	40	4	1	-	41	4
1952–53	34	3	8	-	42	3
1953–54	28	6	4	-	32	6
1954–55	34	3	2	-	36	3
1955–56	40	1	1	-	41	1
	189	18	16	-	205	18

WALTER WHITE

Born: Hurlford, 15 May 1882
Died: Fulham, 8 July 1950

Walter White began with local clubs Britannia, Portland, Thistle, Kilmarnock and Hurlford Thistle. The Wanderers secured his signature from Hurlford in May 1902 and he was a regular inside-forward in the team that was relegated a year later. Having played in the 1904 FA Cup Final, 'Wattie' came to prominence the following season when he hit 24 goals as the Wanderers won promotion to Division One. His haul included three hat-tricks, and his form continued the following season in the top flight. He was ever-present in 1905–06, and only Albert Shepherd scored

more goals. In April 1907 White won the first of two Scottish caps, against England at Newcastle in a 1–1 draw, his second coming a year later in the same fixture before 125,000 spectators in Glasgow, another 1–1 draw. The Wanderers suffered relegation in 1907–08 and they struggled at the start of the following season. White played his last game in a defeat at Derby County in October 1908, joining Everton along with centre-half Bob Clifford. White made 43 League appearances and scored 10 goals for the Goodison club, helping them to runners'-up spot in the League in 1909 and the FA Cup semi-finals a year later. In October 1910 White joined Fulham and remained at Craven Cottage until his retirement in 1923, having played 203 first-class games for them. He is the oldest player to have appeared for Fulham being 40 years nine months in his last game in February 1923. He had a benefit game against Queen's Park Rangers in January 1926.

	League		FA Cup		Total	
	A	G	A	G	A	G
1902–03	21	3	1	-	22	3
1903–04	30	8	6	2	36	10
1904–05	33	24	4	1	37	25
1905–06	38	25	1	-	39	25
1906–07	36	14	4	-	40	14
1907–08	32	13	5	2	37	15
1908–09	6	1	-	-	6	1
	196	88	21	5	217	93

MIKE WHITLOW

Born: Northwich, 13 January 1968

Mike Whitlow joined the club as an apprentice but failed to make the first team and was released, joining Witton Albion in 1987. Primarily a left-back, although capable of playing at centre-half and in midfield, Whitlow then joined Leeds United in November 1988 for £20,000. He played 77 times for the Elland Road club, helping them to win promotion from the Second Division in 1990 and, in March 1992, he moved to Leicester City for a £250,000 fee. He was a regular in the Leicester line up and a member of the sides that won promotion in 1994 and 1996 and the League Cup-winning side of 1997. Whitlow played 180 games for Leicester before rejoining the Wanderers for £700,000 in September 1997, making his debut in a scoreless home draw with Manchester United. He played in the club's Play-off semi-final against Ipswich in 2000, being sent off in the dramatic defeat, and also made a Wembley appearance for the club in the FA Cup semi-final defeat to Aston Villa. He was injured for most of

2000–01 but recovered to make a substitute appearance in the Play-off Final success against Preston North End at Cardiff. Whitlow helped the club settle in the Premier League, making his final appearance against Middlesbrough at the Reebok in May 2003 as the Wanderers won to secure their place at that level. He joined Sheffield United for 17 appearances before moving to Notts County, where he became player-coach. He made 24 appearances for the Magpies and was at Meadow Lane until 2007. Whitlow joined Derby County's youth academy as a coach before being appointed head of youth development at Mansfield Town in May 2009.

	League		FA Cup		FL Cup		Total	
	A	G	A	G	A	G	A	G
1997–98	13	-	1	-	3	-	17	-
1998–99	27/1	-	1	-	3/1	-	31/2	-
1999–2000	37/2	1	5	-	7	-	49/2	1
2000–01	7/4	1	1	-	-	-	8/4	1
2001–02	28/1	-	1	-	-/1	-	29/2	-
2002–03	14/3	-	1/1	-	-	-	15/4	-
	126/11	2	10/1	-	13/2	-	149/14	2

MARK WINSTANLEY

Born: St Helens, 22 January 1968

Mark Winstanley graduated through the Wanderers' youth ranks after he had been spotted playing for his home-town team of Newton-le-Willows. He had the opportunity of going into rugby league but chose football and was taken on a YTS scheme while John McGovern was in charge. Winstanley was originally a left-back but was switched to centre-half by youth coach Walter Joyce. After some impressive displays in the Central League side, Winstanley, made his League debut at Bournemouth in March 1986, replacing the injured Mark Came. During the club's relegation season of 1986–87 Winstanley's appearances were limited as Came and Dave Sutton held down the defensive

	League		FA Cup		FL Cup		Sherpa Van Trophy		Anglo–Italian Cup		Total	
	A	G	A	G	A	G	A	G	A	G	A	G
1985–86	3	-	-	-	-	-	-	-	-	-	3	-
1986–87	12/1	-	-	-	2	-	1	-	-	-	15/1	-
1987–88	8	1	-	-	-	-	-	-	-	-	8	1
1988–89	44	-	3	-	2	-	8	3	-	-	57	3
1989–90	45	1	1	-	8	-	4	-	-	-	58	1
1990–91	32	-	4	-	3	-	2	-	-	-	41	
1991–92	27	-	1	-	-/1	-	1	-	-	-	29/1	-
1992–93	27/2	1	5	-	4	-	3	-	-	-	39/2	1
1993–94	19/2	-	5	-	-	-	-	-	5	-	29/2	-
	217/5	3	19	-	19/1	-	19	3	5	-	279/6	6

FRANK WORTHINGTON

Born: Halifax, 23 November 1948

Frank Worthington became a cult hero at Bolton during the late 1970s in what was a relatively short career with the club. He hailed from a footballing family – older brothers Dave and Bob, who had long League careers, were both full-backs. Frank, however, was a flamboyant centre-forward. He had something of a 'bad boy' image after brushes with authority, but his skill was unquestionable. He turned professional with Huddersfield Town in November 1966 and made 171 League appearances for the Terriers, scoring 42 goals and helping them win the Second Division Championship in 1970 under Ian Greaves. In August 1972 he moved to Leicester City for £80,000, and it was while at Filbert Street that he won his eight full England caps, along with Under-23 and Football League honours. Liverpool almost took him to Anfield but he failed a medical, and his next move was to the Wanderers, on loan, in September 1977 after 72 goals in 210 League games for Leicester. Worthington scored on his Wanderers debut against Stoke at Burnden and was signed permanently for a club record £90,000 by his former Huddersfield boss Ian Greaves. He helped the club to win the Second Division Championship in

berths. Injury to Sutton saw Winstanley play in the final five games of the 1987–88 season, including the promotion-winning final day game at Wrexham. It was also against Wrexham, in February 1989, that he netted two goals in a 3–1 Sherpa Van Trophy game win, one being a spectacular 25-yard drive, and he appeared in the Bolton's Wembley win that season against Torquay United. He played a big part in the Wanderers' Second Division promotion success in 1992–93 but missed the latter part of the season through injury, with Alan Stubbs taking over the role. Winstanley's final game for the Wanderers came in a 1–1 draw at Leicester City in May 1994, and that summer he joined Burnley. He played 152 League game for the Clarets, having a loan spell at Shrewsbury Town in September 1988 before joining Preston North End in March 1999. The following July he moved to Shrewsbury, where he played 33 League games, and he ended his League career at Carlisle United in 2002. Winstanley moved into non-League football with Southport and after retiring from the game worked for Warburton's Bakery in Bolton.

1978, scoring the winning goal at Blackburn that secured promotion, and the following season he was the leading scorer in the First Division. His televised goal against Ipswich Town at Burnden in April 1979 won the Goal of the Season award. Worthington spent the summer of 1979 with Philadelphia Fury in the NASL but failed to find his form after returning. He played his last game for the club in a scoreless home draw with Arsenal and in October 1979 joined Birmingham City for £150,000. He was top scorer at St Andrew's and had summer loan spells with Mjällby and Tampa Bay Rowdies before joining Leeds United in 1982 for £100,000. He later spent time with Sunderland, Brighton, Tranmere – where he became player-manager – Preston North End and Stockport County. The summer of 1988 was spent in South Africa and he then pulled on the shirt of Galway United, Stalybridge Celtic, Weymouth, Radcliffe

Borough, Guiseley, Hinckley Town, Cemaes Bay and Halifax Town before going on the after-dinner speaking circuit. At 60 years old Worthington made a welcome appearance at the Reebok Stadium in Jussi Jääskeläinen's testimonial legends game in August 2009.

	League		FA Cup		FL Cup		Total	
	A	G	A	G	A	G	A	G
1977–78	34/1	11	4	1	-	-	38/1	12
1978–79	42	24	1	-	2	2	45	26
1979–80	5/2	-	-	-	-/1	-	5/3	-
	81/3	35	5	1	2/1	2	88/4	38

CHARLIE WRIGHT

Born: Glasgow, 11 December 1938

One of the biggest characters to have been seen at Burnden Park, Charlie Wright served the Wanderers as a player, coach and manager. The Glaswegian began his career with Rangers, keeping goal in their reserve team in 28 games before being given a free transfer. He moved into the Football League with Workington, signing for them in June 1958 and going on to play 123 League games. During his time in the North West he completed his national service, and in 1960, while stationed in Hong Kong, he represented the island against Peru, saving a penalty and becoming the colony's Player of the Year. In February 1963 Wright joined Grimsby Town and appeared in 129 games before moving to Charlton Athletic three years later. He won rave reviews at The Valley, not only for his goalkeeping prowess but also his humour and ability to entertain the crowd, which included such stunts as having a smoke while play was at the other end of the pitch. It was something of a surprise when he was released after 195 games in June 1971, and Jimmy Armfield stepped in quickly to secure his signature. Wright was ever present in the Wanderers' first-ever Third Division season as the club

recorded their best goals-against record since 1925. In 1973 he won a Third Division Championship medal but soon afterwards retired due to continual injury problems, Barry Siddall becoming the Wanderers' regular 'keeper. Wright took over as the youth team coach at Burnden before joining York City as manager, where he served for three years. He returned to the Wanderers in August 1981 as reserve-team coach, later progressing to first-team coach and manager in February 1985 after the departure of John McGovern. He left the club in December 1985 and moved to London, where he ran a café (see 'Managers').

	League		FA Cup		FL Cup		Total	
	A	G	A	G	A	G	A	G
1971–72	46	-	4	-	6	-	56	-
1972–73	42	-	9	-	2	-	53	-
	88	-	13	-	8	-	109	-

MANAGERS

JOHN SOMERVILLE 1908–10

Popular former player John Somerville was Bolton Wanderers' first secretary-manager, being appointed at the start of 1908–09 season. He had joined the club from his native Ayr in March 1890 and played in the 1894 FA Cup Final, helping the club to promotion to Division One in 1899. As a right-back he was a member of the club's immaculate defensive line-up and went on to play 293 first-class games for the club. He had become secretary, alongside his playing duties in 1898, and was well versed in the running of the club. He oversaw a number of changes in playing personnel in his first season, with the likes of Albert Shepherd, Bob Clifford and Wattie White leaving the club to be replaced with Jimmy Hogan, Billy Hunter and Billy Hughes. In his first season the club won the Second Division Championship Trophy, returning to the top flight after just one season's

absence. Unfortunately, the following season proved to be a complete contrast as Somerville found those same players incapable of performing at the higher level. In January 1910, with the Wanderers at the foot of the First Division and ousted from the FA Cup by Second Division Stockport, Somerville was relieved of the manager's position but remained as secretary until the end of the season with his contract being terminated in July 1910. He went on to become a Football League linesman, having served the club for 20 years and passed away in March 1917 aged 49.

WILL SETTLE 1910–15

Will Settle's association with the club came from his father, Mr Miles Settle JP, who became a director of the club in 1895 in the year that Burnden Park was opened and the club became a Limited Company. Both men were involved in the control of Settle, Speakman & Company, coal merchants. After three years on the board, Miles Settle was succeeded by his son, who served in the same capacity until January 1910 when he was appointed manager. He could do little to prevent the Wanderers falling into Division Two at the end of his first season in office but, with the aid of trainer George Eccles and assistant Peter Bullough, Settle guided the Trotters to promotion at the first attempt. Investment in the team, in an attempt to keep the club in the top flight, was heavy. The likes of Fay, Donaldson, Bentley, Seddon, Lillycrop, Gimblett and Glendenning were all secured under Settle's management. It was, however, the discovery of the left-wing pairing of Ted Vizard and Joe Smith

that was to prove to be invaluable to the club. Settle kept a tight rein on the finances and in 1912 sold Tom Barber to Aston Villa, the profits of which went to pay for the roofing of the Great Lever Stand. After two seasons back in the First Division, both of which saw the Wanderers finish in the top eight and make a profit of £4,000, Settle was rewarded with a contract for a further five years. He guided the club to sixth place in the First Division in 1914 and to the FA Cup semi-finals a year later. Wartime football then replaced the League and Cup, with Settle ending his 17-year association with the club under something of a cloud after he found certain responsibilities taken from him. He left the town in 1918 and made his home in Caernarfon where he died in September 1941, aged 73.

TOM MATHER 1915–19

Tom Mather's record as manager of Bolton Wanderers is difficult to quantify due to the fact that all the games under his charge were played during World War One and as such were not considered to be official games. Chorley-born Mather joined the club during Will Settle's stewardship and acted as secretary before being appointed manager-secretary in 1915. In many respects his term in office was one of the most difficult in the club's history as there were many occasions in which he did not know if he would be able to field a full team. Although he remained, in name, as manager until 1919, he was rarely seen at Burnden Park due to the fact that he had been called up by the Royal Navy, his duties being carried out by his assistant Charles Foweraker. In February 1919 the Bolton directors placed the management of the team in the hands of Ted Vizard as an interim measure to get the club through the remaining war games. This no doubt gave Vizard an insight into a job that he was later to carry out at other clubs after his playing days were over. After the war, Mather returned to football as secretary-manager of Southend United and in October 1923 became manager of Stoke City. In 1933 he guided them to the Second Division Championship, and two years later he was appointed manager of Newcastle United. He left St James' in

1939, and after World War Two he managed Leicester City and Kilmarnock before retiring to Stoke where he died in March 1957.

CHARLES FOWERAKER
1919–44

Charles Foweraker is not only the longest-serving of the club's managers but also the most successful. He entered the world of football in 1895 when he was employed as a part-time checker when Burnden Park opened while employed in the goods section of the old Lancashire & Yorkshire Railway Company. He later became assistant to Tom Mather and in 1915 became secretary, pro-tem, when Mather was called up. He ran the club during World War One and, in July 1919, was appointed secretary-manager on a salary of £400 per annum. He was in charge of Bolton throughout the club's most successful period, during the 1920s when the Trotters won three FA Cup Finals at Wembley and were serious contenders for

the League Championship. Whether he knew the technical side of the game as well as some of his players was debatable. He had no experience of playing to a high level, but his success as a manager was due to his ability to handle the players and to the numerous contacts that he made over the years. Foweraker became one of the most influential personalities in the progress and development of the club. The game carried him and the players into many corners of Europe and into the company of kings. He was presented to Edward VIII, who distributed the FA Cup-winners' medals in 1929, as Prince of Wales, he met George V on two occasions and was also presented to King Alfonso of Spain when the club were on a short Spanish tour. He was awarded the FA's long service medal, awarded only to secretaries with 21 or more years service, and also received the Lancashire FA's equivalent, also serving as a vice-president on that body from 1922. His days at Burnden were not all success, for the Wanderers were relegated in 1933. Foweraker, however, made some astute signings and the absence from the top flight lasted just two seasons. In May 1938 his fondness for cigars and the esteem in which he was held in by his own players was recognised when they presented him with a silver cigar case prior to a game organised in Brighton for the benefit of the King. In August 1939, with war looming, he had two teams prepared to visit Chelsea in case a sudden call on players in the Territorial Army decimated his chosen side. In the circumstances he did not need to call on the second team, but when war was declared he continued to work for the club on a voluntary basis until football returned and money was forthcoming. He spent many solitary days at Burnden Park with no electricity or water supplies. After the club's closure, he struggled and schemed to get the club re-opened, and his battle proved successful in January 1941. He felt the urge to keep the club actively engaged in whatever football was available as it would be to the Wanderers' long-term advantage. He was assisted in this by experienced players such as George Hunt and Harry Hubbick who were both working in munitions and mining. He strongly believed in the development of players under military age, and from this belief came another Bolton Wanderers hero in Nat Lofthouse. In August 1944, Foweraker retired through ill-health, having completed 49 years continuous service with the club. He passed away at his home in Bolton in July 1950, aged 73.

WALTER ROWLEY 1944–50

Walter Rowley was a student of Foweraker's, having both played and coached under him. He was promoted from coach to secretary-manager in August 1944. As a player, Rowley joined Bolton from Oldham Athletic in August 1912. A polished wing-half or centre-half, he served the club well until he was forced to retire through injury in May 1925. He was appointed coach to the reserves and was first-team coach at the outbreak of war. His opening years in charge were encouraging, the Football League War Cup being won at the end of his first season, with the club finishing third in the Football League North and reaching the FA Cup semi-finals in his second season. When normal League football returned things proved more difficult. Despite having a number of good young players, the older stalwarts had seen their best years taken away by the war. Rowley therefore had the unenviable task of ending the Bolton careers of such great players as Ray Westwood, George Hunt, Harry Hubbick

and Albert Geldard. Funds to buy new players proved to be hard to find as the Burnden disaster was to be a drain on the club's income. Money that was spent in an attempt to improve the club's First Division position proved unsuccessful in the majority of cases, but the club made steady if not dramatic progress under Rowley's charge. In October 1950 he resigned due to ill health and was awarded life membership of the club for services rendered in his 38 years as player, coach and secretary-manager. He later returned to management with Middlesbrough and Shrewsbury Town and passed away in 1976.

BILL RIDDING 1951–68

Bill Ridding was one of the last of the old school of secretary-managers. He was born a farmer's son in Heswall, on the Wirral, and played professionally as a centre-forward or inside-right. He scored 13 goals in 17 League appearances for Tranmere before joining Manchester City in 1929. He

played only nine League games for City before making the short journey to join Manchester United in 1931. He played 42 League games, scoring 14 goals, before spells with Northampton Town and Tranmere Rovers, ending his League career at Oldham Athletic in 1935. He was aged just 24 when he retired, a double cartilage injury forcing him to stop playing, and he took a job as a tram conductor while taking his qualifications as a physiotherapist and chiropodist, and he also became Tranmere's A team trainer. He later became the club's trainer and manager after the death of Jimmy Morton. Ridding's association with Bolton Wanderers began in 1946 when Walter Rowley appointed him as trainer and, upon Rowley's resignation in 1950, Ridding was put in temporary charge. In the same year he was appointed trainer to the England team for the World Cup in Brazil. In February 1951 he was appointed secretary-manager of the club and also continued to act as trainer until the appointment of Bert Sproston. Ridding was always a popular figure, but his two appearances on the national stage were

marred in some small degree by everyone outside Bolton rooting for the other team. In 1953, he led the Wanderers to the FA Cup Final against Blackpool, where everyone wanted Stanley Matthews to win a Cup-winners' medal, and five years later the Wanderers took on a post-Munich Manchester United side, and on this occasion Ridding returned victorious. The abolition of the maximum wage in 1961 made it difficult for Ridding to hold on to the home-grown players that were coming through the ranks and to keep the club's better players. After relegation from the top flight in 1964 the club's finances continued to decline, and in August 1968 he relinquished the manager's chair when second only to Matt Busby as the League's longest-serving manager. He joined Lancashire Cricket Club as physiotherapist and passed away in September 1981, aged 70.

NAT LOFTHOUSE OBE 1968–70, 1971 & 1985

The club's most successful goalscorer was appointed temporary manager after the departure of Bill Ridding in August 1968. His appointment as manager was confirmed the following December with another former player, Teddy Rothwell, becoming secretary. Having been with the club since 1939, first as a player and then, after his retirement in 1960, as coach, his managerial career got off to a good start with an undefeated four-game start to the season. Unfortunately, the same issues that had beset Ridding were still there and, with no money to secure new players, Lofthouse began to rely on youngsters which was to prove too much. The club continued to flirt with relegation to the Third Division for the first time and, under his own admission, Lofthouse wanted to move away from team management to more of a general manager's role. In November 1970 Jimmy McIlroy took over team affairs, but this proved to be a short-lived arrangement, with Lofthouse again taking over. In January 1971 he again stepped aside to allow Jimmy Meadows to take over team affairs. Lofthouse's last act was to select the club's youngest-ever League side which defeated a strong Sheffield United side at Burnden, but unfortunately it proved to be the last win of that disastrous season. By April 1971, Meadows had also left, leaving Lofthouse with the unenviable task of leading the club in their first ever relegation into Division Three. He was relieved to hand over the reigns to Jimmy Armfield and was appointed the Wanderers chief scout and could take some satisfaction from the youngsters that he left behind that would prove to be the cornerstone of future success. His 33-year association with the club came to an end in 1972 but he returned six years later to become manager of the Burnden Executive Club without the pressures of team management. In December 1985, he was again to take on the job he least wanted, being in charge as an interim measure to

assist the club for one game, a 2–1 home win over Chesterfield, while a successor to Charlie Wright was recruited. In October 1986 he became the club's president, in December 1989 a freeman of Bolton, and in 1994 appeared in the New Year's Honours list and was presented with an OBE in recognition of his services to the game. After his death in January 2011 there was a large turnout for the funeral of Bolton's greatest sporting hero.

JIMMY McILROY MBE 1970

Jimmy McIlroy's tenure lasted just 18 days to become the club's shortest-serving manager. He had been appointed chief coach and aide to manager Nat Lofthouse in August 1970 and was appointed team manager on 4 November 1970 with assistance from coaches Jim Conway and Eddie Hopkinson. McIlroy had won 55 international caps for Northern Ireland and had seen service as an inside-forward for both Burnley and Stoke City. When his playing days ended he became manager of Oldham Athletic before joining Stoke as chief coach. He resigned his position there in 1969 and was out of the game until

joining the Wanderers. His first game in charge of Bolton was a 1–0 home defeat by Norwich City, followed by a 2–0 reverse at Millwall. After 18 days he parted company with the club looking to accept offers for any players to relieve the financial pressure. In the 2011 New Year's Honours list he received an MBE for his services to football and to charity.

JIMMY MEADOWS 1971

Jimmy Meadows took over as team manager on 15 January 1971, returning to the town of his birth from the position of chief coach at Blackpool. As a player, he was a full-back and began with Bolton YMCA and progressed to League football with Southport. He joined Manchester City in 1951, and while at Maine Road he became an England international, playing in a 7–2 win over Scotland at Wembley in April 1955. His management career began at Stockport County where he had won promotion from the Fourth Division in 1967, but he left Edgeley Park in 1969 to join Blackpool. In his 11-week spell at Burnden he received transfer requests from John Hulme, Roy Greaves and John

Ritson and sold Terry Wharton and Paul Fletcher. Meadows recruited former Olympic athlete Joe Lancaster in an attempt to boost the club's training programmes, but morale was at a low ebb. On 6 April 1971 he resigned, having seen the team slump to the bottom of the Second Division after a 4–0 defeat at Queen's Park Rangers. The other 10 games under his charge had failed to produce a win and the team had scored only four goals. He found success in his next managerial post when he won the Fourth Division Championship with Southport in 1973 before returning to Stockport County where he was in charge for the 1974–75 season. He died in January 1994.

JIMMY ARMFIELD 1971–74

Jimmy Armfield was given the opportunity to revive Bolton's fortunes in what was his first managerial appointment after retiring as a player. He had played 568 League games for his only club, Blackpool, and led England on 15 occasions. Following his display in the 1962 World Cup Finals in Chile he was voted the finest right-back in the world and was also a member of England's 1966 World Cup-winning squad. Armfield was appointed the Wanderers manager on 19 May 1971, 18 days after the club's final game of a disastrous season that had seen them drop into the Third Division for the first time ever. His first task was to restore the club's traditional colours of white shirts and navy blue shorts and to do away with the all-white kit. With little money to spend, he returned to Bloomfield Road and brought in experienced players in Peter Nicholson, Henry Mowbray and Graeme Rowe and also snapped up goalkeeper Charlie Wright from Charlton Athletic. By the end of his first season in charge he had transformed

IAN GREAVES 1974–80

things to the extent that only 41 goals were conceded, the club's best defensive record since 1925 and, although promotion was not won, the club enjoyed two good Cup runs and a famous League Cup victory over Manchester City. The foundations had been laid, and the rewards were reaped the following year when the club won the Third Division Championship and also reached the fifth round of the FA Cup. The club's youth policy, instigated by Nat Lofthouse, was also starting to produce players. 'Gentleman Jim', always recognisable in his familiar track suit and smoking a pipe, turned down offers from other clubs and made some shrewd signings to add to the home grown talent that helped the club settle quickly at Second Division level. He eventually gave way to an offer to manage Leeds United in September 1974, leaving Burnden in the knowledge that he had lifted the Trotters into a new and exciting period of their history. He took Leeds to the 1975 European Cup Final, something that had eluded their former manager, Don Revie, and returned the club to order after its whirlwind affair with Brian Clough. He left Elland Road in 1978 and turned to journalism and is a regular commentator/summariser on BBC Radio

Four months after walking out of Huddersfield Town after a boardroom power battle, Ian Greaves came to Burnden in August 1974 as assistant to Jimmy Armfield. As a player Greaves began with Buxton before joining Manchester United in May 1953. He played in the final 14 games of the 1955–56 season in which United became League champions and also in the 1958 FA Cup Final against the Wanderers. He went on to make 67 League appearances as a full-back before moving to Lincoln City in December 1960. He ended his playing career with Oldham Athletic, his home-town club, in 1962 and turned to coaching. He became Huddersfield Town manager in 1968 and two years later led them to the Second Division Championship but could not prevent them slipping to the Third Division by the time he left in 1974. Armfield recommended his assistant for the manager's job, and Greaves was appointed four hours before a home game against Orient on 5 October 1974. The team, chosen by Armfield, won 2–0, and he went on to blood a number of youngsters as the club finished mid-table before the club's fortunes really took off. He led the club to the League Cup semi-finals in 1977, at the time the club's best in the competition, and a year later, after two near misses, to the Second Division Championship. He won Manager of the Month awards in January 1975, November

1976, August 1977 and October 1977 and won the Second Division Manager of the Season in 1977–78. Unfortunately, the Wanderers failed to establish themselves in the top flight, and Greaves was to suffer the same experience he had previously encountered at Huddersfield. He kept the club up in 1978–79, doing the double over Manchester United, but the following season proved too much. He was sacked in January 1980, just 48 hours after the club had reached the fifth round of the FA Cup but placed bottom of the First Division. Greaves broke the club's transfer record four times, but the final one, Len Cantello, proved ineffective and no doubt hastened his downfall. He retained strong connections with the players he left behind, with many becoming managers in their own right in later years. He returned to management with Oxford United and Wolverhampton Wanderers before becoming assistant manager at Hereford United. In January 1983 he took over the reigns at Mansfield Town and led them to promotion from Division Four in 1986, and a year later to success at Wembley in the Freight Rover Trophy. He left by mutual consent in February 1988 and remained in the game by scouting for a number of clubs. He passed away in January 2009 in Ainsworth, near Bolton, aged 76.

STAN ANDERSON
1980–81

Horden-born Stan Anderson had been Ian Greaves's assistant since the departure of George Mulhall to Bradford City in November 1978. He became caretaker manager after the departure of Greaves, and his position was made permanent in February 1980 despite failing to win a game while caretaker. He secured a major scalp in his first full game in charge when the Wanderers defeated European Cup

holders Nottingham Forest 1–0 at Burnden in what was only the second victory of the season. In his playing days between 1952 and 1966 he made over 500 League appearances as a wing-half for Sunderland, Newcastle and Middlesbrough, was capped twice by England and was in the 1962 World Cup Finals squad. He was manager of Middlesbrough between 1966 and 1973, winning promotion from the Third Division during that time, and then spent a year in charge of AEK Athens. After a spell as assistant manager at Queen's Park Rangers he joined Doncaster Rovers, spending four years in charge at Belle Vue before joining Bolton. Although it was inevitable that the club would suffer relegation from the top flight at the end of the 1979–80 season, expectations the following season were high as Anderson had made additions to the squad. Results did not go as expected, and speculation was rife when George Mulhall returned to the club as assistant in March 1981. In May 1981 Anderson was relieved of his duties with two years of his contract still to run after Mulhall's return had seen results improve to take the club away from the relegation zone.

GEORGE MULHALL
1981-82

George Mulhall had previously been at Burnden as Ian Greaves's assistant in the successful years between 1974 and 1978 before leaving to become manager at Bradford City. He returned as assistant to Stan Anderson in March 1981 and took over the reigns in June that year. As a player, the Falkirk-born outside-left had played for Aberdeen, Sunderland, Cape Town City and Morton, winning three international caps for his country. He began his coaching career at Halifax Town in October 1971, becoming manager in June 1972 before joining the Wanderers. He left Burnden in November 1978 to replace former Wanderer John Napier at Bradford City. He returned to take over a club in turmoil with six players released on free transfers and six available for transfer as a cost-cutting exercise began to take its toll. Mulhall's season in charge proved to be difficult, and he claimed to be embarrassed at some of the team's performances, especially a 7–1 defeat at Queen's Park Rangers. The Wanderers managed to stay in the Second Division by

the skin of their teeth, winning two home games in the last week of the season and having Cardiff to thank as they lost at home. The financial situation worsened, and Mulhall was forced to add Paul Jones to the nine players he had decided were to leave the club at the end of the season. In June 1982 he left the club as the Wanderers stated their intent to advertise for a player-manager. Mulhall later scouted for Ipswich Town and in 1985 spent two years at Tranmere Rovers as assistant to Frank Worthington. He continued to work in the game as a scout with both Halifax, where he had a spell as joint manager, and at Huddersfield Town.

JOHN McGOVERN
1982-85

John McGovern's credentials as a player were impeccable, and he was handed the role of player-manager after being allowed to leave Nottingham Forest on a free transfer, despite having 14 months left on his contract at the City Ground. Over 500 League appearances under his belt with Hartlepool, Derby County, Leeds United and Forest had seen him win two European Cups, two League Championships and two League Cups under Brian Clough. He was also the youngest player, when aged 19, to have played in all four divisions of the Football League. Prior to his appointment, other names had been considered. Speculation included Mike Channon and John Wile, but it was the name of Pele that attracted the most attention. The tradition and reputation of the club proved to be a handicap throughout McGovern's reign as manager. His inexperience in handling players perhaps had a lot to do with the club losing their Second Division status at the end of his first season in charge. In reality, he had taken over a squad that had

just missed out going down the previous season, and there was little money to improve the situation. The Montrose-born midfielder did his best to raise funds, running a marathon, organising supporter's evenings and individual kit sponsor schemes. He got together a good bunch of young players and they made a decent start in Division Three but, with nothing available to build a team around them, they faltered and finished mid table. The following season saw the club at the wrong end of the Third Division and in January 1985 McGovern parted company with the club having played only 16 League games in his spell. He later went into business in Tenerife before returning to have spells in charge at Chorley, Rotherham United, Hull City and Woking and as assistant manager at Plymouth. He is now an after-dinner speaker and a pundit on BBC Radio Nottingham.

CHARLIE WRIGHT 1985

After a distinguished career as a goalkeeper, which included two years at Bolton and a Third Division Championship medal, Glasgow-born Charlie Wright turned to coaching, retiring from League football in 1973 after suffering a back injury. The former Hong

Kong international took charge of the youth team at Burnden, and his effervescent character made him popular and he progressed to become chief coach before leaving to join York City as manager in 1977. He had little success at Bootham Crescent, and in March 1980 he was sacked. He returned to Burnden in July 1981, taking charge of the reserves and working with the club's goalkeepers. In November 1983 he became first-team coach, succeeding Walter Joyce, who switched to the reserves and, after John McGovern's departure in January 1985, he was put in temporary charge. In three weeks Wright steered the team to five consecutive victories, their best winning sequence in almost six years and, despite a number of applications from experienced managers, he was named Bolton manager on 7 February 1985 with Walter Joyce appointed his assistant. Unfortunately, the form did not last with only one success in the next 10 games leaving the club precariously placed at the seasons end. For the opening of the 1985–86 season Wright invested in experience, with David Cross, Sam Allardyce, Dave Sutton and Asa Hartford all signing, but the team continued to struggle. A first-round FA Cup defeat at Fourth Division Wrexham, four League games without a goal and a game before the lowest League attendance at Burnden led to the inevitable. In

December 1985 Wright left the club, along with Joyce, by mutual consent moving south to run a café in the Greenwich area of London.

PHIL NEAL 1985–92

Phil Neal was appointed as player-manager on 18 December 1985 and won his first game in charge against Doncaster Rovers at Burnden. Neal was one of the most 'decorated' players in the English game having won 50 England caps, eight League Championships, four European Cups, four League Cups and a UEFA Cup in a career with Northampton Town and Liverpool that had amassed 635 League appearances. The former full-back turned down offers from clubs higher in the Football League and appointed his former Liverpool teammate Colin Irwin as his assistant, making the club's managerial set up one of the most inexperienced in their history. His first term in charge was indifferent as the club once again managed to remain in Division Three by a whisker, although there was some consolation in a first visit to Wembley since 1958 for the Freight Rover Trophy Final. Unfortunately, past triumphs were not repeated as Bristol City ran out 3–0 winners and it was the same nucleus of players that carried the club into the following season. Neal caused a sensation in September 1986 with the publication of his book, *Life at the Kop*. In it he claimed he had been 'stabbed in the back' at Liverpool and claimed that 'a shambles' had awaited him on his appointment at Burnden and pointed the finger at his predecessors. On the field the team continued to struggle and paid for their inconsistencies with relegation for the first time to Division Four after a Play-off with Aldershot. Neal announced his retirement from playing but was persuaded to change his mind by new coach Mick Brown, formerly on Manchester United's staff, whose experience was second to none. Within 12 months the new managerial team had transformed the team and made the first step back up the ladder with promotion on the final day of the season. In 1989 the team consolidated and returned to Wembley, defeating Torquay United 4–1 in the Sherpa Van Trophy Final, and there was a feel-good factor around the club. Neal took the club to the Third Division Play-offs in 1990 and 1991 only to miss out on each occasion. In 1991–92 the team did well in the FA Cup, reaching the fifth round, but struggled in the League, and less than a week after the final game of the season Neal, who was the ninth longest-serving manager in the Football League, left the club. After a rocky start, Neal brought stability and a measure of success to the club, but the fact that the club was carrying a large squad along with the pressure of poor results and declining attendances brought the inevitable. Neal

returned to club management with Coventry City in October 1993 until being sacked in February 1995. He was involved in the England set up under Graham Taylor and took over at Cardiff City in February 1996 but left in October that year to become assistant to Steve Coppell at Manchester City. He became caretaker manager for a period until the appointment of Frank Clark. Barry Fry appointed him as assistant at Peterborough at the start of the 1997–98 season but was axed the following March. He has, since then, worked in the media.

BRUCE RIOCH 1992–95

Bruce Rioch was appointed manager in May 1992 and quickly began to strengthen the squad with players who were to become a major influence such as Keith Branagan and John McGinlay. In his playing days, Rioch became the first Scottish captain to be born in England, winning 24 caps along with a First Division Championship medal with Derby County in 1975. He also saw

service with over 600 games for Luton Town where he won the Fourth Division Championship in 1968, Aston Villa, where he won the Second Division in 1972, Everton, Birmingham, Sheffield United, Seattle and Torquay. In July 1982 he became player-manager at Torquay, moving to Seattle Storm in February 1985. He returned to England and was appointed manager at Middlesbrough in February 1986, guiding them to promotion from the Third Division a year later. This was followed by a second successive promotion to the First Division via the Play-offs, but they lasted only one season at the top level, and he was sacked in March 1990. He made a quick return to management with Millwall, taking them to the Second Division Play-offs in 1991 but left in March 1992. He led the Wanderers to promotion from the Second Division in 1993, and in the same season the club enjoyed plenty of national coverage with a run to the fifth round of the FA Cup that included a third round replay win over Liverpool at Anfield. In 1993–94 he consolidated the club's place in the First Division and took the Wanderers to the sixth round of the FA Cup, their best effort in the competition at the time since 1959. Once again it was on two fronts that Rioch led the club to success in 1995. The Wanderers reached the Coca-Cola Cup Final for the first time, going down 2–1 to Liverpool at Wembley, and then the Play-off success over Reading that won a return to the top flight for the first time since 1980. The Play-off win at Wembley proved to be Rioch's last game in charge as he left to take over at Arsenal and in his only season at Highbury took them into Europe and started to transform their line-up with the signing of Dennis Bergkamp. After leaving Arsenal he worked as assistant manager to Stewart Houston at Queen's Park Rangers before taking the helm at Norwich, Wigan and Odense. In

June 2008 he took over at Aalborg, guiding them into the Champions League group stage before leaving in October 2008.

ROY McFARLAND 1995–96

After the departure of Bruce Rioch, his assistant Colin Todd was put in charge, along with another former Derby County teammate Roy McFarland. As a player he made over 500 appearances as a central-defender for Tranmere Rovers, Derby County and Bradford City. At the Baseball Ground he won a Second Division Championship medal in 1969 and First Division Championships in 1972 and 1975 along with 28 full caps for England. He began his managerial career at Bradford City, taking over from George Mulhall as player-manager in May 1981. He helped them to the runners'-up spot in the Fourth Division in 1982 and returned to Derby as a coach, becoming assistant manager during Arthur Cox's reign and became manager in October 1993. He was in charge for two seasons, losing the Division One Play-off Final to Leicester City and in June 1995 he joined the Wanderers. The club found things difficult in that initial Premier League season but during his spell at Burnden the Wanderers managed just two League victories, one of those ironically coming against Rioch's Arsenal. After a 4–2 defeat at Sheffield Wednesday on New Year's Day 1996, McFarland left

the club by mutual consent. He took charge at Cambridge United in November 1996 where he won promotion from the Third Division in 1999 and took over at Torquay United in July 2001 but resigned the following April. From June 2003 to March 2007 he was manager of Chesterfield and, in 2009, took over from Nigel Clough at Burton Albion to guide them into the Football League before leaving at the end of that season.

COLIN TODD 1995–99

Colin Todd joined the Wanderers in the summer of 1992 as coach to Bruce Rioch and was to be part of three promotions and two relegations during his time at the club and was in charge during the move from Burnden to the Reebok Stadium. As a player he came through the ranks at Sunderland before joining Derby County in February 1971. He went on to win two League titles at Derby, partnering Roy McFarland in the centre of the defence. He won the PFA Players Player of the Year trophy in 1975 and clocked up more than 600 appearances along with 27 full England appearances. After leaving Derby in 1978 he played for Everton, Birmingham City, Nottingham Forest, Oxford United, where he won the Second Division Championship, Vancouver Whitecaps and Luton Town. He began coaching at Whitley Bay and was coach at Middlesbrough under Bruce Rioch when they won promotion from the Third Division in 1987 and from the Second a year later. As manager he took Boro to the Second Division Play-offs in 1991 and, after a spell at Bradford City, was re-united with Rioch at Burnden. He was coach during the promotion campaigns of 1993 and 1995, and after a spell in dual charge with Roy McFarland, took sole charge in January 1996. He could do little to prevent the Wanderers suffering relegation from

the Premiership in 1996, during which time Ian Porterfield was coach. Todd appointed Phil Brown as his coach for the start of the 1996–97 season and Bolton went on to win the Second Division Championship in record-breaking style. Unfortunately, it was again a one season spell in the top flight when the club were relegated on the last day of the season on goal difference having amassed 40 points. He took the club to the Play-offs in 1999, but the club made a poor start to the following season and Todd left the club in September 1999 to be replaced by Phil Brown who took over as caretaker. Todd later managed Swindon Town, Derby County, Bradford City, Randers FC (Denmark) and Darlington, where he left in September 2009.

SAM ALLARDYCE
1999–2007

Sam Allardyce was appointed manager of the club on his 45th birthday, 19 October 1999, and he began with a 2–2 draw against Crewe Alexandra at the Reebok

Stadium on the same evening. Phil Brown was appointed his assistant after he had won four of the five games he had been in temporary charge of. As a player he joined the Wanderers as a centre-half and came through the ranks to make his League debut for the club in November 1973, going on to win a Second Division Championship medal in 1978. He played 214 first-class games for the club before joining Sunderland in July 1980 and later having spells with Millwall, Tampa Bay, Coventry City and Huddersfield Town before rejoining the Wanderers in 1985. He spent one season back at the club before joining Preston, where he helped them win promotion from Division Four in 1987. He became player-coach at West Brom in February 1989, and he was there two years before becoming player-manager at Limerick, where he guided them to promotion in 1992. He joined Preston as coach-assistant manager before becoming manager at Blackpool in July 1994 where he led them to the Second Division Play-offs in 1996. He took over at Notts County, winning the 1998 Third Division title where they became the first post-war side to win promotion by mid-March. In his first season in charge at the Reebok Stadium the Wanderers reached the semi-finals of both the Worthington Cup (League Cup) and the FA Cup, the latter for the first time since winning the competition in 1958, and to the First Division Play-offs. In 2000–01 he took the club back into the Premier League with a 3–0 win over Preston in the Play-off Final at Cardiff and then moulded together a team that held on to top-flight status. In 2004 he took the club back to Cardiff, this time for a Carling Cup Final that saw Middlesbrough win 2–1, and the following season the club finished sixth to qualify for the UEFA Cup for the first

time in the club's history. The club again qualified for the UEFA Cup with a seventh finishing position in 2007 with Allardyce being in charge for the last time in a 2–2 draw at Chelsea in April 2007. The following month he was unveiled as Newcastle United's manager but remained at St James' only until the following January. He returned to management in December 2008 when he took over at Blackburn Rovers, helping them keep their Premier League status until he was relieved of his duties by new owners in December 2010.

SAMMY LEE 2007

Liverpool-born Sammy Lee had a distinguished playing career as a midfield player, winning Championship medals at Anfield in 1982, 1983 and 1984 and European Cup-winners' medals in 1981 and 1984 along with 14 full England caps. He later played for Queen's Park Rangers, Osasuna and Southampton before joining Bolton in 1990. He played only four games for The Trotters before suffering injury that ended his career. He joined the Liverpool coaching staff in 1993 and became a part-

time coach with England before leaving Anfield to join the National set up full time in 2004. He joined Bolton as assistant to Sam Allardyce in June 2005 and took over as manager after his departure appointing Frank McParland as assistant. Sammy set about changing the style of play and brought in 11 players during the summer. Unfortunately, the club won only one of his 11 League games in charge, against Reading at the Reebok and in October 2007 he was sacked. He rejoined Liverpool in May 2008 as assistant manager to Rafael Benitez and remained in that role under Roy Hodgson and Kenny Dalglish.

GARY MEGSON 2007–09

As a player Gary Megson had been a defensive midfielder, clocking up over 500 appearances for Plymouth Argyle, Everton, Sheffield Wednesday, Nottingham Forest, Newcastle United, Manchester City, Norwich City, Lincoln City and Shrewsbury Town between 1977 and 1995. He began his managerial career at Norwich City and followed this with spells at Blackpool, Stockport County and Stoke City. He took over at West Brom in March

2000, taking them into the Premier League in 2002, and although they were relegated he mounted a successful promotion campaign the following season. In October 2004 he was dismissed and in January 2005 took over at Nottingham Forest but could not prevent them from dropping into League One, and he resigned in February 2006. After a spell coaching at Stoke City he took over at Leicester City in September 2007 but his term there lasted just 41 days before he joined the Wanderers. He took over with the club at the bottom of the Premier League with five points from 10 games, appointing Chris Evans as his assistant, and his first League success came against Manchester United in what was Bolton's first home win against them since 1978. The club reached the last 16 of the UEFA Cup but went out to Sporting Lisbon when he selected a weakened side, but 11 points from the final five games of the season secured a 16th-place finish. During the summer of 2008 he made a number of signings, including Johan Elmander for a club-record 10 million

Euros, and the club kept away from the relegation scrap with a 13th-place finish. The club made a poor start to the 2009–10 season but recovered to climb as high as 13th by the end of October. A run of just one win in nine games plunged them back into trouble, culminating in losing a two goal lead at home to Hull in the final game of the year. He was relieved of his duties the following day. In February 2011 he was appointed manager of League One side Sheffield Wednesday.

OWEN COYLE 2010–

Owen Coyle became the ninth manager to have also played for the club when he was appointed in January 2010. He had scored 23 goals in 55 starts for the Wanderers between 1993 and 1995 when he was a member of the side that won promotion to Premier League for the first time. He also won his only Republic of Ireland international cap while with Bolton and also played for Dumbarton, Clydebank, Airdrieonians, Dundee United, Motherwell, Dunfermline, Ross County, Falkirk (where he was also co-manager

with John Hughes), Airdrie United (where he was also assistant manager to Sandy Stewart) and St Johnstone in a career that saw him score over 250 goals. He began his managerial career in April 2005 at St Johnstone, guiding them to the semi-finals of the Scottish League Cup and FA Cup the following season. In 2007 Saints just missed out on promotion to the Scottish Premier League and in November 2007 he moved south to join Burnley. In 2008–09 Burnley reached the semi-finals of the League Cup, losing narrowly to Spurs and won promotion to the Premier League in the Play-off Final at Wembley. Burnley started well in the Premier League, including a defeat of Manchester United at Turf Moor but struggled away from home. After joining the Wanderers, along with assistant Sandy Stewart, Coyle registered his first win against his former club at the end of January 2010 and guided the club to safety while Burnley suffered relegation. The following season he took the club to Wembley for the FA Cup semi-final and steered the team to some consistent home performances.

Pre-League FA Cup

Match No.	Round	Date		Venue	Opponents		Result		Scorers		Attendance
1881-82											
1	1	Oct	22	H	Eagley	D	5-5		Atherton, Gleaves, Struthers, OG 2		
2	R	Nov	12	A	Eagley	W	1-0		Steel		
3	2		19	A	Blackburn Rovers	L	2-6		Atherton, Struthers		
											Appearances
									Two own-goals		Goals
1882-83											
4	1	Nov	4	H	Bootle	W	6-1		Struthers 5, Steel		
5	2		30	H	Liverpool Ramb	W	3-0		Struthers 2, OG		
6	3	Jan	6	H	Druids	D	0-0				
7	R		22	H	Druids	D	1-1*		Atherton		
8	R		29	N†	Druids	L	0-1				
											Appearances
									One own-goal		Goals
1883-84											
9	1	Nov	10	H	Bolton Olympic	W	9-0		Davenport, Struthers 3, Steel 2, Gleaves, Howarth, Scholes		
10	2	Dec	1	H	Bolton Assoc	W	3-0		Steel 2, Struthers		
11	3		29	H	Irwell Springs	W	8-1		Davenport 2, Fallon 2, Steel 2, Struthers, OG		
12	4		19	A	Notts County	D	2-2*		Davenport, Fallon		
13	R	Jan	2	H	Notts County	L	1-2		Vaughan		
											Appearances
									One own-goal		Goals
1884-85			Drawn against Preston Zingari but both clubs withdrew due to professional argument with the FA.									
1885-86											
14	1	Oct	17	H	Eagley	W	6-0		Gregory, Fallon 2, Hough, Bullough, OG		
15	2	Nov	21	A	Rawtenstall ^	D	3-3				
16	3	Dec	5	H	Preston North End #	L	2-3		Davenport, Struthers		
											Appearances
									One own-goal		Goals
1886-87											
17	1	Oct	30	H	South Shore	W	5-3		Hewitson, Struthers, Howarth Davenport 2		
18	2	Nov	13	A	Third Lanark	W	3-2		Hewitson 2, Struthers		
19	3	Dec	11	A	Darwen	L	3-4		Davenport, Howarth, Struthers		
											Appearances
											Goals
1887-88											
20	1	Oct	15	H	Everton §	W	1-0		Roberts		
21	R		29	A	Everton	D	2-2		Brogan, Roberts		
22	R	Nov	12	H	Everton	D	1-1		Brogan		
23	R		19	A	Everton ‡	L	1-2		Davenport		
24	2	Dec	10	A	Preston North End	L	1-9		Howarth		
											Appearances
											Goals

* After extra-time; N† Played at Wrexham; ^ No record of team/goalscorers. Game played by reserves due to first team having a previous engagement. Rawtenstall disqualified for professionalism and for their pitch being too small; # Both Bolton and Preston disqualified for professionalism; § Replay after protest by Everton that Bolton fielded ineligible players; ‡ Everton disqualified for fielding ineligigble players.

Amerton J	Bullough P	Brogan J	Christie J	Cox W	Davenport JK	Devlin J	Fallon I	Fowler J	Glaister J	Gregory J	Hay T	Hewitson J	Holden	Hough	Howarth P	Howarth T	Jones E	Kennedy J	McKernon J	Naylor T	Owen R	Parkinson J	Parkinson DW	Powell J	Roberts R	Robertson J	Scholes J	Steel W	Struthers WG	Trainer J	Unsworth W	Vaughan J	Ward	Wilson TR	Young J
10					2			4							6		3								11		9	8						1	
10					2		7	4							6		3								11		9	8				5		1	
10					2		7	4							6		3								11		9	8				5		1	
3					3		2	3							3		3								3		3	3				2	3		
2								1																1	2										
		9	6					7	5							11	4		2						10			8						1	3
		9	6					7	5							11	4		2						10			8						1	3
		9	6					7	5								4		2			11			10			8						1	3
		9	6					7	5								4		2						10			8						1	3
11		9	6	3				7	5								4		2						10			8						1	
11		9	6					7	5								4		2						10			8						1	
		5	5	5	1			5	5								2	5	5							1	5	5				5	4		
1																										1	7								
		6	7						5	1					9		4		2				3		11	10		8							
		6	7						5	1					9		4		2				3			10		8				11			
		6	7						5	1					9		4		2				3			10		8				11			
		6	7						5	1							4		2		9		3			10		8				11			
		6	7						5	1							4		2		9		3			10		8				11			
		5	5						5	5					3		5		5	2			5			1	5	5				4			
		4	3						1						1											1	6	5				1			
5								7	6		8				2	10							4									9			
			8						4		7				5	10							3	2	6				11	1					
1			1	1					2	2					2	2							2	1	1				1	1		1			
1			1						2		1				1															1					
4				8								10	2			11		3			7			6			5	9	1						
6				7									2	9		11		3			8			4			5	10	1						
6				7									2			11		3			8			4			5	10	1						
3				3								2	3			3		3			3			3			3	3	3						
				3									3			2												3							
6	8			7												11		3		2				4			5	10			1				
6	8			7												11		3	9	2	10			4			5				1				
6	8			7												11		3	9	2	10			4			5				1				
6	8			7												11		3	9	2	10			4			5				1				
6	8			7												11				2				4			5	10			1				
5	5			5												5		4	3	5	3			5			5	2			5				
	2			1												1								2											

Bateson played number 1 in Match 14; Baxendale played number 9 in Match 24; Bradley played number 11 in March 14; T. Dawson played number 7 in Match 1; Gent played number 3 in Match 14; Henderson played number 9 in Match 19; Nelson played number 5 in Match 1; G. Owen played number 9 in Match 20; W. Parkinson played number 9 in Match 16; Pearson played number 3 in Match 24.

The Wanderers' first-ever Football League game against Derby County, advertised as a 3.15 kick-off, started half an hour after the scheduled time when The Rams arrived late. Bolton's first international player, Kenny Davenport, scored Bolton's first League goal after two minutes play. Bolton found themselves 3–0 up after just five minutes but ended up losing the game 6–3.

Match No.	Date		Venue	Opponents	Result		Scorers	Attendance
1	Sep	8	H	Derby County	L	3-6	Davenport 2, Brogan	3,000
2		15	H	Burnley	L	3-4	Brogan, Davenport, Cooper	4,000
3		22	A	Preston North End	L	1-3	Weir	5,000
4		29	H	Everton	W	6-2	Davenport 2, Tyrer 2, Milne 2	5,000
5	Oct	6	A	Burnley	L	1-4	Roberts	4,000
6		13	H	Stoke	W	2-1	Milne, own-goal	5,000
7		20	H	Aston Villa	L	2-3	Weir, Barbour	8,000
8	Nov	3	A	Everton	L	1-2	Barbour	8,000
9		5	A	West Bromwich Albion	W	5-1	Barbour 2, Milne, Brogan, Weir	4,000
10		10	A	Wolverhampton Wanderers	L	2-3	Brogan, McGuinness	2,000
11		17	A	West Bromwich Albion	L	1-2	Bullough	3,500
12		24	H	Preston North End	L	2-5	Weir, Brogan	10,000
13	Dec	8	A	Blackburn Rovers	D	4-4	Scowcroft, Brogan 2, Milne	4,000
14		22	H	Accrington	W	4-1	Weir 3, Owen	5,000
15		26	A	Derby County	W	3-2	Brogan, Davenport, Milne	3,500
16		29	H	Wolverhampton Wanderers	W	2-1	Weir, own-goal	5,500
17	Jan	12	A	Aston Villa	L	2-6	Barbour 2	2,000
18		19	A	Stoke	D	2-2	Owen, Brogan	6,000
19		26	H	Blackburn Rovers	W	3-2	Weir 2, Owen	6,000
20	Mar	5	A	Notts County	W	4-0	Brogan 2, Barbour, Davenport	3,000
21		9	H	Notts County	W	7-3	Turner, Brogan, Barbour 2, Davenport 3	3,000
22		23	A	Accrington	W	3-2	Brogan, Roberts, Davenport	3,000
							Appearances	
							2 own-goals	Goals

FA Cup

Q1	Oct	6	A	Hurst	D	0-0		
Q2		31	H	West Manchester	W	9-0	J. Turner 3, Simmers 2, Knowles 2, Whittle, own-goal	
Q3	Nov	17	A	Linfield Athletic	L	0-4		

Q1: Hurst scratched from the replay.

All three games played by the reserve team.

		Appearances
	1 own-goal	Goals

Player appearances grid (shirt numbers worn per match):

Harrison C.E.	Robinson B.	Michael J.	Roberts R.	Weir D.	Balbough P.A.	Davenport J.K.	Milne J.	Cooper T.	Barbour A.	Brogan J.	Parkinson J.	Tyrer H.	Jones D.	Simmers W.	Flitcroft W.	Gillam S.G.	Scorecroft J.	Siddons E.	Mercer D.	McGuinness H.	Dyer F.	Owen G.	Turner J.A.	Moores	Haydock	Jackson	Greenhalgh	Pearson	Rushton	Knowles	Turner R.	Whittle
1	2	3	4	5	6	7	8	9	10	11																						
1		2	6	4		5	10	9	8	7	3	11																				
1	2		6	5	4		8	10		9	7		11	3																		
1	2		6	4		8	10		9	7		11	3	5																		
1	2		6	4		8	10		9	7		11	3	5																		
1	2	3	6	4	5	10	8		9	7		11																				
1	2		6	5	4	8	10		9	7		11			3																	
	2	3	5	4		8	10		9	7		11				1	6															
1	2		4	5		8	10		9	7		11					6	3														
1	2		6	5	4	8	10			7		11						3	9													
	2		6	9	4	8	10			7	1	11			3		5															
	2		6	9		8	10			7		11			3	1	5			4												
1			6	4		8	10			7		11	3		2		5				9											
1	2		6	9	4	8	10			7			3				5					11										
1	2		6	9	4	8	10			7			3				5					11										
1	2		6	9	4	8	10			7		11	3				5															
1	2		6	4		8	10		9	7			3				5					11										
1			6	9	4	8	5			7		11	3	2			10															
1	2		6	11	4	8	5		9	7			3				10															
1	2		6	11	4	8	5		9	7			3				10															
1	3		6	10	4	8	5		9	7			2				11															
1			6	10	4	8	5		9	7			3	2			11															
19	18	2	22	22	15	22	22	3	14	22	2	14	12	2	7	2	9	1	1	1	1	7	2	0	0	0	0	0	0	0	0	0
		2	10	1	11	6	1	9	13	2			1				1			1		3	1									

Cup / other appearances grid:

Harrison C.E.	Robinson B.	Michael J.	Roberts R.	Weir D.	Balbough P.A.	Davenport J.K.	Milne J.	Cooper T.	Barbour A.	Brogan J.	Parkinson J.	Tyrer H.	Jones D.	Simmers W.	Flitcroft W.	Gillam S.G.	Scorecroft J.	Siddons E.	Mercer D.	McGuinness H.	Dyer F.	Owen G.	Turner J.A.	Moores	Haydock	Jackson	Greenhalgh	Pearson	Rushton	Knowles	Turner R.	Whittle
						5																10	1	2	3	4	6	7	8	9	11	
															5							10	1	2	3	4	6	7	8	9	11	
															5							10	1	2	3	4	6	7	8	9	11	
					1										2							3	3	3	3	3	3	3	3	3		
															2							3								2	1	

League Table

	P	W	D	L	F	A	Pts
Preston North End	22	18	4	0	74	15	40
Aston Villa	22	12	5	5	61	43	29
Wolverhampton W	22	12	4	6	51	37	28
Blackburn Rovers	22	10	6	6	66	45	26
Bolton Wanderers	22	10	2	10	63	59	22
West Bromwich Albion	22	10	2	10	40	46	22
Accrington	22	6	8	8	48	48	20
Everton	22	9	2	11	35	47	20
Burnley	22	7	3	12	42	62	17
Derby County	22	7	2	13	41	61	16
Notts County	22	5	2	15	40	73	12
Stoke	22	4	4	14	26	51	12

Division One

Match No.	Date		Venue	Opponents	Result		Scorers	Attendance
1	Sep	14	H	Accrington	L	2-4	Weir, Parkinson	5,000
2		21	H	Everton	L	3-4	Brogan, Milne, Barbour	4,500
3		28	A	Everton	L	0-3		10,000
4	Oct	12	H	Preston North End	L	2-6	Bullough, Davenport	10,000
5		19	A	Stoke	W	1-0	Barbour	3,000
6		26	H	Notts County	L	0-4		5,000
7	Nov	4	A	West Bromwich Albion	L	3-6	Davenport, Brogan, Weir	4,813
8		9	H	Blackburn Rovers	W	3-2	Davenport, Milne, Brogan	7,500
9		16	H	Aston Villa	W	2-0	Davenport 2	8,000
10		23	A	Preston North End	L	1-3	Weir	8,000
11		30	H	Derby County	W	7-1	Cassidy 4, Brogan, McNee, Davenport	5,000
12	Dec	7	H	West Bromwich Albion	W	7-0	Weir 2, Brogan, Davenport 2, Bullough, Cassidy	3,500
13		21	A	Blackburn Rovers	L	1-7	Cassidy	6,000
14		26	A	Derby County	L	2-3	Brogan, Weir	4,500
15	Jan	4	A	Accrington	L	1-3	Cassidy	2,000
16		11	A	Notts County	W	5-3	Brogan, Weir 2, McNee, Cassidy	4,000
17		25	A	Aston Villa	W	2-1	Cassidy, Weir	5,000
18	Feb	8	H	Stoke	W	5-0	Cassidy 3, Weir, Brogan	5,000
19		24	H	Wolverhampton Wanderers	W	4-1	Weir, McNee 2, Turner	3,000
20	Mar	1	A	Burnley	L	0-7		
21		15	A	Wolverhampton Wanderers	L	1-5	Cassidy	3,000
22		17	H	Burnley	D	2-2	Milne, Jones	3,000

Bolton claimed the defeat in game 6 was 0-3, not 0-4.

Appearances

Goals

FA Cup

R1	Jan	18	H	Distillery	W	10-2	Weir 4, Cassidy 2, Davenport 2, 2 unknown	2,000
R2	Feb	1	H	Sheffield United	W	13-0	Cassidy 5, Weir 4, Brogan 3, Robinson	3,750
R3		15	A	Preston North End	W	3-2	Weir 2, Brogan	12,000
SF	Mar	8	N	Sheffield Wednesday	L	1-2	McNee	15,000

SF at Perry Barr, Birmingham.

Appearances

2 unknown scorers

Goals

	Harrison C.E.	Robinson B.	Jones D.	Bullough P.A.	Milne J.	Roberts R.	Brogan J.	Davenport J.K.	Weir D.	Parkinson J.	Turner J.A.	Flitcroft W.	Barbour A.	Coupar T.	McWhirter A.	McKee J.	Pearson J.	Cassidy J.	Sutcliffe J.W.	Woods F.	Rushton W.	Haydock J.
	1	2	3	4	5	6	7	8	9	10	11											
	1	6	3	4	5		7	8	10		11	2	9									
	1	2	3	4	5	6	7	8			10		9	11								
	1	3	2	4	5		11	7	9			8		6	10							
	1	3	2	4	5		8	7	10			9		6	11							
		3	2	4	5		8	7	10	1		9		6	11							
		3	2		5	6	8	7	10	1		11	4	9								
		3	2	4	5	6	8	7	10	1		11		9								
		2	3	4	5	6	8	7	10	1		11		9								
		3	2	4	5	6	8	7	10	1		11		9								
		3	2	4	5	6	8	7	10			11		9	1							
		3	2	4		6	8	7	10	1			5	11	9							
		3	2	4	5	6	8	7	10			11		9	1							
		2	3	4		6	7	5	10	1			8	11	9							
			3	4		6	7	5	10	1		11		9		2	8					
		2	3	4		6	8	7	10	1		11		9		5						
		2	3	4		6	8	5	10	1		11		9			7					
			3	4	8		9	7	6	1	11	10			5		2					
		3			5	6	8	7	10	1		11		9		4	2					
		2		4	7	6	8		5	1	10	11		9		3						
		2	3	4	7	6		8	5	1	10	11		9								
	5	19	21	20	17	17	21	21	21	16	6	1	5	2	4	19	1	15	2	5	2	2
		1	2	3			8	8	11	1	1		2			4		13				

	Harrison C.E.	Robinson B.	Jones D.	Bullough P.A.	Milne J.	Roberts R.	Brogan J.	Davenport J.K.	Weir D.	Parkinson J.	Turner J.A.	Flitcroft W.	Barbour A.	Coupar T.	McWhirter A.	McKee J.	Pearson J.	Cassidy J.	Sutcliffe J.W.	Woods F.	Rushton W.	Haydock J.
		3	4		6	8	5	10	1			11		9				7	2			
	2	3	4		6	8	5	10	1			11		9				7				
	2	3	4		6	8	5	10	1			11		9	7							
	2	3	4		6	8	5	10	1			11		9	7							
	3	4	4		4	4	4	4	4			4		4	2			2	1			
	1						4	2	10			1		7								

League Table

	P	W	D	L	F	A	Pts
Preston North End	22	15	3	4	71	30	33
Everton	22	14	3	5	65	40	31
Blackburn Rovers	22	12	3	7	78	41	27
Wolverhampton W	22	10	5	7	51	38	25
West Bromwich Albion	22	11	3	8	47	50	25
Accrington	22	9	6	7	53	56	24
Derby County	22	9	3	10	43	55	21
Aston Villa	22	7	5	10	43	51	19
Bolton Wanderers	22	9	1	12	54	65	19
Notts County	22	6	5	11	43	51	17
Burnley	22	4	5	13	36	65	13
Stoke	22	3	4	15	27	69	10

1890-91

Division One

Did you know that?

On the 6th September 1890 the Wanderers took to the field in red-and-white-quartered jerseys for the first League game of the season against Notts County. Two goals from Jim Munro and one each from Kenny Davenport and Bob Roberts secured a 4–2 Pikes Lane victory. Notts sported blue-and-white-striped jerseys.

Match No.	Date	Venue	Opponents	Result		Scorers	Attendance
1	Sep 6	H	Notts County	W	4-2	Roberts, Munro 2, Davenport	6,000
2	13	H	Derby County	W	3-1	Barbour, Davenport 2	10,000
3	20	H	Everton	L	0-5		12,000
4	27	A	Preston North End	L	0-1		6,000
5	Oct 2	A	Notts County	L	1-3	Cassidy	6,000
6	4	H	Aston Villa	W	4-0	McNee, Brogan, Turner, Bullough	5,000
7	11	A	Burnley	W	2-1	Barbour, McNee	7,000
8	18	A	Everton	L	0-2		12,000
9	25	H	Sunderland	L	2-5	Brogan 2	5,000
10	Nov 3	A	West Bromwich Albion	W	4-2	Munro, McNee 2, Barbour	1,506
11	8	A	Wolverhampton Wanderers	L	0-1		3,000
12	15	H	Preston North End	W	1-0	Davenport	11,000
13	22	A	Aston Villa	L	0-5		10,000
14	Dec 13	H	Accrington	W	6-0	Cassidy 2, Barbour 3, Munro	2,000
15	26	A	Derby County	D	1-1	McNee	2,500
16	29	H	Wolverhampton Wanderers	W	6-0	Turner, McNee 3, Gardiner, Cassidy	4,000
17	Jan 10	A	Accrington	L	1-2	Cassidy	1,500
18	Feb 10	A	Sunderland	L	0-2		6,000
19	Mar 7	A	Blackburn Rovers	W	2-0	Davenport, Turner	6,000
20	14	H	West Bromwich Albion	W	7-1	Turner, Munro 2, Cassidy 2, Brogan, McNee	4,000
21	21	H	Burnley	W	1-0	Cassidy	6,000
22	28	H	Blackburn Rovers	W	2-0	Munro 2	14,000
							Appearances
							Goals

FA Cup

R1	Jan 24	A	Accrington	L	1-5	Cassidy	
							Appearances
							Goals

Appearances grid (shirt numbers per match). Player columns left to right:

Parkinson L.	Somerville J.	Jones D.	Paton A.	Barbour A.	Roberts R.	Davenport J.K.	Brogan J.	Cassidy J.	McAlea J.	Munro J.	Sutcliffe J.W.	Jarrett R.H.	Robinson B.	Russell W.	Bullough P.A.	Turner J.A.	Gardiner H.
1	2	3	4	5	6	7	8	9	10	11							
1	2	3	4	5	6	7	8	9	10	11							
1	2	3	4	5	6	7	8	9	10	11							
	2	3	4		6	5	8	9	10	11	1	7					
		3	4		6	5	8	9	10	11	1	7	2				
1		3	5		6	7	8	9	10				2	4	11		
		3	4	9	6	5	8		10	11	1	7					
	2	3	4	9	6	5	8		10	11	1	7					
	2	3	4		6		8	9	10	11	1	7					5
	2	3	5	9		8			10	11	1		4	6	7		
	2	3	4	9		8			10	11	1	7		6			5
	2	3	4	9	6	7	8		10	11	1						5
	2	3	4	7	6	8		9	10	11	1						5
	2	3	4	7		8	9		10	11	1			6			5
	2	3	4	7	6	8		9	10		1					11	5
	2	3	4	7	6	8		9	10		1					11	5
	2	3	4	7	6	8		9	10	11	1						5
	2	3	4	7	6	8		9	10	11	1						5
	2	3	4		6	5	8	9	10	7	1					11	
	2	3	4		6		8	9	10	7	1					11	5
	2		4		6		8	9	10	7	1			3		11	5
	2	3	4		6		8	9	10	7	1					11	5
4	**19**	**21**	**22**	**14**	**19**	**12**	**21**	**16**	**22**	**19**	**18**	**5**	**1**	**3**	**2**	**12**	**12**
					6	1	5	4	8	9	8				1	4	1

Cup (appearances / goals):

Parkinson L.	Somerville J.	Jones D.	Paton A.	Barbour A.	Roberts R.	Davenport J.K.	Brogan J.	Cassidy J.	McAlea J.	Munro J.	Sutcliffe J.W.	Jarrett R.H.	Robinson B.	Russell W.	Bullough P.A.	Turner J.A.	Gardiner H.
	2	3	4	7			8	10	11	9	1				6	5	
	1	1	1	1			1	1	1	1	1				1	1	
							1										

League Table

	P	W	D	L	F	A	Pts
Everton	22	14	1	7	63	29	29
Preston North End	22	12	3	7	44	23	27
Notts County	22	11	4	7	52	35	26
Wolverhampton W	22	12	2	8	39	50	26
Bolton Wanderers	22	12	1	9	47	34	25
Blackburn Rovers	22	11	2	9	52	43	24
Sunderland	22	10	5	7	51	31	23
Burnley	22	9	3	10	52	63	21
Aston Villa	22	7	4	11	45	58	18
Accrington	22	6	4	12	28	50	16
Derby County	22	7	1	14	47	81	15
West Bromwich Albion	22	5	2	15	34	57	12

Division One

The first penalty awarded in a game involving the Wanderers came in September 1891 at Pikes Lane. Auld converted the kick for Sunderland after 'keeper James Sutcliffe had kicked Hannah, but Bolton went on to win 4–3 although the Wearsiders went on to win the League title.

Match No.	Date		Venue	Opponents	Result		Scorers	Attendance
1	Sep	5	A	Darwen	W	2-1	McNee, Cassidy	7,000
2		12	H	Darwen	W	1-0	Brogan	7,000
3		19	H	Sunderland	W	4-3	McNee, McFettridge, Cassidy 2	8,000
4		26	H	Preston North End	W	3-0	McFettridge, Cassidy, McNee	12,000
5	Oct	1	A	Notts County	L	0-2		3,000
6		3	H	Accrington	L	3-4	McFettridge, Cassidy 2	5,000
7		10	A	Aston Villa	W	2-1	Munro 2	3,000
8		17	H	Everton	W	1-0	Cassidy	10,000
9		24	H	Burnley	W	2-0	Munro, Cassidy	8,000
10		31	H	Blackburn Rovers	W	4-2	McNee, Turner, Cassidy, Munro	12,000
11	Nov	2	A	West Bromwich Albion	W	2-0	Turner, Munro	6,700
12		7	A	Accrington	W	3-0	Munro 2, McNee	5,000
13		14	H	Stoke	D	1-1	Jones	3,000
14		21	A	Blackburn Rovers	L	0-4		9,000
15		28	A	Preston North End	L	0-4		5,000
16	Dec	5	H	Wolverhampton Wanderers	W	3-0	Cassidy 2, Munro	5,000
17		12	A	Stoke	W	1-0	McFettridge	1,000
18		19	H	West Bromwich Albion	D	1-1	Munro	5,000
19		26	A	Derby County	L	2-3	Munro, McNee	5,000
20	Jan	1	H	Derby County	W	3-1	Munro, Cassidy, McFettridge	8,000
21	Mar	1	A	Sunderland	L	1-4	Munro	5,000
22		5	A	Burnley	W	2-1	Cassidy, Bentley	4,000
23		26	H	Notts County	W	2-0	Cassidy, McNee	6,000
24	Apr	2	H	Aston Villa	L	1-2	Bentley	10,000
25		16	A	Wolverhampton Wanderers	W	2-1	Bentley, Cassidy	1,200
26		18	A	Everton	W	5-2	Cassidy 3, Gardiner, Bentley	11,500
							Appearances	
							Goals	

FA Cup

R1	Jan 23	A	Sheffield Wednesday	L	1-4	Jones	17,000
						Appearances	
						Goals	

246

	Sutcliffe J.W.	Somerville J.	Jones D.	Paull A.	Gardiner H.	Turner J.A.	Munro J.	Brogan J.	Cassidy J.	McNee J.	McFettridge D.	Roberts R.	Barbour A.	Chinnale J.E.	Barnley H.	Russell W.	Davenport J.K.
	1	2	3	4	5	6	7	8	9	10	11						
	1	2	3	4	5	6	7	8	9	10	11						
	1	2	3	4	5	6	7	8	9	10	11						
	1	2	3	4	5	7			9	10	11	6	8				
	1	2	3	4	5	8	7		9	10	11	6					
	1	2	3	4	5		7	8	9	10	11	6					
	1	2	3	4	5		7	8	9	10	11	6					
	1	2	3	4	5		7	8	9	10	11	6					
	1	2	3	4	5	6	7	8	9	10	11						
	1	2	3	4	5	8	7		9	10	11	6					
	1	2	3	4	5	8	7		9	10	11	6					
	1	2	3	4	5	6	7	8	9	10	11						
	1	2	3	4	5	8	7		9	10	11	6					
	1	2	3	4	5	6	7	8	9	10	11						
	1	2	3	4	5	8	7		9	10	11	6					
	1	2	3	4	5	8	7		9	10	11	6					
	1	2	3	4	5	8	7		9	10	11	6					
	1	2	3	4	5	8	7		9	10	11	6					
	1	2	3	4	5	6	8		9	10	11		7				
	1	2	3	4	5	6	7	8	9	10	11						
	1	2	3	4	5	8	7		9	10				11	6		
	1	2	3	4	5	8	7		9	10				11	6		
	1	2	3	4	5	8	7		9	10				11	6		
	1	2	3	4	5	8	7		9	10	6			11			
	1	2	3	4	5	8	7		9	10	6			11			
	26	26	26	26	23	25	10	26	26	23	13	1	1	5	3	0	
		1		1	2	12	1	18	7	5			4				

	Sutcliffe J.W.	Somerville J.	Jones D.	Paull A.	Gardiner H.	Turner J.A.	Munro J.	Brogan J.	Cassidy J.	McNee J.	McFettridge D.	Roberts R.	Barbour A.	Chinnale J.E.	Barnley H.	Russell W.	Davenport J.K.
	1	2	3	4			9	7	8		10	11	6			5	
	1	1	1	1			1	1	1		1	1	1			1	
		1															

League Table

	P	W	D	L	F	A	Pts
Sunderland	26	21	0	5	93	36	42
Preston North End	26	18	1	7	61	31	37
Bolton Wanderers	26	17	2	7	51	37	36
Aston Villa	26	15	0	11	89	56	30
Everton	26	12	4	10	49	49	28
Wolverhampton W	26	11	4	11	59	46	26
Burnley	26	11	4	11	49	45	26
Notts County	26	11	4	11	55	51	26
Blackburn Rovers	26	10	6	10	58	65	26
Derby County	26	10	4	12	46	52	24
Accrington	26	8	4	14	40	78	20
West Bromwich Albion	26	6	6	14	51	58	18
Stoke	26	5	4	17	38	61	14
Darwen	26	4	3	19	38	112	11

Division One

Match No.	Date		Venue	Opponents		Result	Scorers	Attendance
1	Sep	3	A	Preston North End	L	1-2	Gardiner	4,000
2		10	H	West Bromwich Albion	W	3-1	Wilson, McNee, Dickenson	8,000
3		17	H	Sheffield Wednesday	W	1-0	Dickenson	6,000
4		24	H	Aston Villa	W	5-0	Cassidy 3, Willocks 2	7,000
5	Oct	1	H	Wolverhampton Wanderers	W	3-1	Cassidy 2, Davenport	9,000
6		6	A	Notts County	D	2-2	McNee, Cassidy	8,000
7		8	A	Accrington	D	1-1	Willocks	3,000
8		15	H	Stoke	D	4-4	Dickenson 3, Wilson	3,000
9		20	A	Nottingham Forest	L	0-2		4,000
10		22	A	Wolverhampton Wanderers	W	2-1	Willocks 2	5,000
11		29	H	Everton	W	4-1	Willocks, Cassidy, Wilson, own-goal	6,000
12	Nov	5	A	Sheffield Wednesday	L	2-4	Wilson, Dickenson	15,000
13		7	A	West Bromwich Albion	L	0-1		4,000
14		19	H	Preston North End	L	2-4	Gardiner, Willocks	7,000
15		26	A	Blackburn Rovers	L	0-3		7,000
16	Dec	3	H	Newton Heath	W	4-1	Bentley 2, Wilson, Cassidy	2,500
17		10	A	Newton Heath	L	0-1		4,000
18		24	A	Aston Villa	D	1-1	McNee	3,000
19		26	A	Derby County	D	1-1	Willocks	7,000
20	Jan	2	A	Derby County	L	0-3		5,000
21		14	A	Stoke	L	0-6		6,000
22	Feb	11	A	Burnley	L	0-3		6,000
23		14	A	Sunderland	D	3-3	Weir 2, Dickenson	6,000
24		25	H	Burnley	W	1-0	own-goal	5,000
25	Mar	4	H	Accrington	W	5-2	Weir 3, Bentley, Paton	4,000
26		18	H	Blackburn Rovers	W	2-1	Dickenson, Weir	6,000
27		25	H	Notts County	W	4-1	Bentley 2, Cassidy, own-goal	4,000
28		31	H	Nottingham Forest	W	3-1	Paton, Dickenson, Wilson	9,000
29	Apr	1	H	Sunderland	W	2-1	Bentley, Weir	13,000
30		3	A	Everton	L	0-3		20,000

Appearances

3 own-goals
Goals

FA Cup

R1	Jan	21	H	Wolverhampton Wanderers	D	1-1	Wilson	10,000
rep		28	A	Wolverhampton Wanderers	L	1-2	McNee	18,000

R1 a.e.t.

Appearances

Goals

Sutcliffe J.W.	Somerville J.	Jones D.	Paton A.	Gardner H.	McFettridge D.	Munro J.	Willocks D.	Cassidy J.	Bentley H.	Dickenson J.	Turner J.A.	Wilson J.	McKee J.	Matthew H.	Davenport J.K.	Tannahill R.	Weir D.	Bullough P.A.
1	2	3	4	5	6	7	8	9	10	11								
1	2	3	4	5		7	9		11	6	8	10						
1	2	3	4	5			9	7	11	6	8	10						
1		3	4	5		8	9		11	2	7	10	6					
1		3	4	5		8	9		11	2		10	6	7				
1		3	4	5		8	9		11	2	7	10	6					
1	2	3	4	5		8	9		11	6	7	10						
1	2	3	4	5		8	9		11	6	7	10						
1	2	3	4	5		8	9		11	6	7	10						
1	2	3	4			8	9		11	6	7	10	5					
1	2	3	4			8	9		11	6	7	10	5					
1	2	3	4			8	9		11	6	7	10	5					
1	2	3	4			8	9		11	6	7	10	5					
1	2	3	4	5		8	9		11	6	7	10						
1	2	3	4	5			9	8	11	10	7		6					
1	2	3	4	5		8	9	11		6	7	10						
1	2	3	4	5		8	9	11		6	7	10						
1	2	3	4	5		8	9		11	6	7	10						
1	2	3	4	5		8	9		11	6	7	10						
1	2	3	4	5	8		9	11		6	7	10						
1	2	3	4	5		7	8	9		11	6		10					
1	2	3	4	5	6		8			11		10		7	9			
1	2	3	4	5			8	10	11	6	7				9			
1	2	3	4	5			8	10	11	6	7				9			
1	2	3	4	5			8	10	11	6	7				9			
1		3	4	5			8	10	11	6	7				9	2		
1	2	3	4	5			8	10	11	6	7				9			
1	2	3	4	5		7	9		10	11	6	8						
1	2	3	4		5	8		10	11	6	7				9			
1	2	3	4		5	8		10	11	6	7				9			
30	26	30	30	24	2	6	21	27	14	26	29	26	20	8	1	1	8	1
	2	2				8	9	6	9		6	3		1		7		

Sutcliffe J.W.	Somerville J.	Jones D.	Paton A.	Gardner H.	McFettridge D.	Munro J.	Willocks D.	Cassidy J.	Bentley H.	Dickenson J.	Turner J.A.	Wilson J.	McKee J.	Matthew H.	Davenport J.K.	Tannahill R.	Weir D.	Bullough P.A.
1	2	3	4	5			8	9		11	6	7	10					
1	2	3	4	5			8	9		11	6	7	10					
2	2	2	2	2			2	2		2	2	2	2					
												1	1					

Match No.	Date		Venue	Opponents		Result	Scorers	Attendance
1	Sep	2	H	Stoke	W	4-1	Cassidy, Bentley 2, McArthur	7,000
2		9	A	Wolverhampton Wanderers	L	1-2	McArthur	4,500
3		16	H	Blackburn Rovers	W	2-1	Cassidy, Hughes	8,000
4		23	A	Sheffield United	L	2-4	Cassidy, McArthur	6,500
5		30	H	Preston North End	L	0-3		10,000
6	Oct	5	A	Nottingham Forest	L	0-1		7,000
7		7	A	Darwen	W	1-0	Weir	3,000
8		14	H	Sheffield United	L	0-1		6,000
9		21	H	Wolverhampton Wanderers	W	2-0	Cassidy, McArthur	4,000
10		28	A	Darwen	W	3-1	Dickenson, Weir, Gardiner	3,000
11	Nov	4	A	Preston North End	L	0-1		7,000
12		6	A	West Bromwich Albion	L	2-5	Cassidy, McArthur	4,000
13		18	H	Aston Villa	L	0-1		700
14	Dec	2	A	Blackburn Rovers	W	1-0	McArthur	5,000
15		9	H	Newton Heath	W	2-0	Paton, Cassidy	6,000
16		16	A	Sheffield Wednesday	L	1-2	Cassidy	5,000
17		25	H	Sheffield Wednesday	D	1-1	Cassidy	6,000
18		26	A	Derby County	L	1-6	Tannahill	10,500
19		30	A	Sunderland	L	1-2	Ferguson	5,000
20	Jan	1	H	Derby County	D	1-1	Ferguson	7,000
21		6	H	Burnley	W	2-0	Ferguson, Weir	1,500
22		13	A	Stoke	L	0-5		4,000
23	Feb	3	A	Burnley	L	1-2	Tannahill	5,000
24	Mar	3	A	Aston Villa	W	3-2	Bentley, Dickenson, Cassidy	8,000
25		23	H	Nottingham Forest	D	1-1	Cassidy	9,000
26		24	A	Newton Heath	D	2-2	Cassidy, Tannahill	10,000
27		26	A	Everton	L	2-3	Wilson, Bentley	25,000
28	Apr	7	H	West Bromwich Albion	L	0-3		2,000
29		16	H	Everton	L	0-1		1,000
30		23	H	Sunderland	W	2-0	Bentley, Hughes	6,000
							Appearances	
							Goals	

FA Cup

	Date		Venue	Opponents		Result	Scorers	Attendance
R1	Jan	27	A	Small Heath	W	4-3	Cassidy 2, Wilson 2	7,000
R2	Feb	10	A	Newcastle United	W	2-1	Hughes, Turner	10,000
R3		24	H	Liverpool	W	3-0	Cassidy, Dickenson 2	20,000
SF	Mar	10	N	Sheffield Wednesday	W	2-1	Bentley 2	20,000
F		31	N	Notts County	L	1-4	Cassidy	37,000

SF at Fallowfield, Manchester. Final at Goodison Park, Liverpool.   Appearances
                                                                                                                                   Goals

Appearances / line-up grid (player positions per match):

Sutcliffe J.W.	Somerville J.	Jones D.	Paton A.	Weir D.	Turner J.A.	Wilson J.	Cassidy J.	McArthur W.	Hughes A.	Bentley H.	Gardiner H.	Dickenson J.	Willocks D.	Tannahill R.	Ferguson G.	Shuttleworth T.	Lever A.	Gilligan A.	Lawson R.R.
1	2	3	4	5	6	7	8	9	10	11									
1	2	3	4	5	6	7	8	9	10	11									
1	2		4	3	6	7	8	9	10	11	5								
1	2		4	3	6	7	8	9		10	5	11							
1	2	3	4	5	6	7	10	9	8	11									
1	2	3	4	5	6	7	8	9		10		11							
1	2	3	4	5	6	7	8		10		11	9							
1	2	3	4		6			8	9		10	5	11		7				
1	2	3	4	10	6			8	9			5	11		7				
1	2	3	4	10	6			8	9			5	11		7				
1	2	3	4	10	6			8	9			5	11		7				
1	2	3	4	10	6			8	9			5	11		7				
1	2	3	4		6			8	9	10		5	11		7				
1	2	3	4		6			9			11	5		8	7	10			
1	2	3		6			8	9			5	11		7	10				
		3	4	2	6			8	9			11	5		7	10	1		
1	2	3		4	6			9			5	11	8	7	10				
1	2	3		4	11	6			8	9			5		7				
1		3		2	6			8			9	4	6	10	11	8	7		
1	2	3	4		6			9			5	10		11	8	7			
1	2	3	4	6			8	9			5	10		11	7				
1		3		2			9	4	6	10			11	8	7		5		
1	2	3		4	9			5	11		8	7	6		10				
1	2	3	4	6			9			5	11		7	10	8				
29	**25**	**28**	**21**	**24**	**24**	**10**	**29**	**19**	**15**	**21**	**18**	**16**	**11**	**23**	**13**	**1**	**1**	**1**	**1**
		1	3		1	11	6	2	5	1	2			3	3				

Sutcliffe J.W.	Somerville J.	Jones D.	Paton A.	Weir D.	Turner J.A.	Wilson J.	Cassidy J.	McArthur W.	Hughes A.	Bentley H.	Gardiner H.	Dickenson J.	Willocks D.	Tannahill R.	Ferguson G.	Shuttleworth T.	Lever A.	Gilligan A.	Lawson R.R.
1		3	4	2	6	8	9		5	11				7	10				
1	2	3	4	10	6	8	9		5	11				7					
1	2	3	4		6		9		5	11	10	7	8						
1	2	3	4		6		9		5	11	10	7	8						
1	2	3	4			7	9		5	11	6	10		8					
5	**4**	**5**	**5**	**2**	**4**	**3**	**5**		**5**	**5**	**1**	**3**	**2**	**5**	**1**				
		1	2	4		1	2			2									

League Table

	P	W	D	L	F	A	Pts
Aston Villa	30	19	6	5	84	42	44
Sunderland	30	17	4	9	72	44	38
Derby County	30	16	4	10	73	62	36
Blackburn Rovers	30	16	2	12	69	53	34
Burnley	30	15	4	11	61	51	34
Everton	30	15	3	12	90	57	33
Nottingham Forest	30	14	4	12	57	48	32
West Bromwich Albion	30	14	4	12	66	59	32
Wolverhampton W	30	14	3	13	52	63	31
Sheffield United	30	13	5	12	47	61	31
Stoke	30	13	3	14	65	79	29
Sheffield Wednesday	30	9	8	13	48	57	26
Bolton Wanderers	30	10	4	16	38	52	24
Preston North End	30	10	3	17	44	56	23
Darwen	30	7	5	18	37	83	19
Newton Heath	30	6	2	22	36	72	14

1894-95

Match No.	Date	Venue	Opponents	Result		Scorers	Attendance
1	Sep 1	H	Stoke	D	2-2	Bentley, Jones	6000
2	8	A	Small Heath	L	0-2		5000
3	13	A	Liverpool	W	2-1	Cassidy, Tannahill	6000
4	15	H	Preston North End	L	1-2	Settle	10000
5	22	A	Sheffield Wednesday	L	1-2	Andrews	8000
6	29	H	Sunderland	W	4-1	Paton, Henderson, Cassidy, Settle	13000
7	Oct 6	A	Everton	L	1-3	Henderson	14000
8	13	A	Blackburn Rovers	L	1-2	Henderson	8000
9	20	H	Burnley	D	1-1	Andrews	5000
10	27	A	Wolverhampton Wanderers	L	2-4	Lawson 2	6000
11	Nov 3	H	Blackburn Rovers	L	1-3	Paton	8000
12	5	A	West Bromwich Albion	D	1-1	Andrews	3500
13	17	A	Sunderland	L	0-4		8500
14	24	H	Small Heath	L	1-2	Cassidy	4000
15	Dec 1	A	Preston North End	D	2-2	Lyden, Henderson	5000
16	8	A	Everton	L	1-3	Henderson	12000
17	15	H	Wolverhampton Wanderers	W	6-1	Henderson 3, Sommerville, Settle, McGinn	3000
18	25	H	Liverpool	W	1-0	Settle	8000
19	26	A	Derby County	D	2-2	Paton, McGinn	6000
20	Jan 1	H	Derby County	W	6-0	Henderson 4, McGinn, Cassidy	8000
21	5	A	Burnley	L	0-1		5000
22	7	H	Sheffield Wednesday	D	2-2	Paton 2	1,500
23	12	A	Stoke	L	0-5		2500
24	14	H	Sheffield United	W	6-2	Cassidy 2, Spence 2, Paton, Tannahill	8000
25	26	A	Aston Villa	L	1-2	McGeachan	5000
26	Mar 16	A	Nottingham Forest	D	3-3	Cassidy 2, McGeachan	4000
27	23	H	Aston Villa	W	4-3	Bentley, Henderson 2, Turnbull	7000
28	Apr 12	A	Nottingham Forest	W	4-1	Joyce 2, Cassidy, Turnbull	10000
29	13	H	West Bromwich Albion	W	5-0	Joyce, Turnbull 3, Freebairn	10000
30	15	A	Sheffield United	L	0-5		7500
						Appearances	
						Goals	

FA Cup

R1	Feb 2	H	Woolwich Arsenal	W	1-0	Jones	7,000
R2	16	H	Bury	W	1-0	Cassidy	14,444
R3	Mar 2	A	Sunderland	L	1-2	Cassidy	16,000
						Appearances	
						Goals	

252

Player appearance / goals grid (column headers, left to right):

Sutcliffe J.W. · Somerville J. · Jones D. · Paton A. · Stevenson J. · Freebairn A. · Tannahill R. · Cassidy J. · Henderson C. · Andrews W. · Bentley J. · Weir D. · Ferguson G. · Miller J. · Settle J. · Docherty J. · Spiers A. · Lawson R.R. · McGinn J. · Bracelin J. · Guest A. · McGeachan J. · Lyden J. · Shuttleworth T. · Joyce W. · Martin J. · Turnbull P.

Sut	Som	Jon	Pat	Ste	Fre	Tan	Cas	Hen	And	Ben	Wei	Fer	Mil	Set	Doc	Spi	Law	McG	Bra	Gue	McGe	Lyd	Shu	Joy	Mar	Tur
1	2	3	4	5		6	7	8	9	10	11															
1	2		4			6	7	8	9	10	11	3	5													
1	2		4			6	7	11	9	8		3		5	10											
1	2		4			6	7	11	9	8		3		5	10											
1	2	3	4			6	7	8	9	10	11		5													
1	2	3	4				7	11	9	8		6		5	10											
1	2	3	4			6	7	11	9	8			5		10											
1	2	3	5	4		6	7	11	9	8					10											
1	2	3	4			6	7		9	10		11				5	8									
1	2	3	4			6		11	9							5					5	8	1			
1	2	3	4			6	7	11	9									10			5	8				
1	2	3	4			6	7	11	9		8							10			5					
1	2	3	4			6	7	11	9		8							10			5					
1	2	3	4			6	7	11	9		8							10			5					
1	2	3	4			6	7	11	9		8							10			5					
1	2	3	4			6	7	11	9		8							10			5					
1	2		4			6	7	11		3								9	8	10	5					
1	2	3	4			6	7	11			9		8					10			5					
1	2	3	5			6	7	11	9			4						8	10		5					
1	2	3	4			6	7		9		10		11	8							5					
1	2	3	4			6		11	8	10											5			9	7	
1	2	3	4			6		7	8	11											5			9		10
1	2	3	4			6	7	11	8												5			9		10
1	2	3	4			6		11	8												5			9	7	10
1	2	3	4			6		11	8												5			9	7	10

Totals (appearances):

29	29	26	30	2	29	25	26	28	12	4	11	2	8	13	2	4	1	15	1	1	16	3	1	5	3	4

Goals:

| 1 | 1 | 6 | | 1 | 2 | 9 | 14 | 3 | 2 | | 4 | | 2 | | 2 | 3 | | 2 | 1 | | 3 | | | 5 | | |

Secondary grid:

Sut	Som	Jon	Pat	Ste	Fre	Tan	Cas	Hen	And	Ben	Wei	Fer	Mil	Set	Doc	Spi	Law	McG	Bra	Gue	McGe	Lyd	Shu	Joy	Mar	Tur
1	2	3	4			6	7	11						5	10		8					9					
1	2	3	4			6	7	8		11		9		10							5					
1	2	3	4			6	7	8	9	10		11									5					
3	3	3	3			3	3	3	1	1	1		2	1	2	1					3					
			1					2																		

League Table

	P	W	D	L	F	A	Pts
Sunderland	30	21	5	4	80	37	47
Everton	30	18	6	6	82	50	42
Aston Villa	30	17	5	8	82	43	39
Preston North End	30	15	5	10	62	46	35
Blackburn Rovers	30	11	10	9	59	49	32
Sheffield United	30	14	4	12	57	55	32
Nottingham Forest	30	13	5	12	50	56	31
Sheffield Wednesday	30	12	4	14	50	55	28
Burnley	30	11	4	15	44	56	26
Bolton Wanderers	30	9	7	14	61	62	25
Wolverhampton W	30	9	7	14	43	63	25
Small Heath	30	9	7	14	50	74	25
West Bromwich Albion	30	10	4	16	51	66	24
Stoke	30	9	6	15	50	67	24
Derby County	30	7	9	14	45	68	23
Liverpool	30	7	8	15	51	70	22

1895-96

Division One

Manager:

Match No.	Date	Venue	Opponents	Result	Scorers	Attendance
1	Sep 2	A	Stoke	L	0-2		7,000
2	7	A	Bury	W	3-0	McGeachan, Brown, Paton	15,000
3	14	H	Everton	W	3-1	Martin, Cassidy, Joyce	14,000
4	21	H	Burnley	W	1-0	Gunn	8,000
5	28	A	Small Heath	W	2-1	Brown, Wright	4,000
6	Oct 5	H	Bury	L	2-4	Joyce 2	8,000
7	12	A	Burnley	W	2-1	Brown, Joyce	4,000
8	19	H	Nottingham Forest	W	2-1	Tannahill, Wright	7,000
9	26	H	Stoke	W	3-1	Joyce 2, Brown	9,000
10	Nov 2	A	Sheffield Wednesday	D	1-1	Joyce	10,000
11	4	A	West Bromwich Albion	W	3-2	McGeachan, Joyce 2	3,500
12	9	A	Preston North End	L	0-1		10,000
13	23	A	Sunderland	L	0-1		5,000
14	30	H	Blackburn Rovers	D	1-1	Brown	10,000
15	Dec 7	A	Blackburn Rovers	L	2-3	Cassidy, Joyce	5,000
16	14	A	Aston Villa	L	0-2		8,000
17	21	H	Sunderland	W	1-0	Joyce	10,000
18	26	A	Derby County	L	1-2	Jack	12,000
19	30	A	Sheffield United	L	0-1		5,000
20	Jan 1	H	Derby County	W	2-1	Gunn 2	18,000
21	4	H	Wolverhampton Wanderers	W	4-0	Tannahill, Joyce, Cassidy, Paton	7,000
22	11	A	Nottingham Forest	D	0-0		6,000
23	Feb 22	H	Small Heath	W	4-1	Gunn 2, Paton, Vail	8,000
24	Mar 7	H	Aston Villa	D	2-2	Wright, Cassidy	14,364
25	14	H	Preston North End	W	1-0	Jack	8,814
26	Apr 3	H	Sheffield United	W	4-1	Paton, Tannahill, Jack, Nicoll	
27	4	H	West Bromwich Albion	W	2-1	Cassidy, Jack	8,000
28	6	H	Everton	D	1-1	Cassidy	15,000
29	11	A	Wolverhampton Wanderers	L	0-5		4,000
30	25	H	Sheffield Wednesday	W	2-0	Jack, Cassidy	6,000

Appearances
Goals

FA Cup

	Date	Venue	Opponents	Result	Scorers	Attendance
R1	Feb 1	A	Crewe Alexandra	W	4-0	Brown, Gunn, Tannahill, Wright	5,000
R2	15	A	Blackpool	W	2-0	Cassidy, Wright	5,00
R3	29	H	Bury	W	2-0	Wright, Gunn	16,39
SF	Mar 21	N	Sheffield Wednesday	D	1-1	Tannahill	30,000
rep	28	N	Sheffield Wednesday	L	1-3	Tannahill	16,00

SF at Goodison Park, Liverpool.
SF replay at the Town Ground, Nottingham.

Appearances
Goal

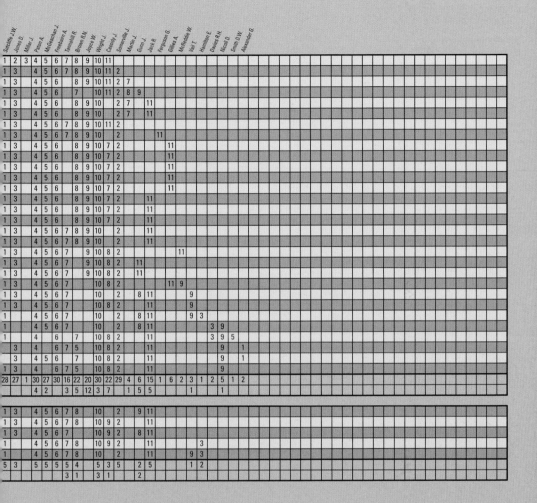

1896-97

The Wanderers faced 'Double' winners elect Aston Villa twice in the space of five days in March 1897. Two Robert Jack goals gave them a half-time advantage at Perry Bar before Villa came back to hit six without reply. Villa then came to Burnden and won 2–1. Bolton, who had led the League at Christmas, slumped by winning just two of their final 10 League games.

Match No.	Date	Venue	Opponents	Result		Scorers	Attendance
1	Sep 5	A	Sunderland	D	1-1	Jack	6,000
2	7	A	Liverpool	W	2-0	Nicoll, Jack	15,000
3	12	H	Blackburn Rovers	D	0-0		5,000
4	19	A	Stoke	W	3-2	Thomson, Nicoll, Clare (own-goal)	5,000
5	26	H	Sunderland	W	1-0	Jones	10,000
6	Oct 3	H	Preston North End	W	3-1	Wright, Jack, Gilligan	14,000
7	10	H	Bury	W	2-0	Paton, Nicoll	15,000
8	17	A	Blackburn Rovers	L	0-1		10,000
9	24	H	Stoke	W	4-0	Jack 2, Thomson, Gilligan	5,000
10	31	A	Bury	D	2-2	Jack, Darroch (own-goal)	14,000
11	Nov 2	A	West Bromwich Albion	L	0-1		5,200
12	14	A	Everton	W	3-2	Thomson, Wright, Gilligan	12,000
13	21	A	Preston North End	W	3-2	Wright, Gilligan, Thomson	10,000
14	Dec 7	H	Everton	W	2-0	Jack, Gilligan	3,000
15	19	H	West Bromwich Albion	D	2-2	Nicoll, Gilligan	9,000
16	26	A	Derby County	L	0-1		15,000
17	29	A	Sheffield United	L	0-1		11,000
18	Jan 1	H	Liverpool	L	1-4	Jack	20,000
19	16	A	Nottingham Forest	L	0-2		6,000
20	Feb 6	H	Burnley	W	2-0	Cassidy, Jack	5,000
21	27	A	Sheffield Wednesday	D	0-0		8,000
22	Mar 6	H	Derby County	L	1-3	Joyce	12,000
23	13	H	Burnley	W	2-1	Miller, Wright	4,000
24	20	H	Nottingham Forest	D	0-0		5,000
25	22	A	Aston Villa	L	2-6	Jack 2	8,000
26	27	H	Aston Villa	L	1-2	McGeachan	8,000
27	Apr 5	H	Wolverhampton Wanderers	L	1-2	Nicoll	4,000
28	10	H	Sheffield Wednesday	W	2-1	Cassidy, Miller	2,000
29	16	H	Sheffield United	L	0-2		7,000
30	20	A	Wolverhampton Wanderers	L	0-4		3,000

Appearances

2 own-goals | Goals

FA Cup

R1	Jan 30	A	Grimsby Town	D	0-0		10,000
rep	Feb 8	H	Grimsby Town	D	3-3	Cassidy, Thomson, Jones	7,000
rep2	11	N	Grimsby Town	W	3-2	Joyce 2, Jones	10,000
R2	13	A	Derby County	L	1-4	Brown	13,750

R1 replay after extra-time. | Appearances

R1 replay 2 at Bramall Lane, Sheffield. | Goals

Appearance Grid

Sutcliffe J.W.	Somerville J.	Jones D.	Paton A.	McGeachan J.	Freebairn A.	Thomson W.	Gilligan A.	Nicoll D.	Wright J.	Jack R.	Brown R.H.	Scott S.	Miller T.A.	Smith D.W.	Cassidy J.	Joyce W.	Scotchbrook F.	Tamblin R.	Davies R.H.	Hiles A.
2	3	4	5	6	7	8	9	10	11											
2	3	4	5	6	7	8	9	10	11											
2	3	4	5	6	7	8	9	10	11											
2	3	4	5	6	7	8	9	10	11											
2	3	4	5	6	7	8	9	10	11											
2	3	4	5	6	7	8	9	10	11											
2	3	4	5	6	7	8	9	10	11											
2	3	4	5	6	7	8	9	10	11											
2	3	4	5	6	7	8	9	10	11											
2	3	5		6	7	8	9	10	11	4										
2	3	4	5	6	7	8	9	10	11											
2		4	5	6	7	8	9	10	11	3										
2	3	4	5	6	7	8	9	10	11											
2	3	4	5	6	7	8	9	10	11											
2	3	4	5	6	7	8	9	10	11											
2	3	4	5	6	7	8	9	10	11											
2	3	4	5	6	7	8		10		11			9							
2	3	4	5	6	7		9	10	11				8	1						
2	3	4	5	6	7	8	9	10	11											
2	3	4	5	6	7		10		11				8	9						
2		4		6		7		11	5	3	8		9		10					
2		4		6			11	10	5	3	9		8	7						
2		5	6	7			11	10	4	3	9	1	8							
2	4	5	6	7				10	11	3	9		8							
2		4		6			10	8	11		3	9	5			7				
	4	5	6				10	8	11		2		7	9			3			
2		4		6		8	9	10	11		3		5			7				
5	3	4		6		10			11		2	7		8	9					
2	3	4	5	6		8		10	11			2	7			9				
	3	4	5	6		8	9	10	11			2	7						1	
28	22	29	24	30	22	22	27	26	28	4	10	10	2	9	5	1	2	1	1	
											1	1	1	4	6	5	4	11		2	2 1

Sutcliffe J.W.	Somerville J.	Jones D.	Paton A.	McGeachan J.	Freebairn A.	Thomson W.	Gilligan A.	Nicoll D.	Wright J.	Jack R.	Brown R.H.	Scott S.	Miller T.A.	Smith D.W.	Cassidy J.	Joyce W.	Scotchbrook F.	Tamblin R.	Davies R.H.	Hiles A.
2	3	4	5	6	7	8		10		11			9							
2	3	4	5	6	7		10		11			1	8	9						
2	3	4	5	6	7		10		11				8	9						
2	3	4	5	6		10			11	7			8	9						
4	4	4	4	4	3	2	3		4	1		1	1	3	3					
	2			1						1				1	2					

League Table

	P	W	D	L	F	A	Pts
Aston Villa	30	21	5	4	73	38	47
Sheffield United	30	13	10	7	42	29	36
Derby County	30	16	4	10	70	50	36
Preston North End	30	11	12	7	55	40	34
Liverpool	30	12	9	9	46	38	33
Sheffield Wednesday	30	10	11	9	42	37	31
Everton	30	14	3	13	62	57	31
Bolton Wanderers	30	12	6	12	40	43	30
Bury	30	10	10	10	39	44	30
Wolverhampton W	30	11	6	13	45	41	28
Nottingham Forest	30	9	8	13	44	49	26
West Bromwich Albion	30	10	6	14	33	56	26
Stoke	30	11	3	16	48	59	25
Blackburn Rovers	30	11	3	16	35	62	25
Sunderland	30	7	9	14	34	47	23
Burnley	30	6	7	17	43	61	19

Did you know that?

A club record of five consecutive League games without a goal was set during January and February 1898. This was not equalled until 1990, but the 28 League goals scored throughout 1897–98 still stands as the lowest total by the club in a season.

Match No.	Date	Venue	Opponents	Result		Scorers	Attendance
1	Sep 4	A	Everton	L	1-2	Thomson	25,00
2	11	A	Blackburn Rovers	W	3-1	Nicoll, Gilligan, Jack	7,00
3	18	H	Notts County	W	1-0	T. Miller	9,00
4	25	H	Preston North End	W	1-0	Cassidy	10,00
5	Oct 2	A	Aston Villa	L	2-3	Jack, Wright	20,00
6	9	H	Sheffield Wednesday	L	0-3		6,00
7	16	A	Preston North End	D	0-0		6,00
8	23	H	Nottingham Forest	W	2-0	T. Miller, Jack	5,00
9	30	H	Sunderland	W	1-0	Cassidy	10,00
10	Nov 1	A	West Bromwich Albion	L	0-2		8,20
11	6	A	Notts County	W	2-1	T. Miller, Jack	8,00
12	13	H	Stoke	W	2-1	Paton (pen), T Miller	5,00
13	20	H	Aston Villa	W	2-0	Wright, Cassidy	15,00
14	27	A	Sheffield Wednesday	L	0-3		5,00
15	Dec 11	A	Bury	L	1-2	Cassidy	7,00
16	25	H	Liverpool	L	0-2		9,00
17	27	A	Derby County	L	0-1		15,00
18	Jan 1	H	Derby County	D	3-3	T. Miller, Wright 2	12,00
19	3	H	Bury	D	0-0		4,00
20	8	A	Nottingham Forest	L	0-2		8,00
21	15	A	Stoke	L	0-2		5,00
22	Feb 7	A	Sheffield United	L	0-4		5,00
23	22	A	Sunderland	L	0-2		6,00
24	Mar 12	H	Wolverhampton Wanderers	W	2-1	Cassidy 2	4,00
25	19	A	Liverpool	D	1-1	Gilligan	7,00
26	26	H	Everton	W	1-0	Nicoll	3,00
27	Apr 2	H	West Bromwich Albion	W	2-0	Fitchett, Nicoll	5,00
28	8	H	Sheffield United	L	0-1		19,35
29	9	A	Wolverhampton Wanderers	L	0-2		4,00
30	14	H	Blackburn Rovers	L	1-2	Cassidy	

Appearances
Goal

FA Cup

	Date	Venue	Opponents	Result		Scorers	Attendance
R1	Jan 29	A	Luton Town	W	1-0	Cassidy	4,50
R2	Feb 12	H	Manchester City	W	1-0	T. Miller	14,00
R3	26	H	Southampton	D	0-0		15,00
rep	Mar 2	A	Southampton	L	0-4		15,00

Appearances
Goals

Player appearances and goals grid (players listed as column headers, left to right): Willie J.W., Somerville J., Jonas D., Platon A., McGlachan J., Freeborn A., Miller T.A., Gilligan A., Thomson W., Wright J., Jack R., Brown B.N., Nicoll D., Cassidy J., Scott S., Tatum W., Miller J., Scorchbrook F., Davies R.H., Fitchett J., Lee J., Gregory J., Chorlton H.H., Lockhart G., Halley W.

Willie J.W.	Somerville J.	Jonas D.	Platon A.	McGlachan J.	Freeborn A.	Miller T.A.	Gilligan A.	Thomson W.	Wright J.	Jack R.	Brown B.N.	Nicoll D.	Cassidy J.	Scott S.	Tatum W.	Miller J.	Scorchbrook F.	Davies R.H.	Fitchett J.	Lee J.	Gregory J.	Chorlton H.H.	Lockhart G.	Halley W.
2	3	4	5	6	7	8	9	10	11															
2	3	4		6		8	7	10	11	5	9													
2	3	4		6	9	8	7	10	11	5														
2	3	4	5	6		8	7	10	11			9												
2	3	4		6	7	8		10	11		9	5												
2	3	4		6		8	7	10		5	9	11												
2		4		6	9	8	7	10	11	5				3										
2		4		6	9	8		10	11	5			7	3										
2		4		6	9	8		10	11	5			7	3	1									
2		4		6	9			10	11	5	8		7	3	1									
2		4		6	9	8		10	11	5			7	3										
2		4		6	9	8		10	11	5			7	3										
2		4		6	9	8		10	11	5			7	3										
2		4		6	9	8		10	11	5			7	3										
2	3	4		6	9	8		10	11				7		5									
2	3	4		6	9	8	7		11	5			10											
2	3	4		6	8	11		10		5			7		9									
2	3	4		6	8	11		10		5			7		9									
2	3	4		6	8	11	7	10			5				9									
2	3			6	8	11	7	10			9	5	4											
2	3			6	8	11			5	10	7		9	4										
2		4		6	8	9		10	11	5			7			3								
2	3			6	7	8		10	11	5				9		4								
2				6	9	8	7			5		10			3	4	1		11					
2				6		8	7			5		9			3	4		11	10					
2				6		8	7		5	10	9				3	4		11						
2				6		8	7		5	10	9				3	4		11						
2				6		8	7		5	10	9				3	4		11						
2		4		6		8	7		11	5	10	9				1			3					
	2	4		6			8	11		9	7		5			1			10		3			
29	**15**	**22**	**2**	**30**	**21**	**28**	**15**	**22**	**19**	**23**	**11**	**24**	**9**	**2**	**8**	**1**	**6**	**6**	**3**	**5**	**2**	**1**	**1**	
	1				5	2	1		4	4			3	7				1						

Willie J.W.	Somerville J.	Jonas D.	Platon A.	McGlachan J.	Freeborn A.	Miller T.A.	Gilligan A.	Thomson W.	Wright J.	Jack R.	Brown B.N.	Nicoll D.	Cassidy J.	Scott S.	Tatum W.	Miller J.	Scorchbrook F.	Davies R.H.	Fitchett J.	Lee J.	Gregory J.	Chorlton H.H.	Lockhart G.	Halley W.
2		4		6	9	8		10	11	5			7				3							
2	3	4		6	9	8		10	11	5			7											
2	3			6	9	8		10	11	5			7					4						
2	3	4		6	9	11	7	10		5				8										
4	**3**	**3**		**4**	**4**	**4**	**1**	**4**	**3**	**4**			**3**	**1**			**1**	**1**						
		1											1											

League Table

	P	W	D	L	F	A	Pts
Sheffield United	30	17	8	5	56	31	42
Sunderland	30	16	5	9	43	30	37
Wolverhampton W	30	14	7	9	57	41	35
Everton	30	13	9	8	48	39	35
Sheffield Wednesday	30	15	3	12	51	42	33
Aston Villa	30	14	5	11	61	51	33
West Bromwich Albion	30	11	10	9	44	45	32
Nottingham Forest	30	11	9	10	47	49	31
Liverpool	30	11	6	13	48	45	28
Derby County	30	11	6	13	57	61	28
Bolton Wanderers	30	11	4	15	28	41	26
Preston North End	30	8	8	14	35	43	24
Notts County	30	8	8	14	36	46	24
Bury	30	8	8	14	39	51	24
Blackburn Rovers	30	7	10	13	39	54	24
Stoke	30	8	8	14	35	55	24

Match No.	Date	Venue	Opponents	Result		Scorers	Attendance
1	Sep 3	H	West Bromwich Albion	D	3-3	Nicoll, Wright, Miller	8,0
2	10	A	Blackburn Rovers	L	1-4	Miller	8,00
3	17	H	Sheffield Wednesday	D	0-0		7,0
4	24	A	Sunderland	D	0-0		18,00
5	Oct 1	H	Wolverhampton Wanderers	W	2-1	Wright 2	6,00
6	8	A	Everton	L	0-1		10,0
7	15	H	Notts County	L	0-1		5,00
8	22	A	Stoke	W	3-2	Miller, Freebairn, Nicoll	4,0
9	29	A	Aston Villa	L	1-2	A. Gilligan	17,40
10	Nov 5	A	Burnley	L	0-2		4,00
11	12	H	Sheffield United	W	3-0	A. Gilligan 2, Jack	9,00
12	19	A	Newcastle United	L	1-4	Miller	16,00
13	26	H	Preston North End	D	2-2	A. Gilligan, Miller	5,00
14	Dec 3	A	Liverpool	L	0-2		10,00
15	10	H	Nottingham Forest	L	0-2		4,00
16	17	H	Bury	L	0-1		8,00
17	26	A	Derby County	D	1-1	Barlow	8,00
18	31	A	West Bromwich Albion	L	0-1		2,00
19	Jan 3	H	Burnley	W	2-0	Brown, Jack	8,00
20	7	H	Blackburn Rovers	L	0-2		8,00
21	14	A	Sheffield Wednesday	L	0-1		6,00
22	21	H	Sunderland	W	6-1	A. Gilligan 2, Brown 2, Barlow, Barnes	9,00
23	Feb 18	H	Stoke	L	0-2		10,00
24	25	H	Everton	L	2-4	Barlow 2	6,00
25	Mar 11	A	Sheffield United	L	1-3	Morgan	8,00
26	18	H	Newcastle United	D	0-0		5,00
27	31	A	Derby County	W	2-1	Morgan, Barlow	8,00
28	Apr 1	H	Liverpool	W	2-1	McAteer, Morgan	12,00
29	3	A	Notts County	L	1-2	McAteer	8,00
30	4	A	Wolverhampton Wanderers	L	0-1		7,00
31	8	A	Nottingham Forest	W	2-1	Morgan 2	4,50
32	15	A	Bury	L	1-3	McAteer	7,00
33	17	H	Aston Villa	D	0-0		7,00
34	29	A	Preston North End	W	1-0	Morgan	2,50

Appearances
Goals

FA Cup

R1	Jan 28	A	Wolverhampton Wanderers	D	0-0		13,54
rep	Feb 1	H	Wolverhampton Wanderers	L	0-1		4,05

Appearances

Player appearance / line-up grid (shirt numbers by player and match)

Somerville J.	Lockhart G.	Fitchett J.	Brown R.N.	Freebairn A.	Thomson W.	Miller T.A.	Nicol D.	Wright J.	Jack R.	Davies R.H.	Gilligan A.	Gregory J.	Sutcliffe J.W.	Barlow T.H.	Davies W.H.	Carr S.R.	Oreston H.H.	McKay P.	Bolton R.	Paton A.	Barnes G.	Howcroft H.	McAleer T.	Gilligan W.	Marshall T.	Morgan H.	Hynds T.	Hanson J.
2	3	4	5	6	7	8	9	10	11																			
	3	4	5	6		8	9	10	2	7	11																	
2	3	7	5	6		8	9	10						8	1	11												
2	3	7	5	6		8	9	10		11			1	4														
2	3		5	6		8	9	10		11			1	4	7													
2	3		5	6		8	9	10		11			1	4	7													
2	3		5	6		8		9		7			1	10	4	11												
2	3		5	6	7	8	9		11				1	10	4													
2	3		5	6	7	8	9		11				1	10	4													
2	3		5	6	7	8	9		11					10	4													
2			5	6	7	8	9		11	3			1	10	4													
2			5	6	7	8	9		11	3			1	10	4													
2			5	6	7	8	9		11	3			1	10	4													
2			5	6	7	8	9		11	3			1	10	4													
2			5	6	7	8			11	3			1	10	4		9											
2	3		8	4					11				1	10	5	7	9		6									
2			8	6					11	3	7		1	10	5				4	9								
2			9	6					11	3	8		1	10	5				4	7								
2			9	6		10			11	3	8		1		5				4	7								
2			9	6		10			11	3			1		5				8	4	7							
2	3		9	6					11				1	10					7	4	5							
2	3		9	5					11				1	10					7	4		6						
2	3		5						11				1	10					7	4		6	8	9				
2	3		5			7			11				1	10	4		8					6		9				
	3		8	6			9		11	2			1	10	4									7	5			
	3			6			9			2			1	10	4				11					7	5	8		
	3	4	9	6					11	2	8		1	10										7	5			
	3	4		6					11	2	8		1	10							9			7	5			
	3	4		6					11	2	8		1	10							9			7	5			
	3			6			9		11	2	8		1		4				10		5			7				
	3	4		6					11	2	8		1	10							9			7	5			
	3	4	10	6					11	2	8		1								9			7	5			
3		4		6					11	2	8		1	10							9			7	5			
3		4	9	6					11	2	8		1	10							5			7				
25	23	11	27	33	8	17	16	7	27	20	28	1	31	16	21	2	3	3	2	5	9	3	8	3	1	12	8	1
		3	1		5	2	3	2		6				5						1		3					6		

Somerville J.	Lockhart G.	Fitchett J.	Brown R.N.	Freebairn A.	Thomson W.	Miller T.A.	Nicol D.	Wright J.	Jack R.	Davies R.H.	Gilligan A.	Gregory J.	Sutcliffe J.W.	Barlow T.H.	Davies W.H.	Carr S.R.	Oreston H.H.	McKay P.	Bolton R.	Paton A.	Barnes G.	Howcroft H.	McAleer T.	Gilligan W.	Marshall T.	Morgan H.	Hynds T.	Hanson J.
2	3	4	9	6					11				1	10										7	5			
2	3			6			9		11				1	10					4					7	5			
2	2	1	1	2			1		2				2	2					1					2	2			

League Table

	P	W	D	L	F	A	Pts
Aston Villa	34	19	7	8	76	40	45
Liverpool	34	19	5	10	49	33	43
Burnley	34	15	9	10	45	47	39
Everton	34	15	8	11	48	41	38
Notts County	34	12	13	9	47	51	37
Blackburn Rovers	34	14	8	12	60	52	36
Sunderland	34	15	6	13	41	41	36
Wolverhampton W	34	14	7	13	54	48	35
Derby County	34	12	11	11	62	57	35
Bury	34	14	7	13	48	49	35
Nottingham Forest	34	11	11	12	42	42	33
Stoke	34	13	7	14	47	52	33
Newcastle United	34	11	8	15	49	48	30
West Bromwich Albion	34	12	6	16	42	57	30
Preston North End	34	10	9	15	44	47	29
Sheffield United	34	9	11	14	45	51	29
Bolton Wanderers	34	9	7	18	37	51	25
Sheffield Wednesday	34	8	8	18	32	61	24

Division Two

Match No.	Date		Venue	Opponents	Result		Scorers	Attendance
1	Sep	2	A	Loughborough	W	3-2	Bell, McAteer, Jack	5,0
2		9	H	Newton Heath	W	2-1	Bell 2	6,0
3		16	A	Sheffield Wednesday	L	1-2	Massey (own-goal)	10,0
4		23	H	Lincoln City	W	4-0	Gilligan, Bell, Fitchett, Somerville	3,0
5		30	A	Small Heath	D	0-0		10,0
6	Oct	14	A	Grimsby Town	D	0-0		5,0
7		21	H	Woolwich Arsenal	W	1-0	Barlow	4,0
8	Nov	4	H	Leicester Fosse	D	2-2	Bell, Morgan	5,0
9		11	A	Luton Town	W	2-0	Barlow 2	
10		25	A	Walsall	D	2-2	Barlow, Picken	4,0
11	Dec	2	H	Middlesbrough	W	3-0	Brown, Jack, Fitchett	3,0
12		6	A	Chesterfield	D	3-3	Jack, Barlow, Picken	
13		16	A	Gainsborough Trinity	D	1-1	Barlow	
14		23	A	Burton Swifts	W	5-2	Bell 2, Morgan, Picken, Freebairn	
15		26	A	Barnsley	W	6-1	Picken, Freebairn, Hanson 3, Morgan	2,5
16		30	H	Loughborough	W	7-0	Hanson 2, Morgan, Bell 3, McAteer	3,0
17	Jan	1	H	New Brighton Tower	W	2-1	Bell 2	8,0
18		2	H	Burslem Port Vale	W	5-0	McAteer 3, Jack 2	2,5
19		6	A	Newton Heath	W	2-1	Picken, Morgan	6,0
20		13	H	Sheffield Wednesday	W	1-0	Jack	12,3
21		20	A	Lincoln City	L	0-1		4,0
22	Feb	3	H	Small Heath	D	1-1	Fitchett	6,2
23		17	H	Grimsby Town	L	1-2	Gilligan	4,1
24		24	A	Woolwich Arsenal	W	1-0	Bell	5,0
25	Mar	10	A	Leicester Fosse	D	0-0		12,0
26		17	A	Luton Town	W	3-0	Jack, Morgan, own-goal	3,6
27		31	H	Walsall	W	2-0	R. Brown, Bell	3,5
28	Apr	7	A	Middlesbrough	W	3-0	Morgan, Hanson, Bell	7,0
29		13	H	Barnsley	W	2-0	Bell, Morgan	8,0
30		14	H	Chesterfield	W	3-0	Picken, Gilligan, Morgan	7,3
31		16	A	New Brighton Tower	L	1-3	Picken	6,0
32		21	H	Gainsborough Trinity	W	3-0	Chorlton 2, Bell	4,3
33		23	A	Burslem Port Vale	W	2-0	Bell 2	4
34		28	H	Burton Swifts	W	5-0	Bell 4, Morgan	2,3
								Appearance
							2 own-goals	Goa

FA Cup

R1	Jan	27	A	Sheffield Wednesday	L	0-1		12,3
								Appearance

	Sutcliffe J.W.	Halley W.	Lockhart G.	Brown R.N.	McAdam T.	Freebairn A.	Morgan H.	Gilligan A.	Bell S.J.T.	Barlow T.H.	Jack R.	Picken J.B.	Somerville J.	Fitchett J.	Hanson J.	Jones L.	Scotchbrook F.	Brown W.G.	Walker W.H.	Anthony A.	Chorlton H.H.
	1	2	3	4	5	6	7	8	9	10	11										
	1	2	3	4	5	6	7		9	10	11	8									
	1	3		5		6	7	8	9	10		11	2	4							
	1	3		6		4		7	9	8			2	5	10	11					
	1	3		5		6	8	11	9	10			2	4	7						
	1	3		5		6	8	11	9	10			2	4		7					
	1	3		7	5	6	8	11	9	10			2	4							
	1	3		5	9	6	8	11	7	10			2	4							
	1	3		4	5	6	8	7	9	10	11		2								
	1	3		5		6	8	7	9	10		11	2	4							
	1	3		5		6	8	7	9	10	11		2	4							
	1	3		5		6		7		10	11	8	2		9		4				
	1	3		4	5	6	7	10	9	8	11		2								
	1			5		6	7		9	10	11	3	2	4	8						
	1				5	6	7		9		11	10	2	4	8		3				
	1		5	6	7		9		11	10	2	4	8				3				
	1			5	6	7		9		11	10	2	4	8			3				
	1		5	6	7		9		11	10	2	4	8				3				
	1	3		5	6	7		9		11	10	2	4	8			3				
	1	3	6	5			7		9	11	10	2	4	8			3				
	1		6	5			7		9	11	10	2	4	8			3				
	1	2		5	6	7		9		11	10		4	8			3				
	1	2	4	5		7	11	9			10		6	8			3				
	1	2		5		10		8		11	9		4	7		6	3				
		2		5		7		9		11	10		4	8		6	3	1			
	1	2		5		6	7	8	9		11	10		4				3			
	1	2		5		6	7	8	9		11	10		4				3			
	1	2		5		6	7	11	9			10		4	8			3			
	1	2		5		6	7	11	9			10		4	8			3			
	1	2		5		6	7	11	9			10		4	8			3			
	1	2		5		6	7	11	9			10		4	8			3			
	1	2		7		6			9			10		4	8			3		5	11
	1	2		7	4	6			9			10			8			3		5	11
	1			4	6	7			9			10	2		8			3		5	11
	33	27	2	27	17	29	30	20	32	14	19	25	20	27	22	2	3	18	1	3	3
		2	5	2	10	3	23	6	7	7	1	3	6					2			
	1	2		6	5		7		9		11	10		4	8			3			
	1	1		1	1		1		1	1		1	1		1			1			

Division One

Match No.	Date		Venue	Opponents	Result		Scorers	Attendance
1	Sep	1	H	Derby County	L	0-1		10,872
2		8	A	Sheffield Wednesday	L	0-1		14,000
3		15	A	Notts County	L	1-3	McAteer (pen)	10,000
4		22	H	Preston North End	D	1-1	Tracey	8,000
5		29	A	Wolverhampton Wanderers	D	1-1	Tracey	6,000
6	Oct	6	H	Aston Villa	W	1-0	L. Bell	12,231
7		13	A	Liverpool	L	1-2	L. Bell	10,000
8		20	H	Newcastle United	W	3-2	Tracey 2, McKie	17,810
9		27	A	Sheffield United	W	2-0	L. Bell, McKie	10,000
10	Nov	3	H	Manchester City	D	0-0		20,634
11		10	A	Bury	L	0-3		10,000
12		12	A	Stoke	L	1-2	Picken	2,000
13		24	A	Blackburn Rovers	L	0-2		4,000
14	Dec	1	H	Stoke	W	1-0	McKie	5,171
15		8	A	West Bromwich Albion	L	2-7	Tracey, McKie	6,000
16		15	H	Everton	W	1-0	L. Bell	6,474
17		25	A	Nottingham Forest	L	0-3		10,000
18		26	A	Aston Villa	L	0-3		20,000
19		29	A	Derby County	L	2-4	Picken, L Bell	8,000
20	Jan	1	H	Nottingham Forest	W	4-2	R. Brown, Hanson, Freebairn, L. Bell	13,900
21		2	H	Sunderland	D	0-0		16,000
22		5	H	Sheffield Wednesday	D	1-1	Freebairn	9,144
23	Feb	16	H	Liverpool	W	1-0	L. Bell	9,461
24	Mar	2	A	Sheffield United	D	0-0		2,017
25		9	A	Manchester City	D	1-1	McKie	14,000
26		16	H	Bury	W	3-2	L. Bell, McAteer, Picken	15,000
27		23	A	Preston North End	W	3-1	Picken 2, McKie	7,000
28		27	A	Newcastle United	L	0-3		16,000
29		30	H	Blackburn Rovers	W	1-0	Tracey	6,053
30	Apr	5	H	Notts County	L	0-1		15,617
31		8	A	Sunderland	L	1-5	McKie	10,000
32		13	H	West Bromwich Albion	W	3-2	Barlow, McKie, R. Brown	5,536
33		20	A	Everton	W	3-2	Barlow 2, Picken	9,000
34		29	H	Wolverhampton Wanderers	W	1-0	Picken	4,000
							Appearances	
							Goals	

FA Cup

R1	Feb	9	H	Derby County	W	1-0	L. Bell	13,171
R2		23	H	Reading	L	0-1		11,592
							Appearances	
							Goals	

League appearance and goals grid (player columns, left to right):

	llsop H.	Barlow T.H.	Bell F.	Ball S.L.T.	Brown R.N.	Brown W.G.	Burnson J.	Calderbank J.	Chorlton H.H.	Fisher J.	Freebairn A.	Halby W.	Hanson J.	Hasam R.	Hodgkiss W.	Jack R.	Low J.H.	McBaer T.	McKie J.	Morgan H.	Oneck C.	Picken J.B.	Smith G.T.	Somerville J.	Sutcliffe J.W.	Tracey W.M.	Waller W.H.	Woolfall T.
			9	5	3				4	6	2	8				11				7		10			1			
			9		3	6			4		2	8					5		7			10			1	11		
			9		3			4		6	2						5	8	7			10			1	11		
	10			3		4				6	2						5	9	7		8				1	11		
	10	7							4	6	2						5	9			8			1		11	3
	10	7							4	6							5	9			8	2	1		11	3	
	10	7							4	6	2						5	9			8		1		11	3	
	10	7							4	6	2						5	9			8				11	1	3
	10	7							4	6	2						5	9			8		1		11	3	
	10	7							4	6	2						5	9			8		1		11	3	
	10	7					4			6	2						5	9			8		1		11	3	
	10	7								6	2				4		5	9			8		1		11	3	
		7		2				4		6				10			5	9			8		1		11	3	
	10	7	4	2						6							5	9			8		1		11	3	
	10	7		2				4		6							5	9			8		1		11	3	
	10	4	7		2							5	6					9			8		1		11	3	
	10		7	4	2					6	1						5	9			8				11	3	
		4	7	5	2					6	1							9		10	8				11	3	
		4	7		2					6	10						5	9			8				11	1	3
		7	4	2						6	8						5	9			10				11	1	3
		7		2					4	6	8						5	9			10				11	1	3
		7		2					4	6	8						5	9			10				11	1	3
	10	7		3					4	6							5	9			8	2	1		11		
	10	7		2					4	6							5	9			8		1		11	3	
	10	7		2					4	6							5	9			8		1		11	3	
	10	7							4	6							5	9			8	2	1		11	3	
	10	7							4	6							5	9	3		8	2	1		11		
	10	7	6						2	4							5	9			8	3	1		11		
	10	7			6				4		1						5	9	3		8		2		11		
	10	7		2	6				4								5	9	3		8		1		11		
		7	11		6				4	8							5	9	3		10		2		1		
	10	7	11		6				4								5	9	3		8		2		1		
	10	7	11		6				4	5								9	3		8		2		1		
8		7	11	2	6			5	4									9	3		10				1		
1	23	3	33	10	19	6	3	1	22	29	12	10	1	1	2	1	29	32	4	7	34	1	9	26	29	5	21
	3		8	2					2	1							2	8			7					6	

Goals / substitutes section:

		7		3					4	6	8						5	9			10			2	1	11	
		8		2						6						4	5	9			10	7		1	11	3	
		2		2				1	2		1					1	2	2			2	1	1	2	2	1	
		1																										

League Table

	P	W	D	L	F	A	Pts
Liverpool	34	19	7	8	59	35	45
Sunderland	34	15	13	6	57	26	43
Notts County	34	18	4	12	54	46	40
Nottingham Forest	34	16	7	11	53	36	39
Bury	34	16	7	11	53	37	39
Newcastle United	34	14	10	10	42	37	38
Everton	34	16	5	13	55	42	37
Sheffield Wednesday	34	13	10	11	52	42	36
Blackburn Rovers	34	12	9	13	39	47	33
Bolton Wanderers	34	13	7	14	39	55	33
Manchester City	34	13	6	15	48	58	32
Derby County	34	12	7	15	55	42	31
Wolverhampton W	34	9	13	12	39	55	31
Sheffield United	34	12	7	15	35	52	31
Aston Villa	34	10	10	14	45	51	30
Stoke	34	11	5	18	46	57	27
Preston North End	34	9	7	18	49	75	25
West Bromwich Albion	34	7	8	19	35	62	22

1901-02

Division One

Match No.	Date		Venue	Opponents	Result		Scorers	Attendance
1	Sep	7	A	Small Heath	L	0-2		15,000
2		14	H	Derby County	W	2-1	L. Bell, Picken	10,429
3		21	A	Sheffield Wednesday	L	1-5	L. Bell	8,000
4		28	H	Notts County	D	1-1	Tracey	9,040
5	Oct	5	H	Grimsby Town	W	4-0	L. Bell 2, Picken 2	5,277
6		12	A	Manchester City	L	0-1		16,000
7		19	H	Wolverhampton Wanderers	D	2-2	L. Bell, Picken	9,100
8		26	A	Liverpool	D	1-1	Barlow	15,000
9	Nov	2	H	Newcastle United	W	3-1	Williams 2, L. Bell	12,173
10		9	A	Aston Villa	L	0-1		15,000
11		23	A	Nottingham Forest	L	1-4	Picken	4,000
12		30	H	Bury	D	2-2	Barlow, Williams	16,292
13	Dec	7	A	Blackburn Rovers	L	0-2		2,000
14		14	H	Stoke	W	2-1	Barlow, Taylor	3,919
15		21	A	Everton	L	0-1		13,000
16		28	H	Sunderland	D	0-0		5,848
17	Jan	1	H	Manchester City	D	3-3	Bannister, L. Bell, Williams	20,000
18		2	H	Nottingham Forest	W	3-0	McKie, Picken, Williams	11,000
19		4	H	Small Heath	W	4-0	McKie 3, Williams	6,583
20		11	A	Derby County	W	2-1	Barlow, L. Bell	6,000
21		18	H	Sheffield Wednesday	W	3-1	Bannister (pen), L. Bell, Freebairn	10,506
22	Feb	1	A	Grimsby Town	L	1-4	Picken	5,000
23		15	A	Wolverhampton Wanderers	W	2-1	Barlow, Picken	5,000
24		22	H	Liverpool	W	1-0	McKie	12,000
25	Mar	1	A	Newcastle United	L	1-4	Picken	18,000
26		8	H	Aston Villa	D	2-2	McKie, Stokes	10,000
27		28	H	Sheffield United	W	1-0	McKie	18,000
28		29	A	Bury	D	2-2	Barlow 2	12,000
29		31	A	Notts County	L	1-2	Stokes	18,000
30	Apr	5	H	Blackburn Rovers	W	4-0	Barlow 2, McKie, Picken	5,784
31		7	A	Sheffield United	L	0-2		3,000
32		12	A	Stoke	L	0-4		4,000
33		19	H	Everton	L	1-3	Barlow	9,715
34		26	A	Sunderland	L	1-2	Worthington	6,000

Appearances
Goals

FA Cup

	Date		Venue	Opponents	Result		Scorers	Attendance
R1	Jan	25	A	Wolverhampton Wanderers	W	2-0	McKie, Williams	16,103
R2	Feb	8	A	Sheffield United	L	1-2	McKie	13,009

Appearances
Goals

Player appearances and goals grid

Sutcliffe J.W.	Brown W.G.	Struthers R.	Fitchett J.	Freebairn A.	Brunson A.	Bell S.J.T.	Picken J.B.	McKie J.	Barlow T.H.	Tracey W.M.	Ostick C.	Brown R.N.	Hanson J.	McAteer T.	Ashley H.	Neyland M.	Taylor R.	Bell F.	Williams H.	Bannister W.	Halliday J.F.	Worthington J.	Nicoll D.	Stokes D.	Woollat T.
1	2	3	4	5	6	7	8	9	10	11															
1	2		4		6	7	8	9	10	11	3	5													
		2	4		6	7	8	9		11	3		1	5	10										
1	2		4		6	7	8			11	3	5			10	9									
1	2		4		6	7	8	9		11	3				10		5								
1	2		4		6	7	8	9		11	3				10		5								
1	2				6	7	8	9		11	3	5			10			4							
1	2		4			7	8	9	10		3	5					6		11						
1	2		4			7	8	9	10		3	5					6		11						
1	2					7		9	10	11	3			5			6	4	8						
1	2		4			7	8	9	10		3	5					6		11						
1	2		4			7	8	9	10		3	5					6		11						
	2					7	8	9	10				4	1			6		11	5	3				
1	2			4		7	8	9	10		3						6			5		11			
1	2			4		7	8	9	10		3						6			5		11			
1	2			4		7	8	9	10		3						6		11	5					
1				4		7	8	9	10		3						6		11	5	2				
1				4		7	8	9	10		3						6		11	5	2				
1				4		7	8	9	10		3						6		11	5	2				
1	2			4		7	8	9	10		3	6								11	5				
1	2			4		7	8	9	10		3						6			11	5				
1	2			4			8	9	10	11		6								5	3		7		
1	2			4			8	9	10	11							6			5	3		7		
	2			4			8	9	10	11		1	5				6			3			7		
	2			4			8	9	10	11	5	1			6					3			7		
1	2			4	6		8	9	10	11										5	3		7		
1				4	6		8	9	10	11	3									5	2		7		
1				4	6		8	9	10	11	3									5	2		7		
1				4	6		8	9	10		3			5					11	2			7		
1				4	6		8	9	10		3			5					11	2			7		
1				4			8	9	10		6								11	5	2		7		
	6			4				9	10			3	8	1						5	2	11	7		
	8		4	6				9			11	3		1						5	2	10	7		
28	24	3	10	23	12	22	32	33	28	15	27	12	6	5	5	2	19	2	15	18	16	3	2	12	0
			1				9	8	8	10	3							1		6	2		1	2	

Sutcliffe J.W.	Brown W.G.	Struthers R.	Fitchett J.	Freebairn A.	Brunson A.	Bell S.J.T.	Picken J.B.	McKie J.	Barlow T.H.	Tracey W.M.	Ostick C.	Brown R.N.	Hanson J.	McAteer T.	Ashley H.	Neyland M.	Taylor R.	Bell F.	Williams H.	Bannister W.	Halliday J.F.	Worthington J.	Nicoll D.	Stokes D.	Woollat T.
1	2				6		7	8	9	10							4		11	5	3				
1			4	6			8	9	10	7									11	5	2		3		
2	1		1	2		1	2	2	2	1							1		2	2	2		1		
					2													1							

League Table

	P	W	D	L	F	A	Pts
Sunderland	34	19	6	9	50	35	44
Everton	34	17	7	10	53	35	41
Newcastle United	34	14	9	11	48	34	37
Blackburn Rovers	34	15	6	13	52	48	36
Nottingham Forest	34	13	9	12	43	43	35
Derby County	34	13	9	12	39	41	35
Bury	34	13	8	13	44	38	34
Aston Villa	34	13	8	13	42	40	34
Sheffield Wednesday	34	13	8	13	48	52	34
Sheffield United	34	13	7	14	53	48	33
Liverpool	34	10	12	12	42	38	32
Bolton Wanderers	34	12	8	14	51	56	32
Notts County	34	14	4	16	51	57	32
Wolverhampton W	34	13	6	15	46	57	32
Grimsby Town	34	13	6	15	44	60	32
Stoke	34	11	9	14	45	55	31
Small Heath	34	11	8	15	47	45	30
Manchester City	34	11	6	17	42	58	28

Match No.	Date		Venue	Opponents	Result		Scorers	Attendance
1	Sep	6	H	Sheffield Wednesday	L	0-2		15,000
2		13	A	West Bromwich Albion	L	1-2	McKie	8,000
3		20	H	Notts County	L	0-1		10,000
4		27	A	Derby County	L	0-5		12,000
5	Oct	4	A	Middlesbrough	L	3-4	Stokes, McKie, Tracey	6,000
6		11	H	Newcastle United	L	0-2		10,738
7		18	A	Wolverhampton Wanderers	L	1-3	Tracey	3,000
8		25	H	Liverpool	D	1-1	Bell	9,336
9	Nov	1	H	Everton	L	1-3	Greenhalgh	10,000
10		8	A	Grimsby Town	D	1-1	Stokes	3,000
11		15	A	Aston Villa	L	2-4	Bannister, Stokes	10,000
12		22	H	Nottingham Forest	D	1-1	Hanson	5,000
13		29	A	Bury	L	0-3		12,000
14	Dec	6	H	Blackburn Rovers	L	1-2	Knowles	9,000
15		13	A	Sunderland	L	1-3	Knowles	5,000
16		20	H	Stoke	L	2-3	Knowles, Bell	8,000
17		25	A	Liverpool	L	1-5	Freebairn	20,000
18		26	A	Sheffield United	L	1-7	Bell	14,000
19		27	A	Everton	L	1-3	McKie	20,000
20	Jan	2	H	Grimsby Town	L	0-1		16,000
21		3	A	Sheffield Wednesday	L	0-3		13,000
22		10	H	West Bromwich Albion	L	0-1		12,000
23		17	A	Notts County	W	3-1	Hanson, Marsh, Taylor	5,000
24		24	H	Derby County	W	2-0	Taylor, Marsh	10,000
25		31	H	Middlesbrough	W	2-1	Marsh, Taylor	10,000
26	Feb	14	H	Wolverhampton Wanderers	W	4-1	Marsh 2, White, Bell	2,000
27		28	H	Sheffield United	W	1-0	Marsh	14,000
28	Mar	14	H	Aston Villa	L	0-1		10,000
29		21	A	Nottingham Forest	W	2-1	White, Marsh	7,000
30		28	H	Bury	W	1-0	Marsh	10,000
31	Apr	4	A	Blackburn Rovers	L	2-4	Taylor 2	8,000
32		11	H	Sunderland	W	2-0	White, Marsh	11,793
33		13	A	Newcastle United	L	0-2		15,000
34		18	A	Stoke	L	0-2		4,000
							Appearances	
							Goals	

FA Cup

R1	Feb	7	A	Bristol City	L	0-5		7,750
							Appearances	

268

Player appearances and goals grid (shirt numbers by match; player columns left → right):

Thompson F.T.	Brown W.G.	Halliday J.F.	Greenhalgh S.	Bannister W.	Boyd J.	Soales D.	Hanson J.	McKie J.	Picken J.B.	Tracey W.M.	Freebairn A.	Osrick C.	Taylor R.	White W.	McKay D.	Bell S.I.T.	Williams H.	Marsh S.	Wright J.	Grime J.	Smethers R.	McCaffery W.	Knowles J.H.	Davies D.	Strang T.	McWilliams P.	Broomfield H.C.	Morgan W.	Marshall T.
1	2	3	4	5	6	7	8	9	10	11																			
1	2	3		6	5		7	8	9	10	11	4																	
1	2		5			7	9		10	11	4	3	6	8															
1	2		5			7	9		10	11	4	3	6	8															
1	2	3	5			7	10	9	8	11	4		6																
1	2	3	6	5		7		9	8	11	4				10														
1	2	3	6	5	4	7	8		10	11				9															
1	2	3	5		4	7	9		10			6			8	11													
1	2	3	5		4	7						6	11		8		9	10											
	2		5			7		11	8		4		6				9	10	1	3									
	2		5			7		9	8		4		6					10	1	3	11								
	2		6		5	7		8			9	4						10	1	3	11								
1	2		6		5	7		8				4			9			10	1	3	11								
1	2		5			9		7			4		6						10	3	11	8							
1	2		6		5			8	9		4				10				11	3	7								
1	2		6		5			7	9		4								11	3	10	8							
1	2		5	6			4	2	11	8	10		9						3										
1		2	5		6			4	11	8	10		9						3										
	1	2	5		6			4	11	8	10		9						3										
1		2	5		6			4	11	8	10								3										
	2		5		6				11	4		8		7		9	10		3				1						
	2		5		6				11	4		8		7		9	10		3	11			1						
	2		5		6				4			8		7		9	10		3		1		1						
	2	5		6					11	8				7		9	10		3		1			4					
	2	5		6					11	8						9	10		3		1		4	7					
	2	5		6					11	8						9	10		3		1		4	7					
	2	5		6			4			11	8					9	10		3			1			7				
	2	5		6				10		4				11	8		9		3	7	1								
	2	5		6						11	8		7		9	10		3	4				1						
20	24	11	30	10	20	16	18	15	10	12	23	8	22	21	7	13	1	15	19	3	24	8	3	6	3	1	5	3	3
		1	1		3	2	3		2	1		5	3			4			9							3				

FA Cup:

Thompson F.T.	Brown W.G.	Halliday J.F.	Greenhalgh S.	Bannister W.	Boyd J.	Soales D.	Hanson J.	McKie J.	Picken J.B.	Tracey W.M.	Freebairn A.	Osrick C.	Taylor R.	White W.	McKay D.	Bell S.I.T.	Williams H.	Marsh S.	Wright J.	Grime J.
1		2	5		6		7		4	11	8	10			9				3	
1		1	1		1		1		1	1	1	1			1				1	

League Table

	P	W	D	L	F	A	Pts
Sheffield Wednesday	34	19	4	11	54	36	42
Aston Villa	34	19	3	12	61	40	41
Sunderland	34	16	9	9	51	36	41
Sheffield United	34	17	5	12	58	44	39
Liverpool	34	17	4	13	68	49	38
Stoke	34	15	7	12	46	38	37
West Bromwich Albion	34	16	4	14	54	53	36
Bury	34	16	3	15	54	43	35
Derby County	34	16	3	15	50	47	35
Nottingham Forest	34	14	7	13	49	47	35
Wolverhampton W	34	14	5	15	48	57	33
Everton	34	13	6	15	45	47	32
Middlesbrough	34	14	4	16	41	50	32
Newcastle United	34	14	4	16	41	51	32
Notts County	34	12	7	15	41	49	31
Blackburn Rovers	34	12	5	17	44	63	29
Grimsby Town	34	8	9	17	43	62	25
Bolton Wanderers	34	8	3	23	37	73	19

1903-04

Second Division Wanderers reached their second FA Cup Final by defeating two Southern League clubs and two First Division clubs en route. Reading, who had knocked the Wanderers out in 1901, and Southern League champions Southampton were accounted for before Sheffield United and Derby County suffered the same fate until the Cup eluded Bolton in the Final against Manchester City.

Match No.	Date		Venue	Opponents	Result		Scorers	Attendance
1	Sep	1	H	Burton United	W	3-0	White 2, Barlow	
2		7	A	Burslem Port Vale	W	3-2	Marsh, Freebairn, Gardner	3,000
3		12	A	Burnley	D	0-0		6,000
4		19	H	Preston North End	L	0-2		13,603
5		26	A	Grimsby Town	D	0-0		5,000
6	Oct	3	H	Leicester Fosse	W	3-1	Wright 2, Marsh	7,000
7		10	A	Blackpool	W	4-1	Stokes 2, Marsh, White	6,000
8		17	A	Gainsborough Trinity	W	5-0	Marsh 3, Wright 2	8,000
9		24	A	Burton United	L	1-2	Taylor	
10		31	H	Bristol City	D	1-1	White	10,000
11	Nov	7	A	Manchester United	D	0-0		30,000
12		14	A	Glossop	L	0-1		5,000
13		21	A	Bradford City	D	3-3	White, Taylor 2	10,000
14		28	H	Woolwich Arsenal	W	2-1	Marsh, Heaton	5,000
15	Dec	12	H	Lincoln City	L	1-2	White	6,000
16		19	A	Stockport County	L	2-3	Marsh, Stokes	3,000
17		25	H	Barnsley	W	5-1	Marsh 3, Wright, Yenson	12,000
18		26	H	Chesterfield	W	4-0	Greenhalgh, Stokes, Taylor, Boyd	10,000
19	Jan	1	H	Blackpool	W	3-0	Marsh, Stokes, Yenson	11,000
20		2	A	Burslem Port Vale	W	5-0	Stokes, Yenson, Marsh, Greenhalgh, Taylor	5,000
21		9	H	Burnley	D	1-1	Yenson	9,000
22		16	A	Preston North End	L	1-3	White	10,000
23		23	H	Grimsby Town	W	4-0	Taylor, Marsh 2, Stokes	5,000
24		30	A	Leicester Fosse	D	2-2	Boyd, Marsh	4,000
25	Feb	13	A	Gainsborough Trinity	L	1-3	Taylor	2,000
26		27	A	Bristol City	L	0-2		5,000
27	Mar	12	A	Glossop	D	3-3	White, Stokes, Yenson	
28		26	A	Woolwich Arsenal	L	0-3		20,000
29	Apr	4	A	Barnsley	L	0-1		3,000
30		9	A	Lincoln City	L	0-1		
31		11	H	Bradford City	W	1-0	Seymour (own-goal)	10,000
32		13	A	Chesterfield	D	1-1	Taylor	1,500
33		16	H	Stockport County	L	0-1		6,000
34		25	H	Manchester United	D	0-0		10,000
								Appearances
							1 own-goal	Goals

FA Cup

R1	Feb	6	A	Reading	D	1-1	Marsh	10,000
rep		10	H	Reading	W	3-2	Freebairn, Marsh, Yenson	10,082
R2		20	H	Southampton	W	4-1	Marsh 2, White 2	12,000
R3	Mar	5	A	Sheffield United	W	2-0	Marsh, Yenson	29,984
SF		19	N	Derby County	W	1-0	Taylor	20,187
F	Apr	23	N	Manchester City	L	0-1		61,374

SF at Molineux, Final at the Crystal Palace.

Appearances
Goals

Davies D.	Ostick C.	Struthers R.	Freebairn A.	Greenhalgh S.	Boyd J.	Stokes D.	White W.	Marsh S.	Barlow T.H.	Gardner A.	Brown W.G.	Warburton F.	Wright J.	Taylor R.	Yenson W.	Shaw J.	Heaton S.	Hanson J.	Clifford R.	Leigh J.	Broomfield H.C.	Foster J.	Robertson J.N.
1	2	3	4	5	6	7	8	9	10	11													
1	2	3	4	5	6	7	8	9	10	11													
1		3	4	5	6	7	8	9	10	11	2												
1		3	4	5	6	7	8	9	10	11	2												
1		3	4	5	6	7	8			11	2	9	10										
1		3	4	5	6	7	8	9		11	2		10										
1		3	4	5	6	7	8	9			2		10	11									
1		3	4	5	6	7	8	9			2		10	11									
1		3	4	5	6	7	8	9			2		10	11									
1	2	3			6	7	8	9		11			10	4	5								
1		3		5	6	11	8	9			2		10	4		7							
1		3		5	6	11		9	10		2		8	4		7							
1		3	4	5	6	7	8	10			2			11			9						
1		3	4	5	6	7	8	10			2			11			9						
1		3	4	5	6	7	8	10		11	2						9						
1	2	3	4	5	6	11	8	9					10			7							
1	2	3		5	6	7		8					10	11	9			4					
1	2	3		5	6	7		8					10	11	9			4					
1	2	3		5	6	7	4	8						11	9			10					
1	2	3		5	6	7	10	8						11	9			4					
1	2	3		5	6	7	10	8						11	9			4					
1	2	3		5	6	7	10	8						11	9				4				
1	2	3		5	6	7	10	8						11	9				4				
1	2	3		5	6	7	10	8						11	9				4				
1		3		5	6	7	10				2		8	11	9				4				
1	2			5	6		10	8			3			11	9				4	7			
		3		5		7	8				2		10	11	9				4		1	6	
1		3	6	5		7	10	8			2			11	9				4				
1		3	4			7	10	8			2			11		9			5			6	
1		3	4	5		7	10	8			2			11			9		6				
1		3	4	5		7	10				2		8	11	9				6				
1		3			6			8			2		10	11	9			4	5	7			
1		3				7	10	8			2			11	9			5	4				6
1	2	3	6	5		7	10	8						11	9				4				
33	14	33	18	30	27	32	30	30	5	8	21	1	15	26	17	4	4	7	13	2	1	2	1
			1	2	2	8	8	16	1	1			5	8	5		1						

Davies D.	Ostick C.	Struthers R.	Freebairn A.	Greenhalgh S.	Boyd J.	Stokes D.	White W.	Marsh S.	Barlow T.H.	Gardner A.	Brown W.G.	Warburton F.	Wright J.	Taylor R.	Yenson W.	Shaw J.	Heaton S.	Hanson J.	Clifford R.
1	2	3	4	5	6	7	10	8						11	9				
1		3	4	5	6	7	10	8			2			11	9				
1	2	3	4	5	6	7	10	8						11	9				
1		3	4	5	6	7	10	8			2			11	9				
1		3	4	5	6	7	10	8			2			11	9				
1		3	6	5		7	10	8			2			11	9				4
6	2	6	6	6	5	6	6	6			4			6	6				1
			1				2	5						1	2				

League Table

	P	W	D	L	F	A	Pts
Preston North End	34	20	10	4	62	24	50
Woolwich Arsenal	34	21	7	6	91	22	49
Manchester United	34	20	8	6	65	33	48
Bristol City	34	18	6	10	73	41	42
Burnley	34	15	9	10	50	55	39
Grimsby Town	34	14	8	12	50	49	36
Bolton Wanderers	34	12	10	12	59	41	34
Barnsley	34	11	10	13	38	57	32
Gainsborough Trinity	34	14	3	17	53	60	31
Bradford City	34	12	7	15	45	59	31
Chesterfield	34	11	8	15	37	45	30
Lincoln City	34	11	8	15	41	58	30
Burslem Port Vale	34	10	9	15	54	52	29
Burton United	34	11	7	16	45	61	29
Blackpool	34	11	5	18	40	67	27
Stockport County	34	8	11	15	40	72	27
Glossop	34	10	6	18	57	64	26
Leicester Fosse	34	6	10	18	42	82	22

Did you know that?

A run of almost six months undefeated away from home helped secure the Wanderers promotion from Division Two. After losing at Bradford at the end of October 1904, it was not until the final away game the following April, at Barnsley, that a loss was suffered on away territory. By then the runners'-up spot had been secured at the expense of Manchester United.

Match No.	Date		Venue	Opponents	Result		Scorers	Attendance
1	Sep	3	A	Bristol City	W	4-3	Marsh 2, Yenson, Clifford	12,000
2		10	H	Burnley	W	4-0	White, Marsh 2, Yenson	12,000
3		17	A	Manchester United	W	2-1	White 2	35,000
4		24	H	Grimsby Town	W	4-1	R. Taylor, White 3 (1 pen)	10,000
5	Oct	1	A	Glossop	W	2-1	Stokes, White	2,500
6		8	H	Blackpool	W	3-0	R. Taylor, Marsh, Greenhalgh	10,000
7		15	A	Chesterfield	L	0-1		3,000
8		22	H	Doncaster Rovers	W	2-0	R. Taylor, Yenson	7,000
9		29	A	Bradford City	L	1-2	Marsh	10,000
10	Nov	5	H	Gainsborough Trinity	W	5-1	White 2, Marsh 2, Greenhalgh	6,000
11		12	H	Lincoln City	W	4-1	Shepherd, Boyd, White, Wilson	12,000
12		19	H	Burton United	W	7-1	Marsh 3, White 3, Shepherd	9,000
13	Dec	3	H	Liverpool	W	2-0	Marsh 2 (1 pen)	25,000
14		10	A	Doncaster Rovers	W	4-0	White 3, Shepherd	1,000
15		17	A	Burslem Port Vale	W	2-1	White (pen), Wilson	3,000
16		24	H	West Bromwich Albion	W	2-1	Marsh, Wilson	9,000
17		26	A	Lincoln City	W	2-0	White, Marsh	7,000
18		27	A	Leicester Fosse	W	4-2	Stokes, White 2, Marsh	8,000
19		31	H	Bristol City	W	3-1	Shepherd 2, Marsh	18,000
20	Jan	2	H	Barnsley	W	2-1	Shepherd 2	
21		3	H	Manchester United	L	2-4	Shepherd, Marsh	40,000
22		7	A	Burnley	W	1-0	R. Taylor	8,000
23		21	A	Grimsby Town	D	2-2	Marsh, Shepherd	3,000
24		28	H	Glossop	W	4-0	Featherstone, Marsh, White, Boyd	5,000
25	Feb	11	H	Chesterfield	W	4-3	Marsh 2 (1 pen), Wilson, Shepherd	10,000
26		25	H	Bradford City	W	2-0	Marsh 2	8,000
27	Mar	18	A	Burton United	W	1-0	Stokes	2,000
28		25	H	Leicester Fosse	L	0-1		5,000
29	Apr	1	A	Liverpool	D	1-1	Stokes	20,000
30		12	A	Gainsborough Trinity	W	4-0	Shepherd 2, White, Marsh	
31		15	H	Burslem Port Vale	W	3-1	White 2, Shepherd	12,000
32		21	A	Blackpool	W	2-0	Stokes, Shepherd	10,000
33		22	A	West Bromwich Albion	W	1-0	Shepherd	5,000
34		24	A	Barnsley	L	1-2	Marsh	8,000
							Appearances	
							Goals	

FA Cup

R1	Feb	4	H	Bristol Rovers	D	1-1	Marsh	10,000
rep		8	A	Bristol Rovers	W	3-0	Stokes, Shepherd, Pudan (own-goal)	8,000
R2		18	A	Manchester City	W	2-1	Shepherd, White	37,448
R3	Mar	4	H	Newcastle United	L	0-2		20,000
							Appearances	
						1 own-goal	Goals	

Player appearance and goals chart (column headers, left to right):

Davies D. · Gozick C. · Struthers R. · Clifford R. · Greenhalgh S. · Boyd J. · Stokes D. · Marsh S. · Yarwton W. · White W. · Taylor R. · Shaw J. · Bromfield H.C. · Taylor A. · Abbott H. · Shepherd A. · Wilson T.C. · Eccles G.S. · Featherstone T. · McEwan M.

Davies D.	Gozick C.	Struthers R.	Clifford R.	Greenhalgh S.	Boyd J.	Stokes D.	Marsh S.	Yarwton W.	White W.	Taylor R.	Shaw J.	Bromfield H.C.	Taylor A.	Abbott H.	Shepherd A.	Wilson T.C.	Eccles G.S.	Featherstone T.	McEwan M.
1	2	3	4	5	6	7	8	9	10	11									
1	2	3	4	5	6	7	8	9	10	11									
1	2	3	4	5	6	7	8	9	10	11									
1	2	3	4	5	6	7		9	10	11	8								
	2		4	5	6	7		9	10	11	8	1	3						
	2	3	4	5	6	7	8	9	10	11		1							
	2	3	4	5	6		8	9	10	11	7	1							
	2	3	4	5	6	7	8	9		11		1		10					
	2	3	6	5	4	7	8	9	10	11		1							
1	2	3	4	5	6	7	8		10						9	11			
1	2	3	4	5	6	7	8		10						9	11			
1	2	3	4	5	6	7	8		10						9	11			
1	2	3	4	5	6	7	8		10						9	11			
1	2	3	4	5	6	7	8		10						9	11			
1	2	3	4	5		7	8		10	6					9	11			
1		3	4	5	6	7	8		10						9	11	2		
1		3	4	5	6	7	8		10						9	11	2		
1		3	4	5	6	7	8		10	11					9		2		
1		3	2	5	6	7	8		10	11	4				9				
1	2	3	4	5	6		8		10	11					9		7		
1		3	4	5	6	7	8		10	11					9		2		
1		3	2		4	7	8	5	10	6					9	11			
1		3	4	5	6	7	8		10						9	11	2		
1	2	3	4	5	6	7	8		10							11		9	
1		3	4	5		7	8		10	6			2		9	11			
1		3		5	6	7	8		10	4			2		9				11
	2	3	4	5	6	7	8		10			1			9	11			
	2	3	4	5	6	7	8		10			1			9	11			
	2	3	4	5	6	7	8		10			1			9	11			
	2	3	4	5	6	7	8		10			1			9	11			
	2	3	4		6	7	8	5	10			1			9	11			
	2	3	4	5	6	7	8		10			1			9	11			
	2	3		5	6	7	8		10	4		1			9	11			
21	**24**	**33**	**32**	**32**	**32**	**32**	**32**	**11**	**33**	**19**	**4**	**13**	**3**	**1**	**24**	**19**	**6**	**2**	**1**
		1	2	2	5	26	3	24	4				15	4		1			

FA Cup:

Davies D.	Gozick C.	Struthers R.	Clifford R.	Greenhalgh S.	Boyd J.	Stokes D.	Marsh S.	Yarwton W.	White W.	Taylor R.	Shaw J.	Bromfield H.C.	Taylor A.	Abbott H.	Shepherd A.	Wilson T.C.	Eccles G.S.	Featherstone T.	McEwan M.
1	2	3	4	5	6	7	8		10						9	11			
1		3	4	5		7	8		10	6			2		9	11			
1		3	4	5	6	7	8		10				2		9	11			
1		3	4	5	6	7	8		10				2		9	11			
4	**1**	**4**	**4**	**4**	**3**	**4**	**4**	**0**	**4**	**1**	**0**	**0**	**3**	**0**	**4**	**4**	**0**	**0**	**0**
	2				1	1							1						

League Table

	P	W	D	L	F	A	Pts
Liverpool	34	27	4	3	93	25	58
Bolton Wanderers	34	27	2	5	87	32	56
Manchester United	34	24	5	5	81	30	53
Bristol City	34	19	4	11	66	45	42
Chesterfield	34	14	11	9	44	35	39
Gainsborough Trinity	34	14	8	12	61	58	36
Barnsley	34	14	5	15	38	56	33
Bradford City	34	12	8	14	45	49	32
Lincoln City	34	12	7	15	42	40	31
West Bromwich Albion	34	13	4	17	56	48	30
Burnley	34	12	6	16	43	52	30
Glossop	34	10	10	14	37	46	30
Grimsby Town	34	11	8	15	33	46	30
Leicester Fosse	34	11	7	16	40	55	29
Blackpool	34	9	10	15	36	48	28
Burslem Port Vale	34	10	7	17	47	72	27
Burton United	34	8	4	22	30	84	20
Doncaster Rovers	34	3	2	29	23	81	8

Division One

Match No.	Date		Venue	Opponents	Result		Scorers	Attendance
1	Sep	2	H	Sheffield United	L	1-2	Wilson	19,000
2		9	A	Notts County	D	3-3	Marsh, Greenhalgh, White	4,000
3		16	H	Stoke	L	1-2	Marsh	20,000
4		23	A	Wolverhampton Wanderers	L	0-2		5,000
5		30	A	Woolwich Arsenal	D	0-0		20,000
6	Oct	7	H	Blackburn Rovers	W	1-0	Shepherd	24,000
7		14	A	Sunderland	D	3-3	Shepherd 2, McEwan	6,000
8		21	H	Birmingham	L	0-1		20,000
9		28	A	Everton	L	1-3	White	17,000
10	Nov	4	H	Derby County	W	5-0	Shepherd, Marsh 3, White	18,000
11		11	A	Sheffield Wednesday	W	2-1	McEwan, Stokes	8,000
12		18	H	Nottingham Forest	W	6-0	Shepherd 4, Marsh, White	8,000
13		25	A	Manchester City	L	1-3	Shepherd	35,000
14	Dec	2	H	Bury	W	4-0	McEwan, Marsh, White 2	25,000
15		9	A	Middlesbrough	D	4-4	White 2, Shepherd 2	3,000
16		16	H	Preston North End	L	1-2	Shepherd	25,000
17		23	A	Newcastle United	L	1-2	Stokes	20,000
18		25	A	Liverpool	D	2-2	Shepherd 2	22,000
19		26	A	Aston Villa	D	1-1	White	40,000
20		30	A	Sheffield United	L	2-5	Stokes, Shepherd	6,000
21	Jan	1	H	Woolwich Arsenal	W	6-1	White 2, Marsh 2, Shepherd, McEwan	21,000
22		2	H	Aston Villa	W	4-1	White, Stokes, Marsh, Shepherd	30,000
23		20	A	Stoke	W	2-1	Marsh, White	5,000
24		27	H	Wolverhampton Wanderers	W	3-2	Shepherd, White, Jones (own-goal)	12,000
25	Feb	3	H	Notts County	W	2-0	Shepherd 2	10,000
26		17	H	Sunderland	W	6-2	Clifford, Shepherd 4, White	18,000
27	Mar	3	H	Everton	W	3-2	White 2, McEwan	22,000
28		10	A	Derby County	W	1-0	McEwan	7,000
29		17	H	Sheffield Wednesday	W	1-0	Marsh	25,000
30		24	A	Nottingham Forest	L	0-4		5,000
31		26	A	Birmingham	W	5-2	White 2, Atkinson, Stokes 2	10,000
32		31	H	Manchester City	L	1-3	White	37,000
33	Apr	2	A	Blackburn Rovers	L	1-4	White	5,000
34		7	A	Bury	L	1-2	White	20,000
35		14	H	Middlesbrough	W	2-1	White 2	18,000
36		16	H	Liverpool	W	3-2	Shepherd 2, McEwan	23,000
37		21	A	Preston North End	L	0-3		5,000
38		28	H	Newcastle United	D	1-1	White	15,000

Appearances
Goals

1 own-goal

FA Cup

R1	Jan 13	A	Middlesbrough	L	0-3		22,000

Appearances

	Davies D.	Gavait C.	Struthers R.	Clifford R.	Greenhalgh S.	Boyd J.	Stokes D.	Marsh S.	Shepherd A.	White W.	Wilson T.	Branstone H.	Taylor R.	McEwan M.	Robertson J.N.	Gaskell A.	Napier S.	Broomfield H.	Freebairn A.	Beckett C.	Woodenholme T.	King H.	Lawrie H.	Atkinson J.	Stanley J.
	1	2	3	4	5	6	7	8	9	10	11														
	1		3		5	6	7	8	9	10		2	4	11											
	1		3		5	6	7	8	9	10		2	4	11											
	1		3		5	6	7			10		2		11	4	8	9								
			3			6	7	8	9	10		2		11	4			1	5						
			3			6	7	8	9	10		2		11	4			1	5						
			3			6	7	8	9	10		2		11	4			1	5						
	1		3			6	7	8	9	10		2		11	4				5						
	1		3			6	7	8	9	10		2		11	4				5						
	1		3	5		6	7	8	9	10		2		11	4										
	1		3	5		6	7	8	9	10		2		11	4										
	1		3	5		6	7	8	9	10		2		11	4										
	1		3	5		6	7	8	9	10		2		11	4										
	1		3	5		6	7	8	9	10		2		11	4										
	1		3	5		6	7		9	10		2		11	4		8								
	1		3	5		6	7	8	9	10		2		11	4										
	1		3	5		6	7	8	9	10		2		11					4						
	1		3	5		6	7	8	9	10		2		11					4						
	1		3	5		6	7	8	9	10		2		11					4						
	1		3	5		6	7	8	9	10		2		11					4						
	1			5		6	7	8	9	10		2		11					4	3					
	1			3		6	7	8	9	10		2	5	11					4						
	1	3		5		6	7	8		10		2		11			9		4						
	1	3		5		6	7	8		10		2		11					4						
	1		3			6	7	8	9	10		2	5	11					4						
	1		3	4		6	7	8	9	10		2	5	11											
	1	3		5		6	7	8	9	10		2		11	4										
	1		3	4		6	7	8	9	10		2	5	11											
	1	3		5		6	7	8		10		2	5	11											
	1			4		6	7	8	9	10		2	5	11	4										
	1	3		4		6	7		9	10		2		11	4										
	1			4		6	7	8	9	10		2	5	11					3						
	1	3		4		6	7	8		10		2	5	11					3						
	1	3		4		6	7	8	9			2	5	11					3				8		
	1	3		4		6	7		9	10		2	5	11									8		
	1	3		4		6	7	8		10		2	5	11		9									
	1	3	5			6	7			10		2	9	11	8				4						
	1		3			6	7			10		2	8	11	4				5						
	1		3			6	7	9		10		2	8	11	4				5						
	1					6	7	8	9	10		2	5	11	4					3					
App	35	4	28	27	4	38	38	33	31	38	1	37	16	37	14	5	4	3	11	1	6	1	3	2	1
Gls			1	1		6	12	26	25	1		7										1			

FA Cup

	Davies D.	Gavait C.	Struthers R.	Clifford R.	Greenhalgh S.	Boyd J.	Stokes D.	Marsh S.	Shepherd A.	White W.	Wilson T.	Branstone H.	Taylor R.	McEwan M.	Robertson J.N.	Gaskell A.	Napier S.	Broomfield H.	Freebairn A.	Beckett C.	Woodenholme T.	King H.	Lawrie H.	Atkinson J.	Stanley J.
	1		3			6	7	8	9	10		2	5	11					4						
	1			1		1	1	1	1	1		1	1	1					1						

League Table

	P	W	D	L	F	A	Pts
Liverpool	38	23	5	10	79	46	51
Preston North End	38	17	13	8	54	39	47
Sheffield Wednesday	38	18	8	12	63	52	44
Newcastle United	38	18	7	13	74	48	43
Manchester City	38	19	5	14	73	54	43
Bolton Wanderers	38	17	7	14	81	67	41
Birmingham	38	17	7	14	65	59	41
Aston Villa	38	17	6	15	72	56	40
Blackburn Rovers	38	16	8	14	54	52	40
Stoke	38	16	7	15	54	55	39
Everton	38	15	7	16	70	66	37
Woolwich Arsenal	38	15	7	16	62	64	37
Sheffield United	38	15	6	17	57	62	36
Sunderland	38	15	5	18	61	70	35
Derby County	38	14	7	17	39	58	35
Notts County	38	11	12	15	55	71	34
Bury	38	11	10	17	57	74	32
Middlesbrough	38	10	11	17	56	71	31
Nottingham Forest	38	13	5	20	58	79	31
Wolverhampton W	38	8	7	23	58	99	23

Division One

Did you know that?

Newly crowned League champions Newcastle United were defeated 4–2 at Burnden Park in the penultimate game of the season. The Wanderers had suffered throughout the campaign with injuries and they managed to field their first-choice forward line for that game for only the second time during the season.

Match No.	Date		Venue	Opponents	Result		Scorers	Attendance
1	Sep	1	A	Notts County	D	0-0		5,000
2		8	H	Sheffield United	W	6-1	White, McEwan, Shepherd 3, Cameron	20,000
3		15	H	Derby County	W	1-0	Boyd	22,000
4		22	A	Manchester United	W	2-1	Shepherd, White	40,000
5		29	H	Stoke	D	1-1	Shepherd	18,000
6	Oct	6	A	Blackburn Rovers	W	3-2	White, Cameron, Clifford	10,000
7		13	H	Sunderland	W	1-0	White	16,000
8		20	A	Birmingham	L	2-4	Shepherd 2	15,000
9		27	H	Everton	L	1-3	Shepherd	22,000
10	Nov	3	A	Woolwich Arsenal	D	2-2	Clifford, Cameron	18,000
11		10	H	Sheffield Wednesday	D	0-0		15,000
12		17	A	Bury	W	3-2	Stokes, Marsh 2	14,000
13		24	H	Manchester City	D	1-1	Shepherd	20,000
14	Dec	1	A	Middlesbrough	D	0-0		15,000
15		8	A	Preston North End	L	1-3	Stokes	12,000
16		15	A	Newcastle United	L	0-4		25,000
17		22	H	Aston Villa	L	1-2	Dempsey	18,000
18		24	A	Stoke	L	0-3		7,000
19		26	A	Liverpool	W	2-0	Owen, Stokes	25,000
20		29	H	Notts County	D	0-0		6,000
21	Jan	1	H	Liverpool	W	3-0	Stokes, Gaskell, Owen	30,000
22		2	H	Preston North End	W	3-0	Shepherd 2, White	15,000
23		5	A	Sheffield United	L	1-2	White	7,000
24		19	A	Derby County	W	1-0	Shepherd	7,000
25		26	H	Manchester United	L	0-1		24,670
26	Feb	9	H	Blackburn Rovers	W	5-2	Clifford, Owen 2, White, Shepherd	12,000
27		16	A	Sunderland	W	2-1	Shepherd, Weaver	10,000
28	Mar	2	A	Everton	L	0-1		15,000
29		9	H	Bury	W	1-0	White	10,000
30		11	H	Birmingham	L	2-3	Owen, White	5,000
31		16	A	Sheffield Wednesday	L	0-2		10,000
32		27	H	Woolwich Arsenal	W	3-0	White 2, Shepherd	5,000
33		29	H	Bristol City	L	1-2	White	20,000
34		30	A	Manchester City	D	1-1	Stokes	36,000
35	Apr	2	A	Bristol City	W	2-1	Marsh, Boyd	10,000
36		6	H	Middlesbrough	W	1-0	Marsh	6,507
37		20	H	Newcastle United	W	4-2	Marsh 2, White, Gaskell	4,000
38		27	A	Aston Villa	W	2-0	Shepherd, White	10,000
							Appearances	
							Goals	

FA Cup

R1	Jan	12	H	Brighton & Hove Albion	W	3-1	Stokes, Clifford, Shepherd	19,330
R2	Feb	2	H	Aston Villa	W	2-0	Shepherd 2	40,367
R3		23	A	Everton	D	0-0		52,455
rep		27	H	Everton	L	0-3		54,470
							Appearances	
							Goals	

Appearance Grid

	Davies D.	Beavenstock H.	Struthers R.	Gaskell A.	Clifford R.	Boyd J.	Stokes D.	Cameron W.S.	Shepherd A.S.	White W.	McEwan M.	Dempsey E.	Broomfield H.	Stanley J.	Marsh S.	Wolstenholme T.	Banks W.E.	Taylor R.	Owen J.R.	Edmondson J.H.	Atkinson J.	Weaver W.	Slater J.	Thorp J.	Freebairn A.	Ryder G.
	1	2	3	4	5	6	7	8	9	10	11															
	1	2	3	4	5	6	7	8	9	10	11															
	1	2	3	4	5	6	7	8	9	10	11															
	1	2	3	4	5	6	7	8	9	10	11															
	1	2	3	4	5	6	7	8	9	10	11															
	1	2	3	4	5	6	7		9	10	11	8														
		2	3	4	5	6	7		9	10	11	8	1													
	1	2	3	4	5	6	7	8	9	10	11															
	1	2	3	4	5	6	7		9	10	11	8														
		2		4	5	6	11	10	9	8	7		1	3												
		2		4	5	6	7	8	9	10	11		1	3												
	1	2		4	5	6	7		9	10	11			3	8											
	1	2		4	5	6	7		9	10	11			3	8											
	1	2		4	5		7			10	11			3	8	6	9									
	1	2		4	5		7			10	11			3	8	6	9									
		2		4	5	6	7			10	11		1	3	8		9									
		2		4	5	6	7	8		10	11		1	3			9									
		2			5	6	7	8		10	11		1	3	4		9									
	1	2		4	5	6	7		9		11			3	8				10							
	1	2		4	5	6	7		9		11			3	8				10							
		2		4	5	6	7		9	10	11			3					8	1						
		2		4	5	6	7		9	10	11			3					8	1						
		2		4	5	6	7		9	10	11			3					8	1						
		2		4	5	6		9	7		11			3	8				10	1						
		2		4		6		9		10	11	7		3					8	1	5					
		2		4	5	6		9		10	11			3	7				8	1						
		2		4	5	6		9		10	11			3					8	1		7				
		2		4	5	6		9			10			3					8	1			11			
		2		4		6	7	9		10	11			3					8	1		3		5		
		2		4	5	6	7			10	11	9		3					8	1						
		2		4	5	6	7		9	10	11			3					8	1						
		2		4	5	6	7		9	10	11			3					8	1						
		2		4	5		7			10	11			3	8				9	1			6			
		2		4	5	6	7							3	8				9	1		11			10	
		2		4	5		7							3	8		6	9	1			11			10	
		2		4	5	6	7		9	10	11			3	8				1							
		2		4	5	6	7		9	10	11			3	8				1							
Apps	14	38	9	37	36	34	33	14	21	36	35	7	6	27	15	3	2	2	19	18	1	4	2	2	1	2
Goals		2		3	2	5	3	16	14	1	1		6						5			1				

	Davies D.	Beavenstock H.	Struthers R.	Gaskell A.	Clifford R.	Boyd J.	Stokes D.	Cameron W.S.	Shepherd A.S.	White W.	McEwan M.	Dempsey E.	Broomfield H.	Stanley J.	Marsh S.	Wolstenholme T.	Banks W.E.	Taylor R.	Owen J.R.	Edmondson J.H.	Atkinson J.	Weaver W.	Slater J.	Thorp J.	Freebairn A.	Ryder G.
	1	2		4	5	6	7		9	10	11			3					8							
		2		4	5	6	7		9	10	11			3					8	1						
		2		4	5	6	7		9	10	11			3					8	1						
		2		4	5	6	7	9		10	11			3					8	1						
Apps	1	4		4	4	4	4	1	3	4	4			4					4	3						
Goals							1		1					3												

League Table

	P	W	D	L	F	A	Pts
Newcastle United	38	22	7	9	74	46	51
Bristol City	38	20	8	10	66	47	48
Everton	38	20	5	13	70	46	45
Sheffield United	38	17	11	10	57	55	45
Aston Villa	38	19	6	13	78	52	44
Bolton Wanderers	38	18	8	12	59	47	44
Woolwich Arsenal	38	20	4	14	66	59	44
Manchester United	38	17	8	13	53	56	42
Birmingham	38	15	8	15	52	52	38
Sunderland	38	14	9	15	65	66	37
Middlesbrough	38	15	6	17	56	63	36
Blackburn Rovers	38	14	7	17	56	59	35
Sheffield Wednesday	38	12	11	15	49	60	35
Preston North End	38	14	7	17	44	57	35
Liverpool	38	13	7	18	64	65	33
Bury	38	13	6	19	58	68	32
Manchester City	38	10	12	16	53	77	32
Notts County	38	8	15	15	46	50	31
Derby County	38	9	9	20	41	59	27
Stoke	38	8	10	20	41	64	26

Did you know that?

The Wanderers were relegated from the top flight for the third time when they lost a winner-takes-all final game to rivals Notts County. Having drawn with champions Manchester United three days previous, Bolton needed just a point from the Magpies to secure safety. County won 1–0 and victory at Chelsea saved them to send Bolton down with Birmingham.

Match No.	Date	Venue	Opponents	Result		Scorers	Attendance
1	Sep 7	H	Bury	L	3-6	Shepherd 3	20,000
2	14	A	Aston Villa	L	0-2		18,000
3	21	H	Liverpool	L	0-4		10,000
4	28	A	Middlesbrough	W	1-0	Shepherd	15,000
5	Oct 5	H	Sheffield United	D	1-1	White	11,345
6	12	A	Chelsea	W	3-1	White 3	30,000
7	19	H	Nottingham Forest	W	1-0	Owen	14,200
8	26	A	Manchester United	L	1-2	Boyd	40,000
9	Nov 2	H	Blackburn Rovers	W	3-1	Owen, Shepherd, White	7,000
10	9	A	Newcastle United	L	0-3		18,000
11	16	A	Birmingham	L	1-2	White	15,000
12	23	H	Everton	W	3-0	White 2, Shepherd	5,000
13	30	A	Sunderland	W	2-1	Shepherd 2	8,000
14	Dec 7	H	Woolwich Arsenal	W	3-1	Shepherd 3	12,000
15	14	A	Sheffield Wednesday	L	2-5	White, Shepherd	5,000
16	21	H	Bristol City	L	1-2	Shepherd	6,000
17	25	A	Preston North End	L	0-2		14,000
18	26	A	Manchester City	L	0-1		35,000
19	28	A	Notts County	W	1-0	Shepherd	6,000
20	30	A	Sheffield United	L	0-1		10,000
21	Jan 1	H	Manchester City	W	2-0	Shepherd, Jee	25,000
22	2	H	Preston North End	W	2-0	Owen, Cameron	18,000
23	4	A	Bury	D	2-2	Cameron, Owen	12,000
24	18	A	Liverpool	L	0-1		20,000
25	25	H	Middlesbrough	D	1-1	Owen	10,000
26	Feb 8	H	Chelsea	L	1-2	White	15,000
27	15	A	Nottingham Forest	L	0-1		6,000
28	29	A	Blackburn Rovers	L	2-3	Shepherd, McEwan	10,000
29	Mar 14	H	Birmingham	W	1-0	Marsh	13,047
30	21	A	Everton	L	1-2	Shepherd	15,000
31	28	H	Sunderland	L	2-3	White, McClarence	19,779
32	Apr 1	H	Newcastle United	W	4-0	White, Shepherd 3	18,000
33	4	A	Woolwich Arsenal	D	1-1	Shepherd	10,000
34	11	H	Sheffield Wednesday	W	2-1	Shepherd, Stokes	17,000
35	17	H	Aston Villa	W	3-1	Shepherd 2, McClarence	20,000
36	18	A	Bristol City	L	0-2		14,000
37	22	H	Manchester United	D	2-2	White, Shepherd	18,000
38	25	H	Notts County	L	0-1		15,000
						Appearances	
						Goals	

FA Cup

R1	Jan 11	H	Woking	W	5-0	Cameron, Stokes, Owen, White, McEwan	8,000
R2	Feb 1	A	Notts County	D	1-1	McEwan	18,000
rep	5	H	Notts County	W	2-1	Cameron, White	17,445
R3	22	H	Everton	D	3-3	Marsh 3	31,113
rep	26	A	Everton	L	1-3	Greenhalgh	32,000

R2 replay and R3 replay a.e.t.

Appearances
Goals

Player column key (left-to-right across the grid):

1 Edmondson J.H. · 2 Beverstock H. · 3 Stanley J. · 4 Gaskell A. · 5 Clifford R. · 6 Boyd J. · 7 Stokes D. · 8 Marsh S. · 9 Shepherd A. · 10 Whitall W. · 11 McEwan M. · 12 Ryder G. · 13 Greenhalgh S. · 14 Slater J. · 15 Owen J.R. · 16 Cannon W.S. · 17 Jee J. · 18 Davies D. · 19 Tierney H. · 20 Evans W.P. · 21 Robinson F. · 22 Stuart W. · 23 McClarence J.P.

1	2	3	4	5	6	7	8	9	10	11	12	13	14	15	16	17	18	19	20	21	22	23
1	2	3	4	5	6	7	8	9	10	11												
1	2	3	4	5	6	7	8	9		11	10											
1	2	3	4	5	6	7	8	9	10	11												
1	2	3		5	6	7	8	9	10	11			4									
1		3		5	6	7		9	10	11		8	4	2								
1		3	4	5	6	7	8	9		11				2	10							
1		3		5	6	7	8	9		11			4	2	10							
1		3		5	6	7		9	10	11		8	4	2								
1		3		5	6	7		9	10	11		8	4	2								
1		3		5	6	7		9	10	11		8	4	2								
1	2	3		5		7		9	10	11		8	4			6						
1	2	3		5		7		9	10	11		8	4									
1	2	3		5	6	7		9	10	11		8	4									
1	2	4	3		6	7		9	10			5		8	11							
1	2	3	4		6	7		9	10			5		8	11							
1	2	3		5	6	7		9	10	11		8	4									
1	2		4		6	7		9	10	11		5		3	8							
1	2		4			7		9	10	11		5		3	8	6						
1	2		4			7		9	10	11		5		3	8	6						
1	2			5	6	7		9	10			8	4	3	11							
1	2			5	6	7		9	10			8	4	3	11							
	2			5	6	7		9	10	11		8	4	3			1					
	2			5	6	7		9	10	11		8	4	3			1					
1	2		4		6	7		9	10	11		5		3								8
	2		4	5		7		9		11		8		3	10	6	1					
		8	2		6	7		9		11			4	3			1	5	10			
	2		4	5	6	7		9		11				3	10		1					8
	2			5	6	7	8	9	10	11			4	3			1					
	2			5	6	7	8	9		11			4	3	10		1					
	2			5	6	7	8		10	11			4	3			1					9
		3		5	6	7		9	10	11			4	2			1					8
		3	4	5	6	7		9		11				2	10		1					8
		3		5	6	7		9	10	11			4	2			1					8
		3	4	5	6	7		9	10	11				2			1					8
		3	4	5	6	7		9	10	11				2			1					8
		3	4	5	6	7		9	10	11				2			1					8
		3	4	5	6	7		9	10	11				2			1					8
24	**24**	**23**	**18**	**33**	**34**	**38**	**9**	**29**	**32**	**32**	**2**	**28**	**27**	**22**	**12**	**6**	**13**	**1**	**1**	**1**	**1**	**8**
				1	1	1	25	13	1				5	2	1							2

Cup appearances:

1	2	3	4	5	6	7	8	9	10	11	12	13	14	15	16	17	18	19	20	21	22	23
1	2			5	6	7		9	10	11		8	4	3								
1	2			5	6	7		9	10	11		8	4	3								
1	2			5	6	7		9		11		8	4	3	10							
	2			5	6	7	8	9		11			4	3			1		10			
	2			5	6	7			10	11		9	4	3			1					
3	5			5	5	5	2		5	5		5	5	3	4		1					2
						1	3			2		2		1	1							2

League Table

	P	W	D	L	F	A	Pts
Manchester United	38	23	6	9	81	48	52
Aston Villa	38	17	9	12	77	59	43
Manchester City	38	16	11	11	62	54	43
Newcastle United	38	15	12	11	65	54	42
Sheffield Wednesday	38	19	4	15	73	64	42
Middlesbrough	38	17	7	14	54	45	41
Bury	38	14	11	13	58	61	39
Liverpool	38	16	6	16	68	61	38
Nottingham Forest	38	13	11	14	59	62	37
Bristol City	38	12	12	14	58	61	36
Everton	38	15	6	17	58	64	36
Preston North End	38	12	12	14	47	53	36
Chelsea	38	14	8	16	53	62	36
Blackburn Rovers	38	12	12	14	51	63	36
Woolwich Arsenal	38	12	12	14	51	63	36
Sunderland	38	16	3	19	78	75	35
Sheffield United	38	12	11	15	52	58	35
Notts County	38	13	8	17	39	51	34
Bolton Wanderers	38	14	5	19	52	58	33
Birmingham	38	9	12	17	40	60	30

1908-09

Division Two

Manager: J. Somerville

Match No.	Date	Venue	Opponents	Result		Scorers	Attendance
1	Sep 2	A	Birmingham	L	0-2		8,000
2	5	A	Barnsley	W	1-0	McClarence	6,000
3	12	H	Gainsborough Trinity	W	4-0	Baverstock, McClarence 2, White	
4	14	H	Hull City	W	1-0	Stuart	12,000
5	15	H	West Bromwich Albion	D	1-1	Owen	12,000
6	19	A	Tottenham Hotspur	L	1-2	Woods	8,000
7	26	H	Grimsby Town	W	2-0	Shepherd, McClarence	6,000
8	Oct 3	A	Hull City	L	0-2		10,000
9	10	H	Fulham	D	0-0		12,000
10	17	A	Derby County	L	0-1		6,000
11	24	H	Burnley	W	2-1	Woods, McEwan	7,000
12	31	A	Blackpool	W	2-1	Shepherd, Barber	6,000
13	Nov 7	H	Bradford Park Avenue	L	0-1		8,000
14	14	A	Chesterfield	W	2-0	Hogan 2	3,000
15	21	H	Wolverhampton Wanderers	D	1-1	Shepherd	8,000
16	28	A	Glossop	W	2-0	Hogan 2	3,000
17	Dec 5	H	Oldham Athletic	W	3-0	Greenhalgh, Hughes, Hogan	10,000
18	12	A	Stockport County	L	0-1		6,000
19	19	H	Clapton Orient	W	2-0	Hughes 2	5,000
20	25	H	Leeds City	W	2-0	Hogan, Hughes	20,000
21	26	A	Leeds City	W	2-1	Hughes, Stokes	10,000
22	Jan 1	H	Birmingham	W	2-1	Hughes, Hogan	23,000
23	2	H	Barnsley	W	3-0	Owen 2, Hughes	18,000
24	9	A	Gainsborough Trinity	L	1-2	Greenhalgh	2,000
25	23	H	Tottenham Hotspur	L	0-1		10,000
26	30	A	Grimsby Town	L	0-1		3,000
27	Feb 13	A	Fulham	W	2-1	Hughes, Hogan	18,000
28	20	H	Chesterfield	W	4-0	Hunter, Barber, Owen, Hughes	10,000
29	27	A	Burnley	W	2-1	Hughes, Hunter	7,000
30	Mar 6	H	Blackpool	W	3-1	Owen 2, Hunter	6,000
31	13	A	Bradford Park Avenue	W	2-1	Greenhalgh, Hogan	10,000
32	27	A	Wolverhampton Wanderers	W	2-1	Hogan, Hughes	7,000
33	Apr 3	H	Glossop	W	2-0	Owen 2	15,400
34	10	A	Oldham Athletic	D	1-1	Hogan	30,000
35	12	A	West Bromwich Albion	L	0-2		30,000
36	17	H	Stockport County	W	4-1	Hughes 2, Hunter 2	8,000
37	24	A	Clapton Orient	W	2-0	Hughes 2	10,000
38	30	H	Derby County	W	1-0	Hughes	30,000
						Appearances	
						Goals	

FA Cup

R1	Jan 16	A	West Bromwich Albion	L	1-3	Hunter	19,164
						Appearances	
						Goals	

Appearance grid — column headers (players):

Edmondson J.H. · Baverstock H. · Slater J. · Greenhalgh S. · Clifford R. · Boyd J. · Stokes D. · McClarence J.P. · Shepherd A. · White W. · McEwan M. · Stanley J. · Gaskell A. · Griffins D. · Stuart W. · Owen J.R. · Whiteside E. · Woods S. · Marsh S. · Craven R. · Grundy W.A. · Barber T. · Slant W. · Hogan J. · Hughes W. · Hunter W.B. · Robinson W.S. · Whiteside J. · Smith J.

Edm	Bav	Sla	Gre	Cli	Boy	Sto	McC	She	Whi	McE	Sta	Gas	Gri	Stu	Owe	WhE	Woo	Mar	Cra	Gru	Bar	Sln	Hog	Hug	Hun	Rob	WhJ	Smi
1	2	3	4	5	6	7	8	9	10	11																		
1	2			5	6		8	9	10	11	3	4	7															
1	2		6	5		9		8	11		3	4	7	10														
1	2		6	5		11	9		8		3	4	7	10														
1	2		6	5		7	8				3	4		10	9	11												
1	2		6	5		7			11		3	4		10	9	8												
1	2		6	5		7	10	9			3	4			8	11												
1	2		5		6	7		9	10		3	4			8	11												
1	2	3	5		6	7	8			11		4			10				9									
1	2	3	4	5				9	10	11		7			8					6								
1	2	3	6	5		7		9		11		4			8					10								
1	2	3	6	5		7		9		11		4			8					10								
1	2	3	6	5		7		9		11		4			8					10								
1	2	3	5			11		9				4			10		8				6	7						
1	2	3	5			7		9		11		4			10		8				6							
1	2	3	5			7				11		4			10		9			6		8						
1	2	3	5			7				11		4			10					6		8	9					
1	2	3	5			7				11		4			10					6		8	9					
1	2	3	5			7				11		4			10					6		8	9					
1	2	3	5			7				11		4			10					6		8	9					
1	2	3	5			7				11		4			10					6		8	9					
1	2	3	5			7				11		4			10					6		8	9					
1	2	3	5			7				11		4			10					6		8	9					
1	2	3	5			7				11		4								6		8	9	10				
1	2	3	5			7				11					4					6		8	9	10				
1	2	3				7				11		5			4		9			6		8		10				
1	2	3	5			7						4			10					6		8	9	11				
1	2	3				7						4			10					6		8	9	11	5			
1	2	3										4			10					6		8	9	11	5	7		
1	6	3				7						4			10					2		8	9	11	5			
1		2	6			7					3	4			10							8	9	11	5			
1	2	3	6			7						4			10							8	9	11	5			
1	2	3	6			7						4			10							8	9	11	5			
1	2	3	6			7						4			10							8	9		5		11	
1	2	3				7						4			10					6		8	9	11	5			
1	2	3	5			7						4			6		10					8	9	11				
1	2	3	6			7						4			10							8	9	11	5			
38	**37**	**31**	**32**	**11**	**4**	**34**	**7**	**10**	**6**	**21**	**8**	**35**	**4**	**5**	**26**	**1**	**4**	**7**	**2**	**2**	**20**	**2**	**24**	**21**	**14**	**10**	**1**	**1**
	1		3			1	4	3	1	1		8		2							2		11	16	5			

Edm	Bav	Sla	Gre	Cli	Boy	Sto	McC	She	Whi	McE	Sta	Gas	Gri	Stu	Owe	WhE	Woo	Mar	Cra	Gru	Bar	Sln	Hog	Hug	Hun	Rob	WhJ	Smi
1	2	3	5			7				11		4			6							8	9	10				
1	1	1	1			1				1		1			1							1	1	1				1

1909-10

Division One

Manager: J. Somerville/W. Settle

Did you know that?

On New Year's Day Bolton were 3–0 up inside 35 minutes against Notts County at Burnden, despite finding themselves bottom of the First Division. Two goals from Gordon Jones and one from John Owen seemed to have made it a happy start to 1910, but County hit back to win 4–3. This was to be one of a club record 10 home League defeats in a season.

Match No.	Date		Venue	Opponents	Result		Scorers	Attendance
1	Sep	1	A	Newcastle United	L	0-1		25,000
2		4	H	Aston Villa	L	1-2	Hughes	20,000
3		6	H	Liverpool	L	1-2	Hogan	12,000
4		7	A	Newcastle United	L	0-4		15,000
5		11	A	Sheffield United	D	2-2	Hughes, Hunter	5,000
6		18	H	Woolwich Arsenal	W	3-0	Hunter, Hughes, Marsh	14,000
7		25	A	Middlesbrough	W	2-1	Hughes 2	12,000
8	Oct	2	A	Chelsea	L	2-3	Hogan, Hunter	25,000
9		9	H	Blackburn Rovers	L	1-2	Hunter	16,000
10		16	A	Nottingham Forest	L	0-2		10,000
11		23	H	Sunderland	W	2-1	Lockett, Hunter	8,000
12		30	H	Everton	L	1-3	Lockett	20,000
13	Nov	6	H	Manchester United	L	2-3	Hunter, Lockett	20,000
14		13	A	Bradford City	L	0-1		16,000
15		27	A	Bristol City	L	0-1		6,000
16	Dec	4	H	Bury	L	1-3	Hunter	20,000
17		11	A	Tottenham Hotspur	D	1-1	Baverstock (pen)	20,000
18		18	H	Preston North End	W	3-1	Hughes, Baverstock 2 (2 pens)	10,000
19		25	A	Liverpool	L	0-3		25,000
20	Jan	1	H	Notts County	L	3-4	Jones 2, Owen	20,000
21		3	H	Sheffield Wednesday	L	0-2		16,000
22		8	A	Aston Villa	L	1-3	Hunter	17,000
23		22	H	Sheffield United	W	1-0	McEwan (pen)	7,000
24		29	A	Woolwich Arsenal	L	0-2		5,000
25	Feb	5	H	Middlesbrough	D	1-1	Jones	6,000
26		12	H	Chelsea	W	5-2	McEwan 2 (1 pen), Hunter 2, Lockett	8,000
27		19	H	Bradford City	D	1-1	Jones	10,000
28		26	H	Nottingham Forest	W	2-1	Hughes, Barber	8,000
29	Mar	5	A	Sunderland	L	0-3		10,000
30		12	H	Everton	L	0-1		8,000
31		19	A	Manchester United	L	0-5		20,000
32		26	A	Blackburn Rovers	L	2-4	Hughes 2	10,000
33		28	A	Notts County	D	0-0		9,000
34	Apr	2	A	Sheffield Wednesday	D	0-0		10,000
35		9	H	Bristol City	W	4-2	Jones, Hughes 2, Stokes	4,000
36		16	A	Bury	W	2-1	Jones, Hughes	8,000
37		23	H	Tottenham Hotspur	L	0-2		5,000
38		30	A	Preston North End	L	0-1		5,000

Appearances
Goals

FA Cup

R1	Jan	15	A	Stockport County	L	1-4	Hogan	8,000

Appearances
Goals

Player columns (rotated headers, left to right):

Edmondson J.H. · Slater J. · Stanley J. · Gaskell A. · Robinson W.S. · Barker T. · Stokes D. · Hogan J. · Hughes W. · Owen J.B. · McEwan M. · Greenhalgh S. · Hunter W.B. · Barecroft H. · Smith J. · Woods S. · Lockett H. · Marsh S. · Freebury J.H. · Davies D. · Wilkinson H. · Whiteside J. · Whiteside E. · Adamson H.M. · Edmonds H. · Jones G. · Stuart W. · Stott W. · Putnam J. · Hilton H.

1	2	3	4	5	6	7	8	9	10	11																			
1	2	3	4	5		7	8	9		10	6	11																	
1	2		4	5		7	8	9			6	11	3	10															
1	2			5	6	7	8			11	4		3		9	10													
1	3		4	5		7		9			6	11	2			10	8												
1		3			6	7	10	9			5	11	2				8	4											
1		3			6	7	10	9			5	11	2				8	4											
		3			6	7	10	9			5	11	2				8	4	1										
1		3		5	6	7	10	9				11	2				8	4											
1		3				7	8	9	10		5	11	2					4		6									
1		3	4		6	7		9		11	5	10	2			8													
1	3		4	6		7		9		11	5	10	2			8													
1	3		4		6	7			10	11	5	9	2			8													
1	3		4		6				11	5	9	2			10	8				7									
1	3		4		6		10			11	5	9	2			8				7									
1	3		4			10	9	6		7	5	11	2			8													
1	3				10	9	5	7			11	2			8	4					6								
1	3		5			9	4	7		11	2	10			8						6								
	3		5	10		9	4	7			11	2			8						6	1							
1	3		5				10	7	5	11	2			8	4					6				9					
1	2		5	6		10	9		7				11		8	4	3				6			8					
1	3		5					7		11	2			8	4					6		9	10						
1		5		7		9	10	11			2				4	3				6		8							
1		5		7		10	6	11		9	2				4	3						8							
1		5		7		9	10	11			2				4	3				6		8							
1		5				9		7		11	2			10	4	3				6		8							
1		5				9		7		11				10	4	3				6		8	2						
		5	10			9		7		11	2				4	3				6		8							
		5	10			9		7		11	2				4	3				6	1	8							
			10		8			7	5	11	2				4	3				6	1	9							
				7		8	10	11	5	9	2				4	3				6	1								
1				7		9	10	11	5		2					3				6		8				4			
1				7		9	10	11	5		2				4	3				6		8							
1				7		9	10		5	11	2				4	3				6		8							
1				7		9	4		5		2	11				3				6		8					10		
1				7		9	4		5		2	11				3				6		8					10		
1				7		9	4		5		2	11				3				6		8					10		
1		5		7		9	4			11	2				3				6	6	8					10			
33	16	8	10	19	15	24	14	31	19	26	23	28	34	6	1	16	21	22	1	1	2	8	13	4	17	1	1	1	4
				1	1	2	12	1	3			10	3				4	1					6						

1	3			5	6		10			7		11	2			8			4				9						
1	1			1	1		1			1		1	1			1			1				1						
								1																					

League Table

	P	W	D	L	F	A	Pts
Aston Villa	38	23	7	8	84	42	53
Liverpool	38	21	6	11	78	57	48
Blackburn Rovers	38	18	9	11	73	55	45
Newcastle United	38	19	7	12	70	56	45
Manchester United	38	19	7	12	69	61	45
Sheffield United	38	16	10	12	62	41	42
Bradford City	38	17	8	13	64	47	42
Sunderland	38	18	5	15	66	51	41
Notts County	38	15	10	13	67	59	40
Everton	38	16	8	14	51	56	40
Sheffield Wednesday	38	15	9	14	60	63	39
Preston North End	38	15	5	18	52	58	35
Bury	38	12	9	17	62	66	33
Nottingham Forest	38	11	11	16	54	72	33
Tottenham Hotspur	38	11	10	17	53	69	32
Bristol City	38	12	8	18	45	60	32
Middlesbrough	38	11	9	18	56	73	31
Woolwich Arsenal	38	11	9	18	37	67	31
Chelsea	38	11	7	20	47	70	29
Bolton Wanderers	38	9	6	23	44	71	24

1910-11

Division Two

Manager: W. Settle

Match No.	Date	Venue	Opponents	Result		Scorers	Attendance
1	Sep 1	H	Stockport County	D	2-2	Greenhalgh, Hewitt	6,000
2	3	A	Leicester Fosse	L	0-5		10,000
3	5	H	West Bromwich Albion	W	3-1	Hughes 3	8,000
4	10	H	Hull City	W	2-1	Hughes, Hewitt	10,000
5	17	A	Wolverhampton Wanderers	L	0-3		10,000
6	24	H	Fulham	W	2-0	Hewitt, Hughes	5,000
7	Oct 1	A	Chelsea	L	0-3		20,000
8	8	H	Bradford Park Avenue	W	1-0	Smith	5,000
9	15	A	Clapton Orient	D	0-0		12,000
10	22	H	Burnley	D	1-1	Shinton	6,000
11	29	A	Blackpool	D	1-1	Hughes	6,000
12	Nov 5	H	Gainsborough Trinity	W	3-0	Hilton, Smith 2	5,000
13	12	A	Glossop	W	2-1	Greenhalgh, Vizard	2,000
14	19	H	Leeds City	W	3-0	Vizard, Greenhalgh, Hilton	9,435
15	26	A	Lincoln City	W	3-1	Barber, Vizard, Stokes	5,000
16	Dec 3	H	Huddersfield Town	W	3-1	Hughes 3	5,000
17	10	A	Huddersfield Town	D	1-1	Hughes	4,000
18	17	A	Derby County	D	2-2	Feebery, Vizard	5,000
19	24	H	Birmingham	W	5-1	Hilton, Stokes, Hughes 3 (1 pen)	8,000
20	26	A	West Bromwich Albion	L	0-2		20,000
21	31	H	Leicester Fosse	W	6-2	Hughes 3, Smith 2, Greenhalgh	9,300
22	Jan 2	H	Barnsley	W	4-0	Hughes 2, Smith, Barber	10,000
23	7	A	Hull City	D	1-1	Smith	10,000
24	21	H	Wolverhampton Wanderers	W	4-1	Hilton 2, Stokes, Smith	5,000
25	28	A	Fulham	L	0-2		15,000
26	Feb 11	A	Bradford Park Avenue	D	1-1	Smith	8,000
27	18	H	Clapton Orient	W	2-0	Hughes, Hilton	11,000
28	25	H	Stockport County	W	1-0	Hughes	5,000
29	Mar 4	H	Blackpool	W	1-0	Smith	14,000
30	11	A	Gainsborough Trinity	L	0-1		3,000
31	18	H	Glossop	W	4-0	J. Whiteside, Barber, Smith, Hilton	10,000
32	20	A	Burnley	W	3-1	Barber 2, Hilton	5,000
33	25	A	Leeds City	L	0-1		15,000
34	Apr 1	H	Lincoln City	W	3-1	Hilton, Hughes, Greenhalgh	10,000
35	17	A	Barnsley	D	0-0		
36	22	H	Derby County	W	2-1	Hilton, Marsh	15,000
37	26	H	Chelsea	W	2-0	Hilton 2	40,000
38	29	A	Birmingham	L	1-2	Hilton	15,000
						Appearances	
						Goals	

FA Cup

R1	Jan 14	H	Chesterfield	L	0-2		6,193
						Appearances	

284

Player appearances and goals grid (shirt numbers worn each match):

Edmonds H.	Beverstock H.	Freebury J.H.	Owen J.R.	Greenhalgh S.	Adamson H.M.	Stokes D.	Jones G.	Shelton F.	Hewitt J.	Hunter W.B.	Robinson W.S.	Slater J.	Kay G.	Whiteside E.	Hughes W.	Hilton H.	Smith J.	Starr W.	Edmondson J.H.	Barber T.	Marsh S.	Vizard E.T.	Newton S.	Whiteside J.
1	2	3	4	5	6	7	8	9	10	11														
1	2	3		5	6	7	8	9	10	11	4													
1	2		4		7			8				3	5	6	9	10	11							
1	2		4		7			8				3	5	6	9	10	11							
1	2		4		7			8				3	5	6	9	10	11							
1	4			5	7			8				3		6	9	10	11	2						
	2		4		7		8		10			5	3		6	9		11	1					
	3	4		5		7		8		11					6	9	10	2	1					
	3			5		7		8	9	11					6		10	2	1	4				
	3			5		7		8	9	11					6		10	2	1	4				
	3	6		5		7		8		11						9	10	2	1	4				
	3	6		5		7									9	8	10	2	1		4	11		
	3	4		5		7								6	9	8	10	2	1			11		
	3	4		5		7								6	9	8	10	2	1			11		
	3	4		5		7								6	9	8		2	1		10	11		
	3	4		5		7								6	9	8	10	2	1			11		
	3	4		5		7								6	9	8		2	1		10	11		
	3	6		5		7									9	8	11	2	1	10				
	3	4		5		7									9	8	11	2	1	10				
	3			5		7								6	9	8	10	2	1	4		11		
	3			5		7								6	9	8	10	2	1	4		11		
	3			5		7								6	9	8	10	2	1	4		11		
	3			5		7								6	9	8	10	2	1	4		11		
	3			5		7								6	9	8	10	2	1	4		11		
	3			5											6	8	10	2	1	9	4	11		7
	3			5											6	8	10	2	1	9	4	11		7
	3			5						11					6	8	10	2	1	9	4			7
	3			5											6	8	10	2	1	9	4			7
	3			5		7									9	8	10	2	1		4	11		
		3		5		7									9	8	10	2	1		9	4	11	
	3			5		7									9	8	10	2	1		9	4	11	
		3		5		7									9	8	10	2	1		9	4	11	

Totals (appearances):

| 6 | 36 | 19 | 4 | 36 | 2 | 34 | 2 | 7 | 11 | 7 | 2 | 5 | 3 | 30 | 28 | 30 | 32 | 32 | 31 | 17 | 16 | 23 | 1 | 4 |

Goals:

| | 1 | | | 5 | | 3 | | | 1 | 3 | | | | | | 21 | 13 | 11 | | 5 | 1 | 4 | | 1 |

(FA Cup appearances / goals):

| 3 | | | | 5 | | 7 | | | | | | | | | 9 | 8 | 10 | 2 | 1 | 6 | 4 | 11 | | |
| 1 | | | | 1 | | 1 | | | | | | | | | 1 | 1 | 1 | 1 | 1 | 1 | 1 | 1 | | |

1911-12

Division One

Manager: W. Settle

Match No.	Date		Venue	Opponents	Result		Scorers	Attendance
1	Sep	2	H	Newcastle United	L	0-2		25,314
2		4	H	Liverpool	W	2-1	Bentley, Hilton	15,000
3		9	A	Sheffield United	W	5-0	Hilton, Bentley 2, Smith 2	10,000
4		16	H	Oldham Athletic	W	2-1	Hilton, Greenhalgh	25,402
5		23	A	Preston North End	W	2-1	Greenhalgh, Bentley	10,000
6		30	A	Bradford City	L	0-1		20,000
7	Oct	7	H	Woolwich Arsenal	D	2-2	Hilton, Barber	20,354
8		14	A	Manchester City	L	1-3	Smith	35,000
9		21	H	Everton	L	1-2	Smith	10,000
10		28	A	West Bromwich Albion	D	0-0		20,000
11	Nov	4	H	Sunderland	W	3-0	Vizard, Bentley, Smith	20,000
12		11	A	Blackburn Rovers	L	0-2		20,000
13		18	H	Sheffield Wednesday	W	4-2	Smith 2, Hilton, Stokes	17,590
14		25	A	Bury	W	3-1	Smith 2, Hilton	12,000
15	Dec	2	H	Middlesbrough	W	1-0	Smith	24,585
16		9	A	Notts County	L	2-3	Smith 2	12,000
17		16	H	Tottenham Hotspur	W	1-0	Barber	18,152
18		23	A	Manchester United	L	0-2		30,000
19		25	A	Liverpool	L	0-1		25,000
20		30	A	Newcastle United	L	2-5	Smith, Bentley	35,000
21	Jan	1	H	Aston Villa	W	3-0	Smith, Fay, Vizard	38,389
22		6	H	Sheffield United	L	0-3		6,000
23		20	A	Oldham Athletic	L	1-3	Smith	5,000
24		27	H	Preston North End	W	3-0	Feebery 2 (2 pens), Barber	17,000
25	Feb	10	A	Woolwich Arsenal	L	0-3		12,000
26		14	H	Bradford City	W	2-0	Smith, Hogan	13,174
27		17	H	Manchester City	W	2-1	Bentley, Stokes	13,000
28		28	A	Everton	L	0-1		15,000
29	Mar	2	H	West Bromwich Albion	W	2-0	Smith, Stokes	9,980
30		9	A	Sunderland	W	1-0	Smith	10,000
31		16	H	Blackburn Rovers	W	2-0	Fay, Barber	30,175
32		23	A	Sheffield Wednesday	W	1-0	Smith	10,000
33		30	H	Bury	W	1-0	Smith	15,882
34	Apr	5	A	Aston Villa	W	1-0	Hogan	20,000
35		6	A	Middlesbrough	L	0-1		5,000
36		13	H	Notts County	W	3-0	Hogan 2, Smith	12,735
37		20	A	Tottenham Hotspur	L	0-1		15,000
38		27	H	Manchester United	D	1-1	Smith	17,935

Appearances

Goals

FA Cup

R1	Jan	13	H	Woolwich Arsenal	W	1-0	Smith	24,854
R2	Feb	3	H	Blackpool	W	1-0	Bentley	18,651
R3		24	H	Barnsley	L	1-2	Smith	34,598

Appearances

Goals

Player columns (left to right): Edmondson J.H., Slater W., Bavenstock H., Barber T., Greenhalgh S., Whiteside E., Staites D., Hilton H., Bentley A., Smith J., Vizard E.T., Slater J., Newman S., Hunter W.B., Fay J.A., Freebairn J.H., Marsh S., Hughes W.H., Egerton W.N., Gimblett G.S., Jones G., Tyldesley J.D., Hogan J.

Edm	SlaW	Bav	Bar	Gre	Whi	Sta	Hil	Ben	Smi	Viz	SlaJ	New	Hun	Fay	Fre	Mar	Hug	Ege	Gim	Jon	Tyl	Hog
1	2	3	4	5	6	7	8	9	10	11												
1	2	3	4	5	6	7	8	9	10	11												
1			2	4	5	6	7	8	9	10	11	3										
			2	4	5	6	7	8	9	10	11	3	1									
			2	4	5	6	7	8	9	10		3	1		11							
			2	6	5		7	8	9	10		3	1		11	4						
			2	4	5	6	7	8	9	10		3	1		11							
	2			6	5		7	8	9	10	11	3	1		4							
1		2	6			8	9	10	11			7	5	3	4							
	2	6			7	8	9	10	11			1	5	3	4							
	2	6			7	8	9	10	11			1	5	3	4							
3	2	6			7	8	9	10	11			1	5		4							
	2	6			7	8	9	10	11			1	5	3	4							
	2	6			7	8	9	10	11			1	5	3	4							
	2	4		6	7	8	9	10	11			1	5	3								
	2	4		6	7	8	9	10	11			1	5	3								
	2	10	4	6	7		9		11			1	5	3	8							
		8	4	6	7		9	10	11	2	1		5	3								
1		4		6	7		9	10	11	2			5	3		8						
1	2		4	6	7		9	10	11				5	3		8						
1	2		6		7		9	10	11				5	3			4	8				
1	2		6		7		9	10	11				5	3			4	8				
	2	4		6	7		9	10	11				5	3			8		1			
	2	10	4	6	7		9	11					5	3		8			1			
	2	4		6	7		9	10	11				5	3					1	8		
1		2	4		6	7		9	10	11				5	3					8		
1		2	4	5	6	7		9	10	11					3					8		
1		6	10		2	7			4	11				5	3	9		8				
1	2		6		11	7		10						5	3	9		4		8		
1	2		6			7			10	11				5	3	9		4		8		
1	2		6			7			10	11				5	3	9		4		8		
1	2		6			7			10	11				5	3	9		4		8		
1	2		6			7			10	11				5	3	9		4		8		
1		2	6			7			10	11				5	3	9		4		8		
1	2		6			7			10	11				5	3	9		4		8		
1	2	3	6			7			10	11				5		9		4		8		
1	2	3	6			7			10	11						9		4	5	8		
1	2	3	6	5		7			10	11						9		4		8		
21	**16**	**26**	**38**	**13**	**19**	**37**	**16**	**27**	**37**	**33**	**8**	**14**	**4**	**29**	**26**	**7**	**13**	**2**	**13**	**3**	**3**	**13**
		4	2		3	6	7	22	2					2	2							4

Edm	SlaW	Bav	Bar	Gre	Whi	Sta	Hil	Ben	Smi	Viz	SlaJ	New	Hun	Fay	Fre	Mar	Hug	Ege	Gim	Jon	Tyl	Hog
	2	4		6	7		9	10	11				5	3		8			1			
	2	4		6	7		9	10	11				5	3					1	8		
1		2	4		6	7		9	10	11				5	3					8		
1		3	3		3	3		3	3	3				3	3		1			2	2	
					1	2																

League Table

	P	W	D	L	F	A	Pts
Blackburn Rovers	38	20	9	9	60	43	49
Everton	38	20	6	12	46	42	46
Newcastle United	38	18	8	12	64	50	44
Bolton Wanderers	38	20	3	15	54	43	43
Sheffield Wednesday	38	16	9	13	69	49	41
Aston Villa	38	17	7	14	76	63	41
Middlesbrough	38	16	8	14	56	45	40
Sunderland	38	14	11	13	58	51	39
West Bromwich Albion	38	15	9	14	43	47	39
Woolwich Arsenal	38	15	8	15	55	59	38
Bradford City	38	15	8	15	46	50	38
Tottenham Hotspur	38	14	9	15	53	53	37
Manchester United	38	13	11	14	45	60	37
Sheffield United	38	13	10	15	63	56	36
Manchester City	38	13	9	16	56	58	35
Notts County	38	14	7	17	46	63	35
Liverpool	38	12	10	16	49	55	34
Oldham Athletic	38	12	10	16	46	54	34
Preston North End	38	13	7	18	40	57	33
Bury	38	6	9	23	32	59	21

1912-13

Division One

Manager: W. Settle

Match No.	Date		Venue	Opponents	Result		Scorers	Attendance
1	Sep	2	H	Newcastle United	L	1-2	Vizard	32,000
2		7	H	Chelsea	W	1-0	Jones	21,666
3		11	A	Newcastle United	L	1-2	Jones	15,000
4		14	A	Woolwich Arsenal	W	2-1	Smith, Jones	15,000
5		21	H	Bradford City	W	2-0	Hogan, Vizard	20,303
6		28	A	Manchester City	L	0-2		33,000
7	Oct	5	H	West Bromwich Albion	W	2-1	Smith, Vizard	24,000
8		12	A	Everton	W	3-2	Jones, Barber, Donaldson	20,000
9		19	H	Sheffield Wednesday	W	3-0	Smith, Barber, Worrall (own-goal)	19,855
10		26	A	Blackburn Rovers	L	0-6		20,000
11	Nov	2	H	Derby County	D	1-1	Jones	17,360
12		9	A	Tottenham Hotspur	W	1-0	Smith	20,000
13		16	H	Middlesbrough	W	3-2	Smith, Bentley 2	8,058
14		23	A	Notts County	L	0-1		8,000
15		30	H	Manchester United	W	2-1	Smith, Bentley	17,257
16	Dec	7	A	Aston Villa	D	1-1	Smith	20,000
17		14	H	Liverpool	D	1-1	Smith	12,755
18		21	A	Sunderland	L	1-2	Greenhalgh	20,000
19		26	A	Sheffield United	W	2-0	Bentley, Donaldson	20,000
20		28	A	Chelsea	W	3-2	Smith, Greenhalgh, Hughes	30,000
21	Jan	1	H	Sheffield United	W	4-2	Jones, Smith 2, Bentley	30,000
22		4	H	Woolwich Arsenal	W	5-1	Donaldson, Jones, Bentley, Smith, Feebery (pen)	9,819
23		18	A	Bradford City	L	1-4	Bentley	8,000
24		25	H	Manchester City	D	2-2	Smith, Bentley	25,000
25	Feb	8	A	West Bromwich Albion	D	2-2	Weir 2	18,000
26		15	H	Everton	D	0-0		19,986
27		24	A	Sheffield Wednesday	D	2-2	Smith, Feebery	10,000
28	Mar	1	H	Blackburn Rovers	D	1-1	Smith	25,822
29		8	A	Derby County	D	3-3	Feebery (pen), Smith, Greenhalgh	10,000
30		15	H	Tottenham Hotspur	W	2-0	Feebery, Smith	14,968
31		21	H	Oldham Athletic	W	3-0	Feebery (pen), Smith 2	35,000
32		22	A	Middlesbrough	L	0-4		8,000
33		25	A	Oldham Athletic	W	3-2	Jones 2, Smith	9,500
34		29	H	Notts County	D	0-0		16,580
35	Apr	5	A	Manchester United	L	1-2	Smith	20,000
36		12	H	Aston Villa	L	2-3	Smith, Hughes	20,838
37		19	H	Liverpool	L	0-5		14,000
38		26	H	Sunderland	L	1-3	Jones	11,857

Appearances

1 own-goal   Goals

FA Cup

R1	Jan	11	A	Oldham Athletic	L	0-2		22,232

Appearances

Player appearance and goal grid (shirt numbers by player column). Column headers (read vertically):

1. Colmendson J.H.
2. Bavenstock H.
3. Fanbury J.H.
4. Greenhalgh S.
5. Fox J.A.
6. Barber T.
7. Stokes D.
8. Hogan J.
9. Jones E.
10. Smith J.
11. Vizard E.T.
12. Donaldson A.P.
13. Bentley A.
14. Thomas J.
15. Tyldesley J.D.
16. Wheaside E.
17. Jennings W.
18. Grindart G.S.
19. Slater J.
20. Stott W.
21. Hughes W.H.
22. Rowley W.J.
23. Weir A.
24. Hilton H.
25. Guendenning R.

1	2	3	4	5	6	7	8	9	10	11	12	13	14	15	16	17	18	19	20	21	22	23	24	25
1	2	3	4	5	6	7	8	9	10	11														
1	2	3	4	5	6			9	10	11	7	8												
1	2	3	4	5	6			9	10	11	7	8												
1	2	3	4	5	6			9	10	11	7	8												
1	2	3	4	5	6		10	9		11	7	8												
1	2	3	4	5	6		10	9		11	7	8												
1	2	3	4	5				9	10	11	7	8	6											
1	2	3	4	5	8			9	10	11	7		6											
1	2	3	4	5	8			9	10	11	7		6											
	2	3	4	5	8			9	10	11	7			1	6									
	2		5		8			9	10	11	7			1	6	3	4							
1		2	5		4			8	10	11	7	9			6	3								
1		2	5				11		8	10	7	9			6	4	3							
1		2	4	5					10	7	9	8			6		3							
1		2	5			7		9	10	11		8			6			3						
1		2	5					8	10	11	7	9			6	4	3							
1		2	5					8	10	11	7	9			6	4	3							
1		3		8				10	11	7	9				6		4		2					
1		2	5					8	10	11	7	9			6	3	4							
1		3	5		8			10	11	7	9	6			1	6		4		2	9				
1		3	5			8		10	11	7	9			6		4	2							
1		3	5				8	10	11	7	9	6	1		4	2								
	3	5			7		8	10	11	9	6	1		4	2									
1	3		5		7		8	10	11	9		6		4	2									
1	2	3		7	8	11		9		6		4			5	10								
1	2	3		7	8	11		9		6		4			5	10								
1	2	3		7	8	10	11		6			9	5											
1	2	3	4		7	9	10	11		6			5	8										
1	2	3	5		7	8	10	11		6	4		9											
1	2	3	5		7	8	10		6		9		4											
1	3		5		11	8	10	7	9		6		2		4									
1	3			11	8	10	7		6		2	9	5	4										
	2	3		11	8	10	7	9		1	6		5	4										
	2	3		7	8	10	11	9	1	6		5	4											
1	2	3		8	10	7		6	11		9	5		4										
1	2	3	5	11	8	10	7		6		9		4											
1	2	3	5	11	8	10	7		6		9		4											

Totals (appearances):

32	25	35	30	14	12	18	3	37	33	31	27	24	7	6	25	5	15	3	8	7	9	2	1	9

Goals:

	5	3		2			1	10	22	3	3	8							2		2			

Cup (appearances / goals):

1		3	5				7		8	10	11		9		6		4		2					
1		1	1				1		1	1	1		1		1		1		1					

League Table

	P	W	D	L	F	A	Pts
Sunderland	38	25	4	9	86	43	54
Aston Villa	38	19	12	7	86	52	50
Sheffield Wednesday	38	21	7	10	75	55	49
Manchester United	38	19	8	11	69	43	46
Blackburn Rovers	38	16	13	9	79	43	45
Manchester City	38	18	8	12	53	37	44
Derby County	38	17	8	13	69	66	42
Bolton Wanderers	38	16	10	12	62	63	42
Oldham Athletic	38	14	14	10	50	55	42
West Bromwich Albion	38	13	12	13	57	50	38
Everton	38	15	7	16	48	54	37
Liverpool	38	16	5	17	61	71	37
Bradford City	38	12	11	15	50	60	35
Newcastle United	38	13	8	17	47	47	34
Sheffield United	38	14	6	18	56	70	34
Middlesbrough	38	11	10	17	55	69	32
Tottenham Hotspur	38	12	6	20	45	72	30
Chelsea	38	11	6	21	51	73	28
Notts County	38	7	9	22	28	56	23
Woolwich Arsenal	38	3	12	23	26	74	18

Division One

Manager: W. Settle

Match No.	Date		Venue	Opponents	Result	Scorers	Attendance
1	Sep	1	H	Sheffield Wednesday	L	0-1	30,000
2		6	H	Oldham Athletic	W	6-2	Lillycrop 2, J. Smith, Feebery, Jones, Vizard	25,000
3		13	A	Manchester United	W	1-0	Lillycrop	40,000
4		20	H	Burnley	D	0-0		29,865
5		27	A	Preston North End	D	1-1	Lillycrop	17,000
6	Oct	4	H	Newcastle United	W	3-1	Lillycrop, Vizard, J. Smith	30,248
7		11	A	Liverpool	L	1-2	Vizard	15,000
8		18	H	Aston Villa	W	3-0	Rowley, Fay, Donaldson	30,310
9		25	A	Middlesbrough	W	3-2	Lillycrop, J. Smith 2	12,000
10	Nov	1	H	Sheffield United	W	3-1	Lillycrop 2, J. Smith	24,526
11		8	A	Derby County	D	3-3	Jones 2, J. Smith	15,000
12		15	H	Manchester City	W	3-0	J. Smith, Jones 2	22,257
13		22	A	Bradford City	L	1-5	Lillycrop	15,000
14		29	H	Blackburn Rovers	W	1-0	Lillycrop	53,747
15	Dec	6	A	Sunderland	L	2-3	Feebery, Lillycrop	10,000
16		13	H	Everton	D	0-0		19,297
17		20	A	West Bromwich Albion	D	1-1	Lillycrop	15,000
18		27	A	Oldham Athletic	L	0-2		13,000
19		29	A	Sheffield Wednesday	D	1-1	Lillycrop	8,000
20	Jan	1	H	Tottenham Hotspur	W	3-0	Lillycrop 2, Fay	36,000
21		3	H	Manchester United	W	6-1	J. Smith 4, Lillycrop, Jones	32,306
22		17	A	Burnley	D	2-2	J. Smith, Donaldson	25,000
23		24	H	Preston North End	L	0-3		22,560
24	Feb	7	A	Newcastle United	L	3-4	Lillycrop, Feebery 2 (1 pen)	20,000
25		11	H	Chelsea	D	1-1	Lillycrop	15,000
26		14	H	Liverpool	W	2-1	Lillycrop 2	16,527
27		25	A	Aston Villa	L	0-3		15,000
28		28	H	Middlesbrough	D	1-1	Jones	16,455
29	Mar	7	H	West Bromwich Albion	W	1-0	Jones	14,649
30		14	H	Derby County	W	3-1	Vizard 2, Stokes	13,808
31		21	A	Manchester City	W	1-0	Vizard	30,000
32		28	H	Bradford City	W	3-0	J. Smith 3	14,380
33	Apr	4	A	Blackburn Rovers	L	2-3	Lillycrop 2	25,000
34		6	A	Sheffield United	L	0-2		5,000
35		10	A	Tottenham Hotspur	L	0-3		40,000
36		11	H	Sunderland	W	2-1	J. Smith 2	27,243
37		13	A	Chelsea	L	1-2	H. Smith	30,000
38		18	A	Everton	D	1-1	Lillycrop	15,000

Appearances
Goals

FA Cup

	Date		Venue	Opponents	Result	Scorers	Attendance
R1	Jan	10	H	Port Vale	W	3-0	J. Smith, Donaldson, Lillycrop	18,975
R2		31	H	Swindon Town	W	4-2	J. Smith 3, Jones	50,558
R3	Feb	21	A	Burnley	L	0-3		32,734

Appearances
Goals

League statistics grid (shirt numbers by player and match):

Edmondson J.H.	Baverstock H.	Feebery J.H.	Glendenning R.	Greenhalgh S.	Whiteside E.	Donaldson A.P.	Jones E.	Lillycrop G.B.	Smith J.	Vizard E.T.	Rowley W.J.	Thomas J.	Gimblett G.S.	Fay J.A.	Tyldesley J.D.	Baverstock J.J.	Heslop T.W.	Stott W.	Jennings W.	Seddon J.	Stokes D.	Smith H.	Hanley C.B.	Lockhart A.	Sidlow E.
	2	3	4	5	6	7	8	9	10	11															
	2	3	4			7	8	9	10	11	5	6													
	2	3				7	8	9	10	11	5	6	4												
	2	3				7	8	9	10	11	5	6	4												
	2	3	4			7	8	9	10	11		6		5											
	2	3	4			7	8	9	10	11		6		5											
	2	3	4			7	8	9	10	11		6		5											
	2	3	4			7	8		10	11	5	6		9											
	2	3	4			7	8	9	10	11	5	6			1										
1	2	3	4			7	8	9	10	11		6		5											
	2	3	4			7	8	9	10	11		6		5											
	2	3	4			7	8	9	10	11		6		5											
	2	3	4			7	8	9	10	11	6			5											
	2	3	4			7	8	9	10	11		6		5											
	2	3	4			7	8	9	10	11		6		5	1	6									
1	2	3	4			7	8	9	10	11				5		6									
	2	3	4			7	8	9	10	11		6		5		6									
1	2	3	4			7	8	9	10	11				5											
		3	4			7	8	9	10	11	6			5		2									
1	2	3	4			7	8	9	10	11	6			5											
	2	3	4			7	8	9	10	11	6			5											
1		3	4			7	8	9	10	11	6			5		2									
1		2	4			7	8	9		11	5			6			10	3							
1		2	4	6	7	8	9		11	5						10	3								
	2	3	4			7	8	9	10	11	6			5											
	2	3	4				8	9	10	11	6						5	7							
	2	3	4			7	8	9	10	11	5	6													
	2	3	4				9	10	11	5						6		7	8						
	2	3	4			7		9	10		5					6		8	11						
1	2	3	4			7		9	10		5					6		11	8						
		4			8	9		6			5				2	3	7	10		11	1				
	3	4				9	10		6			5			2		7	8		11	1				
	2	4			7		9	10		5					3	11	8			1					
	2	3	4			7	8	9	10	11		5				6					1				
	2	3	4				8	9	10		5					6	7	11			1				
	2	3	4			7	8	9	10		5					6		11			1				
.9	31	37	36	1	2	33	32	37	35	31	24	13	2	27	1	2	6	4	10	1	7	8	1	2	6
	4			2	8	24	17	5	1		2								1	1					
	2	3	4			7	8	9	10	11	6			5											
	2	3	4			7	8	9	10	11	6			5											
	2	3	4			7	8	9	10	11	6			5											
3	3	3	3			3	3	3	3	3	3			3											
						1	1	1	4																

Division One
Manager: W. Settle

Match No.	Date	Venue	Opponents	Result		Scorers	Attendance
1	Sep 2	A	Liverpool	L	3-4	Jones 2, Smith	15,000
2	5	A	Oldham Athletic	L	3-5	Vizard, Smith, Fay	12,000
3	7	H	Blackburn Rovers	W	3-2	Lillycrop 2, Smith	23,000
4	12	H	Manchester United	W	3-0	Lillycrop 2, Smith	10,000
5	19	H	Manchester City	L	2-3	Vizard, Smith	21,658
6	26	A	Blackburn Rovers	D	2-2	Vizard, Lillycrop	22,000
7	Oct 3	H	Notts County	L	1-2	Lillycrop	14,113
8	7	A	Bradford Park Avenue	W	2-1	Smith 2	8,000
9	10	A	Sunderland	L	3-4	Smith 2, Vizard	10,000
10	17	H	Sheffield Wednesday	L	0-3		15,000
11	24	A	West Bromwich Albion	L	0-3		5,000
12	31	H	Everton	D	0-0		10,000
13	Nov 7	A	Chelsea	L	1-2	Lillycrop	25,000
14	14	H	Bradford City	L	3-5	Stokes, Smith 2 (1 pen)	5,000
15	21	A	Burnley	L	0-5		10,000
16	28	H	Tottenham Hotspur	W	4-2	Hilton, Roberts, Smith 2 (2 pens)	8,000
17	Dec 5	A	Newcastle United	W	2-1	Wallace, Roberts	6,000
18	12	H	Middlesbrough	W	4-0	Hilton, Stokes, Rowley, Smith	9,646
19	19	A	Sheffield United	L	1-3	Hilton	5,000
20	25	H	Liverpool	L	0-1		17,000
21	26	A	Aston Villa	W	7-1	Smith 4 (1 pen), Roberts 2, Hilton	30,000
22	Jan 1	H	Aston Villa	D	2-2	Stokes, Smith	20,000
23	2	H	Oldham Athletic	W	2-0	Roberts, Smith (pen)	20,000
24	16	A	Manchester United	L	1-4	Smith	8,000
25	23	A	Manchester City	L	1-2	Smith	25,000
26	Feb 27	H	West Bromwich Albion	D	1-1	Smith (pen)	8,900
27	Mar 1	A	Sheffield Wednesday	L	0-7		5,000
28	10	H	Sunderland	D	1-1	Jones	8,000
29	13	H	Burnley	W	3-1	Jones 2, Smith	13,612
30	17	A	Notts County	D	0-0		5,000
31	20	A	Bradford City	L	2-4	Roberts, Jones	8,000
32	22	A	Everton	L	3-5	Roberts, Buchan, Smith	5,000
33	Apr 2	H	Bradford Park Avenue	W	3-2	Roberts 2, Smith	15,000
34	3	A	Tottenham Hotspur	L	2-4	Smith 2 (1 pen)	15,000
35	10	H	Newcastle United	D	0-0		15,000
36	14	H	Chelsea	W	3-1	Roberts, Smith, Vizard	10,000
37	17	A	Middlesbrough	D	0-0		8,000
38	26	H	Sheffield United	L	0-1		12,000

Appearances

Goals

FA Cup

	Date	Venue	Opponents	Result		Scorers	Attendance
R1	Jan 9	H	Notts County	W	2-1	Smith, Hilton	17,871
R2	30	H	Millwall	D	0-0		22,418
rep	Feb 6	A	Millwall	D	2-2	Vizard, Smith (pen)	24,801
rep2	13	H	Millwall	W	4-1	Jones 2, Vizard 2	20,962
R3	20	H	Burnley	W	2-1	Smith 2	42,932
R4	Mar 6	H	Hull City	W	4-2	Vizard, Jones, Smith 2 (2 pens)	24,379
SF	27	N	Sheffield United	L	1-2	Smith	22,404

R2, R2 replay and R3 after extra-time.

SF at Ewood Park, Blackburn.

Appearances

Goals

Player columns (left to right): Edmondson J.H., Baverstock H., Feebury J.H., Glendenning R., Fay J., Jennings W., Donaldson A., Jones E., Lillycrop G., Smith J., Vizard E.T., Toone P., Rowley W.J., Stokes D., Sidlow E., Thomas J., Seddon J., Roberts F., Wilson G., Buckin T.M., Hilton H., Wallace W., Heslop T.W., Kidd J.

Edm	Bav	Fee	Gle	Fay	Jen	Don	Jon	Lil	Smi	Viz	Too	Row	Sto	Sid	Tho	Sed	Rob	Wil	Buc	Hil	Wal	Hes	Kid
1	2	3	4	5	6	7	8	9	10	11													
1	2	3	4	5	6	7	8	9	10	11													
	2		4	5	3	7	8	9	10	11	1	6											
	2		4	5	3		8	9	10	11	1	6	7										
	2		4	5	3		8	9	10	11	1	6	7										
	2		4	5	3		8	9	10	11		7	1	6									
	2		4	5	3		8	9	10	11		6	7	1									
	2		4	6	3	7		9	10	11		1				5	8						
	2		4	6	3	7		9	10	11		1				5	8						
	2	3		4	6	7		9	10	11						5	8						
	2	3		5	6		8	9	10	11		4	7										
1	2		4	6				10	11		5	7				8	3	9					
	2		4	6			9	10	11		5	7				8	3						
1	2		4	6			9	10	11		5	7				8	3						
1	2	3	4	5		9		6	11		7					8		10					
	3	4			7			10	11		5		1	6		9	2		8				
	3	4						10	11		5		1	6		9	2		8	7			
	3	4						10	11		5	7	1	6		9	2		8				
	3	4						10	11		5	7	1			9	2		8				
	3	4						10	11		5		1	6		9	2		8	7			
	3	4						10	11		5	7	1	6		9	2		8				
	3	4			6			10	11		5	7	1			9	2		8				
2			4		6			10	11		5	7	1			9	3		8				
2			4					10	11		5	7	1			9	3		8		6		
1		3	4		6	7		10	11		5					9	2		8				
1		3		4		7	8	9	10	11		5			6		2						
1		3		4		7	8	9	10	11		5			6		2						
1	2		4				8		10	11		5	7		6		9	3					
1	2				6		8		10	11		5	7		4		9	3					
	2				6		8		10	11		5	7		4		9	3		1			
	3				6		8		10	11		5	7		4		9	2		1			
1	2		4		6				10	11		5	7			6	9	3		1			
1	2		4		6	7	8		10	11		5					9	3		1			
2		4			6	7	8		10	11		5					9	3		1			
2			4	6	7	8		10	11		5						9	3		1			
2			4	6	7	8		10	11		5						9	3		1			
2		4	5	6		8		10	11		7						9	3		1			
2		4	5	6	7	8		10	11								9	3		1			
3	27	16	28	22	24	15	21	15	38	38	3	29	21	13	10	6	28	26	3	10	2	1	9
	1						6	7	29	5		1	3				10			1	4	1	

Edm	Bav	Fee	Gle	Fay	Jen	Don	Jon	Lil	Smi	Viz	Too	Row	Sto	Sid	Tho	Sed	Rob	Wil	Buc	Hil	Wal	Hes	Kid
	2		4					10	11		5	7	1	6		9	3		8				
1		3	4		6			10	11		5	7				9	2		8				
1		3	4				8	10	11		5	7		6		9	2						
1		3	4				8	10	11		5	7		6		9	2						
1		3	4				8	10	11		5	7		6		9	2						
1	2		4				8	10	11		5	7		6		9	3						
1			4		3		8	10	11		5	7		6		9	2						
6	2	4	7		2		5		7	7		7	1	6		7	7		2				
					3		7	4									1						

Lancashire Section

Manager:

12th in the Lancashire Section Principal Tournament, 4th in the Subsidiary Tournament Northern Division

The effect of World War One struck the club when, in July 1916, Harold Greenhalgh, who was 23 years old, fell while fighting in Picardy. The full-back had played in the club's first 18 games of the season, the last being in a 3–1 defeat at Southport Central on New Year's Day.

Match No.	Date		Venue	Opponents	Result		Scorers	Attendance
1	Sep	4	H	Liverpool	D	1-1	T Buchan	3,000
2		11	A	Bury	L	2-4	Foulkes, Roberts	6,000
3		18	H	Manchester United	L	3-5	T Buchan 2, Foulkes	2,000
4		25	A	Blackpool	L	1-2	Mather	5,000
5	Oct	2	H	Southport Central	L	0-7		
6		9	A	Oldham Athletic	L	2-6	J Buchan, J Smith	4,000
7		16	H	Everton	L	3-4	T Buchan 2, Mather	2,000
8		23	A	Rochdale	W	4-2	J Smith (pen), Roberts 2, Hampson	4,000
9		30	A	Manchester City	W	2-1	Jennings 2	
10	Nov	6	H	Stoke	W	2-1	T Buchan, J Smith (pen)	3,000
11		13	A	Burnley	L	0-3		5,000
12		20	H	Preston North End	W	1-0	J Smith	2,000
13		27	A	Stockport County	L	2-4	J Smith 2	
14	Dec	4	A	Liverpool	D	3-3	T Buchan, Roberts, J Smith	5,000
15		11	H	Bury	L	1-2	J Smith	
16		18	A	Manchester United	L	0-1		6,000
17		25	H	Blackpool	L	0-2		8,000
18	Jan	1	A	Southport Central	L	1-3	Hulme	3,000
19		8	H	Oldham Athletic	L	1-6	J Smith	
20		15	A	Everton	L	1-2	J Smith	15,000
21		22	H	Rochdale	W	3-0	Roberts 2, Lillycrop	3,000
22		29	H	Manchester City	W	4-2	J Smith 2 (1 pen), Roberts, Lillycrop	
23	Feb	5	A	Stoke	D	1-1	J Smith	
24		12	H	Burnley	W	3-0	Roberts, J Smith, Lillycrop	
25		19	A	Preston North End	W	3-1	J Smith, Roberts, Lillycrop	
26	Mar	4	A	Burnley	L	1-3	H Smith	
27		11	H	Preston North End	L	1-6	J Smith	
28		18	H	Southport Central	W	2-0	Lillycrop, Vizard	
29		25	A	Blackpool	L	1-3	T Buchan	
30	Apr	1	H	Bury	W	4-3	J Smith 3 (1 pen), Roberts	6,000
31		8	H	Burnley	W	2-0	J Smith, Vizard	
32		15	A	Preston North End	D	1-1	Vizard	
33		21	A	Bury	L	2-4	Roberts, Vizard	
34		22	A	Southport Central	W	1-0	J Smith	
35		24	H	Stockport County	W	4-2	Roberts 3, J Smith	
36		29	H	Blackpool	L	1-2	Waller	

Matches 26-34 & 36 were in the Lancashire Section Subsidiary Tournament.

Appearances

Goals

Lansdale J	Greenhalgh H	Shipperbottom F	Glendenning R	Rowley W	Entwistle W	Waller W	Buchan TM	Heamandhaigh T	Derret T	Gray G	Hotharsall H	Fowkes R	Roberts F	Lovett W	Kay T	Mather W	Garmon A	Hulme W	Buchan J	Sloan JR	Smith J	Hurst G	Hampson J	Jennings W	Hallows C	Lillicrop G	Hatfield A	Heslop T	Donaldson A	Vizard ET	Wilson G	Baverstock R	Hilton H	Hodgkiss J	Smith H	Garrett FH
1	2	3	4	5	6	7	8	9	10	11																										
1	2	3			6	7	4		11	5	8	9	10																							
	2	3	4	5	6	7	9		10	11					1	8																				
	2	3		5	6	7		10	11	4					1	8	8																			
	2	3	4	5			8		11			1					6	7	9	10																
1	2	10	4		6		9		11				8	5								3	7													
1	2			5	6		8		11			9			4						10	3	7													
1	2			5	6		8		11			9			4							3	7	10												
1	2			5	6		8			9					4						10	3	7	11												
1	2	5			6		8			9					4						10	3	7	11												
1	2	6		5			8			9					4						10	3	7	11												
	2	6		5			1			11			9			4					10	3	7			8										
1	2			5			8		11			9			4						10	3					6	7								
1	2	6		5			8			9					4						10	3						7	11							
1	2		4	5			8			9											10	3					6	7	11							
1	4	10		5			9		11								6					3					8	7		2						
	4						8			9		1					6				10	3	7				5		11	2						
	6			5			8			9		1									10	3	7	11			4		11	2						
		4					5			9							6				10	3			8						2	7	1	11		
		4	5				6			9											10	3			8				11		2	7	1			
		4	5				6			9											10	3	11		8				11		2	7	1			
		4	5				6			9											10	3			8				11		2	7	1			
		4	5				6			9											10	3			8				11		2	7	1			
		4	5				6			9											10	3			8				11		2	7	1			
			5				6			9							4					3	7	11						2	8	1	10			
			5				6			9											10	3	7				4		11		2	8	1			
1			4	5			6			9							3				10					8			11		2	7				
			4	5			6			9							2				10	3				8			11			1	7			
			4	5			6			9											10	3				8			11	2		1	7			
				5			6			9							4				10	3							11	2	8	1	7			
				5			6			9							4				10	3							11	2	8	1	7			
				5			6			7	9						4				10	3							11	2		1	8			
				5			6			9							4				10	3	7						11	2		1	8	2		
			4	5			6			9							3				10		7		11							1	8			
				5		7	6			9						8	4				10	3		11						2		1				
14	18	13	16	31	10	6	35	1	3	12	2	3	29	2	5	3	2	22	1	1	27	28	13	3	4	10	1	6	3	17	3	15	11	16	9	1
							1	8				2	14				2				22	1	1			5				4				1		

Lancashire Section

Manager:

10th in the Lancashire Section Principal Tournament, 8th in the Subsidiary Tournament

On 6 April 1917, Good Friday, the Wanderers played two games. In the morning they lost 2–0 at Stockport in the Lancashire Section Primary Competition and in the afternoon won 2–1 at Oldham in the Subsidiary Competition. Nine players took part in both games and, just for good measure, a day later Bury were defeated 3–2 at Gigg Lane.

Match No.	Date		Venue	Opponents	Result		Scorers	Attendance
1	Sep	2	A	Liverpool	L	1-3	Geddes	
2		9	H	Southport Central	D	1-1	Buchan	
3		16	A	Bury	L	0-2		
4		23	H	Stoke	W	9-2	Smith 6 (1 pen), Sharp 2, Vizard	
5		30	A	Southport Central	L	0-3		
6	Oct	7	H	Blackburn Rovers	D	0-0		
7		14	A	Manchester City	L	0-1		
8		21	H	Everton	L	1-3	Smith	
9		28	A	Rochdale	W	6-0	Smith 4 (1 pen), Buchan 2	
10	Nov	4	H	Blackpool	W	4-1	Smith, Sharp, Vizard 2	
11		11	H	Port Vale	W	3-2	Smith, Buchan 2	
12		18	A	Oldham Athletic	L	1-2	Sharp	
13		25	H	Preston North End	W	6-2	Smith 4, Buchan, Vizard	
14	Dec	2	A	Burnley	D	2-2	Smith, Jones	
15		9	H	Manchester United	W	5-1	Jones, Buchan 2, Smith 2	
16		30	H	Bury	L	2-3	Nuttall 2	
17	Jan	1	A	Oldham Athletic	L	0-3		
18		6	A	Stoke	L	0-7		
19		13	H	Southport Central	D	0-0		
20		20	A	Blackburn Rovers	L	1-5	Pickup	
21		27	H	Manchester City	D	2-2	Heslop, Buchan	
22	Feb	3	A	Everton	L	0-1		
23		10	A	Rochdale	L	1-3	Appleton	
24		17	A	Blackpool	L	3-5	Brookes, Jones, Winterburn	
25		24	A	Port Vale	L	0-2		
26	Mar	3	H	Oldham Athletic	D	2-2	Gimblett, Sharp	
27		10	A	Preston North End	W	2-1	Geddes, Pickup	
28		17	H	Burnley	W	3-1	Jones 2, Keenan	
29		24	A	Manchester United	L	3-6	Jones, Geddes 2	
30		31	H	Rochdale	L	0-1		
31	Apr	6	A	Stockport County	L	0-2		
32		6	A	Oldham Athletic	W	2-1	Hulme, Cavanagh (og)	
33		7	A	Bury	W	3-2	Geddes 2, Davies	
34		14	A	Rochdale	L	1-5	Stanley	
35		21	H	Bury	W	6-0	Fay 4, Davies, Geddes	
36		28	H	Liverpool	W	1-0	Geddes	

Matches 17,30 & 32-35 were in the Lancashire Section Subsidiary Tournament.

One own goal

Appearances

Goals

Hodgkiss J	Hulme W	Hirst G	Jones A	Nuttall J	Buchan TM	Pickup JH	Sharp S	Geddes R	Smith J	Vizard ET	Hamer J	Johnson H	Farnworth J	Heslop TW	Gimblett GS	Wray J	Hallows C	Keenan H	Haslam G	Nuttall W	Livesey F	Bradbury H	Garside J	Johnson F	Glendenning R	McMillan F	Clayton P	Lane J	Appleton L	Shufflebottom F	Holgate WJ	Hilton J	Stanley G	Brooks J	Winterburn A	Fay J	Hayes R	Smith H	Davies W	Hodson J
1	2	3	4	5	6	7	8	9	10	11																															
1	5	3	4		6	7		9	10	11	2	8																												
1	5	3	4	6	8	7		9	10	11	2																													
1	4	3			6	7	8	9	10	11			2	5																											
1	4	3		5	6	7	8	9	10	11			2																												
1	2			3	6	7	8	9	10	11				5	4																										
1	2			3	6	7	8		10	11				5	4	9																									
1	2			3	6	7	8		10	11				5	4	9																									
1	6	3		2	9	7	8		10					5	4		11																								
1	6	3		2	9	7	8		10	11				5	4																										
1		3		2	9	7	8		10	11				6	4			5																								
1		3		2	9	7	8		10	11				6	4			5																								
1		3	8	2	9	7			10	11				6	4			5																								
1		3	8	2	9	7			10	11				6	4			5																								
1		3	8	2	9	7			10	11				6	4			5																								
1		3	10	2	9	7									4			11	5	6	8																					
1		3	10	2	9	7									6				5	4	8	11																				
1		3	9	2	6	7														5	4	8		10	11																		
1		3		2	10	7									6	8			5						4	9	11																
1		3	8	2	9	7									10	4			5						6		11																
1		3			9	7									8	4			5	2		11						6	10													
1		3			9	7									10	4			5			11						6		8	2												
1		3	8		10	7									6				5									4		9	2	11									
		3	8	2		7													5						4			6					1	9	10	11					
		3	8	2	9	7													5										6					1	4	10	11					
		3		2	4	7	8												5										6					1	9	10	11					
1		3		2	4	7		9											5										6							10	11	8				
1		3	8	2	4	7		9											5										6							10	11					
1		3	8	2	4	7		9											5										6							10			11			
1				2	4	7		9		11								5										6						8					3	10	
1				2	4	7		9											5										6						8		11			10	3
1	8	6		2	4	7		9											5																				11			10	3
1	8			2	4	7		9											5										6								11			10	3
1		6		2	9	7													5										4						8		11			10	3
1		3		2	4	7		9											5										6								11	8		10	
1		3		2	4	7		9	10	11								5										6									8				
3	12	30	15	31	35	36	11	15	16	16	2	1	2	18	14	2	2	26	4	3	3	1	1	3	1	2	15	1	2	2	1	3	6	6	10	3	1	1	6	4
	1		6		9	2	5	8	20	4				1	1			1		2									1				1	1	1	4			2	

Lancashire Section

Manager:

Match No.	Date		Venue	Opponents	Result		Scorers	Attendance
1	Sep	1	H	Stoke	L	2-5	Pilkington, Geddes	
2		8	A	Stoke	L	2-6	Kelly, Geddes	
3		15	H	Liverpool	L	0-3		
4		22	A	Liverpool	L	0-6		
5		29	H	Bury	W	4-1	W Davies, Hilton 2, Winterburn	
6	Oct	6	A	Bury	D	1-1	W Davies	
7		13	H	Southport Central	D	1-1	Winterburn	
8		20	A	Southport Central	L	2-6	W Davies, Buchan	
9		27	A	Burnley	L	1-2	Heathcote	
10	Nov	3	H	Burnley	W	8-0	Heathcote, Clayton 2, Rutter, Geddes, Winterburn 2 (1 pen), one og	
11		10	A	Manchester United	W	3-1	Geddes 2, Winterburn	
12		17	H	Manchester United	W	4-2	W Davies, Heathcote, Geddes, one og	
13		24	A	Stockport County	W	3-2	Winterburn, W Davies, Pickup	
14	Dec	1	H	Stockport County	L	1-3	W Davies	
15		8	A	Oldham Athletic	L	3-6	Rutter, W Davies, Heathcote	
16		15	H	Oldham Athletic	L	3-5	Geddes, Heathcote, one og	
17		22	H	Port Vale	L	0-2		
18		25	A	Bury	D	2-2	Buchan, Geddes	
19		29	A	Port Vale	W	2-1	Smith, Geddes	
20	Jan	1	H	Bury	W	4-0	Smith 2, Buchan, Geddes	
21		5	H	Blackburn Rovers	W	5-2	Smith, Buchan 3, Pickup	
22		12	A	Blackburn Rovers	W	3-1	Winterburn 2, Heathcote	
23		19	A	Preston North End	L	0-2		
24		26	H	Preston North End	W	4-0	Heathcote 2, Barrett, Winterburn	
25	Feb	2	A	Blackpool	W	5-0	W Davies 2, Pickup, Heathcote, A Davies	
26		9	H	Blackpool	D	1-1	Geddes	
27		16	H	Manchester City	W	1-0	Heathcote	
28		23	A	Manchester City	W	1-0	W Davies	
29	Mar	2	H	Rochdale	D	1-1	Winterburn	
30		9	A	Rochdale	L	2-5	Winterburn, Hurst	
31		16	H	Everton	L	2-3	Winterburn, Pickup	
32		23	A	Everton	W	3-2	Heathcote 2, Pickup	
33		30	H	Oldham Athletic	W	2-0	Winterburn, Geddes	
34	Apr	6	A	Oldham Athletic	L	1-2	Heathcote	
35		13	H	Rochdale	W	2-1	J Nuttall, Winterburn	
36		22	A	Rochdale	L	0-4		

Matches 18, 20 & 33-36 were in the Lancashire Section Subsidiary Compeition

Three own goals

Appearances

Goals

Makin W	Nuttall J	Hurst G	Mather W	Wilson J	Clayton P	Geddes R	Davies W	Pilkington F	Rutter M	Winterburn A	Hilton J	Hodson J	Pickup JH	Kiely P	Ellison W	Beverstock AM	Fay J	Burnan TM	Pasquill E	Cousins W	Hilton H	Heathcote J	Vizard ET	Thomas J	Glover W	Davies A	Nuttall W	Young A	Livesey J	Seddon J	Smith J	Kay T	Rowley W	Barrett H	Hulme W	Hodgkiss JH	Abrams L	Longworth B	Clunis A	Greenhalgh H
1	2	3	4	5	6	7	8	9	10	11																														
	2			5	4	9	10			6	11	1	3	7	8																									
	3			4	9	10			11			7	8	1			2	5	6																					
	2			5	4	7	10			11			3		8	1		9	6																					
	2	3			5		10			6	11			9	1			7		4	8																			
		2			5		10			6	11	3			9	1		7	8	4																				
	2				5		10	9	6	11	3				1			8	7	4																				
	3				5	9	10			6	11				1		4		2	8	7																			
	5	3			6	8	10			11					1		4		2		7	9																		
	2	3			6	9	10		8	11					1		4				7	5																		
	5	2				9	10			6	11	3	8		1		4				7																			
	5	2				9	10			6	11	3	7		1		4				8																			
	2	3			6	9	10		5	11			7		1		4				8																			
	2	3			4	9	10		6	11			7		1		5				8																			
	5	2			6		10		9	11	3	7		1			4				8																			
	5					9	10		6	11	3	7		1			4	2			8																			
	2	4					10		6	11	3	7					9				8		1	5																
	2	3			9				6			7		1			11				8				4	5	10													
	2				9	8			6	11	3	7		1			4				8								5	10										
	2				9				6		3	7		8			11				6				4	10	1	5												
	2								3	7	1		9				8	11			6				5	10	4													
	2	3				10		6	11			7		1			4				8				5								9							
	2				10		6	11	3	7		1				9	4				8				5															
	2				10		6	11	3	7		1				4				8				5								9								
	2				10		6	11	3	7		1				4				8				5								9								
	2			9	10		6	11	3	7		1				4				8				5																
	2			9	10		6	11	3	7		1				4				8				5																
	2	3			10		6	11		7		1			5	4				8													9							
	2				10		6	11	3	7		1				4				8													9	5						
	2	5			10		6	11	3	7	9	1				4				8																				
	2	3			10		4	11		7	9				5				8													1	6							
	2			9		6	11		3	7	10			5	4				8														1							
	2	10		9		6	11		3					4				8				5											1	7					
	2	9			6	11		3		10				4				8				5											1	7		8			
	2			9		6	11		3	7				4				10				5											1	8			9		
	2	8			6	11		3		4	10							7				5											1	9					
1	35	17	3	3	13	20	28	2	32	33	1	24	25	9	25	1	4	34	4	7	2	27	3	1	1	12	1	1	1	3	3	1	2	5	1	6	1	2	1	1
1			2	12	10	1	2	14				1	5	1				6			2	13				1					4			1							

1918-19

Lancashire Section

Manager:

Match No.	Date		Venue	Opponents	Result		Scorers	Attendance
1	Sep	7	A	Blackpool	W	4-1	W Davies, Rutter, Ashurst 2	
2		14	H	Blackpool	W	2-1	Lythgoe 2	
3		21	A	Stockport County	D	2-2	Buchan, Winterburn	
4		28	H	Stockport County	W	3-1	Heathcote 2, Winterburn	
5	Oct	5	A	Bury	W	5-1	Cooper, Heathcote, Winterburn 2, A Davies	
6		12	H	Bury	W	3-1	W Davies, Buchan 2	
7		19	A	Liverpool	L	1-6	Heathcote	
8		26	H	Liverpool	D	2-2	Heathcote (pen), Geddes	
9	Nov	2	H	Burnley	W	2-1	Heathcote (pen), Buchan	
10		9	A	Burnley	W	4-0	Pickup, Heathcote, W Davies, Winterburn	
11		16	H	Southport Vulcan	W	3-2	W Davies, Heathcote 2	
12		23	A	Southport Vulcan	D	0-0		
13		30	H	Manchester United	W	3-1	W Davies 2, Jennings	
14	Dec	7	A	Manchester United	L	0-1		
15		14	H	Stoke	D	1-1	Lord	
16		21	H	Stoke	L	1-7	Roberts	
17		25	A	Bury	L	0-1		
18		28	A	Port Vale	L	1-3	Roberts	
19	Jan	1	H	Bury	W	2-1	Roberts, Heathcote	
20		11	A	Blackburn Rovers	W	3-2	Winterburn 2, Morris	
21		18	H	Blackburn Rovers	W	3-0	Seddon 2, P Hilton	
22		25	H	Preston North End	L	2-4	Morris, Buchan	
23	Feb	1	A	Preston North End	D	0-0		
24		8	H	Rochdale	W	3-2	A Davies, H Hilton, Roberts	
25		15	A	Rochdale	D	2-2	Vizard, Roberts	
26		22	A	Everton	L	1-4	Vizard	
27	Mar	1	H	Everton	L	3-6	Roberts 2, Rowley	
28		8	H	Oldham Athletic	L	1-3	Roberts	
29		15	H	Oldham Athletic	W	2-1	Smith, Roberts	
30		22	A	Manchester City	W	2-1	Roberts 2	
31		29	H	Manchester City	W	3-1	Roberts, Smith, Vizard	
32	Apr	5	A	Oldham Athletic	L	1-4	Buchan	
33		12	H	Oldham Athletic	W	3-1	Roberts 3	
34		18	H	Port Vale	W	2-1	Roberts, Vizard	
35		19	A	Rochdale	W	2-1	Roberts (pen), Feebury	
36		26	H	Rochdale	W	2-1	Rutter, Roberts (pen)	

Matches 5,6,32,33,35 and 36 were in the Lancashire Section Subsidiary Tournament and the Lancashire Cup.

Appearances

Goals

	Hodgkiss JH	Nuttall J	Hodson J	Buckim TM	Dawes A	Butler M	Pickup JH	Heathcote J	Ashurst R	Davies W	Winterburn A	Lythgoe J	Cooper E	Fitton W	Boardman E	Hurst G	Geddes R	Lawrence J	Elliston W	Colbourn J	Thomas J	Jennings W	Spaby J	Lord J	Roberts F	Rowley W	Bleasley J	Clayton P	Fay J	Smith J	Seddon J	Morris R	Kelly P	Hilton P	Hulme W	Hinton H	Hazard ET	Woods J	Donaldson A	Freebury J	Hughes J	Longworth B
	1	2	3	4	5	6	7	8	9	10	11																															
	1	2	3	4	5	6	7	8		10	11	9																														
	1	2	3	4	5	6	7	8	9	10	11																															
	1	2	3	4	5	6	7	8	9	10	11																															
	1	2	3	4	5	6	7	8		10	11		9																													
	1	2	3	4	5	6	7	8		10	11			9																												
	1	2	3	4	5	6	7	8		10	11				9																											
	1		3	4	5	6	7	8		10						2	9	11																								
			3	4	5	6	7	8		10						2	9	11	1																							
		2		4	5	6	7	8		10	11					3			1	9																						
	1	2		9	5	6	7	8		10	11					3					4																					
	1	5	2	4		6	7	8		10	11					3				9																						
	1		3	4	5	6	7	8		10	11					2						9																				
	1		3	4	5	6	7	8		10	11					2				9																						
	1	2	3	4	5	6		8			11							7					9	10																		
	1		3	4	5	6	7	8		10	11					2									9																	
	1		3		5	6	7	8		10	11					2									9	4																
	1	8	3		5	6	7			10	11					2									9	4																
	1		3			6	7	8			11					2									9	4		5	10													
	1		3			6	7				11					2									9	4				5	8	10										
	1		3	4		6	7				11					2														5	9	10	8									
	1		3	4		6	7	8			11					2									9					5		10										
	1	3		4		6	7				11					2									9					5		10				8						
	1	3		4	5	6	7									2									9							10				8	11					
	1	2	3	4	5	6	7			10															9											8	11					
		2	3	4	5	6	7			10															9										1	8	11					
			3	4		6	7			10						2									9	5									1	8	11					
	1		3		5	6	7	8		10	11					2									9	4																
	1		3		5	6																8			9	4							10				11	7		2		
	1		3		5	6	7																		9	4							10			8	11			2		
	1		3		5	6																			9	4							10			8	11	7		2		
	1		3	8	5	10																6			9	4											11	7		2		
			3	8	5																	6			9	4							10				11	7	1	2		
			3	8	5	6	7																		9	4							10				11		1	2		
			3	8	5	6	7			10															9	4											11		1	2		
			3		5	6	7			10	11											6			9	4													1	2		8
	28	16	32	27	29	34	31	19	3	17	27	1	2	1	1	18	2	3	2	3	1	5	1	1	19	11	1	2	1	5	4	3	5	1	2	8	11	5	4	8	1	1
			6	6	2	1	10	2		2	7	2	1			1				1		1			18	1				2	2	2				1			1	4		1

1919-20

Division One

Manager: C. Foweraker

Match No.	Date	Venue	Opponents	Result		Scorers	Attendance
1	Aug 30	H	Bradford Park Avenue	L	1-2	Roberts	17,540
2	Sep 1	H	Burnley	D	1-1	Roberts	20,255
3	6	A	Bradford Park Avenue	L	0-2		15,000
4	10	A	Burnley	L	1-2	Smith	14,000
5	13	A	Manchester City	W	4-1	Rowley, Smith 2, Roberts	30,000
6	17	A	Middlesbrough	W	3-1	Smith 3	20,000
7	20	H	Manchester City	W	6-2	Roberts 2, Feebery, Smith 2, Davies	24,616
8	27	A	Derby County	W	2-1	Smith, Feebery	15,000
9	Oct 4	H	Derby County	W	3-0	Roberts, Smith, Feebery (pen)	26,010
10	11	A	West Bromwich Albion	L	1-4	Feebery (pen)	30,000
11	18	H	West Bromwich Albion	L	1-2	Roberts	24,000
12	25	A	Sunderland	L	0-2		20,000
13	Nov 1	H	Sunderland	W	1-0	Rowley	30,514
14	8	A	Arsenal	D	2-2	Vizard, Buchan	30,000
15	15	H	Arsenal	D	2-2	Jennings, Buchan	20,565
16	22	A	Everton	D	3-3	Buchan, Stokes, Herbert	25,000
17	29	H	Everton	L	0-2		17,183
18	Dec 6	A	Bradford City	W	1-0	Roberts	10,000
19	13	H	Bradford City	D	1-1	Buchan	20,000
20	20	A	Blackburn Rovers	D	2-2	Roberts, Herbert	15,000
21	25	H	Preston North End	W	4-1	Buchan 3, Herbert	20,000
22	26	A	Preston North End	D	1-1	Broadhurst (own-goal)	25,000
23	27	H	Blackburn Rovers	W	2-1	Roberts, Buchan	32,564
24	Jan 1	A	Sheffield Wednesday	W	2-0	Roberts 2	26,244
25	3	H	Notts County	W	1-0	Roberts	18,471
26	17	A	Notts County	D	2-2	Seddon, Vizard	20,000
27	24	H	Liverpool	L	0-3		26,298
28	Feb 4	A	Liverpool	L	0-2		30,000
29	7	H	Chelsea	L	1-2	Vizard	28,377
30	14	A	Chelsea	W	3-2	Roberts, Smith 2	50,000
31	21	H	Newcastle United	L	0-3		23,625
32	28	A	Newcastle United	W	1-0	Roberts	40,000
33	Mar 13	H	Aston Villa	W	2-1	Roberts 2 (2 pens)	16,000
34	20	A	Oldham Athletic	L	0-2		20,000
35	27	H	Oldham Athletic	W	1-0	Smith	26,000
36	Apr 3	A	Manchester United	D	1-1	Roberts	40,000
37	5	A	Sheffield Wednesday	W	2-0	Roberts, Smith	15,000
38	7	A	Aston Villa	W	6-3	Smith 2, Roberts 3 (1 pen), Vizard	25,000
39	10	H	Manchester United	L	3-5	Herbert, Smith, Roberts	15,090
40	17	A	Sheffield United	L	2-3	Roberts, Smith	25,000
41	24	H	Sheffield United	W	1-0	Roberts	35,000
42	May 1	H	Middlesbrough	W	2-1	Roberts, Herbert	26,781

Appearances

1 own-goal   Goals

FA Cup

	Date	Venue	Opponents	Result			Attendance
R1	Jan 10	A	Chelsea	L	0-1		35,398

Appearances

Player columns (left to right):

Hughes J. · Rowley W.J. · Watson A.G. · Hulme W. · Seddon J. · Jennings W. · Donaldson A.P. · Buchan T.M. · Rogers F. · Smith J. · Vizard E.T. · Drabble F. · Hotson J. · Longworth B. · Feebery J.H. · Davies A. · Fay J.A. · Pickup J.H. · Howarth J.M. · Winterburn A. · Hilton H. · Baverstock H. · Stokes D. · Herbert W.E. · Gimblett G.S. · Cartman H.R. · Jones J.

Hughes	Rowley	Watson	Hulme	Seddon	Jennings	Donaldson	Buchan	Rogers	Smith	Vizard	Drabble	Hotson	Longworth	Feebery	Davies	Fay	Pickup	Howarth	Winterburn	Hilton	Baverstock	Stokes	Herbert	Gimblett	Cartman	Jones
1	2	3	4	5	6	7	8	9	10	11																
	2	3	4	5	6	7	8	9	10	11	1															
4	2	8		5	6	7	9		10	11	1	3														
	2			5	6	7	8	9	10	11	1	3	4													
	4	2			6	7	8	9	10	11	1				3	5										
	4	2			6	7	8	9	10	11	1				3	5										
	4	2			6	7	8	9	10	11	1				3	5										
	4	2			6	7	8	9	10	11	1				3	5										
	4	2			6	7	8	9	10	11	1				3	5										
1	4	2			6		8	9	10	11					3	5	7									
	4	2		5	6	7	10	9							3	8		1	11							
	4	2		5	6	7	10	9		11	1				3	8										
	4	2		5	6	7	8	9	10	11	1				3											
1	4	2			6	7	10	9		11					3	5				8						
	4	2		5	6	7	10	9		11	1				3	8										
	4				6			10	9	11	1				3	5					2	7	8			
					6			10	9	11	1				3	5					2	7	8	4		
		4	6					10	9						3	5					2	7	8		11	
		4	6					10	9	11	1				3	5					2	7	8			
		4	6					10	9	11	1				3	5					2	7	8			
		4	6		7			10	9	11	1				3	5					2		8			
		4	6					10	9	11	1				3	5					2	7	8	4		
6					7			10	9	11	1				3	5							8	4		
	2		4		6	7		10	9	11	1				3	5							8			
	2		4	6				10	9	11	1				3	5						7	8			
	2		4		7	6	9	10	11	1					3	5							8			
	2		4	6	7	8		10	11	1					3	5							9			
		4	6		7	10	9			11	1				3	5					2		8			
1	4			5	6	7	8	9	10	11					3						2					
		4	9		7	6	8	10	11	1	3					5					2					
		4	9		7	6	8	10	11	1	3					5					2					
1			4	6	7	8	9	10	11			3				5					2					
1	2		4	6		8	9	10	11		3					5					7					
1	6		4		7	8	9	10	11		3					5					2					
1	4	2				6	9	10	11						5							7	8		3	
1	4	2			7	6	9	10	11						5							8			3	
1	4	2			7	6	9	10	11						5							8			3	
1	4	2				6	9	10	11						5							7	8		3	
1	4	2				6	9	10	11						5							7	8		3	
1	5			6	7	4	9	10	11							2							8		3	
	5			6	7	4	9	10	11	1						2							8	11	3	
	5			6	7	4	9	10			1					2							8		3	
13	**26**	**25**	**3**	**24**	**34**	**30**	**42**	**40**	**27**	**39**	**28**	**7**	**1**	**25**	**8**	**25**	**1**	**1**	**1**	**17**	**11**	**21**	**2**	**2**	**8**	
	2			1	1		8	26	18	4				4	1						1	5				

Hughes	Rowley	Watson	Hulme	Seddon	Jennings	Donaldson	Buchan	Rogers	Smith	Vizard	Drabble	Hotson	Longworth	Feebery	Davies	Fay	Pickup	Howarth	Winterburn	Hilton	Baverstock	Stokes	Herbert	Gimblett	Cartman	Jones
	2		4	6	7		9	10	11			3			5					8						
	1		1	1	1		1	1	1			1			1					1						

League Table

	P	W	D	L	F	A	Pts
West Bromwich Albion	42	28	4	10	104	47	60
Burnley	42	21	9	12	65	59	51
Chelsea	42	22	5	15	56	51	49
Liverpool	42	19	10	13	59	44	48
Sunderland	42	22	4	16	72	59	48
Bolton Wanderers	42	19	9	14	72	65	47
Manchester City	42	18	9	15	71	62	45
Newcastle United	42	17	9	16	44	39	43
Aston Villa	42	18	6	18	75	73	42
Arsenal	42	15	12	15	56	58	42
Bradford Park Avenue	42	15	12	15	60	63	42
Manchester United	42	13	14	15	54	50	40
Middlesbrough	42	15	10	17	61	65	40
Sheffield United	42	16	8	18	59	69	40
Bradford City	42	14	11	17	54	63	39
Everton	42	12	14	16	69	68	38
Oldham Athletic	42	15	8	19	49	52	38
Derby County	42	13	12	17	47	57	38
Preston North End	42	14	10	18	57	73	38
Blackburn Rovers	42	13	11	18	64	77	37
Notts County	42	12	12	18	56	74	36
Sheffield Wednesday	42	7	9	26	28	64	23

1920-21

Division One

Manager: C. Foweraker

Match No.	Date		Venue	Opponents	Result		Scorers	Attendance
1	Aug	28	A	Manchester United	W	3-2	Roberts 2, Guy	50,000
2	Sep	1	A	Chelsea	L	0-1		30,000
3		4	H	Manchester United	D	1-1	Smith	32,239
4		6	H	Chelsea	W	3-1	Roberts 2, Smith	35,000
5		11	H	West Bromwich Albion	W	3-0	Smith 2, Roberts	41,584
6		15	H	Aston Villa	W	5-0	Roberts 2, Buchan, Smith 2	48,000
7		18	A	West Bromwich Albion	L	1-2	Herbert	30,000
8		25	H	Manchester City	W	3-0	Smith 2, Roberts	41,317
9	Oct	2	A	Manchester City	L	1-3	Smith	40,000
10		9	A	Arsenal	D	0-0		35,000
11		16	H	Arsenal	D	1-1	Smith	29,180
12		23	A	Middlesbrough	L	1-4	Smith	25,000
13		30	H	Middlesbrough	W	6-2	Buchan, Smith 3, Roberts 2	30,938
14	Nov	6	A	Derby County	D	0-0		15,000
15		13	H	Derby County	W	1-0	Seddon	26,155
16		20	A	Blackburn Rovers	D	2-2	Smith, Roberts	35,000
17		27	H	Blackburn Rovers	W	2-1	Roberts 2	32,560
18	Dec	4	A	Huddersfield Town	D	0-0		15,000
19		11	H	Huddersfield Town	W	3-1	Smith, Herbert, Roberts	26,331
20		18	A	Tottenham Hotspur	L	2-5	Smith, Rowley	30,000
21		25	H	Sunderland	W	6-2	Smith 4, Seddon, Roberts	41,000
22		27	A	Sunderland	D	0-0		45,000
23	Jan	1	H	Tottenham Hotspur	W	1-0	Smith	53,430
24		15	A	Oldham Athletic	D	0-0		10,000
25		22	H	Oldham Athletic	D	1-1	Smith	28,376
26	Feb	5	H	Bradford City	D	1-1	Smith	24,771
27		12	A	Preston North End	W	2-1	Roberts 2	20,000
28		16	A	Bradford City	D	2-2	Roberts, Smith	15,000
29		26	A	Burnley	L	1-3	Roberts	40,000
30	Mar	5	H	Burnley	D	1-1	Smith	54,809
31		12	A	Sheffield United	D	2-2	Roberts 2	30,000
32		19	H	Sheffield United	D	2-2	Smith, Vizard	23,403
33		25	H	Everton	W	4-2	Jack, Roberts, Smith 2	42,000
34		26	H	Bradford Park Avenue	W	2-0	Jack 2	24,808
35		28	A	Everton	W	3-2	Vizard, Smith, Roberts	40,000
36	Apr	2	A	Bradford Park Avenue	L	1-2	Smith	15,000
37		4	H	Preston North End	W	3-0	Roberts, Smith, Walsh	30,000
38		9	H	Newcastle United	W	3-1	Smith 3	23,061
39		16	A	Newcastle United	L	0-1		30,000
40		23	H	Liverpool	W	1-0	Smith	31,681
41		30	A	Liverpool	W	3-2	Smith 2, Jack	35,000
42	May	7	A	Aston Villa	L	0-2		15,000

Appearances
Goals

FA Cup

R1	Jan	8	A	Preston North End	L	0-2		27,000

Appearances

Player appearance grid (Bolton Wanderers), column headers (left to right):

Hilton W.F.W · Elvey J.R · Jones J · Rowley W.J · Seddon J · Jennings W · Donaldson A.P · Guy G · Roberts F · Smith J · Buckan T.M · Herbert W.E · Hughes J · Barwnbick H · Wright S · Vizard E.T · Fay J.A · Watson A.G · Walsh T · Moss A.E · Cartman H.R · Longworth B · Mellor F · Jack D.B.N · Hodson J · Dreblde F

Hilton	Elvey	Jones	Rowley	Seddon	Jennings	Donaldson	Guy	Roberts	Smith	Buckan	Herbert	Hughes	Barwnbick	Wright	Vizard	Fay	Watson	Walsh	Moss	Cartman	Longworth	Mellor	Jack	Hodson	Dreblde
1	2	3	4	5	6	7	8	9	10	11															
1	2	3	4	5	6	7		9	10	11															
1	2	3	4	5	6	7		9	10	11	8														
		3	4		6	7		9	10	11	8	1	2	5											
		3	4		6	7		9	10	11	8	1	2	5											
		3	4		6	7		9	10	11	8	1	2	5											
		3	4		6	7		9	10	11	8	1	2	5											
		3	4	5	6	7		9	10	11	8	1	2												
		3	4	5	6	7		9	10	11	8	1	2												
		3	4		6	7		9	10		8	1	2	5	11										
		3	5		6	7		9	10	4	8	1	2		11										
		3	4	5	6	7		9	10		8	1	2		11										
		3	4		6	7		9	10	8		1	2		11	5									
		3		4	6	7		9		10		1			11	5	2	8							
		3	4	5	6	7		9	10	8		1	2		11										
		3	4		6	7		9	10	8		1	2		11	5									
		3	4		6	7		9	10	8		1	2		11	5									
		3				7		9	10	4	8	1	2			5				6	11				
		3	4	6		7		9	10	11	8	1	2			5									
		3		6		7		9	10	8		1	2		11	5				4					
		3		6		7		9	10	8		1	2		11	5				4					
		3		4		7		9	10	6		1	2		11	5					8				
		3		5		7		9	10	6		1			11		2				4		8		
		3		5		7		9	10	6		1			11		2				4		8		
		3		4		7		9	10	6		1	2	5	11								8		
		3		5		7		8	10	6		1	2							11	4		9		
		3		5				8	10	6		1	2		11						4		7		
1		3		5				8	10	6			2		11			9			4		7		
1		3						8	10	6			2		11	5		9			4		7		
1		3		5				8	10	6					11		2	9			4		7		
		3		5				8	10	6		1	2		11			9			4		7		
1				5				8	10	6			2		11			9			4		7	3	
				5				8	10	6			2		11			9			4		7	3	1
1				5				8	10	6			2		11			9			4		7	3	
				5				8	10	6		1	2		11			9			4		7	3	
1				5				9	10	6					11		2	7			4		8	3	
1				5				9	10	6			2							7	4	11	8	3	
1	2			5				8	10	6					11			9			4		7	3	
1				5				9	10	6			2		11					7	4		8	3	
1				5				9	10	6			2		11					7	4		8	3	
1				5				9	10	6			2		11					7	4		8	3	
14	**3**	**33**	**16**	**32**	**18**	**27**	**2**	**42**	**41**	**40**	**12**	**27**	**33**	**6**	**29**	**11**	**5**	**12**	**1**	**6**	**20**	**2**	**19**	**10**	**1**
			1	2			1	24	38	2	2				2					1			4		

Additional section:

Hilton	Elvey	Jones	Rowley	Seddon	Jennings	Donaldson	Guy	Roberts	Smith	Buckan	Herbert	Hughes	Barwnbick	Wright	Vizard	Fay	Watson	Walsh	Moss	Cartman	Longworth	Mellor	Jack	Hodson	Dreblde
		3	4			7		9	10	6		1	2		11	5					8				
		1	1			1		1	1	1		1	1		1	1					1				

Division One

Manager: C. Foweraker

Match No.	Date	Venue	Opponents	Result		Scorers	Attendance
1	Aug 27	H	Preston North End	D	2-2	J. Smith 2 (1 pen)	39,993
2	29	A	Tottenham Hotspur	W	2-1	J. Smith (pen), Vizard	40,000
3	Sep 3	A	Preston North End	L	1-3	Jack	
4	5	H	Tottenham Hotspur	W	1-0	Vizard	40,000
5	10	H	Bradford City	D	3-3	Jack 2, Roberts	28,418
6	17	A	Bradford City	L	3-4	Jack 2, J. Smith	25,000
7	24	H	Huddersfield Town	W	3-1	Jack, J. Smith, Roberts	27,621
8	Oct 1	A	Huddersfield Town	L	0-3		15,000
9	8	A	Cardiff City	W	2-1	Buchan, Jack	40,000
10	15	H	Cardiff City	L	1-2	Roberts	25,486
11	22	A	Birmingham	D	1-1	Roberts	20,000
12	29	H	Birmingham	L	1-2	Roberts	21,567
13	Nov 5	A	West Bromwich Albion	W	1-0	Jack	30,000
14	12	H	West Bromwich Albion	W	2-0	Vizard, Roberts	20,207
15	19	H	Arsenal	W	1-0	Jack	20,000
16	Dec 3	A	Manchester City	W	3-2	Jack, Roberts 2	29,000
17	10	H	Manchester City	W	5-0	Roberts 2, Jack 2, J. Smith	34,789
18	12	A	Arsenal	D	1-1	Jack	10,000
19	17	A	Blackburn Rovers	W	2-1	Roberts, Jack	25,000
20	24	H	Blackburn Rovers	D	1-1	Jack	33,018
21	26	A	Oldham Athletic	D	0-0		30,000
22	31	A	Everton	L	0-1		35,000
23	Jan 2	H	Oldham Athletic	W	5-1	Roberts, Jack 3, J. Smith (pen)	36,000
24	14	H	Everton	W	1-0	Jack	17,559
25	18	A	Chelsea	W	3-0	Buchan, J. Smith 2 (1 pen)	17,000
26	21	H	Chelsea	L	0-2		19,636
27	Feb 4	H	Sheffield United	W	3-1	Roberts 2, Jack	7,408
28	11	A	Sheffield United	L	0-1		30,000
29	18	H	Burnley	L	0-1		24,164
30	25	A	Burnley	L	0-2		25,000
31	Mar 4	H	Newcastle United	W	3-2	Roberts, J. Smith (pen), Bradley (own-goal)	20,512
32	11	A	Newcastle United	L	1-2	J. Smith	30,000
33	18	A	Liverpool	W	2-0	Jack, J. Smith (pen)	30,000
34	25	H	Liverpool	L	1-3	J. Smith	30,000
35	Apr 1	A	Manchester United	W	1-0	J. Smith	30,000
36	8	H	Manchester United	W	1-0	Jack	11,244
37	14	A	Sunderland	L	2-6	Roberts, J. Smith (pen)	15,000
38	15	A	Aston Villa	L	1-2	Roberts	25,000
39	17	H	Sunderland	D	1-1	J. Smith	30,000
40	22	H	Aston Villa	W	1-0	Roberts	20,000
41	29	A	Middlesbrough	L	2-4	Jack, J. Smith	12,000
42	May 6	H	Middlesbrough	W	4-2	Jack, J. Smith, Rowley, Butler	13,049
							Appearances
						1 own-goal	Goals

FA Cup

R1	Jan 7	H	Bury	W	1-0	Vizard	42,831
R2	28	H	Manchester City	L	1-3	Roberts	66,442
							Appearances
							Goals

Team appearance / goals grid (Bolton Wanderers, Football League Division One)

Player columns (left to right):
Pym R.H. · Dewy J.R. · Hodson J. · Longworth B. · Seddon J. · Jennings W. · Herbert W.E. · Jack D.B.N. · Roberts F. · Smith J. · Vizard E.T. · Buchan T.M. · Carman H.R. · Wright S. · Jones J. · Nuttall H. · Watson A.G. · Hinton F. · Longo J.P. · Baverstock H. · Mellor F. · Rowley W.J. · Lowe J. · Haworth R. · Roberts E. · Donaldson A. · Butler W. · Smith C.F. · Chambers F. · Keatley J.S. · Simpson H. · Walsh T.

Pym	Dewy	Hodson	Longworth	Seddon	Jennings	Herbert	Jack	RobertsF	SmithJ	Vizard	Buchan	Carman	Wright	Jones	Nuttall	Watson	Hinton	Longo	Baverstock	Mellor	Rowley	Lowe	Haworth	RobertsE	Donaldson	Butler	SmithCF	Chambers	Keatley	Simpson	Walsh
1	2	3	4	5	6	7	8	9	10	11																					
1	2	3	4	5			8	9	10	11	6	7																			
1	2	3	4				8	9	10	11	6	7	5																		
1	2			7	5	6	8	9	10	11		3	4																		
1	2			7	5	6	8	9	10	11		3	4																		
1			4	5	6		8	9	10	11		7					3		2												
	2			4	5	6	8	9	10	11				3			1	7													
			4	5	6		8	9	10			7					3		1	2	11		4	7							
				5	6		8	9				11	10	7			3		2	1			4								
				5	6		8	9	10	11				7	4	3		2	1												
				5	6		8	9	10	11				7	4	3		2	1												
		3	4	5			8	9	10	11	6	7					1				2										
			4	5			8	9	10	11	6	7					1				2										
			4	5			8	9	10	11	6	7					1				2										
			4			6	8	9	10	11	6						3				5		2	7							
			4				8	9	10	11	6						3				5		2	7							
			4				8	9	10	11	6						3				5		2	7							
			4				8	9						5	3								2		7						
			4			6	8	9	10	11		7					3				5		2								
			4			6	8	9	10	11							3				5		2	7							
1			4	5	6			9	10	11	8	7					3						2								
			4	5	6			9						10			3				11	2		7	8						
1			4	5	6		8	9	10	11		7					3						2	7							
1			4		6		8	9	10	11							3						2	7		5					
1		3	4				8	9	10	11	6						3						2			7	5	2			
1			4	5				9	10	11											7	2			8	3					
1			4				8	9	10	11						6					5	2			7	3					
1			4	5			8	9	10	11						6						2			7	3					
1			4				8	9	10	11						6						2			7	5	3				
1			4	5			8	9	10		11					3	6						2			7					
1			4	5			8	9															2			7		3	11		
1			4	5			8	9	10	11						3	6						2			7					
1			4	5			8	9	10	11	6						3						2			7					
1	2		4				8	9	10	11	6										5					3	7				
1	2		4	5			8	9	10	11	6															3	7				
1			4	5			8		10	11	6						3						2			7				9	
1			4				8		10							3	6				5	7	2			9				11	

Totals (appearances):
| 23 | 8 | 5 | 38 | 27 | 20 | 1 | 39 | 39 | 39 | 35 | 22 | 13 | 4 | 29 | 10 | 5 | 19 | 1 | 1 | 1 | 13 | 4 | 29 | 4 | 8 | 13 | 3 | 5 | 1 | 2 | 1 |

Goals:
| | | | | | | | 24 | 18 | 18 | 3 | 2 | | | | | | 1 | | | | | | | | | 1 | | | | | |

FA Cup section:
			4		6		8	9	10	11		3					1				5		2			7					
			4	5	6		8	9	10	11		3					1				2		7								
			2	1	2		2	2	2	2		2					2				1		2			2					
							1		1																						

League Table

	P	W	D	L	F	A	Pts
Liverpool	42	22	13	7	63	36	57
Tottenham Hotspur	42	21	9	12	65	39	51
Burnley	42	22	5	15	72	54	49
Cardiff City	42	19	10	13	61	53	48
Aston Villa	42	22	3	17	74	55	47
Bolton Wanderers	42	20	7	15	68	59	47
Newcastle United	42	18	10	14	59	45	46
Middlesbrough	42	16	14	12	79	69	46
Chelsea	42	17	12	13	40	43	46
Manchester City	42	18	9	15	65	70	45
Sheffield United	42	15	10	17	59	54	40
Sunderland	42	16	8	18	60	62	40
West Bromwich Albion	42	15	10	17	51	63	40
Huddersfield Town	42	15	9	18	53	54	39
Blackburn Rovers	42	13	12	17	54	57	38
Preston North End	42	13	12	17	42	65	38
Arsenal	42	15	7	20	47	56	37
Birmingham	42	15	7	20	48	60	37
Oldham Athletic	42	13	11	18	38	50	37
Everton	42	12	12	18	57	55	36
Bradford City	42	11	10	21	48	72	32
Manchester United	42	8	12	22	41	73	28

1922-23

Division One

Manager: C. Foweraker

Match No.	Date		Venue	Opponents	Result		Scorers	Attendance
1	Aug	26	A	Preston North End	L	1-3	Flood	25,000
2	Sep	2	H	Preston North End	D	1-1	F. Roberts	28,140
3		4	H	Oldham Athletic	W	3-1	Flood, J. Smith (pen), Rowley	30,000
4		9	H	Sunderland	D	1-1	Vizard	25,000
5		11	A	Oldham Athletic	L	1-3	J. Smith	18,396
6		16	A	Sunderland	L	1-5	J. Smith	28,000
7		23	H	Birmingham	W	3-0	Vizard, J. Smith 2	17,680
8		30	A	Birmingham	L	0-2		25,000
9	Oct	5	A	Nottingham Forest	D	1-1	J. Smith	12,000
10		7	H	Huddersfield Town	W	1-0	Jack	20,069
11		14	H	Huddersfield Town	W	2-0	J. Smith, Jack	12,000
12		21	A	Aston Villa	L	0-2		25,000
13		28	H	Aston Villa	W	3-0	Butler, Walsh, Buchan	25,000
14	Nov	4	H	Stoke	D	1-1	J. Smith	14,725
15		11	A	Stoke	L	0-2		16,000
16		18	A	Manchester City	L	0-2		30,000
17		25	H	Manchester City	W	2-1	Jack, J.R. Smith	28,611
18	Dec	2	A	West Bromwich Albion	D	1-1	J. Smith	15,000
19		9	H	West Bromwich Albion	W	3-0	Jack 3	21,625
20		16	A	Blackburn Rovers	L	0-1		16,000
21		23	H	Blackburn Rovers	W	3-0	J. Smith 2, Jack	20,360
22		25	H	Arsenal	W	4-1	J.R. Smith, Butler, J. Smith, Jack	32,000
23		26	A	Arsenal	L	0-5		35,000
24		30	H	Cardiff City	D	0-0		15,829
25	Jan	2	H	Nottingham Forest	W	4-2	J. Smith 4	16,000
26		6	A	Cardiff City	L	0-1		20,000
27		20	H	Sheffield United	D	1-1	J.R. Smith	19,225
28		27	A	Sheffield United	D	2-2	Walsh, Jack	25,000
29	Feb	10	H	Burnley	W	2-1	J. Smith, Jack	15,630
30		17	A	Tottenham Hotspur	W	1-0	Jones	30,000
31	Mar	3	A	Liverpool	L	0-3		20,000
32		12	A	Burnley	L	1-2	Jennings	6,000
33		17	H	Newcastle United	W	1-0	Walsh	22,050
34		30	H	Everton	L	0-2		37,000
35		31	H	Middlesbrough	D	1-1	J.R. Smith	14,358
36	Apr	2	A	Everton	D	1-1	Jones	40,000
37		7	A	Middlesbrough	W	2-1	Jack, J.R. Smith	12,000
38		11	H	Tottenham Hotspur	L	0-2		15,000
39		14	H	Chelsea	D	1-1	J.R. Smith	12,895
40		16	A	Newcastle United	L	0-1		20,000
41		18	H	Liverpool	D	1-1	J.R. Smith	15,000
42		21	A	Chelsea	L	0-3		30,000
							Appearances	
							Goals	

FA Cup

R1	Jan	13	A	Norwich City	W	2-0	J. Smith, J.R. Smith	15,286
R2	Feb	3	H	Leeds United	W	3-1	Jack 2, J. Smith	43,341
R3		24	A	Huddersfield Town	D	1-1	Jack	39,442
rep		28	H	Huddersfield Town	W	1-0	Jack	61,609
R4	Mar	10	A	Charlton Athletic	W	1-0	Jack	41,033
SF		24	N	Sheffield United	W	1-0	Jack	72,000
F	Apr	28	N	West Ham United	W	2-0	Jack, J.R. Smith	126,047

SF at Old Trafford, Manchester. Final at Wembley Stadium.

Appearances
Goals

	Pym R.H.	Harwood R.	Thirkell P.	Longworth B.	Smith C.F.	Jennings W.	Roberts F.	Jack D.B.N.	Flood C.W.	Smith J.	Vizard E.T.	Rowley W.J.	Butler W.	Nuttall H.	Johnston J.B.	Seddon J.	Finney A.	Buchan T.M.	Crewe W.	Walsh T.	Wright W.B.	Roberts E.F.	Smith J.R.	Howarth N.	Nevens J.	Jones J.L.M.	Matthews V.E.	Chambers F.	Lowe J.	Simpson H.
	1	2	3	4	5	6	7	8	9	10	11																			
	1	2	3	4		6	9	8		10	11	5	7																	
	1	2	3	4		6	7	8	9	10	11	5																		
	1	2	3	4		6	7	8	9	10	11	5																		
	1	2	3			6	7	8	9	10	11	5		4																
	1		3			6	9	8		10	11	5	7	4	2															
	1	2	3			6	9	8		10	11	4	7			5														
	1	2					9	8		10	11	4	7			5	3	6												
	1		3				8	9	10	11	2	7				5		6	4											
	1						8	9	10	11	2	7				5	3	6	4											
	1						8	9	10	11	2	7				5	3	6	4											
	1						8	9	10	11	2	7				5	3	6	4											
	1					6		8		10	11	2	7			5	3	4		9										
	1			5		6		8		10	11	2	7				3	4		9										
	1					6		8		10	11	2	7			5	3	4		9										
	1			4		6		8		10	11	2	7			5	3			9										
	1	2				6		8		10	11	5		4			3			7	9									
	1	3				6		8		10	11	2	7	4						9	5									
	1	2	3	4			8			10	11		7	6		5		9												
	1	2	3			6		8		10	11	4	7			5				9										
	1					6			10	11	2	7	4		5	3				9			8							
	1	2	3			6		8		11	5	7							10	9			4							
	1	2				6		8		11		7				3	4		9	10			5							
	1		3			6		8		10	11		7	4		5		9						2						
	1	2				6		8		10	11			4		5	3			9						7				
	1		3			6		8		10	11			4						9	7	5	2							
	1	2				6		8						4			3		9	10			5	7				11		
	1	2				6		8						4			3			10	9		5	7				11		
	1	2						8				5					3				10		9	4	6	7			11	
	1	2						8		10		5		4			3						9		6	7			11	
	1	2						8		10	11	5	7	4			3						9			6				
	1	2						8		10	11	5				6	3						9			7			4	
	1	2				6		8		10	11	4	7			5	3						9							
Totals	42	30	14	5	4	32	8	41	8	37	38	33	30	20	1	16	26	9	4	7	6	1	22	2	7	9	2	2	1	5
Goals			1	1		11	2	17	2	1	2					1		3					7			2				

	Pym R.H.	Harwood R.	Thirkell P.	Longworth B.	Smith C.F.	Jennings W.	Roberts F.	Jack D.B.N.	Flood C.W.	Smith J.	Vizard E.T.	Rowley W.J.	Butler W.	Nuttall H.	Johnston J.B.	Seddon J.	Finney A.	Buchan T.M.	Crewe W.	Walsh T.	Wright W.B.	Roberts E.F.	Smith J.R.	Howarth N.	Nevens J.	Jones J.L.M.	Matthews V.E.	Chambers F.	Lowe J.	Simpson H.
	1	2				6		8		10	11	4	7			5	3						9							
	1	2	3			6		8		10	11	4	7			5							9							
	1					6		8		10	11	2	7	4		5	3						9							
	1	2				6		8		10	11	5	7	4			3						9							
	1					6		8		10	11	2	7	4		5	3						9							
	1	2				6		8		10	11		7	4		5	3						9							
	7	5	1			7		7		7	7	5	7	5		6	6						7							
						7		2															2							

League Table

	P	W	D	L	F	A	Pts
Liverpool	42	26	8	8	70	31	60
Sunderland	42	22	10	10	72	54	54
Huddersfield Town	42	21	11	10	60	32	53
Newcastle United	42	18	12	12	45	37	48
Everton	42	20	7	15	63	59	47
Aston Villa	42	18	10	14	64	51	46
West Bromwich Albion	42	17	11	14	58	49	45
Manchester City	42	17	11	14	50	49	45
Cardiff City	42	18	7	17	73	59	43
Sheffield United	42	16	10	16	68	64	42
Arsenal	42	16	10	16	61	62	42
Tottenham Hotspur	42	17	7	18	50	50	41
Bolton Wanderers	42	14	12	16	50	58	40
Blackburn Rovers	42	14	12	16	47	62	40
Burnley	42	16	6	20	58	59	38
Preston North End	42	13	11	18	60	64	37
Birmingham	42	13	11	18	41	57	37
Middlesbrough	42	13	10	19	57	63	36
Chelsea	42	9	18	15	45	53	36
Nottingham Forest	42	13	8	21	41	70	34
Stoke	42	10	10	22	47	67	30
Oldham Athletic	42	10	10	22	35	65	30

Division One

Manager: C. Foweraker

Match No.	Date		Venue	Opponents	Result	Scorers	Attendance
1	Aug	25	A	Cardiff City	L	2-3	D. Jack 2	35,000
2		27	A	Sheffield United	D	0-0		18,000
3	Sep	1	H	Cardiff City	D	2-2	J. Smith 2 (1 pen)	20,013
4		3	H	Sheffield United	W	4-2	J.R. Smith 3, Nuttall	25,000
5		8	A	Manchester City	D	1-1	J.R. Smith	40,000
6		10	A	Birmingham	W	3-0	J.R. Smith 2, D. Jack	15,000
7		12	A	Newcastle United	L	0-1		30,000
8		15	H	Manchester City	D	0-0		28,173
9		22	A	Tottenham Hotspur	D	0-0		40,000
10		29	H	Tottenham Hotspur	W	3-1	J.R. Smith, D. Jack 2	23,464
11	Oct	6	A	Sunderland	D	2-2	J.R. Smith 2	20,000
12		13	A	Sunderland	W	1-0	Nuttall	27,000
13		20	H	Arsenal	L	1-2	J.R. Smith	19,240
14		27	A	Arsenal	D	0-0		25,000
15	Nov	3	A	Chelsea	D	0-0		30,000
16		10	H	Chelsea	W	4-0	J. Smith, D. Jack 3	17,153
17		17	H	Huddersfield Town	W	3-1	J. Smith, J.R. Smith, D. Jack	17,630
18		24	A	Huddersfield Town	L	0-1		15,000
19	Dec	1	H	West Ham United	D	1-1	Bishop (own-goal)	22,592
20		8	A	West Ham United	W	1-0	D. Jack	30,000
21		15	H	Notts County	W	7-1	J. Smith 2, D. Jack 2, J.R. Smith, Butler 2	16,272
22		22	A	Notts County	D	1-1	J. Smith	10,000
23		25	H	West Bromwich Albion	W	2-0	J. Smith, J.R. Smith	35,000
24		26	A	West Bromwich Albion	W	5-0	D. Jack 3, J. Smith, J.R. Smith	35,000
25		29	H	Everton	W	2-0	Vizard, D. Jack	20,832
26	Jan	1	H	Birmingham	D	1-1	J. Smith	35,000
27		5	A	Everton	D	2-2	J. Smith, D. Jack	35,000
28		19	A	Aston Villa	W	1-0	J.R. Smith	26,972
29		26	A	Aston Villa	L	0-1		50,000
30	Feb	9	A	Liverpool	L	1-3	J. Smith	20,000
31		16	H	Nottingham Forest	W	4-0	D. Jack 2, Howarth, J.R. Smith	12,327
32		23	A	Nottingham Forest	L	0-1		11,000
33	Mar	1	H	Burnley	D	0-0		9,886
34		12	H	Liverpool	W	4-1	J. Smith 2, J.R. Smith, D. Jack	10,000
35		15	A	Middlesbrough	W	2-1	Simpson, R. Jack	15,000
36		22	H	Middlesbrough	W	2-0	D. Jack 2	13,608
37		29	A	Preston North End	W	2-0	D. Jack, R. Jack	17,729
38	Apr	1	A	Burnley	L	0-1		6,000
39		5	H	Preston North End	D	0-0		14,845
40		12	A	Blackburn Rovers	L	1-3	J. Smith	10,000
41		18	H	Newcastle United	L	0-1		20,000
42		19	H	Blackburn Rovers	W	3-0	Jones, J. Smith (pen), D. Jack	15,000

Appearances

1 own-goal   Goals

FA Cup

	Date		Venue	Opponents	Result	Scorers	Attendance
R1	Jan	12	A	Hull City	D	2-2	J.R. Smith, D. Jack	28,603
rep		16	H	Hull City	W	4-0	J.R. Smith 2, D. Jack 2	40,315
R2	Feb	2	H	Liverpool	L	1-4	J.R. Smith	51,596

Appearances

Goals

Player appearance and goals chart (shirt numbers shown per match):

Match	Pym R.H.	Haworth R.	Finney A.	Nuttall H.	Seddon J.	Jennings W.	Butler W.	Jack D.B.N.	Smith J.R.	Smith J.	Vizard E.T.	Howarth N.	Rowley W.J.	Walsh T.	Hinton W.F.W.	Chambers F.	Baggett W.J.	Longworth B.	Jack R.R.	Boston H.J.	Simpson H.	Wright W.B.	Jones J.L.M.
1	1	2	3	4	5	6	7	8	9	10	11												
2	1	2	3	4	5	6	7	8	9	10	11												
3	1	2	3	4	5		7	8	9	10	11	6											
4	1	2	3	4			7	8	9	10	11	6	5										
5	1	2	3	4	5	6	7	8	9	10	11												
6	1	2	3	4	5	6	7	8	9	10	11												
7	1	2	3	4	5	6	7	8	9	10	11												
8	1	2	3	4	5	6	7	8		10	11			9									
9	1	2	3	4	5	6	7	8	9	10	11												
10		2	3	4	5	6	7	8	9	10	11				1								
11	1	2	3	4	5	6	7	8	9	10	11												
12	1	2	3	4	5	6	7	8	9	10	11												
13	1		3	4	5	6	7		9	10	11					2	8						
14	1		3	4	5	6	7	8	9	10	11					2							
15	1	2	3	4			7	8		10	11				5								
16	1	2	3	4	5	6	7	8	9	10	11												
17	1	2	3	4	5	6	7	8	9	10	11												
18	1	2	3	4	5		7	8	9	10	11	6											
19	1	2	3			7	8	9	10	11	6								4				
20	1	2	3				6	7		9	10	11	5					4	8				
21	1	2	3		5	6	7	8	9	10	11							4					
22	1	2	3		5	6	7	8	9	10	11							4					
23	1	2	3		5	6	7	8	9	10	11							4					
24	1	2	3			6	7	8	9	10	11		5					4					
25	1	2	3		5	6	7	8	9	10	11							4					
26	1	2	3			6		8	9	10	11		5					4	7				
27	1	2	3		5	6	7	8	9	10	11							4					
28	1	2	3			6	7	8	9	10	11		5					4					
29	1	2	3				8	9	10		6	5						4	7	11			
30	1	2	3	4		6		8	9	10	11	5							7				
31	1	2	3	4		6	7	8	9	10	11		5										
32	1	2	3	4	5		7	8		10		6							9	11			
33	1	2	3	4	5		7	8		10	11	6							9				
34	1	2	3	4	5	6	7	8			11								9			10	
35	1	2	3	4	5	6	7	8			11								9			10	
36	1		3	4	5	6	7	8			11					2			9			10	
37	1		3	4	5					10	11	6				2	8	9	7				
38	1		3	4	5	6	7	8			10	11				2		9					
39	1		3	4		6		8		10	11		5			2			7			9	
Apps	41	36	42	30	29	34	36	39	32	39	40	8	14	2	1	5	2	12	7	6	2	4	1
Goals		2			2	24	17	16	1	1						2		1					1

FA Cup:

Match	Pym R.H.	Haworth R.	Finney A.	Nuttall H.	Seddon J.	Jennings W.	Butler W.	Jack D.B.N.	Smith J.R.	Smith J.	Vizard E.T.	Howarth N.	Rowley W.J.	Walsh T.	Hinton W.F.W.	Chambers F.	Baggett W.J.	Longworth B.	Jack R.R.	Boston H.J.	Simpson H.	Wright W.B.	Jones J.L.M.
1	1	2	3		5	6		8	9	10	11							4	7				
2	1	2	3		5	6	7	8	9	10	11							4					
3	1	2	3		5	6	7	8	9	10	11							4					
Apps	3	3	3		3	3	2	3	3	3	3							3	1				
Goals								3	4														

League Table

	P	W	D	L	F	A	Pts
Huddersfield Town	42	23	11	8	60	33	57
Cardiff City	42	22	13	7	61	34	57
Sunderland	42	22	9	11	71	54	53
Bolton Wanderers	42	18	14	10	68	34	50
Sheffield United	42	19	12	11	69	49	50
Aston Villa	42	18	13	11	52	37	49
Everton	42	18	13	11	62	53	49
Blackburn Rovers	42	17	11	14	54	50	45
Newcastle United	42	17	10	15	60	54	44
Notts County	42	14	14	14	44	49	42
Manchester City	42	15	12	15	54	71	42
Liverpool	42	15	11	16	49	48	41
West Ham United	42	13	15	14	40	43	41
Birmingham	42	13	13	16	41	49	39
Tottenham Hotspur	42	12	14	16	50	56	38
West Bromwich Albion	42	12	14	16	51	62	38
Burnley	42	12	12	18	55	60	36
Preston North End	42	12	10	20	52	67	34
Arsenal	42	12	9	21	40	63	33
Nottingham Forest	42	10	12	20	42	64	32
Chelsea	42	9	14	19	31	53	32
Middlesbrough	42	7	8	27	37	60	22

1924-25

Division One

Manager: C. Foweraker

Match No.	Date		Venue	Opponents	Result		Scorers	Attendance
1	Aug	30	A	Tottenham Hotspur	L	0-3		40,000
2	Sep	1	H	West Bromwich Albion	D	1-1	D. Jack	25,000
3		6	H	Bury	D	3-3	Cassidy 2, J. Smith	36,255
4		8	A	Birmingham	L	0-1		12,000
5		13	H	Notts County	W	1-0	J. Smith (pen)	15,393
6		20	A	Everton	D	2-2	J.R. Smith, D. Jack	35,000
7		27	H	Sunderland	L	1-2	D. Jack	30,853
8	Oct	4	A	Cardiff City	W	2-1	J. Smith, D. Jack	30,000
9		11	H	Preston North End	W	6-1	Vizard, D. Jack 2, J. Smith 2, Cassidy	21,946
10		18	A	Burnley	D	0-0		
11		25	A	Manchester City	D	2-2	J. Smith 2 (1 pen)	50,000
12	Nov	1	H	Arsenal	W	4-1	J.R. Smith 2, D. Jack 2	17,815
13		8	A	Aston Villa	D	2-2	J.R. Smith, J. Smith	25,000
14		15	H	Huddersfield Town	W	1-0	Cassidy	32,291
15		22	H	Blackburn Rovers	W	2-0	J. Smith, Eatock	12,000
16		29	H	West Ham United	W	5-0	J.R. Smith 3, Cassidy 2	25,977
17	Dec	6	A	Sheffield United	L	0-2		25,000
18		13	H	Newcastle United	W	3-2	J.R. Smith 2, D. Jack	17,100
19		20	A	Liverpool	D	0-0		25,000
20		25	H	Nottingham Forest	W	1-0	J.R. Smith	31,000
21		26	A	Nottingham Forest	D	1-1	Wright	21,000
22		27	H	Tottenham Hotspur	W	3-0	D. Jack, J. Smith (pen), J.R. Smith	14,168
23	Jan	1	H	Birmingham	W	3-0	J. Smith 2, D. Jack	27,000
24		3	A	Bury	L	0-1		35,000
25		17	A	Notts County	W	1-0	D. Jack	14,000
26		24	H	Everton	W	1-0	D. Jack	21,769
27	Feb	7	H	Cardiff City	W	3-0	Vizard 2, D. Jack	17,374
28		11	A	Sunderland	L	0-1		7,000
29		14	A	Preston North End	L	0-1		12,000
30		21	H	Burnley	W	5-0	J. Smith 2, Cassidy, D. Jack 2	20,468
31		28	H	Manchester City	W	4-2	J. Smith 3, D. Jack	26,769
32	Mar	7	A	Arsenal	L	0-1		20,000
33		14	H	Aston Villa	W	4-0	J. Smith 2, D. Jack 2	18,900
34		21	A	Huddersfield Town	D	0-0		30,000
35	Apr	4	A	West Ham United	D	1-1	Vizard	20,000
36		10	H	Leeds United	W	1-0	J.R. Smith	24,000
37		11	H	Sheffield United	W	3-1	D. Jack, J. Smith 2 (1 pen)	21,824
38		14	A	Leeds United	L	1-2	J. Smith (pen)	30,000
39		18	A	Newcastle United	W	1-0	D. Jack	7,000
40		22	H	Blackburn Rovers	W	6-0	D. Jack 4, J.R. Smith, J. Smith	14,000
41		25	H	Liverpool	W	2-0	D. Jack, J. Smith (pen)	18,249
42	May	2	A	West Bromwich Albion	D	0-0		15,000
							Appearances	
							Goals	

FA Cup

R1	Jan	10	H	Huddersfield Town	W	3-0	D. Jack, J. Smith (pen), Vizard	50,412
R2		31	A	Tottenham Hotspur	D	1-1	J. Smith	52,631
rep	Feb	4	H	Tottenham Hotspur	L	0-1		51,774
							Appearances	
							Goals	

Appearances and goals grid (players in column headers, match positions in cells):

Pym R.H.	Haworth R.	Finney A.	Nuttall H.	Rowley W.J.	Jennings W.	Butler W.	Jack D.B.N.	Cassidy J.	Smith J.	Vizard E.T.	Matthews V.E.	Seddon J.	Smith J.R.	Blaton H.J.	Eatock T.	Howarth N.	Davies R.I.	Wright W.B.	Greenhalgh H.W.	Forbes J.	Bourne J.T.	Jack R.R.	Chambers F.
1	2	3	4	5	6	7	8	9	10	11													
1	2	3	4		6	7	8	9	10	11	5												
1	2	3	4	5	6	7	8	9	10	11													
1	2	3	4	5	6	7	8	9	10	11													
1		3	4	2		7	8	10	6	11		5	9										
1		3	4	2		7	8	10	6	11		5	9										
1		3	4	2		7	8	10	6	11		5	9										
1		3	4	2	6		8	9	10	11		5		7									
1		3	4	2	6		8	9	10	11		5		7									
1	2	3	4	5	6	7	8	9	10	11													
1	2	3	4		6	7	8		10			5	9		11								
1	2	3	4		6	7	8	9	10	11		5											
1	2	3	4		6	7	8	9	10	11		5											
1	2	3	4		6	7	8		10			5	9		11								
1	2	3	4		6	7	8	9	10			5			11								
1	2	3	4		6	7	8		10			5	9		11								
1	2	3	4		6	7	8		10			5	9		11								
1	2	3	4		6	7	8		10			5	9		11								
1	2	3	4			7	8					5	9		11	6	10						
1	2	3	4			7	8					5	9		11	6		10					
1	2	3	4	5		7	8						9		11	6		10					
1	2	3	4			7	8		10	11		5	9		11	6							
1	2	3	4			7	8		10	11		5	9			6							
1	2	3		4		7	8		10	11		5	9			6							
1		3	4			7	8	9	10	11		5				6							2
1		3	4			7	8		10	11		5				6	9						2
1	2		4			7	8	9	10	11						6			3	5			
1	2		4			7	8	9	10			5				6		11	3				
1	2		4			7	8	9	10	11		5				6			3				
1	2		4				8	9	10	11		5		7		6			3				
	2		4				8	9	10	11		5		7		6			3			1	
1	2		4				8	9	10	11		5		7		6			3				
	2		4			7		9	10	11		5				6			3		8	1	
1	2		4			7		9	10	11		5				6			3		8		
	2	3	4		6	7		9	10	11		5									8	1	
39	35	31	41	11	23	33	42	22	36	31	1	35	21	9	10	16	2	4	13	1	3	3	0
							26	7	24	4			13	1					1				

FA Cup:

Pym R.H.	Haworth R.	Finney A.	Nuttall H.	Rowley W.J.	Jennings W.	Butler W.	Jack D.B.N.	Cassidy J.	Smith J.	Vizard E.T.	Matthews V.E.	Seddon J.	Smith J.R.	Blaton H.J.	Eatock T.	Howarth N.	Davies R.I.	Wright W.B.	Greenhalgh H.W.	Forbes J.	Bourne J.T.	Jack R.R.	Chambers F.
1		3	4			7	8		10	11		5	9			6							2
1	2	3	4			7	8		10	11		5	9			6							
1	2	3	4			7	8		10	11		5	9			6							
3	2	3	3			3	3		3	3		3	3			3							1
									1			2	1										

League Table

	P	W	D	L	F	A	Pts
Huddersfield Town	42	21	16	5	69	28	58
West Bromwich Albion	42	23	10	9	58	34	56
Bolton Wanderers	42	22	11	9	76	34	55
Liverpool	42	20	10	12	63	55	50
Bury	42	17	15	10	54	51	49
Newcastle United	42	16	16	10	61	42	48
Sunderland	42	19	10	13	64	51	48
Birmingham	42	17	12	13	49	53	46
Notts County	42	16	13	13	42	31	45
Manchester City	42	17	9	16	76	68	43
Cardiff City	42	16	11	15	56	51	43
Tottenham Hotspur	42	15	12	15	52	43	42
West Ham United	42	15	12	15	62	60	42
Sheffield United	42	13	13	16	55	63	39
Aston Villa	42	13	13	16	58	71	39
Blackburn Rovers	42	11	13	18	53	66	35
Everton	42	12	11	19	40	60	35
Leeds United	42	11	12	19	46	59	34
Burnley	42	11	12	19	46	75	34
Arsenal	42	14	5	23	46	58	33
Preston North End	42	10	6	26	37	74	26
Nottingham Forest	42	6	12	24	29	65	24

Division One

Manager: C. Foweraker

Match No.	Date		Venue	Opponents	Result		Scorers	Attendance
1	Aug	29	H	Newcastle United	D	2-2	J. Smith, D. Jack	30,998
2		31	A	Leeds United	L	1-2	Vizard	24,188
3	Sep	5	A	Bury	W	5-0	J.R. Smith 2, J. Smith 2 (1 pen), D. Jack	23,093
4		7	H	Leeds United	W	1-0	J. Smith	23,343
5		9	A	Burnley	D	1-1	Butler	14,295
6		12	A	Notts County	L	0-3		18,587
7		16	H	Burnley	W	4-2	D. Jack, J.R. Smith, J. Smith 2	16,647
8		19	H	Aston Villa	L	1-3	Vizard	16,982
9		26	A	Leicester City	L	2-5	J.R. Smith, D. Jack	23,820
10	Oct	3	H	West Ham United	W	1-0	D. Jack	20,923
11		10	A	Arsenal	W	3-2	Vizard 3	41,076
12		17	H	Blackburn Rovers	D	2-2	J. Smith (pen), Baggett	19,468
13		24	A	Sunderland	L	1-2	J. Smith (pen)	23,516
14		31	H	West Bromwich Albion	D	2-2	Howarth, D. Jack	17,063
15	Nov	7	A	Birmingham	W	1-0	Baggett	22,134
16		14	H	Manchester City	W	5-1	D. Jack 2, Vizard, J. Smith, Baggett	22,326
17		21	A	Tottenham Hotspur	W	3-2	Baggett, D. Jack, Vizard	26,792
18		28	H	Cardiff City	L	0-1		21,520
19	Dec	5	A	Sheffield United	L	0-2		20,014
20		12	H	Huddersfield Town	W	6-1	Butler, J. Smith 2, D. Jack, J.R. Smith 2	25,823
21		19	A	Everton	L	1-2	Butler	26,400
22		25	A	Manchester United	L	1-2	D. Jack	38,503
23	Jan	1	H	Birmingham	W	5-3	D. Jack, Vizard, J.R. Smith 3	22,240
24		2	A	Newcastle United	L	1-5	Vizard	34,136
25		16	H	Bury	W	3-2	Baggett, Vizard, J.R. Smith	36,654
26		23	H	Notts County	W	2-1	J.R. Smith 2	15,507
27	Feb	6	H	Leicester City	D	2-2	J. Smith 2 (2 pens)	17,939
28		13	A	West Ham United	L	0-6		24,062
29		27	A	Blackburn Rovers	L	0-3		21,346
30	Mar	13	A	West Bromwich Albion	W	3-0	Baggett 2, R. Jack	15,833
31		17	H	Manchester United	W	3-1	Roberts 2, Baggett	10,794
32		29	A	Manchester City	D	1-1	Vizard	21,720
33	Apr	2	H	Liverpool	L	0-1		30,298
34		3	H	Tottenham Hotspur	D	1-1	Vizard	21,364
35		5	A	Liverpool	D	2-2	Boston, R. Jack	21,398
36		7	H	Sunderland	W	3-2	D. Jack 2, R. Jack	12,076
37		10	A	Cardiff City	W	1-0	R. Jack	13,787
38		12	A	Huddersfield Town	L	0-3		20,829
39		17	H	Sheffield United	W	2-1	Butler, J. Smith (pen)	13,133
40		26	A	Aston Villa	D	2-2	Butler, Vizard	13,093
41		28	H	Arsenal	D	1-1	J. Smith	22,198
42	May	1	H	Everton	L	0-2		11,883

Appearances
Goals

FA Cup

	Date		Venue	Opponents	Result		Scorers	Attendance
R3	Jan	9	A	Accrington Stanley	W	1-0	D. Jack	32,875
R4		30	A	Bournemouth	D	2-2	J.R. Smith, D. Jack	10,165
rep	Feb	3	H	Bournemouth	W	6-2	Boston, J. Smith 2, D. Jack, J.R. Smith 2	24,798
R5		20	H	South Shields	W	3-0	J. Smith (pen), D. Jack, J.R. Smith	48,166
R6	Mar	6	A	Nottingham Forest	D	2-2	Butler 2	26,216
rep		10	H	Nottingham Forest	D	0-0		29,752
rep2		15	N	Nottingham Forest	W	1-0	J. Smith	30,952
SF		27	N	Swansea Town	W	3-0	Baggett, J. Smith 2 (1 pen)	25,476
F	Apr	24	N	Manchester City	W	1-0	D. Jack	91,447

R6 replay a.e.t.
R6 replay 2 at Old Trafford. SF at White Hart Lane. Final at Wembley Stadium.

Appearances
Goals

Player columns (left to right):

Pym R.H. · Haworth R. · Finney A. · Nuttall H. · Seddon J. · Jennings W. · Butler W. · Jack D.B.N. · Smith J.R. · Smith J. · Vizard E.T. · Howarth N. · Greenhalgh H.W. · Cope J.W. · Baggett W.J. · Jones J.L.M. · Eatock T. · Thornborough E.H. · Boston H.J. · Round J.H. · Forbes J. · Wrigstaffe J.T. · Roberts C.L. · Picken A.H. · Jack R.R. · Yates W. · Davies R.J.

League Table

	P	W	D	L	F	A	Pts
Huddersfield Town	42	23	11	8	92	60	57
Arsenal	42	22	8	12	87	63	52
Sunderland	42	21	6	15	96	80	48
Bury	42	20	7	15	85	77	47
Sheffield United	42	19	8	15	102	82	46
Aston Villa	42	16	12	14	86	76	44
Liverpool	42	14	16	12	70	63	44
Bolton Wanderers	42	17	10	15	75	76	44
Manchester United	42	19	6	17	66	73	44
Newcastle United	42	16	10	16	84	75	42
Everton	42	12	18	12	72	70	42
Blackburn Rovers	42	15	11	16	91	80	41
West Bromwich Albion	42	16	8	18	79	78	40
Birmingham	42	16	8	18	66	81	40
Tottenham Hotspur	42	15	9	18	66	79	39
Cardiff City	42	16	7	19	61	76	39
Leicester City	42	14	10	18	70	80	38
West Ham United	42	15	7	20	63	76	37
Leeds United	42	14	8	20	64	76	36
Burnley	42	13	10	19	85	108	36
Manchester City	42	12	11	19	89	100	35
Notts County	42	13	7	22	54	74	33

Division One

Manager: C. Foweraker

Match No.	Date		Venue	Opponents	Result	Scorers	Attendance
1	Aug	28	A	Leeds United	W 5-2	J. Smith (pen), D. Jack, J.R. Smith 3	23,699
2	Sep	1	A	Arsenal	L 1-2	Butler	23,002
3		4	H	Newcastle United	W 2-1	D. Jack, J.R. Smith	25,049
4		6	H	Arsenal	D 2-2	J.R. Smith, D. Jack	19,717
5		11	A	Burnley	L 3-4	Baggett 2, D. Jack	23,730
6		18	H	Cardiff City	W 2-0	Vizard, D. Jack	18,737
7		25	A	Aston Villa	W 4-3	Vizard, Jakeman (own-goal), D. Jack, J.R. Smith	20,696
8	Oct	2	A	Birmingham	W 1-0	D. Jack (pen)	20,006
9		9	H	Manchester United	W 4-0	J.R. Smith, Wright 2, Butler	17,869
10		16	A	West Bromwich Albion	D 1-1	Wright	16,622
11		23	H	Bury	D 2-2	Butler, Wright	39,258
12		30	A	Tottenham Hotspur	L 0-1		29,999
13	Nov	6	H	West Ham United	W 2-0	D. Jack, J. Smith	13,934
14		13	A	Sheffield Wednesday	L 1-2	J. Smith	21,033
15		20	H	Leicester City	W 2-0	Butler, D. Jack	15,255
16		27	A	Everton	D 1-1	J.R. Smith	28,091
17	Dec	4	H	Blackburn Rovers	W 5-1	D. Jack, Butler, J. Smith, Vizard 2	25,614
18		11	A	Huddersfield Town	L 0-1		24,667
19		18	H	Sunderland	D 2-2	J. Smith 2	24,232
20		25	H	Derby County	W 3-1	Butler 3 (1 pen)	31,533
21		27	A	Derby County	L 0-2		30,559
22		28	A	Liverpool	L 2-3	J. Smith, R. Jack	14,802
23	Jan	1	H	Liverpool	W 2-1	J.R. Smith 2	34,573
24		15	A	Leeds United	W 3-0	Vizard, D. Jack, J.R. Smith	19,149
25		22	A	Newcastle United	L 0-1		57,431
26	Feb	5	A	Cardiff City	L 0-1		12,721
27		12	H	Aston Villa	L 0-2		17,745
28		26	A	Manchester United	D 0-0		29,618
29	Mar	5	H	West Bromwich Albion	D 1-1	Vizard	12,954
30		9	H	Burnley	W 3-1	D. Jack, W. Roberts 2	13,331
31		12	A	Bury	L 0-2		30,532
32		19	H	Tottenham Hotspur	D 2-2	W. Roberts 2	17,762
33		26	A	West Ham United	D 4-4	Vizard, D. Jack 2, Gibson	17,752
34	Apr	2	H	Sheffield Wednesday	W 3-2	Blackmore, Marsden (own-goal), Butler	16,195
35		4	A	Birmingham	L 1-6	Gibson	6,301
36		9	A	Leicester City	W 1-0	Blackmore	20,768
37		15	H	Sheffield United	W 4-1	Gibson 2, Butler, D. Jack	23,149
38		16	H	Everton	W 5-0	J.R. Smith, Gibson 3, Vizard	26,381
39		18	A	Sheffield United	D 1-1	Blackmore	12,893
40		19	A	Sunderland	L 2-6	Gibson, J.R. Smith	14,316
41		23	A	Blackburn Rovers	W 3-0	Vizard, D. Jack, Gibson	14,816
42		30	H	Huddersfield Town	W 4-0	Wright 3, Seddon	21,229
							Appearances
						2 own-goals	Goals

FA Cup

	Date		Venue	Opponents	Result	Scorers	Attendance
R3	Jan	8	A	Blackpool	W 3-1	J.R. Smith 3	16,297
R4		29	A	Leeds United	D 0-0		42,694
rep	Feb	2	H	Leeds United	W 3-0	Wright, D. Jack, J.R. Smith	46,686
R5		19	H	Cardiff City	L 0-2		49,465
							Appearances
							Goals

Bolton Wanderers — Season Appearance Chart (1926–27)

Pym R.H.	Haworth R.	Greenhalgh H.W.	Nuttall H.	Seddon J.	Jennings W.	Butler W.	Jack D.B.N.	Smith J.R.	Smith J.	Vizard E.T.	Roberts C.L.	Yates W.	Wagstaffe J.T.	Baggett W.J.	Thornborough E.	Picken A.H.	Finney A.	Cope J.W.	Wright W.B.	Boston H.J.	Jack R.R.	Gill J.J.	Round J.H.	Gibson G.B.	Roberts W.D.	Blackmore H.A.
1	2	3	4	5	6	7	8	9	10	11																
1	2	3	4	5	6	7	8	9	11	10																
	2		4	5	6	7	10	9		11			1	3	8											
	2		4	5		7	10	9					1	3	8	6	11									
	2		4	5		7	10	9		11			1	3	8	6										
1		2	6	5		7	8	9		11								3	4	10						
1		2	6	5		7	8	9		11								3	4	10						
1		2	6	5		7	8	9		11								3	4	10						
1		2	6	5		7	8	9		11								3	4	10						
1		2	6	5		7	8	9		11								3	4	10						
1		2	6	5		7	8	9		11								3	4	10						
1		2	6	5		7	8	9					10					11	3	4						
1		2	6	5		7	8	9	10	11								3	4							
1		2	6	5		7	8	9	10	11								3	4							
1	2		6	5		7	8	9	10	11								3	4							
1		2	6	5			8	9		11								3	4		7						
1		2	6	5		7	8	9	10	11								3	4							
1		2	6	5		7	8	9	10									3	4							
1		2	6	5		7	8	9	10							11	3	4								
1	2		6	5		7	8	9	10							11	3	4								
1	2		6	5		7	8		10							11	3	4		9						
1		2	6			7	8	9	10							5	11	3	4							
1		2	6	5		7	10	9		11								3	4		8						
	2	6	5			7	10	9		11								3	4		8	1					
1		2	4			7	8	9								6		3	10		11		5				
1	2				6	7	8	9		11						4		3	10				5				
1	2	4			6	7		9		11								3	10	8	5						
1	2		5	6		7	8	9		11								3	4					10			
1	2		5	6			8			11								3	4	7				10	9		
1	2		5	6			8			11								3	4	7				10	9		
1	2	3		5	6		8			11						4								10	9		
1	2	3	4	5		7	8			11						6								10	9		
1		2	4			7	8									6		3	11		5			10	9		
1		2				7	8									6		3	4	11	1	5		10		9	
1		2	4	5		7			8							6		3		11				10		9	
1		2	4	5		7		8								6		3		11				10		9	
1		2	4	5		7			9	11						6		3		8				10			
1		2	4	5		7				11						6		3		8				10		9	
1	2	3		5		7	8	9								6			4	11				10			
1	2	3	6		5	7	8			11									4					10		9	
1		2	4	5		7	8	9								6		3		11				10			
37	**14**	**34**	**35**	**35**	**10**	**39**	**38**	**32**	**12**	**29**	**2**	**3**	**3**	**15**	**6**	**33**	**26**	**17**	**3**	**5**	**2**	**5**	**14**	**5**	**5**	
					1		10	16	13	7					9		2		7	1			9	4	3	

Pym R.H.	Haworth R.	Greenhalgh H.W.	Nuttall H.	Seddon J.	Jennings W.	Butler W.	Jack D.B.N.	Smith J.R.	Smith J.	Vizard E.T.	Roberts C.L.	Yates W.	Wagstaffe J.T.	Baggett W.J.	Thornborough E.	Picken A.H.	Finney A.	Cope J.W.	Wright W.B.	Boston H.J.	Jack R.R.	Gill J.J.	Round J.H.	Gibson G.B.	Roberts W.D.	Blackmore H.A.
1		2	6	5		7	8	9	10	11								3	4							
1		2	4	5		7	8	9	10	11						6		3								
1		2	4	5		7	8	9		11						6		3	10								
1		2	6			7	8	9	10	11						5		3	4								
4		**4**	**4**	**3**		**4**	**4**	**4**	**3**	**4**						**3**		**4**	**2**	**1**						
							1	4										1								

1927-28

Division One

Manager: C. Foweraker

Match No.	Date	Venue	Opponents	Result		Scorers	Attendance
1	Aug 27	A	Cardiff City	L	1-2	Smith	24,107
2	Sep 3	H	Blackburn Rovers	W	3-1	Smith 2, Picken	25,711
3	5	H	Everton	D	1-1	R. Jack	18,734
4	10	A	Bury	L	0-1		24,593
5	14	A	Everton	D	2-2	Butler, Picken	22,726
6	17	A	Sheffield Wednesday	L	0-3		19,111
7	24	H	Middlesbrough	D	0-0		21,720
8	Oct 1	A	Birmingham	D	1-1	D. Jack	15,988
9	8	H	Newcastle United	L	1-2	D. Jack	30,676
10	15	A	Huddersfield Town	L	0-1		19,818
11	22	H	Liverpool	W	2-1	Vizard, Blackmore	12,024
12	29	A	Arsenal	W	2-1	Gibson, Vizard	35,787
13	Nov 5	H	Burnley	W	7-1	Blackmore 4 (1 pen), D. Jack 3	14,340
14	12	A	Leicester City	L	2-4	Wright, Blackmore	21,249
15	19	H	Portsmouth	W	3-1	D. Jack, Wright, Blackmore	14,302
16	26	A	Sunderland	D	1-1	D. Jack	20,406
17	Dec 10	A	West Ham United	L	0-2		18,926
18	17	H	Aston Villa	W	3-1	Finney, Smith, Vizard	14,852
19	24	A	Sheffield United	L	3-4	D. Jack 3	10,503
20	26	H	Tottenham Hotspur	W	4-1	D. Jack 2, Nuttall, Gibson	25,229
21	31	H	Cardiff City	W	2-1	D. Jack, Blackmore	15,745
22	Jan 2	H	Derby County	L	1-3	Gibson	23,569
23	7	A	Blackburn Rovers	W	6-1	D. Jack 2, Gibson 2, Smith 2	14,660
24	21	H	Bury	W	2-1	D. Jack, Smith	32,497
25	Feb 4	A	Middlesbrough	W	5-2	D. Jack 2, Smith, Butler, Murphy	21,109
26	6	A	Tottenham Hotspur	W	2-1	Smith 2	18,183
27	11	H	Birmingham	W	3-2	D. Jack 2, Gibson	11,747
28	18	A	Newcastle United	D	2-2	D. Jack, Murphy	28,932
29	25	H	Huddersfield Town	L	0-1		44,082
30	29	H	Sheffield Wednesday	W	2-0	D. Jack 2	9,786
31	Mar 3	A	Liverpool	L	2-4	D. Jack, Gibson	37,115
32	10	A	Arsenal	D	1-1	R. Jack	15,546
33	17	A	Burnley	D	2-2	Butler, McClelland	15,865
34	24	H	Leicester City	D	3-3	McClelland 2, Butler	18,142
35	31	A	Portsmouth	L	0-1		21,846
36	Apr 6	H	Manchester United	W	3-2	McClelland, Vizard, Round	23,795
37	7	H	Sunderland	L	1-2	McClelland (pen)	18,064
38	9	A	Manchester United	L	1-2	McClelland	28,590
39	14	A	Derby County	L	0-1		12,378
40	21	H	West Ham United	W	4-0	McClelland, Murphy, Butler, Nuttall	8,520
41	28	A	Aston Villa	D	2-2	Gibson, Boston	22,895
42	May 5	H	Sheffield United	D	1-1	McClelland	7,958
						Appearances	
						Goals	

FA Cup

R3	Jan 14	H	Luton Town	W	2-1	Butler, Smith	20,266
R4	28	A	Stoke City	L	2-4	Round, Murphy	23,050
						Appearances	
						Goals	

Pym R.H.	Greenhalgh H.W.	Finney A.	Nuttall H.	Seddon J.	Thornborough E.H.	Butler W.	Jack D.B.N.	Smith J.R.	Gibson G.B.	Vizard E.T.	Picken A.H.	Jack R.R.	Haworth R.	Wright W.B.	Cope J.W.	Wagstaffe J.T.	Jennings W.	Beaton H.J.	Blackmore H.A.	Round J.H.	Gill J.J.	Murphy L.	Gough H.	McClelland J.
	2	3	4	5	6	7	8	9	10	11														
	2	3	4	5	6	7	8	9	10		11													
	2	3	4	5	6	7		9	10		11	8												
		3	4	5	6	7		9	10		11		2	8										
		3		5	6	7		9	10		11		2	8	4									
		3	6	5		7		9	10		11		2	8	4									
			4	5		8		9	10		11					3	6	7						
		3	4	5	6	7	8		10		11		2						9					
		3	4	5	6	7	8		10		11		2						9					
		3	4		6	7	8		10	11			2						9	5				
		3			6	7	8		10	11					4			2	9	5				
		3	6			7	8		10	11					4			2	9	5				
		3	6			7	8		10	11					4			2	9	5				
		3	6			7	8			11	10				4			2	9	5				
		3	6			7	8			11	10				4			2	9	5	1			
		3	6			7	8	9		11	10				4			2		5	1			
		3	6			7	8	9		11	10				4			2		5	1			
		3	6			7	8			11					4			2		5	1			
		3	6			7	8	9	10	11			2		4					5	1			
			6			7	8		10	11			2		4	3			9	5	1			
		3	6			7	8		10	11			2		4				9	5	1			
		3	6	2		7	8		10	11					4				9	5	1			
			6			7	8	9	10		11		2		4	3				5	1			
						7	8	9	10			2	6	4	3					5	1	11		
		3	6			7	8	9	10			2		4						5	1	11		
		3				7	8	9	10			2	6	4						5	1	11		
		3	6			7	8	9	10			2		4						5	1	11		
		3	4	5		7	8	9	10			2	6							1		11		
		3	4	5		7	8	9	10			2	6							1		11		
		3	4			7	8			9			2	6						5	1	11		
		3	6	5		7	8		10			9	2		4					1		11		
			6	5		8			10			9	2		4	3	7			11	1			
		3	6	5		7	8		10				2		4					11	1	9		
			2	5		7	8		10	11			6		4	3					1		9	
			4	5		7	8		10			2	6			3				11			9	
	3	4				7			10	11	8	2	6		5						9			
			5			7	8		10	11		2	6	4		3				1			9	
	3		6	7					10			2		4			11	9	5				8	
	3	6	5						10	11	8	2		4		7							9	
		6	5			7	8		10			2		4	3					11			9	
	3	6	5			8			10			2		4		7				11			9	
	3	4	5	6		8			10			2		7						11			9	
3	33	36	21	12	39	33	18	38	18	9	6	28	16	28	1	18	6	12	21	17	14	4	10	
	1	2			5	24	10	8	4	2	2		2			1	8	1		3		8		
						6	7	8	9	10			2	11	4		3			5	1			
	3	6				7	8	9	10			2	4						5	1	11			
	1	1			1	2	2	2	2			2	1	2		1			2	2	1			
							1		1											1	1			

League Table

	P	W	D	L	F	A	Pts
Everton	42	20	13	9	102	66	53
Huddersfield Town	42	22	7	13	91	68	51
Leicester City	42	18	12	12	96	72	48
Derby County	42	17	10	15	96	83	44
Bury	42	20	4	18	80	80	44
Cardiff City	42	17	10	15	70	80	44
Bolton Wanderers	42	16	11	15	81	66	43
Aston Villa	42	17	9	16	78	73	43
Newcastle United	42	15	13	14	79	81	43
Arsenal	42	13	15	14	82	86	41
Birmingham	42	13	15	14	70	75	41
Blackburn Rovers	42	16	9	17	66	78	41
Sheffield United	42	15	10	17	79	86	40
Sheffield Wednesday	42	13	13	16	81	78	39
Sunderland	42	15	9	18	74	76	39
Liverpool	42	13	13	16	84	87	39
West Ham United	42	14	11	17	81	88	39
Manchester United	42	16	7	19	72	80	39
Burnley	42	16	7	19	82	98	39
Portsmouth	42	16	7	19	66	90	39
Tottenham Hotspur	42	15	8	19	74	86	38
Middlesbrough	42	11	15	16	81	88	37

Division One

Manager: C. Foweraker

Match No.	Date		Venue	Opponents	Result		Scorers	Attendance
1	Aug	25	H	Everton	L	2-3	Gibson 2	34,63
2		27	A	Huddersfield Town	L	1-4	Murphy	15,71
3	Sep	1	A	Arsenal	L	0-2		35,12
4		3	H	Huddersfield Town	D	1-1	D. Jack	15,53
5		8	H	Blackburn Rovers	L	0-3		15,63
6		15	A	Sunderland	L	0-4		29,61
7		22	H	Derby County	W	3-0	Murphy, Blackmore 2	20,40
8		29	A	Sheffield Wednesday	D	0-0		25,09
9	Oct	6	H	Bury	L	0-1		37,18
10		13	H	Portsmouth	W	4-2	Butler, Blackmore 3	16,10
11		20	A	Aston Villa	W	5-3	Butler, Gibson, Blackmore 3	29,82
12		27	H	Sheffield United	W	3-1	Gibson 3	18,80
13	Nov	3	A	Manchester United	D	1-1	Murphy	31,18
14		10	H	Leeds United	W	4-1	McClelland, Gibson, Blackmore 2	16,30
15		17	A	Liverpool	L	0-3		27,90
16		24	H	West Ham United	W	4-1	Murphy, Kean, Blackmore 2	12,37
17	Dec	1	A	Newcastle United	L	1-4	McClelland	31,42
18		8	H	Burnley	L	0-1		17,22
19		15	A	Cardiff City	D	1-1	Vizard	11,28
20		22	H	Leicester City	W	5-0	Butler, McClelland, Gibson, Blackmore 2	16,03
21		25	A	Birmingham	W	2-0	Blackmore, McClelland	31,35
22		26	H	Birmingham	W	6-2	Butler, Blackmore 3, Gibson 2	22,11
23		29	A	Everton	L	0-3		34,44
24	Jan	1	H	Cardiff City	W	1-0	Blackmore	33,65
25		5	H	Arsenal	L	1-2	Gibson	17,59
26		19	A	Blackburn Rovers	W	3-1	McClelland, Blackmore, Gibson	22,03
27	Feb	2	A	Derby County	L	1-2	Wright	9,31
28		9	H	Sheffield Wednesday	D	2-2	Blackmore 2	18,80
29		20	H	Sunderland	D	2-2	McClelland, Blackmore	11,31
30		23	A	Portsmouth	D	4-4	Gibson 2, Blackmore, Butler	15,06
31	Mar	9	A	Sheffield United	D	1-1	Blackmore	23,92
32		16	H	Manchester United	D	1-1	Wright	17,35
33		29	A	Manchester City	L	1-5	Butler	45,83
34		30	H	Liverpool	D	0-0		20,46
35	Apr	1	H	Manchester City	D	1-1	Gibson	21,95
36		6	A	West Ham United	L	0-3		20,97
37		13	H	Newcastle United	W	1-0	Blackmore	10,46
38		17	H	Aston Villa	W	3-1	McClelland, Gibson, Vizard	10,27
39		20	A	Burnley	L	1-3	Blackmore	14,58
40		29	A	Leeds United	D	2-2	Blackmore 2	12,87
41	May	1	A	Bury	W	4-3	McClelland 2, Gibson, Vizard	9,41
42		4	A	Leicester City	L	1-6	Blackmore	19,91
							Appearance	
							Goal	

FA Cup

R3	Jan	12	H	Oldham Athletic	W	2-0	Gibson, Blackmore	34,49
R4		26	A	Liverpool	D	0-0		55,05
rep		30	H	Liverpool	W	5-2	Butler, McClelland, Gibson, Blackmore 2	41,80
R5	Feb	16	A	Leicester City	W	2-1	Seddon, Blackmore	30,59
R6	Mar	2	A	Blackburn Rovers	D	1-1	Blackmore	62,52
rep		6	H	Blackburn Rovers	W	2-1	Butler 2	65,29
SF		23	N	Huddersfield Town	W	3-1	Butler, Gibson, Blackmore	39,00
F	Apr	27	N	Portsmouth	W	2-0	Butler, Blackmore	92,57

R4 replay a.e.t. SF at Anfield, Liverpool. Final at Wembley Stadium.

Appearance
Goal

Appearance & goals grid (player columns, by match):

	Pim R.H.	Haworth R.	Finney A.	Cope J.W.	Round J.H.	Nuttall H.	Butler W.	Jack D.B.N.	McClelland J.	Gibson G.B.	Murphy L.	Jennings W.	Wright W.B.	Gill J.J.	Wizard E.T.	Greenhalgh H.W.	Thornborough E.H.	Kean R.W.	Seddon J.	Blackmore H.A.	Boston H.J.	Cook W.L.	Jack R.R.	Wagstaffe J.T.
1	1	2	3	4	5	6	7	8	9	10	11													
	1	2		4	5		7	8	9	10	11	3	6											
		2	3		4		7	8	9	10		5	6	1	11									
	1	2	3		5	4	7	8	9	10	11		6											
	1	2			5	4	7	8	9	10	11						3	6						
	1	2				4	7	8	9	10	11						3	6	5					
		2	3				6	7		8	10	11						4	5	9				
		2	3				6	7		8	10	11						4	5	9				
		2	3				6	7	8		10	11						4	5	9				
		2	3				6	7		8	10	11						4	5	9				
		2	3				6	7		8	10	11						4	5	9				
		2	3				6	7		8	10	11						4	5	9				
		2	3				6	7		8	10	11						4	5	9				
		2	3				6			8	10	11							5	9	7			
		2	3	4			6			8	10	11							5	9	7			
		2	3				6	7		8	10	11							4	5	9			
		2	3				6	7		8		11	10						4	5	9			
		2	3				6	7		8	10	11							4	5	9			
		2	3				6	7		8	10				11				4	5	9			
		2	3				6	7		8	10								4	5	9	11		
		2	3				6	7		8	10									5	9	11		
		2	3	4			6	7		8	10										9	11		
		2	3				6	7		8	10									5	9	11		
		2						7			10						6	4	5	9		11	8	
		2	3					7		8	10						6	4	5	9		11		
		2						7		8	10	9	1			3	6	4	5			11		
		2	3				6	7		8	10							4		9		11		
		2					6	7		8	10							4	5	9		11	3	
		2		5	6	7		8		10		3						4		9		11		
		2	3		5			7		8	10			1				4		9		11		
		2	3	5				7			10		8					6	4		9		11		
		2	3	5	6	7		8		10								4		9		11		
		2					6	7		8	10	3						4	5	9		11		
		2					6	7		8	10	3						4	5	9		11		
		2	3				6	7		8	10	11			1			4	5	9				
		2	3	4	5			7		8	10				1	11	6			9				
		2	3		5	6	7		8	10					1	11	4			9				
		2			5			8				3	10	1	11	6	4			9	7			
			3			7		8	10			2		1	11	6	4			9				
			3		5		7		8	10		2		1	11	6	4			9				
		2		4	5			7	10	11	3	8	1			6				9				
Apps	2	40	32	6	13	31	38	7	39	40	19	9	8	10	7	3	14	32	26	35	3	16	1	1
Goals					6	1		9	17	4			2				3			1	30			

	Pim R.H.	Haworth R.	Finney A.	Cope J.W.	Round J.H.	Nuttall H.	Butler W.	Jack D.B.N.	McClelland J.	Gibson G.B.	Murphy L.	Jennings W.	Wright W.B.	Gill J.J.	Wizard E.T.	Greenhalgh H.W.	Thornborough E.H.	Kean R.W.	Seddon J.	Blackmore H.A.	Boston H.J.	Cook W.L.	Jack R.R.	Wagstaffe J.T.
		2	3				6	7		8	10							4	5	9		11		
		2					6	7		8	10				3			4	5	9		11		
		2	3				6	7		8	10							4	5	9		11		
		2	3				6	7		8	10							4	5	9		11		
		2	3				6	7		8	10							4	5	9		11		
		2	3				6	7		8	10							4	5	9		11		
		2	3				6	7		8	10							4	5	9		11		
		2	3				6	7		8	10							4	5	9		11		
		8	7				8	8		8	8						1		8	8	8		8	
							5			1	3									1	7			

League Table

	P	W	D	L	F	A	Pts
Sheffield Wednesday	42	21	10	11	86	62	52
Leicester City	42	21	9	12	96	67	51
Aston Villa	42	23	4	15	98	81	50
Sunderland	42	20	7	15	93	75	47
Liverpool	42	17	12	13	90	64	46
Derby County	42	18	10	14	86	71	46
Blackburn Rovers	42	17	11	14	72	63	45
Manchester City	42	18	9	15	95	86	45
Arsenal	42	16	13	13	77	72	45
Newcastle United	42	19	6	17	70	72	44
Sheffield United	42	15	11	16	86	85	41
Manchester United	42	14	13	15	66	76	41
Leeds United	42	16	9	17	71	84	41
Bolton Wanderers	42	14	12	16	73	80	40
Birmingham	42	15	10	17	68	77	40
Huddersfield Town	42	14	11	17	70	61	39
West Ham United	42	15	9	18	86	96	39
Everton	42	17	4	21	63	75	38
Burnley	42	15	8	19	81	103	38
Portsmouth	42	15	6	21	56	80	36
Bury	42	12	7	23	62	99	31
Cardiff City	42	8	13	21	43	59	29

1929-30

Division One

Manager: C. Foweraker

Match No.	Date	Venue	Opponents	Result		Scorers	Attendance
1	Aug 31	A	Everton	D	3-3	Butler, Blackmore 2	40,80
2	Sep 2	A	Sheffield Wednesday	L	0-1		26,48
3	7	H	Derby County	L	1-2	Blackmore	20,91
4	14	A	Manchester City	L	0-2		36,97
5	18	H	Middlesbrough	D	2-2	McClelland, Bryan	13,76
6	21	H	Portsmouth	W	2-1	Blackmore 2	13,49
7	25	H	Sheffield Wednesday	L	1-3	Gibson	11,13
8	28	A	Arsenal	W	2-1	Blackmore, Wright	42,72
9	Oct 5	H	Aston Villa	W	3-0	Blackmore, Wright 2	19,18
10	12	A	Leeds United	L	1-2	Wright	29,74
11	19	H	Blackburn Rovers	W	2-1	Blackmore, Rankin (own-goal)	25,75
12	26	A	Newcastle United	W	3-2	Blackmore 2, Gibson	28,63
13	Nov 2	H	Sheffield United	W	2-1	Butler, Gibson	15,06
14	9	A	Liverpool	L	0-3		29,07
15	16	H	Birmingham	D	0-0		15,92
16	23	A	Leicester City	L	2-5	Butler, Blackmore	15,33
17	30	H	Grimsby Town	L	2-3	Gibson, Wright	8,50
18	Dec 7	A	Manchester United	D	1-1	Blackmore	5,65
19	14	H	West Ham United	W	4-1	Nuttall, Cook 3	11,42
20	21	A	Huddersfield Town	W	2-0	Blackmore, McKay	12,62
21	25	H	Burnley	D	1-1	Gibson	21,53
22	26	A	Burnley	D	2-2	McKay, Blackmore	27,51
23	28	H	Everton	W	5-0	Blackmore 4, Gibson	15,92
24	Jan 1	H	Huddersfield Town	W	7-1	Butler 3, Blackmore 2, Gibson, Cook	27,35
25	4	A	Derby County	L	1-2	Blackmore	16,50
26	18	H	Manchester City	L	1-2	Blackmore	42,54
27	Feb 1	H	Arsenal	D	0-0		27,33
28	5	A	Portsmouth	L	0-3		13,15
29	8	A	Aston Villa	L	0-2		26,23
30	15	H	Leeds United	W	4-2	Gibson 3, Milsom	18,10
31	22	A	Blackburn Rovers	L	1-3	Gibson	19,38
32	Mar 1	H	Manchester United	W	4-1	Butler, Blackmore 2, Cook	19,71
33	8	A	Sheffield United	W	3-2	Blackmore 2, Cook	21,03
34	15	H	Liverpool	L	0-2		14,33
35	22	A	Birmingham	L	1-3	Gibson	18,28
36	29	H	Leicester City	W	1-0	Wright	13,64
37	Apr 5	A	Grimsby Town	D	1-1	Milsom	12,08
38	9	H	Newcastle United	D	1-1	Milsom	6,99
39	18	H	Sunderland	W	3-0	McKay, Blackmore 2	16,33
40	19	A	West Ham United	L	3-5	McKay, Blackmore, Gibson	12,83
41	21	A	Sunderland	L	1-4	McKay	28,07
42	May 3	A	Middlesbrough	L	1-3	Blackmore	9,81

Appearance

1 own-goal Goa

FA Cup

R3	Jan 11	A	Birmingham	L	0-1		36,01

Appearance

Player appearance and goals chart (shirt numbers per match):

Hill R.H.	Haworth R.	Finney A.	Keen F.W.	Seddon J.	Nuttall H.	Butler W.	McClelland J.	Blackmore H.A.	Gibson G.B.	Cook W.L.	Thornborough E.H.	Wright W.B.	Bryan J.	Vizard E.T.	Gill L.J.A.	Round J.H.	Jennings W.	McKay W.	Howarth H.	Wagstaffe J.T.	Milsom J.	Jones R.H.	Perry H.
2	3	4	5	6	7	8	9	10	11														
2	3	4	5		7	8	9	10	11	6													
2	3	4	5			7	9	10	11	6	8												
2	3	4	5	6		7	9	10	11		8												
2	3	4	5	6		8	9	10	11				7										
2	3	4	5	6	7	8	9	10	11														
2	3	5		6		8	9	10	7	4		11											
2	3	4	5	6		7	9	10			8		11	1									
2	3	4	5	6			9	10	7		8		11	1									
2	3	4		6			9	10	7		8		11	1	5								
2	3	4	5		6		9	10	11		8			1									
2	3	4	5	6	7		9	10	11		8			1									
2	3	4	5	6	7		9	10	11		8			1									
2	3	4	5		7		9	10	11		8			1	6								
2	3	4	5	6	7		9	10	11		8			1									
2	3	4	5	6	7		9	10	11		8			1									
2	3	5		6	7		9	10	11	4	8			1									
2	3	4	5	6	7		9	10	11		8			1									
2	3	4	5	6	7		9	10	11								8						
2	3	4	5	6	7		9	10	11								8						
2	3	4	5	6	7		9	10	11								8						
2	3	4	5	6	7		9	10	11								8						
2	3	4		6	7		9	10	11						5		8						
2	3	4		6	7		9	10	11						5		8						
2	3	4	5	6	7		9	10	11								8						
2					7		9	10	11				6				8	4	3				
2	3	4	5	6	7		9	10	11								8						
2	3	4	5	6	7		9	10	11								8						
2	3	4	5	6	7		9	10	11								8						
2	3	4	5	6	7		9	10	11							1	8						
2	3	4		6	7			10	11						5		8		9				
2	3	4		6	7			10	11						5		8		9				
2		4	5		7		9	10	11				6				8		3				
2		4	5		7		9	10	11				6				8		3				
2		4	5		7		9	10	11				6				8		3				
2	3	4	5		7		9	10	11				6				8				1		
2	3	4	5		7		9	10	11				8					6			1		
2	3		5		7			10	11				8					4		9	1	6	
2	3		5		7			10	11				8					4		9	1	6	
2	3	4	5		7		9	10	11								8				1	6	
2	3	4	5		7		9	10	11				5				8				1	6	
2	3	4	5		7		9	10	11	6							8					1	
2	3	4		6	7		9	10	11								8					1	5
42	38	39	32	27	35	8	38	42	41	5	21	1	4	11	7	1	22	4	4	4	7	5	
		1	7	1			30	13	6					6	1		5				3		

Hill R.H.	Haworth R.	Finney A.	Keen F.W.	Seddon J.	Nuttall H.	Butler W.	McClelland J.	Blackmore H.A.	Gibson G.B.	Cook W.L.	Thornborough E.H.	Wright W.B.	Bryan J.	Vizard E.T.	Gill L.J.A.	Round J.H.	Jennings W.	McKay W.	Howarth H.	Wagstaffe J.T.	Milsom J.	Jones R.H.	Perry H.
2		4	5	6	7			10	11				9				8		3				
1		1	1	1	1			1	1				1				1		1				

League Table

	P	W	D	L	F	A	Pts
Sheffield Wednesday	42	26	8	8	105	57	60
Derby County	42	21	8	13	90	82	50
Manchester City	42	19	9	14	91	81	47
Aston Villa	42	21	5	16	92	83	47
Leeds United	42	20	6	16	79	63	46
Blackburn Rovers	42	19	7	16	99	93	45
West Ham United	42	19	5	18	86	79	43
Leicester City	42	17	9	16	86	90	43
Sunderland	42	18	7	17	76	80	43
Huddersfield Town	42	17	9	16	63	69	43
Birmingham	42	16	9	17	67	62	41
Liverpool	42	16	9	17	63	79	41
Portsmouth	42	15	10	17	66	62	40
Arsenal	42	14	11	17	78	66	39
Bolton Wanderers	42	15	9	18	74	74	39
Middlesbrough	42	16	6	20	82	84	38
Manchester United	42	15	8	19	67	88	38
Grimsby Town	42	15	7	20	73	89	37
Newcastle United	42	15	7	20	71	92	37
Sheffield United	42	15	6	21	91	96	36
Burnley	42	14	8	20	79	97	36
Everton	42	12	11	19	80	92	35

Division One

Manager: C. Foweraker

Match No.	Date		Venue	Opponents	Result		Scorers	Attendance
1	Aug	30	H	Middlesbrough	W	3-0	McKay, Cook, Blackmore	14,94
2	Sep	1	H	Arsenal	L	1-4	Cook	20,68
3		6	A	Huddersfield Town	L	2-3	Gibson, McKay	15,01
4		10	A	Liverpool	L	2-7	Milsom, Gibson	20,80
5		13	H	Aston Villa	D	1-1	Blackmore	17,20
6		20	A	Chelsea	W	1-0	Blackmore	48,34
7		27	H	Newcastle United	L	0-3		17,98
8	Oct	4	A	Sheffield Wednesday	L	0-1		21,31
9		11	H	Grimsby Town	W	4-2	Cook, Nuttall (pen), Blackmore 2	14,97
10		18	H	Blackpool	W	1-0	Butler	26,65
11		25	A	Blackburn Rovers	D	2-2	Blackmore, Cook	18,64
12	Nov	1	H	Derby County	L	1-2	Goslin	15,57
13		8	A	Sheffield United	L	0-2		19,64
14		15	H	Sunderland	D	2-2	Gibson, Cook	10,83
15		22	A	Manchester City	L	0-3		23,48
16		29	H	Birmingham	W	2-0	Tait, Blackmore	15,36
17	Dec	6	A	Leeds United	L	1-3	Tait	7,59
18		13	H	Portsmouth	W	3-1	Cook 2, Butler	13,34
19		20	A	Leicester City	L	1-2	Blackmore	12,66
20		25	H	Manchester United	W	3-1	Blackmore 2, Gibson	22,26
21		26	A	Manchester United	D	1-1	Blackmore	12,74
22		27	A	Middlesbrough	L	0-3		16,08
23	Jan	3	H	Huddersfield Town	W	1-0	McKay	15,66
24		14	H	Liverpool	W	2-0	Gibson, Blackmore	10,36
25		17	A	Aston Villa	L	1-3	Blackmore	21,95
26		31	A	Newcastle United	L	0-4		9,15
27	Feb	4	H	Chelsea	D	1-1	Blackmore	9,67
28		7	H	Sheffield Wednesday	D	2-2	Tait, Blackmore	19,59
29		17	A	Grimsby Town	L	1-4	Tait	5,74
30		21	A	Blackpool	D	3-3	Butler 2, Blackmore	16,69
31		28	H	Blackburn Rovers	D	1-1	Blackmore	9,46
32	Mar	7	A	Derby County	L	1-4	Blackmore	8,84
33		14	H	Sheffield United	W	6-2	Butler, Blackmore 3, Gibson 2	13,11
34		21	A	Sunderland	L	1-3	Blackmore	17,14
35		28	H	Manchester City	D	1-1	Blackmore (pen)	17,33
36	Apr	3	A	West Ham United	W	4-1	Milsom 2, Gibson, Blackmore	19,11
37		4	A	Birmingham	W	2-0	Gibson, Westwood	18,08
38		6	H	West Ham United	W	4-2	Gibson, Blackmore, Butler, Cadwell (own-goal)	20,22
39		11	H	Leeds United	W	2-0	Butler, Blackmore	15,43
40		18	A	Portsmouth	L	0-1		12,51
41		25	H	Leicester City	W	4-1	Blackmore, Gibson 2, Butler	8,96
42	May	2	A	Arsenal	L	0-5		35,40
								Appearance
							1 own-goal	Goa

FA Cup

R3	Jan	10	H	Carlisle United	W	1-0	Blackmore	23,02
R4		24	H	Sunderland	D	1-1	Blackmore	36,60
rep		28	A	Sunderland	L	1-3	Blackmore	46,00
								Appearance
								Goa

Player appearance grid (shirt numbers per match). Column headers (left to right):

Pym R.H. · Haworth R. · Finney A. · Keen F.W. · Seddon J. · Nuttall H. · Butler W. · McKay W. · Blackmore H.A. · Gibson G.E. · Cook W.L. · Haworth H. · Jones R. · Goslin H.A. · Milsom J. · Wright W.B. · Davin M. · Wagstaffe J.T. · Tait T. · Gorringe F.C. · Rimmer J.W. · Taylor G. · Vizard E.T. · Church H.B. · Westwood R.W.

Pym	HawR	Fin	Keen	Sed	Nut	But	McK	Bla	Gib	Cook	HawH	Jon	Gos	Mil	Wri	Dav	Wag	Tait	Gor	Rim	Tay	Viz	Chu	Wes
1	2	3	4	5	6	7	8	9	10	11														
1	2	3	4		6	7	8	9	10	11	5													
	2	3	4		6	7	8	9	10	11	5	1												
1	2	3		5	6	7	8		10	11			4	9										
	2	3		5	7	10	9		11			1	4		6	8								
	2	3		5	7	10	9		11			1	4		6	8								
	2	3	5		7	10	9		11			1	4		6	8								
	2	3		5	6	7	8	9	10	11		1	4											
	2	3		5	6	7	8	9	10	11		1	4											
	2	3		5	6	7	8	9	10	11		1	4											
	2	3		5	6	7	8	9	10	11		1	4											
	2	3		5		7	8	9	10	11		1	4		6									
	2				7	10	9	8	11	5		1	4		6		3							
	2				7	10	9	8	11	5		1	4		6		3							
	2	3		5	7	9		8	11	6		1	4		10									
	2	3	4	5	6	7		10	8	11		1			9									
	2	3	4	5		10	8	7		1			6		9			9	11						
	2	3	4		5	7	8	10	11			1	6		9									
	2	3	4		5	7	8	10	11			1	6		9									
	2	3		5	6	7	8	9	10	11		1	4											
	2	3		5	6	7	8	9		11		1	4							10				
	2	3		5		7	8	10				1	4		6			9		11				
	3		5		7	8	9			4	1			6			2		11	10				
	3		5		7	8	9	10	11	4	1	2		6			2							
	3		5	4	7		9	8		1	2			6				10	11					
	3		5		7		10	8			4		6		2	9		11	1					
	3			7	4	9	10			5		6		2	8		11	1						
	3		5		7	8	9	10			1	4		6		2						11		
	3			7		9	10		5	1	4	8	6		2						11			
	3			7		9	10		5	1	4	8	6		2						11			
	3			7		9	10		5	1	4	8	6		2						11			
	3			7		9	10		5	1	4	8	6		2						11			
	3		8		9	10		5	1	4		6		2		7						11		
	3			7		9	10		5	1	4		6		2		8					11		
3	29	39	9	21	20	41	28	40	35	26	15	37	33	6	32	3	14	9	1	6	2	3	2	8
					1	8	3	27	12	7				1	3		4							1

Cup matches:

Pym	HawR	Fin	Keen	Sed	Nut	But	McK	Bla	Gib	Cook	HawH	Jon	Gos	Mil	Wri	Dav	Wag	Tait	Gor	Rim	Tay	Viz	Chu	Wes
	2	3		5	6	7	8	9	10	11		1	4											
	2	3		5	6	7	8	9	10	11		1	4											
	2	3		5	6	7		9	10	11		1	4		8									
3	3	3		3	3	3	2	3	3	3		3	3		1									
									3															

League Table

	P	W	D	L	F	A	Pts
Arsenal	42	28	10	4	127	59	66
Aston Villa	42	25	9	8	128	78	59
Sheffield Wednesday	42	22	8	12	102	75	52
Portsmouth	42	18	13	11	84	67	49
Huddersfield Town	42	18	12	12	81	65	48
Derby County	42	18	10	14	94	79	46
Middlesbrough	42	19	8	15	98	90	46
Manchester City	42	18	10	14	75	70	46
Liverpool	42	15	12	15	86	85	42
Blackburn Rovers	42	17	8	17	83	84	42
Sunderland	42	16	9	17	89	85	41
Chelsea	42	15	10	17	64	67	40
Grimsby Town	42	17	5	20	82	87	39
Bolton Wanderers	42	15	9	18	68	81	39
Sheffield United	42	14	10	18	78	84	38
Leicester City	42	16	6	20	80	95	38
Newcastle United	42	15	6	21	78	87	36
West Ham United	42	14	8	20	79	94	36
Birmingham	42	13	10	19	55	70	36
Blackpool	42	11	10	21	71	125	32
Leeds United	42	12	7	23	68	81	31
Manchester United	42	7	8	27	53	115	22

Division One

Manager: C. Foweraker

Did you know that?

In November 1931 the Wanderers defeated Liverpool 8–1 in a Lancashire Cup tie at Burnden, with Billy Butler scoring four of the goals. The Anfield club visited Burnden for the final First Division game of the season and were again on the end of an 8–1 hammering. This time it was Jack Milsom who grabbed four goals.

Match No.	Date		Venue	Opponents	Result		Scorers	Attendance
1	Aug	29	H	West Ham United	L	0-1		15,740
2	Sep	2	A	Liverpool	D	2-2	Gibson, Westwood	20,090
3		5	A	Sheffield Wednesday	L	1-7	Blackmore	14,544
4		9	H	Grimsby Town	W	5-3	Westwood 2, Blackmore 2, Gibson	9,700
5		12	H	Portsmouth	W	4-0	Blackmore, Butler 2, Walters	12,258
6		15	A	Grimsby Town	L	0-2		10,857
7		19	H	Middlesbrough	W	4-2	Blackmore 3, Wagstaffe	14,180
8		26	A	Huddersfield Town	L	0-2		12,901
9	Oct	3	H	Newcastle United	W	2-1	Blackmore, Davidson (own-goal)	13,833
10		10	A	Aston Villa	L	1-2	Gibson	39,673
11		17	A	Arsenal	D	1-1	Blackmore	42,141
12		24	H	West Bromwich Albion	W	1-0	Westwood	19,695
13		31	A	Birmingham	D	2-2	Gibson, Butler	16,163
14	Nov	7	H	Sunderland	W	3-1	Blackmore 2, Butler	14,928
15		14	A	Sheffield United	L	0-4		15,057
16		21	H	Blackburn Rovers	W	3-1	Imrie (own-goal), Butler 2	18,164
17		28	A	Derby County	L	1-5	Butler	9,786
18	Dec	5	H	Blackpool	L	1-2	Cook	14,294
19		12	A	Manchester City	L	1-2	Westwood	20,283
20		19	H	Everton	W	2-1	Milsom 2	33,619
21		25	H	Leicester City	W	1-0	Blackmore	32,544
22		26	A	Leicester City	W	3-1	Taylor 2, Milsom	24,675
23	Jan	1	H	Chelsea	W	1-0	Milsom	28,232
24		2	A	West Ham United	L	1-3	Gibson	15,997
25		16	H	Sheffield Wednesday	L	2-4	Gibson, Blackmore	9,694
26		30	A	Middlesbrough	L	1-3	Gibson	10,502
27	Feb	6	H	Huddersfield Town	L	1-2	Griffiths	11,876
28		17	A	Newcastle United	L	1-3	Butler	22,618
29		20	H	Aston Villa	W	2-1	Milsom 2	12,682
30	Mar	2	H	Arsenal	W	1-0	Milsom	20,922
31		5	A	West Bromwich Albion	L	0-3		16,050
32		9	A	Portsmouth	L	2-3	Wright, Cook	7,974
33		12	H	Birmingham	W	5-1	Cook 2, Gibson 2, Milsom	11,003
34		19	A	Sunderland	L	0-3		21,765
35		25	A	Chelsea	L	0-3		38,515
36		26	H	Sheffield United	W	3-1	Milsom 3	13,737
37	Apr	2	A	Blackburn Rovers	L	1-3	Binns (own-goal)	12,100
38		9	H	Derby County	L	1-2	Milsom	7,722
39		16	A	Blackpool	W	3-0	Milsom 3	16,890
40		23	H	Manchester City	D	1-1	Wright	8,680
41		30	A	Everton	L	0-1		28,546
42	May	7	H	Liverpool	W	8-1	Milsom 4, Edmed, Westwood 2, Wilson	9,209

Appearances

3 own-goals   Goals

FA Cup

R3	Jan	9	A	Preston North End	D	0-0		29,052
rep		13	H	Preston North End	L	2-5	Blackmore, Gibson	32,862

Appearances

Goals

Jones R.	Wagstaffe J.T.	Finney A.	Goslin H.A.	Seddon J.	Wright W.B.	Cook W.L.	Milsom J.	Blackmore H.A.	Gibson G.B.	Westwood R.W.	Nicholson G.	Howarth H.	McKay W.	Boyle M.J.	Nuttall H.	Butler W.	Walters T.C.	Duckworth T.C.	Rimmer J.W.	Griffiths T.P.	Taylor G.	Wilson F.W.	Edmed R.A.
1	2	3	4	5	6	7	8	9	10	11													
1	2	3			6	7		9	10	11	4	5	8										
1		3			6	7		9	10	11	4	5	8	2									
1	2	3			6			9	10	11	4				5	7	8						
1	2	3			6	11		9	10		4				5	7	8						
1	2				6	11		9	10		4	5				7	8	3					
1	2				6	11		9	10		4				5	7	8	3					
1	2				6	11		9	10		4				5	7	8	3					
1	2	3	6		8	11		9	10		4				5	7							
1	2	3	4	5	8			9	10		6					7			11				
1	2	3			6	8		9	10	11	4				5	7							
1	2	3			6	8		9	10	11	4				5	7							
1	2	3			6	8		9	10	11	4				5	7							
1	2	3			6	8		9	10	11	4				5	7							
1		3	2		6	8		9	10	11			4		5	7							
1	2	3			6	8		9	10	11	4				5	7							
1	2	3			6	8		9	10	11	4				5	7							
1	2	3			6	8		9	10	11	4				5	7							
1	2	3				8	9		10	11	4		6		5	7							
1	2	3	4				9	8	10	11					6	7				5			
1	2	3	4				9	8	10	11					6	7				5			
1	2	3			6		9		8	11	4					7				5	10		
1		3			6		9		8	11	4			2		7				5	10		
1		3			6	7	9		8	11	4			2						5	10		
1			4			7		9	10	11				2	6			3		5		8	
1	2	3	4	6		11		9	10							7				5		8	
1	2	3	4			11	9		8						6	7				5	10		
1	2	3	4				9		10				8		6	7			11	5			
1		3			6	11	9		8		4					7		2		5	10		
1		3			6	11	9		8		4					7		2		5	10		
1		3			6	11		9	8		4					7		2		5	10		
1		3			10	11	9		8		4				6	7		2		5			
1		3			10	11	9		8		4				6	7		2		5			
1		3			10	11	9		8		4				6	7		2		5			
1		3			10	11	9		8		4		6			7		2		5			
1		3			10	11	9		8		4		6			7		2		5			
1		3			10	11	9		8		4		6			7		2		5			
1		3			10		9		8	11	4		6			7		2		5			
1		3				11	9		8			6	4			7		2		5	10		
1		3			8	11	9					6	4			7		2		5	10		
1		3			10	11	9		8			6	4			7		2		5			
1		3				11	9			10		6	4					2		5		8	7
42	23	38	10	3	33	34	22	23	40	21	30	7	13	4	22	36	5	18	2	23	9	3	1
	1				2	4	19	13	9	7						8	1			1	2	1	1

1	2	3	4				9		8	11					6	7				5	10		
1	2	3			6	11		9	8				4			7				5	10		
2	2	2	1		1	1	1	1	2	1			1		1	2				2	2		
								1	1														

League Table

	P	W	D	L	F	A	Pts
Everton	42	26	4	12	116	64	56
Arsenal	42	22	10	10	90	48	54
Sheffield Wednesday	42	22	6	14	96	82	50
Huddersfield Town	42	19	10	13	80	63	48
Aston Villa	42	19	8	15	104	72	46
West Bromwich Albion	42	20	6	16	77	55	46
Sheffield United	42	20	6	16	80	75	46
Portsmouth	42	19	7	16	62	62	45
Birmingham	42	18	8	16	78	67	44
Liverpool	42	19	6	17	81	93	44
Newcastle United	42	18	6	18	80	87	42
Chelsea	42	16	8	18	69	73	40
Sunderland	42	15	10	17	67	73	40
Manchester City	42	13	12	17	83	73	38
Derby County	42	14	10	18	71	75	38
Blackburn Rovers	42	16	6	20	89	95	38
Bolton Wanderers	42	17	4	21	72	80	38
Middlesbrough	42	15	8	19	64	89	38
Leicester City	42	15	7	20	74	94	37
Blackpool	42	12	9	21	65	102	33
Grimsby Town	42	13	6	23	67	98	32
West Ham United	42	12	7	23	62	107	31

1932-33

Division One

Manager: C. Foweraker

Match No.	Date		Venue	Opponents		Result	Scorers	Attendance
1	Aug	27	H	Newcastle United	D	2-2	Butler, Wright	16,245
2		29	A	Wolverhampton Wanderers	L	1-4	Butler	28,197
3	Sep	3	A	Aston Villa	L	1-6	T. Griffiths	31,296
4		5	H	Wolverhampton Wanderers	W	2-0	Cook, Butler	11,353
5		10	H	Middlesbrough	W	4-3	Milsom, McKay, Gibson, Butler	12,035
6		17	A	Arsenal	L	2-3	Milsom, Westwood	42,395
7		24	A	Liverpool	W	1-0	Westwood	26,019
8	Oct	1	H	Leicester City	W	5-0	Gibson, Westwood 2, Milsom, Cook	12,342
9		8	A	Portsmouth	L	1-2	Westwood	17,397
10		15	H	Chelsea	L	2-3	Milsom 2	15,021
11		22	H	Manchester City	W	2-1	T. Griffiths, Milsom	14,468
12		29	A	Sunderland	L	4-7	Gibson 2, Butler 2	10,182
13	Nov	5	H	Blackburn Rovers	W	4-2	Milsom, Butler 2, T. Griffiths	20,225
14		12	A	Derby County	L	1-4	Milsom	14,922
15		19	H	Blackpool	W	1-0	Milsom	14,468
16		26	A	Everton	D	2-2	T. Griffiths, Goslin	27,529
17	Dec	3	H	Birmingham	D	2-2	Goslin, Gibson	8,970
18		10	A	West Bromwich Albion	L	0-4		12,778
19		17	H	Sheffield Wednesday	W	3-0	Milsom 3	11,409
20		24	A	Leeds United	L	3-4	Westwood 2, Nicholson	15,804
21		26	H	Huddersfield Town	W	2-1	Butler, Milsom	23,967
22		27	A	Huddersfield Town	L	1-2	T. Griffiths	19,797
23		31	A	Newcastle United	L	1-3	Milsom	18,101
24	Jan	2	H	Sheffield United	D	3-3	Goslin, McKay, Gibson	15,360
25		7	H	Aston Villa	L	0-1		17,624
26		21	A	Middlesbrough	L	1-2	Milsom	9,256
27	Feb	1	A	Arsenal	L	0-4		13,401
28		4	H	Liverpool	D	3-3	Milsom, Cook, Westwood	11,314
29		11	A	Leicester City	L	0-2		14,178
30		22	H	Portsmouth	W	4-1	Gibson, Westwood, Milsom 2	5,320
31		25	A	Chelsea	D	1-1	Gibson	12,590
32	Mar	8	A	Manchester City	L	1-2	Milsom	19,144
33		11	H	Sunderland	D	0-0		10,353
34		18	A	Blackburn Rovers	L	2-3	Rimmer 2	10,423
35		25	H	Derby County	D	1-1	Milsom	9,585
36	Apr	1	A	Blackpool	W	3-1	McKay, Rimmer 2	15,849
37		8	H	Everton	L	2-4	Milsom, Rimmer	12,112
38		15	A	Birmingham	L	1-2	Butler	13,541
39		17	A	Sheffield United	L	2-3	Milsom, McKay	9,410
40		22	H	West Bromwich Albion	D	2-2	Goslin, Westwood	11,647
41		29	A	Sheffield Wednesday	L	0-2		4,810
42	May	6	H	Leeds United	W	5-0	Milsom 3, Westwood 2	10,048
							Appearances	
							Goals	

FA Cup

R3	Jan	14	A	Charlton Athletic	W	5-1	T. Griffiths, Gibson, Cook 2, Milsom	17,402
R4		28	H	Grimsby Town	W	2-1	T. Griffiths, Butler	25,866
R5	Feb	18	H	Manchester City	L	2-4	Westwood, Milsom	69,912
							Appearances	
							Goals	

Appearances grid (player columns, left to right): Jones R., Duckworth T.C., Finney A., McKay W., Griffths T.P., Howarth H., Butler W., Gleson G.B., Wright W.B., Westwood R.W., Cook W.L., Matson J., Griffths J., Nicholson G., Gowin H.A., Rimmer J.W., Boyle M.J., Smith R., Church H.B., Edmed R.A., Watson G., Wilson F.W., Eastham G.R., Atkinson J.E.

Jones R.	Duckw. T.C.	Finney A.	McKay W.	Griff. T.P.	Howarth H.	Butler W.	Gleson G.B.	Wright W.B.	Westwood R.W.	Cook W.L.	Matson J.	Griff. J.	Nichol. G.	Gowin H.A.	Rimmer J.W.	Boyle M.J.	Smith R.	Church H.B.	Edmed R.A.	Watson G.	Wilson F.W.	Eastham G.R.	Atkin. J.E.
1	2	3	4	5	6	7	8	9	10	11													
1	2	3	4	5	6	7	8	9	10	11													
1	2	3	4	5	6	7	8			10	11	9											
1		3		5	7	8	6	10	11	9	2	4											
1		3	4	5	7	8	6	10	11	9	2												
1		3		5	6	7	8	10	11	9	2	4											
1		3		5	6	7	8	10	11	9	2	4											
1		3		5	6	7	8	10	11	9	2	4											
1		3		5	6	7	8	10	11	9	2	4											
1		3		5	6	7	8	10	11	9	2	4											
1		3		5	6	7	8	10	11	9	2	4											
1		3		5	6	7	8	10	11	9	2	4											
1		3		5	6	7	8	10	11	9	2	4											
1		3	4	5	6	7	8	10	11	9	2												
1		3	6	5		7	8	10		9	2		4	11									
1		3	6	5		7	8	10		9	2		4	11									
1		3		5		8	6	10	7	9	2		4	11									
1		3		5		7		6	10	9	2	8	4	11									
1		3		5		7		6	10	9	2	8	4	11									
1		3		5		7		6		10	9	2	8	4	11								
1		3			5	7	10	6			9		8	4	11	2							
1		3	9		5	7	10	6				8		4	11	2							
1		3			5	7	10	6		11	9	2	8	4									
1			4	5		7	10	6		11	9	2		8		3							
1		3	6	5		7	8	10	11	9		4			2								
		3	6	5		7	8	10	11	9		4		2		1							
		3		5	6		8	10		9		4	11	2		1	7						
	2	3		5	6		8	10		9		4	11			1	7						
	2	3		5	6	7	8	10		9		4	11			1							
	2	3	4		6	8		10		9		5	11			1	7						
	2	3	6		5	7		10		9		4	11			1		8					
	2	3	6		5			10	7	9		4	11			1		8					
	2	3	6		5			10	7	9		4	11			1			8				
		3	6		5			10	7	9		4	11	2		1			8				
		3	6		5			10	7	9		4	11	2		1			8				
	2	3	6		5	7		10		9		4	11			1			8				
		3	6			7		10	8	9		4	5	11	2	1							
		3	6			7		10		9		4	8	11	2	1				5			
		3	6			7		10		9		4	8	11		1		2		5			
		3	8		6	7		10		9		4		11		2	1			5			
27	**10**	**41**	**22**	**25**	**30**	**35**	**27**	**13**	**37**	**26**	**39**	**21**	**21**	**26**	**23**	**9**	**3**	**15**	**3**	**2**	**1**	**3**	**3**
		4	5			10	8	1	12	3	25		1	4	5								

FA Cup:

Jones R.	Duckw. T.C.	Finney A.	McKay W.	Griff. T.P.	Howarth H.	Butler W.	Gleson G.B.	Wright W.B.	Westwood R.W.	Cook W.L.	Matson J.	Griff. J.	Nichol. G.	Gowin H.A.	Rimmer J.W.	Boyle M.J.	Smith R.	Church H.B.	Edmed R.A.	Watson G.	Wilson F.W.	Eastham G.R.	Atkin. J.E.
1		3		5	6	7	10			11	9	2	4	8									
1		3	4	5		7	10	6		11	9			8	2								
	2	3		5	6	8	10	11					4			1	7						
2	1	3	1	3	2	3	3	1	1	2	3	1	1	3	1	1	1						
			2		1	1			1	2	2												

League Table

	P	W	D	L	F	A	Pts
Arsenal	42	25	8	9	118	61	58
Aston Villa	42	23	8	11	92	67	54
Sheffield Wednesday	42	21	9	12	80	68	51
West Bromwich Albion	42	20	9	13	83	70	49
Newcastle United	42	22	5	15	71	63	49
Huddersfield Town	42	18	11	13	66	53	47
Derby County	42	15	14	13	76	69	44
Leeds United	42	15	14	13	59	62	44
Portsmouth	42	18	7	17	74	76	43
Sheffield United	42	17	9	16	74	80	43
Everton	42	16	9	17	81	74	41
Sunderland	42	15	10	17	63	80	40
Birmingham	42	14	11	17	57	57	39
Liverpool	42	14	11	17	79	84	39
Blackburn Rovers	42	14	10	18	76	102	38
Manchester City	42	16	5	21	68	71	37
Middlesbrough	42	14	9	19	63	73	37
Chelsea	42	14	7	21	63	73	35
Leicester City	42	11	13	18	75	89	35
Wolverhampton W	42	13	9	20	80	96	35
Bolton Wanderers	42	12	9	21	78	92	33
Blackpool	42	14	5	23	69	85	33

Division Two

Manager: C. Foweraker

Did you know that?

G.T Taylor became the third Bolton player to miss a penalty in as many games during February 1934. His miss came in a home defeat to Preston after Harry Goslin and Jack Milsom had missed in games against Burnley and Oldham respectively.

Match No.	Date	Venue	Opponents	Result		Scorers	Attendance
1	Aug 26	A	West Ham United	L	2-4	Hughes, McKay	24,825
2	29	A	Grimsby Town	W	3-2	Westwood 2, Milsom	9,961
3	Sep 2	H	Plymouth Argyle	W	2-0	Hughes, Westwood	11,388
4	4	H	Grimsby Town	L	0-4		9,370
5	9	A	Manchester United	W	5-1	Milsom 2, Hughes, McKay, Cook	21,779
6	16	H	Bury	W	2-0	McKay, Westwood	18,982
7	23	H	Brentford	W	3-2	Westwood, Milsom 2 (1 pen)	9,894
8	30	H	Burnley	W	3-1	Westwood 2, McKay	12,672
9	Oct 7	H	Oldham Athletic	W	1-0	Atkinson	14,206
10	14	A	Preston North End	D	1-1	Cameron	20,054
11	21	A	Hull City	L	0-1		16,167
12	28	H	Fulham	W	3-1	Cook, Milsom, Westwood	14,190
13	Nov 4	A	Southampton	L	0-1		15,084
14	11	H	Blackpool	L	1-2	McKay (pen)	19,947
15	18	A	Bradford City	L	1-5	Westwood	10,223
16	25	H	Port Vale	W	3-0	Milsom 3 (1 pen)	14,925
17	Dec 2	A	Notts County	W	2-1	Rimmer, Milsom (pen)	11,279
18	9	H	Swansea Town	W	2-1	Rimmer, Westwood	12,595
19	16	A	Millwall	L	1-2	Rimmer	10,181
20	23	H	Lincoln City	L	1-2	Milsom	9,174
21	25	A	Bradford Park Avenue	W	4-1	Cameron, Milsom, Westwood 2	17,527
22	30	H	West Ham United	W	5-1	Milsom 4 (1 pen), Westwood	9,551
23	Jan 1	H	Bradford Park Avenue	L	0-1		19,433
24	2	A	Bury	D	1-1	Westwood	17,969
25	6	A	Plymouth Argyle	L	0-3		18,348
26	20	H	Manchester United	W	3-1	Westwood, G.T. Taylor, Goslin (pen)	11,887
27	Feb 3	A	Brentford	L	1-3	Westwood	16,037
28	10	H	Burnley	W	4-1	G.T. Taylor, Milsom 2, Westwood	13,214
29	20	A	Oldham Athletic	W	3-1	Eastham 2, G.T. Taylor	7,604
30	24	H	Preston North End	L	0-2		27,435
31	Mar 7	H	Hull City	D	3-3	Rimmer, G.T. Taylor, Milsom	5,175
32	10	A	Fulham	W	2-0	Eastham, Milsom	18,636
33	17	H	Southampton	W	2-0	Milsom 2 (1 pen)	11,029
34	24	A	Blackpool	D	1-1	G.T. Taylor	17,464
35	30	H	Nottingham Forest	D	1-1	G.T. Taylor	16,526
36	31	H	Bradford City	W	3-0	Goslin (pen), Eastham, Westwood	15,270
37	Apr 2	A	Nottingham Forest	D	2-2	G.T. Taylor, Westwood	13,444
38	7	A	Port Vale	D	0-0		9,923
39	14	H	Notts County	W	1-0	Eastham	11,652
40	21	A	Swansea Town	D	0-0		10,569
41	28	H	Millwall	W	5-0	G.T. Taylor 2, Milsom, Westwood 2	13,268
42	May 5	A	Lincoln City	D	2-2	E. Jones, Finney	6,412
						Appearances	
						Goals	

FA Cup

R3	Jan 13	H	Halifax Town	W	3-1	Cook 2, Westwood	24,885
R4	27	A	Brighton & Hove Albion	D	1-1	Westwood	25,535
rep	31	H	Brighton & Hove Albion	W	6-1	Milsom 3, Westwood, G.T. Taylor, Cameron	24,047
R5	Feb 17	A	Liverpool	W	3-0	G.T. Taylor, Milsom, Westwood	54,912
R6	Mar 3	H	Portsmouth	L	0-3		52,181
						Appearances	
						Goals	

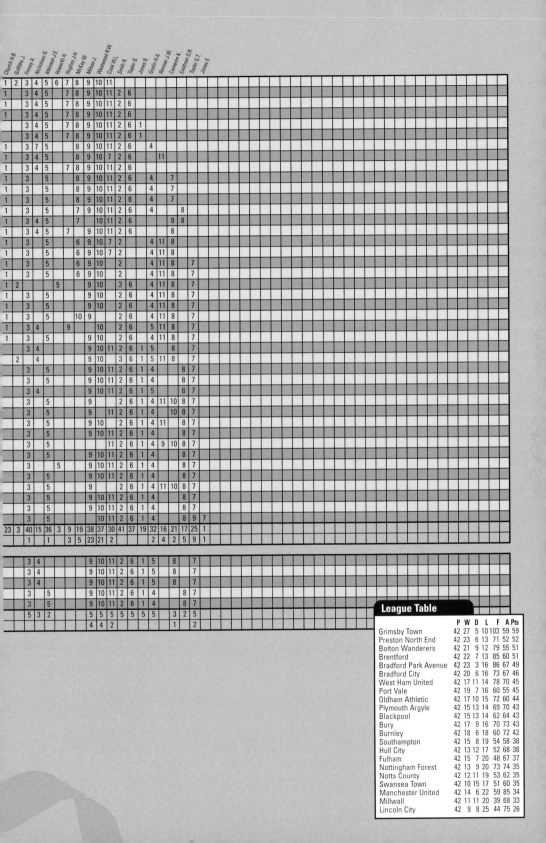

Player columns (left to right): Church H.B., Griffiths J., Finney A., Nicholson G., Atkinson J.E., Howarth H., Hughes J.H., McKay W., Milson J., Westwood R.W., Cook W.L., Smith R., Taylor G., Jones R., Goslin H.A., Rimmer J.W., Cameron K., Eastham G.R., Taylor G.T., Jones E.

Appearances total row:
23 | 3 | 40 | 15 | 36 | 3 | 9 | 19 | 38 | 37 | 30 | 41 | 37 | 19 | 32 | 16 | 21 | 17 | 25 | 1

Goals total row:
1 | | 1 | | | | 3 | 5 | 23 | 21 | 2 | | | | 2 | 4 | 2 | 5 | 9 | 1

League Table

	P	W	D	L	F	A	Pts
Grimsby Town	42	27	5	10	103	59	59
Preston North End	42	23	6	13	71	52	52
Bolton Wanderers	42	21	9	12	79	55	51
Brentford	42	22	7	13	85	60	51
Bradford Park Avenue	42	23	3	16	86	67	49
Bradford City	42	20	6	16	73	67	46
West Ham United	42	17	11	14	78	70	45
Port Vale	42	19	7	16	60	55	45
Oldham Athletic	42	17	10	15	72	60	44
Plymouth Argyle	42	15	13	14	69	70	43
Blackpool	42	15	13	14	62	64	43
Bury	42	17	9	16	70	73	43
Burnley	42	18	6	18	60	72	42
Southampton	42	15	8	19	54	58	38
Hull City	42	13	12	17	52	68	38
Fulham	42	15	7	20	48	67	37
Nottingham Forest	42	13	9	20	73	74	35
Notts County	42	12	11	19	53	62	35
Swansea Town	42	10	15	17	51	60	35
Manchester United	42	14	6	22	59	85	34
Millwall	42	11	11	20	39	68	33
Lincoln City	42	9	8	25	44	75	26

Division Two

Manager: C. Foweraker

Match No.	Date	Venue	Opponents	Result		Scorers	Attendance
1	Aug 25	A	Oldham Athletic	W	4-1	Westwood, Milsom 2, Cook	12,842
2	Sep 1	H	Bury	W	2-0	Milsom, Fairhurst (own-goal)	18,186
3	3	H	Manchester United	W	3-1	Milsom (pen), Atkinson, Vose (own-goal)	16,238
4	8	H	Southampton	W	4-0	Milsom 2, Westwood 2	15,383
5	12	A	Manchester United	W	3-0	Milsom, Westwood, Eastham	24,760
6	15	A	Notts County	W	2-0	Milsom 2	13,783
7	22	H	Bradford City	W	3-0	Eastham, Cook, Westwood	14,181
8	29	A	Sheffield United	L	2-6	Cameron, Milsom	12,788
9	Oct 6	H	Barnsley	W	8-0	Westwood 4, G.T. Taylor 2, Shotton (own-goal), Milsom	15,009
10	13	A	Port Vale	W	3-1	Westwood, Milsom 2 (1 pen)	16,839
11	20	A	Hull City	W	2-0	Rimmer, Milsom	12,758
12	27	H	Nottingham Forest	L	2-3	Milsom, Westwood	21,298
13	Nov 3	A	Brentford	L	0-1		22,322
14	10	H	Fulham	W	4-0	Cook, Westwood 2, Chambers	19,612
15	17	A	Bradford Park Avenue	L	0-4		12,627
16	24	H	Plymouth Argyle	W	3-2	Westwood 2, Milsom	18,210
17	Dec 1	A	Norwich City	W	3-2	Rimmer, G.T. Taylor, Westwood	20,556
18	8	H	Newcastle United	W	1-0	G.T. Taylor	22,170
19	15	A	West Ham United	L	1-4	Atkinson	27,489
20	22	H	Blackpool	W	4-2	Milson 2 (1 pen), Westwood 2	22,255
21	25	A	Burnley	L	1-2	Milsom	26,518
22	29	H	Oldham Athletic	W	2-0	Eastham, Westwood	16,859
23	Jan 2	H	Burnley	W	7-0	Milsom 4 (1 pen), Westwood, Goslin, Eastham	19,354
24	5	A	Bury	L	1-2	Eastham	31,032
25	19	A	Southampton	W	2-1	Milsom, Westwood	16,525
26	30	H	Notts County	W	5-1	Westwood, Rimmer, Milsom 2, G.T. Taylor	8,220
27	Feb 2	A	Bradford City	D	1-1	Rimmer	9,023
28	9	H	Sheffield United	D	1-1	Goslin	23,976
29	23	H	Port Vale	W	2-0	G.T. Taylor, Milsom	18,897
30	Mar 6	H	Hull City	L	1-2	Westwood	13,715
31	9	A	Nottingham Forest	W	1-0	Westwood	16,269
32	23	A	Fulham	L	1-2	Hindson (own-goal)	21,747
33	30	H	Bradford Park Avenue	L	1-2	G.T. Taylor	19,357
34	Apr 6	A	Plymouth Argyle	L	0-1		16,238
35	10	A	Barnsley	D	1-1	Eastham	13,171
36	13	H	Norwich City	W	4-0	Westwood, Milsom 2, Cook	16,218
37	19	H	Swansea Town	W	1-0	Cook	26,583
38	20	A	Newcastle United	W	3-1	Westwood 2, Milsom	28,277
39	22	A	Swansea Town	L	1-2	Cook	19,693
40	27	A	West Ham United	W	3-1	Walton, Westwood 2	34,909
41	May 1	H	Brentford	W	2-0	Milsom, G.T. Taylor	46,554
42	4	A	Blackpool	D	1-1	Westwood	25,550

	Appearances
4 own-goals	Goals

FA Cup

	Date	Venue	Opponents	Result		Scorers	Attendance
R3	Jan 12	A	Northampton Town	W	2-0	Milsom, Cook	17962
R4	26	A	Plymouth Argyle	W	4-1	Milsom 2, Westwood, Rae (own-goal)	31,403
R5	Feb 16	A	Tottenham Hotspur	D	1-1	Atkinson	70,347
rep	20	H	Tottenham Hotspur	D	1-1	Westwood	47,453
rep2	25	N	Tottenham Hotspur	W	2-0	Westwood, Walton	22,692
R6	Mar 2	A	Everton	W	2-1	Eastham, Milsom	67,096
SF	16	N	West Bromwich Albion	D	1-1	Walton	49,605
rep	20	N	West Bromwich Albion	L	0-2		49,110

R5 replay a.e.t. R5 replay 2 at Villa Park.
SF at Elland Road, Leeds. SF replay at the Victoria Ground, Stoke.

	Appearances
1 own-goal	Goals

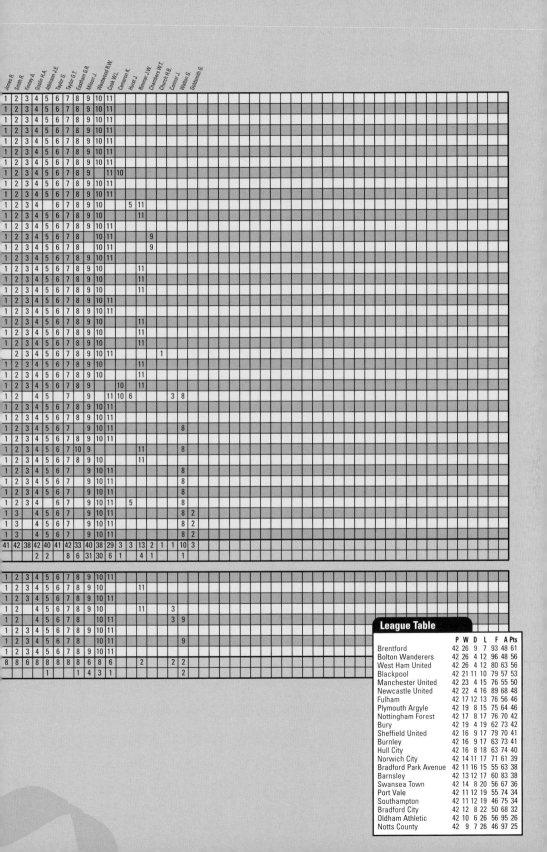

Player columns (left to right): Jones R., Smith R., Finney A., Goslin H.A., Atkinson J.E., Taylor G., Taylor G.T., Eastham G.R., Milson J., Westwood R.W., Cook W.L., Cameron K., Hurst J., Rimmer J.W., Chambers W.T., Church H.B., Connor J., Walton G., Goldsmith G.

Appearance totals (bottom of first block):

| 41 | 42 | 38 | 42 | 40 | 41 | 42 | 33 | 40 | 38 | 29 | 3 | 3 | 13 | 2 | 1 | 1 | 10 | 3 |

League Table

	P	W	D	L	F	A	Pts
Brentford	42	26	9	7	93	48	61
Bolton Wanderers	42	26	4	12	96	48	56
West Ham United	42	26	4	12	80	63	56
Blackpool	42	21	11	10	79	57	53
Manchester United	42	23	4	15	76	55	50
Newcastle United	42	22	4	16	89	68	48
Fulham	42	17	12	13	76	56	46
Plymouth Argyle	42	19	8	15	75	64	46
Nottingham Forest	42	17	8	17	76	70	42
Bury	42	19	4	19	62	73	42
Sheffield United	42	16	9	17	79	70	41
Burnley	42	16	9	17	63	73	41
Hull City	42	16	8	18	63	74	40
Norwich City	42	14	11	17	71	61	39
Bradford Park Avenue	42	11	16	15	55	63	38
Barnsley	42	13	12	17	60	83	38
Swansea Town	42	14	8	20	56	67	36
Port Vale	42	11	12	19	55	74	34
Southampton	42	11	12	19	46	75	34
Bradford City	42	12	8	22	50	68	32
Oldham Athletic	42	10	6	26	56	95	26
Notts County	42	9	7	26	46	97	25

Match No.	Date		Venue	Opponents		Result	Scorers	Attendance
1	Aug	31	H	Brentford	L	0-2		31,949
2	Sep	2	H	Sheffield Wednesday	D	1-1	Eastham	21,655
3		7	A	Derby County	L	0-4		25,716
4		9	A	Sheffield Wednesday	D	2-2	Westwood, Goslin	12,912
5		14	H	Everton	W	2-0	Milsom, Cook	28,391
6		21	A	Grimsby Town	L	1-3	G.T. Taylor	12,768
7		28	A	Huddersfield Town	D	0-0		22,564
8	Oct	5	H	Middlesbrough	W	3-1	Milsom, G.T. Taylor, Eastham	29,910
9		12	A	Aston Villa	W	2-1	Milsom 2	36,297
10		19	H	Liverpool	D	0-0		19,322
11		26	A	Chelsea	L	1-2	Milsom	36,080
12	Nov	2	H	Blackburn Rovers	W	3-1	Milsom, Cook, Westwood	28,981
13		9	A	Stoke City	W	2-1	Westwood 2	21,771
14		16	A	Manchester City	D	3-3	Westwood 2, Milsom	45,809
15		23	A	Leeds United	L	2-5	Cook 2	22,973
16		30	H	Birmingham	W	2-0	Cook, Milsom	21,684
17	Dec	7	A	Sunderland	L	2-7	Eastham, Westwood	27,375
18		14	A	West Bromwich Albion	W	3-1	Westwood, Milsom, Cook	21,736
19		25	H	Wolverhampton Wanderers	L	0-3		30,438
20		26	A	Wolverhampton Wanderers	D	3-3	Westwood, Milsom 2	35,672
21		28	A	Brentford	L	0-4		27,156
22	Jan	1	H	Portsmouth	W	4-0	Milsom 2, Westwood 2	28,300
23		4	H	Derby County	L	0-2		31,392
24		22	A	Everton	D	3-3	G.T. Taylor 3	14,562
25		29	H	Grimsby Town	W	4-0	G.T. Taylor, Westwood, Cook, Currier	10,068
26	Feb	1	H	Huddersfield Town	L	1-2	Eastham	30,852
27		8	A	Middlesbrough	D	0-0		18,377
28		15	H	Aston Villa	W	4-3	Westwood, Currier 2, Rimmer	30,834
29		22	A	Liverpool	D	1-1	Currier	24,543
30		29	H	Stoke City	L	1-2	Goslin	14,906
31	Mar	7	A	Birmingham	D	0-0		20,170
32		14	H	Chelsea	L	2-3	Milsom, O'Hare (own-goal)	18,925
33		21	A	Manchester City	L	0-7		40,779
34		28	H	Leeds United	W	3-0	Milsom, Westwood, Eastham	21,289
35	Apr	1	A	Arsenal	D	1-1	Milsom	10,485
36		4	A	Blackburn Rovers	W	3-0	Milsom 2, Westwood	13,779
37		10	H	Preston North End	D	1-1	Milsom	35,992
38		11	H	Sunderland	W	2-1	Milsom, Atkinson	32,306
39		13	A	Preston North End	L	0-1		25,996
40		18	A	West Bromwich Albion	D	2-2	Currier, Westwood	27,468
41		29	H	Arsenal	W	2-1	G.T. Taylor, Goslin	29,479
42	May	2	A	Portsmouth	L	1-2	Hurst	13,314
								Appearances
							1 own-goal	Goals

FA Cup

R3	Jan	11	A	Blackburn Rovers	D	1-1	Woods	41,000
rep		15	H	Blackburn Rovers	L	0-1		40,800

Replay a.e.t.

	Appearances
	Goals

Player appearance grid (shirt numbers by match). Column headers read vertically:

Jones R.H.	Smith R.	Finney A.	Grosvr H.A.	Atkinson J.E.	Taylor G.	Taylor G.T.	Eastham G.R.	Milsom J.	Westwood R.W.	Cook W.L.	Wason G.	Goldman G.	Connor J.	Kirkman G.	Hurst G.J.	Swift F.V.	Clark T.G.	Tennant J.W.	Connor J.	Rimmer J.W.	Woodward T.	Nicholson C.	Woods C.
1	2	3	4	5	6	7	8	9	10	11													
1	2	3	4	5	6	7	8		10	11	9												
1	2	3	4	5	6	7	8	9	10	11													
1		3	4	5	6	7		9	10	11	8				2								
1		3	4	5	6	7		9	10	11	8				2								
1		3	4	5	6	7		9	10	11	8				2								
1		3	4	5	6	7	10	9		11	8				2								
1		3	4	5	6	7	8	9	10	11					2								
1		3	4	5	6	7	8	9	10	11					2								
1		3	4	5	6	7	10	9		11	8				2								
1		3	4	5	6	7	8	9	10	11					2								
1		3	4	5	6	7	8	9	10	11					2								
1		3	4	5	6	7	8	9	10	11					2								
1		3	4	5	6	7	8	9	10	11					2								
1		3	4	5	6	7	8	9	10	11					2								
1		3	4	5	6	7	8	9	10	11					2								
1		3	4	5	6	7	8	9	10	11					2								
1		3	4	5	6	7	8	9	10	11					2								
1	2		4	5	6	7	8	9	10	11		3											
1	2		4	5	6	7	8	9	10	11		3											
1		3	2		6	7	8	9	10	11					4	5							
1		3	2		6	7	8	9	10	11				5	1			4						
	2		5		6	7	8	9	10	11					1		4	3					
		3	4	5	6	7	8		10	11					1		2						
		3	4	5		7	8		10	11					1		2	9					
		3	4	5		7	8		10	11					1	6	2	9					
		3	4	5	6	7	8		10	11					1		2	9					
		3	4	5		7	8		10					6	1		2	9	11				
		3	4	5		7	8		10					6	1		2	9	11				
		3	4	5		6	8		10						1		2	9	11		7		
		3	4	5		6	8	9	10	7					1		2		11				
		3	4	5		6	8	9	10	7					1		2		11				
			5		6	8	9	10	7		2				1		3		11		4		
		3	4	5	6	7	11	9	10		8				1		2						
		3	4	5	6	7	11	9	10		8				1		2						
		3	4	5	6	7		9	10		8				1		2		11				
		3	4	5	6	7		9	10		8				1		2		11				
		3	4	5	6	7		9	10		8				1		2		11				
		3	4	5		6	8	9	10	7					1		2		11				
		3	4	5	6	7			10		8				1		2	9	11				
		3	4	5	6	7		9	10		8				1		2		11				
		3	4		6	7	8	9	10					5	1		2		11				
21	**3**	**40**	**41**	**39**	**34**	**42**	**34**	**40**	**31**	**13**	**16**	**2**	**1**	**5**	**21**	**3**	**20**	**7**	**13**	**1**	**1**	**0**	
	3	1			7	5	20	16	7				1				5	1					

Supplementary section:

Jones R.H.	Smith R.	Finney A.	Grosvr H.A.	Atkinson J.E.	Taylor G.	Taylor G.T.	Eastham G.R.	Milsom J.	Westwood R.W.	Cook W.L.	Wason G.	Goldman G.	Connor J.	Kirkman G.	Hurst G.J.	Swift F.V.	Clark T.G.
	3	2	5	6	7	8		10	11					1	4		9
	3	2	5	6	7	8		10	11					1	4		9
	2	2	2	2	2	2		2	2					2	2		2
																	1

League Table

	P	W	D	L	F	A	Pts
Sunderland	42	25	6	11	109	74	56
Derby County	42	18	12	12	61	52	48
Huddersfield Town	42	18	12	12	59	56	48
Stoke City	42	20	7	15	57	57	47
Brentford	42	17	12	13	81	60	46
Arsenal	42	15	15	12	78	48	45
Preston North End	42	18	8	16	67	64	44
Chelsea	42	15	13	14	65	72	43
Manchester City	42	17	8	17	68	60	42
Portsmouth	42	17	8	17	54	67	42
Leeds United	42	15	11	16	66	64	41
Birmingham	42	15	11	16	61	63	41
Bolton Wanderers	42	14	13	15	67	76	41
Middlesbrough	42	15	10	17	84	70	40
Wolverhampton W	42	15	10	17	77	76	40
Everton	42	13	13	16	89	89	39
Grimsby Town	42	17	5	20	65	73	39
West Bromwich Albion	42	16	6	20	89	88	38
Liverpool	42	13	12	17	60	64	38
Sheffield Wednesday	42	13	12	17	63	77	38
Aston Villa	42	13	9	20	81	110	35
Blackburn Rovers	42	12	9	21	55	96	33

1936-37

Division One
Manager: C. Foweraker

Did you know that?

G.T. Taylor ended a consecutive run of 290 first-class appearances for Notts County and Bolton when a twisted knee forced him to miss a 3–1 home defeat to Derby County in October 1936. The sequence had begun on 12 April 1930 for Notts County at Southampton.

Match No.	Date		Venue	Opponents	Result		Scorers	Attendance
1	Aug	29	A	Brentford	D	2-2	Currier 2	27,524
2		31	A	Preston North End	W	2-1	Goslin, G.T. Taylor	23,449
3	Sep	5	H	Grimsby Town	L	1-2	Betwood (own-goal)	21,207
4		7	H	Preston North End	D	0-0		17,622
5		12	H	Everton	L	1-2	Westwood	18,029
6		19	A	Huddersfield Town	L	0-2		15,992
7		26	H	Sunderland	D	1-1	Milsom	28,453
8	Oct	3	A	Wolverhampton Wanderers	W	3-2	Westwood 2, Rimmer	28,100
9		10	H	Derby County	L	1-3	Milsom	27,893
10		17	A	Liverpool	D	0-0		21,701
11		24	H	Leeds United	W	2-1	Milsom, Hurst	20,411
12		31	A	Birmingham	D	1-1	Howe	23,288
13	Nov	7	H	Middlesbrough	L	1-3	Howe	18,264
14		14	A	West Bromwich Albion	W	2-0	Milsom, Rimmer	20,125
15		21	H	Manchester City	L	0-2		32,003
16		28	A	Portsmouth	D	1-1	Milsom	18,259
17	Dec	5	H	Chelsea	W	2-1	Milsom 2	13,439
18		12	A	Stoke City	D	2-2	Milsom 2	8,469
19		19	H	Charlton Athletic	W	2-1	Milsom, Westwood	25,202
20		25	A	Manchester United	L	0-1		47,658
21		26	H	Brentford	D	2-2	Milsom, Westwood	36,962
22		28	H	Manchester United	L	0-4		11,801
23	Jan	1	H	Arsenal	L	0-5		42,171
24		2	A	Grimsby Town	L	1-3	Howe	9,719
25		9	A	Everton	L	2-3	G.T. Taylor, Halford	24,422
26		23	H	Huddersfield Town	D	2-2	Milsom, Goslin (pen)	15,746
27	Feb	6	H	Wolverhampton Wanderers	L	1-2	Anderson	19,576
28		10	A	Sunderland	L	0-3		10,975
29		13	A	Derby County	L	0-3		23,046
30		24	H	Liverpool	L	0-1		15,960
31		27	A	Leeds United	D	2-2	Howe, Calder	15,090
32	Mar	6	H	Birmingham	D	0-0		21,572
33		13	A	Middlesbrough	L	0-2		20,025
34		20	H	West Bromwich Albion	W	4-1	Goslin (pen), Westwood, Calder 2	20,268
35		26	H	Sheffield Wednesday	W	1-0	Milsom	26,780
36		27	A	Manchester City	D	2-2	Calder, Howe	51,714
37		29	A	Sheffield Wednesday	L	0-2		30,859
38	Apr	3	H	Portsmouth	W	1-0	Howe	22,552
39		10	A	Chelsea	W	1-0	G.T. Taylor	23,271
40		17	A	Stoke City	D	0-0		16,962
41		24	A	Charlton Athletic	L	0-1		23,684
42	May	1	A	Arsenal	D	0-0		22,875
								Appearances
							1 own-goal	Goals

FA Cup

R3	Jan	16	A	West Ham United	D	0-0		42,300
rep		20	H	West Ham United	W	1-0	Halford	21,539
R4		30	H	Norwich City	D	1-1	Westwood	24,791
rep	Feb	4	H	Norwich City	W	2-1	Anderson, Milsom	30,108
R5		20	H	Manchester City	L	0-5		60,979
R4 replay a.e.t.								Appearances
								Goals

336

Player columns (left to right): Jones R.H., Tennant J.W., Firney A., Goslin H.A., Atkinson J.E., Taylor G., Taylor G.T., Ainstey G.E., Currier J., Westwood R.W., Halford D., Swift F., Hurst J., Corner J., Rimmer J.W., Clark T.C., Eastham G.R., Hanson S., Milsom J., Bower R.W.C., Winton G., Howe D., Anderson A.J., Winter D.T., Hubbick H., Carruthers A.N., Calder J.

League Table

	P	W	D	L	F	A	Pts
Manchester City	42	22	13	7	107	61	57
Charlton Athletic	42	21	12	9	58	49	54
Arsenal	42	18	16	8	80	49	52
Derby County	42	21	7	14	96	90	49
Wolverhampton W	42	21	5	16	84	67	47
Brentford	42	18	10	14	82	78	46
Middlesbrough	42	19	8	15	74	71	46
Sunderland	42	19	6	17	89	87	44
Portsmouth	42	17	10	15	62	66	44
Stoke City	42	15	12	15	72	57	42
Birmingham	42	13	15	14	64	60	41
Grimsby Town	42	17	7	18	86	81	41
Chelsea	42	14	13	15	52	55	41
Preston North End	42	14	13	15	56	67	41
Huddersfield Town	42	12	15	15	62	64	39
West Bromwich Albion	42	16	6	20	77	98	38
Everton	42	14	9	19	81	78	37
Liverpool	42	12	11	19	62	84	35
Leeds United	42	15	4	23	60	80	34
Bolton Wanderers	42	10	14	18	43	66	34
Manchester United	42	10	12	20	55	78	32
Sheffield Wednesday	42	9	12	21	53	69	30

1937-38

Division One
Manager: C. Foweraker

Did you know that?

A home defeat to Derby County in January 1937 was christened as Derby's benefit game. The original game commenced on Christmas Day but was abandoned through fog, with Bolton winning 2–0. The re-arranged match not only saw County take the points but also half of the gate receipts which under League rules they were entitled to.

Match No.	Date	Venue	Opponents	Result		Scorers	Attendance
1	Aug 28	H	Brentford	W	2-0	Milsom, Westwood	31,572
2	30	A	Blackpool	D	2-2	Westwood, Milsom	24,929
3	Sep 4	A	Grimsby Town	W	1-0	G. Taylor	10,642
4	6	H	Blackpool	W	3-0	Grosvenor 2, Westwood	23,606
5	11	A	Huddersfield Town	L	0-1		20,758
6	15	H	Arsenal	W	1-0	Westwood	39,750
7	18	H	Everton	L	1-2	Westwood	35,691
8	25	A	Wolverhampton Wanderers	D	1-1	Carruthers	36,995
9	Oct 2	H	Leicester City	W	6-1	Goslin 2, Milsom, Carruthers, Westwood 2	26,498
10	9	A	Sunderland	L	1-3	Tennant	29,932
11	16	H	Preston North End	L	1-4	Westwood	37,911
12	23	A	Charlton Athletic	D	1-1	Goslin (pen)	24,000
13	30	H	Chelsea	D	5-5	Westwood 3, Calder, Grosvenor	22,293
14	Nov 6	A	West Bromwich Albion	W	4-2	Calder 3, Westwood	20,485
15	13	H	Stoke City	W	1-0	Westwood	29,870
16	20	A	Leeds United	D	1-1	Westwood	23,687
17	27	H	Birmingham	D	1-1	Goslin	21,999
18	Dec 4	A	Portsmouth	D	1-1	Westwood	14,508
19	11	H	Liverpool	D	0-0		15,073
20	18	A	Middlesbrough	W	2-1	Hardwick (own-goal), Milsom	21,407
21	27	A	Derby County	L	2-4	Westwood, Currier	31,679
22	Jan 1	A	Brentford	D	1-1	Carruthers	23,210
23	15	H	Grimsby Town	W	3-1	Westwood 3	14,342
24	22	H	Derby County	L	0-2		26,351
25	26	A	Huddersfield Town	W	2-0	Calder 2	9,722
26	29	A	Everton	L	1-4	Calder	25,848
27	Feb 5	H	Wolverhampton Wanderers	L	1-2	Grosvenor	38,101
28	12	A	Leicester City	D	1-1	Howe	15,069
29	19	H	Sunderland	D	1-1	Milsom	23,943
30	26	A	Preston North End	D	2-2	Anderson 2	29,335
31	Mar 5	H	Charlton Athletic	W	1-0	Howe	23,051
32	12	A	Chelsea	D	0-0		38,171
33	19	H	West Bromwich Albion	W	3-0	Hunt, Westwood 2	23,098
34	26	A	Stoke City	L	2-3	Jones, Currier	19,431
35	Apr 2	H	Leeds United	D	0-0		18,492
36	9	A	Birmingham	L	0-2		19,889
37	15	A	Manchester City	W	2-1	Westwood, Carruthers	53,328
38	16	H	Portsmouth	D	1-1	Goslin (pen)	21,854
39	18	H	Manchester City	W	2-1	Currier, Grosvenor	29,872
40	23	A	Liverpool	L	1-2	Currier	26,370
41	30	H	Middlesbrough	W	3-1	Woodward, Howe, Westwood	12,164
42	May 7	A	Arsenal	L	0-5		40,500

				Appearances
			1 own-goal	Goals

FA Cup

R3	Jan 8	A	Arsenal	L	1-3	Carruthers	64,244

				Appearances
				Goals

Player columns (left to right): Swift F.V · Tennant J.W · Hubbick H · Goslin H.A · Atkinson J.E · Taylor G · Taylor G.T · Grosvenor A.T · Milsom J · Westwood R.W · Anderson A.J · Howe D · Carruthers A.N · Winter D.T · Calder J · Connor J · Hurst G.J · Curran J · Hanson S · Roberts J.H · Woodward T · Jones J.H · Hunt G.S · Rothwell E · Halford D

Swift	Tennant	Hubbick	Goslin	Atkinson	Taylor G	Taylor GT	Grosvenor	Milsom	Westwood	Anderson	Howe	Carruthers	Winter	Calder	Connor	Hurst	Curran	Hanson	Roberts	Woodward	Jones	Hunt	Rothwell	Halford
1	2	3	4	5	6	7	8	9	10	11														
1	2	3	4	5	6	7	8	9	10	11														
1	2	3	4	5	6	7		9	10	11		8												
1	2	3	4	5	6	7	8	9	10	11														
1	2	3	4	5	6	7	8	9	10	11														
1	2	3	4	5	6	7	8	9	10	11														
1	2	3	4	5	6		8	9	10	11			7											
1	2	3	4	5	6		8	9	10	11			7											
1	2	3	4	5	6		8	9	10	11			7											
1	2	3	4	5	6		8	9	10	11			7											
1		3	4	5	6		8		10	11			7	2	9									
1			4	5			8		10	11			7	2		3	6							
1	2		4	5			8		10	11			7		9	3	6							
1	2	3	4	5			8		10	11					9		6							
1	2	3	4	5	6		8		10	11			7		9									
1	2	3	4	5			8		10	11			7		9									
1	2	3	4	5	6		8	9	10	11			7											
1		3	4	5	6		8	9	10	11			7	2										
1	2	3	4	5	6		8		10	11			7											
1	2	3	4	5	6		8	9	10	11			7											
1	2	3	4	5	6		8		10	11			7			9								
1	2	3	4	5	6		8		10	11			7		9									
1	2	3	4	5	6		8		10	11			7		9									
1	2	3	4	5			8					11	10		9		6							
1	2	3	4	5	6		8		10	11			7		9									
1	2	3	4	5			8		10	11			7		9									
1	2	3	4	5			8					11	10			3	5	9	1		7			
	2	3		5	6		4	7	10	11	8				9				1					
	2	3		5	6		4	9		11	10	7							1		7			
	2	3	4	5	6		8		10	11								9		11				
1	2	3	4	5	6		8					10	7					9		11				
	2	3	4	5	6		8			10				7				9	1	11	9			
	2	3	4	5	6		8			10								9	1	11	9	7		
	2	3	4	5	6		8		10	11			7						1		9			
	2	3	4				6		10		8	7		5					1	11	9			
	2	3	4	5	6		8								9	1		7			10	11		
	2	3			6		8			11				5	9	1		7			10			
	2	3			6		8		10	11				5	9	1		7						
	2	3	4				6		8		10	11		5	9	1		7						
28	38	40	40	37	37	6	41	17	33	34	14	25	3	14	3	9	7	14	1	6	6	5	3	1
1			5		1		5	5	23	2	3	4		7		4					1	1	1	

Swift	Tennant	Hubbick	Goslin	Atkinson	Taylor G	Taylor GT	Grosvenor	Milsom	Westwood	Anderson	Howe	Carruthers	Winter	Calder	Connor	Hurst	Curran	Hanson	Roberts	Woodward	Jones	Hunt	Rothwell	Halford
1	2	3	4	5	6		8	9	10	11			7											
1	1	1	1	1	1		1	1	1	1			1											
													1											

League Table

	P	W	D	L	F	A	Pts
Arsenal	42	21	10	11	77	44	52
Wolverhampton W	42	20	11	11	72	49	51
Preston North End	42	16	17	9	64	44	49
Charlton Athletic	42	16	14	12	65	51	46
Middlesbrough	42	19	8	15	72	65	46
Brentford	42	18	9	15	69	59	45
Bolton Wanderers	42	15	15	12	64	60	45
Sunderland	42	14	16	12	55	57	44
Leeds United	42	14	15	13	64	69	43
Chelsea	42	14	13	15	65	65	41
Liverpool	42	15	11	16	65	71	41
Blackpool	42	16	8	18	61	66	40
Derby County	42	15	10	17	66	87	40
Everton	42	16	7	19	79	75	39
Huddersfield Town	42	17	5	20	55	68	39
Leicester City	42	14	11	17	54	75	39
Stoke City	42	13	12	17	58	59	38
Birmingham	42	10	18	14	58	62	38
Portsmouth	42	13	12	17	62	68	38
Grimsby Town	42	13	12	17	51	68	38
Manchester City	42	14	8	20	80	77	36
West Bromwich Albion	42	14	8	20	74	91	36

1938-39

Division One

Manager: C. Foweraker

Match No.	Date		Venue	Opponents	Result		Scorers	Attendance
1	Aug	27	H	Charlton Athletic	W	2-1	Hunt, Anderson	21,809
2		31	A	Manchester United	D	2-2	Hunt 2	37,950
3	Sep	3	A	Portsmouth	L	1-2	Grosvenor	28,452
4		5	H	Chelsea	L	0-2		19,616
5		10	A	Leeds United	W	2-1	Woodward, Hunt	20,381
6		17	H	Liverpool	W	3-1	Roberts, Hunt 2	22,409
7		24	A	Leicester City	D	0-0		18,263
8	Oct	1	H	Middlesbrough	W	4-1	Westwood 2, Roberts, Rothwell	28,505
9		8	A	Birmingham	W	2-0	Westwood, Hunt	21,855
10		15	H	Everton	W	4-2	Roberts 3, Woodward	57,989
11		22	A	Huddersfield Town	L	1-2	Roberts	18,027
12		29	H	Arsenal	D	1-1	Woodward	46,611
13	Nov	5	A	Brentford	D	2-2	Westwood, Hunt	24,594
14		12	H	Blackpool	L	0-1		35,782
15		19	A	Derby County	L	0-3		26,062
16		26	H	Grimsby Town	D	1-1	Currier	16,229
17	Dec	3	A	Sunderland	D	2-2	Howe, Hunt	17,815
18		10	H	Aston Villa	L	1-2	Currier	22,552
19		17	A	Wolverhampton Wanderers	D	1-1	Howe	19,316
20		24	A	Charlton Athletic	L	1-2	Howe	6,590
21		27	H	Preston North End	D	2-2	Roberts, Howe	38,240
22		31	H	Portsmouth	W	5-1	Hunt 2, Goslin (pen), Grosvenor, Roberts	15,679
23	Jan	2	H	Stoke City	L	1-3	Roberts	24,767
24		14	H	Leeds United	D	2-2	Goslin 2 (1 pen)	14,893
25		25	A	Liverpool	W	2-1	Hunt, Sinclair	17,705
26		28	A	Leicester City	W	4-0	Hunt, Howe 2, Sinclair	18,621
27	Feb	4	A	Middlesbrough	W	2-1	Sinclair 2	16,416
28		18	A	Everton	L	1-2	Geldard	38,961
29		22	H	Birmingham	W	3-0	Hunt 2, Howe	11,696
30		25	H	Huddersfield Town	W	3-2	Howe, Hunt 2	19,332
31	Mar	4	A	Arsenal	L	1-3	Hunt	29,814
32		11	H	Brentford	D	1-1	Hunt	15,161
33		18	A	Blackpool	D	0-0		18,896
34		25	H	Derby County	W	2-1	Westwood, Hunt	20,543
35	Apr	1	A	Grimsby Town	D	1-1	Hunt	8,558
36		8	H	Sunderland	W	2-1	Westwood, Hunt	22,692
37		10	A	Stoke City	L	1-4	Hunt	29,042
38		15	A	Aston Villa	W	3-1	Currier, Sinclair, Cobley (own-goal)	23,160
39		22	H	Wolverhampton Wanderers	D	0-0		23,976
40		26	H	Preston North End	L	0-2		15,353
41		29	H	Manchester United	D	0-0		10,314
42	May	6	A	Chelsea	D	1-1	Howe	18,232
								Appearances
							1 own-goal	Goals

FA Cup

R3	Jan	7	A	Middlesbrough	D	0-0		32,790
rep		11	H	Middlesbrough	D	0-0		16,981
rep2		16	N	Middlesbrough	L	0-1		25,577

Replay a.e.t. Replay 2 at Elland Road, Leeds.

Appearances

Player columns (left to right):

Goodall E.I. · Tennant J.W. · Hubbick H. · Goslin H.A. · Atkinson J.E. · Taylor G. · Godard A. · Grosvenor A.T. · Hurst G.S. · Howe D. · Anderson A.J. · Woodward T. · Forrest E. · Winter D.T. · Roberts J.H. · Rothwell E. · Hanson S. · Currier J. · Westwood R.W. · Hurst G.I. · Connor J. · Sinclair T.McK · Marsh F.K. · Sidebottom W.

Did you know that?

The first game after the declaration of war was a friendly with Manchester United at Burnden. The game resulted in a 2–2 draw before a gate of 4,830 the Bolton side being chosen from members of staff in the Bolton Artillery.

Match No.	Date	Venue	Opponents	Result		Scorers	Attendance
1	Aug 26	A	Chelsea	L	2-3	Howe, Westwood	33,902
2	28	A	Stoke City	W	2-1	Hunt, Rothwell	13,151
3	Sep 2	H	Portsmouth	W	2-1	Hubbick, Howe	12,992

Football League season abandoned after three games

Appearances

Goals

North West Regional League

Match No.	Date	Venue	Opponents	Result	Scorers	Attendance
1	Aug 26	A	Chelsea	2-3	Howe, Westwood	33,902
2	28	A	Stoke City	2-1	Hunt, Rothwell	13,151
3	Sep 2	H	Portsmouth	2-1	Hubbick, Howe	12,992
4	Oct 21	A	Burnley	1-1	Hubbick (pen)	3,000
5	28	H	Carlisle United	4-1	Hunt 2, Rothwell, Butler	2,000
6	Nov 11	A	Oldham Athletic	2-2	Rothwell, Butler	8,254
7	18	H	Rochdale	4-0	Hunt 2, Cunliffe 2	2,113
8	25	A	Blackburn Rovers	1-3	Walton	1,221
9	Dec 2	H	Blackpool	3-1	Howe 2, Cunliffe	2,777
10	23	H	Southport	2-1	Connor(pen), Cunliffe	1,033
11	Jan 6	A	Accrington	1-1	Hunt	3,000
12	13	H	Oldham Athletic	3-0	Hunt, Connor (pen), Burgess	1,000
13	20	A	Bury	1-4	Connor (pen)	3,045
14	Feb 24	A	Carlisle United	3-2	Connor (pen), Burgess 2	2,000
15	Mar 16	A	Rochdale	2-2	Woodward, Burgess	3,000
16	22	A	Barrow	2-4	Hunt, Burgess	3,000
17	23	H	Blackburn Rovers	2-0	Rothwell, Sidebottom	3,490
18	30	H	Blackpool	1-3	Burgess	6,000
19	Apr 6	H	Barrow	2-0	Hunt 2	2,000
20	10	H	Burnley	5-1	Hunt 3, Cunliffe, Chadwick	700
21	13	H	Preston North End	1-0	Sidebottom	2,000
22	Apr 20	A	Blackburn Rovers	1-5	Hunt	7,451
23	27	H	Blackburn Rovers	1-3	Hanks	1,500
24	May 4	A	Preston North End	3-1	Chadwick 2, Sidebottom	2,000
25	11	H	Bury	0-1		950
26	13	H	Southport	8-1	Sidebottom 4, Jones 2, Hunt, Chadwick	1,500
27	18	H	Accrington	4-1	Hunt 2 (1 pen), Sidebottom 2	500

4th in the North West Regional League

Appearances

Games 1 to 3 in the (abandoned) Football League

Goals

Games 4 to 21, 24 to 27 in the North West Regional League

Games 22 and 23 in the League War Cup

Player appearance and goalscoring grid.

Column headers (reading left to right): *Hanson S, Winter D, Hubick H, Goslin HA, Hirst J, Taylor G, Gallard A, Howe D, Hunt GS, Westwood RW, Rothwell E, Eastwood E, Whalley H, Adamson JE, Conner J, Butler S, Burgess AC, Sidebottom W, Richardson N, Cunliffe JN, Woodward T, Watton G, Jones WEA, Forrest E, Goodall EJ, Chadwick C, Grosvenor A, Hanks CW, Graham RE*

Upper block

Hanson S	Winter D	Hubick H	Goslin HA	Hirst J	Taylor G	Gallard A	Howe D	Hunt GS	Westwood RW	Rothwell E	Eastwood E
1	2	3	4	5	6	7	8	9	10	11	
1	2	3	4	5	6	7	8	9	10	11	
1	2	3	4	5	6	7	8	9	10	11	
3	3	3	3	3	3	3	3	3	3	3	
	1							2	1	1	1

Lower block

Hanson S	Winter D	Hubick H	Goslin HA	Hirst J	Taylor G	Gallard A	Howe D	Hunt GS	Westwood RW	Rothwell E	Eastwood E	Whalley H	Adamson JE	Conner J	Butler S	Burgess AC	Sidebottom W	Richardson N	Cunliffe JN	Woodward T	Watton G	Jones WEA	Forrest E	Goodall EJ	Chadwick C	Grosvenor A	Hanks CW	Graham RE
1	2	3	4	5	6	7	8	9	10	11																		
1	2	3	4	5	6	7	8	9	10	11																		
1	2	3	4	5	6	7	8	9	10	11																		
		3				1		9			11	2	4	5	6	7	8	10										
		3				1		9			11	2	4	5	6	7	8	10										
		3				1		9			11	2	5		6	7		10	4	8								
		3				1		9			11	2	5		6	7		10	4	8								
		3				1		9				2	5		6			10	4	8	7	11						
1	2	3		5	6		10	9				4					11		8			7						
		3		6		1		9				2	4	5	11		10		8		7							
		3			6	1		9				2	4	5	11	7	10		8									
		3				1		9				2	4	5	6		10	11	8		7							
		3				1		9				2	4	5	6		10	11	8		7							
		3		6		1		9				2	4	5	11	7	10		8									
		3				1		9				2	4	5	6		10	11	8	7								
		3						1		9		2	4	5	3		10	11	8		7	6						
1		3						11				2	6	5		9	10	8	7				4					
		3				1		9				2	4	5	6		10	11	8	7								
		3				1		9				2	4	5	6		10	11	8		7							
		3				1		9				2	4	5	6		10		8	7				11				
		3				1		9				2	4	5	6		11		8	7				10				
		3				1		9				2		5	6		11	4	10	7					8			
		3				1		9				2		5	6		10	4			7				8	11		
		3				1		9				2		5	6		10		8		7				11		4	
		3				1		9				2		5	6		10		8		7					11	4	
		3				1		9				2		5	6		10		8		7				11		4	
		3				1		9				2	6	5			10		8		7				11		4	
5	4	26	3	5	6	25	4	26	3	8	23	19	20	21	4	11	24	5	21	7	1	11	1	1	5	2	2	4
2		1				4	16	1	4			4	2	6	9		5	1	1	2		4			1			

1940-41

Football League North

Did you know that?

26th in the Football League North

Nat Lofthouse wore a Wanderers shirt for the first time on 22 March 1941. At 15 years, 207 days old the striker who was to become a legend scored his side's fourth and fifth goals in a 5–1 defeat of Bury at Burnden.

Match No.	Date		Venue	Opponents	Result		Scorers	Attendance
1	Jan	4	H	Oldham Athletic	W	2-1	Eastham, Butler	2,038
2		11	A	Oldham Athletic	W	5-3e	Hunt 4 (1 pen), Eastham	2,800
3		18	H	Manchester United	W	3-2	Chadwick, Goslin, Howe	2,146
4		25	A	Manchester United	L	1-4	Cunliffe	2,649
5	Feb	1	H	Bradford City	W	6-0	Hunt 3, Chadwick, Sidebottom, Butler	3,210
6		8	H	Bradford City	W	3-1	Cunliffe 2, Finan (pen)	1,567
7		15	H	Burnley	W	3-1	Hunt 2, Finan (pen)	3,820
8		22	A	Burnley	D	2-2	Hunt, Chadwick	2,400
9	Mar	1	H	Preston North End	L	1-4	Hunt	7,838
10		8	A	Preston North End	L	0-2		9,000
11		15	A	Bury	L	1-4	Hunt	2,437
12		22	H	Bury	W	5-1	Lofthouse 2, Cload, Connor, Johnson	1,587
13		29	A	Southport	L	1-2	Sidebottom	1,800
14	Apr	12	A	Burnley	D	2-2	Lofthouse 2	3,729
15		14	H	Burnley	L	0-2		1,500
16		19	A	Rochdale	W	3-1	Sidebottom, Lofthouse 2	800
17		26	H	Blackburn Rovers	W	2-0	Sidebottom, Lofthouse	1,441
18	May	10	A	Chester	L	0-8		1,500
19		17	H	Manchester City	D	1-1	Lofthouse	1,500
20		24	A	Manchester City	L	4-6	Chadwick, Howe 2, Johnson	1,500
21		31	H	Oldham Athletic	W	3-1	Grainger, Lofthouse 2	1,000
22	Jun	7	A	Oldham Athletic	L	2-3	Knight, Lofthouse	1,000

Games 1 to 4, 11 to 22 in the Football League North — Appearances

Games 5 to 10 in the Football League War Cup — Goals

Games 1 to 4 also counted as Lancashire Cup ties

Game 2 ended with Bolton losing 1-2. Extra time was played to settle the Lancashire Cup tie

Game 6 was due to be played at Bradford but was played at home by arrangement

Goodall EJ	Banks R	Hubick H	Martindale L	Eastwood E	Comer J	Cunliffe JN	Eastham GR	Sidebottom W	Taylor G	Butler S	Baton R	Hurst J	Hunt GS	Winter DT	Goslin HA	Atkinson JE	Chadwick C	Howe D	Rothwell E	Finan RJ	Johnson IWH	Pugh SJ	Heslop N	Grimsditch SW	Lofthouse N	Coad H	Mann D	O'Neil W	Houghton W	Barker H	Berry J	Grealing G	Richardson A	Smith JD	Hanson S	Cooper JE	Morriston ER	Clancy D	Granger R	Galon JW	Pearson TU	Burgess A	Pryde RI	Ryder R	Knight J	Leyland EC	Platt E
1	2	3	4	5	6	7	8	9	10	11																																					
	2	3	4		6	8	7	10		11	1	5	9																																		
1		3			6		8	11					9	2	4	5	7	10																													
		3		2	6		8	11				1	9		4	5	7		10																												
	2	3	4		6		10			11	1		9			5	7			8																											
	2	3	4		6		10			11	1		9			5	7			8																											
	2	3	4		6		10			11	1		9			5	7			8																											
	2	3	4		6			11			1		9			5	7			8	10																										
	2	3	4		6		8		10	11	1		9			5	7																														
	2	3			6		8		10	11	1		9			5	7					4																									
	2	3			6			8		11	1		9			5						7	10	4																							
	2	3			6			8							4							5		7	10		1	9	11																		
		3					8								4							5					1	9	11	2	6	7	10														
	2	3			6			10							4							5		8	1	9		11									7										
	2	3			6			10							4							5		11	1	9											7	8									
	2	3			6		8								4	7						5		10	1	9			11																		
	2	3			6			10							4		8					5		1	9	11									4	7											
	4	3			6			8				2			5	7								9	11									1	10												
	2	3			6										5									10	9									1	4	7	8	11									
	2	3			6										4	5	7		10			8			9									1					11								
	2	3			5			4								8						6			9									1		7			11	10							
	2	3					8								4						1	9																			5	7	10	6	11
2	19	22	2	7	20	7	3	15	1	8	9	2	19	2	3	19	10	2	2	7	6	1	3	7	11	6	1	1	1	1	2	1	1	1	3	2	1	3	1	1	1	1	1	1	1	1	1
			1	3	2	4		2					12		1		4	3						2	2						11	1									1						

Football League North

Did you know that?

34th in Football League North (First Competition)

A game schedule to take place at Bradford City on 25 March had to be cancelled when only two players, Nat Lofthouse and Harry Hubbick, could be recruited with the release of guest players in the services being impossible.

£1,000 PRISONERS OF WAR FUND
(Waterworks Ambulance and Mobile First-Aid Party Depot Effort)

BOLTON WANDERERS
versus R.A.F. XI

Burnden Park, Wednesday, May 27th, 1942
(By kind permission of Bolton Wanderers F. & A. Co., Ltd.)

Match No.	Date		Venue	Opponents	Result		Scorers	Attendance
1	Aug 30		A	Bury	D	4-4	Lofthouse, Chadwick, WH Johnson, Bacuzzi (og)	2
2	Sep	6	H	Bury	W	2-1	Jones, Goslin	2,646
3		13	H	Halifax Town	D	1-1	Hunt	1,869
4		20	A	Halifax Town	L	0-2		4,000
5		27	H	Blackburn Rovers	D	2-2	Myers, Hunt	1,986
6	Oct	4	A	Blackburn Rovers	D	3-3	Chadwick, Hunt 2	2,500
7		11	H	Blackpool	L	2-6	Hunt 2	5,203
8		18	A	Blackpool	L	1-2	Hunt	3,000
9		25	H	Oldham Athletic	L	3-5	Rothwell, Hunt 2	1,600
10	Nov	1	A	Oldham Athletic	L	0-2		2,000
11		8	A	Burnley	L	1-2	Chadwick (pen)	3,000
12		15	H	Burnley	W	3-1	Wright, Hunt 2	2,000
13		22	H	Rochdale	D	3-3	Knight, Lofthouse, G Eastham	2,684
14		29	A	Rochdale	L	0-1		1,500
15	Dec	6	A	Preston North End	L	2-4	Wright, Chadwick	1,500
16		13	H	Preston North End	L	2-6	Knight, Chadwick (pen)	2,000
17		20	A	Southport	L	2-3	Wright 2	2,700
18		25	H	Southport	W	4-0	Burgess, Hunt 2, Myers	4,086
19		27	A	Manchester United	L	1-3	Hunt	5,000
20	Jan	3	H	Manchester United	D	2-2	Chadwick 2	2,500
21		10	H	Chester	W	1-0	Knight	2,673
22		17	A	Chester	L	1-3	Speak	1,000
23	Feb	14	A	Stoke City	L	1-3	Franklin (og)	3,224
24		28	H	York City	W	4-3	Knight 2, Hunt (pen), JW Johnson	2,109
25	Mar	14	H	Bradford City	W	4-0	Lofthouse, Hunt, Knight, Morris	2,624
26		21	H	Stoke City	D	1-1	Morris	4,371
27		28	A	York City	L	1-2	Hunt	3,700
28	Apr	4	A	Halifax Town	D	2-2	Morris, Lofthouse	2,000
29		6	H	Sheffield Wednesday	D	3-3	Knight, Hunt (pen), Lofthouse	2,000
30		11	A	Blackpool	L	1-7	Hunt	4,000
31		18	H	Blackpool	W	2-1	Knight, Hunt (pen), Lofthouse	3,760
32		25	A	Bury	L	0-2		1,222
33	May	2	H	Bury	W	2-1	Lofthouse, Gallon	2,900

Games 1 to 18 were in the Football League North (1st Compeititon)
Games 19 to 33 were in the Football League North (2nd Compeititon)   Two own goals
Games 19 to 27 were also in the Football League War Cup
Games 30 and 31 were also for the Lancashire Cup

Appearances
Goals

Also played: RR Newton (game 29, at 1), E Platt (11, 11), JJ Robinson (27,1), W Schofield (11 and 12, at 1),
J Shields (24,9), J Shore (31 and 32, at 6), J Shuttleworth (29,5) K Speak (21 at 6, 22 at 11, 1 goal), AW Steen (22 and 23 at 7),
E Walker (29,11), H Whalley (25,4), GK Whitehead (21 and 31 at 1), DT Winter (19,2), J Wright (5,7).

Smith JD	Banks R	Hubrick H	Hunt GS	Atkinson JE	Connor J	Chadwick C	Knight J	Lofthouse N	Johnson WH	Cloud H	Foster R	Godin HA	Jones WEA	Morrison ER	Brown W	Myers J	Brown J	Hanks CW	Forrest E	McCormick JM	Rothwell E	Mangham W	Hurst J	Jackson J	Eastham H	Eastham GR	Wright H	Grimsditch SW	Hanson S	Catterall G	Swinburne TA	Howe D	Burgess AC	Marsh R	Martindale L	Johnson JW	Boulter LM	Beesdon J	Haslam AD	Morris J	Cross RM	Beardsman EC	Gallon JW	McEwan W	Eastwood E	Russell DW	Mawdsley LAC
1	2	3	4	5	6	7	8	9	10	11																																					
	2	3	9	5	6	11	8		10		1	4	7																																		
	2	3	4	5	6		8	9	10	11																																					
	2	3	4	5	6		8	9		11			7	1	10																																
1	2	3	4	5	6	11	8									10	9																														
	2	3	10	5		11	8	9		1			7				4																														
1	2	3	9	5	6	11	8		4				7				10																														
1	2	3	9	5	6	11	8		4				7				10																														
1	2	3	9	5		11							7				8	4	6	10																											
	3	9	5	6		8							1	7	10		4				11	2																									
	2	3	8		6	7	10													4				5	9																						
	2	3	9	5			10													4					6		7	8	11																		
	2	3		5	6		10	9												4							7	8	11	1																	
	2		8		5		10							4						7			6					9				11				1	3										
	2	3	8	5	6	7														4					9			10	11	1																	
	2	3	9		5	7	8								10					4							11				1	6															
	2	3	9	5		8									10					4						6		11				1				7											
	2	3	9		6		8							4					5								7					1	10	11													
		3	9	5	6		7		8					4														1	10	11																		
	2	3	4		5	11	8		6				7	10	9													1																			
	2	3	4		5		8								10	7										9																					
	2	3	9		5		8		6																			1											4	10							
	2	3	9		5	11			6											4								1											8	10							
	2	3	4		5	11	10		6																	8		1											7								
		3	8	5		11	10	9	6																			1								2	7										
		3	8	5		11	10	9	6				4													7		1								2	7										
		3	8			10			2																								6										4	5	11	8	
		3	4		7	10	9	6																				1											2	8	5	11					
		3	8					10	9	6																7											2	7						4			
		3	8	6		11	10	9																5	7		1									2			7						4		
		3	9			11	8															1				7		2								10			4	5						
		3	8			11	10	9	4																	1		2									7			5							
		3				11	8	9	6									7								1										2			10				4	5			
5	22	32	31	18	21	20	30	12	19	3	3	6	9	2	6	5	4	4	1	7	2	1	2	4	2	5	6	11	1	1	4	1	3	2	2	6	1	1	8	4	2	1	5	1	1	3	3
		20		7	8	6	1			1	1			2						1				1	4			1					1			3			1								

1942-43

Football League North

Did you know that?

46th in Football League North (First Competition) and 33rd in the Second Competition

The first occasion that Nat Lofthouse and Tom Finney played in the same team came in October 1942. Finney guested for the Wanderers in a 2–1 win at Burnley, where Lofthouse scored both goals. The pair were to play together for England after the war.

Match No.	Date		Venue	Opponents	Result		Scorers	Attendance
1	Aug	29	A	Bury	L	3-4	Hunt (pen), Gee 2	2,485
2	Sep	5	H	Bury	L	2-3	Harker, Chadwick	1,185
3		12	H	Southport	L	1-3	Hunt	1,885
4		19	A	Southport	L	2-6	Lofthouse, Hunt	2,000
5		26	A	Manchester City	L	0-2		4,000
6	Oct	3	H	Manchester City	W	2-1	Hunt, Chadwick	3,736
7		10	A	Blackpool	L	0-2		4,000
8		17	A	Blackpool	L	0-2		4,982
9		24	H	Burnley	W	7-4	W Johnson, Lofthouse, Rothwell, Chadwick 3, Hunt	2,664
10		31	A	Burnley	W	2-1	Lofthouse 2	3,000
11	Nov	7	H	Blackburn Rovers	D	3-3	Lofthouse 2, Hunt	3,748
12		14	A	Blackburn Rovers	L	2-4	Lofthouse 2	2,000
13		21	A	Oldham Athletic	L	1-3	Chadwick (pen)	2,000
14		28	H	Oldham Athletic	D	1-1	Lofthouse	2,990
15	Dec	5	H	Rochdale	D	4-4	Chadwick, Watson, Hughes, Wharton	873
16		12	A	Rochdale	L	1-3	Tate	1,000
17		19	H	Manchester United	L	0-2		1,578
18		25	A	Manchester United	L	0-4		6,000
19		26	H	Manchester City	L	2-4	Hunt, Chadwick	8,171
20	Jan	2	A	Manchester City	L	0-2		3,000
21		9	A	Oldham Athletic	D	3-3	Wharton, Lofthouse, Gillies	1,000
22		16	H	Oldham Athletic	W	5-0	Hunt 4 (2 pens), Chadwick	2,374
23		23	H	Burnley	W	4-1	Hunt 2, Colclough, Wharton	3,863
24		30	A	Burnley	W	1-0	Colclough	2,000
25	Feb	6	H	Blackburn Rovers	W	3-1	Hunt 3 (1 pen)	4,501
26		13	A	Blackburn Rovers	L	1-7	Chadwick	3,000
27		20	H	Blackpool	D	1-1	Chadwick	9,000
28		27	A	Blackpool	L	0-5		5,000
29	Mar	6	H	Burnley	W	4-1	Lofthouse 3, Chadwick	2,900
30		13	A	Burnley	L	1-4	Chadwick	2,000
31	Apr	3	A	Blackburn Rovers	W	3-1	W Johnson, Lofthouse, Wright	2,800
32		10	H	Blackburn Rovers	L	0-1		2,971
33		17	H	Chester	W	3-1	Chadwick 2, Gillies	2,000
34		24	H	Liverpool	L	3-6	W Johnson, Knight, Hunt	7,566
35	May	1	A	Liverpool	L	0-4		10,000

Games 1 to 18 were Football League North (1st Competition)   **Appearances**
Games 19 to 35 were Football League North (2nd Competition)   **Goals**
Games 19 to 28 were also in the Football League War Cup
Games 31, 32, 34 and 35 were also Lancashire Cup games

Also played: L Lievesley (game 2 and 3, at 2), R Marsh (11,4), JM McCormick (12,4), T Middleton (25 and 28, at 8), W Moir (35,7), RG Savage (1,1), H Stephan (32,8), FW West (1,5).

Bradshaw EC	Hubbick H	Harker J	Johnson WH	Gee H	Hunt GS	Lofthouse N	Chadwick C	Wharton JE	Grimsditch S	Russell DW	Cross RM	Maudsley RC	Davies JK	Burgess AC	Bray J	Haslam AD	Parker LT	Ittwil WJ	Crozier J	Gorman WE	Connor JE	Gelderd A	Johnson JW	Wright H	John WR	Watson J	Gillies MM	Knight J	Rothwell E	Banks R	Atkinson JE	Finney T	Boften R	Hopkins RW	Hughes GE	Hall J	Galton JW	Power GF	Tate N	Gorman R	Murphy D	Colclough W	Taylor G	Charlesworth S	Longman FH	Braddon S	Crossley J
2	3	4		6	7	8	9	10	11																																						
	3	9		7	8		10	11	1	4	5	6																																			
	3			7	9		11	10		4	6	5		1	2	8																															
	3	6		7	4	9	11	10		5						1	2	8																													
	3	6			9		10			4						1	2	5	7	8	11																										
	3	6		4	9	11	10			5							8		1	2			7																								
	3	6		4	9	11	10			5							8		1	2			7																								
	3	6		8	9		7											2			1	4	5	10	11																							
	3	6		8	9	7	11											4			1		5		10	2																					
	3	6		8	9	11	10											2			1		5				4	7																			
	3	6		10	9	11				5								2			1		5									1	7	8												
	3	6			9	11				8								2		7	1		5										10													
	3	6			9	11	10	4										2		7	1		5										8													
	3	6		4	9	7	11											2		8			5											1	10											
	3	6		10	9	11	7											2			4	5											8	1												
	3	6		10	9	11	7											2			4	5														1	8									
	3	6		4	9	11	7											2				5											10			1	8									
	3			9		7	11									4		2	6			8	5										10			1										
	3	10		9		8	7									4		2	11			6	5													1										
	3	6		9		10	7											2		11	5											8	1		4										
	3	6		10	9	11	7											2			4		5										1	8										
	3			10	9	11	7											2			4	8	5										1				6								
	3	10		9		11	7											2		11		2	5										1				6	8							
	3			10	9	11	7											2			4		5										1				6	8							
	3			9		10	7											2		11	4		5										1				6								
	3			9		8	7											2		11	4		5										1				6	10							
	3			9		10	7											2		11		8	5										1				6	4							
	3				9		7											2		11			11	5										1				6	4							
	3	10		8	9	7												2		11		5											1		4		6								
	3			8	9	7												2		11		5										10		1		4		6							
	3	10		8	9	7												2		11		4											1				6	5							
	3	10		4	9	7												2		11		5											1				6		1						
	3	8		9		7														11		4		10													6	5	1	2						
	3	10		8	9															11		4	7														6	5	1	2						
	3	6		4	9	10														11		2			5																1			8		
1	35	2	25	4	31	25	31	26	1	3	2	8	1	1	1	1	3	2	3	28	3	1	6	13	5	6	23	4	2	10	1	1	3	5	2	16	3	3	7	2	9	3	4	2	1		
	1		3	2	17	14	15	3													1			1	2	1	1										1				1			2				

Football League North

Match No.	Date	Venue	Opponents	Result		Scorers	Attendance
1	Aug 28	A	Burnley	L	0-4		1,700
2	Sep 4	H	Burnley	L	0-2		2,945
3	11	H	Blackburn Rovers	L	1-4	Currier	2,661
4	18	A	Blackburn Rovers	L	1-3	Wright	3,000
5	25	H	Manchester City	W	4-1	Chadwick (pen), Woodward, Currier, Lofthouse	2,756
6	Oct 2	A	Manchester City	L	0-4		3,000
7	9	H	Southport	W	3-1	Currier, R Smith, Woodward	2,771
8	16	A	Southport	L	0-2		3,000
9	23	H	Blackpool	L	1-2	Woodward	10,243
10	30	A	Blackpool	W	2-1	Lofthouse, Currier	7,000
11	Nov 6	A	Bury	W	3-2	Chadwick, Lofthouse 2	5,000
12	13	H	Bury	L	2-4	Woodward, Marshall	4,546
13	20	H	Oldham Athletic	W	3-0	Lofthouse 2, Shankly	3,644
14	27	A	Oldham Athletic	L	2-4	Lofthouse, Hurst (og)	2,000
15	Dec 4	A	Huddersfield Town	L	0-2		3,091
16	11	H	Huddersfield Town	L	0-4		4,125
17	18	A	Manchester United	L	1-3	Gorman	4,800
18	25	H	Manchester United	L	1-3	Woodward	10,696
19	27	A	Rochdale	L	0-5		3,000
20	Jan 1	H	Rochdale	D	2-2	Lofthouse, Currier	6,766
21	8	H	Burnley	W	2-1	Lofthouse, Woodward	5,423
22	15	A	Burnley	L	1-5	Currier	3,000
23	22	A	Blackpool	L	0-6		8,000
24	29	H	Blackpool	L	1-2	Knight	10,254
25	Feb 5	A	Blackburn Rovers	L	0-2		3,000
26	12	H	Blackburn Rovers	W	4-1	Middlebrough 2, Johnson, Currier	6,208
27	19	H	Southport	W	5-1	Currier 4, Middlebrough	4,888
28	26	A	Southport	L	0-2		2,000
29	Mar 4	H	Bury	W	6-1	Johnson, Lofthouse 2, Currier, Berry, Hamlett (pen)	2,750
30	11	A	Bury	L	2-5	Wright, Taylor	2,126
31	18	A	Wrexham	D	3-3	Hamlett (pen), Currier, Lofthouse	5,000
32	25	H	Wrexham	D	1-1	Jones(og)	5,335
33	Apr 1	H	Manchester United	W	3-0	Middlebrough 2, Currier	5,791
34	8	A	Manchester United	L	2-3	Currier 2	13,044
35	10	H	Bury	W	3-2	Rothwell, McClelland 2	7,021
36	15	A	Bury	D	1-1e	Woodward	4,187
37	22	H	Stockport County	W	4-2	Hamlett (pen), Carter, Lofthouse 2	5,003
38	29	A	Stockport County	W	2-1	Lofthouse, Woodward	3,500
39	May 6	A	Liverpool	L	1-3	Currier	16,591
40	13	H	Liverpool	L	2-3	Lofthouse, Hughes (og)	10,254

Games 1 to 18 were in the Football League North (1st Competition)

Games 19 to 39 were in the Football League North (2nd Competition)

Games 19 to 28 were also in the Football League War Cup

Games 33 to 40 were also for the Lancashire Cup games

Game 36 was lost 0-1 after 90 minutes; extra time played for the Lancashire Cup

Three own goals

Appearances

Goals

	Grimsditch SW	Gorman WC	Hublick H	Woodburn J	Murphy D	Taylor G	Chadwick C	Woodburn T	Currier J	Johnson WH	Wright H	Lancaster JW	Gillies MM	Smith K	Hall HHC	Anderson J	Windsor F	Lathouse N	Rothwell E	Rigby E	Smith RAG	Conner J	Knight J	Marshall D	Shandly W	Berry J	Foxton JD	Sullivan A	Middlebrough A	Higham H	Rimmer J	Marsh R	MacFarlane R	Smith G	Speak K	Winter DT	Harrison FH	Hamnett TL	Owens JG	Whalley H	Liddle J	McClelland C	Carter DF	Hughes AL	Smith JR	Watson A
1	2	3	4	5	6	7	8	9	10	11																																				
	2	3	4	6	10	7			9	8	11	1	5																																	
	2	3		5	6	7	10	9	4	11	1	1		8																																
	2	3		5	6		10	8		11					1	4	7	9																												
	2	3		5	6	7	10	8		11					1	4		9																												
	2	3		5	6	7	10	8	4						1			9	11																											
	2	3		6	7	10	9	4	11						1					5	8																									
	2	3		6	7	10	9	4	11						1						5	8																								
	2	3		6	11	10	9	4				7			1					5		8																								
	2	3	6			7	8	4	11						1			9	5					10																						
	2	3	5	6	7		8	4	11						1			9						10																						
	2	3	5		7	8	9	6							1									10	4	11																				
	2	3	5	6	7		8	11							1			9						10	4																					
	2	3	6		7	8	10	11							1			9	5								4																			
	2	3		6	7	8									1			9	5					10	4	11																				
	2	3	5		7	8	4	6	11						1									10			9																			
4	3		5	6	7	10	8		11						1			9										2																		
	2	3	5	6	7	10	8								1											9		1	4	11																
	2	3	6		7	10	8	4	11						1			9	5																											
	2	3	5		10	7	8	4							1			9													6	11														
4	3		10	6		7		8			5			1			9													11	2														
	2	3	5	6		7	8	10							9											1					11	4														
	2	3	6		11	7		8							1			9							10									4	5										
		3		6	11	7	9	4							1							5	8	10										2												
	2	3	11	6		7		4							1			9					8	10										5												
		3	6			7	8	4	11						1									10			9							2												
		3		6		7	8	4	11		5				1									10			9							2												
		3	5	6		7	8	4	11						1									10			9							2												
750	2	3		6		7	8	4	11					1				9						10											5											
		3	5	6		7	8	4	11					1				9						10										2												
	2	3	6			7	8	4						1				9						10										5		4										
	2	3				7	8	4	11						9									10										5		6	1									
4	3				7	8	6	11						1				9						10			9							5				2								
	2	3	6			7	8	4	11						9																			5					1	10						
	2	3				7	8	6						9	11										4			1						5						10						
	2	3		6		7	9	4						9																				5						10		11	1	8	
	2	3		6		7	8	4					1	9																				5						10	11				
	2	3		6		7	8	10					1	9																				5		4		11							
	2	3		6		7	8	10					1	9																				5		4		11							
1	35	40	2	24	28	19	36	34	23	2	3	2	1	25	2	6	1	2	4	8	2	10	3	1	6	1	3	1	1	1	3	3	1	18	1	5	2	7	1	1	1	1			
	1			1	2	8	17	2	2					16	1			1		1	1	1	1			5								3				2	1							

1944-45

9th in Football League North First Competition, 15th in the Second Competiton

In August 1944 secretary-manager Charles Foweraker retired through ill-health and handed the reigns over to Walter Rowley. Foweraker, who had taken over in July 1919, was the longest-serving and most successful manager in the club's history.

OFFICIAL PROGRAMME
BOLTON WANDERERS
FOOTBALL & ATHLETIC CO., LTD.

FOOTBALL LEAGUE (NORTH) CUP
FINAL TIE

Bolton Wanderers
v.
Manchester United

AT BURNDEN PARK, BOLTON
Saturday, 19th May, 1945

KICK-OFF 3-0 P.M.   PROGRAMME 2D.

Match No.	Date	Venue	Opponents	Result		Scorers	Attendance
1	Aug 26	H	Halifax Town	D	0-0		6,504
2	Sep 2	A	Halifax Town	L	0-2		4,000
3	9	A	Blackpool	W	2-1	Hanson, Johnson	8,000
4	16	H	Blackpool	W	1-0	Hamlett (pen)	10,148
5	23	H	Blackburn Rovers	D	0-0		7,057
6	30	A	Blackburn Rovers	L	1-2	Barrass	5,000
7	Oct 7	A	Rochdale	D	2-2	Barrass, Middlebrough	4,100
8	14	H	Rochdale	D	0-0		4,752
9	21	A	Burnley	L	3-6	Hunt 2, Middlesbrough	4,500
10	28	H	Burnley	W	4-0	Middlebrough, Woodward, Barrass, McClelland	3,458
11	Nov 4	A	Accrington Stanley	D	3-3	Barrass 2, Hunt	4,301
12	11	A	Accrington Stanley	W	3-2	Barrass, Hunt, Middlebrough	3,500
13	18	A	Preston North End	W	3-2	Hunt, Barrass 2	4,000
14	25	H	Preston North End	D	0-0		6,950
15	Dec 2	H	Southport	W	3-1	Middlebrough, McClelland, Barrass	3,621
16	9	H	Southport	W	2-0	Barrass 2	3,000
17	16	A	Oldham Athletic	W	5-0	Lofthouse 2,Barrass,Rothwell,Hamlett (pen)	3,000
18	23	H	Oldham Athletic	W	2-1	Lofthouse, Woodward	9,271
19	26	H	Stockport County	W	2-0	Lofthouse, Barrass	2,934
20	30	A	Stockport County	L	0-2		3,000
21	Jan 6	A	Everton	L	1-2	Lofthouse	18,123
22	13	H	Everton	L	1-3	Lofthouse	14,204
23	27	A	Southport	W	4-3	Hunt, Barrass, Murphy, Lofthouse	1,800
24	Feb 3	A	Tranmere Rovers	W	4-1	Lofthouse 3, Hunt	2,500
25	10	H	Tranmere Rovers	W	6-1	Lofthouse 4, Barrass 2	6,273
26	17	H	Liverpool	W	2-1	Woodward, Moir	11,494
27	24	A	Liverpool	D	1-1	Barrass	20,966
28	Mar 3	A	Crewe Alexandra	L	1-4	Lofthouse	5,059
29	10	H	Southport	W	6-1	Lofthouse 3, Woodward, Murphy, Hamlett	8,745
30	17	H	Bury	D	3-3	Hunt, Lofthouse, Barrass	10,503
31	24	H	Accrington Stanley	D	0-0		14,214
32	31	A	Accrington Stanley	W	4-0	Lofthouse 2, Murphy, Woodward	11,721
33	Apr 2	A	Bury	L	0-1		9,314
34	7	A	Blackpool	W	4-1	Lofthouse 4	20,000
35	14	H	Blackpool	L	1-2	Lofthouse	13,613
36	21	H	Newcastle United	W	3-0	Barrass, Lofthouse 2	25,924
37	28	A	Newcastle United	L	2-4e	Hunt, Lofthouse	38,704
38	May 5	A	Wolverhampton W.	D	2-2	Barrass, Butler	29,861
39	12	H	Wolverhampton W.	W	2-1	Moir, Hunt	29,683
40	19	H	Manchester United	W	1-0	Lofthouse	40,785
41	26	A	Manchester United	D	2-2	Barrass 2	57,395
42	Jun 2	A	Chelsea	W	2-1	Hunt, Hamlett (pen)	45,000

Games 1-18 inclusive were Football League - Northern Section (1st Comp.) comprising 54 clubs.   Appearances
Games 19-41 inclusive were Football League - Northern Section (2nd Comp.), comprising 54 clubs.   Goals
Games 19-27 & 29 inclusive were Football League War Cup (North), Qualifying Comp., Bolton finished 13th out of 32 qualifiers.
Games 30-41 also counted towards Football League War Cup (North), Games 40 & 41 being the final.
Games 30 & 33 also counted as Lancashire Cup 1st round games.
Game 42 was the Football League War Cup, North v South Final.

Player appearance / batting-order grid (columns = players, rows = matches):

Hall HHC	Winter DT	Hublick H	Johnson WH	Harnett TL	Taylor G	Muir W	Woodward T	Hunt GS	Barraze WM	Hanson AJ	Rigby E	Lofthouse N	McClelland C	Gillies MM	Fielding W	Milne JL	Wheatley H	Threlfall JR	Foxton JD	Middlesborough A	McCormick JM	Berry J	Conner J	Murphy D	Topping H	Rothwell E	Dailey H	Koffman SJ	Butler S	Jones S	Knight J
1	2	3	4	5	6	7	8	9	10	11																					
1		3	4	2	6		7	8		11	5	9	10																		
1		3	4	2	6		7	8	10	11		9			1	5															
		3	4	2	6		7	8	10	11		9			1	5															
		3	8	5			7	9	10				11		1		6	2	4												
1		3	4	2	6		7	11	10										5	9	8										
1		3	4	2			7	8	10				11						5	9	6										
1		3		5			7	8	10				11				2	4	9	6											
1		3		2	4		7	8	10				11						9				5	6							
1		3		2	4		7	8	10				11						9				5	6							
		3	4	5			7	8	10				11		1				9					6	2						
	2	3	4	5		7	11	8	10			9			1									6							
		3	4	5			7	8	10				11		1				9					6	2						
		3		5	4		7	8	10				11		1				9					6	2						
		3		5	4		7	8	10			9	11		1									6	2						
		3		5	4		7	8	10			9			1									6	2				11		
		3		5			7	4	10			9			1									6	2				11	8	
		3		5	4		7	8	10			9			1									6	2				11		
		3		5	4		7	8	10			9			1									6	2				11		
		3		2	4		7	8	10			9	11	5	1									6							
		3		5			7	8	10			9			1			2						6					11		
		3		5			7	8	10			9	11		1	4								6	2						
		3		5	4		7	8	10			9	11		1									6	2						
		3		5	4		7	8	10			9			1			2						6					11		
		3		2	4	7	11	8	10			9			1								5	6							
	2	3		5	4		7	8	10			9			1	4								6					11		
		3		2	4		7	8				9	10		1				11				5	6							
		3		5	4		7	8	10			9			1		2			11				6							
		3		5			7	8	10			9	11		1	4		2						6							
	2	3		5			7	8	10			9			1	4								6					11		
		3		5	4		7	8	10			9			1			2						6					11		
		3		2			7		5			9	10		1		4							6						11	8
		3		5	4	11	7	8	10			9			1									6	2						
	2	3		5	4		7	8	10			9			1									6					11		
		3		5	4		7	8	10			9			1			2						6					11		
	2	3		5	4		7	8	10			9			1									6					11		
		3		5	4		7	8	10			9			1			2						6					11		
		3		5	4	9	7	8	10						1			2						6					11		
		3		5	4		7	8	10			9			1			2						6					11		
		3		5	4		7	8	10			9			1			2						6							
8	6	42	11	42	30	6	42	41	40	5	1	31	16	2	34	3	2	14	5	9	2	1	6	33	12	4	1	2	9	1	1
		1	4		2	5	11	22	1			30	2				5								3		1			1	

Match No.	Date		Venue	Opponents		Result		Scorers	Attendance
1	Aug	25	A	Everton		L	2-3	Lofthouse, Barrass	24,898
2		29	A	Liverpool		D	2-2	Howe, Lofthouse	17,437
3	Sep	1	H	Everton		W	3-1	Lofthouse, Woodward, Howe	16,683
4		8	H	Burnley		W	2-0	Lofhouse, Hamlett (pen)	16,652
5		12	A	Blackpool		D	1-1	Lofthouse	15,207
6		15	H	Burnley		D	2-2	Lofthouse, Sullivan	9,212
7		22	H	Preston North End		D	0-0		17,983
8		29	A	Preston North End		W	2-1	Hunt, Moir	14,000
9	Oct	6	A	Leeds United		L	1-2	Hunt	11,836
10		13	H	Leeds United		W	6-0	Howe, Lofthouse 2, Moir 2, Hunt	17,770
11		20	H	Manchester United		D	1-1	Woodward	23,829
12		27	A	Manchester United		L	1-2	Lofthouse	27,472
13	Nov	3	A	Sunderland		L	0-1		13,381
14		10	H	Sunderland		L	1-2	Barrass	18,336
15		17	H	Sheffield United		L	1-4	Hunt	19,391
16		24	A	Sheffield United		W	3-2	Hunt, Hamlett (pen), Lofthouse	19,832
17	Dec	1	A	Middlesbrough		L	0-1		16,666
18		8	H	Middlesbrough		W	2-1	Geldard, Westwood	16,812
19		15	H	Stoke City		D	2-2	Westwood, Hamlett	25,100
20		22	H	Stoke City		L	1-4	Barrass	12,974
21		25	A	Grimsby Town		W	2-0	Geldard, Moir	10,075
22		29	H	Blackpool		D	1-1	Lofthouse	28,775
23	Jan	1	H	Grimsby Town		D	0-0		20,953
24		12	H	Bury		W	1-0	Moir	25,064
25		19	A	Bury		W	2-0	Howe 2	14,451
26	Feb	2	H	Blackburn Rovers		L	1-2	Lofthouse	14,169
27		16	A	Bradford Park Ave		W	5-0	Lofthouse 3, Howe, Hamlett (pen)	20,358
28		20	A	Blackburn Rovers		W	1-0	Barrass	4,400
29		23	A	Manchester City		L	0-1		25,000
30	Mar	13	H	Bradford Park Ave		D	0-0		5,162
31		16	A	Newcastle United		W	4-3	Lofthouse, Moir 2, Westwood	30,000
32		27	H	Manchester City		W	3-1	Lofthouse, Barrass, Hamlett (pen)	17,500
33		30	H	Sheffield Wednesday		W	2-1	Barrass, Moir	20,531
34	Apr	1	A	Sheffield Wednesday		D	0-0		13,500
35		6	H	Huddersfield Town		W	2-1	Lofthouse 2	15,000
36		10	H	Newcastle United		L	0-1		9,380
37		13	H	Huddersfield Town		D	1-1	Lofthouse	11,996
38		19	A	Chesterfield		W	2-1	Hamlett (pen), Woodward	25,000
39		20	H	Barnsley		W	2-0	Hunt, Moir	10,000
40		22	H	Chesterfield		W	1-0	Hamlett (pen)	24,000
41		27	A	Barnsley		W	3-0	Barrass 2, Hunt	12,000
42		29	H	Liverpool		W	1-0	Roberts	18,000
									Appearances
									Goals

FA Cup

3.1	Jan	5	H	Blackburn Rovers		W	1-0	Moir	26,307
3.2		9	A	Blackburn Rovers		W	3-1	Westwood 2, Hunt	16,800
4.1		26	H	Liverpool		W	5-0	Lofthouse 2, Westwood 3	39,682
4.2		30	A	Liverpool		L	0-2		35,000
5.1	Feb	9	H	Middlesbrough		W	1-0	Westwood	43,453
5.2		13	A	Middlesbrough		D	1-1	Hunt	51,612
6.1	Mar	2	A	Stoke City		W	2-0	Westwood 2	50,735
6.2		9	H	Stoke City		D	0-0		65,419
SF		23	N	Charlton Atheltic		L	0-2		69,500

Ties played over two legs this season

SF at Villa Park, Birmingham

Appearances

Goals

Football appearances and goals grid (players as columns, matches as rows).

Fielding W	Threlfall JR	Hrublick H	Taylor G	Hamlet TL	Murphy D	Woodward T	Hunt GS	Lofthouse N	Barrass MW	Dove D	Moir W	Roberts JH	Sinclair TM	Tomlinson F	Sullivan A	Neal C	Hurst J	Hanson S	Hanks C	Gibfard A	Westwood RW	Atkinson JE	Rothwell E	Aspinall J	Forrest E
1	2	3	4	5	6	7	8	9	10	11															
1	2	3	4	5	6	7	8	9	10	11															
1	2	3	4	5	6	7	8	9	10	11															
1	2	3		5	6		8	9	10	4	7	11													
1	2	3			6			9	5	4	7	10	8	11											
1	2	3		5	6			9	10	4	7		8		11										
1	2	3		5	6	7	9		10	4	11			8											
1	2	3		5	6	7	8	9	10	4	11														
1	2	3		5	6	7	8	9	10	4	11														
1	2	3	4	5	6	7	8	9			10	11													
1	2	3	4	5	6	7	8	9			10	11													
	2	3		5	6	7	8	9	10		11					1	4								
1	2	3		5	6		8	9			7	10		11			4								
1	2	3		5	6	7	8	9	10		11						4								
1	2	3		5	6	7	8	9	10		11						4								
	2	3		5	6		8	9	10			11					4	1		7					
	2	3		5	6		8	9	10			7					4	1	11						
	2	3		5	6		8	9				11					4	1		7	10				
	2	3		5	6	11	8	9									4	1		7	10				
	2	3	4	5	6		8	9	11								1	1		7	10				
	2	3		5	6	11	8		9			10					4	1		7					
	2	3		5	6	11	8		9			10					4	1		7					
		3			2	6		8				11	9				4	1		7	10	5			
	2	3		5	6			9	10	8	11						4	1		7					
	2	3		4	6	11	8	9			10						1	1		7		5			
	2	3		5	6	11		9		8							4	1		7		11			
	2	3		5	6	11		9		8							4	1			10		7		
	2	3		5	6	11		9		8	10						4	1		7					
		3		2	6			9		8	11						4	1		7	10	5			
	2	3		5	6	11		9	10	4	8						4	1		7					
	2	3		5	6	11	9		10	4	8						1	1		7					
		3			6		8	9	10	4							5	1		7				2	11
	2	3			6	11		9	10	4	8						1	1	7		5				
	2	3			7			9	11	4	8						1	1			10	5	6		
		3	2				9	8	4	11							1	1	7	10	5		6		
		3	2		11		9		4	8							1	1	7	10	5		6		
	2	3		5		7	9		10	8	11						4	1					6		
		3	2		7	9		11	4	8							5	1		10			6		
		3	2			9		11	4	7	8						5	1		10			6		
		3	2			9		11	4	7	8						5	1		10			6		
14	34	42	6	38	35	26	29	34	28	29	32	6	3	2	1	1	23	27	2	19	13	7	2	1	8
				7		3	7	20	8	6	9	1			1				2	3					

Fielding W	Threlfall JR	Hrublick H	Taylor G	Hamlet TL	Murphy D	Woodward T	Hunt GS	Lofthouse N	Barrass MW	Dove D	Moir W	Roberts JH	Sinclair TM	Tomlinson F	Sullivan A	Neal C	Hurst J	Hanson S	Hanks C	Gibfard A	Westwood RW	Atkinson JE	Rothwell E	Aspinall J	Forrest E
	2	3		5	6	11	8			9							4	1		7	10				
		3		2	6	11	8			9							4	1		7	10	5			
	2	3		5	6	11			9		8						4	1		7	10				
	2	3		4	6	11		9		8							1	1		7	10	5			
	2	3		5	6	11		9		8							4	1		7	10				
	2	3		5	6		9			8	11						4	1		7	10				
	2	3		5	6	7		9		8	11						4	1			10				
	2	3		5	6	11		9		8							4	1		7	10				
	2	3		5	6	11		9		8							4	1		7	10				
	8	9		9	9	8	3	6		7	4						8	9		8	9	2			
						2	2			1								8							

Division One

Manager: W. Rowley

The BOLTON WANDERERS
Football & Athletic Co. Ltd.

2D.   OFFICIAL PROGRAMME   2D.

BOLTON WANDERERS
versus
MANCHESTER CITY
AT BURNDEN PARK, BOLTON
Wed., 30th Oct., 1946
KICK-OFF 2-45 P.M.

NEXT HOME MATCHES:

Match No.	Date		Venue	Opponents	Result		Scorers	Attendance
1	Aug	31	A	Chelsea	L	3-4	Lofthouse 2, Forrest	62,850
2	Sep	2	A	Stoke City	W	2-1	Woodward, Westwood	22,559
3		7	H	Portsmouth	W	1-0	Moir	33,597
4		11	H	Stoke City	W	3-2	Roberts, Barrass 2	26,366
5		14	H	Liverpool	L	1-3	Woodward	35,861
6		16	A	Preston North End	W	4-0	Lofthouse 2, Westwood, Roberts	32,536
7		21	A	Leeds United	L	0-4		25,739
8		28	H	Grimsby Town	L	1-2	Hamlett (pen)	30,547
9	Oct	5	A	Charlton Athletic	L	0-2		33,859
10		12	H	Middlesbrough	D	1-1	Lofthouse	32,000
11		19	A	Everton	L	1-2	Roberts	45,104
12		26	H	Blackpool	D	1-1	Westwood	35,896
13	Nov	2	A	Brentford	L	0-1		23,782
14		9	H	Blackburn Rovers	D	0-0		31,727
15		16	A	Aston Villa	D	1-1	Lofthouse	40,399
16		23	H	Derby County	W	5-1	Woodward, Moir 2, Lofthouse 2	28,127
17		30	A	Arsenal	D	2-2	Woodward, Roberts	42,522
18	Dec	7	H	Huddersfield Town	W	4-0	Moir, Lofthouse, Roberts, Gillies	21,975
19		14	A	Wolverhampton Wanderers	L	0-5		37,775
20		21	H	Sunderland	L	0-1		19,757
21		25	H	Manchester United	D	2-2	Woodward, Lofthouse	30,511
22		26	A	Manchester United	L	0-1		57,446
23		28	H	Chelsea	D	1-1	Hamlett (pen)	36,048
24	Jan	1	H	Preston North End	L	1-2	Lofthouse	47,040
25		4	A	Portsmouth	L	0-2		25,221
26		18	A	Liverpool	W	3-0	Lofthouse, Moir, Barrass	49,820
27	Feb	1	A	Grimsby Town	D	2-2	Lofthouse, Hamlett (pen)	11,467
28		3	H	Leeds United	W	2-0	Woodward, Hamlett	4,280
29		15	A	Middlesbrough	L	1-3	Hamlett (pen)	31,437
30		19	H	Charlton Athletic	L	0-1		16,489
31		22	H	Everton	L	0-2		21,080
32	Mar	1	A	Blackpool	W	1-0	Woodward	20,356
33		15	H	Blackburn Rovers	L	1-2	Moir	31,262
34		22	H	Aston Villa	W	2-1	Lofthouse, Moir	26,417
35		29	A	Derby County	W	3-1	Lofthouse, Westwood, Hamlett (pen)	18,767
36	Apr	4	H	Sheffield United	W	3-2	Hamlett, Roberts (pen), Lofthouse	34,109
37		5	A	Arsenal	L	1-3	Wrigglesworth	34,398
38		7	A	Sheffield United	L	2-4	Lofthouse, Moir	29,170
39		12	A	Huddersfield Town	L	0-1		21,639
40		19	H	Wolverhampton Wanderers	L	0-3		34,419
41		26	A	Sunderland	L	1-3	Lofthouse	19,359
42	May	10	H	Brentford	W	1-0	Hamlett (pen)	19,887

Appearances
Goals

FA Cup

R3	Jan	11	H	Stockport County	W	5-1	Lofthouse 2, Geldard, Barrass, Woodward	30,024
R4		25	H	Manchester City	D	3-3	Lofthouse, Barrass, Wrigglesworth	41,286
rep		29	A	Manchester City	L	0-1		39,355

Appearances
Goals

Player appearance and goals grid (shirt numbers by match):

	Hanson S	Threlfall J.R	Hubbick H	Howe D	Hamlet T.L	Forrest E	Woodward T	Moir W	Linthouse N	Westwood R.W	Rothwell E	Atkinson J.E	Roberts J.H	Barrass M.W	Hunt G.S	Geldard A	Aspinall J	Banks R	Gillies M.M	Hurst J	Murphy D	Wrightlesworth W	Burgess A.C	Middlebrough A
	1	2	3	4	5	6	7	8	9	10	11													
	1	2	3	4	5	6	7	8	9	10	11													
	1	2	3	4	5	6	7	8	9	10	11													
	1		3	4	2	6	7	11	9			5	8	10										
	1		3	4	2	6	7	11	9			5		10	8									
	1		3	4	2	6	7		9	11		5	8	10										
	1		3	4	2	6	7		9	11		5	8	10										
	1		3	4	2	6	7		9	11		5	8	10										
	1			4	2	6	7		9	10		5		8	11	3								
	1			4	2	6	7		9	10		5		8	11	3								
	1			4	2	6	7		9	10	11	5	8			3								
	1		3	4	2	6			9	10	11	5	8						7					
	1		3	4	2	6			11	9	10		5	8					7					
	1		3	8	2	6	11		9	10		5			7				4					
	1		3	8	2	6	7		9	10	11	5							4					
	1		3		2	6	7	10	9		11	5	8						4					
	1		3		2	6	7	10	9		11	5	8						4					
	1		3		2	6	7	10	9		11	5	8						4					
	1		3		2	6	7	10	9		11	5	8						4					
	1		3		2	6	7	10	9		11	5	8			4								
	1		3		2	6	7	10	9	11		5	8						4					
	1		3		2	6	7	10	9	11		5	8						4					
	1		3		2	10	7		9	11			8						4	5	6			
	1		3		2	6	7		9	11			8	10					4	5				
	1		3	8	2	6	7	11	9	10		5							4					
	1		3		5	6	7	8	9				10				2	4				11		
	1		3	10	5	6	7	8	9			2						4				11		
	1		3	4	5	6	7	8	9			2	10									11		
	1		3	10	5	6	11	8	9			2	7					4						
	1		3		5	6	11	8	9	10		2	7					4						
	1		3	6	5			7	8	9	10	2						4				11		
	1		3	10	5	6	7	8	9			2						4				11		
	1		3	10	5	6	7	8	9			2						4				11		
	1		3		5	6	7	8	9	10		2						4				11		
	1		3		5	6	7	8	9	10		2						4				11		
	1		3		5	6	7	8	9	10		2						4				11		
	1			8	2	6	7	9		10		5	3					4				11		
	1		3		5	6	7	8	9	10		2						4				11		
	1				2	6	7	8	9	10		5	3					4				11		
	1				2	6	11	8	9	10		5	3			7		4						
	1				2	6	11	8	9	10		5	3			7		4						
	1				2	6	11	7		10		5	3					4					8	9
Apps	42	3	34	23	42	41	40	31	40	29	11	25	32	8	3	9	2	2	27	3	1	12	1	1
Goals			8	1	7	8	18	4				6	3			1			1					

Cup matches:

	Hanson S	Threlfall J.R	Hubbick H	Howe D	Hamlet T.L	Forrest E	Woodward T	Moir W	Linthouse N	Westwood R.W	Rothwell E	Atkinson J.E	Roberts J.H	Barrass M.W	Hunt G.S	Geldard A	Aspinall J	Banks R	Gillies M.M	Hurst J	Murphy D	Wrightlesworth W	Burgess A.C	Middlebrough A
	1		3		5	6	11	8	9				10				7	2	4					
	1		3		5	6	7	8	9				10					2	4			11		
	1		3	10	5	6	7	8	9			2						4				11		
Apps	3		3	1	3	3	3	3	3			1	2			1	2	3	2					
Goals					1		3					2	1						1					

<table>

League Table

	P	W	D	L	F	A	Pts
Liverpool	42	25	7	10	84	52	57
Manchester United	42	22	12	8	95	54	56
Wolverhampton W	42	25	6	11	98	56	56
Stoke City	42	24	7	11	90	53	55
Blackpool	42	22	6	14	71	70	50
Sheffield United	42	21	7	14	89	75	49
Preston North End	42	18	11	13	76	74	47
Aston Villa	42	18	9	15	67	53	45
Sunderland	42	18	8	16	65	66	44
Everton	42	17	9	16	62	67	43
Middlesbrough	42	17	8	17	73	68	42
Portsmouth	42	16	9	17	66	60	41
Arsenal	42	16	9	17	72	70	41
Derby County	42	18	5	19	73	79	41
Chelsea	42	16	7	19	69	84	39
Grimsby Town	42	13	12	17	61	82	38
Blackburn Rovers	42	14	8	20	45	53	36
Bolton Wanderers	42	13	8	21	57	69	34
Charlton Athletic	42	11	12	19	57	71	34
Huddersfield Town	42	13	7	22	53	79	33
Brentford	42	9	7	26	45	88	25
Leeds United	42	6	6	30	45	90	18

1947-48

Division One

Manager: W. Rowley

Match No.	Date	Venue	Opponents		Result	Scorers	Attendance
1	Aug 23	H	Stoke City	L	0-1		31,189
2	25	A	Preston North End	L	0-1		33,901
3	30	A	Burnley	L	0-2		35,835
4	Sep 1	H	Preston North End	L	1-2	Woodward	31,867
5	6	H	Portsmouth	W	4-0	Burgess 2, Middlebrough, Flewin (own-goal)	26,597
6	10	A	Arsenal	L	0-2		46,969
7	13	A	Chelsea	D	1-1	Howe	41,242
8	20	A	Liverpool	D	0-0		43,920
9	27	H	Middlesbrough	L	1-3	Woodward	30,641
10	Oct 4	A	Charlton Athletic	L	1-2	Rothwell	31,284
11	11	H	Huddersfield Town	L	1-5	Lofthouse	27,590
12	18	A	Derby County	L	1-2	Lofthouse	24,134
13	25	H	Blackpool	W	1-0	Lofthouse	45,037
14	Nov 1	A	Blackburn Rovers	L	0-4		31,721
15	8	H	Sunderland	W	3-1	Moir 2, Hamlett (pen)	26,729
16	15	A	Aston Villa	L	1-3	Bradley	43,531
17	22	H	Manchester City	W	2-1	Lofthouse 2	28,883
18	29	A	Grimsby Town	W	2-0	Lofthouse 2	11,901
19	Dec 6	H	Wolverhampton Wanderers	W	3-2	Lofthouse 2, Moir	28,438
20	13	A	Everton	L	0-2		33,458
21	20	A	Stoke City	L	0-2		23,469
22	25	A	Sheffield United	L	1-2	Lofthouse	36,670
23	27	H	Sheffield United	L	2-3	Barrass 2	29,262
24	Jan 1	H	Arsenal	L	0-1		30,028
25	3	H	Burnley	D	1-1	Barrass	43,442
26	17	A	Portsmouth	L	0-2		25,347
27	24	A	Sunderland	W	2-1	Lofthouse, Bradley	24,326
28	31	H	Chelsea	W	2-1	Lofthouse, Moir	24,232
29	Feb 7	H	Liverpool	W	3-0	Howe (pen), Barrass, Lofthouse	22,895
30	14	A	Middlesbrough	L	1-4	Howe (pen)	24,234
31	21	A	Charlton Athletic	W	1-0	Lofthouse	16,792
32	28	A	Huddersfield Town	W	2-1	Moir, Barrass	14,273
33	Mar 20	H	Blackburn Rovers	W	1-0	Woodward	34,520
34	26	A	Manchester United	W	2-0	Woodward, Barrass	72,840
35	29	H	Manchester United	L	0-1		46,322
36	Apr 3	H	Aston Villa	W	1-0	Burgess	26,403
37	5	A	Blackpool	D	1-1	Lofthouse	25,050
38	10	A	Manchester City	W	2-0	Lofthouse 2	36,409
39	17	H	Grimsby Town	W	2-0	Lofthouse, Bradley	23,378
40	21	H	Derby County	L	0-3		25,938
41	24	A	Wolverhampton Wanderers	L	0-1		25,751
42	May 1	H	Everton	D	0-0		17,391
							Appearances
						1 own-goal	Goals

FA Cup

R3	Jan 10	H	Tottenham Hotspur	L	0-2		37,075
a.e.t.							Appearances

358

Appearance / Team-sheet Grid

	Hanson S.	Roberts J.H.	Crook W.	Gillies M.M.	Hamlet T.L.	Murphy D.	Woodward T.	Moir W.	Lithhouse N.	Westwood R.W.	McShane H.	Forrest E.	Jackson J.	Barrass M.W.	Lees A.	Wrigglesworth W.	Burgess A.C.	Middlebrough A.	Howe D.	Rothwell E.	Banks R.	Atkinson J.E.	Bradley J.	Ely R.	Aspinall J.	Dillon V.	Banks T.	Grimm J.
1	1	2	3	4	5	6	7	8	9	10	11																	
2	1	2	3	4	5	6	7	8	9	10	11																	
3	1	2	3	4	5		7		9		11	6	8	10														
4	1	2	3	4		6	7		9	10				8	5	11												
5	1	2	3	5		6	7			10	11	4					8	9										
6	1	2	3	5		6	7			10	11	4					8	9										
7	1	2	3	4	5	6	7			10	11	9					8											
8	1	2	3	4	5	6	7		9	10	11						8											
9	1	2	3	4	5	6	7			10	11				9	8												
10	1	2	3	5		6	7		9	10	11	4					8											
11	1	2	3	4	5		7		9	10	11	6					8											
12	1		3			6	7		9		11	4					8			2	5	10						
13	1		3			7	11	9			4						6	8	2	5	10							
14	1		3			7	11	9			4						6	8	2	5	10							
15	1	2		5		7	11	9			4						6	8	3		10							
16	1	2		5		7	11	9			4						6	8	3		10							
17	1		3	5		7	11	9			4	8					6		2		10							
18	1	2	3	5		7	11	9			4	8					6				10							
19	1	2	3	5		7	11	9			4	8					6				10							
20	1	2	3	5		7	11	9			4	8					6				10							
21		2	3	5		7	11	9			4	8					6				10	1						
22	1	2	3	5		7	11	9			4		8				6				10							
23	1	2	3	5		7	11	9			4	8					6				10							
24	1	2	3			7	11	9			4	8					6			5	10							
25	1	2	3			7		9		11	4	8					6			5	10							
26	1	2	3	5		7	11	8			4				9	6					10							
27	1	2	3	5		6	7	11	9			8			4						10							
28	1	2	3	5		6	7	11	9			8			4						10							
29	1	2	3	5		6	7	11	9			8			4						10							
30	1	2	3	5		6	7	11	9			8			4						10							
31	1	2		5			7	11	9			8			4				3		10	6						
32	1	2			5	6	7	11				8			4	9	3				10							
33	1	2	6	5			7	11	9			8			4		3				10							
34	1	2		5			7		9		11	8			4		3				10							
35	1	2		5		6	7	11	9			8	10		4		3											
36	1	2		5			7	11	9			10	8		4		3					6						
37	1	2		5			7	11	9			10	8		4		3					6						
38	1	2		5			7	11	9			8			4		3	10				6						
39	1	3		5	2		7	11			8				4						10	6	9					
40	1				2		11			6	8		5		4						10		9	3	7			
41	1	2		5			7	11				6	8		4		3	10					9					
App	41	37	28	25	21	18	40	31	34	11	12	23	6	23	2	4	4	33	8	16	5	28	1	5	3	1	1	
Gls			1		4	5	18						6							3	1	3	1				3	
FA Cup	1	2	3			7	11	9			4		8				6			5	10							
	1	1	1			1	1	1			1		1				1			1	1							

League Table

	P	W	D	L	F	A	Pts
Arsenal	42	23	13	6	81	32	59
Manchester United	42	19	14	9	81	48	52
Burnley	42	20	12	10	56	43	52
Derby County	42	19	12	11	77	57	50
Wolverhampton W	42	19	9	14	83	70	47
Aston Villa	42	19	9	14	65	57	47
Preston North End	42	20	7	15	67	68	47
Portsmouth	42	19	7	16	68	50	45
Blackpool	42	17	10	15	57	41	44
Manchester City	42	15	12	15	52	47	42
Liverpool	42	16	10	16	65	61	42
Sheffield United	42	16	10	16	65	70	42
Charlton Athletic	42	17	6	19	57	66	40
Everton	42	17	6	19	52	66	40
Stoke City	42	14	10	18	41	55	38
Middlesbrough	42	14	9	19	71	73	37
Bolton Wanderers	42	16	5	21	46	58	37
Chelsea	42	14	9	19	53	71	37
Huddersfield Town	42	12	12	18	51	60	36
Sunderland	42	13	10	19	56	67	36
Blackburn Rovers	42	11	10	21	54	72	32
Grimsby Town	42	8	6	28	45	111	22

1948-49

Division One

Manager: W. Rowley

Match No.	Date		Venue	Opponents	Result		Scorers	Attendance
1	Aug	21	A	Sunderland	L	0-2		47,854
2		25	H	Aston Villa	W	3-0	Bradley, Dillon 2	24,774
3		28	H	Wolverhampton Wanderers	L	0-5		35,878
4		30	A	Aston Villa	W	4-2	Moir 4 (1 pen)	26,890
5	Sep	4	A	Chelsea	D	2-2	Howe (pen), McShane	42,971
6		6	H	Huddersfield Town	L	1-2	Jackson	25,332
7		11	A	Liverpool	W	1-0	McShane	56,561
8		15	A	Huddersfield Town	W	2-0	Moir 2	16,046
9		18	H	Blackpool	D	2-2	Moir, Hernon	46,779
10		25	A	Derby County	L	0-1		33,972
11	Oct	2	H	Arsenal	W	1-0	Howe	45,228
12		9	H	Birmingham City	D	0-0		45,494
13		16	A	Middlesbrough	L	0-5		28,628
14		23	H	Newcastle United	L	1-5	Moir	39,071
15		30	A	Portsmouth	D	0-0		29,760
16	Nov	6	H	Manchester City	W	5-1	Moir, Barrass 4 (1 pen)	40,089
17		13	A	Charlton Athletic	W	4-1	Barrass, Moir 2, Woodward	37,047
18		20	H	Stoke City	W	2-1	Moir, Barrass	37,249
19		27	A	Burnley	L	0-3		37,291
20	Dec	4	H	Preston North End	W	5-3	Bradley 2, Moir 2, Barrass	40,140
21		11	A	Everton	L	0-1		40,407
22		18	H	Sunderland	W	4-1	Moir, Lofthouse 2, Bradley	24,309
23		25	A	Sheffield United	D	1-1	Bradley	39,676
24		27	H	Sheffield United	W	6-1	Moir 4, Lofthouse 2	42,630
25	Jan	1	A	Wolverhampton Wanderers	L	0-2		27,110
26		22	H	Liverpool	L	0-3		35,668
27	Feb	12	A	Blackpool	L	0-1		23,210
28		19	H	Derby County	W	4-0	Woodward, Moir, Lofthouse, Bradley	37,948
29		26	A	Arsenal	L	0-5		50,263
30	Mar	5	A	Birmingham City	D	0-0		20,730
31		12	H	Middlesbrough	W	4-1	Moir 3 (1 pen), Lofthouse	28,783
32		19	A	Stoke City	L	0-4		24,350
33		26	H	Burnley	L	0-1		26,593
34	Apr	2	A	Manchester City	L	0-1		27,241
35		9	H	Charlton Athletic	D	2-2	Bradley 2	20,371
36		15	H	Manchester United	L	0-1		47,157
37		16	A	Newcastle United	D	1-1	Moir	39,999
38		18	H	Manchester United	L	0-3		50,504
39		23	H	Portsmouth	L	1-2	Roberts	31,063
40		30	A	Preston North End	D	1-1	Lofthouse	33,495
41	May	4	H	Chelsea	D	1-1	Roberts	19,084
42		7	H	Everton	W	1-0	Moir	22,725
							Appearances	
							Goals	

FA Cup								
R3	Jan	8	A	Aston Villa	D	1-1	Bradley	53,459
rep		15	H	Aston Villa	D	0-0		38,706
rep2		17	A	Aston Villa	L	1-2	Lofthouse	49,709

All three games a.e.t.

							Appearances	
							Goals	

360

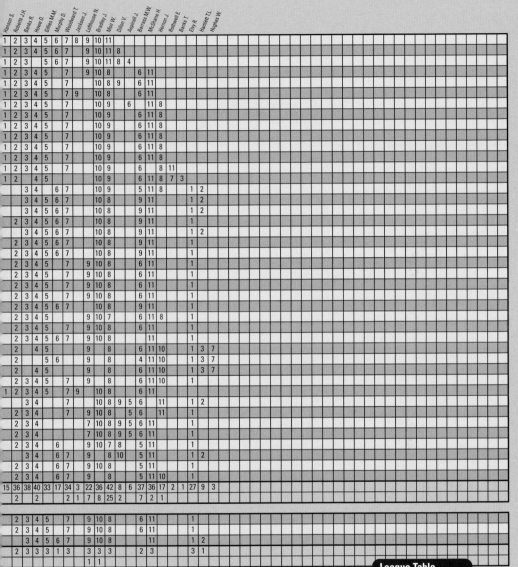

Division One

Manager: W. Rowley

Match No.	Date	Venue	Opponents	Result		Scorers	Attendance
1	Aug 20	H	Stoke City	W	4-0	Bradley 2, Lofthouse, Moir	32,222
2	24	A	Manchester United	L	0-3		42,515
3	27	A	Burnley	L	1-2	Woodward	31,581
4	31	H	Manchester United	L	1-2	McShane	39,226
5	Sep 3	H	Sunderland	W	2-1	Howe (pen), Moir	32,092
6	5	H	Derby County	D	0-0		29,558
7	10	A	Liverpool	D	1-1	Bradley	44,212
8	17	H	Arsenal	D	2-2	Roberts (pen), Barrass	33,867
9	24	A	Portsmouth	D	1-1	Lofthouse	35,188
10	Oct 1	A	Birmingham City	D	0-0		33,142
11	8	H	Huddersfield Town	L	1-2	Lofthouse	31,048
12	15	A	Everton	D	0-0		38,421
13	22	H	Middlesbrough	L	1-2	Murphy	30,095
14	29	A	Blackpool	L	0-2		23,233
15	Nov 5	H	Newcastle United	D	2-2	Howe, Lofthouse	31,728
16	12	A	Fulham	L	0-3		30,197
17	19	H	Manchester City	W	3-0	Roberts (pen), Lofthouse 2	35,376
18	26	A	Charlton Athletic	D	0-0		19,755
19	Dec 3	H	Aston Villa	D	1-1	Barrass	22,861
20	10	A	Wolverhampton Wanderers	D	1-1	Bradley	30,768
21	17	H	Stoke City	L	2-3	Moir, Bradley	17,031
22	24	H	Burnley	L	0-1		34,461
23	26	H	West Bromwich Albion	W	3-0	Moir 2, Bradley	38,764
24	27	A	West Bromwich Albion	L	1-2	Bradley	41,746
25	31	A	Sunderland	L	0-2		38,135
26	Jan 14	H	Liverpool	W	3-2	Howe, Bradley, McShane	41,507
27	21	A	Arsenal	D	1-1	Moir	47,493
28	Feb 4	H	Portsmouth	W	1-0	Lofthouse	32,441
29	18	H	Birmingham City	W	1-0	Roberts (pen)	30,383
30	25	A	Huddersfield Town	L	0-2		12,352
31	Mar 8	H	Everton	L	1-2	Lofthouse	14,807
32	11	A	Manchester City	D	1-1	Lofthouse	43,764
33	18	H	Charlton Athletic	W	3-0	Howe (pen), Moir, Langton	24,895
34	25	A	Newcastle United	L	1-3	Moir	33,752
35	Apr 1	H	Fulham	W	2-1	Moir, Lofthouse	23,658
36	7	A	Chelsea	D	1-1	McShane	52,985
37	8	A	Middlesbrough	L	0-2		21,674
38	10	H	Chelsea	W	1-0	Hernon	24,441
39	15	H	Blackpool	D	0-0		25,800
40	22	A	Aston Villa	L	0-3		29,820
41	29	H	Wolverhampton Wanderers	L	2-4	Howe (pen), McShane	16,336
42	May 6	A	Derby County	L	0-4		14,622
						Appearances	
						Goals	

FA Cup

R3	Jan 7	A	Coventry City	W	2-1	Lofthouse, Langton	29,090
R4	28	A	Leeds United	D	1-1	Lofthouse	51,488
rep	Feb 1	H	Leeds United	L	2-3	Lofthouse, McShane	29,440

R4 replay a.e.t.

						Appearances	
						Goals	

Elvy R.	Roberts J.H.	Kinsell T.H.	Howe D.	Gillies M.M.	Barrass M.W.	Woodward T.	Moir W.	Lofthouse N.	Bradley J.	McShane H.	Hanson S.	Hernon J.	Jackson J.	Banks R.	Murphy D.	Hughes W.	Banks T.	Dillon V.	Langton R.	Aspinall J.	Corfield E.	Bingley W.	Webster H.
1	2	3	4	5	6	7	8	9	10	11													
1	2	3	4	5	6	7	8	9	10	11													
1	2	3	4	5	6	7	8	9	10	11													
	2	3	4	5	6	7	8	9		11	1	10											
	2	3	4	5	6		8	9	10	11	1	7											
	2	3	4	5	6		7		10	11	1	8	9										
		3	4	5					10	11	1	8	9	2	6	7							
	2		4	5	9			7	10	11	1	8		3	6								
	2	3	4	5		7		9	10	11	1	8			6								
	2	3	4	5		7		9	10	11	1	8			6								
	2	3	4	5		7	8	9	10	11	1				6								
		3	4	5			8	9		11	1	10		2	6	7							
		3	4	5	9		8			11	1	10		2	6	7							
	2		4	5			7	9	10	11	1				6		3	8					
	2		8	5	4		7	9		11	1	10			6		3						
	2		8	5	4		7	9		11	1	10			6		3						
	2	3	8	5	4			9	10	7	1				6				11				
	2	3	8	5	4			9	10	7	1				6				11				
	2	3	8	5	4			9	10	7	1				6				11				
	2	3		5	4		8	9	10	7	1				6				11				
	2	3		5	4		8		10	7	1				6			9	11				
	2			5	4		8		10	7	1			3	6			9	11				
	2		6	5	4		8	9	10	7	1			3					11				
	2			5	4		8	9	10	7	1			3	6				11				
	2		4	5	9		8	7	10		1			3	6				11				
	2		6	5	4		8	9	10	7	1			3					11				
	2		6	5	4		8	9	10	7	1			3					11				
	2		6		4		8	9	10	7	1			3					11	5			
	2		6	5	4		8	9	10	7	1			3					11				
	2		6	5	4				10	7	1			3				9	11		8		
			6	5	4			9	10	7	1			2					11		8	3	
			6	5	4		8	9			1	10		2	3				11				7
	2		6	5	4		8	9		7	1	10		3					11				
	2		6	5	4		8	9		11	1	10		3		7							
	2		6	5	4		8	9		7	1	10		3					11				
	2		6	5	4		8	9		7	1	10		3					11				
	2		6	5	4		8	9		7	1	10			3				11				
	2		6	5	4			9	8	7	1	10		3					11				
	2		6	5	4					11	1	10		3		7		9					8
	2		6	5	4		8	9		11	1	10				7						3	
	2		3	5	4		8	9		7	1	10			6				11				
	2		6	5	4		8	9		7	1	10		3					11				
3	37	17	38	41	36	7	31	35	27	40	39	22	2	22	21	6	3	5	23	1	2	2	2
	3		5		2	1	9	10	8	4		1			1				1				

Elvy R.	Roberts J.H.	Kinsell T.H.	Howe D.	Gillies M.M.	Barrass M.W.	Woodward T.	Moir W.	Lofthouse N.	Bradley J.	McShane H.	Hanson S.	Hernon J.	Jackson J.	Banks R.	Murphy D.	Hughes W.	Banks T.	Dillon V.	Langton R.	Aspinall J.	Corfield E.	Bingley W.	Webster H.
	2		6	5	4		8	9	10	7	1			3					11				
	2		6	5	4		8	9	10	7	1			3					11				
	2		6	5	4		8	9	10	7	1			3					11				
	3		3	3	3		3	3	3	3	3			3					3				
								3		1									1				

League Table

	P	W	D	L	F	A	Pts
Portsmouth	42	22	9	11	74	38	53
Wolverhampton W	42	20	13	9	76	49	53
Sunderland	42	21	10	11	83	62	52
Manchester United	42	18	14	10	69	44	50
Newcastle United	42	19	12	11	77	55	50
Arsenal	42	19	11	12	79	55	49
Blackpool	42	17	15	10	46	35	49
Liverpool	42	17	14	11	64	54	48
Middlesbrough	42	20	7	15	59	48	47
Burnley	42	16	13	13	40	40	45
Derby County	42	17	10	15	69	61	44
Aston Villa	42	15	12	15	61	61	42
Chelsea	42	12	16	14	58	65	40
West Bromwich Albion	42	14	12	16	47	53	40
Huddersfield Town	42	14	9	19	52	73	37
Bolton Wanderers	42	10	14	18	45	59	34
Fulham	42	10	14	18	41	54	34
Everton	42	10	14	18	42	66	34
Stoke City	42	11	12	19	45	75	34
Charlton Athletic	42	13	6	23	53	65	32
Manchester City	42	8	13	21	36	68	29
Birmingham City	42	7	14	21	31	67	28

Division One

Manager: W. Rowley until 17 October 1950, then W. Ridding from 7 February 1951

Did you know that?

A Willie Moir goal earned the Wanderers a 1–0 win at Aston Villa in September 1950, ending a club record run of 36 away League games without a win stretching back to November 1948.

Match No.	Date	Venue	Opponents	Result		Scorers	Attendance
1	Aug 19	A	Charlton Athletic	L	3-4	Lofthouse 3	30,487
2	23	H	Tottenham Hotspur	L	1-4	Langton	21,745
3	26	H	Manchester United	W	1-0	Lofthouse	40,759
4	28	A	Tottenham Hotspur	L	2-4	Moir 2	44,246
5	Sep 2	A	Wolverhampton Wanderers	L	1-7	Moir	46,794
6	4	H	Chelsea	W	1-0	Hughes	25,457
7	9	H	Sunderland	L	1-2	Webster	30,745
8	16	A	Aston Villa	W	1-0	Moir	32,817
9	23	H	Derby County	W	3-0	Howe (pen), Lofthouse, Webster	36,745
10	30	A	Liverpool	D	3-3	Moir, Lofthouse, Webster	44,534
11	Oct 7	H	Portsmouth	W	4-0	Lofthouse 2, Webster 2	36,995
12	14	A	Everton	D	1-1	Moir	53,421
13	21	H	Newcastle United	L	0-2		49,213
14	28	A	Huddersfield Town	W	4-0	Howe (pen), Moir, Lofthouse, Webster	30,989
15	Nov 4	H	Stoke City	D	1-1	Webster	34,244
16	11	A	West Bromwich Albion	W	1-0	Kennedy (own-goal)	28,816
17	18	H	Middlesbrough	L	0-2		37,296
18	25	A	Sheffield Wednesday	W	4-3	Lofthouse 2, Webster 2	37,053
19	Dec 2	H	Arsenal	W	3-0	Moir, Langton 2	43,484
20	9	A	Burnley	L	0-2		31,124
21	16	H	Charlton Athletic	W	3-0	Moir, Webster 2	19,207
22	23	A	Manchester United	W	3-2	Lofthouse 2, Webster	37,235
23	25	A	Fulham	W	1-0	Lofthouse	21,712
24	26	H	Fulham	L	0-1		43,116
25	Jan 13	A	Sunderland	W	2-1	Moir, Webster	47,197
26	20	H	Aston Villa	W	1-0	Moss (own-goal)	29,233
27	Feb 3	A	Derby County	D	2-2	Lofthouse, Webster	19,879
28	10	H	Burnley	D	1-1	Howe (pen)	35,540
29	17	H	Liverpool	W	2-1	Howe, Lofthouse	34,807
30	24	A	Portsmouth	L	1-2	Lofthouse	27,222
31	Mar 3	H	Everton	W	2-0	Codd, Langton	36,752
32	17	H	Huddersfield Town	W	4-0	Lofthouse, Langton (pen), Webster, Wheeler	29,796
33	23	A	Blackpool	L	0-2		33,627
34	24	A	Stoke City	L	1-2	Lofthouse	20,682
35	26	H	Blackpool	L	1-2	Langton	42,265
36	31	H	West Bromwich Albion	L	0-2		21,860
37	Apr 7	A	Middlesbrough	D	1-1	Moir	24,243
38	14	H	Sheffield Wednesday	L	0-1		19,956
39	18	A	Newcastle United	W	1-0	Lofthouse	39,099
40	21	A	Arsenal	D	1-1	Lofthouse	42,040
41	28	H	Wolverhampton Wanderers	W	2-1	Moir, Codd	26,775
42	May 5	A	Chelsea	L	0-4		38,928

						Appearances
					2 own-goals	Goals

FA Cup

R3	Jan 6	H	York City	W	2-0	Lofthouse, Langton	26,652
R4	27	A	Newcastle United	L	2-3	Moir 2	68,659

						Appearances
						Goals

Appearances & Goals

Hanson S.	Roberts J.H.	Banks R.	Barrass M.W.	Gillis M.M.	Howe D.	McShane H.	Mion W.	Lofthouse N.	Bradley J.	Langton R.	Bell E.	Banks T.	Herron J.	Murphy D.	Hughes W.	Dillon V.	Webster H.	Ball J.	Kennedy G.M.	Edwards G.B.	Beards A.	Mathiewsoon R.	Gold R.W.	Wheeler J.E.	Corfield E.
1	2	3	4	5	6	7	8	9	10	11															
1	2	3	4	5	6	7	8	9		11	10														
1		2	4	5	6	7	8	9		11		3	10												
1		2	4	5	6	7	8	9		11		3	10												
1		2	4	5	6	7	8	9		11		3	10												
1		3	4	5	2		8			11				6	7	9	10								
1		3	4	5	2		8	9		11				6	7		10								
1		3	5		4		8	9		11				6	7		10		2						
1			5		4		8	9		11					6		7	10	2	3					
1			5		4		8	9		11					6		7	10	2	3					
1			5		4		8	9							6		7	10	2	3	11				
1			5		4		8	9		11					6		7	10	2	3					
1					4		8	9		11					6		7	10	2	3		5			
1			5		4		8	9		11					6		7	10	2	3					
1			5		4		8	9		11					6		7	10	2	3					
1			5		4		8	9		11					6		7	10	2	3					
1			5		4		8			11					6		7	10	2	3			9		
1			5		4		8	9		11					6		7	10	2	3					
1			5		4		8	9		11					6		7	10	2	3					
1			5		4		8	9		11					6		7	10	2	3					
1			5		4		8	9		11					6		7	10	2	3					
1			5		4		8			11					6		7	10	2	3			9		
1			5		4		8	9		11					6		7	10	2	3					
1		3	5		4		8	9		11					6		7	10	2						
1		3	5		4		8	9					11		6		7	10	2						
1		3	5		4		8	9		11					6		7	10	2						
1			5		4		8			11					3		7	10	2		6			8	
1			5		4		8	9		11					3		7	10	2		6			8	
1			5		3		8			11							7	10	2		6			9	4
1			5		3		8	9		11							7	10	2		6				4
1			5		3		8	9		11								10	2		6		7	4	
1			5		3		8	9		11								10	2		6		7	4	
1			5		4	10	9			11					3		7		2		6			8	
1			5		4	10	9			11					3		7		2		6			8	
1			5		4	10	9			11					3		7		2		6			8	
1			5		4	10	9			11					3		7		2		6			8	
1			5		3		8	9		11							10	2		6		7	4	
1			5		3		8	9		11							10	2		6		7	4	
1			5		3	10	9			11								2		6		7	4	8
1			5		3	10	9			11								2		6		7	4	8
42	**2**	**11**	**38**	**14**	**42**	**5**	**41**	**38**	**1**	**40**	**1**	**3**	**4**	**9**	**31**	**1**	**31**	**35**	**17**	**30**	**1**	**1**	**9**	**13**	**2**
				4				12		21			6		1			15					2	1	

Hanson S.	Roberts J.H.	Banks R.	Barrass M.W.	Gillis M.M.	Howe D.	McShane H.	Mion W.	Lofthouse N.	Bradley J.	Langton R.	Bell E.	Banks T.	Herron J.	Murphy D.	Hughes W.	Dillon V.	Webster H.	Ball J.	Kennedy G.M.	Edwards G.B.	Beards A.	Mathiewsoon R.	Gold R.W.	Wheeler J.E.	Corfield E.
1			5		4		8	9		11					6		7	10	2	3					
1		3	5		4		8	9		11					6		7	10	2						
2		1	2		2		2	2		2					2		2	2	2	1					
								2		1								1							

League Table

	P	W	D	L	F	A	Pts
Tottenham Hotspur	42	25	10	7	82	44	60
Manchester United	42	24	8	10	74	40	56
Blackpool	42	20	10	12	79	53	50
Newcastle United	42	18	13	11	62	53	49
Arsenal	42	19	9	14	73	56	47
Middlesbrough	42	18	11	13	76	65	47
Portsmouth	42	16	15	11	71	68	47
Bolton Wanderers	42	19	7	16	64	61	45
Liverpool	42	16	11	15	53	59	43
Burnley	42	14	14	14	48	43	42
Derby County	42	16	8	18	81	75	40
Sunderland	42	12	16	14	63	73	40
Stoke City	42	13	14	15	50	59	40
Wolverhampton W	42	15	8	19	74	61	38
Aston Villa	42	12	13	17	66	68	37
West Bromwich Albion	42	13	11	18	53	61	37
Charlton Athletic	42	14	9	19	63	80	37
Fulham	42	13	11	18	52	68	37
Huddersfield Town	42	15	6	21	64	92	36
Chelsea	42	12	8	22	53	65	32
Sheffield Wednesday	42	12	8	22	64	83	32
Everton	42	12	8	22	48	86	32

Division One

Manager: W. Ridding

Match No.	Date	Venue	Opponents	Result		Scorers	Attendance
1	Aug 18	H	Aston Villa	W	5-2	Moir, Lofthouse, Webster 2, Langton (pen)	30,253
2	22	H	Newcastle United	D	0-0		39,942
3	25	A	Stoke City	W	2-1	Lofthouse, Webster	22,442
4	29	A	Newcastle United	W	1-0	Moir	49,587
5	Sep 1	H	Manchester United	W	1-0	Lofthouse	55,477
6	3	H	Middlesbrough	W	3-1	Moir, Webster, Codd	33,811
7	8	A	Tottenham Hotspur	L	1-2	Langton (pen)	61,838
8	15	H	Preston North End	D	1-1	Webster	46,523
9	22	A	Burnley	W	3-1	Wheeler, Moir, Webster	37,196
10	29	H	Charlton Athletic	W	2-1	Moir, Webster	37,719
11	Oct 6	H	Sunderland	D	1-1	Lofthouse	43,887
12	13	A	Wolverhampton Wanderers	L	1-5	Lofthouse	38,413
13	20	H	Huddersfield Town	W	2-1	Langton (pen), Codd	33,670
14	27	A	Chelsea	W	3-1	Langton 2, Codd	45,287
15	Nov 3	H	Portsmouth	L	0-3		26,299
16	10	A	Liverpool	D	1-1	Wheeler	49,537
17	17	H	Blackpool	W	1-0	Garrett (own-goal)	38,990
18	24	A	Arsenal	L	2-4	Moir, Webster	50,790
19	Dec 1	H	Manchester City	W	2-1	Lofthouse, Howe	43,405
20	8	A	Derby County	L	2-5	Lofthouse, Howe	23,838
21	15	A	Aston Villa	D	1-1	Howe	28,907
22	22	H	Stoke City	D	1-1	Moir	19,235
23	25	H	West Bromwich Albion	W	3-2	Moir 2 (1 pen), Lofthouse	32,562
24	26	A	West Bromwich Albion	L	2-3	Moir, Lofthouse	37,698
25	29	A	Manchester United	L	0-1		55,073
26	Jan 5	H	Tottenham Hotspur	D	1-1	Langton (pen)	46,354
27	19	A	Preston North End	D	2-2	Lofthouse, Langton	38,646
28	26	H	Burnley	L	1-4	Hassall	38,149
29	Feb 2	H	Derby County	L	1-2	Holden	26,596
30	9	A	Charlton Athletic	L	0-1		23,480
31	16	A	Sunderland	W	2-0	Moir, Holden	43,397
32	Mar 1	H	Wolverhampton Wanderers	D	2-2	Moir, Lofthouse	33,294
33	8	A	Huddersfield Town	W	2-0	Moir, Lofthouse	24,045
34	15	H	Chelsea	W	3-0	Lofthouse, Holden, Hassall	31,448
35	22	A	Portsmouth	L	0-3		31,135
36	29	H	Liverpool	D	1-1	Wheeler	17,459
37	Apr 5	A	Blackpool	L	0-1		17,374
38	11	A	Fulham	W	2-1	Wheeler, Moir	38,304
39	12	H	Arsenal	W	2-1	Moir, Lofthouse	47,940
40	14	H	Fulham	W	2-1	Lofthouse, Holden	29,461
41	19	A	Manchester City	W	3-0	Moir, Lofthouse, Hassall	28,388
42	23	A	Middlesbrough	L	0-2		23,591
							Appearances
						1 own-goal	Goals

FA Cup

R3	Jan 3	A	West Bromwich Albion	L	0-4		37,900
							Appearances

Player appearance grid (shirt numbers by match). Column headers read vertically:

Hanson S.	Ball J.	Higgins G.	Wheeler J.E.	Barrass M.W.	Edwards G.B.	Hughes W.	Moir W.	Lofthouse N.	Webster H.	Langton R.	Gold R.W.	Parry R.A.	Gillies M.M.	Corfield E.	Howe D.	Holden A.D.	Banks R.	Hassall H.W.	Greaves K.J.	Bell E.
1	2	3	4	5	6	7	8	9	10	11										
1	2	3	4	5	6	7	8		10	11	9									
1	2	3	4	5	6	7	8	9	10	11										
1	2	3	4	5	6		8	9	10	11	7									
1	2	3	4	5	6		8	9	10	11	7									
1	2	3	4	5	6		8	9	10	11	7									
1	2	3	4	5	6		8	9	10	11	7									
1	2	3	4	5	6		8	9	10	11	7									
1	2	3	4	5	6		8	9	10	11	7									
1	2	3	4	5	6		8	9	10	11	7									
1	2	3	4	5	6		8	9	10	11	7									
1	2	3	4	5	6		8	9		11	7	10								
1	2	3	4		6		8			11	9	10	5	7						
1	2	3	4	5	6		8	9	10		7				11					
1	2	3	4	5	6		8	9	10		7				11					
1	2	3	4	5	6		8	9								10	7			
1	2	3	4	5	6		8	9								10	7			
1	2	3	4	5	6		8	9								10	7			
1	2	3	4	5	6		8	9								10	7			
1	2	3	4	5	6		8	9								10	7			
1	2	3	4		6		8	9	10	11		5				7				
1	2	3	4		6		8	9	10	11		5			10	7				
1	2		4	5	6		8	9		11						7		10		4
1	2	3	8	5		9				7					6	11		10	1	4
		3		5	6		8		9	11					7			10	1	4
	2	3	4	5	6		8	9		11					7			10		1
1	2	3	8	5				9			7				6	11		10		4
1	2	3	8	5				9			7				6	11		10		4
1	2		4	5	6		8	9		11						7		10		4
1	2	3	4	5	6		8	9		11						7		10		
1	2	3	4	5	6		8	9		11						7		10		
1	2	3	4	5	6		8	9		11						7		10		
1		3	4	5	6		8	9		11			2			7		10		
1		3	4	5	6		8		9	11			2			7		10		
1	2	3	9	5	6		8			11						7		10		4
1	2	3	4	5	6		8	9		11						7		10		
1	2	3	4	5	6		8	9			11					7		10		
1	2	3	4	5	6		8	9								7		10		
1	2	3	4	5	6		8	9	11							7		10		
1	2	3	4	5	6		8	9	11							7		10		
40	**39**	**40**	**40**	**37**	**40**	**3**	**39**	**38**	**21**	**35**	**18**	**2**	**5**	**2**	**10**	**25**	**4**	**17**	**2**	**5**
			4				16	18	8	5	3				3	4		3		

Lower grid (cup):

Hanson S.	Ball J.	Higgins G.	Wheeler J.E.	Barrass M.W.	Edwards G.B.	Hughes W.	Moir W.	Lofthouse N.	Webster H.	Langton R.	Gold R.W.	Parry R.A.	Gillies M.M.	Corfield E.	Howe D.	Holden A.D.	Banks R.	Hassall H.W.	Greaves K.J.	Bell E.
1	2	3	4	5	6		8	9	10	11						7				
1	1	1	1	1	1		1	1	1	1						1				

League Table

	P	W	D	L	F	A	Pts
Manchester United	42	23	11	8	95	52	57
Tottenham Hotspur	42	22	9	11	76	51	53
Arsenal	42	21	11	10	80	61	53
Portsmouth	42	20	8	14	68	58	48
Bolton Wanderers	42	19	10	13	65	61	48
Aston Villa	42	19	9	14	79	70	47
Preston North End	42	17	12	13	74	54	46
Newcastle United	42	18	9	15	98	73	45
Blackpool	42	18	9	15	64	64	45
Charlton Athletic	42	17	10	15	68	63	44
Liverpool	42	12	19	11	57	61	43
Sunderland	42	15	12	15	70	61	42
West Bromwich Albion	42	14	13	15	74	77	41
Burnley	42	15	10	17	56	63	40
Manchester City	42	13	13	16	58	61	39
Wolverhampton W	42	12	14	16	73	73	38
Derby County	42	15	7	20	63	80	37
Middlesbrough	42	15	6	21	64	88	36
Chelsea	42	14	8	20	52	72	36
Stoke City	42	12	7	23	49	88	31
Huddersfield Town	42	10	8	24	49	82	28
Fulham	42	8	11	23	58	77	27

Division One

Manager: W. Ridding

Match No.	Date		Venue	Opponents	Result		Scorers	Attendance
1	Aug	23	H	Derby County	W	2-0	Holden, Langton	35,551
2		25	A	Wolverhampton Wanderers	L	1-3	Moir	32,449
3		30	A	Blackpool	L	0-3		31,317
4	Sep	1	H	Wolverhampton Wanderers	W	2-1	Moir, Hassall	28,057
5		6	H	Chelsea	D	1-1	Lofthouse	29,877
6		10	A	Charlton Athletic	L	0-2		14,900
7		13	A	Manchester United	L	0-1		42,370
8		20	H	Portsmouth	L	0-5		29,590
9		27	A	Middlesbrough	W	2-1	Moir, Hassall	26,679
10	Oct	4	A	Aston Villa	D	1-1	Beards	32,242
11		11	H	Liverpool	D	2-2	Lofthouse 2	38,450
12		18	A	Manchester City	W	2-1	Lofthouse, Langton	42,369
13		25	H	Stoke City	W	2-1	Moir 2	28,295
14	Nov	1	A	Preston North End	D	2-2	Hassall, Langton (pen)	37,848
15		8	H	Burnley	L	1-2	Lofthouse	37,603
16		15	A	Tottenham Hotspur	D	1-1	Lofthouse	31,442
17		22	H	Sheffield Wednesday	D	1-1	Moir	34,435
18	Dec	6	H	Newcastle United	W	4-2	Moir, Lofthouse, Hassall 2	28,577
19		13	A	West Bromwich Albion	W	1-0	Beards	16,148
20		20	A	Derby County	L	3-4	Moir, Lofthouse, Hassall	12,884
21		25	H	Arsenal	L	4-6	Moir 2, Lofthouse 2	45,432
22	Jan	1	H	Charlton Athletic	L	1-2	Holden	32,614
23		3	H	Blackpool	W	4-0	Wheeler 3, Moir	36,572
24		17	A	Chelsea	L	0-1		36,572
25		24	H	Manchester United	W	2-1	Moir 2	46,818
26	Feb	7	A	Portsmouth	L	1-3	Parry	25,240
27		18	H	Middlesbrough	W	5-3	Lofthouse 3, Hassall, Hughes	15,041
28		21	H	Aston Villa	D	0-0		34,446
29	Mar	4	A	Liverpool	D	0-0		24,999
30		7	H	Manchester City	W	1-0	Lofthouse	39,585
31		11	A	Cardiff City	L	0-1		31,099
32		14	A	Stoke City	W	2-1	Lofthouse, Webster	28,070
33		25	H	Preston North End	L	0-3		22,173
34		28	A	Burnley	W	1-0	Moir	20,392
35	Apr	3	A	Sunderland	W	5-0	Lofthouse 3 (1 pen), Langton, Neill	34,862
36		4	H	Tottenham Hotspur	L	2-3	Moir 2	40,185
37		6	A	Sunderland	L	0-2		32,227
38		11	A	Sheffield Wednesday	D	1-1	Lofthouse	39,893
39		15	A	Arsenal	L	1-4	Moir	35,381
40		18	H	Cardiff City	L	0-1		18,037
41		22	H	West Bromwich Albion	L	0-1		17,189
42		25	A	Newcastle United	W	3-2	Lofthouse 3 (1 pen)	34,824
							Appearances	
							Goals	

FA Cup

	Date		Venue	Opponents	Result		Scorers	Attendance
R3	Jan	14	H	Fulham	W	3-1	Holden, Moir, Lofthouse	32,235
R4		31	H	Notts County	D	1-1	Lofthouse	40,048
rep	Feb	5	A	Notts County	D	2-2	Moir 2	33,668
rep2		9	N	Notts County	W	1-0	Lofthouse	23,171
R5		14	A	Luton Town	W	1-0	Lofthouse	23,735
R6		28	A	Gateshead	W	1-0	Lofthouse	17,692
SF	Mar	21	N	Everton	W	4-3	Lofthouse 2, Moir, Holden	75,213
F	May	2	N	Blackpool	L	3-4	Moir, Bell, Lofthouse	100,000

R4 replay a.e.t., R4 replay 2 at Hillsborough, Sheffield.
SF at Maine Road, Machester. Final at Wembley Stadium.

Appearances
Goals

Hanson S.	Ball J.	Higgins G.	Wheeler J.E.	Barrass M.W.	Edwards G.B.	Holden A.D.	Moir W.	Lofthouse N.	Hassall H.W.	Langton R.	Webster H.	Banks R.	Bell E.	Parry R.A.	Neill T.K.	Beards A.	Codd R.W.	Hartle L.R.	Matthewson R.	Banks T.	Hughes W.	Pilling V.J.	Higgins J.O.	McIlwaine M.	Gubbins R.G.
1	2	3	4	5	6	7	8	9	10	11															
1	2	3	4	5	6	7	8	9	10	11															
1	2	3	4	5	6	7	8	9	11		10														
1	2	3	4	5	6	7	8	9	10		11														
1	2	3	4	5	6	7	8	9	10		11														
1	2	3	4	5	6	7	8	9	10			11													
1	2	3	4	5	6	7	10	9					8	11											
1	2	3	4	5	6	7	11	9					8	10											
1	2	3	4	5		7	8	9	10						6	11									
1	2	3	4	5		7	8		10						6	11	9								
1	2	3	4	5		7	8	9	10						6	11									
1	2	3	4	5		7	8	9	10	11					6										
1	2	3	4	5		7	8	9	10	11					6										
1	2	3	4	5		7	8	9	10	11					6										
1	2	3	4	5		7	8	9	10	11					6										
1	2	3	4	5		7	8	9	10						6	11									
1	2	3	4	5		7	8	9	10						6	11									
1	2	3	4	5		7	8	9	10						6	11									
1	2	3	4	5		7	8	9	10						6	11									
1	2	3	4	5		7	8	9	10						6	11									
1	2	3	4	5		7	8	9		11	10				6										
1		3	4	5	6	7	8	9			10					11		2							
1		3	9	4		7	8							10	6	11		2	5						
1		3	4	5		7	8	9		11			6	10				2							
1		3	4	5		7	8	9	10	11			6					2							
1	2		4				8	9	10					11	6			5		3	7				
1		3	4	5			8	9	10	11			6					2			7				
1		3	4	5			8	9	10				6	11				2			7				
1			4	5				9	10				6	8			7	2		3		11			
1			4	5			8	9	10		11		6					2		3		7			
1				5				9	10	11			6	8	4			2		3		7			
1		3		5				9		11	8		6	10	4			2				7			
1			9	5		7	8		10	11		3	6		4			2							
1			4			7	9		10	11		3	6	8				2					5		
1				5		7	8	9	10	11		3	6		4			2							
1				5		7	8	9	10	11		3	6		4			2							
1				5	6			9	10	11		3		8	4			2				7			
1				5	6	7	8	9	10			3		11				2						4	
1	2				6	7	9			11		3		10	4								5	8	
1	2				6		9		10			3		8	4				5		7	11			
1	2		4	5	6	7	8	9	10	11		3													
1	2		4	5		7		9		11		3	6	8											10
42	26	28	34	38	14	33	37	36	33	20	7	11	15	15	23	10	2	17	2	4	4	6	2	2	1
			3			2	17	22	7	4	1			1	1	2					1				

1		3	4	5		7	8	9		11			6	10				2							
1			4	5		7	8	9	10	11		3	6					2							
1			4	5		7	8	9	10	11		3	6					2							
1			4	5		7	8	9	10	11		3	6					2							
1		3	4	5		7	8	9	10	11			6					2							
1		3	4	5		7	8	9	10	11			6					2							
1		3	4	5		7	8	9	10	11			6					2							
1	2		4	5		7	8	9	10	11		3	6												
8	1	4	8	8		8	8	8	7	8		4	8	1				7							
						2	5	8					1												

League Table

	P	W	D	L	F	A	Pts
Arsenal	42	21	12	9	97	64	54
Preston North End	42	21	12	9	85	60	54
Wolverhampton W	42	19	13	10	86	63	51
West Bromwich Albion	42	21	8	13	66	60	50
Charlton Athletic	42	19	11	12	77	63	49
Burnley	42	18	12	12	67	52	48
Blackpool	42	19	9	14	71	70	47
Manchester United	42	18	10	14	69	72	46
Sunderland	42	15	13	14	68	82	43
Tottenham Hotspur	42	15	11	16	78	69	41
Aston Villa	42	14	13	15	63	61	41
Cardiff City	42	14	12	16	54	46	40
Middlesbrough	42	14	11	17	70	77	39
Bolton Wanderers	42	15	9	18	61	69	39
Portsmouth	42	14	10	18	74	83	38
Newcastle United	42	14	9	19	59	70	37
Liverpool	42	14	8	20	61	82	36
Sheffield Wednesday	42	12	11	19	62	72	35
Chelsea	42	12	11	19	56	66	35
Manchester City	42	14	7	21	72	87	35
Stoke City	42	12	10	20	53	66	34
Derby County	42	11	10	21	59	74	32

Division One

Manager: W. Ridding

Match No.	Date		Venue	Opponents	Result		Scorers	Attendance
1	Aug	22	A	West Bromwich Albion	D	1-1	Moir	28,975
2		26	H	Middlesbrough	W	3-2	Hassall 2 (1 pen), Webster	29,502
3		29	H	Liverpool	W	2-0	Moir, Webster	27,258
4	Sep	2	A	Middlesbrough	L	2-3	Wheeler, Hassall	25,458
5		5	A	Newcastle United	W	3-2	Hassall (pen), Webster 2	61,321
6		9	H	Sheffield Wednesday	W	2-1	Moir, Hassall (pen)	31,143
7		12	H	Manchester United	D	0-0		48,591
8		16	A	Sheffield Wednesday	L	1-2	Hassall	26,025
9		19	A	Cardiff City	D	1-1	Hassall	35,788
10		26	A	Preston North End	L	1-3	Moir	39,553
11	Oct	3	H	Tottenham Hotspur	W	2-0	Hassall, Lofthouse	39,842
12		10	H	Manchester City	W	3-2	Moir, Allcock 2	34,443
13		17	A	Sunderland	W	2-1	Wheeler, Lofthouse	45,358
14		24	H	Wolverhampton Wanderers	D	1-1	Moir	40,027
15		31	A	Aston Villa	D	2-2	Moir, Lofthouse	25,325
16	Nov	7	H	Portsmouth	W	6-1	Holden, Lofthouse 2, Hassall 3 (1 pen)	22,441
17		14	A	Arsenal	L	3-4	Moir, Hassall (pen), Wheeler	52,319
18		21	H	Chelsea	D	2-2	Wheeler, Lofthouse	30,635
19		28	A	Blackpool	D	0-0		29,464
20	Dec	5	H	Huddersfield Town	D	0-0		36,077
21		12	A	Sheffield United	L	0-3		27,769
22		19	H	West Bromwich Albion	W	2-1	Wheeler, Lofthouse	32,246
23		25	A	Charlton Athletic	L	0-1		19,226
24		26	H	Charlton Athletic	W	3-1	Wheeler, Moir, Lofthouse	36,065
25	Jan	1	H	Sheffield United	W	2-1	Lofthouse, Caldwell (own-goal)	37,484
26		2	A	Liverpool	W	2-1	Moir, Stevens	44,383
27		16	H	Newcastle United	D	2-2	Moir, Lofthouse	29,476
28		23	A	Manchester United	W	5-1	Moir, Parry 2, Lofthouse 2	48,505
29	Feb	6	H	Cardiff City	W	3-0	Moir, Stevens, Lofthouse	30,777
30		13	H	Preston North End	L	0-2		44,639
31		27	A	Manchester City	L	0-3		39,340
32	Mar	3	A	Tottenham Hotspur	L	2-3	Moir, Lofthouse	16,720
33		6	H	Sunderland	W	3-1	Moir, Parry, Stevens	36,379
34		20	H	Aston Villa	W	3-0	Hassall 2, Stevens	26,292
35		24	A	Wolverhampton Wanderers	D	1-1	Lofthouse	19,617
36		27	H	Portsmouth	L	2-3	Moir, Parry	22,784
37	Apr	3	H	Arsenal	W	3-1	Moir, Hassall (pen), Lofthouse	30,525
38		10	A	Chelsea	L	0-2		49,433
39		16	H	Burnley	D	0-0		34,394
40		17	H	Blackpool	W	3-2	Moir, Hassall, Lofthouse	40,291
41		19	A	Burnley	D	1-1	Parry	25,857
42		24	A	Huddersfield Town	L	1-2	Parry	25,635
								Appearances
							1 own-goal	Goals

FA Cup

R3	Jan	9	H	Liverpool	W	1-0	Moir	45,340
R4		30	A	Headington United	W	4-2	Moir, Parry, Lofthouse, Stevens	16,600
R5	Feb	20	H	Portsmouth	D	0-0		53,883
rep		24	A	Portsmouth	W	2-1	Moir 2	45,806
R6	Mar	13	A	Sheffield Wednesday	D	1-1	Moir	65,000
rep		17	H	Sheffield Wednesday	L	0-2		52,568
								Appearances
								Goals

Hanson S.	Ball J.	Higgins G.	Wheeler J.E.	Barrass M.W.	Bell E.	Holden A.D.	Moir W.	Codd R.W.	Hassall H.W.	Parry R.A.	Banks T.	Webster H.	Lofthouse N.	Stevens D.	Allcock T.	Neill T.K.	Higgins J.O.	Beards A.	Grieves K.J.	Hennin D.	Edwards G.B.
1	2	3	4	5	6	7	8	9	10	11											
1	2		4	5	6	7	8		10	11	3	9									
1	2		4	5	6	7	8		10	11	3	9									
1	2		4	5	6	7	8		10	11	3	9									
1	2		4	5	6	7	8		10	11	3	9									
1	2		4	5	6	7	8		10	11	3	9									
1	2		4	5	6	7	8		10	11	3		9								
1	2		4	5	6	7	8		10	11	3		9								
1	2		4	5	6	7	8		10	11	3		9								
1	2		4	5	6	7	8			11	3		9	10							
1	2		4	5	6	7	8		10	11	3		9								
1	2		4	5	6	7	10			11	3	9			8						
1	2		4	5	6	7	10			11	3		9		8						
1	2		4	5	6	7	8		10	11	3		9								
1	2		4	5	6	7	8		10	11	3		9								
1	2			5	6	7	8		10	11	3		9			4					
1	2		9	5	6	7	8		10	11	3					4					
1	2		4	5		7	8		10	11	3		9			6					
1	2		4	5	6	7	8		10	11	3		9								
1	2		4		6	7	8		10	11	3		9				5				
1	2			5	6	7	10			11	3		9		8	4					
1	2		4	5	6	7	8			10	3		9					11			
1	2		4	5	6	7	8			10	3		9					11			
1	2		4	5	6	7	8			10	3		9					11			
1	2		4	5	6	7	8			11	3		9	10							
1	2		9	5	6	7	8			11	3			10		4					
1	2		4	5	6	7	8			11	3		9	10							
1	2		4	5	6	7	8			11	3		9	10							
1	2		4	5	6	7	8			11	3		9	10							
	2		4	5	6	7	8	9	10	11	3								1		
	2				6	7	8			11	3		9	10		4	5		1		
1	2					7	8		10	11	3		9				5			4	6
1	2				6	7	8			11	3		9	10			5			4	
1	2			5	6	7			10	11			9	8						4	3
1	2			5	6	7	8		10	11	3		9							4	
1	2			5	6	7	8		10	11	3		9							4	
1	2			5	6	7	8		10	11	3		9							4	
1	2			5	6	7	8		10	11	3		9							4	
1	2			5	6	7	8		10	11	3		9							4	
1	2			5	6	7	8		10		3		9	11						4	
1	2			5	6	7			8	11	3		9	10						4	
1	2			5	6	7			8	11	3		9	10						4	
40	42	1	28	38	40	42	39	2	28	41	40	6	32	12	3	6	4	3	2	11	2
			6			1	18		16	6		4	17	4	2						

1	2		4	5	6	7	8			11	3		9	10							
1	2		4	5	6	7	8			11	3		9	10							
1	2		4	5	6	7	8			11	3		9	10							
1	2		4	5	6	7	8			11	3		9	10							
1	2			5	6	7	8			11	3		9	10						4	
1	2			5	6	7	8			11	3		9	10						4	
6	6		4	6	6	6	6			6	6		6	6						2	
							5			1			1	1							

League Table

	P	W	D	L	F	A	Pts
Wolverhampton W	42	25	7	10	96	56	57
West Bromwich Albion	42	22	9	11	86	63	53
Huddersfield Town	42	20	11	11	78	61	51
Manchester United	42	18	12	12	73	58	48
Bolton Wanderers	42	18	12	12	75	60	48
Blackpool	42	19	10	13	80	69	48
Burnley	42	21	4	17	78	67	46
Chelsea	42	16	12	14	74	68	44
Charlton Athletic	42	19	6	17	75	77	44
Cardiff City	42	18	8	16	51	71	44
Preston North End	42	19	5	18	87	58	43
Arsenal	42	15	13	14	75	73	43
Aston Villa	42	16	9	17	70	68	41
Portsmouth	42	14	11	17	81	89	39
Newcastle United	42	14	10	18	72	77	38
Tottenham Hotspur	42	16	5	21	65	76	37
Manchester City	42	14	9	19	62	77	37
Sunderland	42	14	8	20	81	89	36
Sheffield Wednesday	42	15	6	21	70	91	36
Sheffield United	42	11	11	20	69	90	33
Middlesbrough	42	10	10	22	60	91	30
Liverpool	42	9	10	23	68	97	28

Division One

Manager: W. Ridding

Match No.	Date	Venue	Opponents	Result		Scorers	Attendance
1	Aug 21	H	Charlton Athletic	W	3-2	Lofthouse, Hassall, Webster	34,526
2	23	A	Blackpool	W	3-2	Lofthouse, Webster 2	33,915
3	28	A	Chelsea	L	2-3	Moir, Parry	52,756
4	Sep 1	H	Blackpool	W	3-0	Lofthouse, Hassall, Edwards	47,013
5	4	A	Huddersfield Town	L	0-2		28,726
6	6	H	Portsmouth	W	3-1	Lofthouse 2, Hassall	26,629
7	11	H	Manchester United	D	1-1	Lofthouse	50,708
8	15	A	Portsmouth	L	0-1		24,113
9	18	A	Wolverhampton Wanderers	W	2-1	Hassall, Parry	40,899
10	25	H	Aston Villa	D	3-3	Wheeler, Moir, Lofthouse	28,335
11	Oct 2	A	Sunderland	D	1-1	Hassall	50,486
12	9	H	Leicester City	W	4-1	Moir 2, Lofthouse, Hassall	34,358
13	16	A	Burnley	L	0-2		30,016
14	23	H	Manchester City	D	2-2	Wheeler, Lofthouse	29,841
15	30	A	Cardiff City	D	2-2	Parry, Hassall	31,698
16	Nov 6	H	Arsenal	D	2-2	Moir, Parry	31,223
17	13	A	West Bromwich Albion	D	0-0		34,961
18	20	H	Newcastle United	W	2-1	Hassall (pen), Webster	25,936
19	27	A	Everton	D	0-0		43,681
20	Dec 11	H	Sheffield United	L	0-2		22,947
21	18	A	Charlton Athletic	L	0-2		16,491
22	25	H	Tottenham Hotspur	L	1-2	Stevens	25,978
23	27	A	Tottenham Hotspur	L	0-2		41,063
24	Jan 1	H	Chelsea	L	2-5	Barrass 2	30,998
25	22	A	Manchester United	D	1-1	Stevens	41,719
26	Feb 5	H	Wolverhampton Wanderers	W	6-1	Moir, Webster, Bell, Parry 3	37,427
27	12	A	Aston Villa	L	0-3		21,447
28	Mar 2	H	Sunderland	W	3-0	Moir, Lofthouse, Webster	17,190
29	5	H	Sheffield United	W	1-0	Lofthouse	26,837
30	9	H	Preston North End	W	2-1	Lofthouse, Webster	19,250
31	16	A	Manchester City	L	2-4	Lofthouse, Barrass (pen)	27,742
32	19	H	Cardiff City	D	0-0		25,321
33	26	A	Arsenal	L	0-3		32,852
34	Apr 2	H	West Bromwich Albion	L	2-4	Parry, Allcock	17,715
35	8	H	Sheffield Wednesday	D	2-2	Moir, Barrass	22,909
36	9	A	Preston North End	D	2-2	Parry, Wheeler	25,213
37	11	A	Sheffield Wednesday	L	2-3	Lofthouse 2	16,569
38	16	H	Everton	W	2-0	Stevens, Barrass (pen)	26,722
39	23	A	Newcastle United	D	0-0		48,194
40	27	H	Huddersfield Town	W	1-0	Holden	16,184
41	30	H	Burnley	L	0-1		20,671
42	May 4	A	Leicester City	L	0-4		12,223
						Appearances	
						Goals	

FA Cup

R3	Jan 8	H	Millwall	W	3-1	Moir 2 (1 pen), Parry	33,597
R4	29	A	Birmingham City	L	1-2	Moir	56,800
						Appearances	
						Goals	

Bolton Wanderers — Football League Division One, 1954–55

Hanson S.	Ball J.	Banks T.	Wheeler J.E.	Barrass M.W.	Edwards G.B.	Holden A.D.	Mori W.	Lofthouse N.	Hassall H.W.	Webster H.	Parry R.A.	Bell E.	Birch B.	Stevens D.	Hennin D.	Bingley W.	Gubbins R.G.	Higgins J.D.	Pilling V.	Greaves K.J.	Neill T.K.	Allcock T.	Barnard A.
1	2	3	4	5	6	7	8	9	10	11													
1	2	3	4	5	6	7	8	9	10	11													
1	2	3	4	5	6	7	8	9	10		11												
1	2	3	4	5	6	7	8	9	10	11													
1	2	3	4	5	6	7	8	9	10		11												
1	2	3	4	5	6	7	8	9	10	11													
1	2	3	4	5	6	7	8	9	10	11													
1	2	3	4	5	6	7	8	9	10	11													
1	2	3	9	5	6	7	8			10	11	4											
1	2	3	4	5			8	9	10		11	6	7										
1	2	3		5	6		8	10		9	11	4	7										
1	2	3	4	5	6	7	8	9	10		11												
1	2	3	4	5	6	7	8	9	10	11													
1	2	3	4	5		7	8	9	10		11	6											
1	2	3	4	5		7	8	9	10		11	6											
1	2	3	4	5		7	8	9	10		11	6											
1	2	3		5	6	7	8	9	10		11	4											
1	2	3		5	6	7	8		10	9	11	4											
1	2	3		5	6	7	8		10		11	4			9								
1	2	3		5	6	7	8	9	10		11		4										
1	2			5	6	7	8			11	9			10	4	3							
1	2		9	5	6	7	8			11				10	4	3							
1	2		4	5	6	7		9		10				8		3	11						
1	2		4	10	6			9		11				8	3		5	7					
1	2		4	5	3	7	8	9			11	6		10									
1	2		4	5	3	11	7	9		8	10	6											
	2		4	5	3	11	7	9		8	10	6							1				
1	2		4	5	3	11	7	9		8		6		10									
1	2		4	5	3	11	7	9		8		6		10									
1	2		4	5	3	11	7	9		8		6		10									
1	2		4	5	3	11	7	9		8		6		10									
1	2			5	3	11	7	9		8	10	4		6									
1	2		4	5	3	7		8	9	10	11	6											
1	2		4	5	3	7		9	11	6	10			8									
	2		4	5	3	7	8	9		10	6			11					1				
	2		4	5	3	7		9		8	10	6		11					1				
	2		4	5	3	7		9	8	10				11					1	6			
	2	3	8	5	6	7		9							10	4	11		1				
	2	3	8		6	7		9							10	4	11	5	1				
	2	3		5	6	7		9	10						8	4	11		1				
	2	3	8	5		7		9	10							4	11		1	6			
	2	3	8	5	6	7		9							10	4	11		1				
33	42	25	34	40	38	39	32	31	24	21	28	21	2	14	9	4	9	2	1	8	3	1	1
			3	5	1	1	8	15	8	7	9	1		3			1						

Hanson S.	Ball J.	Banks T.	Wheeler J.E.	Barrass M.W.	Edwards G.B.	Holden A.D.	Mori W.	Lofthouse N.	Hassall H.W.	Webster H.	Parry R.A.	Bell E.	Birch B.	Stevens D.	Hennin D.	Bingley W.	Gubbins R.G.	Higgins J.D.	Pilling V.	Greaves K.J.	Neill T.K.	Allcock T.	Barnard A.
1	2		4	5	3	7	8	9			11	6		10									
1	2		4	5	3	7	8	9			11	6		10									
2	2		2	2	2	2	2	2			2	2		2									
					3						1												

League Table

	P	W	D	L	F	A	Pts
Chelsea	42	20	12	10	81	57	52
Wolverhampton W	42	19	10	13	89	70	48
Portsmouth	42	18	12	12	74	62	48
Sunderland	42	15	18	9	64	54	48
Manchester United	42	20	7	15	84	74	47
Aston Villa	42	20	7	15	72	73	47
Manchester City	42	18	10	14	76	69	46
Newcastle United	42	17	9	16	89	77	43
Arsenal	42	17	9	16	69	63	43
Burnley	42	17	9	16	51	48	43
Everton	42	16	10	16	62	68	42
Huddersfield Town	42	14	13	15	63	68	41
Sheffield United	42	17	7	18	70	86	41
Preston North End	42	16	8	18	83	64	40
Charlton Athletic	42	15	10	17	76	75	40
Tottenham Hotspur	42	16	8	18	72	73	40
West Bromwich Albion	42	16	8	18	76	96	40
Bolton Wanderers	42	13	13	16	62	69	39
Blackpool	42	14	10	18	60	64	38
Cardiff City	42	13	11	18	62	76	37
Leicester City	42	12	11	19	74	86	35
Sheffield Wednesday	42	8	10	24	63	100	26

1955-56

Division One
Manager: W. Ridding

Did you know that?

In February 1956 16-year-old Joe Dean became the youngest-ever First Division 'keeper when he made his Bolton debut in a 4–2 defeat at Wolverhampton Wanderers. Unfortunately, Dean did not finish the game as he had to leave the field for stitches to a wound, with Nat Lofthouse taking over in goal.

BOLTON WANDERERS
Football & Athletic Co. Ltd.

WINNERS OF THE
FOOTBALL ASSOCIATION CUP 1923, 1926 & 1929
F.A. Cup Finalists 1894, 1904, 1953
FOOTBALL LEAGUE (NORTH) CUP 1944-45
LANCS CUP 1885-6, 1890-1, 1911-2, 1921-2, 1924-5, 1926-7, 1931-2,
1934-5, 1947-8
MANCHESTER CUP 1894-5, 1903-4, 1908-9, 1920-1, 1921-2, 1935-6
RICHARDSON CUP 1928-9, 1930-1, WEST LANCS CUP 1930-1, 1935-1
CENTRAL LEAGUE CHAMPIONS 1934-5

Telephone: BOLTON 885   Telegrams: "WANDERERS, BOLTON"

DIRECTORS:
E. GERRARD, J.P. (Chairman), H. WARBURTON (Vice-Chairman),
C. H. BANKS, F. DUXBURY, ESQ. J. ENTWISTLE, J.P., W. HAYWARD,
S. BROUGHTON
W. RIDDING (Manager)   HAROLD ABBOTTS (Secretary)

1955-56 SEASON

FUTURE EVENTS AT BURNDEN PARK :
Football League   Central League
Jan. 14—Portsmouth .... 3.30   Jan. 21—Stoke City
C. H. BANKS ....   Feb. 4—Wolverhampton W. 3.0
Feb. 18—Tottenham H. ...... 3.0   Feb. 25—Burnley

CANTEEN TEA 4d. COFFEE 5d. HAM SANDWICH 6d.

3rd ROUND F.A. CUP
Wed. Jan. 11—HUDDERSFIELD TOWN
OFFICIAL PROGRAMME   **3d.**

Match No.	Date		Venue	Opponents	Result		Scorers	Attendance
1	Aug	20	A	Chelsea	W	2-0	Stevens, Holden	44,454
2		27	H	Charlton Athletic	L	1-3	Lofthouse	25,989
3		31	A	Cardiff City	L	0-1		26,973
4	Sep	3	H	Arsenal	W	4-1	Lofthouse 3, Parry	26,324
5		7	A	Cardiff City	W	4-0	Lofthouse, Stevens, Parry 2	25,012
6		10	A	Portsmouth	D	3-3	Lofthouse 2, Stevens	30,904
7		17	H	Sunderland	L	0-3		33,178
8		24	A	Aston Villa	W	2-0	Lofthouse 2	28,418
9	Oct	1	A	Wolverhampton Wanderers	W	2-1	Stevens, Webster	34,134
10		8	A	Tottenham Hotspur	W	3-0	Lofthouse, Gubbins 2	35,237
11		15	H	Everton	D	1-1	Stevens	32,999
12		22	A	Burnley	L	0-2		23,839
13		29	H	Luton Town	W	4-0	Lofthouse 2, Holden 2	26,794
14	Nov	5	A	West Bromwich Albion	L	0-2		23,651
15		12	H	Manchester United	W	3-1	Lofthouse 2, Parry	41,829
16		19	A	Sheffield United	W	3-1	Lofthouse 2, Holden	21,002
17		26	H	Preston North End	D	0-0		32,630
18	Dec	3	A	Newcastle United	L	0-3		36,856
19		10	H	Birmingham City	W	6-0	Lofthouse 4, Wheeler, Stevens	15,793
20		17	H	Chelsea	W	4-0	Lofthouse 3, Gubbins	24,129
21		24	A	Charlton Athletic	L	1-3	Parry	18,746
22		26	H	Manchester City	L	1-3	Hartle	43,947
23		27	A	Manchester City	L	0-2		38,407
24		31	A	Arsenal	L	1-3	Lofthouse	43,757
25	Jan	2	H	Huddersfield Town	D	2-2	Lofthouse, Parry (pen)	39,524
26		14	H	Portsmouth	W	4-0	Gubbins, Parry, Lofthouse, Edwards	24,093
27		21	A	Sunderland	D	0-0		38,871
28	Feb	11	A	Wolverhampton Wanderers	L	2-4	Lofthouse, Stevens	24,919
29		18	H	Aston Villa	W	1-0	Lofthouse	19,737
30		25	A	Everton	L	0-1		47,293
31	Mar	3	H	Sheffield United	W	2-1	Lofthouse, Stevens	20,521
32		10	A	Luton Town	D	0-0		20,432
33		17	H	West Bromwich Albion	W	4-0	Lofthouse 2, Stevens 2	23,603
34		21	H	Tottenham Hotspur	W	3-2	Barrass 2 (1 pen), Edwards	10,942
35		24	A	Manchester United	L	0-1		46,346
36		30	A	Blackpool	D	0-0		34,764
37		31	H	Burnley	L	0-1		29,488
38	Apr	2	H	Blackpool	L	1-3	Allcock	39,208
39		7	A	Preston North End	W	1-0	Gubbins	18,834
40		14	H	Newcastle United	W	3-2	Stevens, Neill, Gubbins	17,378
41		21	A	Birmingham City	L	2-5	Stevens 2	29,640
42		28	A	Huddersfield Town	L	1-3	Lofthouse	18,877
							Appearances	
							Goals	

FA Cup

R3	Jan	11	H	Huddersfield Town	W	3-0	Lofthouse, Stevens, Neill	20,862
R4		28	H	Sheffield United	L	1-2	Hartle	47,105
							Appearances	
							Goals	

374

Appearance / Team Selection Grid

Greaves K.J.	Ball J.	Banks T.	Wheeler J.E.	Barrass M.W.	Edwards G.B.	Holden A.D.	Moir W.	Lofthouse N.	Stevens D.	Parry R.A.	Hartle L.R.	Allcock T.	Gubbins R.G.	Birch B.	Webster H.	Higgins J.O.	Hanson S.	Neill T.K.	Dean J.	Bannister N.	Hennin D.	Threlfall J.	Barnard A.
1	2	3	4	5	6	7	8	9	10	11													
1	2	3	4	5	6	7	8	9	10	11													
1		3	4	5	6	7		9	10		2	8		11									
1		3	4	5	6	7		9	8	10	2			11									
1		3	4	5	6	7		9	8	10	2			11									
1		3	4	5	6	7		9	8	10	2			11									
1		3	4	5	6	7		9	8	10	2			11									
1		3	4	5	6	7		9	8	10	2		11										
1		3	4	5	6	7		9	8	10	2		11										
1		3	4	5	6	7		9	8	10	2			11									
1		3	4	5	6	7		9	8	10	2			11									
1		3	4	5	6	7		9	8	10	2			11									
1		3	4	5	6	7		9	8	10	2			11									
1		3	4	5	6	7		9	8	10	2			11									
1		3	4	5	6	7		9	8	10	2			11									
1		3	4	5	6	7		9	8	10	2			11									
1		3	4		6	7		9	8	10	2			11	5								
1		3	4		6	7		9	8	10	2			11	5								
1		3	4		6	7		9	8	10	2			11	5								
		3	4		6	7		9	8	10	2			11	5	1							
		3	4		6	7		9	8	10	2			11	5	1							
1		3			6	7		9	8	10	2			11	5		4						
1		3		5	6	7		9	8	10	2			11	4								
		3	4	5	6	7		9	8	10	2			11				1					
1		3	4	5	6	7		9	8	10	2		11										
1		3	4	5	6	7		9	8	10	2	11											
1		3	4	5	6	7		9	8	10	2			11									
1		3	4	5	6	7		9	8	10	2			11									
1		3	4	5	6	7		9	8		2		10	11									
1		3	4	5	6	7		9	8		2		10	11									
1		3	4	5	6	7		9	8		2		10	11									
1		3	4	5	6	7		9	8	10	2			11									
1		3	4	5	6	7		9	8	10	2			11									
1		3	4	5	6	7		9	8			2		10	11								
1	3	9	5	6	7				8	10	2			11					4				
1		3	4		6	7			9		2	8	10	11	5								
		9		6	7				2	8	11			5		10			4	3			
1			4		6	7			2	9	10	11		5	8				3				
		4		6	7		8		2	9	11			5	10	1			3				
1		3	4	5	6			9	8		2		11				10	7					
		3	4	5	6			9	8	10	2	11		7							1		
37	**2**	**39**	**40**	**32**	**42**	**40**	**2**	**36**	**39**	**33**	**40**	**5**	**34**	**11**	**2**	**10**	**2**	**6**	**2**	**2**	**2**	**3**	**1**
				1	2	2	4	32	13	7		1	1	6		1		1					

Greaves K.J.	Ball J.	Banks T.	Wheeler J.E.	Barrass M.W.	Edwards G.B.	Holden A.D.	Moir W.	Lofthouse N.	Stevens D.	Parry R.A.	Hartle L.R.	Allcock T.	Gubbins R.G.	Birch B.	Webster H.	Higgins J.O.	Hanson S.	Neill T.K.	Dean J.	Bannister N.	Hennin D.	Threlfall J.	Barnard A.
		3	4		6	7		9	8	10	2			11		1	5						
1		3		5	6	7		9	8	10	2			11			4						
1		2	1	1	2	2		2	2	2	2		2			1	2						
						1	1			1							1						

Division One

Manager: W. Ridding

Match No.	Date		Venue	Opponents	Result		Scorers	Attendance
1	Aug	18	H	Blackpool	W	4-1	Lofthouse 3, Stevens	33,310
2		22	A	Sunderland	L	0-3		33,307
3		25	A	Everton	D	2-2	Lofthouse 2	40,816
4	Sep	1	H	Tottenham Hotspur	W	1-0	Lofthouse	30,889
5		5	H	Sunderland	W	2-1	Lofthouse 2	33,786
6		8	A	Leeds United	L	2-3	Lofthouse, Holden	40,010
7		12	H	Charlton Athletic	W	2-0	Lofthouse, Holden	19,846
8		15	H	Cardiff City	W	2-0	Lofthouse, Parry	28,738
9		20	A	Charlton Athletic	L	1-2	Lofthouse	13,649
10		22	H	Wolverhampton Wanderers	L	0-3		35,720
11		29	A	Aston Villa	D	0-0		34,402
12	Oct	6	A	Birmingham City	D	0-0		29,614
13		13	H	West Bromwich Albion	D	1-1	Stevens	24,969
14		20	A	Preston North End	D	2-2	Lofthouse, Stevens	26,994
15		27	H	Chelsea	D	2-2	Stevens, Gubbins	21,299
16	Nov	3	A	Sheffield Wednesday	W	2-1	Gubbins, Allcock	23,968
17		10	H	Manchester United	W	2-0	Allcock, Holden	39,922
18		17	A	Arsenal	L	0-3		33,377
19		24	H	Burnley	W	3-0	Stevens, Parry, Gubbins	26,062
20	Dec	1	A	Portsmouth	D	1-1	Stevens	19,021
21		8	H	Newcastle United	W	3-1	Lofthouse 2, Webster	25,131
22		15	H	Blackpool	L	2-4	Stevens, Lofthouse	17,556
23		25	A	Manchester City	W	3-1	Stevens, Lofthouse 2	19,731
24		26	H	Manchester City	W	1-0	Stevens	20,856
25		29	A	Tottenham Hotspur	L	0-4		42,030
26	Jan	12	H	Leeds United	W	5-3	Holden, Gubbins, Lofthouse 2, Dunn (own-goal)	25,705
27		19	A	Cardiff City	L	0-2		12,810
28	Feb	2	A	Wolverhampton Wanderers	L	2-3	Stevens, Webster	30,520
29		9	H	Aston Villa	D	0-0		21,012
30		20	H	Birmingham City	W	3-1	Lofthouse, Parry, Warhurst (own-goal)	11,284
31		23	A	Chelsea	D	2-2	Hennin, Lofthouse	13,647
32	Mar	2	H	Preston North End	L	2-3	Stevens, Lofthouse	37,090
33		9	H	Newcastle United	L	0-4		34,073
34		16	H	Sheffield Wednesday	W	3-2	Lofthouse, Ball, Hennin	18,424
35		25	A	Manchester United	W	2-0	Parry, Foulkes (own-goal)	61,101
36		30	H	Arsenal	W	2-1	Stevens, Lofthouse	23,897
37	Apr	6	A	Burnley	L	0-1		23,250
38		13	H	Portsmouth	D	1-1	Parry	16,969
39		19	H	Luton Town	D	2-2	Lofthouse 2	18,666
40		20	A	West Bromwich Albion	L	2-3	Stevens, Birch	18,351
41		22	A	Luton Town	L	0-1		13,396
42		27	H	Everton	D	1-1	Lofthouse	16,016
								Appearances
							3 own-goals	Goals

FA Cup

R3	Jan	5	H	Blackpool	L	2-3	Hennin (pen), Gubbins	42,515
								Appearances
								Goals

Hopkinson E.	Hartle L.R.	Banks T.	Hennin D.	Barrass M.W.	Edwards G.B.	Holden A.D.	Stevens D.	Lofthouse N.	Parry R.A.	Gubbins R.G.	Higgins J.O.	Ball J.	Allcock T.	Neill T.K.	Bailey D.	Birch B.	Webster H.	Threlfall J.	Ball E.	Riley B.F.	Edisbury W.	Stanley G.	Edwards M.
1	2	3	4	5	6	7	8	9	10	11													
1	2	3	4	5	6	7	8	9	10	11													
1	2	3	4		6	7	8	9	10	11	5												
1	2	3	4		6	7	8	9	10	11	5												
1	2	3	4		6	7	8	9	10	11	5												
1	2	3	4		6	7	8	9	10	11	5												
1	2		4		6	7	8	9	10	11	5	3											
1	2		4		6	7	8	9	10	11	5	3											
1	2		4		6	7	8	9	10	11	5	3											
1	2		4		6	7	8	9	10	11	5	3											
1	2	3	4		6	7		9	11		5		8	10									
1	2	3	4		6	7		9	11		5		8	10									
1	2	3	4		6	7	10	9	11		5		8										
1	2	3	4		6	7	10	9			5		8		11								
1	2	3	4		6	11	8			10	5		9			7							
1	2	3	4		6	7			10	11	5		9				8						
1	2	3	4		6	7	8		10	11	5		9										
1	2	3	4		6	7	8		10	11	5		9										
1	2	3	4		6	7	8		10	11	5		9										
1	2	3	4		6	7	8			11	5		9				10						
1	2	3	4		6	7	8	9		11	5						10						
1	2	3	4		6	7	8	9	10	11	5												
1	2		4		6	7	8	9	10	11	5							3					
1	2		4		6	7	8	9		11	5		10					3					
1	2		4		6	7	8	9		11	5		10					3					
1	2		4		6	7	8	9		11	5						10	3					
1	2		4		6	7	8	9		11	5						10	3					
1	2		4		6	7	8	9	11		5						10	3					
1	2		4		6	7	8	9	11		5						10	3					
1	2		4		3	7	8	9	10	11	5								6				
1	2		4		3	7	8	9	10	11	5								6				
1	2		4		5	7	8	9	10	11								3	6				
1	2		4		5	7	8	9	11	10		3							6				
1	2		4		5	7	8	9		10		3							6	11			
1	2		4		5	7	8	9	10	11		3							6				
1	2		4		5	7	8	9	10	11		3							6				
1	2		4		5	7	8	9	10	11		3							6				
1	2		4		5	7	8	9	10	11									6		3		
1	2	3	4		5	11	8	9	10							7			6				
1	2				5	11	8	9	10							7		3	6			4	
1		3			5	11	8	9				2				7	10		6			4	
1	2	3			5	11	8	9					10			7						4	6
2	41	21	39	2	42	42	39	36	31	32	29	10	13	2	1	5	8	9	12	1	1	3	1
			2			4	13	28	5	4		1	2			1	2						

1	2		4		6	7	8	9	10	11	5							3					
1	1		1		1	1	1	1	1	1	1							1					
			1							1													

League Table

	P	W	D	L	F	A	Pts
Manchester United	42	28	8	6	103	54	64
Tottenham Hotspur	42	22	12	8	104	56	56
Preston North End	42	23	10	9	84	56	56
Blackpool	42	22	9	11	93	65	53
Arsenal	42	21	8	13	85	69	50
Wolverhampton W	42	20	8	14	94	70	48
Burnley	42	18	10	14	56	50	46
Leeds United	42	15	14	13	72	63	44
Bolton Wanderers	42	16	12	14	65	65	44
Aston Villa	42	14	15	13	65	55	43
West Bromwich Albion	42	14	14	14	59	61	42
Chelsea	42	13	13	16	73	73	39
Birmingham City	42	15	9	18	69	69	39
Sheffield Wednesday	42	16	6	20	82	88	38
Everton	42	14	10	18	61	79	38
Luton Town	42	14	9	19	58	76	37
Newcastle United	42	14	8	20	67	87	36
Manchester City	42	13	9	20	78	88	35
Portsmouth	42	10	13	19	62	92	33
Sunderland	42	12	8	22	67	88	32
Cardiff City	42	10	9	23	53	88	29
Charlton Athletic	42	9	4	29	62	120	22

1957-58

Division One
Manager: W. Ridding

BOLTON WANDERERS
FOOTBALL CLUB

BURNDEN PARK · · · BOLTON

OFFICIAL PROGRAMME 3"

SEASON 1957-58
Wed. Jan. 29th-YORK CITY
F.A. CUP—4th ROUND REPLAY
NEXT MATCH—SATURDAY, FEB. 1st
LEEDS UNITED.   Kick-off 3-8 p.m.

Match No.	Date		Venue	Opponents	Result		Scorers	Attendance
1	Aug	24	A	Luton Town	L	0-1		17,591
2		28	A	Wolverhampton Wanderers	L	1-6	Lofthouse	30,796
3		31	H	Blackpool	W	3-0	Stevens, Allcock 2	31,491
4	Sep	4	H	Wolverhampton Wanderers	D	1-1	Stevens	25,845
5		7	A	Leicester City	W	3-2	Holden, Stevens, Lofthouse	30,033
6		11	H	Sunderland	D	2-2	Parry, Allcock	17,647
7		14	H	Manchester United	W	4-0	Stevens, Lofthouse, Parry (pen), Birch	48,003
8		18	A	Sunderland	W	2-1	Lofthouse, Parry	30,021
9		21	A	Leeds United	L	1-2	Parry (pen)	18,379
10		28	H	Portsmouth	W	1-0	Stevens	13,184
11	Oct	5	A	Arsenal	L	0-1		20,212
12		12	A	West Bromwich Albion	D	2-2	Sanders (own-goal), Stevens	31,370
13		19	H	Tottenham Hotspur	W	3-2	Lofthouse 2, Parry	20,381
14		26	A	Birmingham City	L	1-5	Parry	26,225
15	Nov	2	H	Sheffield Wednesday	W	5-4	Holden, Lofthouse 2, Parry, Birch	18,072
16		9	A	Manchester City	L	1-2	Birch	34,147
17		16	H	Nottingham Forest	W	2-0	Holden, Lofthouse	24,562
18		23	A	Preston North End	L	0-3		28,036
19		30	H	Chelsea	D	3-3	Stevens 2, Parry	18,815
20	Dec	7	A	Newcastle United	W	2-1	Lofthouse, Parry	29,888
21		14	H	Burnley	W	2-1	Stevens, Parry	20,197
22		21	H	Luton Town	L	1-2	Hennin	16,754
23		25	A	Everton	D	1-1	Birch	29,584
24		26	H	Everton	L	1-5	Lofthouse	23,462
25		28	A	Blackpool	W	3-2	Lofthouse, Parry, Armfield (own-goal)	19,858
26	Jan	11	H	Leicester City	L	2-3	Stevens, Parry	17,884
27		18	A	Manchester United	L	2-7	Stevens, Lofthouse	41,360
28	Feb	1	H	Leeds United	L	0-2		18,558
29		8	A	Portsmouth	D	2-2	Parry, Hennin	21,950
30		18	A	Arsenal	W	2-1	Lofthouse, Gubbins	28,425
31		22	H	West Bromwich Albion	D	2-2	Stevens, Gubbins	19,132
32	Mar	8	H	Birmingham City	W	1-0	Lofthouse	18,309
33		12	A	Tottenham Hotspur	L	1-4	Parry	22,978
34		15	A	Sheffield Wednesday	L	0-1		24,085
35		29	A	Nottingham Forest	D	0-0		24,060
36	Apr	4	H	Aston Villa	W	4-0	Stevens, Hennin 3 (1 pen)	19,026
37		5	H	Manchester City	L	0-2		27,733
38		8	A	Aston Villa	L	0-4		32,745
39		12	A	Chelsea	D	2-2	Gubbins, Ball (pen)	27,994
40		19	H	Newcastle United	D	1-1	Lofthouse	19,284
41		21	H	Preston North End	L	0-4		24,067
42		26	A	Burnley	L	1-3	Lofthouse	17,419
								Appearances
							2 own-goals	Goals

FA Cup

R3	Jan	4	A	Preston North End		3-0	Stevens, Parry 2	32,641
R4		25	A	York City		0-0		23,460
rep		29	H	York City		3-0	Birch, Allcock 2	34,062
R5	Feb	15	H	Stoke City		3-1	Lofthouse, Stevens, Parry	56,667
R6	Mar	1	H	Wolverhampton Wanderers		2-1	Stevens, Parry	56,306
SF		22	N	Blackburn Rovers		2-1	Gubbins 2	74,800
F	May	3	N	Manchester United		2-0	Lofthouse 2	100,000

SF at Maine Road, Manchester. Final at Wembley Stadium.

Appearances

Goals

Appearance and goals grid (Bolton Wanderers, season 1957–58):

Hopkinson E.	Hartle L.R.	Banks T.	Ball E.	Higgins J.O.	Edwards G.B.	Holden A.D.	Stevens D.	Lofthouse N.	Parry R.A.	Gubbins R.G.	Hennin D.	Birch B.	Allcock T.	Ball J.	Edwards M.	Deare J.	Rion B.F.	Gratty J.G.	Edsbury W.	Stanley G.	Hill F.	Deakin P.
	2	3	4	5	6	7	8	9	10	11												
	2	3	4	5	6	7	8	9	10	11												
	2	3		5	6	11	8		10		4	7	9									
	2		6	5	3	11	8		10		4	7	9									
		6	5	3	11	8	7	10	4		9	2										
		6	5	3	11	8	7	10	4		9	2										
		6	5	3	11	8	9	10	4	7												
	2		6	5	3	11		9	10	4	7	8										
	2		6	5	3	11		9	10	4	7	8										
	2		5	3	11	8	9	10	4	7		6										
	2		5	3	11			10	8	4	7	6										
	2	3		5	6	11	8	9	10	4	7											
	2	3		5	6	7	8	9	10	4				1	11							
	2	3		5	6	7	8	9	10	4				11								
	2	3		5	6	11	8	9	10	4	7											
	2		5	3	11	8	9	10	4	7				1		6						
	2		5	3	11	8	9	10	4	7						6						
	2		5	3	11	8	9	10	4	7						6						
	2		5	3	11	8	9	10	4	7						6						
	2		5	6	11	8	9	10	4	7							3					
	2	3		5	6	11	8	9	10	4	7											
	2	3		5	6	11	8	9	10	4	7											
	2	3		5	6	11	8	9	10	4	7											
	2	3		5	6	11	8	9	10		7							4				
	2	3		5		8		9	10	4	7				11		6					
	2	3		5	6	11	8	9	10	7	4											
	2	3		5	6		8		10	4	7				11							
	2	3		5	6		8		10	11	7	9					4					
	2	3		5	6		8	9	10	11	4	7										
	2	3		5	6	7	8	9	10	11	4											
	2	3		5	6		11	4	7													
	2	3		5	6	11	8	9	10		7					1		4				
	2	3		5	6	11	8	9	10		7					1		4				
	2	3		5	6	11	8		10	9	4	7					1					
	2	3		5	6	11	8		10	9	4	7					1					
	2	3		5	6	11	8			10	9	7					1		4			
	2	3		5	6	11	8			10	9	7					1		4			
	2	3		5	6	11	8			9	7					1		4	10			
	2			5	6	11	8			9	7	3					4		10			
	2	3		5	6			9	10	11	7					1		4	8			
	2	3		5	6	11	8	9	10		7							4				
	2	3		5	6	11	8	9	10	4	7											
3	39	28	8	42	41	37	37	31	38	15	32	34	9	4	2	9	4	4	1	11	1	2
				3	13	17	14	3	5	4	3	1										

Hopkinson E.	Hartle L.R.	Banks T.	Ball E.	Higgins J.O.	Edwards G.B.	Holden A.D.	Stevens D.	Lofthouse N.	Parry R.A.	Gubbins R.G.	Hennin D.	Birch B.	Allcock T.	Ball J.	Edwards M.	Deare J.	Rion B.F.	Gratty J.G.	Edsbury W.	Stanley G.	Hill F.	Deakin P.
	2	3		5	6	11	8	9	10		4	7										
	2	3		5		11	8	9	10		7					6		4				
	2	3		5		11	8		10	7	9					6		4				
	2	3		5	6	11	8	9	10		4	7										
	2	3		5	6	11	8	9	10		4	7										
	1	2	3		5	6	11	8		10	9	4	7									
	1	2	3		5	6	11	8	9	10		4	7									
7	7		7	5	7	7	5	7	1	5	7	1				2		2				
				3	3	4	2		1	2												

1958-59

Division One

Manager: W. Ridding

Did you know that?

In October 1958 the Wanderers added the Charity Shield to the FA Cup in the trophy cabinet by defeating League champions Wolverhampton Wanderers 4–1 at Burnden Park. Nat Lofthouse, who scored two of the goals, had to have a stint in goal when Joe Dean had to have time off the field with a shoulder injury.

Match No.	Date		Venue	Opponents	Result		Scorers	Attendance
1	Aug	23	H	Leeds United	W	4-0	Birch, Parry, Lofthouse 2	25,92
2		27	A	Manchester City	D	3-3	Birch, Parry (pen), Lofthouse	40,84
3		30	A	West Bromwich Albion	D	1-1	G.B. Edwards	37,24
4	Sep	3	H	Manchester City	W	4-1	Birch, Stevens, Lofthouse, Parry	39,72
5		6	H	Birmingham City	W	2-0	G.B. Edwards, Lofthouse	24,70
6		9	A	Arsenal	L	1-6	Parry (pen)	45,27
7		13	A	Luton Town	D	0-0		19,69
8		17	H	Arsenal	W	2-1	Birch, Lofthouse	42,20
9		20	H	Nottingham Forest	W	3-2	Stevens, Lofthouse 2	28,48
10		27	H	Burnley	L	1-2	Lofthouse	32,35
11	Oct	4	A	Preston North End	D	0-0		28,76
12		11	A	Chelsea	W	1-0	Lofthouse	49,22
13		18	H	Blackpool	W	4-0	Stevens, Holden, Hill 2 (1 pen)	37,04
14		25	A	Aston Villa	L	1-2	Stevens	28,74
15	Nov	1	H	West Ham United	L	0-2		31,06
16		8	A	Tottenham Hotspur	D	1-1	Lofthouse	39,82
17		15	H	Manchester United	W	6-3	G.B. Edwards, Stevens 2, Parry (pen), Gubbins 2	33,35
18		22	A	Wolverhampton Wanderers	W	2-1	Stevens, Lofthouse	33,48
19		29	H	Portsmouth	W	2-1	Stevens, Lofthouse	20,62
20	Dec	6	A	Blackburn Rovers	D	1-1	Stevens	38,02
21		13	H	Newcastle United	D	1-1	Stevens	23,02
22		20	A	Leeds United	W	4-3	G.B. Edwards, Lofthouse 2, Gibson (own-goal)	28,53
23		26	A	Everton	L	0-1		61,69
24		27	H	Everton	L	0-3		37,26
25	Jan	3	H	West Bromwich Albion	W	2-1	Lofthouse 2	27,84
26		31	H	Luton Town	W	4-2	Lofthouse 3, Holden	27,78
27	Feb	7	A	Nottingham Forest	L	0-3		29,70
28		21	H	Preston North End	W	2-1	Birch, Hill	16,47
29	Mar	4	H	Chelsea	W	6-0	Lofthouse 2, Parry, Hill 3 (1 pen)	24,25
30		7	A	Blackpool	L	0-4		21,07
31		18	H	Aston Villa	L	1-3	Lofthouse	21,80
32		21	A	West Ham United	L	3-4	Stevens, Parry, Hill	27,72
33		27	H	Leicester City	D	3-3	Ogilvie (own-goal), Stevens, Lofthouse	21,21
34		28	A	Tottenham Hotspur	W	4-1	Parry 2, Stevens, Baker (own-goal)	21,38
35		30	A	Leicester City	D	0-0		20,32
36	Apr	4	A	Manchester United	L	0-3		61,52
37		8	A	Birmingham City	W	3-1	Birch, Riley, Lofthouse	24,60
38		11	H	Wolverhampton Wanderers	D	2-2	Lofthouse, Parry (pen)	26,01
39		14	A	Burnley	W	1-0	Lofthouse	23,66
40		18	A	Portsmouth	W	1-0	Lofthouse	14,16
41		22	A	Newcastle United	L	0-2		17,45
42		25	H	Blackburn Rovers	W	3-1	Lofthouse, Parry 2 (1 pen)	18,26
								Appearance
							3 own-goals	Goal

FA Cup

	Date		Venue	Opponents	Result		Scorers	Attendance
R3	Jan	10	A	Scunthorpe United	w	2-0	Lofthouse 2	23,70
R4		24	A	Wolverhampton Wanderers	W	2-1	Lofthouse, Parry (pen)	55,62
R5	Feb	14	H	Preston North End	D	2-2	Birch, Parry	58,69
rep		18	A	Preston North End	D	1-1	Holden	36,86
rep2		23	N	Preston North End	W	1-0	Lofthouse	51,09
R6		28	A	Nottingham Forest	L	1-2	Birch	44,41

R5 replay a.e.t. R5 replay 2 at Ewood Park.

								Appearance
								Goal

380

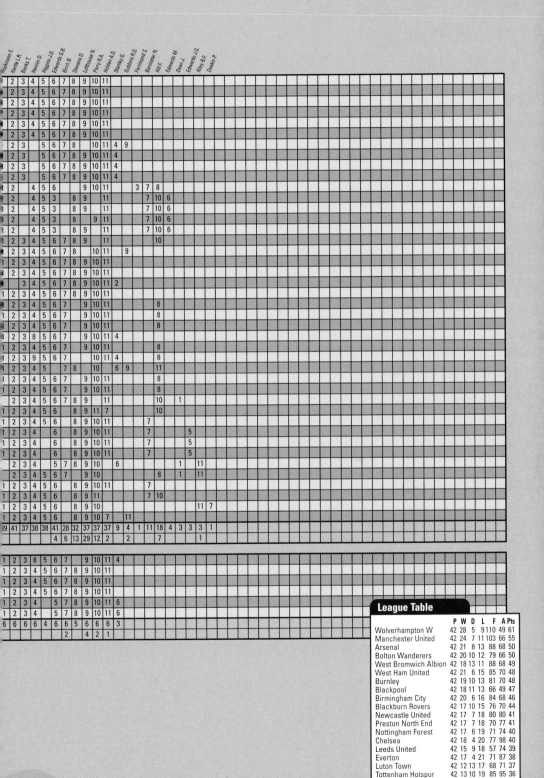

BOLTON WANDERERS FOOTBALL CLUB

BURNDEN PARK, BOLTON

SEASON 1959-60

FOOTBALL LEAGUE—DIVISION I.
Wednesday, Aug. 26th
WANDERERS v. BLACKBURN ROVERS

OFFICIAL PROGRAMME 3"

Match No.	Date	Venue	Opponents	Result		Scorers	Attendance
1	Aug 22	A	Blackpool	L	2-3	Hill, Parry (pen)	29,21
2	26	H	Blackburn Rovers	L	0-3		42,32
3	29	H	Everton	W	2-1	Stevens, Parry	26,79
4	31	A	Blackburn Rovers	L	0-1		39,03
5	Sep 5	A	Luton Town	D	0-0		15,60
6	9	H	Arsenal	L	0-1		32,57
7	12	H	West Ham United	W	5-1	Banks, Stevens, Hill, Bannister 2	24,24
8	15	A	Arsenal	L	1-2	McCullough (own-goal)	38,63
9	19	H	Fulham	W	3-2	Stevens, Hill, Lampe (own-goal)	24,75
10	26	A	Nottingham Forest	L	0-2		28,93
11	Oct 3	H	Sheffield Wednesday	W	1-0	Parry	23,99
12	10	A	Chelsea	W	2-0	Parry, Hill	28,70
13	17	H	West Bromwich Albion	D	0-0		22,58
14	24	A	Newcastle United	W	2-0	Parry 2	34,679
15	31	H	Leeds United	D	1-1	Hennin	20,18
16	Nov 7	A	Tottenham Hotspur	W	2-0	Stevens, Parry	41,90
17	14	H	Manchester United	D	1-1	Stevens	37,892
18	21	A	Preston North End	L	0-1		28,72
19	28	H	Leicester City	W	3-1	Stevens, Hartle (pen), Parry	19,834
20	Dec 5	A	Burnley	L	0-4		26,51
21	12	H	Birmingham City	W	4-1	Holden, Stevens, Parry 2	16,074
22	19	H	Blackpool	L	0-3		17,30
23	26	H	Wolverhampton Wanderers	W	2-1	Hartle (pen), Stevens	36,039
24	28	A	Wolverhampton Wanderers	W	1-0	Birch	28,42
25	Jan 2	A	Everton	W	1-0	Stevens	37,51
26	23	H	West Ham United	W	2-1	Stevens, Parry	21,155
27	Feb 6	A	Fulham	D	1-1	Birch	24,74
28	13	H	Nottingham Forest	D	1-1	Stanley	16,218
29	24	A	Sheffield Wednesday	L	0-1		34,46
30	27	H	Burnley	W	2-1	Hartle, Birch	28,772
31	Mar 5	A	West Bromwich Albion	D	1-1	Holden	23,707
32	9	H	Luton Town	D	2-2	Hill, Birch	14,79
33	12	H	Newcastle United	L	1-4	Stevens	24,648
34	19	A	Birmingham City	W	5-2	Stevens, Hill 2, Bannister, Hartle (pen)	24,183
35	26	H	Tottenham Hotspur	W	2-1	Holden, Parry	31,106
36	Apr 2	A	Manchester United	L	0-2		45,482
37	9	H	Preston North End	W	2-1	Hartle (pen), Stevens	30,816
38	15	A	Manchester City	L	0-1		50,053
39	16	A	Leeds United	L	0-1		19,272
40	18	H	Manchester City	W	3-1	Holden, Stevens, Birch	35,59
41	23	H	Chelsea	W	2-0	Hill, Birch	19,432
42	30	A	Leicester City	W	2-1	Deakin 2	19,527
							Appearances
						2 own-goals	Goals

FA Cup

R3	Jan 9	A	Bury	D	1-1	Parry	35,000
rep	13	H	Bury	W	4-2	Stevens, Parry 2, Birch	43,616
R4	30	A	West Bromwich Albion	L	0-2		36,207

R3 replay a.e.t.

Appearances
Goals

Appearances and goals grid (player columns, left to right):

Hopkinson E. · Hartle L.R. · Banks T. · Hennin D. · Higgins J.O. · Edwards G.B. · Holden A.D. · Stevens D. · Gubbins R.G. · Hill F. · Parry R.A. · Stanley G. · Birch B. · Bannister N. · Edwards M. · Dean J. · Farrimond S. · Deakin P. · Pythian E.R. · Bollands J.F. · Ousby R. · Cunliffe J.G.

Hop	Hart	Ban	Hen	Hig	EdG	Hol	Ste	Gub	Hill	Par	Sta	Bir	Ban	EdM	Dea	Far	Dea	Pyt	Bol	Ous	Cun
1	2	3	4	5	6	7	8	9	10	11											
1	2	3	4	5	6	7	8	9	10	11											
1	3	2	5	6	11	8		9	10	4	7										
1	3	2	5	6	11	8		9	10	4	7										
1	3	2	5	6	11	9		8	10	4	7										
1	3	2	5	6	11	9		8	10	4	7										
1	3	2	5	6	11	9		8	10	4		7									
1	3	2	5	6	11	9		8	10	4		7									
1	3	2	5	6	11	9		8	10	4		7									
1	2	3	4	5	6	11	9		8	10		7									
1	2	3	4	5	6	11	9		8	10		7									
1	2	3	4	5	6	11			8	10		7	9								
1	2	3	4	5	6	11	9		8	10		7		1							
1	2		9	5	6	11		8	10	4	7				3						
1	2		9	5	6	11		8	10	4	7				3						
1	2			5	6	11	9		8	10	4	7			3						
1	2			5	6	11	9		8	10	4	7			3						
1	2			5		11	9		8	10	4	7		6	3						
1	2			5		11	9		8	10	4	7		6	3						
1	2			5		11	9		8	10	4	7		6	3						
1	2		4	5		11	9		8	10	6	7			3						
1	2		4	5		11	9		8	10	6	7			3						
1	2		4	5		11	9		8	10	6	7			3						
1	2		4	5		11	9		8	10	6	7			3						
1	2		4	5		11	9		8	10	6	7			3						
1	2		4	5		11	9		8	10	6	7			3						
1	2		4	5		11	10			6	9	7			3	8					
	2		4	5		11	10			6	9	7		1	3	8					
	2		4	5		11	10		8		6	7		1	3		9				
	2		4	5		11	9		10		6	7			3	8		1			
	2		4	5		11	9		10		6	7			3	8		1			
	2		4	5		11	9			8	10	6	7		3			1			
	2	6		5		11	9		8	10	4	7			3			1			
	2	3				11	9		8	10	4	7				1	5	6			
	2	3				11	9		8	10	4	7				1	5	6			
	2	3				11	9		8	10	4	7				1	5	6			
	2	3		5		11	9		8		4	7			10	1		6			
	2	3		5		11	9		8	10	4	7				1		6			
	2			5		11	9		8	10	4	7			3	1		6			
	2			5		11	9		8		4	7			3	10	1	6			
	2			5		11	9		8		4	7			3	10	1	6			
	2	3		5		11	9		8		4	7			10	1		6			
26	35	20	27	39	17	42	39	2	40	33	36	30	12	4	3	23	8	1	13	3	9
	5	1	1			4	14		8	12	1	6	3				2				

Hop	Hart	Ban	Hen	Hig	EdG	Hol	Ste	Gub	Hill	Par	Sta	Bir	Ban	EdM	Dea	Far	Dea	Pyt	Bol	Ous	Cun
1	2		4	5		11	9		8	10	6	7			3						
1	2		4	5		11	9		8	10	6	7			3						
1	2		4	5		11	9		8	10	6	7			3						
3	3		3	3		3	3		3	3	3	3			3						
							1			3		1									

League Table

	P	W	D	L	F	A	Pts
Burnley	42	24	7	11	85	61	55
Wolverhampton W	42	24	6	12	106	67	54
Tottenham Hotspur	42	21	11	10	86	50	53
West Bromwich Albion	42	19	11	12	83	57	49
Sheffield Wednesday	42	19	11	12	80	59	49
Bolton Wanderers	42	20	8	14	59	51	48
Manchester United	42	19	7	16	102	80	45
Newcastle United	42	18	8	16	82	78	44
Preston North End	42	16	12	14	79	76	44
Fulham	42	17	10	15	73	80	44
Blackpool	42	15	10	17	59	71	40
Leicester City	42	13	13	16	66	75	39
Arsenal	42	15	9	18	68	80	39
West Ham United	42	16	6	20	75	91	38
Everton	42	13	11	18	73	78	37
Manchester City	42	17	3	22	78	84	37
Blackburn Rovers	42	16	5	21	60	70	37
Chelsea	42	14	9	19	76	91	37
Birmingham City	42	13	10	19	63	80	36
Nottingham Forest	42	13	9	20	50	74	35
Leeds United	42	12	10	20	65	92	34
Luton Town	42	9	12	21	50	73	30

Division One

Manager: W. Ridding

Match No.	Date		Venue	Opponents	Result		Scorers	Attendance
1	Aug	20	H	Birmingham City	D	2-2	Birch, Parry	20,543
2		24	H	Wolverhampton Wanderers	L	0-2		20,132
3		27	A	West Ham United	L	1-2	Deakin	24,283
4		31	A	Wolverhampton Wanderers	L	1-3	Banks	37,313
5	Sep	3	H	Chelsea	W	4-1	G.B. Edwards, Holden, McAdams 2	21,609
6		7	H	Tottenham Hotspur	L	1-2	McAdams	41,565
7		10	A	Blackpool	W	1-0	Hill	17,166
8		14	A	Tottenham Hotspur	L	1-3	McAdams	43,559
9		17	H	Everton	L	3-4	McAdams, Parry, Hill	30,405
10		24	A	Blackburn Rovers	L	1-3	Hartle (pen)	29,236
11	Oct	1	H	Manchester United	D	1-1	McAdams	39,197
12		8	A	West Bromwich Albion	L	0-1		18,672
13		15	A	Cardiff City	W	1-0	Lofthouse	22,672
14		22	H	Fulham	L	0-3		19,816
15		29	A	Sheffield Wednesday	L	0-2		25,708
16	Nov	5	H	Manchester City	W	3-1	Stanley, Lofthouse, Lee	34,005
17		12	A	Nottingham Forest	D	2-2	Lofthouse, Iley (own-goal)	18,812
18		19	H	Burnley	L	3-5	McAdams 2, Lee	23,830
19	Dec	3	H	Newcastle United	W	2-1	M. Edwards, Stevens	12,922
20		10	A	Arsenal	L	1-5	McAdams	30,598
21		17	A	Birmingham City	D	2-2	Stevens 2	19,051
22		24	H	Leicester City	W	2-0	Deakin, Stevens	11,534
23		26	A	Leicester City	L	0-2		23,806
24		31	H	West Ham United	W	3-1	Birch, McAdams, Stevens	15,931
25	Jan	14	A	Chelsea	D	1-1	McAdams	20,461
26		21	H	Blackpool	W	3-1	McAdams, Stanley (pen), Stevens	15,909
27	Feb	4	A	Everton	W	2-1	McAdams 2 (1 pen)	35,654
28		11	H	Blackburn Rovers	D	0-0		16,183
29		18	A	Manchester United	L	1-3	McAdams	38,146
30		25	A	West Bromwich Albion	L	2-3	Stevens, Bannister	15,171
31	Mar	4	H	Cardiff City	W	3-0	Holden, Stevens 2	21,815
32		11	A	Fulham	D	2-2	Holden, Phythian	18,794
33		18	H	Sheffield Wednesday	L	0-1		19,418
34		25	A	Manchester City	D	0-0		21,816
35	Apr	1	H	Arsenal	D	1-1	Neill (own-goal)	18,618
36		3	H	Aston Villa	W	3-0	McAdams 3	21,721
37		4	A	Aston Villa	L	0-4		15,732
38		8	A	Burnley	L	0-2		22,998
39		15	H	Nottingham Forest	W	3-1	Hartle, Birch, Hill	18,601
40		18	A	Preston North End	D	0-0		17,786
41		22	A	Newcastle United	L	1-4	Pilkington	18,820
42		29	H	Preston North End	D	1-1	Stevens	12,637
								Appearances
							2 own-goals	Goals

FA Cup

R3	Jan	7	A	Hull City	W	1-0	Stevens	18,771
R4		28	H	Blackburn Rovers	D	3-3	Stanley (pen), McAdams, Stevens	29,804
rep	Feb	1	A	Blackburn Rovers	L	0-4		31,000
								Appearances
								Goals

League Cup

R1	Oct	10	A	Hull City	D	0-0		11,980
rep		19	H	Hull City	W	5-1	Birch, Hill 2, McAdams 2	10,781
R2		26	H	Grimsby Town	W	6-2	Hill, Stevens, Lofthouse, Keeble (own-goal)	7,992
R3	Nov	14	A	Darlington	W	2-1	Hartle, Holden	21,023
R4	Dec	20	H	Rotherham United	L	0-2		6,594
								Appearances
							1 own-goal	Goals

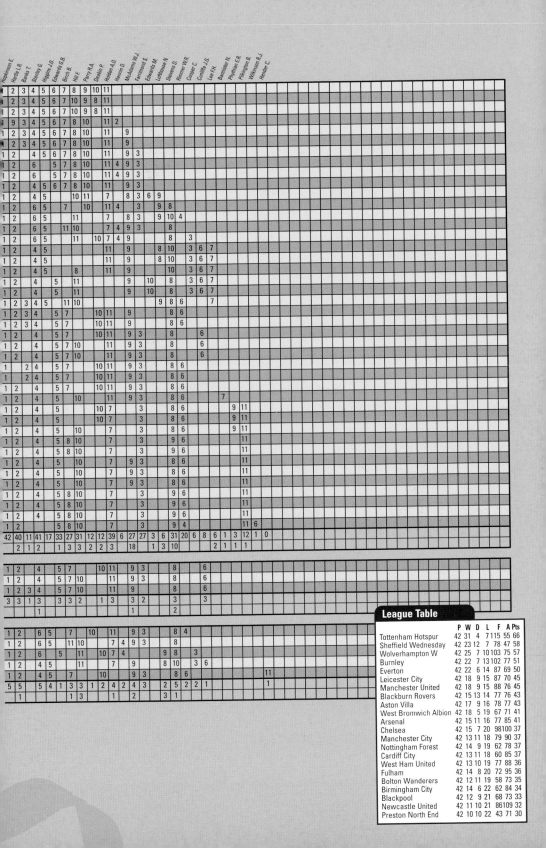

League Table

	P	W	D	L	F	A	Pts
Tottenham Hotspur	42	31	4	7	115	55	66
Sheffield Wednesday	42	23	12	7	78	47	58
Wolverhampton W	42	25	7	10	103	75	57
Burnley	42	22	7	13	102	77	51
Everton	42	22	6	14	87	69	50
Leicester City	42	18	9	15	87	70	45
Manchester United	42	18	9	15	88	76	45
Blackburn Rovers	42	15	13	14	77	76	43
Aston Villa	42	17	9	16	78	77	43
West Bromwich Albion	42	18	5	19	67	71	41
Arsenal	42	15	11	16	77	85	41
Chelsea	42	15	7	20	98	100	37
Manchester City	42	13	11	18	79	90	37
Nottingham Forest	42	14	9	19	62	78	37
Cardiff City	42	13	11	18	60	85	37
West Ham United	42	13	10	19	77	88	36
Fulham	42	14	8	20	72	95	36
Bolton Wanderers	42	12	11	19	58	73	35
Birmingham City	42	14	6	22	62	84	34
Blackpool	42	12	9	21	68	73	33
Newcastle United	42	11	10	21	86	109	32
Preston North End	42	10	10	22	43	71	30

Did you know that?

In March 1962 the Wanderers received a then record fee of £35,000 for inside forward Dennis Stevens. He had won a Cup-winners' medal with the club in 1958 and went on to win the League Championship with Everton in 1963.

Match No.	Date		Venue	Opponents	Result		Scorers	Attendance
1	Aug	19	H	Ipswich Town	D	0-0		16,70
2		23	A	Sheffield Wednesday	L	2-4	Holden, McAdams (pen)	35,46
3		26	A	Burnley	L	1-3	Threlfall	24,18
4		30	H	Sheffield Wednesday	W	4-3	Holden, McAdams, Hill 2	19,55
5	Sep	2	H	Arsenal	W	2-1	McAdams 2	18,41
6		6	A	Fulham	D	2-2	Hill 2	12,63
7		9	A	Cardiff City	W	2-1	Holden, McAdams	22,07
8		16	A	Manchester City	L	1-2	Stevens	27,27
9		20	H	Fulham	L	2-3	Stevens, Phythian	16,74
10		23	H	West Bromwich Albion	W	3-2	Hill, Pilkington, Phythian	14,15
11		30	A	Birmingham City	L	1-2	Stevens	17,21
12	Oct	9	H	Tottenham Hotspur	L	1-2	Hill	24,72
13		14	A	Blackpool	L	1-2	McAdams	22,06
14		21	H	Wolverhampton Wanderers	W	1-0	Stevens	14,75
15		28	A	Manchester United	W	3-0	McAdams, Hill, Pilkington	31,44
16	Nov	4	H	Sheffield United	W	2-0	Hartle, Coldwell (own-goal)	12,56
17		11	A	Chelsea	L	0-1		12,40
18		18	H	Aston Villa	D	1-1	McAdams	13,19
19		25	A	Nottingham Forest	W	1-0	Hill	23,91
20	Dec	2	H	Blackburn Rovers	D	1-1	Holden	12,85
21		9	A	West Ham United	L	0-1		19,49
22		16	A	Ipswich Town	L	1-2	Holden	16,58
23		26	A	Everton	L	0-1		45,46
24	Jan	13	A	Arsenal	W	2-1	Holden, Stevens	33,45
25		20	H	Cardiff City	D	1-1	Stevens	11,23
26	Feb	3	H	Manchester City	L	0-2		18,45
27		10	A	West Bromwich Albion	L	2-6	Hartle, Hill	20,22
28		17	H	Birmingham City	W	3-2	Stevens, Hill, Hennessey (own-goal)	13,30
29		24	A	Tottenham Hotspur	D	2-2	Hill 2	36,47
30	Mar	3	H	Blackpool	D	0-0		14,83
31		10	A	Wolverhampton Wanderers	L	1-5	Holden	18,88
32		17	H	Manchester United	W	1-0	Pilkington	34,36
33		24	A	Sheffield United	L	1-3	Pilkington	18,32
34		31	H	Chelsea	W	4-2	Holden, McGarry, Davies, Harris (own-goal)	15,49
35	Apr	4	H	Everton	D	1-1	Rimmer	20,42
36		7	A	Aston Villa	L	0-3		23,57
37		11	H	Burnley	D	0-0		26,615
38		14	H	Nottingham Forest	W	6-1	Rimmer, Holden, Hill, Birch, Davies, McGarry	12,89
39		21	A	Blackburn Rovers	W	3-2	Holden, Hill, McGarry (pen)	15,45
40		23	H	Leicester City	W	1-0	Davies	19,26
41		24	A	Leicester City	D	1-1	McGarry	14,09
42		28	H	West Ham United	W	1-0	Holden	17,333
							Appearances	
							3 own-goals	Goals

FA Cup

R3	Jan	6	A	Manchester United	L	1-2	Stevens	42,202
							Appearances	
								Goals

League Cup

R1	Sep	13	H	Sunderland	D	1-1	Stevens	13,125
rep		25	A	Sunderland	L	0-1		19,557
							Appearances	
								Goals

Player appearance grid (shirt numbers by match):

Match	Hopkinson E.	Harris J.R.	Farrimond S.	Rimmer W.R.	Edwards G.B.	Wilkinson R.J.	Holden A.D.	Stevens D.	McAdams W.J.	Hill F.	Pilkington B.	Stanley G.	Cunliffe J.G.	Birch B.	Phythian E.R.	Sleight G.	Lee F.H.	Deakin P.	McGarry R.J.	Davies R.W.	Hatton D.H.
1	1	2	3	4	5	6	7	8	9	10	11										
2	1	2	3	4	5	6	7	8	9	10	11										
3	1		3	6	5		7	8	9	10	11	2	4								
4	1	2	3	6	5		7	8	9	10	11		4								
5	1	2	3	6	5		7	8	9	10	11		4								
6	1	2	3	6	5		7	8	9	10	11		4								
7	1	2	3	4	5			8		10				6	7	9	11				
8	1	2	3	4	5			8		10				6	7	9	11				
9	1	2	3	6	5			8		10	11		4	7	9						
10	1	2	3	6	5			8	9	10	11		4		7						
11	1	2	3	6	5			8	9	10	11		4		7						
12	1	2	3	6	5			8	9	10	11		4		7						
13	1	2	3	6	5		7	8	9	10		4			11						
14	1	2	3	6	5		7	8	9	10	11	4									
15	1	2	3	6	5		7	8	9		11	4						10			
16	1	2	3	6	5		7	8	9	10	11	4									
17	1	2	3	6	5		7	8	9	10	11	4									
18	1	2	3	6	5		7	8	9	10	11	4									
19	1	2	3	6	5		7	8		10	11	4			9						
20	1	2	3	6	5		7	8		10					11	9					
21	1	2	3	6	5		7		9	10	11	4		8							
22	1	2	3	6	5		7		9	10	11	4		8							
23	1	2	3	6	5		7		9	10	11	4			8						
24	1	2	3	6	5			9		10	11	4		7	8						
25	1	2	3	6	5			9		8	11	4		7				10			
26	1	2	3	6	5			9		8	11	4		7				10			
27	1	2	3	6	5		7	9			8	11	4					10			
28	1	2	3	6	5			7			8	11	4					10	9		
29	1	2	3	6	5			7			8	11	4					10	9		
30	1	2	3	6	5			7			8	11	4					10	9		
31	1	2	3	6	5			7			8	11	4					10	9		
32	1	2	3	6	5			7			8	11	4					10	9		
33	1	2	3	6	5		7				8	11	4					10	9		
34	1	2	3	6	5			11			8		4		7			10	9		
35	1	2	3	6	5			11			8		4		7			10	9		
36	1	2	3	6	5			11			8		4		7			10	9		
37	1	2	3	6	5		7				8	11						10	9	4	
38	1	2	3	6	5		7				8	11						10	9	4	
Apps	42	41	42	42	42	2	32	30	17	41	35	26	11	2	12	6	2	5	3	15	12	2
Goals	2			2			11	7	8	14	4	1			1	2				4	3	

Cup appearances (sub-grids):

	1	2	3	6	5		7	9		10	11	4						8			
Apps	1	1	1	1	1		1	1		1	1	1						1			
Goals					1																

	1	2	3	6	5			8	9	10	11		4		7						
	1	2	3		5			8		10				6	7	9	11			4	
	2	2	2	1	2			2	1	2	1		1	1	2	1	1			1	

League Table

	P	W	D	L	F	A	Pts
Ipswich Town	42	24	8	10	93	67	56
Burnley	42	21	11	10	101	67	53
Tottenham Hotspur	42	21	10	11	88	69	52
Everton	42	20	11	11	88	54	51
Sheffield United	42	19	9	14	61	69	47
Sheffield Wednesday	42	20	6	16	72	58	46
Aston Villa	42	18	8	16	65	56	44
West Ham United	42	17	10	15	76	82	44
West Bromwich Albion	42	15	13	14	83	67	43
Arsenal	42	16	11	15	71	72	43
Bolton Wanderers	42	16	10	16	62	66	42
Manchester City	42	17	7	18	78	81	41
Blackpool	42	15	11	16	70	75	41
Leicester City	42	17	6	19	72	71	40
Manchester United	42	15	9	18	72	75	39
Blackburn Rovers	42	14	11	17	50	58	39
Birmingham City	42	14	10	18	65	81	38
Wolverhampton W	42	13	10	19	73	86	36
Nottingham Forest	42	13	10	19	63	79	36
Fulham	42	13	7	22	66	74	33
Cardiff City	42	9	14	19	50	81	32
Chelsea	42	9	10	23	63	94	28

1962-63

Division One

Manager: W. Ridding

BOLTON WANDERERS FOOTBALL CLUB

BURNDEN PARK · · · BOLTON

OFFICIAL PROGRAMME 3ᵈ

Match No.	Date		Venue	Opponents	Result		Scorers	Attendance
1	Aug	18	A	Sheffield Wednesday	D	1-1	Davies	28,036
2		22	H	Burnley	D	2-2	Rimmer, Davies	28,897
3		25	H	Fulham	W	1-0	Hill	16,666
4		28	A	Burnley	L	1-2	Pilkington	27,529
5	Sep	1	A	Leicester City	L	1-4	Norman (own-goal)	19,113
6		5	H	Manchester United	W	3-0	Pilkington (pen), Hill, Davies	45,097
7		8	H	Ipswich Town	L	1-3	Holden	17,790
8		12	A	Manchester United	L	0-3		37,951
9		15	H	Everton	L	0-2		27,404
10		22	A	West Bromwich Albion	L	4-5	Lee 3 (2 pens), Davies	18,209
11		29	H	Arsenal	W	3-0	Lee 2 (1 pen), McGarry	16,634
12	Oct	6	A	Liverpool	L	0-1		41,115
13		13	H	Wolverhampton Wanderers	W	3-0	Pilkington, Lee 2	27,838
14		20	A	Sheffield United	L	1-4	Davies	19,862
15		27	H	Nottingham Forest	W	1-0	Lee	13,614
16	Nov	3	A	West Ham United	W	2-1	McGarry 2	19,885
17		10	H	Manchester City	W	3-1	Lee 2 (1 pen), Davies	21,700
18		17	A	Blackpool	L	1-3	Lee	12,930
19		24	H	Blackburn Rovers	D	0-0		26,868
20	Dec	1	A	Aston Villa	L	0-5		34,075
21		8	H	Tottenham Hotspur	W	1-0	Deakin	20,737
22	Feb	16	A	Arsenal	L	2-3	Hill, Butler	25,203
23	Mar	9	H	Sheffield United	W	3-2	Hill 3	12,925
24		16	A	Nottingham Forest	L	0-1		16,294
25		20	A	Wolverhampton Wanderers	L	0-4		17,648
26		23	H	West Ham United	W	3-0	Russell, Butler, Lee	19,177
27		25	H	West Bromwich Albion	L	1-2	Davies	14,997
28		29	A	Blackburn Rovers	L	0-5		11,533
29	Apr	3	A	Birmingham City	D	2-2	Hill, Birch	13,200
30		6	H	Blackpool	W	3-0	Hartle, Rimmer, Birch	14,584
31		12	A	Leyton Orient	W	1-0	Butler (pen)	15,389
32		13	A	Manchester City	L	1-2	Deakin	18,551
33		15	H	Leyton Orient	L	0-1		16,752
34		20	H	Aston Villa	W	4-1	Davies 2, Deakin, Butler	13,411
35		24	H	Birmingham City	D	0-0		12,949
36		27	A	Tottenham Hotspur	L	1-4	Deakin	40,965
37	May	1	H	Fulham	L	1-2	Deakin	10,896
38		4	A	Everton	L	0-1		52,047
39		6	H	Sheffield Wednesday	L	0-4		12,905
40		11	H	Leicester City	W	2-0	Deakin, Russell	10,734
41		13	H	Liverpool	W	1-0	Pilkington	15,837
42		17	A	Ipswich Town	L	1-4	Davies	19,088
								Appearances
							1 own-goal	Goals

FA Cup

R3	Mar	6	A	Sheffield United	L	1-3	Lee	27,184
								Appearances
								Goals

League Cup

R2	Sep	26	A	Norwich City	L	0-4		19,258
								Appearances

Player columns (left to right):

Hopkinson E. · Hartle L.R. · Farrimond S. · Threlfall J. · Edwards G.B. · Rimmer W.R. · Holden A.D. · Hill F. · Davies R.W. · Deakin P. · Pilkington B. · McGarry P.J. · Cooper C. · Hatton D.H. · Stanley G. · Cunliffe J.G. · Lee F.H. · Birch B. · Hulme J. · Butler D.A. · Bromley B. · Taylor G. · Russell W. · Smith A. · Lennard D. · Goulden A.E. · Oxoby R.

Hpk	Hrt	Far	Thr	Edw	Rim	Hol	Hil	Dav	Dea	Pil	McG	Coo	Hat	Sta	Cun	Lee	Bir	Hul	But	Bro	Tay	Rus	Smi	Len	Gou	Oxo
1	2	3	4	5	6	7	8	9	10	11																
1	2	3	4	5	6	7	8	9	10	11																
1	2	3	4	5	6	7	8	9	10	11																
1	2	3	4	5	6	7	8	9	10	11																
1	2	3	4	5	6	7	8	9		11	10															
1	2	3	4	5	6	7	8	9		11	10															
1	2	3	4	5	6	7	8	9		11	10															
1	2		4	5		7	8	9	10	11		3	6													
1		3		5			8	9	10					4	2	6	7	11								
1	2	3		5	4	11	10	9								6	7					8				
1	2	3		5	6	11	8	9						4		7			10							
1	2	3		5	6	11	8	9						4		7			10							
1	2	3		5	6		8	9						4		7			11	10						
1	2	3	4	5	6			9	8	11	10					7										
1	2	3			6		8	9						4		7	5		11	10						
1	2	3		5	6		8	9						4		7			11	10						
1	2	3		5	6		8	9						4		7			11	10						
1	2	3		5	6		8	9						4		7			11	10						
1	2	3		5	6		8	9	10					4		7			11							
1	2	3		5	6		8	9	10					4		7			11							
1	2	3		5	6		8	9	10					4		7			11							
1	2	3		5	6		8	9						4		7			11			10				
1	2	3		5	6		8	9						4		7			11			10				
1	2	3		5	6			9						4		7			11			10	8			
1	2	3		5	6		10	9						4		7			11			8				
1	2	3		5	6		10	9						4		7			11			8				
1	2	3		5	6		10	9						4		7			11			8				
	2	3		5	4		10	9								7			11			8	1	6		
1	2	3		5	4		10	9								7			11			8		6		
1	2	3		5	4		10	9								7			11			8		6		
	2		5	4		10	9	8								7			11				1	6	3	
	2		5	4		10	9			3						7	11					8	1	6		
1	2		5	4			9	10		3						7			11			8		6		
1	2		5	4			9	10		3						7			11			8		6		
1	2		5	6		10		8	11	3	4					7			9							
1	2		5	6		10	9	8	11	3	4					7										
1	2		5	6		10		8	11	3	4					7			9							
1	2		5	6		10	9		11	3	4					7			8		7					
1	2		5	6		7	9	10	11	3	4								8							
1	2		5	6		7	9	10	11	3	4								8							
1	2		5	6		8	9	10	11	3	4			7												
39	**41**	**30**	**9**	**41**	**40**	**11**	**38**	**40**	**19**	**22**	**12**	**1**	**14**	**23**	**2**	**23**	**11**	**1**	**16**	**3**	**1**	**14**	**3**	**7**	**1**	**0**
	1			2	1	7	10	6	4	3				12	2		4					2				

F.A. Cup

Hpk	Hrt	Far	Thr	Edw	Rim	Hol	Hil	Dav	Dea	Pil	McG	Coo	Hat	Sta	Cun	Lee	Bir	Hul	But
1	2	3		5	6		8	9	10					4		7			11
1	1	1		1	1		1	1						1		1			1
																	1		

Football League Cup

Hpk	Hrt	Far	Thr	Edw	Rim	Hol	Hil	Dav	Dea	Pil	McG	Cooper	Hatton	Stanley	Cunliffe	Lee	Russell
1	2	3					8			11	10		4		6	9	5
1	1	1					1			1	1		1		1	1	1

League Table

	P	W	D	L	F	A	Pts
Everton	42	25	11	6	84	42	61
Tottenham Hotspur	42	23	9	10	111	62	55
Burnley	42	22	10	10	78	57	54
Leicester City	42	20	12	10	79	53	52
Wolverhampton W	42	20	10	12	93	65	50
Sheffield Wednesday	42	19	10	13	77	63	48
Arsenal	42	18	10	14	86	77	46
Liverpool	42	17	10	15	71	59	44
Nottingham Forest	42	17	10	15	67	69	44
Sheffield United	42	16	12	14	58	60	44
Blackburn Rovers	42	15	12	15	79	71	42
West Ham United	42	14	12	16	73	69	40
Blackpool	42	13	14	15	58	64	40
West Bromwich Albion	42	16	7	19	71	79	39
Aston Villa	42	15	8	19	62	68	38
Fulham	42	14	10	18	50	71	38
Ipswich Town	42	12	11	19	59	78	35
Bolton Wanderers	42	15	5	22	55	75	35
Manchester United	42	12	10	20	67	81	34
Birmingham City	42	10	13	19	63	90	33
Manchester City	42	10	11	21	58	102	31
Leyton Orient	42	6	9	27	37	81	21

1963-64

Division One

Manager: W. Ridding

Did you know that?

The Wanderers longest unbroken period in the top flight of 29 years came to an end on the final weekend of the season. Going into their final game against Wolverhampton Wanderers at Burnden Park, held on a Friday evening to avoid a clash with the local Holcombe Brook races, they knew a win would guarantee safety. A 4–0 defeat followed by Birmingham's home win over Sheffield United the following day proved disasterous.

Match No.	Date		Venue	Opponents	Result		Scorers	Attendance
1	Aug	24	A	Birmingham City	L	1-2	Davies	24,817
2		31	H	West Bromwich Albion	L	1-2	Hill	14,398
3	Sep	4	H	Everton	L	1-3	Rimmer	34,093
4		7	A	Arsenal	L	3-4	Bromley, Davies 2	26,016
5		11	A	Everton	L	0-2		48,301
6		14	H	Leicester City	D	0-0		12,753
7		18	H	Ipswich Town	W	6-0	Pilkington, Davies 2, Lennard 2, Taylor	12,917
8		21	A	Nottingham Forest	L	1-3	Taylor	23,712
9		28	A	Fulham	L	1-3	Lee	17,345
10	Oct	1	A	Ipswich Town	W	3-1	Butler, Taylor 2	11,363
11		5	H	Manchester United	L	0-1		36,183
12		9	A	Blackburn Rovers	L	0-3		18,675
13		12	H	Stoke City	L	3-4	Lee 2 (1 pen), Butler	17,560
14		19	A	Wolverhampton Wanderers	D	2-2	Butler, Pilkington	19,420
15		26	H	Blackpool	D	1-1	Rimmer	14,359
16	Nov	2	A	Aston Villa	L	0-3		18,847
17		9	H	Liverpool	L	1-2	Hatton	24,049
18		16	A	Sheffield United	W	1-0	Deakin	21,518
19		23	H	West Ham United	D	1-1	Lee (pen)	11,041
20		30	A	Chelsea	L	0-4		19,969
21	Dec	7	H	Tottenham Hotspur	L	1-3	Davies	18,394
22		14	H	Birmingham City	L	0-2		9,663
23		21	A	West Bromwich Albion	D	1-1	Deakin	10,705
24		26	A	Sheffield Wednesday	L	0-3		30,532
25		28	H	Sheffield Wednesday	W	3-0	Lee, Davies, Deakin	12,376
26	Jan	11	H	Arsenal	D	1-1	Lee	14,830
27		18	A	Leicester City	L	0-1		15,902
28	Feb	1	H	Nottingham Forest	L	2-3	Lee 2 (1 pen)	10,770
29		8	H	Fulham	W	2-1	Robson (own-goal), Taylor	9,615
30		19	A	Manchester United	L	0-5		33,426
31		22	A	Stoke City	W	1-0	Lee	20,419
32		29	H	Blackburn Rovers	L	0-5		18,343
33	Mar	7	A	Blackpool	L	0-2		12,242
34		20	A	Liverpool	L	0-2		38,583
35		28	H	Aston Villa	D	1-1	Davison	8,348
36		30	H	Burnley	W	2-1	Hatton, Lee	14,112
37		31	A	Burnley	D	1-1	Hatton	12,554
38	Apr	4	A	West Ham United	W	3-2	Taylor, Lee, Bromley	19,398
39		8	H	Sheffield United	W	3-0	Hill, Lee, Bromley	16,905
40		11	H	Chelsea	W	1-0	Bromley	18,868
41		18	A	Tottenham Hotspur	L	0-1		32,507
42		24	H	Wolverhampton Wanderers	L	0-4		27,808
								Appearances
							1 own-goal	Goals

FA Cup

R3	Jan	4	A	Bath City	D	1-1	Lee (pen)	12779
rep		8	H	Bath City	W	3-0	Taylor, Lee (pen), Davies	26983
R4		25	H	Preston North End	D	2-2	Deakin 2	39234
rep		27	A	Preston North End	L	1-2	Edwards	38290
								Appearances
								Goals

League Cup

R2	Sep	25	A	Sheffield United	W	2-1	Lee 2	9,805
R3	Oct	29	A	Stoke City	L	0-3		11,825
								Appearances
								Goals

Column headers (left to right): Hopkinson E., Harris L.R., Farmmond S., Stanley G., Edwards G.B., Rimmer W.R., Lee F.H., Russell W., Davies R.W., Hill F., Pilkington B., Lennard D., Birch B., Deakin P., Hulme J., Butler D.A., Bromley B., Smith A., Hatton D.H., Taylor G., Redrow W.E., Dawson J.H., Cooper C.

1	2	3	4	5	6	7	8	9	10	11													
1	2	3	4	5	6	7	8	9	10	11													
1	2	3		5	4			9	10	11	6	7	8										
1	2	3			4			9	10	11	6			5	7	8							
	2				4			9	10	11	6			5	7	8	1	3					
	2				4			9	10	11	6			5	7	8	1	3					
	2				4			9	10	11	6			5	7		1	3	8				
	2				4			9	10	11	6			5	7		1	3	8				
	2			4	8		9				6	7		5	11		1	3	10				
	2			4	8		9				6	7		5	11		1	3	10				
	2			4	8		9				6	7		5	11		1	3	10				
	2		4			8		9			11	6		5	7		1	3	10				
	2			4	9						11	6		5	7	8	1	3	10				
	2			4	8		9				6	7	10	5	7		1	3					
	2			4	8		9				6	7	10	5	11		1						
1	2	3				7					6		10	5	11	8		4		9			
1	2	3			8		9				6		10	5	11			4			7		
1	2	3			11		9				6		10	5		8		4			7		
1	2	3			11		9				6		10	5		8		4			7		
1	2	3			8			11			6			5		10		4		9	7		
1	2	3	4	5			9	8	11	6		10						7					
1	2	3	4	5		8	9	10	11	6	6							7					
1	2	3			8		9	11			6		10	5				4			7		
1	2	3			8		9	11			6		10	5				4			7		
	2	3	5		8		9	11			6		10			1	4				7		
1	2	3		5	8			7			6		10			9		4	11				
1	2	3		5	4	8			7		6		10			9			11				
1	2	3		6		8	9						5		10	4	11			7			
1	2	3	4	5		8			10		6		9					11	7				
1	2	3	4	5		8			10		6		9					11	7				
1	2	3			8	9			10		6		7				4	11					
	3			5	8	9			10		6		7				4	11				2	
1	2	3		5		7			10		6		8				9	11					4
1	2	3		5	4	8			10		6						9	11	7				
1	2	3		5	4	8			10		6						9	11	7				
1	2	3		5	6	9			10							8		4	11	7			
1	2	3		5	6	9			10							8		4	11	7			
1	2	3		5	4	9			10		6					8			11	7			
1	2	3		5	4	9			10		6					8			11	7			
1	2	3		5	4	9			10		6					8			11	7			
1	2	3		5	4	9					6					8		10	11	7			
31	41	31	7	23	24	34	5	23	29	13	37	5	18	20	14	18	11	29	24	2	21	2	
				2	12		7	2	2	2		3		3	4		3	6		1			

1	2	3		5		8		9	11		6		10				4			7			
1	2	3		5		8		9	11		6		10				4	7					
1		3		5	4	7		9	8		6		10				2	11					
1		3		5	4	7		9	8		6		10				2	11					
4	2	4		4	2	4		4	4		4		4				4	4		1			
				1		2		1			2							1					

	2		4		6	8		9	11	7				5				1	3	10			
1	2		4	6				9			7	10	5	11				3	8				
1	2		2	1	1	1		2	1	1		1	1	2	1		1	2	2				
					2																		

1964-65

Division Two
Manager: W. Ridding

Match No.	Date		Venue	Opponents	Result		Scorers	Attendance
1	Aug	22	A	Huddersfield Town	D	1-1	Davies	12,657
2		26	A	Southampton	L	2-3	Lee, Davies	17,240
3		29	H	Coventry City	L	1-3	Davies	15,969
4	Sep	2	H	Southampton	W	3-0	Davies 3	10,943
5		5	A	Cardiff City	W	3-1	Charter (own-goal), Hill, Fry	13,501
6		7	A	Middlesbrough	L	2-5	Hill, Bromley	22,670
7		12	H	Preston North End	W	5-1	Lee, Hill 2, Davies 2	18,186
8		16	H	Middlesbrough	W	4-2	Lee 2 (1 pen), Hill, Bromley	13,912
9		19	A	Ipswich Town	W	4-1	Lee 2, Thrower (own-goal), Elsworthy (own-goal)	12,558
10		26	H	Plymouth Argyle	W	6-1	Hill 2, Davies 2, Bromley, Taylor	13,670
11		28	A	Leyton Orient	L	1-3	Lee	11,385
12	Oct	2	A	Bury	L	1-2	Lee (pen)	23,321
13		10	H	Crystal Palace	W	3-0	Lee, Hill, Davies	13,671
14		17	A	Norwich City	L	2-3	Lee, Butler (own-goal)	18,065
15		24	H	Rotherham United	W	2-0	Lee (pen), Taylor	14,173
16		31	A	Swansea Town	L	0-2		10,651
17	Nov	7	H	Derby County	W	3-1	Lee, Davies, Bromley	12,903
18		14	A	Swindon Town	W	3-1	Lee 2, Davies	14,445
19		21	H	Portsmouth	W	3-2	Lee, Hill, Davies	13,181
20		28	A	Manchester City	W	4-2	Lee 2 (1 pen), Davies 2	21,895
21	Dec	15	H	Huddersfield Town	W	1-0	Hill	11,782
22		19	A	Coventry City	D	0-0		23,384
23		26	H	Northampton Town	D	0-0		24,487
24	Jan	16	A	Preston North End	D	2-2	Hill, Davies	19,187
25		23	H	Ipswich Town	D	0-0		13,557
26	Feb	6	A	Plymouth Argyle	W	3-1	Lee, Bromley, Taylor	14,553
27		13	H	Bury	L	0-1		16,726
28		27	H	Norwich City	W	5-2	Lee, Hill, Davies 2, Taylor	14,130
29	Mar	2	A	Northampton Town	L	0-4		15,515
30		6	A	Charlton Athletic	W	3-1	Lee (pen), Bromley, Butler	8,634
31		13	H	Swansea Town	W	2-1	Lee, Hill	14,027
32		20	A	Derby County	W	3-2	Lee, Hill, Taylor	16,178
33		26	H	Swindon Town	D	1-1	Lee (pen)	20,731
34		29	H	Charlton Athletic	D	1-1	Rimmer	19,563
35	Apr	3	A	Portsmouth	L	0-3		11,214
36		7	A	Crystal Palace	L	0-2		14,022
37		10	H	Manchester City	W	4-0	Hill, Davies 2, Bromley	14,546
38		16	A	Newcastle United	L	0-2		59,960
39		17	A	Rotherham United	D	0-0		7,685
40		19	H	Newcastle United	D	1-1	Butler	15,979
41		24	H	Leyton Orient	D	0-0		9,016
42		28	H	Cardiff City	W	1-0	Hatton	6,498
							Appearances	
							4 own-goals	Goals

FA Cup

R3	Jan	9	H	Workington	W	4-1	Hill, Butler, Davies 2	14,743
R4		30	A	Preston North End	W	2-1	Lee (pen), Davies	33,553
R5	Feb	20	H	Liverpool	L	0-1		57,207
							Appearances	
								Goals

League Cup

R2	Sep	23	H	Blackburn Rovers	L	1-5	Davies	17,335
							Appearances	
								Goals

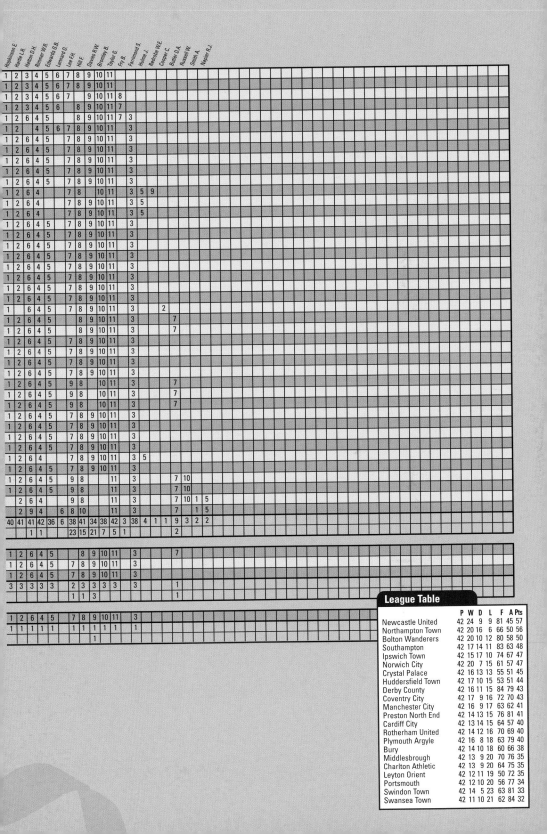

Appearance & Goal Chart

Hopkinson E.	Harris L.R.	Hatton D.H.	Rimmer W.R.	Edwards G.B.	Leonard D.	Lee F.H.	Hill F.	Davies R.W.	Bromley B.	Taylor G.	Fry B.	Farrimond S.	Hulme J.	Redrobe W.E.	Cooper C.	Butler D.A.	Russell W.	Smith A.	Napier F.H.
1	2	3	4	5	6	7	8	9	10	11									
1	2	3	4	5	6	7	8	9	10	11									
1	2	3	4	5	6	7		9	10	11	8								
1	2	3	4	5	6		8	9	10	11	7								
1	2	6	4	5			8	9	10	11	7	3							
1	2		4	5	6	7	8	9	10	11		3							
1	2	6	4	5		7	8	9	10	11		3							
1	2	6	4	5		7	8	9	10	11		3							
1	2	6	4	5		7	8	9	10	11		3							
1	2	6	4	5		7	8	9	10	11		3							
1	2	6	4	5		7	8	9	10	11		3							
1	2	6	4			7	8		10	11		3	5	9					
1	2	6	4			7	8	9	10	11		3	5						
1	2	6	4			7	8	9	10	11		3	5						
1	2	6	4	5		7	8	9	10	11		3							
1	2	6	4	5		7	8	9	10	11		3							
1	2	6	4	5		7	8	9	10	11		3							
1	2	6	4	5		7	8	9	10	11		3							
1	2	6	4	5		7	8	9	10	11		3							
1	2	6	4	5		7	8	9	10	11		3							
1	2	6	4	5		7	8	9	10	11		3							
1		6	4	5		7	8	9	10	11		3			2				
1	2	6	4	5			8	9	10	11		3				7			
1	2	6	4	5			8	9	10	11		3				7			
1	2	6	4	5		7	8	9	10	11		3							
1	2	6	4	5		7	8	9	10	11		3							
1	2	6	4	5		7	8	9	10	11		3							
1	2	6	4	5		7	8	9	10	11		3							
1	2	6	4	5		9	8		10	11		3				7			
1	2	6	4	5		9	8		10	11		3				7			
1	2	6	4	5		9	8		10	11		3				7			
1	2	6	4	5		7	8	9	10	11		3							
1	2	6	4	5		7	8	9	10	11		3							
1	2	6	4	5		7	8	9	10	11		3							
1	2	6	4	5		7	8	9	10	11		3							
1	2	6	4			7	8	9	10	11		3	5						
1	2	6	4	5		7	8	9	10	11		3							
1	2	6	4	5		9	8			11		3				7	10		
1	2	6	4	5		9	8			11		3				7	10		
	2	6	4			9	8			11		3				7	10	1	5
	2	9	4		6	8		10		11		3				7		1	5
40	**41**	**41**	**42**	**36**	**6**	**38**	**41**	**34**	**38**	**42**	**3**	**38**	**4**	**1**	**1**	**9**	**3**	**2**	**2**
	1	1				23	15	21	7	5	1			2					

F.A. Cup

Hopkinson E.	Harris L.R.	Hatton D.H.	Rimmer W.R.	Edwards G.B.	Leonard D.	Lee F.H.	Hill F.	Davies R.W.	Bromley B.	Taylor G.	Fry B.	Farrimond S.	Hulme J.	Redrobe W.E.	Cooper C.	Butler D.A.	Russell W.	Smith A.	Napier F.H.
1	2	6	4	5			8	9	10	11		3				7			
1	2	6	4	5		7	8	9	10	11		3							
1	2	6	4	5		7	8	9	10	11		3							
3	**3**	**3**	**3**	**3**		**2**	**3**	**3**	**3**	**3**		**3**				**1**			
								1	1	3				1					

Football League Cup

Hopkinson E.	Harris L.R.	Hatton D.H.	Rimmer W.R.	Edwards G.B.	Leonard D.	Lee F.H.	Hill F.	Davies R.W.	Bromley B.	Taylor G.	Fry B.	Farrimond S.	Hulme J.	Redrobe W.E.	Cooper C.	Butler D.A.	Russell W.	Smith A.	Napier F.H.
1	2	6	4	5		7	8	9	10	11		3							
1	**1**	**1**	**1**	**1**		**1**	**1**	**1**	**1**	**1**		**1**							
									1										

League Table

	P	W	D	L	F	A	Pts
Newcastle United	42	24	9	9	81	45	57
Northampton Town	42	20	16	6	66	50	56
Bolton Wanderers	42	20	10	12	80	58	50
Southampton	42	17	14	11	83	63	48
Ipswich Town	42	15	17	10	74	67	47
Norwich City	42	20	7	15	61	57	47
Crystal Palace	42	16	13	13	55	51	45
Huddersfield Town	42	17	10	15	53	51	44
Derby County	42	16	11	15	84	79	43
Coventry City	42	17	9	16	72	70	43
Manchester City	42	16	9	17	63	62	41
Preston North End	42	14	13	15	76	81	41
Cardiff City	42	13	14	15	64	57	40
Rotherham United	42	14	12	16	70	69	40
Plymouth Argyle	42	16	8	18	63	79	40
Bury	42	14	10	18	60	66	38
Middlesbrough	42	13	9	20	70	76	35
Charlton Athletic	42	13	9	20	64	75	35
Leyton Orient	42	12	11	19	50	72	35
Portsmouth	42	12	10	20	56	77	34
Swindon Town	42	14	5	23	63	81	33
Swansea Town	42	11	10	21	62	84	32

1965-66

Division Two

Manager: W. Ridding

Match No.	Date		Venue	Opponents	Result		Scorers	Attendance
1	Aug	21	H	Charlton Athletic	W	4-2	Rimmer, Lee 2 (1 pen), Bonds (own-goal)	12,744
2		25	A	Crystal Palace	D	1-1	Bromley	20,784
3		28	A	Plymouth Argyle	W	3-1	Davies 2, Taylor	16,444
4	Sep	1	H	Crystal Palace	W	3-0	Lee (pen), Davies, Taylor	15,617
5		4	H	Portsmouth	W	2-0	Lee, Hill	12,107
6		7	A	Huddersfield Town	L	0-1		24,532
7		15	H	Huddersfield Town	D	1-1	Butler	16,614
8		18	A	Ipswich Town	L	0-2		12,775
9		25	H	Birmingham City	L	1-2	Hill	12,117
10	Oct	2	A	Leyton Orient	L	0-1		7,774
11		9	H	Southampton	L	2-3	Greaves 2	12,511
12		16	A	Derby County	L	0-2		11,418
13		23	H	Cardiff City	W	2-1	Davies, Taylor	11,088
14		30	A	Carlisle United	D	1-1	Hill	11,114
15	Nov	6	H	Coventry City	W	4-2	Davies 2, Bromley, Butler	13,499
16		13	A	Bristol City	D	2-2	Ford (own-goal), Davies	19,912
17		16	A	Bury	D	1-1	Hill	12,686
18		20	H	Manchester City	W	1-0	Hatton	22,927
19		27	A	Rotherham United	L	1-2	Redrobe	9,785
20	Dec	4	H	Wolverhampton Wanderers	W	2-1	Hill, Davies	12,276
21		11	A	Norwich City	L	0-3		14,363
22		18	H	Derby County	L	0-1		8,578
23	Jan	1	A	Southampton	L	1-5	Lee	18,807
24		8	H	Bristol City	L	1-2	Lee (pen)	10,405
25		29	A	Charlton Athletic	W	1-0	Bromley	10,227
26	Feb	5	H	Plymouth Argyle	L	0-1		10,705
27		19	A	Portsmouth	L	0-1		11,995
28		26	H	Bury	W	2-1	Lee, Hill	12,528
29	Mar	5	A	Cardiff City	D	1-1	Davies	8,951
30		12	H	Ipswich Town	W	3-1	Lee, Hill, Davies	9,180
31		16	H	Preston North End	L	1-3	Davies	13,961
32		19	A	Birmingham City	W	1-0	Lee	13,770
33		26	H	Leyton Orient	W	2-0	Rimmer, Lee (pen)	8,713
34	Apr	2	A	Coventry City	D	2-2	Lee, Taylor	19,461
35		11	H	Middlesbrough	W	6-0	Lee, Hill, Davies, Bromley, Taylor 2	11,948
36		12	A	Middlesbrough	D	1-1	Greaves	11,384
37		16	A	Manchester City	L	1-4	Taylor	29,459
38		19	A	Preston North End	W	1-0	Hatton	11,231
39		25	H	Rotherham United	L	1-3	Davies	10,622
40		30	A	Wolverhampton Wanderers	L	1-3	Taylor	15,770
41	May	4	H	Carlisle United	W	4-0	Hatton 2, Lee, Taylor	6,536
42		7	H	Norwich City	D	1-1	Rimmer	7,420
							Appearances	
							Sub appearances	
					2 own-goals		Goals	

FA Cup

R3	Jan	22	H	West Bromwich Albion	W	3-0	Lee 2, Bromley	24,425
R4	Feb	12	H	Preston North End	D	1-1	Davies	35,680
rep		14	A	Preston North End	L	2-3	Lee, Davies	31,131
							Appearances	
							Goals	

League Cup

R2	Sep	22	H	Aldershot	W	3-0	Lee 2, Davies	8,329
R3	Oct	13	A	Grimsby Town	L	2-4	Butler, Greaves	8,824
							Appearances	
							Goals	

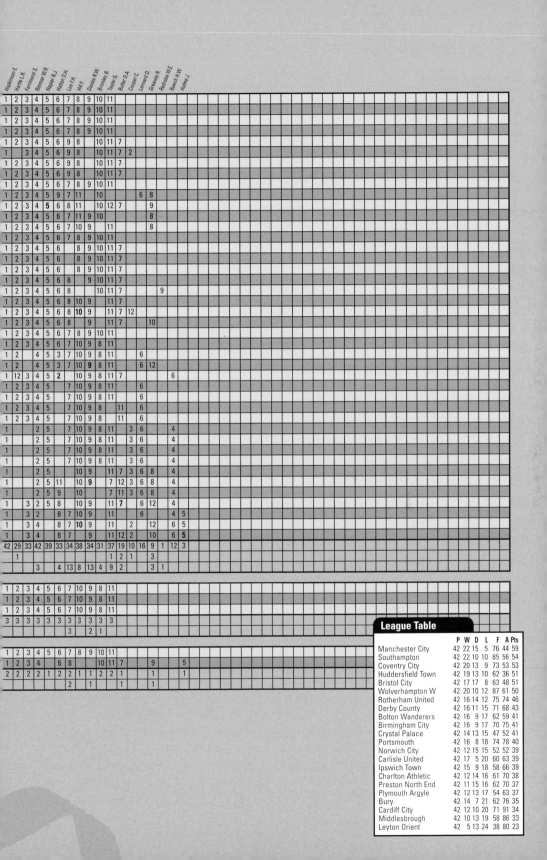

League Table

	P	W	D	L	F	A	Pts
Manchester City	42	22	15	5	76	44	59
Southampton	42	22	10	10	85	56	54
Coventry City	42	20	13	9	73	53	53
Huddersfield Town	42	19	13	10	62	36	51
Bristol City	42	17	17	8	63	48	51
Wolverhampton W	42	20	10	12	87	61	50
Rotherham United	42	16	14	12	75	74	46
Derby County	42	16	11	15	71	68	43
Bolton Wanderers	42	16	9	17	62	59	41
Birmingham City	42	16	9	17	70	75	41
Crystal Palace	42	14	13	15	47	52	41
Portsmouth	42	16	8	18	74	78	40
Norwich City	42	12	15	15	52	52	39
Carlisle United	42	17	5	20	60	63	39
Ipswich Town	42	15	9	18	58	66	39
Charlton Athletic	42	12	14	16	61	70	38
Preston North End	42	11	15	16	62	70	37
Plymouth Argyle	42	12	13	17	54	63	37
Bury	42	14	7	21	62	76	35
Cardiff City	42	12	10	20	71	91	34
Middlesbrough	42	10	13	19	58	86	33
Leyton Orient	42	5	13	24	38	80	23

Division Two

Manager: W. Ridding

Match No.	Date	Venue	Opponents	Result		Scorers	Attendance
1	Aug 20	A	Charlton Athletic	W	1-0	Davies	10,429
2	24	H	Rotherham United	D	2-2	Davies, Hill	14,389
3	27	H	Derby County	W	3-1	Napier, Lee (pen), Bromley	11,656
4	30	H	Rotherham United	W	1-0	Taylor	11,943
5	Sep 3	A	Crystal Palace	L	2-3	Rimmer, Greaves	16,578
6	7	H	Carlisle United	W	3-0	Davies 3	15,282
7	10	H	Huddersfield Town	W	1-0	Lee	17,600
8	17	A	Cardiff City	W	5-2	Lee 2 (1 pen), Davies 2, Murray (own-goal)	7,594
9	24	H	Wolverhampton Wanderers	D	0-0		21,149
10	Oct 1	A	Ipswich Town	D	2-2	Lee, Davies	16,019
11	8	H	Preston North End	W	4-2	Davies 3, Cranston (own-goal)	20,239
12	14	A	Bury	L	1-2	Davies	21,545
13	22	H	Coventry City	D	1-1	Byrom	14,561
14	29	A	Norwich City	L	0-1		12,593
15	Nov 5	H	Birmingham City	W	3-1	Rimmer, Lee, Byrom	10,030
16	12	A	Portsmouth	L	1-2	Lee	12,665
17	19	H	Hull City	W	2-1	Lee 2 (1 pen)	14,950
18	26	A	Plymouth Argyle	L	0-2		13,665
19	Dec 3	H	Northampton Town	L	1-2	Byrom	10,352
20	10	A	Millwall	L	0-2		13,222
21	17	H	Charlton Athletic	W	2-1	Lee (pen), Bromley	7,911
22	26	A	Bristol City	D	1-1	Lee	16,724
23	31	A	Derby County	D	2-2	Bromley, Byrom	14,619
24	Jan 14	A	Huddersfield Town	L	1-2	Byrom	18,176
25	21	H	Cardiff City	W	3-1	Rimmer, Lee, Byrom	9,071
26	Feb 4	A	Wolverhampton Wanderers	L	2-5	Bromley 2	24,015
27	11	H	Ipswich Town	D	1-1	Taylor	12,565
28	25	A	Preston North End	W	3-1	Lee 3 (1 pen)	16,067
29	Mar 4	H	Norwich City	D	1-1	Farrimond	12,483
30	11	H	Crystal Palace	D	0-0		9,784
31	18	A	Coventry City	D	1-1	Phillips	28,674
32	25	A	Bury	W	3-1	Lee, R.Hatton 2	20,320
33	27	H	Blackburn Rovers	L	0-1		21,740
34	Apr 1	A	Birmingham City	D	2-2	Lee, Isherwood (own-goal)	18,187
35	8	H	Portsmouth	L	0-1		11,281
36	15	H	Hull City	D	1-1	Lee	16,480
37	19	H	Bristol City	D	0-0		8,647
38	22	H	Plymouth Argyle	L	1-2	Phillips	7,427
39	25	A	Blackburn Rovers	D	0-0		12,403
40	29	A	Northampton Town	L	1-2	Lee	9,387
41	May 6	H	Millwall	W	5-0	Napier, Lee 2 (1 pen), Bromley, Lennard	6,502
42	13	A	Carlisle United	L	1-6	Lee	7,732
						Appearances	
						Sub appearances	
						3 own-goals	Goals

FA Cup

R3	Jan 28	H	Crewe Alexandra	W	1-0	Lee (pen)	23,730
R4	Feb 18	H	Arsenal	D	0-0		31,870
rep	22	A	Arsenal	L	0-3		47,050
						Appearances	
						Sub appearances	
							Goals

League Cup

R2	Sep 14	A	Manchester City	L	1-3	Lee	9,006
						Appearances	
							Goals

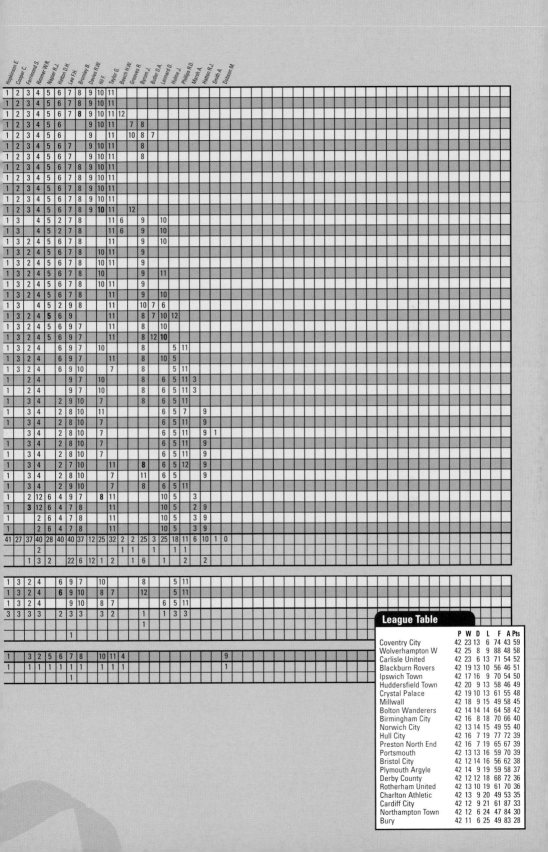

	Hopkinson E.	Cooper C.	Farrimond S.	Rimmer W.R.	Napier R.J.	Hatton D.H.	Lee F.H.	Bromley B.	Davies R.W.	Hill F.	Taylor G.	Beech H.W.	Greaves R.	Byrom J.	Butler D.A.	Lennard D.	Hulme J.	Phillips R.D.	Marsh A.	Hatton R.J.	Smith A.	Dobson M.
	1	2	3	4	5	6	7	8	9	10	11											
	1	2	3	4	5	6	7	8	9	10	11											
	1	2	3	4	5	6	7	8	9	10	11	12										
	1	2	3	4	5	6			9	10	11		7	8								
	1	2	3	4	5	6			9		11		10	8	7							
	1	2	3	4	5	6	7		9	10	11			8								
	1	2	3	4	5	6	7		9	10	11			8								
	1	2	3	4	5	6	7	8	9	10	11											
	1	2	3	4	5	6	7	8	9	10	11											
	1	2	3	4	5	6	7	8	9	10	11											
	1	2	3	4	5	6	7	8	9	10	11											
	1	2	3	4	5	6	7	8	9	10	11		12									
	1	3		4	5	2	7	8		11	6		9		10							
	1	3		4	5	2	7	8		11	6		9		10							
	1	3	2	4	5	6	7	8		11			9		10							
	1	3	2	4	5	6	7	8	10	11			9									
	1	3	2	4	5	6	7	8	10	11			9									
	1	3	2	4	5	6	7	8	10				9		11							
	1	3	2	4	5	6	7	8	10	11			9									
	1	3	2	4	5	6	7	8		11			9		10							
	1	3		4	5	2	9	8		11			10	7	6							
	1	3	2	4	5	6	9			11			8	7	10	12						
	1	3	2	4	5	6	9	7		11			8		10							
	1	3	2	4	5	6	9	7		11			8	12	10							
	1	3	2	4		6	9	7	10				8				5	11				
	1	3	2	4		6	9	7		11			8				10	5				
	1	3	2	4		6	9	10		7			8					5	11			
	1		2	4			9	7	10				8		6		5	11	3			
	1		2	4			9	7	10				8		6		5	11	3			
	1		3	4		2	9	10		7			8		6		5	11				
	1		3	4		2	8	10		11				6	5	7			9			
	1		3	4		2	8	10		7				6	5	11						
			3	4		2	8	10		7				6	5	11			9	1		
	1		3	4		2	8	10		7				6	5	11			9			
	1		3	4		2	8	10		7				6	5	11			9			
	1		3	4		2	7		11				8		6	5	12		9			
	1		3	4		2	8	10			7		11		6	5			9			
	1		3	4		2	9	10			7		8		6	5	11					
	1		2	12	6	4	9	7		8	11				10	5		3				
	1		3	12	6	4	7	8		11					10	5		2	9			
	1		2	6	4	7	8		11						10	5		3	9			
	1		2	6	4	7	8		11						10	5		3	9			
	41	27	37	40	28	40	40	37	12	25	32	2	2	25	3	25	18	11	6	10	1	0
		2									1	1		1		1	1					
		1	3	2		22	6	12	1	2		1	6		1		2		2	2		

	1	3	2	4		6	9	7		10			8				5	11				
	1	3	2	4		6	9	10		8	7		12				5	11				
	1	3	2	4			9	10		8	7				6	5	11					
	3	3	3	3		2	3	3		3	2		1		1	3	3					
									1													
				1																		

	1		3	2	5	6	7	8		10	11	4						9				
	1		1	1	1	1	1		1	1	1							1				
				1																		

BOLTON WANDERERS FOOTBALL CLUB

BURNDEN PARK, BOLTON

OFFICIAL PROGRAMME 6D.

SEASON 1967-68 — LEAGUE CUP—2nd ROUND REPLAY
WEDNESDAY, SEPTEMBER 27th, 1967
BOLTON WANDERERS v. LIVERPOOL

Match No.	Date		Venue	Opponents	Result		Scorers	Attendance
1	Aug	19	A	Birmingham City	L	0-4		23,537
2		23	H	Hull City	W	6-1	Lee 2, Taylor 2, Byrom 2	9,653
3		26	H	Cardiff City	D	1-1	Lee	10,654
4		30	A	Hull City	W	2-1	Lee, Byrom	15,776
5	Sep	2	H	Huddersfield Town	W	3-1	Lee 2, Byrom	11,544
6		6	H	Millwall	D	1-1	Lee	11,360
7		9	A	Ipswich Town	D	1-1	Lee	14,903
8		16	H	Carlisle United	L	2-3	Greaves, Bromley	12,809
9		23	A	Blackburn Rovers	L	1-2	Byrom	19,393
10		30	H	Blackpool	L	1-2	Phillips	16,695
11	Oct	7	A	Queen's Park Rangers	L	0-1		16,848
12		14	H	Norwich City	W	2-0	Bromley, Byrom	8,503
13		21	A	Rotherham United	D	2-2	Greaves, Byrom	7,229
14		28	H	Derby County	W	5-3	Greaves, Byrom 2, Williams 2	12,631
15	Nov	4	A	Preston North End	D	1-1	Taylor	19,796
16		18	A	Portsmouth	L	0-3		21,437
17		22	H	Charlton Athletic	W	2-0	Williams, Wharton	12,043
18		25	H	Aston Villa	L	2-3	Hill, Deakin (own-goal)	13,064
19	Dec	2	A	Crystal Palace	W	3-0	Taylor, Wharton 2 (1 pen)	15,780
20		9	H	Plymouth Argyle	L	1-2	Taylor	9,505
21		16	H	Birmingham City	D	1-1	Greaves	10,468
22		23	A	Cardiff City	W	3-1	Taylor, Greaves, Carver (own-goal)	11,082
23		26	H	Middlesbrough	W	2-0	Rimmer, Wharton	16,076
24		30	A	Middlesbrough	W	2-1	Rimmer, Horner (own-goal)	29,217
25	Jan	6	A	Huddersfield Town	D	1-1	Hill	14,147
26		20	A	Carlisle United	L	0-3		11,065
27	Feb	3	H	Blackburn Rovers	W	2-1	Williams 2	17,334
28		10	A	Blackpool	D	1-1	Taylor (pen)	19,183
29		16	A	Millwall	L	0-3		12,457
30		24	H	Queen's Park Rangers	D	1-1	Hulme	14,956
31	Mar	2	A	Norwich City	L	1-3	Taylor	14,694
32		9	A	Ipswich Town	L	1-2	Greaves	8,695
33		16	H	Rotherham United	L	0-2		8,682
34		23	A	Derby County	L	1-2	Greaves	16,054
35		30	H	Preston North End	D	0-0		14,664
36	Apr	2	A	Bristol City	D	1-1	Greaves	11,047
37		6	A	Charlton Athletic	L	0-2		10,571
38		13	H	Portsmouth	L	1-2	Smith (own-goal)	7,833
39		17	H	Bristol City	W	1-0	Greaves	7,289
40		20	A	Aston Villa	D	1-1	Taylor	16,860
41		27	H	Crystal Palace	D	2-2	Greaves, Hulme	6,768
42	May	4	A	Plymouth Argyle	W	2-1	Hill, Wharton (pen)	5,371

							Appearances
							Sub appearances
						4 own-goals	Goals

FA Cup

R3	Jan 27	A	Nottingham Forest	L	2-4	Taylor, Hulme	37,229

| | | | | | | Appearances |
| | | | | | | Goals |

League Cup

R2	Sep 13	A	Liverpool	D	1-1	Lee	45,957
rep	27	H	Liverpool	W	3-2	Hill, Taylor 2	30,669
R3	Oct 11	A	West Ham United	L	1-4	Byrom	20,450

| | | | | | | Appearances |
| | | | | | | Goals |

Appearances and goals grid (player columns, left to right):

	Hopkinson E.	Marsh A.	Farrimond S.	Greaves R.	Hatton D.H.	Lennard D.H.	Lee F.H.	Bromley B.	Hatton R.J.	Hill F.	Taylor G.	Byrom J.	Smith A.	Cooper C.	Hulme J.	Butler D.A.	Phillips R.D.	Rixon J.A.	Williams G.C.	Rimmer W.R.	Wharton T.J.	Roberts G.M.
1	1	2	3	4	5	6	7	8	9	10	11											
2	1	2	3	4	5	6	7		9	10	11	8										
3	1	2	3	4	5	6	7		9	10	11	8										
4		2	3	4	5	6	7		9	10	11	8	1									
5		2	3	4	5	6	7		**9**	10	11	8	1	12								
6	1	2	3	4	5	6	7	8		10	11	9										
7	1		3	4	2	6		7	8		10	11	9		5							
8	1	**2**	3	4	6			7	8	12	10	11	9		5							
9	1	12	3	4	2	6	7	8	**9**		11	10		5								
10	1		3	4	2	6		8		10		9		5	7	11						
11	1		3	8	2		7		10	11	9		5					4	6			
12	1		3	8	2	11			10	7	9		5					4	6			
13	1		3	8	2		7		10	11	9		5					4	6			
14	1		3	8	2				10	11	9		5					4	6	7		
15	1		3	6		12		8		10	11	**9**		2	5			4		7		
16	1		3					8	9	10	11			2	5		12	**4**	6	7		
17	1		3					8	9	10	11			2	5			4	6	7		
18	1		3					8	9	10	11			2	5			4	6	7		
19	1		3					8	9	10	11			2	5			4	6	7		
20	1		3	9	6			8		11				2	5			4	10	7		
21	1		3	9	6			8		11				2	5			4	10	7		
22	1		3	9	6			8		11				2	5			4	10	7		
23	1		3	9	6			8		11				2	5			4	10	7		
24	1		3	9	6			8		11				2	5			4	10	7		
25	1	12	3	9				8		11				2	5		6	4	10	**7**		
26	1		3	12	9			8		11				2	5			4	10	**7**		
27	1		3	7	6			8		11				2	5			4	10			
28	1		3	7	6			8		11	9			2	5			4	10			
29	1		3	9	6		12		7	11	8			2	**5**			4	10			
30	1	6	3	5				7	8	11	9			2				4	10			
31	1		3	9	6			8		11				2	5		7	4	10			
32	1		3		5		8	9	10	7			2		11	12	4	6				
33	1		3	9	6	10		8		11			2	5			7	4				
34	1		3	9	6	10			11	9			2	5			4	8				
35	1		3	9	6	10			11	8			2	5			4	7				
36	1		3	9	6	10			11	8				5			4	2	7			
37	1		3	9	6		10		8	11				5		2	4		7			
38	1		3	9	6		10		8	11			2	5		2	4		7			
39	1		3	9	6		10		8	11				5			4		7			
40	1		3	9	6		10		8	11				5		2	4		7			
41	1			9	6		10		8	11				5		2	4		**7**	3		
Apps	40	8	41	36	35	15	9	21	13	36	41	23	2	22	34	1	3	7	31	24	19	1
Sub	2		1			1	1							1					1	2		
Goals	10			8	2		3	9	9			2			1			5	2	5		

FA Cup:

	Hopkinson E.	Marsh A.	Farrimond S.	Greaves R.	Hatton D.H.	Lennard D.H.	Lee F.H.	Bromley B.	Hatton R.J.	Hill F.	Taylor G.	Byrom J.	Smith A.	Cooper C.	Hulme J.	Butler D.A.	Phillips R.D.	Rixon J.A.	Williams G.C.	Rimmer W.R.	Wharton T.J.	Roberts G.M.
	1		3	10			7		8	11	9		2	5				4	6			
	1		1	1			1		1	1	1		1	1				1	1			

League Cup:

	Hopkinson E.	Marsh A.	Farrimond S.	Greaves R.	Hatton D.H.	Lennard D.H.	Lee F.H.	Bromley B.	Hatton R.J.	Hill F.	Taylor G.	Byrom J.	Smith A.	Cooper C.	Hulme J.	Butler D.A.	Phillips R.D.	Rixon J.A.	Williams G.C.	Rimmer W.R.	Wharton T.J.	Roberts G.M.
	1	2	3	4	6		7	8		10	11	9		5								
	1		3	4	2	6	7	8		10	11	9		5								
	1		3	6	2			8		10	11	9		5			4	7				
	3	1	3	3	3	1	2	3		3	3	3		3			1	1				
					1					1	2	1										

League Table

	P	W	D	L	F	A	Pts
Ipswich Town	42	22	15	5	79	44	59
Queen's Park Rangers	42	25	8	9	67	36	58
Blackpool	42	24	10	8	71	43	58
Birmingham City	42	19	14	9	83	51	52
Portsmouth	42	18	13	11	68	55	49
Middlesbrough	42	17	12	13	60	54	46
Millwall	42	14	17	11	62	50	45
Blackburn Rovers	42	16	11	15	56	49	43
Norwich City	42	16	11	15	60	65	43
Carlisle United	42	14	13	15	58	52	41
Crystal Palace	42	14	11	17	56	56	39
Bolton Wanderers	42	13	13	16	60	63	39
Cardiff City	42	13	12	17	60	66	38
Huddersfield Town	42	13	12	17	46	61	38
Charlton Athletic	42	12	13	17	63	68	37
Aston Villa	42	15	7	20	54	64	37
Hull City	42	12	13	17	58	73	37
Derby County	42	13	10	19	71	78	36
Bristol City	42	13	10	19	48	62	36
Preston North End	42	12	11	19	43	65	35
Rotherham United	42	10	11	21	42	76	31
Plymouth Argyle	42	9	9	24	38	72	27

Division Two

Manager: N. Lofthouse

Season 1968-69
League—Second Division

Saturday, Aug. 31st, 1968

OFFICIAL PROGRAMME 9ᵈ

WANDERERS v. SHEFFIELD UNITED

Match No.	Date		Venue	Opponents	Result		Scorers	Attendance
1	Aug	10	A	Oxford United	D	1-1	Williams	11,427
2		17	H	Bury	W	2-0	Greaves, Bromley	16,627
3		20	A	Bristol City	D	2-2	Wharton 2	17,353
4		24	A	Fulham	W	2-0	Hulme, Hill	12,830
5		26	A	Millwall	L	1-3	Wharton	15,655
6		31	H	Sheffield United	W	4-2	Greaves 3, Wharton (pen)	14,636
7	Sep	7	A	Blackpool	L	0-1		22,688
8		14	H	Blackburn Rovers	D	1-1	Bromley	16,097
9		18	H	Aston Villa	W	4-1	Greaves 2, Hill, Hulme	14,513
10		21	A	Hull City	L	0-1		13,487
11		28	H	Derby County	L	1-2	Wharton	15,202
12	Oct	5	A	Carlisle United	D	1-1	Hill	8,846
13		9	H	Millwall	L	0-4		12,715
14		12	H	Charlton Athletic	W	3-0	Greaves, Hill, Curtis (own-goal)	9,060
15		19	A	Cardiff City	W	2-0	Wharton, Taylor	12,026
16		26	A	Huddersfield Town	L	2-3	Wharton (pen), Hill	12,431
17	Nov	2	A	Crystal Palace	L	1-2	Fletcher	13,027
18		16	A	Middlesbrough	D	0-0		18,458
19		23	H	Birmingham City	D	0-0		7,175
20		30	A	Preston North End	W	4-1	Byrom 2, Rimmer, Williams	15,252
21	Dec	4	H	Norwich City	D	1-1	Byrom	9,842
22		7	H	Portsmouth	W	1-0	Taylor	7,805
23		14	A	Charlton Athletic	D	2-2	Williams, Fletcher	9,270
24		21	A	Cardiff City	L	1-2	Wharton	8,895
25		26	H	Carlisle United	L	0-1		13,922
26	Jan	11	H	Crystal Palace	D	2-2	Greaves 2	9,082
27		18	A	Norwich City	L	0-2		11,997
28	Feb	1	H	Middlesbrough	D	0-0		7,658
29		22	A	Portsmouth	D	2-2	Wharton, Taylor	16,500
30	Mar	1	H	Oxford United	D	1-1	Byrom	6,707
31		4	A	Huddersfield Town	L	0-3		8,614
32		7	A	Bury	L	1-2	Williams	11,755
33		15	H	Fulham	W	3-2	Conway (own-goal), Rimmer, Taylor	8,323
34		22	A	Sheffield United	L	2-5	Hill, Phillips	12,467
35		25	A	Birmingham City	L	0-5		20,454
36		29	H	Blackpool	L	1-4	Taylor (pen)	9,264
37	Apr	5	A	Derby County	L	1-5	Greaves	30,684
38		7	H	Bristol City	W	1-0	Byrom	8,172
39		8	A	Aston Villa	D	1-1	Hulme	25,442
40		12	H	Hull City	W	1-0	Phillips	5,106
41		16	H	Preston North End	D	0-0		8,028
42		19	A	Blackburn Rovers	W	3-2	Greaves, Wharton, Bryom	8,178
							Appearances	
							Sub appearances	
						2 own-goals	Goals	

FA Cup

R3	Jan	4	H	Northampton Town	W	2-1	Fletcher, Greaves	12,632
R4		25	H	Bristol Rovers	L	1-2	Williams	16,707
							Appearances	
							Sub appearances	
							Goals	

League Cup

R2	Sep	4	A	West Ham United	L	2-7	Wharton (pen), Taylor	24,737
							Appearances	
							Goals	

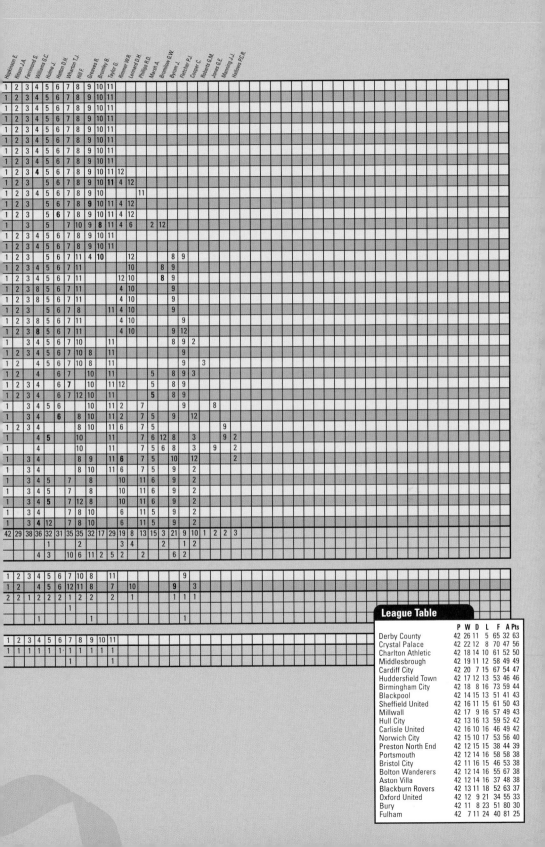

League Table

	P	W	D	L	F	A	Pts
Derby County	42	26	11	5	65	32	63
Crystal Palace	42	22	12	8	70	47	56
Charlton Athletic	42	18	14	10	61	52	50
Middlesbrough	42	19	11	12	58	49	49
Cardiff City	42	20	7	15	67	54	47
Huddersfield Town	42	17	12	13	53	46	46
Birmingham City	42	18	8	16	73	59	44
Blackpool	42	14	15	13	51	41	43
Sheffield United	42	16	11	15	61	50	43
Millwall	42	17	9	16	57	49	43
Hull City	42	13	16	13	59	52	42
Carlisle United	42	16	10	16	46	49	42
Norwich City	42	15	10	17	53	56	40
Preston North End	42	12	15	15	38	44	39
Portsmouth	42	12	14	16	58	58	38
Bristol City	42	11	16	15	46	53	38
Bolton Wanderers	42	12	14	16	55	67	38
Aston Villa	42	12	14	16	37	48	38
Blackburn Rovers	42	13	11	18	52	63	37
Oxford United	42	12	9	21	34	55	33
Bury	42	11	8	23	51	80	30
Fulham	42	7	11	24	40	81	25

Division Two

Manager: N. Lofthouse

Match No.	Date		Venue	Opponents	Result		Scorers	Attendance
1	Aug	9	H	Millwall	W	4-1	Byrom 3, Greaves	10,402
2		16	A	Watford	D	0-0		15,975
3		20	A	Leicester City	D	2-2	Wharton (pen), Phillips	27,673
4		23	H	Preston North End	W	2-0	Phillips, Wharton (pen)	15,009
5		26	A	Carlisle United	L	1-2	Wharton	11,682
6		30	A	Cardiff City	L	1-2	Wharton	21,048
7	Sep	6	H	Birmingham City	W	2-0	Taylor, Byrom	11,303
8		13	A	Hull City	L	2-4	Greaves, Byrom	10,646
9		17	H	Aston Villa	W	2-1	Byrom, Greaves	11,700
10		20	H	Portsmouth	L	0-1		10,579
11		27	A	Huddersfield Town	L	0-1		12,326
12	Oct	4	H	Swindon Town	L	0-1		9,372
13		8	H	Watford	L	2-3	Hurley, Seddon	7,443
14		11	A	Middlesbrough	L	0-4		14,020
15		18	H	Oxford United	D	1-1	Byrom	7,030
16		25	A	Blackpool	D	1-1	Manning	17,179
17	Nov	1	H	Bristol City	W	3-1	Byrom, Wharton, Rooks (own-goal)	6,757
18		8	A	Blackburn Rovers	L	1-3	Wharton	13,175
19		12	H	Leicester City	L	2-3	Taylor, Wharton (pen)	7,219
20		15	H	Sheffield United	D	0-0		7,992
21		19	A	Aston Villa	L	0-3		22,951
22		22	A	Norwich City	L	0-1		10,809
23		29	H	Queen's Park Rangers	W	6-4	Manning 2, Byrom 2, Taylor, Wharton	7,253
24	Dec	6	A	Charlton Athletic	D	1-1	Byrom	7,644
25		13	H	Hull City	W	2-1	Byrom 2	7,059
26		26	A	Preston North End	W	3-1	Manning, Byrom, Hurley	23,934
27	Jan	10	H	Portsmouth	D	1-1	Byrom	10,464
28		17	H	Huddersfield Town	D	1-1	Byrom	14,272
29		31	A	Swindon Town	L	2-3	Wharton, Manning	18,564
30	Feb	11	H	Middlesbrough	W	2-1	Hunt, Hurley	9,928
31		14	H	Millwall	L	0-2		9,881
32		21	H	Blackpool	L	0-2		14,431
33		24	A	Birmingham City	L	0-2		19,489
34		28	A	Oxford United	L	1-3	Byrom	9,627
35	Mar	14	A	Queen's Park Rangers	W	4-0	Hunt 2, Greaves, Byrom	13,596
36		18	H	Cardiff City	L	0-1		10,434
37		21	H	Charlton Athletic	D	1-1	Hunt	8,367
38		27	A	Bristol City	D	2-2	Hulme, Byrom	17,298
39		28	A	Sheffield United	W	1-0	Byrom	18,539
40		30	H	Blackburn Rovers	W	1-0	Hunt	18,032
41	Apr	4	H	Carlisle United	D	0-0		9,120
42		9	H	Norwich City	D	0-0		7,164
							Appearances	
							Sub appearances	
						1 own-goal	Goals	

FA Cup

R3	Jan	3	H	Watford	L	1-2	Greaves	22,447
							Appearances	
							Goals	

League Cup

R1	Aug	13	H	Rochdale	W	6-3	Byrom 3, Wharton (pen), Greaves 2	10,097
R2	Sep	3	H	Rotherham United	D	0-0		11,043
rep		9	A	Rotherham United	D	3-3	Hulme, Byrom 2	7,924
rep2		11	A	Rotherham United	L	0-1		9,018
R2 replay a.e.t.							Appearances	
							Sub appearances	
							Goals	

Player columns (left to right):

Hopkinson E. · Rison J.A. · Hallows P.C.R. · Rimmer W.R. · Hurley C. · Marsh A. · Wharton T.J. · Byrom J. · Greaves R. · Hatton D.H. · Phillip R.D. · Fletcher P.J. · Taylor G. · Seddon I.W. · Hulme J. · Williams G.C. · Roberts G.M. · Manning J.J. · Harfern J. · Boswell A.H. · Hunt R. · Farrimond S. · Duffey C.P. · McAllister D.

Appearances / totals row:

| 20 | 39 | 26 | 36 | 28 | 37 | 38 | 40 | 37 | 6 | 13 | 4 | 28 | 13 | 15 | 17 | 3 | 14 | 1 | 22 | 17 | 5 | 2 | 1 |

Goals row:

| | | 3 | | 9 | 20 | 4 | | 2 | | 3 | 1 | 1 | | 5 | | | 5 | | | | | | |

Division Two

Manager: N. Lofthouse until 2 November 1970, J. McIlroy 3 to 20 November 1970, N. Lofthouse until 14 January 1971, J. Meadows 15 January to 6 April 1971, N. Lofthouse until May 1971

Match No.	Date		Venue	Opponents	Result		Scorers	Attendance
1	Aug	15	H	Luton Town	W	4-2	Wharton 3 (2 pens), Greaves	11,664
2		19	H	Sheffield Wednesday	W	2-1	Ritson, Hunt	13,462
3		22	A	Portsmouth	L	0-4		15,743
4		29	H	Queen's Park Rangers	D	2-2	Williams, Wharton (pen)	11,242
5	Sep	2	A	Sheffield Wednesday	D	1-1	Hunt	12,240
6		5	A	Hull City	L	0-1		16,290
7		12	A	Cardiff City	L	0-2		11,086
8		19	A	Blackburn Rovers	W	2-0	Taylor, Byrom	10,421
9		26	H	Oxford United	L	0-2		9,095
10		30	H	Orient	L	0-1		7,165
11	Oct	3	A	Sunderland	L	1-4	Fletcher	15,972
12		10	H	Charlton Athletic	W	4-0	Fletcher, Byrom 2, Taylor	7,937
13		17	A	Luton Town	L	0-2		19,055
14		20	A	Sheffield United	D	2-2	Hulme, Phillips	18,216
15		24	H	Bristol City	W	1-0	Williams	7,749
16		31	A	Leicester City	L	0-1		24,623
17	Nov	7	H	Norwich City	L	0-1		7,201
18		14	A	Millwall	L	0-2		6,410
19		21	H	Birmingham City	W	3-0	Hunt 3	7,432
20		28	A	Watford	D	1-1	Manning	12,020
21	Dec	5	H	Swindon Town	L	0-3		7,826
22		12	A	Middlesbrough	L	0-1		12,873
23		19	H	Portsmouth	D	1-1	Manning	5,813
24		26	H	Carlisle United	L	0-1		11,132
25	Jan	9	A	Orient	L	1-3	Redfern	6,580
26		16	H	Sheffield United	W	2-1	Seddon, Fletcher	10,146
27		30	H	Watford	L	0-1		10,239
28	Feb	6	A	Swindon Town	L	1-3	Hunt	15,325
29		13	H	Middlesbrough	L	0-3		9,877
30		20	A	Birmingham City	L	0-4		25,600
31		27	H	Leicester City	L	0-3		8,663
32	Mar	6	A	Bristol City	D	1-1	Waldron	10,550
33		13	H	Millwall	D	1-1	G. Jones	6,308
34		20	A	Norwich City	L	1-2	G. Jones (pen)	9,051
35		27	H	Hull City	D	0-0		8,759
36	Apr	3	A	Queen's Park Rangers	L	0-4		8,613
37		7	A	Cardiff City	L	0-1		21,282
38		10	H	Carlisle United	L	0-3		8,038
39		12	H	Sunderland	L	1-3	Hunt	5,937
40		17	A	Charlton Athletic	L	1-4	Greaves	10,295
41		24	H	Blackburn Rovers	D	1-1	Goodwin (own-goal)	7,195
42	May	1	A	Oxford United	D	1-1	Hunt	7,357

Appearances	
Sub appearances	
1 own-goal	Goals

FA Cup

R3	Jan	2	A	York City	L	0-2		10,113

Appearances	
Sub appearances	

FL Cup

R2	Sep	9	H	Blackburn Rovers	W	1-0	Fletcher	12,000
R3	Oct	7	H	Leicester City	D	1-1	Manning	8,623
rep.		12	A	Leicester City	L	0-1		18,068

Appearances	
Sub appearances	
	Goals

Player columns (left to right):

Clarke P.A. · Ritson J.A. · Farnimand S. · Williams G.C. · Hulme J. · Rimmell W.R. · Wharton T.J. · Byrom J. · Hunt R. · Greaves R. · Taylor G. · Hurley C.J. · Boswell A.H. · Hallows P.C.R. · Seddon I.W. · Fletcher P.J. · Phillips R.D. · McAllister D. · Jones G.E. · Waldron A. · Marsh A. · Manning J.J. · Redfern J. · Jones P.B. · Duffey C.P.

Clarke	Ritson	Farnim.	Williams	Hulme	Rimmell	Wharton	Byrom	Hunt	Greaves	Taylor	Hurley	Boswell	Hallows	Seddon	Fletcher	Phillips	McAllister	Jones GE	Waldron	Marsh	Manning	Redfern	Jones PB	Duffey
1	2	3	4	5	6	7	8	9	10	11														
1	2	3	4	5	6	7	8	9	10	11														
1	2	3	4	5	6	7	8	9	10	11	12													
		3	4	5	6	7	8	9	10	11		1	2											
		3	4	5	6	7	8	9	10	11		1	2											
		3		5	6		8	10	7	11		1	2	4	9	12								
		3	4		6		8	10	11			1	2	9		5	7							
		3	4	5	6		10	8	7	11		1	2	9										
		3	4	5	6		10	8	7	11		1	2	9	12									
		3		5	6			10		12		1	2	8	9	11		7	4					
		3		5	6			10		7		1	2	8	9	11		4						
	2	3	4	6		8				11	5	1		7	10			9						
	2	3	4	6		8				11	5	1		7	10			9						
	2	3	4	6	10	8				7	5	1		9	11									
	2	3	4	6	10	8				7	5	1		9	11									
	2	3	4	6	10	8				7	5	1		9	11									
	2	3	4	6	8		10				5	1		12	11		7	9						
	2	3	4	5	6		10					1		8	11	7	12	9						
	2		4	6		7		8	10	11	5	1						9	3					
	2		4	6		7		8	10	11	5	1						9	3					
	2		4	6		7		8	10	11	5	1						9	3					
	2		4	6		7		8	10	11	5	1		12				9	3					
	2		4	5	6	12	8		10			1		11		7		9	3					
			4	5	6		8		10		1	2		9	11	7		3						
	2		4	5	6			10			1			8	9	11	7		3	12				
	2			5						1		8	9	11		10	4	3	7	6				
	2		5	12			6			1		8	9	11		10	4	3	7					
	2		4			8	6			5	1		7	9	11		10	12	3					
	2					8	6			5	1		7	9	11		10	3	12	4				
	2		4			8				5	1			9	11	10	7	12	3					
1	2			5		8		6				12	10	7		4		9	3	11				
1	2		9	5		8		6				7	10			4		11	3					
1	2		9	5		8	12	6				10		7	4			3	11					
1	2		9	5		8		6				10		7	4			3	11					
1	2		9	5		8	12	6				10		7	4			3	11					
1	2		9	5		8	4	6				10		7				3	11					
1	2			5	10	8	4				12		11	6	9			3	7					
1	2			5		8	4					10	11	6	9	12		3	7					
1				5		8	4			2	12		11	6	9	10		3	7					
1	2			5		8						10		6	9	4		3	7	11				
	2			5			12		8	1		10				9	4	3	7	6	11			
	2			5			9	10	8	1		12				11	4	3	7	6				
13	32	18	24	37	27	9	22	22	34	19	13	29	11	17	20	20	5	22	14	11	24	13	4	2
				1			1	1			1		1	2	1	4		3	1		2			
	1		2	1			4	3	8	2	2			1	3	1		2	1	2		1		

League Cup / FA Cup sub-tables:

	2		4	5	6		8		10			1		12	9	11		7			3			
	1		1	1	1		1		1			1		1	1			1			1			
														1										

		3	4		6			8	10	11		1	2			9		5	7					
	2	3	4	6	8		12			7	5	1		10	11			9						
	2	3	4	6			8	12		11	5	1		7	10			9						
	2	3	3	2	2		1	1	1	3	2	3	1	3	2	1	1	2						
							1	1																
														1				1						

League Table

	P	W	D	L	F	A	Pts
Leicester City	42	23	13	6	57	30	59
Sheffield United	42	21	14	7	73	39	56
Cardiff City	42	20	13	9	64	41	53
Carlisle United	42	20	13	9	65	43	53
Hull City	42	19	13	10	54	41	51
Luton Town	42	18	13	11	62	43	49
Middlesbrough	42	17	14	11	60	43	48
Millwall	42	19	9	14	59	42	47
Birmingham City	42	17	12	13	58	48	46
Norwich City	42	15	14	13	54	52	44
Queen's Park Rangers	42	16	11	15	58	53	43
Swindon Town	42	15	12	15	61	51	42
Sunderland	42	15	12	15	52	54	42
Oxford United	42	14	14	14	41	48	42
Sheffield Wednesday	42	12	12	18	51	69	36
Portsmouth	42	10	14	18	46	61	34
Orient	42	9	16	17	29	51	34
Watford	42	10	13	19	38	60	33
Bristol City	42	10	11	21	46	64	31
Charlton Athletic	42	8	14	20	41	65	30
Blackburn Rovers	42	6	15	21	37	69	27
Bolton Wanderers	42	7	10	25	35	74	24

Division Three

Manager: J. Armfield

BOLTON WANDERERS
SEASON 1971-72

LEAGUE CUP – THIRD ROUND
MANCHESTER CITY
TUESDAY, 5th OCTOBER, 1971
Kick-off 7-30 p.m.
Official Programme 5p

Match No.	Date		Venue	Opponents	Result		Scorers	Attendance
1	Aug	14	A	Oldham Athletic	D	2-2	Byrom 2	14,372
2		21	H	Bournemouth	D	0-0		8,962
3		28	A	Notts County	W	2-1	Hunt 2	15,658
4	Sep	4	H	Aston Villa	W	2-0	Hunt, Byrom	11,470
5		11	A	Blackburn Rovers	W	3-0	Hunt, Byrom 2	13,938
6		18	H	York City	L	0-1		12,192
7		24	A	Tranmere Rovers	D	0-0		6,988
8		29	H	Halifax Town	D	1-1	Greaves	9,304
9	Oct	2	A	Mansfield Town	W	2-0	Greaves, G. Jones	8,751
10		9	A	Port Vale	D	1-1	Nicholson	6,394
11		12	A	Plymouth Argyle	L	0-2		13,336
12		16	H	Oldham Athletic	W	2-1	Ritson (pen), Greaves	13,302
13		23	H	Swansea City	D	0-0		11,242
14		30	A	Bristol Rovers	L	0-2		11,532
15	Nov	6	A	Wrexham	L	0-2		8,953
16		13	A	Chesterfield	L	1-2	Hunt	9,423
17		26	A	Shrewsbury Town	L	0-1		6,605
18	Dec	4	H	Brighton & Hove Alb.	D	1-1	Greaves	5,209
19		18	A	Aston Villa	L	2-3	Seddon, Waldron	27,767
20		27	H	Barnsley	D	0-0		6,973
21	Jan	1	A	York City	D	0-0		4,467
22		8	H	Notts County	L	1-2	Byrom	8,096
23		22	A	Halifax Town	W	1-0	Hunt	3,919
24		29	H	Plymouth Argyle	W	2-1	Greaves, Seddon	5,856
25	Feb	12	A	Swansea City	L	2-3	Greaves, Byrom	4,962
26		19	H	Bristol Rovers	D	0-0		5,819
27		26	A	Wrexham	W	2-1	Hunt 2	3,851
28	Mar	4	H	Chesterfield	W	1-0	R. Wright	5,607
29		11	H	Port Vale	W	3-0	Nicholson, Hunt, McMahon	5,956
30		15	A	Bradford City	D	0-0		7,818
31		18	A	Bournemouth	W	2-1	Hunt 2	15,123
32		22	H	Walsall	L	0-1		6,786
33		25	H	Blackburn Rovers	W	1-0	G. Jones	11,026
34		27	A	Mansfield Town	L	0-1		5,398
35	Apr	1	A	Barnsley	L	0-1		3,925
36		3	H	Tranmere Rovers	W	1-0	Byrom	6,216
37		8	A	Walsall	D	1-1	Byrom	4,735
38		12	H	Rochdale	W	2-1	Byrom, P. Jones	5,773
39		15	H	Shrewsbury Town	W	2-0	Greaves (pen), Phillips	5,447
40		19	A	Torquay United	W	2-0	Byrom, G. Jones	5,193
41		22	A	Brighton & Hove Alb.	D	1-1	G. Jones (pen)	25,074
42		24	A	Rochdale	D	2-2	G. Jones, Phillips	4,826
43		29	H	Rotherham United	D	2-2	Phillips 2	5,345
44	May	2	A	Rotherham United	L	0-2		3,945
45		5	A	Torquay United	D	1-1	McAllister	2,081
46		10	A	Bradford City	W	3-0	McAllister, Lee, R. Wright	2,468

Appearances
Sub appearances
Goals

FA Cup

R1	Nov	20	H	Bangor City	W	3-0	Ritson (pen), Nicholson, Duffey	6,252
R2	Dec	11	N	Rossendale United	W	4-1	Greaves 3, Byrom	12,100
R3	Jan	15	H	Torquay United	W	2-1	Hunt, Greaves	7,551
R4	Feb	5	A	Chelsea	L	0-3		38,066

R2 played at Gigg Lane, Bury.

Appearances
Sub appearances
Goals

FL Cup

R1	Aug	18	A	Bradford City	D	1-1	Byrom	5,742
rep		25	H	Bradford City	W	2-1	Redfern, Phillips	8,256
R2	Sep	7	A	Huddersfield Town	W	2-0	Greaves 2	10,131
R3	Oct	5	H	Manchester City	W	3-0	G. Jones 3 (1 pen)	42,039
R4		27	A	Chelsea	D	1-1	Rowe	27,679
rep	Nov	8	H	Chelsea	L	0-6		29,805

Appearances
Sub appearances
Goals

	Wright C.G.	Ritson J.A.	Mowbray H.	Nicholson P.	Hulme J.	Rimmer W.R.	Rowe G.E.	Hunt R.	Greaves R.	Byron J.	Jones G.E.	Radfern J.	Denton R.W.	Jones P.B.	Sudden I.W.	Waldron A.	Phillips R.D.	Duffey C.P.	Hallows P.C.R.	McAllister D.	Law F.S.	Wight R.L.	McMahon K.
	1	2	3	4	5	6	7	**8**	9	10	11	12											
	1	2	3	4	5	6		8	10	9	8	11	7										
	1	2		4	5	6		8	10	11	9		3	7									
	1	2		4	5	6		8	10	11	9		3	**7**	12								
	1	2	3	4	5	6		8	10	11	9			7									
	1	2	3	4	5	6		8	10	11	9			7	12								
	1	2	3	4	5	6		8	10	11	9	12		7									
	1	2	3	4	5	6	12	8	10	11	9			7									
	1	2	3		5	6	7		10	11	9				8	**4**							
	1	2	3	7	5	6		12	10	11	9				8	**4**							
	1	2	3	4	5	6		8	10	11	9		7	12									
	1	2	3	7	5	6			10	11	9				8	**4**	12						
	1	2	3	7	5	6	12		10	**11**	9				8	4							
	1	2	3	7	5	11			**10**		9				12	8	4						
	1	2	3	7	5	6	11	12	10		9				8		4						
	1	2	3	**5**		6		8	9		11	7	12		10	4							
	1	2	3	7		6		8		9			5	10	4		11						
	1	2	3			6			10	7			5	8	4		11						
	1		3	7		6		8		9			5	10	4		11	2	12				
	1		12	**6**				10	7	9		3	5	8	4		11	2					
	1		7	6			10	9	11				5	8	4			2	3	12			
	1		2	6			8	9	11	7			5	10	4			3					
	1	2		6			8	9	11	7			5	10	4			3					
	1		3	4	6			7	9	10	11		5	8				2					
	1		3	7		6		8	9	10	11		5		4			2					
	1		3	7		6		8	9	10			5		4			2	11	12			
	1		3	6			8	9	10	12			5		4			2	**11**	7			
	1		3	4		6		8	9	12	10		5		4			2	11	**7**			
	1		**3**	4		6		8	9		11		5		12			2	10	7			
	1		2			6		8	9	7	11		5		4	10		3					
	1		2		6			8		7	11		5		4	10		**3**	12	9			
	1	2	3	10		6		8	9	**7**			5		4				12				
	1	2	3	4		6		8	9	7	11		5			10							
	1	2	3	4		6		8	9	7	11		5			10							
	1	2	3	4		6		8	9	7	11		5			10							
	1	2		4		6		**8**		9	11		5			10		3					
	1	2		**4**		6			10	9			5		7	11		3	12				
	1	2		**4**		6		8		10	9		5		7	11		3	12				
	1	2		4		6		8	9		11		5			10		3	7				
	1	2		4		6			9	11			5	10	7			3	8				
	1	2		4		6			9	11			5	10			7	3	8				
	1	2		4		6				11			5	10				3	9	8			
Apps	46	32	30	40	22	39	4	33	38	37	41	2	3	37	18	27	13	4	3	21	2	10	4
		1					2	2		1	1	2	1		1	3	1		1		1	4	2
	1		2					11	7	11	5			1	2	1	4		2	1	2	1	

League Table

	P	W	D	L	F	A	Pts
Aston Villa	46	32	6	8	85	32	70
Brighton & Hove Albion	46	27	11	8	82	47	65
Bournemouth	46	23	16	7	73	37	62
Notts County	46	25	12	9	74	44	62
Rotherham United	46	20	15	11	69	52	55
Bristol Rovers	46	21	12	13	75	56	54
Bolton Wanderers	46	17	16	13	51	41	50
Plymouth Argyle	46	20	10	16	74	64	50
Walsall	46	15	18	13	62	57	48
Blackburn Rovers	46	19	9	18	54	57	47
Oldham Athletic	46	17	11	18	59	63	45
Shrewsbury Town	46	17	10	19	73	65	44
Chesterfield	46	18	8	20	57	57	44
Swansea City	46	17	10	19	46	59	44
Port Vale	46	13	15	18	43	59	41
Wrexham	46	16	8	22	59	63	40
Halifax Town	46	13	12	21	48	61	38
Rochdale	46	12	13	21	57	83	37
York City	46	12	12	22	57	66	36
Tranmere Rovers	46	10	16	20	50	71	36
Mansfield Town	46	8	20	18	41	63	36
Barnsley	46	9	18	19	32	64	36
Torquay United	46	10	12	24	41	69	32
Bradford City	46	11	10	25	45	77	32

Division Three

Manager: J. Armfield

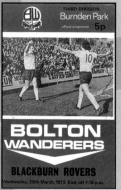

Match No.	Date	Venue	Opponents	Result		Scorers	Attendance
1	Aug 12	H	Bournemouth	W	3-0	Byrom 2, Machin (own-goal)	7,133
2	19	A	Notts County	L	0-1		11,129
3	26	A	Oldham Athletic	W	2-1	R. Wright, Phillips	7,019
4	28	A	Brentford	L	1-2	Byrom	11,800
5	Sep 2	A	Blackburn Rovers	W	3-0	Byrom, R. Wright, Phillips	9,546
6	9	H	Plymouth Argyle	W	2-0	Byrom, G. Jones (pen)	5,515
7	16	A	Grimsby Town	L	0-2		8,678
8	19	A	Bristol Rovers	D	1-1	G. Jones (pen)	9,572
9	23	H	Tranmere Rovers	W	2-0	G. Jones (pen), R Wright	6,139
10	27	H	Chesterfield	W	1-0	Waldron	6,532
11	30	A	Halifax Town	D	1-1	P. Jones	4,664
12	Oct 7	A	Walsall	L	2-3	P. Jones, Greaves	7,631
13	11	H	Swansea City	W	3-0	Byrom 2, G. Jones	6,112
14	14	H	Scunthorpe United	D	0-0		7,175
15	21	A	Rochdale	D	2-2	Byrom, Nicholson	7,165
16	28	H	Southend United	D	1-1	Phillips	7,342
17	30	A	Wrexham	W	3-1	G. Jones, Phillips, Lee	5,547
18	Nov 4	A	Chesterfield	W	1-0	Lee	6,576
19	11	H	Bristol Rovers	W	2-0	Byrom, Lee	8,419
20	25	H	Rotherham United	W	2-1	Byrom, G. Jones	7,980
21	Dec 2	A	Watford	L	1-2	Byrom	7,349
22	16	A	Charlton Athletic	W	3-2	P. Jones, Byrom, G. Jones	6,789
23	23	H	Port Vale	W	2-0	Byrom, G. Jones	12,354
24	26	A	Tranmere Rovers	D	1-1	G. Jones	14,356
25	30	H	Notts County	D	2-2	Byrom, Lee	17,575
26	Jan 6	A	Oldham Athletic	L	0-2		19,745
27	27	A	Plymouth Argyle	L	0-1		8,592
28	30	H	Wrexham	W	1-0	P. Jones	16,732
29	Feb 10	H	Grimsby Town	W	2-0	G. Jones, Waldron	16,588
30	17	A	Bournemouth	L	0-2		18,384
31	20	A	Charlton Athletic	W	3-0	Nicholson, P. Jones, Phillips	18,146
32	Mar 3	H	Walsall	W	3-1	P. Jones, Byrom, G. Jones	14,924
33	5	A	York City	W	1-0	Lee	9,032
34	10	A	Scunthorpe United	D	1-1	G. Jones	4,424
35	17	H	Rochdale	W	2-1	Byrom, G. Jones	17,870
36	21	H	Shrewsbury Town	W	2-0	Lee, Redfern	18,193
37	24	H	Southend United	D	1-1	P. Jones	8,046
38	28	H	Blackburn Rovers	L	0-1		33,010
39	31	A	Rotherham United	L	0-1		6,506
40	Apr 4	A	Swansea City	W	3-2	Byrom, Whatmore 2	3,096
41	7	H	Watford	D	1-1	Lee (pen)	17,462
42	13	A	Shrewsbury Town	W	2-0	Byrom, G. Jones	6,574
43	16	A	Halifax Town	W	3-0	Lee 3	20,062
44	21	H	York City	W	3-0	Nicholson, Lee 2	19,999
45	23	A	Port Vale	D	2-2	Nicholson, Byrom	14,168
46	28	H	Brentford	W	2-0	Nicholson, Byrom	21,646

						Appearances
						Sub appearances
					1 own-goal	Goals

FA Cup

R1	Nov 18	H	Chester	D	1-1	Byrom	9,620
rep	22	A	Chester	W	1-0	G. Jones	7,611
R2	Dec 9	A	Shrewsbury Town	W	3-0	Phillips, Lee, Ritson	8,403
R3	Jan 13	A	Charlton Athletic	D	1-1	Lee	10,688
rep	17	H	Charlton Athletic	W	4-0	Nicholson, Greaves 2, G. Jones	21,195
R4	Feb 3	H	Cardiff City	D	2-2	G. Jones, Ritson	24,729
rep	7	A	Cardiff City	D	1-1	.G. Jones	14,849
rep2	12	N	Cardiff City	W	1-0	Lee	6,609
R5	24	H	Luton Town	L	0-1		39,556

R4 replay a.e.t. R4 replay 2 at The Hawthorns, West Bromwich.

						Appearances
						Sub appearances
						Goals

FL Cup

R1	Aug 16	H	Oldham Athletic	W	3-0	Byrom, G. Jones 2	7,947
R2	Sep 6	A	Sheffield Wednesday	L	0-2		15,903

						Appearances
						Sub appearances
						Goals

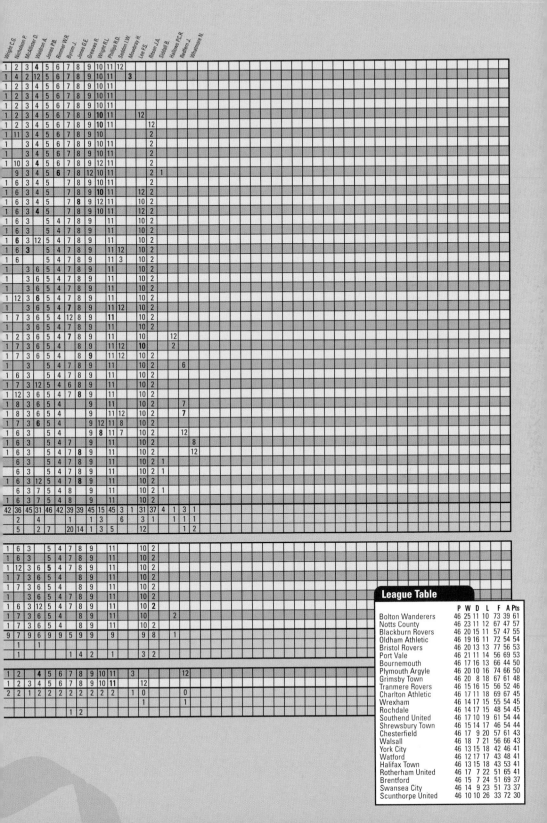

League Table

	P	W	D	L	F	A	Pts
Bolton Wanderers	46	25	11	10	73	39	61
Notts County	46	23	11	12	67	47	57
Blackburn Rovers	46	20	15	11	57	47	55
Oldham Athletic	46	19	16	11	72	54	54
Bristol Rovers	46	20	13	13	77	56	53
Port Vale	46	21	11	14	56	69	53
Bournemouth	46	17	16	13	66	44	50
Plymouth Argyle	46	20	10	16	74	66	50
Grimsby Town	46	20	8	18	67	61	48
Tranmere Rovers	46	15	16	15	56	52	46
Charlton Athletic	46	17	11	18	69	67	45
Wrexham	46	14	17	15	55	54	45
Rochdale	46	14	17	15	48	54	45
Southend United	46	17	10	19	61	54	44
Shrewsbury Town	46	15	14	17	46	54	44
Chesterfield	46	17	9	20	57	61	43
Walsall	46	18	7	21	56	66	43
York City	46	13	15	18	42	46	41
Watford	46	12	17	17	43	48	41
Halifax Town	46	13	15	18	43	53	41
Rotherham United	46	17	7	22	51	65	41
Brentford	46	15	7	24	51	69	37
Swansea City	46	14	9	23	51	73	37
Scunthorpe United	46	10	10	26	33	72	30

1973-74

Division Two

Manager: J. Armfield

Match No.	Date	Venue	Opponents	Result		Scorers	Attendance
1	Aug 25	A	Bristol City	L	0-1		13,288
2	Sep 1	H	Hull City	W	1-0	Greaves	12,708
3	8	A	Portsmouth	W	2-0	Byrom 2	13,367
4	11	H	Orient	D	1-1	Byrom	16,761
5	15	H	Crystal Palace	W	2-0	Lee, Byrom	18,392
6	22	A	Fulham	L	0-1		9,556
7	29	H	Nottingham Forest	W	1-0	Byrom	15,101
8	Oct 6	A	Carlisle United	L	0-1		8,365
9	13	H	Aston Villa	L	1-2	Whatmore	19,206
10	20	H	Millwall	L	0-1		13,002
11	22	A	Orient	L	0-3		11,702
12	27	A	West Bromwich Albion	D	0-0		15,604
13	Nov 3	H	Oxford United	W	2-1	Shuker (own-goal), Byrom	12,709
14	10	A	Luton Town	L	1-2	Whatmore	9,628
15	13	A	Sunderland	L	0-3		26,454
16	17	H	Notts County	L	1-3	Greaves	11,850
17	24	A	Cardiff City	L	0-1		9,606
18	Dec 5	H	Sunderland	W	1-0	Whatmore	8,425
19	8	A	Preston North End	L	1-2	Byrom	14,715
20	15	H	Swindon Town	W	2-0	Byrom, Whatmore	8,846
21	22	A	Nottingham Forest	L	2-3	Byrom, G. Jones	9,498
22	26	H	Blackpool	D	1-1	Suddaby (own-goal)	18,150
23	29	H	Portsmouth	W	4-0	G. Jones (pen), Byrom, Whatmore 2	13,684
24	Jan 1	H	Hull City	D	0-0		12,210
25	12	A	Crystal Palace	D	0-0		15,804
26	20	H	Bristol City	W	2-1	Merrick (own-goal), Greaves	23,315
27	Feb 3	A	Swindon Town	D	2-2	Whatmore 2	8,835
28	16	H	Sheffield Wednesday	W	4-2	Ritson, Byrom 2, G. Jones	13,405
29	23	H	Carlisle United	W	2-0	Byrom, G. Jones (pen)	16,675
30	27	A	Aston Villa	D	1-1	Byrom	18,952
31	Mar 2	A	Blackpool	W	2-0	G. Jones, Ritson	18,575
32	9	H	West Bromwich Albion	D	1-1	Byrom	17,760
33	16	A	Millwall	L	1-2	Byrom	6,419
34	23	H	Luton Town	W	1-0	Greaves	15,616
35	30	A	Oxford United	W	2-0	Whatmore, Byrom	6,223
36	Apr 2	H	Fulham	D	0-0		18,636
37	6	H	Cardiff City	D	1-1	Waldron	14,857
38	9	A	Middlesbrough	D	0-0		28,143
39	13	A	Notts County	D	0-0		8,349
40	15	H	Middlesbrough	W	2-1	Byrom, G. Jones	22,246
41	20	H	Preston North End	L	0-2		17,273
42	27	A	Sheffield Wednesday	L	0-1		23,264

							Appearances
							Sub appearances
						1 own-goal	Goals

FA Cup

R3	Jan 6	H	Stoke City	W	3-2	Byrom 3	39,138
R4	26	A	Southampton	D	3-3	Byrom 2, G. Jones (pen)	20,265
rep	30	H	Southampton	L	0-2		21,788

R4 replay a.e.t.

							Appearances
							Sub appearances
							Goals

FL Cup

R1	Aug 28	H	Preston North End	D	1-1	Byrom	17,101
rep	Sep 3	A	Preston North End	W	2-0	Lee 2	18,571
R2	Oct 10	A	Rochdale	W	4-0	Lee 2, P. Jones, Waldron	7,241
R3	31	A	Millwall	D	1-1	P. Jones	9,281
rep	Nov 6	H	Millwall	L	1-2	Greaves	13,501

R1 replay a.e.t.

							Appearances
							Sub appearances
							Goals

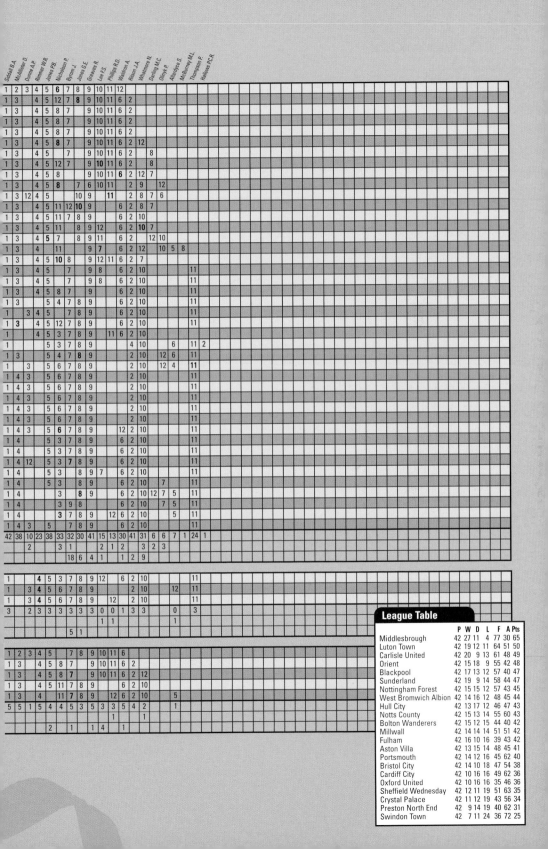

Players (column headers): Sudall B.A., McAllister D., Dunne A.P., Rimmer W.R., Jones P.B., Nicholson P., Byrom J., Jones G.E., Greaves R., Lee F.S., Phillips R.D., Waldron A., Ritson L.A., Whatmore N., Darling M.C., Dmyk P., Allardyce S., McBurney M.L., Thompson P., Hatlow P.C.R.

1	2	3	4	5	6	7	8	9	10	11	12								
1	3		4	5	12	7	8	9	10	11	6	2							
1	3		4	5	8	7		9	10	11	6	2							
1	3		4	5	8	7		9	10	11	6	2							
1	3		4	5	8	7		9	10	11	6	2							
1	3		4	5	8	7		9	10	11	6	2	12						
1	3		4	5	12	7		9	10	11	6	2	8						
1	3		4	5	8			9	10	11	6	2	12	7					
1	3		4	5	8			7	6	10	11		2	9		12			
1	3	12	4	5				10	9		11		2	8	7	6			
1	3		4	5	11	12	10	9			6	2	8	7					
1	3		4	5	11	7	8	9			6	2	10						
1	3		4	5	11		8	9	12		6	2	10	7					
1	3		4	5	7		8	9	11		6	2		12	10				
1	3		4		11			9	7		6	2	12		10	5	8		
1	3		4	5	10	8		9	12	11	6	2	7						
1	3		4	5		7		9	8		6	2	10					11	
1	3		4	5		7		9	8		6	2	10					11	
1	3		4	5	8	7		9			6	2	10					11	
1	3			5	4	7	8	9			6	2	10					11	
1		3	4	5		7	8	9			6	2	10					11	
1	3		4	5	12	7	8	9			6	2	10					11	
1		4	5	3	7	8	9		11	6	2	10						11	
1			5	3	7	8	9			4	10			6		11	2		
1	3		5	4	7	8	9			2	10		12	6		11			
1		3		5	6	7	8	9		2	10		12	4		11			
1	4	3		5	6	7	8	9		2	10					11			
1	4	3		5	6	7	8	9		2	10					11			
1	4	3		5	6	7	8	9		2	10					11			
1	4	3		5	6	7	8	9		2	10					11			
1	4			5	6	7	8	9		2	10					11			
1	4	3		5	6	7	8	9		12	2	10					11		
1	4			5	3	7	8	9		6	2	10					11		
1	4			5	3	7	8	9		6	2	10					11		
1	4	12		5	3	7	8	9		6	2	10					11		
1	4			5	3		8	9	7		6	2	10					11	
1	4			5	3		8	9		6	2	10		7				11	
1	4				3	9	8			6	2	10		7	5			11	
1	4			3	7	8	9		12	6	2	10			5			11	
1	4	3		5		7	8	9		6	2	10					11		
42	38	10	23	38	33	32	30	41	15	13	30	41	31	6	6	7	1	24	1
	2			3	1			2	1	2		3	2	3					
				18	6	4	1		1	2	9								

1		4	5	3	7	8	9	12		6	2	10					11		
1		3	4	5	6	7	8	9			2	10				12	11		
1		3	4	5	6	7	8	9		12	2	10					11		
3		2	3	3	3	3	3	0	0	1	3	3				0	3		
								1	1							1			
				5	1														

1	2	3	4	5		7	8	9	10	11	6								
1	3		4	5	8	7		9	10	11	6	2							
1	3		4	5	8	7		9	10	11	6	2	12						
1	3		4	5	11	7	8	9			6	2	10						
1	3		4		11	7	8	9		12	6	2	10			5			
5	5	1	5	4	4	5	3	5	3	3	5	4	2			1			
								1			1								
			2		1		1	4		1									

League Table

	P	W	D	L	F	A	Pts
Middlesbrough	42	27	11	4	77	30	65
Luton Town	42	19	12	11	64	51	50
Carlisle United	42	20	9	13	61	48	49
Orient	42	15	18	9	55	42	48
Blackpool	42	17	13	12	57	40	47
Sunderland	42	19	9	14	58	44	47
Nottingham Forest	42	15	15	12	57	43	45
West Bromwich Albion	42	14	16	12	48	45	44
Hull City	42	13	17	12	46	47	43
Notts County	42	15	13	14	55	60	43
Bolton Wanderers	42	15	12	15	44	40	42
Millwall	42	14	14	14	51	51	42
Fulham	42	16	10	16	39	43	42
Aston Villa	42	13	15	14	48	45	41
Portsmouth	42	14	12	16	45	62	40
Bristol City	42	14	10	18	47	54	38
Cardiff City	42	10	16	16	49	62	36
Oxford United	42	10	16	16	35	46	36
Sheffield Wednesday	42	12	11	19	51	63	35
Crystal Palace	42	11	12	19	43	56	34
Preston North End	42	9	14	19	40	62	31
Swindon Town	42	7	11	24	36	72	25

Division Two

Manager: J. Armfield until 30 September 1974, I. Greaves from 5 October 1974

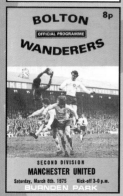

BOLTON WANDERERS 8p
OFFICIAL PROGRAMME

SECOND DIVISION
MANCHESTER UNITED
Saturday, March 8th. 1975   Kick-off 3-0 p.m.
BURNDEN PARK

Match No.	Date		Venue	Opponents	Result		Scorers	Attendance
1	Aug	17	H	Portsmouth	W	3-0	P. Jones 2, Byrom	12,776
2		24	A	Blackpool	L	1-2	Whatmore	15,513
3		31	H	Aston Villa	W	1-0	P. Jones	12,976
4	Sep	7	A	Bristol City	L	1-2	Ritson	9,263
5		14	H	Sheffield Wednesday	L	0-1		14,597
6		21	A	Sunderland	D	0-0		28,453
7		25	A	Manchester United	L	0-3		47,084
8		28	H	Notts County	D	1-1	Whatmore	10,045
9	Oct	5	H	Orient	W	2-0	Greaves, P. Jones	9,769
10		12	A	Hull City	L	0-2		7,353
11		19	H	Cardiff City	W	2-1	Curran 2	9,439
12		22	A	Blackpool	D	0-0		12,574
13		26	A	York City	W	3-1	Lee, Curran, Allardyce	8,804
14	Nov	2	H	Nottingham Forest	W	2-0	Curran, Smith	12,395
15		9	A	Millwall	D	1-1	Curran	7,136
16		12	A	Oldham Athletic	D	1-1	Curran	14,667
17		16	H	Southampton	W	3-2	Lee, Byrom 2	14,348
18		23	A	Norwich City	L	0-2		18,649
19		30	A	Bristol Rovers	L	0-1		9,369
20	Dec	7	H	West Bromwich Albion	L	0-1		12,315
21		14	A	Portsmouth	L	0-2		7,612
22		21	H	Oxford United	W	3-1	Greaves, Curran, Nicholson	9,588
23		26	A	Sheffield Wednesday	W	2-0	Lee, Curran	17,153
24		28	H	Fulham	D	0-0		14,703
25	Jan	18	H	Bristol Rovers	W	5-1	Byrom 2, Lee 2, Curran	11,432
26	Feb	1	H	Millwall	W	2-0	Lee, Byrom	12,920
27		4	A	Oldham Athletic	L	0-1		16,363
28		8	A	Nottingham Forest	W	3-2	Byrom 2, Curran	11,922
29		15	H	Norwich City	D	0-0		15,506
30		22	A	Southampton	W	1-0	Curran	18,339
31	Mar	5	A	Aston Villa	D	0-0		39,322
32		8	H	Manchester United	L	0-1		37,759
33		15	A	Notts County	D	1-1	Byrom	8,196
34		22	H	Bristol City	L	0-2		11,066
35		28	A	Fulham	L	1-2	Byrom	9,453
36		29	A	Oxford United	L	1-2	Whatmore	6,742
37		31	H	Sunderland	L	0-2		18,220
38	Apr	5	H	York City	D	1-1	P. Jones (pen)	7,876
39		8	A	West Bromwich Albion	W	1-0	Thompson	7,937
40		12	A	Orient	D	0-0		5,478
41		19	H	Hull City	D	1-1	Allardyce	8,208
42		26	A	Cardiff City	W	2-1	Nicholson, Allardyce	6,396

Appearances
Sub appearances
Goals

FA Cup

R3	Jan	4	H	West Bromwich Albion	D	0-0		17,305
rep		8	A	West Bromwich Albion	L	0-4		21,210

Appearances
Sub appearances

FL Cup

R2	Sep	11	H	Norwich City	D	0-0		11,205
rep		17	A	Norwich City	L	1-3	P. Jones	14,417

Appearances
Sub appearances
Goals

Appearances & Goals Grid

Sudall B.A.	Ritson J.A.	Dunne A.P.	Nicholson P.	Jones P.B.	McAllister D.	Byrom J.	Waldon A.	Lee F.S.	Whatmore N.	Thompson P.	Greaves R.	Jones O.E.	Taylor S.J.	Curran H.P.	Phillips R.D.	Reed P.	Rimmer W.R.	Olinyk P.	Allardyce S.	Smith B.	Smith S.	Walsh M.T.
1	2	3	4	5	6	7	8	9	10	11												
1	2	3	4	5	6	7	**8**	12	10	11	9											
1	2	3	4	5	6	7		10	11	9	8											
1	2	3	4	5	6	7		10	11	9	**8**	12										
1	2	3	4	5	6	7			11	9		8	10									
1	2	3	4	5	6		7		11	9		8	10									
1	2	3	4	5	6				11	9		8	10									
1	2	3	4	5	6	10		7	11	9		8										
1	2	3	4	5	6	7		10	11	9		8		12								
1		3	2	5	6	7		10	11	9		8		4	12							
1	2		3	5	6		10		11	9		8		4								
1	2			3	5	6		10		11	9		8		4		7					
1	**3**		4	5	6			10		11	9		8					12	7			
1	2	3	4	5	6			10		11	9		8						7			
1	2	3	4	5	6			10		11	9		8		12				**7**			
1	2	3	4	5	6			9		11	10		8		12				**7**			
1	2	3	4	5	6	7		9		11	10	8										
1		3	4	5	2	7		9		11	10		8			6						
1		3	4	5	2	**7**		10		8		12	9	11		6						
1	2		4	5	3			9		11	10	**7**	8			6	12					
1	2	3	4	**5**				9		11	10	12	8			6		7				
1	2		3	5				9	12	11	**10**		8		7	6			4			
1	2		3	5		6	7	9		11			8			10			4			
1	2		3	5	6	7		9		11			8			10			4			
1	2	3	4	5	6	7		9		11			8			10						
1	2	3	4	5	6	7		9		11			8			10						
1	**2**	3	4	5	6	7		9	12	11			8			10						
1	**3**	2	5		6	7		9		11	4		8			10			12			
1	2	3		5		7		9		11	4		8			10		6				
1	2	3	12	5		7		9		11	4		8			**10**		6				
1	2	3		5		7		9		11	4		8			10		6				
1	2	3		5		7		9		11	4		8	12		**10**		6				
1	2	3		5		7		9		11	4		8			10		6				
1	2	3		5		7		9	12	11	4		**8**			10		6				
1	2	3	4	5		7			9	11		8				10		6				
1	2	3	4	**5**		7			9	11	12		8			10		6				
1	2	3	4	5					9	11	7		**8**	12		10		6				
1	2	3	4	5		7		12	9	11			**8**			10		6				
1	2	**3**	4	5				8	9	11			12			10		6		7		
1			4	5				8	9	11		7				10		6		3		
1	2		**4**	5				9		11		8		12		10		6	7	3		
1	2	3	4	5				9		11		8		12		10		6		**7**		
42	38	34	36	42	26	28	2	29	14	41	29	5	3	32	4	24	2	1	17	6	3	4
	1							2	3		1	1	2	3	2	3	1		1	1		1
	1		2	5		10		6	3	1	2			11					3	1		

Sudall B.A.	Ritson J.A.	Dunne A.P.	Nicholson P.	Jones P.B.	McAllister D.	Byrom J.	Waldon A.	Lee F.S.	Whatmore N.	Thompson P.	Greaves R.	Jones O.E.	Taylor S.J.	Curran H.P.	Phillips R.D.	Reed P.	Rimmer W.R.	Olinyk P.	Allardyce S.	Smith B.	Smith S.	Walsh M.T.
1	2		3	5	6			9		11	10	7		8		4						
1	2		3	5	**6**	12		9		11	10	7		8		4						
2	2		2	2	2	0		2		2	2	2		2		2						
																						1

Sudall B.A.	Ritson J.A.	Dunne A.P.	Nicholson P.	Jones P.B.	McAllister D.	Byrom J.	Waldon A.	Lee F.S.	Whatmore N.	Thompson P.	Greaves R.	Jones O.E.	Taylor S.J.	Curran H.P.	Phillips R.D.	Reed P.	Rimmer W.R.	Olinyk P.	Allardyce S.	Smith B.	Smith S.	Walsh M.T.
1	2	3	4	5	6	7		**10**	11	9	8			12								
1	2	3	4	5		7		8	11	9			10		6							
2	2	2	2	2	1	2		2	2	2	2		1	1								
													1									
		1																				

League Table

	P	W	D	L	F	A	Pts
Manchester United	42	26	9	7	66	30	61
Aston Villa	42	25	8	9	79	32	58
Norwich City	42	20	13	9	58	37	53
Sunderland	42	19	13	10	65	35	51
Bristol City	42	21	8	13	47	33	50
West Bromwich Albion	42	18	9	15	54	42	45
Blackpool	42	14	17	11	38	33	45
Hull City	42	15	14	13	40	53	44
Fulham	42	13	16	13	44	39	42
Bolton Wanderers	42	15	12	15	45	41	42
Oxford United	42	15	12	15	41	51	42
Orient	42	11	20	11	28	39	42
Southampton	42	15	11	16	53	54	41
Notts County	42	12	16	14	49	59	40
York City	42	14	10	18	51	55	38
Nottingham Forest	42	12	14	16	43	55	38
Portsmouth	42	12	13	17	44	54	37
Oldham Athletic	42	10	15	17	40	48	35
Bristol Rovers	42	12	11	19	42	64	35
Millwall	42	10	12	20	44	56	32
Cardiff City	42	9	14	19	36	62	32
Sheffield Wednesday	42	5	11	26	29	64	21

Match No.	Date		Venue	Opponents	Result		Scorers	Attendance
1	Aug	16	A	Bristol City	L	0-1		10,510
2		20	A	Oxford United	L	0-2		5,277
3		23	H	Fulham	D	2-2	G. Jones, Byrom	8,786
4		30	A	York City	W	2-1	P. Jones, G. Jones	5,640
5	Sep	6	H	Southampton	W	3-0	Curran, G. Jones, Byrom	9,188
6		13	A	Luton Town	W	2-0	P. Futcher (own-goal), Curran	11,217
7		20	H	Orient	D	1-1	Greaves	10,218
8		23	A	Bristol Rovers	D	2-2	P. Jones, Greaves	7,992
9		27	A	Nottingham Forest	W	2-1	Whatmore, P. Jones (pen)	10,775
10	Oct	4	H	Charlton Athletic	W	5-0	Whatmore 2, Ritson, Byrom 2	9,895
11		11	A	Plymouth Argyle	W	3-2	Whatmore 2, Reid	14,595
12		18	H	Notts County	W	2-1	Allardyce, Whatmore	16,080
13		25	A	Hull City	D	2-2	Byrom, G. Jones	7,369
14	Nov	1	H	Blackpool	W	1-0	Ritson	17,274
15		4	H	Portsmouth	W	4-1	P. Jones, G. Jones 2, Whatmore	18,538
16		8	A	Blackburn Rovers	D	1-1	G. Jones	24,480
17		15	H	Carlisle United	D	0-0		14,556
18		22	A	Notts County	D	1-1	G. Jones	12,964
19		29	H	West Bromwich Albion	L	1-2	Greaves	18,710
20	Dec	6	A	Chelsea	W	1-0	Greaves	20,896
21		13	A	Fulham	W	2-1	Whatmore, G. Jones	8,720
22		20	H	Bristol City	W	1-0	Whatmore	18,505
23		26	A	Oldham Athletic	L	1-2	Whatmore	24,537
24		27	H	Sunderland	W	2-1	Allardyce, Byrom	42,680
25	Jan	17	A	Southampton	D	0-0		20,363
26		27	H	Luton Town	W	3-0	G. Jones, Byrom, Allardyce	21,358
27	Feb	7	A	Portsmouth	W	1-0	Went (own-goal)	8,958
28		21	A	Carlisle United	L	2-3	Reid, Allardyce	12,809
29		28	H	Hull City	W	1-0	Thompson	21,781
30	Mar	2	H	Oxford United	L	0-1		22,340
31		6	A	Blackpool	D	1-1	G. Jones	18,548
32		13	H	Plymouth Argyle	D	0-0		21,147
33		20	A	West Bromwich Albion	L	0-2		25,319
34		23	H	Blackburn Rovers	L	0-1		24,780
35		27	H	Chelsea	W	2-1	Hay (own-goal), G. Wilkins (own-goal)	20,817
36	Apr	3	A	Nottingham Forest	D	0-0		21,464
37		10	A	Orient	D	0-0		6,294
38		13	H	York City	L	1-2	Nicholson	19,048
39		17	H	Oldham Athletic	W	4-0	Greaves 2, P. Jones 2 (2 pens)	22,455
40		19	A	Sunderland	L	1-2	Allardyce	51,943
41		24	A	Charlton Athletic	W	4-0	Whatmore, Greaves, Byrom 2	14,415
42		28	H	Bristol Rovers	W	3-1	Nicholson, Byrom 2	12,815

	Appearances
	Sub appearances
3 own-goals	Goals

FA Cup

R3	Jan	3	A	Brentford	D	0-0		12,450
rep		6	H	Brentford	W	2-0	Whatmore 2	18,538
R4		24	A	Huddersfield Town	W	1-0	Reid	27,824
R5	Feb	14	H	Newcastle United	D	3-3	G. Jones, P. Jones, Allardyce	46,584
rep		18	A	Newcastle United	D	0-0		50,381
rep2		23	N	Newcastle United	L	1-2	G. Jones	42,280

R5 replay a.e.t. R5 replay 2 at Elland Road, Leeds.

	Appearances
	Sub appearances
	Goals

FL Cup

R2	Sep	10	A	Coventry City	L	1-3	Byrom	12,743

	Appearances
	Goals

Players (column headers, left to right):
Siddall B.A. · Ritson J.A. · Dunne A.P. · Greaves R. · Jones P.B. · Walsh M.T. · Bryon J. · Curran H.P. · Jones G.E. · Reid P. · Thompson P. · Nicholson P. · Allardyce S. · Waldron A. · Whatmore N. · Taylor S.J. · Smith B. · Morgan W.

Appearances grid

Siddall	Ritson	Dunne	Greaves	Jones P.B.	Walsh	Bryon	Curran	Jones G.E.	Reid	Thompson	Nicholson	Allardyce	Waldron	Whatmore	Taylor	Smith	Morgan
1	2	3	4	5	6	7	8	9	10	11							
1	2	3	4	5	6	7	8	**9**	10	11	12						
1	2	3	4	5		7	8	9	10	11		6					
1	2	3	4	5		7	8	9	10	11		6					
1	2	3	4	5		7	8	9	10	11		6					
1	2			4	5		7	8	9	10	11	3	6				
1	2	3	4	5		7	**8**	9	10	11		6	12				
1	2	3	4	5		7		9	10	11		6		8			
1		3	4	5		7		9	10	11	2	6		8			
1	2	3	4	5	12	7		**9**	10	11	2	6		8			
1	2	3	4	5				9	10	11		6	7	8			
1	2	3	4	5		7		9	10	11		6		8			
1	2	3	4	5		7		9	10	11		6		8			
1	2	3	4	5		7		9	10	11		6		8			
1	2	3	4	5		7		9	10	11		6		8			
1	2	3	4	5		**7**	12	9	10	11		6		8			
1	2	3	4	5				9	10	11	7	6		8			
1	2	3	4	5			**9**		10	11		6	7	8	12		
1	2	3	4	5				9	10	11		6	7	8			
1	2	3	4	5			9		10	**11**		6	7	8	12		
1	2	3	4	5			12	9	10			6	7	8	**11**		
1	2	3	4	5			12	9	10			6	**7**	8	11		
1	2	3	4	5		7		9	10	11		6		8			
1	2	3	4	5		**7**		9	10	11	12	6		8			
1	2	3	4	5		7		9	10	11		6		8			
1	2	3	4			7		9	10	11	5	6		8			
1	2	3	4	5	12	**7**		9	10	11		6		8			
1		3	4	5			9	10	11	2	6	**8**	12	7			
1	**2**	3	4	5	12		9	10	11		6	7		8			
1		3	4	5	2	7		9	10	11		6		8		12	
1		3	4	5			9	10	11	2	6		8			7	
1		3	4	5				10	11	2	6	**8**	12	9	7		
1		3	4	5		9		10	11	2	6		8			7	
1			4	5	3	9		12	10	**11**	2	6		8		7	
1	2	**3**	4	5		11		9	10		12	6		8		7	
1	2		4	5		11		9	10		3	6		8		7	
1			4	5	2	12		**9**	10	11	3	6		8		7	
1			4	5	2	12		**9**	10	11	3	6		8		7	
1	2		4	5		9		10	11	3	6		8			7	
1	2		4	5		9		10	11	3	6		8			7	
42	**32**	**35**	**42**	**41**	**6**	**29**	**8**	**36**	**42**	**38**	**15**	**40**	**6**	**35**	**0**	**5**	**10**
	3		7	6		10	2	11	2	1	2	5		11			

F.A. Cup

Siddall	Ritson	Dunne	Greaves	Jones P.B.	Walsh	Bryon	Curran	Jones G.E.	Reid	Thompson	Nicholson	Allardyce	Waldron	Whatmore	Taylor	Smith	Morgan
1	2	3	4	5		7		9	10	11		6		8			
1	2	3	4	5		7		9	10	**11**		6		8	12		
1	2	3	4	5		7		9	10	11		6		8			
1	2	3	4	5		7		9	10	11		6		8			
1	**2**	3	4			12	7		9	10		5	6	11	8		
6	6	6	6	5	0	6		6	6	5	1	6	1	6	0		
			1									1					
		1				2	1		1		2						

League Cup

Siddall	Ritson	Dunne	Greaves	Jones P.B.	Walsh	Bryon	Curran	Jones G.E.	Reid	Thompson	Nicholson	Allardyce	Waldron	Whatmore	Taylor	Smith	Morgan
1	2	3	4	5		7	8	9	10	11		6					
1	1	1	1	1		1	1	1	1	1		1					
				1													

League Table

	P	W	D	L	F	A	Pts
Sunderland	42	24	8	10	67	36	56
Bristol City	42	19	15	8	59	35	53
West Bromwich Albion	42	20	13	9	50	33	53
Bolton Wanderers	42	20	12	10	64	38	52
Notts County	42	19	11	12	60	41	49
Southampton	42	21	7	14	66	50	49
Luton Town	42	19	10	13	61	51	48
Nottingham Forest	42	17	12	13	55	40	46
Charlton Athletic	42	15	12	15	61	72	42
Blackpool	42	14	14	14	40	49	42
Chelsea	42	12	16	14	53	54	40
Fulham	42	13	14	15	45	47	40
Orient	42	13	14	15	37	39	40
Hull City	42	14	11	17	45	49	39
Blackburn Rovers	42	12	14	16	45	50	38
Plymouth Argyle	42	13	12	17	48	54	38
Oldham Athletic	42	13	12	17	57	68	38
Bristol Rovers	42	11	16	15	38	50	38
Carlisle United	42	12	13	17	45	59	37
Oxford United	42	11	11	20	39	59	33
York City	42	10	8	24	39	71	28
Portsmouth	42	9	7	26	32	61	25

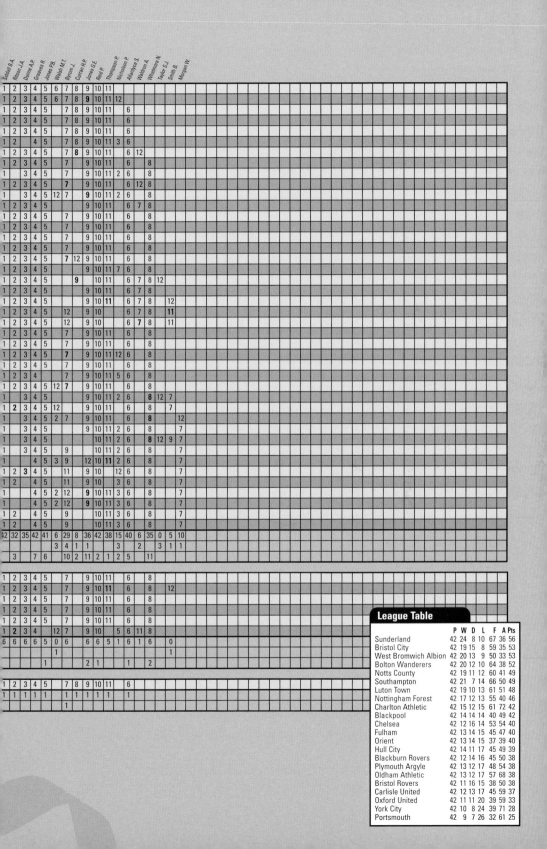

Division Two

Manager: I. Greaves

Match No.	Date		Venue	Opponents		Result	Scorers	Attendance
1	Aug	21	A	Blackburn Rovers	L	1-3	Reid	14,368
2		24	H	Orient	W	2-0	P. Jones (pen), Taylor	11,600
3		28	H	Millwall	W	3-1	Taylor 2, Smith	13,628
4	Sep	4	A	Notts County	W	1-0	P. Jones	9,266
5		11	H	Hull City	W	5-1	Whatmore, P. Jones 2, Taylor 2	12,495
6		18	A	Chelsea	L	1-2	Taylor	24,835
7		25	A	Plymouth Argyle	D	1-1	Mariner (own-goal)	12,564
8	Oct	2	H	Blackpool	L	0-3		18,680
9		9	A	Cardiff City	L	2-3	P. Jones (pen), Taylor	11,007
10		16	H	Bristol Rovers	W	1-0	P. Jones (pen)	12,771
11		23	A	Oldham Athletic	D	2-2	Greaves, Taylor	15,811
12		30	H	Fulham	W	2-1	Whatmore, Allardyce	24,228
13	Nov	6	A	Carlisle United	W	1-0	P. Jones	8,811
14		9	H	Burnley	W	2-1	Taylor, Reid	20,681
15		20	A	Southampton	W	3-1	Whatmore, Taylor 2	17,611
16		27	H	Charlton Athletic	W	1-0	Allardyce	17,842
17	Dec	15	A	Hereford United	D	3-3	Whatmore, Allardyce, Greaves	5,025
18		18	A	Wolverhampton Wanderers	L	0-1		18,444
19		21	H	Luton Town	W	2-1	Whatmore, Greaves	17,475
20		27	H	Nottingham Forest	D	1-1	Whatmore	31,313
21		28	A	Sheffield United	W	3-2	Whatmore 2, Taylor	25,503
22	Jan	3	A	Fulham	W	2-0	Whatmore, Taylor	12,594
23		22	H	Blackburn Rovers	W	3-1	Whatmore 2, Reid	28,525
24	Feb	5	A	Millwall	L	0-3		10,461
25		12	H	Notts County	W	4-0	Richards (own-goal), P. Jones, Whatmore, Morgan	21,171
26		19	A	Hull City	D	2-2	Reid, Whatmore	9,913
27		26	H	Chelsea	D	2-2	Whatmore, G. Jones	31,600
28	Mar	5	H	Plymouth Argyle	W	3-0	Whatmore 2, P. Jones (pen)	18,496
29		12	A	Blackpool	L	0-1		23,659
30		15	A	Orient	D	2-2	Greaves, G. Jones	5,413
31		22	H	Carlisle United	L	3-4	Allardyce, Whatmore 2	18,471
32	Apr	2	A	Oldham Athletic	W	3-0	Taylor, Allardyce, Whatmore	18,130
33		6	A	Nottingham Forest	L	1-3	P. Jones	24,580
34		9	H	Sheffield United	L	1-2	Taylor	19,576
35		12	H	Burnley	D	0-0		20,342
36		16	H	Southampton	W	3-0	Whatmore 2, P. Jones	20,095
37		22	A	Charlton Athletic	D	1-1	Whatmore	10,517
38		30	H	Hereford United	W	3-1	Hughes (own-goal), Allardyce, Taylor	18,874
39	May	7	A	Luton Town	D	1-1	Reid	11,164
40		10	H	Cardiff City	W	2-1	Whatmore, G. Jones	22,060
41		14	H	Wolverhampton Wanderers	L	0-1		35,603
42		17	A	Bristol Rovers	D	2-2	Whatmore 2	6,991

Appearances
Sub appearances
3 own-goals · Goals

FA Cup

R3	Jan	8	A	West Ham United	L	1-2	Waldron	24,147

Appearances
Sub appearances
Goals

FL Cup

R2	Sep	1	A	Bradford City	W	2-1	Whatmore 2	7,479
R3		22	A	Fulham	D	2-2	Greaves, Reid	14,961
rep	Oct	5	H	Fulham	d	2-2	Taylor, Walsh	15,010
rep2		18	N	Fulham	W	2-1	P. Jones, Whatmore	9,315
R4		26	A	Swansea City	D	1-1	Taylor	14,000
rep	Nov	2	H	Swansea City	W	5-1	Morgan, Greaves, Taylor 2, Whatmore	14,955
R5	Dec	1	A	Derby County	W	2-1	Whatmore, Morgan	26,734
SF1	Jan	18	A	Everton	D	1-1	Whatmore	54,032
SF2	Feb	15	H	Everton	L	0-1		50,413

R3 replay a.e.t. R3 replay 2 at St Andrews, Birmingham.

Appearances
Sub appearances
Goals

Anglo-Scottish Cup

Gp	Aug	7	H	Blackpool	D	0-0		9,402
Gp		10	H	Blackburn Rovers	W	2-0	Morgan, Byrom	7,054
Gp		14	A	Burnley	L	0-1		9,028
QF1	Sep	14	H	Partick Thistle	D	0-0		10,329
QF2		29	A	Partick Thistle	L	0-1		6,000

Appearances
Sub appearances
Goals

iddall B.A.	Ritson J.A.	Dunne A.P.	Graves R.	Jones P.B.	Allardyce S.	Morgan W.	Jones G.E.	Whatmore N.	Reid P.	Thompson P.	Smith B.	Taylor S.J.	Walsh M.T.	McDonagh J.M.	Nicholson P.	Waldron A.	Curran H.P.	Train R.	Carter M.	Byrom J.
	2	3	4	5	6	7	8	**9**	10	11	12									
	2	**3**	4	5	6	7	8		10		11	9	12							
	2	3	4	5	6	7	**8**	12	10		11	9								
	2	3	4	5	6	7		8	10	12	**11**	9								
	2	3	4	5	6	7		8	10	11		9								
	2	3	4	5	6	7		8	10	11		9								
	2	3	4	5	6	7		8	10	11		9								
		3	4	5	6	7		8	10	**11**	12	9		1	2					
			4	5	6	7		**8**	10		11	9	3	1	2	12				
		3	4	5	6	7		8	10			9		1	2	11				
		3	4	5	6	7		8	10			9		1	2	11				
		3	4	5	6	7		8	10			9		1	2	11				
		3	4	5	6	7		8	10		11	9	12	1	2					
			4	5	6	7		**8**	10		11	9	3	1	2		12			
		3	4	5	6	7		8	10		11	9		1	2					
		3	4	5	6	7		8	10		11	9		1	2					
		3	4	5	6	7		8	10		11	9		1	2					
		3	4	5	6	7		8	10		11	9		1	2					
		3	4	5	6	7		8	10	12	**11**	9		1	2					
		3	**4**	5	6	7		8	10		11	9		1	2		12			
		3		5	6	**7**		8	10	12	11	9		1	2	4				
		3	4	5	6	7		8	10		11	9		1	2					
		3	4	5	6	7		8	10			9		1	2	11				
		3	4	5	6	7	9	8	10					1	2	11	12			
		3	**4**	5	6	7	9	8	10	12				1	2	11				
		3	4	5	6	7	9	8	10					1	2	11				
		3	4	5	6	7	9	8	10					1	2	11				
		3	4	5	6	7	9	8	10				12	1	2	11				
		3	4	5	6	7	9	8	10					1	2	**11**		12		
			4	5	6	7	9	8	10				3	1	2			11		
			4	5	6	7	**9**	8	10	12			3	1	2			11		
		3	4	5	6	7	12	8	10			9		1	**2**			11		
	2	3	4	5	6	7	12	8	10			**9**		1				11		
		3	4	5	6	**7**	12	8	10			9		1	2			11		
		3	4	5	6		12	8	10	7		9		1	2			11		
	2		4	5		7		8	10			9	6	1	3			11		
	2		4	5	6	7		8	10			9		1	3			11		
	2		4	5	6	7		8	10			9		1	3			11		
	2		4	5	6	7		8	10			9		1	3			11		
	2		4	5	6	7	9	8	10					1	3			11		
	2		4	5	6	7	9	8	10					1	3			11		
	2		4	5	6	7	**9**	8	10			12		1	3			11		
7	15	31	41	42	41	41	14	40	42	6	14	30	5	35	34	11	0	13	0	0
							4	1		5	2	1	3			1	3	1		
		4	11	6	1	3	25	5		1	16									

		3	4	**5**		7		8	10		11	9	6	1	2	12				
		1	1	1		1		1	1		1	1	1	1	1	0				
																1				
																1				

1	2		4	5	6	7		8	10		11	9	3							
1	2	3	4	5	6	7		8	10	11		9								
			4	5	6	7		8	10		11	9	3	1	2					
			4	5	6	7		8	10			9	3	1	2	11				
		3	4	5	6			8	10		7	9		1	2	11				
		3	4	5	6	7		8	10			9		1	2	**11**			12	
		3	4	5	6	7		8	10		11	9		1	2					
		3	4	5		7		8	10		**11**	9	6	1	2	12				
		3	4	5	6	7	9	8	10					1	2	11				
2	2	6	9	9	8	8	1	9	9	1	5	8	4	7	7	4			0	
																1			1	
			2	1		2		6	1			4	1							

1	2	3	4	5	6	7	9	**8**	10	12										11
1	2	3	4	5	6	7				11	10						9			8
1	2		4	5	6	7			10	11			3				9			8
1	2	3	4	5	6	7		8	10	11		9								
	2	3	4		6	7		8	10	11		9	5	1						
4	5	4	5	4	5	5	1	3	4	4	1	2	2	1			2			3
										1										
						1														1

League Table

	P	W	D	L	F	A	Pts
Wolverhampton W	42	22	13	7	84	45	57
Chelsea	42	21	13	8	73	53	55
Nottingham Forest	42	21	10	11	77	43	52
Bolton Wanderers	42	20	11	11	75	54	51
Blackpool	42	17	17	8	58	42	51
Luton Town	42	21	6	15	67	48	48
Charlton Athletic	42	16	16	10	71	58	48
Notts County	42	19	10	13	65	60	48
Southampton	42	17	10	15	72	67	44
Millwall	42	15	13	14	57	53	43
Sheffield United	42	14	12	16	54	63	40
Blackburn Rovers	42	15	9	18	42	54	39
Oldham Athletic	42	14	10	18	52	64	38
Hull City	42	10	17	15	45	53	37
Bristol Rovers	42	12	13	17	53	68	37
Burnley	42	11	14	17	46	64	36
Fulham	42	11	13	18	54	61	35
Cardiff City	42	12	10	20	56	67	34
Orient	42	9	16	17	37	55	34
Carlisle United	42	11	12	19	49	75	34
Plymouth Argyle	42	8	16	18	46	65	32
Hereford United	42	8	15	19	57	78	31

Division Two

Manager: I. Greaves

Match No.	Date	Venue	Opponents	Result		Scorers	Attendance
1	Aug 20	A	Burnley	W	1-0	Greaves	14,71
2	23	H	Millwall	W	2-1	Allardyce, Whatmore	14,87
3	27	H	Sheffield United	W	2-1	Reid, Whatmore	16,84
4	Sep 3	A	Hull City	D	0-0		10,10
5	10	H	Oldham Athletic	W	1-0	Whatmore	16,03
6	17	A	Sunderland	W	2-0	Whatmore, Reid	30,34
7	24	A	Crystal Palace	L	1-2	Whatmore	23,60
8	Oct 1	H	Stoke City	D	1-1	Worthington	20,799
9	3	H	Blackburn Rovers	W	4-2	Reid, Allardyce, Greaves 2	18,24
10	8	A	Brighton & Hove Alb.	W	2-1	Reid, Greaves (pen)	27,43
11	15	H	Mansfield Town	W	2-0	Worthington 2	18,93
12	22	A	Southampton	D	2-2	Worthington, Morgan	27,29
13	29	H	Luton Town	W	2-1	Morgan, Worthington	20,11
14	Nov 5	A	Orient	D	1-1	Greaves (pen)	7,54
15	12	H	Charlton Athletic	W	2-1	Whatmore, Wood (own-goal)	15,97
16	19	A	Bristol Rovers	W	1-0	Waldron	7,87
17	26	H	Tottenham Hotspur	W	1-0	Greaves	32,26
18	Dec 3	A	Fulham	L	0-2		8,16
19	10	H	Cardiff City	W	6-3	P. Jones 2, Reid, Whatmore, Walsh, Morgan	16,09
20	17	A	Charlton Athletic	L	1-2	Whatmore	12,80
21	26	H	Notts County	W	2-0	Allardyce, Whatmore	22,64
22	27	A	Blackpool	W	2-0	Worthington, Whatmore	25,78
23	31	A	Millwall	L	0-1		6,72
24	Jan 2	H	Burnley	L	1-2	Whatmore	26,33
25	14	A	Sheffield United	W	5-1	Reid, Worthington, Nicholson, Greaves (pen), Whatmore	22,60
26	21	A	Hull City	W	1-0	Whatmore	18,25
27	Feb 18	A	Oldham Athletic	D	2-2	Reid, Whatmore	20,81
28	25	A	Stoke City	D	0-0		19,28
29	Mar 4	H	Brighton & Hove Alb.	D	1-1	Reid	21,40
30	7	H	Sunderland	W	2-0	Whatmore, Morgan	20,97
31	11	A	Mansfield Town	W	1-0	Ritson	12,32
32	18	A	Southampton	D	0-0		23,77
33	21	A	Luton Town	L	1-2	P. Jones	8,30
34	25	H	Blackpool	W	2-1	Reid, P. Jones	20,50
35	27	A	Notts County	D	1-1	Whatmore	15,71
36	Apr 1	H	Orient	W	2-0	Allardyce, Whatmore	17,95
37	8	A	Tottenham Hotspur	L	0-1		50,09
38	15	H	Bristol Rovers	W	3-0	Whatmore, Worthington 2	20,39
39	18	H	Crystal Palace	W	2-0	Whatmore, Worthington	23,98
40	22	A	Cardiff City	L	0-1		12,56
41	26	A	Blackburn Rovers	W	1-0	Worthington	27,83
42	29	H	Fulham	D	0-0		34,11
						Appearances	
						Sub appearances	
					1 own-goal	Goals	

FA Cup

R3	Jan 7	A	Tottenham Hotspur	D	2-2	Greaves (pen), Whatmore	43,731
rep	10	H	Tottenham Hotspur	W	2-1	Ritson, G. Jones	31,314
R4	Feb 6	H	Mansfield Town	W	1-0	Worthington	23,830
R5	27	A	Middlesbrough	L	0-2		36,662
R3 replay a.e.t.						Appearances	
						Sub appearances	
						Goals	

FL Cup

R2	Aug 31	H	Lincoln City	W	1-0	Waldron	11,467
R3	Oct 25	H	Peterborough United	W	3-1	Greaves, Allardyce, Whatmore (pen)	14,990
R4	Nov 30	H	Leeds United	L	1-3	G. Jones	33,766
						Appearances	
						Sub appearances	
						Goals	

Anglo-Scottish Cup

Gp	Aug 6	H	Burnley	W	1-0	Train	8,250
Gp	10	A	Blackburn Rovers	L	0-2		6,757
Gp	13	A	Blackpool	W	1-0	Greaves (pen)	8,158
Did not qualify for knock-out stages.						Appearances	
						Goals	

McDonagh J.M.	Clements A.P.	Dunne A.P.	Greaves R.	Walsh M.T.	Allardyce S.	Morgan W.	Whatmore N.	Train R.	Reid P.	Thompson P.	Ritson J.A.	Taylor S.J.	Waldron A.	Jones G.E.	Nicholson P.	Worthington F.S.	Jones P.B.	Gowling A.E.	Graham M.A.	Thompson C.D.
	2	3	4	5	6	7	8	9	10	11										
		3	4	5	6	7	8	9	10	11	2									
		3	4	5	6	7	8	9	10		2	11								
		3		5	6	7	8	9	10		2		4	11						
		3		5	6	7	8	9	10		2		4	11						
			4	5	6	7	8	9	10		2			11	3					
		3	4	5	6	7	8	9	10					11	2					
		3	4	5	6	7	8	9	10						2	11				
		3	4	5	6	7	8	9	10						2	11				
		3	4	5	6	7	8	9	10						2	11				
		3	4	5	6	7	8	9	**10**				12		2	11				
		3	4	5	6	7	8	9	10						2	11				
		3	4	5	6	7	8	9	10						2	11				
		3	4	5	6	**7**	8	9					10		2	11	12			
		3	4	5	6	7	8	9					10		2	11	12			
		3	4	9	6	7	8						10		2	11	5			
		3	4	9	6	7	8						10		2	11	5			
		3	4	9	6	7	8		10						2	11	5			
		3	4	9	6	7	8	12	10						2	11	5			
		3	4	9	6	7	8		10						2	11	5			
		3	4		6	7	8	9	10						2	11	5			
		3	4	12	6	7	8	9	10						2	11	5			
			4	5	6	7	8	9	10		3				2	11				
			4	5	6	7	8	9	10		3				2	11				
			4	5	6	7	8	9	10		2				3	11				
			4	5	6	7	8	9	10		2				3	11				
			4	3	6	7	8	9	10		2					11	5			
			4	3	6	7	8	**9**	10		2				12	11	5			
			4	3	6	7	8		10		2			9		11	5			
			4	3	6	7	8		10		2			9	12	11	**5**			
		3	4	6		7	8		10		2					11	5	9	12	
			4	3	6	7	8		10		2					11	5	9		
		2	4	3	6	7	8	9	10							**11**	5	12		
		3	4	5	6	7	8	**9**	10							12	2	11		
		3	4	5	6	7	8		10							11	2	9		
		3	4	5	6	7	8		10	12						11	2	**9**		
		3	4	5	6	7	8	9	10							11	2			
		3	4	5	6	7	8	9	10							11	2			
		3	4	5	6	7	8	9	10		2					11				
		3	4	5	6	7	8	9	10		2					11				
		3	4	5	6	**7**	8	9	10		2					11		12		
		3	4	5	6		8	9	10		2					11		7		
2	1	32	40	40	41	41	42	31	38	2	19	1	6	6	21	34	19	6	0	0
				1				1		1			1		2	1	2	2	1	
			7	1	4	4	19		9		1		1		1	11	4			

McDonagh J.M.	Clements A.P.	Dunne A.P.	Greaves R.	Walsh M.T.	Allardyce S.	Morgan W.	Whatmore N.	Train R.	Reid P.	Thompson P.	Ritson J.A.	Taylor S.J.	Waldron A.	Jones G.E.	Nicholson P.	Worthington F.S.	Jones P.B.	Gowling A.E.	Graham M.A.	Thompson C.D.
			4	3	6	7	8	9	10		2				12	11	**5**			
			4	5	6	7	8	9	10		2			12	3	11				
			4	5	6	7	8	9	10		2				3	11				
			4	9	6	7	8		**10**		2			12	3	11	5			
4			4	4	4	4	4	3	4		4			0	3	4	2			
														2	1					
			1				1				1			1		1				

McDonagh J.M.	Clements A.P.	Dunne A.P.	Greaves R.	Walsh M.T.	Allardyce S.	Morgan W.	Whatmore N.	Train R.	Reid P.	Thompson P.	Ritson J.A.	Taylor S.J.	Waldron A.	Jones G.E.	Nicholson P.	Worthington F.S.	Jones P.B.	Gowling A.E.	Graham M.A.	Thompson C.D.
		3		5	6	7	8	9	10		2	**11**	4	12						
		3	4	5	6	7	8	9	10						2					11
		3	4	9	6		8		10	7				11	2		5			
3		3	2	3	3	2	3	2	3	1	1	1	1	1	2		1			1
														1						
			1		1		1						1	1						

McDonagh J.M.	Clements A.P.	Dunne A.P.	Greaves R.	Walsh M.T.	Allardyce S.	Morgan W.	Whatmore N.	Train R.	Reid P.	Thompson P.	Ritson J.A.	Taylor S.J.
		3	4	5	6		8	7	10	11	2	9
	2	3	4	5	6		8	7	10	11		9
	2	3	4	5	6		8	7	10	11		9
3	2	3	3	3	3		3	3	3	3	1	3
			1									

League Table

	P	W	D	L	F	A	Pts
Bolton Wanderers	42	24	10	8	63	33	58
Southampton	42	22	13	7	70	39	57
Tottenham Hotspur	42	20	16	6	83	49	56
Brighton & Hove Albion	42	22	12	8	63	38	56
Blackburn Rovers	42	16	13	13	56	60	45
Sunderland	42	14	16	12	67	59	44
Stoke City	42	16	10	16	53	49	42
Oldham Athletic	42	13	16	13	54	58	42
Crystal Palace	42	13	15	14	50	47	41
Fulham	42	14	13	15	49	49	41
Burnley	42	15	10	17	56	64	40
Sheffield United	42	16	8	18	62	73	40
Luton Town	42	14	10	18	54	52	38
Orient	42	10	18	14	43	49	38
Notts County	42	11	16	15	54	62	38
Millwall	42	12	14	16	49	57	38
Charlton Athletic	42	13	12	17	55	68	38
Bristol Rovers	42	13	12	17	61	77	38
Cardiff City	42	13	12	17	51	71	38
Blackpool	42	12	13	17	59	60	37
Mansfield Town	42	10	11	21	49	69	31
Hull City	42	8	12	22	34	52	28

Division One

Manager: I. Greaves

Match No.	Date		Venue	Opponents		Result	Scorers	Attendance
1	Aug	19	H	Bristol City	L	1-2	Gowling	21,355
2		22	A	Southampton	D	2-2	Worthington 2	21,059
3		26	A	West Bromwich Albion	L	0-4		23,237
4	Sep	2	H	Birmingham City	D	2-2	Worthington 2 (1 pen)	20,234
5		9	H	Derby County	W	2-1	Gowling 2	20,331
6		16	A	Arsenal	L	0-1		31,024
7		23	H	Norwich City	W	3-2	Whatmore, Worthington 2	19,901
8		30	A	Liverpool	L	0-3		47,099
9	Oct	7	H	Leeds United	W	3-1	Worthington, Morgan, Smith	27,751
10		14	A	Chelsea	L	3-4	Gowling 2, Worthington (pen)	19,879
11		21	H	Manchester City	D	2-2	Gowling, Worthington	32,249
12		28	A	Tottenham Hotspur	L	0-2		37,337
13	Nov	4	H	Coventry City	D	0-0		22,379
14		11	A	Bristol City	L	1-4	Walsh	18,168
15		18	H	West Bromwich Albion	L	0-1		22,278
16		21	A	Birmingham City	L	0-3		21,643
17		25	H	Nottingham Forest	L	0-1		25,692
18	Dec	2	A	Queen's Park Rangers	W	3-1	Gowling, Worthington 2	11,635
19		9	H	Wolverhampton Wanderers	W	3-1	Greaves, Gowling, Worthington (pen)	21,006
20		16	A	Ipswich Town	L	0-3		16,953
21		22	H	Manchester United	W	3-0	Worthington 2, Gowling	32,390
22		26	A	Middlesbrough	D	1-1	Worthington	20,125
23	Feb	3	A	Norwich City	D	0-0		15,369
24		24	H	Chelsea	W	2-1	Burke, McNab	19,457
25	Mar	3	A	Manchester City	L	1-2	Worthington	41,127
26		7	A	Aston Villa	L	0-3		28,053
27		17	A	Coventry City	D	2-2	Worthington, McNab	15,231
28		21	A	Derby County	L	0-3		15,227
29		24	H	Southampton	W	2-0	Gowling 2	19,879
30		26	H	Arsenal	W	4-2	Worthington 2 (2 pens), Gowling 2	20,704
31		31	A	Nottingham Forest	D	1-1	Gowling	29,015
32	Apr	3	H	Everton	W	3-1	Morgan, Whatmore, P. Jones	27,263
33		7	A	Queen's Park Rangers	W	2-1	Worthington, Gowling	21,119
34		11	A	Manchester United	W	2-1	Worthington 2	49,617
35		14	H	Middlesbrough	D	0-0		22,621
36		16	A	Everton	L	0-1		31,214
37		21	H	Ipswich Town	L	2-3	Worthington, Allardyce	20,073
38		25	A	Leeds United	L	1-5	McNab	20,218
39		28	A	Wolverhampton Wanderers	D	1-1	Whatmore	18,125
40	May	1	H	Liverpool	L	1-4	Souness (own-goal)	35,200
41		5	H	Aston Villa	D	0-0		17,394
42		8	H	Tottenham Hotspur	L	1-3	Worthington	17,879

	Appearances
	Sub appearances
1 own-goal	Goals

FA Cup

R3	Jan	9	A	Bristol City	L	1-3	Smith	17,392

	Appearances
	Goals

FL Cup

R2	Aug	29	H	Chelsea	W	2-1	Worthington 2 (1 pen)	10,449
R3	Oct	4	A	Exeter City	L	1-2	Gowling	9,151

	Appearances
	Sub appearances
	Goals

Anglo-Scottish Cup

Gp	Aug	5	A	Sunderland	L	0-2		7,260
Gp		8	H	Sheffield United	W	1-0	Whatmore	6,042
Gp		12	H	Oldham Athletic	D	0-0		5,418

Did not qualify for knock-out stages.

	Appearances
	Sub appearances
	Goals

Player appearance grid (column headers, left to right):

McDonagh J.M. · Nicholson P. · Walsh M.T. · Greaves R. · Jones P.B. · Aldridge S. · Morgan W. · Whatmore N. · Gowling A.E. · Worthington F.S. · Train R. · Dunne A.P. · Jones G.E. · Burke D.I. · Smith B. · Graham M.A. · Reid P. · McNab N. · Nowak T. · Poole T. · Thompson C.D. · Moores A.C.

McDonagh	Nicholson	Walsh	Greaves	Jones P.B.	Aldridge	Morgan	Whatmore	Gowling	Worthington	Train	Dunne	Jones G.E.	Burke	Smith	Graham	Reid	McNab	Nowak	Poole	Thompson	Moores
1	2	3	4	5	**6**	7	8	9	10	11	12										
1	**2**	5	4	12	6	7	8	9	10	11	3										
1		5	4	**2**	6	7	8	9	10	11	3	12									
1		5	4		6	7	8	9	10	11			3	2							
1	2	5	4			7	8	9	10	**11**	3		6		12						
1	2	5	4	6		7	8	9	10		3				11						
1	2	**5**	4	6	12	7	8	9	10		3				11						
1	2	5	4	6		7	8	9	10		3				11						
1		5	4	2	6	7		**9**	10		12				3	11	8				
1		5	4	2	6	7	12	**9**	10						3	11	8				
1	2	5	4		6	7		9	10						3	11	8				
1	2	5	4	6		7		9	10			3			8	11					
1	2	5	4			7		9	10			3			8	11					
1	2	5	4			7	12	9	10			**3**			8	11					
1	2	6	4	5		7		9	10			3			8	11					
1	2	3	4	5	6	7		9	10						8	11					
1	2	6	4	5		7		9	10			3			8	11					
1	2	6	4	5		7		9	10			3			8	11					
1	2	6	4	5		7		9	10			3			8	11					
1	2	6	4	5		7		9	10			3			8	11					
1	2	6	4	5		7		9	10			3			8	11					
1	2	6	4	5		7	9		10			3		8		11					
1	2	6	4	5		7		9	10			3		8		11					
1	2	6	4	5		7	12	9	10			3		**8**		11					
1	2	6	4	5		7	12	9	10			3		**8**		11					
1	2	6	4	5	8	7		9	10			**3**	12			11					
1	2	6	4	**5**	8	7	12	9	10			3				11					
1	2	6	4	5		7	8	9	10			3				11					
1	2	6	4	5		7	8	9	10			3				11					
1	2	6	4	5		7	8	9	10			3				11					
1	2	6	4	5		7	8	9	10			3				11					
1	**2**	6	4	5		7	8	9	10			3				11	12				
1		6	4	5		7	8	9	10			3		2	11						
1		6	4	5	12	7	8	9	10			**3**		2	11						
1		3	4	5	6	7	8	9	10					2	11						
1	2	3		**5**	6	7	8	9	10					11		4	12				
1		6	4		5	7	8		10		3	2	9		11						
1	2	6	4		5	7	8		10	3			11		9						
1	2	6	4		5	7	8		10	3			11		9						
1	2	6	4		5	7	8		10		3	11			9						
1	2	6	4		5		8		10	**3**	11	12			9	7					
42	34	42	41	31	18	41	23	36	42	5	24	0	19	9	18	14	22	1	0	0	0
		1	2		6						2	1	1		2		1	1			
	1	1	1	1	2	3	15	24				1		1		3					

McD	Nic	Wal	Gre	JPB	Ald	Mor	Wha	Gow	Wor	Tra	Dun	JGE	Bur	Smi	Gra	Rei	McN	Now	Poo	Tho	Moo
1	2	6	4	5		7		9	10			3			8		11				
1	1	1	1	1		1		1	1			1			1		1				

McD	Nic	Wal	Gre	JPB	Ald	Mor	Wha	Gow	Wor	Tra	Dun	JGE	Bur	Smi	Gra	Rei	McN	Now	Poo	Tho	Moo
1		5	4		6	7	8	9	10	11			3	2							
		5	4		6	7	8	9	10			3	**2**		12			1	11		
1		2	2			2	2	2	2	1		2	2		0			1	1		
															1						
				1	2																

McD	Nic	Wal	Gre	JPB	Ald	Mor	Wha	Gow	Wor	Tra	Dun	JGE	Bur	Smi	Gra	Rei	McN	Now	Poo	Tho	Moo
1	2	3	4	5	6		8	9	11	7					10				12		
1		3	4	5	6		8	9	11		12		7	2	**10**						
1	2	3	4	5	6		8	9	10	7			11								
3	2	3	3	3	3		3	3	3	2	0		2	1	2			0			
											1							1			
			1																		

League Table

	P	W	D	L	F	A	Pts
Liverpool	42	30	8	4	85	16	68
Nottingham Forest	42	21	18	3	61	26	60
West Bromwich Albion	42	24	11	7	72	35	59
Everton	42	17	17	8	52	40	51
Leeds United	42	18	14	10	70	52	50
Ipswich Town	42	20	9	13	63	49	49
Arsenal	42	17	14	11	61	48	48
Aston Villa	42	15	16	11	59	49	46
Manchester United	42	15	15	12	60	63	45
Coventry City	42	14	16	12	58	68	44
Tottenham Hotspur	42	13	15	14	48	61	41
Middlesbrough	42	15	10	17	57	50	40
Bristol City	42	15	10	17	47	51	40
Southampton	42	12	16	14	47	53	40
Manchester City	42	13	13	16	58	56	39
Norwich City	42	7	23	12	51	57	37
Bolton Wanderers	42	12	11	19	54	75	35
Wolverhampton W	42	13	8	21	44	68	34
Derby County	42	10	11	21	44	71	31
Queen's Park Rangers	42	6	13	23	45	73	25
Birmingham City	42	6	10	26	37	64	22
Chelsea	42	5	10	27	44	92	20

Division One

Manager: I. Greaves until 26 January 1980, S. Anderson from February 1980

Match No.	Date	Venue	Opponents	Result		Scorers	Attendance
1	Aug 18	H	Aston Villa	D	1-1	Whatmore	19,795
2	21	A	Liverpool	D	0-0		45,900
3	25	H	Southampton	W	2-1	McNab, Whatmore	17,417
4	Sep 1	A	Brighton & Hove Alb.	L	1-3	Walsh	20,171
5	8	H	West Bromwich Albion	D	0-0		17,033
6	15	A	Coventry City	L	1-3	Morgan	15,355
7	22	H	Leeds United	D	1-1	Allardyce	21,724
8	29	A	Norwich City	L	1-2	Whatmore	16,500
9	Oct 6	A	Derby County	L	0-4		16,810
10	9	H	Liverpool	D	1-1	Whatmore	25,571
11	13	H	Arsenal	D	0-0		17,032
12	20	A	Nottingham Forest	L	2-5	Thompson, Morgan (pen)	24,564
13	27	H	Crystal Palace	D	1-1	Gowling	15,132
14	Nov 3	A	Aston Villa	L	1-3	Whatmore	24,744
15	10	A	Tottenham Hotspur	L	0-2		33,155
16	17	H	Manchester City	L	0-1		25,515
17	24	A	Stoke City	L	0-1		15,435
18	Dec 1	H	Bristol City	D	1-1	Greaves	12,074
19	8	A	Wolverhampton Wanderers	L	1-3	Whatmore	20,169
20	15	H	Ipswich Town	L	0-1		10,929
21	21	A	Middlesbrough	L	1-3	Morgan (pen)	11,813
22	26	H	Everton	D	1-1	Carter	18,220
23	29	A	Southampton	L	0-2		21,607
24	Jan 12	H	Brighton & Hove Alb.	L	0-2		13,963
25	Feb 9	A	Leeds United	D	2-2	Whatmore, Greaves	16,428
26	23	A	Arsenal	L	0-2		24,383
27	27	A	Manchester United	L	0-2		47,546
28	Mar 1	H	Nottingham Forest	W	1-0	Whatmore	16,164
29	8	A	Crystal Palace	L	1-3	Jones	18,728
30	11	H	Norwich City	W	1-0	Whatmore	10,442
31	15	H	Derby County	L	1-2	Reid	13,236
32	18	A	West Bromwich Albion	D	4-4	Carter 2, Reid, Whatmore	11,721
33	22	H	Tottenham Hotspur	W	2-1	Carter, Whatmore	14,734
34	29	A	Manchester City	D	2-2	Whatmore, Reid (pen)	33,500
35	Apr 5	A	Everton	L	1-3	Whatmore	28,030
36	7	H	Manchester United	L	1-3	Whatmore	31,902
37	8	H	Middlesbrough	D	2-2	Nowak, Whatmore	10,613
38	12	A	Bristol City	L	1-2	Allardyce	13,584
39	15	H	Coventry City	D	1-1	Wilson	8,995
40	19	H	Stoke City	W	2-1	Carter, Whatmore	11,304
41	26	A	Ipswich Town	L	0-1		21,447
42	May 3	H	Wolverhampton Wanderers	D	0-0		11,710
						Appearances	
						Sub appearances	
						Goals	

FA Cup

	Date	Venue	Opponents	Result		Scorers	Attendance
R3	Jan 5	A	Sunderland	W	1-0	Whatmore	24,464
R4	26	H	Halifax Town	W	2-0	Greaves, Whatmore	21,085
R5	Feb 16	H	Arsenal	D	1-1	Allardyce	23,530
rep	19	A	Arsenal	L	0-3		40,140
						Appearances	
						Sub appearances	
						Goals	

FL Cup

	Date	Venue	Opponents	Result		Scorers	Attendance
R2/1	Aug 28	H	Southend United	L	1-2	Gowling	7,861
R2/2	Sep 3	A	Southend United	D	0-0		9,140
						Appearances	
						Sub appearances	
						Goals	

Anglo-Scottish Cup

	Date	Venue	Opponents	Result		Scorers	Attendance
Gp	Aug 2	H	Bury	D	2-2	Gowling, McNab	5,697
Gp	4	A	Oldham Athletic	W	3-1	Nowak, Whatmore 2	4,518
Gp	7	H	Sunderland	W	2-0	Whatmore, McNab	3,685
QF1	Sep 19	A	St Mirren	L	2-4	Worthington, Nowak	5,500
QF2	Oct 2	H	St Mirren	W	2-1	Allardyce 2	7,856
QF2 a.e.t.; St Mirren won on aggregate.						Appearances	
						Sub appearances	
						Goals	

McDonagh J.M.	Clement D.T.	Nicholson P.	Greaves R.	Jones P.B.	Walsh M.T.	Nowak T.	Whatmore N.	Gowling A.E.	Cantello L.	McNab N.	Burke D.I.	Worthington F.S.	Morgan W.	Thompson C.D.	Allardyce S.	Carter M.	Graham M.A.	Reid P.	Wilson P.	Bennett M.	Hoggan D.M.
1	2	3	4	5	6	7	8	9	10	11											
1	2	3	4	5	6		8	9	10	11	7										
1	2	3	4	5	6	7	8	9	10	11											
1	2		4	5	6	12	**8**	9	10	11	3	**7**									
1	2	3	4	5	6		8	9	10		11	12	7								
1	2	**3**	4	5	6		8	9	10		11		7	12							
1	2		4		6		12	8	**10**	11	3	9	7		5						
1	2		4		6		11	9	8		3	10	7		5						
1	2		4		6		8	**9**	12	11	3	10	7		5						
1	2	10		5	**6**		8	9			3	12	7	11	4						
1	2	10		5	6		8				3	9	7	11	4						
1	**2**	10		5	6		8	9		12	3		7	11	4						
1		2		5	6		8	9	10		3		7	11	4						
1		2	12	5	6		8	9	10		3		7	11	**4**						
1	2		4	5	6		8	9		10	3		7	11							
1	2		4	5	6		8	9	10	11	3		7								
1	**2**	3	4	5	6		8	9	10	11	12		7								
1		2	4	5	6		8	**9**	10	11	3		7			12					
1		3	4	5	6		8		10		11		7		2	9					
1		2	4	5	6		8	9	10		3		**7**	11		12					
1		11	4		6		8	9	**10**		3		7		5	12	2				
1	2		4		6		**8**	9	10	11	3		7		5	12					
1	2	3	4		6	7		9	10		12			**11**	5	8					
1	2	3	4		6		8	**9**	10				7		5	12		11			
1	2		4		3		8	6	10		12		7		5	**9**		11			
1	2	4		5	6	7	8				3			9				11	10		
1	2	4		5	6	9	8				3		7					11	10		
1	2	4		5	6	7	8				**3**			9		12		11	10		
1	**2**	4		5	6	7	8				3			9			12	11	10		
1	2	3		5	6	7	8		**4**					9		12		11	10		
1	2	3		5	6	7	8		4					**9**		12		11	10		
1	2	3		5	6	7	8		4							9		11	10		
1	2	3		5	6	7	8		4							9		11	10		
1	2	3		**5**	6	7	8		4							9		11	10	12	
1	2	**3**		5	6	7	8		4							9		11	10	12	
1				5	6	7	8		4							9	2	11	10	3	
1				5	6	7	8		**4**		3			12		9	2	11	10		
1				5	6	7	**8**								12	9	2	11	10	3	4
1				5	6	7	8									9	2	11	10	3	4
1		4			6	7	8								5	9	2	11	10	3	
1		4		5	6		8	11	7							9	2		10	3	
1		3			6	7	8		4						5	9	2		10	11	12
42	29	30	20	32	42	19	40	24	30	11	24		21	13	16	14	8	17	17	6	2
			1			1	1		1	1	3			2	1	8	1			2	1
			2	1	1	1	16	1		1			3	1	2	5		3	1		

McDonagh J.M.	Clement D.T.	Nicholson P.	Greaves R.	Jones P.B.	Walsh M.T.	Nowak T.	Whatmore N.	Gowling A.E.	Cantello L.	McNab N.	Burke D.I.	Worthington F.S.	Morgan W.	Thompson C.D.	Allardyce S.	Carter M.	Graham M.A.	Reid P.	Wilson P.	Bennett M.	Hoggan D.M.
1	2	3	4		6		8	9	10				7		5			11			
1		2	4		6		8			10	3		7		5	9		11			
1	2		4		3		8	6	10		12		7		5	**9**		11			
1	2		4		3		8	6	10				7	12	**5**	9		11			
4	3	2	4		4		4	3	3	1	1		4	0	4	3		4			
											1			1							
			1				2								1						

McDonagh J.M.	Clement D.T.	Nicholson P.	Greaves R.	Jones P.B.	Walsh M.T.	Nowak T.	Whatmore N.	Gowling A.E.	Cantello L.	McNab N.	Burke D.I.	Worthington F.S.	Morgan W.	Thompson C.D.	Allardyce S.	Carter M.	Graham M.A.	Reid P.	Wilson P.	Bennett M.	Hoggan D.M.
1	2	3	4	5	6	**7**	8	9	10	11			12								
1	2		4	5	6		**8**	9	10	11	3	12	7								
2	2	1	2	2	2	1	2	2	2	2	1	0	1								
												1	1								
								1													

McDonagh J.M.	Clement D.T.	Nicholson P.	Greaves R.	Jones P.B.	Walsh M.T.	Nowak T.	Whatmore N.	Gowling A.E.	Cantello L.	McNab N.	Burke D.I.	Worthington F.S.	Morgan W.	Thompson C.D.	Allardyce S.	Carter M.	Graham M.A.	Reid P.	Wilson P.	Bennett M.	Hoggan D.M.
1	2	3	4	5	6	7	8	9		11	10				12						
1	2	3	4	5	6	7	8	9	**10**	11	12										
1	2	3	4	5	6	7	8	9		11	10										
1	**2**	12		5		7	8		10	11	3	9		4	6						
1		2	4		6		8	**9**		11	3	10	7	12	5						
5	4	4	4	4	4	4	5	4	2	5	4	2	1	1	2						
		1									1			1	1						
						2	3	1		2		1			2						

League Table

	P	W	D	L	F	A	Pts
Liverpool	42	25	10	7	81	30	60
Manchester United	42	24	10	8	65	35	58
Ipswich Town	42	22	9	11	68	39	53
Arsenal	42	18	16	8	52	36	52
Nottingham Forest	42	20	8	14	63	43	48
Wolverhampton W	42	19	9	14	58	47	47
Aston Villa	42	16	14	12	51	50	46
Southampton	42	18	9	15	65	53	45
Middlesbrough	42	16	12	14	50	44	44
West Bromwich Albion	42	11	19	12	54	50	41
Leeds United	42	13	14	15	46	50	40
Norwich City	42	13	14	15	58	66	40
Crystal Palace	42	12	16	14	41	50	40
Tottenham Hotspur	42	15	10	17	52	62	40
Coventry City	42	16	7	19	56	66	39
Brighton & Hove Albion	42	11	15	16	47	57	37
Manchester City	42	12	13	17	43	66	37
Stoke City	42	13	10	19	44	58	36
Everton	42	9	17	16	43	51	35
Bristol City	42	9	13	20	37	66	31
Derby County	42	11	8	23	47	67	30
Bolton Wanderers	42	5	15	22	38	73	25

Division Two

Manager: S. Anderson

Did you know that?

Goals from Mick Carter and Brian Kidd earned the Wanderers a 2–1 win at Shrewsbury Town in October 1980 to end a run of 28 away League games without success, the last victory being at Manchester United by the same score.

Match No.	Date	Venue	Opponents	Result		Scorers	Attendance
1	Aug 16	A	Notts County	L	1-2	Whatmore	7,459
2	19	H	Sheffield Wednesday	D	0-0		15,926
3	23	H	Newcastle United	W	4-0	Kidd 3, Whatmore	11,835
4	30	A	Derby County	L	0-1		17,378
5	Sep 6	H	Bristol Rovers	W	2-0	Griffiths (own-goal), Gowling (pen)	8,712
6	13	A	Cardiff City	D	1-1	Walsh	6,649
7	20	H	Swansea City	L	1-4	Whatmore	9,419
8	27	A	Oldham Athletic	D	1-1	Cantello	10,174
9	Oct 4	H	Chelsea	L	2-3	Thompson, Gowling	11,888
10	7	A	Shrewsbury Town	W	2-1	Carter, Kidd	5,077
11	11	A	Queen's Park Rangers	L	1-3	Kidd	8,641
12	18	H	Bristol City	D	1-1	Gowling	8,988
13	21	H	Preston North End	W	2-1	Carter, Whatmore	10,713
14	25	A	West Ham United	L	1-2	Kidd	25,277
15	Nov 1	H	Cambridge United	W	6-1	Kidd 3, Whatmore, Hoggan, Cantello	8,016
16	8	A	Watford	L	1-3	Hoggan	11,290
17	11	A	Sheffield Wednesday	L	0-2		16,262
18	22	H	Grimsby Town	D	1-1	Hoggan	9,031
19	25	H	Notts County	W	3-0	Wilson 2, Kidd	7,344
20	29	A	Luton Town	D	2-2	Whatmore 2	8,300
21	Dec 6	H	Orient	W	3-1	Whatmore, Kidd 2	8,228
22	13	A	Bristol City	L	1-3	Gowling (pen)	7,384
23	19	H	Queen's Park Rangers	L	1-2	Gowling	6,315
24	26	A	Wrexham	W	1-0	Whatmore	7,635
25	27	H	Blackburn Rovers	L	1-2	Hoggan	18,184
26	Jan 10	A	Grimsby Town	L	0-4		9,320
27	24	H	Derby County	W	3-1	Gowling 2, Thomas	9,937
28	31	A	Newcastle United	L	1-2	Bennett	19,108
29	Feb 7	H	Cardiff City	W	4-2	Thomas 2, Wilson, Nikolic	8,115
30	14	A	Bristol Rovers	L	1-2	Gowling	5,368
31	24	H	Oldham Athletic	W	2-0	Whatmore, Thomas	9,641
32	28	A	Swansea City	L	0-3		9,468
33	Mar 7	A	Chelsea	L	0-2		12,948
34	14	H	Shrewsbury Town	L	0-2		7,900
35	24	A	Preston North End	W	2-1	Reid, Gowling	8,505
36	28	H	West Ham United	D	1-1	Whatmore	13,271
37	Apr 4	A	Cambridge United	W	3-2	Reid, Nikolic, Whatmore	4,512
38	11	H	Watford	W	2-1	Thomas, Whatmore	8,461
39	18	A	Blackburn Rovers	D	0-0		16,357
40	20	H	Wrexham	D	1-1	Kidd (pen)	6,194
41	26	A	Orient	D	2-2	Gowling, Whatmore	3,824
42	May 2	H	Luton Town	L	0-3		7,268
						Appearances	
						Sub appearances	
					1 own-goal	Goals	

FA Cup

R3	Jan 3	A	Nottingham Forest	D	3-3	Hoggan 2, Whatmore	22,520
rep	6	H	Nottingham Forest	L	0-1		22,799
R3 replay a.e.t.						Appearances	
						Sub appearances	
						Goals	

FL Cup

R2/1	Aug 26	H	Crystal Palace	L	0-3		9,913
R2/2	Sep 2	A	Crystal Palace	L	1-2	Kidd	14,764
						Appearances	
						Sub appearances	
						Goals	

Player appearance and scoring grid (shirt numbers worn per match). Column headers (left to right):

Peacock D. · Graham M.A. · Burke D.I. · Wilson P. · Jones P.B. · Walsh M.T. · Goodup A.E. · Whitmore N. · Carter M. · Kidd R. · Camstio L. · Clement D.T. · Hoggan D.M. · McElhinney G.M.A. · Novak T. · Poole T. · Thompson C.D. · Nicholl D. · Nicholson P. · Reid P. · Moores J.C. · Thomas J.W. · Brennan I. · Bennett M.

Pea	Gra	Bur	Wil	Jon	Wal	Goo	Whi	Car	Kid	Cam	Cle	Hog	McE	Nov	Poo	Tho	Nic	Nic	Rei	Moo	Tho	Bre	Ben
1	2	3	4	5	6	7	8	9	10	11													
1	2	3	4	5	6	7	8	9	10	11													
1	2	3	4	5	6	7	8	9	10	11													
1		3		5	6	7	8	9	10	4	2	11											
1		3	12	6		7	8	9	10	4	2	11	5										
1		3	12	5	6		9	8		10	4	2	11		7								
1		3	9		6	5	8		10	4	2	11		7									
	2	3		5	6	9	8		10	4		11			1	7							
	2	3		5	6	9	8		10	4		12			1	7	11						
12	3	7	5	6	9		8	10	4			1		11	2								
	3	7	5	6	9	8		11	10	4			1			2							
2	11		5	6	9		8	10	4			1			3	7							
2	3		5	6	11	8	9	10	4			1				7							
2	3		5	6	11	8	9	10	4			1				7							
	3		5	6	11	8	9	10	4		12	1			2	7							
	3		5	6	11	8		10	4		9	1			2	7							
2	3	12	5	6	11	8		10				9			1	4	7						
2	3		5	6	4	8	9	10		11		1				7	12						
2		4	5	6	11	8		10			9	3	1				7						
2		4	5	6	11	8		10			9	3	1			7							
2		4	5	6	11	8		10			9	3	1			7		12					
2		4	5	6	11	8		10			9	3	1			7		12	6				
2	3	4	5	8		11	8		10		9	6	1	12		7							
2		4		11	8		10		9	3	1		5	7				6					
1	2		4		11		12	10		9	3			7			8	5	6				
1	2		4		5		10		9	3			7	12			8	6	11				
1	2		4	5	11		10		9	3		12	7				8	6					
1	2		4	5		8		10		9	3			7				8	6	11			
1	2		4	5		11			9	3			7				8	6	10				
	2	12	5		11	8			9	3			7				10	6	4				
2	4		5		11	8			9	3			7				10	6					
2	4		5		11	8		9	3			1	12	7			10	6					
	2			5	11	8		10	4		12	3		1	7			9		6			
2	3			5	11	8		10	4		12	6		1	7			9					
		5	3	11	8		12	6		10			1		7	2	4		9				
		5	3	11	8			6		10			1		7	2	4		9				
		5	3	11	8			6		10			1		7	2	4		9				
	6	5	3	11	8		12			10			1		7	2	4		9				
		5	3	11	8			6		10			1		7	2	4		9				
		5		11	8		12	6		10			1		7	2	4		9	3			
		5	3	11	8			6		10			1		7	2	4		9	12			
1			5	6	11	8	12			4					7	2	10		9	3			
13	**26**	**22**	**18**	**35**	**30**	**41**	**36**	**12**	**30**	**25**	**4**	**29**	**17**	**2**	**29**	**3**	**21**	**18**	**18**	**0**	**15**	**12**	**6**
	1		4						2	3					4		3	1			1	2	1
	3		1	10	14	2	13	2		4			1	2		2		5		1			

Cup block A:

1	2		4	**5**		11	8		10						9	6			7	12		3	
1	2		4		11	8		10						9	3			7	5			6	
2	2		2	1		2	2		2					2	2			2	1		2		
																		1					
						1									2								

Cup block B:

1	2	3	**4**	5	6	7	8	9	10			11		12									
1		3	**5**	6	7	8	9	10	4	2	11		12										
2	1	2	1	2	2	2	2	2	2	1	1	2		0									
													2										
						1																	

League Table

	P	W	D	L	F	A	Pts
West Ham United	42	28	10	4	79	29	66
Notts County	42	18	17	7	49	38	53
Swansea City	42	18	14	10	64	44	50
Blackburn Rovers	42	16	18	8	42	29	50
Luton Town	42	18	12	12	61	46	48
Derby County	42	15	15	12	57	52	45
Grimsby Town	42	15	15	12	44	42	45
Queen's Park Rangers	42	15	13	14	56	46	43
Watford	42	16	11	15	50	45	43
Sheffield Wednesday	42	17	8	17	53	51	42
Newcastle United	42	14	14	14	30	45	42
Chelsea	42	14	12	16	46	41	40
Cambridge United	42	17	6	19	53	65	40
Shrewsbury Town	42	11	17	14	46	47	39
Oldham Athletic	42	12	15	15	39	48	39
Wrexham	42	12	14	16	43	45	38
Orient	42	13	12	17	52	56	38
Bolton Wanderers	42	14	10	18	61	66	38
Cardiff City	42	12	12	18	44	60	36
Preston North End	42	11	14	17	41	62	36
Bristol City	42	7	16	19	29	51	30
Bristol Rovers	42	5	13	24	34	65	23

1981-82

Division Two

Manager: G. Mulhall

Did you know that?

In October 1981 John Thomas scored the Wanderers' 5,000th goal in League football, but unfortunately it was not enough as Grimsby Town ran out 2–1 winners on a Burnden Park pitch that had had under-soil heating installed during the close season.

Match No.	Date		Venue	Opponents	Result		Scorers	Attendance
1	Aug	29	A	Chelsea	L	0-2		16,606
2	Sep	5	H	Luton Town	L	1-2	Gowling	6,911
3		12	A	Barnsley	L	0-3		13,844
4		19	H	Oldham Athletic	L	0-2		7,222
5		23	A	Derby County	W	2-0	Thompson, McElhinney	12,066
6		26	A	Rotherham United	L	0-2		6,998
7		29	H	Newcastle United	W	1-0	Thompson	6,429
8	Oct	3	H	Grimsby Town	L	1-2	Thomas	7,217
9		10	H	Leicester City	L	0-3		7,361
10		17	A	Cardiff City	L	1-2	Cantello	3,879
11		24	H	Cambridge United	L	3-4	Henry 2, Kidd	5,751
12		31	A	Norwich City	D	0-0		12,991
13	Nov	7	H	Watford	W	2-0	Henry, Thompson	7,066
14		14	A	Shrewsbury Town	L	0-2		4,062
15		21	H	Orient	W	1-0	Carter	5,737
16		24	A	Luton Town	L	0-2		8,889
17		28	A	Crystal Palace	L	0-1		8,839
18	Dec	5	H	Queen's Park Rangers	W	1-0	Hoggan	6,076
19		19	H	Charlton Athletic	W	2-0	Henry, Chandler	5,484
20		28	H	Blackburn Rovers	D	2-2	Thompson, Henry	16,577
21	Jan	16	H	Chelsea	D	2-2	Foster, Henry	7,278
22		30	A	Oldham Athletic	D	1-1	Thompson	9,271
23	Feb	3	A	Newcastle United	L	0-2		14,761
24		6	H	Barnsley	W	2-1	Henry, Thompson	11,680
25		16	A	Sheffield Wednesday	W	1-0	Foster	16,355
26		20	H	Rotherham United	L	0-1		9,466
27		27	A	Leicester City	L	0-1		10,678
28	Mar	2	A	Grimsby Town	D	1-1	Henry	6,525
29		6	H	Cardiff City	W	1-0	Jones (pen)	6,269
30		9	A	Wrexham	L	1-2	Thompson	3,220
31		13	A	Cambridge United	L	1-2	Henry	3,430
32		20	H	Norwich City	L	0-1		6,199
33		27	A	Watford	L	0-3		12,937
34	Apr	3	H	Shrewsbury Town	D	1-1	Thompson	5,833
35		10	A	Wrexham	W	2-0	Henry (pen), Reid	6,221
36		12	A	Blackburn Rovers	W	2-0	Thompson 2	11,912
37		17	A	Orient	L	0-3		2,851
38		24	H	Crystal Palace	D	0-0		6,280
39		28	A	Charlton Athletic	L	0-1		3,379
40	May	1	A	Queen's Park Rangers	L	1-7	Henry (pen)	10,002
41		4	H	Derby County	W	3-2	Thompson 2, Henry	5,226
42		8	H	Sheffield Wednesday	W	3-1	Chandler, Gowling, Henry	13,656
							Appearances	
							Sub appearances	
							Goals	

FA Cup

R3	Jan	2	H	Derby County	W	3-1	Gowling, Foster, Thompson	9,534
R4		23	A	Crystal Palace	L	0-1		9,719
							Appearances	
							Sub appearances	
							Goals	

FL Cup

R1/1	Sep	1	H	Oldham Athletic	W	2-1	Kidd, Thomas	5,156
R1/2		15	A	Oldham Athletic	L	2-4	Thompson, Berry	4,779
R1/2 a.e.t.							Appearances	
							Sub appearances	
							Goals	

FL Group Cup

Gp	Aug	15	H	Shrewsbury Town	L	0-2		2,513
Gp		18	A	Bury	D	2-2	Nikolic, Hoggan	2,892
Gp		22	A	Chester	W	2-1	Hoggan, Thompson	1,291
Did not qualify for knock-out stage.							Appearances	
							Sub appearances	
							Goals	

McDonagh J.M.	Nicholson P.	Brennan I.	McElhinney G.M.A.	Jones P.B.	Gowling A.E.	Thomas J.W.	Thompson C.D.	Hoggan D.M.	Cantello L.	Reid P.	Bennett M.	Kidd B.	Nikolic D.	Henry A.	Carter M.	Hebberd T.N.	Peacock D.	Chandler J.G.	Whitworth S.J.	Foster W.P.	Bailey I.C.	Langley G.R.	Doyle M.	Berry M.	Whatmore N.
1	2	3	4	5	6	7	8	9	10	11															
1	2		4	5	6	7		9	10	11	3	8													
1	2		4	5	6		12	9	**10**	11	3	8	7												
1	12	4		5	6		7	9	**10**		3	8		2	11										
1	2		5		6		7	9	10		3	8		4		11									
			5	2	6		7	9	10		3			4	8	11	1								
			5	2	6		7	9	10		3			4	8	11	1								
			5	2	6	12	7	**9**	10		3			4	8	11	1								
1			**5**	2	6	12	9		10		3	8		4		11		7							
1		3		5	6		9		10		2	8		4		11		7							
1		**3**		5	6	9		10			11	8		4				7	2	12					
1				5	6		11	9	10		3	8		4				7	2						
1				5	6		11	9	10		3	8		4				7	2						
1				5	6		11	9	10		3	**8**		4	12			7	2						
1			6	5			**8**	11	10					4	9			7	2	12	3				
1			6	5			**8**	11	10					4	9			7	2	12	3				
1				5	6		12	11	10					4	9			**7**	2	8	3				
1				5	6			11	10					4	9			7	2	8	3				
1			6	5	9		11		10					4				7	2	8	3				
1			6	5	9		11		**10**		3			4	8			7	2			12			
1			6	5	9		11				3			4				7	2	8		10			
1				5	9		11	12	10		3			4				**7**	2	8			6		
1				5	9		**11**	7	10		3			4	12				2	8			6		
1				5	9		11	10			3			4				7	2	8			6		
1				5	9		11	12	**10**		3			4				7	2	8			6		
1			6	5	9			11	10		3			4				7	2	8					
1				5	6		11		10		3			4	9			7	2	8					
1	3			5	9		11		10					4				7	2	8			6		
1				5	9		11		10		3			4				7	2	8			6		
1	12			5	9		11		**10**		3			4				7	2	8			6		
1	3			5	9		11				10			4				7	2			12	**6**	8	
1			6	5	9			10			3			4				7	2	8		11			
1			6	5	9			10			3			4				7	2	8		**11**		12	
1			6	5	9		11		8	10	3			**4**				7	2			12			
1				5	6		**11**	12	8	10	3			4				7	2	9					
1				5	6		11		8	10	3			4				7	2	9					
1				5	6		11	12	8	10	3			4				7		**9**				2	
1			12	5	6		11		**8**	10	3			4				7	2	9					
1			**2**	5	6		11	7	8	10	3			4				12		9					
1				5	6		11	2	8	10	3			4	9			7							
1				5	9		11	8		10	3			4				7	2				6		
1				5	9		11	8		10	3			4				7	2				6		
39	6	4	18	41	40	3	34	25	34	12	35	10	1	39	11	6	3	32	29	20	5	3	10	2	0
	2		1			2	2	4							2			1		3		3		1	
			1	1	2	1	12	1	1	1		1		13	1			2		2					

1			6	5	9		11				3			4				7	2	8		10			
1			6	5	9		11	12			3			4				7	2	8		**10**			
2			2	2	2		2	0			2			2				2	2	2		2			
								1																	
					1		1													1					

1	2		4	5	6	7		9	10	11	3	8													
1	2	4		5	6		10	9			3	8	**7**		11									12	
2	2	1	1	2	2	1	1	2	1	1	2	2	1		1									0	
																								1	
						1	1					1												1	

1	2	3		5	6	7		12	10	11			**4**							9					8
1	3			5	6	7		9	10	11			**4**		12									2	8
1	12	3	5		6	7	8	9	10	11	14		4											**2**	
3	2	2	1	2	3	3	1	2	3	3			3							1				2	2
	1							1			1				1										
							1	2					1												

League Table

	P	W	D	L	F	A	Pts
Luton Town	42	25	13	4	86	46	88
Watford	42	23	11	8	76	42	80
Norwich City	42	22	5	15	64	50	71
Sheffield Wednesday	42	20	10	12	55	51	70
Queen's Park Rangers	42	21	6	15	65	43	69
Barnsley	42	19	10	13	59	41	67
Rotherham United	42	20	7	15	66	54	67
Leicester City	42	18	12	12	56	48	66
Newcastle United	42	18	8	16	52	50	62
Blackburn Rovers	42	16	11	15	47	43	59
Oldham Athletic	42	15	14	13	50	51	59
Chelsea	42	15	12	15	60	60	57
Charlton Athletic	42	13	12	17	50	65	51
Cambridge United	42	13	9	20	48	53	48
Crystal Palace	42	13	9	20	34	45	48
Derby County	42	12	12	18	53	68	48
Grimsby Town	42	11	13	18	53	65	46
Shrewsbury Town	42	11	13	18	37	57	46
Bolton Wanderers	42	13	7	22	39	61	46
Cardiff City	42	12	8	22	45	61	44
Wrexham	42	11	11	20	40	56	44
Orient	42	10	9	23	36	61	39

1982-83

Division Two

Manager: J. McGovern

Did you know that?

On 15 January 1983 the Wanderers defeated Burnley 3–0 at Burnden Park, with one of the goals coming from goalkeeper Jim McDonagh. The Irish international had gone close on a couple of occasions in the strong wind, and he finally caught out the Clarets' 'keeper Billy O'Rourke with a long clearance.

Match No.	Date	Venue	Opponents	Result		Scorers	Attendance
1	Aug 28	A	Burnley	D	0-0		10,527
2	Sep 4	H	Newcastle United	W	3-1	Henry 2 (1 pen), Reid	17,738
3	7	A	Sheffield Wednesday	L	1-3	Henry	17,307
4	11	A	Fulham	L	0-4		5,688
5	18	H	Wolverhampton Wanderers	L	0-1		9,264
6	25	A	Grimsby Town	L	0-1		7,583
7	28	H	Oldham Athletic	L	2-3	Henry, Moores	5,605
8	Oct 2	H	Crystal Palace	W	1-0	Hoggan	5,804
9	9	H	Rotherham United	D	2-2	C. Thompson, Moores	6,577
10	16	A	Middlesbrough	L	0-1		5,529
11	23	H	Barnsley	L	0-2		7,339
12	30	A	Queen's Park Rangers	L	0-1		9,363
13	Nov 6	H	Shrewsbury Town	L	1-4	Henry (pen)	4,879
14	13	A	Derby County	D	0-0		10,999
15	20	A	Blackburn Rovers	D	1-1	Chandler	7,428
16	27	H	Leicester City	W	3-1	Foster, Doyle, C. Thompson	5,060
17	Dec 4	A	Cambridge United	D	0-0		2,622
18	11	H	Charlton Athletic	W	4-1	Whatmore 2, Chandler, Foster	5,645
19	18	A	Chelsea	L	1-2	Henry	6,903
20	27	H	Carlisle United	W	1-0	Jones	8,171
21	28	A	Leeds United	D	1-1	Whatmore	16,180
22	Jan 1	H	Blackburn Rovers	W	1-0	Henry	11,481
23	3	A	Newcastle United	D	2-2	Foster, C. Thompson	23,533
24	15	H	Burnley	W	3-0	Henry, Hoggan, McDonagh	8,894
25	22	A	Oldham Athletic	W	3-2	C. Thompson, Chandler, Foster	8,510
26	Feb 5	H	Fulham	L	0-1		6,748
27	19	A	Rotherham United	D	1-1	Chandler	5,646
28	22	A	Crystal Palace	L	0-3		4,456
29	26	H	Middlesbrough	W	3-1	Deakin, Hoggan 2	5,598
30	Mar 5	A	Barnsley	L	1-3	Rudge	10,403
31	12	H	Queen's Park Rangers	W	3-2	Doyle, Henry, Rudge	6,373
32	19	A	Shrewsbury Town	L	0-1		4,163
33	26	H	Derby County	L	0-2		7,041
34	Apr 2	H	Leeds United	L	1-2	Rudge	10,784
35	5	A	Carlisle United	L	0-5		5,615
36	9	H	Sheffield Wednesday	L	0-2		6,408
37	16	A	Wolverhampton Wanderers	D	0-0		12,723
38	23	H	Cambridge United	W	2-0	Hoggan 2	4,636
39	30	A	Leicester City	D	0-0		13,959
40	May 2	H	Grimsby Town	D	0-0		5,866
41	7	H	Chelsea	L	0-1		8,687
42	14	A	Charlton Athletic	L	1-4	Moores	8,720

Appearances
Sub appearances
Goals

FA Cup

R3	Jan 8	A	Arsenal	L	1-2	Whatmore	22,576

Appearances
Goals

FL Cup

R1/1	Aug 31	A	Carlisle United	D	3-3	Doyle, Hoggan, Moores	4,313
R1/2	Sep 14	H	Carlisle United	W	4-0	Henry 2 (1 pen), Doyle, Moores	4,039
R2/1	Oct 5	H	Watford	L	1-2	Hoggan	5,664
R2/2	26	A	Watford	L	1-2	McGovern	11,520

R2/2 a.e.t.

Appearances
Sub appearances
Goals

Player columns (left to right):
McDonagh J.M. · Whitworth S. · Bennett M. · McGovern J.P. · Joicey P.B. · Doyle M. · Chandler J.G. · Henry A. · Moores I.R. · Reid P. · Hoggan D.M. · Berry N. · McChimney G.M.A. · Rudge S.J. · Deakin R.J. · Thompson C.D. · Foster W.P. · Thompson S.J. · Whitmore N. · Radfearn N.D. · Gray S. · Burrows B. · Joyce W.G.

1	2	3	4	5	6	7	8	9	10	11	12											
1	2	3	4	5	6	7	8	9	10	11												
1	2	3	4	5	6	7	8	9	10	11												
1	2	3	4	5		7	8	9	10	12	11	6										
1	2	3	4	5	6	7	8	9	10		11		12									
1	2	3	4	5		7	8	9	10			6	11									
1	2	3	4	5		7	8	9	10			6	11									
1	2		4	5		7	8		10	11		6	9	3								
1	2		4	5		7	8	10				6	9	3	11	12						
1		2	4	5		7	8	9	10			6		3	11							
1	2	3		5		7	8	9	4	11		6	10									
1		3	4	5			10	9			2	6	8		11	7						
1		3	4	5		12	10	9			2	6	8		11	7						
1	2	12		5	6	7	4		10			8	3		9	11						
1	2		4	5	6	7	8		10			3	11	9								
1	2		4	5	6	7	8		10			3	11	9								
1	2	3		5		7	4		10			6	11	9		8						
1	2			5	6	7	4		10			3	11	9		8						
1			5	6	7	4			10	2		3	11	9		8						
1	2			5	6	7	4		10			3	11	9		8						
1	2			5	6	7	4		10			3	11	9		8						
1	2			5	6	7	4	12	10			3	11	9		8						
1	2	3		5		7	4		10			6	11	9		8						
1	2			5	6	7	4		10			3	11	9		8						
1	2			5	6	7	4	12	10			3	11	9		8						
1	2			5	6	7	4		10			3	11	9		8						
1	2	3		5		7	8		10			6		9	11		4					
1	2	11		5	6	7	4		8			12	3	9			10					
1	2			5	6	7	10		11			8	3	9			4					
1	2			5	6	7	10	12	11			8	3	9			4					
1	2			5	6	7	4	9	11			10	3				8					
1	2			5	6	7		9	10			8	3		11		4					
1	2			5	6	7		9	10	3		8					4	11				
1	2				6	7		9		11	5	8					4	10	3			
1	2				6	7			5			8	3	9			4	11	10	12		
1	2				6			9				5	10	3		8	4	11	7	12		
1	2				6			9	11			5	8	3			4	7	10			
1	2				6	7		9	11			5	8	3			4	10	12			
1	2				6			9	10			5	8	3		12	4	11	7			
1	2				6			9	10			5	8	3			4	11	7			
1	2				6	12		9	10			5	8	3			4	11	7			
1	2				6	8		9	10			5		3		12	4	11	7			

42	38	15	14	33	30	35	31	23	15	27	8	16	21	30	16	21	3	10	10	10	9	5
	1				2		3		1	1		2			3							3
		1	2	4	9	3	1	6			3	1	4	4		3						

1	2	3		5		7	4		10			6	11	9		8						
1	1	1		1		1	1		1			1	1	1		1						
														1								

1	2	3	4	5	6	7	8	9	10	11	12											
1	2	3	4	5	6	7	8	9	10		11											
1	2			4	5		7	8	12	10	11			6	9	3						
1		3	4	5			9	8	11	2	6	10			12	7						
4	3	3	4	4	2	3	3	3	4	3	2	2	2	1	0	1						
							1			1				1								
		1		2		2	2		2													

League Table

	P	W	D	L	F	A	Pts
Queen's Park Rangers	42	26	7	9	77	36	85
Wolverhampton W	42	20	15	7	68	44	75
Leicester City	42	20	10	12	72	44	70
Fulham	42	20	9	13	64	47	69
Newcastle United	42	18	13	11	75	53	67
Sheffield Wednesday	42	16	15	11	60	47	63
Oldham Athletic	42	14	19	9	64	47	61
Leeds United	42	13	21	8	51	46	60
Shrewsbury Town	42	15	14	13	48	48	59
Barnsley	42	14	15	13	57	55	57
Blackburn Rovers	42	15	12	15	58	58	57
Cambridge United	42	13	12	17	42	60	51
Derby County	42	10	19	13	49	58	49
Carlisle United	42	12	12	18	68	70	48
Crystal Palace	42	12	12	18	43	52	48
Middlesbrough	42	11	15	16	46	67	48
Charlton Athletic	42	13	9	20	63	86	48
Chelsea	42	11	14	17	51	61	47
Grimsby Town	42	12	11	19	45	70	47
Rotherham United	42	10	15	17	45	68	45
Burnley	42	12	8	22	56	66	44
Bolton Wanderers	42	11	11	20	42	61	44

1983-84

Division Three

Manager: J. McGovern

Did you know that?

Bolton defeated Chester 3–0 at home in the first round, first leg of the League Cup, only to go down by the same score in the second leg at Sealand Road. Extra-time could not separate the sides, and Chester went through on penalties when the Wanderers missed four consecutive spot-kicks.

Match No.	Date		Venue	Opponents		Result	Scorers	Attendance
1	Aug	27	H	Wimbledon	W	2-0	Rudge, Chandler (pen)	3,992
2	Sep	3	A	Bradford City	W	2-0	Caldwell, Rudge	3,324
3		6	A	Gillingham	L	0-2		3,087
4		10	H	Walsall	W	8-1	Caldwell 5, Deakin, Rudge, Valentine	4,375
5		16	A	Scunthorpe United	L	0-1		4,406
6		24	H	Rotherham United	W	2-0	Caldwell, Redfearn	5,592
7		27	H	Burnley	D	0-0		9,709
8	Oct	1	A	Bristol Rovers	L	1-2	Rudge	5,651
9		8	A	Exeter City	D	2-2	Caldwell 2	3,478
10		15	H	Newport County	L	2-3	Caldwell, Chandler	4,928
11		18	H	Hull City	D	0-0		6,397
12		22	A	Port Vale	W	2-1	Caldwell, Caldwell	4,269
13		29	H	Southend United	W	2-0	Caldwell 2	5,366
14	Nov	2	A	Lincoln City	D	0-0		3,988
15		5	A	Orient	W	3-2	McElhinney, Foster, Joyce	5,859
16		12	A	Plymouth Argyle	L	0-2		4,624
17		26	A	Bournemouth	D	2-2	Chandler, Thompson	3,941
18	Dec	3	H	Brentford	W	1-0	Chandler	5,416
19		17	H	Preston North End	D	2-2	Foster, Chandler	6,245
20		26	A	Wigan Athletic	W	1-0	Chandler	10,045
21		27	H	Oxford United	W	1-0	Chandler	11,059
22		31	A	Sheffield United	L	0-5		14,252
23	Jan	2	H	Millwall	W	2-0	Rudge, Joyce	7,054
24		14	A	Wimbledon	L	0-4		2,955
25		21	H	Scunthorpe United	D	0-0		5,379
26		28	A	Walsall	L	0-1		7,812
27	Feb	4	H	Bristol Rovers	W	3-0	Caldwell 2, Chandler (pen)	5,399
28		6	A	Southend United	W	1-0	Caldwell	1,594
29		11	A	Rotherham United	D	1-1	Rudge	5,043
30		14	H	Lincoln City	L	0-2		5,450
31		25	H	Port Vale	W	2-0	Caldwell 2	5,818
32	Mar	3	A	Hull City	D	1-1	Chandler	6,869
33		6	A	Orient	L	1-2	Chandler	2,449
34		17	H	Exeter City	W	1-0	Foster	5,161
35		24	A	Newport County	W	3-2	Whatmore, Thompson, Joyce	2,436
36		27	H	Bradford City	L	0-2		5,994
37		31	A	Burnley	D	2-2	Thompson, Whatmore	8,359
38	Apr	7	H	Gillingham	L	0-1		4,815
39		14	A	Brentford	L	0-3		3,831
40		16	H	Plymouth Argyle	W	2-1	Chandler (pen), Bell	3,266
41		20	A	Oxford United	L	0-5		9,188
42		21	H	Wigan Athletic	L	0-1		6,142
43		28	A	Bournemouth	L	0-1		3,045
44	May	5	A	Millwall	L	0-3		2,346
45		7	H	Sheffield United	W	3-1	Chandler 2, Caldwell	9,036
46		12	A	Preston North End	L	1-2	Rudge	5,077

Appearances
Sub appearances
Goals

FA Cup

R1	Nov	19	A	Tranmere Rovers	D	2-2	Joyce, Chandler (pen)	5,497
rep		22	H	Tranmere Rovers	W	4-1	Chandler 2 (1 pen), Rudge, Caldwell	6,305
R2	Dec	10	H	Mansfield Town	W	2-0	Foster, Rudge	6,934
R3	Jan	7	H	Sunderland	L	0-3		14,018

R1 replay a.e.t.

Appearances
Sub appearances
Goals

FL Cup

R1/1	Aug	30	H	Chester City	W	3-0	Joyce, Caldwell 2	2,665
R1/2	Sep	14	A	Chester City	L	0-3		1,502

R1/2 a.e.t. Lost 0-2 on penalties.

Appearances
Sub appearances
Goals

Associate Members Cup

R1	Feb	21	A	Burnley	L	1-2	Caldwell	3,355

Appearances
Goals

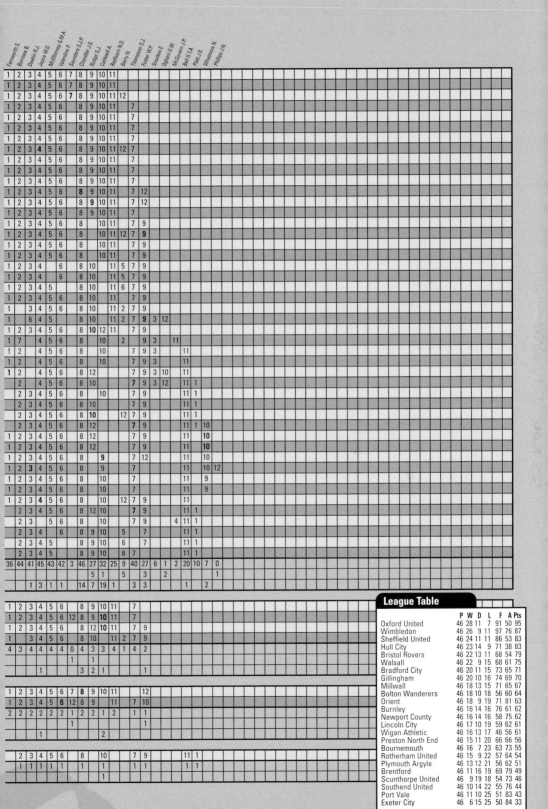

League Table

	P	W	D	L	F	A	Pts
Oxford United	46	28	11	7	91	50	95
Wimbledon	46	26	9	11	97	76	87
Sheffield United	46	24	11	11	86	53	83
Hull City	46	23	14	9	71	38	83
Bristol Rovers	46	22	13	11	68	54	79
Walsall	46	22	9	15	68	61	75
Bradford City	46	20	11	15	73	65	71
Gillingham	46	20	10	16	74	69	70
Millwall	46	18	13	15	71	65	67
Bolton Wanderers	46	18	10	18	56	60	64
Orient	46	18	9	19	71	81	63
Burnley	46	16	14	16	76	61	62
Newport County	46	16	14	16	58	75	62
Lincoln City	46	17	10	19	59	62	61
Wigan Athletic	46	16	13	17	46	56	61
Preston North End	46	15	11	20	66	66	56
Bournemouth	46	16	7	23	63	73	55
Rotherham United	46	15	9	22	57	64	54
Plymouth Argyle	46	13	12	21	56	62	51
Brentford	46	11	16	19	69	79	49
Scunthorpe United	46	9	19	18	54	73	46
Southend United	46	10	14	22	55	76	44
Port Vale	46	11	10	25	51	83	43
Exeter City	46	6	15	25	50	84	33

1984-85

Division Three

Manager: J. McGovern until 7 January 1985, C. Wright from 8 February 1985

Match No.	Date		Venue	Opponents	Result		Scorers	Attendance
1	Aug	25	H	Bristol Rovers	L	0-1		4,469
2	Sep	1	A	Derby County	L	2-3	Caldwell, Chandler (pen)	11,478
3		8	H	Hull City	D	0-0		5,403
4		15	A	Rotherham United	L	1-3	Oghani	3,926
5		18	A	Swansea City	L	1-2	Oghani	3,636
6		22	H	Plymouth Argyle	W	7-2	Caldwell 3, Oghani, Joyce, Chandler 2 (1 pen)	3,876
7		29	A	Doncaster Rovers	L	0-2		4,850
8	Oct	2	H	Walsall	W	3-1	Oghani, Thompson, Caldwell	4,445
9		6	A	Reading	L	1-3	Chandler	3,253
10		13	H	Bournemouth	W	2-1	Foster, Chandler (pen)	4,651
11		20	H	Preston North End	W	4-0	Chandler, Oghani 3	5,691
12		23	A	Bristol City	L	2-3	Foster, Oghani	7,715
13		27	A	Burnley	L	2-3	Oghani 2	6,460
14	Nov	3	H	Lincoln City	W	1-0	Thompson	4,019
15		6	H	York City	W	2-1	Rudge, Oghani (pen)	4,672
16		10	A	Newport County	L	2-3	Foster, Thompson	2,073
17		24	H	Gillingham	L	1-2	Chandler	4,381
18	Dec	1	A	Brentford	L	1-2	Joyce	3,668
19		15	A	Millwall	W	2-0	Caldwell 2	4,544
20		22	H	Cambridge United	D	0-0		4,310
21		26	A	Wigan Athletic	L	0-1		8,871
22		29	A	Bradford City	L	1-2	Caldwell	6,255
23	Jan	1	H	Orient	D	0-0		4,710
24		12	H	Derby County	W	3-0	Caldwell, Chandler 2 (1 pen)	6,491
25		26	A	Rotherham United	W	2-0	Caldwell 2	5,059
26		29	A	Bristol Rovers	W	2-1	Caldwell, Chandler (pen)	3,982
27	Feb	2	H	Doncaster Rovers	W	3-1	Came, Caldwell, Chandler (pen)	5,810
28		9	A	Plymouth Argyle	L	0-2		4,978
29		16	H	Swansea City	D	0-0		5,448
30		23	A	Lincoln City	L	0-2		2,448
31	Mar	2	H	Burnley	L	1-3	Joyce	6,468
32		5	H	Bristol City	L	1-4	Joyce	3,774
33		9	A	Preston North End	L	0-1		5,478
34		16	A	Bournemouth	L	0-4		2,715
35		19	A	Walsall	L	0-1		4,941
36		23	H	Reading	L	1-2	Caldwell	3,627
37		29	A	York City	W	3-0	Jones (own-goal), Phillips, Foster	4,363
38	Apr	2	A	Hull City	D	2-2	Oghani, Joyce	7,863
39		6	H	Wigan Athletic	W	1-0	Chandler (pen)	6,067
40		9	A	Orient	L	3-4	Chandler 2, Rudge	2,197
41		13	H	Newport County	W	3-1	Caldwell 2, Chandler	4,011
42		20	A	Gillingham	W	3-2	Caldwell, Chandler, Oghani	5,132
43		27	H	Brentford	D	1-1	Thompson	4,230
44	May	4	A	Millwall	L	2-5	Oghani 2	7,202
45		6	H	Bradford City	L	0-2		7,712
46		11	A	Cambridge United	W	3-2	Walker, Oghani, Caldwell	1,694

Appearances
Sub appearances
Goals

FA Cup

R1	Nov 17	A	Hull City	L	1-2	Foster	6,424

Appearances
Goals

FL Cup

R1/1	Aug 28	H	Oldham Athletic	W	2-1	Caldwell, Chandler (pen)	3,286
R1/2	Sep 4	A	Oldham Athletic	D	4-4	Oghani 2, Bell, Chandler	4,111
R2/1	25	A	Shrewsbury Town	D	2-2	Chandler, Oghani	3,720
R2/2	Oct 9	H	Shrewsbury Town	W	2-1	Thompson, Chandler	5,445
R3	30	A	Notts County	L	1-6	Foster	4,547

R1/2 a.e.t.

Appearances
Sub appearances
Goals

Freight Rover Trophy

R1/1	Jan 22	H	Crewe Alexandra	W	3-2	Joyce 2, Caldwell	2,345
R1/2	Feb 5	A	Crewe Alexandra	D	0-0		3,303
R2	Mar 12	A	Rochdale	W	1-0	Caldwell	2,650
QF	Apr 16	H	Darlington	W	2-1	Oghani 2	3,769
SF	May 8	H	Mansfield Town	L	1-2	Caldwell	6,706

Appearances
Sub appearances
Goals

Player columns (left to right): Farnworth S., Borrows B., Phillips J.N., Joyce W.G., Barry N., Deakin R.J., Thompson S.J., Chandler J.G., Oghani G.W., Caldwell A., Bell G.T.A., McElhinney G.M.A., Lodge P., Valentine P., Rudge S.J., Foster W.P., Caine M.R., Booth P., Evans A., Bailey I.C., Fitzpatrick P.J., Walker R.A.

Appearance / scoring grid (shirt numbers by match):

1	2	3	4	5	6	7	8	9	10	11											
1	2	3	4		6		8	9	10	11	5	7									
1	2		4		3		8	9	10	11	5	7	6								
1	2		4		3		8	9	10	11	5	7	6	12							
1	2	11	4		3	7		9			5		6	8	10						
1	2	3	4				7	8	9	10	11	5		6							
1	2	3	4			7		8	9	10	11	5		6			12				
1	2	3	4				7	8	9	10	11	5		6							
1	2	3	4				7	8	9	10	11	5		6							
1	2	3	4	5			7	8	9		11			6		10					
1	2	3	4	5			7	8	9		11			6		10					
1	2	3	4	5			7	8	9		11			6		10					
1	2	3	4	5			7	8	9		11			6		10					
1	2	3	4			6	7	8	9		11	12				10	5				
1	2	3	4			6	7		9		11			8	10	5					
1	2	3	4			6	7		9		11		12	8	10	5					
1	2	3	4			6	7	8	9		11			12	10	5					
1	2	3	4			7		8	9		11	5			10	6					
1	2	3	4			7		8		10	11	5			9	6					
1	2	3	4			7		8	12	10	11	5			9	6					
1	2		4		3		8	12	10	11	5		7	9	6						
1	2		4		3		8	9	10	11	5		7	12							
1	2	3	4			7		8	9	10		5	11		6						
1	2	3	4			6	7	8	9	10	11				5						
1	2	3	4			6	7	8	9	10	11				5						
1	2	3	4			6	7	8	9	10	11				5						
1	2	3	4			6	7	8	9	10	11	12			5						
1	2		4		3	7		8		10	11		6	12	9	5					
1	2	3	4			6		8	9	10	11				12	5	7				
1	2	3	4			6		8	9	10	11	7				5					
1	2	3	4			6	7	8	12	10	11				5	9					
1	2	3	4			6		8	7	10	11				5	9					
1	2	3	4			6		8	7	10	11	5		12	9						
1	2	12	4			6	7			11	5	8	10		9	3					
1	2	6	4			7	12		10	11	5	8	9		3						
1	2	6	4			12	7		10	11	5	8	9		3						
1	2	3	4			6	7	12	10		5	8	9		11						
1	2	5	4			6	7	8	10			11	9		3						
1	2	5	4			6	7	8	10	12		11	9		3						
1	2	5	4			6	7	8	10	12		11	9		3						
1	2	3	4			6	7	8	12	10	5	11	9								
1	2	3	4			6	7	8	9	10	5	11	12								
1		3	2			6	7	8	9	10	4	5	11	12							
1						6	7	8	9		4		11	10	5		3	2				
1		12	4			6	7	8	9			11	10	5			3	2			
1		12	4				11	8	9	10		6			5		3	2	7		
46	42	37	45	6	33	34	39	37	29	36	13	4	24	16	24	22	1	4	10	3	1
	3				1		2	4	2		1		2	4	4	1					
	1	5				4	16	16	18				2	4	1				1		

League Table

	P	W	D	L	F	A	Pts
Bradford City	46	28	10	8	77	45	94
Millwall	46	26	12	8	73	42	90
Hull City	46	25	12	9	78	49	87
Gillingham	46	25	8	13	80	62	83
Bristol City	46	24	9	13	74	47	81
Bristol Rovers	46	21	12	13	66	48	75
Derby County	46	19	13	14	65	54	70
York City	46	20	9	17	70	57	69
Reading	46	19	12	15	68	62	69
Bournemouth	46	19	11	16	57	46	68
Walsall	46	18	13	15	58	52	67
Rotherham United	46	18	11	17	55	55	65
Brentford	46	16	14	16	62	64	62
Doncaster Rovers	46	17	8	21	72	74	59
Plymouth Argyle	46	15	14	17	62	65	59
Wigan Athletic	46	15	14	17	60	64	59
Bolton Wanderers	46	16	6	24	69	75	54
Newport County	46	13	13	20	55	67	52
Lincoln City	46	11	18	17	50	51	51
Swansea City	46	12	11	23	53	80	47
Burnley	46	11	13	22	60	73	46
Orient	46	11	13	22	51	76	46
Preston North End	46	13	7	26	51	100	46
Cambridge United	46	4	9	33	37	95	21

1985-86

Division Three

Manager: C. Wright until 6 December 1985, N. Lofthouse
(caretaker) 6 to 17 December 1985, P. Neal 18 December 1985

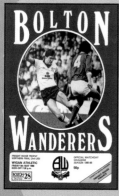

Match No.	Date	Venue	Opponents	Result		Scorers	Attendance
1	Aug 17	H	Rotherham United	D	1-1	Caldwell	5,129
2	24	A	Doncaster Rovers	D	1-1	Cross	3,414
3	26	H	Bury	L	1-4	Cross	8,772
4	31	A	Gillingham	L	1-2	Cross	2,773
5	Sep 7	H	Wolverhampton Wanderers	W	4-1	Thompson 2 (1 pen), Cross 2	4,986
6	14	A	Walsall	L	0-2		4,532
7	17	H	Lincoln City	D	1-1	Thompson	3,928
8	21	A	Newport County	W	1-0	Oghani	2,212
9	28	H	Plymouth Argyle	W	3-1	Joyce, Caldwell, Rudge	4,270
10	Oct 1	A	York City	L	0-3		4,680
11	5	A	Reading	L	0-1		8,164
12	12	H	Brentford	L	1-2	Joyce	4,106
13	19	H	Swansea City	D	1-1	Thompson (pen)	3,558
14	22	A	Bristol Rovers	L	1-2	Caldwell	4,308
15	26	A	Cardiff City	W	1-0	Bell	2,502
16	Nov 2	H	Bournemouth	W	1-0	Thompson	3,800
17	5	H	Darlington	L	0-3		2,902
18	9	A	Notts County	L	0-1		4,497
19	23	H	Derby County	L	0-1		5,887
20	30	A	Bristol City	L	0-2		6,253
21	Dec 14	H	Chesterfield	W	2-1	Thompson, Hartford	3,621
22	21	A	Doncaster Rovers	W	2-0	Cross 2	4,546
23	26	A	Blackpool	D	1-1	Cross	9,473
24	Jan 1	H	Wigan Athletic	L	1-2	Thompson (pen)	9,252
25	11	H	Gillingham	L	0-1		5,232
26	18	A	Rotherham United	L	0-4		3,821
27	25	H	Walsall	W	3-1	Caldwell, Bell, Oghani	4,088
28	Feb 1	A	Wolverhampton Wanderers	W	2-0	Rudge, Oghani	3,110
29	4	H	Bristol Rovers	L	0-2		3,672
30	8	A	Swansea City	L	1-3	Hartford	4,242
31	22	H	Newport County	W	4-0	Caldwell 2, Oghani, Ripley	4,063
32	25	H	Bury	L	1-2	Caldwell (pen)	6,006
33	Mar 4	H	York City	D	1-1	Hartford	3,589
34	8	H	Reading	W	2-0	Caldwell (pen), Joyce	4,903
35	14	A	Brentford	D	1-1	Sutton	3,284
36	18	A	Bournemouth	L	1-2	Oghani	2,063
37	22	H	Cardiff City	W	5-0	Joyce, Came, Neal, Oghani, Caldwell	4,114
38	25	A	Lincoln City	D	1-1	Neal	2,329
39	29	A	Wigan Athletic	W	3-1	Hartford, Gavin, Caldwell	8,009
40	31	H	Blackpool	L	1-3	Thompson	7,878
41	Apr 12	H	Notts County	W	1-0	Phillips	4,688
42	19	A	Derby County	L	1-2	Hartford	12,232
43	22	A	Plymouth Argyle	L	1-4	Sutton	12,183
44	24	A	Darlington	W	1-0	Oghani	1,870
45	26	H	Bristol City	L	0-4		4,493
46	May 3	A	Chesterfield	L	0-3		3,183

Appearances
Sub appearances
Goals

FA Cup

R1	Nov 16	A	Wrexham	L	1-3	Thompson	2,738

Appearances
Sub appearances
Goals

FL Cup

R1/1	Aug 20	H	Stockport County	W	4-1	Hartford, Cross 2, Bell	3,311
R1/2	Sep 3	H	Stockport County	D	1-1	Caldwell	2,573
R2/1	25	A	Nottingham Forest	L	0-4		10,530
R2/2	Oct 8	H	Nottingham Forest	L	0-3		4,010

R1/2 played at Burnden Park by arrangement, Stockport's ground under repair.

Appearances
Sub appearances
Goals

Freight Rover Trophy

R1	Jan 20	A	Stockport County	D	2-2	Came, Caldwell	1,874
R1	28	H	Crewe Alexandra	W	1-0	Oghani	2,428
QF	Mar 11	H	Tranmere Rovers	W	2-1	Caldwell, Oghani	3,865
SF	May 1	A	Darlington	W	3-0	Oghani, Caldwell, Hartford	3,771
Fn1	6	A	Wigan Athletic	W	1-0	Caldwell	6,975
Fn2	9	H	Wigan Athletic	W	2-1	Oghani, Caldwell	12,120
F	24	N	Bristol City	L	0-3		54,000

Final at Wembley Stadium.

Appearances
Sub appearances
Goals

Player columns (diagonal headers):
Farnworth S. · Joyce W.G. · Phillips J.N. · Rudge S.J. · Sutton D.W. · Carine M.R. · Thompson S.J. · Caldwell A. · Cross D. · Harford R.A. · Bell G.T.A. · Walker R.A. · Scott D.E. · Allardyce S. · Oghani G.W. · Fitzpatrick P.J. · Entwistle W.P. · Neal P.G. · Felgate D.W. · Ripley S.E. · Winstanley M.A. · Gavin M.W. · Derby J.T. · Ring M.P. · Roberts D.

1	2	3	**4**	5	6	7	8	9	10	11	12													
1	4	3		5		7	**8**	9	10	11		2	6	12										
1	4	3		5		7	8	9	10	**11**		2	6	12										
1	2		4	5		**7**	8	9	10	11		3	6	12										
1	4			5	7	**8**	9	10		12	3	6	11	2										
1	4			5	7	8	9	10			3	6	11	2										
1			5	4	8	9	10	11	7	3	6		2											
1		8	5	4		9	10	7		3	6	11	2											
1	7		5	4	8		10		11	3	6		2											
1	7	**9**	5	4	8		10	12		3	6	11	2											
1	4	3		5	7	8	9	10	12		**2**	6	11											
1	4	3		5	**7**		9	10	11	12		6	8	2										
1	2	3		5	4	**8**	9	10	7	12	6		11											
1	2	3		5	4	8	**9**	10	11	7	6			12										
1	2	3			5	4	8		10	11	7	5	6		9									
1	2	3			4	8	12	10	10	11	7	5	6		**9**									
1	2	3			**4**	12	8	10	11	7	5	6		9										
1	2	3			5	4	8		10	7		6	11		9									
1	4	3	9	6	5		12		10	11		2		8	**7**									
1	2		4	6	5		8		10	**11**	12	3		9	7									
1	4		6	5	7	8	9	10	11		2		3											
1	4		12	6	5	7	8	**9**	10	11		2			3									
1	6			5	4	8	7	9	10	11		2			3									
1	6		4	5		8	7	9	10	**11**		2		12	3									
1	6	3		5		**8**	7	9	10	11		2		12	4									
1		3	7	6	5			9	10	11		2		8	4									
1		3	7	6	5	4	9		10	11		2		8										
1	10	3	7	6	5	4	9		11			2		8										
1	11	**3**	7	6	5	4	9		10			2		8	12									
1		7	6	5	**4**	9		10	11		2		8	12	3									
	6	3		4	5		9		10	11		2		8		1	7							
	6	3		4	5		9		10	11		2		8		7	1							
	6	3		4	5		9		10		2		8		7	1	11							
	6	3		4	5		9		10	12		2		8		7	1	**11**						
	3		4	5		9		10	11		2		8		7	1	6							
	3		4		**9**		10	11		2		8	12	7	1	6	5							
6	3	12	4	5		9		10	11		2		8		7	1								
	6	3		4	5	11	9		10		2		8		7	1								
	3		4		6	9		10	12		**2**		8		7	1		5	11					
	3		4			9			8			7	1	5	11	2	12							
	3		4	5	6	**9**		10		2		8		7	1		11		12					
	3		4	5	6		10		2		8		7	1		11		9						
	3		4	5	6	**9**		10	12		2		8		7	1		11						
	3		4	5			10	9		2		8		7	1		11							
1	3		4	5			10	6		2		8		9		7	1	11	7					
	3		4	5	6	9		10	12		2		8		7	1		**11**						

31	31	33	13	32	35	38	19	46	30	6	43	14	31	10	5	20	15	5	3	8	2	1	0	
		2				2	1		6	5			5	1	3				2					
4	1	2	2	1	8	10	8	5	2		7		2		1		1							

1	4	3	12		5	7			10	11		6		8	2	**9**								
1	1	1	0		1	1			1	1		1		1	1	1	1							
		1																						
				1																				

1	4	3		5	**6**	7	8	9	10	11		2		12										
1	**4**		5	7	12	9	10		11	3	6	8	2											
1	12		**8**	5	4		9	10	7		3	6	11	2										
1	4	3		5	7	8	9	10		6	11	2												
4	3	2	1	4	4	4	3	4	2	1	3	3	4	3										
	1											1												
				1	2	1	1																	

	3	**7**	6	5		9		10	11		2		8		12	4								
1		3	7	6	5	4	9		10		2		8		12				11					
	6	3		4	5		9		10	11		2		8		7	1							
	3		4	5	6	9		10		2		8		7	1		11							
	3		4	5	6	9		10		2		8		7	1		11							
	3		4	5	6	9		10		2		8		7	1		11							
	3		4	5	**6**	9		10	12		2		8		7			11						
3	1	7	2	7	7	5	7		7	2		7		7		6	4		4			1		
					1												2							
				1		5		1				4												

Did you know that?

The Wanderers suffered 10 home League defeats to equal a club record and leave them in a relegation Play-off place. Aldershot ran out 3–2 aggregate winners after extra-time in the second leg to send the Wanderers into the Fourth Division for the first time in their history.

Match No.	Date	Venue	Opponents	Result		Scorers	Attendance
1	Aug 23	H	Swindon Town	L	1-2	Oghani	5,684
2	30	A	Bristol Rovers	L	0-1		4,092
3	Sep 6	H	Darlington	W	4-3	Elliott, Thompson, Oghani, Joyce	3,952
4	13	A	Bournemouth	L	1-2	Caldwell	3,031
5	16	A	Fulham	L	2-4	Elliott, Thompson	2,434
6	20	A	Port Vale	W	3-0	Caldwell, Elliott, Joyce	4,872
7	26	A	Wigan Athletic	L	1-2	Joyce	4,986
8	30	H	Chesterfield	L	1-2	Caldwell	3,931
9	Oct 4	H	Notts County	D	1-1	Oghani	4,248
10	11	A	Walsall	D	3-3	Thompson (pen), Caldwell, Elliott	4,677
11	18	A	Rotherham United	L	0-1		3,430
12	21	H	Blackpool	W	1-0	Thompson	6,534
13	25	H	Chester City	D	1-1	Elliott	4,607
14	Nov 1	A	Brentford	W	2-1	Gavin, Thompson	3,522
15	4	A	Middlesbrough	D	0-0		10,096
16	8	H	Newport County	L	0-1		4,530
17	22	A	Mansfield Town	D	2-2	Caldwell, Joyce	3,096
18	29	H	York City	W	3-1	Hartford, Caldwell 2	4,528
19	Dec 13	H	Gillingham	W	3-0	Caldwell 2, Gavin	4,867
20	20	A	Bristol City	L	1-4	Elliott	8,028
21	26	H	Bury	L	2-3	Thompson, Oghani	10,135
22	27	A	Doncaster Rovers	L	0-3		3,301
23	Jan 3	H	Mansfield Town	L	0-1		5,058
24	17	H	Bristol Rovers	D	2-2	Sutton, Caldwell	4,087
25	31	H	Bournemouth	L	0-1		4,219
26	Feb 3	A	Carlisle United	D	0-0		2,535
27	7	H	Fulham	W	3-2	Joyce, Thompson, Caldwell	4,128
28	14	A	Port Vale	D	1-1	Elliott	3,628
29	18	A	Darlington	W	1-0	Elliott	1,464
30	28	A	Chesterfield	D	0-0		3,202
31	Mar 3	H	Brentford	L	0-2		3,563
32	7	A	Chester City	D	0-0		2,764
33	14	H	Rotherham United	D	0-0		3,748
34	17	A	Blackpool	D	1-1	Sutton	4,717
35	21	H	Walsall	W	1-0	Elliott	4,308
36	24	A	Swindon Town	L	0-2		8,110
37	28	A	Notts County	D	0-0		4,776
38	Apr 4	A	Newport County	L	1-2	Stevens	1,193
39	7	H	Wigan Athletic	L	1-2	Hartford (pen)	5,321
40	11	H	Middlesbrough	L	0-1		5,858
41	18	A	Carlisle United	W	2-0	Neal, Stevens	4,241
42	20	A	Bury	D	0-0		4,969
43	25	H	Bristol City	D	0-0		4,414
44	May 2	A	York City	L	1-2	Hartford	4,079
45	4	H	Doncaster Rovers	L	0-1		4,838
46	9	A	Gillingham	L	0-1		5,561
						Appearances	
						Sub appearances	
						Goals	

Play-offs

SF1	14	A	Aldershot	L	0-1		4,164
SF2	17	H	Aldershot	D	2-2	Caldwell 2 (1 pen)	7,445
SF2 a.e.t.							
						Appearances	
						Sub appearances	
						Goals	

FA Cup

R1	Nov 15	A	Halifax Town	D	1-1	Oghani	3,370
rep	18	H	Halifax Town	D	1-1	Caldwell	4,652
rep2	24	A	Halifax Town	W	3-1	Thompson, Caldwell, Gavin	3,338
R2	Dec 6	H	Tranmere Rovers	W	2-0	Caldwell, Thompson	6,193
R3	Jan 10	A	Coventry City	L	0-3		12,044
						Appearances	
						Sub appearances	
						Goals	

FL Cup

R1/1	Aug 26	A	Bury	L	1-2	Ross (own-goal)	3,217
R1/2	Sep 2	H	Bury	D	0-0		4,330
						Appearances	
						Sub appearances	
					1 own-goal		

Freight Rover Trophy

PR	Dec 2	H	Blackpool	W	1-0	Gavin	3,395
PR	16	A	Burnley	W	2-0	Oghani, Darby	1,464
R1	Jan 27	H	Burnley	W	2-1	Allen, Caldwell	3,698
QF	Feb 10	H	Chester City	L	1-2	Came	3,900
						Appearances	
						Sub appearances	
						Goals	

Appearances and goals grid (players across the top):

Salmon M.B. · Neal P.G. · Phillips J.N. · Darby J.T. · Scott D.E. · Thompson S.J. · Gavin M.W. · Sutton D.W. · Elliott S.B. · Hartford R.A. · Oghani G.W. · Joyce W.G. · Winstanley M.A. · Carne M.R. · Cadwell A. · Mullineux L.J. · Falgate D.W. · Atkinson P.G. · Matthews N. · Stevens I.D. · Brookman N.A. · Allen P.R. · Farnworth S. · Griffin P.

Sa	Ne	Ph	Da	Sc	Th	Ga	Su	El	Ha	Og	Jo	Wi	Ca	Cd	Mu	Fa	At	Ma	St	Br	Al	Fw	Gr
1	2	3	4	5	6	7	8	9	10	11	12												
1	2	10	12		6		8	9		11	4	3	5	7									
1	2	10			6	7	8	9		11	4	3	5										
1	2	11	12		6	7	8	9			4	3	5	10									
1	2	11	6			8	7		9		4	3	5	10	12								
1	2	11	6			8	7		9		12	4	3	5	10								
1	2	12	6			8				10	11	4	3	5	9	7							
1	2	11	6		8		3			10	7	4	12	5	9								
1	2	11	6		8	12	3	7	10			4		5	9								
1		11	6	2	8	4	3	7	10				5	9									
1		3	6	2	8	11	5	9	10	7	4												
1		3	6	2	8	11	5	9	10	7	4	12											
1		3	6	2	8	11	9	10	7	4		5											
1		3	6	2	8	11	9	10	7	4		5	12										
1	12	3	6	2	8	11	9	10		4		5	7										
1	2	3		6	8	11	10	9	4			5	7										
1	2	3		6	8	11	9	10	4			5	7										
1	2	3		6	8	11	10	9	4			5	7										
1	12	3	2	6	8	11	10	9	4			5	7										
1	2	3		6	8	11	10	9	4			5	7										
1		3	10	2	8	11	5		4	6	9	7											
1		3	10	2	8	11	5	9	4	6	7												
1		3	10	2	8	11	5	9	4	6	7												
5		3	10	2	8	11	9	4	6	7	1												
		3	5	2	8	11	9	4	6	7	1	10											
		3		2	8	11	5	9	10	4	6	1	7										
		3		2	8	11	5	9	10	7	4	6	1	12									
		3	11	2	8	5	9	10	4	6	7	1											
		3	12	2	8	11	5	9	10	4	6	7	1										
		3	8	2		11	5	9	10	4	6	7	1										
	2		3	12	11	5	9	10	4	6	7	1											
		8	2	12	11	5	9	10	4	3	6	7	1										
4			2	8	11	5	9	10		3	6		1	7	12								
		3	2	8	11	5	9	10	4		6	12	1	7									
	2		8	11	5	9	10	4	3	6		1	7										
	2		3	8	11	5	9	10	4		6	7	1	12									
	2		3	12	11	5	9	10	4		6		1	7	8								
	2		3		11	5	9	10	4		6		1	12	8								
	2		3	12		5	9	10	4		6	7	1	8	11								
	2		3	8	11		9	10	4	5	6	7	1			12							
	2		3	8	11		9	10	4	5	6	7	1										
26	26	33	24	36	39	40	30	38	35	17	43	12	42	32	1	20	2	1	5	4	0	0	0
	2	1	4		5	1				2	1	1	1	3	1		3	1					
1				7	2	2	9	3	4	5				11			2						

Substitute / goal sub-sections:

Sa	Ne	Ph	Da	Sc	Th	Ga	Su	El	Ha	Og	Jo	Wi	Ca	Cd	Mu	Fa	At	Ma	St	Br	Al	Fw	Gr
	2		3	8	11	5	9	10	4		6	7	1										
	2		3	8	11	5	9	10	4		6	7	1	12									
	2		2	2	2	2	2	2		2		2	2	2		2		0					
																		1					
															2								

		3	6	2	8	11		9	10	12	4		5	7							1		
1	2	3	6		8	11		9	10	12	4		5	7									
1	2	3		6	8	11	9	10	12	4		5	7										
1	2	3		6	8	11		9	10		4		5	7									
1		3	2	6	8	11	5		10	12	4		9	7									
4	3	5	3	4	4	5	5	1	4	5	0		5	5					1				
											4												
		2	1				1				1			3									

1	2	3	4		6	7	8	9		11	10	5											
1	2	11	7		6		8	9		12	4	3	5	10	14								
2	2	2	2		2	1	2	2		1	2	2	1	1	0								
											1				1								

1		3	2	6	8	11		9	10	12	4		5	7									
1		3	10	2	8	11	5		9		6		7			4		12					
1		3	10	2	8	11	5		9			6	7			4							
1	5	3	10	2	8	11	5		9		4		6	7									
4	1	4	4	4	4	4	2	2	1	2	2	1	3	4			2		0				
									1										1				
		1		1						1		1	1					1					

Match No.	Date	Venue	Opponents	Result		Scorers	Attendance
1	Aug 15	H	Crewe Alexandra	D	1-1	Henshaw	4,792
2	22	H	Cardiff City	W	1-0	Chandler	4,530
3	29	A	Scarborough	L	0-4		4,462
4	31	H	Peterborough Utd.	W	2-0	Thomas (pen), Thompson	3,746
5	Sep 5	A	Hereford United	W	3-0	Thomas 2, Morgan	2,541
6	12	H	Halifax Town	W	2-0	Henshaw, Shaw (own-goal)	4,445
7	15	A	Scunthorpe United	D	1-1	Morgan	2,501
8	19	A	Torquay United	L	1-2	Savage	2,247
9	26	H	Hartlepool United	L	1-2	Came	4,398
10	Oct 3	H	Wolverhampton Wanderers	W	1-0	Thomas (pen)	3,833
11	10	A	Darlington	L	0-1		1,763
12	17	H	Carlisle United	W	5-0	Brookman 2, Darby, Elliott, Wright (own-goal)	4,184
13	20	H	Exeter City	W	1-0	Came	4,165
14	24	A	Rochdale	D	2-2	Thomas 2 (1 pen)	4,294
15	31	H	Swansea City	D	1-1	Thompson	4,607
16	Nov 3	A	Newport County	W	1-0	Elliott	1,566
17	7	H	Leyton Orient	W	1-0	Thomas	5,189
18	21	A	Burnley	L	1-2	Thomas	7,489
19	28	H	Cambridge United	D	2-2	Thomas 2 (1 pen)	4,294
20	Dec 11	A	Colchester United	L	0-3		1,743
21	15	A	Tranmere Rovers	L	0-2		3,064
22	19	H	Wrexham	W	2-0	Thompson, Morgan	3,701
23	26	A	Hartlepool United	D	0-0		4,102
24	28	H	Stockport County	W	2-1	Storer, Morgan	6,607
25	Jan 1	H	Scarborough	W	3-1	Came, Thomas, Thompson	6,295
26	12	A	Halifax Town	D	0-0		2,663
27	16	H	Torquay United	L	1-2	Came	5,993
28	30	A	Peterborough Utd.	W	4-0	Thomas 3 (2 pens), Brookman	3,412
29	Feb 6	H	Hereford United	W	1-0	Savage	4,559
30	12	A	Stockport County	W	2-1	Brookman, Morgan	4,814
31	20	A	Crewe Alexandra	L	1-2	Morgan	4,340
32	27	A	Wolverhampton Wanderers	L	0-4		12,430
33	Mar 1	H	Tranmere Rovers	W	2-0	Thompson, Thomas	3,979
34	5	A	Carlisle United	W	2-0	Thomas (pen), Brookman	2,760
35	11	H	Darlington	D	1-1	Brookman	4,948
36	18	A	Swansea City	L	0-1		3,980
37	26	H	Rochdale	D	0-0		4,173
38	Apr 2	A	Leyton Orient	W	2-1	Darby, May	4,537
39	4	H	Burnley	W	2-1	May, Thompson	9,921
40	9	A	Exeter City	D	1-1	Thomas	1,962
41	15	A	Cardiff City	L	0-1		6,703
42	19	H	Scunthorpe United	D	0-0		6,669
43	23	H	Newport County	W	6-0	Thomas 3 (1 pen), Morgan, Winstanley, Thompson	4,357
44	29	A	Cambridge United	D	2-2	Thomas, Savage	2,063
45	May 2	H	Colchester United	W	4-0	Thomas, Savage, Came, Chandler	5,540
46	7	A	Wrexham	W	1-0	Savage	5,977
						Appearances	
						Sub appearances	
						2 own-goals	Goals

FA Cup

R1	Nov 14	A	Burnley	W	1-0	Thomas (pen)	10,788
R2	Dec 5	A	Wrexham	W	2-1	Thomas 2	4,703
R3	Jan 9	A	Barnsley	L	1-3	Stevens	9,667
						Appearances	
						Goals	

FL Cup

R1/1	Aug 18	A	Wigan Athletic	W	3-2	Morgan 2, Chandler	4,115
R1/2	25	H	Wigan Athletic	L	1-3	Thomas	5,847
						Appearances	
						Sub appearances	
						Goals	

Sherpa Van Trophy

PR	Oct 13	H	Preston North End	D	0-0		3,478
PR	Nov 24	A	Stockport County	W	3-1	Thomas 2, Brookman	2,123
R1	Jan 19	A	Bury	L	0-1		3,796
						Appearances	
						Sub appearances	
						Goals	

League Table

	P	W	D	L	F	A	Pts
Wolverhampton W	46	27	9	10	82	43	90
Cardiff City	46	24	13	9	66	41	85
Bolton Wanderers	46	22	12	12	66	42	78
Scunthorpe United	46	20	17	9	76	51	77
Torquay United	46	21	14	11	66	41	77
Swansea City	46	20	10	16	62	56	70
Peterborough United	46	20	10	16	52	53	70
Leyton Orient	46	19	12	15	85	63	69
Colchester United	46	19	10	17	47	51	67
Burnley	46	20	7	19	57	62	67
Wrexham	46	20	6	20	69	58	66
Scarborough	46	17	14	15	56	48	65
Darlington	46	18	11	17	71	69	65
Tranmere Rovers	46	19	9	18	61	53	64
Cambridge United	46	16	13	17	50	52	61
Hartlepool United	46	15	14	17	50	57	59
Crewe Alexandra	46	13	19	14	57	53	58
Halifax Town	46	14	14	18	54	59	55
Hereford United	46	14	12	20	41	59	54
Stockport County	46	12	15	19	44	58	51
Rochdale	46	11	15	20	47	76	48
Exeter City	46	11	13	22	53	68	46
Carlisle United	46	12	8	26	57	86	44
Newport County	46	6	7	33	35	105	25

Match No.	Date		Venue	Opponents	Result		Scorers	Attendance
1	Aug	27	A	Southend United	L	0-2		4,075
2	Sep	3	H	Cardiff City	W	4-0	Thomas, Henshaw, Darby 2	4,831
3		10	A	Reading	D	1-1	Thomas	4,660
4		17	H	Bristol Rovers	D	1-1	Brown	4,821
5		20	H	Fulham	W	3-2	Savage, Thompson, Morgan	4,289
6		24	A	Aldershot	W	3-0	Stevens 2, Brookman	2,127
7	Oct	1	H	Sheffield United	W	2-0	Thompson 2 (1 pen)	9,345
8		4	A	Swansea City	L	0-1		3,283
9		8	A	Blackpool	D	2-2	Morgan, Thompson (pen)	7,106
10		15	A	Port Vale	L	1-2	Brookman	7,985
11		22	H	Wolverhampton Wanderers	L	1-2	Morgan	8,174
12		25	A	Wigan Athletic	D	1-1	Brookman	4,438
13		29	H	Chesterfield	W	5-0	Brown 2, Morgan 2, Stevens	4,783
14	Nov	5	A	Bristol City	D	1-1	Morgan	8,802
15		8	A	Huddersfield Town	W	1-0	Morgan	7,802
16		12	H	Bury	L	2-4	Brown, Thompson	7,897
17		26	H	Northampton Town	W	2-1	Stevens, Brookman	4,446
18	Dec	3	A	Brentford	L	0-3		4,600
19		17	H	Chester City	L	0-1		4,318
20		26	A	Preston North End	L	1-3	Savage	12,124
21		31	A	Notts County	L	0-2		5,096
22	Jan	2	H	Mansfield Town	D	0-0		4,936
23		6	H	Gillingham	W	2-1	Stevens, Thompson (pen)	4,178
24		14	A	Cardiff City	L	0-1		4,212
25		21	H	Reading	D	1-1	Henshaw	5,172
26		28	A	Bristol Rovers	L	0-2		5,311
27	Feb	4	A	Sheffield United	L	0-4		11,162
28		11	H	Swansea City	W	1-0	Savage	4,178
29		18	A	Blackpool	L	0-2		5,552
30	Mar	4	A	Wolverhampton Wanderers	L	0-1		13,521
31		11	H	Bristol City	W	2-0	Darby 2	4,423
32		14	A	Chesterfield	D	1-1	Thompson	2,877
33		18	H	Southend United	D	0-0		3,505
34		25	A	Mansfield Town	D	1-1	Savage	3,256
35		27	H	Preston North End	W	1-0	Thompson	10,281
36	Apr	1	A	Chester City	D	0-0		3,225
37		4	A	Gillingham	W	1-0	Thomas	3,096
38		8	H	Notts County	D	3-3	Thomas, Thompson, Morgan	4,521
39		15	A	Fulham	D	1-1	Morgan	4,950
40		22	H	Aldershot	W	1-0	Savage	4,407
41		25	H	Port Vale	D	1-1	Chandler	5,296
42		29	A	Bury	D	0-0		4,393
43	May	1	H	Huddersfield Town	W	3-1	Chandler, Morgan, Thomas	5,511
44		6	A	Brentford	W	4-2	Thomas 2, Darby, Savage	4,627
45		9	H	Wigan Athletic	D	1-1	Storer	6,166
46		13	A	Northampton Town	W	3-2	Thomas 2, Storer	3,655
							Appearances	
							Sub appearances	
							Goals	

FA Cup

R1	Nov	19	H	Chesterfield	D	0-0		4,840
rep		28	A	Chesterfield	W	3-2	Stevens, Storer, Darby	4,168
R2	Dec	10	H	Port Vale	L	1-2	Keeley	7,499
							Appearances	
							Sub appearances	
							Goals	

FL Cup

R1/1	Aug	30	H	Chester City	W	1-0	Darby	3,535
R1/2	Sep	7	A	Chester City	L	1-3	Cowdrill	3,784
							Appearances	
							Sub appearances	
							Goals	

Sherpa Van Trophy

PR	Dec	6	H	Preston North End	W	1-0	Thompson (pen)	2,690
PR		20	A	Bury	L	0-1		2,032
R1	Jan	17	A	Preston North End	W	1-0	Darby	5,569
QF	Feb	21	H	Wrexham	W	3-1	Winstanley 2, Savage	3,833
SF	Mar	21	A	Crewe Alexandra	W	2-1	Winstanley, Brown	5,928
Fn1	Apr	11	H	Blackpool	W	1-0	Darby	10,345
Fn2		18	A	Blackpool	D	1-1	Thompson (pen)	9,027
F	May	28	N	Torquay United	W	4-1	Darby, Morrison (own-goal), Crombie, Morgan	46,513

QF, SF and Fn2 a.e.t. Final at Wembley Stadium.

1 own-goal	Appearances
	Sub appearances
	Goals

Player appearance grid: Felgate D.W., Brown P., Conaghi B.J., Darby J.T., Carne M.R., Winstanley M.A., Brookman N.A., Thompson S.J., Stevens J.D., Elliott S.B., Sarage R.J., Hanstow G., Thomas J.W., Kasley G.M., Crombie E.M., Morgan T.J., Steer S.J., Neal P.S., Chandler J.G., Jemson M.B., Barnes P.S., Jeffrey M.R.

League Table

	P	W	D	L	F	A	Pts
Wolverhampton W	46	26	14	6	96	49	92
Sheffield United	46	25	9	12	93	54	84
Port Vale	46	24	12	10	78	48	84
Fulham	46	22	9	15	69	67	75
Bristol Rovers	46	19	17	10	67	51	74
Preston North End	46	19	15	12	79	60	72
Brentford	46	18	14	14	66	61	68
Chester City	46	19	11	16	64	61	68
Notts County	46	18	13	15	64	54	67
Bolton Wanderers	46	16	16	14	58	54	64
Bristol City	46	18	9	19	53	55	63
Swansea City	46	15	16	15	51	53	61
Bury	46	16	13	17	55	67	61
Huddersfield Town	46	17	9	20	63	73	60
Mansfield Town	46	14	17	15	48	52	59
Cardiff City	46	14	15	17	44	56	57
Wigan Athletic	46	14	14	18	55	53	56
Reading	46	15	11	20	68	72	56
Blackpool	46	14	13	19	56	59	55
Northampton Town	46	16	6	24	66	76	54
Southend United	46	13	15	18	56	75	54
Chesterfield	46	14	7	25	51	86	49
Gillingham	46	12	4	30	47	81	40
Aldershot	46	8	13	25	48	78	37

Match No.	Date		Venue	Opponents	Result		Scorers	Attendance
1	Aug	19	A	Cardiff City	W	2-0	Philliskirk, Darby	4,376
2		26	H	Fulham	D	0-0		5,524
3	Sep	2	A	Huddersfield Town	D	1-1	Crombie	7,872
4		9	H	Bristol Rovers	W	1-0	Reeves	5,913
5		16	A	Rotherham United	L	0-1		6,846
6		23	H	Leyton Orient	W	2-1	Cowdrill, Philliskirk	5,951
7		26	A	Notts County	L	1-2	Philliskirk	5,392
8		30	H	Mansfield Town	D	1-1	Winstanley	5,797
9	Oct	7	H	Wigan Athletic	W	3-2	Philliskirk (pen), Darby 2	6,462
10		14	A	Crewe Alexandra	D	2-2	Reeves 2	4,284
11		17	A	Brentford	W	2-1	Reeves 2	4,537
12		21	H	Chester City	W	1-0	Philliskirk	6,496
13		28	A	Preston North End	W	4-1	Philliskirk, Thompson, Darby, Kelly (own-goal)	9,135
14		31	H	Walsall	D	1-1	Darby	7,363
15	Nov	4	H	Swansea City	D	0-0		6,618
16		11	A	Bristol City	D	1-1	Brown	11,994
17		25	A	Birmingham City	L	0-1		8,081
18	Dec	2	H	Northampton Town	L	0-3		5,501
19		16	A	Shrewsbury Town	D	3-3	Thompson 2, Philliskirk	3,443
20		26	H	Blackpool	W	2-0	Darby, Cowdrill	9,944
21		30	H	Bury	W	3-1	Reeves 2, Storer	10,628
22	Jan	6	A	Tranmere Rovers	W	3-1	Cowdrill, Darby, Storer	8,273
23		13	A	Fulham	D	2-2	Pike, Storer	4,523
24		20	H	Cardiff City	W	3-1	Philliskirk 2 (1 pen), Comstive	7,017
25		28	A	Bristol Rovers	D	1-1	Philliskirk	7,722
26	Feb	10	H	Rotherham United	L	0-2		7,728
27		17	A	Northampton Town	W	2-0	Darby, Thompson	3,432
28		24	H	Birmingham City	W	3-1	Reeves 2, Thompson	7,681
29	Mar	3	A	Reading	L	0-2		4,461
30		6	A	Mansfield Town	W	1-0	Darby	3,334
31		10	H	Notts County	W	3-0	Darby, Philliskirk, Reeves	8,420
32		16	A	Wigan Athletic	L	0-2		6,850
33		20	H	Crewe Alexandra	D	0-0		7,241
34		24	H	Brentford	L	0-1		6,156
35		27	A	Leyton Orient	D	0-0		3,296
36		31	A	Chester City	L	0-2		2,738
37	Apr	3	H	Reading	W	3-0	Philliskirk 2, Thompson	4,679
38		7	H	Preston North End	W	2-1	Philliskirk 2	8,266
39		10	A	Walsall	L	1-2	Philliskirk (pen)	3,376
40		14	H	Tranmere Rovers	D	1-1	Storer	9,070
41		16	A	Blackpool	L	1-2	Philliskirk	6,435
42		21	H	Shrewsbury Town	L	0-1		5,665
43		24	A	Bury	L	0-2		6,551
44		28	A	Bristol City	W	1-0	Green	11,098
45	May	1	H	Huddersfield Town	D	2-2	Green, Philliskirk (pen)	8,550
46		5	A	Swansea City	D	0-0		5,623
							Appearances	
							Sub appearances	
						1 own-goal	Goals	

Play-offs

1	May	13	H	Notts County	D	1-1	Philliskirk (pen)	15,105
2		16	A	Notts County	L	0-2		15,200
							Appearances	
							Sub appearances	
							Goals	

FA Cup

R1	Nov	18	A	Blackpool	L	1-2	Crombie	7,309
							Appearances	
							Sub appearances	
							Goals	

FL Cup

R1/1	Aug	22	A	Rochdale	L	1-2	Thompson (pen)	3,464
R1/2		29	H	Rochdale	W	5-1	Philliskirk, Reeves, Savage, Cowdrill, Darby	4,637
R2/1	Sep	19	H	Watford	W	2-1	Philliskirk 2	6,856
R2/2	Oct	3	A	Watford	D	1-1	Comstive	8,452
R3		24	A	Swindon Town	D	3-3	Henshaw, Philliskirk, Came	8,318
rep	Nov	7	H	Swindon Town	D	1-1	Brown	11,533
rep2		14	H	Swindon Town	D	1-1	Philliskirk (pen)	14,126
rep3		21	A	Swindon Town	L	1-2	Came	11,238

R3 replay, replay 2 and replay 3 a.e.t.

							Appearances	
							Sub appearances	
							Goals	

Leyland Daf Cup

PR	Nov	28	H	Crewe Alexandra	W	2-0	Darby, Brookman	3,868
PR	Dec	5	A	Wigan Athletic	L	0-1		2,306
R1	Jan	9	H	Lincoln City	W	2-1	Reeves 2	4,420
QF		31	H	Rotherham United	W	1-0	Storer	6,838
SF	Feb	20	A	Tranmere Rovers	L	1-2	Philliskirk	9,315
							Appearances	
							Sub appearances	
							Goals	

Player columns (left to right):
Rose K.P., Brown P., Cowdrill B.J., Savage R.J., Cramlee D.M., Winstanley M.A., Storer S.J., Thompson S.J., Reeves D.E., Philliskirk A., Darby J.T., Felgate D.W., Henshaw G., Jeffrey M.R., Comstive P.T., Chandler J.G., Steavens J.D., Carne M.R., Hughes P., Brookman N.A., Pike M.R., Gregory J.C., Green S.P., Neal P.G.

1	2	3	4	5	6	7	8	9	10	11													
	2	3	4	5	6	7	8	9	10	11	1												
	2	3	4	5	6	7	8	9	10	11	1	12											
1	2	3	4	5	6	7	8	9	10	11			12										
1	2	3	4	5	6	7	8	9	10	11		12	14										
1	2	3		5	6	7	8	9	10	11		12		4									
1	2	3		5	6		8	9	10	11		7		4									
1	2	3		5	6		8	9	10	11		7		4									
	2	3		5	6	7	8	9	10	11	1			4	12								
	2	3		5	6	7	8	9	10	11	1			4									
	2	3		5	6	7	8	9	10	11	1			4									
	2	3		5	6	7	8	9	10	11	1	12		4									
	2	3		5	6		8		10	11	1	7		4		9							
	2	3		5	6		8		10	11	1	7		4		9							
	2	3		5	6		8		10	11	1	7	12	4		9							
	2	3		5	6		8	9	10	11	1	7		4									
	2	3		5	6		8			11	1	7	10	4			9	12	14				
	2	3		5	6		8		10	11	1	7				9	4	12					
	2			5	6	7	8	9	10	11	1	4						3					
	2	14		5	6	7	8	9	10	11	1			4		12		3					
	2	4		5	6	7	8	9	10	11	1							3					
	2	4		5	6	7	8	9	10	11	1							3					
	2			5	6	7	8	9	10	11	1	14		4		12		3					
	2	3		6		7	8	9	10	11	1			4		5							
	2	3		6		7	8	9	10	11	1			4		5							
	2	3		6		7	8	9	10	11	1			4		5							
	2	3	12	5	6		7	8	9	10	11	1		4									
	2	3	12	5	6	7	8	9	10	11	1			4		14							
	2	3		6		7	8	9	10	11	1			4		5							
	2	3	12	6		7	8	9	10	11	1			4		5							
	2	3		6		7	8	9	10	11	1			4		5			12				
	2	3	12	6		7	8	9	10	11	1			4		5			14				
	2	3		5	6	7	8	9	10	11	1			4									
	2	3		5	6	7	8	9	10	11	1			4		12			8				
	2	3	4	5	6	7	8	9	10	11	1								12				
	2	3	4	5	6	7	8	9	10	11	1								4				
	2	3		5	6	7	8	9	10	11	1			12	14			4					
	2	3		6		7	8	9	10	11	1			4		5			12				
	2	3		5	6	7	8	9	10	11	1			4									
	2	3		5	6	7	8	9	10	11	1			4					12				
	2	3		6		7	8	9	10	11	1					5			4				
	2	3		6		7	8	9	10	11	1					5		12	4				
	2	3	12	6		7	8	9	10	11	1					5			4				
	2	3		6		7	8	9	10	11	1					5			4				
6	46	43	7	36	43	38	45	41	45	46	40	9	1	30	0	3	15	1	0	5	2	4	0
		1	3	2								5	3	1	1	1	4	1	2		5	1	
1	3			1	1	4	6	10	18	10			1				1			2			

	2	3				6	7	8	9	10	11	1		12			5				4		
	2	3		12	6	7	8	9	10	11	1			5					14	4			
	2	2		0	2	2	2	2	2	2	2		0		2			0	2				
							1						1					1					
								1															

	2	3		5	6	12	8	9	10	11	1	7		4			14						
	1	1		1	1		1	0	1	1	1	1		1			0						
								1						1									
		1																					

1	2	3	4	5	6	7	8	9	10	11		12											
	2	3	4	5	6	7	8	9	10	11	1												
1	2	3		5	6	7	8	9	10	11		4											
	2	3		5	6		8	9	10	11	1	7	4										
	2	3		5	6		8	9	10	11	1	7	4	12		14							
	2	3		5	6		8	9	10	11	1	7	14	4		12							
	2	3		5	6		8	9	10	11	1	7	4										
	2	3		5	6		8			11	1	10	4			14	9	7			12		
2	8	8	2	8	8	4	8	7	7	8	6	4	1	5	0	1	1				1		
									1	1		1	1	2					1				
	1	1	1			1	1	5	1		1		1		2								

	2	3		5	6		8			11	1	7					9	4	10				
	2	3		5	6	12	8		10	11	1	7				9		4					
	2			5	6	7	8	9	10	11	1	12		4					3				
	2	3		5		7	8	9	10	11	1			4		6							
	2	3		5	6		8	9	10	11	1			4									
	5	4		5	4	3	5	4	3	5	5	2		3			3	1	2	1			
									1														
						1		2	1	1							1						

League Table

	P	W	D	L	F	A	Pts
Bristol Rovers	46	26	15	5	71	35	93
Bristol City	46	27	10	9	76	40	91
Notts County	46	25	12	9	73	53	87
Tranmere Rovers	46	23	11	12	86	49	80
Bury	46	21	11	14	70	49	74
Bolton Wanderers	46	18	15	13	59	48	69
Birmingham City	46	18	12	16	60	59	66
Huddersfield Town	46	17	14	15	61	62	65
Rotherham United	46	17	13	16	71	62	64
Reading	46	15	19	12	57	53	64
Shrewsbury Town	46	16	15	15	59	54	63
Crewe Alexandra	46	15	17	14	56	53	62
Brentford	46	18	7	21	66	66	61
Leyton Orient	46	16	10	20	52	56	58
Mansfield Town	46	16	7	23	50	65	55
Chester City	46	13	15	18	43	55	54
Swansea City	46	14	12	20	45	63	54
Wigan Athletic	46	13	14	19	48	64	53
Preston North End	46	14	10	22	65	79	52
Fulham	46	12	15	19	55	66	51
Cardiff City	46	12	14	20	51	70	50
Northampton Town	46	11	14	21	51	68	47
Blackpool	46	10	16	20	49	73	46
Walsall	46	9	14	23	40	72	41

Division Three

Manager: P. Neal

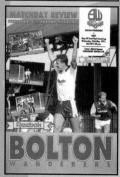

Match No.	Date	Venue	Opponents	Result		Scorers	Attendance
1	Aug 25	A	Shrewsbury Town	W	1-0	Storer	4,608
2	Sep 1	H	Bradford City	L	0-1		7,031
3	8	A	Huddersfield Town	L	0-4		5,419
4	15	H	Crewe Alexandra	W	3-2	Philliskirk, Green, Darby	4,933
5	18	H	Preston North End	L	1-2	Darby	5,844
6	22	A	Brentford	L	2-4	Green, Reeves	5,077
7	28	A	Wigan Athletic	L	1-2	Philliskirk (pen)	4,366
8	Oct 2	H	Mansfield Town	D	1-1	Reeves	3,631
9	6	H	Stoke City	L	0-1		8,521
10	13	A	Bury	D	2-2	Thompson, Philliskirk (pen)	5,634
11	20	A	Leyton Orient	W	1-0	Storer	4,121
12	23	H	Rotherham United	D	0-0		4,692
13	27	H	Swansea City	W	1-0	Philliskirk	4,158
14	Nov 3	A	Chester City	W	2-0	Reeves, Philliskirk	2,553
15	10	H	Reading	W	3-1	Thompson 2 (1 pen), Reeves	4,648
16	24	A	Grimsby Town	W	1-0	Green	6,240
17	Dec 1	H	Tranmere Rovers	W	2-1	Green, Philliskirk	6,941
18	15	H	Fulham	W	1-0	Philliskirk	3,466
19	22	H	Cambridge United	D	2-2	Storer, Thompson	5,800
20	26	A	Southend United	D	1-1	Green	7,539
21	29	A	Birmingham City	W	3-1	Philliskirk, Darby, Reeves	7,318
22	Jan 1	H	Bournemouth	W	4-1	Darby, Comstive 2, Philliskirk (pen)	7,639
23	12	A	Bradford City	D	1-1	Philliskirk	8,764
24	19	A	Shrewsbury Town	W	1-0	Thompson	6,164
25	Feb 2	A	Preston North End	W	2-1	Philliskirk 2 (1 pen)	9,844
26	5	A	Brentford	W	1-0	Evans (own-goal)	6,731
27	9	H	Huddersfield Town	D	1-1	Philliskirk	7,947
28	13	H	Exeter City	W	1-0	Reeves	5,532
29	16	A	Grimsby Town	D	0-0		10,318
30	23	A	Reading	W	1-0	Cowdrill	5,997
31	Mar 1	A	Tranmere Rovers	D	1-1	Patterson	10,076
32	9	H	Fulham	W	3-0	Philliskirk 2 (1 pen), Patterson	7,316
33	12	A	Mansfield Town	L	0-4		3,611
34	16	H	Wigan Athletic	W	2-1	Reeves, Darby	7,812
35	19	H	Bury	L	1-3	Green	9,006
36	23	A	Stoke City	D	2-2	Darby, Storer	13,869
37	26	A	Exeter City	L	1-2	Reeves	4,009
38	30	H	Southend United	W	1-0	Darby	10,666
39	Apr 2	A	Cambridge United	L	1-2	Philliskirk	7,763
40	7	H	Birmingham City	W	3-1	Philliskirk, Darby, Cunningham	11,280
41	13	A	Bournemouth	L	0-1		7,159
42	16	A	Crewe Alexandra	W	3-1	Philliskirk 2 (1 pen), Reeves	4,419
43	20	H	Leyton Orient	W	1-0	Reeves	7,926
44	27	A	Rotherham United	D	2-2	Cunningham 2	8,045
45	May 4	A	Swansea City	W	2-1	Darby, Storer	4,713
46	11	H	Chester City	W	1-0	Cunningham	12,826

Appearances
Sub appearances
Goals

Play-offs

1/1	May 19	A	Bury	D	1-1	Philliskirk (pen)	8,000
1/2	22	H	Bury	W	1-0	Philliskirk	19,198
F	Jun 1	N	Tranmere Rovers	L	0-1		30,217

Final a.e.t., at Wembley Stadium.

Appearances
Sub appearances
Goals

FA Cup

R1	Nov 17	A	Witton Albion	W	2-1	Darby, Comstive	3,790
R2	Dec 11	A	Chesterfield	W	4-3	Reeves, Philliskirk, Thompson, Storer	4,836
R3	Jan 5	A	Barrow	W	1-0	Philliskirk	11,475
R4	26	A	Manchester United	L	0-1		43,293

Appearances
Sub appearances
Goals

FL Cup

R1/1	Aug 29	A	Huddersfield Town	W	3-0	Darby 2, Philliskirk (pen)	4,444
R1/2	Sep 4	H	Huddersfield Town	W	2-1	Stubbs, Darby	3,101
R2/1	26	A	Coventry City	L	2-4	Philliskirk 2	6,193
R2/2	Oct 9	H	Coventry City	L	2-3	Philliskirk 2 (1 pen)	5,222

Appearances
Sub appearances
Goals

Leyland Daf Cup

PR	Nov 6	H	Tranmere Rovers	W	1-0	Reeves	3,178
PR	Dec 18	A	Blackpool	L	0-3		2,579

Appearances
Sub appearances
Goals

Appearances & Goals Chart

Folgate D.W.	Brown P.	Burke D.I.	Cowdrill B.J.	Came M.R.	Westaley M.A.	Green S.P.	Thompson S.P.	Reeves D.E.	Philiskirk A.	Darby J.T.	Storer S.J.	Stubbs A.	Comstive P.T.	Crombie D.M.	Housman G.	Seagraves M.	Lee S.	Stevens I.D.	Patterson M.A.	Cunningham A.E.
1	2	3	**4**	5	6	7	8	9	10	11	12									
1	2	3	**4**	5	6	7	8	9	10	11	12	14								
1	2	3		6	4		8	9	10	11	7	5	12							
1	2	3	**5**		6	4	8	9	10	11	7	12								
1	2	3			4	8	9	10	11	7	5		6							
1	2	3			4	8	9	10		12	5	**11**	6	7						
1	2	**3**		6	4	8	9	10	11	7				5						
1	2	3		6	4	8	9	10	11	7				5						
1	2	**3**	12		6	4	8	9	10	11				5	7	14				
1	2	3			6	4	8	12	10	11	5				7	**9**				
1	2	3			6	4	8	9	10	11	5				7					
1	2	3			6	4	8	12	10	11	5				7	14				
1	2	3			6	4	**9**	10	11	7	5		14			12				
1	2	3			6	4	8	9	10	11	7				5					
1	2	3			6	10	8	**9**		11	7		4			5	12			
1	2	3			6	8		9	10	11	7		4			5				
1	2	3			6	4	8	9	10	11	**7**		4			5				
1	2	3			6		8	9	10	11	7		4			5				
1	2	3	5	6	12	8	9	10	11	**7**	14	4				5				
1	2	3	5	6		8	9	10	11	7		4								
1	2	3	5	6		8	9	10	11	7		**4**					12			
1	2	3		6	12	8	9	10	**11**	7				5		4				
1	2	3		6		7	8	9	10	11				5		4				
1	2	3		6	7	8	9	10	11					5		4				
1	2	3		6	7	8	9	10		12				5		4				
1	2	3		6	7	8	9	10	11					5		4				
1	2	3		6	7	8	9	10	**11**	12	14			5		4				
1	2	3		6	7	8	9	10	11					5		4				
1	2	3		6	7	8	9	10	11					5		4				
1	2	3		6	7	8	9	10	11					5		4				
1	2	3		6	7	8	9	10	11					5		4				
1	2	3		6	7	8	9	10	11					5		4				
1	2	3		6	7	8	9	10	**11**	12	14			5		4				
1	2	3		6	7	8	9	10	11					5		4				
1	2	3		6	7	8	9		11	10	12			5		4				
1	2	14	3		7	8	9		11	10	6	12		5		**4**				
1	2	3			12	8	9	10	11	7				5						
1	2	3			12	8	9	10	11	**7**	6	4		5						
1	2	3			7	8		11	12	6				5					4	9
1	2	3			7	8		11	12	6				5						9
1		3	4		7	8	12	10	11	2	6	14		5						9
1	2	3			14	8	12	10	11	7	6			5					4	9
1	2	3			14	8	12	10	11	**7**	6			5					4	9
1	2	3				8	12	10	11	7	6			5					4	9
1	2	3				8	12	10	11	7	6	**4**		5						9
1	2	3			12	8		10	11	7	6	4		5						9
46	**45**	**13**	**35**	**8**	**32**	**33**	**45**	**36**	**43**	**45**	**30**	**16**	**12**	**2**	**1**	**32**	**4**	**1**	**18**	**9**
	1	1		8		8			5	7	6		3				4	1		
		1		6	5	10	19	9	5		2							2	4	

Folgate D.W.	Brown P.	Burke D.I.	Cowdrill B.J.	Came M.R.	Westaley M.A.	Green S.P.	Thompson S.P.	Reeves D.E.	Philiskirk A.	Darby J.T.	Storer S.J.	Stubbs A.	Comstive P.T.	Crombie D.M.	Housman G.	Seagraves M.	Lee S.	Stevens I.D.	Patterson M.A.	Cunningham A.E.
1	2		3			12	8		10	11	7	**6**	4			5				9
1	2		3				8		10	11	7	6	4			5				9
1	2		3			14	8	12	10	11	7	6	4			5				**9**
3	3		3			0	3	0	3	3	3	3	3			3				3
						2			1											
									2											

Folgate D.W.	Brown P.	Burke D.I.	Cowdrill B.J.	Came M.R.	Westaley M.A.	Green S.P.	Thompson S.P.	Reeves D.E.	Philiskirk A.	Darby J.T.	Storer S.J.	Stubbs A.	Comstive P.T.	Crombie D.M.	Housman G.	Seagraves M.	Lee S.	Stevens I.D.	Patterson M.A.	Cunningham A.E.
1	2		3		6	10	8		9	11	7		12			**4**	5			
1	2		3	5	6	4	8	9	10	11	7									
1	2		3	5	6		4	8	9	10	11	7			5	6				
1	2		3		6	12	8	9	10	11	**7**		4			5				
4	4		3	2	4	3	4	3	4	4	3	4	2		1	1	2			
								1								1				
				1	1	2	1	1	1	1										

Folgate D.W.	Brown P.	Burke D.I.	Cowdrill B.J.	Came M.R.	Westaley M.A.	Green S.P.	Thompson S.P.	Reeves D.E.	Philiskirk A.	Darby J.T.	Storer S.J.	Stubbs A.	Comstive P.T.	Crombie D.M.	Housman G.	Seagraves M.	Lee S.	Stevens I.D.	Patterson M.A.	Cunningham A.E.
1	2	3	4	5	6	7	8	9	10	11										
1	2	3		12	6	4	8	9	10	11	7	5								
1	2	3			4	8	9	10	11	7		5		6						
1	2		3		6	4	8		10	11	12	5				7	9			
4	4	3	2	1	3	4	4	3	4	2	1	1	1	1		1	1			
	1																			
					5	3			1											

Folgate D.W.	Brown P.	Burke D.I.	Cowdrill B.J.	Came M.R.	Westaley M.A.	Green S.P.	Thompson S.P.	Reeves D.E.	Philiskirk A.	Darby J.T.	Storer S.J.	Stubbs A.	Comstive P.T.	Crombie D.M.	Housman G.	Seagraves M.	Lee S.	Stevens I.D.	Patterson M.A.	Cunningham A.E.
1	2		3		6	4	8	9	10	11	7					5				
1	2		3	5	6	**4**	8	9	10	11	7	12								
2	2		2	1	2	2	2	2	2	2	2	0		1		1				
									1											
									1											

League Table

	P	W	D	L	F	A	Pts
Cambridge United	46	25	11	10	75	45	86
Southend United	46	26	7	13	67	51	85
Grimsby Town	46	24	11	11	66	34	83
Bolton Wanderers	46	24	11	11	64	50	83
Tranmere Rovers	46	23	9	14	64	46	78
Brentford	46	21	13	12	59	47	76
Bury	46	20	13	13	67	56	73
Bradford City	46	20	10	16	62	54	70
Bournemouth	46	19	13	14	58	58	70
Wigan Athletic	46	20	9	17	71	54	69
Huddersfield Town	46	18	13	15	57	51	67
Birmingham City	46	16	17	13	45	49	65
Leyton Orient	46	18	10	18	55	58	64
Stoke City	46	16	12	18	55	59	60
Reading	46	17	8	21	53	66	59
Exeter City	46	16	9	21	58	52	57
Preston North End	46	15	11	20	54	67	56
Shrewsbury Town	46	14	10	22	61	68	52
Chester City	46	14	9	23	46	58	51
Swansea City	46	13	9	24	49	72	48
Fulham	46	10	16	20	41	56	46
Crewe Alexandra	46	11	11	24	62	80	44
Rotherham United	46	10	12	24	50	87	42
Mansfield Town	46	8	14	24	42	63	38

Division Three

Manager: P. Neal

Match No.	Date		Venue	Opponents		Result	Scorers	Attendance
1	Aug	17	H	Huddersfield Town	D	1-1	Philliskirk	7,606
2		24	A	Swansea City	D	1-1	Reeves	3,578
3		31	H	Leyton Orient	W	1-0	Reeves	5,058
4	Sep	3	A	Darlington	L	2-3	Philliskirk, Reeves	3,384
5		7	H	West Bromwich Albion	W	3-0	Philliskirk 2, M. Brown	7,980
6		14	A	Bournemouth	W	2-1	Reeves, P. Brown	5,690
7		17	A	Bradford City	D	4-4	Darby 2, Patterson (pen), Reeves	5,669
8		21	H	Wigan Athletic	D	1-1	Darby	6,923
9		28	A	Brentford	L	2-3	Reeves, Darby	5,658
10	Oct	5	H	Torquay United	W	1-0	Green	5,092
11		12	A	Stoke City	L	0-2		12,420
12		19	H	Fulham	L	0-3		5,152
13		26	A	Chester City	W	1-0	Darby	1,867
14	Nov	2	H	Reading	D	1-1	Philliskirk (pen)	3,632
15		5	A	Stockport County	D	2-2	Philliskirk 2 (1 pen)	5,036
16		9	A	Bury	D	1-1	M. Brown	5,886
17		23	H	Preston North End	W	1-0	Reeves	7,033
18		30	A	Shrewsbury Town	W	3-1	Philliskirk (pen), Kelly, Reeves	3,937
19	Dec	14	H	Hull City	W	1-0	Philliskirk (pen)	5,273
20		26	A	Leyton Orient	L	1-2	Green	4,896
21		28	A	Huddersfield Town	L	0-1		11,884
22	Jan	1	H	Darlington	W	2-0	Fisher, Philliskirk	5,841
23		11	A	Exeter City	D	2-2	Philliskirk, Walker	3,336
24		18	A	Hartlepool United	D	2-2	Walker, Darby	6,129
25	Feb	1	A	Fulham	D	1-1	Walker	3,804
26		8	H	Chester City	D	0-0		6,609
27		11	H	Shrewsbury Town	W	1-0	Walker	5,276
28		22	H	Exeter City	L	1-2	Walker	5,631
29		29	A	Peterborough Utd.	L	0-1		6,270
30	Mar	3	A	Hartlepool United	W	4-0	Kelly, Walker 2, M. Brown	2,244
31		10	H	Stockport County	D	0-0		7,365
32		14	A	Reading	L	0-1		3,515
33		17	H	Birmingham City	D	1-1	P. Brown	7,329
34		21	H	Bury	W	2-1	Walker 2	7,619
35		24	H	Peterborough Utd.	W	2-1	Walker, Charlery (own-goal)	5,421
36		28	A	Preston North End	L	1-2	Philliskirk	7,327
37		31	H	Bournemouth	L	0-2		4,955
38	Apr	4	A	West Bromwich Albion	D	2-2	Walker, Stubbs	10,287
39		7	A	Swansea City	D	0-0		3,535
40		11	H	Bradford City	D	1-1	Walker	4,892
41		14	A	Birmingham City	L	1-2	Walker	14,440
42		18	H	Wigan Athletic	D	1-1	Spooner	3,357
43		20	H	Brentford	L	1-2	Walker	4,382
44		25	A	Torquay United	L	0-2		2,178
45		29	A	Hull City	L	0-2		3,997
46	May	2	H	Stoke City	W	3-1	Patterson, Seagraves, Walker	10,000

	Appearances
	Sub appearances
1 own-goal	Goals

FA Cup

	Date		Venue	Opponents		Result	Scorers	Attendance
R1	Nov	17	N	Emley	W	3-0	Reeves 2, Philliskirk	9,035
R2	Dec	7	H	Bradford City	W	3-1	Burke, Reeves, Philliskirk (pen)	7,129
R3	Jan	4	H	Reading	W	2-0	Philliskirk 2	7,301
R4		25	H	Brighton & Hove Albion	W	2-1	Walker, Philliskirk (pen)	12,636
R5	Feb	16	H	Southampton	D	2-2	Walker, Green	20,136
rep		26	A	Southampton	L	2-3	Walker, Darby	18,009

R1 played at Leeds Road. R5 replay a.e.t.

	Appearances
	Sub appearances
	Goals

FL Cup

	Date		Venue	Opponents		Result	Scorers	Attendance
R1/1	Aug	20	H	York City	D	2-2	Philliskirk, Darby	3,017
R1/2		27	A	York City	W	2-1	Darby, Patterson	2,757
R2/1	Sep	25	A	Nottingham Forest	L	0-4		19,936
R2/2	Oct	8	H	Nottingham Forest	L	2-5	Darby, Kelly	5,469

	Appearances
	Sub appearances
	Goals

Autoglass Trophy

	Date		Venue	Opponents		Result	Scorers	Attendance
PR	Nov	19	A	Preston North End	L	1-2	Reeves	2,709
PR	Dec	10	H	Rochdale	W	4-1	Reeves 3, Philliskirk	1,507
R1	Jan	14	A	Crewe Alexandra	L	0-2		2,155

	Appearances
	Sub appearances
	Goals

Player columns (left to right):
Feigans D.W., Brown P., Cowdrill B.J., Kelly A.G., Seagraves M., Stubbs A., Green S.P., Thompson S.J., Reeves D.E., Philliskirk A., Darby J.T., Brown M.A., Rose K.P., Burke D.I., Stoner S.J., Winstanley M.A., Patterson M.A., Jeffrey M.R., Dibble A.G., Carne M.R., Kennedy A.J., Fisher N.J., Walter A.F., Spooner N.M., Payton G.J., Charnley J.C., Maxwell A.E., Lydiate J.L., Comstive P.T.

League Table

	P	W	D	L	F	A	Pts
Brentford	46	25	7	14	81	55	82
Birmingham City	46	23	12	11	69	52	81
Huddersfield Town	46	22	12	12	59	38	78
Stoke City	46	21	14	11	69	49	77
Stockport County	46	22	10	14	75	51	76
Peterborough United	46	20	14	12	65	58	74
West Bromwich Albion	46	19	14	13	64	49	71
Bournemouth	46	20	11	15	52	48	71
Fulham	46	19	13	14	57	53	70
Leyton Orient	46	18	11	17	62	52	65
Hartlepool United	46	18	11	17	57	57	65
Reading	46	16	13	17	59	62	61
Bolton Wanderers	46	14	17	15	57	56	59
Hull City	46	16	11	19	54	54	59
Wigan Athletic	46	15	14	17	58	64	59
Bradford City	46	13	19	14	62	61	58
Preston North End	46	15	12	19	61	72	57
Chester City	46	14	14	18	56	59	56
Swansea City	46	14	14	18	55	65	56
Exeter City	46	14	11	21	57	80	53
Bury	46	13	12	21	55	74	51
Shrewsbury Town	46	12	11	23	53	68	47
Torquay United	46	13	8	25	42	68	47
Darlington	46	10	7	29	56	90	37

1992-93

Division Two
Manager: B. Rioch

Match No.	Date		Venue	Opponents	Result		Scorers	Attendance
1	Aug	15	H	Huddersfield Town	W	2-0	Walker, Darby	7,897
2		22	A	Brighton & Hove Alb.	L	1-2	Walker	6,205
3		29	A	Reading	W	2-1	Seagraves, Walker	4,877
4	Sep	1	H	Blackpool	W	3-0	Philliskirk, Walker, Green	7,291
5		5	A	Stoke City	D	0-0		14,252
6		12	A	Rotherham United	L	1-2	P. Brown	5,227
7		15	H	West Bromwich Albion	L	0-2		8,531
8		19	H	Bournemouth	D	1-1	Philliskirk	4,623
9		26	A	Plymouth Argyle	L	1-2	Darby	6,829
10	Oct	3	A	Leyton Orient	L	0-1		3,946
11		10	H	Hartlepool United	L	1-2	Green	5,097
12		17	A	Chester City	D	2-2	Reeves, McGinlay	3,394
13		24	H	Hull City	W	2-0	McGinlay, Patterson	4,136
14		31	A	Preston North End	D	2-2	Green, Stubbs	7,013
15	Nov	3	H	Exeter City	W	3-1	Spooner, Walker 2	2,431
16		7	H	Port Vale	D	1-1	McGinlay	7,349
17		21	A	Fulham	W	4-1	Walker 2, Stubbs, Lee	4,049
18		28	A	Burnley	W	4-0	Lee, Walker 2 (1 pen), P. Brown	11,438
19	Dec	19	H	Bradford City	W	5-0	Seagraves, McGinlay 2, Lee, Walker	6,887
20		26	H	Wigan Athletic	W	2-1	Walker	11,493
21		28	A	Swansea City	W	2-1	P. Brown, McGinlay	7,220
22	Jan	9	A	West Bromwich Albion	L	1-3	Walker (pen)	14,581
23		16	H	Plymouth Argyle	W	3-1	Walker, Seagraves, Morrison (own-goal)	8,256
24		27	A	Reading	W	2-1	Walker, Lee	4,640
25		30	H	Brighton & Hove Alb.	L	0-1		8,929
26	Feb	6	A	Huddersfield Town	D	1-1	Walker	8,858
27		9	A	Stockport County	L	0-2		7,363
28		20	A	Blackpool	D	1-1	McGinlay (pen)	8,054
29		27	A	Hartlepool United	W	2-0	McGinlay, Green	2,756
30	Mar	6	A	Leyton Orient	W	1-0	Walker	7,763
31		9	H	Mansfield Town	W	2-1	Walker 2	6,557
32		13	A	Port Vale	D	0-0		11,055
33		20	H	Exeter City	W	4-1	McGinlay 2, Walker, Kelly	6,815
34		23	A	Burnley	W	1-0	McGinlay	15,085
35		27	H	Fulham	W	1-0	Walker	8,402
36		30	H	Rotherham United	W	2-0	Walker 2 (1 pen)	7,985
37	Apr	3	A	Mansfield Town	D	1-1	Seagraves	5,366
38		6	H	Stockport County	W	2-1	Walker, McGinlay	13,773
39		10	A	Wigan Athletic	W	2-0	Kelly, Walker	5,408
40		12	H	Swansea City	W	3-1	Green 2, Lee	10,854
41		17	A	Bradford City	L	1-2	McGinlay	9,813
42		24	A	Chester City	W	5-0	P. Brown, Seagraves, Patterson, McGinlay, Winstanley	8,514
43		27	A	Bournemouth	W	2-1	Darby, P. Brown	4,434
44		30	A	Hull City	W	2-1	Windass (own-goal), McGinlay	8,785
45	May	4	H	Stoke City	W	1-0	Darby	19,238
46		8	H	Preston North End	W	1-0	McGinlay (pen)	21,720

							Appearances
							Sub appearances
						2 own-goals	Goals

FA Cup

R1	Nov	14	H	Sutton Coldfield Town	W	2-1	Reeves, Walker	5,345
R2	Dec	5	H	Rochdale	W	4-0	McAteer, McGinlay 2, Walker	6,876
R3	Jan	3	H	Liverpool	D	2-2	McGinlay, Seagraves	21,502
rep		13	A	Liverpool	W	2-0	McGinlay, Walker	34,790
R4		24	A	Wolverhampton Wanderers	W	2-0	Green, McGinlay	19,120
R5	Feb	13	A	Derby County	L	1-3	Walker	20,289

							Appearances
							Sub appearances
							Goals

FL Cup

R1/1	Aug	18	H	Port Vale	W	2-1	Stubbs, Green	3,282
R1/2		25	A	Port Vale	D	1-1	Walker	4,870
R2/1	Sep	22	H	Wimbledon	L	1-3	Stubbs	5,049
R2/2	Oct	6	A	Wimbledon	W	1-0	Philliskirk	1,987

							Appearances
							Sub appearances
							Goals

Autoglass Trophy

R1	Dec	1	A	Rochdale	D	0-0		1,348
R1		8	H	Bury	D	1-1	McGinlay	3,278
R2	Jan	19	A	Darlington	W	4-3	Walker 2, Lee, Kelly	1,265
QF	Feb	2	A	Huddersfield Town	L	0-3		2,996

R2 a.e.t.

							Appearances
							Sub appearances
							Goals

Player Appearances Grid

...agan K.G	Brown P.	Burke D.I.	Derby J.T.	Seagraves M.	Winstanley M.A.	Brown M.A.	Stubbs A.	Walker A.F.	Philliskirk A.	Patterson M.A.	Reeves D.E.	Green S.P.	Kelly A.G.	Caine M.R.	Foster N.J.	Oliver D.	McGinlay J.	Seymour N.M.	Lydiate J.L.	Lee D.M.	McAteer J.W.	Storer S.J.	Parkinson G.A.	Roscoe A.R.
2	3	4	5	6	**7**	8	9	10	11	12	14													
2	3	4	5	6	12	8	9	10	11	**7**														
2	3	4	5	6		8	9	10	**11**		7	12												
2	3	4	5	6		8	9	10			7	11												
2	3	4	5	6	12	8	9	**10**			7	11												
2	3	4	5	6		8	9	**10**		12	7	11	14											
2	**3**	4		6	9	8			12	10	7	11	5											
2	**3**	4		6	9	8			14	12	10	7	11	5										
2	3	12		6		8	9	10	11		7	4	**5**	14										
2		4		6		5		10	11		7		8	3	9									
	4			6		10		9	11		7		**8**	3	12	2	5							
		6		10			11	12	7	4		**8**	3	9	2	5								
3		6		8		11	10	7	4			9	2	5										
3		12	6	**4**	8	14	11	10	7			9	2	5										
3		5	6		8	9		11	10	7			2		4									
3		5	6		8	9		11	10	7		12	**2**		4									
2	3		5	6		8	9		11	**10**	7	14		12		4								
2	3		5	6			9		11		**7**	8		10		4	12							
2	3		5	6			9		11		7	8		10		4								
2	3		5	6	12		9		11		**7**	8		10		4								
2	3		5	6			9		11		7	8		10		4								
2	3		5	6	14		9		11		**7**	8		10		4	12							
2	3		5	6	12		9		11		**7**	8		10		4								
2	3		5	6			9		11		7	8		10		4								
2	3		5		6		9		11	12	**7**	8		10		4								
2	3	7	5	6			9		11		**10**	8				4		14						
2	3		5	6		12			11	9	7	8		10		4		14						
2	3			6			11	9	12			10	5	4	8	**7**								
2	3			6	9		11		7			10	5	4	8									
2	3		5		6	9		11		7			10		4	8								
2	3	12	5		6	9		11		**7**	14		10		4	8								
2	3	10	5		6	9		11	12	7					4	8								
2	3		5		6	9		11		7			10		4	8								
2	3		5		6	9		11		7			10		4	8								
2	3		5		6	9		11	12	7			10		**4**	8								
2	3	11	5		6	9				7			10		4	8								
2	3	**11**	5		6	9			12	7			10		4	8								
2	3		5		6	9		**11**		7			10		4	8		12						
2	3		5		6	9		11		7			10		4	8								
2	3		5	12	6	**9**		11		7			10		4	8		14						
2	3		5	9	6			11		7			10		4	8								
2	3	12	5	14	6			11		**9**	7		10		4	8								
2	3	**9**	5		6			11		12	7		10		4	8								
2	3	**9**	5		6			11		7			10		4	8								
2	3	**9**	5		6			11		12	7		10		4	8								
2	3	**9**	5		6			11		12	7		10		4	8								
6	40	43	18	36	27	4	37	31	9	35	10	33	33	3	3	31	6	6	32	19	1	0	0	
		3	1	2	2	5	1	1	2	4	8	3	1	1		3			2	2	2			
5		4	5	1		2	26	2	2	1	6	2		16	1		5							

...agan K.G	Brown P.	Burke D.I.	Derby J.T.	Seagraves M.	Winstanley M.A.	Brown M.A.	Stubbs A.	Walker A.F.	Philliskirk A.	Patterson M.A.	Reeves D.E.	Green S.P.	Kelly A.G.	Caine M.R.	Foster N.J.	Oliver D.	McGinlay J.	Seymour N.M.	Lydiate J.L.	Lee D.M.	McAteer J.W.	Storer S.J.	Parkinson G.A.	Roscoe A.R.
	3		5	6		8	9		11	10	7	12				2	4							
2	3		5	6			9		**11**	12	7	8				10			4					
2	3		5	6			9		11		7	8				10		4						
2	3		5	6			9		11		7	8				10		4						
2	3		5	6			**9**		11	12	7	8				10		4						
2	3			6	9			11								10	5	4	8	7				
5	6		5		5		2	6		6	1	5	4			5	1	2	4	2	1			
							2			1														
		1			4			1	1			5				1								

...agan K.G	Brown P.	Burke D.I.	Derby J.T.	Seagraves M.	Winstanley M.A.	Brown M.A.	Stubbs A.	Walker A.F.	Philliskirk A.	Patterson M.A.	Reeves D.E.	Green S.P.	Kelly A.G.	Caine M.R.	Foster N.J.	Oliver D.	McGinlay J.	Seymour N.M.	Lydiate J.L.	Lee D.M.	McAteer J.W.	Storer S.J.	Parkinson G.A.	Roscoe A.R.
2	3	4	5	6		**8**	9	10	11	12	7													
2	3	4	5	6	12	8	9	**10**	11		7													
2	3		6		8	9	10	11			7	4	5											
	4		6		10		9	11			7		8	3		2	5							
3	3	3	2	4	0	4	3	4	4	0	4	1	1	1		1	1							
		1				1				1														
		2	1	1			1																	

...agan K.G	Brown P.	Burke D.I.	Derby J.T.	Seagraves M.	Winstanley M.A.	Brown M.A.	Stubbs A.	Walker A.F.	Philliskirk A.	Patterson M.A.	Reeves D.E.	Green S.P.	Kelly A.G.	Caine M.R.	Foster N.J.	Oliver D.	McGinlay J.	Seymour N.M.	Lydiate J.L.	Lee D.M.	McAteer J.W.	Storer S.J.	Parkinson G.A.	Roscoe A.R.
2	3		5	6			9		11		**7**	8				10		4			12			
2	3			6	12	9		11		7						10	5	8	4					
2	3		5	6			9	11	14	**7**	8					10		4		12				
2	3	12	5		6	9		**11**			8					10		4	14	7				
4	4	0	3	3		1	4		4	0	3	3				4	1	4	1	1	0			
			1			1				1							1	1						
				2						1						1			1					

League Table

	P	W	D	L	F	A	Pts
Stoke City	46	27	12	7	73	34	93
Bolton Wanderers	46	27	9	10	80	41	90
Port Vale	46	26	11	9	79	44	89
West Bromwich Albion	46	25	10	11	88	54	85
Swansea City	46	20	13	13	65	47	73
Stockport County	46	19	15	12	81	57	72
Leyton Orient	46	21	9	16	69	53	72
Reading	46	18	15	13	66	51	69
Brighton & Hove Albion	46	20	9	17	63	59	69
Bradford City	46	18	14	14	69	67	68
Rotherham United	46	17	14	15	60	60	65
Fulham	46	16	17	13	57	55	65
Burnley	46	15	16	15	57	59	61
Plymouth Argyle	46	16	12	18	59	64	60
Huddersfield Town	46	17	9	20	54	61	60
Hartlepool United	46	14	12	20	42	60	54
Bournemouth	46	12	17	17	45	52	53
Blackpool	46	12	15	19	63	75	51
Exeter City	46	11	17	18	54	69	50
Hull City	46	13	11	22	46	69	50
Preston North End	46	13	8	25	65	94	47
Mansfield Town	46	11	11	24	52	80	44
Wigan Athletic	46	10	11	25	43	72	41
Chester City	46	8	5	33	49	102	29

Match No.	Date		Venue	Opponents	Result		Scorers	Attendance
1	Aug	14	A	Grimsby Town	D	0-0		8,59
2		21	H	Stoke City	D	1-1	Coyle	11,32
3		28	A	Charlton Athletic	L	0-3		7,57
4		31	H	Oxford United	W	1-0	McGinlay	8,23
5	Sep	11	A	Luton Town	W	2-0	McGinlay 2	7,18
6		18	H	Leicester City	L	1-2	McGinlay (pen)	12,04
7		26	H	Nottingham Forest	W	4-3	Lee 2, Thompson, Patterson	10,57
8	Oct	2	A	Bristol City	L	0-2		7,70
9		9	A	Tranmere Rovers	L	1-2	Brown	10,12
10		16	H	Millwall	W	4-0	McGinlay 2, McAteer, Lee	9,38
11		19	A	Birmingham City	L	1-2	Thompson	12,07
12		23	A	Watford	L	3-4	McAteer, Lee, Thompson	7,49
13		30	H	Derby County	L	0-2		11,46
14	Nov	2	H	Peterborough Utd.	D	1-1	McGinlay	7,05
15		6	A	West Bromwich Albion	D	2-2	Green, McAteer	15,70
16		21	A	Middlesbrough	W	1-0	McGinlay	6,82
17		24	H	Crystal Palace	W	1-0	McGinlay	7,48
18		27	A	Barnsley	D	1-1	Coyle	6,75
19	Dec	7	A	West Bromwich Albion	D	1-1	Coyle	9,27
20		11	A	Oxford United	W	2-0	Kelly, Thompson	5,55
21		18	H	Grimsby Town	D	1-1	Coyle	9,43
22		27	H	Sunderland	D	0-0		18,49
23		28	A	Portsmouth	D	0-0		14,27
24	Jan	1	H	Notts County	W	4-2	Fleck, Green, Thompson, Devlin (own-goal)	11,04
25		3	A	Wolverhampton Wanderers	L	0-1		24,05
26		12	A	Southend United	W	2-0	Stubbs, McGinlay	4,96
27		15	A	Millwall	L	0-1		9,77
28		23	H	Tranmere Rovers	W	2-1	McGinlay 2	11,55
29	Feb	5	H	Watford	W	3-1	Coyle, Watson (own-goal), McGinlay (pen)	10,15
30		12	A	Derby County	L	0-2		16,69
31		22	A	Stoke City	L	0-1		14,25
32		26	A	Crystal Palace	D	1-1	Coyle	17,24
33	Mar	5	H	Charlton Athletic	W	3-2	McGinlay 3 (1 pen)	13,02
34		19	A	Nottingham Forest	L	2-3	Brown, Green	23,84
35		26	H	Bristol City	D	2-2	Lee, Coyle	10,22
36		29	H	Wolverhampton Wanderers	L	1-3	McGinlay	12,40
37	Apr	2	A	Sunderland	L	0-2		18,57
38		4	H	Portsmouth	D	1-1	McGinlay	9,56
39		9	A	Notts County	L	1-2	McGinlay	7,27
40		12	A	Southend United	L	0-2		7,14
41		16	A	Peterborough Utd.	W	3-2	Walker 2, Welsh (own-goal)	6,61
42		23	H	Middlesbrough	W	4-1	McGinlay 3, Green	9,22
43		30	H	Birmingham City	D	1-1	Walker	13,60.
44	May	3	A	Leicester City	D	1-1	McGinlay	18,14
45		5	A	Luton Town	W	2-1	McGinlay, Thompson	7,10.
46		8	H	Barnsley	L	2-3	Seagraves, McGinlay	11,66

Appearances
Sub appearances
Three own-goal   Goals

FA Cup

	Date		Venue	Opponents	Result		Scorers	Attendance
R1	Nov	13	H	Gretna	W	3-2	McGinlay, Coyle 2	6,447
R2	Dec	4	A	Lincoln City	W	3-1	Thompson, Brown, Coyle	6,250
R3	Jan	8	A	Everton	D	1-1	Patterson	21,07.
rep		19	A	Everton	W	3-2	McGinlay, Stubbs, Coyle	34,65.
R4		31	H	Arsenal	D	2-2	McAteer, Coyle	18,89
rep	Feb	9	A	Arsenal	W	3-1	McGinlay, McAteer, Walker	33,86.
R5		20	H	Aston Villa	W	1-0	Stubbs	18,81
R6	Mar	12	H	Oldham Athletic	L	0-1		20,32

R1 played at home by arrangement. R3 replay and R4 replay a.e.t.

Appearances
Sub appearances
Goals

FL Cup

	Date		Venue	Opponents	Result		Scorers	Attendance
R1/1	Aug	17	H	Bury	L	0-2		6,45.
R1/2		24	A	Bury	W	2-0	Coyle, McGinlay	4,52.
R2/1	Sep	21	H	Sheffield Wednesday	D	1-1	Kelly (pen)	11,59.
R2/2	Oct	6	A	Sheffield Wednesday	L	0-1		16,19.

R1/2 won 3-0 on penalties, a.e.t.

Appearances
Sub appearances
Goals

Anglo Italian Cup

	Date		Venue	Opponents	Result		Scorers	Attendance
PR	Sep	7	A	Tranmere Rovers	W	2-1	McGinlay, Coyle	2,78.
PR		14	H	Sunderland	W	2-0	Coyle 2	3,460
Gp	Oct	12	H	Ancona	W	5-0	McGinlay 2, Thompson, McAteer, Phillips	3,448
Gp	Nov	9	H	Brescia	D	3-3	Coyle, McGinlay, Green	3,02.
Gp		16	A	Pisa	D	1-1	Phillips	1,000
Gp	Dec	22	A	Ascoli	D	1-1	Seagraves	1,000

Did not qualify for semi-finals.

Appearances
Sub appearances
Goals

Branagan K.G. · Brown P. · Phillips J.N. · Kelly A.G. · Burke D.I. · Winstanley M.A. · Lee D.M. · McAteer J.W. · Coyle O.C. · McGinlay J. · Thompson A. · Green S.P. · Stubbs A. · Patterson M.A. · Darby J.T. · Seagraves M. · Davison A.J. · Hoult R. · Fleck R.W. · Parkinson G.A. · Walker A.F. · Lydiate J.J. · Fulton S. · Roscoe A.R. · Walton M.A. · Fisher N.J. · Spooner N.M. · Whittaker S.

League Table

	P	W	D	L	F	A	Pts
Crystal Palace	46	27	9	10	73	46	90
Nottingham Forest	46	23	14	9	74	49	83
Millwall	46	19	17	10	58	49	74
Leicester City	46	19	16	11	72	59	73
Tranmere Rovers	46	21	9	16	69	53	72
Derby County	46	20	11	15	73	68	71
Notts County	46	20	8	18	65	69	68
Wolverhampton W	46	17	17	12	60	47	68
Middlesbrough	46	18	13	15	66	54	67
Stoke City	46	18	13	15	57	59	67
Charlton Athletic	46	19	8	19	61	58	65
Sunderland	46	19	8	19	54	57	65
Bristol City	46	16	16	14	47	50	64
Bolton Wanderers	46	15	14	17	63	64	59
Southend United	46	17	8	21	63	67	59
Grimsby Town	46	13	20	13	52	47	59
Portsmouth	46	15	13	18	52	58	58
Barnsley	46	16	7	23	55	67	55
Watford	46	15	9	22	66	80	54
Luton Town	46	14	11	21	56	60	53
West Bromwich Albion	46	13	12	21	60	69	51
Birmingham City	46	13	12	21	52	69	51
Oxford United	46	13	10	23	54	75	49
Peterborough United	46	8	13	25	48	76	37

1994-95

Division One

Manager: B. Rioch

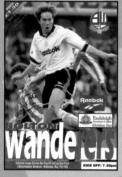

Match No.	Date		Venue	Opponents		Result	Scorers	Attendance
1	Aug	13	A	Grimsby Town	D	3-3	Paatelainen 2, McGinlay (pen)	8,393
2		20	H	Bristol City	L	0-2		12,127
3		27	A	Middlesbrough	L	0-1		19,570
4		30	H	Millwall	W	1-0	Patterson	9,519
5	Sep	3	H	Stoke City	W	4-0	McGinlay (pen), McAteer 2, Paatelainen	11,515
6		10	A	Sheffield United	L	1-3	McGinlay	14,116
7		13	A	Luton Town	W	3-0	McGinlay 2, Sneekes	5,764
8		17	H	Portsmouth	D	1-1	McGinlay	11,284
9		24	A	Southend United	L	1-2	Sneekes	4,507
10	Oct	1	H	Derby County	W	1-0	McGinlay	12,015
11		8	A	Burnley	D	2-2	McGinlay, Coleman	16,687
12		16	H	Oldham Athletic	D	2-2	Paatelainen, Lee	11,106
13		22	A	Port Vale	D	1-1	Green	10,005
14		29	H	Watford	W	3-0	Paatelainen, McGinlay 2 (1 pen)	10,483
15	Nov	1	H	Swindon Town	W	3-0	Coleman, Thompson, De Freitas	10,046
16		5	A	Charlton Athletic	W	2-1	Sneekes 2	9,783
17		19	H	Notts County	W	2-0	De Freitas, Paatelainen	11,698
18		23	A	Wolverhampton Wanderers	L	1-3	Paatelainen	25,903
19		26	A	Barnsley	L	0-3		8,507
20	Dec	6	H	Port Vale	W	1-0	Patterson	10,324
21		10	A	Bristol City	W	1-0	Patterson	6,144
22		17	H	Grimsby Town	D	3-3	Coyle 2, Lee	10,522
23		26	A	Sunderland	D	1-1	Paatelainen	18,758
24		27	H	Tranmere Rovers	W	1-0	Thompson	16,782
25		31	A	West Bromwich Albion	L	0-1		18,184
26	Jan	2	H	Reading	W	1-0	Coleman	14,705
27		14	A	Watford	D	0-0		9,113
28		21	H	Charlton Athletic	W	5-1	McGinlay 2, McAteer, Coyle, Paatelainen	10,516
29	Feb	4	A	Wolverhampton Wanderers	W	5-1	Sneekes, Coleman, Phillips, Coyle, Thompson	16,96
30		7	A	Notts County	D	1-1	Coyle	7,553
31		18	H	Barnsley	W	2-1	Thompson, Sneekes	12,463
32		26	A	Derby County	L	1-2	McAteer	11,003
33	Mar	4	H	Southend United	W	3-0	Thompson, Lee, McAteer	10,766
34		11	A	Middlesbrough	W	1-0	Paatelainen	18,370
35		19	A	Millwall	W	1-0	McGinlay	6,108
36		22	H	Sheffield United	D	1-1	Stubbs	16,756
37		25	A	Portsmouth	D	1-1	Paatelainen	7,765
38	Apr	5	H	Swindon Town	W	1-0	Thompson	8,100
39		8	H	West Bromwich Albion	W	1-0	Thompson (pen)	16,207
40		11	H	Luton Town	D	0-0		13,619
41		14	A	Tranmere Rovers	L	0-1		15,559
42		17	H	Sunderland	W	1-0	McGinlay	15,030
43		21	A	Reading	L	1-2	Lee	13,223
44		29	A	Oldham Athletic	L	1-3	McGinlay	11,901
45	May	3	A	Stoke City	D	1-1	McGinlay	15,547
46		7	H	Burnley	D	1-1	Paatelainen	16,853

Appearances
Sub appearances
Goals

Play-offs

	Date		Venue	Opponents		Result	Scorers	Attendance
SF1	May	14	A	Wolverhampton Wanderers	L	1-2	McAteer	26,153
SF2		17	H	Wolverhampton Wanderers	W	2-0	McGinlay 2	20,041
F		29	N	Reading	W	4-3	De Freitas 2, Coyle, Paatelainen	64,107

SF2 and Final a.e.t.

Appearances
Sub appearances
Goals

FA Cup

	Date		Venue	Opponents		Result	Scorers	Attendance
R3	Jan	7	A	Portsmouth	L	1-3	Sneekes	9,721

Appearances
Sub appearances
Goals

FL Cup

	Date		Venue	Opponents		Result	Scorers	Attendance
R2/1	Sep	21	A	Ipswich Town	W	3-0	McAteer, McGinlay, Thompson	7,787
R2/2	Oct	5	H	Ipswich Town	W	1-0	Sneekes	8,212
R3		25	A	Sheffield United	W	2-1	Paatelainen, Scott (own-goal)	6,939
R4	Nov	30	A	West Ham United	W	3-1	McGinlay 2 (1 pen), Lee	18,190
R5	Jan	11	H	Norwich City	W	1-0	Lee	17,029
SF1	Feb	12	A	Swindon Town	L	1-2	Stubbs	15,341
SF2	Mar	8	H	Swindon Town	W	3-1	McAteer, Paatelainen, McGinlay	19,851
F	Apr	2	N	Liverpool	L	1-2	Thompson	75,595

Final at Wembley Stadium.

Appearances
Sub appearances
1 own-goal   Goals

League Table

	P	W	D	L	F	A	Pts
Middlesbrough	46	23	13	10	67	40	82
Reading	46	23	10	13	58	44	79
Bolton Wanderers	46	21	14	11	67	45	77
Wolverhampton W	46	21	13	12	77	61	76
Tranmere Rovers	46	22	10	14	67	58	76
Barnsley	46	20	12	14	63	52	72
Watford	46	19	13	14	52	46	70
Sheffield United	46	17	17	12	74	55	68
Derby County	46	18	12	16	66	51	66
Grimsby Town	46	17	14	15	62	56	65
Stoke City	46	16	15	15	50	53	63
Millwall	46	16	14	16	60	60	62
Southend United	46	18	8	20	54	73	62
Oldham Athletic	46	16	13	17	60	60	61
Charlton Athletic	46	16	11	19	58	66	59
Luton Town	46	15	13	18	61	64	58
Port Vale	46	15	13	18	58	64	58
Portsmouth	46	15	13	18	53	63	58
West Bromwich Albion	46	16	10	20	51	57	58
Sunderland	46	12	18	16	41	45	54
Swindon Town	46	12	12	22	54	73	48
Burnley	46	11	13	22	49	74	46
Bristol City	46	11	12	23	42	63	45
Notts County	46	9	13	24	45	66	40

Premiership

Manager: C. Todd/R. McFarland until 2 January 1996, C. Todd from 2 January 1996

Match No.	Date		Venue	Opponents		Result	Scorers	Attendance
1	Aug	19	A	Wimbledon	L	2-3	Thompson (pen), De Freitas	9,317
2		22	H	Newcastle United	L	1-3	Bergsson	20,243
3		26	H	Blackburn Rovers	W	2-1	De Freitas, Stubbs	20,253
4		30	A	Aston Villa	L	0-1		31,770
5	Sep	9	H	Middlesbrough	D	1-1	McGinlay	18,376
6		16	A	Manchester United	L	0-3		32,812
7		23	A	Liverpool	L	2-5	Todd, Patterson (pen)	40,104
8		30	H	Queen's Park Rangers	L	0-1		17,362
9	Oct	14	H	Everton	D	1-1	Paatelainen	20,427
10		21	A	Nottingham Forest	L	2-3	Sneekes, De Freitas	25,426
11		30	A	Arsenal	W	1-0	McGinlay	18,682
12	Nov	4	A	Manchester City	L	0-1		28,397
13		18	H	West Ham United	L	0-3		19,047
14		22	A	Chelsea	L	2-3	Curcic, Green	17,495
15		25	A	Southampton	L	0-1		14,404
16	Dec	2	H	Nottingham Forest	D	1-1	De Freitas	17,342
17		9	H	Liverpool	L	0-1		21,042
18		16	A	Queen's Park Rangers	L	1-2	Sellars	11,456
19		23	A	Tottenham Hotspur	D	2-2	Green, Bergsson	30,702
20		27	H	Leeds United	L	0-2		18,414
21		30	H	Coventry City	L	1-2	McGinlay	16,678
22	Jan	1	A	Sheffield Wednesday	L	2-4	Curcic, Taggart	24,872
23		13	H	Wimbledon	W	1-0	McGinlay (pen)	16,216
24		20	A	Newcastle United	L	1-2	Bergsson	36,543
25	Feb	3	A	Blackburn Rovers	L	1-3	Green	30,419
26		10	H	Aston Villa	L	0-2		18,099
27		17	A	Middlesbrough	W	4-1	Blake, Coleman, De Freitas, Lee	29,354
28		25	H	Manchester United	L	0-6		21,381
29	Mar	2	A	Leeds United	W	1-0	Bergsson	30,106
30		16	A	Coventry City	W	2-0	Stubbs 2	17,226
31		20	H	Tottenham Hotspur	L	2-3	Stubbs, Sellars	17,829
32		23	H	Sheffield Wednesday	W	2-1	Sellars, Curcic	18,368
33		30	H	Manchester City	D	1-1	McGinlay	21,050
34	Apr	6	A	Everton	L	0-3		37,974
35		8	H	Chelsea	W	2-1	McGinlay, Curcic	18,021
36		13	H	West Ham United	L	0-1		23,086
37		27	H	Southampton	L	0-1		18,795
38	May	5	A	Arsenal	L	1-2	Todd	38,104

Appearances
Sub appearances
Goals

FA Cup

	Date		Venue	Opponents		Result	Scorers	Attendance
R3	Jan	6	A	Bradford City	W	3-0	McGinlay, Curcic 2	10,265
R4	Feb	14	H	Leeds United	L	0-1		16,694

Appearances
Sub appearances
Goals

FL Cup

	Date		Venue	Opponents		Result	Scorers	Attendance
R2/1	Sep	19	H	Brentford	W	1-0	Sneekes	5,243
R2/2	Oct	3	A	Brentford	W	3-2	Patterson, McGinlay, Thompson	4,861
R3		25	H	Leicester City	D	0-0		9,166
rep	Nov	8	A	Leicester City	W	3-2	McGinlay, Sneekes, Curcic	14,884
R4		29	A	Norwich City	D	0-0		13,820
rep	Dec	20	H	Norwich City	D	0-0		8,736

R4 replay lost 2-3 on penalties, a.e.t.

Appearances
Sub appearances
Goals

Player appearance grid

Column headers (left to right):
Barragan K.G., Bergsson G., Phillips J.N., McAteer J.W., Fairclough C.H., Stubbs A., Green S.P., Patterson M.A., Paatelainen M.M.P., De Freitas F., Thompson A., Lee D.M., Coyle O.C., Sneekes R., McGinlay J., Taggart G.P., Todd A.J.J., McAnespie S., Curcic S., Sellars S., Blake N.A., Burnett W., Strong G., Coleman S., Davison A.J., Ward G.J., Taylor S.J., Small B., Whittaker S.

1	2	3	4	5	6	7	8	9	10	11	12	13	14	15	16	17	18	19	20	21	22	23	24	25	26	27	28	29
1	2	3	4	5	6	7	8	9	10	11	12	13																
1	2	3	4	5	6	7	8		10	11	13	9	12															
1	2	3	4	5	6	7	8		10	11	12	9																
1	2	3	4	5	6		7	8		9	11	13		12	10													
1	4	3		5		2	8		9	11		12	7	10	6													
1	4	3		5	13	2	12		9	11	7		8	10	6													
1	6	3		5		2	4		9	11	7	12	8	10		13												
1	5	3		6		4			9	11	7		8	10			2											
1	4	3		5	6	12	8	9		11	13		7	10			2											
1	4	3		5	6		8	9	12	11	13		7	10			2											
1	4	3		5	6	13	12	9		11	7			10			2	8										
1	4	3		5	6	14	12	9	13	11	7			10			2	8										
1	6	3		5		12	4			11	7		8	9		13	2	10										
1	4	3		5		2	8			11			9	6	7			10										
1	4	3		5		2	8			11			9	6	7			10										
1	4	3		5		2			9	11			10	6	7			8										
1	4	3		5		2	12		9				10	6	7		8	11										
1	4	3		5		2			9				10	6	7	12	8	11										
1	4	3		5		2				13			12	10	6	7		8	11	9								
1	4	3		5		2				13			7	10	6			8	11	9	12							
1		3	5		2								7	10	6	4		8	11	9								
1		3		6	2				13				7	10	5	4		8	11	9	12							
1	5	3		6	2		9				12		7	10				4	11	8								
1	5	3		6	2	12				7			8	10		13	14	4	11	9								
1	4	3		5	6	2	9				13		7	10				8	11	12								
1	4	3		5	6	2		9	12				7	13				8	11	10								
1		3		5		2		9	11	7								4	8	10		6						
1		3		5		2		9	11	7			12					4	8	10		6						
1	4	3		5	8	2	9	12										7	11	10		6						
1	4	3		5	8	2	9	12										7	11	10		6						
	4	3		5	8	2	9	14	13				12					7	11	10		6	1					
	2	3		5	8		9	11										10		4	7		6	1				
	2	3		5	8	12	13	9	11									10		4	7	14	6		1			
	4	3		5	8	2	9	12										10		7	11	13	6		1			
	2	3		5	8			11										10		4	7	9	6		1	12		
	2	3		5	8		12	11										10		4	7	9	6		1			
	2	3	5		8		13	9	11	12								10		4	7		6		1			
1	5			8				9		12								10		7	2	4	11	13		6		3
Apps																												
31	34	37	4	33	24	26	12	12	17	23	9	2	14	29	11	9	7	28	22	14	0	0	12	2	5	0	1	0
	1		5	4	3	10	3	9	3	3	3	3				3	2			4	1	1			1			
4			4	3	1	1	5	1	1			1	6	1	2		4	3	1			1						

Cup competition sections

1		3		5	6	2				7	10	4						8	11	9								
1		3		5	6	2		13	9	11	7							12	4	8			10					
2		2		2	2	2		0	1	1	1							1	1	2			2	1	2			
					1													1										
																		1		2								

1	6	3		5		2	4		9	11	7	12	8	10			13											
1	6	3		5	9	12	4			11	7		8	10		13	2											
1	4	3		5	6		8	9	13	11	12		7	10			2											
1	4	3		5	6	13	12				11	7	8	9			2	10										
1	4	3		5		2	8			11			9	6	7			10										
1	4	3		5		2	11		9				10	6	7		8									12		
6	6	6		6	3	3	5	1	2	5	3	0	4	6	2	2	3	3								0		
					2	1		1		1	1						2									1		
					1			1					2	2			1											

Division One

Manager: C. Todd

Club records tumbled in the final season at Burnden Park as the Wanderers secured the First Division Championship. Most wins in a season (28), most home wins (18), fewest defeats in a season (4), fewest away defeats (3), most goals scored in a season (100), most goals scored away from home (40), most points in a season (98) and finally equalling a record of scoring in 24 consecutive League games that was set in the club's opening Football League seasons in 1888 and 1889.

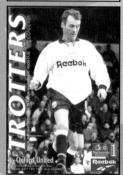

Match No.	Date		Venue	Opponents	Result		Scorers	Attendance
1	Aug	17	A	Port Vale	D	1-1	Thompson	10,057
2		20	H	Manchester City	W	1-0	Frandsen	18,257
3		24	H	Norwich City	W	3-1	Blake 2, Johansen	13,507
4	Sep	1	A	Queen's Park Rangers	W	2-1	McGinlay, Thompson	11,225
5		7	A	Southend United	L	2-5	Blake, McGinlay	4,475
6		10	H	Grimsby Town	W	6-1	Johansen 2, Blake, Lee, Fairclough, Taylor	12,448
7		14	H	Portsmouth	W	2-0	Blake, Fairclough	14,248
8		21	A	Bradford City	W	4-2	Thompson, Blake 2, Frandsen	12,034
9		28	H	Stoke City	D	1-1	Blake	16,195
10	Oct	2	A	Wolverhampton Wanderers	W	2-1	McGinlay 2	26,540
11		12	H	Oldham Athletic	W	3-1	Johansen, McGinlay 2	14,813
12		15	H	Tranmere Rovers	W	1-0	Sellars	14,136
13		19	A	Charlton Athletic	D	3-3	McGinlay 2 (1 pen), Blake	11,091
14		25	A	Barnsley	D	2-2	McGinlay (pen), De Zeeuw (own-goal)	9,413
15		29	A	Reading	W	2-1	Sellars, McGinlay	12,677
16	Nov	2	H	Huddersfield Town	W	2-0	Thompson, McGinlay	15,865
17		13	A	Birmingham City	L	1-3	Sheridan	17,033
18		16	H	Crystal Palace	D	2-2	Sheridan, McGinlay (pen)	16,892
19		19	A	Oxford United	D	0-0		7,517
20		22	A	Sheffield United	D	1-1	Blake	17,069
21		30	H	Barnsley	D	2-2	Blake, Thompson	16,852
22	Dec	8	A	West Bromwich Albion	D	2-2	Frandsen, Fairclough	13,082
23		14	A	Ipswich Town	L	1-2	Bergsson	13,314
24		22	A	Swindon Town	D	2-2	Green, McGinlay	8,948
25		26	A	Grimsby Town	W	2-1	Taggart, Blake	8,185
26		28	H	Southend United	W	3-1	Sellars 2, McGinlay (pen)	16,357
27	Jan	1	H	Bradford City	W	2-1	Lee, Sellars	16,192
28		11	A	Portsmouth	W	3-0	Blake 2, Johansen	10,467
29		18	H	Wolverhampton Wanderers	W	3-0	McGinlay, Curle (own-goal), Blake	18,980
30		29	A	Stoke City	W	2-1	Pollock, McGinlay	15,645
31	Feb	1	H	Birmingham City	W	2-1	Pollock, McGinlay (pen)	16,737
32		8	A	Reading	L	2-3	Thompson, McGinlay	10,739
33		15	H	Sheffield United	D	2-2	Paatelainen, Fairclough	17,922
34		22	A	Huddersfield Town	W	2-1	Fairclough, Taggart	16,061
35	Mar	2	H	West Bromwich Albion	W	1-0	Blake	13,258
36		4	H	Crystal Palace	D	1-1	Fairclough	16,035
37		8	H	Swindon Town	W	7-0	Thompson, Frandsen, Pollock, Bergsson 2, McGinlay, Blake	13,981
38		15	A	Ipswich Town	W	1-0	McGinlay	16,187
39		18	H	Port Vale	W	4-2	Frandsen, Glover (own-goal), Fairclough, Blake	14,150
40		22	A	Norwich City	W	1-0	Sellars	17,585
41	Apr	5	H	Queen's Park Rangers	W	2-1	Fairclough, McGinlay	19,198
42		9	A	Manchester City	W	2-1	Paatelainen, Sellars	28,026
43		12	H	Oxford United	W	4-0	Thompson 2, Sellars, Blake	15,994
44		19	A	Oldham Athletic	D	0-0		10,702
45		25	H	Charlton Athletic	W	4-1	Thompson, Taggart, McGinlay 2 (1 pen)	22,030
46	May	4	A	Tranmere Rovers	D	2-2	McGinlay, Pollock	14,309

	Appearances
	Sub appearances
3 own-goals	Goals

FA Cup

R3	Jan	21	A	Luton Town	D	1-1	Pollock	7,414
rep		25	H	Luton Town	W	6-2	McGinlay, Blake 2, Thompson, Pollock, Green	9,713
R4	Feb	4	H	Chesterfield	L	2-3	Taylor, Green	10,852

	Appearances
	Sub appearances
	Goals

FL Cup

R2/1	Sep	18	A	Bristol City	D	0-0		6,351
R2/2		24	H	Bristol City	W	3-1	McGinlay, Blake, Thompson	6,367
R3	Oct	22	H	Chelsea	W	2-1	McGinlay, Blake	16,867
R4	Nov	27	H	Tottenham Hotspur	W	6-1	McGinlay 3 (1 pen), Taggart, Blake, Taylor	18,621
R5	Jan	8	H	Wimbledon	L	0-2		16,968

R2/2 a.e.t.

	Appearances
	Sub appearances
	Goals

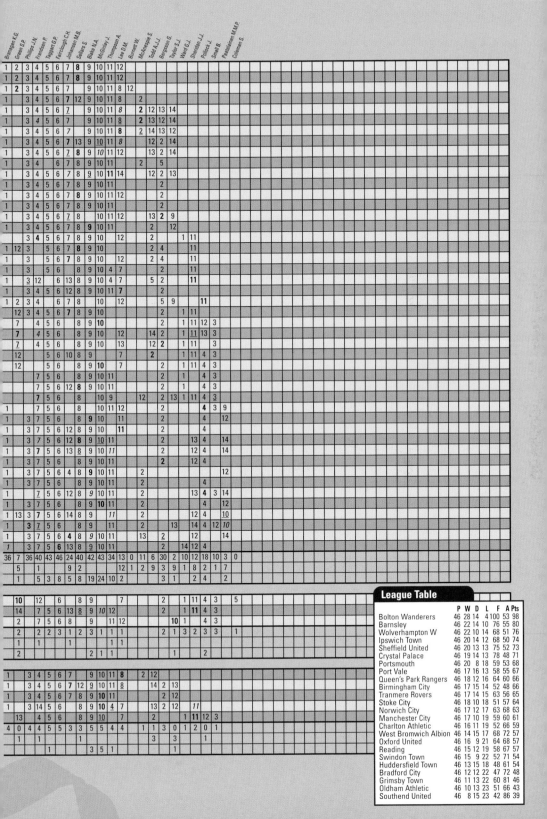

League Table

	P	W	D	L	F	A	Pts
Bolton Wanderers	46	28	14	4	100	53	98
Barnsley	46	22	14	10	76	55	80
Wolverhampton W	46	22	10	14	68	51	76
Ipswich Town	46	20	14	12	68	50	74
Sheffield United	46	20	13	13	75	52	73
Crystal Palace	46	19	14	13	78	48	71
Portsmouth	46	20	8	18	59	53	68
Port Vale	46	17	16	13	58	55	67
Queen's Park Rangers	46	18	12	16	64	60	66
Birmingham City	46	17	15	14	52	48	66
Tranmere Rovers	46	17	14	15	63	56	65
Stoke City	46	18	10	18	51	57	64
Norwich City	46	17	12	17	63	68	63
Manchester City	46	17	10	19	59	60	61
Charlton Athletic	46	16	11	19	52	66	59
West Bromwich Albion	46	14	15	17	68	72	57
Oxford United	46	16	9	21	64	68	57
Reading	46	15	12	19	58	67	57
Swindon Town	46	15	9	22	52	71	54
Huddersfield Town	46	13	15	18	48	61	54
Bradford City	46	12	12	22	47	72	48
Grimsby Town	46	11	13	22	60	81	46
Oldham Athletic	46	10	13	23	51	66	43
Southend United	46	8	15	23	42	86	39

1997-98

Premiership

Manager: C. Todd

Match No.	Date		Venue	Opponents	Result		Scorers	Attendance
1	Aug	9	A	Southampton	W	1-0	Blake	15,206
2		23	A	Coventry City	D	2-2	Blake 2	16,633
3		27	A	Barnsley	L	1-2	Beardsley	18,236
4	Sep	1	H	Everton	D	0-0		23,131
5		13	A	Arsenal	L	1-4	Thompson	38,138
6		20	H	Manchester United	D	0-0		25,000
7		23	H	Tottenham Hotspur	D	1-1	Thompson (pen)	23,433
8		27	A	Crystal Palace	D	2-2	Beardsley, Johansen	17,134
9	Oct	4	H	Aston Villa	L	0-1		24,196
10		18	A	West Ham United	L	0-3		24,865
11		26	H	Chelsea	W	1-0	Holdsworth	24,080
12	Nov	1	H	Liverpool	D	1-1	Blake	25,000
13		8	A	Sheffield Wednesday	L	0-5		25,027
14		22	A	Leicester City	D	0-0		20,464
15		29	H	Wimbledon	W	1-0	Blake	22,703
16	Dec	1	H	Newcastle United	W	1-0	Blake	24,494
17		6	A	Blackburn Rovers	L	1-3	Frandsen	25,503
18		14	H	Derby County	D	3-3	Thompson (pen), Blake, Pollock	23,027
19		20	A	Leeds United	L	0-2		31,163
20		26	H	Barnsley	D	1-1	Bergsson	25,000
21		28	A	Everton	L	2-3	Bergsson, Sellars	37,149
22	Jan	10	H	Southampton	D	0-0		23,333
23		17	A	Newcastle United	L	1-2	Blake	36,767
24		31	H	Coventry City	L	1-5	Sellars	25,000
25	Feb	7	A	Manchester United	D	1-1	Taylor	55,156
26		21	H	West Ham United	D	1-1	Blake	25,000
27	Mar	1	A	Tottenham Hotspur	L	0-1		29,032
28		7	A	Liverpool	L	1-2	Thompson	44,532
29		14	H	Sheffield Wednesday	W	3-2	Frandsen, Blake, Thompson (pen)	24,847
30		28	H	Leicester City	W	2-0	Thompson 2	25,000
31		31	H	Arsenal	L	0-1		25,000
32	Apr	4	A	Wimbledon	D	0-0		11,356
33		11	H	Blackburn Rovers	W	2-1	Holdsworth, Taylor	25,000
34		13	A	Derby County	L	0-4		29,126
35		18	H	Leeds United	L	2-3	Thompson, Fish	25,000
36		25	A	Aston Villa	W	3-1	Cox, Taylor, Blake	38,392
37	May	2	H	Crystal Palace	W	5-2	Blake, Fish, Phillips, Thompson, Holdsworth	24,449
38		10	A	Chelsea	L	0-2		34,845

Appearances
Sub appearances
Goals

FA Cup

R3	Jan	3	A	Barnsley	L	0-1		15,042

Appearances
Sub appearances

FL Cup

R2/1	Sep	16	A	Leyton Orient	W	3-1	Todd, Frandsen, McGinlay	4,128
R2/2		30	H	Leyton Orient	D	4-4	Blake 2, McGinlay (pen), Gunnlaugsson	6,444
R3	Oct	14	H	Wimbledon	W	2-0	Pollock, McAllister (own-goal)	9,875
R4	Nov	18	A	Middlesbrough	L	1-2	Thompson	22,801

R3 and R4 a.e.t.

Appearances
Sub appearances

1 own-goal   Goals

Column headers (players):
Branagan K.G. · Cox N.J. · Elliott R.J. · Pollock J. · Taggart G.P. · Bergsson G. · Frandsen P. · Sellars S. · Blake N.A. · McGinlay J. · Thompson A. · Phillips J.N. · Beardsley P.A. · Johansen M.B. · McAnespie S. · Todd A.J.J. · Gunnlaugsson A.B. · Strong G. · Whitlow M.W. · Fish M.A. · Holdsworth D.C. · Carr F.A. · Ward G.I. · Fairclough C.H. · Taylor R. · Sheridan J.J. · Solako J.A. · Anjorlee H. · Gudjonsson G.

League Table

	P	W	D	L	F	A	Pts
Arsenal	38	23	9	6	68	33	78
Manchester United	38	23	8	7	73	26	77
Liverpool	38	18	11	9	68	42	65
Chelsea	38	20	3	15	71	43	63
Leeds United	38	17	8	13	57	46	59
Blackburn Rovers	38	16	10	12	57	52	58
Aston Villa	38	17	6	15	49	48	57
West Ham United	38	16	8	14	56	57	56
Derby County	38	16	7	15	52	49	55
Leicester City	38	13	14	11	51	41	53
Coventry City	38	12	16	10	46	44	52
Southampton	38	14	6	18	50	55	48
Newcastle United	38	11	11	16	35	44	44
Tottenham Hotspur	38	11	11	16	44	56	44
Wimbledon	38	10	14	14	34	46	44
Sheffield Wednesday	38	12	8	18	52	67	44
Everton	38	9	13	16	41	56	40
Bolton Wanderers	38	9	13	16	41	61	40
Barnsley	38	10	5	23	37	82	35
Crystal Palace	38	8	9	21	37	71	33

1998-99

Division One

Manager: C. Todd

Did you know that?

Arnar Gunnlaugsson scored the Wanderers 6,000th League goal during a 2–2 draw at Bradford City in August 1998. The following month the Icelandic striker went on a run of scoring in seven consecutive League games.

Match No.	Date		Venue	Opponents		Result	Scorers	Attendance
1	Aug	8	A	Crystal Palace	D	2-2	Holdsworth, Gunnlaugsson	19,029
2		15	H	Grimsby Town	W	2-0	Blake, Holdsworth (pen)	16,584
3		23	A	Bradford City	D	2-2	Gunnlaugsson, Blake	13,163
4		29	H	Sheffield United	D	2-2	Strong, Blake	18,263
5	Sep	8	A	West Bromwich Albion	W	3-2	Gunnlaugsson, Blake, Gardner	15,789
6		12	H	Birmingham City	W	3-1	R. Taylor 2, Frandsen	19,637
7		19	A	Crewe Alexandra	D	4-4	Gunnlaugsson 2, R. Taylor, Frandsen	5,744
8		26	H	Huddersfield Town	W	3-0	Frandsen, Blake, Gunnlaugsson	20,971
9		29	H	Swindon Town	W	2-1	Blake, Gunnlaugsson	16,497
10	Oct	3	A	Barnsley	D	2-2	Gunnlaugsson, Johansen	17,382
11		17	H	Oxford United	D	1-1	Frandsen	17,064
12		20	H	Watford	L	1-2	Gunnlaugsson	15,921
13		23	A	Bristol City	L	1-2	Gunnlaugsson	12,026
14	Nov	1	H	Sunderland	L	0-3		21,676
15		4	H	Port Vale	W	3-1	R. Taylor, Frandsen, Gunnlaugsson	14,324
16		7	A	Queen's Park Rangers	L	0-2		11,814
17		14	H	Tranmere Rovers	D	2-2	Johansen, Holdsworth (pen)	16,564
18		21	A	Ipswich Town	W	1-0	R. Taylor	17,225
19		24	A	Stockport County	W	1-0	R. Taylor	8,520
20		28	H	Bury	W	4-0	Johansen 2, Gunnlaugsson 2	21,028
21	Dec	5	A	Wolverhampton Wanderers	D	1-1	R. Taylor	22,537
22		12	A	Tranmere Rovers	D	1-1	R. Taylor	6,959
23		19	A	Portsmouth	W	3-1	R. Taylor, Frandsen, Holdsworth	15,981
24		26	H	Bradford City	D	0-0		24,625
25		28	A	Port Vale	W	2-0	Sellars, Holdsworth (pen)	8,201
26	Jan	10	H	Crystal Palace	W	3-0	R. Taylor, Johansen, Jensen	15,410
27		16	A	Sheffield United	W	2-1	Holdsworth 2	15,787
28		30	H	Norwich City	W	2-0	Holdsworth, Cox	18,766
29	Feb	6	A	Grimsby Town	W	1-0	Holdsworth	8,674
30		13	H	West Bromwich Albion	W	2-1	R. Taylor, Cox	20,657
31		21	A	Birmingham City	D	0-0		26,051
32		27	A	Crewe Alexandra	L	1-3	Holdsworth (pen)	19,437
33	Mar	2	A	Huddersfield Town	L	2-3	Holdsworth, Johansen	13,867
34		6	A	Swindon Town	D	3-3	Fish, Jensen, Gudjohnsen	8,392
35		9	H	Barnsley	D	3-3	Sellars, Holdsworth (pen), Gudjohnsen	16,537
36		13	H	Queen's Park Rangers	W	2-1	R. Taylor 2	17,919
37		20	A	Sunderland	L	1-3	Frandsen	41,505
38	Apr	3	A	Oxford United	D	0-0		7,547
39		5	H	Stockport County	L	1-2	R. Taylor	18,587
40		10	A	Watford	L	0-2		13,001
41		13	H	Bristol City	W	1-0	Gudjohnsen	14,459
42		17	A	Ipswich Town	W	2-0	R. Taylor, Gudjohnsen	19,894
43		20	A	Norwich City	D	2-2	Cox, Frandsen	11,137
44		23	A	Bury	L	1-2	Cox	7,680
45		30	H	Wolverhampton Wanderers	D	1-1	Gardner	20,208
46	May	9	A	Portsmouth	W	2-0	Johansen, Gudjohnsen	16,015
							Appearances	
							Sub appearances	
							Goals	

Play-offs

SF1	May 16		H	Ipswich Town	W	1-0	Johansen	18,295
SF2	19		A	Ipswich Town	L	3-4	R. Taylor 2, Frandsen	21,755
F	31		N	Watford	L	0-2		70,343

SF2 won on away goals, a.e.t. Score at 90 minutes 2-3.

							Appearances	
							Sub appearances	
							Goals	

FA Cup

R3	Jan 2		H	Wolverhampton Wanderers	L	1-2	Sellars	18,269
							Appearances	
							Sub appearances	
							Goals	

FL Cup

R1/1	Aug 11		H	Hartlepool United	W	1-0	R. Taylor	6,429
R1/2	25		A	Hartlepool United	W	3-0	Blake 3	3,185
R2/1	Sep 15		H	Hull City	W	3-1	Phillips, Gunnlaugsson, Frandsen	7,544
R2/2	22		A	Hull City	W	3-2	Jensen, Johansen, Gardner	4,226
R3	Oct 27		A	Norwich City	D	1-1	Elliott	14,189
R4	Nov 10		H	Wimbledon	L	1-2	Jensen	7,868

R3 won 3-1 on penalties, a.e.t.

							Appearances	
							Sub appearances	
							Goals	

Player columns (left to right):

Jaaskelainen J.A., Cox N.J., Phillips J.N., Todd A.J.J., Bergsson G., Fish M.A., Jensen C.W., Frandsen P., Blake N.A., Holdsworth D.C., Sellars S., Johansen M.B., Gunnlaugsson A.B., Whitlow M.W., Strong G., Taylor R., Taylor S.J., Gardner R.W., Gudjohnsen E.S., Branagan K.G., Aljofree H., Elliott R.J., Newsome J., Warhurst P., Hansen B.J.N., Banks S., Fullarton J.

Appearance/totals row:

| 34 | 42 | 14 | 18 | 15 | 36 | 44 | 44 | 11 | 22 | 22 | 40 | 22 | 27 | 4 | 32 | 0 | 19 | 8 | 3 | 1 | 14 | 6 | 17 | 1 | 9 | 1 |

League Table

	P	W	D	L	F	A	Pts
Sunderland	46	31	12	3	91	28	105
Bradford City	46	26	9	11	82	47	87
Ipswich Town	46	26	8	12	69	32	86
Birmingham City	46	23	12	11	66	37	81
Watford	46	21	14	11	65	56	77
Bolton Wanderers	46	20	16	10	78	59	76
Wolverhampton W	46	19	16	11	64	43	73
Sheffield United	46	18	13	15	71	66	67
Norwich City	46	15	17	14	62	61	62
Huddersfield Town	46	15	16	15	62	71	61
Grimsby Town	46	17	10	19	40	52	61
West Bromwich Albion	46	16	11	19	69	76	59
Barnsley	46	14	17	15	59	56	59
Crystal Palace	46	14	16	16	58	71	58
Tranmere Rovers	46	12	20	14	63	61	56
Stockport County	46	12	17	17	49	60	53
Swindon Town	46	13	11	22	59	81	50
Crewe Alexandra	46	12	12	22	54	78	48
Portsmouth	46	11	14	21	57	73	47
Queen's Park Rangers	46	12	11	23	52	61	47
Port Vale	46	13	8	25	45	75	47
Bury	46	10	17	19	35	60	47
Oxford United	46	10	14	22	48	71	44
Bristol City	46	9	15	22	57	80	42

1999-2000

Division One

Manager: C. Todd until 22 September 1999, S. Allardyce from 19 October 1999

Did you know that?

Gareth Farelly was brought in on loan from Everton by Sam Allardyce, and he scored just 82 seconds into his debut in a 2–1 win at Sheffield United.

Match No.	Date		Venue	Opponents	Result		Scorers	Attendance
1	Aug	7	A	Tranmere Rovers	D	0-0		7,674
2		14	H	Queen's Park Rangers	W	2-1	Holdsworth (pen), Gudjohnsen	13,019
3		21	A	Ipswich Town	L	0-1		17,696
4		28	H	Manchester City	L	0-1		21,671
5	Sep	5	H	Birmingham City	D	3-3	Frandsen 2, Holdsworth (pen)	11,668
6		11	A	Charlton Athletic	L	1-2	Johansen	19,028
7		18	H	Barnsley	D	2-2	Tuttle (own-goal), Gardner	14,621
8		25	H	Nottingham Forest	W	3-2	Gardner, Holdsworth (pen), Cox	14,978
9	Oct	2	A	Swindon Town	W	4-0	Cox, Holdsworth, Gardner, Elliott	6,711
10		9	A	Wolverhampton Wanderers	L	0-1		18,665
11		16	H	Huddersfield Town	W	1-0	Gardner	16,603
12		19	H	Crewe Alexandra	D	2-2	Gudjohnsen, Holdsworth	12,676
13		24	A	Norwich City	L	1-2	Gardner	12,468
14		27	A	Nottingham Forest	D	1-1	Gudjohnsen	15,572
15		30	H	Swindon Town	W	2-0	Taylor, Hansen	12,486
16	Nov	6	H	Crystal Palace	W	2-0	Gudjohnsen, Jensen	12,744
17		14	A	Sheffield United	W	2-1	Farrelly, Hansen	10,013
18		20	H	Grimsby Town	W	2-0	Hansen 2	12,415
19		23	A	Fulham	D	1-1	Gudjohnsen	9,642
20		27	A	Portsmouth	D	0-0		10,431
21	Dec	4	H	Tranmere Rovers	L	2-3	Gudjohnsen, Taylor	13,534
22		7	A	Blackburn Rovers	L	1-3	Elliott	21,046
23		18	A	Stockport County	L	0-1		13,285
24		28	H	West Bromwich Albion	D	1-1	Jensen	16,269
25	Jan	3	A	Walsall	L	0-2		6,873
26		15	A	Queen's Park Rangers	W	1-0	Jensen	11,396
27		22	H	Ipswich Town	D	1-1	Holdsworth	13,266
28	Feb	5	H	Blackburn Rovers	W	3-1	Bergsson, Johansen, Gudjohnsen	17,687
29		8	A	Port Vale	W	1-0	Gudjohnsen	5,092
30		12	A	Birmingham City	L	1-2	Johnston	18,426
31		22	A	Portsmouth	W	3-0	Taylor, Jensen, Elliott	12,672
32		26	A	Barnsley	D	1-1	Holdsworth (pen)	14,604
33	Mar	4	H	Charlton Athletic	L	0-2		13,788
34		7	A	Crystal Palace	D	0-0		15,236
35		11	H	Fulham	W	3-1	Holdsworth 2 (1 pen), Gudjohnsen	12,761
36		14	A	Stockport County	D	0-0		6,412
37		18	A	Grimsby Town	W	1-0	Bergsson	5,289
38		21	H	Sheffield United	W	2-0	Johnston, O'Kane	11,891
39		25	H	Port Vale	W	2-1	Gudjohnsen, Johnston	12,292
40	Apr	5	A	Manchester City	L	0-2		32,927
41		8	H	Walsall	W	4-3	Johansen (pen), Hansen 2, Phillips	11,777
42		15	A	West Bromwich Albion	D	4-4	Hansen, Gudjohnsen, Bergsson 2	12,802
43		22	A	Huddersfield Town	W	3-0	Hansen 2, Whitlow	16,404
44		29	A	Crewe Alexandra	W	3-1	Gudjohnsen, Holdsworth (pen), Jensen	8,015
45	May	3	A	Wolverhampton Wanderers	W	2-1	Jensen, Gudjohnsen	18,871
46		7	H	Norwich City	W	1-0	Holdsworth	17,987
							Appearances	
							Sub appearances	
							Goals	

Play-offs

	Date		Venue	Opponents	Result		Scorers	Attendance
SF1	May	14	H	Ipswich Town	D	2-2	Holdsworth, Gudjohnsen	18,814
SF2		17	A	Ipswich Town	L	3-5	Holdsworth 2, Johnston	21,543
SF2 a.e.t.								
							Appearances	
							Sub appearances	
							Goals	

FA Cup

	Date		Venue	Opponents	Result		Scorers	Attendance
R3	Dec	21	H	Cardiff City	W	1-0	Gudjohnsen	5,734
R4	Jan	8	A	Grimsby Town	W	2-0	Gudjohnsen, Hansen	4,270
R5		29	A	Cambridge United	W	3-1	Taylor 2, Gudjohnsen	7,523
R6	Feb	19	H	Charlton Athletic	W	1-0	Gudjohnsen	20,131
SF	Apr	2	N	Aston Villa	D	0-0		62,828
SF at Wembley; lost 1-4 on penalties, a.e.t.								
							Appearances	
							Sub appearances	
							Goals	

FL Cup

	Date		Venue	Opponents	Result		Scorers	Attendance
R1/1	Aug	10	A	Darlington	D	1-1	Frandsen	5,361
R1/2		24	H	Darlington	W	5-3	Gudjohnsen, Gardner, Taylor, Frandsen, Johansen (pen)	4,991
R2/1	Sep	14	A	Gillingham	W	4-1	Cox, Gudjohnsen 2, Bergsson	4,996
R2/2		21	H	Gillingham	W	2-0	Hansen, Holdsworth	3,673
R3	Oct	13	H	Derby County	W	2-1	Fish, Johansen	20,242
R4	Nov	30	H	Sheffield Wednesday	W	1-0	Elliott	12,543
R5	Dec	14	H	Wimbledon	W	2-1	Gudjohnsen, Johansen (pen)	9,463
SF1	Jan	12	H	Tranmere Rovers	L	0-1		13,303
SF2		26	A	Tranmere Rovers	L	0-3		15,834
							Appearances	
							Sub appearances	
							Goals	

462

League Table

	P	W	D	L	F	A	Pts
Charlton Athletic	46	27	10	9	79	45	91
Manchester City	46	26	11	9	78	40	89
Ipswich Town	46	25	12	9	71	42	87
Barnsley	46	24	10	12	88	67	82
Birmingham City	46	22	11	13	65	44	77
Bolton Wanderers	46	21	13	12	69	50	76
Wolverhampton W	46	21	11	14	64	48	74
Huddersfield Town	46	21	11	14	62	49	74
Fulham	46	17	16	13	49	41	67
Queen's Park Rangers	46	16	18	12	62	53	66
Blackburn Rovers	46	15	17	14	55	51	62
Norwich City	46	14	15	17	45	50	57
Tranmere Rovers	46	15	12	19	57	68	57
Nottingham Forest	46	14	14	18	53	55	56
Crystal Palace	46	13	15	18	57	67	54
Sheffield United	46	13	15	18	59	71	54
Stockport County	46	13	15	18	55	67	54
Portsmouth	46	13	12	21	55	66	51
Crewe Alexandra	46	14	9	23	46	67	51
Grimsby Town	46	13	12	21	41	67	51
West Bromwich Albion	46	10	19	17	43	60	49
Walsall	46	11	13	22	52	77	46
Port Vale	46	7	15	24	48	69	36
Swindon Town	46	8	12	26	38	77	36

Players

Banegan K.G., Cox N.J., Whitlow M.W., Frandsen P., Todd A.J.J., Strong G., Johansen M.B., Jensen C.W., Gudjohnsen E.S., Hansen B.J.N., Gardner R.W., Holdsworth D.C., Allonee H., Phillips J.N., Taylor R., Elliott R.J., Bergsson G., Warhurst P., Fish M.A., Jaaskelainen J.A., Farrelly G., O'Kane J.A., Holden D.T.J., Pass F., Holloway D., Ritchie P.S., Banks S., Johnston A., Kapelaun M., Nolan K.A.J., Simon L.R., Potter L.

Division One

Manager: S. Allardyce

Match No.	Date		Venue	Opponents		Result	Scorers	Attendance
1	Aug	12	H	Burnley	D	1-1	Frandsen (pen)	20,662
2		19	A	West Bromwich Albion	W	2-0	Rankin, Farrelly	17,316
3		26	H	Preston North End	W	2-0	Rankin, Ricketts	19,954
4		28	A	Tranmere Rovers	W	1-0	Whitlow	9,530
5	Sep	9	A	Huddersfield Town	W	3-2	Holdsworth, Ricketts 2	12,248
6		12	A	Grimsby Town	W	1-0	Ricketts	3,732
7		16	H	Portsmouth	W	2-0	Holdsworth, Ricketts	14,113
8		23	A	Blackburn Rovers	D	1-1	Hansen	23,660
9		30	H	Fulham	L	0-2		19,924
10	Oct	6	A	Gillingham	D	2-2	Hansen, O'Kane	9,311
11		14	H	Wolverhampton Wanderers	W	2-1	Holdsworth, Bergsson	15,585
12		17	H	Nottingham Forest	D	0-0		13,017
13		21	A	Stockport County	L	3-4	Marshall 2, Ricketts	8,266
14		24	A	Watford	L	0-1		11,799
15		28	H	Crystal Palace	D	3-3	Bergsson, Ricketts, Frandsen	12,872
16		31	H	Queen's Park Rangers	W	3-1	Bergsson, Elliott, Ricketts	10,180
17	Nov	4	A	Birmingham City	D	1-1	Ricketts	20,043
18		11	A	Barnsley	W	2-0	Ricketts, Gardner	13,406
19		18	A	Norwich City	W	2-0	Ricketts, Bergsson	15,224
20		25	A	Sheffield United	L	0-1		14,962
21	Dec	3	H	Watford	W	2-1	Gardner, Marshall	13,904
22		9	H	Crewe Alexandra	W	4-1	Frandsen, Marshall, Bergsson, Nolan	12,836
23		16	A	Wimbledon	W	1-0	Holdsworth	6,076
24		23	A	Burnley	W	2-0	Ricketts 2	18,552
25		26	H	Sheffield Wednesday	W	2-0	Holdsworth, Hendry	21,316
26		30	H	West Bromwich Albion	L	0-1		18,986
27	Jan	1	A	Preston North End	W	2-0	Farrelly, Ricketts	15,863
28		13	A	Tranmere Rovers	W	2-0	Hansen, Hill (own-goal)	15,493
29		20	A	Sheffield Wednesday	W	3-0	Gardner, Ricketts, Marshall	17,638
30	Feb	3	A	Queen's Park Rangers	D	1-1	Frandsen	10,283
31		10	H	Huddersfield Town	D	2-2	Bergsson, Frandsen	14,866
32		13	A	Portsmouth	W	2-1	Ricketts, Frandsen	11,337
33		20	H	Grimsby Town	D	2-2	Bergsson, Hansen	24,249
34		23	H	Blackburn Rovers	L	1-4	Ricketts	20,017
35	Mar	4	A	Fulham	D	1-1	Frandsen	16,468
36		10	H	Gillingham	D	3-3	Frandsen, Patterson (own-goal), Holdsworth	13,161
37		17	A	Nottingham Forest	W	2-0	Holdsworth, Farrelly	22,162
38		31	H	Wimbledon	D	2-2	Elliott, Hendry	14,562
39	Apr	3	A	Stockport County	D	1-1	Hendry	12,492
40		13	H	Birmingham City	D	2-2	Bergsson, Holdsworth	15,025
41		16	A	Crystal Palace	W	2-0	Marshall, Kolinko (own-goal)	16,268
42		18	A	Crewe Alexandra	L	1-2	Holdsworth	8,054
43		21	H	Norwich City	W	1-0	Holdsworth	17,967
44		28	A	Barnsley	W	1-0	Ricketts	13,979
45	May	1	A	Wolverhampton Wanderers	W	2-0	Holdsworth, Ricketts	16,242
46		6	H	Sheffield United	D	1-1	Holden	14,836

Appearances
Sub appearances
3 own-goals   Goals

Play-offs

	Date		Venue	Opponents		Result	Scorers	Attendance
SF1	May	13	A	West Bromwich Albion	D	2-2	Bergsson, Frandsen (pen)	18,167
SF2		17	H	West Bromwich Albion	W	3-0	Bergsson, Gardner, Ricketts	23,515
F		28	N	Preston North End	W	3-0	Farrelly, Ricketts, Gardner	54,328

Final at the Millennium Stadium, Cardiff

Appearances
Sub appearances
Goals

FA Cup

	Date		Venue	Opponents		Result	Scorers	Attendance
R3	Jan	6	H	Yeovil Town	W	2-1	O'Kane, Ricketts	11,161
R4		28	H	Scunthorpe United	W	5-1	Holdsworth 3, Nolan 2	11,737
R5	Feb	17	H	Blackburn Rovers	D	1-1	Ricketts	22,048
rep	Mar	7	A	Blackburn Rovers	L	0-3		20,318

Appearances
Sub appearances
Goals

FL Cup

	Date		Venue	Opponents		Result	Scorers	Attendance
R1/1	Aug	22	H	Macclesfield Town	W	1-0	Holdsworth	4,957
R1/2	Sep	5	A	Macclesfield Town	L	1-3	Ricketts	2,235

Appearances
Sub appearances
Goals

League Table

	P	W	D	L	F	A	Pts
Fulham	46	30	11	5	90	32	101
Blackburn Rovers	46	26	13	7	76	39	91
Bolton Wanderers	46	24	15	7	76	45	87
Preston North End	46	23	9	14	64	52	78
Birmingham City	46	23	9	14	59	48	78
West Bromwich Albion	46	21	11	14	60	52	74
Burnley	46	21	9	16	50	54	72
Wimbledon	46	17	18	11	71	50	69
Watford	46	20	9	17	76	67	69
Sheffield United	46	19	11	16	52	49	68
Nottingham Forest	46	20	8	18	55	53	68
Wolverhampton W	46	14	13	19	45	48	55
Gillingham	46	13	16	17	61	66	55
Crewe Alexandra	46	15	10	21	47	62	55
Norwich City	46	14	12	20	46	58	54
Barnsley	46	15	9	22	49	62	54
Sheffield Wednesday	46	15	8	23	52	71	53
Grimsby Town	46	14	10	22	43	62	52
Stockport County	46	11	18	17	58	65	51
Portsmouth	46	10	19	17	47	59	49
Crystal Palace	46	12	13	21	57	70	49
Huddersfield Town	46	11	15	20	48	57	48
Queen's Park Rangers	46	7	19	20	45	75	40
Tranmere Rovers	46	9	11	26	46	77	38

Premiership

Manager: S. Allardyce

Match No.	Date	Venue	Opponents	Result		Scorers	Attendance
1	Aug 18	A	Leicester City	W	5-0	Nolan 2, Ricketts, Frandsen 2	19,987
2	21	H	Middlesbrough	W	1-0	Ricketts	20,747
3	27	H	Liverpool	W	2-1	Ricketts, Holdsworth	27,205
4	Sep 8	A	Leeds United	D	0-0		40,153
5	15	H	Southampton	L	0-1		24,378
6	19	A	Blackburn Rovers	D	1-1	Wallace	25,949
7	22	A	Arsenal	D	1-1	Ricketts	38,014
8	29	H	Sunderland	L	0-2		24,520
9	Oct 13	H	Newcastle United	L	0-4		25,631
10	20	A	Manchester United	W	2-1	Nolan, Ricketts	67,559
11	27	A	Aston Villa	L	2-3	Ricketts 2	33,599
12	Nov 3	H	Everton	D	2-2	Frandsen, Ricketts	27,343
13	18	A	Ipswich Town	W	2-1	Bergsson, Ricketts	22,335
14	24	H	Fulham	D	0-0		23,848
15	Dec 3	H	Tottenham Hotspur	L	2-3	Ricketts, Wallace	32,971
16	8	A	Derby County	L	0-1		25,712
17	15	H	Charlton Athletic	D	0-0		20,834
18	23	A	Chelsea	L	1-5	Nolan	34,063
19	26	H	Leeds United	L	0-3		27,060
20	29	H	Leicester City	D	2-2	Nolan, Ricketts	23,037
21	Jan 1	A	Liverpool	D	1-1	Nolan	43,710
22	12	H	Chelsea	D	2-2	Ricketts, Nolan	23,891
23	19	A	Middlesbrough	D	1-1	Hansen	26,104
24	29	H	Manchester United	L	0-4		27,350
25	Feb 2	A	Newcastle United	L	2-3	Gardner, Southall	52,094
26	9	H	West Ham United	W	1-0	Gardner	24,342
27	23	A	Southampton	D	0-0		31,380
28	Mar 2	H	Blackburn Rovers	D	1-1	Wallace	27,203
29	5	A	Sunderland	L	0-1		43,011
30	16	H	Derby County	L	1-3	Gardner	25,893
31	23	A	Charlton Athletic	W	2-1	Djorkaeff 2	26,358
32	30	H	Aston Villa	W	3-2	Delaney (own-goal), Bobic, Nolan	24,600
33	Apr 1	A	Everton	L	1-3	N'Gotty	39,784
34	6	H	Ipswich Town	W	4-1	Bobic 3, Djorkaeff	25,817
35	20	H	Tottenham Hotspur	D	1-1	Holdsworth	25,817
36	23	A	Fulham	L	0-3		18,107
37	29	H	Arsenal	L	0-2		27,351
38	May 11	A	West Ham United	L	1-2	Djorkaeff	35,546

Appearances
Sub appearances
1 own-goal
Goals

FA Cup

R3	Jan 16	A	Stockport County	W	4-1	Bergsson, Fradin (own-goal), Pedersen, Ricketts	5,821
R4	Feb 5	A	Tottenham Hotspur	L	0-4		27,093

Appearances
Sub appearances
Goals

FL Cup

R2	Sep 11	H	Walsall	W	4-3	Ricketts, Holdsworth, Nishizawa, Pedersen	5,761
R3	Oct 8	H	Nottingham Forest	W	1-0	Wallace	6,881
R4	Nov 27	H	Southampton	D	2-2	Holdsworth (pen), Ricketts	8,404
R5	Dec 11	A	Tottenham Hotspur	L	0-6		28,430

R2 a.e.t. R4 won 6-5 on penalties, a.e.t.

Appearances
Sub appearances
Goals

Player columns (left to right):
Jaaskelainen L.A., Barness A., Charlton S.T., Warhurst P., Bergsson G., Whitlow M.W., Nolan K.A.J., Frandsen P., Ricketts M.B., Hansen B.J.N., Gardner R.W., Southall L.N., Marshall L.P., Pedersen H., Holdsworth D.C., Diawara D., Farrelly G., Richardson L.N., Wallace R.S., N'Gotty B., Johnson J., Banks S., Poole K., Hendry E.C.J., Bobic F., Tofting S., Djorkaeff Y., Espartero M., Konstantinidis K., Smith J., Holden D.T.I., Norris D.M., Nishizawa A., Vlander J., Taylor C.K.W., Buchanan W.B.

Appearance / line-up grid for the season (Bolton Wanderers)

League Table	P	W	D	L	F	A	Pts
Arsenal	38	26	9	3	79	36	87
Liverpool	38	24	8	6	67	30	80
Manchester United	38	24	5	9	87	45	77
Newcastle United	38	21	8	9	74	52	71
Leeds United	38	18	12	8	53	37	66
Chelsea	38	17	13	8	66	38	64
West Ham United	38	15	8	15	48	57	53
Aston Villa	38	12	14	12	46	47	50
Tottenham Hotspur	38	14	8	16	49	53	50
Blackburn Rovers	38	12	10	16	55	51	46
Southampton	38	12	9	17	46	54	45
Middlesbrough	38	12	9	17	35	47	45
Fulham	38	10	14	14	36	44	44
Charlton Athletic	38	10	14	14	38	49	44
Everton	38	11	10	17	45	57	43
Bolton Wanderers	38	9	13	16	44	62	40
Sunderland	38	10	10	18	29	51	40
Ipswich Town	38	9	9	20	41	64	36
Derby County	38	8	6	24	33	63	30
Leicester City	38	5	13	20	30	64	28

Premiership

Manager: S. Allardyce

Match No.	Date	Venue	Opponents	Result		Scorers	Attendance
1	Aug 17	A	Fulham	L	1-4	Ricketts (pen)	16,338
2	24	H	Charlton Athletic	L	1-2	Djorkaeff	21,753
3	Sep 1	W	Aston Villa	W	1-0	Ricketts (pen)	22,501
4	11	A	Manchester United	W	1-0	Nolan	67,623
5	14	H	Liverpool	L	2-3	Gardner, Campo	27,328
6	21	A	Arsenal	L	1-2	Farrelly	37,974
7	28	H	Southampton	D	1-1	Djorkaeff	22,692
8	Oct 5	A	Middlesbrough	L	0-2		31,005
9	20	A	Tottenham Hotspur	L	1-3	Djorkaeff	35,909
10	28	H	Sunderland	D	1-1	Babb (own-goal)	23,036
11	Nov 2	A	Birmingham City	L	1-3	Okocha	27,224
12	9	H	West Bromwich Albion	D	1-1	Frandsen	23,630
13	17	A	Leeds United	W	4-2	Pedersen 2, Djorkaeff, Ricketts (pen)	36,627
14	23	H	Chelsea	D	1-1	Pedersen	25,076
15	30	A	Manchester City	L	0-2		34,860
16	Dec 7	H	Blackburn Rovers	D	1-1	Okocha	24,556
17	16	H	Leeds United	L	0-3		23,201
18	21	A	West Ham United	D	1-1	Ricketts	34,892
19	26	H	Newcastle United	W	4-3	Ricketts 2, Okocha, Gardner	27,314
20	28	A	Everton	D	0-0		39,480
21	Jan 1	A	Aston Villa	L	0-2		31,838
22	11	H	Fulham	D	0-0		25,156
23	18	A	Charlton Athletic	D	1-1	Djorkaeff	26,057
24	22	A	Newcastle United	L	0-1		52,005
25	28	H	Everton	L	1-2	Bergsson	25,119
26	Feb 1	H	Birmingham City	W	4-2	Cunningham (own-goal), Djorkaeff, Pedersen, Facey	24,288
27	8	A	West Bromwich Albion	D	1-1	Pedersen	26,933
28	22	H	Manchester United	D	1-1	N'Gotty	27,409
29	Mar 8	A	Liverpool	L	0-2		41,462
30	15	A	Sunderland	W	2-0	Okocha, Pedersen	42,124
31	24	H	Tottenham Hotspur	W	1-0	Okocha (pen)	23,084
32	Apr 5	A	Manchester City	W	2-0	Pedersen, Campo	26,919
33	12	A	Chelsea	L	0-1		39,852
34	19	H	West Ham United	W	1-0	Okocha	27,160
35	21	A	Blackburn Rovers	D	0-0		28,862
36	26	H	Arsenal	D	2-2	Djorkaeff, Keown (own-goal)	27,253
37	May 3	A	Southampton	D	0-0		30,951
38	11	H	Middlesbrough	W	2-1	Frandsen, Okocha	27,241

	Appearances
	Sub appearances
3 own-goals	Goals

FA Cup

	Date	Venue	Opponents	Result		Scorers	Attendance
R3	Jan 4	H	Sunderland	D	1-1	Ricketts	10,123
rep	14	A	Sunderland	L	0-2		14,550

Replay a.e.t.

	Appearances
	Sub appearances
	Goals

FL Cup

	Date	Venue	Opponents	Result		Scorers	Attendance
R2	Oct 2	H	Bury	L	0-1		12,621

	Appearances
	Sub appearances

Player columns (left to right):

Jaaskelainen J.A · Mendy B · Charlton S.T · Fransden P · Bergsson G · N'Gotty B · Nolan K.A.J · Djorkaeff Y · Ricketts M.B · Obucha A.A · Gardner R.W · Pedersen H · Warhurst P · Whitlow M.W · Barness A · Walters J.R · Holdsworth D.C · Campo R.L · Livesey D.R · Farrelly G · Tofting S · Johnson J · Facey D.M · Bulent A · Balasita V.S · Aicha P-Y · Lanille F · Poole K · Holdsworth D.G · Smith J · Armstrong C.P · Hunt N.B

Appearance totals row:

38 20 27 34 31 23 15 36 13 26 31 31 5 14 21 0 5 28 0 6 2 0 1 0 1 0 10 0 0 0 0 0

Premiership

Manager: S. Allardyce

Match No.	Date		Venue	Opponents	Result		Scorers	Attendance
1	Aug	16	A	Manchester United	L	0-4		67,647
2		23	H	Blackburn Rovers	D	2-2	Davies, Djorkaeff (pen)	27,423
3		26	A	Portsmouth	L	0-4		20,113
4		30	H	Charlton Athletic	D	0-0		23,098
5	Sep	13	H	Middlesbrough	W	2-0	N'Gotty, Davies	26,419
6		20	A	Newcastle United	D	0-0		52,014
7		27	H	Wolverhampton Wanderers	D	1-1	Davies	27,043
8	Oct	5	A	Aston Villa	D	1-1	Nolan	30,229
9		18	A	Manchester City	L	2-6	Campo, Nolan	47,101
10		25	H	Birmingham City	L	0-1		25,023
11	Nov	1	A	Tottenham Hotspur	W	1-0	Nolan	35,191
12		8	H	Southampton	D	0-0		25,619
13		22	A	Leeds United	W	2-0	Davies, Giannakopoulos	36,558
14		29	H	Everton	W	2-0	Frandsen, Djorkaeff	27,350
15	Dec	6	A	Fulham	L	1-2	Davies	14,393
16		13	A	Chelsea	W	2-1	N'Gotty, Terry (own-goal)	40,491
17		20	H	Arsenal	D	1-1	Pedersen	28,003
18		26	A	Liverpool	L	1-3	Pedersen	42,987
19		28	H	Leicester City	D	2-2	Thatcher (own-goal), Campo	28,353
20	Jan	7	A	Manchester United	L	1-2	G. Neville (own-goal)	27,668
21		10	A	Blackburn Rovers	W	4-3	Nolan 2, Giannakopoulos, Djorkaeff	23,538
22		17	H	Portsmouth	W	1-0	Davies	26,558
23		31	A	Charlton Athletic	W	2-1	Nolan, Pedersen	26,249
24	Feb	7	H	Liverpool	D	2-2	Hunt, Djorkaeff	27,552
25		10	A	Leicester City	D	1-1	Walker (own-goal)	26,674
26		21	H	Manchester City	L	1-3	Nolan	27,301
27	Mar	6	A	Birmingham City	L	0-2		28,003
28		13	H	Chelsea	L	0-2		26,717
29		20	A	Arsenal	L	1-2	Campo	38,053
30		28	H	Newcastle United	W	1-0	Pedersen	27,360
31	Apr	3	A	Middlesbrough	L	0-2		30,107
32		10	A	Aston Villa	D	2-2	Pedersen, Davies	26,374
33		12	A	Wolverhampton Wanderers	W	2-1	Pedersen, Davies	28,695
34		17	H	Tottenham Hotspur	W	2-0	Campo, Pedersen	26,440
35		24	A	Southampton	W	2-1	Nolan, Davies	31,712
36	May	2	H	Leeds United	W	4-1	Djorkaeff 2, Harte (own-goal), Nolan	27,420
37		8	A	Everton	W	2-1	Djorkaeff 2	40,190
38		15	H	Fulham	L	0-2		27,383

Appearances
Sub appearances
4 own-goals   Goals

FA Cup

R3	Jan	3	A	Tranmere Rovers	D	1-1	Nolan	10,587
rep		13	H	Tranmere Rovers	L	1-2	Shakes	8,759

Replay a.e.t.

Appearances
Sub appearances
Goals

FL Cup

R2	Sep	24	H	Walsall	W	3-1	Nolan, Jardel 2	5,680
R3	Oct	28	H	Gillingham	W	2-0	Pedersen, Giannakopoulos	5,646
R4	Dec	3	A	Liverpool	W	3-2	Okocha, Djorkaeff (pen), Jardel	33,185
R5		16	H	Southampton	W	1-0	Pedersen	13,957
SF1	Jan	21	H	Aston Villa	W	5-2	N'Gotty, Nolan, Okocha 2, Giannakopoulos	16,302
SF2		27	A	Aston Villa	L	0-2		36,883
F	Feb	29	N	Middlesbrough	L	1-2	Davies	72,634

R5 a.e.t.

Final at the Millennium Stadium, Cardiff.

Appearances
Sub appearances
Goals

Ribeiro MJ de A played as Jardel.

League Table

	P	W	D	L	F	A	Pts
Arsenal	38	26	12	0	73	26	90
Chelsea	38	24	7	7	67	30	79
Manchester United	38	23	6	9	64	35	75
Liverpool	38	16	12	10	55	37	60
Newcastle United	38	13	17	8	52	40	56
Aston Villa	38	15	11	12	48	44	56
Charlton Athletic	38	14	11	13	51	51	53
Bolton Wanderers	38	14	11	13	48	56	53
Fulham	38	14	10	14	52	46	52
Birmingham City	38	12	14	12	43	48	50
Middlesbrough	38	13	9	16	44	52	48
Southampton	38	12	11	15	44	45	47
Portsmouth	38	12	9	17	47	54	45
Tottenham Hotspur	38	13	6	19	47	57	45
Blackburn Rovers	38	12	8	18	51	59	44
Manchester City	38	9	14	15	55	54	41
Everton	38	9	12	17	45	57	39
Leicester City	38	6	15	17	48	65	33
Leeds United	38	8	9	21	40	79	33
Wolverhampton W	38	7	12	19	38	77	33

Premiership

Manager: S. Allardyce

Match No.	Date	Venue	Opponents		Result	Scorers	Attendance
1	Aug 14	H	Charlton Athletic	W	4-1	Okocha 2, Pedersen 2	24,100
2	21	A	Fulham	L	0-2		17,541
3	25	A	Southampton	W	2-1	Pedersen, Okocha (pen)	30,713
4	29	H	Liverpool	W	1-0	Davies	27,880
5	Sep 11	H	Manchester United	D	2-2	Nolan, Ferdinand	27,766
6	18	A	Arsenal	D	2-2	Pedersen, Jaidi	37,010
7	25	H	Birmingham City	D	1-1	Jaidi	23,692
8	Oct 2	A	West Bromwich Albion	L	1-2	Giannakopoulos	23,849
9	16	H	Crystal Palace	W	1-0	Davies	25,501
10	23	A	Tottenham Hotspur	W	2-1	Pedersen, Jaidi	36,025
11	31	H	Newcastle United	W	2-1	Davies, Diouf	27,196
12	Nov 7	A	Middlesbrough	D	1-1	Pedersen	29,656
13	13	H	Aston Villa	L	1-2	Diouf	25,779
14	20	A	Chelsea	D	2-2	Davies, Jaidi	42,203
15	27	H	Portsmouth	L	0-1		25,008
16	Dec 4	H	Everton	L	2-3	Davies 2	35,929
17	11	A	Norwich City	L	2-3	Okocha (pen), Hierro	23,549
18	18	H	Manchester City	L	0-1		27,274
19	26	A	Manchester United	L	0-2		67,867
20	28	H	Blackburn Rovers	L	0-1		27,038
21	Jan 1	H	West Bromwich Albion	D	1-1	Diouf	25,205
22	4	A	Birmingham City	W	2-1	Nolan, Diouf	27,177
23	15	H	Arsenal	W	1-0	Giannakopoulos	27,514
24	24	A	Blackburn Rovers	W	1-0	Diouf	20,056
25	Feb 1	H	Tottenham Hotspur	W	3-1	Davies, Ben Haim, Diouf (pen)	24,780
26	5	A	Crystal Palace	W	1-0	Nolan	23,163
27	12	H	Middlesbrough	D	0-0		24,322
28	27	A	Newcastle United	L	1-2	Giannakopoulos	50,430
29	Mar 7	A	Manchester City	W	1-0	Diouf	43,050
30	19	H	Norwich City	W	1-0	Giannakopoulos	25,081
31	Apr 2	A	Liverpool	L	0-1		43,755
32	9	H	Fulham	W	3-1	Nolan, Okocha (pen), Giannakopoulos	25,493
33	16	A	Charlton Athletic	W	2-1	Okocha (pen), Diouf	26,708
34	19	H	Southampton	D	1-1	Giannakopoulos	25,125
35	23	A	Aston Villa	D	1-1	Speed	36,053
36	30	H	Chelsea	L	0-2		27,653
37	May 7	A	Portsmouth	D	1-1	Diouf	20,188
38	15	H	Everton	W	3-2	Davies, Giannakopoulos, Jaidi	27,701
						Appearances	
						Sub appearances	
						Goals	

FA Cup

	Date	Venue	Opponents		Result	Scorers	Attendance
R3	Jan 8	A	Ipswich Town	W	3-1	Pedersen 2, Giannakopoulos	20,080
R4	30	A	Oldham Athletic	W	1-0	Vaz Te	12,029
R5	Feb 19	H	Fulham	W	1-0	Davies	16,151
R6	Mar 12	H	Arsenal	L	0-1		23,523
						Appearances	
						Sub appearances	
						Goals	

FL Cup

	Date	Venue	Opponents		Result	Scorers	Attendance
R2	Sep 21	A	Yeovil Town	W	2-0	Julio Cesar, Pedersen	8,047
R3	Oct 27	H	Tottenham Hotspur	L	3-4	King (own-goal), Okocha (pen), Ferdinand	18,037
R3 a.e.t.						Appearances	
						Sub appearances	
				1 own-goal		Goals	

Santos-Correia JC played as Julio Cesar.

League Table

	P	W	D	L	F	A	Pts
Chelsea	38	29	8	1	72	15	95
Arsenal	38	25	8	5	87	36	83
Manchester United	38	22	11	5	58	26	77
Everton	38	18	7	13	45	46	61
Liverpool	38	17	7	14	52	41	58
Bolton Wanderers	38	16	10	12	49	44	58
Middlesbrough	38	14	13	11	53	46	55
Manchester City	38	13	13	12	47	39	52
Tottenham Hotspur	38	14	10	14	47	41	52
Aston Villa	38	12	11	15	45	52	47
Charlton Athletic	38	12	10	16	42	58	46
Birmingham City	38	11	12	15	40	46	45
Fulham	38	12	8	18	52	60	44
Newcastle United	38	10	14	14	47	57	44
Blackburn Rovers	38	9	15	14	32	43	42
Portsmouth	38	10	9	19	43	59	39
West Bromwich Albion	38	6	16	16	36	61	34
Crystal Palace	38	7	12	19	41	62	33
Norwich City	38	7	12	19	42	77	33
Southampton	38	6	14	18	45	66	32

Premiership

Manager: S. Allardyce

Match No.	Date	Venue	Opponents	Result		Scorers	Attendance
1	Aug 13	A	Aston Villa	D	2-2	Campo, Davies	33,263
2	21	H	Everton	L	0-1		25,608
3	24	H	Newcastle United	W	2-0	Diouf, Giannakopoulos	25,904
4	27	A	West Ham United	W	2-1	Campo, Nolan	31,629
5	Sep 11	H	Blackburn Rovers	D	0-0		24,405
6	18	A	Manchester City	W	1-0	Speed (pen)	43,137
7	24	H	Portsmouth	W	1-0	Nolan	23,134
8	Oct 2	A	Wigan Athletic	L	1-2	Jaidi	20,553
9	15	A	Chelsea	L	1-5	Giannakopoulos	41,775
10	23	H	West Bromwich Albion	W	2-0	Nolan, Nakata	25,151
11	29	A	Charlton Athletic	W	1-0	Nolan	26,175
12	Nov 7	H	Tottenham Hotspur	W	1-0	Nolan	24,634
13	27	A	Fulham	L	1-2	Legwinski (own-goal)	19,768
14	Dec 3	H	Arsenal	W	2-0	Giannakopoulos, Diagne-Faye	26,792
15	10	H	Aston Villa	D	1-1	Diouf	23,646
16	17	A	Everton	W	4-0	Davies, Giannakopoulos 2, Speed (pen)	34,500
17	26	A	Sunderland	D	0-0		32,232
18	31	A	Manchester United	L	1-4	Speed	67,858
19	Jan 2	H	Liverpool	D	2-2	Jaidi, Diouf	27,604
20	14	A	Blackburn Rovers	D	0-0		18,180
21	21	H	Manchester City	W	2-0	Nolan, Borgetti	26,466
22	Feb 1	A	Portsmouth	D	1-1	Fadiga	19,128
23	4	H	Wigan Athletic	D	1-1	Giannakopoulos	25,345
24	11	A	Arsenal	D	1-1	Nolan	38,193
25	26	H	Fulham	W	2-1	Hulguson (own-goal), Nolan	23,104
26	Mar 4	A	Newcastle United	L	1-3	Davies	52,012
27	11	H	West Ham United	W	4-1	Speed, Pedersen, Giannakopoulos 2	24,461
28	18	H	Sunderland	W	2-0	Nolan, Davies	23,568
29	26	A	Middlesbrough	L	3-4	Jaidi, Okocha, Giannakopoulos	25,971
30	Apr 1	H	Manchester United	L	1-2	Davies	27,718
31	4	A	Birmingham City	L	0-1		26,493
32	9	A	Liverpool	L	0-1		44,194
33	15	H	Chelsea	L	0-2		27,266
34	17	A	West Bromwich Albion	D	0-0		23,181
35	22	H	Charlton Athletic	W	4-1	Davies 2, Vaz Te, Borgetti	24,713
36	30	A	Tottenham Hotspur	L	0-1		36,179
37	May 3	H	Middlesbrough	D	1-1	Vaz Te	22,733
38	7	H	Birmingham City	W	1-0	Vaz Te	26,275
						Appearances	
						Sub appearances	
					2 own-goals	Goals	

FA Cup

	Date	Venue	Opponents	Result		Scorers	Attendance
R3	Jan 7	A	Watford	W	3-0	Vaz Te, Giannakopoulos, Borgetti	13,239
R4	28	H	Arsenal	W	1-0	Giannakopoulos	13,326
R5	Feb 18	H	West Ham United	D	0-0		17,120
rep	Mar 15	A	West Ham United	L	1-2	Davies	24,685
R5 replay a.e.t.						Appearances	
						Sub appearances	
						Goals	

FL Cup

	Date	Venue	Opponents	Result		Scorers	Attendance
R3	Oct 26	H	West Ham United	W	1-0	Borgetti	10,927
R4	Nov 30	H	Leicester City	W	2-1	Vaz Te, Borgetti	13,067
R5	Dec 20	A	Wigan Athletic	L	0-2		13,401
R4 a.e.t.						Appearances	
						Sub appearances	
						Goals	

UEFA Cup

	Date	Venue	Opponents	Result		Scorers	Attendance
R1/1	Sep 15	H	Lokomotiv Plovdiv		2-1	Diouf, Borgetti	19,723
R1/2	29	A	Lokomotiv Plovdiv		2-1	Tunchev (own-goal), Nolan	14,000
Gp	Oct 20	A	Besiktas		1-1	Borgetti	17,027
Gp	Nov 3	H	Zenit St Petersburg		1-0	Nolan	15,905
Gp	24	A	Vitoria Guimaraes		1-1	Vaz Te	20,000
Gp	Dec 14	H	Sevilla		1-1	N'Gotty	15,623
R3/1	Feb 15	H	Olympique Marseille		0-0		19,288
R3/2	23	A	Olympique Marseille		1-2	Giannakopoulos	38,351
						Appearances	
						Sub appearances	
					1 own-goal	Goals	

Column headers (player names, read vertically):
Jaaskelainen J.A., Hunt N.B., Gardner R.W., Campo R.I., Jaidi R.B.A., Ben Haim T., Nolan K.A.J., Speed G.A., Davies K.C., Pedersen H., Diouf E.H.O., Okocha A.A., Giannakopoulos S., Vaz Te R.J., Diagne-Faye A., Borgetti J.F., N'Gotty B., Nakata H., O'Brien J.M., Fernandes F., Fadiga K., Djetou M.O., Jansen M.B., Fojut J., Ashton S.S., Sissons R.M.J., Walker I.M.

Appearance totals row:
38, 12, 27, 8, 15, 32, 35, 29, 37, 15, 17, 18, 29, 6, 23, 5, 27, 14, 22, 0, 5, 1, 3, 0, 0, 0, 0

League Table

	P	W	D	L	F	A	Pts
Chelsea	38	29	4	5	72	22	91
Manchester United	38	25	8	5	72	34	83
Liverpool	38	25	7	6	57	25	82
Arsenal	38	20	7	11	68	31	67
Tottenham Hotspur	38	18	11	9	53	38	65
Blackburn Rovers	38	19	6	13	51	42	63
Newcastle United	38	17	7	14	47	42	58
Bolton Wanderers	38	15	11	12	49	41	56
West Ham United	38	16	7	15	52	55	55
Wigan Athletic	38	15	6	17	45	52	51
Everton	38	14	8	16	34	49	50
Fulham	38	14	6	18	48	58	48
Charlton Athletic	38	13	8	17	41	55	47
Middlesbrough	38	12	9	17	48	58	45
Manchester City	38	13	4	21	43	48	43
Aston Villa	38	10	12	16	42	55	42
Portsmouth	38	10	8	20	37	62	38
Birmingham City	38	8	10	20	28	50	34
West Bromwich Albion	38	7	9	22	31	58	30
Sunderland	38	3	6	29	26	69	15

2006-07

Premiership

Manager: S. Allardyce until 29 April 2007, S. Lee from 1 May 2007

Match No.	Date		Venue	Opponents	Result		Scorers	Attendance
1	Aug	19	H	Tottenham Hotspur	W	2-0	Campo, Davies	22,899
2		23	A	Fulham	D	1-1	Diouf (pen)	18,559
3		26	A	Charlton Athletic	L	0-2		23,638
4	Sep	9	H	Watford	W	1-0	Speed (pen)	21,140
5		16	H	Middlesbrough	D	0-0		21,164
6		25	A	Portsmouth	W	1-0	Nolan	19,105
7		30	H	Liverpool	W	2-0	Campo, Speed	25,061
8	Oct	15	A	Newcastle United	W	2-1	Diouf 2	48,145
9		22	A	Blackburn Rovers	W	1-0	Campo	27,662
10		28	H	Manchester United	L	0-4		27,229
11	Nov	4	H	Wigan Athletic	L	0-1		21,255
12		11	A	Sheffield United	D	2-2	Davies, Diouf	28,294
13		18	A	Everton	L	0-1		34,417
14		25	H	Arsenal	W	3-1	Diagne-Faye, Anelka 2	24,409
15		29	H	Chelsea	L	0-1		23,559
16	Dec	2	A	Reading	L	0-1		23,556
17		9	H	West Ham United	W	4-0	Davies 2, Diouf, Anelka	22,283
18		16	A	Aston Villa	W	1-0	Speed (pen)	27,450
19		23	A	Manchester City	W	2-0	Anelka 2	40,157
20		26	H	Newcastle United	W	2-1	Ramage (own-goal), Anelka	26,437
21		30	H	Portsmouth	W	3-2	Campo, Diagne-Faye, Anelka	22,447
22	Jan	1	A	Liverpool	L	0-3		41,370
23		13	H	Manchester City	D	0-0		22,334
24		20	A	Middlesbrough	L	1-5	Nolan	24,614
25		31	H	Charlton Athletic	D	1-1	Pedersen	22,357
26	Feb	3	A	Watford	W	1-0	Anelka	18,722
27		11	H	Fulham	W	2-1	Nolan, Speed (pen)	24,919
28		25	A	Tottenham Hotspur	L	1-4	Speed (pen)	35,747
29	Mar	4	H	Blackburn Rovers	L	1-2	Anelka	21,743
30		17	A	Manchester United	L	1-4	Speed (pen)	76,058
31		31	H	Sheffield United	W	1-0	Davies	24,312
32	Apr	7	A	Wigan Athletic	W	3-1	Anelka, Teimourian 2	18,610
33		9	H	Everton	D	1-1	Davies	25,179
34		14	A	Arsenal	L	1-2	Anelka	60,101
35		21	H	Reading	L	1-3	Shorey (own-goal)	23,533
36		28	A	Chelsea	D	2-2	Davies, Michalik	41,105
37	May	5	A	West Ham United	L	1-3	Speed	34,404
38		13	H	Aston Villa	D	2-2	Speed, Davies	26,255

Appearances
Sub appearances
2 own-goals   Goals

FA Cup

	Date		Venue	Opponents	Result		Scorers	Attendance
R3	Jan	6	A	Doncaster Rovers	W	4-0	Davies, Tal, Teimourian 2	14,297
R4		28	A	Arsenal	D	1-1	Nolan	59,778
rep	Feb	14	H	Arsenal	L	1-3	Meite	21,088

R4 replay a.e.t.

Appearances
Sub appearances
Goals

FL Cup

	Date		Venue	Opponents	Result		Scorers	Attendance
R2	Sep	19	A	Walsall	W	3-1	Campo, Nolan, Anelka	6,243
R3	Oct	25	A	Charlton Athletic	L	0-1		10,788

Appearances
Sub appearances
Goals

Player columns (left to right):
Jaaskelainen J.A. · Hunt N.B. · Fortune Q. · Campo R.I. · Meite A. · Ben Haim T. · Nolan K.A.J. · Speed G.A. · Davies K.C. · Vaz Te R.J. · Diouf E.H.D. · Giannakopoulos S. · Diagne-Faye A. · Pedersen H. · Tal I. · Anelka N. · Tamoudrani A. · Smith J.A.R. · Gardner R.W. · Thompson D.A. · Michalik L. · Sinclair J.A. · Martin C. · Walker I.M. · Augustyin B.S. · Fojut J.

League Table

	P	W	D	L	F	A	Pts
Manchester United	38	28	5	5	83	27	89
Chelsea	38	24	11	3	64	24	83
Liverpool	38	20	8	10	57	27	68
Arsenal	38	19	11	8	63	35	68
Tottenham Hotspur	38	17	9	12	57	54	60
Everton	38	15	13	10	52	36	58
Bolton Wanderers	38	16	8	14	47	52	56
Reading	38	16	7	15	52	47	55
Portsmouth	38	14	12	12	45	42	54
Blackburn Rovers	38	15	7	16	52	54	52
Aston Villa	38	11	17	10	43	41	50
Middlesbrough	38	12	10	16	44	49	46
Newcastle United	38	11	10	17	38	47	43
Manchester City	38	11	9	18	29	44	42
West Ham United	38	12	5	21	35	59	41
Fulham	38	8	15	15	38	60	39
Wigan Athletic	38	10	8	20	37	59	38
Sheffield United	38	10	8	20	32	55	38
Charlton Athletic	38	8	10	20	34	60	34
Watford	38	5	13	20	29	59	28

Premiership

Manager: S. Lee until 9 October 2007, G. Megson from 24 October 2007

Did you know that?

In December 2007 the Wanderers defeated Wigan Athletic 4–1 at the Reebok Stadium to register their 100th Premier League win. Nicolas Anelka missed a 24th-minute penalty but made up for it with an 89th-minute goal to secure the best win of the season.

Match No.	Date	Venue	Opponents	Result		Scorers	Attendance
1	Aug 11	H	Newcastle United	L	1-3	Anelka	25,414
2	15	A	Fulham	L	1-2	Helguson	21,102
3	18	A	Portsmouth	L	1-3	Anelka	17,108
4	25	H	Reading	W	3-0	Speed, Anelka, Braaten	20,023
5	Sep 1	H	Everton	L	1-2	Anelka	22,064
6	15	A	Birmingham City	L	0-1		28,124
7	23	H	Tottenham Hotspur	D	1-1	Campo	20,308
8	29	A	Derby County	D	1-1	Anelka	31,503
9	Oct 7	H	Chelsea	L	0-1		20,059
10	20	A	Arsenal	L	0-2		59,442
11	28	H	Aston Villa	D	1-1	Anelka	18,413
12	Nov 4	A	West Ham United	D	1-1	Nolan	33,867
13	11	H	Middlesbrough	D	0-0		17,624
14	24	H	Manchester United	W	1-0	Anelka	25,028
15	Dec 2	A	Liverpool	L	0-4		43,270
16	9	H	Wigan Athletic	W	4-1	Scharner (own-goal), Nolan, Davies, Anelka	20,309
17	15	A	Manchester City	L	2-4	Nolan, Diouf	40,506
18	22	H	Birmingham City	W	3-0	Anelka 2, Diouf	19,111
19	26	A	Everton	L	0-2		38,918
20	29	A	Sunderland	L	1-3	Diouf	42,058
21	Jan 2	H	Derby County	W	1-0	Giannakopoulos	17,014
22	13	H	Blackburn Rovers	L	1-2	Nolan	18,315
23	19	A	Newcastle United	D	0-0		52,250
24	29	A	Fulham	D	0-0		17,732
25	Feb 2	A	Reading	W	2-0	Nolan, Helguson	21,893
26	9	H	Portsmouth	L	0-1		18,544
27	24	A	Blackburn Rovers	L	1-4	Davies	23,995
28	Mar 2	H	Liverpool	L	1-3	Cohen	24,004
29	16	H	Wigan Athletic	L	0-1		17,055
30	19	A	Manchester United	L	0-2		75,476
31	22	H	Manchester City	D	0-0		22,633
32	29	H	Arsenal	L	2-3	Taylor 2	22,431
33	Apr 5	A	Aston Villa	L	0-4		37,773
34	12	H	West Ham United	W	1-0	Davies	23,043
35	19	A	Middlesbrough	W	1-0	McCann	25,037
36	26	A	Tottenham Hotspur	D	1-1	Giannakopoulos	36,176
37	May 3	H	Sunderland	W	2-0	Diouf, Murphy (own-goal)	25,053
38	11	A	Chelsea	D	1-1	Taylor	41,755

		Appearances
		Sub appearances
	2 own-goals	Goals

FA Cup

	Date	Venue	Opponents	Result		Scorers	Attendance
R3	Jan 5	H	Sheffield United	L	0-1		15,286

	Appearances
	Sub appearances

FL Cup

	Date	Venue	Opponents	Result		Scorers	Attendance
R3	Sep 26	A	Fulham	W	2-1	Guthrie, Giannakopoulos	10,500
R4	Oct 31	H	Manchester City	L	0-1		15,510
R3 a.e.t.							

	Appearances
	Sub appearances
	Goals

UEFA Cup

	Date	Venue	Opponents	Result		Scorers	Attendance
R1/1	Sep 20	A	Rabotnicki Kometal	D	1-1	Meite	8,500
R1/2	Oct 4	H	Rabotnicki Kometal	W	1-0	Anelka	18,932
Gp	25	H	Sporting Braga	D	1-1	Diouf	10,848
Gp	Nov 8	A	Bayern Munich	D	2-2	Davies, Gardner	66,000
Gp	29	H	Aris Salonika	D	1-1	Giannakopoulos	10,229
Gp	Dec 6	A	Red Star Belgrade	W	1-0	McCann	30,689
R3/1	Feb 14	H	Atletico Madrid	W	1-0	Diouf	26,163
R3/2	21	A	Atletico Madrid	D	0-0		27,590
R4/1	Mar 6	H	Sporting Lisbon	D	1-1	McCann	25,664
R4/2	13	A	Sporting Lisbon	L	0-1		22,031

	Appearances
	Sub appearances
	Goals

League Table

	P	W	D	L	F	A	Pts
Manchester United	38	27	6	5	80	22	87
Chelsea	38	25	10	3	65	26	85
Arsenal	38	24	11	3	74	31	83
Liverpool	38	21	13	4	67	28	76
Everton	38	19	8	11	55	33	65
Aston Villa	38	16	12	10	71	51	60
Blackburn Rovers	38	15	13	10	50	48	58
Portsmouth	38	16	9	13	48	40	57
Manchester City	38	15	10	13	45	53	55
West Ham United	38	13	10	15	42	50	49
Tottenham Hotspur	38	11	13	14	66	61	46
Newcastle United	38	11	10	17	45	65	43
Middlesbrough	38	10	12	16	43	53	42
Wigan Athletic	38	10	10	18	34	51	40
Sunderland	38	11	6	21	36	59	39
Bolton Wanderers	38	9	10	19	36	54	37
Fulham	38	8	12	18	38	60	36
Reading	38	10	6	22	41	66	36
Birmingham City	38	8	11	19	46	62	35
Derby County	38	1	8	29	20	89	11

Match No.	Date	Venue	Opponents	Result		Scorers	Attendance
1	Aug 16	H	Stoke City	W	3-1	Steinsson, K. Davies, Elmander	22,717
2	23	A	Newcastle United	L	0-1		47,711
3	30	H	West Bromwich Albion	D	0-0		20,387
4	Sep 13	A	Fulham	L	1-2	K. Davies	23,656
5	20	H	Arsenal	L	1-3	K. Davies	22,694
6	27	A	Manchester United	L	0-2		75,484
7	Oct 5	A	West Ham United	W	3-1	Cahill, K. Davies, Taylor	33,715
8	18	H	Blackburn Rovers	D	0-0		24,778
9	26	A	Tottenham Hotspur	L	0-2		35,507
10	29	H	Everton	L	0-1		21,692
11	Nov 2	H	Manchester City	W	2-0	Gardner, Dunne (own-goal)	21,095
12	8	A	Hull City	W	1-0	Taylor	24,903
13	15	H	Liverpool	L	0-2		24,893
14	22	A	Middlesbrough	W	3-1	Steinsson, Elmander, Taylor	24,487
15	29	A	Sunderland	W	4-1	Cahill, Elmander 2, Taylor	35,457
16	Dec 6	H	Chelsea	L	0-2		22,023
17	13	A	Aston Villa	L	2-4	K. Davies, Elmander	35,134
18	20	H	Portsmouth	W	2-1	Taylor, Gardner	19,884
19	26	A	Liverpool	L	0-3		43,548
20	28	H	Wigan Athletic	L	0-1		23,726
21	Jan 10	A	Arsenal	L	0-1		60,068
22	17	H	Manchester United	L	0-1		26,021
23	28	A	Blackburn Rovers	D	2-2	K. Davies, Taylor	25,205
24	31	H	Tottenham Hotspur	W	3-2	K. Davies 2, Puygrenier	21,575
25	Feb 7	A	Everton	L	0-3		33,791
26	21	H	West Ham United	W	2-1	K. Davies, Taylor	21,245
27	Mar 1	H	Newcastle United	W	1-0	Gardner	20,763
28	4	A	Stoke City	L	0-2		26,319
29	14	H	Fulham	L	1-3	K. Davies	22,117
30	21	A	West Bromwich Albion	D	1-1	Taylor	25,530
31	Apr 4	H	Middlesbrough	W	4-1	Cahill, K. Davies, Taylor, Gardner	20,819
32	11	A	Chelsea	L	3-4	A. O'Brien, Taylor, Basham	41,096
33	18	A	Portsmouth	L	0-1		20,158
34	25	H	Aston Villa	D	1-1	Cohen	21,709
35	May 2	A	Wigan Athletic	D	0-0		18,655
36	9	H	Sunderland	D	0-0		24,005
37	16	H	Hull City	D	1-1	Steinsson	25,085
38	24	A	Manchester City	L	0-1		47,202

	Appearances
	Sub appearances
1 own-goal	Goals

FA Cup

	Date	Venue	Opponents	Result		Scorers	Attendance
R3	Jan 3	A	Sunderland	L	1-2	Smolarek	20,685

	Appearances
	Sub appearances
	Goals

FL Cup

	Date	Venue	Opponents	Result		Scorers	Attendance
R2	Aug 26	H	Northampton Town	L	1-2	Nolan	7,136

	Appearances
	Sub appearances
	Goals

Column headers (players):

Jaaskelainen J.A. · Steinsson G.R. · Samuel J.L. · O'Brien J.M. · O'Brien A.J. · Cahill G.J. · Nolan K.A.J. · Muamba F.N. · Davies K.C. · Elmander J.E.C. · Taylor M.S. · McCann G.P. · Gardner R.W. · Mustapha R.R. · Shimo D.O. · Helguson H. · Smolarek E. · Vaz Te R.J. · Basham C.P. · Obadeyi T.A. · Makukula A. · Puygrenier S.N. · Davies M.N. · Cohen T.

Jaa	Ste	Sam	O'B(J)	O'B(A)	Cah	Nol	Mua	Dav(K)	Elm	Tay	McC	Gar	Mus	Shi	Hel	Smo	Vaz	Bas	Oba	Mak	Puy	Dav(M)	Coh
1	2	3	4	5	6	7	8	9	**10**	11	12												
1	2	3	*4*	5	6	7	8	*9*		**11**	12	13	14										
1	2	3	**4**	5		10	8	9			7	11	12	6										
1	2	3	4	5		10	8	9			**7**	11	12	6	13									
1	2	3	*4*	5		10	*8*	9			13	11	12	6		**7**	14							
1	2	3		5	6	7	8	9	**10**		4	**11**			13	12								
1	2	3	13	5	6	7	8	9	**10**	12	4	11												
1	2	3	13	5	6	7	**8**	9	10	*11*	4	12	14											
1	2	3		5	6	7	8	9	**10**	11	4	12	13											
1	2	3		5	6	7	8	9		11	4					4								
1	2	3		5	6	7	8	9		11	4	12	**10**											
1	2	3		5	6		8	9	**10**	11	4	7			12									
1	2	3		5	6	7	**8**	9	10	**11**	4	12			13									
1	2	3		5	6	7	8	9	10	**11**	4	13			12									
1	2	3		5	6	7	8	9	**10**	**11**	4	12		13										
1	2	3		5	6	7	**8**	9	10	**11**	4	12			13									
1	2	3		5	6	7	12	9	10	11	4	**8**												
1	2	**3**		5	6	7	8	12	*9*	**11**	4	10	14		13									
1	2	3		5		**7**	12	9	10	11	4	*8*	13	6			14							
1		3		5		8	9	**10**	7	4	11	*12*	6		2	13								
1	2	3		5	6		4	9		11		8			7	12	**10**	13						
1	2	3			6	7	4	9		11					8		**10**	5	12					
1	2	3		13	6		4	9		11		8			12		**10**	5	7					
1	7	3		2	6		**4**	9		11			14		12	13	*10*	5	8					
1	2	3		12	6		13	9	*10*	11	4	8						**5**	7					
1	2	3		5	6		**8**	9	*10*	11	4	12			13				7					
1	2	3		5	6		**8**	9	10	11	4	12					13		7					
1	2	3		5	6		12	9	10	11	4	8	13						**7**					
1	2	3			6		8	9	**10**	7	4	11	12	13				**5**						
1	2	3		6			8	9	**10**	7	4	11		12				13				14	7	
1	2	3		**5**	6		8	9	10	11	4				13				12		**7**			
1	2	3		5	6		8	9	10	11	4			12				13			12	**7**		
1	2	3		6			8	9	*10*	**11**	4			13	5			12	14		7			
1	2	3		14	6		8	9	*10*	**11**	4			13	5			12			7			
38	37	38	5	30	33	20	33	37	30	33	30	18	2	9	0	1	0	4	0	4	5	8	3
			2		4		5	1				1	3	11	15	1	1	11	2	7	3	2	2	1
	3			1	3		11	5	10		4				1			1		1		1	

Jaa	Ste	Sam	O'B(J)	O'B(A)	Cah	Nol	Mua	Dav(K)	Elm	Tay	McC	Gar	Mus	Shi	Hel	Smo	Vaz	Bas	Oba	Mak	Puy	Dav(M)	Coh
1	2	3		5		7	4	**9**	10	11		8	13	6		12							
1	1	1		1		1	1	1	1	1		1	0	1		0							
												1		0		1							
														1									

Jaa	Ste	Sam	O'B(J)	O'B(A)	Cah	Nol	Mua	Dav(K)	Elm	Tay	McC	Gar	Mus	Shi	Hel	Smo	Vaz	Bas	Oba	Mak	Puy	Dav(M)	Coh
1	2	*3*	4	12	6	13	8	14		7	11	**10**	5	9									
1	1	1	1	0	1	0	1	0		1	1	1	1	1									
				1		1		1					1										
				1		1																	

League Table

	P	W	D	L	F	A	Pts
Manchester United	38	28	6	4	68	24	90
Liverpool	38	25	11	2	77	27	86
Chelsea	38	25	8	5	68	24	83
Arsenal	38	20	12	6	68	37	72
Everton	38	17	12	9	55	37	63
Aston Villa	38	17	11	10	54	48	62
Fulham	38	14	11	13	39	34	53
Tottenham Hotspur	38	14	9	15	45	45	51
West Ham United	38	14	9	15	42	45	51
Manchester City	38	15	5	18	58	50	50
Wigan Athletic	38	12	9	17	34	45	45
Stoke City	38	12	9	17	38	55	45
Bolton Wanderers	38	11	8	19	41	53	41
Portsmouth	38	10	11	17	38	57	41
Blackburn Rovers	38	10	11	17	40	60	41
Sunderland	38	9	9	20	34	54	36
Hull City	38	8	11	19	39	64	35
Newcastle United	38	7	13	18	40	59	34
Middlesbrough	38	7	11	20	28	57	32
West Bromwich Albion	38	8	8	22	36	67	32

2009-10

Premiership

Manager: G. Megson

Did you know that?

When the Wanderers defeated Burnley 1–0 in the Premier League at the Reebok Stadium in January 2010 it was the first time they had kept a clean sheet since May 2009, a run of 22 League games. The club record was set in 1902–03 when 27 games were played without keeping a clean sheet.

Match No.	Date		Venue	Opponents		Result	Scorers	Attendance
1	Aug	15	H	Sunderland	L	0-1		22,247
2		22	A	Hull City	L	0-1		22,999
3		29	H	Liverpool	L	2-3	K. Davies, Cohen	23,284
4	Sep	12	A	Portsmouth	W	3-2	Cahill, Taylor (pen), Cohen	17,564
5		19	H	Stoke City	D	1-1	Taylor (pen)	20,265
6		26	A	Birmingham City	W	2-1	Lee, Cohen	28,671
7	Oct	3	H	Tottenham Hotspur	D	2-2	K. Davies, Gardner	21,305
8		17	A	Manchester United	L	1-2	Taylor	75,103
9		25	H	Everton	W	3-2	Cahill, Lee, Klasnic	21,547
10		31	H	Chelsea	L	0-4		22,680
11	Nov	7	A	Aston Villa	L	1-5	Elmander	38,101
12		22	H	Blackburn Rovers	L	0-2		21,777
13		28	A	Fulham	D	1-1	Klasnic	23,554
14	Dec	5	A	Wolverhampton Wanderers	L	1-2	Elmander	27,362
15		12	H	Manchester City	D	3-3	Cahill, Klasnic 2	22,735
16		15	H	West Ham United	W	3-1	Cahill, Lee, Klasnic	17,849
17		26	A	Burnley	D	1-1	Taylor	21,761
18		29	H	Hull City	D	2-2	K. Davies, Klasnic	20,696
19	Jan	17	H	Arsenal	L	0-2		23,893
20		20	A	Arsenal	L	2-4	Cahill, Taylor (pen)	59,084
21		26	H	Burnley	W	1-0	Lee	23,986
22		30	A	Liverpool	L	0-2		43,413
23	Feb	6	H	Fulham	D	0-0		22,289
24		9	A	Manchester City	L	0-2		42,016
25		17	A	Wigan Athletic	D	0-0		18,089
26		21	A	Blackburn Rovers	L	0-3		23,888
27		27	H	Wolverhampton Wanderers	W	1-0	Knight	21,261
28	Mar	6	A	West Ham United	W	2-1	K. Davies, Wilshere	33,824
29		9	A	Sunderland	L	0-4		36,087
30		13	H	Wigan Athletic	W	4-0	Muamba, K. Davies (pen), Elmander, Taylor	20,053
31		20	A	Everton	L	0-2		36,503
32		27	H	Manchester United	L	0-4		25,370
33	Apr	3	H	Aston Villa	L	0-1		21,111
34		13	A	Chelsea	L	0-1		40,539
35		17	A	Stoke City	W	2-1	Taylor 2	27,250
36		24	H	Portsmouth	D	2-2	K. Davies, Klasnic	20,526
37	May	1	A	Tottenham Hotspur	L	0-1		35,852
38		9	H	Birmingham City	W	2-1	K. Davies, Klasnic	22,863

Appearances
Sub appearances
Goals

FA Cup

R3	Jan	2	H	Lincoln City	W	4-0	Swaibu (own-goal), Cahill, Lee, M. Davies	11,193
R4		23	H	Sheffield United	W	2-0	Elmander, Steinsson	14,572
R5	Feb	14	H	Tottenham Hotspur	D	1-1	K. Davies	13,596
rep		24	A	Tottenham Hotspur	L	0-4		31,436

Appearances
Sub appearances
1 own-goal · Goals

FL Cup

R2	Aug	25	A	Tranmere Rovers	W	1-0	M. Davies	5,381
R3	Sep	22	H	West Ham United	W	3-1	Cahill, K. Davies, Elmander	8,050
R4	Oct	28	A	Chelsea	L	0-4		41,538

R3 a.e.t.

Appearances
Sub appearances
Goals

482

Players (columns left to right): Jääskeläinen J.A., Ricketts S.D., Robinson P.P., Mouutta F.N., Knighy Y., Cahil G.J., McCann G.P., Davis S., Davies K.C., Elmander J.E.C., Taylor M.S., Lee C.Y., Weird D.C., Davies M.N., Samuel J.L., Cohen T., Basham C.P., Steinsson G.R., Muangona R.R., Klasnic I., Gardner R.W., O'Brien A.J., Weiss V., Wilshere J.A.G., Holden S., Al-Habsi A.A.H.

Jääskeläinen J.A.	Ricketts S.D.	Robinson P.P.	Mouutta F.N.	Knighy Y.	Cahil G.J.	McCann G.P.	Davis S.	Davies K.C.	Elmander J.E.C.	Taylor M.S.	Lee C.Y.	Weird D.C.	Davies M.N.	Samuel J.L.	Cohen T.	Basham C.P.	Steinsson G.R.	Muangona R.R.	Klasnic I.	Gardner R.W.	O'Brien A.J.	Weiss V.	Wilshere J.A.G.	Holden S.	Al-Habsi A.A.H.
1	2	3	4		5	6	**7**	8	9	**10**	11	12	13												
1	2	3	**4**		5	6		8	9	**10**	11	12	14	7	13										
1	2		4	5	6		8	9	**10**	11				3	7	12	13	14							
1	**2**		4	5	6	14		9		11			10	3	**8**	13	7		12						
1	2		4	5	6	8		9		11				3	10		**7**		13	12					
1	2		4	5	6	13		9		11	12			3	7				**10**	8					
1	2		**4**	5	6			9		11	10		13	3	7				14	8					
1	2		4	5	6			9		11	**10**		13	3	7	14			12	8					
1	2		4	5	6			9		11	10			3	7	13			12	**8**					
1	2	13	4	5	6			9	10		11			14	3	8	**7**			12					
1	**2**	3	4	5	6			9	12	11	10				7		13			8					
1			4	6	**7**			9	**10**	11	13		14	3					12	**8**	5				
1		12		6	4			9		11			13	3	**7**			2		**10**	8	5			
1				6	4				12	11	10			3	7			2		9	8	5			
1		3	4	5	6			9	12	11	7		13		8			2		**10**					
1		3	4	5	6			9		**11**	7				8	13	2			**10**	12				
1		3		5	6			9		11	7		12		8	4	2			**10**	13				
1		3	4	5	6	12		9		11	7				8				**10**						
1		**4**	5	6	12			9	14	11	7				8		2			**10**	13				
1	14	**3**	4	5	6	12		9		11	7				8		2			13					
1	3		4	5	6			9	12	**11**	7				8		2		**10**	13		14			
1	3		4	5	6			9	14	**11**	7		10		**8**		2			12		13			
1	2	3	4	5				9	13	**11**	7		10		8	12			**6**	14					
1	6	3	4	5				9	10	13	7		12		8		2					**11**			
1	6	3	4	5				9	10	**11**	7				13		2		8		12	14			
1	6	**3**	4	5				9	10	**11**	7		12				2		14	8	13				
1	6	3	4	5				9	**10**	13	7						2		12		14	**11**	8		
1	6	3	4	5				9	**10**	13	7				8		2			12					
1	6	3	**4**	5				9	10	14	7						2		13	8		12	11		
1		3	4	5				**9**	10	12	7				8		2		14		6	13	11		
1	12	3	4	5				9	**10**	13	7		14		8		2				6		**11**		
1	2		4	5	6			9	**10**	14	7				3	8			12				**11**		
1	2	3	4	5	6			9	**10**	14	7					8			12		13	11			
1	2	3	4	5	6			9	12	11	7					8			13			**10**			
1	**2**	3	4	5	6			9		11	**7**		14			8			12		13	10			
1		3	4	5	6			9	13	11	12		14			2		**10**	**7**	**8**					
1		3	4	5	6			9	12	11	13					2		**10**	14		7	8			
1		3	4	5	6			9		11	12					2		10	14		**7**	**8**	13		
38	25	24	35	35	29	5	3	37	15	29	27	0	5	12	26	2	25	0	12	11	6	3	13	1	0
	2	1	1			6			10	8	7	2	12	1	1	6	2	1	15	10		10	1	1	
		1	1	5			7	3	8	4		3			8	1			1						

Jääskeläinen J.A.	Ricketts S.D.	Robinson P.P.	Mouutta F.N.	Knighy Y.	Cahil G.J.	McCann G.P.	Davis S.	Davies K.C.	Elmander J.E.C.	Taylor M.S.	Lee C.Y.	Weird D.C.	Davies M.N.	Samuel J.L.	Cohen T.	Basham C.P.	Steinsson G.R.	Muangona R.R.	Klasnic I.	Gardner R.W.	O'Brien A.J.	Weiss V.	Wilshere J.A.G.	Holden S.	Al-Habsi A.A.H.
	3	**4**		6				9	13	11	7		12		14		2		**10**	8	5			1	
1	2		4	5	6			*9*	12		11		3	8	13	7	14	**10**							
1	6	3	4	5				9	10	*11*	7		13	14	2		8	12							
1	2		**4**	5				13	11	14			3	7		12	**9**	8	6		10				
3	3	2	4	3	2	0	0	3	1	3	3	0	0	2	2	0	3	0	3	3	2	0	0	1	1
								3		1		2		2	1		2		1						
			1				1	1		1		1		1			1								

Jääskeläinen J.A.	Ricketts S.D.	Robinson P.P.	Mouutta F.N.	Knighy Y.	Cahil G.J.	McCann G.P.	Davis S.	Davies K.C.	Elmander J.E.C.	Taylor M.S.	Lee C.Y.	Weird D.C.	Davies M.N.	Samuel J.L.	Cohen T.	Basham C.P.	Steinsson G.R.	Muangona R.R.	Klasnic I.	Gardner R.W.	O'Brien A.J.	Weiss V.	Wilshere J.A.G.	Holden S.	Al-Habsi A.A.H.
1	2		4	5	6	13	8	9	10	11	12		**7**	3											
1	2		4	5	6	7		9	13	11	12		3	14					**10**	**8**					
	2		4	5	6			12	11				9	3		13	7		**10**	8				1	
2	3		3	3	3	1	1	2	1	2	1	0	2	3	0		1	2	2	0				1	
					1			2		2				1	1										
			1				1	1					1												

League Table

	P	W	D	L	F	A	Pts
Chelsea	38	27	5	6	103	32	86
Manchester United	38	27	4	7	86	28	85
Arsenal	38	23	6	9	83	41	75
Tottenham Hotspur	38	21	7	10	67	41	70
Manchester City	38	18	13	7	73	45	67
Aston Villa	38	17	13	8	52	39	64
Liverpool	38	18	9	11	61	35	63
Everton	38	16	13	9	60	49	61
Birmingham City	38	13	11	14	38	47	50
Blackburn Rovers	38	13	11	14	41	55	50
Stoke City	38	11	14	13	34	48	47
Fulham	38	12	10	16	39	46	46
Sunderland	38	11	11	16	48	56	44
Bolton Wanderers	38	10	9	19	42	67	39
Wolverhampton W	38	9	11	18	32	56	38
Wigan Athletic	38	9	9	20	37	79	36
West Ham United	38	8	11	19	47	66	35
Burnley	38	8	6	24	42	82	30
Hull City	38	6	12	20	34	75	30
Portsmouth	38	7	7	24	34	66	18

Match No.	Date	Venue	Opponents	Result		Scorers	Attendance
1	Aug 14	H	Fulham	D	0-0		20,352
2	21	A	West Ham United	W	3-1	Upson (og), Elmander 2	32,533
3	29	H	Birmingham City	D	2-2	K Davies (pen), Blake	18,139
4	Sep 11	A	Arsenal	L	1-4	Elmander	59,876
5	18	A	Aston Villa	D	1-1	K Davies	34,655
6	26	H	Manchester United	D	2-2	Knight, Petrov	23,926
7	Oct 2	A	West Bromwich Albion	D	1-1	Elmander	22,846
8	16	H	Stoke City	W	2-1	Lee, Klasnic	22,975
9	23	A	Wigan Athletic	D	1-1	Elmander	17,100
10	31	H	Liverpool	L	0-1		25,171
11	Nov 6	H	Tottenham Hotspur	W	4-2	K Davies 2 (1 pen), Steinsson, Petrov	20,255
12	10	A	Everton	D	1-1	Klasnic	31,808
13	13	A	Wolverhampton Wanderers	W	3-2	Stearman (og), Elmander, Holden	27,508
14	20	H	Newcastle United	W	5-1	K Davies 2 (2 pens), Lee, Elmander 2	22,203
15	27	H	Blackpool	D	2-2	Petrov, M Davies	25,851
16	Dec 4	A	Manchester City	L	0-1		46,860
17	12	H	Blackburn Rovers	W	2-1	Muamba, Holden	24,471
18	18	A	Sunderland	L	0-1		35,101
19	26	H	West Bromwich Albion	W	2-0	Taylor, Elmander	23,413
20	29	A	Chelsea	L	0-1		40,982
21	Jan 1	A	Liverpool	L	1-2	K Davies	35,400
22	5	H	Wigan Athletic	D	1-1	Moreno	18,852
23	15	A	Stoke City	L	0-2		26,809
24	24	H	Chelsea	L	0-4		22,837
25	Feb 2	H	Wolverhampton Wanderers	W	1-0	Sturridge	18,944
26	5	A	Tottenham Hotspur	L	1-2	Sturridge	36,197
27	13	H	Everton	W	2-0	Cahill, Sturridge	22,986
28	26	A	Newcastle United	D	1-1	Sturridge	48,062
29	Mar 5	A	Aston Villa	W	3-2	Cahill 2, Klasnic	22,533
30	19	A	Manchester United	L	0-1		75,486
31	Apr 2	A	Birmingham City	L	1-2	Elmander	26,142
32	9	H	West Ham United	W	3-0	Sturridge 2, Lee	25,857
33	24	H	Arsenal	W	2-1	Sturridge, Cohen	26,881
34	27	A	Fulham	L	0-3		23,222
35	30	A	Blackburn Rovers	L	0-1		28,985
36	May 7	H	Sunderland	L	1-2	Klasnic	22,597
37	14	A	Blackpool	L	3-4	K Davies, Taylor, Sturridge	15,979
38	22	H	Manchester City	L	0-2		26,285
						Appearances	
						Sub appearances	
						Goals	

FA Cup

	Date	Venue	Opponents	Result		Scorers	Attendance
R3	Jan 8	H	York City	W	2-0	K Davies, Elmander	13,120
R4	29	H	Wigan Athletic	D	0-0		14,950
rep	Feb 16	A	Wigan Athletic	W	1-0	Klasnic	7,515
R5	20	A	Fulham	W	1-0	Klasnic	19,571
R6	Mar 12	A	Birmingham City	W	3-2	Elmander, K Davies (pen), Lee	23,699
SF	Apr 17	N	Stoke City	L	0-5		75,064
						Appearances	
						Sub appearances	
						Goals	

FL Cup

	Date	Venue	Opponents	Result		Scorers	Attendance
R2	Aug 24	A	Southampton	W	1-0	Klasnic	10,251
R3	Sep 21	A	Burnley	L	0-1		17,602
R3 a.e.t.						Appearances	
						Sub appearances	
						Goals	

League Table

HONOURS AND RECORDS

LEAGUE HIGHS AND LOWS

Most Points in a Season	98	1996–97
Most Home Wins in a Season	18	1924–25, 1972–73, 1992–93, 1996–97
Most Home Draws in a Season	11	1979–80
Most Home Losses in a Season	10	1909–10, 1963–64, 1970–71, 1986–87, 1995–96
Most Home Goals Scored in a Season	63	1934–35
Most Home Goals Conceded in a Season	35	1952–53, 1957–58, 1963–64
Most Away Wins in a Season	14	2000–01 (15 inc Play-off)
Most Away Draws in a Season	10	1986–87, 1996–97, 1998–99
Most Away Losses in a Season	18	1984–85
Most Away Goals Scored in a Season	40	1996–97 (41 2000–01 inc Play-offs)
Most Away Goals Conceded in a Season	59	1932–33
Most Wins in a Season	28	1996–97
Most Draws in a Season	17	1991–92
Most Losses in a Season	25	1970–71, 1995–96
Most Goals Scored in a Season	100	1996–97
Most Goals Conceded in a Season	92	1932–33
Least Home Wins in a Season	5	1979–80
Least Home Draws in a Season	0	1888–89, 1890–91, 1904–05
Least Home Losses in a Season	0	1910–11, 1920–21
Least Home Goals Scored in a Season	18	1893–94, 1897–98, 1902–03
Least Home Goals Conceded in a Season	7	1899–1900
Least Away Wins in a Season	0	1949–50, 1979–80
Least Away Draws in a Season	0	1889–90, 1891–92
Least Away Losses in a Season	3	1899–1900, 1904–05, 1996–97
Least Away Goals Scored in a Season	10	1897–98
Least Away Goals Conceded in a Season	16	1904–05
Least Wins in a Season	5	1979–80
Least Draws in a Season	1	1889–90, 1890–91
Least Losses in a Season	4	1899–1900, 1996–97
Least Goals Scored in a Season	28	1897–98
Least Goals Conceded in a Season	25	1899–1900

MOST CONSECUTIVE:

Wins	11	1904–05
Home Wins	17	1924–25
Away Wins	6	1999–2000/2000–01
Draws	6	1912–13
Losses	11	1901–02/1902–03
Home Losses	4	1902–03, 2004–05

The Wanderers team of 1904–05 with the most concecutive wins in the club's history.

Away Losses	11	1979–80, 1984–85
Games Without Scoring	5	1897–98, 1989–90
Games With Scoring	24	1888–89, 1889–90, 1996–97
Run Without Defeat	23	1990–91
Run Without a Draw	27	1911–12
Run Without a Win	26	1901–02/1902–03
Home Games Without a Win	11	1902–03
Away Games Without a Win	36	1948–49/1950–51
Games Without Conceding a Goal	7	1899–1900
Games Conceding a Goal	27	1901–02/1902–03
Unbeaten Home Games	27	1919–20/1920–21
Unbeaten Away Games	11	1904–05

RECORD VICTORIES:

LEAGUE:
Home: 8–0 v Barnsley, Division Two, 6 October 1934
Away: 7–1 v Aston Villa, Division One, 26 December 1914

FA CUP
Home: 13–0 v Sheffield United, second round, 1 February 1890
Away: 5–1 v Charlton Athletic, third round, 14 January 1933

LEAGUE CUP
Home: 6–1 v Tottenham Hotspur, fourth round, 27 November 1996
Away: 4–0 v Rochdale, second round, 10 October 1973

The Wanderers' record-breaking team of 1996–97.

RECORD DEFEATS:

LEAGUE:

Home: 0–6 v Manchester United, Premier League, 25 February 1996

Away: 0–7 v Burnley, Division One, 1 March 1890
v Sheffield Wednesday, Division One, 1 March 1915
v Manchester City, Division One, 21 March 1936

FA CUP:

Home: 0–5 v Bristol City, first round, 7 February 1903
v Manchester City, fifth round, 20 February 1937

Away: 1–9 v Preston North End, second round, 10 December 1887

LEAGUE CUP:

Home: 0–6 v Chelsea, fourth-round replay, 8 November 1971

Away: 0–6 v Tottenham Hotspur, fifth round, 11 December 2001

GATE RECORDS (RECORDED):

Record Attendance: Highest:

Home

Burnden Park, 69,912 v Manchester City (FA Cup fifth round) 18 February 1933

Reebok Stadium, 28,353 v Leicester City (Premier League) 28 December 2003

Away
76,058 v Manchester United (Premier League) 17 March 2007

Lowest:
Home
Burnden Park: 1,507 v Rochdale (Autoglass Trophy) 10 December 1991
2,902 v Darlington (Division Three) 5 November 1985
Reebok Stadium: 3,673 v Gillingham (League Cup second round) 21 September 1999
10,180 v Queen's Park Rangers (Division One) 21 October 2000
Away
1,000 v Pisa (Anglo-Italian Cup) 16 November 1993
v Ascoli (Anglo-Italian Cup) 22 December 1993
1,193 v Newport County (Division Three) 4 April 1987

Record Receipts: £537,185 v Manchester United (Premier League) 28 October 2006

OTHER RECORDS (PLAYERS):

Appearances: Eddie Hopkinson 578 (1956–69) (519 League)
Goalscorer: Nat Lofthouse 285 (1945–60) (255 League)
Goals in a Season: Joe Smith 38 (1920–21) (All League)
Goals in a Match:
Billy Struthers 5 (6–1 v Bootle, FA
Cup 4 November 1882)
Jim Cassidy 5 (13–0 v Sheffield
United, FA Cup 1 February 1890)
Tony Caldwell 5 (8–1 v Walsall,
Division Three 10 September 1983)
Most Capped:
Ricardo Gardner (Jamaica 59
appearances (105 in total))
Record Transfer Fee Paid:
£8.2 million, Johan Elmander
(Toulouse July 2008)
Record Transfer Fee Received: £15
million, Nicolas Anelka (Chelsea
January 2008)
Youngest Player:
Ray Parry, 15 years 267 days v
Wolves 13 October 1951
Oldest Player:
Peter Shilton, 45 years 239 days v
Wolves 15 May 1995

Peter Shilton. The
Wanderers' eldest player.

FOOTBALL LEAGUE AND PREMIERSHIP RECORD:

FA Premier League: 1995–96, 1997–98, 2001–02 to date.

Division One: 1888–89 to 1898–99, 1900–01 to 1902–03, 1905–06 to 1907–08, 1909–10, 1911–12 to 1932–33, 1935–36 to 1963–64, 1978–79 to 1979–80.

Division One (Formerly Division Two): 1899–1900, 1903–04 to 1904–05, 1908–09, 1910–11, 1933–34 to 1934–35, 1964–65 to 1970–71, 1973–74 to 1977–78, 1980–81 to 1982–83, 1993–94 to 1994–95, 1996–97, 1998–99 to 2000–01.

Division Two (Formerly Division Three): 1971–72 to 1972–73, 1983–84 to 1986–87, 1988–89 to 1992–93.

Division Three (Formerly Division Four): 1987–88.

Highest Finishing position: Third, 1892, 1921, 1925 (Division One)

Division One/Two Champions: 1909, 1978, 1997

Runners Up/Promoted via Play-offs: 1900, 1905, 1911, 1935, 1995, 2001

Division Two/Three Champions: 1973

Runners Up: 1993

Division Three/Four Promotion: 1988

FA Cup Winners: 1923, 1926, 1929, 1958

FA Cup Runners-up: 1894, 1904, 1953

League Cup Runners-up: 1995, 2004

Sherpa Van Trophy Winners: 1989

Freight Rover Trophy Runners-up: 1986

FA Charity Shield Winners: 1958

Lancashire Cup Winners: 1886, 1891, 1912, 1922, 1925, 1927, 1932, 1934, 1939 (joint winners), 1948, 1988, 1990

Manchester Cup Winners: 1895, 1906, 1909, 1921, 1922, 1938, 1954, 1961, 1963

Central League Champions: 1955, 1995

FA Premier League Reserve North Champions: 2007

FA CUP RECORD

	PL	W	D	L	F	A
HOME	178	98	40	40	367	191
AWAY	172	61	46	65	240	272
NEUTRAL	32	17	2	13	42	39
TOTAL	**382**	**176**	**88**	**118**	**649**	**502**

LEAGUE CUP RECORD

	PL	W	D	L	F	A
HOME	87	49	14	24	162	115
AWAY	83	29	19	35	117	149
NEUTRAL	3	1	0	2	4	5
TOTAL	**173**	**79**	**33**	**61**	**283**	**269**

Football League Record 1888 To Date

		Pld.	HOME					AWAY					Pts.	Pos.	Div.
			W	D	L	F	A	W	D	L	F	A			
1	1888–89	22	6	0	5	35	30	4	2	5	28	29	22	5	1
2	1889–90	22	6	1	4	37	24	3	0	8	17	41	19	9	1
3	1890–91	22	9	0	2	36	14	3	1	7	11	20	25	5	1
4	1891–92	26	9	2	2	29	14	8	0	5	22	23	36	3	1
5	1892–93	30	12	1	2	43	21	1	5	9	13	34	32	5	1
6	1893–94	30	7	3	5	18	14	3	1	11	20	38	24	13	1
7	1894–95	30	8	3	4	45	23	1	4	10	16	39	25	10	1
8	1895–96	30	12	2	1	34	14	4	3	8	15	23	37	4	1
9	1896–97	30	7	3	5	22	18	5	3	7	18	25	30	8	1
10	1897–98	30	9	2	4	18	13	2	2	11	10	28	26	11	1
11	1898–99	34	6	5	6	24	21	3	2	12	13	30	25	17	1
12	1899–1900	34	14	2	1	47	7	8	6	3	32	18	52	2	2
13	1900–01	34	10	5	2	21	12	3	2	12	18	43	33	10	1
14	1901–02	34	10	6	1	38	17	2	2	13	13	39	32	12	1
15	1902–03	34	6	2	9	18	20	2	1	14	19	53	19	18	1
16	1903–04	34	10	3	4	38	11	2	7	8	21	30	34	7	2
17	1904–05	34	15	0	2	53	16	12	2	3	34	16	56	2	2
18	1905–06	38	13	1	5	51	22	4	6	9	30	45	41	6	1
19	1906–07	38	10	4	5	35	18	8	4	7	24	29	44	6	1
20	1907–08	38	10	3	6	35	26	4	2	13	17	32	33	19	1
21	1908–09	38	14	3	2	37	8	10	1	8	22	20	52	1	2
22	1909–10	38	7	2	10	31	34	2	4	13	13	37	24	20	1
23	1910–11	38	17	2	0	53	12	4	7	8	16	28	51	2	2
24	1911–12	38	14	2	3	35	15	6	1	12	19	28	43	4	1
25	1912–13	38	10	6	3	36	20	6	4	9	26	43	42	8	1
26	1913–14	38	13	4	2	41	14	3	6	10	24	38	42	6	1
27	1914–15	38	8	5	6	35	27	3	3	13	33	57	30	17	1
28	1919–20	42	11	3	7	35	29	8	6	7	37	36	47	6	1
29	1920–21	42	15	6	0	53	17	4	8	9	24	36	52	3	1
30	1921–22	42	12	4	5	40	24	8	3	10	28	35	47	6	1
31	1922–23	42	11	8	2	36	17	3	4	14	14	41	40	13	1
32	1923–24	42	13	6	2	45	13	5	8	8	23	21	50	4	1
33	1924–25	42	18	2	1	61	13	4	9	8	15	21	55	3	1
34	1925–26	42	11	6	4	46	31	6	4	11	29	45	44	8	1
35	1926–27	42	15	5	1	54	19	4	5	12	30	43	48	4	1
36	1927–28	42	12	5	4	47	26	4	6	11	34	40	43	7	1

		Pld.	HOME					AWAY					Pts.	Pos.	Div.
			W	D	L	F	A	W	D	L	F	A			
37	1928–29	42	10	6	5	44	25	4	6	11	29	55	40	14	1
38	1929–30	42	11	5	5	46	24	4	4	13	28	50	39	15	1
39	1930–31	42	12	6	3	45	26	3	3	15	23	55	39	14	1
40	1931–32	42	15	1	5	51	25	2	3	16	21	55	38	17	1
41	1932–33	42	10	7	4	49	33	2	2	17	29	59	33	21	1
42	1933–34	42	14	2	5	45	22	7	7	7	34	33	51	3	2
43	1934–35	42	17	1	3	63	15	9	3	9	33	33	56	2	2
44	1935–36	42	11	4	6	41	27	3	9	9	26	49	41	13	1
45	1936–37	42	6	6	9	22	33	4	8	9	21	33	34	20	1
46	1937–38	42	11	6	4	38	22	4	9	8	26	38	45	7	1
47	1938–39	42	10	6	5	39	25	5	9	7	28	33	45	8	1
48	1946–47	42	8	5	8	30	28	5	3	13	27	41	34	18	1
49	1947–48	42	11	2	8	29	25	5	3	13	17	33	37	17	1
50	1948–49	42	10	4	7	43	32	4	6	11	16	36	38	14	1
51	1949–50	42	10	5	6	34	22	0	9	12	11	37	34	16	1
52	1950–51	42	11	2	8	31	20	8	5	8	33	41	45	8	1
53	1951–52	42	11	7	3	35	26	8	3	10	30	35	48	5	1
54	1952–53	42	9	4	8	39	35	6	5	10	22	34	39	14	1
55	1953–54	42	14	6	1	45	20	4	6	11	30	40	48	5	1
56	1954–55	42	11	6	4	45	29	2	7	12	17	40	39	18	1
57	1955–56	42	13	3	5	50	24	5	4	12	21	34	43	8	1
58	1956–57	42	13	6	2	42	23	3	6	12	23	42	44	9	1
59	1957–58	42	9	5	7	38	35	5	5	11	27	52	38	15	1
60	1958–59	42	14	3	4	56	30	6	7	8	23	36	50	4	1
61	1959–60	42	12	5	4	37	27	8	3	10	22	24	48	6	1
62	1960–61	42	9	5	7	38	29	3	6	12	20	44	35	18	1
63	1961–62	42	11	7	3	35	22	5	3	13	27	44	42	11	1
64	1962–63	42	13	3	5	35	18	2	2	17	20	57	35	18	1
65	1963–64	42	6	5	10	30	35	4	3	14	18	45	28	21	1
66	1964–65	42	13	6	2	46	17	7	4	10	34	41	50	3	2
67	1965–66	42	12	2	7	43	25	4	7	10	19	34	41	9	2
68	1966–67	42	10	7	4	36	19	4	7	10	28	39	42	9	2
69	1967–68	42	8	6	7	37	28	5	7	9	23	35	39	12	2
70	1968–69	42	8	7	6	29	26	4	7	10	26	41	38	17	2
71	1969–70	42	9	6	6	31	23	3	6	12	23	38	36	16	2
72	1970–71	42	6	5	10	22	31	1	5	15	13	43	24	22	2
73	1971–72	46	11	8	4	25	13	6	8	9	26	28	50	7	3
74	1972–73	46	18	4	1	44	9	7	7	9	29	30	61	1	3
75	1973–74	42	12	5	4	30	17	3	7	11	14	23	42	11	2
76	1974–75	42	9	7	5	27	16	6	5	10	18	25	42	10	2
77	1975–76	42	12	5	4	36	14	8	7	6	28	24	52	4	2
78	1976–77	42	15	2	4	46	21	5	9	7	29	33	51	4	2
79	1977–78	42	16	4	1	39	14	8	6	7	24	19	58	1	2
80	1978–79	42	10	5	6	36	28	2	6	13	18	47	35	17	1

			HOME				AWAY							
		Pld.	W	D	L	F	A	W	D	L	F	A	Pts.	Pos.	Div.
81	1979–80	42	5	11	5	19	21	0	4	17	19	52	25	22	1
82	1980–81	42	10	5	6	40	27	4	5	12	21	39	38	18	2
83	1981–82	42	10	4	7	28	24	3	3	15	11	37	46	19	2
84	1982–83	42	10	2	9	30	26	1	9	11	12	35	44	22	2
85	1983–84	46	13	4	6	36	17	5	6	12	20	43	64	10	3
86	1984–85	46	12	5	6	38	22	4	1	18	31	53	54	17	3
87	1985–86	46	10	4	9	35	30	5	4	14	19	38	53	18	3
88	1986–87*	48	8	6	10	31	28	2	10	12	17	33	45	21	3
89	1987–88	46	15	6	2	42	12	7	6	10	24	30	78	3	4
90	1988–89	46	12	8	3	42	23	4	8	11	16	31	64	10	3
91	1989–90*	48	12	8	4	33	20	6	8	10	27	31	69	6	3
92	1990–91*	49	15	5	4	34	18	10	7	8	32	34	83	4	3
93	1991–92	46	10	9	4	26	19	4	8	11	31	37	59	13	3
94	1992–93	46	18	2	3	48	14	9	7	7	32	27	90	2	2
95	1993–94	46	10	8	5	40	31	5	6	12	23	33	59	14	1
96	1994–95*	49	17	6	1	45	13	6	8	11	29	37	77	3	1
97	1995–96	38	5	4	10	16	31	3	1	15	23	40	29	20	PL
98	1996–97	46	18	4	1	60	20	10	10	3	40	33	98	1	1
99	1997–98	38	7	8	4	25	22	2	5	12	16	39	40	18	PL
100	1998–99*	49	14	6	4	45	25	7	10	8	37	40	76	6	1
101	1999–2000*	48	14	6	4	45	28	7	8	9	29	29	76	6	1
102	2000–01*	49	11	10	3	43	28	15	6	4	41	19	87	3	1
103	2001–02	38	5	7	7	20	31	4	6	9	24	31	40	16	PL
104	2002–03	38	7	8	4	27	24	3	6	10	14	27	44	17	PL
105	2003–04	38	6	8	5	24	21	8	3	8	24	35	53	8	PL
106	2004–05	38	9	5	5	25	18	7	5	7	24	26	58	6	PL
107	2005–06	38	11	5	3	29	13	4	6	9	20	28	56	8	PL
108	2006–07	38	9	5	5	26	20	7	3	9	21	32	56	7	PL
109	2007–08	38	7	5	7	23	18	2	5	12	13	36	37	16	PL
110	2008–09	38	7	5	7	21	21	4	3	12	20	32	41	13	PL
111	2009–10	38	6	6	7	26	31	4	3	12	16	36	39	14	PL
112	2010–11	38	10	5	4	34	24	2	5	12	18	32	46	14	PL
		4502	1214	519	516	4120	2452	529	566	1158	2576	4017	5026		

	Pld.	W	D	L	F	A
Play-offs	18	6	5	7	29	28

1986–87: Aldershot 1 – Bolton 0, Bolton 2 – Aldershot 2 (Aet)
1989–90: Bolton 1 – Notts Co 1, Notts Co 2 – Bolton 0
1990–91: Bury 1 – Bolton 1, Bolton 1 – Bury 0, Bolton 0 – Tranmere 1 (Aet)
1994–95: Wolves 2 – Bolton 1, Bolton 2 – Wolves 0 (Aet), Bolton 4 – Reading 3 (Aet)
1998–99: Bolton 1 – Ipswich 0, Ipswich 4 – Bolton 3 (Aet), Bolton 0 – Watford 2
1999–2000: Bolton 2 – Ipswich 2, Ipswich 5 – Bolton 3 (Aet)
2000–01: West Brom 2 – Bolton 2, Bolton 3 – West Brom 0, Bolton 3 – Preston 0

FOOTBALL LEAGUE RECORD (DIVISIONAL SPLIT) TO END 2010–11

	HOME							AWAY							NEUTRAL					
	PL	W	D	L	F	A	Pts	PL	W	D	L	F	A	Pts	PL	W	D	L	F	A
DIVISION ONE (PREMIER FROM 92/93)	1382	715	324	343	2552	1663	1843	1382	292	311	779	1558	2727	945						
DIVISION TWO (INC 11P/OS) (DIV ONE FROM 1992–93) (CHAMPIONSHIP FROM 2003/04)	588	345	126	117	1134	564	910	588	166	175	247	707	870	558	3	2	0	1	7	5
DIVISION THREE (INC 7 P/OS) (DIV TWO FROM 1992–93) (LEAGUE ONE FROM 2003–04)	256	139	63	54	392	213	446	256	62	74	120	280	384	246	1	0	0	1	0	1
DIVISION FOUR (DIV THREE FROM 1992–93) (LEAGUE TWO FROM 2003–04)	23	15	6	2	42	12	51	23	7	6	10	24	30	27						
TOTAL	2249	1214	519	516	4120	2452	3250	2249	527	566	1156	2569	4011	1776	4	2	0	2	7	6

TOTALS

	PL	W	D	L	F	A	Pts
DIVISION ONE	2764	1007	635	1122	4110	4390	2788
DIVISION TWO	1179	513	301	365	1848	1439	1468
DIVISION THREE	513	201	137	175	672	598	692
DIVISION FOUR	46	22	12	12	66	42	78
TOTAL	**4502**	**1743**	**1085**	**1674**	**6696**	**6469**	**5026**

FOOTBALL LEAGUE RECORD. PIKES LANE/BURNDEN PARK/REEBOK STADIUM SPLIT TO END 2010–11

		PL	W	D	L	F	A	Pts
PIKES LANE	**DIVISION ONE**	91	57	10	24	243	140	239
BURNDEN PARK	**DIVISION ONE** (PREMIER FROM 1992–93)	1082	574	247	261	2029	1280	1285
	DIVISION TWO (INC 1P/OS) (DIV ONE FROM 1992–93)	516	306	104	106	1001	483	778
	DIVISION THREE (INC 3P/OS) (DIV TWO FROM 1992–93)	256	139	63	54	392	213	446
	DIVISION FOUR (DIV THREE FROM 1992–93)	23	15	6	2	42	12	51
REEBOK STADIUM	**PREMIER LEAGUE**	209	84	67	58	280	243	319
	FIRST DIVISION (INC 3 P/O)	72	39	22	11	133	81	132
BURNDEN	TOTAL	1877	1034	420	423	3464	1988	2560
REEBOK	TOTAL	281	123	89	69	413	324	451
	TOTAL	**2249**	**1214**	**519**	**516**	**4120**	**2452**	**3250**

Football League
Opponents 1888 To Date

	OPPONENTS	HOME						AWAY						TOTAL					
		PL	W	D	L	F	A	PL	W	D	L	F	A	PL	W	D	L	F	A
1	ACCRINGTON	5	3	0	2	20	11	5	2	1	2	9	8	10	5	1	4	29	19
2	ALDERSHOT	2	1	1	0	3	2	2	1	0	1	3	1	4	2	1	1	6	3
3	ARSENAL	58	28	15	15	101	76	58	7	16	35	57	131	116	35	31	50	158	207
4	ASTON VILLA	75	38	18	19	141	81	75	16	19	40	95	162	150	54	37	59	236	243
5	BARNSLEY	16	9	5	2	40	17	16	3	6	7	18	23	32	12	11	9	58	40
6	BIRMINGHAM CITY	58	33	18	7	123	56	58	13	14	31	63	102	116	46	32	38	186	158
7	BLACKBURN ROVERS	72	37	18	17	120	84	72	20	15	37	98	145	144	57	33	54	218	229
8	BLACKPOOL	43	23	9	11	73	44	43	11	15	17	52	61	86	34	24	28	125	105
9	BOURNEMOUTH	9	4	2	3	11	7	9	3	1	5	10	16	18	7	3	8	21	23
10	BRADFORD PA	7	3	0	4	8	8	7	3	1	3	10	12	14	6	1	7	18	20
11	BRADFORD CITY	20	9	7	4	33	18	20	4	6	10	34	45	40	13	13	14	67	63
12	BRENTFORD	16	8	3	5	22	17	16	2	4	10	17	34	32	10	7	15	39	51
13	BRIGHTON & HA	4	0	2	2	2	5	4	1	1	2	5	7	8	1	3	4	7	12
14	BRISTOL CITY	25	11	6	8	30	30	25	3	8	14	26	46	50	14	14	22	56	76
15	BRISTOL ROVERS	13	8	3	2	23	8	13	2	4	7	12	19	26	10	7	9	35	27
16	BURNLEY	56	26	17	13	98	56	56	14	13	29	57	97	112	40	30	42	155	153
17	BURTON UNITED	3	3	0	0	15	1	3	2	0	1	7	4	6	5	0	1	22	5
18	BURY	31	17	4	10	57	46	31	6	10	15	41	50	62	23	14	25	98	96
19	CAMBRIDGE UNITED	6	2	3	1	15	9	6	2	2	2	10	10	12	4	5	3	25	19
20	CARDIFF CITY	32	20	6	6	61	25	32	12	5	15	39	37	64	32	11	21	100	62
21	CARLISLE UNITED	12	6	2	4	22	11	12	2	3	7	9	23	24	8	5	11	31	34
22	CHARLTON ATHLETIC	37	26	6	5	82	32	37	11	7	19	45	59	74	37	13	24	127	91
23	CHELSEA	53	22	14	17	91	78	53	12	13	28	63	95	106	34	27	45	154	173
24	CHESTER CITY	6	3	2	1	8	2	6	2	3	1	5	4	12	5	5	2	13	6
25	CHESTERFIELD	9	8	0	1	25	6	9	2	4	3	9	11	18	10	4	4	34	17
26	COLCHESTER UNITED	1	1	0	0	4	0	1	0	0	1	0	3	2	1	0	1	4	3
27	COVENTRY CITY	7	1	3	3	9	14	7	1	5	1	10	10	14	2	8	4	19	24
28	CREWE ALEXANDRA	6	2	3	1	11	9	6	2	2	2	14	12	12	4	5	3	25	21
29	CRYSTAL PALACE	17	10	7	0	33	12	17	3	7	7	18	23	34	13	14	7	51	35
30	DARLINGTON	4	2	1	1	7	7	4	2	0	2	4	4	8	4	1	3	11	11
31	DARWEN	2	2	0	0	2	0	2	2	0	0	5	2	4	4	0	0	7	2
32	DERBY COUNTY	57	31	6	20	111	76	57	8	12	37	62	132	114	39	18	57	173	208
33	DONCASTER ROVERS	4	3	0	1	7	2	4	1	1	2	5	6	8	4	1	3	12	8
34	EVERTON	68	27	13	28	103	99	68	9	18	41	76	127	136	36	31	69	179	226
35	EXETER CITY	5	4	0	1	8	3	5	1	3	1	9	8	10	5	3	2	17	11
36	FULHAM	37	18	11	8	49	37	37	9	10	18	42	62	74	27	21	26	91	99

	OPPONENTS	HOME						AWAY						TOTAL					
		PL	W	D	L	F	A	PL	W	D	L	F	A	PL	W	D	L	F	A
37	GAINSBOROUGH	5	5	0	0	20	1	5	1	1	3	7	7	10	6	1	3	27	8
38	GILLINGHAM	6	2	1	3	9	8	6	2	1	3	7	9	12	4	2	6	16	17
39	GLOSSOP	4	3	0	1	10	1	4	3	1	0	9	5	8	6	1	1	19	6
40	GRIMSBY TOWN	27	13	7	7	58	32	27	8	10	9	27	38	54	21	17	16	85	70
41	HALIFAX TOWN	3	2	1	0	6	1	3	1	2	0	2	1	6	3	3	0	8	2
42	HARTLEPOOL UNITED	3	0	1	2	4	6	3	2	1	0	6	0	6	2	2	2	10	6
43	HEREFORD UNITED	2	2	0	0	4	1	2	1	1	0	6	3	4	3	1	0	10	4
44	HUDDERSFIELD TOWN	42	25	10	7	86	42	42	10	8	24	38	59	84	35	18	31	124	101
45	HULL CITY	20	12	7	1	33	14	20	4	8	8	18	25	40	16	15	9	51	39
46	IPSWICH TOWN	15	5	5	5	25	17	15	5	2	8	22	28	30	10	7	13	47	45
47	LEEDS UNITED	26	16	4	6	55	28	26	7	6	13	41	53	52	23	10	19	96	81
48	LEICESTER CITY	30	17	7	6	73	37	30	6	11	13	35	56	60	23	18	19	108	93
49	LINCOLN CITY	8	4	1	3	15	9	8	2	3	3	8	8	16	6	4	6	23	17
50	LIVERPOOL	58	25	13	20	83	77	58	10	16	32	55	110	116	35	29	52	138	187
51	LOUGHBOROUGH	1	1	0	0	7	0	1	1	0	0	3	2	2	2	0	0	10	2
52	LUTON TOWN	15	9	3	3	31	18	15	4	5	6	14	13	30	13	8	9	45	31
53	MANCHESTER CITY	55	28	15	12	104	63	55	13	10	32	62	103	110	41	25	44	166	166
54	MANCHESTER UNITED	58	25	15	18	96	80	58	16	10	32	60	104	116	41	25	50	156	184
55	MANSFIELD TOWN	7	3	3	1	8	4	7	2	3	2	6	9	14	5	6	3	14	13
56	MIDDLESBROUGH	54	33	15	6	113	57	54	16	12	26	67	100	108	49	27	32	180	157
57	MILLWALL	14	10	2	2	32	10	14	1	1	12	7	30	28	11	3	14	39	40
58	NEW BRIGHTON	1	1	0	0	2	1	1	0	0	1	1	3	2	1	0	1	3	4
59	NEWCASTLE UNITED	55	29	12	14	92	80	55	12	7	36	53	111	110	41	19	50	145	191
60	NEWPORT COUNTY	5	3	0	2	15	5	5	3	0	2	8	7	10	6	0	4	23	12
61	NORTHAMPTON TOWN	4	1	1	2	3	6	4	2	0	2	6	8	8	3	1	4	9	14
62	NORWICH CITY	17	10	5	2	26	10	17	3	3	11	16	28	34	13	8	13	42	38
63	NOTTS COUNTY	38	21	8	9	76	40	38	10	13	15	44	50	76	31	21	24	120	90
64	NOTTINGHAM FOREST	35	22	9	4	72	32	35	7	9	19	35	64	70	29	18	23	107	96
65	OLDHAM ATHLETIC	22	17	3	2	51	17	22	4	9	9	29	38	44	21	12	11	80	55
66	ORIENT	20	14	4	2	27	8	20	4	7	9	18	28	40	18	11	11	45	36
67	OXFORD UNITED	10	5	3	2	14	8	10	2	4	4	8	14	20	7	7	6	22	22
68	PETERBOROUGH UTD	3	2	1	0	5	2	3	2	0	1	7	3	6	4	1	1	12	5
69	PLYMOUTH ARGYLE	14	10	1	3	35	14	14	4	1	9	14	25	28	14	2	12	49	39
70	PORTSMOUTH	46	32	6	8	99	40	46	8	15	23	45	75	92	40	21	31	144	115
71	PORT VALE	15	13	2	0	40	7	15	7	7	1	22	13	30	20	9	1	62	20
72	PRESTON NORTH END	59	26	13	20	94	84	59	17	17	25	76	88	118	43	30	45	170	172
73	QPR	12	8	2	2	25	17	12	4	1	7	14	23	24	12	3	9	39	40
74	READING	11	7	2	2	20	10	11	3	1	7	10	15	22	10	3	9	30	25
75	ROCHDALE	3	2	1	0	4	2	3	0	3	0	6	6	6	2	4	0	10	8
76	ROTHERHAM UNITED	15	5	6	4	18	16	15	1	5	9	10	24	30	6	11	13	28	40
77	SCARBOROUGH	1	1	0	0	3	1	1	0	0	1	0	4	2	1	0	1	3	5
78	SCUNTHORPE UNITED	3	0	3	0	0	0	3	0	2	1	2	3	6	0	5	1	2	3
79	SHEFFIELD UNITED	54	34	12	8	117	60	54	11	10	33	68	125	108	45	22	41	185	185
80	SHEFFIELD WEDS	49	26	11	12	79	63	49	8	10	31	44	100	98	34	21	43	123	163

Gary Cahill scores the Wanderers first goal in a 3–2 defeat of Aston Villa at the Reebok Stadium in March 2011. It was the 150th League game between the clubs, with Bolton having played Villa more than any other club in the League.

	OPPONENTS	HOME						AWAY						TOTAL					
		PL	W	D	L	F	A	PL	W	D	L	F	A	PL	W	D	L	F	A
81	SHREWSBURY TOWN	8	4	1	3	8	8	8	4	1	3	11	9	16	8	2	6	19	17
82	SOUTHAMPTON	16	8	5	3	26	10	16	6	5	5	18	20	32	14	10	8	44	30
83	SOUTHEND UNITED	7	4	2	1	10	4	7	2	2	3	8	11	14	6	4	4	18	15
84	STOCKPORT COUNTY	9	3	3	3	12	10	9	3	2	4	11	13	18	6	5	7	23	23
85	STOKE CITY	39	19	12	8	73	46	39	12	6	21	37	78	78	31	18	29	110	124
86	SUNDERLAND	65	35	16	14	115	72	65	11	13	41	68	149	130	46	29	55	183	221
87	SWANSEA CITY	14	7	6	1	16	9	14	3	3	8	13	22	28	10	9	9	29	31
88	SWINDON TOWN	9	5	1	3	18	8	9	3	3	3	18	16	18	8	4	6	36	24
89	TORQUAY UNITED	3	2	0	1	4	2	3	0	1	2	2	5	6	2	1	3	6	7
90	TOTTENHAM HOTSPUR	43	25	7	11	76	52	43	9	7	27	43	81	86	34	14	38	119	133
91	TRANMERE ROVERS	11	8	2	1	18	8	11	2	6	3	10	11	22	10	8	4	28	19
92	WALSALL	9	7	1	1	25	9	9	0	3	6	9	17	18	7	4	7	34	26
93	WATFORD	10	6	1	3	17	10	10	1	3	6	7	16	20	7	4	9	24	26
94	WEST BROMWICH ALB	67	33	19	15	120	66	67	15	25	27	96	123	134	48	44	42	216	189
95	WEST HAM UNITED	28	21	4	3	67	21	28	9	4	15	43	61	56	30	8	18	110	82
96	WIGAN ATHLETIC	15	6	4	5	22	16	15	4	5	6	15	15	30	10	9	11	37	31
97	WIMBLEDON	4	3	1	0	6	2	4	1	1	2	3	7	8	4	2	2	9	9
98	WOLVERHAMPTON W	59	34	11	14	113	71	59	13	10	36	64	137	118	47	21	50	177	208
99	WREXHAM	5	3	1	1	6	3	5	4	0	1	8	4	10	7	1	2	14	7
100	YORK CITY	7	3	2	2	11	7	7	4	1	2	10	7	14	7	3	4	21	14

Bolton Wanderers in Europe

Anglo-Italian Cup

7 September 1993
Tranmere Rovers 1 Bolton Wanderers 2
While a visit to Prenton Park may not constitute a European game in many supporters' eyes, the competition was set up on a group basis with the most successful English sides going on to play Italian opposition. Aidan Davison produced his best-ever performance in a Wanderers goalkeeping shirt, making no less than 11 one-to-one saves, as Tranmere did everything but win the game. John McGinlay got a touch to Mark Patterson's angled shot to put Bolton ahead in the 23rd minute, and Owen Coyle increased the lead two minutes from the interval. Chris Malkin finally beat Davison to make it a tense last 10 minutes.

Davison, Parkinson, Phillips, Green, Darby, Winstanley, Lee, Fulton, Coyle, McGinlay, Patterson. Subs: Thompson, Lydiate, Branagan.
Attendance 2,786

Owen Coyle scores against Sunderland.

Aidan Davison – his best performance in the Anglo-Italian.

14 September 1993
Bolton Wanderers 2 Sunderland 0
Two superbly taken headers from Owen Coyle secured a place in the international stage of the competition. Manager Bruce Rioch admitted to not seeing Coyle play before signing him but knew of his goalscoring record. Once again Aidan Davison produced a sterling performance in goal as he had done the previous week. Coyle headed home Gary Parkinson's cross in the 74th minute and followed this up by putting away Scott Green's 86th-minute cross.

Davison, Parkinson, Phillips, Roscoe, Seagraves, Winstanley, Green, Fulton, Coyle, Thompson, Patterson. Subs: Lydiate, Fisher, Branagan. *Attendance 3,460*

12 October 1993
Bolton Wanderers 5 Ancona 0
The international stage of the competition got off to a great start in what was technically the club's first competitive game against European opposition, organised for clubs in the

Alan Thompson scores against Ancona.

second tier of the English and Italian League's. John McGinlay put the Wanderers ahead in the 11th minute, and when Jason McAteer hustled his way in for a second 12 minutes after the break it was going to be a case of how many? David Lee supplied a superb cross for Alan Thompson to head the third on 62 minutes, and he then turned provider for McGinlay to net his second. Jimmy Phillips then got in on the act, poaching a fifth from Scott Green's miskick eight minutes from time. The Italians hardly offered a threat, with Keith Branagan restricted to routine operations, especially after they had been reduced to 10 men after the dismissal of Felice Centofani for a foul on Jason McAteer.

Branagan, Brown, Phillips, Kelly, Seagraves, Stubbs, Lee, McAteer (Green), Thompson, McGinlay, Patterson. Subs: Winstanley, Parkinson, Coyle, Davison.
Attendance 3,448

9 November 1993
Bolton Wanderers 3 Brescia 3
Top Italian referee Pierre Luigi Collina put the Wanderers into a flattering match winning position when he awarded them a penalty for handball just two minutes from time. He overturned the decision after consulting his linesman in a touchline rumpus, but Bolton could have no complaints after receiving a footballing lesson from Gheorghe Hagi and his Brescia teammates. Gabriell Ambrosetti put the Italians ahead in the third minute when he was set up by Hagi who threatened to make it an exhibition. Owen Coyle got Bolton back into it after 39 minutes, and he then set up John McGinlay to put the Wanderers ahead three minutes after the interval. A 35-yard Hagi free-kick that slipped through Davison's grasp levelled things before Ambrosetti put the Italians into

Pisa – Bolton's first competitive European away fixture.

the lead. Scott Green fired home a 74th-minute equaliser to keep up Wanderers unbeaten run in the competition.

Davison, Parkinson, Phillips, Green, Stubbs, Winstanley, Lee, (Thompson), McAteer, Coyle, McGinlay, Patterson (Fulton). Subs: Burke, Seagraves, Hoult.
Attendance 3.021

16 November 1993
Pisa 1 Bolton Wanderers 1

The Wanderers looked anything but European newcomers in their first competitive game on foreign soil. Playing a continental style three central-defenders, they went ahead in the 23rd minute when Jimmy Phillips struck a venomous 20-yarder into the roof of the net. Pisa levelled just before half-time when Luca Mattei was on hand to find the net from close range. The Wanderers did not produce much in the way of goalscoring opportunities, but the locals were left fascinated by the 20-minute chant of 'We are the one and only Wanderers' from the 500 travellers that only stopped at the final whistle.

Davison, Brown, Phillips, Kelly, Seagraves, Winstanley, McAteer, Stubbs, Coyle (Lee), McGinlay, Thompson. Subs: Green, Fulton, Burke, Hoult.
Attendance 1,000

22 December 1993
Ascoli 1 Bolton Wanderers 1

Referee Peter Foakes needed a police escort from the pitch as the Wanderers Anglo-Italian adventure ended in controversy. Italian players pushed and aimed kicks at the official in furious protest over his handling of the game that ended in a 1–1 draw when Mark Seagraves snatched a dramatic late equaliser. Pedro Troglio gave Ascoli the lead in the 52nd minute and looked to have gone further behind when Oliver Bierhoff struck, only for the referee to disallow the effort sparking a lack of discipline in the Italian side. In injury time Seagraves got onto the end of Tony Kelly's free-kick, and Wanderers' only shot on target was enough to square it and extend the team's unbeaten run to 13 games. Despite being unbeaten in the competition, it was Notts County who topped the English group and they went on to face Brescia in the Final at Wembley.

Hoult, Parkinson, Phillips, Kelly, Seagraves, Winstanley, McAteer, Stubbs, Coyle (Green), Fleck, Thompson. Subs: Brown, Patterson, Lee, Davison.
Attendance 1,000

Anglo-Italian Cup Record

	PL	W	D	L	F	A
Home	3	2	1	0	10	3
Away	3	1	2	0	4	3
Total	6	3	3	0	14	6

El Hadji Diouf scores the club's first UEFA
Cup goal against Plovdiv at The Reebok.

UEFA Cup

2005–06
First round first leg
15 September 2005
Bolton Wanderers 2 Lokomotive Plovdiv 1

The Wanderers much anticipated first taste of major European competition threatened to turn
sour when the Bulgarians plundered a 27th-minute goal against the run of play. Plovdiv, who
had come though the qualifiers to reach the first-round stage, let themselves down with their
dubious tactics which got worse after Boban Janchevski put them ahead. Their gamesmanship
proved to be their undoing when George Iliev went down holding his ankle after a tackle by
Kevin Nolan. Having already kicked the ball out a number of times when they had feigned
injury, Nolan set up an attack which culminated in Nicky Hunt delivering a quality cross for El
Hadji Diouf to score with a stunning diving header after 72 minutes. Fielding a side from 11
different countries in the starting line up, Bolton had their best spell of the game after
equalising, but it was not until two minutes into injury time that they grabbed a winner that
gave them a slender first-leg lead. The goal was constructed and scored by new signings.
Substitute, Fabrice Fernandes, making his debut, crossed for another debutant, Hidetoshi
Nakata to head on to Jared Borgetti and the Mexican netted his first goal for the club to give
them a fighting chance of progressing to the group stages.

Bolton: Jääskeläinen, Hunt, Jaidi, N'Gotty, Pedersen (Borgetti), Okoacha (Nolan), Campo,
Nakata, Giannakopoulos (Fernandes), Diouf, Gardner. Subs: Davies, O'Brien, Faye, Walker.
Plovdiv: Kolev, Ivanov, Kotev, Giordani, Tunchev, Iliev (Vundev), Dimitrov, Krizmanic, Petrov,
Halimi (Georgiev), Janchevski (Stoynev). Subs: Zlatinski, Mihailov, Hristev, Kamburov.
Attendance: 19,723

First round second leg
29 September 2005
Lokomotive Plovdiv 1 Bolton Wanderers 2
(Aggregate: Bolton Wanderers 4 Lokomotive Plovdiv 2)

The Wanderers left it late to qualify for the group stages of the UEFA Cup. Trailing 1–0 with
just 11 minutes to go, they came from behind, just as they had done at The Reebok Stadium
in the first leg two weeks earlier, to make it a memorable night at the Naftex Stadium in
Burgas on the Black Sea coast. Plovdiv, playing a home game on neutral territory due to
their home stadium not having passed the UEFA standards, took the lead six minutes into
the second half when Georgi Iliev hit an unstoppable 30-yarder that threatened to knock
the Wanderers out on the away goals rule. The home supporters celebrated by lighting
flares, an act that was to get them fined by UEFA. Sam Allardyce made seven changes to the
side that had defeated Portsmouth in the Premiership five days earlier, giving Ian Walker,

Kevin Nolan celebrates his winner in Bulgaria against Plovdiv.

Joey O'Brien, Fabrice Fernandes and Jared Borgetti their first starts of the season, but it was not until the introductions of the substitutions that Bolton got onto the front foot. Eleven minutes from time the Wanderers got lucky. With over 2,000 supporters behind them, Lokomotive full-back Alexander Tunchev turned Henrik Pedersen's cross into his own net and from then on there was only going to be one winner. Four minutes later the tie was made safe when Kevin Nolan struck a first-time shot from the edge of the penalty area to finish off a superb move that involved Henrik Pedersen and Kevin Davies. Late on, Ian Walker produced a stunning save to deny Iliev and that ensured that the Wanderers would be involved in at least four more European ties against different opponents.

Bolton: Walker, Ben Haim, N'Gotty, Faye, Pedersen, Giannakopoulos, Fernandes (Nolan), O'Brien (Nakata), Okocha, Diouf, Borgetti (Davies). Subs: Fojut, Vaz Te, Gardner, Jääskeläinen.
Plovdiv: Kolev, Ivanov, Kotev, Giordani, Tunchev, Iliev, Dimitrov, Krizmanich (Halimi), Petrov, Vandev (Stoneyev), Janchevski. Subs: Mihailov, Georgiev, Hristev, Zlatinov, Kamburov.
Attendance: 14,000

Group H stages, match one
20 October 2005
Besiktas 1 Bolton Wanderers 1
The Inönü Stadium in Istanbul was an intimidating and hostile environment for the Wanderers to open their group phase. Most of the crowd assembled an hour before the kick-off to guarantee a fiery reception to the Wanderers as they warmed up and to the few hundred followers that had made the trip to Turkey. Much was expected from the Turkish side who had been champions in 2003, and they got off to the best possible start. There was only seven minutes on the clock when Brazilian striker Ailton blasted a 20-yard shot past Ian Walker. This only increased the noise level and Bolton looked vulnerable to the Turks

blistering pace up front. Having made seven changes to the side that had lost 5–1 at Chelsea the previous Saturday, mainly due to injuries, they needed something to get a foothold back into the game and it arrived in the 28th minute. Jared Borgetti grabbed his

Jared Borgetti celebrates his goal against Besiktas.

503

second goal in the competition when he got onto the end of a cross from El Hadji Diouf, finishing off a move he had started himself, and from then on the pressure was on the home side. The goal from Borgetti proved to be a catalyst to a solid performance from the Wanderers, with Khalilou Fadiga producing what was his best performance in a Bolton shirt and 19-year-old Joey O'Brien solid in midfield. Indeed, the Wanderers came close to winning the tie when Diouf found the net after 71 minutes only to have the goal ruled out for offside. At the final whistle the unhappy Besiktas fans turned on their own team and directors in protest at their decline over the previous two years.

Bolton: Walker, Ben Haim, Faye, Jaidi, Gardner, Fernandes (Nolan), Nakata, O'Brien, Fadiga, Diouf, Borgetti. Subs: Davies, N'Gotty, Vaz Te, Fojut, Pedersen, Jääskeläinen.
Besiktas: Cordoba, Havutcu, Toraman (Zan), (Dogan), Atan, Dursun, Hassan, Avci, Kleberson, Akim, Metim (Uzulmez), Ailton. Subs: Gunes, Veysel, Cihan, Dursun, Sahin.
Attendance: 17,027

Group H stages, match two
3 November 2005
Bolton Wanderers 1 Zenit St Petersburg 0
Two magnificent late saves from Jussi Jääskeläinen made sure that a first-half goal from captain Kevin Nolan earned maximum points that left the Wanderers on top of the group and within touching distance of the last 32. The game became farcical when torrential rain that had fallen almost incessantly for the previous two days continued throughout the game. It made for atrocious playing conditions and the rain washed away the green dye used to cover the smaller pitch markings used in the Premier League, so much so that players took throw-ins while standing in the playing area! There can be little doubt that if it had been a domestic game that it would have been abandoned. The Wanderers made just two changes to the side that had won at Charlton the previous Saturday, and the victory over the Russian's extended the unbeaten run to five games, the previous four having been won without conceding a goal. The only goal came in the 24th minute. Bruno N'Gotty's free-kick fell to Stelios Giannakopoulos in a crowded penalty area and his shot was only parried by 'keeper, Kamil Contofalsky, the ball falling to Nolan who prodded home the rebound. It was the first time that the Wanderers had scored first in their UEFA Cup campaign. The Russians did not lie down, and they showed plenty of class that might have produced a different result but for the conditions. Jääskeläinen produced the first of his match-winning saves in the 77th minute when he denied Egor Denisov. In injury-time Zenit skipper Andrey Arshavin pounced, but the Finn produced a match-winning reaction save.

Bolton: Jaasskelainen, O'Brien, Ben Haim, N'Gotty, Gardner, Faye, Giannakopoulos, Nakata (Okocha), Speed, Nolan (Diouf), Davies (Borgetti). Subs: Walker, Jaidi, Vaz Te, Fojut.

Jay Jay Okocha makes a splash against Zenit.

Zenit St Petersburg: Contofalsky, Flachbart, Hagen, Vjestica, Skrtel (Gorshkov), Anyukov, Sumulikoski, Denisov, Vlasov (Kozlov), Kerzhakov, Arshavin. Subs: Malafeev, Cadikovsky, Poskus, Kozhanov, Stroev.
Attendance: 15,905

Group H stages, match three
24 November 2005
Vitoria Guimaraes 1 Bolton Wanderers 1

Ricardo Vaz Te stepped up to the plate for the Wanderers when Sam Allardyce threw him into the fray with just three minutes of the game remaining when they were trailing by a single goal. There were just five minutes remaining when Vitoria's Polish striker, Mrek Saganowski, broke the deadlock and threatened to inflict the Wanderers first defeat in the competition. He became the first player to breach Bolton's defence for six games, 618 minutes, Ailton's goal for Besiktas being the last goal conceded. It was Bolton's last throw of the dice when Vaz Te took to the field, but the Portugese Under-20 international took it

Ricardo Vaz Te after scoring his late equaliser in Guimaraes.

all in his stride to equalise within a minute of taking the field. Taking a pass from El Hadji Diouf on the edge of the penalty area, he let fly with a powerful right-foot shot that left Pavia stranded and sent 3,000 travelling Bolton fans into party mode. It was yet another never-say-die performance from the Wanderers, despite a poor first-half show, coming from behind for the fourth time in the competition and being ably led by Kevin Nolan who was playing his first game since being officially installed as club captain.

Bolton: Jääskeläinen, O'Brien, Ben Haim, N'Gotty, Gardner, Nolan, Okocha (Vaz Te), Faye, Nakata (Speed), Giannakopoulos, Borgetti (Diouf). Subs: Walker, Jaidi, Hunt, Fadiga.
Vitoria Guimaraes: Pavia, Sergio, Cleber, Dragoner, Matias, Svard, Flavio, Neca (Sergio), Benachour, Saganowski, Dario (Targino). Subs: Freitas, Moreno, Geromel, Manoel, Zezinho.
Attendance: 20,000

Group H stages, match four
14 December 2005
Bolton Wanderers 1 Sevilla 1

Bruno N'Gotty grabbed his first goal in almost two years to secure the Wanderers place in the last 32 of the UEFA Cup. The result left them as the only unbeaten team in the group, and the point staved off a late challenge from Besiktas to pip them. Bolton made six changes to the side that had faced Aston Villa in the Premiership while Sevilla, second favourites to win the competition, fielded just three players who had faced Barcelona the previous weekend. The Spaniards came closest in the first half when Luis Fabiano hit the post, but it was half-time

Bruno N'Gotty scores against Sevilla.

substitute N'Gotty who fired Bolton in front after 65 minutes. Sevilla introduced their big names and were rewarded with an equaliser from Adriano in the 74th minute and both teams secured their passage through to the knockout stages.

Bolton: Walker, Hunt, Ben Haim, Jaidi, Gardner (N'Gotty), Diouf, Fadiga, Faye (Speed), Okocha, Nakata, Davies (Vaz Te). Subs: Nolan, Speed, Giannakopoulos, Borgetti, Jääskeläinen.

Sevilla: Notario, Crespo, Prieto, Alfaro, Dragutinovic, Lopez (Adriano), Ruiz (Ocio), Marti, Puerta, Kepa (Saviola), Fabiano. Subs: Kanoute, Navas, Capel, Palop.

Attendance: 15,623

Group H

	PL	W	D	L	F	A	Pts
Sevilla	4	2	1	1	8	4	7
Zenit St Petersburg	4	2	1	1	5	4	7
Bolton Wanderers	4	1	3	0	4	3	6
Besiktas	4	1	2	1	5	6	5
Vitoria Guimaraes	4	0	1	3	4	9	1

Third round first leg
15 February 2006
Bolton Wanderers 0 Marseille 0

Bolton were frustrated by a well-organised and impressive Marseille side, but more so by the Portugese referee, Olegario Benquerenca, who turned down no less than four penalty appeals, including one blatant handball by Frederic Dehu. Even rival boss, Jean Fernandez, admitted that Jay Jay Okocha's 37th-minute cross should have resulted in a penalty for the Wanderers, the defender knocking the ball out for a corner with his hand. The French side relied on a counter-attacking game, and lone striker Mamadou Niang was always a threat. Five minutes into the second half he capitalised on a rare mistake by Bruno N'Gotty to have a free run on goal. Jussi Jääskeläinen went down at his feet to deny the Senegalese striker and make sure that the Wanderers remained unbeaten in the competition. At the other end, former Manchester United 'keeper, Fabien Barthez, was also in good form with his best save coming as early as the seventh minute to keep out an Okocha rocket.

Bolton: Jääskeläinen, O'Brien, Ben Haim, N'Gotty, Gardner, Nolan, Faye, Okocha (Speed) Davies, Borgetti (Vaz Te), Giannakopoulos. Subs: Hunt, Jaidi, Perez, Fojut, Walker.

Marseille: Barthez, Ferreira, Beye, Dehu, Cesar, Taiwo, Nasri (Giminez), Cana, Oruma, Ribery, Niang (Cantareil). Subs: Delfim, Meite, Covelli, Deruda, Carrasso.

Third round second leg
23 February 2006
Marseille 2 Bolton Wanderers 1
(Aggregate: Marseille 2 Bolton Wanderers 1)

Bolton's first foray into major European competition ended in disappointment at The Stade Velodrome but not before giving the former 1993 European champions a fright. Needing a score draw at least to go through, they got off to a great start after 25 minutes when Stelios Giannakopoulos pounced to capitalise when Fabien Barthez dropped a cross from Jay Jay Okocha,

Stelios Giannakopoulos puts Bolton ahead in Marseille.

silencing the fanatical home crowd. The Wanderers thought they had increased their lead in the 39th minute when Abdoulaye Faye had a goal ruled out by a debateable offside decision. The game turned on the stroke of half-time when a poor clearance from Bruno N'Gotty fell to Samir Nasri who crossed for Frank Ribery to head the equaliser. The impetus changed and Marseille came out for the second half a changed team. The French side took the lead with what turned out to be the deciding goal in the 68th minute when Tal Ben Haim attempted to intercept Habib Beye's cross only to turn the ball past Jussi Jääskeläinen and into his own net. And so the European adventure came to an end, but the players remained upbeat and determined that it would not be the last time that the club would be involved in the competition.

Bolton: Jääskeläinen, O'Brien, Ben Haim, N'Gotty, Gardner, Nolan, Okocha, Faye (Pedersen), (Borgetti), Speed (Vaz Te), Giannakopoulos, Davies. Subs: Hunt, Nakata, Jaidi, Walker.
Marseille: Barthez, Ferreira (Deruda), Meite, Dehu, Beye, Taiwo, Cana (Civelli), Nasri, Oruma, Ribery (Cantareil), Niang. Subs: Luis, Giminez, Begeorgi, Carrasso.
Attendance: 38,351

2007–08
First round first leg
22 September 2007
Rabotnicki Kometal 1 Bolton Wanderers 1

The Wanderers found the going hard on their visit to Macedonia for the group qualifying game. After creating, and missing, a host of chances they fell behind in the 52nd minute when a mistake from Gerald Cid led to Nemanja Milisavievic giving the Skopje side the lead. The home side, unbeaten in ten domestic and European games were happy to add overacting and feigning injury to their repertoire despite causing a nervous Wanderers defence some hairy moments. At the other end both El Hadi Diouf and Nicolas Anelka missed good

Abdoulaye Meite stabs home the equaliser at Rabotnicki.

chances, Diouf spooning the ball over from eight yards and the Frenchman rounding the 'keeper only to put the ball into the side netting. With just seven minutes remaining Abdoulaye Meite rescued Bolton. He grabbed his second goal for the club from close range after the home side's 'keeper Filip Madzovski had spilled Anelka's free-kick to silence the home crowd and put the Wanderers into the driving seat with a precious away goal.

Bolton: Jääskeläinen, Hunt (J. O'Brien), Meite, Cid (A. O'Brien), Gardner, McCann (Braaten), Davies, Nolan, Speed, Diouf, Anelka. Subs: Alonso, Teimourian, Guthrie, Al-Habsi.
Rabotnicki: Madzovski, Bosinovski, Vajs, Stanisic, Lukman, Demiri, Nedzipi, Gligorov, Osmani (Pejcic), Trickovski (Selim), Milisavievic. Subs: Gjorevski, Idrizi, Sabani, Pacovski.
Attendance: 8,500

First round second leg
4 October 2007
Bolton Wanderers 1 Rabotnicki Kometal 0
(Aggregate: Rabotnicki Kometal 1 Bolton Wanderers 2)
The Wanderers made it through to the group stages thanks to a 67th-minute goal from Nicolas Anelka. The striker had been on the pitch just 80 seconds when he scored with his first touch. The Frenchman took the captain's armband after replacing Kevin Davies and rose superbly at the back post to head home a cross from Stelios Giannkopoulos for his sixth goal of the season. Anelka claimed it was the first time he had ever scored with his first touch, but more importantly the win stretched Bolton's unbeaten run to five games to take

some of the pressure off manager Sammy Lee. Lee had made seven changes to the side that had drawn at Derby in the Premiership the previous weekend. One was forced, Ivan Campo not having been registered for the competition, Ricardo Gardner, Abdoulaye Faye, Nicolas Anelka and El Hadji Diouf all dropped to the bench while Gary Speed and Kevin Nolan were rested. The win was more convincing than the score suggests, with Bolton creating a number of chances that were wasted, the best of which fell to Giannakopoulos, a half-time replacement for Alonso, who rounded the

'Captain' Anelka after scoring the winner against Rabotnicki at The Reebok.

'keeper but saw his effort cleared off the line. The Greek international made up for that minutes later with his pin-point cross for Anelka.

Bolton: Jääskeläinen, J. Obrien, A. O'Brien, Michalik, Cid, McCann, Braaten (Diouf), Alonso (Giannakopoulos), Guthrie, Wilhelmsson, Davies (Anelka). Subs: Teimourian, Meite, Gardner, Al-Habsi.
Rabotnicki: Pacouski, Kovacevic, Vajs, Stanisic, Lukman (Bozinivski), Demini, Nedzipi, Gligorov, Milisavievic, Trickovski (Pejcic), Osmani. Subs: Velkovski, Idrizi, Lazarevski, Mikajlovic.
Attendance: 18,932

Group F stages, match one
25 October 2007
Bolton Wanderers 1 SC Braga 1

Wanderers' new boss Gary Megson, appointed the previous afternoon, was denied a winning start when a late equaliser cost two home points in the opening group game. It was caretaker Archie Knox who issued the instructions on the night, with Megson taking a back seat before a disappointing crowd at the Reebok Stadium. Bolton struggled to impose themselves against the Portugese but still created chances before the interval, the best of which fell to Kevin Davies, who headed Nicolas Anelka's cross over the bar. The introduction of El Hadji Diouf changed things in the 62nd minute. The crowd chanted a chorus of 'you don't know what you're doing' as he replaced the hard-working Danny Guthrie, but he had been on the field just four minutes when he headed home a pin-point cross from Davies to put Bolton into the driving seat. It appeared that the points had been secured until they let their guard drop in the 86th minute, allowing in Brazilian striker Jailson, on loan from Benfica, to get onto the end of a deep cross to shoot past Jussi Jääskeläinen and earn Braga a share of the spoils. The focus immediately returned to the Premier League after the game and the visit of Aston Villa, with the Wanderers lying bottom with just five points from 10 games.

Bolton: Jääskeläinen, Hunt, A. O'Brien, Meite, Cid, McCann, Davies, Guthrie (Diouf), Speed, Gardner (Teimourian), Anelka. Subs: Al-Habsi, J. O'Brien, Nolan, Braaten, Alonso.
Braga: Santos, Pereira, Jorge, Rodriguez, Peixoto, Andres Madrid (Jailson), Vandinho, Castanheira (Stelvio), Jorginho, Linz, Wender (Manuel). Subs: Dabi, Tomas, Fernandes, Anilton.
Attendance: 10,848

Group F stages, match two
8 November 2007
Bayern Munich 2 Bolton Wanderers 2

Gary Megson repeated his claim that progress in Europe came a poor second to the prime objective of keeping the Wanderers in the Premiership but the weakened team, with only five players included that played against West Ham the previous weekend, made it a memorable night for the club and its supporters. The 4,000 who had followed the club to Munich to see the Wanderers take on the Bundesliga leaders were in heaven when, after only eight minutes, Ricardo Gardner latched on to Danny Guthrie's through ball to chip the ball

Ricardo Gardner puts the Wanderers ahead in Munich.

over Oliver Kahn for his first goal since Boxing Day 2002. The Wanderers then had to defend in numbers after that early breakthrough but Kevin Davies went close to increasing the lead in the 29th minute with a shot that went narrowly wide. A minute later Bayern levelled when Lokas Podolski drove a shot low into the net after being set up by Franck Ribery. Ali Al-Habsi, making only his second appearance for the club, was working overtime and he produced a magnificent save to deny Bastian Schweinsteiger just before the interval. He could do little to prevent Bayern going ahead in the 49th minute when Ribery and Podolski again combined for the latter to grab his second from close range. Bolton began to get stretched by the German's pace as they looked to keep up their unbeaten start to the season. The Omani 'keeper produced a stunning save to deny Ribery on the hour as the German's thought they had done enough to secure the game. The Allianz Arena was stunned eight minutes from time when Kevin Nolan got the better of Christian Lell to set up Davies to smash home the equaliser with his first goal of the season. The makeshift Wanderers side had pulled off a major shock to produce their best-ever result in European football.

The team that drew at Bayern Munich. Back. Al-Habsi, A. O'Brien, Michalik, Nolan, Cid, Braaten. Front. Davies, Gardner, Alonso, McCann, Guthrie.

Bolton: Al-Habsi, McCann, Michalik, A. O'Brien, Cid, Nolan, Braaten (Teimourian), Guthrie, Alonso (Giannakopoulos), Gardner, Davies. Subs: Sissons, Sinclair, Speed, Harsanyi, Walker.

Bayern Munich: Khan, Lell, Lucio, Van Buyten, Jansen, Schweinsteiger (Altintop), Van Bommel, Otti, Ribery (Kroos), Podolski (Toni), Klose. Subs: Ze Roberto, Schlaudraff, Rensing. *Attendance: 66,000*

Group F stages, match three
29 November 2007
Bolton Wanderers 1 Aris Thessaloniki 1
It was Stelios Giannakopoulos who came to the Wanderers rescue with a 93rd-minute strike to earn a point that kept them in the hunt to qualify, for the midfielder had failed to start in any of the Wanderers Premier League games so far but made the most of the chance given to him against his fellow countrymen. The game came five days after an impressive home win against Manchester United in the Premier League, but the performance left a lot

Stelios Giannakopoulos scores against Aris.

to be desired. Although there were four changes to the side, it was Aris who took the initiative and went ahead in the 44th minute. Abdoulaye Meite's header fell to Calvo who volleyed past Jussi Jääskeläinen to send their 1,500 supporters wild with delight. The Wanderers had chances to level, Andy O'Brien seeing a header crash against the bar and Kevin Davies having a close-range shot straight at the 'keeper. The introduction of El Hadji Diouf and Nicolas Anelka brightened things up, but things became frustrating as chances came and went. At the other end Jääskeläinen made a spectacular save from a 30-yard strike from Garcia, but just as Aris thought they had booked their passage through to the last 32, Stelios maintained the Wanderers' unbeaten home record in Europe.

Bolton: Jääskeläinen, Hunt, A. O'Brien, Meite, Cid, McCann (Alonso), Giannakopoulos, Nolan, Guthrie, Wilhelmsson (Diouf), Davies (Anelka). Subs: Michalik, Samuel, Teimourian, Al-Habsi.

Aris Thessaloniki: Chalklas, Neto, Papadopoulos, Ronaldo, Karampelas, Nempegleras, Garcia (Gogolos), Prittas, Calvo (Javito), Koke (Kyriakos), Siston. Subs: Kelemen, Koulucheris, Sanchon, Aurielo.
Attendance 10,229

Group F stages, match four
6 December 2007
Red Star Belgrade 0 Bolton Wanderers 1
The Wanderers put one foot into the last 32 when a scratch side became the first English team to win at the home of the former European champions. The result left them at the top of the group but they now had to wait for a fortnight for the final group games to be played.

It was a performance that showed plenty of control and composure with the winning goal coming on the stroke of half-time to silence the Marakana crowd except for the small band of 400 Bolton supporters who made themselves heard in the vast bowl. It was Gavin McCann, with his first goal for the club, that secured the precious victory. He fired in an angled shot from the edge of the penalty area and the ball flew into the net off the 'keeper's right-hand post. The goal capped a tireless performance in midfield. Ali Al-Habsi again produced a European performance of quality with a number of

Gavin McCann hits the winner in Belgrade.

511

stunning first-half saves but found he had little to do after the interval as the home crowd took to giving their own players the bird with piercing whistles. Braga produced a 2–0 win over Red Star to go above the Wanderers, but there was relief when Bayern hammered Aris 6–0 to not only send Bolton through but put their draw at the Allianz into perspective.

Bolton: Al-Habsi, Hunt, Meite, Michalik, Samuel, McCann, Giannakopoulos, Teimourian, Speed, Wilhelmsson, Braaten (Sinclair). Subs: Guthrie, Harsanyi, Cassidy, Sissons, Woolfe, Walker.
Red Star: Randelovic, Basta, Tutoric, Bajalica, Bronowicki (Anelkovic), Milovanovic, Lukas, Milijas (Burzanovic), Molina, Koroman, Jestrovic (F. Dordevic). Subs: V. Dordevic, Catillo, Banovic.
Attendance: 30,689
Group F

	PL	W	D	L	F	A	Pts
Bayern Munich	4	2	2	0	12	5	8
Braga	4	1	3	0	5	3	6
Bolton Wanderers	4	1	3	0	5	4	6
Aris	4	1	2	1	5	8	5
Red Star Belgrade	4	0	0	4	2	9	0

Third round first leg
14 February 2008
Bolton Wanderers 1 Atletico Madrid 0
The club's best-ever home crowd for a European game saw the Wanderers, lying three points above the relegation zone, defeat the fourth-best team in Spain in a match that was marred with controversy. The victory showcased Bolton's increasing organisation and spirit under Gary Megson, and they took advantage of a second-half dismissal to give themselves a first-leg lead and hope of progressing further. The turning point came in the 73rd minute when Sergio Aguero was sent off for spitting, and a minute later Bolton grabbed what turned out to be the winning goal. Matt Taylor, playing his first European tie and a constant problem to the Madrid defence, fired in an effort that bounced off a defender and fell to El Hadji Diouf who finished clinically with his fifth goal of the season. The nine times Spanish champions came closest to scoring when Diego Forlan clipped the outside of the post with a shot, but the Wanderers' work ethic had them riled and they found chances hard to come by. The atmosphere in the stadium made it a special European night and set up an intriguing second leg the following week.

Bolton: Jääskeläinen, Hunt, Samuel, Campo, A. O'Brien, Cahill, Nolan, Guthrie (Giannakopoulos), Taylor, Davies, Diouf. Subs: Meite, Teimourian, Vaz Te, J. O'Brien, Sinclair, Al-Habsi.

El Hadji Diouf grabs the winner against Atletico.

Atletico: Abbiati, Antonio Lopez, Pernia, Luis Perea, Pablo Ibanez, Santana, Maxi Rodriguez, Reyes (Aguero), Simao (Jurado), Forlan, Mista (Miguel). Subs: Eller, Rodriguez Rivas, Dominguez, Falcon.
Attendance: 26,163

Third round second leg
21 February 2008
Atletico Madrid 0 Bolton Wanderers 0
(Aggregate Bolton Wanderers 1 Atletico Madrid 0)
Against all the odds, the Wanderers produced a magnificent rearguard action to hold Atletico to a scoreless draw in the Vicente Calderon and march into the last 16 of the competition to surpass the achievement of two years previous when they went out at this stage. The Spaniards had attempted to get at the Wanderers, putting details of the team's travel itinerary on their website, and warned the officials to be tough against a perceived physical threat. The hostile atmosphere in the stadium was no surprise, and the Spaniards created opportunities that went begging. Bolton stood firm throughout and, despite Atletico's dominance as they desperately tried to level the aggregate, Jussi Jääskeläinen was never seriously tested. At the other end it was not until late in the game the Bolton created opportunities with substitutes Ivan Campo and El Hadji Diouf going close. Ten minutes from time Atletico appealed for a penalty as Diego Forlan's cross hit Jlloyd Samuel, but the Wanderers breathed a sigh of relief as the referee waved play on. Almost 4,000 Wanderers supporters, situated on the top tier of the stadium were jubilant, but unfortunately celebrations were marred for some of them when fighting broke out with the police.

Bolton: Jääskeläinen, Hunt, Cahill, A.O'Brien (Meite), Samuel, Giannakopoulos (Diouf), Nolan, J. O'Brien, McCann (Campo), Taylor, Davies. Subs: Teimourian, Alonso, Vaz Te, Al-Habsi.
Atletico:Abbiati, Antonio Lopez, Perea, Pablo Ibanez (Mista), Pernia, Luis Garcia (De las Cuevas) Cleber Santana, Jurado, Maxi Rodriguez, Reyes, Forlan. Subs: Eller, De Castro, Quillo, Dominguez, Falcon.
Attendance: 27,590

Fourth round first leg
6 March 2008
Bolton Wanderers 1 Sporting Lisbon 1
The Wanderers were left with it all to do in the second leg after Sporting hit back with an away goal to make them favourites in the second leg. Things got off to a great start for Bolton, who were backed by an enthusiastic Reebok crowd. Having got themselves on top they took the lead in the 26th minute when Heidar Helguson and Kevin Davies combined from Nicky Hunt's free-kick to set up Gavin McCann. The midfielder, without a domestic goal to his name for the club, netted his second in the competition by calmly sliding the ball beyond Rui Patricio in the Sporting goal. Chances continued to come and go. Both McCann and Matt Taylor missed the target from good positions and Helguson hit the bar with a header early in the second half. The visitors became more of a threat late in the game. In the 68th minute substitute Romagnoli shot against the bar, and two minutes later the Portuguese levelled. Simon Vukcevic linked with

Rodrigo Tiui to get behind the Wanderers defence and slip the ball past Ali Al-Habsi. A booking for McCann meant he would miss the second leg, while Wanderers manager was left to complain that the Israeli referee, Alon Yefet, had let Sporting off the hook when he has missed a blatant handball outside his area by 'keeper Rui Patricio early in the game.

Bolton: Al-Habsi, Hunt, A. O'Brien, Cahill, Gardner, Campo (Teimourian), Davies, J. O'Brien (Guthrie), McCann, Taylor, Helguson (Giannakopoulos). Subs: Samuel, Meite, Vaz Te, Walker.
Sporting: Rui Patricio, Abel Ferreira (Romagnoli), Tonel, Polga, Grimi, Pereirinha, Veloso, Joao Moutinho, Izmailov (Gladstone), Tiui (Adrien Silva), Vukcevic. Subs: Stojkovic, Pedro Silva, Purovic, Farnerud.
Attendance: 25,664

Fourth round second leg
13 March 2008
Sporting Lisbon 1 Bolton Wanderers 0
(Aggregate: Bolton Wanderers 1 Sporting Lisbon 2)
The Wanderers bowed out of the UEFA Cup when a goal from Bruno Pereirinha five minutes from time gave Sporting a narrow win in the Jose Alvalade Stadium to deny Bolton a place in the quarter-finals. Manager Gary Megson defended his decision to rest a number of first-team regulars in preparation for the following weekend's Premier League game at Wigan Athletic. He considered the starting line up, including six full internationals and four Under-21 internationals, to be capable of getting a result. The Wanderers had to score to have any chance of going through, and they frustrated the home side with their direct approach to the game. Neither 'keeper had much to do until late in the game when Bolton had to go for broke in their attempt to find the net and, in doing so, the game opened up. Unfortunately, despite their great effort, Rui Patricio in the Sporting goal was never really tested while at the other end it was Ali Al-Habsi who produced some great saves late in the game to keep the Wanderers in with a shout. One small consolation was the fact that the Wanderers had the distinction of being the last English side left in the competition after Tottenham and Everton had been eliminated the previous evening.

Bolton: Al-Habsi, Hunt, Samuel, Teimourian (Braaten), Cahill, Meite, J. O'Brien, Guthrie, Helguson (Woolfe), Vaz Te, Giannakopoulos. Subs: Harsanyi, jamieson, Sinclair, Sisson, Walker.
Sporting: Rui Patricio, Anderson Polga, Tonel, Grimi, Abel Ferreira, Izmailov (Gladstone), Vukcevic (Tiui), Pereirinha, Joao Moutinho, Romagnoli, (Silva), Liedson. Subs: Ronny, Yannick, Farnerud, Stojkovic.
Attendance: 22,031

UEFA Cup Record

	PL	W	D	L	F	A
Home	9	4	5	0	9	5
Away	9	2	5	2	9	9
Total	18	6	10	2	18	14

Bolton in Other Cups

The Lancashire Cup

Right from the inception of the Lancashire Senior Cup in 1879–80 Bolton Wanderers took part, with their first opponents in that inaugural season being Bolton All Saints. Although now seen as a relatively minor competition, it is a competition that had a long and interesting history, with the Wanderers having played their part, winning the magnificent trophy on no fewer than 12 occasions.

The Lancashire FA, formed in September 1878, saw the competition as its flagship, and in February 1880 the trophy was commissioned with a design by Monk Brothers of Bolton being accepted. The cost of the trophy, which stands 39in tall, amounted to £160.

It was Darwen who won the first competition, and it was not until 1886 when the Wanderers got their hands on the trophy for the first time when they defeated Blackburn Rovers at Deepdale before 7,000. It was seen as just revenge for an incident that had occurred in the previous season's competition.

The Wanderers had triumphed 5–1 against Rovers in the semi-final at Darwen in April 1885, but Rovers protested that Bolton had fielded four ineligible players. At the time the rule was that a player had to have two years' residential qualification, the same as in the FA Cup, before being eligible. The Welsh contingent of Powell, Vaughan, Roberts and Jones were the 'culprits', and the Wanderers Secretary did not contest the protest which saw them expelled and Rovers going on to win the trophy for the fourth time.

Only Jimmy Brogan survived from the winning 1886 team in the next success. That came in April 1891 against Darwen at Anfield, with Brogan scoring one of the goals in a 3–1 success.

The competition caught the public's support, and in March 1893 there were rowdy scenes at Gigg Lane when Bolton went to face holders Bury in a second-round tie. Reports said that anything between 16,000 to 20,000 people were present, and with such a crush there were several pitch encroachments. The Wanderers were winning the game 3–1 when a supporter ran on the pitch and attacked Jimmy Turner after he had had an altercation with Bury's Arthur Wilkinson. With only an hour played the game was abandoned, and it was re-played at Burnden, with the Wanderers winning 1–0. The Final was reached that season, but it was Preston who ran out winners at Ewood Park.

It was not until 1911–12 that the Wanderers won the trophy again. A crowd of 11,000 were at Burnden to see Burnley take the lead before two Alf Bentley goals helped them on their way to a 4–1 success.

The Cup kings of the 1920s matched their nationwide success of three FA Cup wins by securing the Lancashire trophy on the same number of occasions during the decade. A crowd of 15,912 were at Gigg Lane to see the home side go ahead in May 1922, before two goals from Frank Roberts and a Joe Smith penalty won the trophy. After the game, the Bolton players and officials travelled back in a special tram car and were welcomed by large crowds.

The trophy was again secured in 1925 when Blackpool were beaten at Burnden Park thanks to a last minute Harry Nuttall goal. Nine of the FA Cup-winning side took to the field before a crowd of 11,292 with Harry Greenhalgh replacing Bob Howarth and Joe Cassidy in for John Smith.

In May 1927 a full-strength line up defeated Bury at Burnden Park, with John Smith netting the only goal before 13,229 to take the club to a third success in six seasons. For Ted Vizard it was his fourth winners' medal with the club, having been a member of the 1911–12 winning team.

The Wanderers did not get their hands on the trophy again until May 1932. They had qualified for the Final by winning each round in a replay. In the third round, after a 1–1 draw at Liverpool, the holders were thrashed 8–1 at Burnden, and Bolton repeated the scoring feat against the Reds in the final First Division game of the season. In the Final, Manchester City were the opponents at Maine Road, the home side twice taking the lead before the Wanderers came back to equalise before half-time thanks to goals from Billy McKay and George Gibson. A goal from Willie Cook secured a 3–2 win before 15,386 with Billy Butler picking up his fourth winners' medal.

Bolton reached the Final the following season, but in May 1933 Liverpool gained revenge for the previous season's mauling by winning the trophy by 2–1 at Anfield, Ray Westwood's goal not being enough. Everton's players and officials were in the crowd that afternoon to show off the FA Cup which was displayed alongside the Lancashire Cup.

The Wanderers made it three Finals in a row when they faced Oldham Athletic in the Final at Maine Road in May 1934. The Wanderers had just missed out on promotion from the second division and were facing a team from the same division. Goals from George Eastham, G.T. Taylor and a Ray Westwood brace won the trophy by 4–2. Stalwart Alex Finney matched his former teammates by winning his fourth winners' medal in the competition.

The crowd at Maine Road was 6,173 and the Lancashire FA were worried about the declining attendances in the competition, having warned clubs by letter about their concerns from a playing and financial view. The majority of the games were played in mid-week throughout the winter, and in an attempt to re-vitalise the competition it was expanded to allow six non-League clubs to take part. Games also switched to Saturday afternoons, leaving Football League clubs little option other than to field their reserves.

In 1935–36 Rossendale United put the Wanderers out of the competition in extra-time after a replay at Burnden. Blackpool ran out winners that season for the first time in their history, with former Wanderer Joe Smith having taken over as manager at the start of the season.

Preston North End were Bolton's opponents in the Final of 1938–39. A crowd of 5,850 at Deepdale saw George Hunt put the Wanderers ahead before Alex Millar levelled late on. A replay was set to take place early the following season, but in the event it never took place due to the outbreak of war and so the trophy was shared.

Programme from the 1948 Cup success at Southport.

During the war years the competition was played on a two-legged basis, with most of the games taking place on Saturday afternoons. The Wanderers' record during this time was poor, with just one final appearance in the 1943–44 season when Liverpool ran out 6–3 winners on aggregate. In 1946–47 Bolton's first-round tie with Manchester City became a marathon when it went to four games before Bolton ran out winners. Interest in the competition that season ended in the semi-finals when Bury won 4–3 on aggregate.

The trophy came back to Burnden for the 10th time in May 1948. A crowd of 10,734 were at Haig Avenue to watch a full-strength Bolton side defeat Southport 5–1. A first-half hat-trick from Willie Moir set Bolton on their way, and second-half goals from Jack Bradley and John Jackson completed the rout.

The competition in terms of success became barren for the club for the next 40 years. In October 1953 a first-round tie with Preston at Deepdale attracted over 12,000 for the first game played after the installation of the floodlighting system. The home side ran out 3–0 winners. In April 1955 the Wanderers again faced Preston, this time in the second round. After a drawn game the club requested that they be allowed to field the A team in the replay but were refused permission. In the event, nine B team players took to the field along with two reserves, Preston winning 1–0. The Wanderers were warned as to their future conduct in relation to the competition.

Season 1964–65 again saw Bolton involved in a marathon tie. This time it was against Blackpool, in the first round, with the Seasiders winning through at the fourth attempt. Defeats at Morecambe in October 1966, Barrow in November 1967 and against Chorley in November 1971 and October 1972 proved to low points in the clubs participation in the competition.

The team that defeated Preston in 1990 to secure the trophy.Back Row, Came, Brown, Green, Cowdrill, Reeves, Philliskiirk, Felgate. Front, Burke, Storer, Winstanley, Darby, Thompson.

In April 1974 the Wanderers lost in the semi-finals to eventual winners, Manchester City, but it was to be the last game in the competition for eight years. There had been growing discontent within most of the clubs in relation to organising the fixtures within an already busy schedule, and it was not revived until 1982 as a pre-season competition. The tournament was sponsored by the Isle of Man Tourist Board, with teams placed in two groups and a bonus point being awarded for scoring three or more goals in a game. The group winners would play in the Final.

The club's record in the pre-season competition was poor, with just four victories in 18 games over six seasons. In 1988 the club reached the Final after defeating Rochdale on penalties in the final group game after both clubs had finished with identical records. In the Final they faced Preston at Burnden, and a crowd of 5,757 saw a John Thomas goal win the trophy for Bolton.

In 1990 the Wanderers were successful for the 12th time in the competition when Preston were again defeated at Burnden. A crowd of 4,585 saw two David Reeves goals win the tie by 2–1. The club continued to use the competition as part of the pre-season preparations until 1994 when, for the first time in The Lancashire Cup competition's history, the name of Bolton Wanderers was missing.

The competition continued without Bolton's participation, and between 1999 and 2003 there was no competition due to a lack of interest. It was revived for 2004–05, with clubs' reserve sides taking part, Rochdale ending the Wanderers' interest in the semi-finals at Leyland.

Bolton reached the Final of the 2006–07 competition, the game taking place as a pre-season game at the start of the following season, with Blackburn running out 6–2 winners before a crowd of 189 at Leyland, the crowd being the lowest ever for a Lancashire Cup Final. In 2008–09 the Wanderers faced Manchester United in the Final, again at Leyland, but went down to a single-goal defeat.

Bolton Wanderers in the Lancashire Cup

Season	Date	Opponents	Venue	Round	Result
1879–80	11 Oct	Bolton All Saints	H	1	5–2
	29 Nov	Blackburn Rovers	A	2	0–4
1880–81	30 Oct	Irwell Springs	H	1	7–1
	20 Nov	Great Harwood	A	2	2–0
	5 Feb	Great Lever	A	3	3–2
	27 Feb	Blackburn Park Road	H	4	1–1
	12 Mar	Blackburn Park Road	A	4R	1–6
1881–82	5 Nov	Blackburn Park Road	H	1	10–4
	10 Dec	Low Moor	A	2	13–0
	7 Jan	Lower Darwen	H	3	9–0
	11 Feb	Accrington	A	4	3–7
1882–83	1 Nov	Egerton	A	1	6–2
	15 Nov	Bradshaw	H	2	9–2
	20 Dec	Rishton	A	3	2–2
	20 Jan	Rishton	H	3R	10–1
	3 Feb	Peel Bank Rovers	H	4	7–0
	17 Feb	Darwen St Johns	H	5	5–1
	17 Mar	Blackburn Rovers	At Darwen	SF	1–4
1883–84	29 Sep	Darwen Old Wanderers	H	1	1–2
1884–85	4 Oct	Hurst Park Road	H	1	10–1
	18 Oct	Lowerhouse	H	2	6–1
	29 Nov	Great Lever	H	3	5–2
	10 Jan	Low Moor	H	4	3–0
	31 Jan	Darwen Old Wanderers	H	5	3–1
	11 Apr	Blackburn Rovers	At Darwen	SF	5–1
	(Bolton Disqualified for fielding ineligible players)				
1885–86	10 Oct	Burnley Wanderers	A	1	0–0
	21 Oct	Burnley Wanderers	H	1R	7–0
	7 Nov	South Shore	A	2	3–0
	5 Dec	Blackburn Olympic	H	3	11–2
	19 Dec	Blackpool St Johns	A	4	9–1
	13 Feb	Darwen	A	SF	2–1
	17 Apr	Blackburn Rovers	At Preston	Final	1–0
1886–87	9 Oct	Wigan	H	1	14–0
	6 Nov	Burnley	A	2	5–1

	4 Dec	Rossendale (result later declared void)	A	3	8–1
	14 Dec	Irwell Springs (aban. result stands)	A	3	4–1
	19 Feb	Padiham	At Preston	SF	4–1
	26 Mar	Preston North End	H	Final	0–3
1887–88	1 Oct	Bells Temperance	H	1	10–1
	26 Nov	Burnley Union Star	A	2	0–5
1888–89	29 Sep	Halliwell	A	1	1–8
1889–90	2 Nov	Accrington	H	1	4–2
	14 Dec	Darwen	A	2	2–4
1890–91	7 Feb	Higher Walton	A	1	2–1
	21 Feb	Everton	H	2	6–0
	11 Apr	Blackburn Rovers	At Hyde Road	SF	2–0
	15 Apr	Darwen	At Anfield	Final	3–1
1891–92	6 Feb	Rossendale	H	1	4–1
	20 Feb	Blackburn Rovers	A	2	2–3
1892–93	18 Feb	Accrington	H	1	4–0
	11 Mar	Bury	A	2	3–1
		(Game Unfinished due to Crowd invasion)			
	27 Mar	Bury	H	2	1–0
	8 Apr	Ardwick	H	SF	5–1
	22 Apr	Preston North End	At Blackburn	Final	0–2
1893–94	20 Jan	Preston North End	H	1	4–1
	17 Feb	Darwen	A	2	5–4
	17 Mar	Accrington	At Everton	SF	1–0
	14 Apr	Everton	At Hyde Road	Final	1–2
1894–95	19 Jan	Newton Heath	H	1	2–1
	9 Feb	Everton	H	2	1–3
1895–96	18 Jan	Burnley	H	1	1–2
1896–97	5 Dec	Nelson	H	1	3–0
	23 Jan	Liverpool	A	2	2–2
	15 Feb	Liverpool	H	2R	2–0
	20 Feb	Manchester City	A	SF	1–2
1897–98	4 Dec	Nelson	H	1	3–3
	7 Dec	Nelson	A	1R	1–0
	22 Jan	Everton	A	2	2–1
	19 Feb	Newton Heath	At Hyde Road	SF	1–4
1898–99	5 Dec	Blackpool	H	1	1–0
	11 Feb	Burnley	H	2	3–2
	4 Mar	Blackburn Rovers	A	SF	2–1
	25 Mar	Bury	At Burnden Park	Final	1–3
1899–1900	9 Dec	Newton Heath	H	1	2–3
1900–01	1 Oct	Preston North End	H	1	5–0
	22 Oct	Burnley	A	2	0–5

1901–02	30 Sep	Bury	H	1	2–1
	21 Oct	Burnley	H	2	1–1
	4 Nov	Burnley	A	2R	2–3
1902–03	29 Sep	Barrow	A	1	4–2
	20 Oct	Bury	H	2	2–2
	27 Oct	Bury	A	2R	1–2
1903–04	9 Jan	St Helens Town	A	1	1–1
	13 Jan	St Helens Town	H	1R	0–1
1904–05	10 Oct	Manchester United	H	1	4–2
	9 Jan	Bury	H	2	5–1
	13 Feb	Everton	A	SF	1–2
1905–06	18 Sep	Burnley	H	1	4–0
	2 Oct	Blackburn rovers	H	2	5–2
	16 Oct	Bury	A	SF	1–2
1906–07	1 Oct	Manchester City	H	1	4–3
	15 Oct	Darwen	H	2	3–0
	5 Nov	Blackburn Rovers	At Clayton	SF	0–2
1907–08	30 Sep	Blackburn Rovers	A	1	4–3
	14 Oct	Manchester United	A	2	0–2
1908–09	12 Oct	Manchester United	H	1	0–3
1909–10	11 Oct	Oldham Athletic	H	1	1–2
1910–11	10 Oct	Bury	H	1	3–2
	24 Oct	Blackburn Rovers	H	2	0–4
1911–12	10 Oct	Nelson	A	1	4–2
	23 Oct	Barrow	H	2	1–0
	20 Nov	Manchester United	H	SF	2–1
	13 Dec	Burnley	At Burnden Park	Final	4–1
1912–13	7 Oct	Southport Central	H	1	2–1
	21 Oct	Manchester United	H	2	0–3
1913–14	6 Oct	Preston North End	H	2	3–1
	20 Oct	Rochdale	A	3	2–3
1914–15	5 Oct	Preston North End	A	2	0–1
1915–16 to 1917–18			No Competition		
1918–1919	5 Oct	Bury	A		5–1
	12 Oct	Bury	H		3–1
	5 Apr	Oldham Athletic	A		1–4
	12 Apr	Oldham Athletic	H		3–1
	19 Apr	Rochdale	A		2–1
	26 Apr	Rochdale	H		2–1
		(Run on a League basis, failed to qualify for semi-finals)			
1919–20	Nov 22	Everton	A		3–3
	Nov 29	Everton	H		0–2
	Jan 24	Liverpool	H		0–3

	Feb 4	Liverpool	A		0–2
		(Run on a League basis, failed to qualify for semi-finals)			
1920–21	25 Mar	Everton	H		4–2
	28 Mar	Everton	A		3–2
	23 Apr	Liverpool	H		1–0
	30 Apr	Liverpool	A		3–2
		(League games counted as qualifiers)			
	9 May	Bury	H	SF	4–2
	14 May	Manchester City	At Old Trafford	Final	1–2
1921–22	31 Dec	Everton	A	Qualifier	0–1
	14 Jan	Everton	H	Qualifier	1–0
	18 Mar	Liverpool	A	Qualifier	2–0
	25 Mar	Liverpool	H	Qualifier	1–3
		(League games counted as qualifiers)			
	26 Apr	Everton	H	Play-offs	6–0
	3 May	Liverpool	H	Play-offs	3–1
	8 May	Manchester City	At Old Trafford	SF	0–0
	13 May	Manchester City	At Bury	SF R	1–0
	17 May	Bury	At Bury	Final	3–1
1922–23	3 Mar	Liverpool	A	Qualifier	0–3
	30 Mar	Everton	H	Qualifier	0–2
	2 Apr	Everton	A	Qualifier	1–1
	18 Apr	Liverpool	H	Qualifier	1–1
		(League games counted as qualifiers)			
1923–24	24 Sep	Burnley	A	2	0–2
1924–25	15 Oct	Stockport County	H	2	4–0
	5 Nov	Southport Central	H	3	3–1
	10 Dec	Everton	At Old Trafford	SF	4–1
	21 Jan	Blackpool	At Burnden Park	Final	2–1
1925–26	3 Nov	Nelson	A	2	6–0
	30 Nov	Oldham Athletic	A	3	0–3
1926–27	6 Oct	Everton	A	2	2–1
	2 Nov	Burnley	A	3	3–0
	29 Nov	Manchester City	A	SF	6–1
	14 May	Bury	At Burnden Park	Final	1–0
1927–28	27 Sep	Burnley	A	2	3–1
	17 Oct	Preston North End	A	3	6–3
	30 Nov	Bury	H	SF	0–2
1928–29	19 Sep	Manchester City	A	2	1–1
	17 Oct	Manchester City	H	2R	3–1
	7 Nov	Liverpool	A	3	2–2
	21 Nov	Liverpool	H	3R	7–2
	12 Dec	Manchester United	H	SF	2–2

	3 Apr	Manchester United	A	SF R	0–1	
1929–30	9 Sep	Blackburn Rovers	A	2	2–1	
	30 Oct	Manchester United	A	3	1–6	
1930–31	8 Oct	Manchester City	H	2	2–1	
	3 Nov	Blackburn Rovers	A	3	1–2	
1931–32	7 Oct	Accrington Stanley	A	2	0–0	
	19 Oct	Accrington Stanley	H	2R	4–1	
	4 Nov	Liverpool	A	3	1–1	
	11 Nov	Liverpool	H	3R	8–1	
	20 Apr	Blackpool	A	SF	1–1	
	4 May	Blackpool	H	SF R	5–1	
	14 May	Manchester City	At Maine Road	Final	3–2	
1932–33	20 Sep	Southport	A	1	2–1	
	18 Oct	Oldham Athletic	A	2	1–0	
	4 Mar	Preston North End	H	SF	4–2	
	13 May	Liverpool	At Anfield	Final	1–2	
1933–34	18 Sep	Burnley	H	1	3–0	
	4 Oct	Accrington Stanley	H	2	5–2	
	15 Nov	Manchester City	H	SF	3–2	
	12 May	Oldham Athletic	At Maine Road	Final	4–2	
1934–35	10 Sep	Preston North End	A	1	1–5	
1935–36	2 Sep	Rossendale	A	1	1–1	
	8 Oct	Rossendale	A	1R	0–1	AET
1936–37	28 Sep	Preston North End	A	1	2–2	
	28 Oct	Preston North End	H	1R	2–1	
	16 Nov	Barrow	A	2	5–2	
	3 May	Blackburn Rovers	H	SF	0–1	
1937–38	30 Mar	New Brighton	H	1	5–1	
	27 Apr	Southport	A	2	1–1	
	9 May	Southport	A	2R	1–3	
1938–39	5 Oct	Blackpool	A	1	1–0	
	25 Oct	Bury	A	2	2–1	
	11 Feb	Manchester City	H	SF	4–0	
	10 May	Preston North End	At Deepdale	Final	1–1	
		(No replay due to war – Trophy Shared)				
1939–40	4 Nov	Liverpool	H	1	1–3	
1940–41	4 Jan	Oldham Athletic	H	1 1st Leg	2–1	
	11 Jan	Oldham Athletic	A	1 2nd Leg	5–3	AET
	18 Jan	Manchester United	H	2 1st Leg	3–2	
	25 Jan	Manchester United	A	2 2nd Leg	1–4	
1941–42	11 Apr	Blackpool	A	1 1st Leg	1–7	
	18 Apr	Blackpool	H	2 2nd Leg	2–1	
1942–43		Manchester City (Manchester City scratched)	1			

	Date	Opponent	Venue	Round	Score	Notes
	3 Apr	Blackburn Rovers	A	2 1st Leg	3–1	
	10 Apr	Blackburn Rovers	H	2 2nd Leg	0–1	
	24 Apr	Liverpool	H	SF 1st Leg	3–6	
	1 May	Liverpool	A	SF 2nd Leg	0–4	
1943–44	1 Apr	Manchester United	H	1 1st Leg	3–0	
	8 Apr	Manchester United	A	1 2nd Leg	2–3	
	10 Apr	Bury	H	2 1st Leg	3–2	
	15 Apr	Bury	A	2 2nd Leg	1–1	AET
	22 Apr	Stockport County	H	SF 1st Leg	4–2	
	29 Apr	Stockport County	A	SF 2nd Leg	2–1	
	6 May	Liverpool	A	F 1st Leg	1–3	
	13 May	Liverpool	H	F 2nd Leg	2–3	
1944–45	17 Mar	Bury	H	1 1st Leg	3–3	
	2 Apr	Bury	A	1 2nd Leg	0–1	
1945–46	3 Sep	Accrington Stanley	H	1 1st Leg	2–0	
	25 Sep	Accrington Stanley	A	1 2nd Leg	0–1	
	11 Mar	Liverpool	A	2	1–3	
1946–47	16 Oct	Manchester City	A	1 1st Leg	1–0	
	30 Oct	Manchester City	H	1 2nd Leg	2–3	AET
	6 Nov	Manchester City	A	1 R	0–0	AET
	27 Nov	Manchester City	A	1 2R	2–1	
	4 Dec	Chester	A	2 1st Leg	2–1	
	11 Dec	Chester	H	2 2nd Leg	3–0	
	7 May	Bury	H	SF 1st Leg	3–1	
	14 May	Bury	A	SF 2nd Leg	0–3	AET
1947–48	7 Oct	Everton	A	1	4–3	
	4 Nov	Bury	A	2	3–2	
	28 Apr	Blackburn Rovers	H	SF	1–0	AET
	8 May	Southport	At Haig Avenue	Final	5–1	
1948–49	27 Oct	Accrington Stanley	H	1	3–1	
	24 Nov	Manchester United	H	2	2–4	
1949–50	5 Oct	Accrington Stanley	H	1	4–1	
	8 Feb	Rochdale	H	2	0–1	
1950–51	25 Oct	Manchester United	H	1	2–3	
1951–52	24 Oct	Manchester United	H	1	1–0	
	20 Feb	Burnley	A	2	1–2	
1952–53	1 Oct	Bury	H	1	2–2	
	14 Oct	Bury	A	1R	3–1	
	24 Feb	Preston North End	A	2	0–1	
1953–54	21 Oct	Preston North End	A	1	0–3	
1954–55	23 Nov	Bury	A	1	1–0	
	16 Mar	Preston North End	H	2	2–2	AET
	4 Apr	Preston North End	A	2R	0–1	

1955–56	24 Oct	Rochdale	A	1	1–1	
	15 Feb	Rochdale	A	1R	0–2	
1956–57	12 Mar	Bury	A	1	2–5	
1957–58	6 Nov	Manchester United	A	1	1–3	
1958–59	27 Oct	Bury	H	1	3–2	
	11 Feb	Liverpool	A	2	0–3	
1959–60	9 Dec	Preston North End	H	1	2–5	
1960–61	7 Dec	Manchester United	A	1	1–3	
1961–62	23 Oct	Manchester City	A	1	4–3	
	12 Apr	Blackburn Rovers	A	2	1–4	
1962–63	14 Nov	Bury	H	1	4–0	
		Liverpool	A. Not played	2		
		(Competition abandoned due to weather)				
1963–64	30 Oct	Blackburn Rovers	H	3	1–1	
	21 Nov	Blackburn Rovers	A	3R	0–3	
1964–65	28 Oct	Blackpool	H	1	1–1	
	3 Nov	Blackpool	A	1R	1–1	AET
	17 Nov	Blackpool	A	1 2R	2–2	AET
	27 Jan	Blackpool	H	1 3R	1–2	
1965–66	4 Jan	Bury	A	1	0–0	
	21 Mar	Bury	H	1R	1–2	
1966–67	11 Oct	Morecambe	A	1	0–2	
1967–68	20 Nov	Barrow	A	2	1–4	
1968–69	15 Oct	Bury	H	2	4–1	
	11 Dec	Manchester City	H	3	1–2	
1969–70	21 Oct	Manchester United	H	2	1–2	
1970–71	19 Oct	Manchester City	A	2	1–2	
1971–72	2 Nov	Chorley	A	1	0–2	
1972–73	25 Oct	Chorley	H	2	0–1	
1973–74	15 Oct	Rochdale	H	1	4–0	
	12 Feb	Blackpool	H	2	1–0	
	30 Apr	Manchester City	H	SF	1–3	AET

1974–75 to 1981–82   No competition

(Competition re-introduced under the sponsorship of the Isle of Man Tourist Board as a pre–season competition)

1982–83	14 Aug	Preston North End	A		2–3
	17 Aug	Blackburn Rovers	H		0–1
	21 Aug	Blackpool	A		2–2
1983–84	13 Aug	Rochdale	A		3–3
	16 Aug	Wigan Athletic	A		0–0
	20 Aug	Bury	H		2–3
1984–85	11 Aug	Preston North End	A		1–1
	14 Aug	Blackburn Rovers	H		1–1

	18 Aug	Bury	A		4–3	
1985–86	3 Aug	Rochdale	H		2–0	
	6 Aug	Bury	H		1–0	
	10 Aug	Burnley	A		0–4	
1986–87	9 Aug	Preston North End	H		0–0	
	12 Aug	Burnley	A		3–2	
	16 Aug	Wigan Athletic	H		3–4	
1987–88	1 Aug	Blackburn Rovers	H		1–2	
	4 Aug	Blackpool	A		0–0	
	7 Aug	Burnley	H		1–1	
1988–89	6 Aug	Bury	H		1–0	
	11 Aug	Wigan Athletic	At Oldham Athletic		1–0	
	13Aug	Rochdale	H		1–1	
		(Bolton win 5–4 on Penalties)				
	16 Aug	Preston North End	H	Final	1–0	
1989–90	5 Aug	Burnley	A		2–2	
	8 Aug	Wigan Athletic	A		0–1	
	12 Aug	Blackburn Rovers	H		3–1	
1990–91	11 Aug	Wigan Athletic	A		0–0	
	14 Aug	Blackpool	H		2–0	
	18 Aug	Burnley	H		3–0	
	21 Aug	Preston North End	H	Final	2–1	
1991–92	5 Aug	Rochdale	H		0–1	
	7 Aug	Blackpool	A		2–1	
	10 Aug	Wigan Athletic	H		0–1	
1992–93	27 Jul	Bury	H		0–0	
	1 Aug	Rochdale	H		0–0	
1993–94	23 Jul	Rochdale	A		4–3	
	27 Jul	Burnley	A		1–0	
	30 Jul	Blackpool	H		1–3	
1994–95 to 1998–99			Did not enter			
1999–2000 to 2003–04			No competition			
2004–05	16 Aug	Preston North End	H	1	2–2	5–4 on pens
	12 Jan	Rochdale	H	SF	0–1	
2005–06	22 Aug	Blackburn Rovers	H	1	1–1	3–2 on pens
	20 Mar	Preston North End	H	SF	1–4	
2006–07	20 Sept	Manchester United	H	1	1–0	
	7 May	Accrington Stanley	A	SF	1–1	5–4 on pens
	31 July	Blackburn Rovers	Leyland	Final	2–6	
2007–08	12 Nov	Rochdale	H	1	1–0	
	18 Jan	Blackburn Rovers	H	2	2–0	
	24 Apr	Manchester United	H	SF	1–2	
2008–09	7 Feb	Morecambe	A	2	3–0	

	5 May	Blackburn Rovers	H	SF	2–2	5–4 on pens
	17 Aug	Manchester United	Leyland	Final	0–1	
2009–10	1 Feb	Liverpool	H	2	0–2	
2010–11	26 Oct	Accrington Stanley	H	2	2–3	

THE MANCHESTER CUP

The Manchester Senior Cup was instituted in 1885, the first winners being Hurst who defeated Newton Heath in the Final.

Bolton first entered the competition in 1891–92 when they reached the Final only to lose out to the holders Ardwick by 4–1 in a game that was held at Newton Heath. The Final was again reached the following season, but on this occasion Newton Heath ran out winners.

The first occasion that the trophy ended up in the Burnden trophy cabinet was in 1894–95 when Bury were defeated 3–2 at Hyde Road after a drawn game. It was not until 1906 that the trophy was again secured but by then the competition had seen most senior clubs fielding their reserves owing to the calls of the League, FA and Lancashire Cup ties.

Success came in 1909, 1921 and 1922. The 1922 competition saw Bolton defeat Eccles United at Old Trafford before 15,000 to add the Trophy to the Lancashire Cup that had been won three days earlier at Bury.

The next three times that the trophy came back to Bolton was in 1938, 1954 and 1961 all against Manchester United. From 1959 the Association selected two teams from their membership to play in the Final such was the lack of interest. The last occasion that Bolton won the trophy was by these means when they were selected to play Oldham Athletic at Boundary Park in 1963, going on to win 3–1.

The 1906 team parading the Manchester Cup that was secured by defeating Bury in the Final.

Programme from the 1963 Cup Final success at Oldham Athletic.

During the 1970s it was competed for by non-League members of the association and not held at all from 1980 until 1999. Then it was re-introduced for professional clubs reserve sides in 1999 but it wasn't until the 2003–04 season that the Wanderers took part again. The competition, held on a single group basis, sees drawn games settled on penalties after 90 minutes and the top two teams Play-off in the Final.

The club reached the Final in four consecutive seasons between 2008 and 2011, twice losing narrowly to Manchester United at Old Trafford, again to United and to Manchester City at the Reebok Stadium.

Bolton Wanderers in the Manchester Cup

Season	Date	Opponents	Venue	Round	Result	
1891–92	13 Feb	Stockport County	A	1	2–1	
	12 Mar	Newton Heath	At Ardwick	SF	3–1	
	23 Apr	Ardwick	At Newton Heath	Final	1–4	
1892–93	27 Feb	Stockport County	H	1	4–1	
	21 Mar	Heywood Central	At Bury	SF	3–2	
	15 Apr	Newton Heath	At Ardwick	Final	1–2	
1893–94	3 Feb	Newton Heath	H	1	3–2	AET
	3 Mar	Heywood Central	At Bury	SF	1–2	
1894–95	26 Jan	Newton Heath	A	1	4–0	
	23 Feb	Manchester City	At Bury	SF	2–2	
	9 Mar	Manchester City	At Hyde Road	SF R	2–1	
	30 Mar	Bury	At Newton Heath	Final	0–0	
	8 Apr	Bury	At Hyde Road	Final R	3–2	
1895–96	26 Jan	Manchester City	A	1	0–1	
1896–97	16 Jan	Fairfield	H	1	3–0	
	17 Mar	Stalybridge Rovers	At Hyde Road	SF	1–1	
	29 Mar	Stalybridge Rovers	At Hyde Road	SF R	4–3	AET
	3 Apr	Bury	At Hyde Road	F	1–3	
1897–98	5 Feb	Stockport County	A	1	1–2	
1898–99	8 Feb	Manchester City	H	1	3–9	

1899–1900	19 Feb	Rochdale	H	1	3–0	
	12 Mar	Manchester City	A	SF	5–3	
	4 Apr	Bury	At Hyde Road	Final	0–2	
1900–01	13 Mar	Manchester City	A	1	0–2	
1901–02	3 Mar	Bury	H	1	2–0	
	9 Apr	Newton Heath	At Hyde Road	SF	1–1	
	14 Apr	Newton Heath	At Hyde Road	SF R	0–1	
1902–03	24 Feb	Stalybridge Rovers	A	1	0–1	
1903–04	30 Mar	Bury	At Clayton	SF	1–1	
	26 Apr	Bury	At Clayton	SF R	0–4	
1904–05	23 Jan	Bury	A	1	1–1	
	6 Feb	Bury	H	1R	1–2	
1905–06	23 Jan	Manchester City	H	1	1–1	
	30 Jan	Manchester City	A	1R	1–1	
	12 Feb	Manchester City	At Clayton	1 2R	1–1	AET
	19 Feb	Manchester City	At Weaste	1 3R	1–0	
	9 Mar	Stockport County	H	SF	4–1	
	30 Mar	Bury	At Clayton	Final	3–0	
1906–07	18 Mar	Stockport County	A	1	0–0	
	17 Apr	Stockport County	H	1R	1–2	
1907–08	2 Dec	Stockport County	H	1	2–2	
	2 Mar	Stockport County	A	1R	1–4	
1908–09	25 Jan	Glossop	A	1	3–1	
	15 Mar	Manchester City	H	SF	1–0	
	29 Apr	Stockport County	At Hyde Road	Final	3–0	
1909–10	27 Nov	Northern Nomads	H	1	1–2	
1910–11	3 Oct	Stockport County	A	1	0–3	
1911–12	16 Oct	Glossop	H	1	3–1	
	12 Feb	Manchester United	At Hyde Road	SF	0–4	
1912–13	10 Feb	Hurst	H	1	3–1	
	12 Mar	Rochdale	H	SF	1–1	
	1 Apr	Rochdale	A	SF R	2–1	
	21 Apr	Manchester United	At Hyde Road	Final	1–4	
1913–14	10 Feb	Hurst	A	1	0–2	
1914–15	10 Feb	Bury	H	1	2–2	
	2 Mar	Bury	A	1R	3–2	
	15 Mar	Stockport County	A	2	0–3	
1915–16 to 1918–19			No competition			
1919–20	24 Mar	Stalybridge	H	1	3–2	
	12 Apr	Manchester United	A	SF	2–5	
1920–21	14 Mar	New Moss Colliery	H	1	4–1	
	11 Apr	Stalybridge Celtic	A	2	2–2	
	19 Apr	Stalybridge Celtic	H	2R	6–0	

	2 May	Mossley	H	SF	8–0	
	11 May	Manchester United	H	Final	2–0	
1921–22	28 Feb	Rochdale	H	1	2–1	
	28 Mar	Stalybridge Celtic	H	2	2–0	
	1 May	Stockport County	A	SF	4–4	
	10 May	Stockport County	H	SF R	6–0	
	20 May	Eccles United	At Old Trafford	Final	3–1	
1922–23	7 Feb	Mossley	H	1	6–0	
	10 Apr	Stockport County	A	2	0–2	
1923–24	20 Feb	Eccles United	H	1	8–2	
	26 Mar	Stalybridge Celtic	H	2	2–1	
	30 Apr	Manchester United	A	SF	0–4	
1924–25	25 Feb	Mossley	H	1	4–0	
	24 Mar	Bury	A	2	1–3	
1925–26	10 Feb	Eccles United	H	1	9–0	
	22 Mar	Stockport County	A	2	1–2	
1926–27	16 Mar	Crewe Alexandra	A	1	1–5	
1927–28	21 Mar	Wigan Borough	H	3	1–4	
1928–29	11 Mar	Manchester United	H	3	4–1	
	10 Apr	Manchester North End	H	SF	1–0	
	11 May	Manchester City	A	F	0–2	
1929–30	12 Feb	Wigan Borough	A	1	0–1	
1930–31	25 Feb	Bury	H	3	0–0	
	25 Mar	Bury	A	3R	1–2	AET
1931–32	16 Mar	Oldham Athletic	H	3	1–2	
1932–33	8 Mar	Bury	H	1	2–3	
1933–34	25 Apr	Manchester United	A	SF	0–4	
1934–35	13 Mar	Oldham Athletic	H	1	1–0	
	24 Apr	Bury	A	SF	2–2	
	29 Feb	Bury	H	SF R	0–3	
1935–36	18 Mar	Manchester United	A	SF	0–3	
1936–37	14 Apr	Manchester United	A	SF	0–1	
1937–38	23 Mar	Manchester City	A	SF	1–1	
	2 May	Manchester City	H	SF R	1–0	
	14 May	Manchester United	A	Final	2–1	
1938–39	14 Mar	Bury	A	1	0–5	
1939–40 to 1945–46			No competition			
1946–47		Manchester City	A	SF		
			Competition Abandoned			
1947–48	13 Mar	Oldham Athletic	A	SF	2–1	
	5 May	Manchester United	H	F	1–3	AET
1948–49	25 Apr	Manchester United	H	1	1–0	
	9 May	Manchester City	A	SF	0–0	

	14 May	Manchester City	H	SF R	0–2	
1949–50	19 Apr	Manchester City	H	SF	0–1	AET
1950–51	4 Mar	Manchester United	H	1	2–0	
	23 Mar	Oldham Athletic	H	SF	1–2	
1951–52	27 Feb	Manchester United	A	SF	0–0	
	26 Mar	Manchester United	H	SF R	1–0	
		Bury	A	Final	1–2	
1952–53	15 Apr	Bury	H	1	2–1	
	22 Apr	Manchester United	A	SF	1–0	
	4 May	Oldham Athletic	A	Final	1–3	
1953–54	31 Mar	Oldham Athletic	H	SF	1–0	
	26 Apr	Manchester United	A	Final	1–0	
1954–55	26 Oct	Bury	A	1	1–1	
	10 Nov	Bury	H	1R	3–4	
1955–56	30 Apr	Manchester City	H	1	5–0	

Competition abandoned

1956–57	29 Apr	Oldham Athletic	H	SF	2–4	
1957–58	18 Mar	Manchester City	A	SF	0–1	
1958–59		did not enter				
1959–60		did not enter				
1960–61	13 Nov	Manchester United	A	Final	1–0	
1961–62		did not enter				
1962–63	20 May	Oldham Athletic	A	Final	3–1	
1963–64		did not enter				
1964–65		did not enter				
2003–04	25 Sep	Manchester United	A	Q	1–1	3–5 on pens
	1 Oct	Manchester City	H	Q	2–1	
	12 Nov	Oldham Athletic	H	Q	1–3	
	19 Nov	Bury	A	Q	2–3	
2004–05	29 Sep	Oldham Athletic	A	Q	0–0	4–2 on pens
	29 Nov	Bury	H	Q	1–0	
	21 Dec	Manchester City	A	Q	1–1	4–3 on pens
	17 Jan	Manchester United	H	Q	1–2	
2005–06		did not enter				
2006–07	12 Oct	Manchester United	H	Q	0–1	
	24 Oct	Oldham Athletic	A	Q	0–6	
	17 Jan	Manchester City	H	Q	1–4	
	28 Feb	Stockport County	H	Q	1–0	
	2 May	Bury	A	Q	2–1	
2007–08	13 Aug	Manchester City	A	Q	2–1	
	17 Oct	Oldham Athletic	H	Q	3–0	
	31 Jan	Manchester United	A	Q	2–3	
	14 Apr	Bury	H	Q	3–2	

	1 May	Stockport County	A	Q	0–0	
	12 May	Manchester United	A	Final	0–2	
2008–09	11 Aug	Manchester City	H	Q	2–2	5–4 on pens
	30 Oct	Manchester United	A	Q	0–0	9–8 on pens
	10 Nov	Stockport County	H	Q	2–1	
	17 Feb	Oldham Athletic	H	Q	4–1	
	28 Apr	Bury	A	Q	2–0	
	12 May	Manchester United	H	Final	0–1	
2009–10	26 Oct	Oldham Athletic	A	Q	1–2	
	14 Dec	Manchester United	H	Q	2–2	3–2 on pens
	2 Mar	Bury	H	Q	2–1	
	16 Mar	Manchester City	A	Q	1–1	5–4 on pens
	19 Apr	Stockport County	A	Q	2–0	
	6 May	Manchester City	H	Final	0–1	
2010–11	17 Aug	Manchester City	H	Q	2–1	
	23 Sep	Manchester United	A	Q	0–4	
	9 Nov	Rochdale	A	Q	3–0	
	18 Jan	Oldham Athletic	H	Q	4–1	
	22 Mar	Bury	H	Q	5–1	
	5 May	Stockport County	H	Q	3–0	
	16 May	Manchester United	A	Q	1–3	

BOLTON WANDERERS IN THE FA YOUTH CUP

Season	Opponents	Venue	Round	Result
1952–53	Bury	H	2	1–3
1953–54	Manchester City	A	1	5–5
	Manchester City	H	1R	4–5
1954–55	Bury	H	2	2–2
	Bury	A	2R	6–0
	Huddersfield Town	A	3	6–0
	Sunderland	A	4	1–0
	West Bromwich Albion	A	5	1–3
1955–56	Blackburn Rovers	H	2	1–0
	Liverpool	A	3	2–1
	Everton	H	4	4–0
	Wolverhampton Wanderers	H	5	2–0
	Manchester United	A	SF1	1–1
	Manchester United	H	SF2	0–3
1956–57	Manchester City	A	1	4–2
	Everton	H	2	0–1

BOLTON WANDERERS

Football & Athletic Co. Ltd.

F.A. Youth
Challenge Cup - 2nd Leg

BOLTON WANDERERS v
MANCHESTER UNITED

Future Events at Burnden Park

Tues. April	24	Aston Villa (Central League)	3-0	p.m.
Thurs. „	26	Prestwich Cup Final	6-30	„
Fri. „	27	Marshall Cup Final	6-30	„
		...dersfield T. (Central League)	3-0	„
		...on Combination	6-30	„
		...nchester C. (Man. Cup)	3-0	„
		...dwick Cup Final	6-30	„

...y, 23rd April, 1956

...Programme **2**d.

1957–58	Preston North End	A	1	5–0
	Huddersfield Town	H	2	3–2
	Everton	A	3	1–1
	Everton	H	3R	1–0
	Sheffield United	A	4	4–1
	Wolverhampton Wanderers	A	5	1–1
	Wolverhampton Wanderers	H	5R	1–3
1958–59	Preston North End	H	1	3–1
	Liverpool	A	2	0–0
	Liverpool	H	2R	3–0
	Blackburn Rovers	A	3	1–5
1959–60	Hyde United	A	1	5–2
	Barrow	A	2	6–0
	Manchester City	A	3	2–4
1960–61	Blackburn Rovers	H	1	3–0
	Huddersfield Town	A	2	6–2
	Everton	A	3	1–4
1961–62	Burnley	A	1	1–3
1962–63	Tranmere Rovers	A	2	2–1
	Newcastle United	A	3	0–1
1963–64	Preston North End	A	2	0–3
1964–65	Bury	A	2	1–1
	Bury	H	2R	3–0
	Leeds United	H	3	0–2
1965–66	Burnley	A	2	0–4
1966–67	Port Vale	H	1	1–1
	Port Vale	A	1R	0–1
1967–68	Tranmere Rovers	A	1	0–2
1968–69	Wigan Athletic	A	1	3–1
	Blackburn Rovers	A	2	2–3
1969–70	Wigan Athletic	H	1	2–0
	Preston North End	H	2	2–1
	Bury	A	3	2–0
	Rotherham United	A	4	0–1
1970–71	Tranmere Rovers	H	2	2–0
	Manchester United	A	3	0–2
1971–72	Barrow	A	2	6–0
	Halifax Town	H	3	6–0
	Leeds United	H	4	1–0
	Arsenal	H	5	0–1
1972–73	Wolverhampton Wanderers	A	2	0–0
	Wolverhampton Wanderers	H	2R	6–1
	Burnley	H	3	3–0
	Ipswich Town	H	4	1–1

	Ipswich Town	A	4R	0–1	
1973–74	Derby County	H	2	2–3	
1974–75	Liverpool	A	2	1–2	
1975–76	Tranmere Rovers	A	1	1–0	
	Wrexham	H	2	2–0	
	Rotherham United	A	3	0–1	
1976–77	Rochdale	A	1	2–0	
	Manchester United	H	2	3–0	
	Leicester City	A	3	3–2	
	Middlesbrough	A	4	1–2	
1977–78	Oldham Athletic	H	2	2–3	
1978–79	Sheffield Wednesday	A	2	2–2	
	Sheffield Wednesday	H	2R	2–1	
	Leeds United	H	3	1–1	
	Leeds United	A	3R	1–3	
1979–80	Rotherham United	H	2	3–1	
	Sheffield Wednesday	H	3	0–2	
1980–81	Notts County	H	2	4–0	
	Manchester United	H	3	2–4	
1981–82	Leeds United	H	2	1–1	
	Leeds United	A	2R	0–2	AET
1982–83	Liverpool	H	2	2–2	
	Liverpool	A	2R	1–0	
	Sunderland	H	3	0–1	
1983–84	Blackpool	A	2	2–4	
1984–85	Burnley	A	2	0–2	
1985–86	Hull City	H	1	3–1	
	Rotherham United	A	2	0–3	
1986–87	Oldham Athletic	A	1	2–2	
	Oldham Athletic	H	1R	1–2	
1987–88	Hull City	H	1	0–1	
1988–89	Marine	A	1q–f	3–0	
	Huddersfield Town	A	1	1–1	
	Huddersfield Town	H	1R	1–2	
1989–90	Halifax Town	A	1 q–f	0–2	
1990–91	Preston North End	H	prel	4–1	
	Marine	H	1 q–f	5–1	
	Accrington Stanley	A	2 q–f	3–0	
	Oldham Athletic	H	1	3–3	
	Oldham Athletic	A	1R	0–2	
1991–92	Yorkshire Amateurs	A	prel	2–1	
	Warrington Town	A	1 q–f	2–0	
	Shrewsbury Town	A	2 q–f	0–1	
1992–93	Warrington Town	A	prel	2–1	
	Salford	H	1 q–f	5–3	

	Stockport County	H	2 q–f	0–1	
1993–94	Marine	H	prel	3–1	
	Rochdale	H	1 q–f	1–2	
1994–95	Chadderton	A	prel	1–1	
	Chadderton	H	prel r	4–2	
	Bury	A	1 q–f	0–4	
1995–96	Marine	A	prel	2–1	
	Chester	A	1 q–f	2–1	
	Southport	A	2 q–f	2–3	
1996–97	Mansfield Town	H	prel	3–0	
	Farsley Celtic	A	1 q–f	4–1	
	Lincoln City	A	2 q–f	0–0	
	Lincoln City	H	2 q–f r	2–0	
	Derby County	H	1	5–0	
	Sheffield United	H	2	1–1	
	Sheffield United	A	2R	5–4	AET
	Everton	H	3	1–2	
1997–98	Scarborough	H	1	1–2	
1998–99	Barnsley	H	3	0–0	
	Barnsley	A	3R	3–2	
	Millwall	A	4	0–4	
1999–2000	Port Vale	H	3	1–0	
	Leicester City	H	4	2–1	
	Southampton	H	5	0–1	
2000–01	Swindon Town	H	3	2–1	
	Sheffield Wednesday	H	4	1–1	
	Sheffield Wednesday	A	4R	2–2	AET. 5–4 on pens
	Blackburn Rovers	A	5	0–3	
2001–02	Bradford City	H	3	2–1	
	Tottenham Hotspur	H	4	1–2	
2002–03	Cambridge United	H	3	0–1	
2003–04	Norwich City	A	3	0–1	
2004–05	Blackburn Rovers	H	3	2–3	
2005–06	Bristol City	A	3	1–0	
	Crewe Alexandra	H	4	1–0	AET
	Southampton	H	5	0–1	
2006–07	Sheffield Wednesday	A	3	2–0	
	Sunderland	A	4	1–2	
2007–08	West Ham United	A	3	2–0	
	Port Vale	H	4	2–3	AET
2008–09	Doncaster Rovers	H	3	2–0	
	Hull City	H	4	4–0	
	Nottingham Forest	A	5	1–0	
	Liverpool	A	6	2–4	
2009–10	Bournemouth	H	3	3–1	
	Fulham	H	4	2–2	AET. 3–5 on pens
2010–11	Crewe Alexandra	H	3	1–2	

OTHER GAMES

All friendly matches unless shown otherwise

Season	Date	Opponents	Venue	Result
1879–80	27 Dec	Turton	A	1–2
	3 Jan	Great Lever	A	6–0
	10 Jan	Great Lever	H	0–0
	24 Jan	Eagley	A	4–2
	31 Jan	Bolton Olympic	H	3–2
	14 Feb	Turton	H	1–4
	21 Feb	Accrington	A	2–1
	28 Feb	Halliwell	H	4–2
	6 Mar	Blackburn Olympic	H	3–1
	27 Mar	Astley Bridge	A	4–4
	3 Apr	Bolton Olympic	A	3–5
	17 Apr	Blackburn Olympic	A	2–3
	24 Apr	Darwen (played at Bolton Rugby Club)		3–3
1880–81	9 Oct	Blackburn Rovers	A	0–7
	16 Oct	Accrington	A	1–12
	23 Oct	Eagley	H	5–2
	6 Nov	Preston North End	A	7–2
	27 Nov	Earlstown	H	8–1
	11 Dec	Turton	H	1–1
	18 Dec	Eagley	A	1–4
	8 Jan	Preston North End	H	4–0
	22 Jan	Northwich	A	2–1
	27 Jan	Accrington	A	1–8
	12 Feb	Turton	H	3–2
	5 Mar	Blackburn Olympic	H	2–1
	19 Mar	Northwich	H	1–1
	26 Mar	Manchester Wanderers	H	10–0
	2 Apr	Blackburn Rovers	H	3–5
	9 Apr	Blackburn Olympic	A	1–3
	15 Apr	Blackpool	A	3–3
	18 Apr	Edinburgh Hibernians	H	3–4
1881–82	10 Sep	Great Lever	H	9–0
	17 Sep	All Saints (Bolton & District)	H	3–3
	24 Sep	Blackburn Park Road	A	3–0
	1 Oct	Blackburn Rovers	H	2–2
	8 Oct	Bootle	A	7–1
	15 Oct	Astley Bridge	H	8–1
	29 Oct	Edinburgh Hibernians	A	0–3
	26 Nov	Manchester Wanderers	A	11–0
	30 Nov	Liverpool	H	13–1
	14 Dec	Macclesfield	H	12–0
	17 Dec	Vale of Leven	H	3–1
	24 Dec	Notts Rangers	H	9–0
	31 Dec	3rd Lanark RV	H	4–1

	2 Jan	Dumbarton	H	2–3
	14 Jan	Great Lever	H	11–1
	21 Jan	Blackburn Park Road	H	5–1
	28 Jan	Eagley	H	4–3
	4 Feb	Manchester Wanderers	H	15–0
	18 Feb	Darwen	A	2–2
	25 Feb	Turton	A	4–0
	4 Mar	Nottingham Forest	A	1–2
	11 Mar	Darwen	H	2–2
	18 Mar	Turton	H	4–0
	25 Mar	Accrington	H	2–3
	1 Apr	Turton (Played at Eagley)		8–3
		(Bolton Charity Cup first round)		
	8 Apr	Vale of Leven	H	0–1
	10 Apr	Edinburgh Hibernians	H	1–3
	15 Apr	Astley Bridge	A	5–3
	17 Apr	Bootle	H	12–0
	22 Apr	Halliwell (Bolton Charity Cup semi-final)	H	9–1
	26 Apr	Blackburn Olympic	H	4–0
	6 May	Astley Bridge (Bolton Charity Cup Final)	H	3–3
	10 May	Devlin's Team (Devlin Benefit)	H	2–7
	20 May	Astley Bridge (At Bolton Rugby Club)		6–1
		(Bolton Charity Cup Final)		
	27 May	Witton	H	4–1
1882–83	9 Sep	Turton	H	3–1
	16 Sep	Wednesbury Old Athletic	H	1–3
	23 Sep	Staveley	H	4–1
	30 Sep	Great Lever	H	5–1
	7 Oct	Druids	A	5–2
	14 Oct	Darwen	H	1–1
	21 Oct	Accrington	A	3–3
	28 Oct	Glasgow Rangers	H	1–0
	6 Nov	Sheffield Wanderers	H	9–0
	11 Nov	Nottingham Forest	H	9–0
	18 Nov	Darwen	A	2–3
	25 Nov	Eagley	A	7–1
	6 Dec	Co-operative Employees	A	8–0
	9 Dec	Great Lever (Played at High Street)		1–1
	16 Dec	Kilmarnock Portland	H	9–0
	23 Dec	Northwich Victoria	H	8–0
	26 Dec	Nottingham Forest	A	1–3
	30 Dec	Halliwell	H	14–2
	1 Jan	Dumbarton	H	0–2
	13 Jan	Paisley St Mirren	H	8–2
	27 Jan	Accrington	H	4–8
	10 Feb	Accrington	A	2–4
	26 Feb	Wednesbury Old Athletic	H	6–0
	3 Mar	Everton	A	8–1
	5 Mar	Walsall Swifts	H	2–1
	10 Mar	Church	H	7–0

	21 Mar	Oxford University	H	2–2
	24 Mar	Druids	H	6–0
	26 Mar	3rd Lanark RV	H	3–0
	31 Mar	Paisley St Mirren	A	4–3
	7 Apr	Great Lever (Played at Halliwell)		4–1
		(Bolton Charity Cup first round)		
	14 Apr	Blackburn Rovers	H	6–3
	21 Apr	Turton	A	4–1
	24 Apr	Eagley	H	3–2
	28 Apr	Turton(Bolton Charity Cup semi-final)	H	3–0
	30 Apr	North of England	H	4–2
	5 May	Edinburgh University	H	2–1
	12 May	Gilnow Rangers	H	3–0
		(Bolton Charity Cup Final)		
	15 May	Blackburn–Darwen–Bolton Select	H	2–1
		(Fowler Benefit)		
1883–84	25 Aug	Astley Bridge	A	4–3
	1 Sep	Oswestry	H	8–0
	8 Sep	Staveley	H	4–2
	15 Sep	Birmingham St Georges	H	4–2
	22 Sep	Padiham	H	6–1
	29 Sep	Northwich Victoria	A	1–3
	6 Oct	Walsall Swifts	H	2–2
	13 Oct	Preston North End	H	1–1
	20 Oct	Darwen	A	0–1
	27 Oct	Accrington	H	5–1
	3 Nov	Blackburn Rovers	A	0–0
	12 Nov	Staveley	H	7–2
	17 Nov	Bolton Association	H	1–1
	19 Nov	West Bromwich Albion	H	3–1
	24 Nov	Turton	A	4–1
	13 Dec	Blackburn Park Road	A	3–2
	15 Dec	Liverpool Ramblers	H	11–1
	22 Dec	Wednesbury Old Athletic	A	1–0
	1 Jan	Heart Of Midlothian	H	4–1
	2 Jan	Sheffield Wednesday	H	4–1
	5 Jan	Halliwell	H	2–1
	12 Jan	Darwen	H	4–0
	17 Jan	Blackpool (Abandoned after 15 mins)	A	0–0
		(Tom Howarth Broken Leg)		
	9 Feb	Accrington (Howarth Benefit)	A	0–1
	23 Feb	Bolton & District	H	7–1
	1 Mar	Walsall Town	H	5–1
	8 Mar	Wednesbury Town	H	10–0
	10 Mar	Blackburn Olympic	H	2–3
	15 Mar	Glasgow Rangers	H	1–1
	22 Mar	Accrington	H	7–0
	29 Mar	Wednesbury Old Athletic	H	2–1
	5 Apr	Walsall Swifts	A	2–1
	7 Apr	Aston Villa	A	1–0

	11 Apr	Halliwell	A	1–1
	12 Apr	3rd Lanark RV	H	1–1
	14 Apr	Edinburgh Hibernians	H	1–1
	19 Apr	Preston North End	A	2–1
	26 Apr	Halliwell	H	3–0
	3 May	Aston Villa	H	2–1
	10 May	Great Lever	H	0–1
	17 May	Astley Bridge	H	2–0
	24 May	Walsall Swifts	H	5–0
1884–85	1 Sep	Padiham	H	3–4
	6 Sep	Burnley	H	3–1
	9 Sep	Padiham	A	2–4
	13 Sep	Staveley	H	7–1
	20 Sep	Walsall Town	H	5–1
	27 Sep	Sheffield Wednesday	H	2–1
	4 Oct	Aston Villa	A	2–1
	11 Oct	Astley Bridge	H	7–3
	18 Oct	Accrington	A	3–4
	25 Oc	Padiham	H	7–0
	27 Oct	Burnley	A	2–0
	1 Nov	Halliwell	H	3–1
	3 Nov	Burnley	H	3–1
	8 Nov	Clitheroe	H	6–1
	10 Nov	Burslem Port Vale	A	6–1
	15 Nov	Preston North End	A	1–4
	22 Nov	Aston Villa	H	4–1
	6 Dec	Preston North End	H	2–2
	13 Dec	Blackburn Rovers	H	3–2
	19 Dec	Old Corinthians	H	7–0
	20 Dec	Blackburn Olympic	A	1–2
	25 Dec	Burnley	A	2–3
	27 Dec	Walsall Swifts	H	2–0
	1 Jan	Paisley St Mirren	H	2–2
	2 Jan	Cambuslang	H	2–0
	3 Jan	St Bernards	H	7–0
	17 Jan	Halliwell	A	3–2
	24 Jan	Sheffield Wednesday	A	6–2
	2 Feb	Burnley	H	1–2
	4 Feb	Everton	H	7–0
	7 Feb	Astley Bridge	H	4–0
	14 Feb	Accrington	H	1–3
	16 Feb	Burnley	A	2–3
	17 Feb	Darwen	H	3–0
	21 Feb	Derby County	H	4–1
	28 Feb	Blackburn Olympic	H	6–0
	7 Mar	Stoke	A	3–0
	9 Mar	Astley Bridge	A	7–2
	14 Mar	Notts County	H	4–2
	16 Mar	Wigan	A	9–1
	21 Mar	Accrington	H	2–2

	25 Mar	Bolton Association	H	4–0
	28 Mar	Burnley	H	4–0
	3 Apr	Kilmarnock	H	8–1
	4 Apr	Renton	H	2–1
	7 Apr	Battlefield	H	5–3
	18 Apr	Astley Bridge (At Halliwell)		3–1
		(Bolton Charity Cup semi-final)		
	20 Apr	Wolverhampton Wanderers	H	3–1
	25 Apr	West Bromwich Albion	A	1–0
	27 Apr	Wolverhampton Wanderers	A	1–0
	2 May	Great Lever	H	2–1
	9 May	Great Lever (Bolton Charity Cup Final)	H	5–1
	16 May	Great Lever	A	1–1
	18 May	Blackburn Rovers	A	4–1
	23 May	Accrington	H	1–0
	26 May	Everton	A	2–1
	29 May	Arbroath	A	3–0
	30 May	Old Boys (Dundee)	A	4–3
	1 Jun	3rd Lanark RV	A	3–3
1885–86	15 Aug	Padiham	A	1–1
	22 Aug	Church	A	6–1
	29 Aug	Aston Villa	H	7–2
	3 Sep	Turton	H	6–0
	5 Sep	Astley Bridge	H	7–0
	12 Sep	Walsall Town	H	5–0
	19 Sep	Burnley	H	2–1
	21 Sep	South Shore	A	3–0
	26 Sep	Notts Rangers	H	4–2
	28 Sep	Stoke	A	4–2
	3 Oct	Preston North End	H	1–3
	10 Oct	Wolverhampton Wanderers	A	2–0
	17 Oct	Everton	A	4–1
	19 Oct	Blackburn Olympic	H	7–0
	24 Oct	Accrington	H	2–0
	31 Oct	Accrington	A	5–2
	2 Nov	Derby Junction	H	11–0
	2 Nov	Wigan	A	3–0
	7 Nov	Corinthians (At Kennington Oval)		2–0
	14 Nov	Preston North End	A	0–5
	21 Nov	Burnley	A	2–2
	23 Nov	Stoke	H	11–0
	25 Nov	Everton	H	10–0
	28 Nov	Birmingham Excelsior	A	12–2
	12 Dec	Aston Villa	A	3–4
	19 Dec	Walsall Swifts	A	4–0
	25 Dec	Great Lever	A	2–1
		(Abandoned, fighting in crowd of 10,000)		
	26 Dec	Notts County	A	3–3
	28 Dec	West Bromwich Albion	A	0–0
	1 Jan	Derby County	H	1–1

	2 Jan	Great Lever	H	7–1
	4 Jan	Blackburn Rovers	H	5–3
	9 Jan	Padiham	H	0–1
	9 Jan	Accrington	A	0–5
	16 Jan	Birmingham St Georges	H	7–1
	23 Jan	Nottingham Forest	A	7–0
	25 Jan	Burslem Port Vale	A	4–0
	30 Jan	Darwen	H	3–4
	6 Feb	Wolverhampton Wanderers	H	5–0
	8 Feb	Burnley	H	3–0
	13 Feb	Witton	H	4–0
	20 Feb	Blackburn Rovers	A	3–1
	27 Feb	Halliwell	H	7–1
	6 Mar	Darwen	A	6–1
	9 Mar	Staveley	A	6–0
	13 Mar	Derby County	H	7–0
	15 Mar	Burslem Port Vale	A	0–0
	20 Mar	Blackburn Rovers	H	5–2
	22 Mar	Aston Villa	A	1–3
	27 Mar	Grimsby Town	A	1–1
	29 Mar	Burnley	A	2–3
	3 Apr	Notts County	H	6–1
	5 Apr	Stoke	A	1–0
	7 Apr	Church	A	3–1
	9 Apr	Glasgow Rangers	A	3–2
	10 Apr	Heart of Midlothian (Opening of Tynecastle)	A	1–4
	12 Apr	Accrington	H	4–0
	23 Apr	Edinburgh Hibernians	H	6–2
	24 Apr	Battlefield	H	2–1
	26 Apr	Heart of Midlothian	H	2–2
	27 Apr	Derby County	A	1–1
	1 May	Halliwell (Bolton Charity Cup)	A	4–1
	8 May	Derby County (Derby Charity Cup)	A	2–0
1886–87	31 Jul	Crewe & District	A	6–1
	14 Aug	Everton	A	3–1
	21 Aug	Burnley	H	5–1
	23 Aug	Astley Bridge	A	7–0
	27 Aug	Cowlairs	A	0–4
	28 Aug	Edinburgh Hibernians	A	2–3
	4 Sep	Preston North End	A	1–2
	11 Sep	Druids	H	7–1
	18 Sep	Walsall Town	H	5–2
	25 Sep	Wolverhampton Wanderers	H	9–0
	27 Sep	Burslem Port Vale	A	0–3
	2 Oct	Accrington	A	2–1
	13 Oct	Burnley	A	4–3
	16 Oct	Blackburn Rovers	A	2–6

23 Oct	West Bromwich Albion	H	1–0	
28 Oct	Heart of Midlothian	A	2–2	
1 Nov	Wigan	A	6–0	
8 Nov	Blackburn Rovers	H	5–4	
20 Nov	Preston North End	H	3–2	
27 Nov	Derby County	H	2–0	
6 Dec	Stoke	A	1–1	
18 Dec	Burnley	H	2–2	
25 Dec	Preston North End	A	1–12	
28 Dec	West Bromwich Albion	A	3–1	
1 Jan	Glasgow Rangers	H	3–2	
3 Jan	Heart of Midlothian	H	3–2	
4 Jan	Cowlairs	H	3–1	
8 Jan	Mitchell St Georges	H	6–1	
22 Jan	Blackburn Olympic	H	6–0	
29 Jan	Burslem Port Vale	A	2–3	
5 Feb	Blackburn Rovers	H	2–2	
12 Feb	Stoke	H	4–0	
14 Feb	Blackburn Rovers	A	5–1	
26 Feb	Accrington	H	2–2	
5 Mar	Burnley	A	0–6	
5 Mar	Derby County	A	0–3	
12 Mar	Halliwell	A	3–2	
16 Mar	Middlesbrough	A	5–2	
19 Mar	Preston North End	H	3–0	
2 Apr	Halliwell	H	4–4	
4 Apr	Blackburn Olympic	A	2–1	
8 Apr	Edinburgh Hibernians	H	1–1	
9 Apr	3rd Lanark RV	H	2–1	
11 Apr	Renton	H	3–3	
16 Apr	Mitchell St Georges	A	2–0	
18 Apr	Bootle	A	1–0	
23 Apr	Bury	A	6–0	
25 Apr	Burnley	A	0–1	
30 Apr	Newton Heath	A	5–0	
7 May	Halliwell (Bolton Charity Cup semi-final)	A	1–1	
14 May	Darwen	H	3–2	
16 May	Halliwell (Bolton Charity Cup semi-final replay)	H	1–2	
21 May	Everton	A	0–5	
25 May	Crewe Alexandra	A	1–2	
28 May	West Bromwich Albion	A	0–2	
30 May	Halliwell	H	2–0	
20 Jun	Halliwell (Charity game)	H	1–1	
1887–88	6 Aug	Accrington (At Raikes Hall Gardens Blackpool. Part of illuminations weekend)		2–4
	27 Aug	Earlstown (Engineers Strike Fund)	A	5–4

29 Aug	Astley Bridge	A	3–0
3 Sep	Lockwood Bros	H	0–1
5 Sep	Wolverhampton Wanderers	A	1–1
10 Sep	Hyde	A	8–2
13 Sep	Bootle	A	2–3
17 Sep	Burnley	H	1–4
24 Sep	West Bromwich Albion	H	1–1
26 Sep	Burslem Port Vale	A	4–1
28 Sep	Newton Heath	A	1–2
	(Manchester Royal Jubilee Exhibition)		
8 Oct	Accrington	H	1–1
12 Oct	Northwich Victoria	A	1–1
22 Oct	Derby County	A	0–3
5 Nov	Grimsby Town	A	0–2
7 Nov	West Bromwich Albion	A	0–6
26 Nov	Halliwell	H	4–3
3 Dec	Walsall Town	H	6–1
12 Dec	Burnley	H	4–3
17 Dec	Halliwell	A	0–2
24 Dec	Witton	H	2–4
26 Dec	Bootle	A	2–1
27 Dec	Nottingham Forest	A	2–3
31 Dec	Kilmarnock	H	2–0
3 Jan	Paisley Abercorn	H	0–2
4 Jan	Heart of Midlothian	H	3–1
7 Jan	Newton Heath	A	1–0
14 Jan	Accrington	A	1–3
21 Jan	Halliwell	H	3–4
28 Jan	Lincoln City	A	3–4
4 Feb	Bootle	H	2–1
11 Feb	Mitchell St Georges	A	2–3
14 Feb	Notts County	A	3–0
18 Feb	Blackburn Rovers	H	4–1
25 Feb	Darwen	A	2–3
3 Mar	Preston North End	A	1–5
5 Mar	Stoke	A	5–1
10 Mar	Derby County	H	5–5
17 Mar	Halliwell	A	1–4
24 Mar	Burnley	A	1–3
30 Mar	Mitchell St Georges	H	3–4
31 Mar	Nottingham Forest	H	3–1
7 Apr	Blackburn Rovers	A	0–6
14 Apr	Preston North End	H	1–4
17 Apr	Fletcher Street Men	H	1–1
21 Apr	Darwen	H	3–3
23 Apr	Newton Heath	A	3–3
25 Apr	Middlesbrough	A	0–1
28 Apr	Accrington	H	1–1
30 Apr	Astley Bridge (At Halliwell)		4–2
	(Bolton Charity Cup semi-final)		

	2 May	Everton	A	0–4
	5 May	Burnley	H	4–1
	7 May	Lancashire (Steel Benefit)	H	2–1
	12 May	Aston Villa	H	4–3
	19 May	Halliwell	H	3–1
	21 May	Blackburn Rovers(At Eaton Hall Fete, Chester)		4–2
	9 Jun	Farnworth Standard	H	5–1
		(Bolton Charity Cup Final)		
1888–89	1 Sep	Newton Heath	A	0–1
	2 Sep	Gorton Villa	A	2–0
	17 Sep	Astley Bridge	A	1–0
	24 Sep	Bootle	A	3–1
	16 Oct	Port Vale	A	1–3
	27 Oct	Bootle	H	4–0
	28 Nov	Blackpool	A	4–2
	1 Dec	Grimsby Town	A	0–3
	15 Dec	Sunderland	H	10–1
	25 Dec	Battlefield	H	5–3
	27 Dec	Nottingham Forest	A	4–1
	31 Dec	Partick Thistle	H	6–1
	1 Jan	Cambuslang	H	4–3
	2 Jan	Glasgow Rangers	H	1–1
	5 Jan	Sunderland Albion	A	3–1
	2 Feb	Newton Heath	H	3–1
	9 Feb	Burmley	A	1–2
	16 feb	Sunderland	A	3–4
	23 Feb	Burnley	H	2–1
	2 Mar	Halliwell	A	3–1
	16 Mar	Grimsby Town	H	5–3
	25 Mar	Bootle	A	1–0
	30 Mar	Lincoln City	A	3–2
	6 Apr	Preston North End	H	5–1
	8 Apr	Stoke	A	2–2
	13 Apr	Halliwell	H	4–2
	19 Apr	Glasgow Celtic	H	2–0
	20 Apr	Wolverhampton Wanderers	H	2–1
	22 Apr	Battlefield	H	5–0
	23 Apr	Rotherham	A	3–4
	27 Apr	Heywood Central	A	1–4
	1 May	Blackpool	A	4–2
	4 May	Sunderland Albion	A	0–1
	4 May	Kearsley	H	4–0
		(Bolton Charity Cup semi-final)		
	6 May	Everton	A	0–1
	8 May	Blackburn Rovers	H	2–0
	11 May	Hyde	A	2–3
	18 May	Preston North End	A	2–2
	20 May	Blackburn Rovers	A	1–1
	23 May	Glasgow Celtic	A	1–5
	24 May	Glasgow Thistle	A	6–1

	25 May	Dumfries Wanderers	A	3–8
	30 May	Everton	A	2–2
	30 May	Heywood Central	A	3–2
		(Bolton Charity Cup Final)		
1889–90	2 Sep	Southport High Park	A	5–0
	4 Sep	Blackpool	A	4–0
	7 Sep	Newton Heath	A	1–1
	9 Sep	Bootle	A	1–3
	16 Sep	Chester	A	3–1
	23 Sep	Port Vale	A	0–2
	30 Sep	Birmingham St Georges	A	1–3
	5 Oct	Sunderland	H	2–3
	19 Nov	Sheffield United	A	2–0
	25 Dec	Battlefield	H	9–1
	28 Dec	Burnley	H	6–3
	1 Jan	Birmingham St Georges	H	7–2
	2 Jan	Glasgow Rangers	H	4–0
	18 Feb	Rotherham	A	3–0
	22 Feb	Preston North End	H	2–4
	22 Mar	Middlesbrough Ironopolis	A	2–1
	29 Mar	Burnley	A	3–1
	4 Apr	Glasgow Celtic	H	4–0
	5 Apr	London Caledonians	H	2–0
	7 Apr	Sunderland	A	1–0
	8 Apr	Stockton	A	4–1
	12 Apr	Preston North End	H	2–1
	19 Apr	Bootle	A	7–0
	21 Apr	Rhos & District	A	5–0
	24 Apr	Everton	H	0–0
	26 Apr	Preston North End	A	0–5
	28 Apr	Stoke	A	0–3
	30 Apr	Middlesbrough Ironopolis	A	0–2
	3 May	Southport Central	A	2–0
	9 May	St Bernards	A	2–1
	10 May	Glasgow Celtic	A	2–2
	13 May	West Manchester	A	0–0
	17 May	Newton Heath	A	1–1
	19 May	Everton	A	0–1
	24 May	Sunderland	A	0–1
1890–91	1 Sep	Bootle	A	3–2
	3 Sep	Southport High Park	A	2–1
	8 Sep	Ardwick	A	5–1
	22 Sep	Port Vale	A	6–1
	1 Nov	Derby County	A	3–1
	17 Nov	Sheffield United	A	1–2
	27 Nov	Nottingham Forest	A	1–7
	29 Nov	Sheffield Wednesday	H	3–0
	3 Dec	Blackpool	A	1–2
	6 Dec	Sheffield Wednesday	A	6–3
	25 Dec	Hurlford	H	9–2

	27 Dec	Chirk	H	0–0
	1 Jan	Nottingham Forest	H	3–0
	2 Jan	Paisley St Mirren	H	1–1
	3 Jan	Burnley	H	1–1
	31 Jan	Everton	A	0–1
	28 Feb	Everton	A	1–4
	27 Mar	Glasgow Celtic	H	2–2
	30 Mar	Linfield Athletic	A	1–0
	31 Mar	UlsterVille	A	1–1
	4 Apr	Preston North End	H	2–0
	6 Apr	Burnley	A	1–2
	13 Apr	Stoke	A	0–1
	15 Apr	Middlesbrough Ironopolis	A	1–2
	18 Apr	Glasgow Celtic	A	0–2
	27 Apr	International XI	H	1–2
	29 Apr	Halliwell	H	4–0
	30 Apr	Grimsby Town	A	0–0
	2 May	Bury	H	2–0
1891–92	3 Sep	Preston North End	A	2–4
	7 Sep	Newton Heath	A	2–0
	9 Sep	The Canadians	H	1–1
	21 Sep	Sheffield United	A	3–4
	14 Oct	Accrington	A	1–1
	12 Nov	Nottingham Forest	A	0–5
	25 Dec	Newton Heath	H	6–3
	2 Jan	Sheffield United	H	3–3
	4 Jan	Kilmarnock	H	6–1
	9 Jan	Ardwick	A	3–0
	30 Jan	Everton	H	1–1
	10 Feb	The Aladdin Pantomime Company	H	
	13 Feb	Darwen	A	5–0
	24 Feb	Lytham	A	1–1
	19 Mar	Small Heath	A	0–7
	7 Apr	Gorton Villa	A	2–1
	9 Apr	Preston North End	H	3–1
	15 Apr	Nottingham Forest	H	1–0
	25 Apr	Leicester	A	2–0
	26 Apr	Arsenal	A	2–3
	27 Apr	Chatham	A	1–1
	28 Apr	Sheffield Wednesday	A	1–1
	30 Apr	Bury	A	2–5
1892–93	1 Sep	Everton	A	2–4
	5 Sep	Lancashire XI	H	3–5
	6 Sep	Bury	A	1–0
	19 Sep	Darwen	H	2–5
	21 Sep	Preston North End	A	3–2
	27 Sep	Darwen	A	0–4
	9 Nov	Blackpool	A	3–0
	12 Nov	Ardwick	A	0–3
	28 Nov	Sheffield United	A	0–1

	17 Dec	Crewe Alexandra	H	9–1
	31 Dec	The Corinthians	H	2–1
	3 Jan	Bury	H	3–4
	7 Jan	Newcastle United	A	1–3
	23 Jan	Blackburn Rovers (At Swinton RLFC)		1–1
	4 Feb	Small Heath	A	3–4
	8 Feb	Bolton Wednesday	H	9–2
	24 Apr	Liverpool	A	1–1
	25 Apr	Heywood Central	A	2–1
	29 Apr	Sheffield United	H	3–0
1893–94	4 Sep	Ardwick	A	5–0
	6 Sep	Horwich	A	3–1
	11 Sep	Everton	A	0–3
	18 Sep	Farnworth Standard	A	4–1
	11 Nov	Southport Central	A	5–1
	23 Nov	Southampton	A	5–0
	24 Nov	Bournemouth	A	4–1
	25 Nov	The Corinthians	A	1–2
	20 Dec	Preston North End	H	3–4
	28 Apr	Blackburn Rovers	H	0–4
	30 Apr	Halliwell Rovers	A	4–0
1894–95	3 Sep	Darwen	H	3–0
	6 Sep	South Shore	A	4–2
	18 Sep	Darwen	A	1–1
	26 Sep	Manchester City	A	3–2
	17 Oct	Bolton Wednesday	H	8–0
	24 Oct	Bolton Wednesday Rovers	H	5–0
	6 Nov	Millwall Athletic	A	1–5
	7 Nov	New Brompton	A	4–1
	8 Nov	Southampton	A	2–5
	9 Nov	Bournemouth	A	5–0
	10 Nov	The Corinthians	A	4–5
	23 Jan	Blackpool	A	1–2
	13 Mar	Bolton Wednesday	H	10–0
	27 Apr	Chorley	A	0–2
1895–96	11 Sep	Preston North End	H	0–1
	18 Sep	Bolton Wednesday	H	7–0
	24 Sep	Bradford & District	A	7–2
	26 Sep	Southport Central	A	1–2
	23 Oct	Bolton Wednesday Rovers	H	13–2
	11 Nov	Bolton Shop Assistants	H	9–1
	25 Dec	Liverpool	H	0–0
	8 Feb	Glasgow Celtic	A	1–4
	16 Apr	Ayr	A	3–2
	18 Apr	Clyde	A	3–0
	20 Apr	Morton	A	1–0
	21 Apr	St Bernards	A	2–2
	29 Apr	Halliwell Rovers	H	5–0
	30 Apr	Turton	A	0–0
1896–97	1 Sep	Southport Central	A	1–0

	3 Sep	Preston North End	A	0–3
	9 Sep	Bury	H	4–0
	16 Sep	Darwen	H	0–1
	22 Sep	Darwen	A	1–4
	29 Sep	Oldham County	A	2–1
	12 Dec	The Corinthians	A	1–4
	15 Dec	Rochdale	A	1–3
	25 Dec	Motherwell	H	6–0
	2 Jan	Bury	H	2–1
	9 Jan	West Bromwich Albion	H	2–2
	31 Mar	Halliwell Rovers	A	2–1
	12 Apr	Everton	H	8–0
	28 Apr	West Manchester	A	1–2
1897–98	1 Sep	Bury	H	0–0
	6 Sep	Bradford	A	3–0
	7 Sep	Stalybridge Rovers	A	2–0
	20 Sep	Liverpool	A	1–3
	11 Oct	Liverpool	H	4–2
	5 Jan	S.H. Woods University XI	H	4–0
	23 Mar	Wigan County	A	2–1
	11 Apr	The Corinthians	A	3–3
	12 Apr	Dundee	H	0–0
	23 Apr	Heart of Midlothian	H	0–0
	25 Apr	Liverpool	A	1–1
	26 Apr	St Helens	A	1–2
	30 Apr	Tottenham Hotspur	A	2–2
1898–99	1 Sep	Wigan County	A	3–0
	19 Sep	Liverpool	A	2–3
	27 Sep	Stockport	A	6–1
	26 Apr	Bolton Amateurs	H	5–1
1899–1900	4 Sep	Burnley	A	0–0
	5 Sep	Bury	A	2–2
	18 Sep	Bury	H	3–2
	7 Oct	New Brighton	A	0–1
	28 Oct	The Kaffirs	H	13–3
	18 Nov	Tottenham Hotspur	A	0–4
	17 Apr	Hunslet	A	1–1
1900–01	12 Sep	Manchester City	H	2–0
	17 Sep	Burnley	A	1–3
	17 Nov	Belfast Distillery	A	6–1
	14 Jan	Bury	H	1–1
	18 Mar	Blackpool	A	2–3
	6 Apr	Glasgow Rangers	H	2–0
	25 Apr	Shrewsbury Town	A	3–1
1901–02	2 Sep	Bradford	A	3–1
	10 Sep	Bury	A	1–5
	15 Mar	Bohemians	A	4–2
	1 Apr	Brierley Hill	A	3–1
	21 Apr	Barrow	A	3–1
	3 May	Preston North End	H	2–4

1902–03	1 Sep	Barrow	A	2–1
	9 Sep	Manchester City	A	1–3
	21 Feb	Kidderminster	A	4–1
	7 Mar	Third Lanark	A	2–0
	10 Apr	Third Lanark	H	1–0
	22 Apr	Northwich Victoria	A	7–0
1903–04	1 Apr	Third Lanark	H	2–0
	28 Apr	Bolton St Lukes	A	2–1
1904–05	12 Sep	Wrexham	A	3–0
	11 Mar	Corinthians	A	1–1
	29 Apr	Bolton St Lukes	A	8–2
1905–06	11 Sep	Brierley Hill	A	4–1
	24 Feb	West Ham	A	3–5
	28 Mar	Northern Nomads	H	0–2
	8 Apr	Pendlebury	A	0–1
	20 Apr	Glasgow Celtic	H	1–3
	22 Apr	Blackpool	A	1–1
1906–07	21 Mar	Barnsley	A	1–1
	13 Apr	Corinthians	A	0–0
	15 Apr	Brighton & HA	A	2–2
	25 Apr	Pendlebury	A	0–1
1907–08	18 Sep	Whitchurch	A	3–7
	22 Apr	Eccles Borough	A	0–1
1908–09	9 Nov	Blackburn Rovers	A	1–3
	26 Apr	Woking	A	4–1
	16 May	HBS Hague	A	4–1
	20 May	Sparta Rotterdam	A	3–0
	23 May	Swallows FC	A	6–0
	30 May	A.F.S	A	8–1
	1 Jun	Dordrecht	A	10–1
1910–11	3 Jan	Rest of Lancs	A	0–0
1911–12	9 Apr	Blackpool	A	1–1
	10 Apr	Brierley Hill	A	6–5
1912–13	1 May	Duisberg Spieldaerein	A	5–1
	4 May	Victoria Berliner	A	1–2
	11 May	Weiner	A	3–0
	12 May	Vienna ASC	A	3–0
	15 May	Sports Club Rapid	A	3–3
	16 May	Austria Vienna	A	2–2
	18 May	German Association	A	12–0
1916–17	25 Dec	Preston Garrison RFA	H	2–4
	12 May	Atherton	A	1–5
1917–18	29 Mar	RFA	H	4–0
	27 Apr	Blackpool	A	5–2
1918–19	21 Apr	Derby County	A	1–5
	8 May	Oldham Athletic	A	3–3
	10 May	Oldham Athletic	H	6–2
1919–20	2 Apr	Arsenal	H	4–2
	28 Apr	Dublin Bohemians	H	2–4
1920–21	11 Oct	Bournemouth	A	5–0

	3 Jan	Cardiff City	H	4–2
	19 Feb	Sunderland	A	3–2
	20 Apr	Broughton & District	A	2–1
	27 Apr	International XI	H	4–0
1921–22	30 Aug	Witton Albion	A	2–2
	10 Oct	Swansea	A	2–0
	19 Oct	Northern Nomads	H	3–0
	26 Oct	Bolton Wednesday League	H	6–0
1922–23	25 Sep	Plymouth Argyle	A	0–3
	27 Sep	Exeter City	A	2–0
	5 May	Chorley	A	8–0
	20 May	Servette Geneva	A	2–2
	21 May	Young Boys Berne	A	2–0
	23 May	Norastern Basle	A	2–1
	26 May	La Chaux de Fond	A	5–0
	27 May	Zurich XI	A	5–1
	30 May	Young Boys Berne	A	2–1
	2 Jun	Mullhouse	A	6–0
	3 Jun	Alsace XI	A	3–0
1923–24	9 Oct	Glasgow Celtic	A	1–1
	31 Oct	Bournemouth	A	0–0
	6 Mar	Nuneaton Borough	A	3–2
	8 Mar	Corinthians	A	0–0
	21 Apr	Glasgow Celtic	H	0–0
	23 Apr	Llandudno	A	3–1
	26 Apr	Heart of Midlothian	A	1–1
	29 Apr	Atherton	A	2–1
	4 May	Gutmus	A	3–1
	7 May	Fortuna	A	9–0
	11 May	Sparta Prague	A	3–1
	13 May	Nurnberg	A	4–0
	15 May	Munich	A	3–1
	18 May	Union Club	A	4–0
	19 May	Aberdeen (Played in Leipzig)		3–1
	21 May	Ajax	A	3–1
	25 May	Leeds United (Played in Amsterdam)		3–1
	29 May	Sparta Rotterdam	A	5–1
1924–25	24 Sep	Colwyn Bay	A	5–1
	28 Mar	Manchester City	H	3–0
	8 May	Hakoah	A	2–1
	10 May	MTK Budapest	A	1–1
	14 May	Austrian–Budapest Select	A	4–2
	17 May	Budapest League XI	A	1–3
	21 May	City of Prague	A	0–2
1926–27	28 Mar	Plymouth Argyle	A	1–0
	30 Mar	Exeter City	A	2–3
	5 May	International XI	H	4–7
1927–28	29 Aug	Barry	A	3–1
	25 Apr	Hamilton Academicals	H	4–0
	30 Apr	Atherton	A	4–1

	21 May	Helsingborg	A	3–1
	25 May	Gothenburg	A	2–2
	28 May	Elfsborg	A	4–0
	30 May	Stockholm	A	2–3
	1 Jun	Stockholm XI	A	3–1
	3 Jun	Oslo	A	3–1
1928–29	2 May	Hinckley	A	2–1
	20 May	Cataluna	A	0–4
1929–30	12 May	Macclesfield	A	4–0
1930–31	6 Apr	Brierley Hill Alliance	A	6–2
	27 Apr	Past Players	H	2–1
1932–33	24 Apr	Accrington Stanley	A	4–0
1935–26	9 May	Grimsby Town	A	0–1
1937–38	8 Sep	Morton	A	0–2
	27 Apr	Flint Town	A	2–1
	4 May	Brighton & HA	A	5–1
1938–39	20 Aug	Bury	H	1–2
	19 Sep	Coalville	A	6–1
	12 Apr	Flint Town	A	2–3
	14 May	Norwegian XI	A	4–0
	16 May	Fredrikstad	A	2–1
	18 May	Skien	A	5–1
	21 May	Drammen	A	2–0
	23 May	Stavanger	A	4–0
1939–40	19 Aug	Bury	H	2–1
	16 Sep	Manchester United	H	2–2
	23 Sep	Liverpool	A	0–3
	30 Sep	Blackpool	A	0–2
	7 Oct	Preston North End	A	1–6
	14 Oct	Manchester City	H	2–2
	16 Dec	53rd Field Regiment RA	H	3–3
	25 Dec	Stoke City	H	3–0
	26 Dec	Stoke City	A	5–1
	1 Jan	Preston North End	H	3–1
	17 Feb	Blackpool	A	1–2
	2 Mar	Oldham Athletic	A	2–4
	9 Mar	Sheffield Wednesday	A	3–3
	25 Mar	Liverpool	A	1–0
1940–41	25 De	Blackpool	A	1–3
	28 Dec	Halifax Town	A	1–4
	5 Apr	RAF XI	H	3–3
	2 Jun	RAF Kirkham	H	3–3
	6 Jun	RAF (Played at Blackpool)		1–2
1941–42	27 May	RAF XI	H	2–1
1942–43	27 Mar	RAF	H	7–3
	26 Apr	RAF Paras	H	5–2
1946–47	3 May	Hull City	A	1–0
	17 May	Carlisle United	A	1–4
1947–48	6 Mar	Motherwell	H	3–4
1948–49	5 Feb	Middlesbrough	A	1–1

	6 Apr	Chester	A	3–2
		(Abandoned after 70 mins, bad light)		
	9 May	Norwich City	A	2–0
1949–50	11 Feb	St Mirren	H	4–2
	12 May	Drumcondra	A	2–1
	14 May	Sligo Rovers	A	4–2
	16 May	Derry City	A	3–1
1950–51	7 May	Norwich City	A	2–3
	9 May	Dundee	H	2–1
	14 May	Lucerne	A	3–0
	16 May	Zurich XI	A	0–1
	17 May	Berne	A	1–1
	22 May	Basle	A	0–1
	25 May	Schaafhausen	A	2–0
1951–52	23 Feb	Nottingham Forest	A	3–3
	5 Mar	Dutch XI	A	2–2
	26 Apr	Hibernian	A	2–2
1952–53	9 May	Germany B	A	2–1
	14 May	Germany A	A	0–2
	16 May	German Select	A	1–1
	20 May	Germany B	A	3–3
	24 May	Select XI	A	3–2
	31 May	Dutch XI	A	6–1
1953–54	13 Oct	Bury	A	2–2
	5 May	Dutch XI	A	0–2
	9 May	Bangu de Rio	A	3–0
	12 May	Liege XI	A	2–1
	16 May	Borussia–Rheydt XI	A	1–0
1954–55	7 Aug	Edinburgh Select	A	2–3
	5 Oct	Bury	A	3–2
	19 Apr	Tranmere Rovers	A	2–2
	7 May	Rot–Weiss Essen	A	1–3
	11 May	Schalke 04	A	2–2
	15 May	Athletic Bilbao	A	1–2
	19 May	Royal Antwerp	A	1–2
1955–56	11 Oct	Bury	A	2–2
	31 Oct	Rhyl	A	3–1
	28 Nov	Accrington	A	1–3
	18 Apr	International XI	A	2–3
		(Ken Grieves Benefit at Altrincham)		
	10 May	Larvik Turn	A	3–3
	12 May	Lyn Oslo	A	6–1
	15 May	Brann Bergen	A	4–0
	18 May	Stavanger	A	5–0
1956–57	2 Oct	Bury	A	2–2
	26 Jan	Liverpool	H	5–3
	16 Feb	Heart of Midlothian	A	6–3
	10 Mar	La Gantoise	A	1–1
	23 Apr	All Stars XI (Harold Hassall Benefit)	H	3–0
	29 Apr	Tranmere Rovers	A	2–0

1957–58	14 Oct	Heart of Midlothian	H	1–1
	4 Nov	CDSA Moscow	H	3–1
	28 Nov	Feyenoord	A	0–3
	9 Dec	Blackburn Rovers	H	4–1
	8 May	Fortuna Geleen	A	0–2
	10 May	Dusseldorf–Rot-Weiss Essen Select	A	3–2
	13 May	F C Sochaux	A	0–2
	15 May	Olympique Lyonnais	A	3–2
	21 May	Flamingo de Rio (In Paris)		1–1
	23 May	Racing Club Paris	A	1–2
1958–59	16 May	Southern Transvaal	A	2–1
	20 May	Eastern Transvaal	A	1–2
	23 May	Natal	A	0–1
	27 May	Border FA	A	6–1
	30 May	Western Province	A	3–0
	1 Jun	Northern Transvaal	A	2–1
	6 Jun	South Africa	A	1–0
	13 Jun	South Africa	A	2–1
	17 Jun	Southern Rhodesia	A	5–0
	21 Jun	Northern Rhodesia	A	5–3
1959–60	19 Oct	Hibernian	A	2–5
	17 May	Royal Beerschot	A	1–1
	20 May	Borussia Dortmund	A	1–0
	22 May	VFB Stuttgart	A	3–2
	26 May	Real Betis	A	1–2
	29 May	Borussia Dortmund (In Seville)		2–3
1960–61	14 Aug	Le Havre	A	1–1
	15 Mar	Le Havre	H	4–0
	6 May	Karlsruher	A	2–1
	11 May	Saarbrucken	A	0–1
	13 May	Mestalla	A	0–1
	14 May	Espanyol	A	0–2
1961–62	22 Nov	Saarbrucken	H	4–1
	23 Jan	Barnsley	A	0–2
	27 Jan	Hibernian	A	0–2
	2 May	AEK Athens	A	1–4
	4 May	Loval	A	2–1
	6 May	Panathanaikos	A	1–1
	7 May	Olympiakos	A	2–1
	9 May	Racing Club Paris	A	0–1
1962–63	11 Aug	Middlesbrough	A	2–0
	3 Dec	RFC Liege	H	3–2
	13 Feb	Manchester United (In Cork)		2–4
1963–64	17 Aug	Sunderland	A	4–3
1964–65	10 Aug	Blackburn Rovers	A	1–4
	13 Aug	Blackburn Rovers	H	3–2
1965–66	14 Aug	Crewe Alexandra	A	1–0
1966–67	15 Aug	Manchester City	A	0–0
1967–68	12 Aug	Tranmere Rovers	A	1–3
1968–69	31 Jul	Twente Enschede	A	1–1

	3 Aug	VFR Neuss	A	1–0
	12 Nov	Bremerhaven	H	4–2
	27 Apr	Bremerhaven	A	1–1
	30 Apr	Hvidovre	A	2–0
	2 May	Holbaek	A	2–0
	5 May	South Jutland Alliance	A	4–0
	8 May	Freja Randers	A	4–3
1969–70	26 Jul	Walsall	A	0–1
	30 Jul	Burnley	H	1–1
	2 Aug	Ayr United	A	2–1
	24 Nov	VFR Neuss	H	3–0
	24 Jan	Halifax Town	A	2–0
	6 Feb	Tranmere Rovers	A	1–1
	14 Apr	South Liverpool	A	1–1
1970–71	2 Aug	SPVGG Bayreuth	A	0–0
	4 Aug	Celle	A	2–0
	5 Aug	VFL Osnabruck	A	2–1
	8 Aug	Newcastle United	A	0–3
	23 Jan	Grimsby Town	A	0–2
	1 Mar	Freja Randers	H	2–1
1971–72	31 Jul	Burnley	H	1–0
	7 Aug	Chelsea	H	2–0
	29 Nov	Hvidovre	H	4–0
1972–73	29 Jul	Preston North End	H	2–0
	2 Aug	Bohemians Prague	H	1–1
	5 Aug	Raith Rovers	A	1–2
	2 May	Burnley (Warwick Rimmer Testimonial)	H	3–1
1973–74	1 Aug	Helmond	A	3–0
	4 Aug	Mulheim	A	0–2
	5 Aug	Dordrecht	A	1–2
	11 Aug	Huddersfield	H	0–1
	17 Aug	Blackburn Rovers	H	2–0
1974–75	28 Jul	Erkenschwick	A	1–2
	30 Jul	Gutersloh	A	1–1
	1 Aug	Haltern	A	4–0
	3 Aug	NAC Breda	A	1–1
	7 Aug	Plymouth Argyle	H	1–1
	10 Aug	Blackburn Rovers	H	2–2
	24 Jan	Blackburn Rovers	H	3–1
1975–76	19 Jul	Westphalia Herne	A	2–0
	23 Jul	Homburg	A	3–2
	27 Jul	NAC Breda	A	0–4
	2 Aug	Chesterfield	H	2–1
	5 Aug	Rotherham United	A	2–0
	9 Aug	Wolverhampton Wanderers	A	1–1
	3 May	All Star XI (Roy Greaves Testimonial)	H	1–2
1976–77	24 Jul	Paderborn	A	1–0
	25 Jul	Rot-Weiss Essen	A	1–1
	27 Jul	VFB Rhine	A	2–1
	31 Jul	Westphalia Herne	A	0–1

	7 Aug	Blackpool (Anglo-Scottish Cup)	H	0–0	
	10 Aug	Blackburn Rovers (Anglo-Scottish Cup)	H	2–0	
	14 Aug	Burnley (Anglo-Scottish Cup)	A	0–1	
	14 Sep	Partick Thistle (Anglo-Scottish Cup)	H	0–0	
	29 Sep	Partick Thistle (Anglo-Scottish Cup)	A	0–1	
	28 Jan	Huddersfield Town	A	2–2	
1977–78	23 Jul	Bayreuth	A	1–5	
	26 Jul	VFB Stuttgart	A	1–3	
	28 Jul	Atlas Delmenhorst	A	2–1	
	1 Aug	SV Troisdorf	A	2–3	
	6 Aug	Burnley (Anglo-Scottish Cup)	H	1–0	
	10 Aug	Blackburn Rovers (Anglo-Scottish Cup)	A	0–2	
	13 Aug	Blackpool (Anglo-Scottish Cup)	A	1–0	
	12 May	Liverpool–Everton XI	H	5–5	
		(Peter Thompson Testimonial)			
1978–79	28 Jul	Bradford City	A	2–2	
	1 Aug	Doncaster Rovers	A	1–1	
	5 Aug	Sunderland (Anglo-Scottish Cup)	A	0–2	
	8 Aug	Sheffield United (Anglo-Scottish Cup)	H	1–0	
	12 Aug	Oldham Athletic (Anglo-Scottish Cup)	H	0–0	
	6 Nov	Blackburn Rovers (John Byrom Testimonial)	H	3–4	
1979–80	2 Aug	Bury (Anglo Scottish Cup)	H	2–2	
	4 Aug	Oldham Athletic (Anglo-Scottish Cup)	A	3–1	
	7 Aug	Sunderland (Anglo-Scottish Cup)	H	2–0	
	13 Aug	Ajax Amsterdam	H	1–3	
	11 Sep	Malawi (At Chorley)		3–1	
	19 Sep	St Mirren (Anglo-Scottish Cup)	A	2–4	
	2 Oct	St Mirren (Anglo-Scottish Cup)	H	2–1	AET
1980–81	1 Aug	Darlington	A	0–0	
	5 Aug	Haarlem	A	1–0	
	7 Aug	Sparta Rotterdam	A	2–1	
	9 Aug	Legia Warsaw	H	0–2	
	4 Nov	Haarlem	H	5–0	
	17 Mar	Sparta Rotterdam	H	2–1	
	4 May	Rotherham United	A	0–2	
		(John Breckin Testimonial)			
1981–82	10 Aug	Hartlepool United	A	3–2	
	15 Aug	Shrewsbury Town (Group Cup)	H	0–2	
	18 Aug	Bury (Group Cup)	A	2–2	
	22 Aug	Chester (Group Cup)	A	2–1	
	24 Aug	Birmingham City	H	1–1	
	11 Feb	Nigerian XI	A	1–4	
	11 May	Wigan Athletic (John Brown Testimonial)	A	0–1	
1982–83	6 Aug	Fleetwood Town	A	6–1	
	9 Aug	Morecambe	A	2–0	
	24 Aug	Manchester United	A	2–2	
		(Jim Headridge Testimonial)			
	19 Oct	1978 XI (Peter Nicholson Testimonial)	H	4–0	
	28 Jan	Sunderland	H	0–1	
1983–84	2 Aug	Sligo Rovers	A	2–1	

	4 Aug	Finn Harps	A	2–1
	6 Aug	Carrick Rangers	A	6–0
	8 Aug	Glentoran	A	0–0
	9 Mar	Hamilton Academicals	A	1–3
1984–85	1 Aug	Glenavon	A	2–3
	3 Aug	Portadown	A	4–2
	4 Aug	Linfield	A	2–1
	6 Aug	Moyola Park	A	8–0
	8 Aug	Bangor	A	2–0
	17 Oct	Winsford United	A	6–3
	19 Nov	Hyde United	A	3–3
	8 Dec	Rochdale	A	3–2
1985–86	24 Jul	Chorley	A	0–0
	25 Jul	Macclesfield Town	A	2–1
	27 Jul	Workington	A	0–0
	30 Jul	Southport	A	5–2
1986–87	30 Jul	Morecambe	A	2–0
	2 Aug	Fleetwood Town	A	2–1
	4 Aug	Workington	A	3–0
	20 Feb	Scarborough	A	3–0
1987–88	29 Jul	Port Vale	A	3–2
1989–90	23 Jul	Motherwell (Isle of Man Tournament)		0–1
	25 Jul	Dundalk (Isle of Man Tournament)		1–0
	28 Jul	Swansea City (Isle of Man Tournament)		1–2
	10 Aug	Manchester City	H	0–2
		(Nat Lofthouse Testimonial)		
1990–91	31 Jul	Lancaster City	A	5–1
	7 Aug	Lincoln United	A	3–0
	15 Oct	Manchester City (Fred Hill testimonial)	H	2–1
1991–92	28 Jul	Sunderland (Isle of Man Tournament)		2–2
	29 Jul	Shelbourne (Isle of Man Tournament)		0–0
	2 Aug	Isle of Man (Isle of Man Tournament)		6–0
	7 Jan	Leek Town	A	0–0
1992–93	22 Jul	Atherton LR	A	4–0
	25 Jul	Barnsley	A	2–0
	17 Nov	Manchester City	H	4–2
		(Frank Worthington–Robbie Savage Testimonial)		
1993–94	21 Jul	Atherton LR	A	2–0
	7 Aug	Chorley	A	2–1
1994–95	22 Jul	Atherton LR	A	1–0
	26 Jul	Liverpool	H	4–1
	30 Jul	Dunfermline	A	0–0
		(won 5–4 on penalties)		
	1 Aug	Ross County	A	7–0
	3 Aug	Caledonian Thistle	A	2–0
	6 Aug	St Johnstone	A	3–1
1995–96	28 Jul	Atherton LR	A	1–0
	31 Jul	Queens Park	A	3–0
	2 Aug	Dundee	A	2–2
	5 Aug	Dunfermline	A	2–3

	8 Aug	Aberdeen	H	3–1
	12 Aug	Kilmarnock	A	2–1
1996–97	19 Jul	Atherton LR	A	5–0
	24 Jul	Queen of the South	A	3–1
	27 Jul	Hull City	A	0–1
	31 Jul	Wrexham	A	1–1
	3 Aug	York City	A	2–0
	6 Aug	Rotherham United	A	1–0
	10 Aug	Carlisle United	A	0–1
1997–98	16 Jul	Crewe Alexandra	A	1–2
	19 Jul	Notts County	A	4–3
	22 Jul	Colchester United	A	1–1
	25 Jul	Norwich City	A	1–0
	29 Jul	Bury	A	2–1
	2 Aug	Port Vale	A	2–1
	9 Oct	Rochdale	A	0–2
1998–99	18 Jul	Galway	A	5–0
	21 Jul	Waterford	A	2–3
	24 Jul	Sligo Rovers	A	3–0
	25 Jul	St Patricks Athletic	A	1–0
	1 Aug	Blackpool	A	1–2
	4 Aug	Celtic (Jimmy Phillips Testimonial)	H	1–1
	13 Oct	Leigh RMI	A	2–0
1999–2001	17 Jul	Stoke City	A	1–2
	21 Jul	Blackpool	A	1–1
	24 Jul	Cambridge United	A	1–0
	28 Jul	Wrexham	A	1–0
	1 Aug	Preston North End (abandoned)	H	2–1
2000–01	12 Jul	Brondby	A	1–2
	15 Jul	Lyngby	A	0–6
	17 Jul	Odense	A	1–6
	25 Jul	Indiana Blast	A	2–0
	30 Jul	USA U23	A	0–1
	5 Aug	Bury	A	2–1
	7 Aug	Chester	A	0–0
2001–02	14 Jul	Radcliffe Borough	A	3–1
	30 Jul	Boston United	A	4–3
	31 Jul	Halifax Town	A	1–0
	3 Aug	Athletic Bilbao	H	0–1
	7 Aug	Deportivo Alaves	H	0–1
2002–03	16 Jul	Radcliffe Borough	A	1–1
	21 Jul	Bormio	A	13–0
	24 Jul	Litex Lovech (In Bormio)		2–1
	27 Jul	Inter Milan (In Reggio Emilia)		0–2
	31 Jul	Burnley	A	0–1
	3 Aug	Cardiff City	A	1–2
	8 Aug	Hellas Verona	H	2–0
2003–04	16 Jul	Ballymena United	A	7–1
	19 Jul	Portadown	A	4–0

	23 Jul	Royal Antwerp	H	4–0
	24 Jul	Halifax Town	A	1–2
	29 Jul	Birkikara	A	2–1
	31 Jul	Floriana	A	5–1
	6 Aug	Real Mallorca	H	0–0
	9 Aug	Olympiakos	H	1–1
	3 Sep	Cork City	A	2–0
		(Carl Davenport Testimonial)		
	15 Nov	Sao Paulo	H	3–6
2004–05	14 Jul	Dundee United (At Leyland)		2–0
	17 Jul	Radcliffe Borough	A	3–1
	21 Jul	Sporting Lisbon	A	2–1
	22 Jul	Vitoria Setubal	A	0–3
	24 Jul	Bradford City	A	1–2
		(Wayne Jacobs Testimonial)		
	27 Jul	Oldham Athletic	A	1–0
	28 Jul	Chesterfield	A	0–1
	31 Jul	Sheffield Wednesday	A	2–2
	1 Aug	Inter Milan	H	0–1
	7 Aug	Real Zaragoza	H	1–1
	4 Sep	Seville	A	0–2
2005–06	9 Jul	Rushen United	A	10–0
	20 Jul	Manchester City (Asia Cup, Bangkok)		1–1
		(Won 5–4 on pens)		
	23 Jul	Thailand (Asia Cup, Bangkok)		1–0
	26 Jul	Vissel Kobe	A	1–1
	28 Jul	Kawasaki Frontale	A	1–1
	30 Jul	Hull City	A	0–1
	1 Aug	Bury	A	1–2
	2 Aug	CG Malaga	H	2–1
	6 Aug	Heerenveen	H	1–1
2006–07	22 Jul	Burnley	A	1–2
	29 Jul	Derby County	A	0–2
	8 Aug	Recreativo Huelva (Colombino Cup)	A	2–3
	9 Aug	Seville (Colombino Cup)	A	0–3
	12 Aug	AZ Alkmaar	H	1–3
2007–08	12 Jul	Seongnam (Peace Cup, South Korea)		1–1
	14 Jul	Chivas (Peace Cup, South Korea)		2–0
	17 Jul	Racing Santander (Peace Cup, South Korea)		2–1
	21 Jul	Olympique Lyonnais (Peace Cup Final)		0–1
	25 Jul	Hibernian	A	0–3
	28 Jul	Tranmere Rovers	A	1–0
	1 Aug	Espanyol	H	3–0
	4 Aug	Colchester United	A	2–1
	27 Aug	Radcliffe Borough	A	4–0
2008–09	25 Jul	Rochdale	A	0–0
	26 Jul	Macclesfield Town	A	0–1
	1 Aug	Doncaster Rovers	A	5–0
	2 Aug	Chorley	A	2–0
	4 Aug	Aris Thessaloniki	A	1–1

Bolton win the Carslebrg Cup against Toronto in 2010.

	8 Aug	AEK Athens	A	0–1
2009–10	25 Jul	Borussia Monchengladbach	A	1–1
	28 Jul	FC Den Bosch	A	2–1
	31 Jul	FC Eindhoven	A	2–2
	4 Aug	Heart of Midlothian	A	1–1
	8 Aug	Hibernian	H	0–0
		(Jussi Jääskeläinen Testimonial)		
2010–11	14 Jul	Charlotte Eagles	A	3–0
	17 Jul	Charleston Battery	A	2–0
	21 Jul	Toronto (Carlsberg Cup)	A	1–1
		(Won 4–3 on pens)		
	24 Jul	Rochdale	A	1–1
	28 Jul	Oldham Athletic	A	0–3
	31 Jul	Falkirk	A	0–0
	2 Aug	St Johnstone	A	2–0
	6 Aug	Osasuna	H	2–0
	15 Nov	Cliftonville	A	2–0

Bolton Wanderers Reserves Championship-Winning Seasons

1954–55 Central League

No	Date	Venue	Opponents	Result		Goalscorer
1	21 Aug	A	Blackburn Rovers	L	0–1	
2	25 Aug	H	Derby County	W	2–0	Neill, Codd
3	28 Aug	H	Bury	W	3–0	Codd, Allcock, Neill
4	1 Sep	A	Derby County	W	5–1	Hennin, Stevens 2, Codd, Gubbins
5	4 Sep	H	Huddersfield Town	L	1–2	Stevens
6	11 Sep	A	Manchester United	W	3–0	Stevens, Codd 2
7	13 Sep	A	Sheffield Wednesday	W	3–0	Stevens, Codd, Allcock
8	18 Sep	H	Liverpool	W	2–0	Codd, McIlwaine
9	22 Sep	H	Sheffield Wednesday	W	2–0	Webster, Hennin
10	25 Sep	A	Aston Villa	L	0–1	
11	2 Oct	H	Wolverhampton Wanderers	L	1–2	Stevens
12	9 Oct	A	Leeds United	W	2–0	Stevens, Allcock
13	16 Oct	H	Manchester City	D	1–1	Stevens
14	23 Oct	A	Newcastle United	D	0–0	
15	30 Oct	H	West Bromwich Albion	L	0–1	
16	6 Nov	A	Everton	W	2–0	Stevens, Webster
17	13 Nov	H	Stoke City	W	6–1	Stevens, Hennin 2, Allcock, Webster, Pilling
18	20 Nov	A	Sheffield United	D	2–2	Pollitt, Stevens
19	27 Nov	H	Barnsley	W	1–0	Hennin (pen)
20	4 Dec	A	Burnley	W	2–1	Allcock, Pilling
21	11 Dec	H	Preston North End	W	1–0	Wheeler
22	18 Dec	H	Blackburn Rovers	W	2–1	Parry 2 (1 pen)
23	25 Dec	A	Chesterfield	W	2–1	Pollitt, Gubbins
24	27 Dec	H	Chesterfield	D	0–0	
25	1 Jan	A	Bury	L	0–1	
26	15 Jan	A	Huddersfield Town	D	0–0	
27	5 Feb	A	Liverpool	L	0–1	
28	12 Feb	H	Aston Villa	W	2–0	Gubbins, Hartle
29	19 Feb	H	Manchester United	W	3–1	Gubbins, Allcock, Stevens
30	5 Mar	A	Manchester City	D	2–2	Pollitt, Gubbins
31	12 Mar	H	Newcastle United	W	2–1	Birch, Allcock
32	19 Mar	A	West Bromwich Albion	D	1–1	Stevens
33	23 Mar	H	Leeds United	W	1–0	Pollitt
34	26 Mar	H	Everton	W	3–0	Pollitt 2, Stevens
35	2 Apr	A	Stoke City	W	4–0	Hennin, Gubbins 2, Pollitt

36	8 Apr	A	Blackpool	L	0–1	
37	9 Apr	H	Sheffield United	W	2–1	Hennin, Pollitt
38	11 Apr	H	Blackpool	W	2–1	Hennin (pen), Pollitt
39	16 Apr	A	Barnsley	L	0–3	
40	23 Apr	H	Burnley	W	3–0	Allcock 2, Pollitt
41	30 Apr	A	Preston North End	W	1–0	Allcock
42	2 May	A	Wolverhampton Wanderers	W	1–0	Pollitt

Appearances/goals

Allcock, Terry	36–10	Hartle, Roy	42–1
Bailey, Dennis	5–0	Haydock, Dennis	7–0
Banks, Tommy	9–0	Hennin, Derek	31–8
Barnard, Arthur	12–0	Higgins, John	40–0
Barrass, Malcolm	1–0	McIlwaine, Matt	7–1
Bell, Eric	5–0	Moir, Willie	1–0
Bingley, Walter	29–0	Neill, Tommy	38–2
Birch, Brian	25–1	Oldham, Eric	4–0
Bradley, Warren	7–0	Parry, Ray	8–2
Codd, Ronnie	12–7	Pilling, Vince	15–2
Cunliffe, Graham	5–0	Pollitt, Jack	19–11
Greenwood, Peter	1–0	Stevens, Dennis	29–14
Grieves, Ken	26–0	Webster, Harry	11–3
Gubbins, Ralph	31–7	Wheeler, Johnny	2–1
Hanson, Stan	4–0		

1994–95 Central League

No	Date	Venue	Opponents	Result		Goalscorer
1	17 Aug	A	Nottingham Forest	W	2–0	Coyle 2
2	22 Aug	H	Wolverhampton Wanderers	W	5–1	Coyle 3, Green, Emblen (og)
3	7 Sep	H	Stoke City	D	3–3	Coyle, Thompson 2
4	14 Sep	A	Liverpool	W	1–0	Lee
5	21 Sep	H	Tranmere Rovers	W	5–3	Evans 2, Martindale, Wiggans, Whittaker
6	29 Sep	A	Derby County	L	2–3	Martindale, Cumberbatch
7	11 Oct	A	Coventry City	W	3–1	De Freitas 2, Coyle
8	19 Oct	H	Sheffield United	L	2–3	Martindale, Coyle
9	26 Oct	A	Rotherham United	W	2–1	Fisher, Coyle
10	3 Nov	H	West Bromwich Albion	W	2–1	Whittaker, Coyle
11	8 Nov	H	Manchester United	W	3–1	McAteer, Coyle 2
12	16 Nov	A	Aston Villa	W	2–0	Coyle, Martindale
13	21 Nov	H	Leeds United	W	4–3	Coyle 2, Martindale 2
14	29 Nov	A	Sheffield United	L	0–2	
15	7 Dec	H	Nottingham Forest	W	2–0	Roscoe, Martindale
16	12 Dec	A	Wolverhampton Wanderers	D	2–2	De Freitas, Thompson
17	21 Dec	H	Everton	W	2–1	Martindale, Fisher
18	4 Jan	A	Sunderland	D	1–1	Martindale
19	12 Jan	A	Blackburn Rovers	W	2–0	Coyle 2
20	16 Jan	H	Notts County	W	2–1	Coyle, Cumberbatch
21	1 Feb	A	Manchester United	W	4–2	Martindale 3, Roscoe

The Wanderers line up with the Championship trophy in May 1995 prior to the home game with Coventry City.

22	8 Feb	H	Aston Villa	W	4–3	De Freitas 2, Martindale, McGinlay
23	14 Feb	A	Leeds United	D	0–0	
24	1 Mar	A	Tranmere Rovers	L	1–2	Coyle
25	16 Mar	H	Derby County	L	1–2	Coyle
26	23 Mar	H	Liverpool	W	3–1	Coyle 2 (1 pen), Whittaker
27	30 Mar	A	Stoke City	W	1–0	De Freitas
28	6 Apr	A	Everton	W	2–0	De Freitas, Coyle
29	12 Apr	H	Sunderland	W	1–0	Whittaker
30	18 Apr	A	Notts County	L	0–3	
31	26 Apr	H	Blackburn Rovers	D	0–0	
32	3 May	A	West Bromwich Albion	W	3–1	De Freitas 2, Martindale
33	10 May	H	Coventry City	L	0–4	
34	12 May	H	Rotherham United	W	2–1	Mason 2

Appearances/goals

Aljofree, Hasney	22–0		McGinlay, John	2–1
Anderson, Lee	1–0		McKay, Andy	2–0
Bergsson, Gudni	3–0		Neil, Martin	2–0
Bowman, Matthew	(1)–0		Niemi, Antti	2–0
Coyle, Owen	22–23		Oliveira, Mario	1–0
Cumberbatch, Grant	9(9)–2		Patterson, Mark	11–0
Davison, Aidan	21–0		Powell, Mark	26–0
De Freitas, Fabian	18(1)–9		Proctor, Daniel	1–0
Dreyer, John	4–0		Quinn, Stephen	1(1)–0
Ellis, Peter	2–0		Rawlinson, Mark	1–0
Evans, Robert	3(1)–2		Redmond, Brendan	7(1)–0

Fisher, Neil	24–2	Rhodes, Andy	1–0
Green, Scott	9–1	Roscoe, Andrew	14–2
Hall, David	1–0	Samuel, Gavin	1–0
Heinola, Antti	2–0	Seagraves, Mark	16–0
Kelly, Tony	3–0	Shilton, Peter	2–0
Kernaghan, Alan	2–0	Spooner, Nicky	6–0
Leather, Ian	10–0	Stubbs, Alan	2–0
Lee, David	2–1	Thomas, Glenn	2–0
Lydiate, Jason	11–0	Thompson, Alan	4–3
Maddix, Stuart	1–0	Verveer, Etienne	3–0
Marsh, Neil	(1)–0	Westhead, Mark	8(2)–0
Martindale, Gary	28(1)–14	Whittaker, Stuart	27–4
Mason, Andrew	9(3)–2	Wiggans, Andrew	7(2)–1
McAllister, Mark	1–0	Wright, Jermaine	1–0
McAteer, Jason	2–1	Opponents	0–1
McDonald, Neil	14–0		

2006–07 FA Premier Reserve League North

No	Date	Venue	Opponents	Result		Goalscorer
1	30 Aug	H	Sheffield United	L	1–3	Charlesworth
2	11 Sep	A	Blackburn Rovers	L	0–1	
3	5 Oct	A	Manchester United	L	1–4	Woolfe
4	31 Oct	A	Middlesbrough	L	0–2	
5	8 Nov	A	Wigan Athletic	W	1–0	Nolan (pen)
6	22 Nov	H	Manchester City	W	2–1	L. Thompson, Vaz Te (pen)
7	5 Dec	A	Everton	D	2–2	Charlesworth, Tal (pen)
8	20 Dec	H	Liverpool	W	1–0	Vaz Te
9	24 Jan	H	Blackburn Rovers	W	1–0	Woolfe
10	14 Feb	H	Manchester United	D	0–0	
11	22 Feb	A	Liverpool	L	0–1	
12	5 Mar	A	Newcastle United	D	0–0	
13	14 Mar	H	Middlesbrough	W	2–0	Harsanyi, Wolze
14	21 Mar	H	Wigan Athletic	W	1–0	Granqvist (og)
15	3 Apr	A	Sheffield United	W	2–0	Harsanyi, D. Thompson
16	10 Apr	A	Manchester City	W	2–0	Martin, Giannakopoulos
17	18 Apr	H	Everton	W	2–1	Tal, Giannakopoulos
18	25 Apr	H	Newcastle United	W	3–1	Wolze, Obadeyi (2)

Appearances/goals

Al-Habsi, Ali	9–0	Mountford Sean	1–0
Augustyn, Blazej	15–0	Nolan Kevin	2–1
Basham Chris	12(2)–0	Obadeyi Temitope	3(6)–2
Brooks Tom	1(5)–0	Pedersen Henrik	1–0
Cassidy Matt	9(3)–0	Roddy Michael	1(1)–0
Charlesworth Mark	6–2	Sheridan Sam	1(1)–0
Ellis Mark	5(1)–0	Sinclair James	14(1)–0
Fojut Jaroslaw	9(3)–0	Sissons Rob	11(5)–0
Gardner Ricardo	3–0	Smith Johann	6–0

Wanderers 2006–07 reserve squad.

Gbemie David	6–0	Stott Danny	2–0
Giannakopoulos Stelios	2–2	Tal Idan	6–2
Harsanyi Zoltanl	8–2	Teymourian Andranik	6–0
Howarth Chris	2–0	Thompson Les	8(7)–1
Hunt Nicky	1–0	Thompson David	6–1
Jamieson Scott	13(2)–0	Vaz Te Ricardo	6–2
Kazimierczak Przemyslaw	3–0	Walker Ian	4–0
Lainton Rob	1–0	Wolze Kevin	5(1)–2
Martin Cesar	6–1	Woolfe Nathan	13–2
McDonald Stuart	(1)–0	Opponents	0–1
Michalik Lubomir	2–0		

North/South Final

11 May, Majedski Stadium

Reading 2 Bolton Wanderers 0

Al-Habsi, Gbemie, Jamieson, Cassidy, Augustyn, Fojut, Basham (L. Thompson), Sisssons, Obadeyi, Wolze (Sheridan), Woolfe (Brooks). Subs not used: Ellis, Kazimierczak

Attendance 4,172

BOLTON WANDERERS RESERVES RECORD

The Central League

	PL	W	D	L	F	A	PTS	POS
1911–12	32	9	15	8	46	45	33	6th
1912–13	38	9	13	16	43	50	31	14th
1913–14	38	10	8	20	48	59	28	20th
1914–15	38	16	5	17	70	76	37	10th
1919–20	42	13	8	21	61	106	34	20th
1920–21	42	22	8	12	71	58	52	3rd
1921–22	42	16	12	14	64	57	44	7th

	PL	W	D	L	F	A	PTS	POS
1922–23	42	15	11	16	65	55	41	11th
1923–24	42	21	7	14	71	53	49	7th
1924–25	42	19	11	12	88	57	49	6th
1925–26	42	13	10	19	76	90	36	17th
1926–27	42	15	7	20	70	96	37	15th
1927–28	42	20	3	19	82	76	43	11th
1928–29	42	13	11	18	72	87	37	16th
1929–30	42	17	6	19	86	85	40	10th
1930–31	42	14	12	16	84	83	40	15th
1931–32	42	20	10	12	116	83	50	6th
1932–22	42	16	5	21	73	79	37	16th
1933–34	42	10	8	24	61	92	28	20th
1934–35	42	13	8	21	63	78	34	21st
1935–36	42	17	8	17	83	79	42	13th
1936–37	42	11	12	19	59	83	34	18th
1937–38	42	23	9	10	86	48	55	2nd
1938–39	42	18	10	14	65	64	46	8th
1945–46	40	16	4	20	60	79	36	11th
1946–47	42	16	15	11	85	73	47	7th
1947–48	42	17	6	19	77	83	40	11th
1948–49	42	21	5	16	69	56	47	7th
1949–50	42	18	8	16	67	45	44	9th
1950–51	42	17	9	16	55	59	43	12th
1951–52	42	15	9	18	54	68	39	14th
1952–53	42	16	11	15	60	47	43	9th
1953–54	42	19	9	14	53	35	47	6th
1954–55	42	26	7	9	70	28	59	1st
1955–56	42	14	11	17	44	51	39	15th
1956–57	42	16	9	17	71	74	41	13th
1957–58	42	12	9	21	63	80	33	20th
1958–59	42	16	8	18	78	76	40	13th
1959–60	42	9	11	22	53	97	29	19th
1960–61	42	23	6	13	79	61	52	6th
1961–62	42	16	8	18	74	80	40	13th
1962–63	42	24	6	12	95	61	54	5th
1963–64	42	8	11	23	40	64	27	20th
1964–65	42	10	13	19	51	62	33	16th
1965–66	42	16	7	19	60	76	39	14th
1966–67	42	15	5	22	55	69	35	16th
1967–68	42	11	6	25	41	74	28	20th
1968–69	42	15	6	21	54	74	36	16th
1969–70	42	12	9	21	52	78	33	17th
1970–71	42	16	12	14	73	71	44	9th
1971–72	42	12	14	16	49	57	38	17th
1972–73	42	7	11	24	44	89	25	20th
1973–74	42	12	13	17	62	68	37	16th
1974–75	42	11	15	16	49	61	37	16th

	PL	W	D	L	F	A	PTS	POS
975–76	42	10	9	23	40	72	29	19th
1976–77	42	9	10	23	44	75	28	20th
1977–78	42	14	10	18	57	64	38	15th
1978–79	42	11	13	18	61	83	35	17th
1979–80	42	8	10	24	45	75	26	21st
1980–81	42	9	9	24	40	85	27	20th
1981–82	42	6	9	27	54	109	21	22nd
DIVISION TWO								
1982–83	30	17	4	9	68	50	38	3rd
DIVISION ONE								
1983–84	30	8	3	19	35	68	27	15th
DIVISION TWO								
1984–85	34	15	3	16	62	65	48	8th
1985–86	34	16	5	13	56	48	53	9th
1986–87	32	6	12	14	47	65	30	16th
1987–88	34	14	8	12	55	58	50	7th
1988–89	34	18	8	8	77	52	62	5th
1989–90	34	10	11	13	47	55	41	12th
PONTINS								
DIVISION TWO								
1990–91	34	17	9	8	70	42	60	3rd
DIVISION ONE								
1991–92	34	10	11	13	52	56	41	12th
1992–93	34	15	8	11	48	49	53	5th
1993–94	34	15	10	9	88	65	55	3rd
1994–95	34	22	5	7	69	46	71	1st
1995–96	34	12	9	13	51	52	45	10th
PREMIER								
1996–97	24	7	5	12	31	38	26	12th
DIVISION ONE								
1997–98	24	8	7	9	36	34	31	8th
1998–99	24	8	4	12	25	35	28	10th
FA PREMIER NORTH								
1999–2000	24	6	4	14	22	59	22	11th
AVON INSURANCE PREMIER								
2000–01	24	7	4	13	25	44	25	13th
FA PREMIER NORTH								
2001–02	24	12	3	9	45	40	39	5th
2002–03	28	11	5	12	45	48	38	9th
2003–04	26	3	4	19	22	51	13	14th
2004–05	28	8	9	11	32	41	33	10th
2005–06	28	6	6	16	25	46	24	13th
2006–07	18	10	3	5	21	16	33	1st
2007–08	18	3	4	11	13	32	13	10th
2008–09	20	6	3	11	22	38	21	11th
2009–10	18	5	2	11	24	37	17	10th
2010–11	19	8	3	8	24	32	27	5th

THE INTERNATIONALISTS

FULL INTERNATIONALS

	Career Total Caps at Club	Date	Opponents	Venue	Competition	Result	Goals Scored
ENGLAND							
T. Banks	1	18 May 1958	Ussr	Moscow	FR	1–1	
	2	8 June 1958	Ussr (WC)	Gothenburg	WC	2–2	
	3	11 June 1958	Brazil (WC)	Gothenburg	WC	0–0	
	4	15 June 1958	Austria (WC)	Boras	WC	2–2	
	5	17 June 1958	Ussr (WC)	Gothenburg	WC	0–1	
	6 6	4 October 1958	N. Ireland	Belfast	HI	3–3	
W. Bannister	1 2	22 March 1902	Ireland	Belfast	HI	1–0	
M. Barrass	1	20 October 1951	Wales	Cardiff	HI	1–1	
	2	14 November 1951	N. Ireland	Villa Park	HI	2–0	
	3 3	18 April 1953	Scotland	Wembley	HI	2–2	
W. Butler	1 1	12 April 1924	Scotland	Wembley	HI	1–1	
G. Cahill	1	3 September 2010	Bulgaria (Sub)	Wembley	ECQ	4–0	
	2	9 February 2011	Denmark (Sub)	Copenhagen	FR	2–1	
	3 3	29 March 2011	Ghana	Wembley	FR	1–1	
J.K. Davenport	1	14 March 1885	Wales	Blackburn	HI	1–1	
	2 2	15 March 1890	Ireland	Belfast	HI	9–1	2
K. Davies	1 1	12 October 2010	Montenegro (Sub)	Wembley	ECQ	0–0	
G.R. Eastham	1 1	18 May 1935	Holland	Amsterdam	FR	1–0	
H.W. Hassall	1 5	11 November 1953	N. Ireland	Goodison Park	WCQ	3–1	2
F. Hill	1	20 October 1962	N. Ireland	Belfast	HI	3–1	
	2 2	21 November 1962	Wales	Wembley	HI	4–0	
A.D. Holden	1	11 April 1959	Scotland	Wembley	HI	1–0	
	2	6 May 1959	Italy	Wembley	FR	2–2	
	3	13 May 1959	Brazil	Rio De Janeiro	FR	0–2	
	4	17 May 1959	Peru	Lima	FR	1–4	
	5 5	24 May 1959	Mexico	Mexico City	FR	1–2	
E. Hopkinson	1	19 October 1957	Wales	Cardiff	HI	4–0	
	2	6 November 1957	N. Ireland	Wembley	HI	2–3	
	3	27 November 1957	France	Wembley	FR	4–0	
	4	19 April 1958	Scotland	Glasgow	HI	4–0	
	5	7 May 1958	Portugal	Wembley	FR	2–1	

	Caps at Club	Career Total Date	Opponents	Venue	Competition	Result	Goals Scored
	6	11 May 1958	Yugoslavia	Belgrade	FR	0–5	
	7	11 April 1959	Scotland	Wembley	HI	1–0	
	8	6 May 1959	Italy	Wembley	FR	2–2	
	9	13 May 1959	Brazil	Rio De Janeiro	FR	0–2	
	10	17 May 1959	Peru	Lima	FR	1–4	
	11	24 May 1959	Mexico	Mexico City	FR	1–2	
	12	28 May 1959	Usa	Los Angeles	FR	8–1	
	13	17 October 1959	Wales	Cardiff	HI	1–1	
	14	14	28 October 1959	Sweden	Wembley	FR	2–3	
D. Jack	1	3 March 1924	Wales	Blackburn	HI	1–2	
	2	12 April 1924	Scotland	Wembley	HI	1–1	
	3	17 May 1928	France	Paris	FR	5–1	1
	4	4	19 May 1928	Belgium	Antwerp	FR	3–1	
F.W. Kean	1	9 May 1929	France	Paris	FR	4–1	
	2	9	15 May 1929	Spain	Madrid	FR	3–4	
R. Langton	1	15 April 1950	Scotland	Glasgow	HI	1–0	
	2	11	7 October 1950	N. Ireland	Belfast	HI	4–1	
N. Lofthouse	1	22 November 1950	Yugoslavia	Highbury	FR	2–2	2
	2	20 October 1951	Wales	Cardiff	HI	1–1	
	3	14 November 1951	N. Ireland	Villa Park	HI	2–0	2
	4	29 November 1951	Austria	Wembley	FR	2–2	1
	5	5 April 1952	Scotland	Glasgow	HI	2–1	
	6	18 May 1952	Italy	Florence	FR	1–1	
	7	25 May 1952	Austria	Vienna	FR	3–2	2
	8	28 May 1952	Switzerland	Zurich	FR	3–0	2
	9	4 October 1952	N. Ireland	Belfast	HI	2–2	1
	10	12 November 1952	Wales	Wembley	HI	5–2	2
	11	26 November 1952	Belgium	Wembley	FR	5–0	2
	12	18 April 1953	Scotland	Wembley	HI	2–2	
	13	17 May 1953	Argentina	Buenos Aires	FR	0–0	
	14	24 May 1953	Chile	Santiago	FR	2–1	1
	15	31 May 1953	Uruguay	Montevideo	FR	1–2	
	16	8 June 1953	Usa	New York	FR	6–3	2
	17	10 October 1953	Wales	Cardiff	WCQ	4–1	2
	18	21 October 1953	Rest Of Europe	Wembley	FR	4–4	
	19	11 November 1953	N. Ireland	Goodison Park	HI	3–1	1
	20	17 June 1954	Belgium (WC)	Basle	WC	4–4	2
	21	26 June 1954	Uruguay (WC)	Basle	WC	2–4	1
	22	2 October 1954	N. Ireland	Belfast	HI	2–0	
	23	2 April 1955	Scotland	Wembley	HI	7–2	2
	24	18 May 1955	France	Paris	FR	0–1	
	25	20 May 1955	Spain	Madrid	FR	1–1	
	26	22 May 1955	Portugal	Porto	FR	1–3	
	27	2 October 1955	Denmark	Copenhagen	FR	5–1	2
	28	22 October 1955	Wales	Cardiff	HI	1–1	
	29	30 November 1955	Spain	Wembley	FR	4–1	
	30	14 April 1956	Scotland	Glasgow	HI	1–1	
	31	20 May 1956	Finland (Sub)	Helsinki	FR	5–1	2
	32	22 October 1958	Ussr	Wembley	FR	5–0	1
	33	33	26 November 1958	Wales	Villa Park	HI	2–2	

	Career Total						Goals
	Caps at Club	Date	Opponents	Venue	Competition	Result	Scored
H. Nuttall	1	22 October 1927	Ireland	Belfast	HI	0–2	
	2	28 November 1927	Wales	Turf Moor	HI	1–2	
	3	3	13 April 1929	Scotland	Glasgow	HI	0–1	
R.A. Parry	1	18 November 1959	N. Ireland	Wembley	HI	2–1	1
	2	2	19 April 1960	Scotland	Glasgow	HI	1–1	
R.H. Pym	1	28 February 1925	Wales	Swansea	HI	2–1	
	2	4 April 1925	Scotland	Glasgow	HI	0–2	
	3	3	1 March 1926	Wales	Selhurst Park	HI	1–3	
M. Ricketts	1	1	13 February 2002	Holland	Amsterdam	FR	1–1	
J. Seddon	1	10 May 1923	France	Paris	FR	4–1	
	2	21 May 1923	Sweden	Stockholm	FR	4–2	
	3	24 May 1923	Sweden	Stockholm	FR	3–1	
	4	1 November 1923	Belgium	Antwerp	FR	2–2	
	5	12 February 1927	Wales	Wrexham	HI	3–3	
	6	6	13 April 1929	Scotland	Glasgow	HI	0–1	
A. Shepherd	1	1	7 April 1906	Scotland	Glasgow	HI	1–2	1
J. Smith	1	15 February 1913	Ireland	Belfast	HI	1–2	
	2	16 March 1914	Wales	Cardiff	HI	2–0	1
	3	4 April 1914	Scotland	Glasgow	HI	1–3	
	4	25 October 1919	Ireland	Belfast	HI	1–1	
	5	5	15 March 1920	Wales	Arsenal	HI	1–2	
J.W. Sutcliffe	1	13 March 1893	Wales	Stoke	HI	6–0	
	2	9 March 1895	Ireland	Derby	HI	9–0	
	3	6 April 1895	Scotland	Goodison Park	HI	3–0	
	4	4	30 March 1901	Scotland	Selhurst Park	HI	2–2	
J.A. Turner	1	1	13 March 1893	Wales	Stoke	HI	6–0	
D. Weir	1	2 March 1889	Ireland	Goodison Park	HI	6–1	1
	2	2	13 April 1889	Scotland	Kennington	HI	2–3	1
R. Westwood	1	29 September 1934	Wales	Cardiff	HI	4–0	
	2	6 April 1935	Scotland	Glasgow	HI	0–2	
	3	18 May 1935	Holland	Amsterdam	FR	1–0	
	4	19 October 1935	Ireland	Belfast	HI	3–1	
	5	4 December 1935	Germany	White Hart Lane	FR	3–0	
	6	6	17 October 1935	Wales	Cardiff	HI	1–2	
J.E. Wheeler	1	1	2 October 1954	N. Ireland	Belfast	HI	2–0	
SCOTLAND							
W.L. Cook	1	14 April 1934	England	Wembley	HI	0–3	
	2	20 October 1934	Ireland	Belfast	HI	1–2	
	3	3	21 November 1934	Wales	Aberdeen	HI	3–2	

| | Career Total | | | | | | | Goals |
---	Caps	at Club	Date	Opponents	Venue	Competition	Result	Scored
A. Donaldson	1		28 February 1914	Wales	Glasgow	HI	0–0	
	2		14 March 1914	Ireland	Belfast	HI	1–1	
	3		4 April 1914	England	Glasgow	HI	3–1	
	4		13 March 1920	Ireland	Glasgow	HI	3–0	
	5		10 April 1920	England	Sheffield	HI	4–5	1
	6	6	4 March 1922	Ireland	Glasgow	HI	2–1	
C. Hendry	1		24 March 1901	Belgium	Glasgow	WCQ	2–2	
	2	51	28 March 1901	San Marino	Glasgow	WCQ	4–0	2
A. Johnston	1		29 March 2000	France (Sub)	Glasgow	FR	0–2	
	2	9	30 May 2000	Ireland (Sub)	Dublin	FR	2–1	
J. McGinlay	1		20 April 1994	Austria	Vienna	FR	2–1	1
	2		27 May 1994	Holland	Utrecht	FR	0–3	
	3		12 October 1994	Faroe Islands	Glasgow	ECQ	5–1	1
	4		16 November 1994	Russia	Glasgow	ECQ	1–1	
	5		18 December 1994	Greece	Athens	ECQ	0–1	
	6		29 March 1995	Russia	Moscow	ECQ	0–0	
	7		26 April 1995	San Marino	Serravalle	ECQ	2–0	
	8		7 June 1995	Faroe Islands	Toftir	ECQ	2–0	1
	9		11 October 1995	Sweden	Stockholm	ECQ	0–2	
	10		9 October 1996	Estonia (Abandoned)	Tallinn	WCQ		
	11		10 November 1996	Sweden	Ibrox	WCQ	1–0	1
	12		11 February 1997	Estonia	Monaco	WCQ	0–0	
	13		29 March 1997	Estonia (Sub)	Kilmarnock	WCQ	2–0	
	14	14	2 April 1997	Austria (Sub)	Celtic Park	WCQ	2–0	
P. Ritchie	1		29 March 2000	France	Glasgow	FR	0–2	
	2	6	26 April 2000	Holland	Arnhem	FR	0–0	
W. Moir	1	1	15 April 1950	England	Hampden Park	WCQ	0–1	1
W. White	1		6 April 1907	England	Newcastle	HI	1–1	
	2	2	4 April 1908	England	Glasgow	HI	1–1	

WALES

	Caps	at Club	Date	Opponents	Venue	Competition	Result	Goals Scored
N. Blake	1		24 January 1996	Italy (Sub)	Terni	FR	0–3	
	2		20 August 1997	Turkey	Istanbul	WCQ	4–6	1
	3		5 September 1998	Italy	Liverpool	ECQ	0–2	
	4		10 October 1998	Denmark	Copenhagen	ECQ	2–1	
	5	10	14 October 1998	Belarus	Cardiff	ECQ	3–2	
D. Davies	1		12 March 1904	Scotland	Dundee	HI	1–1	
	2		21 March 1904	Ireland	Bangor	HI	0–1	
	3	3	16 March 1908	England (Sub)	Wrexham	HI	1–7	
R.W. Davies	1		12 October 1963	England	Cardiff	HI	0–4	
	2		3 October 1964	Scotland	Cardiff	HI	3–2	1
	3		21 October 1964	Denmark	Copenhagen	WCQ	0–1	
	4		18 November 1964	England	Wembley	HI	1–2	
	5		9 December 1964	Greece	Athens	WCQ	0–2	
	6		31 March 1965	N. Ireland	Belfast	FR	5–0	

	Career Total						Goals
	Caps at Club	Date	Opponents	Venue	Competition	Result	Scored
	7	30 May 1965	Ussr	Moscow	WCQ	1–2	1
	8	2 October 1965	England	Cardiff	HI	0–0	
	9	27 October 1965	Ussr	Cardiff	WCQ	2–1	
	10	24 November 1965	Scotland	Hampden Park	HI	1–4	
	11	1 December 1965	Denmark	Wrexham	WCQ	4–2	1
	12	30 March 1966	N. Ireland	Cardiff	HI	1–4	1
	13	14 May 1966	Brazil	Rio De Janeiro	FR	1–3	
	14	18 May 1966	Brazil	Rio De Janeiro	FR	0–1	
	15	22 May 1966	Chile (Sub)	Santiago	FR	0–2	
	16 16	22 October 1966	Scotland	Cardiff	HI	1–1	
T.P. Griffiths	1	26 October 1932	Scotland	Edinburgh	HI	5–2	1
	2	16 November 1932	England	Wrexham	HI	0–0	
	3 11	7 December 1932	Ireland	Wrexham	HI	4–1	
W. Jennings	1	28 February 1914	Scotland	Glasgow	HI	0–0	
	2	16 March 1914	England	Cardiff	HI	0–2	
	3	26 February 1920	Scotland	Cardiff	HI	1–1	
	4	5 March 1923	England	Cardiff	HI	2–2	
	5	14 April 1923	Ireland	Wrexham	HI	0–3	
	6	16 February 1924	Scotland	Cardiff	HI	2–0	
	7	3 March 1924	England	Blackburn	HI	2–1	
	8	15 March 1924	Ireland	Belfast	HI	1–0	
	9	30 October 1926	Scotland	Glasgow	HI	0–3	
	10	9 April 1927	Ireland	Cardiff	HI	2–2	
	11 11	27 October 1928	Scotland	Glasgow	HI	2–4	
D. Jones	1	23 February 1989	England	Stoke	HI	1–4	
	2	15 April 1989	Scotland	Wrexham	HI	0–0	
	3	27 April 1989	Ireland	Belfast	HI	3–1	
	4	8 February 1990	Ireland	Shrewsbury	HI	5–2	
	5	15 March 1990	England	Wrexham	HI	1–3	
	6	21 March 1991	Scotland	Wrexham	HI	3–4	
	7	27 February 1992	Ireland	Bangor	HI	1–1	
	8	13 March 1993	England	Stoke	HI	0–6	
	9	12 March 1994	England	Wrexham	HI	1–5	
	10	18 March 1995	England	London	HI	1–1	
	11 13	19 March 1998	Scotland	Motherwell	HI	2–5	
E. Jones	1 7	19 January 1911	Ireland	Wrexham	HI	1–2	1
J. Powell	1 10	17 March 1984	England	Wrexham	HI	0–4	
S. Ricketts	1 35	12 August 2009	Montenegro	Podgorica	FR	1–2	
	2 36	9 September 2009	Russia	Cardiff	WCQ	1–3	
	3 37	14 November 2009	Scotland	Cardiff	FR	3–0	
	4 38	23 May 2010	Croatia	Osijek	FR	0–2	
	5 39	11 August 2010	Luxembourg	Llanelli	FR	5–1	
	6 40	3 September 2010	Montenegro	Podgorica	ECQ	0–1	
	7 41	8 October 2010	Bulgaria	Cardiff	ECQ	0–1	
	8 42	8 February 2011	Ireland	Dublin	Nc	0–3	
J.H. Roberts	1 1	23 May 1949	Belgium	Liege	FR	1–3	

	Career Total						Goals
	Caps at Club	Date	Opponents	Venue	Competition	Result	Scored
R. Roberts	1	21 March 1987	Scotland	Wrexham	HI	0–2	
	2	4 February 1988	England	Crewe	HI	1–5	
	3	10 March 1988	Scotland	Edinburgh	HI	1–5	
	4	23 February 1989	England	Stoke	HI	1–4	
	5	15 April 1989	England	Wrexham	HI	0–0	
	6	22 March 1990	Scotland	Glasgow	HI	0–5	
	7 8	27 February 1992	Ireland	Bangor	HI	1–1	
G. Speed	1	18 August 2004	Latvia	Riga	FR	2–0	
	2	4 September 2004	Azerbaijan	Baku	WCQ	1–1	1
	3	8 September 2004	N. Ireland	Cardiff	WCQ	2–2	
	4	9 October 2004	England	Old Trafford	WCQ	0–2	
	5 85	13 October 2004	Poland	Cardiff	WCQ	2–3	
J. Trainer	1 1	21 March 1987	Scotland	Wrexham	HI	0–2	
J. Vaughan	1 11	17 March 1984	England	Wrexham	HI	0–4	
E.T. Vizard	1	28 January 1911	Ireland	Belfast	HI	2–1	
	2	6 March 1911	Scotland	Cardiff	HI	2–2	
	3	13 March 1911	England	London	HI	0–3	
	4	2 March 1912	Scotland	Edinburgh	HI	0–1	
	5	11 March 1912	England	Wrexham	HI	0–2	
	6	3 March 1913	Scotland	Wrexham	HI	0–0	
	7	19 January 1914	Ireland	Wrexham	HI	1–2	
	8	16 March 1914	England	Cardiff	HI	0–2	
	9	15 March 1920	England	London	HI	2–1	
	10	12 February 1921	Scotland	Aberdeen	HI	1–2	
	11	16 March 1921	England	Cardiff	HI	0–0	
	12	9 April 1921	Ireland	Swansea	HI	2–1	
	13	4 February 1922	Scotland	Wrexham	HI	2–1	
	14	13 March 1922	England	Liverpool	HI	0–1	
	15	5 March 1923	England	Cardiff	HI	2–2	
	16	14 April 1923	Ireland	Wrexham	HI	0–3	
	17	16 February 1924	Scotland	Cardiff	HI	2–0	
	18	3 March 1924	England	Blackburn	HI	2–1	1
	19	15 March 1924	Ireland	Belfast	HI	1–0	
	20	31 October 1925	Scotland	Cardiff	HI	0–3	
	21	1 March 1926	England	London	HI	3–1	
	22 22	30 October 1926	Scotland	Glasgow	HI	0–3	
Northern Ireland							
A. Davison	1 1	24 April 1996	Sweden	Belfast	FR	1–2	
W. Hughes	1 1	7 March 1951	Wales	Belfast	HI	1–2	
W. McAdams	1	8 October 1960	England	Belfast	HI	2–5	2
	2	26 October 1960	West Germany	Belfast	WCQ	3–4	3
	3	9 November 1960	Scotland	Hampden Park	HI	2–5	
	4	12 April 1961	Wales	Belfast	HI	1–5	
	5	25 April 1961	Italy	Bologna	FR	2–3	1
	6	3 May 1961	Greece	Athens	WCQ	1–2	

	Caps	Career Total at Club	Date	Opponents	Venue	Competition	Result	Goals Scored
	7		10 May 1961	West Germany	Berlin	WCQ	1–2	
	8		17 October 1961	Greece	Belfast	WCQ	2–0	
	9	14	22 November 1961	England	Wembley	HI	1–1	
G. McElhinney	1		16 November 1983	West Germany	Hamburg	ECQ	1–0	
	2		13 December 1983	Scotland	Belfast	HI	2–0	
	3		4 April 1984	England	Wembley	HI	0–1	
	4		22 May 1984	Wales	Swansea	HI	1–1	
	5		27 May 1984	Finland	Pori	WCQ	0–1	
	6	6	12 September 1984	Romania	Belfast	WCQ	3–2	
R.J. Napier	1	1	7 May 1966	West Germany	Belfast	FR	0–2	
G. Taggart	1		9 November 1996	Germany	Nuremburg	WCQ	1–1	1
	2		14 December 1996	Albania	Belfast	WCQ	2–0	
	3		22 January 1997	Italy	Palermo	FR	0–2	
	4		11 February 1997	Belgium	Belfast	FR	3–0	
	5		29 March 1997	Portugal	Belfast	WCQ	0–0	
	6		2 April 1997	Ukraine	Kiev	WCQ	1–2	
	7		30 April 1997	Armenia	Erevan	WCQ	0–0	
	8		20 August 1997	Germany	Belfast	WCQ	1–3	
	9		11 October 1997	Portugal	Lisbon	WCQ	0–1	
	10	46	2 June 1998	Spain	Santander	FR	1–4	1

IRELAND

	Caps	Career Total at Club	Date	Opponents	Venue	Competition	Result	Goals Scored
K. Branagan	1	1	11 February 1997	Wales	Cardiff	FR	0–0	
O. Coyle	1	1	20 April 1994	Holland (Sub)	Tilburg	FR	1–0	
A.P. Dunne	1		5 May 1974	Brazil (Sub)	Rio De Janeiro	FR	1–2	
	2		8 May 1974	Uruguay	Montevideo	FR	0–2	
	3		12 May 1974	Chile	Santiago	FR	2–1	
	4		20 November 1974	Turkey	Izmir	ECQ	1–1	
	5		1 March 1975	West Germany B	Dublin	FR	1–0	
	6		11 May 1975	Switzerland	Dublin	ECQ	2–1	
	7		18 May 1975	Ussr	Kiev	ECQ	1–2	
	8		21 May 1975	Switzerland	Berne	ECQ	0–1	
	9	33	29 October 1975	Turkey	Dublin	ECQ	4–0	
G. Farrelly	1	6	6 June 2000	USA	Boston	Nike Cup	1–1	
C. Hurley	1	40	8 June 1969	Hungary	Dublin	WCQ	1–2	
A. Kernaghan	1	12	12 October 1994	Liechtenstein	Dublin	WCQ	4–0	
J. McAteer	1		23 March 1994	Russia	Dublin	FR	0–0	
	2		20 April 1994	Holland (Sub)	Tilburg	FR	1–0	
	3		24 May 1994	Bolivia (Sub)	Dublin	FR	1–0	
	4		5 June 1994	Czech Republic (Sub)	Dublin	FR	1–3	
	5		29 May 1994	Germany	Hannover	FR	2–0	
	6		18 June 1994	Italy (Sub)	New York	WC	1–0	
	7		24 June 1994	Mexico (Sub)	Orlando	WC	1–2	
	8		28 June 1994	Norway	New York	WC	0–0	

	Career Total						Goals
	Caps at Club	Date	Opponents	Venue	Competition	Result	Scored
	9	4 July 1994	Holland (Sub)	Orlando	WC	0–2	
	10	7 September 1994	Latvia	Riga	ECQ	3–0	
	11	12 October 1994	Liechtenstein	Dublin	ECQ	4–0	
	12	16 November 1994	N. Ireland	Belfast	ECQ	4–0	
	13	29 March 1995	N. Ireland (Sub)	Dublin	ECQ	1–1	
	14	14	3 June 1995	Liechtenstein	Vaduz	ECQ	0–0	

J. McDonagh

	Caps at Club	Date	Opponents	Venue	Competition	Result	Scored
	1		9 September 1981	Holland	Rotterdam	WCQ	2–2	
	2		14 October 1981	France	Dublin	WCQ	3–2	
	3		22 May 1982	Chile	Santiago	FR	0–1	
	4		27 May 1982	Brazil	Uderlandia	FR	0–7	
	5		22 September 1982	Holland	Rotterdam	ECQ	1–2	
	6		13 October 1982	Iceland	Dublin	ECQ	2–0	
	7		17 November 1982	Spain	Dublin	ECQ	3–3	
	8		30 March 1983	Malta	Valletta	ECQ	1–0	
	9	13	27 April 1983	Spain	Zaragoza	ECQ	0–2	

J. O'Brien

	Caps at Club	Date	Opponents	Venue	Competition	Result	Scored
	1		1 March 2006	Sweden	Dublin	FR	3–0	
	2		13 October 2007	Germany	Dublin	FR	0–0	
	3	3	17 October 2007	Cyprus	Dublin	ECQ	1–1	

BULGARIA
M. Petrov

	Caps at Club	Date	Opponents	Venue	Competition	Result	Scored
	1		11 August 2010	Russia	St Petersburg	FR	0–1	
	2		3 September 2010	England	Wembley	ECQ	0–4	
	3		7 September 2010	Montenegro	Sofia	ECQ	0–1	
	4		8 October 2010	Wales	Cardiff	ECQ	1–0	
	5		17 November 2010	Serbia	Sofia	FR	0–1	
	6		29 March 2011	Cyprus	Larnaca	FR	1–0	1
	7	84	4 June 2011	Montenegro	Podgorica	ECQ	1–1	

CROATIA
I. Klasnic

	Caps at Club	Date	Opponents	Venue	Competition	Result	Scored
	1		9 September 2009	England (Sub)	Wembley	WCQ	1–5	
	2		8 October 2009	Qatar	Rijeka	FR	3–2	1
	3		14 October 2009	Kazakhstan	Astana	WCQ	2–1	
	4	38	14 November 2009	Liechtenstein (Sub)	Vinkovci	FR	5–0	
	5	39	3 June 2011	Georgia (Sub)	Split	ECQ	2–1	

DENMARK
P. Frandsen

	Caps at Club	Date	Opponents	Venue	Competition	Result	Scored
	1		9 November 1996	France	Copenhagen	FR	1–0	
	2		29 March 1997	Croatia	Zagreb	WCQ	1–1	
	3		30 April 1997	Slovakia (Sub)	Copenhagen	WCQ	4–0	
	4		8 June 1997	Bosnia (Sub)	Copenhagen	WCQ	2–0	
	5		10 September 1997	Croatia	Copenhagen	WCQ	3–1	
	6		25 March 1998	Scotland (Sub)	Glasgow	FR	1–0	
	7		22 April 1998	Norway	Copenhagen	FR	0–2	
	8		28 May 1998	Sweden	Malmo	FR	0–3	
	9		5 June 1998	Cameroon (Sub)	Copenhagen	FR	1–2	
	10		12 June 1998	Saudi Arabia (Sub)	Lens	WC	1–0	
	11		28 June 1998	Nigeria (Sub)	Paris	WC	4–1	
	12		19 August 1998	Czech Republic (Sub)	Prague	FR	0–1	
	13		10 October 1998	Wales	Copenhagen	ECQ	1–2	
	14		14 October 1998	Switzerland	Zurich	ECQ	1–1	
	15		10 June 1999	Wales (Sub)	Liverpool	ECQ	2–0	

	Career Total						Goals
	Caps	at Club	Date	Opponents	Venue	Competition	Result	Scored
	16		16 August 2000	Faroe Islands (Sub)	Torshavn	FR	2–0	
	17		1 September 2001	N. Ireland (Sub)	Copenhagen	WCQ	1–1	
	18		17 April 2002	Israel (Sub)	Copenhagen	FR	3–1	
	19	23	2 April 2003	Bosnia	Copenhagen	ECQ	0–2	
H. Pedersen	1		4 September 2004	Ukraine (Sub)	Copenhagen	WCQ	1–1	
	2	3	9 October 2004	Albania	Tirana	WCQ	2–0	
S. Tofting	1		13 February 2002	Saudi Arabia	Riyadh	FR	1–0	
	2		17 May 2002	Cameroon	Copenhagen	FR	2–1	
	3		26 May 2002	Tunisia	Wakayama	FR	2–1	
	4		1 June 2002	Uruguay	Ulsan	WC	2–1	
	5		6 June 2002	Senegal	Daegu	WC	1–1	
	6		11 June 2002	France	Incheon	WC	2–0	
	7	41	15 June 2002	England	Niigata	WC	0–3	
C. Jensen	1	1	29 March 2000	Portugal (Sub)	Lisbon	FR	1–2	

DR CONGO

K. Lord Ndiwa	1		25 January 2004	Guinea (Sub)	Rades	ANC	1–2	
	2	2	6 June 2004	Uganda	Kampala	FR	0–1	

FINLAND

J. Jääskeläinen	1		25 March 1998	Malta	Valetta	FR	2–0	
	2		19 August 1998	Slovakia (Sub)	Kosice	FR	0–0	
	3		10 February 1999	Poland (Sub)	Valetta	FR	1–1	
	4		28 April 1999	Slovenia (Sub)	Ljubljana	FR	1–1	
	5		16 August 2000	Norway	Helsinki	FR	3–1	
	6		2 September 2000	Albania	Helsinki	WCQ	2–1	
	7		15 November 2000	Ireland	Dublin	FR	0–3	
	8		20 March 2002	South Korea	Cartagena	FR	0–2	
	9		22 May 2002	Latvia (Sub)	Helsinki	FR	2–1	
	10		21 August 2002	Ireland	Helsinki	FR	0–3	
	11		12 February 2003	N. Ireland	Belfast	FR	1–0	
	12		30 April 2003	Iceland	Helsinki	FR	3–0	
	13		7 June 2003	Serbia, Montenegro	Helsinki	ECQ	3–0	
	14		11 June 2003	Italy	Helsinki	ECQ	0–1	
	15		20 August 2003	Denmark	Copenhagen	FR	1–1	
	16		11 October 2003	Canada	Tampere	FR	3–2	
	17		31 March 2004	Malta (Sub)	Valetta	FR	2–1	
	18		17 November 2004	Italy	Messina	FR	0–1	
	19		9 February 2005	Latvia	Nicosia	FR	2–1	
	20		26 March 2005	Czech Republic	Teplice	WCQ	3–4	
	21		2 June 2005	Denmark	Tampere	FR	0–1	
	22		8 June 2005	Holland	Helsinki	WCQ	0–4	
	23		17 August 2005	Macedonia	Skopje	WCQ	3–0	
	24		8 October 2005	Romania	Helsinki	WCQ	0–1	
	25		12 October 2005	Czech Republic	Helsinki	WCQ	0–3	
	26		1 March 2006	Belarus	Paphos	FR	2–2	
	27		25 May 2006	Sweden	Gothenburg	FR	0–0	
	28		16 August 2006	N. Ireland	Helsinki	FR	1–2	
	29		2 September 2006	Poland	Bydgoszcz	ECQ	3–1	
	30		6 September 2006	Portugal	Helsinki	ECQ	1–1	
	31		7 October 2006	Armenia	Yerevan	ECQ	0–0	
	32		11 October 2006	Kazakhstan	Almathy	ECQ	2–0	
	33		15 November 2006	Armenia	Helsinki	ECQ	1–0	
	34		28 March 2007	Azerbaijan	Baku	ECQ	0–1	
	35		2 June 2007	Serbia	Helsinki	ECQ	0–2	
	36		6 June 2007	Belgium	Helsinki	ECQ	2–0	

	Career Total Caps at Club	Date	Opponents	Venue	Competition	Result	Goals Scored
	37	22 August 2007	Kazakhstan	Tampere	ECQ	2–1	
	38	8 September 2007	Serbia	Belgrade	ECQ	0–0	
	39	12 September 2007	Poland	Helsinki	ECQ	0–0	
	40	13 October 2007	Belgium	Brussels	ECQ	0–0	
	41	17 November 2007	Azerbaijan	Helsinki	ECQ	2–1	
	42	21 November 2007	Portugal	Porto	ECQ	0–0	
	43	20 August 2008	Israel	Tampere	FR	2–0	
	44	10 September 2008	Germany	Helsinki	WCQ	3–3	
	45	11 October 2008	Azerbaijan	Helsinki	WCQ	1–0	
	46	15 October 2008	Russia	Moscow	WCQ	0–3	
	47	19 November 2008	Switzerland	St Gallen	FR	0–1	
	48	11 February 2009	Portugal	Algarve	FR	0–1	
	49	28 March 2009	Wales	Cardiff	WCQ	2–0	
	50	6 June 2009	Liechtenstein	Helsinki	WCQ	2–1	
	51	10 June 2009	Russia	Helsinki	WCQ	0–3	
	52	5 September 2009	Azerbaijan	Kankaran	WCQ	2–1	
	53	9 September 2009	Liechtenstein	Vaduz	WCQ	1–1	
	54	10 October 2009	Wales	Helsinki	WCQ	2–1	
	55	14 Octpober 2009	Germany	Hamburg	WCQ	1–1	
	56 56	12 October 2010	Hungary	Helsinki	ECQ	1–2	
M. Paatelainen	1	17 August 1994	Denmark	Copenhagen	FR	1–2	
	2	7 September 1994	Scotland	Helsinki	ECQ	0–2	
	3	12 October 1994	Greece	Salonika	ECQ	0–4	
	4	16 November 1994	Faroes	Helsinki	ECQ	5–0	2
	5	14 December 1994	San Marino	Helsinki	ECQ	4–1	4
	6	26 April 1995	Faroes	Toftir	ECQ	4–0	1
	7	1 June 1995	Denmark (Sub)	Helsinki	FR	0–1	
	8	11 June 1995	Greece	Helsinki	ECQ	2–1	
	9	16 August 1995	Russia	Helsinki	ECQ	0–6	
	10 50	2 April 1997	Azerbaijan	Baku	WCQ	2–1	1
J. Viander	1	4 January 2002	Bahrain	Manama	FR	2–0	
	2 13	10 January 2002	Macedonia	Manama	FR	3–0	

FRANCE

	Career Total Caps at Club	Date	Opponents	Venue	Competition	Result	Goals Scored
N. Anelka	1	11 October 2006	Faroe Islands	Sochaux	ECQ	5–0	1
	2	15 November 2006	Greece (Sub)	St Denis	FR	1–0	
	3	7 February 2007	Argentina	St Denis	FR	1–0	
	4	24 March 2007	Lithuania	Kaunas	ECQ	1–0	1
	5	28 March 2007	Austria	St Denis	FR	1–0	
	6	2 June 2007	Ukraine	St Denis	ECQ	2–0	1
	7	6 June 2007	Georgia	Auxerre	ECQ	1–0	
	8	22 August 2007	Slovakia	Trnava	FR	1–0	
	9	8 September 2007	Italy	Milan	ECQ	0–0	
	10	12 September 2007	Scotland	Paris	ECQ	0–1	
	11	13 October 2007	Faroe Islands	Torshavn	ECQ	6–0	1
	12 43	16 November 2007	Morocco (Sub)	St Denis	FR	2–2	

	Career Total Caps at Club	Date	Opponents	Venue	Competition	Result	Goals Scored
Y. Djorkaeff	1	27 March 2002	Scotland (Sub)	Paris	FR	5–0	
	2	17 April 2002	Russia	Paris	FR	0–0	
	3	18 May 2002	Belgium	Paris	FR	1–2	
	4	26 May 2002	South Korea	Suwon	FR	3–2	
	5	31 May 2002	Senegal	Seoul	WC	0–1	
	6 82	11 June 2002	Denmark (Sub)	Incheon	WC	0–2	

GREECE

	Career Total Caps at Club	Date	Opponents	Venue	Competition	Result	Goals Scored
S. Giannakopoulos	1	20 August 2003	Sweden	Norkoping	FR	2–1	1
	2	6 September 2003	Armenia	Yerevan	ECQ	1–0	
	3	11 October 2003	N. Ireland	Athens	ECQ	1–0	
	4	15 November 2003	Portugal	Aviero	FR	1–1	
	5	31 March 2004	Switzerland	Iraklion	FR	1–0	
	6	28 April 2004	Holland	Eindhoven	FR	0–4	
	7	29 May 2004	Poland	Szczecin	FR	0–1	
	8	3 June 2004	Liechtenstein	Vaduz	FR	2–0	
	9	12 June 2004	Portugal	Porto	EC	2–1	
	10	16 June 2004	Spain	Porto	EC	1–1	
	11	1 July 2004	Czech Republic (Sub)	Porto	EC	1–0	
	12	4 July 2004	Portugal	Lisbon	Ecf	1–0	
	13	18 August 2004	Czech Republic	Prague	FR	0–0	
	14	4 September 2004	Albania (Sub)	Tirana	WCQ	1–2	1
	15	8 September 2004	Turkey	Piraeus	WCQ	0–0	
	16	9 October 2004	Ukraine	Kiev	WCQ	1–1	
	17	9 February 2005	Denmark	Athens	WCQ	2–1	
	18	26 March 2005	Georgia	Tbilisi	WCQ	3–1	1
	19	30 March 2005	Albania	Piraeus	WCQ	2–0	
	20	4 June 2005	Turkey	Istanbul	WCQ	0–0	
	21	8 June 2005	Ukraine	Piraeus	WCQ	0–1	
	22	16 June 2005	Brazil	Leipzig	CC1	0–3	
	23	19 June 2005	Japan	Frankfurt	CC1	0–1	
	24	22 June 2005	Mexico	Frankfurt	CC1	0–0	
	25	17 August 2005	Belgium	Brussels	FR	0–2	
	26	7 September 2005	Kazhakstan	Almaata	WCQ	2–1	1
	27	8 October 2005	Denmark	Copenhagen	WCQ	0–1	
	28	16 November 2005	Hungary	Piraeus	FR	1–2	1
	29	28 February 2006	Belarus	Tsiron	FR	1–0	
	30	1 March 2006	Kazhakstan	Nicosia	FR	2–0	1
	31	25 May 2006	Australia	Sydney	FR	0–1	
	32	16 August 2006	England	Old Trafford	FR	0–4	
	33	7 October 2006	Norway	Athens	ECQ	1–0	
	34	11 October 2006	Bosnia Herzogov'	Zenica	ECQ	4–0	
	35	15 November 2006	France	Paris	FR	0–1	
	36	6 February 2007	South Korea (Sub)	Fulham	FR	0–1	
	37	24 March 2007	Turkey	Piraeus	ECQ	1–4	
	38	2 June 2007	Hungary (Sub)	Heraklion	ECQ	2–0	
	39	6 June 2007	Moldova (Sub)	Heraklion	ECQ	2–1	
	40	13 October 2007	Bosnia–Herz (Sub)	Athens	ECQ	3–2	
	41	17 November 2007	Malta	Athens	ECQ	5–0	
	42	5 February 2008	Czech Republic B	Nicosia	FR	1–0	
	43	26 March 2008	Portugal	Dusseldorf	FR	2–1	
	44	19 May 2008	Cyprus	Patras	FR	2–0	
	45	24 May 2008	Hungary (Sub)	Budapest	FR	3–2	
	46	14 June 2008	Russia (Sub)	Salzburg	EC	0–1	
	47 77	18 June 2008	Spain (Sub)	Salzburg	EC	1–2	

	Caps	Career Total at Club	Date	Opponents	Venue	Competition	Result	Goals Scored
K. Konstantinidis	1		17 April 2002	Czech Republic	Athens	FR	0–0	
	2	33	15 May 2002	Cyprus	Rhodes	FR	3–1	
GUATEMALA								
D. Pezarossi	1		1 May 2004	Panama	Guatamala City	FR	1–2	1
	2		5 May 2004	Haiti	Guatamala City	FR	1–0	
	3		12 June 2004	Surinam	Paramabo	WCQ	1–1	
	4	16	20 June 2004	Surinam	Guatamala City	WCQ	3–1	1
HUNGARY								
A. Bogdan	1	1	3 June 2011	Luxembourg	Luxembourg	FR	1–0	
ICELAND								
G. Bergsson	1		22 April 1995	Chile	Temuco	FR	1–1	
	2		1 June 1995	Sweden	Solna	FR	1–1	
	3		11 June 1995	Hungary	Reykjavic	ECQ	2–1	
	4		16 August 1995	Switzerland	Reykjavic	ECQ	0–2	
	5		11 October 1995	Turkey	Reykjavic	ECQ	0–0	
	6		11 November 1995	Hungary	Budapest	ECQ	0–1	
	7		24 April 1996	Estonia	Tallinn	WCQ	3–0	
	8		1 June 1996	Macedonia	Reykjavic	WCQ	1–1	
	9		5 June 1996	Cyprus	Reykjavic	FR	2–1	
	10		4 September 1996	Czech Republic	Jablonec	FR	1–2	
	11		5 October 1996	Lithuania	Vilnius	WCQ	0–2	
	12		9 October 1996	Romania	Reykjavic	WCQ	0–4	
	13		29 April 1997	Slovakia	Reykjavic	FR	1–3	
	14		7 June 1997	Macedonia	Skopje	WCQ	0–1	
	15		11 June 1997	Lithuania	Reykjavic	WCQ	0–0	
	16		20 July 1997	Norway	Reykjavic	FR	0–1	
	17		20 August 1997	Liechtenstein	Vaduz	WCQ	4–0	
	18		6 September 1997	Ireland	Reykjavic	WCQ	2–4	
	19		29 March 2003	Scotland	Glasgow	ECQ	1–2	
	20		7 June 2003	Faroe Islands	Reykjavic	ECQ	2–1	
	21	80	11 June 2003	Lithuania	Kaunas	ECQ	3–0	
E. Gudjohnsen	1		4 September 1999	Andorra (Sub)	Reykjavic	ECQ	3–0	1
	2		8 September 1999	Ukraine (Sub)	Reykjavic	ECQ	0–1	
	3	4	9 October 1999	France (Sub)	Paris	ECQ	2–3	
A. Gunnlaugsson	1		27 July 1997	Faroe Islands	Reykjavic	FR	1–0	
	2		5 February 1998	Slovenia	Cyprus	FR	2–3	
	3		9 February 1998	Norway	Cyprus	FR	0–1	
	4		5 September 1998	France	Reykjavic	ECQ	1–1	
	5		10 October 1998	Armenia	Yerevan	ECQ	0–0	
	6	28	14 October 1998	Russia	Reykjavic	ECQ	1–0	
H. Helguson	1		6 September 2008	Norway	Oslo	WCQ	2–2	1
	2		10 September 2008	Scotland	Reykjavic	WCQ	1–2	
	3	19	19 November 2008	Malta	Valetta	FR	1–0	1
B. Kristinsson	1		10 March 1999	Luxembourg	Luxembourg	FR	2–1	
	2		27 March 1999	Andorra	Andorra	ECQ	2–0	
	3	58	31 March 1999	Ukraine	Kiev	ECQ	1–1	

	Career Total						Goals
	Caps	at Club	Date	Opponents	Venue	Competition	Result	Scored

	Caps	at Club	Date	Opponents	Venue	Competition	Result	Scored
G. Steinsson	1		26 March 2008	Slovakia	Zlate Moravce	FR	2–1	
	2		20 August 2008	Azerbaijan	Rekjavic	FR	1–1	1
	3		6 September 2008	Norway	Oslo	WCQ	2–2	
	4		10 September 2008	Scotland	Reykjavic	WCQ	1–2	
	5		15 October 2008	Macedonia	Reykjavic	WCQ	1–0	
	6		11 February 2009	Liechtenstein	Vaduz	FR	2–0	
	7		1 April 2009	Scotland	Glasgow	WCQ	1–2	
	8		6 June 2009	Holland	Reykjavic	WCQ	1–2	
	9		10 June 2009	Macedonia	Skopje	WCQ	0–2	
	10		12 August 2009	Slovakia	Reykjavic	FR	1–1	
	11		5 September 2009	Norway	Reykjavic	WCQ	1–1	
	12		9 September 2009	Georgia	Reykjavic	FR	3–1	
	13		13 October 2009	South Africa	Reykjavic	FR	1–0	
	14		14 November 2009	Luxembourg	Luxembourg	FR	1–1	
	15		11 August 2010	Liechtenstein	Reykjavic	FR	1–1	
	16		3 September 2010	Norway	Reykjavic	ECQ	1–2	
	17	38	12 October 2010	Portugal	Reykjaviv	ECQ	1–3	

IRAN

	Caps	at Club	Date	Opponents	Venue	Competition	Result	Scored
A. Teymourian	1		2 September 2006	Korea	Seoul	ACQ	1–1	
	2		6 September 2006	Syria	Damascus	ACQ	2–0	
	3		11 October 2006	Taiwan	Taipei	ACQ	2–0	
	4		15 November 2006	South Korea	Tehran	ACQ	2–0	
	5		7 February 2007	Belarus	Tehran	FR	2–2	
	6		11 July 2007	Uzbekistan	Kuala Lumpur	AC	2–1	
	7		15 July 2007	China	Kuala Lumpur	AC	2–2	
	8		18 July 2007	Malaysia	Kuala Lumpur	AC	2–0	
	9		22 July 2007	South Korea	Kuala Lumpur	AC	0–0	
	10		6 February 2008	Syria	Tehran	WCQ	0–0	
	11		26 March 2008	Kuwait	Kuwait City	WCQ	2–2	
	12		2 June 2008	Uae	Tehran	WCQ	0–0	
	13		14 June 2008	Syria (Sub)	Damascus	WCQ	2–0	
	14	27	22 June 2008	Kuwait	Tehran	WCQ	2–0	

ISRAEL

	Caps	at Club	Date	Opponents	Venue	Competition	Result	Scored
T. Ben Haim	1		18 August 2004	Croatia	Varazdin	FR	0–1	
	2		4 September 2004	France	Paris	WCQ	0–0	
	3		8 September 2004	Cyprus	Tel Aviv	WCQ	2–1	
	4		9 October 2004	Switzerland	Tel Aviv	WCQ	2–2	
	5		17 November 2004	Cyprus	Nicosia	WCQ	2–1	
	6		26 March 2005	Ireland	Tel Aviv	WCQ	1–1	
	7		30 March 2005	France	Tel Aviv	WCQ	1–1	
	8		15 August 2005	Ukraine	Kiev	FR	0–0	
	9		3 September 2005	Switzerland	St Jakob	WCQ	1–1	
	10		7 September 2005	Faroes	Torshaven	WCQ	2–0	
	11		8 October 2005	Faroes	Tel Aviv	WCQ	2–1	
	12		7 October 2006	Russia	Moscow	ECQ	1–1	
	13		15 November 2006	Croatia	Tel Aviv	ECQ	3–4	
	14		7 February 2007	Ukraine	Tel Aviv	FR	1–1	
	15		24 March 2007	England	Tel Aviv	ECQ	0–0	
	16	27	28 March 2007	Estonia	Tel Aviv	ECQ	4–0	
T. Cohen	1		6 February 2008	Romania	Tel Aviv	FR	1–0	

	Caps at Club	Career Total	Date	Opponents	Venue	Competition	Result	Goals Scored
	2		26 March 2008	Chile	Tel Aviv	FR	1–0	
	3		20 August 2008	Finland	Tampere	FR	0–2	
	4		6 September 2008	Switzerland	Tel Aviv	WCQ	2–2	
	5		10 September 2008	Moldova	Chisnau	WCQ	2–1	
	6		28 March 2009	Greece	Tel Aviv	WCQ	1–1	
	7		12 August 2009	N. Ireland	Belfast	FR	1–1	
	8		5 September 2009	Latvia (Sub)	Tel Aviv	WCQ	0–1	
	9		9 September 2009	Luxembourg	Tel Aviv	WCQ	7–0	
	10		10 October 2009	Moldova	Tel Aviv	WCQ	3–1	
	11		14 October 2009	Switzerland	Basle	WCQ	0–0	
	12		3 March 2010	Romania (Sub)	Timisoara	FR	2–0	
	13		2 September 2010	Malta	Tel Aviv	ECQ	3–1	
	14		7 September 2010	Georgia	Tbilisi	ECQ	0–0	
	15		9 October 2010	Croatia	Tel Aviv	ECQ	1–2	
	16	20	12 October 2010	Greece	Piraeus	ECQ	1–2	
I. Tal	1		15 August 2006	Slovenia	Celje	FR	1–1	
	2		7 October 2006	Russia	Moscow	ECQ	1–1	
	3		15 November 2006	Croatia	Tel Aviv	ECQ	3–4	
	4		28 March 2007	Estonia	Tel Aviv	ECQ	4–0	1
	5		2 June 2007	Fyr Macedonia	Skopje	ECQ	2–1	
	6	64	6 June 2007	Andorra	La Vella	ECQ	2–0	

IVORY COAST

	Caps at Club	Career Total	Date	Opponents	Venue	Competition	Result	Goals Scored
A. Meite	1		16 August 2006	Senegal	Tours	FR	0–1	
	2		1 September 2006	Nice	Nice	FR	1–0	
	3		8 October 2006	Gabon	Abidjan	Anq	5–0	
	4		15 November 2006	Sweden	Mans. France	FR	1–0	
	5		6 February 2007	Guinea	Rouen	FR	1–0	
	6		22 August 2007	Egypt	Paris	FR	0–0	
	7		8 September 2007	Gabon	Libreville	Acnq	0–0	
	8		17 October 2007	Austria (Sub)	Innsbruck	FR	2–3	
	9		17 November 2007	Angola	Melun	FR	1–2	
	10		21 January 2008	Nigeria	Sekondi	ACN	1–0	
	11		25 January 2008	Benin	Sekondi	ACN	4–1	
	12		3 February 2008	Guinea	Sekondi	ACN	5–0	
	13		7 February 2008	Egypt	Kumasi	ACN	1–4	
	14		26 March 2008	Tunisia	Bondoufle	FR	0–2	
	15		22 May 2008	Paraguay	Yokohama	K Cup	1–1	
	16		24 May 2008	Japan	Toyota	K Cup	1–0	
	17		1 June 2008	Mozambique	Abidjan	WCQ	1–0	
	18		8 June 2008	Madagascar	Antananarivo	WCQ	0–0	
	19		13 June 2008	Botswana	Gaborne	WCQ	1–1	1
	20	40	22 June 2008	Botswana	Abidjan	WCQ	4–0	

JAMAICA

	Caps at Club	Career Total	Date	Opponents	Venue	Competition	Result	Goals Scored
R. Gardner	1		10 February 1999	Costa Rica	Kingston	FR	1–1	
	2		28 March 1999	Trinidad & Tobago	Port Of Spain	FR	0–2	
	3		31 March 1999	Paraguay	Kingston	FR	3–0	
	4		7 June 1999	Grenada	Port Of Spain	CC	2–1	
	5		10 June 1999	Cuba	Port Of Spain	CC	0–2	
	6		8 September 1999	Usa	Port Of Spain	CC	2–2	2
	7		16 January 2000	New Zealand	China	FR	2–1	

	Career Total Caps at Club	Date	Opponents	Venue	Competition	Result	Goals Scored
	8	8 February 2000	Cayman Islands	Usa	FR	3–0	
	9	12 February 2000	Columbia	Usa	GC	0–1	
	10	14.02 2000	Honduras	USA	GC	0–2	
	11	15.11 2000	El Salvador	San Salvador	WCQ	0–2	
	12	26 January 2000	Bolivia	Miami	FR	3–0	
	13	28.01 2000	Bulgaria	Kingston	FR	0–0	
	14	28 February 2001	Trinidad & Tobago	Kingston	WCQ	1–0	
	15	25 March 2001	Mexico	Mexico City	WCQ	0–4	
	16	25 April 2001	Honduras	Kingston	WCQ	1–1	1
	17	10 June 2001	Cuba	Kingston	FR	4–1	1
	18	16 June 2001	Usa	Kingston	WCQ	0–0	
	19	30 June 2001	Trinidad & Tobago	Port of Spain	WCQ	2–1	
	20	2 September 2001	Mexico	Kingston	WCQ	1–2	
	21	5 September 2001	Honduras	Tegucigalpa	WCQ	0–1	
	22	7 October 2001	Usa	Boston	WCQ	1–2	
	23	20 November 2002	Nigeria	Lagos	FR	0–0	
	24	12 February 2003	Usa	Kingston	FR	1–2	
	25	25 May 2003	Nigeria	Kingston	FR	3–2	
	26	06 July 2003	Cuba	Kingston	FR	1–2	
	27	9 July 2003	Paraguay	Kingston	FR	2–0	
	28	13 July 2003	Columbia	Miami	GC	0–1	
	29	15 July 2003	Guatemala	Miami	GC	2–0	
	30	20 July 2003	Mexico	Mexico City	GC	0–5	
	31	7 September 2003	Australia	Reading	FR	1–2	
	32	12 October 2003	Brazil	Leicester	FR	0–1	
	33	16 November 2003	El Salvador	Kingston	FR	3–0	
	34	31 May 2004	Nigeria	Charlton	FR	0–2	
	35	12 June 2004	Haiti	Miami	WCQ	1–1	
	36	19 June 2004	Haiti	Kingston	WCQ	3–0	
	37	18 August 2004	Usa	Kingston	WCQ	1–1	
	38	4 September 2004	Panama	Kingston	WCQ	1–2	
	39	8 September 2004	El Salvador	San Salvador	WCQ	3–0	
	40	9 October 2004	Panama	Panama City	WCQ	1–1	
	41	13 October 2004	El Salvador	Kingston	WCQ	0–0	
	42	17 November 2004	Usa	Columbus	WCQ	1–1	
	43	9 October 2005	Australia	Fulham	FR	0–5	
	44	26 March 2007	Panama	Kingston	FR	1–1	
	45	18 November 2007	El Salvador	Kingston	FR	3–0	2
	46	6 February 2007	Costa Rica	Kingston	FR	1–1	
	47	3 June 2008	St Vincent & Gren'	Kingston	FR	5–1	1
	48	7 June 2008	Trinidad	Maloya	FR	1–1	
	49	15 June 2008	Bahamas	Kingston	WCQ	7–0	1
	50	18 June 2008	Bahamas	Greenfield	WCQ	6–0	
	51	20 August 2008	Canada	Toronto	WCQ	1–1	
	52	6 September 2008	Mexico	Mexico City	WCQ	0–3	
	53	10 September 2008	Honduras	Sen Pedro Sula	WCQ	0–2	
	54	11 October 2008	Mexico	Kingston	WCQ	1–0	
	55	15 October 2008	Honduras	Kingston	WCQ	1–0	
	56	19 November 2008	Canada	Kingston	WCQ	3–0	
	57	3 July 2009	Canada	Los Angeles	GC	0–1	
	58	7 July 2009	Costa Rica	Columbus	GC	0–1	
	59 105	10 July 2009	El Salvador	Miami	GC	1–0	
J. Johnson	1	7 October 2001	USA (Sub)	Boston	WCQ	1–2	
	2	16 May 2002	USA (Sub)	East Rutherford	FR	0–5	
	3	16 October 2002	Japan (Sub)	Tokyo	FR	1–1	

	Caps at Club	Career Total	Date	Opponents	Venue	Competition	Result	Goals Scored
	4		9 November 2002	Barbados (Sub)	St Georges	GC	1–1	
	5		11 November 2002	Guadeloupe	St Georges	GC	2–0	1
	6		13 November 2002	Grenada	St Georges	GC	4–1	2
	7		20 November 2002	Nigeria (Sub)	Lagos	FR	0–0	
	8		12 February 2003	Usa (Sub)	Kingston	FR	1–2	
	9		26 March 2003	St Lucia (Sub)	Kingston	GC	5–0	
	10		28 March 2003	Martinique(Sub)	Kingston	GC	2–2	
	11		30 March 2003	Haiti	Kingston	GC	3–0	1
	12		20 April 2003	South Africa	Cape Town	FR	0–0	
	13		25 May 2003	Nigeria	Kingston	FR	3–2	1
	14		7 September 2003	Australia	Reading	FR	1–2	
	15		16 November 2003	El Salvador	Kingston	FR	3–0	
	16		18 February 2004	Uruguay (Sub)	Kingston	FR	2–0	1
	17	27	31 March 2004	Honduras (Sub)	Kingston	FR	2–2	
D. Ricketts	1		18 February 2004	Uruguay	Kingston	FR	2–0	
	2		31 March 2004	Honduras	Kingston	FR	2–2	
	3		28 April 2004	Venezuela	Kingston	FR	2–1	
	4		31 May 2004	Nigeria	Charlton	FR	0–2	
	5		2 June 2004	Ireland	Charlton	FR	0–1	
	6		12 June 2004	Haiti	Miami	WCQ	1–1	
	7	13	20 June 2004	Haiti	Kingston	WCQ	3–0	

JAPAN

	Caps at Club	Career Total	Date	Opponents	Venue	Competition	Result	Goals Scored
H. Nakata	1		7 September 2005	Honduras	Myagi	FR	5–4	
	2		8 October 2005	Latvia	Riga	FR	2–2	
	3		12 October 2005	Ukraine	Kiev	FR	0–1	
	4		16 November 2005	Angola	Tokyo	FR	1–0	
	5		1 March 2006	Bosnia H	Germany	FR	2–2	1
	6		30 May 2006	Germany	Leverkusen	FR	2–2	
	7		4 June 2006	Malta	Dusseldorf	FR	1–0	
	8		12 June 2006	Australia	Kaiserslautern	WC	1–3	
	9		18 June 2006	Croatia	Nuremburg	WC	0–0	
	10	77	22 June 2006	Brazil	Dortmund	WC	1–4	
A. Nishizawa	1		7 October 2001	Nigeria	Southampton	FR	0–2	
	2	26	7 November 2001	Italy (Sub)	Saitama	FR	1–1	

MEXICO

	Caps at Club	Career Total	Date	Opponents	Venue	Competition	Result	Goals Scored
J. Borgetti	1		17 August 2005	Costa Rica	Mexico City	WCQ	2–0	1
	2		3 September 2005	Usa	Columbus	WCQ	0–2	
	3		7 September 2005	Panama	Mexico City	WCQ	5–0	1
	4		1 March 2005	Ghana	Dallas	FR	1–0	
	5		27 May 2005	France	Paris	FR	0–1	
	6		1 June 2005	Holland	Eindhoven	FR	1–2	1
	7		11 June 2005	Iran	Nuremburg	WC	3–1	
	8	77	24 June 2005	Argentina	Leipzig	WC	1–2	

NIGERIA

	Caps at Club	Career Total	Date	Opponents	Venue	Competition	Result	Goals Scored
B. Kaku	1		9 October 2004	Gabon (Sub)	Libreville	WCQ	1–1	
	2	5	17 November 2004	South Africa		FR	2–1	

	Career Total						Goals
	Caps	at Club	Date	Opponents	Venue	Competition	Result	Scored

	Caps	at Club	Date	Opponents	Venue	Competition	Result	Scored
A. Okocha	1		29 March 2003	Malawi	Blantyre	ANCQ	1–0	
	2		11 June 2003	Brazil	Abuja	FR	0–3	
	3		27 July 2003	Venezuela	Watford	FR	1–0	
	4		27 January 2004	Morocco	Monastir	ANC	0–1	
	5		31 January 2004	South Africa	Monastir	ANC	4–0	1p
	6		4 February 2004	Benin	Sfax	ANC	2–1	
	7		8 February 2004	Cameroon	Monastir	ANCQF	2–1	1
	8		11 February 2004	Tunisia	Tunis	ANCSF	1–1	1p
	9		13 February 2004	Mali	Monastir	ANC3	2–1	1
	10		2 July 2004	Algeria	Lagos	WCQ	1–0	
	11		5 September 2004	Zimbabwe		WCQ	3–0	
	12		26 March 2005	Gabon	Port Harcourt	WCQ	2–0	1
	13		18 June 2005	Angola	Port Harcourt	WCQ	1–1	1
	14		7 February 2006	Ivory Coast (Sub)	Alexandria	ANC	0–1	
	15	74	9 February 2006	Senegal	Cairo	ANC	1–0	
D. Shittu	1		6 September 2008	South Africa	Port Elizabeth	WCQ	1–0	
	2		11 October 2008	Sierra Leone	Abuja	WCQ	4–1	
	3		19 November 2008	Colombia	Cali	FR	0–1	
	4		11 February 2009	Jamaica	Millwall	FR	0–0	
	5		29 March 2009	Mozambique	Maputo	WCQ	0–0	
	6		10 October 2009	Mozambique (Sub)	Abuja	WCQ	1–0	
	7		6 January 2010	Zambia	Durban	FR	0–0	
	8		16 January 2010	Benin	Benguela	ANC	1–0	
	9		20 January 2010	Mozambique	Lubango	ANC	3–0	
	10		25 January 2010	Zambia	Lubango	Ancqf	0–0	
	11		28 January 2010	Ghana	Luanda	Ancsf	0–1	
	12		30 January 2010	Algeria	Benguela	Anc3	1–0	
	13		25 May 2010	Saudi Arabia	Wattens, Austria	FR	0–0	
	14		6 June 2010	North Korea	Johanesburg	FR	3–1	
	15		12 June 2010	Argentina	Johnnesburg	WC	0–1	
	16		17 June 2010	Greece	Bloemfontein	WC	1–2	
	17		22 June 2010	South Korea	Durban	WC	2–2	
	18	31	11 August 2010	South Korea	Suwon	FR	1–2	

NORWAY

	Caps	at Club	Date	Opponents	Venue	Competition	Result	Scored
D. Braaten	1		22 August 2007	Argentina	Oslo	FR	2–1	
	2		17 October 2007	Bosnia–Herz (Sub)	Sarajevo	ECQ	2–0	
	3	13	6 February 2008	Wales	Wrexham	FR	0–3	

OMAN

	Caps	at Club	Date	Opponents	Venue	Competition	Result	Scored
A. Al-Habsi	1		22 February 2006	Uae	Dubai	ACQ	0–1	
	2		1 March 2006	Jordan	Wattayyah	ACQ	3–0	
	3		1 September 2006	Syria	Muscat	FR	3–0	
	4		6 September 2006	Pakistan	Muscat	ACQ	5–0	
	5		11 October 2006	Uae	Muscat	ACQ	2–1	
	6		15 November 2006	Jordan	Amman	ACQ	0–3	
	7		8 June 2007	Australia	Bangkok	AC	1–1	
	8		12 June 2007	Thailand	Bangkok	AC	0–2	
	9		16 June 2007	Iraq	Bangkok	AC	0–0	
	10		8 October 2007	Nepal	Muscat	WCQ	2–0	
	11		28 October 2007	Nepal	Kathmandu	WCQ	2–0	
	12	66	6 February 2008	Bahrain	Muscat	WCQ	0–1	

Caps at Club	Career Total	Date	Opponents	Venue	Competition	Result	Goals Scored
13		26 March 2008	Thailand	Bangkok	WCQ	1–0	
14		2 June 2008	Japan	Yokohama	WCQ	0–3	
15		7 June 2008	Japan	Muscat	WCQ	1–1	
16		14 June 2008	Bahrain	Manama	WCQ	1–1	
17		22 June 2008	Thailand	Muscat	WCQ	2–1	
18		20 August 2008	Uzbekistan	Muscat	FR	2–0	
19		6 September 2008	Morrocco	Wattayah	FR	0–0	
20		10 September 2008	Zimbabwe	Wattayah	FR	3–2	
21		19 November 2008	Paraguay	Muscat	FR	0–1	
22		22 December 2008	Senegal	Muscat	FR	1–0	
23		4 January 2009	Kuwait	Muscat	GC	0–0	
24		7 January 2009	Iraq	Muscat	GC	4–0	
25		10 January 2009	Bahrain	Muscat	GC	2–0	
26		14 January 2009	Kuwait	Muscat	GC Sf	1–0	
27		17 January 2009	Saudi Arabia	Muscat	GC F	0–0	
28		28 March 2009	Senegal	Seeb	FR	2–0	
29		30 May 2009	Egypt	Muscat	FR	0–1	
30		2 June 2009	South Korea	Dubai	FR	0–0	
31		6 June 2009	Bosnia Herzogovina	Cannes	FR	1–2	
32		12 August 2009	Saudi Arabia	Salalah	FR	2–1	
33		9 September 2009	Qatar	Doha	FR	1–1	
34		14 October 2009	Australia	Melborne	ACQ	0–1	
35		14 November 2009	Australia	Muscat	ACQ	1–2	
36		17 November 2009	Brazil	Muscat	FR	0–2	
37		6 January 2010	Indonesia	Jaakarta	ACQ	2–1	
38	92	3 March 2010	Kuwait	Muscat	ACQ	0–0	

POLAND

E. Smolarek

1		10 September 2008	San Marino	Serraville	WCQ	2–0	1
2		11 October 2008	Czech Republic	Chorzow	WCQ	2–1	
3		15 October 2008	Slovakia	Bratislava	WCQ	1–2	1
4		11 February 2009	Wales (Sub)	V'real St Antonio	FR	1–0	
5	38	1 April 2009	San Marino	Kielce	WCQ	10–0	4

SENEGAL

E.H. Diouf

1		17 November 2004	Algeria	Toulon	FR	2–1	
2		9 February 2005	Cameroon	Creiteil	FR	0–1	
3		26 March 2005	Liberia	Dakar	WCQ	6–1	2.1p
4		5 June 2005	Congo	Brazzaville	WCQ	0–0	
5		18 June 2005	Togo	Dakar	WCQ	2–2	
6		18 August 2005	Ghana	Brentford	FR	0–0	
7		2 September 2005	Zambia	Lusaka	WCQ	1–0	1
8		8 October 2005	Mali	Dakar	WCQ	3–0	1
9		23 January 2006	Zimbabwe	Port Said	ANC	2–0	
10		27 January 2006	Ghana	Port Said	ANC	0–1	
11		31 January 2006	Nigeria	Port Said	ANC	1–2	
12		7 February 2006	Egypt (Sub)	Cairo	ANC	1–2	
13		2 September 2006	Mozambique	Dakar	ANCQ	2–0	
14		7 October 2006	Burkina Faso	Ouagadougu	ANCQ	0–1	
15		21 August 2007	Ghana	Millwall	FR	1–1	1
16		24 March 2007	Tanzania	Dakar	ANCQ	4–0	
17		8 September 2007	Burkina Faso	Dakar	ANCQ	5–1	1
18		12 January 2008	Namibia	Dakar	FR	3–1	

	Career Total						Goals
	Caps at Club	Date	Opponents	Venue	Competition	Result	Scored
	19	23 January 2008	Tunisia	Tamale	ACN	2–2	
	20	27 January 2008	Angola	Tamale	ACN	1–3	
	21	30 May 2008	Algeria	Dakar	WCQ	1–0	
	22	6 June 2008	Gambia	Banjul	WCQ	0–0	
	23	15 June 2008	Liberia	Monrovia	WCQ	2–2	1
	24 33	20 June 2008	Liberia	Dakar	WCQ	3–1	1
K. Fadiga	1	9 February 2005	Cameroon (Sub)	Creiteil	FR	1–0	
	2	25 March 2005	Liberia	Dakar	WCQ	6–1	1
	3	5 June 2005	Congo	Pointe Noire	WCQ	0–0	
	4 9	18 August 2005	Ghana	Brentford	FR	0–0	
A.D. Faye	1	13 November 2005	South Africa	Port Elizabeth	FR	3–2	
	2	23 January 2006	Zimbabwe	Port Said	ANC	2–0	
	3	27 January 2006	Ghana (Sub)	Port Said	ANC	0–1	
	4	9 February 2006	Nigeria	Cairo	ANC	0–1	
	5	23 May 2006	South Korea	Seoul	FR	1–1	1
	6	2 September 2006	Mozambique	Dakar	ANCQ	2–0	
	7 17	7 October 2006	Burkina Faso	Ouagadougou	ANCQ	0–1	

SLOVAKIA

Lubomir Michalik	1	28 March 2007	Ireland (Sub)	Dublin	ECQ	0–1	
	2	17 November 2007	Czech Republic	Prague	ECQ	1–3	
	3 4	21 November 2007	San Marino	Seravalle	ECQ	5–0	1
Vladimir Weiss	1	3 March 2010	Norway	Zilina	FR	0–1	
	2	5 June 2010	Costa Rica	Bratislava	FR	3–0	
	3	15 June 2010	New Zealand	Rustenburg	WC	1–1	
	4	20 June 2010	Paraguay	Bloemfontein	WC	0–2	
	5 11	28 June 2010	Holland	Durban	WC	1–2	

SOUTH AFRICA

M. Fish	1	16 November 1997	Germany	Dusseldorf	FR	0–3	
	2	7 December 1997	Brazil	Johannesburg	FR	1–2	
	3	13 December 1997	Czech Republic	Riyadh	PC	2–2	
	4	15 December 1997	Uae	Riyadh	PC	0–1	
	5	17 December 1997	Uruguay	Riyadh	PC	3–4	
	6	24 January 1998	Namibia	Windhoek	COS	2–3	
	7	8 February 1998	Angola	Bobo Dioulaso	ANC	0–0	
	8	11 February 1998	Ivory Coast	Bobo Dioulaso	ANC	1–1	
	9	22 February 1998	Morroco	Ouagoudougu	ANC	2–1	
	10	25 February 1998	Congo	Ouagoudougu	ANC	2–1	
	11	28 February 1998	Egypt	Ouagoudougu	Ancf	0–2	
	12	20 May 1998	Zambia	Johannesburg	FR	1–1	
	13	25 May 1998	Argentina	Buenos Aires	FR	0–2	
	14	6 June 1998	Iceland	Balersbron	FR	1–1	
	15	12 June 1998	France	Marseille	WC	0–3	
	16	18 June 1998	Denmark	Toulouse	WC	1–1	
	17	24 June 1998	Saudi Arabia	Bordeaux	WC	2–2	
	18	3 October 1998	Angola	Johannesburg	ANCQ	1–0	
	19	16 December 1998	Egypt	Johannesburg	FR	2–1	
	20	23 January 1999	Mauritius	Port Louis	ANCQ	1–1	
	21	27 February 1999	Gabon	Cape Town	ANCQ	4–1	

Career Total							Goals
Caps at Club		Date	Opponents	Venue	Competition	Result	Scored
22		10 April 1999	Gabon	Libreville	ANCQ	0–1	
23		28 April 1999	Denmark	Copenhagen	FR	1–1	
24		5 June 1999	Mauritius	Durban	ANCQ	2–0	
25		16 June 1999	Zimbabwe	Johannesburg	FR	0–1	
26		18 September 1999	Saudi Arabia	Cape Town	AA	1–0	
27		30 September 1999	Saudi Arabia	Riyadh	AA	0–0	
28		23 January 2000	Gabon	Kumasi	ANC	3–1	
29		27 January 2000	Dr Congo	Kumasi	ANC	1–0	
30		2 February 2000	Algeria	Kumasi	ANC	1–1	
31		6 February 2000	Ghana	Kumasi	Ancqf	1–0	
32		10 February 2000	Nigeria	Accra	Ancsf	0–2	
33		3 September 2000	Congo	Pointe Noire	ANCQ	2–1	
34	60	7 October 2000	France	Johannesburg	FR	0–0	

SOUTH KOREA

C.Y. Lee

1		5 September 2009	Australia	Seoul	FR	3–1	
2		14 October 2009	Senegal	Seoul	FR	2–0	
3		14 November 2009	Denmark	Esbjerg	FR	0–0	
4		18 November 2009	Serbia	Craven Cottage	FR	0–1	
5		3 March 2010	Ivory Coast	Loftus Road	FR	2–0	
6		16 May 2010	Ecuador	Seoul	FR	2–0	1
7		24 May 2010	Japan	Saitama	FR	2–0	
8		30 May 2010	Belarus	Kufstein	FR	0–1	
9		3 June 2010	Spain	Innsbruck	FR	0–1	
10		12 June 2010	Greece	Port Elizabeth	WC	2–0	
11		17 June 2010	Argentina	Joburg S City	WC	1–4	1
12		22 June 2010	Nigeria	Durban	WC	2–2	
13		26 June 2010	Uruguay	Port Elizabeth	WC	1–2	1
14		7 September 2010	Iran	Seoul	FR	0–1	
15		12 October 2010	Japan	Seoul	FR	0–0	
16		30 December 2010	Syria	Abu Dhabi	FR	1–0	
17		10 January 2011	Bahrain	Doha	AC	2–1	
18		14 January 2011	Australia	Doha	AC	1–1	
19		18 January 2011	India	Doha	AC	4–1	
20		22 January 2011	Iran	Doha	ACQ	1–0	
21		25 January 2011	Japan	Doha	ACSF	2–2 (Lost on Pens)	
22		28 January 2011	Uzbekistan	Doha	ACPO	3–2	
23		25 March 2011	Honduras	Seoul	FR	4–0	
24		3 June 2011	Serbia	Seoul	FR	2–1	
25	40	7 June 2011	Ghana	Jeonju	FR	2–1	

SWEDEN

J. Elmander

1		11 October 2008	Portugal	Solna	WCQ	0–0	
2		28 March 2009	Portugal	Porto	WCQ	0–0	
3		6 June 2009	Denmark (Sub)	Stockholm	WCQ	0–1	
4		12 August 2009	Finland	Stockholm	FR	1–0	1
6		5 September 2009	Hungary	Budapest	WCQ	2–1	
7		9 September 2009	Malta	Valetta	WCQ	1–0	
8		14 October 2009	Albania	Stockholm	WCQ	4–1	
9		18 November 2009	Italy	Cesena	FR	0–1	
10		3 March 2010	Wales	Cardiff	FR	1–0	1
11		11 August 2010	Scotland	Stockholm	FR	3–0	
12		3 September 2010	Hungary	Stockholm	ECQ	2–0	

	Career Total Caps at Club	Date	Opponents	Venue	Competition	Result	Goals Scored
	13	7 September 2010	San Marino (Sub)	Malmo	ECQ	6–0	
	14	12 October 2010	Holland	Amsterdam	ECQ	1–4	
	15	9 February 2011	Ukraine	Cyprus	FR	1–1	1
	16	29 March 2011	Moldova	Solna	ECQ	2–1	
	17	3 June 2011	Moldova	Chisinau	ECQ	4–1	2
	18 52	7 June 2011	Finland	Solna	ECQ	5–0	
C. Wilhelmsson	1	22 August 2007	Usa	Gothenburg	FR	1–0	
	2	8 September 2007	Denmark	Stockholm	ECQ	0–0	
	3	13 October 2007	Leichtenstein	Vaduz	ECQ	3–0	1
	4	17 October 2007	Northern. Ireland	Stockholm	ECQ	1–1	
	5	17 November 2007	Spain	Madrid	ECQ	0–3	
	6 46	21 November 2007	Latvia	Stockholm	ECQ	2–1	

TRINIDAD & TOBAGO

J. Samuel	1	5 September 2009	Honduras	San Pedro Sula	WCQ	1–4	
	2 2	9 September 2009	Usa	Port Of Spain	WCQ	0–1	

TUNISIA

R. Jaidi	1	18 August 2004	South Africa	Tunis	FR	0–2	
	2	4 September 2004	Morrocco	Rabat	WCQ	1–1	
	3	9 October 2004	Malawi	Blantyre	WCQ	2–2	
	4	26 March 2005	Malawi	Tunis	WCQ	7–0	
	5	4 June 2005	Botswana	Gaborone	WCQ	3–1	
	6	11 June 2005	Guinea	Tunis	WCQ	2–0	
	7	15 June 2005	Argentina	Cologne	CC1	1–2	
	8	18 June 2005	Germany	Cologne	CC1	0–3	
	9	17 August 2005	Kenya	Nairobi	WCQ	1–0	
	10	8 October 2005	Morrocco	Tunis	WCQ	2–2	
	11	22 January 2006	Zambia	Cairo	ANC	4–1	
	12	26 January 2006	South Africa	Cairo	ANC	2–1	
	13	30 January 2006	Giunea	Cairo	ANC	0–3	
	14	4 February 2006	Nigeria	Port Said	ANC	1–1	
	15	1 March 2006	Serbia	Rades	FR	0–1	
	16	30 March 2006	Belarus	Tunis	FR	3–0	
	17	2 June 2006	Uruguay	Tunis	FR	0–0	
	18	14 June 2006	Saudi Arabia	Munich	WC	2–2	1
	19	19 June 2006	Spain	Stuttgart	W	1–3	
	20 92	23 January 2006	Ukraine	Berlin	WC	0–1	

USA

S. Holden	1	3 March 2010	Holland	Amsterdam	FR	1–2	
	2	25 May 2010	Czech Republic	East Hartford	FR	2–4	
	3	29 May 2010	Turkey (Sub)	Phildelphia	FR	2–1	
	4	12 June 2010	England (Sub)	Rustenburg	WC	1–1	
	5	9 October 2010	Poland	Chicago	FR	2–2	
	6 17	12 October 2010	Colombia	Chester	FR	0–0	

YUGOSLAVIA

S. Curcic	1	27 March 2096	Romania	Belgrade	FR	1–0	
	2	24 April 1996	Faroe Islands	Belgrade	WCQ	3–1	
	3	23 May 1996	Mexico	Japan	FR	0–0	
	4 10	26 May 1996	Japan (Sub)	Japan	FR	0–1	

Competition Codes

WC World Cup Finals	HI Home International
EC European Championships	AA Afro.Asian Cup
WCQ World Cup Finals Qualifier	PC Presidents Cup
ECQ European Championship Qualifier	COS Cosafa Castle Cup
ANC African Nations Cup	CC Copa Caribe Cup
ACN African Cup Of Nations	ANCQ African Nations Cup Qualifier
GC Gold Cup	FR Friendly
CC1 Confederations Cup	

UNDER-23

	Career Total						Goals
	Caps	at Club	Date	Opponents	Venue	Competition	Result	Scored
ENGLAND							
F. Hill	1		15 March 1961	W. Germany	Tottenham	FR	4–1	
	2		9 November 1961	Israel	Leeds	FR	7–1	
	3		29 November 1961	Holland	Rotterdam	FR	5–2	
	4		28 February 1962	Scotland	Aberdeen	FR	4–2	
	5		22 March 1962	Turkey	Southampton	FR	4–1	
	6		7 November 1962	Belgium	Plymouth	FR	6–1	
	7		28 November 1962	Greece	Birmingham	FR	5–0	
	8		21 March 1963	Yugoslavia	Manchester	FR	0–0	
	9		29 May 1963	Yugoslavia	Belgrade	FR	4–2	
	10	10	2 June 1963	Romania	Bucharest	FR	0–1	
E. Hopkinson							
	1		19 May 1957	Bulgaria	Sofia	FR	1–2	
	2		26 May 1957	Romania	Bucharest	FR	1–0	
	3		30 May 1957	Czechoslovakia	Bratislava	FR	2–0	
	4		25 September 1957	Bulgaria	Chelsea	FR	6–2	
	5		15 January 1958	Scotland	Everton	FR	3–1	
	6	6	18 March 1959	France	Lyon	FR	1–1	
R. Parry							
	1		16 October 1957	Romania	Wembley	FR	3–2	
	2		18 March 1959	France	Lyon	FR	1–1	
	3		7 May 1959	Italy	Milan	FR	3–0	
	4	4	10 May 1959	West Germany	Bochum	FR	2–2	
D. Stevens							
	1		26 May 1957	Romania	Bucharest	FR	1–0	
	2	2	30 May 1957	Czechoslovakia	Bratislava	FR	2–0	
N. IRELAND							
J. Napier	1	1	22 February 1967	Wales	Belfast	FR	2–1	
WALES							
W. Davies	1		5 December 1962	Scotland	Aberdeen	FR	0–2	
	2		13 November 1963	England	Bristol	FR	1–1	
	3		30 November 1964	Scotland	Wrexham	FR	6–0	
	4	4	10 February 1965	N. Ireland	Cardiff	FR	2–2	
M. Edwards	1		23 April 1958	England	Wrexham	FR	1–2	
	2	2	25 November 1959	Scotland	Wrexham	FR	1–1	

	Caps	at Club	Date	Opponents	Venue	Competition	Result	Goals Scored
PORTUGAL								
R. Vaz Te	1		11 October 2009	Poland	Sandomierz	FR	0–0	
	2	2	3 March 2010	Wales	Fatima	FR	7–2	2

UNDER-21

	Caps	at Club	Date	Opponents	Venue	Competition	Result	Goals Scored
DENMARK								
C. Jensen	1		18 August 1998	Czech Republic	Prague	FR	1–0	
	2		4 September 1998	Belarus	Minsk	ECQ	2–0	1
	3		9 October 1998	Wales	Odense	ECQ	2–2	
	4		13 October 1998	Switzerland	Basle	ECQ	0–2	
	5		9 February 1999	Croatia	Zagreb	FR	0–0	
	6		4 June 1999	Belarus	Odense	ECQ	3–0	
	7		9 June 1999	Wales	Wrexham	ECQ	2–1	
	8	19	8 October 1999	England	Bradford	FR	1–4	
ENGLAND								
N. Hunt	1		17 February 2004	Holland	Hull	FR	2–2	
	2		17 August 2004	Ukraine	Middlesbrough	FR	3–1	
	3		3 September 2004	Austria	Krems	ECQ	2–0	
	4		8 October 2004	Wales	Blackburn	ECQ	2–0	
	5		12 October 2004	Azerbaijan	Baku	ECQ	0–0	
	6		16 November 2004	Spain	Alcaca	FR	0–1	
	7		25 March 2005	Germany	Hull	ECQ	2–2	
	8		16 August 2005	Denmark	Herning	FR	1–0	
	9		2 September 2005	Wales (Sub)	Wrexham	ECQ	4–0	
	10	10	6 September 2005	Germany	Mainz	ECQ	1–1	
F. Muamba	1		19 August 2008	Slovenia (Sub)	Hull	FR	2–1	
	2		6 September 2008	Portugal	Wembley	ECQ	2–0	
	3		14 October 2008	Wales (Sub)	Villa Park	ECQ	2–2	
	4		18 November 2008	Czech Republic	Bramhall Lane	FR	2–0	
	5		27 March 2009	Sandefjord	Oslo	FR	5–0	
	6		31 March 2009	France (Sub)	City Ground	FR	0–2	
	7		8 June 2009	Azerbaijan	Milton Keynes	FR	7–0	
	8		15 June 2009	Finland	Halmstad	EC	2–1	
	9		18 June 2009	Spain	Gothenburg	EC	2–0	
	10		26 June 2009	Sweden	Gothenburg	Ecsf	3–3	
	11		29 June 2009	Germany	Malmo	Ecf	0–4	
	12		4 September 2009	Macedonia	Prilep	ECQ	2–1	
	13		8 September 2009	Greece	Tripoli	ECQ	1–1	
	14		9 October 2009	Macedonia (Sub)	Milton Keynes	ECQ	6–3	
	15		13 November 2009	Portugal	Wembley	ECQ	1–0	
	16		17 November 2009	Lithuania	Vilnius	ECQ	0–0	
	17		3 March 2010	Greece	Doncaster	ECQ	1–2	
	18		3 September 2010	Portugal (Sub)	Barcelos	ECQ	1–0	
	19		8 October 2010	Romania	Norwich	ECQ	2–1	
	20		12 October 2010	Romania	Botosani	ECQ	0–0	
	21		8 February 2011	Italy	Empoli	FR	0–1	
	22	30	24 March 2011	Denmark	Viborg	FR	4–0	
	23		5 June 2011	Norway	Southampton	FR	2–0	
	24		15 June 2011	Ukraine (Sub)	Herning	EC	0–0	
	25	33	19 June 2011	Czech Republic	Viborg	EC	1–2	

| | Career Total | | | | | | | Goals |
	Caps	at Club	Date	Opponents	Venue	Competition	Result	Scored
K. Nolan	1	1	11 February 2003	Italy	Cararra	FR	0–1	
P. Reid	1		27 April 1977	Scotland	Bramall Lane	FR	1–0	
	2		26 May 1977	Finland	Helsinki	ECQ	1–0	
	3		1 June 1977	Norway	Bergen	ECQ	2–1	
	4		12 October 1977	Finland	Hull	ECQ	8–1	
	5		5 April 1978	Italy	Rome	ECQ	0–0	
	6	6	19 April 1978	Yugoslavia	Novi Sad	ECQ	1–2	
D. Sturridge	1	11	24 March 2011	Denmark	Viborg	FR	4–0	1
A. Thompson	1		7 June 1995	Latvia	Burnley	ECQ	4–0	
	2	2	2 September 1995	Portugal	Santa Maria	ECQ	0–2	
J. Wilshere	1	5	3 March 2010	Greece	Doncaster	ECQ	1–2	
NORTHERN IRELAND								
W. Buchanan	1	1	12 February 2002	Germany (Sub)	Belfast	FR	0–1	
FRANCE								
B. Mendy	1		6 September 2002	Cyprus	Limmasol	ECQ	1–0	
	2		11 October 2002	Slovenia	Clemont Fer'nd	ECQ	1–0	
	3		15 October 2002	Malta	Taquali	ECQ	3–0	
	4		28 March 2003	Malta	Lille	ECQ	2–0	
	5	5	1 April 2003	Israel	Trapani	ECQ	3–0	
HUNGARY								
A. Bogdan	1		7 September 2007	San Marino	San Marino	ECQ	6–1	
	2		12 September 2007	Serbia	H	ECQ	2–1	
	3		16 October 2007	Belarus	H	ECQ	0–1	
	4		18 November 2007	Latvia	Riga	ECQ	0–1	
	5	6	5 September 2008	Serbia	Belgrade	ECQ	0–8	
ICELAND								
E. Gudjohnsen	1	1	9 October 1998	Armenia	Yerevan	ECQ	1–3	1
IRELAND								
M. Connolly	1		9 February 2011	Cyprus	Larnaca	FR	0–0	
	2	2	25 March 2011	Portugal	Aguera	FR	0–2	
J. O'Brien	1		8 February 2005	Portugal (Sub)	Rio Maior	FR	0–2	
	2		25 March 2005	Israel (Sub)	Herz Liya	ECQ	1–3	
	3		3 June 2005	Israel	Longford	ECQ	2–2	
	4		16 August 2005	N. Ireland	Lurgan	FR	2–2	
	5		6 September 2005	France	Cork	ECQ	1–2	
	6		7 October 2005	Cyprus	Larnaca	ECQ	1–1	
	7	7	11 October 2005	Switzerland	Dublin	ECQ	0–1	
PORTUGAL								
R. Vaz Te	1		28 February 2006	Italy (Sub)	Agueda	FR	0–1	
	2		25 May 1906	Serbia	Barcelos	ECQ	2–0	
	3		1 September 2006	Latvia	Riga	ECQ	0–2	
	4		5 September 2006	Poland	Pedroso	ECQ	2–0	

Caps	Career Total	Date	Opponents	Venue	Competition	Result	Goals Scored
5		6 October 2006	Russia	Moscow	ECQ	1–4	
6		10 October 2006	Russia	Vila Nova Gaia	ECQ	3–0	
7		14.11.06	Serbia (Sub)	Figueira Da Foz	FR	3–0	1
8		6 February 2007	Estonia	Rio De Janeiro Maior	FR	3–0	
9		8 February 2007	Czech Republic (Sub)	Abrantes	FR	1–1	
10		23 March 2007	Slovakia (Sub)	Amadora	FR	2–0	1
11		27 March 2007	Serbia	Novi Sad	FR	0–2	
12		16 June 2007	Israel	Groningen	EC	4–0	1
13		21 June 2007	Italy	Nijmegan	EC	0–0	
14		5 February 2008	Scotland	Abrantes	FR	2–1	
15		6 February 2008	Sweden	Rio De Janeiro Maior	FR	3–0	
16		19 August 2008	Czech Republic	Tocha	FR	2–3	
17		6 September 2008	England	Wembley	ECQ	0–2	
18	18	9 September 2008	Ireland	Dos Barreiros	ECQ	2–2	1

SLOVAKIA

Z. Harsanyi

1		2 June 2007	Russia	Presov	FR	1–3	
2		5 June 2007	England (Sub)	Norwich	FR	0–5	
3		6 February 2008	Turkey	Antalya	FR	2–3	1
4	4	24 May 2008	Poland	Nowy Sacz	FR	1–2	

SWITZERLAND

B. Dzemaili

| 1 | | 26 March 2008 | Fyr Macedonia | Skopje | FR | 1–2 | |
| 2 | 13 | 23 May 2008 | Holland | Amsterdam | FR | 1–0 | |

WALES

R. Powell

| 1 | 1 | 15 November 2005 | Cyprus | A | | FR | 3–3 | |

B INTERNATIONALS

ENGLAND

E. Bell

| 1 | | 3 March 1954 | Scotland | Roker Park | FR | 1–1 | |
| 2 | 2 | 16 May 1954 | Yugoslavia | Lubljana | FR | 1–2 | |

R. Langton

| 1 | | 11 May 1950 | Italy | Milan | FR | 0–5 | |
| 2 | 2 | 17 May 1950 | Holland | Amsterdam | FR | 0–3 | |

N. Lofthouse

| 1 | 1 | 22 February 1950 | Holland | Newcastle | FR | 1–0 | 1 |

J. Wheeler

1		26 March 1952	Holland	Amsterdam	FR	1–0	
2		22 May 1952	France	Le Havre	FR	1–7	
3		23 March 1955	West Germany	Hillsborough	FR	1–1	
4		19 October 1955	Yugoslavia	Maine Road	FR	5–1	
5	5	29 February 1956	Scotland	Dundee	FR	2–2	

A. Stubbs

| 1 | 1 | 10 May 1994 | N. Ireland | Hillsborough | FR | 4–2 | |

IRELAND

K. Branagan

| 1 | 1 | 13 December 1994 | England | Liverpool | FR | 0–2 | |

O. Coyle

| 1 | 1 | 13 December 1994 | England | Liverpool | FR | 0–2 | |

J. McAteer

| 1 | 1 | 13 December 1994 | England | Liverpool | FR | 0–2 | |

	Caps at Club	Career Total	Date	Opponents	Venue	Competition	Result	Goals Scored
N. IRELAND								
A. Davidson	1	1	26 March 1996	Norway	Coleraine	FR	3–0	
W. Buchanan	1	1	28 April 2004	Serbia, Montenegro	Belfast	FR	0–0	
SCOTLAND								
J. McGinlay	1	1	23 April 1996	Denmark	Nykobing	FR	0–3	
W. Moir	1		11 November 1952	France Espoir	Toulouse	FR	0–0	
	2	2	11 March 1953	England	Easter Road	FR	2–2	

FOOTBALL LEAGUE REP

Under-21

S. Taylor	1	1	19 February 1997	Italian League	A	FR	1–1	

ENGLAND YOUTH INTERNATIONALS

(Under-16-Under-20)

H. Aljofree	1995		F.H. Lee	1961
K. Bartley	2007		M. McGeechan	2007
M. Bennett	1980, 1981		K. Nolan	2000, 2001, 2002
B. Bromley	1964		Y. Novaki	1977
D. Burke	1979		T. Obadeyi	2006, 2007, 2008
R. Coghiel	1984		E. Phythian	1959
J. Dean	1957, 1958		E. Redrobe	1961
T. Eckersley	2008		B. Robinson	1961
R. Ellis	1970		B. Siddall	1973
S. Farrimond	1958		R. Sissons	2004
W. Foster	1982		B. Smith	1973, 1974
K. France	1959		C. Stokes	2007
M. Gillan	2001, 2002		C. Thompson	1978
D. Holden	1998		L. Woodland	2010
D. Jones	1973			

AUSTRALIA

S. Jamieson	2005		A. Mooy	2007

CYPRUS

M. Michail	2007

GERMANY

K. Wolze	2006, 2007, 2008

IRELAND

M. Cassidy	2006		L. Irwin	2010, 2011
J. O'Brien	2004, 2005, 2006		A. Power	2000
M. Roddy	2005		C. Ryan	2001
S. Sheridan	2008			

JAMAICA

C. Taylor	2003

POLAND

B. Augustyn	2006		J. Fojut	2005, 2006
P. Kazimierczak	2006			

PORTUGAL

R. Vaz Te	2005, 2006

SCOTLAND

J. Evans	1998	G. McGregor	2010
M. McLeod	1996	M. Minchella	1997
M. O'halloran	2007, 2010		

SWEDEN

D. Thach	2003

USA

J. Smith	2006, 2007, 2008

WALES

M. Byrne	2004	R. Powell	2003, 2004, 2005

ENGLAND V YOUNG ENGLAND

F. Hill	1961	D. Holden	1959
E. Hopkinson	1959	R. Parry for Young England	1959

FOOTBALL LEAGUE REPRESENTATIVES

J. Ball	1952, 1954	(2)	D.B.N. Jack	1923, 1928, 1929	(3)
T. Banks	1958	(1)	R. Langton	1951, 1952	(3)
W. Bannister	1902	(1)	N. Lofthouse	1951, 1952, 1953, 1954,	
M. Barrass	1952	(2)		1955, 1956, 1957	(14)
E. Bell	1954	(1)	R.A. Parry	1958, 1960	(2)
J. Fay	1912, 1913	(2)	R.H. Pym	1924, 1925	(2)
J. Fitchett	1901, 1902	(2)	A. Shepherd	1906	(1)
H. Gardiner	1892	(1)	D. Stevens	1958	(1)
S. Greenhalgh	1904, 1908, 1910	(4)	D. Stokes	1905, 1907, 1909	(4)
R. Hartle	1959	(1)	J.W. Sutcliffe	1894, 1896, 1897	(3)
H. Hassall	1954, 1955	(2)	R. Westwood	1935, 1936, 1937, 1938	(6)
D. Holden	1959	(1)	J. Wheeler	1955	(1)
E. Hopkinson	1958, 1960	(2)			

UNOFFICIAL INTERNATIONALS

	Date	Opponents	Venue	Result	Goals Scored
ENGLAND					
M. Barrass	20 October 1945	Wales	The Hawthorns	0–1	
	7 July 1956	All Ireland	Dublin	5–3	
J. Fay	20 April 1914	Scottish XI	Shawfield	2–0	
J. Fitchett	25 September 1901	Germany	Hyde Road	10–0	
R. Glendenning	20 April 1914	Scottish XI	Shawfield	2–0	
H. Goslin	2 December 1939	Scotland	Newcastle	2–1	
	4 October 1941	Scotland	Wembley	2–0	
	25 October 1941	Wales	St Andrews	2–1	
S. Hanson	19 June 1950	United States	New York	1–0	
N. Lofthouse	19 June 1950	United States	New York	1–0	

	Date	Opponents	Venue	Result	Goals Scored
	14 May 1953	Buenos Aires	River Plate	1–3	
	21 October 1953	Rest of Europe	Wembley	4–3	
J. Smith	13 May 1916	Scotland	Goodison Park	4–3	1
	26 April 1919	Scotland	Goodison Park	2–2	
	3 May 1919	Scotland	Hampden Park	4–3	
	18 October 1919	Wales	Victoria Ground	2–0	1
	19 June 1920	South Africa	Durban	3–1	1
	26 June 1920	South Africa	Johannesburg	3–0	
	17 July 1920	South Africa	Cape Town	9–1	2
	15 July 1926	Eastern Canada	Montreal	2–1	1
J.W. Sutcliffe	15 March 1999	Scottish XI	Crystal Palace	1–2	
H. Webster	14 July 1951	Australia	Sydney	6–1	3
R. Westwood	21 August 1935	Scotland	Hampden Park	2–4	1

SCOTLAND

	Date	Opponents	Venue	Result	Goals Scored
W. Cook	8 May 1935	England	Highbury	1–0	
A. Donaldson	22 March 1919	Ireland	Ibrox	2–1	
	19 April 1919	Ireland	Windsor Park	0–0	
	26 April 1919	England	Goodison Park	2–2	

WALES

	Date	Opponents	Venue	Result	Goals Scored
D. Jones	21 October 1991	Canada	Wrexham	1–1	
	12 October 1991	Canada	Wrexham	2–1	
R. Roberts	12 October 1991	Canada	Wrexham	2–1	
E.T. Vizard	18 October 1919	England	Victoria Ground	0–2	
D. Winter	5 May 1945	England	Cardiff	2–3	

FOOTBALL LEAGUE

	Date	Opponents	Venue	Result	Goals Scored
J. Atkinson	11 May 1935	Wales–Ireland	Goodison Park	10–2	
G. Eastham	11 May 1935	Wales–Ireland	Goodison Park	10–2	2
R. Smith	11 May 1935	Wales–Ireland	Goodison Park	10–2	
R. Westwood	11 May 1935	Wales–Ireland	Goodison Park	10–2	1

REST OF THE UK

	Date	Opponents	Venue	Result	Goals Scored
N. Lofthouse	5 December 1951	Wales	Cardiff	2–3	

PLAYER RECORDS

	SEASON	LEAGUE			FA CUP			LEAGUE CUP			FRTROVER–AUTO			UEFA CUP ANGLO ITALIAN			TOTAL		
		APS	SUB	GLS	APS	SUB	GLS	APS	SUB	GLS	APS	SUB	GLS	APS	SUB	GLS	APS	SUB	GLS
ABBOTT, H.	1904–05	1															1	0	0
ADAMSON, H.M.	1909–10 to 1910–11	15															15	0	0
AINSLEY, G.E.	1936–37	7															7	0	0
AKIN, B.	2002–03		1		1												2	1	0
ALEXANDER, G.	1895–96	2															2	0	0
ALJOFREE, H.	1997–98 to 1999–2000	6	8			2		4	2								10	12	0
ALLARDYCE, S.	*1973–74 to 1985–86	194	4	21	14	1	2	18		1							226	5	24
ALLCOCK, T.	1953–54 to 1957–58	31		9	1		2										32	0	11
ALLEN, P.	1986–87		1					2		1							2	1	1
AL HABSI, A.	2006–07	10			2			2						4			18	0	0
ALONSO, M.	2007–08	4	3					2						2	1		8	4	0
ALONSO, Marcos	2010–11	4			2	1		2									8	1	0
ANDERSON, A.	1936–37 to 1938–39	52		4	5		1										57	0	5
ANDRE, P.Y.	2002–03		9														0	9	0
ANDREWS, W.	1894–95	12		3	1												13	0	3
ANELKA, N.	2006–07 to 2007–08	53	2	21	2	1	1	1		1				2			58	3	23
ANTHONY, A.	1899–1900	3															3	0	0
ARMSTRONG, C.	2002–03				1												1	0	0
ASHTON, S.	2005–06					1											0	1	0
ASPINALL, J.	1946–47 to 1949–50	14															14	0	0
ASTLEY, H.	1900–01 to 1901–02	6															6	0	0
ATHERTON, J.	PRE-LEAGUE				5		3										5	0	3
ATKINSON, J.	1905–06 to 1906–07	3		1													3	0	1
ATKINSON, JE.	1932–33 to 1947–48	240		4	23		1										263	0	5
ATKINSON, P.	1986–87	2	1														2	1	0
AUGUSTYN, B.	2006		1														0	1	0
BA, I.	2003–04		9		1			5	1								6	10	0
BAGGETT, J.W.	1923–24 to 1926–27	24		10	3		1										27	0	11
BAILEY, D.	1956–57	1															1	0	0
BAILEY, I.C.	*1981–82 to 1984–85	15									1	2					16	2	0

PLAYER	SEASON	LEAGUE APS	LEAGUE SUB	LEAGUE GLS	FA CUP APS	FA CUP SUB	FA CUP GLS	LEAGUE CUP APS	LEAGUE CUP SUB	LEAGUE CUP GLS	FRT/ROVER–AUTO APS	FRT/ROVER–AUTO SUB	FRT/ROVER–AUTO GLS	UEFA CUP / ANGLO ITALIAN APS	UEFA CUP / ANGLO ITALIAN SUB	UEFA CUP / ANGLO ITALIAN GLS	TOTAL APS	TOTAL SUB	TOTAL GLS
BALL, J.	1950–51 to 1957–58	200		2	12												212	0	2
BALLESTA, S.	2002–03	1	5														1	5	0
BANKS, R.	1946–47 to 1952–53	104			14												118	0	0
BANKS, S.	1998–99 to 2002–03	23	1		5			7									35	1	0
BANKS, T.	1947–48 to 1960–61	233		2	22												255	0	2
BANNISTER, N.	1955–56 to 1960–61	26		4													26	0	4
BANNISTER, W.	1901–02 to 1902–03	28		3	2												30	0	3
BARBER, T.	1908–09 to 1912–13	102		14	5												107	0	14
BARBOUR, A.	1888–89 to 1891–92	34		17	1												35	0	17
BARLOW, T.H.	*1898–99 to 1903–04	86		25	4												90	0	25
BARNARD, A.	1954–55 to 1955–56	2															2	0	0
BARNES, J.	1898–99	9		1	2												11	0	1
BARNES, P.	*1987–88	4	1			1											4	2	0
BARNESS, A.	2000–01 to 2004–05	76	20		7	2		9	2								92	24	0
BARRASS, M.W.	1946–47 to 1956–57	329		25	28		2										357	0	27
BASHAM, C.	2008–09	6	13	1		1			1								6	15	1
BATES, W.E.	1906–07	2															2	0	0
BATESON	PRE-LEAGUE				1												1	0	0
BAVERSTOCK, H.	1905–06 to 1921–22	366		4	22												388	0	4
BAVERSTOCK, J.J.	1913–14	2															2	0	0
BAXENDALE	PRE-LEAGUE				1												1	0	0
BEARDS, A.	1950–51 to 1953–54	14		2													14	0	2
BEARDSLEY, P.	1997–98 to 1998–99	14	3	2		1		3									17	4	2
BECKETT, C.	1905–06	1															1	0	0
BEECH, H.W.	1965–66 to 1966–67	14	1					1									15	1	0
BELL, E.	1950–51 to 1957–58	102		1	16		1										118	0	2
BELL, F.	1900–01 to 1901–02	5															5	0	0
BELL, G.	1983–84 to 1985–86	86	6	3	2			7		2	6	1					101	7	5
BELL, L.	1899–1900 to 1902–03	99		44	4		1										103	0	45
BEN HAIM, T.	2004–05 to 2006–07	81	7	1	9			6						7			103	7	1
BENNETT, M.	1979–80 to 1982–83	62	3	1	3			5									70	3	1
BENTLEY, A.	1910–11 to 1912–13	51		15	4		1										55	0	16
BENTLEY, H.	1891–92 to 1894–95	44		17	6		2										50	0	19
BERGSSON, G.	1994–95 to 2002–03	271	9	25	12		1	23	2	1							306	11	27

	SEASON	LEAGUE APS	SUB	GLS	FA CUP APS	SUB	GLS	LEAGUE CUP APS	SUB	GLS	FR/TROVER-AUTO APS	SUB	GLS	UEFA CUP / ANGLO ITALIAN APS	SUB	GLS	TOTAL APS	SUB	GLS
BERRY, N.	1981–82 to 1984–85	25	7		1			4	2	1							30	9	1
BINGLEY, W.	1949–50 to 1954–55	6															6	0	0
BIRCH, B.	1954–55 to 1963–64	165		23	19		4	7		1							191	0	28
BLACKMORE, H.A.	1926–27 to 1931–32	153		111	12		11										165	0	122
BLAKE, N.	1995–96 to 1998–99	102	5	38	6		2	10	1	8							118	6	48
BLAKE, R.	2010–11		8	1	1	1		2									3	9	1
BOBIC, F.	2001–02	14	2	4													14	2	4
BOGDAN, A.	2010–11	3	1		3			2									8	1	0
BOLLANDS, J.F.	1959–60	13															13	0	0
BOLTON, R.	1898–99	2															2	0	0
BOOTH, P.	1984–85	1									1						2	0	0
BORGETTI, J.	2005–06 to 2006–07	5	14	2	1	2	2	2	1	2				4	3	1	12	20	7
BORROWS, B.	1982–83 to 1984–85	95		7	4			7			4						110	0	7
BOSTON, W.J.	1923–24 to 1928–29	37		2	2		1										39	0	3
BOSWELL, A.H.	1969–70 to 1970–71	51			3			2									56	0	0
BOURNE, J.T.	1924–25	3															3	0	0
BOWER, R.W.	1936–37	3															3	0	0
BOYD, J.	1902–03 to 1908–09	189		7	19												208	0	7
BOYLE, M.J.	1931–32 to 1932–33	13		7	1												14	0	7
BRAATEN, D.	2007–08		6		1			1	1					3	2		5	9	0
BRACELIN, J.	1894–95	1		1													1	0	1
BRADLEY	PRE-LEAGUE	1															1	0	0
BRADLEY, J.	1947–48 to 1950–51	92		19	7		1										99	0	20
BRANAGAN, K.	1992–93 to 1999–2000	216			9			33			4			1			263	0	0
BRENNAN, I.	1980–81 to 1981–82	16	1		2			1									19	1	0
BROGAN, J.	1888–89 to 1891–92	74		26	12		6										86	0	32
BROMILOW, G.	1968–69	3	2														3	2	0
BROMLEY, B.	1962–63 to 1968–69	165	1	25	10		1	8									183	1	26
BROOKMAN, N.	1986–87 to 1989–90	47	10	10	5			1			7	1	2				60	11	12
BROOMFIELD, H.	1902–03 to 1906–07	28															28	0	0
BROWN, M.	1991–92 to 1992–93	27	6	3	3			2	1								32	7	3
BROWN, P.	1988–89 to 1993–94	259	2	14	23		1	25		1	21		1	2			330	2	17
BROWN, R.N.	1895–96 to 1901–02	125		12	11		2										136	0	14
BROWN, W.	1899–1900 to 1903–04	106			8												114	0	0

	SEASON	LEAGUE APS	SUB	GLS	FA CUP APS	SUB	GLS	LEAGUE CUP APS	SUB	GLS	FRTROVER–AUTO APS	SUB	GLS	ANGLO ITALIAN / UEFA CUP APS	SUB	GLS	TOTAL APS	SUB	GLS
BRYAN, J.	1929-30	1		1													1	0	1
BUCHAN, T.M.	1914-15 to 1922-23	116		14	1												117	0	14
BUCHANAN, W.B.	2001-02 to 2002-03					1											0	1	0
BULLOUGH, P.A.	1888-89 to 1892-93	38		4	14		1										52	0	5
BURGESS, A.C.	1946-47 to 1947-48	5		3													5	0	3
BURKE, D.I.	*1978-79 to 1993-94	169	6	1	14	1		16	1		7						206	8	2
BURNETT, W.	1995-96 to 1996-97		2														0	2	0
BURNISON, J.	1900-01 to 1901-02	18															18	0	0
BUTLER, D.A.	1962-63 to 1967-68	62	3	11	2		1	2		1							66	3	13
BUTLER, W.	1921-22 to 1932-33	407		65	42		9										449	0	74
BYROM, J.	1966-67 to 1975-76	296	8	113	22	2	7	22	1	10							340	11	130
CAHILL, G.	2007-08	111		11	7		1	4		1				4			126	0	13
CALDER, J.	1936-37 to 1937-38	27		11													27	0	11
CALDERBANK, J.	1900-01	3															3	0	0
CALDWELL, A.	1983-84 to 1986-87	133	8	60	8		4	8	1	4	17	4	10				166	9	78
CALLAGHAN, I.	1987-88	1			1												2	0	0
CAME, M.	1984-85 to 1992-93	192	7	7	16	2	2	15	4	2	23		2				246	13	11
CAMERON, K.	1933-34 to 1934-35	24		3	3		1										27	0	4
CAMERON, W.S.	1906-07 to 1907-08	26		5	5		2										31	0	7
CAMPBELL, A.	2000-01	3	3														3	3	0
CAMPO, I. (RAMOS)	2002-03 to 2007-08	149	23	13	6	1	1	8	3	1				3	1		166	28	14
CANDELLA, V.	2004-05	9	1		1	1											10	2	0
CANTELLO, L.	1979-80 to 1981-82	89	1	3	3			4									96	1	3
CARR, F.	1997-98		5														0	5	0
CARR, S.R.	1898-99	2															2	0	0
CARRUTHERS, A.	1936-37 to 1937-38	26		4	1		1										27	0	5
CARTER, M.	1979-80 to 1981-82	37	12	8	3			3	1								43	13	8
CARTMAN, H.R.	1919-20 to 1921-22	22															22	0	0
CASSIDY, J.	1889-90 to 1897-98	194		84	25		17										219	0	101
CASSIDY, J.	1924-25	22		7													22	0	7
CESAR, J.	2004-05	4	1					2		1							6	1	1
CHAMBERS, F.	1921-22 to 1923-24	12			1												13	0	0
CHAMBERS, W.T.	1934-35	2		1													2	0	1
CHANDLER, J.G.	*1981-82 to 1989-90	170	11	40	7		3	12	1	5	9	1					198	13	48

	SEASON	LEAGUE			FA CUP			LEAGUE CUP			FRT ROVER–AUTO			UEFA CUP ANGLO ITALIAN			TOTAL		
		APS	SUB	GLS	APS	SUB	GLS	APS	SUB	GLS	APS	SUB	GLS	APS	SUB	GLS	APS	SUB	GLS
CHARLTON, S.	2000–01 to 2003–04	111	12		3	1		6	2								120	15	0
CHARNLEY, J.	1991–92	3															3	0	0
CHIRNSIDE, J.E.	1891–92	1															1	0	0
CHORLTON, H.H.	1897–98 to 1900–01	9		2													9	0	2
CHRISTIE, J.	PRE-LEAGUE				5												5	0	0
CHURCH, H.B.	1930–31 to 1934–35	41			1												42	0	0
CID, G.	2007–08	6	1		1									5			13	1	0
CLARK, T.G.	1935–36 to 1936–37	21			2												23	0	0
CLARKE, M.	2000–01	11															11	0	0
CLARKE, P.A.	1970–71	13															13	0	0
CLEMENT, D.T.	1979–80 to 1980–81	33			3			3									39	0	0
CLEMENTS, A.P.	1977–78	1															1	0	0
CLIFFORD, R.	1903–04 to 1908–09	152		5	15		1										167	0	6
CODD, R.W.	1950–51 to 1953–54	31		5													31	0	5
COHEN, T.	2007–08 to 2010–11	35	14	6	4	3		1	1								40	18	6
COLEMAN, S.	1994–95 to 1997–98	34	8	5	2			4									40	0	5
COMSTIVE, P.	1989–90 to 1991–92	45	8	3	3	1	1	6		1	3	1					57	10	5
COMYN - PLATT.C	2003–04 to 2004–05				2	2			2								2	2	0
CONNOR, J.	1934–35 to 1938–39	29			7												36	0	0
COOK, W.L.	1928–29 to 1935–36	234		35	28		5										262	0	40
COOPER, C.	1960–61 to 1968–69	79	4		5			2									86	4	0
COPE, J.W.	1925–26 to 1928–29	79			7												86	0	0
CORFIELD, E.	1949–50 to 1951–52	6															6	0	0
COUPAR, T.	1888–89 to 1889–90	5		1													5	0	1
COWDRILL, B.	1988–89 to 1991–92	122	2	4	8			13		2	14	1					157	3	6
COX, N.	1997–98 to 1999–2000	80	3	7	1	1		9		1							90	4	8
COX, W.	PRE-LEAGUE				5												5	0	0
COYLE, O.C.	1993–94 to 1995–96	37	20	13	8		5	5	3	1				5		4	55	23	23
CRAVEN, R.	1908–09	2															2	0	0
CREWE, W.	1922–23	4															4	0	0
CROMBIE, D.	1987–88 to 1990–91	90	6	1	5		1	11	1		13		1				119	7	3
CROOK, W.	1947–48	28			1												29	0	0
CROSS, D.	1985–86	19	1	8	4			4		2							23	1	10
CUNLIFFE, J.G.	1957–58 to 1962–63	25		5	5			3									33	0	0

	SEASON	LEAGUE			FA CUP			LEAGUE CUP			FRTROVER-AUTO			UEFA CUP ANGLO ITALIAN			TOTAL		
		APS	SUB	GLS	APS	SUB	GLS	APS	SUB	GLS	APS	SUB	GLS	APS	SUB	GLS	APS	SUB	GLS
CUNNINGHAM, T.	1990–91	12		4													12	0	4
CURCIC, S.	1995–96 to 1996–97	28		4	2		2	3		1							33	0	7
CURRAN, H.P.	1974–75 to 1976–77	40	7	13	2			1									43	7	13
CURRIER, J.	1935–36 to 1938–39	26		14													26	0	14
DARBY, J.	1985–86 to 1993–94	263	12	36	19		3	25		8	25	1	5	1			333	13	52
DARLING, M.	1973–74	6	2														6	2	0
DAVENPORT, J.K.	1888–89 to 1892–93	56		25	21		11										77	0	36
DAVIES, A.	1919–20	8		1													8	0	1
DAVIES, D.	1902–03 to 1909–10	123			14												137	0	0
DAVIES, K.	2003–04	281	4	62	17	2	6	12	3	2				12	1	1	322	10	71
DAVIES, M.	2008–09	22	29	1	3	4	1	4		1							29	33	3
DAVIES, R.H.	1895–96 to 1898–99	29			1												30	0	0
DAVIES, R.I.	1924–25 to 1925–26	3															3	0	0
DAVIES, R.W.	1961–62 to 1966–67	155		66	11		6	4		2							170	0	74
DAVIES, W.H.	1898–99	21															21	0	0
DAVIN, M.	1930–31	3															3	0	0
DAVIS, S.	2009–10	3			1												4	0	0
DAVISON, A.	1993–94 to 1996–97	35	2		8									4			47	2	0
DAVISON, J.H.	1963–64	21		1	1												22	0	1
DAWSON, T.	PRE-LEAGUE				1												1	0	0
DEFREITAS, F.	1994–95 to 1995–96	24	18	9	1			2	4								27	22	9
DEAKIN, P.	1957–58 to 1963–64	63		13	7		2	3									73	0	15
DEAKIN, R.J.	1982–83 to 1984–85	104	1	2	6			5			5						120	1	2
DEAN, J.	1955–56 to 1959–60	17															17	0	0
DEMPSEY, E.	1906–07	7		1													7	0	1
DENTON, R.	1971–72	3	1														3	1	0
DEVLIN, J.	PRE-LEAGUE				3												3	0	0
DIAWARA, D.	2001–02	4	5					2									6	5	0
DIBBLE, A.	1991–92	13									1						14	0	0
DICKENSON, J.	1892–93 to 1893–94	42		11	5		2										47	0	13
DILLON, V.	1947–48 to 1950–51	17		2													17	0	2
DIOUF, E.H.	2004–05	102	12	21	3	2		3	2					6	6	3	114	22	24
DJETOU, M.	2005–06	1	2					1	1								2	3	0
DJORKAEFF, Y.	2001–02 to 2003–04	72	3	19	1		1	4	1								77	4	20

PLAYER	SEASON	LEAGUE			FA CUP			LEAGUE CUP			FRT/ROVER-AUTO			UEFA CUP / ANGLO ITALIAN			TOTAL		
		APS	SUB	GLS	APS	SUB	GLS	APS	SUB	GLS	APS	SUB	GLS	APS	SUB	GLS	APS	SUB	GLS
DOBSON, M.	1966–67							1									1	0	0
DOCHERTY, J.	1894–95	2															2	0	0
DONALDSON, A.	1912–13 to 1921–22	139		5	7		1										146	0	6
DOWNEY, C.	2001–02 to 2002–03		1														0	1	0
DOYLE, M.	1981–82 to 1982–83	40		2	2		2										42	0	4
DRABBLE, F	191920 to 1920–21	29			1												30	0	0
DREYER, J.	1994–95	2	2														2	2	0
DUCKWORTH, T.C.	1931–32 to 1932–33	28			1												29	0	0
DUFFEY, C.	1969–70 to 1971–72	8			2	1	1										10	1	1
DUNNE, A.P.	1973–74 to 1978–79	166	4		10			13									189	4	0
DYER, F.	1888–89	1															1	0	0
DZEMAILI, B.	2007–08 to 2008–09					1											0	1	0
EASTHAM, G.R.	1932–33 to 1936–37	114		16	17		1										131	0	17
EATOCK, T.	1924–25 to 1925–26	11		1													11	0	1
ECCLES, G.S.	1904–05	6															6	0	0
EDISBURY, W.	1956–57 to 1957–58	2															2	0	0
EDMED, R.A.	1931–32 to 1932–33	4		1	1												5	0	1
EDMONDS, H.	1909–10 to 1910–11	10															10	0	0
EDMONDSON, J.H.	1906–07 to 1914–15	239			20												259	0	0
EDWARDS, G.B.	1950–51 to 1964–65	482		8	31		1	5									518	0	9
EDWARDS, J.G.	1958–59	3															3	0	0
EDWARDS, M.	1956–57 to 1960–61	14		1													14	0	1
EGERTON, W.	1911–12	2		1	1												3	0	1
ELLIOTT, R.	1997–98 to 2000–01	76	17	5	5	1		4		2							85	18	7
ELLIOTT, S.	1986–87 to 1988–89	59	3	11	6			4			4						73	3	11
ELMANDER, J.	2008–09 to 2010–11	82	10	18	6	5	3	1	4	1							89	19	22
ELVEY, J.R.	1920–21 to 1921–22	11															11	0	0
ELVY, R.	1947–48 to 1949–50	31			3												34	0	0
ENTWISTLE, W.	1985–86	5	3		1							2					6	5	0
ESPARTERO, M.	2001–02		3														0	3	0
EVANS, W.P.	1907–08	1															1	0	0
EVANS, T.	1984–85	4									1						5	0	0
FACEY, D.	2002–03 to 2003–04	1	9	1	4												5	9	0
FADIGA, K.	2004–05 to 2005–06	5	8	1	4	1		1						2			12	9	1

Player	Season	LEAGUE			FA CUP			LEAGUE CUP			FRT/ROVER-AUTO			UEFA CUP/ANGLO ITALIAN			TOTAL		
		APS	SUB	GLS	APS	SUB	GLS	APS	SUB	GLS	APS	SUB	GLS	APS	SUB	GLS	APS	SUB	GLS
FAIRCLOUGH, C.	1995-96 to 1997-98	89	1	8	5			11									105	1	8
FALLON, L.	PRE-LEAGUE				6		5										6		5
FARNWORTH, S.	1983-84 to 1985-86	113			7			11			8						139		
FARRELLY, G.	1999-2000 to 2003-04	64	17	6	6	2		4									74	19	6
FARRIMOND, S.	1958-59 to 1970-71	364	1	1	22			17									403	1	1
FAY, J	1911-12 to 1920-21	128		5	8												136		5
FAYE, A.D.	2005-06 to 2007-08	53	7	3	3			2						7			65	7	3
FEATHERSTONE, F.	1904-05	2		1													2		1
FEEBURY, J.H.	1909-10 to 1919-20	180		16	12												192		16
FELGATE, D.	*1985-86 to 1992-93	245			17			14			24						300		
FERDINAND, L.	2004-05	1	11	1				1	1	1							2	12	2
FERGUSON, G.	1893-94 to 1995-96	16		3	3												19		3
FERNANDES, F.	2005-06	1	1											2	1		3	2	
FINNEY, A.	1922-23 to 1936-37	483		2	47												530		2
FISH, M.	1997-98 to 2000-01	107	1	3	6	1		12		1							125	2	4
FISHER, N.	1990-91 to 1994-95	17	7	1	1			4									22	7	1
FITCHETT, J.	1897-98 to 1901-02	76		4	5												81		4
FITZPATRICK, P.	1984-85 to 1985-86	13	1		1			3			1						18	1	
FLECK, R.	1993-94	6	1	1										1			7	1	1
FLETCHER, P.J.	1968-69 to 1970-71	33	3	5	2		1	3	1	1							38	4	7
FLITCROFT, W.	1888-89 to 1889-90	8															8		
FLOOD, C.W.	1922-23	8		2													8		2
FOJUT, J.	2005-06 to 2008-09		3					1									1	3	
FORBES, J.	1924-25 to 1925-26	3															3		
FORREST, E.	1938-39 to 1947-48	69		1	4												73		1
FORTUNE, Q.	2006-07	5	1		1	1											6	2	
FOSTER, J.	1903-04	2															2		
FOSTER, W.P.	1981-82 to 1984-85	92	13	13	6	1	3	3	3	1	2						103	17	17
FOWLER, J.	PRE-LEAGUE				7												7		
FRANDSEN, P.	*1996-97 to 2003-04	250	21	32	7	4		20	2	4							277	27	36
FREDGAARD, C.	2000-01	1	4														1	4	
FREEBAIRN, A.	1894-95 to 1906-07	286		9	29		1										315		10
FRY, B.	1964-65	3		1													3		1
FULLARTON, J.	1998-99	1															1		

NAME	SEASON	LEAGUE			FA CUP			LEAGUE CUP			FR/ROVER-AUTO			UEFA CUP / ANGLO ITALIAN			TOTAL		
		APS	SUB	GLS	APS	SUB	GLS	APS	SUB	GLS	APS	SUB	GLS	APS	SUB	GLS	APS	SUB	GLS
FULTON, S.	1993-94	4												2	1		6	1	0
GARDINER, H.	1890-91 to 1893-94	80		5	4												84	0	5
GARDNER, A.	1903-04	8		1													8	0	1
GARDNER, W.R.	1998-99	285	59	22	20	4		21	4	2				11		1	337	67	25
GASKELL, A.	1905-06 to 1909-10	105		2	5												110	0	2
GAVIN, M.	1985-86 to 1986-87	50	1	3	6		1				8		1				64	1	5
GEE, J.	1907-08	6		1	1												7	0	1
GELDARD, A.	1938-39 to 1946-47	29		1	10		1										39	0	2
GENT	PRE-LEAGUE				1												1	0	0
GIALLANZA, G.	1997-98		3														0	3	0
GIANNAKOPOULOS, S.S.	2003-04 to 2007-08	86	51	20	12		3	10	4	3				10	4	2	118	59	28
GIBSON, G.B.	1926-27 to 1932-33	236		76	19		5										255	0	81
GILL, J.J.	1926-27 to 1929-30	40			2												42	0	0
GILLAM, S.G.	1888-89	2															2	0	0
GILLIES, A.	1895-96	6															6	0	0
GILLIES, M.	1946-47 to 1951-52	145		1	9												154	0	1
GILLIGAN, A.	1893-94 to 1899-1900	99		17	8												107	0	17
GILLIGAN, W.	1898-99	3															3	0	0
GIMBLETT, G.S.	1911-12 to 1913-14	30			1												31	0	0
GIMBLETT, W.S.	1919-20	2															2	0	0
GLAISTER, J.	PRE-LEAGUE				2												2	0	0
GLEAVES, J.	PRE-LEAGUE				13		2										13	0	2
GLENDENNING, R.	1912-13 to 1914-15	73			10												83	0	0
GOLDSMITH, G.	1934-35 to 1935-36	19															19	0	0
GOODALL, E.I.	1938-39	12															12	0	0
GOPE - FENEPE, J.J.	2000-01		2														0	2	0
GORRINGE, F.C.	1930-31	1															1	0	0
GOSLIN, H.A.	1930-31 to 1938-39	303		23	31												334	0	23
GOUGH, H.	1927-28	4															4	0	0
GOULDEN, A.E.	1962-63	4															4	0	0
GOWLING, A.E.	1977-78 to 1981-82	147	2	28	8		1	8		2							163	2	31
GRAHAM, M.A.	1977-78 to 1980-81	43	3		2			3									48	3	0
GRAY, S.	1982-83	10															10	0	0
GREAVES, R.	1965-66 to 1979-80	487	8	66	39		10	41		9							567	8	85

PLAYER	SEASON	LEAGUE			FA CUP			LEAGUE CUP			FRTROVER–AUTO			UEFA CUP / ANGLO ITALIAN			TOTAL		
		APS	SUB	GLS	APS	SUB	GLS	APS	SUB	GLS	APS	SUB	GLS	APS	SUB	GLS	APS	SUB	GLS
GREEN, S.	1989–90 to 1996–7	171	56	25	20	3	4	19	4	1	8			3	2	1	221	65	31
GREENHALGH	1888–89				3												3	0	0
GREENHALGH, H.W.	1924–25 to 1928–29	70			10												80	0	0
GREENHALGH, S.	*1902–03 to 1913–14	259		19	19		1										278	0	20
GREGORY	PRE-LEAGUE				2		1										2	0	1
GREGORY, J.	1897–98 to 1898–99	6															6	0	0
GREGORY, J.	1989–90	2	6														2	6	0
GRIEVES, K.J.	1951–52 to 1955–56	49			1												50	0	0
GRIFFIN, P.	1986–87											1					0	1	0
GRIFFITHS, D.	1908–09	4															4	0	0
GRIFFITHS, J.	1932–33 to 1933–34	24			1												25	0	0
GRIFFITHS, T.P.	1931–35 to 1932–33	48		6	5		2										53	0	8
GRIME, J.	1902–03	3															3	0	0
GROSVENOR, A.T.	1937–38 to 1938–39	53		7	3												56	0	7
GRUNDY, W.A.	1908–09	2															2	0	0
GUBBINS, R.G.	1952–53 to 1959–60	97		15	4		3										101	0	18
GUDJOHNSEN, E.	1998–99 to 1999–2000	52	7	19	4	1	4	8	1	4							64	9	27
GUEST, A.	1894–95	1															1	0	0
GUNN, J.	1895–96	6		5	2		2										8	0	7
GUNNLAUGSSON, A.	1997–98 to 1998–99	24	18	13	1	1	1	6	3	1							31	22	15
GUTHRIE, D.	2007–08	21	4		1			2		1				6	1		30	5	1
GUY, G.	1920–21	2		1													2	0	1
HALFORD, D.	1936–37 to 1937–38	6		1	2		1										8	0	2
HALLEY, W.	1897–98 to 1900–01	40			1												41	0	0
HALLIDAY, J.F.	1901–02 to 1902–03	27			3												30	0	0
HALLOWS, P.C.R.	1968–69 to 1973–74	45	2	8	2			6									53	2	8
HAMILTON, E.	1895–96	1			2												3	0	0
HAMLETT, T.L.	1946–47 to 1948–49	72		9	13												85	0	9
HANSEN, B.	1998–99 to 2001–02	67	37	15	4	2	1	7	2	1							78	41	17
HANSON, J.	1898–99 to 1903–04	64		9	3												67	0	9
HANSON, S.	1936–37 to 1955–56	384			39												423	0	0
HARRISON, C.E.	1888–89 to 1889–90	24															24	0	0
HARTFORD, A.	1985–86 to 1986–87	83		8	6			4		1	8		1				101	0	10
HARTLE, L.R.	1952–53 to 1965–66	446	1	11	39		1	13		1							498	1	13

NAME	SEASON	LEAGUE			FA CUP			LEAGUE CUP			FRT/ROVER-AUTO			UEFA CUP/ANGLO ITALIAN			TOTAL		
		APS	SUB	GLS	APS	SUB	GLS	APS	SUB	GLS	APS	SUB	GLS	APS	SUB	GLS	APS	SUB	GLS
HASLAM, R.	1900–01	1															1	0	0
HASSALL, H.W.	1951–52 to 1954–55	102		34	7												109	0	34
HATELEY, C.B.	1913–14	1															1	0	0
HATTON, D.H.	1961–62 to 1969–70	231		8	14			14									259	0	8
HATTON, R.J.	1966–67 to 1967–68	23	1	2													23	1	2
HAWORTH, R.	1921–22 to 1930–31	322			35												357	0	0
HAY, T.	PRE-LEAGUE				5												5	0	0
HAYDOCK, J.	1988–89 to 1989–90	2			4												6	0	0
HEATON, S.	1903–04	4		1													4	0	1
HEBBERD, T.N.	1981–82	6															6	0	0
HELGUSON, H.	2007–08 to 2008–09	3	4	2	1									2			6	4	2
HENDER, P.	1960–61	1															1	0	0
HENDERSON	PRE-LEAGUE				1												1	0	0
HENDERSON, C.	1894–95	28		14	1												29	0	14
HENDRY, C.	2000–01 to 2002–03	28		3	1			4									33	0	3
HENNIN, D.	1953–54 to 1960–61	164		8	17		1	2									183	0	9
HENRY, T.	1981–82 to 1982–83	70		22	3			3		2							76	0	24
HENSHAW, G.	1987–88 to 1990–91	49	21	4	4	1	1	8	1		4	2					65	25	5
HERBERT, W.E.	1919–20 to 1921–22	34		7	1												35	0	7
HERNON, J.	1948–49 to 1950–51	43		2													43	0	2
HESLOP, T.W.	1913–14 to 1914–15	7															7	0	0
HEWITSON	PRE-LEAGUE				2		3										2	0	3
HEWITT, J.	1910–11	11		3													11	0	3
HIERRO, F.	2004–05	15	14	1	4			2									21	14	1
HIGGINS, G.	1951–52 to 1953–54	69			4												73	0	0
HIGGINS, J.O.	1952–53 to 1960–61	183			15			4									202	0	0
HILES, A.	1896–97	1															1	0	0
HILL, F.	1957–58 to 1968–69	373	2	74	23		1	14		4							410	2	79
HILTON, H.	1909–10 to 1919–20	62		23	3		1										65	0	24
HINTON, F.	1920–21 to 1923–24	34			2												36	0	0
HODGKISS	1900–01	1															1	0	0
HODSON, J.	1919–20 to 1921–22	22															22	0	0
HOGAN, J.	*1908–09 to 1912–13	54		18	4		1										58	0	19
HOGGAN, D.M.	1979–80 to 1982–83	83	10	11	3		2	7	1	2							93	11	15

NAME	SEASON	LEAGUE APS	SUB	GLS	FA CUP APS	SUB	GLS	LEAGUE CUP APS	SUB	GLS	FRTROVER-AUTO APS	SUB	GLS	UEFA CUP / ANGLO ITALIAN APS	SUB	GLS	TOTAL APS	SUB	GLS
HOLDEN	PRE-LEAGUE				5												5	0	0
HOLDEN, A.D.	1951–52 to 1962–63	419		40	40		3	4		1							463	0	44
HOLDEN, D.	1999–2000 to 2001–02	7	6	1	3	1		3	1								13	8	1
HOLDEN, S.	2009-10	27	1	2	3	1											30	3	2
HOLDSWORTH, DEAN	1997–98 to 2002–03	102	61	42	5	2	3	11	5	4							118	68	49
HOLDSWORTH, DAVID	2002-03							1									1	0	0
HOLLOWAY, D.	1999-2000	3	1														3	1	0
HOPKINSON, E.	1956–57 to 1969–70	519			38			21									578	0	0
HOUGH	PRE-LEAGUE				2		1										2	0	1
HOULT, R.	1993-94	3	1											1			4	1	0
HOWARTH, H.	1929-30 to 1933-34	59			2												61	0	0
HOWARTH, J.M.	1919-20	1															1	0	0
HOWARTH, N.	1922-23 to 1925-26	35		2	3												38	0	2
HOWARTH, P.	PRE-LEAGUE				8		3										8	0	3
HOWARTH, T.	PRE-LEAGUE				6		1										6	0	1
HOWCROFT, H.	1898-99	3			2												5	0	0
HOWE, D.	1936-37 to 1951-52	266		35	20												286	0	35
HOWEY, S.	2003-04	2	1														2	1	0
HUBBICK, H.	1936-37 to 1946-47	128			16												144	0	0
HUGHES, A.	1893-94	15		2	5		1										20	0	3
HUGHES, J.	1919-20 to 1920-21	40			1												41	0	0
HUGHES, J.H.	1933-34	9		3													9	0	3
HUGHES, P.	1987-88 to 1990-91	12	1					1			2						15	1	0
HUGHES, W.	1908-09 to 1912-13	100		51	2												102	0	51
HUGHES, W.	1948-49 to 1952-53	47		2	2												49	0	2
HULME, J.	1962-63 to 1971-72	186	2	7	9		1	18		1							213	2	9
HULME, W.	1919-20	3															3	0	0
HUNT, G.S.	1937-38 to 1946-47	45		24	6		2										51	0	26
HUNT, N.	2000-01	113	15	1	9	3		11			10						143	18	1
HUNT, R.	1969-70 to 1971-72	72	4	24	2	1	1	3	2								77	7	25
HUNTER, W.B.	1908-09 to 1911-12	53		15	2		1										55	0	16
HURLEY, C.J.	1969-70 to 1970-71	41	1	3	1			3									45	1	3
HURST, G.J.	1934-35 to 1946-47	60		2	13												73	0	2
HYNDS, T.	1898-99	8															8	0	0

	SEASON	LEAGUE APS	SUB	GLS	FA CUP APS	SUB	GLS	LEAGUE CUP APS	SUB	GLS	FRTROVER-AUTO APS	SUB	GLS	UEFA CUP / ANGLO ITALIAN APS	SUB	GLS	TOTAL APS	SUB	GLS
JAASKELAINEN, J.	1998–99	457	1		21			19						11			508	1	0
JACK, D.B.N.	1920–21 to 1928–29	295		144	29		17										324	0	161
JACK, R.	1895–96 to 1900–01	110		29	15												125	0	29
JACK, R.R.	1923–24 to 1928–29	29		9	2												31	0	9
JACKSON	PRE-LEAGUE				3												3	0	0
JACKSON, J.	1947–48 to 1949–50	11		1													11	0	1
JAIDI, R.	2004–05 to 2005–06	35	8	8	2	1		3						3			43	9	8
JANSEN, M.	2005–06	3	3			1											3	4	0
JARDEL, M.	2003–04		7		1			3	1	3							4	8	3
JEFFREY, M.	1988–89 to 1991–92	9	6		1			1	2		2	1					13	9	0
JEMSON, N.	1988–89	4	1														4	1	0
JARRETT, R.H.	1890–91	5															5	0	0
JENNINGS, W.	1912–13 to 1929–30	267		2	20												287	0	2
JENSEN, C.	1998–99 to 1999–2000	90	1	8	6			12		2							108	1	10
JOHANSEN, M.	1996–97 to 1999–2000	117	25	17	7	1		16	4	4							140	30	21
JOHNSON, J.	2001–02 to 2003–04	4	8		1	1		3									8	9	0
JOHNSTON	1922–23	1															1	0	0
JOHNSTON, A.	1999–2000	19	2	4	2												21	2	4
JONES	PRE-LEAGUE				2												2	0	0
JONES, D.	1888–89 to 1897–98	228		4	27		4										255	0	8
JONES, E.	1912–13 to 1914–15	90		24	9		4										99	0	28
JONES, E.	1933–34	1		1													1	0	1
JONES, G.	1909–10 to 1911–12	22		6	1												23	0	6
JONES, G.E.	1968–69 to 1978–79	195	8	41	25	2	8	16	1	6							236	11	55
JONES, J.	1899–1900	2															2	0	0
JONES, J.	1919–20 to 1921–22	70															70	0	0
JONES, J.L.M.	1937–38	6		1													6	0	1
JONES, J.L.M.	1922–23 to 1925–26	12		3	3												15	0	3
JONES, P.B.	1970–71 to 1982–83	441	4	38	31		1	30		4							502	4	43
JONES, R.	1929–30 to 1936–37	219		25	25												244	0	0
JOYCE, W.	1894–95 to 1896–97	30		16	3		2										33	0	18
JOYCE, W.G.	1982–83 to 1987–88	182	4	17	11	1	1	14	1	1	9		2				216	5	21
KAKU, B.	2004–05		1					1	1								1	2	0
KAPRIELIAN, M.	1999–2000 to 2000–01		1														0	1	0

SEASON	LEAGUE APS	SUB	GLS	FA CUP APS	SUB	GLS	LEAGUE CUP APS	SUB	GLS	FRT ROVER–AUTO APS	SUB	GLS	UEFA CUP / ANGLO ITALIAN APS	SUB	GLS	TOTAL APS	SUB	GLS
KAY, G. — 1910–11	3															3		0
KEAN, F.W. — 1928–29 to 1930–31	80			9		1										89		1
KEELEY, G. — 1988–89	20			1		1	2									23		1
KEETLEY, J.S. — 1921–22	1															1		0
KELLY, A. — 1991–92 to 1994–95	103	3	5	15	3		9		2	6		1	3			136	6	8
KENNEDY, A. — 1991–92	1															1		0
KENNEDY, J. — PRE-LEAGUE				10												10		0
KENNEDY, G.M. — 1950–51	17			1												18		0
KERNAGHAN, A. — 1994–95	9	2														9	2	0
KIDD, B. — 1980–81 to 1981–82	40	3	14	2			4		2							46	3	16
KIDD, J. — 1914–15	9															9		0
KING, H. — 1905–06	1															1		0
KINSELL, T.H. — 1949–50	17															17		0
KIRKMAN, G. — 1935–36	1															1		0
KLASNIC, I. — 2009–10	12	37	12	8		2	4		1							24	37	15
KONSTANTINIDIS, K. — 2001–02	3															3		0
KNIGHT, Z. — 2009–10	69		2	6	3		5									80	3	2
KNOWLES — 1888–89				3		2										3		2
KNOWLES, J.H. — 1902–03	3	3	3													3	3	3
LANGLEY, G.R. — 1981–82	3	3		2												5	3	0
LANGTON, R. — 1949–50 to 1952–53	118		16	14		2										132		18
LAVILLE, F. — 2002–03 to 2004–05	15															15		0
LAWRIE, H. — 1905–06	3															3		0
LAWSON, R.R. — 1893–94 to 1894–95	2		2													2		2
LEE, C.Y. — 2009–10	52	13	7	6	2	2		3								58	18	9
LEE, D. — 1992–93 to 1996–97	125	31	17	13	2	2	19	1	1	4			3	1		164	35	20
LEE, F.H. — 1960–61 to 1967–68	189		92	13		8	8		6							210		106
LEE, F.S. — 1971–72 to 1974–75	77	8	20	11	2	3	3		4							91	10	27
LEE, J. — 1897–98 to 1898–99	6															6		0
LEE, S. — 1990–91 to 1991–92	4			1												5		0
LEES, A. — 1947–48	2															2		0
LEIGH, J. — 1903–04	2															2		0
LENNARD, D. — 1962–63 to 1968–69	114	5	3	6			1									121	5	3
LEVER, A. — 1893–94	1															1		0

	SEASON	LEAGUE APS	LEAGUE SUB	LEAGUE GLS	FA CUP APS	FA CUP SUB	FA CUP GLS	LEAGUE CUP APS	LEAGUE CUP SUB	LEAGUE CUP GLS	FRT/ROVER-AUTO APS	FRT/ROVER-AUTO SUB	FRT/ROVER-AUTO GLS	UEFA CUP/ANGLO ITALIAN APS	UEFA CUP/ANGLO ITALIAN SUB	UEFA CUP/ANGLO ITALIAN GLS	TOTAL APS	TOTAL SUB	TOTAL GLS
LILLYCROP, G.R.	1913–14 to 1914–15	52		31	3		1										55	0	32
LITTLE, G.	2003–04		4														0	4	0
LIVESEY, D.	2002–03 to 2004–05	2	2		3												4	2	0
LOCKHART, A.	1913–14	2						1									2	0	0
LOCKETT, H.	1909–10	16		4													16	0	4
LOCKHART, G.	1897–98 to 1899–1900	26			2												28	0	0
LODGE, P.	1984–85	4						1									5	0	0
LOFTHOUSE, N.	1946–47 to 1960–61	452		255	49		27	2		3							503	0	285
LONG, J.P.	1921–22	1															1	0	0
LONGWORTH, B.	1919–20 to 1923–24	77			5												82	0	0
LOW, J.	1900–01	1															1	0	0
LOWE, J.	1921–22 to 1922–23	5			1												6	0	0
LYDEN, J.	1894–95	3		1													3	0	1
LYDIATE, J.	1991–92 to 1994–95	29	1		2			4			1						36	1	0
McADAMS, W.J.	1960–61 to 1961–62	44		26	3		1	5		2							52	0	29
McAFFERTY, W.	1902–03	8															8	0	0
McALLISTER, D.	1969–70 to 1974–75	155	1	2	14			7									176	1	2
McANESPIE, S.	1995–96 to 1997–98	19	5					6									25	5	0
McARTHUR, W.	1893–94	19		6													19	0	6
McATEER, J.	1992–93 to 1995–96	112	5	9	11		3	11		2	1	1		4		1	139	6	15
McATEER, T.	1898–99 to 1901–02	59		10	3												62	0	10
McBURNEY, M.L.	1973–74	1															1	0	0
McCANN, G.	2007–08 to 2009–10	56	19	1	4	1								8		2	68	20	3
McCLARENCE, J.P.	1907–08 to 1908–09	15		6													15	0	6
McCLELLAND, J.	1927–28 to 1929–30	57		18	8		1										65	0	19
McDONAGH, J.M.	1976–77 to 1982–83	242		1	13			19									274	0	1
McDONALD, N.	1994–95 to 1995–96	6															6	0	0
McELHINNEY, G.R.	1980–81 to 1984–85	107	2		8			9			1						125	2	2
McEWAN, M.	1904–05 to 1909–10	152		13	12		2										164	0	15
McFETTRIDGE, D.	1891–92 to 1892–93	25		5	2												27	0	5
McGARRY, R.J.	1961–62 to 1962–63	27		7	1												28	0	7
McGEACHAN, J.	1894–95 to 1897–98	69		5	12												81	0	5
McGINN, J.	1894–95	15		3													15	0	3
McGINLAY, J.	1992–93 to 1997–98	183	12	89	16	1	10	23	2	14	4		1	4		4	230	15	118

	SEASON	LEAGUE			FA CUP			LEAGUE CUP			FR/ROVER-AUTO			UEFA CUP ANGLO ITALIAN			TOTAL		
		APS	SUB	GLS	APS	SUB	GLS	APS	SUB	GLS	APS	SUB	GLS	APS	SUB	GLS	APS	SUB	GLS
McGOVERN, J.P.	1982–83 to 1983–84	16			4					1							20	0	1
McGUINESS	1888–89	1		1													1	0	1
McILWAINE, M.	1952–53	2															2	0	0
McKAY, D.	1902–03	7			1												8	0	0
McKAY, P.	1898–99	3															3	0	0
McKAY, W.	1929–30 to 1933–34	104		17	5												109	0	17
McKERNON, J.	PRE-LEAGUE				17												17	0	0
McKIE, J.	1900–01 to 1902–03	81		19	4		1										85	0	20
McMAHON, K.	1971–72	4	2	1													4	2	1
McNAB, N.	1978–79 to 1979–80	33	2	4	2			2									37	2	4
McNEE, J.	1889–90 to 1892–93	87		23	9		2										96	0	25
McREDDIE, W.	1895–96	2															2	0	0
McSHANE, H.	1947–48 to 1950–51	93		6	6		1										99	0	7
McWHIRTER, A.	1889–90	4															4	0	0
McWILLIAMS, P.	1902–03	1															1	0	0
MAKUKULA, A	2008–09	4	2														4	2	0
MANNING, J.J.	1968–69 to 1970–71	27	2	7	1			2		1							30	2	8
MARSH, A.	1966–67 to 1970–71	71	2		1			5									77	2	0
MARSH, F.K.	1938–39	3															3	0	0
MARSH, S.	1902–03 to 1911–12	185		72	16		9										201	0	81
MARSHALL, I.	2000–01 to 2001–02	13	27	6	3			2									18	27	6
MARSHALL, T.	1898–99 to 1902–03	4															4	0	0
MARTIN, C.	2006–07		1														0	1	0
MARTIN, J.	1894–95 to 1895–96	7		1													7	0	1
MATHEWSON, R.	1950–51 to 1952–53	3															3	0	0
MATTHEW, H.	1892–93	8															8	0	0
MATTHEWS, N.	1986–87	1															1	0	0
MATTHEWS, V.E.	1922–23 to 1924–25	3															3	0	0
MAXWELL, A.	1991–92	3															3	0	0
MAY, A.	1987–88	9	1	2													9	1	2
MEITE, A.	2006–07	56			3	1	1	4						5	1	1	68	2	2
MELLOR, F.	1920–21 to 1921–22	2															2	0	0
MENDY, B.	2002–03	20	1		1			1									22	1	0
MERCER	1888–89	1															1	0	0

NAME	SEASON	LEAGUE APS	SUB	GLS	FA CUP APS	SUB	GLS	LEAGUE CUP APS	SUB	GLS	FRT/ROVER–AUTO APS	SUB	GLS	UEFA CUP/ANGLO ITALIAN APS	SUB	GLS	TOTAL APS	SUB	GLS
MICHALIK, L.	2006–07 to 2007–08	8	3		1		1	1	1					3			13	4	1
MIDDLEBROUGH, A.	1946–47 to 1947–48	5		1													5	0	1
MILLAR, J.	1894–95 to 1895–96	9			1												10	0	0
MILLER, J.	1897–98	8			1												9	0	0
MILLER, T.A.	1896–97 to 1898–99	48		12	5		1										53	0	13
MILNE, J.	1888–89 to 1889–90	39		9													39	0	9
MILSOM, J.	1929–30 to 1937–38	235		142	20		11										255	0	153
MITCHELL, J.	1888–89	2															2	0	0
MOIR, W.	1946–47 to 1955–56	325		118	33		16										358	0	134
MOORES	PRE-LEAGUE				3												3	0	0
MOORES, I.R.	1982–83	23	3	3				3	1	2							26	4	5
MOORES, J.C.	1980–81		1														0	1	0
MORGAN, H.	1898–99 to 1900–01	46		16	1												47	0	16
MORGAN, T.	1987–88 to 1989–90	65	12	17	4			2		2	7		1				78	12	20
MORGAN, W.	1902–03	3															3	0	0
MORGAN, W.	1975–76 to 1979–80	154	1	10	10			13	1	2							177	2	12
MORENO, J.	2003–04	1	7						2								1	9	0
MORENO MACHADO, R.	2010–11	4	13	1	1	2		1									6	15	1
MORINI, E.	2000–01 to 2001–02	1	1		1												2	1	0
MOSS, A.E.	1920–21	1															1	0	0
MOWBRAY, H.	1971–72 to 1972–73	31			3			6									40	0	0
MUAMBA, F.	2008 to 2009	100	10	2	10			4									114	10	2
MULLINEUX, I.	1986–87	1	1						1								1	2	0
MUNRO, J.	1890–91 to 1892–93	50		20	2		1										52	0	21
MURPHY, D.	1946–47 to 1950–51	66		1	10												76	0	1
MURPHY, L.	1927–28 to 1928–29	33		7	1		1										34	0	8
NAKATA, H.	2005–06	14	7	1	3			2						5	1		24	8	1
NAPIER, R.J.	1964–65 to 1966–67	69		2	3			2									74	0	2
NAPIER, S.	1905–06	4															4	0	0
NAYLOR, T.	PRE-LEAGUE				3												3	0	0
NEAL, P.	1985–86 to 1988–89	58	8	3	6	1		2	2		7		1				73	12	3
NELSON	PRE-LEAGUE				1												1	0	0
NEILL, T.K.	1952–53 to 1956–57	40		2	2		1										42	0	3
NEWNES, J.	1922–23	7															7	0	0

		LEAGUE			FA CUP			LEAGUE CUP			FRT/ROVER-AUTO			UEFA CUP ANGLO ITALIAN			TOTAL		
	SEASON	APS	SUB	GLS	APS	SUB	GLS	APS	SUB	GLS	APS	SUB	GLS	APS	SUB	GLS	APS	SUB	GLS
NESOME, J.	1998–99	6															6	0	0
NEWTON, S.	1910–11 to 1911–12	15															15	0	0
NEYLAND, M.	1901–02	2															2	0	0
NGOTTY, B.	2001–02 to 2005–06	143	5	4	7			8	2	1				6	1	1	164	8	6
NICHOLSON, G.	1931–32 to 1935–36	67		1	4												71	0	1
NICHOLSON, P.	1971–72 to 1981–82	303	15	12	23	3	2	26									352	18	14
NICOLL, D.	1895–96 to 1901–02	61		11	4												65	0	11
NIKOLIC, D.	1980–81 to 1981–82	22	2	2	2												25	0	2
NISHIZAWA, A.	2001–02							3		1							3	0	1
NOLAN, K.	1999–2000 to 2008–09	259	39	40	13	7	4	10	5	4				9	3	2	291	54	50
NORRIS, D.	2000–01 to 2002–03					1		3	1								4	1	0
NOWAK, T.	1978–79 to 1980–81	22	2	1	1				2								23	4	1
NUTTALL, H.	1921–22 to 1931–32	294		6	32												326	0	6
OAKES, A.	2004–05	1															1	0	0
OBADEYI, T.	2008 to 2009		3														0	3	0
O'BRIEN, A.	2007–08 to 2010–11	68	6		4	1	1	2	1					7	1		81	9	1
O'BRIEN, J.	2004–05 to 2010–11	42	8		4			4	1					10	1		60	10	0
OGHANI, G.	1983–84 to 1986–87	86	13	27	2	4	1	9	2	3	13		7				110	20	38
OKANE, J.	1999–2000 to 2000–01	32	6	2	3	1	1	4									39	7	3
OKOCHA, A.	2002–03 to 2005–06	106	18	14	4	1		7	2	4				6	1		123	22	18
OLINYK, P.	1973–74 to 1974–75	7	3														7	3	0
OLIVER, D.	1992–93	3						1									4	0	0
OSTICK, C.	1900–01 to 1905–06	84			3												87	0	0
OTSEMEBOR, J.	2003–04	1															1	0	0
OWEN, G.	1888–89	7		3	1												8	0	3
OWEN, J.R.	1906–07 to 1910–11	90		19	8		1										98	0	20
OWEN, R.	PRE-LEAGUE				3												3	0	0
OXTOBY, R.	1959–60	3			1												4	0	0
PAATELAINEN, M.M.	1994–95 to 1996–97	61	11	16	1	1		8	1	2							70	13	18
PARKINSON, D.W.	PRE-LEAGUE				3												3	0	0
PARKINSON, G.	1992–93 to 1993–94	1	2											4			5	2	0
PARKINSON, J.	1888–89 to 1890–91	22		1	16												38	0	1
PARKINSON, W.	PRE-LEAGUE				1												1	0	0
PARRY, A.	1929–30	5															5	0	0

NAME	SEASON	LEAGUE			FA CUP			LEAGUE CUP			FRT/OVER-AUTO			UEFA CUP ANGLO ITALIAN			TOTAL		
		APS	SUB	GLS	APS	SUB	GLS	APS	SUB	GLS	APS	SUB	GLS	APS	SUB	GLS	APS	SUB	GLS
PARRY, R.A.	1951–52 to 1960–61	270		68	28		11	1									299	0	79
PASSI, F.	1999–200 to 2000–01	21	18		5	1		4									30	19	0
PATON, A.	1890–91 to 1898–99	215		15	26												241	0	15
PATTERSON, M.	1990–91 to 1995–96	158	11	11	17		1	16	4	2	5			4			200	15	14
PEACOCK, D.	1980–81 to 1981–82	16			2			2									20	0	0
PEARSON, J.	1889–90 2006–07	93	50	22	7	4	3	7	7	4				2	1		109	62	29
PETROV, M.	2010–11	18	10	3	6												24	10	3
PEYTON, G.	1991–92	1															1	0	0
PHILLIPS, J.	*1983–84 to 2000–01	316	18	5	17	3		37	3	1	14			6		2	390	21	8
PHILLIPS, R.D.	1966–67 to 1974–75	135	10	17	13	1	1	12	4	1							160	15	19
PHILLISKIRK, A.	1989–90 to 1992–93	144	2	54	10		7	18		12	8		2				180	2	75
PHYTHIAN, E.R.	1959–60 to 1961–62	10		3	1												11	0	3
PICKEN, A.H.	1925–26 to 1927–28	18		2													18	0	2
PICKEN, J.H.	1899–1900 to 1902–03	101		22	5												106	0	22
PICKUP, J.H.	1919–20	1															1	0	0
PIKE, M.	1989–90	5		1				1									6	0	1
PILKINGTON, B.	1960–61 to 1963–64	82		11	1			3									86	0	11
PILLING, V.	1952–53 to 1954–55	7															7	0	0
PLATT, J.	1983–84	10						1									11	0	0
POLLOCK, J.	1996–97 to 1997–98	43	3	5	4		2	4	1	1							51	4	8
POTTER, L.	1999–2000								1								0	1	0
POOLE, K.	2001–02 to 2004–05	4	1		4			7									15	1	0
POOLE, T.	1980–81	29						1									30	0	0
POWELL, J.	PRE-LEAGUE				6												6	0	0
PULMAN, J.	1909–10	1															1	0	0
PUYGRENIER, S.	2008 to 2009	5	2	1													5	2	1
PYM, R.H.	1921–22 to 1930–31	301			35												336	0	0
RANKIN, I.	2000–01	9	7	2				2									11	7	2
RASIAK, G.	2007–08	2	5														2	5	0
REDFEARN, N.D.	1982–83 to 1983–84	35		1	4			2									41	0	1
REDFERN, J.	1969–70 to 1972–73	19	5	2	3	1	1										22	6	3
REDROBE, W.E.	1963–64 to 1965–66	4		1													4	0	1
REEVES, D.	1989–90 to 1992–93	113	24	29	8	5	5	14	1	1	7		7				142	31	42
REID, P.	1974–75 to 1982–83	222	3	23	17		1	18	1	1							257	4	25

NAME	SEASON	LEAGUE APS	SUB	GLS	FA CUP APS	SUB	GLS	LEAGUE CUP APS	SUB	GLS	FR TROVER-AUTO APS	SUB	GLS	UEFA CUP ANGLO ITALIAN APS	SUB	GLS	TOTAL APS	SUB	GLS
RICHARDSON, L.	2000–01 to 2002–03	5	8		1			3	1								9	9	0
RICKETTS, M.	2000–01 to 2002–03	64	37	39	4	4	4		3	3							68	44	46
RICKETTS, S.	2009–10	39	5		6			5									50	5	0
RIGA, M.	2008–09 to 2010–11	2	16			3		1									3	19	0
RILEY, B.F.	1956–57 to 1958–59	8		1													8	0	1
RIMMER, J.W.	1930–31 to 1936–37	81		16	2												83	0	16
RIMMER, W.R.	1960–61 to 1974–75	462	7	17	30			29									521	7	17
RING, M.	1985–86	1	2														1	2	0
RIPLEY, S.	1985–86	5		1													5	0	1
RITCHIE, P.	1999–2000	15	1		3	1		1									19	2	0
RITSON, J.A.	1967–68 to 1977–78	321	3	9	30		4	24									375	3	13
ROBERTS, C.L.	1925–26 to 1926–27	6		2													6	0	2
ROBERTS, D.	1985–86										1						1	0	0
ROBERTS, E.	1921–22 to 1922–23	5															5	0	0
ROBERTS, F.	1914–15 to 1922–23	157		79	11		1										168	0	80
ROBERTS, G.M.	1967–68 to 1969–70	5															5	0	0
ROBERTS, J.H.	1937–38 to 1950–51	162		19	9												171	0	19
ROBERTS, R.	1888–89 to 1891–92	71		3	14		2										85	0	5
ROBERTS, W.D.	1926–27	5		4													5	0	4
ROBERTSON	PRE-LEAGUE				3												3	0	0
ROBERTSON, J.N.	1903–04 to 1905–06	15															15	0	0
ROBINSON, B.	1888–89 to 1890–91	38			3		1										41	0	1
ROBINSON, P.	2009–10	59	1		7												66	1	0
ROBINSON, W.S.	1908–09 to 1910–11	31			1												32	0	0
ROLLINSON, F.	1907–08	1															1	0	0
ROSCOE, A.	1992–93 to 1994–95	2	1											1	1		3	2	0
ROSE, K.	1989–90 to 1991–92	10						6									16	0	0
ROTHWELL, E.	1937–38 to 1948–49	48		2													48	0	2
ROUND, J.H.	1925–26 to 1929–30	56		1	3		1										59	0	2
ROWE, G.E.	1971–72	4	2					2		1							6	2	1
ROWLEY, W.J.	1912–13 to 1924–25	175		7	16												191	0	7
RUDGE, S.J.	1982–83 to 1985–86	77	13	14	4	2	2	5			5						91	15	16
RUSHTON, W.	1889–90	2			5												7	0	0
RUSSELL, W.	1890–91 to 1891–92	6															6	0	0

		LEAGUE			FA CUP			LEAGUE CUP			FRT/OVER-AUTO			UEFA CUP/ANGLO ITALIAN			TOTAL		
	SEASON	APS	SUB	GLS	APS	SUB	GLS	APS	SUB	GLS	APS	SUB	GLS	APS	SUB	GLS	APS	SUB	GLS
RUSSELL, W.	1962–63 to 1964–65	22		2													22	0	2
RYDER, G.	1906–07 to 1907–08	4															4	0	0
SALAKO, J.	1997–98		7														0	7	0
SALMON M.	1986–87	26			4			2			4						36	0	0
SAMUEL, J.L.	2007–08 to 2010–11	64	7		3			5	1					4			76	7	0
SAUNDERS, S.	1983–84	3	1		1	1											4	2	0
SAVAGE, R.	1987–88 to 1989–90	83	4	11	3			3		1	9		1				98	4	13
SCHOLES, J.	PRE-LEAGUE				2		1										2	0	1
SCOTCHBROOK, F.	1896–97 to 1899–1900	5															5	0	0
SCOTT, D.	1985–86 to 1987–88	121			8			4			14						147	0	0
SCOTT, S.	1896–97 to 1897–98	19															19	0	0
SCOWCROFT, J.	1888–89	9		1	2												11	0	1
SEAGREAVES, M.	1990–91 to 1994–95	155	5	7	17		1	8	1		6			4		1	190	5	9
SEDDON, I.W.	1969–70 to 1971–73	51	13	4	4	1		6									61	15	4
SEDDON, J.	1913–14 to 1931–32	337		4	38		1										375	0	5
SELLARS, S.	1995–96 to 1998–99	106	6	15	5		1	8	1								119	7	16
SETTLE, J.	1894–95	13		4	2												15	0	4
SHAKES, R.	2003–04 to 2004–05				1		1										1	0	1
SHAW, J.	1903–04 to 1904–05	8															8	0	0
SHEPHERD, A.	1904–05 to 1908–09	115		85	8		5										123	0	90
SHERIDAN, J.	1996–97 to 1997–98	24	8	2	2			2									28	8	2
SHILTON, P.	1994–95	1	1														1	1	0
SHINTON, F.	1910–11	7		1													7	0	1
SHITTU, D.	2008–09 to 2010–11	9	1		1	1		1									11	1	1
SHUTTLEWORTH, T.	1893–94 to 1894–95	2															2	0	0
SIDDALL, B.	1972–73 to 1976–77	137			11			10									158	0	0
SIDDONS	1888–89	1															1	0	0
SIDEBOTTOM, W.	1938–39	1															1	0	0
SIDLOW, E.	1913–14 to 1914–15	19			1												20	0	0
SIMM, J.	1947–48	1															1	0	0
SIMMERS, W.	1888–89	2			2		2										4	0	2
SIMPSON, H.	1921–22 to 1923–24	9		1													9	0	1
SINCLAIR, J.	2006–07 to 2008–09		2						1					1			0	3	0
SINCLAIR, T.M.	1938–39	10		5													10	0	5

Name	Season	League APS	League SUB	League GLS	FA Cup APS	FA Cup SUB	FA Cup GLS	League Cup APS	League Cup SUB	League Cup GLS	Frtrover–Auto APS	Frtrover–Auto SUB	Frtrover–Auto GLS	UEFA Cup / Anglo Italian APS	UEFA Cup / Anglo Italian SUB	UEFA Cup / Anglo Italian GLS	Total APS	Total SUB	Total GLS
SISSONS, R.	2005–06 to 2008–09					1											0	1	0
SLATER, J.	1906–07 to 1912–13	92			7												99	0	0
SLEIGHT, G.	1961–62	2			1												3	0	0
SMALL, B.	1995–96 to 1997–98	11	1		3			1									15	1	0
SMITH, A.	1962–63 to 1967–68	19			1												20	0	0
SMITH, B.	1974–75 to 1978–79	43	6	3	2	1	1	5									50	7	4
SMITH, C.F.	1921–22 to 1922–23	7															7	0	0
SMITH, D.W.	1895–96 to 1896–97	3			1												4	0	0
SMITH, G.T.	1900–01	1			1												2	0	0
SMITH, H.	1913–14	8		1													8	0	1
SMITH, J.	1908–09 to 1926–27	449		254	43		23										492	0	277
SMITH, J.	2000–01 to 2003–04	1	1		4			2									7	1	0
SMITH, J.	2006–07		1			1			1								0	3	0
SMITH, J.R.	1922–23 to 1927–28	147		72	27		15										174	0	87
SMITH, R.	1932–33 to 1935–36	89			13												102	0	0
SMITH, S.	1974–75	3															3	0	0
SMOLAREK, E.	2008 to 2009	1	11	1					1								1	12	1
SNEEKES, R.	1994–95 to 1995–96	51	4	7	2		1	11	1	3							64	5	11
SNOOKES, E.	1983–84	6															6	0	0
SOMERVILLE, J.	1890–91 to 1900–01	265		2	28												293	0	2
SOMMER, J.	2000–01				1												1	0	0
SOUTHALL, N.	2001–02 to 2002–03	10	8	1	2			4									16	8	1
SPEED, G.	2004–05 to 2007–08	115	6	14	6			4						5	3		130	9	14
SPENCE, A.	1894–95	4		2	1												5	0	2
SPOONER, N.	1991–92 to 1998–99	22	1	2	3			2			1						27	2	2
STANLEY, G.	1956–57 to 1963–64	141		3	12		1	8									161	0	4
STANLEY, J.	1905–06 to 1909–10	67			4												71	0	0
STATON, L.	1999–2000								1								0	1	0
STEEL, R.	PRE-LEAGUE				14		8										14	0	8
STEEL, W.	PRE-LEAGUE				8												8	0	0
STEINSSON, G.	2007–08	101	2	3	6		1	3									110	2	4
STEVENS, D.	1953–54 to 1961–62	273		90	30		9	7		2							310	0	101
STEVENS, I.	1986–87 to 1990–91	26	22	7	4		2	1	2		3						34	24	9
STEVENSON, J.	1894–95	2															2	0	0

NAME	SEASON	LEAGUE APS	SUB	GLS	FA CUP APS	SUB	GLS	LEAGUE CUP APS	SUB	GLS	FRT/ROVER–AUTO APS	SUB	GLS	UEFA CUP / ANGLO ITALIAN APS	SUB	GLS	TOTAL APS	SUB	GLS
STOKES, D.	1901–02 to 1919–20	387		43	33		3										420	0	46
STORER, S.	1987–88 to 1992–93	100	28	12	7	3	2	9	2		11	5	1				127	38	15
STOTT, W.	1908–09 to 1913–14	63			2												65	0	0
STRANG, T.	1902–03	3															3	0	0
STRONG, G.	1995–96 to 1998–99	10	2	1				8	2								18	4	1
STRUTHERS, R.	1901–02 to 1906–07	130			11												141	0	0
STRUTHERS, W.G.	PRE-LEAGUE				19		18										19	0	18
STUART, W.	1907–08 to 1909–10	7		1													7	0	1
STUBBS, A.	1990–91 to 1995–96	187	21	9	16	2	2	23		4	2	1		4			232	24	15
STURRIDGE, D.	2010–11	11	1	8													11	1	8
SUMMERBEE, N.	2000–01	9	3		3												12	3	0
SUTCLIFFE, J.W.	1889–90 to 1901–02	332			32												364	0	0
SUTTON, D.	1985–86 to 1987–88	100		4	2			5			12						119	0	4
SWIFT, F.	1935–36 to 1937–38	62			3												65	0	0
TAGGART, G.	1995–96 to 1997–98	68	1	4	4			8		1							80	1	5
TAIT, T.	1930–31	9		4	1												10	0	4
TAL, I.	2006–07	4	12	1	1	1		2									7	13	1
TANNAHILL, R.	1892–93 to 1896–97	67		8	13		3										80	0	11
TATHAM, W.	1897–98	2															2	0	0
TAYLOR, A.	1904–05	3			3												6	0	0
TAYLOR, C.	2001–02 to 2003–04					2											0	2	0
TAYLOR, G.	1930–31 to 1938–39	220		3	24												244	0	3
TAYLOR, G.	1962–63 to 1970–71	253	5	41	14		2	14		3							281	5	46
TAYLOR, G.T.	1933–34 to 1937–38	150		27	20		2										170	0	29
TAYLOR, M.	2007–08	100	23	23	5	3		5						3			113	26	23
TAYLOR, R.	1901–02 to 1906–07	104		18	10		1										114	0	19
TAYLOR, R.	*1997–98 to 1999–2000	60	20	23	4	1	2	6	5	2							70	26	27
TAYLOR, S.J.	1974–75 to 1977–78	34	6	16	1			9		4							44	6	20
TAYLOR, S.J.	1995–96 to 1998–99	2	10	1	1		1		4	1							3	14	3
TENNANT, J.W.	1935–36 to 1938–39	99		1	6												105	0	1
TEYMOURIAN, A.	2006–07 to 2007–08	7	13	2	2		2	2	1					2	2		13	16	4
THIRKELL, P.	1922–23	14			1												15	0	0
THOMAS, J.	1912–13 to 1914–15	30			6												36	0	0
THOMAS, J.W.	*1980–81 to 1988–89	89	6	37	2		3	5		2	6	2	2				102	8	44

Player	Season	LEAGUE			FA CUP			LEAGUE CUP			FRTROVER–AUTO			UEFA CUP ANGLO ITALIAN			TOTAL		
		APS	SUB	GLS	APS	SUB	GLS	APS	SUB	GLS	APS	SUB	GLS	APS	SUB	GLS	APS	SUB	GLS
THOME, E.	2003–04	25	1		5			1									31	1	0
THOMPSON, A.	1993–94 to 1997–98	146	14	34	6	2	2	24	1	5				4	1	1	180	18	42
THOMPSON, C.D.	1979–80 to 1982–83	66	7	18	3	1	1	3	1	1							72	9	20
THOMPSON, D.	2006–07	3	5														3	5	0
THOMPSON, F.	1902–03	20			1												21	0	0
THOMPSON, P.	1973–74 to 1977–78	111	6	2	10			5									126	6	2
THOMPSON, S.J.	1982–83 to 1991–92	336	6	49	21	4		27	2	2	32	2					416	6	57
THOMSON, W.	1896–97 to 1898–99	45		5	4		1										49	0	6
THORNBOROUGH, E.H.	1925–26 to 1929–30	69			11												80	0	0
THORP, J.	1906–07	2															2	0	0
THRELFALL, J.	1955–56 to 1962–63	47		1	2												49	0	1
THRELFALL, J.R.	1946–47	3			8												11	0	0
TIERNEY, H.	1907–08	1															1	0	0
TODD, A.J.J.	1995–96 to 1999–2000	69	18	2	1			14	5	1							84	23	3
TOFTING, S.	2001–02 to 2002–03	8	6		2			1									11	6	0
TOONE, P.E.S.	1914–15	3															3	0	0
TRACEY, W.	1900–01 to 1902–03	56		11	3												59	0	11
TRAIN, R.	1976–77 to 1978–79	49	2		3			3									55	2	0
TRAINER, J.	PRE-LEAGUE				4												4	0	0
TURNBULL, P.	1894–95	4		5													4	0	5
TURNER, J.A.	1888–89 to 1893–94	96		8	12		4										108	0	12
TURNER, R.	1888–89	3															3	0	0
TYLDESLEY, J.	1911–12 to 1913–14	10			2												12	0	0
TYRER, H.	1888–89	14		2													14	0	2
UNSWORTH, W.	PRE-LEAGUE				5		5										5	0	5
VAIL, T.	1895–96	3		1	1												4	0	1
VALENTINE, P.	1983–84 to 1984–85	66	2	1	4	1		4			5						79	2	1
VAUGHAN, J.	PRE-LEAGUE				4		1										4	0	1
VAZ TE, R.	2003–04 to 2009–10	10	48	3	5	6	2	3	1	1				1	4	1	19	59	7
VIANDER, J.	2001–02	1															1	0	0
VIZARD, E.T.	1910–11 to 1930–31	467	45	64	45	6											512	0	70
WAGSTAFFE, J.T.	1925–26 to 1931–32	50		1	3												53	0	1
WALDRON, A.	1970–71 to 1977–78	127	14	6	12	2	2	14	1	1							153	17	9
WALKER, A.	1991–92 to 1993–94	61	6	44	9	3	8	3		1	5		2				78	9	55

PLAYER	SEASON	LEAGUE			FA CUP			LEAGUE CUP			FRT–ROVER–AUTO			UEFA CUP / ANGLO ITALIAN			TOTAL		
		APS	SUB	GLS	APS	SUB	GLS	APS	SUB	GLS	APS	SUB	GLS	APS	SUB	GLS	APS	SUB	GLS
WALKER, I.	2005–06	5												3			8	0	0
WALKER, R.	1984–85 to 1985–86	7	5	1							1	1					8	6	1
WALLACE, R.	2001–02	14	5	3	1		1	1	2								16	7	4
WALLACE, W.	1914–15	2		1													2	0	1
WALLER, W.H.	1899–1900 to 1900–01	6															6	0	0
WALSH, M.T.	1974–75 to 1980–81	169	8	4	10	1		13		1							192	9	5
WALSH, T.	1920–21 to 1923–24	22		4													22	0	4
WALTERS, J.	2002–03 to 2003–04	1	4			1											1	5	0
WALTERS, T.C.	1931–32	5		1													5	0	1
WALTON, G.	1932–33 to 1936–37	26		1	2		2										28	0	3
WALTON, M.	1993–94	3															3	0	0
WARBURTON, F.	1903–04	1															1	0	0
WARD	PRE-LEAGUE				3												3	0	0
WARD, D.	2009–10		2														0	2	0
WARD, G.J.	1995–96 to 1998–99	19	3		4			2									25	3	0
WARHURST, P.	1998–99 to 2002–03	83	12		3	2		3	3								89	17	0
WATSON, A.G.	1919–20 to 1921–22	35			1												36	0	0
WEAVER, W.	1906–07	4		1													4	0	1
WEBSTER, H.	1949–50 to 1956–57	98		38	3												101	0	38
WEIR, A.	1912–13	2		2													2	0	2
WEIR, D.	1888–89 to 1894–95	86		31	6		10										92	0	41
WEISS, V.	2009–10	3	10														3	10	0
WESTWOOD, R.W.	1930–31 to 1947–48	301		127	32		17										333	0	144
WHARTON, T.J.	1967–68 to 1970–71	101	1	28	2	1		5		2							108	2	30
WHATMORE, N.	*1972–73 to 1983–84	279	15	107	21		7	22	1	7							322	16	121
WHEATCROFT, P.	2000–01 to 2001–02		2						1								0	3	0
WHEATER, D.	2010–11	5	2		4												9	2	0
WHEELER, J.E.	1950–51 to 1955–56	189		18	16												205	0	18
WHITE, W.	1902–03 to 1908–09	196		88	21		5										217	0	93
WHITESIDE, E.	1908–09 to 1913–14	84			4												88	0	0
WHITESIDE, J.	1908–09 to 1910–11	7		1													7	0	1
WHITLOW, M.	1997–98 to 2002–03	126	11	2	10	1		13	2								149	14	2
WHITTAKER, S.	1993–94 to 1996–97	2	1						1								2	2	0
WHITTLE	1888–89				3		1										3	0	1
WHITWORTH, S.	1981–82 to 1982–83	67			3			3									73	0	0

		LEAGUE			FA CUP			LEAGUE CUP			FRTROVER-AUTO			UEFA CUP ANGLO ITALIAN			TOTAL		
	SEASON	APS	SUB	GLS	APS	SUB	GLS	APS	SUB	GLS	APS	SUB	GLS	APS	SUB	GLS	APS	SUB	GLS
WILHELMSSON, C.	2007–08		7		1									3	1		4	8	0
WILKINSON, H.	1909–10	1			1												2	0	0
WILKINSON, R.J.	1960–61 to 1961–62	3															3	0	0
WILLCOCKS, D.	1892–93 to 1893–94	32		8	4												36	0	8
WILLIAMS, G.C.	1967–68 to 1970–71	108	1	11	4		1	4									116	1	12
WILLIAMS, H.	1901–02 to 1902–03	16		6	2		1										18	0	7
WILSHERE, J.	2009–10	13	1	1													13	1	1
WILSON, F.W.	1931–32 to 1932–33	4		1													4	0	1
WILSON, G.	1914–15	26			7												33	0	0
WILSON, J.	1892–93 to 1893–94	36		7	5		3										41	0	10
WILSON, P.	1979–80 to 1980–81	35	4	4	2			1									38	4	4
WILSON, T.	1904–05 to 1905–06	20		5	4												24	0	5
WILSON, T.R.	PRE-LEAGUE				8												8	0	0
WINSTANLEY, M.	1985–86 to 1993–94	217	5	3	19			19	1		19		3	5			279	6	6
WINTER, D.T.	1936–37 to 1938–39	34			3												37	0	0
WINTERBURN, A.	1919–20	1															1	0	0
WOLSTENHOLME, T.	1905–06 to 1906–07	9		1	1												10	0	1
WOODS, C.	1935–36	2															2	0	0
WOODS, F.	1889–90	5															5	0	0
WOODS, S.	1908–09 to 1909–10	5		2													5	0	2
WOODWARD, T.	1935–36 to 1949–50	152		18	17		1										169	0	19
WOOLFALL, T.	1900–01	21			2												23	0	0
WOOLFE, N.	2007–08 to 2008–09														1		0	1	0
WORTHINGTON, W.	1901–02	3		1													3	0	1
WORTHINGTON, F.S.	1977–78 to 1979–80	81	3	35	5		1	2	1	2							88	4	38
WIGGLESWORTH, W.	1946–47 to 1947–48	13		1	2		1										15	0	2
WRIGHT, C.G.	1971–72 to 1972–73	88			13			8									109	0	0
WRIGHT, J.	1895–96 to 1903–04	119		19	9		3										128	0	22
WRIGHT, R.L.	1971–72 to 1972–73	25	7	5				2									27	7	5
WRIGHT, S.	1920–21 to 1921–22	10															10	0	0
WRIGHT.T	2000–01	3	1														3	1	0
WRIGHT, W.B.	1922–23 to 1932–33	154		21	5		1										159	0	22
YATES, W.	1925–26 to 1926–27	6															6	0	0
YENSON, W.	1925–26 to 1926–27	28		8	6		2										34	0	10
YOUNG, J.	PRE-LEAGUE				4												4	0	0

Roll of Honour

Paul Palgrave
Paul Willis
Barry Holland
Curtis Warburton
Yash Patel
George McDermott
Brian Armitage
Jack Norman Ward
Charlie Sweeney
Justin Paul Hilton
John L. Gorse
Roy Williams
Stephen Denham
Robert John Taylor
John Stott
Norman Peter Maginn
John Coughlin
Ryan Crompton
Marc Crompton
Harry Leek
Graham Marsden
John Pietralski
Robert Wolstoncroft
Lynn Charlton
John Smalley
Ian & Tom Hampson
Andrew Pearce
Mark Heys
Tony Grimshaw
Robert Scholes
Graham Brandwood
Dave Jones
Lewis Charnley
Colin Styan
Bernard Collier
John Davidson
Roy Beardsworth
Mr. James Eckersley
Christopher Tom Jones
David Croughton
John & Samuel Ryan
Michael Hodgkiss
Norman Leigh
Steven Battersby
Andrew Bridges
Adam Fairbanks
Janet R. Marland

William Cowburn
Martin Peter Nisbet
Kenneth & Steven Nisbet
David Thompson
Peter J. Leatham
Paul Strickleton
Melvyn & Neil Woodcock
Ella & Isabella Holliday
John Lloyd
Wayne Lloyd
Brian George Ainsworth
John Cullen
Thomas, Robert & Bethan Carr
Eileen F. Rigby
Thomas Simmons
Mark Dalton
Russell Howarth
Thomas Simmons
Emily Morse
Andy Childs
Lliam S. Heavey
Graham Tyldsley
Mark Hibbert
Roderick James Mark-Bell
Kevan Hanley
David Blundell
Andy & Linda Hayes
R.I.P. Dad (Bill Holden)
David & Carol Marshall
Geoff Kenny
Martin Timothy
Michael Coglan
Terry & Mary Woods
Ray O'Donnell
Stephen Charles Hunt
Emil Anderson
John James Hamer
Graham Edge
Andy Makin
Penny & Neil Wood
Olen Higson
Stephen Monks
Garry Jones Breightmet Bolton
Andrea Lever
Andrew Littlefair
Ian Kennedy
Matthew Wolfenden

Dennis, Daniel & Benny Jensen
Stephen Berry
Norman Entwistle
Jordan Jack Peploe
Mark & Jack Tyldsley
Michael James
Greg Sykes
Andrew Barnes
Simon Nightingale & Family
Stephen Lashmar
John Aspinall
James W. Morgan
David Lomax
Tam & Susan, Falkirk
John Holmes
Aaron Haley
William Mellan
Lynda Wallace Rands
Roy Millichip
Alan Kay
Michael Taylor
Jeff Turner
Richard Savelli
Peter Coglan
John Scaldwell
Joel Burgess
John Grundy

Darren & Ricky Hitching
Steve Caron
James Caron
Matthew Caron
Daniel Caron
Ian Wilson
David Wilson
Anthony Wilson
Keith Wright
Mark Hughes
The Yates Family
Zac Burger South Carolina
Paul S. Worthington
Alan Simkin
Stanley Marshall 1907-2004
Kevin Rainford
C. J. Meadows
Diane Lealand
Dave Phillips, Dalbeattie
The Castley Family, Norfolk
Danilo "Dan" Ronzani (Bologna)
Dave Unsworth (Warrington)
Shaun Irving (Warrington)
Diane Jones
Mike Vickers
Dave Cookson